72 *French Novelists, 1930-1960,* edited by Catharine Savage Brosman (1988)

73 *American Magazine Journalists, 1741-1850,* edited by Sam G. Riley (1988)

74 *American Short-Story Writers Before 1880,* edited by Bobby Ellen Kimbel, with the assistance of William E. Grant (1988)

75 *Contemporary German Fiction Writers, Second Series,* edited by Wolfgang D. Elfe and James Hardin (1988)

76 *Afro-American Writers, 1940-1955,* edited by Trudier Harris (1988)

77 *British Mystery Writers, 1920-1939,* edited by Bernard Benstock and Thomas F. Staley (1988)

78 *American Short-Story Writers, 1880-1910,* edited by Bobby Ellen Kimbel, with the assistance of William E. Grant (1988)

79 *American Magazine Journalists, 1850-1900,* edited by Sam G. Riley (1988)

80 *Restoration and Eighteenth-Century Dramatists, First Series,* edited by Paula R. Backscheider (1989)

81 *Austrian Fiction Writers, 1875-1913,* edited by James Hardin and Donald G. Daviau (1989)

82 *Chicano Writers, First Series,* edited by Francisco A. Lomelí and Carl R. Shirley (1989)

83 *French Novelists Since 1960,* edited by Catharine Savage Brosman (1989)

84 *Restoration and Eighteenth-Century Dramatists, Second Series,* edited by Paula R. Backscheider (1989)

85 *Austrian Fiction Writers After 1914,* edited by James Hardin and Donald G. Daviau (1989)

86 *American Short-Story Writers, 1910-1945, First Series,* edited by Bobby Ellen Kimbel (1989)

87 *British Mystery and Thriller Writers Since 1940, First Series,* edited by Bernard Benstock and Thomas F. Staley (1989)

88 *Canadian Writers, 1920-1959, Second Series,* edited by W. H. New (1989)

89 *Restoration and Eighteenth-Century Dramatists, Third Series,* edited by Paula R. Backscheider (1989)

90 *German Writers in the Age of Goethe, 1789-1832,* edited by James Hardin and Christoph E. Schweitzer (1989)

91 *American Magazine Journalists, 1900-1960, First Series,* edited by Sam G. Riley (1990)

92 *Canadian Writers, 1890-1920,* edited by W. H. New (1990)

93 *British Romantic Poets, 1789-1832, First Series,* edited by John R. Greenfield (1990)

94 *German Writers in the Age of Goethe: Sturm und Drang to Classicism,* edited by James Hardin and Christoph E. Schweitzer (1990)

95 *Eighteenth-Century British Poets, First Series,* edited by John Sitter (1990)

96 *British Romantic Poets, 1789-1832, Second Series,* edited by John R. Greenfield (1990)

97 *German Writers from the Enlightenment to Sturm und Drang, 1720-1764,* edited by James Hardin and Christoph E. Schweitzer (1990)

98 *Modern British Essayists, First Series,* edited by Robert Beum (1990)

99 *Canadian Writers Before 1890,* edited by W. H. New (1990)

100 *Modern British Essayists, Second Series,* edited by Robert Beum (1990)

101 *British Prose Writers, 1660-1800, First Series,* edited by Donald T. Siebert (1991)

102 *American Short-Story Writers, 1910-1945, Second Series,* edited by Bobby Ellen Kimbel (1991)

103 *American Literary Biographers, First Series,* edited by Steven Serafin (1991)

104 *British Prose Writers, 1660-1800, Second Series,* edited by Donald T. Siebert (1991)

105 *American Poets Since World War II, Second Series,* edited by R. S. Gwynn (1991)

106 *British Literary Publishing Houses, 1820-1880,* edited by Patricia J. Anderson and Jonathan Rose (1991)

107 *British Romantic Prose Writers, 1789-1832, First Series,* edited by John R. Greenfield (1991)

108 *Twentieth-Century Spanish Poets, First Series,* edited by Michael L. Perna (1991)

109 *Eighteenth-Century British Poets, Second Series,* edited by John Sitter (1991)

110 *British Romantic Prose Writers, 1789-1832, Second Series,* edited by John R. Greenfield (1991)

111 *American Literary Biographers, Second Series,* edited by Steven Serafin (1991)

112 *British Literary Publishing Houses, 1881-1965,* edited by Jonathan Rose and Patricia J. Anderson (1991)

113 *Modern Latin-American Fiction Writers, First Series,* edited by William Luis (1992)

114 *Twentieth-Century Italian Poets, First Series,* edited by Giovanna Wedel De Stasio, Glauco Cambon, and Antonio Illiano (1992)

115 *Medieval Philosophers,* edited by Jeremiah Hackett (1992)

116 *British Romantic Novelists, 1789-1832,* edited by Bradford K. Mudge (1992)

117 *Twentieth-Century Caribbean and Black African Writers, First Series,* edited by Bernth Lindfors and Reinhard Sander (1992)

118 *Twentieth-Century German Dramatists, 1889-1918,* edited by Wolfgang D. Elfe and James Hardin (1992)

119 *Nineteenth-Century French Fiction Writers: Romanticism and Realism, 1800-1860,* edited by Catharine Savage Brosman (1992)

120 *American Poets Since World War II, Third Series,* edited by R. S. Gwynn (1992)

121 *Seventeenth-Century British Nondramatic Poets, First Series,* edited by M. Thomas Hester (1992)

122 *Chicano Writers, Second Series,* edited by Francisco A. Lomelí and Carl R. Shirley (1992)

123 *Nineteenth-Century French Fiction Writers: Naturalism and Beyond, 1860-1900,* edited by Catharine Savage Brosman (1992)

124 *Twentieth-Century German Dramatists, 1919-1992,* edited by Wolfgang D. Elfe and James Hardin (1992)

125 *Twentieth-Century Caribbean and Black African Writers, Second Series,* edited by Bernth Lindfors and Reinhard Sander (1993)

126 *Seventeenth-Century British Nondramatic Poets, Second Series,* edited by M. Thomas Hester (1993)

127 *American Newspaper Publishers, 1950-1990,* edited by Perry J. Ashley (1993)

128 *Twentieth-Century Italian Poets, Second Series,* edited by Giovanna Wedel De Stasio, Glauco Cambon, and Antonio Illiano (1993)

129 *Nineteenth-Century German Writers, 1841-1900,* edited by James Hardin and Siegfried Mews (1993)

130 *American Short-Story Writers Since World War II,* edited by Patrick Meanor (1993)

131 *Seventeenth-Century British Nondramatic Poets, Third Series,* edited by M. Thomas Hester (1993)

132 *Sixteenth-Century British Nondramatic Writers, First Series,* edited by David A. Richardson (1993)

133 *Nineteenth-Century German Writers to 1840,* edited by James Hardin and Siegfried Mews (1993)

134 *Twentieth-Century Spanish Poets, Second Series,* edited by Jerry Phillips Winfield (1994)

135 *British Short-Fiction Writers, 1880-1914: The Realist Tradition,* edited by William B. Thesing (1994)

136 *Sixteenth-Century British Nondramatic Writers, Second Series,* edited by David A. Richardson (1994)

137 *American Magazine Journalists, 1900-1960, Second Series,* edited by Sam G. Riley (1994)

138 *German Writers and Works of the High Middle Ages: 1170-1280,* edited by James Hardin and Will Hasty (1994)

139 *British Short-Fiction Writers, 1945-1980,* edited by Dean Baldwin (1994)

140 *American Book-Collectors and Bibliographers, First Series,* edited by Joseph Rosenblum (1994)

141 *British Children's Writers, 1880-1914,* edited by Laura M. Zaidman (1994)

142 *Eighteenth-Century British Literary Biographers,* edited by Steven Serafin (1994)

143 *American Novelists Since World War II, Third Series,* edited by James R. Giles and Wanda H. Giles (1994)

144 *Nineteenth-Century British Literary Biographers,* edited by Steven Serafin (1994)

145 *Modern Latin-American Fiction Writers, Second Series,* edited by William Luis and Ann González (1994)

SC

Dictionary of Literary Biography

1 *The American Renaissance in New England,* edited by Joel Myerson (1978)

2 *American Novelists Since World War II,* edited by Jeffrey Helterman and Richard Layman (1978)

3 *Antebellum Writers in New York and the South,* edited by Joel Myerson (1979)

4 *American Writers in Paris, 1920-1939,* edited by Karen Lane Rood (1980)

5 *American Poets Since World War II,* 2 parts, edited by Donald J. Greiner (1980)

6 *American Novelists Since World War II, Second Series,* edited by James E. Kibler Jr. (1980)

7 *Twentieth-Century American Dramatists,* 2 parts, edited by John MacNicholas (1981)

8 *Twentieth-Century American Science-Fiction Writers,* 2 parts, edited by David Cowart and Thomas L. Wymer (1981)

9 *American Novelists, 1910-1945,* 3 parts, edited by James J. Martine (1981)

10 *Modern British Dramatists, 1900-1945,* 2 parts, edited by Stanley Weintraub (1982)

11 *American Humorists, 1800-1950,* 2 parts, edited by Stanley Trachtenberg (1982)

12 *American Realists and Naturalists,* edited by Donald Pizer and Earl N. Harbert (1982)

13 *British Dramatists Since World War II,* 2 parts, edited by Stanley Weintraub (1982)

14 *British Novelists Since 1960,* 2 parts, edited by Jay L. Halio (1983)

15 *British Novelists, 1930-1959,* 2 parts, edited by Bernard Oldsey (1983)

16 *The Beats: Literary Bohemians in Postwar America,* 2 parts, edited by Ann Charters (1983)

17 *Twentieth-Century American Historians,* edited by Clyde N. Wilson (1983)

18 *Victorian Novelists After 1885,* edited by Ira B. Nadel and William E. Fredeman (1983)

19 *British Poets, 1880-1914,* edited by Donald E. Stanford (1983)

20 *British Poets, 1914-1945,* edited by Donald E. Stanford (1983)

21 *Victorian Novelists Before 1885,* edited by Ira B. Nadel and William E. Fredeman (1983)

22 *American Writers for Children, 1900-1960,* edited by John Cech (1983)

23 *American Newspaper Journalists, 1873-1900,* edited by Perry J. Ashley (1983)

24 *American Colonial Writers, 1606-1734,* edited by Emory Elliott (1984)

25 *American Newspaper Journalists, 1901-1925,* edited by Perry J. Ashley (1984)

26 *American Screenwriters,* edited by Robert E. Morsberger, Stephen O. Lesser, and Randall Clark (1984)

27 *Poets of Great Britain and Ireland, 1945-1960,* edited by Vincent B. Sherry Jr. (1984)

28 *Twentieth-Century American-Jewish Fiction Writers,* edited by Daniel Walden (1984)

29 *American Newspaper Journalists, 1926-1950,* edited by Perry J. Ashley (1984)

30 *American Historians, 1607-1865,* edited by Clyde N. Wilson (1984)

31 *American Colonial Writers, 1735-1781,* edited by Emory Elliott (1984)

32 *Victorian Poets Before 1850,* edited by William E. Fredeman and Ira B. Nadel (1984)

33 *Afro-American Fiction Writers After 1955,* edited by Thadious M. Davis and Trudier Harris (1984)

34 *British Novelists, 1890-1929: Traditionalists,* edited by Thomas F. Staley (1985)

35 *Victorian Poets After 1850,* edited by William E. Fredeman and Ira B. Nadel (1985)

36 *British Novelists, 1890-1929: Modernists,* edited by Thomas F. Staley (1985)

37 *American Writers of the Early Republic,* edited by Emory Elliott (1985)

38 *Afro-American Writers After 1955: Dramatists and Prose Writers,* edited by Thadious M. Davis and Trudier Harris (1985)

39 *British Novelists, 1660-1800,* 2 parts, edited by Martin C. Battestin (1985)

40 *Poets of Great Britain and Ireland Since 1960,* 2 parts, edited by Vincent B. Sherry Jr. (1985)

41 *Afro-American Poets Since 1955,* edited by Trudier Harris and Thadious M. Davis (1985)

42 *American Writers for Children Before 1900,* edited by Glenn E. Estes (1985)

43 *American Newspaper Journalists, 1690-1872,* edited by Perry J. Ashley (1986)

44 *American Screenwriters, Second Series,* edited by Randall Clark, Robert E. Morsberger, and Stephen O. Lesser (1986)

45 *American Poets, 1880-1945, First Series,* edited by Peter Quartermain (1986)

46 *American Literary Publishing Houses, 1900-1980: Trade and Paperback,* edited by Peter Dzwonkoski (1986)

47 *American Historians, 1866-1912,* edited by Clyde N. Wilson (1986)

48 *American Poets, 1880-1945, Second Series,* edited by Peter Quartermain (1986)

49 *American Literary Publishing Houses, 1638-1899,* 2 parts, edited by Peter Dzwonkoski (1986)

50 *Afro-American Writers Before the Harlem Renaissance,* edited by Trudier Harris (1986)

51 *Afro-American Writers from the Harlem Renaissance to 1940,* edited by Trudier Harris (1987)

52 *American Writers for Children Since 1960: Fiction,* edited by Glenn E. Estes (1986)

53 *Canadian Writers Since 1960, First Series,* edited by W. H. New (1986)

54 *American Poets, 1880-1945, Third Series,* 2 parts, edited by Peter Quartermain (1987)

55 *Victorian Prose Writers Before 1867,* edited by William B. Thesing (1987)

56 *German Fiction Writers, 1914-1945,* edited by James Hardin (1987)

57 *Victorian Prose Writers After 1867,* edited by William B. Thesing (1987)

58 *Jacobean and Caroline Dramatists,* edited by Fredson Bowers (1987)

59 *American Literary Critics and Scholars, 1800-1850,* edited by John W. Rathbun and Monica M. Grecu (1987)

60 *Canadian Writers Since 1960, Second Series,* edited by W. H. New (1987)

61 *American Writers for Children Since 1960: Poets, Illustrators, and Nonfiction Authors,* edited by Glenn E. Estes (1987)

62 *Elizabethan Dramatists,* edited by Fredson Bowers (1987)

63 *Modern American Critics, 1920-1955,* edited by Gregory S. Jay (1988)

64 *American Literary Critics and Scholars, 1850-1880,* edited by John W. Rathbun and Monica M. Grecu (1988)

65 *French Novelists, 1900-1930,* edited by Catharine Savage Brosman (1988)

66 *German Fiction Writers, 1885-1913,* 2 parts, edited by James Hardin (1988)

67 *Modern American Critics Since 1955,* edited by Gregory S. Jay (1988)

68 *Canadian Writers, 1920-1959, First Series,* edited by W. H. New (1988)

69 *Contemporary German Fiction Writers, First Series,* edited by Wolfgang D. Elfe and James Hardin (1988)

70 *British Mystery Writers, 1860-1919,* edited by Bernard Benstock and Thomas F. Staley (1988)

71 *American Literary Critics and Scholars, 1880-1900,* edited by John W. Rathbun and Monica M. Grecu (1988)

146 *Old and Middle English Literature,* edited by Jeffrey Helterman and Jerome Mitchell (1994)

147 *South Slavic Writers Before World War II,* edited by Vasa D. Mihailovich (1994)

148 *German Writers and Works of the Early Middle Ages: 800-1170,* edited by Will Hasty and James Hardin (1994)

149 *Late Nineteenth- and Early Twentieth-Century British Literary Biographers,* edited by Steven Serafin (1995)

150 *Early Modern Russian Writers, Late Seventeenth and Eighteenth Centuries,* edited by Marcus C. Levitt (1995)

151 *British Prose Writers of the Early Seventeenth Century,* edited by Clayton D. Lein (1995)

152 *American Novelists Since World War II, Fourth Series,* edited by James R. Giles and Wanda H. Giles (1995)

153 *Late-Victorian and Edwardian British Novelists, First Series,* edited by George M. Johnson (1995)

154 *The British Literary Book Trade, 1700-1820,* edited by James K. Bracken and Joel Silver (1995)

155 *Twentieth-Century British Literary Biographers,* edited by Steven Serafin (1995)

156 *British Short-Fiction Writers, 1880-1914: The Romantic Tradition,* edited by William F. Naufftus (1995)

157 *Twentieth-Century Caribbean and Black African Writers, Third Series,* edited by Bernth Lindfors and Reinhard Sander (1995)

158 *British Reform Writers, 1789-1832,* edited by Gary Kelly and Edd Applegate (1995)

159 *British Short-Fiction Writers, 1800-1880,* edited by John R. Greenfield (1996)

160 *British Children's Writers, 1914-1960,* edited by Donald R. Hettinga and Gary D. Schmidt (1996)

161 *British Children's Writers Since 1960, First Series,* edited by Caroline Hunt (1996)

162 *British Short-Fiction Writers, 1915-1945,* edited by John H. Rogers (1996)

163 *British Children's Writers, 1800-1880,* edited by Meena Khorana (1996)

164 *German Baroque Writers, 1580-1660,* edited by James Hardin (1996)

165 *American Poets Since World War II, Fourth Series,* edited by Joseph Conte (1996)

166 *British Travel Writers, 1837-1875,* edited by Barbara Brothers and Julia Gergits (1996)

167 *Sixteenth-Century British Nondramatic Writers, Third Series,* edited by David A. Richardson (1996)

168 *German Baroque Writers, 1661-1730,* edited by James Hardin (1996)

169 *American Poets Since World War II, Fifth Series,* edited by Joseph Conte (1996)

170 *The British Literary Book Trade, 1475-1700,* edited by James K. Bracken and Joel Silver (1996)

171 *Twentieth-Century American Sportswriters,* edited by Richard Orodenker (1996)

172 *Sixteenth-Century British Nondramatic Writers, Fourth Series,* edited by David A. Richardson (1996)

173 *American Novelists Since World War II, Fifth Series,* edited by James R. Giles and Wanda H. Giles (1996)

174 *British Travel Writers, 1876-1909,* edited by Barbara Brothers and Julia Gergits (1997)

175 *Native American Writers of the United States,* edited by Kenneth M. Roemer (1997)

176 *Ancient Greek Authors,* edited by Ward W. Briggs (1997)

177 *Italian Novelists Since World War II, 1945-1965,* edited by Augustus Pallotta (1997)

178 *British Fantasy and Science-Fiction Writers Before World War I,* edited by Darren Harris-Fain (1997)

179 *German Writers of the Renaissance and Reformation, 1280-1580,* edited by James Hardin and Max Reinhart (1997)

180 *Japanese Fiction Writers, 1868-1945,* edited by Van C. Gessel (1997)

181 *South Slavic Writers Since World War II,* edited by Vasa D. Mihailovich (1997)

182 *Japanese Fiction Writers Since World War II,* edited by Van C. Gessel (1997)

183 *American Travel Writers, 1776-1864,* edited by James J. Schramer and Donald Ross (1997)

184 *Nineteenth-Century British Book-Collectors and Bibliographers,* edited by William Baker and Kenneth Womack (1997)

185 *American Literary Journalists, 1945-1995, First Series,* edited by Arthur J. Kaul (1998)

186 *Nineteenth-Century American Western Writers,* edited by Robert L. Gale (1998)

187 *American Book Collectors and Bibliographers, Second Series,* edited by Joseph Rosenblum (1998)

188 *American Book and Magazine Illustrators to 1920,* edited by Steven E. Smith, Catherine A. Hastedt, and Donald H. Dyal (1998)

189 *American Travel Writers, 1850-1915,* edited by Donald Ross and James J. Schramer (1998)

190 *British Reform Writers, 1832-1914,* edited by Gary Kelly and Edd Applegate (1998)

191 *British Novelists Between the Wars,* edited by George M. Johnson (1998)

192 *French Dramatists, 1789-1914,* edited by Barbara T. Cooper (1998)

193 *American Poets Since World War II, Sixth Series,* edited by Joseph Conte (1998)

194 *British Novelists Since 1960, Second Series,* edited by Merritt Moseley (1998)

195 *British Travel Writers, 1910-1939,* edited by Barbara Brothers and Julia Gergits (1998)

196 *Italian Novelists Since World War II, 1965-1995,* edited by Augustus Pallotta (1999)

197 *Late-Victorian and Edwardian British Novelists, Second Series,* edited by George M. Johnson (1999)

198 *Russian Literature in the Age of Pushkin and Gogol: Prose,* edited by Christine A. Rydel (1999)

199 *Victorian Women Poets,* edited by William B. Thesing (1999)

200 *American Women Prose Writers to 1820,* edited by Carla J. Mulford, with Angela Vietto and Amy E. Winans (1999)

201 *Twentieth-Century British Book Collectors and Bibliographers,* edited by William Baker and Kenneth Womack (1999)

202 *Nineteenth-Century American Fiction Writers,* edited by Kent P. Ljungquist (1999)

203 *Medieval Japanese Writers,* edited by Steven D. Carter (1999)

204 *British Travel Writers, 1940-1997,* edited by Barbara Brothers and Julia M. Gergits (1999)

205 *Russian Literature in the Age of Pushkin and Gogol: Poetry and Drama,* edited by Christine A. Rydel (1999)

206 *Twentieth-Century American Western Writers, First Series,* edited by Richard H. Cracroft (1999)

207 *British Novelists Since 1960, Third Series,* edited by Merritt Moseley (1999)

208 *Literature of the French and Occitan Middle Ages: Eleventh to Fifteenth Centuries,* edited by Deborah Sinnreich-Levi and Ian S. Laurie (1999)

209 *Chicano Writers, Third Series,* edited by Francisco A. Lomelí and Carl R. Shirley (1999)

210 *Ernest Hemingway: A Documentary Volume,* edited by Robert W. Trogdon (1999)

211 *Ancient Roman Writers,* edited by Ward W. Briggs (1999)

212 *Twentieth-Century American Western Writers, Second Series,* edited by Richard H. Cracroft (1999)

213 *Pre-Nineteenth-Century British Book Collectors and Bibliographers,* edited by William Baker and Kenneth Womack (1999)

214 *Twentieth-Century Danish Writers,* edited by Marianne Stecher-Hansen (1999)

215 *Twentieth-Century Eastern European Writers, First Series,* edited by Steven Serafin (1999)

216 *British Poets of the Great War: Brooke, Rosenberg, Thomas. A Documentary Volume,* edited by Patrick Quinn (2000)

217 *Nineteenth-Century French Poets,* edited by Robert Beum (2000)

218 *American Short-Story Writers Since World War II, Second Series,* edited by Patrick Meanor and Gwen Crane (2000)

219 *F. Scott Fitzgerald's* The Great Gatsby: *A Documentary Volume,* edited by Matthew J. Bruccoli (2000)

220 *Twentieth-Century Eastern European Writers, Second Series,* edited by Steven Serafin (2000)

221 *American Women Prose Writers, 1870-1920,* edited by Sharon M. Harris, with the assistance of Heidi L. M. Jacobs and Jennifer Putzi (2000)

222 *H. L. Mencken: A Documentary Volume,* edited by Richard J. Schrader (2000)

223 *The American Renaissance in New England, Second Series*, edited by Wesley T. Mott (2000)

224 *Walt Whitman: A Documentary Volume*, edited by Joel Myerson (2000)

225 *South African Writers*, edited by Paul A. Scanlon (2000)

226 *American Hard-Boiled Crime Writers*, edited by George Parker Anderson and Julie B. Anderson (2000)

227 *American Novelists Since World War II, Sixth Series*, edited by James R. Giles and Wanda H. Giles (2000)

228 *Twentieth-Century American Dramatists, Second Series*, edited by Christopher J. Wheatley (2000)

229 *Thomas Wolfe: A Documentary Volume*, edited by Ted Mitchell (2001)

230 *Australian Literature, 1788-1914*, edited by Selina Samuels (2001)

231 *British Novelists Since 1960, Fourth Series*, edited by Merritt Moseley (2001)

232 *Twentieth-Century Eastern European Writers, Third Series*, edited by Steven Serafin (2001)

233 *British and Irish Dramatists Since World War II, Second Series*, edited by John Bull (2001)

234 *American Short-Story Writers Since World War II, Third Series*, edited by Patrick Meanor and Richard E. Lee (2001)

235 *The American Renaissance in New England, Third Series*, edited by Wesley T. Mott (2001)

236 *British Rhetoricians and Logicians, 1500-1660*, edited by Edward A. Malone (2001)

237 *The Beats: A Documentary Volume*, edited by Matt Theado (2001)

238 *Russian Novelists in the Age of Tolstoy and Dostoevsky*, edited by J. Alexander Ogden and Judith E. Kalb (2001)

239 *American Women Prose Writers: 1820-1870*, edited by Amy E. Hudock and Katharine Rodier (2001)

240 *Late Nineteenth- and Early Twentieth-Century British Women Poets*, edited by William B. Thesing (2001)

241 *American Sportswriters and Writers on Sport*, edited by Richard Orodenker (2001)

242 *Twentieth-Century European Cultural Theorists, First Series*, edited by Paul Hansom (2001)

243 *The American Renaissance in New England, Fourth Series*, edited by Wesley T. Mott (2001)

244 *American Short-Story Writers Since World War II, Fourth Series*, edited by Patrick Meanor and Joseph McNicholas (2001)

245 *British and Irish Dramatists Since World War II, Third Series*, edited by John Bull (2001)

246 *Twentieth-Century American Cultural Theorists*, edited by Paul Hansom (2001)

247 *James Joyce: A Documentary Volume*, edited by A. Nicholas Fargnoli (2001)

Dictionary of Literary Biography Documentary Series

1 *Sherwood Anderson, Willa Cather, John Dos Passos, Theodore Dreiser, F. Scott Fitzgerald, Ernest Hemingway, Sinclair Lewis*, edited by Margaret A. Van Antwerp (1982)

2 *James Gould Cozzens, James T. Farrell, William Faulkner, John O'Hara, John Steinbeck, Thomas Wolfe, Richard Wright*, edited by Margaret A. Van Antwerp (1982)

3 *Saul Bellow, Jack Kerouac, Norman Mailer, Vladimir Nabokov, John Updike, Kurt Vonnegut*, edited by Mary Bruccoli (1983)

4 *Tennessee Williams*, edited by Margaret A. Van Antwerp and Sally Johns (1984)

5 *American Transcendentalists*, edited by Joel Myerson (1988)

6 *Hardboiled Mystery Writers: Raymond Chandler, Dashiell Hammett, Ross Macdonald*, edited by Matthew J. Bruccoli and Richard Layman (1989)

7 *Modern American Poets: James Dickey, Robert Frost, Marianne Moore*, edited by Karen L. Rood (1989)

8 *The Black Aesthetic Movement*, edited by Jeffrey Louis Decker (1991)

9 *American Writers of the Vietnam War: W. D. Ehrhart, Larry Heinemann, Tim O'Brien, Walter McDonald, John M. Del Vecchio*, edited by Ronald Baughman (1991)

10 *The Bloomsbury Group*, edited by Edward L. Bishop (1992)

11 *American Proletarian Culture: The Twenties and The Thirties*, edited by Jon Christian Suggs (1993)

12 *Southern Women Writers: Flannery O'Connor, Katherine Anne Porter, Eudora Welty*, edited by Mary Ann Wimsatt and Karen L. Rood (1994)

13 *The House of Scribner, 1846-1904*, edited by John Delaney (1996)

14 *Four Women Writers for Children, 1868-1918*, edited by Caroline C. Hunt (1996)

15 *American Expatriate Writers: Paris in the Twenties*, edited by Matthew J. Bruccoli and Robert W. Trogdon (1997)

16 *The House of Scribner, 1905-1930*, edited by John Delaney (1997)

17 *The House of Scribner, 1931-1984*, edited by John Delaney (1998)

18 *British Poets of The Great War: Sassoon, Graves, Owen*, edited by Patrick Quinn (1999)

19 *James Dickey*, edited by Judith S. Baughman (1999)

See also DLB 210, 216, 219, 222, 224, 229, 237, 247

Dictionary of Literary Biography Yearbooks

1980 edited by Karen L. Rood, Jean W. Ross, and Richard Ziegfeld (1981)

1981 edited by Karen L. Rood, Jean W. Ross, and Richard Ziegfeld (1982)

1982 edited by Richard Ziegfeld; associate editors: Jean W. Ross and Lynne C. Zeigler (1983)

1983 edited by Mary Bruccoli and Jean W. Ross; associate editor Richard Ziegfeld (1984)

1984 edited by Jean W. Ross (1985)

1985 edited by Jean W. Ross (1986)

1986 edited by J. M. Brook (1987)

1988 edited by J. M. Brook (1989)

1989 edited by J. M. Brook (1990)

1990 edited by James W. Hipp (1991)

1991 edited by James W. Hipp (1992)

1992 edited by James W. Hipp (1993)

1993 edited by James W. Hipp, contributing editor George Garrett (1994)

1994 edited by James W. Hipp, contributing editor George Garrett (1995)

1995 edited by James W. Hipp, contributing editor George Garrett (1996)

1996 edited by Samuel W. Bruce and L. Kay Webster, contributing editor George Garrett (1997)

1997 edited by Matthew J. Bruccoli and George Garrett, with the assistance of L. Kay Webster (1998)

1998 edited by Matthew J. Bruccoli, contributing editor George Garrett, with the assistance of D. W. Thomas (1999)

1999 edited by Matthew J. Bruccoli, contributing editor George Garrett, with the assistance of D. W. Thomas (2000)

2000 edited by Matthew J. Bruccoli, contributing editor George Garrett, with the assistance of George Parker Anderson (2001)

Concise Series

Concise Dictionary of American Literary Biography, 7 volumes (1988-1999): *The New Consciousness, 1941-1968; Colonization to the American Renaissance, 1640-1865; Realism, Naturalism, and Local Color, 1865-1917; The Twenties, 1917-1929; The Age of Maturity, 1929-1941; Broadening Views, 1968-1988; Supplement: Modern Writers, 1900-1998.*

Concise Dictionary of British Literary Biography, 8 volumes (1991-1992): *Writers of the Middle Ages and Renaissance Before 1660; Writers of the Restoration and Eighteenth Century, 1660-1789; Writers of the Romantic Period, 1789-1832; Victorian Writers, 1832-1890; Late-Victorian and Edwardian Writers, 1890-1914; Modern Writers, 1914-1945; Writers After World War II, 1945-1960; Contemporary Writers, 1960 to Present.*

Concise Dictionary of World Literary Biography, 10 volumes projected (1999-   ): *Ancient Greek and Roman Writers; German Writers; African, Caribbean, and Latin American Writers; South Slavic and Eastern European Writers.*

James Joyce
A Documentary Volume

James Joyce
A Documentary Volume

Edited by
A. Nicholas Fargnoli
Molloy College

A Bruccoli Clark Layman Book
The Gale Group
Detroit • San Francisco • London • Boston • Woodbridge, Conn.

Printed in the United States of America

The paper used in this publication meets the minimum requirements
of American National Standard for Information Sciences–Permanence
Paper for Printed Library Materials, ANSI Z39.48-1984. ∞™

Library of Congress Cataloging-in-Publication Data

James Joyce: a documentary volume / edited by A. Nicholas Fargnoli.
    p. cm.–(Dictionary of literary biography: v. 247)
"A Bruccoli Clark Layman book."
Includes bibliographical references and index.
ISBN 0-7876-4664-4 (alk. paper)
1. Joyce, James, 1882–1941–Handbooks, manuals, etc. 2. Authors, Irish–20th century–Biography.
3. Joyce, James, 1882–1941–Bibliography. I. Fargnoli, A. Nicholas. II. Series.

PR6019.09 Z633565 2001
823'.912–dc21   2001033995
[B]

10 9 8 7 6 5 4 3 2 1

*To Harriett . . .
and to Giuliana, Alessandro, and Gioia . . .
and
in fond memory of
Philip Lyman (1926–1998)*

Contents

Plan of the Series xxi

Introduction. xxiii

Acknowledgments xxvi

Permissions xxvii

Books by James Joyce 3

James Joyce: A Chronology of His Career and Writings 6

Early Life and Work: *Chamber Music* and *Dubliners* 19

Birth and Family 19

At Clongowes Wood College 21

First Publication 22

> Joyce, excerpt from "Ivy Day in the Committee Room"

Belvedere College 24

University College 29

> Joyce, excerpts from *A Portrait of the Artist as a Young Man*
> Joyce, "Ibsen's New Drama," *Fortnightly Review,* 1 April 1900
> Joyce, "The Day of the Rabblement," 1901

Collecting Epiphanies 43

> Joyce, poem XXXV from *Chamber Music*
> Joyce, excerpt from *Stephen Hero*
> Oliver St. John Gogarty, excerpt from
> *As I Was Going Down Sackville Street*
> Joyce, excerpt from *Ulysses*

A First Trip Abroad 46

> Stanislaus Joyce, excerpt from *My Brother's Keeper*

A First Portrait 46

Epiphanies in Criticism 47

> Harry Levin, excerpt from *James Joyce: A Critical Introduction*
> Robert Scholes and Richard Kain, excerpt from
> *The Workshop of Daedalus*

Robert Adams Day, "Dante, Ibsen, Joyce, Epiphanies, and
the Art of Memory," *James Joyce Quarterly*, Spring 1988

Epicleti, Epiclets, and *Dubliners* 49

Nora Barnacle and a Life Abroad 53

Chamber Music 55

On the Title *Chamber Music* 55

Reviews of *Chamber Music* 56

Thomas Kettle, review, *Freeman's Journal*, 1 June 1907
Arthur Symons, "A Book of Songs," *Nation*, 22 June 1907
Excerpts from reviews of *Dubliners* chosen by Joyce, 1914

Setting Joyce's Poems to Music 58

Publishing *Dubliners* 59

Joyce, "A Curious History," *The Egoist*, 15 January 1914
Arthur Symons letter to Joyce, 29 June 1914

Publishing a Protest 61

Reviews of *Dubliners* 66

The Times Literary Supplement, review, 18 June 1914
Athenæum, review, 20 June 1914
Gerald Gould, review, *The New Statesman*, 27 June 1914
Everyman, review, 3 July 1914
Academy, review, 11 July 1914
Ezra Pound, "'Dubliners' and Mr. James Joyce,"
The Egoist, 15 July 1914
Irish Book Lover, review, November 1914
George Moore letter to Sir Edward Marsh, 3 August 1916

Establishing a Reputation: *A Portrait of the Artist
as a Young Man* **and** *Exiles* 72

Turning *Stephen Hero* into *A Portrait* 72

Bernard Benstock, excerpt from *James Joyce*

Publication in *The Egoist* 76

Ezra Pound letter to Joyce, January 1914
Wyndham Lewis's impressions of serialized novel

Supporting Joyce 76

Ezra Pound letter to A. Llewelyn Roberts, 3 August 1915
Ezra Pound letter to Joyce, 7 September 1915
William Butler Yeats letter to Joyce, 29 July 1915
Ezra Pound, "Mr. James Joyce and the Modern Stage,"
The Drama, February 1916
William Butler Yeats letter to Joyce, 26 August 1917
James Joyce, poem from *Chamber Music*

An English Reader's Response 82

    Jonathan Cape letter to James B. Pinker, 26 January 1916

    Ezra Pound letter to James B. Pinker, 30 January 1916

The First Edition of *A Portrait* 83

    B. W. Huebsch letter to Harriet Shaw Weaver, 16 June 1916

Reviews of *A Portrait of the Artist as a Young Man* 84

    Ezra Pound, "At Last the Novel Appears,"
        The Egoist, February 1917

    "A Study in Garbage," *Everyman,* 23 February 1917

    H. G. Wells, "James Joyce," *Nation,* 24 February 1917

    A. Clutton-Brock, "Wild Youth," *The Times Literary*
        Supplement, 1 March 1917

    A.M., "A Sensitivist," *The Manchester Guardian,* 2 March 1917

    Francis Hackett, "Green Sickness," *The New Republic,* 3 March 1917

    Jane Heap, "James Joyce," *The Little Review,* April 1917

    Margaret Anderson, "Note on Joyce and *A Portrait of the Artist*
        as a Young Man," *The Little Review,* April 1917

    "A Dyspeptic Portrait," *Freeman's Journal,* 7 April 1917

    J. C. Squire, "Mr. James Joyce," *The New Statesman,* 14 April 1917

    Irish Book Lover, review, April–May 1917

    John Quinn, "James Joyce, A New Irish Novelist,"
        Vanity Fair, May 1917

    Ezra Pound, editorial, *The Little Review,* May 1917

    Van Wyck Brooks, review, *The Seven Arts,* May 1917

    John Macy, "James Joyce," *The Dial,* 14 June 1917

    New Age, review, 12 July 1917

    Diego Angeli, review, *The Egoist,* February 1918

    John F. Harris, "A Note on James Joyce," *To-Day,* May 1918

Contemporary Writers Respond. 109

    Padraic Colum, "James Joyce," *Pearson's Magazine,* May 1918

    Hart Crane, "Joyce and Ethics," *The Little Review,* July 1918

    Virginia Woolf, "Modern Novels," *The Times Literary*
        Supplement, 10 April 1919

Exiles 118

Reviews of *Exiles* 118

    J. W. G., "Ibsen in Ireland," *Freeman's Journal,* 15 June 1918

    A. Clutton-Brock, "The Mind to Suffer,"
        The Times Literary Supplement, 25 July 1918

    Scofield Thayer, "James Joyce," *The Dial,* 19 September 1918

    Desmond MacCarthy, review, *The New Statesman,* 21 September 1918

    Francis Hackett, review, *The New Republic,* 12 October 1918

    Padraic Colum, "James Joyce as Dramatist," *Nation,* 12 October 1918

    John Rodker, Israel Solon, Samuel A. Tannenbaum, and j h,
        "*Exiles:* A Discussion of James Joyce's Play,"
        The Little Review, January 1919

    Evelyn Scott, "Contemporary of the Future," *The Dial,* October 1920

Reassessing *Exiles* 142

    Francis Fergusson, "*Exiles* and Ibsen's Work,"
        Hound & Horn, April–June 1932

    Bernard Bandler II, "Joyce's *Exiles,*" *Hound & Horn,*
        January–March 1933

    Padraic Colum, introduction to 1951 edition of *Exiles*

Ulysses 155

The Making of *Ulysses* 155

    Frank Budgen, excerpt from *James Joyce and the Making of Ulysses*

    William Butler Yeats letter to John Quinn, 23 July 1918

Ulysses in *The Little Review* 157

    Ezra Pound letter to Joyce, 22 November 1918

A Reaction to the Censorship of *Ulysses*. 158

    R.H.C., "Readers and Writers," *New Age,* 28 April 1921

    Robert McAlmon, excerpt from *Being Geniuses Together:*
        An Autobiography

    Ezra Pound letter to John Quinn, 19 June 1920

Schema for *Ulysses* 159

Shakespeare and Company 159

    George Bernard Shaw letter to Sylvia Beach, 10 October 1921

An Early Affirmation. 164

    Valéry Larbaud, "The *Ulysses* of James Joyce,"
        Criterion, October 1922

Reviews of *Ulysses* 170

    George Rehm, review, *Chicago Tribune,* 13 February 1922

    Stanislaus Joyce comments on Circe episode, 26 February 1922

    Sisley Huddleston, "*Ulysses,*" *Observer,* 5 March 1922

    George Slocombe, review, *Daily Herald,* 17 March 1922

    S. P. B. Mais, "An Irish Revel: And Some Flappers,"
        Daily Express, 25 March 1922

    Aramis, "The Scandal of *Ulysses,*" *Sporting Times,* 1 April 1922

    J. Middleton Murry, "Mr. Joyce's *Ulysses,*"
        The Nation & Athenæum, 22 April 1922

    Arnold Bennett, "James Joyce's *Ulysses,*" *Outlook,* 29 April 1922

    Joseph Collins, "James Joyce's Amazing Chronicle,"
        The New York Times Book Review, 28 May 1922

    Holbrook Jackson, review, *To-Day,* June 1922

    Edmund Wilson, review, *The New Republic,* 5 July 1922

    Mary Colum, "The Confessions of James Joyce,"
        Freeman, 19 July 1922

    Gilbert Seldes, review, *Nation,* 30 August 1922

    Domini Canis, review, *Dublin Review,* July–September 1922

    C. C. Martindale, S. J., review, *Dublin Review,* October–December 1922

    Shane Leslie, review, *Quarterly Review,* October 1922

Commentary on Joyce and *Ulysses* in the 1920s and 1930s 209

    Ezra Pound, "James Joyce et Pécuchet," *Mercure de France,* June 1922

    Cecil Maitland, "Mr. Joyce and the Catholic Tradition,"
        New Witness, 4 August 1922

    Alfred Noyes, "Rottenness in Literature," *Sunday Chronicle,*
        29 October 1922

    Ford Madox Hueffer, "*Ulysses* and the Handling of Indecencies,"
        English Review, December 1922

    Ernest Boyd, excerpt from *Ireland's Literary Renaissance*

    T. S. Eliot, "*Ulysses,* Order and Myth," *The Dial,* November 1923

    Laurence K. Emery, "The *Ulysses* of Mr. James Joyce,"
        Claxon, Winter 1923–1924

    Ford Madox Ford, "Literary Causeries: vii: So She Went
        into the Garden," *Chicago Tribune Sunday Magazine,* 6 April 1924

    Alec Waugh, "The Neo-Georgians," *Fortnightly,* January 1924

    Edwin Muir, "James Joyce: The Meaning of 'Ulysses,'"
        Calendar of Modern Letters, July 1925

    Edmund Gosse letter to Louis Gillet, 7 June 1924

    Edmund Wilson, "James Joyce as a Poet," *The New Republic,*
        November 1925

    E. M. Forster, excerpt from *Aspects of the Novel*

    Wyndham Lewis, "An Analysis of the Mind of James Joyce,"
        Time and Western Man

    Stuart Gilbert, excerpt from his introduction to
        Letters of James Joyce, volume 1

    John Eglinton, "The Beginnings of Joyce," *Life and Letters,*
        December 1932

The Pirating of *Ulysses* 260

    Protest statement, 2 February 1927

Jung and Joyce. 262

    C. G. Jung letter to Joyce, September 1932

The Circulation of *Ulysses* in England 262

    Paul Léon letter to F. V. Morley, 19 November 1933

Judge Woolsey's Decision. 263

    OPINION A. 110-59 United States of America,
        Libelant V. One Book called "Ulysses"

    Geoffrey Faber letter to Donald Somervell, 5 January 1934

    T. S. Eliot letter to Joyce, 9 January 1934

    "*Ulysses* Pure, Customs 'Goofy,'" *New York Evening Post,*
        7 August 1934

    "Higher Court Holds *Ulysses* Is Not Obscene,"
        New York Herald-Tribune, 8 August 1934

Reviews of the First American Edition of *Ulysses* 269

    Horace Gregory, review, *New York Herald Tribune Books,* 21 January 1934

    Gilbert Seldes, review, *New York Evening Journal,* 27 January 1934

Samuel Harden Church, "A Stableboy's Book,"
    Carnegie Magazine, February 1934

Robert Cantwell, review, *New Outlook,* March 1934

Edwin Baird, review, *Real America,* April 1934

Publication of *Ulysses* in England 277

Allen Lane letter to Ralph Pinker, 29 August 1934

G. W. Stonier, "Leviathan," *The New Statesman and Nation,*
    10 October 1936

"Interpretations of 'Ulysses,'" *The Times Literary Supplement,*
    23 January 1937

George Bernard Shaw letter to the editor of *Picture Post,*
    3 June 1939

Ulysses as a Movie 282

Last Works: *Pomes Penyeach* and *Finnegans Wake* 287

Life and Work, 1923–1939 287

Richard Ellmann, excerpt from introduction to the
    Letters of James Joyce, volume 3
"Finnegan's Wake"

Pomes Penyeach 294

George Russell [Y.O.], review, *Irish Statesman,* 23 July 1927

Edmund Wilson, "New Poems by Joyce," *The New Republic,*
    26 October 1927

Robert Hillyer, excerpt from *New Adelphi,* March 1928

Responses to *Work in Progress* in the 1920s 295

Desmond McCarthy, "Affable Hawk," *The New Statesmen,* 14 May 1927

William Carlos Williams, "A Note on the Recent Work
    of James Joyce," *transition,* November 1927

Padraic Colum, "River Episode from James Joyce's
    Uncompleted Work," *The Dial,* April 1928

"Mr. Joyce's Experiment," *The Times Literary Supplement,*
    20 December 1928

Vladimir Dixon's Letter 302

Cyril Connolly, "The Position of Joyce," *Life and Letters,*
    April 1929

"Triumph of Jabberwocky," *The New York Times,*
    23 August 1929

Arnold Bennett, "Comment on *Anna Livia Plurabelle,*"
    London Evening Standard, 19 September 1929

Michael Stuart, "The Dubliner and his Dowdili
    (A Note on the Sublime)," *transition,* November 1929

Joyce's Poetry and *The Joyce Book* 317

Morton D. Zabel, "The Lyrics of James Joyce," *Poetry,* July 1930

Padraic Colum, "James Joyce as Poet," *The Joyce Book*

Arthur Symons, Epilogue, *The Joyce Book*

Work in Progress in the 1930s 326

Rebecca West, "James Joyce and His Followers,"
New York Herald Tribune Books, 12 January 1930

J. Leon Edel, "The New Writers," *Canadian Forum,* June 1930

G. W. Stonier, "Mr. James Joyce in Progress,"
The New Statesman, 28 June 1930

"Mr. Joyce's Experiment," *The Times Literary Supplement,*
17 July 1930

Sean O'Faolain, letter to the editor, *Criterion,*
October 1930

Stuart Gilbert, "A Footnote to Work in Progress," *New Experiment,*
Spring 1931

Michael Stuart, "Mr. Joyce's Word Creatures," *Symposium,*
October 1931

D. G. Bridson, "Views and Review," *New English Weekly,*
5 January 1933

Eugene Jolas, "Marginalia to James Joyce's *Work in Progress,*"
transition, February 1933

G. W. Stonier, "Joyce Without End," *The New Statesman
and Nation,* 22 September 1934

Reviews of *Finnegans Wake* 343

Paul Rosenfeld, "James Joyce's Jabberwocky,"
The Saturday Review of Literature, 6 May 1939

"The Progress of Mr Joyce," *The Times Literary Supplement,*
6 May 1939

Padraic Colum, review, *The New York Times,* 7 May 1939

Malcolm Muggeridge, review, *Time and Tide,* 20 May 1939

Edwin Muir, review, *Listener,* 11 May 1939

Alfred Kazin, review, *New York Herald Tribune,* 21 May 1939

Richard Aldington, review, *The Atlantic Monthly,* June 1939

Review, *The Irish Times,* 3 June 1939

Mary Colum, "The Old and the New," *The Forum and Century,*
October 1939

Illness and Death 357

"James Joyce Dies; Wrote 'Ulysses,'" *The New York Times,*
13 January 1941

"James Joyce Is Dead at Zurich," *New York Herald Tribune,*
13 January 1941

Tributes 363

Thornton Wilder, "James Joyce, 1882–1941," *Poetry,*
1940–1941

Remembering James Joyce

Eugene Jolas, "My Friend James Joyce," *Partisan Review,*
March–April 1941

Images of an Artist

For Further Reading and Reference. 375

Letters 375

Bibliographies 375

Selected Biographies and Biographical Sources .376

General Criticism, Context, and Interpretation. .380

Criticism and Interpretation by Work. 386

Catalogues and Collections 404

Selected Documentaries and Theatrical and Motion-Picture Adaptations. . . .405

Journals 407

Special Issues 407

Organizations 408

Papers 408

Cumulative Index 411

Plan of the Series

. . . Almost the most prodigious asset of a country, and perhaps its most precious possession, is its native literary product—when that product is fine and noble and enduring.

Mark Twain*

The advisory board, the editors, and the publisher of the *Dictionary of Literary Biography* are joined in endorsing Mark Twain's declaration. The literature of a nation provides an inexhaustible resource of permanent worth. Our purpose is to make literature and its creators better understood and more accessible to students and the reading public, while satisfying the needs of teachers and researchers.

To meet these requirements, *literary biography* has been construed in terms of the author's achievement. The most important thing about a writer is his writing. Accordingly, the entries in *DLB* are career biographies, tracing the development of the author's canon and the evolution of his reputation.

The purpose of *DLB* is not only to provide reliable information in a usable format but also to place the figures in the larger perspective of literary history and to offer appraisals of their accomplishments by qualified scholars.

The publication plan for *DLB* resulted from two years of preparation. The project was proposed to Bruccoli Clark by Frederick G. Ruffner, president of the Gale Research Company, in November 1975. After specimen entries were prepared and typeset, an advisory board was formed to refine the entry format and develop the series rationale. In meetings held during 1976, the publisher, series editors, and advisory board approved the scheme for a comprehensive biographical dictionary of persons who contributed to literature. Editorial work on the first volume began in January 1977, and it was published in 1978. In order to make *DLB* more than a dictionary and to compile volumes that individually have claim to status as literary history, it was decided to organize volumes by topic, period, or

*From an unpublished section of Mark Twain's autobiography, copyright by the Mark Twain Company

genre. Each of these freestanding volumes provides a biographical-bibliographical guide and overview for a particular area of literature. We are convinced that this organization—as opposed to a single alphabet method—constitutes a valuable innovation in the presentation of reference material. The volume plan necessarily requires many decisions for the placement and treatment of authors. Certain figures will be included in separate volumes, but with different entries emphasizing the aspect of his career appropriate to each volume. Ernest Hemingway, for example, is represented in *American Writers in Paris, 1920–1939* by an entry focusing on his expatriate apprenticeship; he is also in *American Novelists, 1910–1945* with an entry surveying his entire career, as well as in *American Short-Story Writers, 1910–1945, Second Series* with an entry concentrating on his short fiction. Each volume includes a cumulative index of the subject authors and articles.

Since 1981 the series has been further augmented by the *DLB Yearbooks,* which update published entries, add new entries to keep the *DLB* current with contemporary activity, and provide articles on literary history. There have also been nineteen *DLB Documentary Series* volumes which provide illustrations, facsimiles, and biographical and critical source materials for figures, works, or groups judged to have particular interest for students. In 1999 the *Documentary Series* was incorporated into the *DLB* volume numbering system beginning with *DLB 210, Ernest Hemingway.*

We define literature as the *intellectual commerce of a nation:* not merely as belles lettres but as that ample and complex process by which ideas are generated, shaped, and transmitted. *DLB* entries are not limited to "creative writers" but extend to other figures who in their time and in their way influenced the mind of a people. Thus the series encompasses historians, journalists, publishers, book collectors, and screenwriters. By this means readers of *DLB* may be aided to perceive literature not as cult scripture in the keeping of intellectual high priests but firmly positioned at the center of a nation's life.

DLB includes the major writers appropriate to each volume and those standing in the ranks behind them. Scholarly and critical counsel has been sought in deciding which minor figures to include and how full their entries should be. Wherever possible, useful references are made to figures who do not warrant separate entries.

Each *DLB* volume has an expert volume editor responsible for planning the volume, selecting the figures for inclusion, and assigning the entries. Volume editors are also responsible for preparing, where appropriate, appendices surveying the major periodicals and literary and intellectual movements for their volumes, as well as lists of further readings. Work on the series as a whole is coordinated at the Bruccoli Clark Layman editorial center in Columbia, South Carolina, where the editorial staff is responsible for accuracy and utility of the published volumes.

One feature that distinguishes *DLB* is the illustration policy–its concern with the iconography of literature. Just as an author is influenced by his surroundings, so is the reader's understanding of the author enhanced by a knowledge of his environment. Therefore *DLB* volumes include not only drawings, paintings, and photographs of authors, often depicting them at various stages in their careers, but also illustrations of their families and places where they lived. Title pages are regularly reproduced in facsimile along with dust jackets for modern authors. The dust jackets are a special feature of *DLB* because they often document better than anything else the way in which an author's work was perceived in its own time. Specimens of the writers' manuscripts and letters are included when feasible.

Samuel Johnson rightly decreed that "The chief glory of every people arises from its authors." The purpose of the *Dictionary of Literary Biography* is to compile literary history in the surest way available to us–by accurate and comprehensive treatment of the lives and work of those who contributed to it.

The *DLB* Advisory Board

Introduction

James Joyce, self-exiled Irish novelist and poet, is one of the most important writers in world literature and arguably the greatest modernist author of the twentieth century. Joyce's influence is perduring and immeasurable. *A Portrait of the Artist as a Young Man* (1916), *Ulysses* (1922), and *Finnegans Wake* (1939) not only belong to but also help define both the modernist and postmodernist canon. Along with other modernist writers such as T. S. Eliot, Virginia Woolf, and Ezra Pound, Joyce forever changed literature.

Joyce's works, which span the first four decades of the twentieth century and which were both condemned and acclaimed, are characterized by unparalleled innovation and ingenuity. The narrative technique of the interior monologue, often called stream of consciousness, was masterfully manipulated by Joyce and is virtually identified with his style of writing. A phrase first used by William James in *Principles of Psychology* (1890), the stream of consciousness was later employed by critics to identify a literary technique that can refer to both a character's inner thoughts and a narrator's style. The interior monologue Joyce adapted from the French novelist Edouard Dujardin, who first used the technique in his 1887 novel, *Les lauriers sont coupés* (translated as *We'll to the Woods No More*). According to Joyce, the one who coined the term *interior monologue* was the French novelist and translator Valéry Larbaud.

Like the stream of consciousness, the interior monologue presents the dynamic and disjointed flow of thought and sense perceptions, but unlike it, some contend, the interior monologue disregards basic rules of syntax and grammar. Though the terms are usually used interchangeably, a slight distinction should be made when applying them to Joyce. It is more precise to associate Joyce with the interior monologue, especially in *Ulysses,* than with the stream of consciousness. The last chapter of the novel, the Penelope episode, is written entirely in the style of the interior monologue and given over completely to Molly Bloom's inner feelings, impressions, and thoughts. Though the stylistic device of the interior monologue can cause difficulties for the reader, it can also provide a rich portrait of a character. It offers a much more direct presentation of a character's most intimate thoughts than traditional narrative techniques.

The influence of Joyce's innovations was apparent upon his contemporaries such as Woolf, William Faulkner, Aldous Huxley, Hermann Broch, Joyce Cary, and Jorge Luis Borges. The interior monologue was particularly helpful to Faulkner in his conception of *The Sound and the Fury* (1929) and *As I Lay Dying* (1930). As Michael Groden points out in "Criticism in New Composition: *Ulysses* and *The Sound and the Fury,*" published in the October 1975 issue of *Twentieth Century Literature,* with the technique of the interior monologue Faulkner in *The Sound and the Fury* was able to resolve problems with characterization that he faced in two earlier novels, *Soldiers' Pay* (1926) and *Mosquitos* (1927). F. Scott Fitzgerald, an author not normally associated with experimental writing, employed the interior monologue in a limited way in chapter 10 of book 2 of *Tender Is the Night* (1934), a chapter on which the whole structure of the novel pivots. Later writers, including Yukio Mishima, Anthony Burgess, William Gaddis, and Thomas Pynchon, have also been influenced by Joyce and his stylistic devices. Any discussion of the stream-of-consciousness or interior monologue technique inevitably includes James Joyce.

Another identifiably Joycean stylistic technique is that of free indirect discourse. Found throughout Joyce's writings, this technique mingles the linguistic traits or voice of a character with that of the narrator, requiring the reader to discern who the speaker is. The opening line of "The Dead," the last short story in *Dubliners,* is an example often cited: "Lily, the caretaker's daughter, was literally run off her feet." That Lily in fact is not "literally run off her feet" is an unmistakable exaggeration reflecting Lily's voice in describing the feverish pitch of her activity; the voice, then, can be attributed to her, once the reader observes her speech patterns, and not to the narrator. In correcting Wyndham Lewis's comments in *Time and Western Man* (1927) on Joyce's *A Portrait of the Artist as a Young Man* and the "inadvertency of diction," Hugh Kenner in *Joyce's Voices* (1978) suggests that "*the narrative idiom need not be that of the narrator's*" and names this technique the Uncle Charles Principle, after Simon Dedalus's uncle in chapter 2 of *A Portrait of the Artist as a Young Man*. Identification of voice is problematic in *Ulysses* and even more so in *Finnegans Wake*. Free indirect discourse is very much a vital part of Joyce's style and an avenue into Joyce's aesthetic achievement.

Joyce's innovative appropriation of literature and mythology, of the religious and theological traditions that formed his thinking, and of the cultural and social environment that shaped his perceptions figures prominently throughout his canon. Nourished by these sources and unbounded by convention, Joyce's creative imagination found expression in new ways that also integrated his musical and linguistic talents. In one of the first critical essays on *Ulysses*, "*Ulysses*, Order and Myth" (1923), T. S. Eliot observed that Joyce's use of myth and Homer's *Odyssey*

> has the importance of a scientific discovery. No one else has built a novel upon such a foundation before. . . . In using the myth, in manipulating a continuous parallel between contemporaneity and antiquity, Mr Joyce is pursuing a method which others must pursue after him. They will not be imitators, any more than the scientist who uses the discoveries of an Einstein in pursuing his own, independent, further investigation. It is simply a way of controlling, of ordering, of giving a shape and a significance to the immense panorama of futility and anarchy which is contemporary history. . . . Instead of narrative method, we may now use the mythical method.

Mythical references and their function in Joyce's works, especially in *Finnegans Wake*, continue to be important areas of critical discussion. The first full-length study of the author's last work, *A Skeleton Key to Finnegans Wake* (1944), by Joseph Campbell and Henry Morton Robinson, emphasized its mythic dimensions. Of course, later critical writings, such as R. J. Schork's *Greek and Hellenic Culture in Joyce* and *Latin and Roman Culture in Joyce* (1997), move beyond the mythic parameters of Campbell and Robinson and elucidate the broader classical allusions and vocabulary operating throughout Joyce's writings, which have been studied from a wide variety of critical angles.

Joyce's Jesuit schooling from his days at Clongowes Wood College in 1888 through his graduation from University College, Dublin, in 1902, where he was awarded a degree in modern languages, furnished him with an education that, in combination with his own literary interests and tastes, contributed to an artistic imagination that revolutionized twentieth-century literature. Joyce's poetics of allusion, his profound sensitivity to sound, and his playfulness with the nuances of words are major characteristics of his writings easily detected in his first published book, *Chamber Music* (1907), a suite of thirty-six lyrical poems. These poems show a sympathy for Elizabethan music and style as well as for symbolist techniques. Joyce's command of language and narrative perspective progressively heighten from *Dubliners* to *Ulysses*, reaching their highest level with the publication of *Finnegans Wake*. Joyce's literary techniques, narrative strategies, musical sensitivities, use of popular culture, linguistic adeptness, and mental acuity culminate in a unique and formidable body of work.

His writings reveal the richness of a fertile mind, for Joyce read widely—and in many languages. Though the list is not exhaustive, the following writers had a major impact on the formation of his thinking and imagination: Giambattista Vico, Giordano Bruno, Aristotle, St. Thomas Aquinas, Dante, Henrik Ibsen, Daniel Defoe, William Shakespeare, William Blake, Jonathan Swift, and John Dowland. The thinking of Vico, the Italian philosopher of jurisprudence, history, and social thought, informs both *Ulysses* and *Finnegans Wake*. In *The New Science* (*Principi di scienza nuova di Giambattista Vico d'intorno alla comune natura nazioni*, third edition, 1744), a highly original study of mythology and the development of society, Vico postulates a cyclical theory of history that consists of three distinct ages: that of the gods, of heroes, and of humans. The last is followed by a *ricorso*, a collapse into chaos that begins the cycle anew. Joyce thoroughly absorbed Vico's insights into language and the recurring patterns of human history; these insights are fundamental to understanding Joyce's use of myth and pattern types in *Ulysses* and *Finnegans Wake*. Vico's notion of recurring patterns and ages relates directly to the structure of *Finnegans Wake*, which opens with a clear reference to the philosopher: "riverrun, past Eve and Adam's, from swerve of shore to bend of bay, brings us by a commodius vicus of recirculation back to Howth Castle and Environs."

The Italian Renaissance philosopher Giordano Bruno also influenced Joyce. A fiercely independent thinker, Bruno undermined philosophical orthodoxy with anti-Aristotelian views. He paid the price for his originality, as he was burned at the stake for heresy in Rome in February 1600.

When Joyce thought of becoming an actor in his late teens, he chose Gordon Brown as a stage name. Joyce also greatly admired the Elizabethan lutenist and composer John Dowland. According to his brother Stanislaus, Joyce copied out many of Dowland's songs. The poems of *Chamber Music* show an indebtedness to Dowland.

Aristotle and Aquinas considerably influenced Joyce's ideas, especially in regard to metaphysics and aesthetics. Aristotle and Aquinas are referred to throughout his works. Joyce pays tribute to these thinkers as early as his broadside "The Holy Office" (1904), in which he attacks the Dublin literati:

> Myself unto myself will give
> This name, Katharsis-Purgative.
> I, who dishevelled ways forsook
> To hold the poets' grammar-book,
> Bringing to tavern and to brothel
> The mind of witty Aristotle,
> Lest bards in the attempt should err
> Must here be my interpreter:
> Wherefore receive now from my lip
> Peripatetic scholarship.
> . . . .
> So distantly I turn to view
> The shamblings of that motley crew,
> Those souls that hate the strength that mine has
> Steeled in the school of old Aquinas.

Joyce's first published article, "Ibsen's New Drama," focused on Ibsen's last play, *When We Dead Awaken.* Joyce was eighteen and a university student at the time the essay was published in the 1 April 1900 issue of the *Fortnightly Review.* Pleased by the article when it came to his attention, Ibsen wrote to his English translator, William Archer, who quickly informed Joyce of the correspondence. A year later Joyce sent Ibsen greetings on the playwright's seventy-third birthday in a letter written in Norwegian that expressed not only Joyce's admiration for Ibsen but confidence in his own artistic vocation.

Dante, as Mary T. Reynolds argues in *Joyce and Dante: The Shaping Imagination* (1981), "is a massive presence" in Joyce's writings. She contends that Joyce's "imagination was saturated with Dante," but that he used him very differently from the way he incorporated elements from Shakespeare and Homer. "Joyce has taken Dante's pattern and epistemology," Reynolds writes, "to reproduce in Dublin a spiritual journey, in conscious emulation of Dante's similar use of Virgil, whose *Aeneid* in turn adapted Homer." The journey motif on one level or another—spiritual or artistic—is clearly present in Joyce's works.

The English novelist and journalist Daniel Defoe appealed to Joyce for his realistic portrayal of life and for his concern with everyday events and common speech patterns. While living in Trieste in 1912, Joyce lectured on Defoe's realism at the Università del Popolo. He also lectured on Blake's idealism. In their introductory note to the incomplete manuscript of Joyce's lecture on Blake published in *The Critical Writings of James Joyce* (1959), Ellsworth Mason and Richard Ellmann comment on Joyce's affinities to these two very

different writers: "Defoe and Blake, in their different ways, were working with the conception of an archetypal man. Robinson Crusoe summarizes a people and a time as Bloom does. Blake's Albion, the universal man who symbolizes eternity, is related to that other giant form, Finnegan, in whose life, death and awakening Joyce finds all human enterprise and aspiration."

A Protestant and ordained priest of the Anglican Church, Swift was born in Dublin, where he served as dean of St. Patrick's Cathedral. Despite his predilection for things English, he nevertheless was a staunch critic of British imperialism and supported social justice, which garnered him the admiration of the Irish. Swift's stylistic and thematic influence on Joyce is particularly evident in *Finnegans Wake.* Swift's idiosyncratic use of language in his *Journal to Stella* (1948) and his unsettling relationships with Esther Johnson and Esther Vanhomrigh found their way into Joyce's portrayal of the emotional, sexual, and psychological conflicts of characters in *Finnegans Wake.*

Between November 1912 and February 1913, Joyce gave a series of lectures on *Hamlet* at the university in Trieste. These lectures, titled "Amleto di G. Shakespeare" (Shakespeare's *Hamlet*), are now lost, but Joyce's notes can be found in the Joyce collection at the Cornell University Library. Shakespearean references are pervasive throughout Joyce, and in the Scylla and Charybdis episode, chapter 9 of *Ulysses,* Joyce devotes a concentrated amount of time on him. In his schema of the novel, Joyce presents Stephen Dedalus as a Hamlet figure.

Dictionary of Literary Biography 247: James Joyce: A Documentary Volume assembles significant published responses to Joyce's works in chronological order with brief introductory remarks and with related material and illustrations. The volume gives the reader a sense of the history of the contemporary criticism of Joyce's writings as his reputation was emerging and should be used in conjunction with reading his works; it does not provide a detailed discussion or interpretation of his texts. Readers familiar with Robert H. Deming's invaluable *James Joyce: The Critical Heritage* (1970) will recognize the indebtedness this volume owes to it, for both make accessible material that might otherwise be unavailable. It is hoped, though, that through its many illustrations and editorial headnotes *DLB 247: James Joyce: A Documentary Volume* will provide a more varied means for the reader to come to terms with Joyce's works.

–A. Nicholas Fargnoli

Acknowledgments

This book was produced by Bruccoli Clark Layman, Inc. Karen L. Rood is senior editor. George Parker Anderson was the in-house editor. He was assisted by Nikki La Rocque.

Production manager is Philip B. Dematteis.

Administrative support was provided by Ann M. Cheschi, Amber L. Coker, and Angi Pleasant.

Accountant is Ann-Marie Holland.

Copyediting supervisor is Sally R. Evans. The copyediting staff includes Phyllis A. Avant, Brenda Carol Blanton, Worthy B. Evans, Melissa D. Hinton, William Tobias Mathes, Rebecca Mayo, Nancy E. Smith, and Elizabeth Jo Ann Sumner. Freelance copyeditor is Brenda Cabra.

Editorial associates are Jennifer Reid and Michael S. Martin.

Database manager is José A. Juarez.

Layout and graphics supervisor is Janet E. Hill. The graphics staff includes Karla Corley Brown and Zoe R. Cook.

Office manager is Kathy Lawler Merlette.

Photography supervisor is Paul Talbot. Photography editor is Scott Nemzek.

Digital photographic copy work was performed by Joseph M. Bruccoli.

The SGML staff includes Jaime All, Frank Graham, Linda Dalton Mullinax, Jason Paddock, and Alex Snead.

Systems manager is Marie L. Parker.

Typesetting supervisor is Kathleen M. Flanagan. The typesetting staff includes Jaime All, Patricia Marie Flanagan, Mark J. McEwan, and Pamela D. Norton. Freelance typesetter is Wanda Adams.

Walter W. Ross did library research. He was assisted by Jaime All, Steven Gross, and the following librarians at the Thomas Cooper Library of the University of South Carolina: circulation department head Tucker Taylor; reference department head Virginia W. Weathers; Brette Barclay, Marilee Birchfield, Paul Cammarata, Gary Geer, Michael Macan, Tom Marcil, Rose Marshall, and Sharon Verba; interlibrary loan department head John Brunswick; and interlibrary loan staff Robert Arndt, Hayden Battle, Barry Bull, Jo Cottingham, Marna Hostetler, Marieum McClary, Erika Peake, and Nelson Rivera.

The editor acknowledges with sincere gratitude the many colleagues and friends whose assistance has made his task much easier: Phillip Ahrens; Laura Barnes; Rockville Camera; Joshua Chapman; Winnie Chen; Cynthia Cox; Kathy Duffy; Anne Dupré; Roger Dupré; Alessandro Fargnoli; Gioia Fargnoli; Giuliana Fargnoli; Harriett Fargnoli; Sidney Feshbach; Sister Elizabeth Gill, O.P.; Michael Patrick Gillespie; Joel Greenberg; Michael Groden; Ciceil Gross; Murray Gross; Carol Kealiher; Robert Joseph Kinpoitner; Laura Linke; Alexandra Lipsky; Philip Lyman; Lucretia Joyce Lyons; Daniel C. Maguire; Robert D. Martin; Rev. Leonard Moloney, S.J.; Sister Patricia A. Morris, O.P.; Sonia Moss; Trisha O'Neill; Brian Quinn; Marie-Anne Rosembert; Myra T. Russel; Joseph Roughan; Martin D. Snyder; Faith Steinberg; and Norman A. Weil.

Special thanks must be given to Conrad Schoeffling and Manju Prasad-Rao of the C. W. Post Library of Long Island University and to the Irish Tourist Board for generously providing many of the illustrations. It must also be mentioned that *James Joyce: The Critical Heritage,* 2 volumes, edited by Robert H. Demming (London: Routledge & Kegan Paul, 1970), was invaluable in the organization and selection of material to be included in this volume.

Acknowledgment is also made to the Council of Trustees, National Library of Ireland, for reproducing the first page of "The Sisters" as it appeared in *The Irish Homestead.*

Permissions

The Atlantic Monthly
Richard Aldington's review of *Finnegans Wake*. Originally published in the June 1939 issue of *The Atlantic Monthly*.

Beinecke Rare Book and Manuscript Library, Yale University
Photos of Joyce as a baby, Joyce by C. P. Curran in 1904, Lucia Joyce as a young woman, and Joyce recuperating after an eye operation in the 1920s.

Belvedere College
Four photos of Joyce, a page from the college roll book, a record of Joyce's election as the prefect of the Sodality of the Blessed Virgin Mary, and pages from an 1898 Whitsunday play program appear courtesy of Belvedere College. Copyright and ownership belong to Belvedere College, Dublin, c/o Society of Jesus.

Carnegie Magazine
Samuel Harden Church, "A Stableboy's Book," *Carnegie Magazine*, VII, 279–281 (February 1934).

Continuum International Publishing Group Inc.
Bernard Benstock, excerpt from *James Joyce* (Copyright © 1985 by Frederick Ungar Publishing Data).

Cornell University, Division of Rare and Manuscript Collections
Clipping from *The Irish Times* mentioning prize awarded Joyce in Feis Ceoil competition; printed announcement of a lecture to be given by Valéry Larbaud; contract with Grant Richards for the publication of *Dubliners*; Royal University of Ireland matriculation certificate; extracts from press notices and reviews of *Dubliners*; extracts from English, American, and Continental reviews of *A Portrait of the Artist as a Young Man*; extracts from press notices and reviews of *Exiles*.

John Dixon
Vladimir Dixon's letter to Joyce, "Dear Mr. Germs Choice," and a photograph of Vladimir Dixon.

T. S. Eliot Estate
T. S. Eliot's 9 January 1934 letter to Joyce.

Ellmann Properties and Penguin Putnam Inc.
Richard Ellman, "Paris 1920–1939," excerpt from introduction to volume 3 of the *Letters of James Joyce*. Used by permission of Viking Penguin, a division of Penguin Putnam Inc., and Ellmann Properties.

Faber and Faber
Geoffrey Faber's 5 January 1934 letter to Donald Somervell.

Indiana University Press
Frank Budgen, excerpt from *James Joyce and the Making of Ulysses*.

Indiana University Press and Gillon Aitken Associates
Hugh Kenner's schema from *Dublin's Joyce* (Bloomington: Indiana University Press, 1956).

The Irish Statesman
Review of *Pomes Penyeach* by George Russell (pseudonym Æ) (23 July 1927).

James Joyce Quarterly
Robert Adams Day, "Dante, Ibsen, Joyce, Epiphanies, and the Art of Memory," *James Joyce Quarterly*, 25 (Spring 1988): 360–361; Arthur Symons, 29 June 1914 letter to Joyce, *James Joyce Quarterly*, 4 (Winter 1967): 98.

Wyndham Lewis Memorial Trust
Wyndham Lewis, "An Analysis of the Mind of James Joyce," *Time and Western Man* (1927)–© Wyndham Lewis and the Estate of the late Mrs. Wyndham Lewis by permission of the Wyndham Lewis Memorial Trust.

Library of Congress
Man Ray's photo of Joyce, circa 1940; photo of Joyce wearing a hat, 27 March 1933; and Hannah Thomas's woodcut of Joyce, 1956.

The Limited Editions Club
Title page, Aeolus drawing, Cyclops drawing, and Nausicaa drawing from *Ulysses* (New York: Limited Editions Club, 1935).

Marquette University,
Patrick and Beatrice Haggerty Museum of Art
Death mask of James Joyce. Courtesy of Patrick and Beatrice Haggerty Museum of Art, Marquette University, Milwaukee, Wisconsin, Gift of Mr. and Mrs. Paul J. Polansky, 77.10. Copyright © 1998 Marquette University.

New Directions Publishing Corporation
Ezra Pound letters to Joyce: 17 and 19 January 1914 (excerpts), 3 August 1915, September 1915 (excerpt), 30 January 1916, 22 November 1918 (excerpt)–from *Pound/Joyce: Letters & Essays,* copyright © 1967 by Ezra Pound. Reprinted by permission of New Directions Publishing Corp.; Harry Levin, excerpt from *James Joyce,* copyright © 1941, 1960 New Directions Publishing Corp. Reprinted by permission of New Directions Publishing Corp.; William Carlos Williams, "A Note on the Recent Work of James Joyce," copyright © 1954 by William Carlos Williams. Reprinted by permission of New Directions Publishing Corp.

The New Republic
Edmund Wilson, "James Joyce as a Poet" (November 1925): 279–280 and Wilson's review of *Pomes Penyeach* (26 October 1927): 268.

New Statesman
Desmond McCarthy, "Affable Hawk," *New Statesman* (14 May 1927). © New Statesman, 2001.

The New York Times
"A New Work by James Joyce," an obituary for Joyce (13 January 1941), and an excerpt from "Triumph of Jabberwocky."

News Int. Associated Services
Times Literary Supplement reviews: A. Clutton-Brock, "Mr. Joyce's Experiment," 20 December 1928; A. Glendinning, "Mr. Joyce's Experiment," 17 July 1930; A. Clutton-Brock, "Interpretations of *Ulysses,*" 23 January 1937; R. Scott-James, "The Progress of Mr. Joyce," 6 May 1939.

Northwestern University Press
Robert Scholes and Richard M. Kain, *The Workshop of Daedalus* (Evanston: Northwestern University Press, 1965), pp. 3–4.

Penguin Putnam Inc.
"Introduction," by Padraic Colum, copyright 1951 by Viking Penguin Inc., renewed, from *Exiles* by Joyce. Used by permission of Viking Penguin, a division of Penguin Putnam Inc.

Poetry
Morton D. Zabel, "The Lyrics of James Joyce," *Poetry* (July 1930).

Photo Researchers, Inc.
Gisele Freund portrait of Joyce. © Gisele Freund/Photo Researchers.

Princeton University Press
Carl Gustave Jung's 27 September 1932 letter to Joyce.

The Society of Authors on behalf of the Bernard Shaw Estate
Bernard Shaw: 10 October 1921 letter to Sylvia Beach and extract from letter to the editor of *Picture Post,* 3 June 1939.

Southern Illinois University
Photos of Joyce at two, Joyce's mother, Joyce with University College friends Clancy and Byrne, Joyce in graduation robes, Nora, the Volta Theatre, Joyce in Zurich, 7 Eccles Street, Joyce with his son George, the Joyce family in Paris, Joyce with Sylvia Beach, and the first page of G. Molyneux Palmer's handwritten setting of CM XXXI. Courtesy of the Croessmann Collection of James Joyce, Special Collections/Morris Library, Southern Illinois University, Carbondale.

TimePix
Photos of Joyce on the 29 January 1934 and the 8 May 1939 covers of *Time.*

Dictionary of Literary Biography® • Volume Two Hundred Forty-Seven

James Joyce
A Documentary Volume

Dictionary of Literary Biography

Books by James Joyce

See also the Joyce entries in *DLB 10: Modern British Dramatists, 1900–1945; DLB 19: British Poets, 1880–1914; DLB 36: British Novelists, 1890–1929: Modernists; DLB 162: British Short-Fiction Writers, 1915–1945; DLB Yearbook: 1982; DLB Yearbook: 1984; DLB Yearbook: 1985;* and *DLB Yearbook: 1997.*

BOOKS: *Chamber Music* (London: Elkin Mathews, 1907; New York: Huebsch, 1918);

Dubliners (London: Richards, 1914; New York: Huebsch, 1916);

A Portrait of the Artist as a Young Man (New York: Huebsch, 1916; London: Egoist Press, 1917);

Exiles: A Play in Three Acts (London: Richards, 1918; New York: Huebsch, 1918); augmented, with notes by Joyce (New York: Viking, 1951);

Ulysses (Paris: Shakespeare & Company, 1922; revised, 1924; London: Egoist Press, 1922; New York: Random House, 1934);

Pomes Penyeach (Paris: Shakespeare & Company, 1927; Princeton: Sylvia Beach, 1931; London: Harmsworth, 1932);

Collected Poems (New York: Black Sun, 1936);

Finnegans Wake (London: Faber & Faber, 1939; New York: Viking, 1939);

Stephen Hero, edited by Theodore Spencer (London: Cape, 1944; New York: New Directions, 1944); augmented, edited by John J. Slocum and Herbert Cahoon (London: Cape, 1956; New York: New Directions, 1956; augmented, New York: New Directions, 1963);

The Early Joyce: The Book Reviews, 1902–1903, edited by Stanislaus Joyce and Ellsworth Mason (Colorado Springs: Mamalujo, 1955);

Epiphanies (Buffalo, N.Y.: Lockwood Memorial Library, University of Buffalo, 1959);

The Critical Writings of James Joyce, edited by Ellsworth Mason and Richard Ellmann (New York: Viking, 1959);

The Workshop of Dedalus: James Joyce and the Materials for "A Portrait of the Artist as a Young Man," edited by Robert Scholes and Richard M. Kain (Evanston, Ill.: Northwestern University Press, 1965);

Giacomo Joyce, edited by Ellmann (New York: Viking, 1968);

Ulysses: A Facsimile of the Manuscript, edited by Clive Driver (New York: Farrar, Straus & Giroux, 1975);

Ulysses Notebooks, edited by Phillip F. Herring (Charlottesville: University of Virginia Press, 1977);

James Joyce in Padua, edited and translated by Louis Berrone (New York: Random House, 1977);

The James Joyce Archive, 63 volumes, edited by Michael Groden, Hans Walter Gabler, David Hayman, A. Walton Litz, and Danis Rose (New York & London: Garland, 1977–1979);

Poems and Epiphanies, edited by Ellmann and Litz (New York: Viking / London: Faber & Faber, 1990);

James Joyce: Poems and Shorter Writings, edited by Ellmann, Litz, and John Whittier-Ferguson (London: Faber & Faber, 1991);

James Joyce: Poems and Exiles, edited, with an introduction and notes, by J. C. C. Mays (London: Penguin, 1992).

Editions and Collections: *Ulysses* (London: Bodley Head, 1936);

Introducing James Joyce, A Selection of Joyce's Prose by T. S. Eliot (London: Faber & Faber, 1942);

The Portable James Joyce, edited by Harry Levin (New York: Viking, 1947);

A Portrait of the Artist as a Young Man, edited by Chester G. Anderson and Richard Ellmann (New York: Viking, 1964);

Dubliners, edited and corrected text by Robert Scholes in consultation with Richard Ellmann (New York: Viking, 1967);

A Portrait of the Artist as a Young Man, with criticism and notes, edited by Chester G. Anderson (New York: Viking, 1968);

Ulysses: A Critical and Synoptic Edition, 3 volumes, edited by Hans Walter Gabler, Wolfhard Steppe, and Claus Melchior (New York & London: Garland, 1984);

Ulysses, edited by Gabler, Steppe, and Melchior (New York: Random House / London: Bodley Head, 1986);

Ulysses, annotated student's edition with introduction and notes by Declan Kibert (London: Penguin, 1992);

Ulysses, republication of 1922 first edition, edited, with an introduction, by Jeri Johnson (Oxford: The World's Classics, Oxford University Press, 1993);

Ulysses, edited by Danis Rose (London: Picador, 1997);

Ulysses, facsimile of the 1926 second edition, with a preface by Stephen James Joyce, introduction by Jacques Aubert, and etchings by Mimmo Paladino (London: Folio Society, 1998).

James Joyce (2 February 1882 – 13 January 1941) (photograph © by Giselle Freund, Photo Researchers)

James Joyce:
A Chronology of His Career and Writings

Accessible references for Joyce's short works are cited in the text or in parentheses. Two short titles are used in the chronology: Critical Writings *for* The Critical Writings of James Joyce *(1959), edited by Ellsworth Mason and Richard Ellmann, and* Letters I, II, *or* III *for the three volumes of the* Letters of James Joyce *(1965–1966), edited by Stuart Gilbert and Ellmann.*

1882

2 February   James Augustine Joyce, the eldest surviving son of John Stanislaus Joyce, who serves in the Office of the Collector of Rates, and Mary (May) Jane Joyce, is born at 41 Brighton Square in the fashionable Dublin suburb of Rathgar. His parents have fifteen children, ten children who survive infancy.

1884

April   The Joyce family moves to 23 Castlewood Avenue, Rathmines, Dublin.

17 December   Stanislaus Joyce is born. James's closest sibling, Stanislaus is the author of *My Brother's Keeper: James Joyce's Early Years* (1958).

1887

May   The Joyces move to 1 Martello Terrace, Bray.

1888

1 September   Joyce enters Clongowes Wood College, a prestigious Jesuit institution in County Kildare.

1891

March   At his confirmation, Joyce chooses "Aloysius" as his saint's name; his full name becomes James Augustine Aloysius Joyce.

June   Joyce is withdrawn from Clongowes because of his family's deteriorating finances.

circa October   Joyce writes "Et Tu, Healy," a poem on Timothy Michael Healy's betrayal of Charles Stewart Parnell, the Irish politician who led the Home Rule Party. Parnell, who was accused of adultery in 1889 and ousted from the leadership of the party the following year, died on 6 October 1891. Fragments of the poem are included in *Letters I* (22 November 1930), *My Brother's Keeper,* and *James Joyce: Poems and Shorter Writings* (1991).

1892

November   The Joyce family moves to Dublin.

1893

6 April   Joyce and his brother enter Belvedere College, a Jesuit day school in Dublin, from which he graduates in 1898.

1894

12 June   Joyce wins the first of many prizes for excellence in state examinations.

1896

The family moves to North Richmond Street, which is described in "Araby," the third story in *Dubliners* (1914).

Joyce writes "Trust Not Appearances" (*Critical Writings*) and translates Horace's ode "*O fons Bandusiae*" into English; the translation was first published in Herbert S. Gorman's *James Joyce* (1939).

1897

Joyce writes a collection of short stories, "Silhouettes," and a collection of poems, "Moods." Neither is extant.

1898

September   Joyce begins attending Royal University (now University College, Dublin), where he studies modern languages. In the years from 1898 to 1904 he writes many prose sketches, which are collected in *Epiphanies* (1956). In the 1898–1899 school year he writes two essays, "Force" and "The Study of Languages" (*Critical Writings*).

1899

Joyce writes "Dark Rosaleen," a musical composition published in the second volume of *James Joyce Archive* (1977), and the essay "Royal Hibernian Academy 'Ecce Homo'" (*Critical Writings*).

1900

Joyce writes poems under the title "Shine and Dark," fragments of which were published in *My Brother's Keeper*. Richard Ellmann in his biography comments, "Most of the fragments that his brother preserved belong to dark rather than to shine."

Joyce translates Paul Verlaine's "Les Sanglots longs" from "Chanson d'automne" into English (Gorman's *James Joyce*).

20 January   Joyce reads "Drama and Life" to the Literary and Historical Society (*Critical Writings*); his defense of the attention paid to the ordinary details of life in contemporary drama provokes outrage among his peers.

1 April   "Ibsen's New Drama," a review of Henrik Ibsen's *When We Dead Awaken,* is published in the *Fortnightly Review* in London (*Critical Writings*).

Summer   Joyce writes two plays, "A Brilliant Career" in prose and "Dream Stuff" in verse. Neither is extant, though a fragment of one song from "Dream Stuff" is published in Ellmann's *James Joyce.*

1901

Joyce writes "The Final Peace" and "The Passionate Poet"; neither poem is extant.

Summer   Joyce translates Gerhart Hauptmann's play *Vor Sonnenaufgang* into English; it is published in *Joyce and Hauptmann: Before Sunrise*, edited by Jill Perkins (San Marino, Cal.: Huntington Library, 1978). He also translates Hauptmann's *Michael Kramer*, which is nonextant.

November   Joyce has his essay "The Day of the Rabblement," in which he attacks the Irish Literary Theatre, privately printed as a pamphlet in Dublin (*Critical Writings*).

1902

1 February   Joyce reads "James Clarence Mangan," a laudatory essay on the Irish poet, to the Literary and Historical Society. The address is published in the May issue of *St. Stephen's* in Dublin (*Critical Writings*).

31 October   Joyce receives his Bachelor of Arts degree from University College.

December   Joyce leaves Dublin for Paris with the intention of studying medicine.

11 December   "An Irish Poet," a review of *Poems and Ballads of William Rooney,* and "George Meredith," a review of Walter Jerrold's *George Meredith: An Essay Towards Appreciation,* are published in the *Daily Express* in Dublin (*Critical Writings*).

1903

29 January   "To-day and To-morrow in Ireland," a review of Stephen Gwynn's book of that title, is published in the *Daily Express* in Dublin (*Critical Writings*).

6 February   "A Suave Philosophy," a review of H. Fielding Hall's *The Soul of a People,* "An Effort at Precision in Thinking," a review of James Anstie's *Colloquies of Common People,* and "Colonial Verses," a review of Clive Phillipps Wolley's *Songs of an English Esau,* are published in the *Daily Express* in Dublin (*Critical Writings*).

21 March   "Catilina," a review of Ibsen's first play, is published in the *Speaker* in London (*Critical Writings*).

26 March   "The Soul of Ireland," a review of Lady Gregory's *Poets and Dreamers,* is published in the *Daily Express* in Dublin (*Critical Writings*).

April   Joyce returns to Dublin because of his mother's illness.

7 April   "The Motor Derby," an interview with French driver Henri Fournier about the upcoming Gordon Bennett Cup Race in Ireland, is published in the *Irish Times* in Dublin (*Critical Writings*).

13 August   Joyce's mother dies.

circa September   Joyce writes a letter to the editor, "Empire Building," which addresses the mistreatment of sailors by Jacques Lebaudy. The letter was first published in *Critical Writings*.

3 September   "A Ne'er-do-Well," a review of Valentine Caryl's book of that title, and "Aristotle on Education," a review of a book of that title edited by John Burnet, are published in the *Daily Express* in Dublin (*Critical Writings*).

17 September   "A Peep into History," a review of John Pollock's *The Popish Plot,* "The Mettle of the Pasture," a review of James Lane Allen's book of that title, and a review of Aquila Kempster's *The Adventures of Prince Aga Mirza* are published in the *Daily Express* in Dublin (*Critical Writings*).

1 October	"A French Religious Novel," a review of Marcelle Tintyre's *The House of Sin,* "Mr. Arnold Graves' New Work," a review of *Clytemnæstra: A Tragedy,* and "Unequal Verse," a review of Frederick Langbridge's *Ballads and Legends,* are published in the *Daily Express* in Dublin (*Critical Writings*).
15 October	"A Neglected Poet," a review of Alfred Ainger's *George Crabbe,* and "Mr. Mason's Novels," a review of A. E. W. Mason's *The Courtship of Morrice Buckler, The Philanderers,* and *Miranda of the Balcony,* are published in the *Daily Express* in Dublin (*Critical Writings*).
30 October	"The Bruno Philosophy," a review of J. Lewis McIntyre's *Giordano Bruno,* is published in the *Daily Express* in Dublin (*Critical Writings*).
12 November	"Humanism," a review of F. S. C. Schiller's *Humanism: Philosophical Essays,* and "Shakespeare Explained!," a review of Albert S. G. Canning's *Shakespeare Studied in Eight Plays,* are published in the *Daily Express* in Dublin (*Critical Writings*).
19 November	A review of T. Baron Russell's *Borlase and Son* is published in the *Daily Express* in Dublin (*Critical Writings*).

1904

	Joyce translates George Moore's *Celibates: Three Short Stories* into Italian (*James Joyce Archive,* volume 2).
January	Joyce writes a fictionalized autobiographical essay, "A Portrait of an Artist." He uses the essay as the basis for his novel, "Stephen Hero," which he begins in 1904 and finishes in 1905. An early version of *A Portrait of the Artist as a Young Man* (1916), *Stephen Hero* was first published in 1944, three years after Joyce's death. "A Portrait of the Artist" was first published in the Spring 1960 issue of the *Yale Review.*
14 May	"Song," poem XXIV of *Chamber Music* (1907), is published in the *Saturday Review* in London.
June	Joyce meets Nora Barnacle. On 16 June 1904 the couple goes walking in Ringsend, a Dublin suburb. Joyce later memorializes the date in *Ulysses.*
30 July	"O Sweetheart," poem XVIII of *Chamber Music,* is published in the *Speaker* in London.
August	"Song," poem VII of *Chamber Music,* is published in *Dana* in Dublin.
13 August	"The Sisters," a story that Joyce revises for *Dubliners,* is published in the *Irish Homestead* in Dublin under the name Stephen Daedalus.
10 September	"Eveline," a story that Joyce revises for *Dubliners,* is published in the *Irish Homestead* in Dublin under the name Stephen Daedalus.
October	Joyce and Nora leave Ireland and arrive in the Austrian city of Pola, where he teaches at the Berlitz school until March of the following year.
8 October	"A Wish," poem VI of *Chamber Music,* is published in the *Speaker* in London.
November	"Two Songs," poems XII and XXVI of *Chamber Music,* are published in *The Venture, An Annual of Art and Literature* in London, the first appearance of Joyce's work in a book.
17 December	"After the Race," a story substantially the same as the version collected in *Dubliners,* is published in the *Irish Homestead* in Dublin under the name Stephen Daedalus.

1905

late 1904 or early 1905	Joyce has his satirical poem "The Holy Office," in which he attacks contemporary writers, privately printed in Pola (*Critical Writings*). The poem may have been printed in Dublin before Joyce left the city, but no copies of such a printing have survived.

March	Joyce and Nora move to Trieste, Austria, where he has found another teaching position.
27 July	The Joyces' son, Giorgio, is born. He later prefers to be called George.
September	*Chamber Music* is rejected for publication by Grant Richards. Three other publishers in London and Dublin also reject the collection.
November	Joyce submits an early manuscript of *Dubliners,* lacking "Two Gallants," "A Little Cloud," and "The Dead," to Grant Richards. More than nine years will pass before the publisher finally brings the work to press.

1906

Joyce continues to work on his stories, writing "Two Gallants" and "A Little Cloud."

| July | Joyce and Nora leave Trieste for Rome, where they stay for seven months; Joyce works in a bank. Joyce begins "The Dead," the last and longest story of *Dubliners,* which he finishes in early 1907. |

1907

March	Joyce and Nora return to Trieste, where they live continuously for the next nine years.
22 March	"Il Fenianismo. L'Ultimo Feniano" is published in *Il Piccolo della Sera* in Trieste; it is translated as "Fenianism: The Last Fenian" in *Critical Writings*.
27 April	Joyce delivers a lecture in Italian, "Irlanda, Isola dei Santi e dei Savi," at the Università Popolare Triestina, Trieste; it is translated as "Ireland, Island of Saints and Sages" in *Critical Writings*.
circa May	Joyce delivers a lecture in Italian, "Giacomo Clarenzio Mangan," a translation of his 1902 essay, at the Università Popolare Triestina in Trieste.
May	*Chamber Music,* a collection of thirty-six poems, is published by Elkin Mathews in London and receives positive reviews. Various poems from the collection are subsequently published during Joyce's lifetime in *The Dublin Book of Irish Verse, 1728–1909* (1909), *Irish Homestead* (17 September 1910), *The Wild Harp* (1913), *Glebe* (February 1914), and *Querschnitt* (Fall 1923).
19 May	"Home Rule Maggiorenne" is published in *Il Piccolo della Sera* in Trieste; it is translated as "Home Rule Comes of Age" in *Critical Writings*.
26 July	The Joyces' daughter, Lucia, is born.
16 September	"L'Irlanda alla Sbarra" is published in *Il Piccolo della Sera* in Trieste; it is translated as "Ireland at the Bar" in *Critical Writings*.
Fall	Joyce discards "Stephen Hero" and begins anew on the manuscript that becomes *A Portrait of the Artist as a Young Man*.

1908

Joyce writes the first three chapters of *A Portrait of the Artist as a Young Man* and then sets them aside.

Joyce writes a melody for "Bid Adieu," poem XI from *Chamber Music;* Edmund Pendleton later writes a piano accompaniment, and the composition is published in 1949 by G. Schirmer (*James Joyce Archive,* volume 2).

Joyce and Nicolò Vidacovich translate J. M. Synge's play *Riders to the Sea* into Italian as *La Cavalcata al Mare* (*James Joyce Archive,* volume 2).

1909

24 March   "Oscar Wilde: Il Poeta di 'Salomé'" is published in *Il Piccolo della S*
                as "Oscar Wilde: The Poet of 'Salomé'" in *Critical Writings*.

5 September   "La Battaglia Fra Bernard Shaw e la Censura. 'Blanco Posnet Sma
                Piccolo della Sera in Trieste; it is translated as "Bernard Shaw's
                Shewing-Up of Blanco Posnet" in *Critical Writings*.

1910

22 December   "La Cometa dell' 'Home Rule'" is published in *Il Piccolo della Sera* in
                Home Rule Comet" in *Critical Writings*.

1911

17 August   Joyce writes a letter to the editor in which he describes his travails wi
                Dubliners and sends copies to many newspapers. "Author and
                version of the letter without the controversial passage Joyce cit
                published in *Northern Whig* in Belfast on 26 August; the whole le
                September issue of *Sinn Féin* in Dublin as "Dubliners, To The I
                letter is included in "A Curious History," published in 1914.

1912

                Joyce takes Italian state examinations to qualify as a teacher. His exam
                lished as *James Joyce in Padua* (1977).

March   Joyce delivers a lecture in Italian, "Verismo ed idealismo nella letteratu
                Foe–William Blake)" at the Università Popolare Triestina in Tries
                lecture was translated as "Daniel Defoe" in *Buffalo Studies* (Winter
                half was translated as "William Blake" in *Critical Writings*.

16 May   "L'Ombra di Parnell" is published in *Il Piccolo della Sera* in Trieste; it i
                Shade of Parnell" in *Critical Writings*.

July   Joyce makes his last visit to Ireland, going to Galway as well as Dublin,
                tember. He leaves when he is unable to secure the publication of *Du*

11 August   "La Città delle Tribù. Ricordi Italiani in un Porto Irlandese" is published
                in Trieste; it is translated as "The City of the Tribes: Italian Echoes
                Critical Writings.

September   Joyce has his satirical poem "Gas from a Burner," in which he attacks publish
                privately printed as a broadside in Trieste (*The Portable James Joyce* and

5 September   "Il Miraggio del Pescatore di Aran. La Valvola dell'Inghilterra in Caso ⌐
                lished in *Il Piccolo della Sera* in Trieste; it is translated as "The Mirage o⌐
                Aran. England's Safety Valve in Case of War" in *Critical Writings*.

10 September   "Politics and Cattle Disease," an editorial, is published in the *Freeman's Journa*
                cal Writings).

Fall   Joyce begins giving a series of twelve lectures on William Shakespeare's *Ham*
                sità Popolare Triestina in Trieste. He begins to write poetry again.

Joyce translates William Butler Yeats's play *The Countess Cathleen* into Italian; the translation is not extant.

ptember   "Watching the Needleboats at San Sabba" is published in *Saturday Review* in London; it is collected in *Pomes Penyeach* (1927).

mber   Joyce receives a letter from Ezra Pound, who has been told of Joyce by Yeats; Pound, whom Joyce will not meet face to face until 1920, is instrumental in getting *A Portrait of the Artist as a Young Man* published.

Joyce keeps a notebook about his relationship with his student Amalia Popper, the daughter of a Jewish businessman, who served as one of the models for Molly Bloom in *Ulyssess;* the notebook is published as *Giacomo Joyce* (1968).

anuary   "A Curious History," a series of letters by Joyce with an introduction by Pound in which the author's difficulties in publishing *Dubliners* are recounted, is published in the *Egoist* in London; it is republished in *Dubliners*.

ebruary   The first of twenty-five installments of *A Portrait of the Artist as a Young Man* is published in the *Egoist,* London; the serialization of the novel runs through 1 September 1915.

rch   Joyce begins work on *Ulysses*.

June   *Dubliners,* a collection of fifteen short stories, is published by Grant Richards in London. Reviews, even those objecting to certain passages and stories or to his subjects, find that Joyce's style, precision of writing, and keen observations on life deserve the highest praise.

ovember   Joyce drafts notes for the play that becomes *Exiles*.

15

Joyce translates Gottfried Keller's poem "Nun hab' ich gar die Rose aufgefressen" into English; the translation is not extant.

ne   Joyce and his family move to Zürich.

916

916–
920   Joyce writes "Dooleysprudence," a poem that Mason and Ellmann assert shows his "pacifist irritation." with all sides in World War I (*Critical Writings*).

Joyce writes two musical compositions, "Whittington Chimes" and "Ça ira," both of which are published in the *James Joyce Archive,* volume 2.

December   *Dubliners* is published in America by B. W. Huebsch in New York.

29 December   *A Portrait of the Artist as a Young Man* is published by B. W. Huebsch in New York.

1917

February   Harriet Shaw Weaver begins anonymous benefaction to James Joyce.

12 February   *A Portrait of the Artist as a Young Man* is published by the Egoist Press in London; it is printed from American sheets in the United States because English printers fear legal action.

May	"A Flower Given to My Daughter," "Flood," "Nightpiece," "Simples," and "Tutto è Sciolto" are published in *Poetry* in Chicago; all five poems are collected in *Pomes Penyeach*, though "Tutto è Sciolto" is substantially revised.
November	"Alone," "On the Beach at Fontana," and "She Weeps Over Rahoon" are published in *Poetry* in Chicago; all three poems are collected in *Pomes Penyeach*.

1918

Joyce sets "Dooleysprudence" to music (*James Joyce Archive*, volume 2).

Joyce translates Felix Béran's poem "Des Weibes Klage" into English as "Lament for the Yeoman" (Ellmann's *James Joyce*).

February	Joyce's translation of Diego Angeli's review of *A Portrait of the Artist as a Young Man*, "Un Romanzo di Gesuiti," is published in *The Egoist* in London.
March	The first of twenty-three installments of *Ulysses* is published in the *Little Review*. The initial thirteen episodes and part of the fourteenth episode of the eighteen-episode novel are published before the New York Society for the Suppression of Vice forces the magazine to cease publication of *Ulysses* with the December 1920 issue.
25 May	*Exiles, A Play in Three Acts* is published by Grant Richards in London and by B. W. Huebsch in New York.

1919

January	U.S. Postal Authorities confiscate and burn the issue of *Little Review* that includes the first part of the Lestrygonians episode from *Ulysses*.
January–February	A fragment of the Nestor episode of *Ulysses* is published in *The Egoist* in London. Brief fragments of the novel, from the Proteus, Hades, and Wandering Rocks episodes, will be published in the March–April, July, September, and December issues.
May	U.S. Postal Authorities confiscate and burn the issue of *Little Review* that includes the first half of the Scylla and Charybdis episode from *Ulysses*.
7 August	*Exiles* is performed in Munich.
15 August	"Bahnhofstrasse" is published in the *Anglo-French Review* in London; the poem is collected in *Pomes Penyeach*.
October	Joyce and his family return to Trieste.

1920

January	U.S. Postal Authorities confiscate the issue of *Little Review* that includes the second half of the Cyclops episode from *Ulysses*.
15 April	"A Memory of the Players in a Mirror at Midnight" is published in *Poesia* in Milan; the poem is collected in *Pomes Penyeach*.
June	Joyce meets Pound for the first time.
July	Joyce and his family move to Paris, where he will meet Adrienne Monnier, Sylvia Beach, T. S. Eliot, Wyndham Lewis, and Valéry Larbaud.
July–August	U.S. Postal Authorities confiscate the issue of *Little Review* that includes the second half of the Nausicaa episode from *Ulysses*.

20 September	The New York Society for the Suppression of Vice lodges a complaint against *Ulysses*, citing the Nausicaa episode.
December	The *Little Review* publishes the first part of the Oxen of the Sun episode, the last installment of *Ulysses* it will publish.

1921

February	The editors of *Little Review* are convicted of publishing obscenity and ordered to cease publication of *Ulysses*.
29 October	Joyce completes the Ithaca episode, the penultimate episode in *Ulysses* but the last to be drafted.

1922

2 February	*Ulysses* is published by Shakespeare and Company in Paris on Joyce's fortieth birthday.
August	Joyce and his family travel to England, where he meets his benefactor Harriet Shaw Weaver.
September	Joyce and his family return to Paris.
12 October	*Ulysses* is printed in France for the Egoist Press of London.

1923

March	Joyce begins "Work in Progress," the working title for *Finnegans Wake*.

1924

January	A new, revised edition of *Ulysses* is published by Shakespeare and Company in Paris.
April	"From Work in Progress," the first fragments of *Finnegans Wake* (pages 383–389 of the 1939 edition), are published in the *transatlantic review* in Paris.

1925

19 February	"From Work in Progress," pages 30–34 of *Finnegans Wake,* is published in *Contact Collection of Contemporary Writers* in Paris.
	Exiles is produced in New York.
Spring	"Letter to Ernest Walsh," a letter of tribute to Ezra Pound, is published in *This Quarter* in Paris (*Critical Writings*).
July	"Fragment of an Unpublished Work," pages 104–125 of *Finnegans Wake,* is published in the *Criterion* in London.
September	*Two Worlds,* edited by Samuel Roth, begins the unauthorized republication of Joyce's new work in New York. In the September and December issues in 1925 and the March, June, and September issues in 1926, *Two Worlds* republishes excerpts from *Criterion, Contact Collection of Contemporary Writers, Navire d'Argent, This Quarter,* and *transatlantic review*.
October	"From Work in Progress," pages 196–216 of *Finnegans Wake,* is published in *Navire d'Argent* in Paris.
Autumn–Winter 1925–1926	"Extract from Work in Progress," pages 169–195 of *Finnegans Wake,* is published in *This Quarter* in Milan.

1926

July	*Two Worlds Monthly* begins the unauthorized publication of a bowdlerized version of *Ulysses* in New York. Fourteen episodes of the novel are published in twelve installments that run until October 1927.

1927

2 February	A statement of protest against the pirating of *Ulysses* by Samuel Roth and *Two Worlds Monthly* is released in Paris. It is signed by 167 artists and writers, including Albert Einstein, T. S. Eliot, Ernest Hemingway, D. H. Lawrence, Thomas Mann, Bertrand Russell, and Virginia Woolf.
April	"Work in Progress," the first of seventeen installments of excerpts from *Finnegans Wake* during the next eleven years, is published in *transition*. The entire first part of the novel, corresponding to pages 3–216 of the 1939 edition, was published in the eight issues of *transition*, from April through November of 1927. Eventually, the first three chapters of Part II and all of Part III were also published in the journal. The fragments that had been previously published were substantially revised when they were republished in *transition;* all of the text that appeared in the journal was revised again before publication in *Finnegans Wake*.
5 July	*Pomes Penyeach,* a collection of thirteen poems, is published by Shakespeare and Company in Paris. Eleven of the poems have been previously published.

1928

9 January	*Work in Progress Volume I,* Part I of *Finnegans Wake,* is printed by Donald Friede in New York. The twenty copies printed were not for sale and were produced only for the purpose of copyrighting the material in the United States. Subsequently, printings of five copies of fragments appearing in *transition* were produced to protect copyright in the United States on 24 July 1928, 15 August 1928, 15 February 1929, and 7 January 1930.
January–February	Letter to the Editor, a letter Joyce wrote for a special number devoted to Thomas Hardy, is published in *Revue Nouvelle* in Paris (*Critical Writings*).
February	"Work in Progress," pages 282–304 of *Finnegans Wake,* is published in *transition*.
March	The first chapter of Part III of *Finnegans Wake,* pages 403–428, is published as "Work in Progress" in *transition.* The next three installments published in the journal–Summer 1928, February 1929, and November 1929–complete Part III of the novel, pages 429–590.
20 October	*Anna Livia Plurabelle*–the final chapter of Part I, pages 196–216, of *Finnegans Wake*–is published by Crosby Gaige in New York. Joyce signed the 850 copies of this limited edition. A British edition was published by Faber & Faber on 12 June 1930.

1929

	A pirated edition of the ninth Shakespeare and Company *Ulysses* is published in New York for Samuel and Max Roth. A portion of the estimated two to three thousand copies printed were seized by the Society for the Suppression of Vice on 5 October.
February	A French translation of *Ulysses* is published by Adrienne Monnier's *La Maison des Amis des Livres.*
March–April	"Omaggio a Svevo," a letter on Italo Svevo, is published in *Solaria* in Florence; it is translated as "Letter on Svevo" in *Critical Writings*.

May	Samuel Beckett and others publish *Our Exagmination Round His Factification for Incamination of Work in Progress,* a defense of Joyce's work that includes some quotations from the work that appear for the first time.
9 August	*Tales Told of Shem and Shaun,* including three fragments from *Finnegans Wake* first published in *transition,* is published by the Black Sun Press in Paris. The fragments are titled "The Mookse and the Gripes," (*Finnegans Wake,* pp. 152–159), "The Muddest Thick That Was Ever Heard Dump" (pp. 282–304), and "The Ondt and the Gracehoper" (pp. 414–419). The English edition omitting "The Muddest Thick That Was Ever Heard Dump" was published by Faber & Faber in London on 1 December 1932.

1930

	Stuart Gilbert's *James Joyce's 'Ulysses,'* a critical study of the novel written with Joyce's assistance, is published.
June	*Haveth Childers Everywhere,* pages 532–554 of *Finnegans Wake,* is published by Henry Babou and Jack Kahane in Paris and by the Fountain Press in New York. The English edition was published on 8 May 1931.
10 December	Joyce's son George marries Helen Kaster Fleischmann, an American divorcée.

1931

Spring	"From Work in Progress," pages 3–29 from *Finnegans Wake,* is published in *New Experiment* in Cambridge, England.
1 May	A French translation of "Anna Livia Plurabelle," completed with Joyce's assistance, is published in *La Nouvelle Revue Française* in Paris.
2 May	The first American edition of *Pomes Penyeach* is printed by Princeton University Press for Sylvia Beach. The fifty copies printed were not for sale and were produced only for the purpose of copyrighting the book in the United States.
4 July	Joyce marries Nora Barnacle in London to ensure the inheritance of their children.
29 December	Joyce's father dies.

1932

15 February	Joyce's grandson Stephen James Joyce is born to George and Helen Joyce.
27 February	"From a Banned Writer to a Banned Singer," a tribute to the Irish tenor John Sullivan, is published in the *New Statesman and Nation* (*Critical Writings*).
March	Joyce's translation of James Stephens's poem "Stephen's Green" into French, "Les Verts de Jacques," is published in *transition* in Paris (Gorman's *James Joyce*). In his 7 May 1932 letter to Stephens, Joyce included translations of the poem into German, Latin, Norwegian, Italian, and French (*Letters I*).
22 May	Joyce writes a humorous commentary on Stanislaus Joyce's preface to the English translation of Italo Svevo's *Senilità;* titled "Ad-Writer," it was included in *Critical Writings*.
29 May	Lucia Joyce is taken to Dr. G. Maillard's clinic at l'Hay-les-Roses, where she is diagnosed with a form of schizophrenia. She remains there for several weeks.
October	*Pomes Penyeach* is printed in France and published by the Obelisk Press in Paris and Desmond Harmsworth in London; the initial letters of the poems are designed and illuminated by Joyce's daughter, Lucia.

	Joyce writes the poem "A Portrait of the Artist as an Ancient Mariner," in which he humorously reflects on the pirating of *Ulysses*. He includes the poem in a 29 October 1932 letter to Harriet Shaw Weaver (Ellmann's *James Joyce*).
30 November	"Ecce Puer," a poem in which Joyce celebrates the birth of his grandson while mourning the death of his father, is published in the *New Republic* (*Collected Poems*).
1 December	*Ulysses,* "specially revised . . . by Stuart Gilbert," is published by the Odyssey Press in Hamburg, Paris, and Bologna.

1933

	Lucia is hospitalized in Nyon near Zurich.
February	"Work in Progress," pages 219–259 of *Finnegans Wake,* is published in *transition*.
6 December	Judge John M. Woolsey decides that *Ulysses* is not obscene and can be published in the United States.

1934

	Lucia is again hospitalized; she is a patient of Carl Jung.
25 January	First authorized American edition of *Ulysses* is published by Random House in New York.
15 February	"Work in Progress," pages 7–10 of *Finnegans Wake,* is published in *Contempo* in Chapel Hill, North Carolina.
23 February	"The Mime of Mick Nick and the Maggies," pages 258–259 of *Finnegans Wake,* is published in *Les Amis de 1914: Bulletin Hebdomadaire de l'Academie de la Coupole* in Paris.
April	Joyce writes "Epilogue to Ibsen's *Ghosts*," a poem inspired by his seeing a performance of an Ibsen play in Paris; the poem is included in Gorman's *James Joyce*.
June	*The Mime of Mick Nick and the Maggies,* pages 219–259 of *Finnegans Wake,* is published by the Servire Press in The Hague.

1935

July	"Work in Progress," pages 260–275 and 304–308 of *Finnegans Wake,* is published in *transition*.
22 October	*Ulysses* is published with six illustrations by Henri Matisse by The Limited Editions Club in New York. Joyce is displeased with the drawings, which Matisse based on Homer's *Odyssey*.

1936

10 August	Joyce includes an untitled children's story in a letter to his grandson (*Letters I*). Titled *The Cat and the Devil,* it was illustrated by Richard Erdoes and published by Dodd, Mead & Company in New York in 1964.
3 October	The first English edition of *Ulysses* actually printed in England is published by Bodley Head in London.
December	*Collected Poems* is published by the Black Sun Press in New York.

1937

February	"Work in Progress," pages 338–355 of *Finnegans Wake,* is published in *transition*.

June	Joyce delivers an address, "Communication de M. James Joyce sur le Droit Moral des Écrivains," to the International PEN Congress held in Paris (*Critical Writings*).
October	*Storiella as She is Syung,* pages 260–275 and 304–308 of *Finnegans Wake,* is published by Corvinus Press in London.

1938

March–June	"A Phoenix Park Nocturne," pages 244–246 of *Finnegans Wake,* is published in *Verve* in Paris.
April–May	"Work in Progress," pages 338–355 of *Finnegans Wake,* is published in *transition*.
13 November	Joyce finishes *Finnegans Wake*.

1939

4 May	*Finnegans Wake* is published by Faber & Faber in London and the Viking Press in New York.
December	The Joyces move from Paris to Saint-Gérand-le-Puy, a small village near Vichy, where they stay for a year before departing for neutral Switzerland.

1940

15 February	Herbert Gorman's biography, *James Joyce,* is published by Farrar & Rinehart in New York; the English edition is published in January 1941 by John Lane, The Bodley Head, London.
December	Joyce, with his wife, Nora, son, and grandson, arrives in Zürich.

1941

10 January	Joyce is hospitalized with acute abdominal pain. He undergoes what is believed to be a successful operation for a perforated duodenal ulcer.
13 January	Joyce dies. He is buried in Fluntern Cemetery outside of Zürich.

Early Life and Work: *Chamber Music* and *Dubliners*

Birth and Family

The eldest surviving child of John Stanislaus and May Joyce, James Augustine Joyce was born on 2 February 1882 in the fashionable Dublin suburb of Rathgar. Joyce's father (1849–1931), like his fictional counterpart Simon Dedalus in A Portrait of the Artist as a Young Man *and* Ulysses, *was born of a well-to-do family in Cork. After graduating from St. Colman's College in Fermoy, he studied medicine at Queens College, Cork, but left before earning a degree. In 1873, he moved to Dublin where he worked as secretary for the Dublin and Chapelizod Distilling Company. His involvement in Dublin politics advanced him to a position in the Office of the Collector of Rates, the office in charge of collecting property taxes. In 1880, he married Mary Jane (May) Murray.*

With the downfall of Charles Stewart Parnell (1846–1891) in 1889 and the merging of the Rates Office by the Dublin City Corporation in 1892, John Joyce lost his job, never to regain full-time employment again. His small pension was far too inadequate to support the demands of a growing family, and part-time work as a solicitor's clerk (like the character Farrington in "Counterparts"), as a political campaign worker (like those in "Ivy Day in the Committee Room"), and as an advertising canvasser for the Freeman's Journal *(like Leopold Bloom in* Ulysses) *was hardly sufficient to supplement his pension. James Joyce clearly had his father in mind as the prototype of Simon Dedalus in chapter V of* A Portrait of the Artist as a Young Man *when Stephen Dedalus ironically lists for his classmate Cranly Mr. Dedalus's many accomplishments: "A medical student, an oarsman, a tenor, an amateur actor, a shouting politician, a small landlord, a small investor, a drinker, a good fellow, a storyteller, somebody's secretary, something in a distillery, a taxgatherer, a bankrupt and at present a praiser of his own past."*

Of the nine other children who survived infancy: Margaret Alice ("Poppie," born 1884), Charles Patrick (1886), George Alfred (1887), Eileen Isabel Mary Xavier Brigid (1889), Mary Kathleen (1890), Eva Mary (1891), Florence Elizabeth (1892), and Mabel Josephine Anne ("Baby," 1893), Joyce was closest to his brother John Stanislaus ("Stannie," 1884), who served as confidant and whetstone for many of the ideas relating to his emergent artis-

tic vision. At Joyce's request, Stanislaus moved to Trieste in October 1905 and began teaching at the same Berlitz School where James was an instructor. By 1920 when James and his family left Trieste to live in Paris, the relationship between the two brothers had changed. Though they corresponded with one another, they were no longer as close as they once had been.

Joyce's birthplace, 41 Brighton Square, Rathgar, a middle-class suburb on the south side of Dublin (courtesy of Irish Tourist Board)

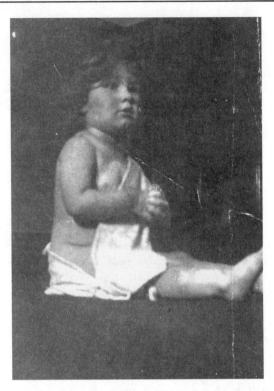

Drawing of Joyce's mother, May Murray Joyce, by Patrick Tuohy (Croessmann Collection of James Joyce, Special Collections/Morris Library, Southern Illinois University, Carbondale)

Joyce as a baby (James Joyce Collection, General Collection, Beinecke Rare Book and Manuscript Library, Yale University)

Joyce at age two (Croessmann Collection of James Joyce, Special Collections/Morris Library, Southern Illinois University Carbondale)

At Clongowes Wood College

When he was six years old, Joyce entered Clongowes Wood College, which he attended as a boarding student from September 1888 to June 1891. At the time, Clongowes was considered the finest Catholic school in Ireland. Joyce was withdrawn from the school because his family could no longer afford the fees.

Clongowes Wood College, a preparatory school founded in 1814 by the Society of Jesus, located west of Dublin in Sallins, County Kildare. The school is the setting for much of the action in the first chapter of A Portrait of the Artist as a Young Man *(courtesy of Irish Tourist Board).*

Joyce with his parents and maternal grandfather, John Murray, on the day he entered Clongowes Wood in September 1888 (courtesy of Ken Monaghan)

Joyce as a student at Clongowes Wood College

He opened the geography to study the lesson; but he could not learn the names of places in America. Still they were all different places that had those different names. They were all in different places and the countries were in continents and the continents were in the world and the world was in the universe.

He turned to the flyleaf of the geography and read what he had written there: himself, his name and where he was.

> Stephen Dedalus
> Class of Elements
> Clongowes Wood College
> Sallins
> County Kildare
> Ireland
> Europe
> The World
> The Universe

That was in his writing: and Fleming one night for a cod had written on the opposite page:

> Stephen Dedalus is my name
> Ireland is my nation.
> Clongowes is my dwellingplace
> And heaven my expectation.

—*A Portrait of the Artist as a Young Man*

First Publication

Fragments of Joyce's earliest work, "Et Tu, Healy," a broadside on the death of the Irish politician Charles Stewart Parnell (1846–1891), appear in Joyce's 22 November 1930 letter to his patron Harriet Shaw Weaver (Letters I, *p. 295),* John J. Slocum and Herbert Cahoon's A Bibliography of James Joyce *(1953), and Stanislaus Joyce's* My Brother's Keeper *(1958). The popular Parnell, who championed the cause of Home Rule for Ireland, was at one time affectionately called "Ireland's uncrowned King" by his staunch supporter Timothy Michael Healy. However, when Parnell's affair with Katharine ("Kitty") O'Shea, the wife of Captain William O'Shea, became a public scandal, Healy led the opposition against Parnell. In "Et Tu, Healy," Joyce at the age of nine seems to have reflected the anger of his father at what he regarded as Ireland's betrayal of Parnell, who he saw as a victim of hypocrisy and narrow-minded prejudices. The poem so impressed Joyce's father that he had it printed to hand out to his friends. He even sent a copy to the Pope.*

Painting of Joyce's father, John Stanislaus Joyce, by Patrick Tuohy

Parnell Monument, Dublin (courtesy of Irish Tourist Board)

The day of Parnell's death, 6 October 1891, came to be observed as Ivy Day by his followers, who pinned sprigs of ivy on their coat lapels in his memory. Joyce alludes to the commemoration in "Ivy Day in the Committee Room," a Dubliners *short story that concludes with the newspaper reporter Joe Hynes reciting a sentimental poem titled "The Death of Parnell"– verse that may echo Joyce's earlier poem.*

    –Sit down, Joe, said Mr O'Connor, we're just talking about the Chief–

    –Aye, aye! said Mr Henchy–

    Mr Hynes sat on the side of the table near Mr Lyons but said nothing.

    –There's one of them, anyhow, said Mr Henchy, that didn't renege him. By God, I'll say for you, Joe! No, by God, you stuck to him like a man!–

    O, Joe, said Mr O'Connor suddenly. Give us that thing you wrote–do you remember? Have you got it on you?–

    –O, aye! said Mr Henchy. Give us that. Did you ever hear that, Crofton? Listen to this now: splendid thing–

    –Go on, said Mr O'Connor. Fire away, Joe–

    Mr Hynes did not seem to remember at once the piece to which they were alluding but after reflecting a while, he said:

    –O, that thing is it . . . Sure, that's old now–

    –Out with it, man! said Mr O'Connor–

    –'Sh, 'sh, said Mr Henchy. Now, Joe!–

    Mr Hynes hesitated a little longer. Then amid the silence he took off his hat, laid it on the table and stood up. He seemed to be rehearsing the piece on his mind. After a rather long pause he announced:

THE DEATH OF PARNELL
6ᵗʰ October, 1891

He cleared his throat once or twice and then began to recite:

He is dead. Our Uncrowned King is dead.
   O, Erin, mourn with grief and woe
For he lies dead whom the fell gang
   Of modern hypocrites laid low.

He lies slain by the coward hounds
   He raised to glory from the mire;
And Erin's hopes and Erin's dreams
   Perish upon her monarch's pyre.

In palace, cabin or in cot
   The Irish heart where'er it be
Is bowed with woe – for he is gone
   Who would have wrought her destiny.

He would have had his Erin famed,
   The green flag gloriously unfurled,
Her statesmen, bards and warriors raised
   Before the nations of the World.

He dreamed (alas, 'twas but a dream!)
   Of Liberty: but as he strove
To clutch that idol, treachery
   Sundered him from the thing he loved.

Shame on the coward, caitiff hands
   That smote their Lord or with a kiss
Betrayed him to the rabble-rout
   Of fawning priests – no friends of his.

May everlasting shame consume
   The memory of those who tried
To befoul and smear th'exalted name
   Of one who spurned them in his pride.

He fell as fall the mighty ones,
   Nobly undaunted to the last,
And death has now united him
   With Erin's heroes of the past.

No sound of strife disturb his sleep!
   Calmly he rests: no human pain
Or high ambition spurs him now
   The peaks of glory to attain.

They had their way: they laid him low:
   But Erin, list, his spirit may
Rise, like the Phœnix from the flames,
   When breaks the dawning of the day,

The day that brings us Freedom's reign.
   And on that day may Erin well
Pledge in the cup she lifts to Joy
   One grief – the memory of Parnell.

    Mr Hynes sat down again on the table. When he had finished his recitation there was silence and then a burst of clapping: even Mr Lyons clapped. The applause continued for a little time. When it had ceased all the auditors drank from their bottles in silence.

    Pok! The cork flew out of Mr Hynes' bottle, but Mr Hynes remained sitting flushed and bareheaded on the table. He did not seem to have heard the invitation.

    –Good man, Joe! said Mr O'Connor, taking out his cigarette papers and pouch the better to hide his emotion–

    –What do you think of that, Crofton? cried Mr Henchy. Isn't that fine? What?–

    Mr Crofton said that it was a very fine piece of writing.

Belvedere College

In 1893 Joyce resumed his studies at Belvedere College, a Jesuit school in Dublin, from which he graduated in 1898. On 25 September 1896, Joyce was elected prefect of the Sodality of the Blessed Virgin Mary, effectively making him captain, or head-boy, of Belvedere College. Joyce wrote both poetry and prose while at Belvedere, though nothing sur-

vives from his collections of poems, "Moods," and short stories, which he titled "Silhouettes," both of which were written in or around 1897. In his last year at the college, Joyce acted in Vice-Versa, *a comedy adapted for the stage by Edward Rose from the novel of the same title by F. Anstey (Thomas Anstey Guthrie).*

Belvedere College

Page from the Belvedere College Roll Book recording the registration of Joyce and his brother Stanislaus on 6 April 1893 (courtesy of Belvedere College, Dublin)

Belvedere College S.J.
Great Denmark St. Dublin

BELVEDERE COLLEGE, Great Denmark Street, is conducted by the Fathers of the Society of Jesus. To parents resident in or near the City of Dublin, who desire to combine in the education of their sons the discipline and teaching of a public school with the very important influences of home life, it offers the advantages of a High Class Grammar School.

The Course of Education comprises the usual Grammar School subjects. In the three Higher Forms boys are prepared for the Intermediate Examinations. Candidates are also prepared for the Entrance Examinations of the College of Surgeons, for Civil Service Examinations, Preliminary Examinations for Solicitors' Apprentices, &c

The School Year is divided into three Terms: First Term, from August till December; Second Term, from December till April; Third Term, from April till July. The Pension for each of these Terms is £3, payable in advance, within the first month of the Term.

Advertisement for Belvedere College (courtesy of Belvedere College, Dublin)

Joyce at Belvedere College, front row, seated far left (courtesy of Belvedere College, Dublin)

Joyce (second row, third from left) and members of the Sodality of the Blessed Virgin Mary at Belvedere College (courtesy of Belvedere College, Dublin)

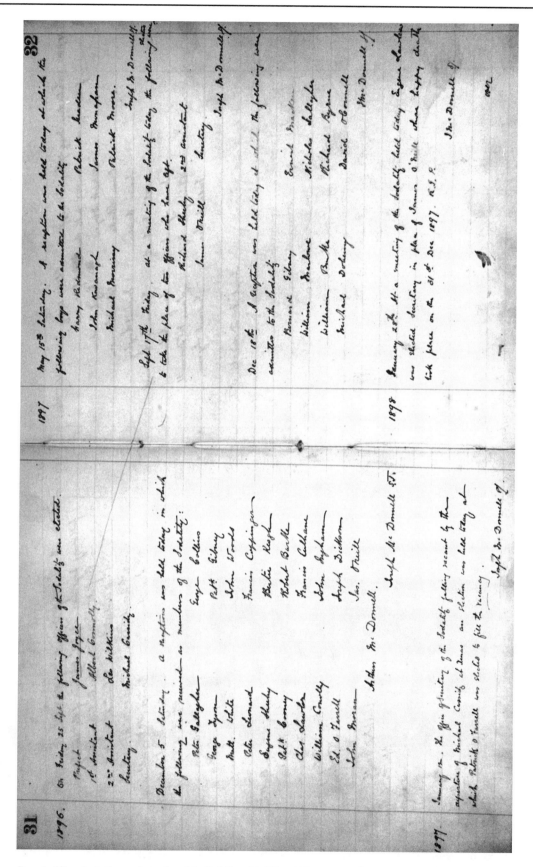

Record of Joyce's election as the prefect of the Sodality of the Blessed Virgin Mary (courtesy of Belvedere College, Dublin)

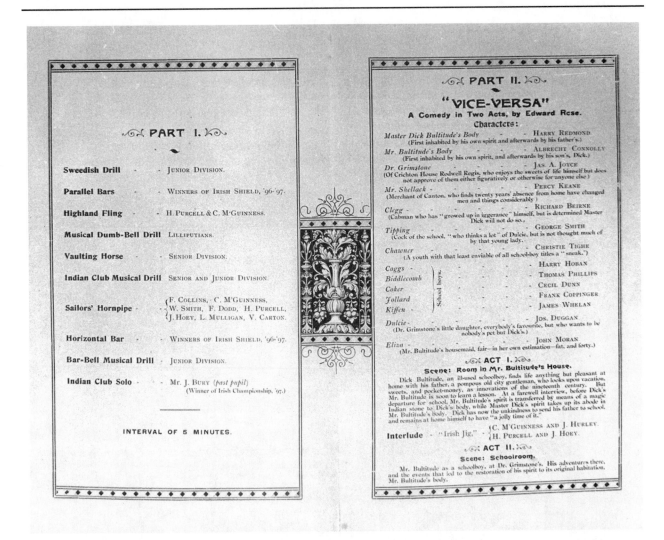

PART I.

Sweedish Drill	Junior Division.
Parallel Bars	Winners of Irish Shield, '96-'97.
Highland Fling	H. Purcell & C. M'Guinness.
Musical Dumb-Bell Drill	Lilliputians.
Vaulting Horse	Senior Division.
Indian Club Musical Drill	Senior and Junior Division.
Sailors' Hornpipe	F. Collins, C. M'Guinness, W. Smith, F. Dodd, H. Purcell, J. Hoey, L. Mulligan, V. Carton.
Horizontal Bar	Winners of Irish Shield, '96-'97.
Bar-Bell Musical Drill	Junior Division.
Indian Club Solo	Mr. J. Bury (*past pupil*) (Winner of Irish Championship, '97.)

INTERVAL OF 5 MINUTES.

PART II.

"VICE-VERSA"

A Comedy in Two Acts, by Edward Rose.

Characters:

Master Dick Bultitude's Body - HARRY REDMOND.
(First inhabited by his own spirit and afterwards by his father's.)

Mr. Bultitude's Body - ALBRECHT CONNOLLY.
(First inhabited by his own spirit, and afterwards by his son's, Dick.)

Dr. Grimstone - JAS. A. JOYCE.
(Of Crichton House Rodwell Regis, who enjoys the sweets of life himself but does not approve of them either figuratively or otherwise for anyone else.)

Mr. Shellack - PERCY KEANE.
(Merchant of Canton, who finds twenty years' absence from home have changed men and things considerably.)

Clegg - RICHARD BEIRNE.
(Cabman who has "growed up in iggerance" himself, but is determined Master Dick will not do so.)

Tipping - GEORGE SMITH.
(Cock of the school, "who thinks a lot" of Dulcie, but is not thought much of by that young lady.)

Chawner - CHRISTIE TIGHE.
(A youth with that least enviable of all school-boy titles a "sneak.")

Coggs - HARRY HOBAN.
Biddlecomb - THOMAS PHILLIPS.
Coker — School boys — CECIL DUNN.
Jollard - FRANK COPPINGER.
Kiffen - JAMES WHELAN.

Dulcie - JOS. DUGGAN.
(Dr. Grimstone's little daughter, everybody's favourite, but who wants to be nobody's pet but Dick's.)

Eliza - JOHN MORAN.
(Mr. Bultitude's housemaid, fair—in her own estimation—fat, and forty.)

ACT I.

Scene: Room in Mr. Bultitude's House.

Dick Bultitude, an ill-used schoolboy, finds life anything but pleasant at home with his father, a pompous old city gentleman, who looks upon vacation, sweets, and pocket-money, as innovations of the nineteenth century. But Mr. Bultitude is soon to learn a lesson. At a farewell interview, before Dick's departure for school, Mr. Bultitude's spirit is transferred by means of a magic Indian stone to Dick's body, while Master Dick's spirit takes up its abode in Mr. Bultitude's body. Dick has now the unkindness to send his father to school, and remains at home himself to have "a jolly time of it."

Interlude - "Irish Jig," C. M'GUINNESS AND J. HURLEY.
H. PURCELL AND J. HOEY.

ACT II.

Scene: Schoolroom.

Mr. Bultitude as a schoolboy, at Dr. Grimstone's. His adventures there, and the events that led to the restoration of his spirit to its original habitation, Mr. Bultitude's body.

Pages from the program for a play in which Joyce performed during Whitsuntide 1898 (courtesy of Belvedere College, Dublin)

Joyce (second row, center, wearing a mortar board) with the other cast members of Vice-Versa *(courtesy of Belvedere College, Dublin)*

University College

In 1898 Joyce attended University College (now a college of the National University of Ireland), which had been founded by John Henry Cardinal Newman in 1853 as the Catholic University of Ireland. With the University Education Act of 1879, the university was reorganized and came under the jurisdiction of the Royal University of Ireland. Although the university changed its name to University College in 1882, Joyce received his degree in modern languages in 1902 through the Royal University of Ireland.

During his university days, Joyce continued with his writing. A few fragments of poems Joyce wrote around 1900, which he titled "Shine and Dark," have been published in Stanislaus Joyce's My Brother's Keeper: James Joyce's Early Years (1958) and Richard Ellmann's James Joyce (1959). The pieces that do remain show that Joyce was imitating a romantic verse style of the time. In the summer of 1900, Joyce wrote two plays, "A Brilliant Career" in prose and "Dream Stuff" in verse; neither work survives.

University College (Croessmann Collection of James Joyce, Special Collections/Morris Library, Southern Illinois University Carbondale)

Joyce (right) with his friends George Clancy (left) and John Francis Byrne (center) during their college days (Croessmann Collection of James Joyce, Special Collections/Morris Library, Southern Illinois University Carbondale)

The Newman House, in which Joyce and his fictional counterpart Stephen Dedalus studied, and its commemorative plaque (courtesy of Faith Steinberg)

The next day he sat at his table in the bare upper room for many hours. Before him lay a new pen, a new bottle of ink and a new emerald exercise. From force of habit he had written at the top of the first page the initial letters of the jesuit motto: A.M.D.G. On the first line of the page appeared the title of the verses he was trying to write: To E– C–. He knew it was right to begin so for he had seen similar titles in the collected poems of Lord Byron. When he had written this title and drawn an ornamental line underneath he fell into a daydream and began to draw diagrams on the cover of the book.

–A Portrait of the Artist as a Young Man

According to Joyce's brother Stanislaus, "The Villanelle of the Temptress" that Joyce incorporates in chapter five of A Portrait of the Artist as a Young Man *to expose the adolescent emotions of Stephen Dedalus was one of the poems he wrote around the turn of the century.*

A flow of desire kindled again his soul and fired and fulfilled all his body. Conscious of his desire she was waking from odorous sleep, the temptress of his villanelle. Her eyes, dark and with a look of languor, were opening to his eyes. Her nakedness yielded to him, radiant, warm odorous and lavish limbed, enfolded him like a shining cloud, enfolded him like water with a liquid life: and like a cloud of vapour or like waters circumfluent in space the liquid letters of speech, symbols of the element of mystery, flowed forth over his brain.

Are you not weary of ardent ways,
Lure of the fallen seraphim?
Tell no more of enchanted days.

Your eyes have set man's heart ablaze
And you have had your will of him.
Are you not weary of ardent ways?

Above the flame the smoke of praise
Goes up from ocean rim to rim.
Tell no more of enchanted days.

Our broken cries and mournful lays
Rise in one eucharistic hymn.
Are you not weary of ardent ways?

While sacrificing hands upraise
The chalice flowing to the brim.
Tell no more of enchanted days.

And still you hold our longing gaze
With languorous look and lavish limb!
Are you not weary of ardent ways?
Tell no more of enchanted days.

–A Portrait of the Artist as a Young Man

Joyce's interest in drama extended to literary criticism. In April of 1900, Joyce's first formal publication, an article on Ibsen's last play, When We Dead Awaken, *appeared in the prestigious* Fortnightly Review *and earned the eighteen-year-old author twelve guineas. In a 23 April 1900 note of appreciation to his English translator, William Archer, Ibsen wrote "I have read, or rather spelt out, a review by Mr James Joyce in the* Fortnightly Review *which is very benevolent ('velvillig') and for which I should greatly like to thank the author if only I had sufficient knowledge of the language" (Letters II, p. 7).*

Ibsen's New Drama
James A. Joyce
Fortnightly Review, n.s., 67 (1 April 1900): 575–590

Twenty years have passed since Henrik Ibsen wrote *A Doll's House*, thereby almost marking an epoch in the history of drama. During those years, his name has gone abroad through the length and breadth of two continents, and has provoked more discussion and criticism than that of any other living man. He has been upheld as a religious reformer, a social reformer, a Semitic lover of righteousness, and as a great dramatist. He has been rigorously denounced as a meddlesome intruder, a defective artist, an incomprehensible mystic, and, in the eloquent words of a certain English critic, 'a muck-ferreting dog'. Through the perplexities of such diverse criticism, the great genius of the man is day by day coming out as a hero comes out amid the earthly trials. The dissonant cries are fainter and more distant, the random praises are rising in steadier and more choral chaunt. Even to the uninterested bystander it must seem significant that the interest attached to this Norwegian has never flagged for over a quarter of a century. It may be questioned whether any man has held so firm an empire over the thinking world in modern times. Not Rousseau; not Emerson; not Carlyle; not any of those giants of whom almost all have passed out of human ken. Ibsen's power over two generations has been enhanced by his own reticence. Seldom, if at all, has he condescended to join battle with his enemies. It would appear as if the storm of fierce debate rarely broke in upon his wonderful calm. The conflicting voices have not influenced his work in the very smallest degree. His output of dramas has been regulated by the utmost order, by a clockwork routine, seldom found in the case of genius. Only once he answered his assailants after their violent attack on *Ghosts*. But from *The Wild Duck* to *John Gabriel Borkman*, his dramas have appeared almost mechanically at intervals of two years. One is apt to overlook the sustained energy which such a plan of campaign demands; but even surprise at this must give way to admiration at the gradual, irresistible advance of this extraordinary man. Eleven plays, all dealing with modern life, have been published. Here is the list: *A Doll's House, Ghosts, An Enemy of the People, The Wild Duck, Rosmersholm, The Lady from the Sea, Hedda Gabler, The Master Builder, Little Eyolf, John Gabriel Borkman,* and lastly–his new drama, published at Copenhagen, December 19th, 1899–*When We Dead Awaken.* This play is already in process of translation into almost a dozen different languages–a fact which speaks volumes for the power of its author. The drama is written in prose, and is in three acts.

To begin an account of a play of Ibsen's is surely no easy matter. The subject is, in one way, so confined, and, in another way, so vast. It is safe to predict that nine-tenths of the notices of this play will open in some such way as the following: 'Arnold Rubek and his wife, Maja, have been married for four years, at the beginning of the play. Their union is, however, unhappy. Each is discontented with the other.' So far as this goes, it is unimpeachable; but then it does not go very far. It does not convey even the most shadowy notion of the relations between Professor Rubek and his wife. It is a bald, clerkly version of countless, indefinable complexities. It is as though the history of a tragic life were to be written down rudely in two columns, one for the pros and the other for the cons. It is only saying what is literally true, to say that, in the three acts of the drama, there has been stated all that is essential to the drama. There is from first to last hardly a superfluous word or phrase. Therefore, the play itself expresses its own ideas as briefly and as concisely as they can be expressed in the dramatic form. It is manifest, then, that a notice cannot give an adequate notion of the drama. This is not the case with the common lot of plays, to which the fullest justice may be meted out in a very limited number of lines. They are for the most part reheated dishes–unoriginal compositions, cheerfully owlish as to heroic insight, living only in their own candid claptrap–in a word, stagey. The most perfunctory curtness is their fittest meed. But in dealing with the work of a man like Ibsen, the task set the reviewer is truly great enough to sink all his courage. All he can hope to do is to link some of the more salient points together in such a way as to suggest rather than to indicate, the intricacies of the plot. Ibsen has attained ere this to such mastery over his art that, with apparently easy dialogue, he presents his men and women passing through different soul-crises. His analytic method is thus made use of to the fullest extent, and into the comparatively short space of two days the life of all his characters is compressed. For instance, though we only see Solness during one night and up to the following evening, we have in reality watched with bated breath the whole course of his life up to the moment when Hilda Wangel enters his house. So

in the play under consideration, when we see Professor Rubek first, he is sitting in a garden chair, reading his morning paper, but by degrees the whole scroll of his life is unrolled before us, and we have the pleasure not of hearing it read out to us, but of reading it for ourselves, piecing the various parts, and going closer to see wherever the writing on the parchment is fainter or less legible.

As I have said, when the play opens, Professor Rubek is sitting in the gardens of a hotel, eating, or rather having finished, his breakfast. In another chair, close beside him, is sitting Maja Rubek, the Professor's wife. The scene is in Norway, a popular health resort near the sea. Through the trees can be seen the town harbour, and the fjord, with steamers plying over it, as it stretches past headland and river-isle out to the sea. Rubek is a famous sculptor, of middle age, and Maja, a woman still young, whose bright eyes have just a shade of sadness in them. These two continue reading their respective papers quietly in the peace of the morning. All looks so idyllic to the careless eye. The lady breaks the silence in a weary, petulant manner by complaining of the deep peace that reigns about them. Arnold lays down his paper with mild expostulation. Then they begin to converse of this thing and that; first of the silence, then of the place and the people, of the railway stations through which they passed the previous night, with their sleepy porters and aimlessly shifting lanterns. From this they proceed to talk of the changes in the people, and of all that has grown up since they were married. Then it is but a little further to the main trouble. In speaking of their married life it speedily appears that the inner view of their relations is hardly as ideal as the outward view might lead one to expect. The depths of these two people are being slowly stirred up. The leaven of prospective drama is gradually discerned working amid the *fin-de-siècle* scene. The lady seems a difficult little person. She complains of the idle promises with which her husband had fed her aspirations.

MAJA. You said you would take me up to a high mountain and show me all the glory of the world.

RUBEK. (*with a slight start*). Did I promise you that, too?

In short, there is something untrue lying at the root of their union. Meanwhile the guests of the hotel, who are taking the baths, pass out of the hotel porch on the right, chatting and laughing men and women. They are informally marshalled by the inspector of the baths. This person is an unmistakable type of the conventional official. He salutes Mr. and Mrs. Rubek, enquiring how they slept. Rubek asks him if any of the guests take their baths by night, as he has seen a white figure moving in the park during the night. Maja scouts the notion, but the inspector says that there is a strange lady, who has rented the pavilion which is to the left, and who is staying there, with one attendant–a Sister of Mercy. As they are talking, the strange lady and her companion pass slowly through the park and enter the pavilion. The incident appears to affect Rubek, and Maja's curiosity is aroused.

MAJA. (*a little hurt and jarred*). Perhaps this lady has been one of your models, Rubek? Search your memory.

RUBEK. (*looks cuttingly at her*). Model?

MAJA. (*with a provoking smile*). In your younger days, I mean. You are said to have had such innumerable models–long ago, of course.

RUBEK. (*in the same tone*). Oh, no, little Frau Maja. I have in reality had only one single model. One and one only for everything I have done.

While this misunderstanding is finding outlet in the foregoing conversation, the inspector, all at once, takes fright at some person who is approaching. He attempts to escape into the hotel, but the high-pitched voice of the person who is approaching arrests him.

ULFHEIM'S voice (*heard outside*). Stop a moment, man. Devil take it all, can't you stop? Why do you always scuttle away from me?

With these words, uttered in strident tones, the second chief actor enters on the scene. He is described as a great bear-killer, thin, tall, of uncertain age, and muscular. He is accompanied by his servant, Lars, and a couple of sporting dogs. Lars does not speak a single word in the play. Ulfheim at present dismisses him with a kick, and approaches Mr. and Mrs. Rubek. He falls into conversation with them, for Rubek is known to him as the celebrated sculptor. On sculpture this savage hunter offers some original remarks.

ULFHEIM . . . We both work in a hard material, madam–both your husband and I. He struggles with his marble blocks, I daresay; and I struggle with tense and quivering bear-sinews. And we both of us win the fight in the end–subdue and master our material. We don't give in until we have got the better of it, though it fight never so hard.

RUBEK. (*deep in thought*). There's a great deal of truth in what you say.

This eccentric creature, perhaps by the force of his own eccentricity, has begun to weave a spell of enchantment about Maja. Each word that he utters tends to wrap the web of his personality still closer about her. The black dress of the Sister of Mercy causes him to grin sardonically. He speaks calmly of all his near friends, whom he has dispatched out of the world.

MAJA. And what did you do for your nearest friends?

ULFHEIM. Shot them, of course.

RUBEK. (*looking at him*). Shot them?

MAJA (*moving her chair back*). Shot them dead?

ULFHEIM (*nods*). I never miss, madam.

However, it turns out that by his nearest friends he means his dogs, and the minds of his hearers are put somewhat more at ease. During their conversation the Sister of Mercy has prepared a slight repast for her mistress at one of the tables outside the pavilion. The unsustaining qualities of the food excite Ulfheim's merriment. He speaks with a lofty disparagement of such effeminate diet. He is a realist in his appetite.

ULFHEIM (*rising*). Spoken like a woman of spirit, madam. Come with me, then! They [his dogs] swallow whole, great, thumping meat bones–gulp them up and then gulp them down again. Oh, it's a regular treat to see them!

On such half-gruesome, half-comic invitation Maja goes out with him, leaving her husband in the company of the strange lady who enters from the pavilion. Almost simultaneously the Professor and the lady recognize each other. The lady has served Rubek as model for the central figure of his famous masterpiece, 'The Resurrection Day'. Having done her work for him, she had fled in an unaccountable manner, leaving no traces behind her. Rubek and she drift into familiar conversation. She asks him who is the lady who has just gone out. He answers, with some hesitation, that she is his wife. Then he asks if she is married. She replies that she is married. He asks her where her husband is at present.

RUBEK. And where is he now?

IRENE. Oh, in a churchyard somewhere or other, with a fine, handsome monument over him; and with a bullet rattling in his skull.

RUBEK. Did he kill himself?

IRENE. Yes, he was good enough to take that off my hands.

RUBEK. Do you not lament his loss, Irene?

IRENE (*not understanding*). Lament? What loss?

RUBEK. Why, the loss of Herr von Satow, of course.

IRENE. His name was not Satow.

RUBEK. Was it not?

IRENE. My second husband is called Satow. He is a Russian.

RUBEK. And where is he?

IRENE. Far away in the Ural Mountains. Among all his goldmines.

RUBEK. So he lives there?

IRENE (*shrugs her shoulders*). Lives? Lives? In reality I have killed him.

RUBEK (*starts*). Killed–!

IRENE. Killed him with a fine sharp dagger which I always have with me in bed–

Rubek begins to understand that there is some meaning hidden beneath these strange words. He begins to think seriously on himself, his art, and on her, passing in review the course of his life since the creation of his masterpiece, 'The Resurrection Day'. He sees that he has not fulfilled the promise of that work, and comes to realize that there is something lacking in his life. He asks Irene how she has lived since they last saw each other. Irene's answer to his query is of great importance, for it strikes the key note of the entire play.

IRENE (*rises slowly from her chair and says quiveringly*). I was dead for many years. They came and bound me–lacing my arms together at my back. Then they lowered me into a grave-vault, with iron bars before the loophole. And with padded walls, so that no one on the earth above could hear the grave-shrieks.

In Irene's allusion to her position as model for the great picture, Ibsen gives further proof of his extraordinary knowledge of women. No other man could have so subtly expressed the nature of the relations between the sculptor and his model, had he even dreamt of them.

IRENE. I exposed myself wholly and unreservedly to your gaze [*more softly*] and never once did you touch me . . . .

* * * *

RUBEK (*looks impressively at her*). I was an artist, Irene.

IRENE (*darkly*). That is just it. That is just it.

Thinking deeper and deeper on himself and on his former attitude towards this woman, it strikes him yet more forcibly that there are great gulfs set between his art and his life, and that even in his art his skill and genius are far from perfect. Since Irene left him he has done nothing but paint portrait busts of townsfolk. Finally, some kind of resolution is enkindled in him, a

resolution to repair his botching, for he does not altogether despair of that. There is just a reminder of the will-glorification of *Brand* in the lines that follow.

RUBEK (*struggling with himself, uncertainly*). If we could, oh, if only we could . . . .

IRENE. Why can we not do what we will?

In fine, the two agree in deeming their present state insufferable. It appears plain to her that Rubek lies under a heavy obligation to her, and with their recognition of this, and the entrance of Maja, fresh from the enchantment of Ulfheim, the first act closes.

RUBEK. When did you begin to seek for me, Irene?

IRENE (*with a touch of jesting bitterness*). From the time when I realized that I had given away to you something rather indispensable. Something one ought never to part with.

RUBEK (*bowing his head*). Yes, that is bitterly true. You gave me three or four years of your youth.

IRENE. More, more than that I gave you–spendthrift as I then was.

RUBEK. Yes, you were prodigal, Irene. You gave me all your naked loveliness–

IRENE. To gaze upon–

RUBEK. And to glorify–

* * * *

IRENE. But you have forgotten the most precious gift.

RUBEK. The most precious . . . what gift was that?

IRENE. I gave you my young living soul. And that gift left me empty within–soulless [*looks at him with a fixed stare*]. It was that I died of, Arnold.

It is evident, even from this mutilated account, that the first act is a masterly one. With no perceptible effort the drama rises, with a methodic natural ease it develops. The trim garden of the nineteenth-century hotel is slowly made the scene of a gradually growing dramatic struggle. Interest has been roused in each of the characters, sufficient to carry the mind into the succeeding act. The situation is not stupidly explained, but the action has set in, and at the close the play has reached a definite stage of progression.

The second act takes place close to a sanatorium on the mountains. A cascade leaps from a rock and flows in steady stream to the right. On the bank some children are playing, laughing and shouting. The time is evening. Rubek is discovered lying on a mound to the left. Maja enters shortly, equipped for hill-climbing. Helping herself with her stick across the stream, she calls out to Rubek and approaches him. He asks how she and her companion are amusing themselves, and questions her as to their hunting. An exquisitely humorous touch enlivens their talk. Rubek asks if they intend hunting the bear near the surrounding locality. She replies with a grand superiority.

MAJA. You don't suppose that bears are to be found in the naked mountains, do you?

The next topic is the uncouth Ulfheim. Maja admires him because he is so ugly—then turns abruptly to her husband saying, pensively, that he also is ugly. The accused pleads his age.

RUBEK (*shrugging his shoulders*). One grows old. One grows old, Frau Maja!

This semi-serious banter leads them on to graver matters. Maja lies at length in the soft heather, and rails gently at the Professor. For the mysteries and claims of art she has somewhat comical disregard.

MAJA (*with a somewhat scornful laugh*). Yes, you are always, always an artist.

and again—

MAJA. . . . Your tendency is to keep yourself to yourself and—think your own thoughts. And, of course, I can't talk properly to you about your affairs. I know nothing about Art and that sort of thing. [*With an impatient gesture.*] And care very little either, for that matter.

She rallies him on the subject of the strange lady, and hints maliciously at the understanding between them. Rubek says that he was only an artist and that she was the source of his inspiration. He confesses that the five years of his married life have been years of intellectual famine for him. He has viewed in their true light his own feelings towards his art.

RUBEK (*smiling*). But that was not precisely what I had in my mind.
MAJA. What then?
RUBEK (*again serious*). It was this—that all the talk about the artist's vocation and artist's mission, and so forth, began to strike me as being very empty and hollow and meaningless at bottom.
MAJA. Then what would you put in its place?
RUBEK. Life, Maja.

The all-important question of their mutual happiness is touched upon, and after a brisk discussion a tacit

agreement to separate is effected. When matters are in this happy condition Irene is descried coming across the heath. She is surrounded by the sportive children and stays awhile among them. Maja jumps up from the grass and goes to her, saying, enigmatically, that her husband requires assistance to 'open a precious casket'. Irene bows and goes towards Rubek, and Maja goes joyfully to seek her hunter. The interview which follows is certainly remarkable, even from a stagey point of view. It constitutes, practically, the substance of the second act, and is of absorbing interest. At the same time it must be added that such a scene would tax the powers of the mimes producing it. Nothing short of a complete realization of the two *rôles* would represent the complex ideas involved in the conversation. When we reflect how few stage artists would have either the intelligence to attempt it or the powers to execute it, we behold a pitiful revelation.

In the interview of these two people on the heath, the whole tenors of their lives are outlined with bold steady strokes. From the first exchange of introductory words each phrase tells a chapter of experiences. Irene alludes to the dark shadow of the Sister of Mercy which follows her everywhere, as the shadow of Arnold's unquiet conscience follows him. When he has half-involuntarily confessed so much, one of the great barriers between them is broken down. Their trust in each other is, to some extent, renewed, and they revert to their past acquaintance. Irene speaks openly of her feelings, of her hate for the sculptor.

IRENE (*again vehemently*). Yes, for you—for the artist who had so lightly and carelessly taken a warm-blooded body, a young human life, and worn the soul out of it—because you needed it for a work of art.

Rubek's transgression has indeed been great. Not merely has he possessed himself of her soul, but he has withheld from its rightful throne the child of her soul. By her child Irene means the statue. To her it seems that this statue is, in a very true and very real sense, born of her. Each day as she saw it grow to its full growth under the hand of the skilful moulder, her inner sense of motherhood for it, of right over it, of love towards it, had become stronger and more confirmed.

IRENE (*changing to a tone full of warmth and feeling*). But that statue in the wet, living clay, that I loved—as it rose up, a vital human creature out of these raw, shapeless masses—for that was our creation, our child. Mine and yours.

It is, in reality, because of her strong feelings that she has kept aloof from Rubek for five years. But when she hears now of what he has done to the child—her child—all her powerful nature rises up against him in resentment. Rubek, in a mental agony, endeavours to explain, while she listens like a tigress whose cub has been wrestled away from her by a thief.

RUBEK. I was young then—with no experience of life. The Resurrection, I thought, would be most beautifully and exquisitely figured as a young unsullied woman—with none of a life's experience—awakening to light and glory without having to put away from her anything ugly and impure.

With larger experience of life he has found it necessary to alter his ideal somewhat, he has made her child no longer a principal, but an intermediary figure. Rubek, turning towards her, sees her just about to stab him. In a fever of terror and thought he rushes into his own defence, pleading madly for the errors he has done. It seems to Irene that he is endeavouring to render his sin poetical, that he is penitent but in a luxury of dolour. The thought that she has given up herself, her whole life, at the bidding of his false art, rankles in her heart with a terrible persistence. She cries out against herself, not loudly, but in deep sorrow.

IRENE (*with apparent self-control*). I should have borne children into the world—many children—real children—not such children as are hidden away in grave-vaults. That was my vocation. I ought never to have served you—poet.

Rubek, in poetic absorption, has no reply, he is musing on the old, happy days. Their dead joys solace him. But Irene is thinking of a certain phrase of his which he had spoken unwittingly. He had declared that he owed her thanks for her assistance in his work. This has been, he had said, a truly blessed *episode* in my life. Rubek's tortured mind cannot bear any more reproaches, too many are heaped upon it already. He begins throwing flowers on the stream, as they used in those bygone days on the lake of Taunitz. He recalls to her the time when they made a boat of leaves, and yoked a white swan to it, in imitation of the boat of Lohengrin. Even here in their sport there lies a hidden meaning.

IRENE. You said I was the swan that drew your boat.
RUBEK. Did I say so? Yes, I daresay I did [*absorbed in the game*]. Just see how the sea-gulls are swimming down the stream!
IRENE (*laughing*). And all your ships have run ashore.

RUBEK (*throwing more leaves into the brook*). I have ships enough in reserve.

While they are playing aimlessly, in a kind of childish despair, Ulfheim and Maja appear across the heath. These two are going to seek adventures on the high tablelands. Maja sings out to her husband a little song which she has composed in her joyful mood. With a sardonic laugh Ulfheim bids Rubek good-night and disappears with his companion up the mountain. All at once Irene and Rubek leap to the same thought. But at that moment the gloomy figure of the Sister of Mercy is seen in the twilight, with her leaden eyes looking at them both. Irene breaks from him, but promises to meet him that night on the heath.

RUBEK. And you will come, Irene?
IRENE. Yes, certainly I will come. Wait for me here.
RUBEK (*repeats dreamily*). Summer night on the upland. With you. With you. [*His eyes meet hers.*] Oh, Irene, that might have been our life. And that we have forfeited, we two.
IRENE. We see the irretrievable only when [*breaks short off*].
RUBEK (*looks inquiringly at her*). When? . . .
IRENE. When we dead awaken.

The third act takes place on a wide plateau, high up on the hills. The ground is rent with yawning clefts. Looking to the right, one sees the range of the summits half-hidden in the moving mists. On the left stands an old, dismantled hut. It is in the early morning, when the skies are the colour of pearl. The day is beginning to break. Maja and Ulfheim come down to the plateau. Their feelings are sufficiently explained by the opening words.

MAJA (*trying to tear herself loose*). Let me go! Let me go, I say!
ULFHEIM. Come, come! are you going to bite now? You're as snappish as a wolf.

When Ulfheim will not cease his annoyances, Maja threatens to run over the crest of the neighbouring ridge. Ulfheim points out that she will dash herself to pieces. He has wisely sent Lars away after the hounds, that he may be uninterrupted. Lars, he says, may be trusted not to find the dogs too soon.

MAJA (*looking angrily at him*). No, I daresay not.
ULFHEIM (*catching at her arm*). For Lars—he knows my—my methods of sport, you see.

Maja, with enforced self-possession, tells him frankly what she thinks of him. Her uncomplimentary observations please the bear-hunter very much. Maja requires all her tact to keep him in order. When she talks of going back to the hotel, he gallantly offers to carry her on his shoulders, for which suggestion he is promptly snubbed. The two are playing as a cat and a bird play. Out of their skirmish one speech of Ulfheim's rises suddenly to arrest attention, as it throws some light on his former life.

ULFHEIM (*with suppressed exasperation*). I once took a young girl–lifted her up from the mire of the streets, and carried her in my arms. Next my heart I carried her. So I would have borne her all through life, lest haply she should dash her foot against a stone . . . . [*with a growling laugh.*] And do you know what I got for my reward?

MAJA. No. What did you get?

ULFHEIM (*looks at her, smiles and nods*). I got the horns! The horns that you can see so plainly. Is not that a comical story, madam bear-murderess?

As an exchange of confidence, Maja tells him her life in summary–and chiefly her married life with Professor Rubek. As a result, these two uncertain souls feel attracted to each other, and Ulfheim states his case in the following characteristic manner:

ULFHEIM. Should not we two tack our poor shreds of life together?

Maja, satisfied that in their vows there will be no promise on his part to show her all the splendours of the earth, or to fill her dwelling-place with art, gives a half-consent by allowing him to carry her down the slope. As they are about to go, Rubek and Irene, who have also spent the night on the heath, approach the same plateau. When Ulfheim asks Rubek if he and madame have ascended by the same pathway, Rubek answers significantly.

RUBEK. Yes, of course [*with a glance at* MAJA]. Henceforth the strange lady and I do not intend our ways to part.

While the musketry of their wit is at work, the elements seem to feel that there is a mighty problem to be solved then and there, and that a great drama is swiftly drawing to a close. The smaller figures of Maja and Ulfheim are grown still smaller in the dawn of the tempest. Their lots are decided in comparative quiet, and we cease to take much interest in them. But the other two hold our gaze, as they stand up silently on the fjaell, engrossing central figures of boundless, human interest. On a sudden, Ulfheim raises his hand impressively towards the heights.

ULFHEIM. But don't you see that the storm is upon us? Don't you hear the blasts of wind?

RUBEK (*listening*). They sound like the prelude to the Resurrection Day.

* * * *

MAJA (*drawing* ULFHEIM *away*). Let us make haste and get down.

As he cannot take more than one person at a time, Ulfheim promises to send aid for Rubek and Irene, and, seizing Maja in his arms, clambers rapidly but warily down the path. On the desolate mountain plateau, in the growing light, the man and the woman are left together–no longer the artist and his model. And the shadow of a great change is stalking close in the morning silence. Then Irene tells Arnold that she will not go back among the men and women she has left; she will not be rescued. She tells him also, for now she may tell all, how she had been tempted to kill him in frenzy when he spoke of their connection as an episode in his life.

RUBEK (*darkly*). And why did you hold your hand?

IRENE. Because it flashed upon me with a sudden horror that you were dead already–long ago.

But, says Rubek, our love is not dead in us, it is active, fervent and strong.

IRENE. The love that belongs to the life of earth–the beautiful, miraculous life of earth–the inscrutable life of earth–that is dead in both of us.

There are, moreover, the difficulties of their former lives. Even here, at the sublimest part of his play, Ibsen is master of himself and his facts. His genius as an artist faces all, shirks nothing. At the close of *The Master Builder*, the greatest touch of all was the horrifying exclamation of one without, 'O! the head is all crushed in.' A lesser artist would have cast a spiritual glamour over the tragedy of Bygmester Solness. In like manner here Irene objects that she has exposed herself as a nude before the vulgar gaze, that Society has cast her out, that all is too late. But Rubek cares for such considerations no more. He flings them all to the wind and decides.

RUBEK (*throwing his arms violently around her*). Then let two of the dead–us two–for once live life to its uttermost, before we go down to our graves again.

IRENE (*with a shriek*). Arnold!

RUBEK. But not here in the half-darkness. Not here with this hideous dank shroud flapping around us!

IRENE (*carried away by passion*). No, no–up in the light and in all the glittering glory! Up to the Peak of Promise!

RUBEK. There we will hold our marriage-feast, Irene–oh! my beloved!

IRENE (*proudly*). The sun may freely look on us, Arnold.

RUBEK. All the powers of light may freely look on us–and all the powers of darkness too [*seizes her hand*]–will you then follow me, oh my grace-given bride!

IRENE (*as though transfigured*). I follow you, freely and gladly, my lord and master!

RUBEK (*drawing her along with him*). We must first pass through the mists, Irene, and then–

IRENE. Yes, through all the mists, and then right up to the summit of the tower that shines in the sunrise.

The mist-clouds close in over the scene. RUBEK *and* IRENE, *hand in hand, climb up over the snowfield to the right and soon disappear among the lower clouds. Keen storm-gusts hurtle and whistle through the air.*

The SISTER OF MERCY *appears upon the rubble-slope to the left. She stops and looks around silently and searchingly.*

MAJA *can be heard singing triumphantly from the depths below.*

MAJA. I am free! I am free! I am free!
No more life in the prison for me!
I am free as a bird! I am free!

Suddenly a sound like thunder is heard from high up on the snowfield, which glides and whirls downwards with rushing speed. RUBEK *and* IRENE *can be dimly discerned as they are whirled along with the masses of snow and buried in them.*

THE SISTER OF MERCY (*gives a shriek, stretches out her arms towards them and cries*), Irene! [*Stands silent a moment, then makes the sign of the cross before her in the air, and says*], Pax Vobiscum!

MAJA'S *triumphant song sounds from still further down below.*

Such is the plot, in a crude and incoherent way, of this new drama. Ibsen's plays do not depend for their interest on the action, or on the incidents. Even the characters, faultlessly drawn though they be, are not the first things in his plays. But the naked drama–either the perception of a great truth, or the opening up of a great question, or a great conflict which is almost independent of the conflicting actors, and has been and is of far-reaching importance–this is what primarily rivets our attention. Ibsen has chosen the average lives in their uncompromising truth for the groundwork of all his later plays. He has abandoned the verse form, and has never sought to embellish his work after the conventional fashion. Even when his dramatic theme reached its zenith he has not sought to trick it out in

gawds or tawdriness. How easy it would have been to have written *An Enemy of the People* on a speciously loftier level–to have replaced the *bourgeois* by the legitimate hero! Critics might then have extolled as grand what they have so often condemned as banal. But the surroundings are nothing to Ibsen. The play is the thing. By the force of his genius, and the indisputable skill which he brings to all his efforts, Ibsen has, for many years, engrossed the attention of the civilized world. Many years more, however, must pass before he will enter his kingdom in jubilation, although, as he stands to-day, all has been done on his part to ensure his own worthiness to enter therein. I do not propose here to examine into every detail of dramaturgy connected with this play, but merely to outline the characterization.

In his characters Ibsen does not repeat himself. In this drama–the last of a long catalogue–he has drawn and differentiated with his customary skill. What a novel creation is Ulfheim! Surely the hand which has drawn him has not yet lost her cunning. Ulfheim is, I think, the newest character in the play. He is a kind of surprise-packet. It is as a result of his novelty that he seems to leap, at first mention, into bodily form. He is superbly wild, primitively impressive. His fierce eyes roll and glare as those of Yégof or Herne. As for Lars, we may dismiss him, for he never opens his mouth. The Sister of Mercy speaks only once in the play, but then with good effect. In silence she follows Irene like a retribution, a voiceless shadow with her own symbolic majesty.

Irene, too, is worthy of her place in the gallery of her compeers. Ibsen's knowledge of humanity is nowhere more obvious than in his portrayal of women. He amazes one by his painful introspection; he seems to know them better than they know themselves. Indeed, if one may say so of an eminently virile man, there is a curious admixture of the woman in his nature. His marvellous accuracy, his faint traces of femininity, his delicacy of swift touch, are perhaps attributable to this admixture. But that he knows women is an incontrovertible fact. He appears to have sounded them to almost unfathomable depths. Beside his portraits the psychological studies of Hardy and Turgénieff, or the exhaustive elaborations of Meredith, seem no more than sciolism. With a deft stroke, in a phrase, in a word, he does what costs them chapters, and does it better. Irene, then, has to face great comparison; but it must be acknowledged that she comes forth of it bravely. Although Ibsen's women are uniformly true, they, of course, present themselves in various lights. Thus Gina Ekdal is, before all else, a comic figure, and Hedda Gabler a tragic one–if such old-world terms may be employed without incongruity. But Irene cannot be so readily classified; the very aloofness from passion, which is not separable from her, forbids classification. She interests us strangely–magnetically, because of her inner power of character. However perfect Ibsen's former creations may be, it is questionable whether any of his women reach to the depth of soul of Irene. She holds our gaze for the sheer force of her intellectual capacity. She is moreover, an intensely spiritual creation–in the truest and widest sense of that. At times she is liable to get beyond us, to soar above us, as she does with Rubek. It will be considered by some as a blemish that she–a woman of fine spirituality–is made an artist's model, and some may even regret that such an episode mars the harmony of the drama. I cannot altogether see the force of this contention; it seems pure irrelevancy. But whatever may be thought of the fact, there is small room for complaint as to the handling of it. Ibsen treats it, as indeed he treats all things, with large insight, artistic restraint, and sympathy. He sees it steadily and whole, as from a great height, with perfect vision and an angelic dispassionateness, with the sight of one who may look on the sun with open eyes. Ibsen is different from the clever purveyor.

Maja fulfills a certain technical function in the play, apart from her individual character. Into the sustained tension she comes as a relief. Her airy freshness is as a breath of keen air. The sense of free, almost flamboyant, life, which is her chief note, counterbalances the austerity of Irene and the dullness of Rubek. Maja has practically the same effect on this play, as Hilda Wangel has on *The Master Builder*. But she does not capture our sympathy so much as Nora Helmer. She is not meant to capture it.

Rubek himself is the chief figure in this drama, and, strangely enough, the most conventional. Certainly, when contrasted with his Napoleonic predecessor, John Gabriel Borkman, he is a mere shadow. It must be borne in mind, however, that Borkman is alive, actively, energetically, restlessly alive, all through the play to the end, when he dies; whereas Arnold Rubek is dead, almost hopelessly dead, until the end, when he comes to life. Notwithstanding this, he is supremely interesting, not because of himself, but because of his dramatic significance. Ibsen's drama, as I have said, is wholly independent of his characters. They may be bores, but the drama in which they live and move is invariably powerful. Not that Rubek is a bore by any means! He is infinitely more interesting in himself than Torvald Helmer or Tesman, both of whom possess certain strongly-marked characteristics. Arnold Rubek is, on the other hand, not intended to be a genius, as perhaps Eljert Lövborg is. Had he been a genius like Eljert he would have understood in a truer way the value of his life. But, as we are to suppose, the facts that he is devoted to his art and that he has attained to a degree of mastery in it–mastery of hand linked with limitation of thought–tell us that there may be lying dormant in him a capacity for greater life, which may be exercised when he, a dead man, shall have risen from among the dead.

The only character whom I have neglected is the inspector of the baths, and I hasten to do him tardy, but

Ibsen's New Drama

[From *The Fortnightly Review* LONDON April 1900].

BY

James A. Joyce

ULYSSES BOOKSHOP
187, High Holborn, London, W. C. 1

Title page for Joyce's article republished as a monograph in March 1930, thirty years after it was initially published in The Fortnightly Review

scant, justice. He is neither more nor less than the average inspector of baths. But he is that.

So much for the characterization, which is at all times profound and interesting. But apart from the characters in the play, there are some noteworthy points in the frequent and extensive side-issues of the line of thought. The most salient of these is what seems, at first sight, nothing more than an accidental scenic feature. I allude to the environment of the drama. One cannot but observe in Ibsen's later work a tendency to get out of closed rooms. Since *Hedda Gabler* this tendency is most marked. The last act of *The Master Builder* and the last act of *John Gabriel Borkman* take place in the open air. But in this play the three acts are *al fresco*. To give heed to such details as these in the drama may be deemed ultra-Boswellian fanaticism. As a matter of fact it is what is barely due to the work of a great artist. And this feature, which is so prominent, does not seem to me altogether without its significance.

Again, there has not been lacking in the last few social dramas a fine pity for men–a note nowhere audible in the uncompromising rigour of the early eighties. Thus in the conversion of Rubek's views as to the girl-figure in his masterpiece, 'The Resurrection Day', there is involved an all-embracing philosophy, a deep sympathy with the cross-purposes and contradictions of life, as they may be reconcilable with a hopeful awakening–when the manifold travail of our poor humanity may have a glorious issue. As to the drama itself, it is doubtful if any good purpose can be served by attempting to criticize it. Many things would tend to prove this. Henrik Ibsen is one of the world's great men before whom criticism can make but feeble show. Appreciation, hearkening is the only true criticism. Further, that species of criticism which calls itself dramatic criticism is a needless adjunct to his plays. When the art of a dramatist is perfect the critic is superfluous. Life is not to be criticized, but to be faced and lived. Again, if any plays demand a stage they are the plays of Ibsen. Not merely is this so because his plays have so much in common with the plays of other men that they were not written to cumber the shelves of a library, but because they are so packed with thought. At some chance expression the mind is tortured with some question, and in a flash long reaches of life are opened up in vista, yet the vision is momentary unless we stay to ponder on it. It is just to prevent excessive pondering that Ibsen requires to be acted. Finally, it is foolish to expect that a problem, which has occupied Ibsen for nearly three years, will unroll smoothly before our eyes on a first or second reading. So it is better to leave the drama to plead for itself. But this at least is clear, that in this play Ibsen has given us nearly the very best of himself. The action is neither hindered by many complexities, as in *The Pillars of Society*, nor harrowing in its simplicity, as in *Ghosts*. We have whimsicality, bordering on extravagance, in the wild Ulfheim, and subtle humour in the sly contempt which Rubek and Maja entertain for each other. But Ibsen has striven to let the drama have perfectly free action. So he has not bestowed his wonted pains on the minor characters. In many of his plays these minor characters are matchless creations. Witness Jacob Engstrand, Tönnesen, and the demonic Molvik! But in this play the minor characters are not allowed to divert our attention.

On the whole, *When We Dead Awaken* may rank with the greatest of the author's work–if, indeed, it be not the greatest. It is described as the last of the series, which began with *A Doll's House*–a grand epilogue to its ten predecessors. Than these dramas, excellent alike in dramaturgic skill, characterization, and supreme interest, the long roll of drama, ancient or modern, has few things better to show.

James A. Joyce

Oliver St. John Gogarty, circa 1899

Oliver St. John Gogarty

A writer in his own right, a surgeon, and a member of the Irish senate, Gogarty was known for his caustic wit and ribald humor. In December 1902, Joyce first met Gogarty at the National Library of Ireland and an immediate but not enduring friendship between the two easily developed. Although for a short period of time in September 1904 Joyce stayed with Gogarty at the Martello Tower in Sandycove (the setting for the opening scene of Ulysses*), Joyce's relationship with his rival began to cool, and by October, when Joyce left for Zurich with Nora Barnacle, his dealings with Gogarty virtually ended. Gogarty is one of the persons Joyce satirizes in his broadside, "The Holy Office" (1904). When Joyce visited Ireland in 1909, the first time since his departure in 1904, Gogarty tried to renew their relationship but to no avail.*

The National Library of Ireland, one of Joyce's favorite places at the turn of the century. It is the setting for two important episodes in the last chapter of A Portrait of the Artist as a Young Man *and for Stephen Dedalus's discussion of Shakespeare in the Scylla and Charybdis episode in* Ulysses *(courtesy of Irish Tourist Board).*

Joyce's intellectual and literary independence often put him at odds with students and teachers. He began to experience a growing dissatisfaction with the literary life of Dublin that he believed was incompatible with his own artistic talents and tastes. When the Irish Literary Theatre, which later became the Abbey Theatre, opened in May 1899 with Yeats's The Countess Cathleen, *Joyce refused to join other students in their condemnation of its heresy.*

Joyce soon became disenchanted with what he regarded as the provincialism of the Irish Literary Theatre. When "The Day of Rabblement" was rejected by St. Stephen's, *a university magazine, he contrived to have it published at his own expense. In the beginning of the essay, Joyce was purposefully cryptic in his allusion to the philosopher Giordano Bruno of Nola (1548–1600), because, according to Stanislaus Joyce, he believed that his readers should be encouraged to think. At the end of the piece, Joyce is likely referring to himself as "the third minister" who is "worthy to carry on the tradition of the old master," Henrik Ibsen.*

The Day of the Rabblement
James A. Joyce
(Dublin: Gerrard Bros., 1901)

No man, said the Nolan, can be a lover of the true or the good unless he abhors the multitude; and the artist, though he may employ the crowd, is very careful to isolate himself. This radical principle of artistic economy applies specially to a time of crisis, and today when the highest form of art has been just preserved by desperate sacrifices, it is strange to see the artist making terms with the rabblement. The Irish Literary Theatre is the latest movement of protest against the sterility and falsehood of the modern stage. Half a century ago the note of protest was uttered in Norway, and since then in several countries long and disheartening battles have been fought against the hosts of prejudice and misinterpretation and ridicule. What triumph there has been here and there is due to stubborn conviction, and every movement that has set out heroically has achieved a little. The Irish Literary Theatre gave out that it was the champion of progress, and proclaimed war against commercialism and vulgarity. It had partly made good its word and was expelling the old devil, when after the first encounter it surrendered to the popular will. Now, your popular devil is more dangerous than your vulgar devil. Bulk and lungs count for something, and he can gild his speech aptly. He has prevailed once more, and the Irish Literary Theatre must now be considered the property of the rabblement of the most belated race in Europe.

It will be interesting to examine here. The official organ of the movement spoke of producing European masterpieces, but the matter went not further. Such a project was absolutely necessary. The censorship is powerless in Dublin, and the directors could have produced *Ghosts* or

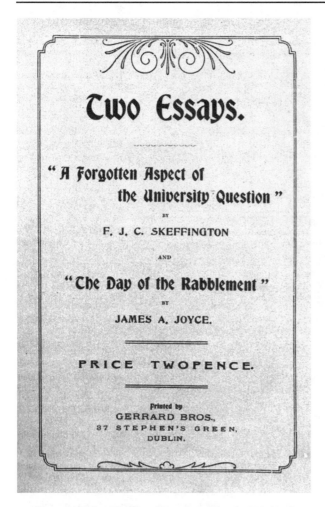

Cover for book published at the expense of Joyce and his friend
Skeffington, who in his essay advocated equal status for women
at the university. Because neither author agreed with the
other's position, they included a preface in which they
asserted that "each writer is responsible only for what
appears under his own name."

The Dominion of Darkness if they chose. Nothing can be done until the forces that dictate public judgement are calmly confronted. But, of course, the directors are shy of presenting Ibsen, Tolstoy or Hauptmann, where even *Countess Cathleen* is pronounced vicious and damnable. Even for a technical reason this project was necessary. A nation which never advanced so far as a miracle-play affords no literary model to the artist, and he must look abroad. Earnest dramatists of the second rank, Sudermann, Björnson, and Giacosa, can write very much better plays than the Irish Literary Theatre has staged. But, of course, the directors would not like to present such improper writers to the uncultivated, much less to the cultivated, rabblement. Accordingly, the rabblement, placid and intensely moral, is enthroned in boxes and galleries amid a hum of approval—*la bestia Tionfante*—and those who think that Echegaray is 'morbid,' and titter coyly when Mélisande lets down her

hair, are not sure but they are the trustees of every intellectual and poetic treasure.

Meanwhile, what of the artists? It is equally unsafe at present to say of Mr. Yeats that he has or has not genius. In aim and form *The Wind among the Reeds* is poetry of the highest order, and *The Adoration of the Magi* (a story which one of the great Russians might have written) shows what Mr. Yeats can do when he breaks with the half-gods. But an aesthete has a floating will, and Mr. Yeats's treacherous instinct of adaptability must be blamed for his recent association with a platform from which even self-respect should have urged him to refrain. Mr. Martyn and Mr. Moore are not writers of much originality. Mr. Martyn, disabled as he is by an incorrigible style, has none of the fierce, hysterical power of Strindberg, whom he suggests at times; and with him one is conscious of a lack of breadth and distinction which outweighs the nobility of certain passages. Mr. Moore, however, has wonderful mimetic ability, and some years ago his books might have entitled him to the place of honour among English novelists. But though *Vain Fortune* (perhaps one should add some of *Esther Waters*) is fine, original work, Mr. Moore is really struggling in the backwash of that tide which has advanced from Flaubert through Jakobsen to D'Annunzio: for two entire eras lie between *Madame Bovary* and *Il Fuoco*. It is plain from *Celibates* and the later novels that Mr. Moore is beginning to draw upon his literary account, and the quest of a new impulse may explain his recent startling conversion. Converts are in the movement now, and Mr. Moore and his island have been fitly admired. But however frankly Mr. Moore may misquote Pater and Turgenieff to defend himself, his new impulse has no kind of relation to the future of art.

In such circumstances it has become imperative to define the position. If an artist courts the favour of the multitude he cannot escape the contagion of its fetichism and deliberate self-deception, and if he joins in a popular movement he does so at his own risk. Therefore, the Irish Literary Theatre by its surrender to the trolls has cut itself adrift from the line of advancement. Until he has freed himself from the mean influences about him—sodden enthusiasm and clever insinuation and every flattering influence of vanity and low ambition—no man is an artist at all. But his true servitude is that he inherits a will broken by doubt and a soul that yields up all its hate to a caress; and the most seeming-independent are those who are the first to reassume their bonds. But Truth deals largely with us. Elsewhere there are men who are worthy to carry on the tradition of the old master who is dying in Christiania. He has already found his successor in the writer of *Michael Kramer,* and the third minister will not be wanting when his hour comes. Even now that hour may be standing by the door.

Painting of Lady Gregory in 1903 by John Butler Yeats (The Granger Collection, New York)

Lady Gregory

Lady Gregory played an instrumental role in the Irish Literary Revival. With William Butler Yeats and Edward Martin, Lady Gregory (née Isabella Augusta Persse) co-founded the Irish Literary Theatre in 1898. In 1904, she helped found the Abbey Theatre. Through association with Yeats, Joyce met Lady Gregory in 1902, the time when he was planning to study medicine in Paris. To financially assist Joyce in his academic endeavors, she introduced him to the editor of the Daily Express, *Ernest V. Longworth, who agreed to having Joyce write book reviews while studying in Paris. Joyce was harshly critical in his review of Lady Gregory's* Poets and Dreamers, *causing Longworth some consternation in deciding to publish it. In* Ulysses, *Joyce has Buck Mulligan poke fun at Stephen Dedalus, when he sarcastically says: "she gets you a job on the paper and then you go and slate her drivel to Jaysus." In his broadside "The Holy Office," Joyce alludes to Lady Gregory as one of Yeats's "giddy dames." The broadside and review clearly reflect Joyce's uncompromising aesthetic values and his attitude toward the Irish Literary Revival and its established figures. To Joyce, Lady Gregory epitomized the kind of artistic expression that he was struggling against.*

In 1902 W. B. Yeats heard Joyce read some of his poems. Joyce sent Yeats the poem he later included as poem XXXV in Chamber Music.

All day I hear the noise of waters
   Making moan,
Sad as the sea-bird is, when going
   Forth alone,
He hears the winds cry to the waters'
   Monotone.

The grey winds, the cold winds are blowing
   Where I go.
I hear the noise of many waters
   Far below.
All day, all night, I hear them flowing
   To and fro.

In his letter to Joyce of 18 December 1902, Yeats complimented the "charming rhythm in the second stanza" but found the poem "a little thin." He told Joyce the poem was the work "of a young man who is practicing his instrument, taking pleasure in the mere handling of the stops" (Letters II, p. 23).

Collecting Epiphanies

Joyce adapted the religious term epiphany to fit his artistic ends and to help define the theory of art that he was developing at this time. The word is derived from the Greek epiphaneia and means a sudden (transitory) manifestation of deity; the term also implies the revelation of a hidden message to benefit others. In Christianity, the Feast of the Epiphany, celebrated on 6 January, commemorates the showing forth of the divinity of Christ to the Magi. Joyce exploited the idea behind the term for literary purposes in his writing of Stephen Hero, Dubliners, A Portrait of the Artist as a Young Man, and Ulysses. For Joyce an epiphany meant a revelatory moment exposing the true character or essence of a person or thing. Only forty of the seventy-one or so epiphanies that Joyce recorded between 1900 and 1903 are extant, and these surviving examples seem to fall within dramatic and lyrical (or narrative) forms.

In My Brother's Keeper, Stanislaus Joyce recalled his brother working on epiphanies in spring 1900 at their home at 32 Glengriff Parade.

Another experimental form which his literary urge took while we were living at this address consisted in the noting of what he called 'epiphanies'—manifestations or revelations. Jim always had a contempt for secrecy, and these notes were in the beginning ironical observations of slips, and little errors and gestures—mere straws in the wind—by which people betrayed the very things they were most careful to conceal. 'Epiphanies' were always brief sketches, hardly ever more than some dozen lines in length, but always very accurately observed and noted, the matter being so slight. (pp. 124–125)

Joyce (second from left, third row) with faculty and classmates in the class of 1902 at University College

Joyce provides an account of the origin of the idea of collecting epiphanies in his first novel, Stephen Hero, *written 1904–1905, which was published after his death in 1944. One evening as he was walking down Eccles Street, Stephen*

heard the following fragment of colloquy out of which he received an impression keen enough to afflict his sensitiveness very severely.

The Young Lady–(drawling discreetly) . . . O, yes . . . I was . . . at the . . . cha . . . pel . . .

The Young Gentleman–(inaudibly) . . . I . . . (again inaudibly) . . . I . . .

The Young Lady–(softly) . . . O . . . but you're . . . ve . . . ry . . . wick . . . ed . . .

This triviality made him think of collecting many such moments together in a book of epiphanies. By an epiphany he meant a sudden spiritual manifestation, whether in the vulgarity of speech or of gesture or in a memorable phase of the mind itself. He believed that it was for the man of letters to record these epiphanies with extreme care, seeing that they themselves are the most delicate and evanescent of moments.

– *Stephen Hero, pp. 210–211*

In his 1937 memoir Oliver St. John Gogarty, *the model for Buck Mulligan in* Ulysses, *tells a story about Joyce's practice of collecting epiphanies. He recalls Joyce meeting with his friends following "an unsuccessful interview" with Lady Gregory, who "had no room for playboys except on the stage."*

. . . So Ulysses had to strike out for himself. Dublin's Dante had to find a way out of his own Inferno. But he had lost the key. James Augustine Joyce slipped politely from the snug with an "Excuse me!"

"Whist! He's gone to put it all down!"

"Put what down?"

"Put *us* down. A chiel's among us takin' notes. And, faith, he'll print it."

Now, that was a new aspect of James Augustine. I was too unsophisticated to know that even outside Lady Gregory's presence, notes made of those contemporary with the growing "Moment" would have a sale value later on, and even an historical interest. . . .

I was trying to recall what spark had been struck or what "folk phrase" Joyce had culled from Ellwood or me that sent him out to make his secret record.

Secrecy of any kind corrupts sincere relations. I don't mind being reported, but to be an unwilling contributor to one of his "Epiphanies" is irritating.

Probably Fr. Darlington had taught him, as an aside in his Latin class–for Joyce knew no Greek–that "Epiphany" meant "a showing forth." So he recorded

*Joyce in graduation robe for University College in 1902 (Croessmann
Collection of James Joyce, Special Collections/Morris Library,
Southern Illinois University, Carbondale)*

under "Epiphany" any showing forth of the mind by which he considered one gave oneself away.

Which of us had endowed him with an "Epiphany" and sent him to the lavatory to take it down?

"John," I said, seeking an ally, "he's codding the pair of us."

But John could not be enlisted to resent.

"A great artist!" he exclaimed, using "artist" in the sense it has in Dublin of a quaint fellow or a great cod: a pleasant and unhypocritical poseur, one who sacrifices his own dignity for his friends' diversion. . . .

"Codding apart, John, why is he taking notes?"

"We're all on the stage–Jayshus, we're all on the stage since the Old Lady threw him out. . . ."

– *As I Was Going Down Sackville Street: A Phantasy in Fact,*
pp. 294–295

In the Proteus episode of Ulysses, *Stephen Dedalus mockingly recalls the epiphanies he once wrote:*

Remember your epiphanies written on green oval leaves, deeply deep, copies to be sent if you died to all the great libraries of the world, including Alexandria? Someone was to read them there after a few thousand years, a mahamanvantara. Pico della Mirandola like. Ay, very like a whale. When one reads these strange pages of one long gone one feels that one is at one with one who once. . . .

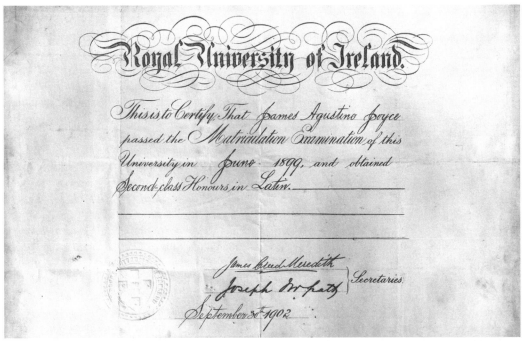

*Joyce's matriculation certificate for his work at University College was awarded through the Royal University of Ireland
(Division of Rare and Manuscript Collections, Carl A. Kroch Library, Cornell University [Robert Scholes,
catalogue of the Cornell Joyce Collection 1374]).*

A First Trip Abroad

With the intention of studying medicine, Joyce left Dublin for Paris in December 1902. According to Stanislaus Joyce in My Brother's Keeper, *Joyce recorded a dream-epiphany while he was living in Paris in 1902–1903, which he later recast in the Circe episode of* Ulysses. *In Joyce's dream the identity of his mother commingles with that of the Blessed Virgin:*

> She comes at night when the city is still, invisible, inaudible, all unsummoned. She comes from her ancient seat to visit the least of her children, mother most venerable, as though he had never been alien to her. She knows the inmost heart; therefore she is gentle, nothing exacting, saying, I am susceptible of change, an imaginative influence in the hearts of my children. Who has pity for you when you are sad among the strangers? Years and years I loved you when you lay in my womb.

Joyce returned to Dublin in April 1903 when he learned that his mother was dying, and by the time of her death in August, Joyce was uncertain of his plans. He continued to write book reviews for Dublin's Daily Express, *which he had been doing while in Paris, and composed the poems that make up* Chamber Music.

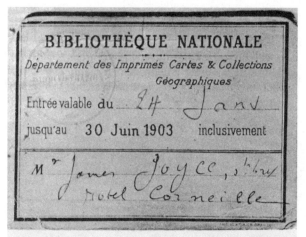

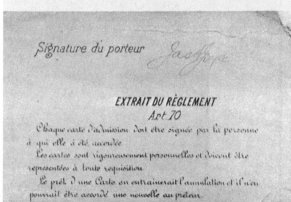

Joyce's card for admission to the Bibliothèque Nationale in Paris (Richard Ellmann's James Joyce, *new and revised edition, 1982)*

Joyce's brother Stanislaus, circa 1904, who was an invaluable confidant and often acted as a whetstone for the author's ideas during his early literary career

A First Portrait

In early 1904, Joyce submitted "A Portrait of the Artist," a fictional and philosophical prose reflection on the evolution of the artist, to the Irish magazine Dana. *Although commissioned by the journal's editors, John Eglinton and Frederick Ryan, the piece was rejected on the grounds that Eglinton found it incomprehensible. Joyce then decided to expand the essay into the novel he called "Stephen Hero," beginning to work on it on his twenty-second birthday, 2 February 1904. Edited by Richard M. Kain and Robert Scholes, "A Portrait of the Artist" was first published in the* Yale Review *(Spring 1960); it has been republished in* The Workshop of Daedalus, *edited by Scholes and Kain, in* A Portrait of the Artist as a Young Man: Text, Criticism, and Notes, *edited by Chester G. Anderson, and in* Poems and Shorter Writings *(1991). "[A] portrait," Joyce writes in the last line of the opening paragraph of the essay, "is not an indentificative paper but rather the curve of an emotion."*

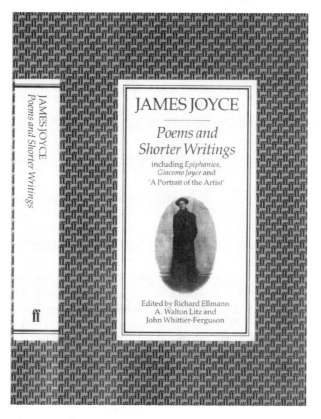

Dust jacket for 1991 book that includes much of Joyce's early work

Epiphanies in Criticism

Harry Levin's James Joyce: A Critical Introduction *(1941) was the first book-length discussion of the author by an American to receive international recognition. Levin also edited and wrote an introduction for* The Portable James Joyce, *a volume that has remained in print since its publication in 1946. Levin asserts that for Joyce an epiphany was "an essentially mystical concept."*

The term "fiction," ever since the novelists of the nineteenth century discovered that truth was stranger, has been misleading. A conscientious pupil of the naturalistic school, Joyce would not invent his material. He would continue to utilize his own experience, though his imagination was to carry him much farther than the naturalists in interpreting and arranging it. The precincts of his observation were restricted, but his perceptions were abnormally acute. He was the sort of person that Henry James advises the novelist to be, "one of those people on whom nothing is lost." The friends of his student days were quick to sense that he went among them taking notes. "So he recorded under Epiphany," says Dr. Gogarty, "any showing forth of the mind by which he considered one gave oneself away." Here, from the squirming model for Buck Mulligan, we have a clinical definition of what was

to Joyce an essentially mystical concept. The writer, no longer hoping to comprehend modern life in its chaotic fullness, was searching for external clues to its inner meaning.

An epiphany is a spiritual manifestation, more especially the original manifestation of Christ to the Magi. There are such moments in store for all of us, Joyce believed, if we but discern them. Sometimes, amid the most encumbered circumstances, it suddenly happens that the veil is lifted, the burthen of the mystery laid bare, and the ultimate secret of things made manifest. Such a sudden intimation was experienced by Marcel Proust, when he had dipped a bit of *madeleine* into a cup of linden tea. Such a momentary vision, perhaps too intimate to be included in the final version of the *Portrait of the Artist,* had once come to Stephen Dedalus, passing through Eccles Street, before "one of those brown brick houses which seem the very incarnation of Irish paralysis." It now seemed to him that the task of the man of letters was to record these delicate and evanescent states of mind, to become a collector of epiphanies. Walking along the beach, in *Ulysses,* he muses upon his own collection, and his youthful resolve to leave copies to all the libraries of the world, including Alexandria.

– James Joyce: A Critical Introduction, pp. 27–29

In their introductory note on the epiphanies in The Workshop of Daedalus *(1965), Robert Scholes and Richard Kain distinguish between two types of epiphanies and argue that the term is often used too loosely in criticism.*

The Epiphanies which have been preserved fall readily into two classes, which correspond, in many respects, to the two facets of Stephen Daedalus' definition in *SH*. In one kind the mind of the writer is most important. These Epiphanies, which may be called narrative (though a case might be made for calling some of them lyric) present for the most part "memorable phases" of Joyce's mind – as he observes, reminisces, or dreams. The Epiphanies of the second kind, which may be called dramatic, dispense with the narrator and focus more on "vulgarity of speech or of gesture." The distinction between the two kinds of Epiphany clearly reflects Joyce's early vision of himself in the world, and his counterpart Stephen in his world: the mind of the artist is "memorable," his companions and environment "vulgar." The conflict between the artist and his crass environment is at the root of the three versions of *A Portrait of the Artist as a Young Man* which Joyce wrote. He quickly outgrew the easy contrast between heroic artist and mean environment, and his view of this conflict grew complex enough in the final version so that critics can now argue as to whether the portrait of Stephen is finally ironic or romantic, hostile or sympathetic. But the early concept of the Epiphany seems to reserve, by definition, the sympathy for the artist's mind and the hostility for the surrounding world.

The relationship to Joyce's art of this term "epiphany," and of the actual Epiphanies which he recorded, has posed some difficult problems. The term has been applied, to *Dubliners* in particular, as if it referred to a principle of art according to which each story in the collection was constructed. If criticism finds the term useful in this sense, critics will no doubt continue to employ it; but they should do so in full awareness that they are using the term quite differently from the way Joyce himself used it. For him it had reference to life only, not to art. An Epiphany was life observed, caught in a kind of camera eye which reproduced a significant moment without comment. An Epiphany could not be constructed, only recorded. But such moments, once recorded, could be placed in an artistic framework and used to enrich with reality a fictional narrative. It is possible that a few Epiphanies were actually so used in *Dubliners,* but up to now not one known Epiphany has been discovered in that collection of stories.

In this excerpt Robert Adams Day discusses how Joyce used his epiphanies in his published work.

Dante, Ibsen, Joyce, Epiphanies, and the Art of Memory
Robert Adams Day
James Joyce Quarterly, 25 (Spring 1988): 357–362

I have been talking about single objects or names or phrases, while Joyce's epiphanies are all of paragraph length–dramatic scenes or speaking pictures. In fact, as I classify them, seventeen are sharply observed reality, eleven are Joyce's own dreams, seven are heavily ornamented static pictures, three are pure fantasy, and two might be called prose poems. But we discover that when Joyce uses them he nearly always trims them considerably–little is actually used beyond a single phrase in most cases; the surrounding details come from elsewhere. This fact leads me to suggest that the early epiphanies are rough diamonds and that Joyce later saw that he had not gotten their essence purified even when he set them down. The essence turns out to be a luminous point in darkness like the epiphanies of all the other modernists or like Dante's God, arbitrary, often grotesque or seemingly inappropriate, but serving to unlock the door of memory and trigger an appropriate and copious flow of words. (I might note that the epiphanies that are used *in extenso* are generally the prose-poems, and are used to represent a relatively immature hero self-indulgently gassing away in relatively immature, and hence rather thin, prose-poetry.)

The youthful critic who reads Dante and Ibsen and who records the epiphanies is the Stephen who in *Stephen Hero* gives the theory of the epiphany, with its wholeness, harmony, and radiance. The theory could not be bettered; but I believe that it was extended meditation on the performance of Dante and Ibsen that led Joyce to pare down the epiphanies to the single points of light that we see in their work and in his own later work. Joyce's practice, with its tiny radiant objective correlatives that trigger huge reverberations in both author and reader, is a recognition that *quidditas* is *claritas,* and that the very strangeness of the *quidditas* may be what best stimulates the memory and controls the imagination. Like the ancient practitioners of the art of memory [. . .] the mature Joyce trusted in the artist's prophetic genius to recognize the essential *quidditas* that would irradiate an epic.

TUESDAY, MAY 17, 1904.

FEIS CEOIL.

SINGING AND PIANOFORTE COMPETITIONS.

Yesterday, the annual competitions in connection with the Feis Ceoil opened in the Antient Concert Rooms. There was a large attendance of the general public, and much interest was taken in the singing and pianoforte playing. It may be remarked that the entries this year show a slight falling off, but this did not take away from the general interest which the festival excites. The vocal competitions for soprano (solo), and tenor (solo), took place in the large hall, whilst the upper hall was set apart for the pianoforte competitors. In the first of these three classes there were 29 entries, in the second 22, and in the third no less than 40.

Soprano Solo—The judge of solo singing was Signor Luigi Denza, Professor R.A.M. The test pieces were as follows :—(a) " Hear ye, Israel," from Mendelssohn's " Elijah " ; (b) an Irish Air—" Lullaby," arranged by Stanford ; and (c) a sight-reading test.

Signor Denza announced the result as follows :—1, Miss Margaret Moriarty, 92 Lower Leeson street ; 2, Miss Katharyn Warwick, 71 University avenue, Belfast; 3, Miss Moll Byrne, 6 Irishtown avenue, Sandycove ; highly commended, Miss Fanny Vincent, Loreto Abbey, Rathfarnham ; Miss Frances Walsh, 15 The Square, Tralee, and 103 Upper Rathmines.

In making the announcement Signor Denza said it gave him great pleasure to be back adjudicating at the Feis. The competition had been a very close one, there being but one mark of difference between the winners of the first and second prizes.

Junior Pianoforte—The test pieces were (a), Nocturne in G major (Field) ; (b), study No. 4 (Scarlatti) ; (c), an easy piece at sight. Prize-winners—1, Miss Annie Tracey, Charlotte street, Dublin, and Miss Elge Kennedy, Monkstown avenue. Both candidates being equal, get a silver medal. 2nd, Miss Charlotte Graham, Ailesbury road, Dublin, and Miss Gertrude E. Coloban, Rathmines road. Each of these candidates was awarded equal marks, and therefore each gets a second. Commended, Miss Norah Ireland, Eglinton avenue, Belfast.

Mr. Franklin Taylor, in announcing the result, said that the standard of merit of the performances had been so equal that a second trial was necessary. Even after the second test no point of difference was noticeable, and two of the youthful pianists were bracketed for equal honours in connection with the first prize. The same state of things prevailed in connection with the second prize, so that two seconds were awarded.

Tenor solo—1, Joseph A. Walsh, 66 Dublin road, Belfast ; 2, Whiston R. Gage, 2 Brighton terrace, Rathgar ; 3, James J. Joyce, 7 St. Peter's terrace, Cabra.

The adjudicator said he awarded second place to Mr. William Rathborne, of 154 Clonliffe road. He placed Mr. W. R. Gage second, and highly commended Mr. Joyce. Mr. Rathborne, however, was disqualified from winning the second prize, he having won it last year, and the awards were, therefore, made in the order given above.

THE CONCERT.

The attendance at the Feis inaugural concert in the Great Hall of the Royal University Buildings last evening did not exactly betoken an overflow . . . . . . Celtic song. The audience

Clipping from The Irish Times, *Dublin, in which it is announced that Joyce was awarded the bronze medal for his singing (Division of Rare and Manuscript Collections, Carl A. Kroch Library, Cornell University [Scholes 1388]*

Epicleti, Epiclets, and *Dubliners*

While Joyce was working on "Stephen Hero," the Irish writer and theosophist George Russell, whose pen name was Æ, asked him to contribute a short story to the weekly Dublin newspaper, the Irish Homestead. *Joyce immediately began "The Sisters," his first* Dubliners *story, which was published on 13 August 1904 under the pseudonym Stephen Daedelus. Two others followed, "Eveline" (10 September 1904) and "After the Race" (17 December 1904). During this time, Joyce, in a letter to his former classmate Constantine Curran, explained his intentions: "I am writing a series of epicleti–ten–for a paper. I have written one. I call the series* Dubliners *to betray the soul of that hemiplegia or paralysis which many consider a city" (Letters I, p. 55).*

The term epicleti *is a Latinized transliteration of the Greek adjective* epicletos *and is related to the Greek noun* epiclesis, *a word that means an invocation or a calling down upon. In the ancient Christian liturgy, the* epiclesis *was an invocation to the Holy Spirit during the sacrament of the mass to descend upon the bread and wine and to transform them into the eucharistic body and blood of Christ. Although no longer used in the Roman Catholic liturgy, the prayer is still part of the Eastern Orthodox tradition. Joyce's precise understanding of the term is uncertain. Its meaning, as Ellmann and others suggest, may be elucidated by a comment that Joyce voiced to his brother Stanislaus. In* My Brother's Keeper, *Stanislaus records the assertion Joyce made about the poetry he was currently writing around 1900: "'Don't you think . . . there is a certain resemblance between the mystery of the Mass and what I am trying to do? I mean that I am trying in my poems to give people some kind of intellectual pleasure or spiritual enjoyment by converting the bread of everyday life into something that has a permanent artistic life of its own . . . for their mental, moral, and spiritual uplift'" (pp. 103–104).*

Epicleti can also mean an imputation or a charge against someone, and its slight variant epicletos *can mean accused or summoned before a court. The Latinized form* epicleti, *then, would either be a genitive singular (e.g., stories of the accused) or a plural adjective (e.g., the accused people, that is, in this case, the accused Dubliners, as Joyce's remarks to Curran seem to indicate). The term may also suggest a trial to which Joyce summons the accused.*

But the basis of the argument–the word itself–may hinge upon a misreading of Joyce's handwriting. In a detailed article titled "The Merry Greeks (With a Farewell to epicleti*)," published in the* James Joyce Quarterly *(vol. 32, Spring and Summer 1995, pp. 597–617), Wolfhard Steppe offers a perceptive analysis of the transmissional history of* epicleti *and the scholarship surrounding it and concludes that what Joyce actually wrote was* epiclets, *meaning little epics, and not* epicleti.

676   THE IRISH HOMESTEAD.   AUGUST 13, 1904.

O, King of Glory, is it not a great change
  Since I was a young man, long, long ago?
When the heat of the sun made my face glow
  As I cut the grass, on a fine cloudless day;
Fair girls laughing
  All through the field raking hay,
Merry in the fragrant morning,
  And the sound of their voices like music in the air.

The bees were after the honey,
  Taking it to their nests among the hay,
Flying against us nimbly and merrily,
  And disappearing from sight with small keen buzz
And the butterflies on the thistles,
  And on the meadow daisies, and from flower to flower,
On light wing lying and rising up,
  Moving through the air—they were fine.

The blackbird and the thrush were in the small nut wood,
  Making sweet music like the songs of the bards,
And the sprightly lark with a song in her little mouth
  Poising herself in the air aloft,
The beautiful thrush was on top of the branch,
  His throat stretched out in melodious song.
And, O, God of Grace, it was fine to be
  In beauteous Ireland at that time!

OUR WEEKLY STORY.

THE SISTERS.

By Stephen Dedalus.

Three nights in succession I had found myself in Great Britain-street at that hour, as if by Providence. Three nights also I had raised my eyes to that lighted square of window and speculated. I seemed to understand that it would occur at night. But in spite of the Providence that had led my feet, and in spite of the reverent curiosity of my eyes, I had discovered nothing. Each night the square was lighted in the same way, faintly and evenly. It was not the light of candles, so far as I could see. Therefore, it had not yet occurred.

On the fourth night at that hour I was in another part of the city. It may have been the same Providence that led me there—a whimsical kind of Providence to take me at a disadvantage. As I went home I wondered was that square of window lighted as before, or did it reveal the ceremonious candles in whose light the Christian must take his last sleep. I was not surprised, then, when at supper I found myself a prophet. Old Cotter and my uncle were talking at the fire, smoking. Old Cotter is the old distiller who owns the batch of prize setters. He used to be very interesting when I knew him first, talking about "faints" and "worms." Now I find him tedious.

While I was eating my stirabout I heard him saying to my uncle:

"Without a doubt. Upper storey—(he tapped an unnecessary hand at his forehead)—gone."

"So they said. I never could see much of it. I thought he was sane enough."

"So he was, at times," said old Cotter.

I sniffed the "was" apprehensively, and gulped down some stirabout.

"Is he better, Uncle John?"

"He's dead."

"O . . . he's dead?"

"Died a few hours ago."

"Who told you?"

"Mr. Cotter here brought us the news. He was passing there."

"Yes, I just happened to be passing, and I noticed the window . . . you know."

"Do you think they will bring him to the chapel?" asked my aunt.

"Oh, no, ma'am. I wouldn't say so."

"Very unlikely," my uncle agreed.

So old Cotter had got the better of me for all my vigilance of three nights. It is often annoying the way people will blunder on what you have elaborately planned for. I was sure he would die at night.

The following morning after breakfast I went down to look at the little house in Great Britain-street. It was an unassuming shop registered under the vague name of "Drapery." The drapery was principally children's boots and umbrellas, and on ordinary days there used to be a notice hanging in the window, which said "Umbrellas recovered." There was no notice visible now, for the shop blinds were drawn down and a crape bouquet was tied to the knocker with white ribbons. Three women of the people and a telegram boy were reading the card pinned on the crape. I also went over and read :—"July 2nd, 189— The Rev. James Flynn (formerly of St. Ita's Church), aged 65 years. R.I.P."

Only sixty-five! He looked much older than that. I often saw him sitting at the fire in the close dark room behind the shop, nearly smothered in his great coat. He seemed to have almost stupefied himself with heat, and the gesture of his large trembling hand to his nostrils had grown automatic. My aunt, who is what they call good-hearted, never went into the shop without bringing him some High Toast, and he used to take the packet of snuff from her hands, gravely inclining his head for sign of thanks. He used to sit in that stuffy room for the greater part of the day from early morning, while Nannie (who is almost stone deaf) read out the newspaper to him. His other sister, Eliza, used to mind the shop. These two old women used to look after him, feed him, and clothe him. The clothing was not difficult, for his ancient, priestly clothes were quite green with age, and his dogskin slippers were everlasting. When he was tired of hearing the news he used to rattle his snuff-box on the arm of his chair to avoid shouting at her, and then he used to make believe to read his Prayer Book. Make believe, because, when Eliza brought him a cup of soup from the kitchen, she had always to waken him.

As I stood looking up at the crape and the card that bore his name I could not realise that he was dead. He seemed like one who could go on living for ever if he only wanted to; his life was so methodical and uneventful. I think he said more to me than to anyone else. He had an egoistic contempt for all women-folk, and suffered all their services to him in polite silence. Of course, neither of his sisters were very intelligent. Nannie, for instance, had been reading out the newspaper to him every day for years, and could read tolerably well, and yet she always spoke of it as the *Freeman's General*. Perhaps he found me more intelligent, and honoured me with words for that reason. Nothing, practically nothing, ever occurred to remind him of his former life (I mean friends or visitors), and still he could remember every detail of it in his own fashion. He had studied at the college in Rome, and he taught me to speak Latin in the Italian way. He often put me through the responses of the Mass, he smiling often and pushing huge pinches of snuff up each nostril alternately. When he smiled he used to uncover his big, discoloured teeth, and let his tongue lie on his lower lip. At first this habit of his used to make me feel uneasy. Then I grew used to it.

The first published version of the story that Joyce later revised as the opening story of Dubliners. *The Irish Homestead was a weekly Dublin newspaper founded in 1895 and associated with the Irish Agricultural Co-operative Movement (National Library of Ireland).*

AUGUST 13, 1904.   THE IRISH HOMESTEAD.   677

That evening my aunt visited the house of mourning and took me with her. It was an oppressive summer evening of faded gold. Nannie received us in the hall, and, as it was no use saying anything to her, my aunt shook hands with her for all. We followed the old woman upstairs and into the dead-room. The room, through the lace end of the blind, was suffused with dusky golden light, amid which the candles looked like pale, thin flames. He had been coffined. Nannie gave the lead, and we three knelt down at the foot of the bed. There was no sound in the room for some minutes except the sound of Nannie's mutterings—for she prays noisily. The fancy came to me that the old priest was smiling as he lay there in his coffin.

But, no. When we rose and went up to the head of the bed I saw that he was not smiling. There he lay solemn and copious in his brown habit, his large hands loosely retaining his rosary. His face was very grey and massive, with distended nostrils and circled with scanty white fur. There was a heavy odour in the room—the flowers.

We sat downstairs in the little room behind the shop, my aunt and I and the two sisters. Nannie sat in a corner and said nothing, but her lips moved from speaker to speaker with a painfully intelligent motion. I said nothing either, being too young, but my aunt spoke a good deal, for she is a bit of a gossip—harmless.

"Ah, well! he's gone!"

"To enjoy his eternal reward, Miss Flynn, I'm sure. He was a good and holy man."

"He was a good man, but, you see . . . he was a disappointed man. . . . You see, his life was, you might say, crossed."

"Ah, yes! I know what you mean."

"Not that he was anyway mad, as you know yourself, but he was always a little queer. Even when we were all growing up together he was queer. One time he didn't speak hardly for a month. You know, he was that kind always."

"Perhaps he read too much, Miss Flynn?"

"O, he read a good deal, but not latterly. But it was his scrupulousness, I think, affected his mind. The duties of the priesthood were too much for him."

"Did he . . . peacefully?"

"O, quite peacefully, ma'am. You couldn't tell when the breath went out of him. He had a beautiful death, God be praised."

"And everything . . . ?"

"Father O'Rourke was in with him yesterday and gave him the Last Sacrament."

"He knew then?"

"Yes; he was quite resigned."

Nannie gave a sleepy nod and looked ashamed.

"Poor Nannie," said her sister, "she's worn out. All the work we had, getting in a woman, and laying him out; and then the coffin and arranging about the funeral. God knows we did all we could, as poor as we are. We wouldn't see him want anything at the last."

"Indeed you were both very kind to him while he lived."

"Ah, poor James; he was no great trouble to us. You wouldn't hear him in the house no more than now. Still I know he's gone and all that. . . . I won't be bringing him in his soup any more, nor Nannie reading him the paper, nor you, ma'am, bringing him his snuff. How he liked that snuff! Poor James!"

"O, yes, you'll miss him in a day or two more than you do now."

Silence invaded the room until memory reawakened it, Eliza speaking slowly—

"It was that chalice he broke. . . . Of course, it was all right. I mean it contained nothing. But still . . . They say it was the boy's fault. But poor James was so nervous, God be merciful to him."

"Yes, Miss Flynn, I heard that . . . about the chalice. . . He . . . his mind was a bit affected by that."

"He began to mope by himself, talking to no one, and wandering about. Often he couldn't be found. One night he was wanted, and they looked high up and low down and couldn't find him. Then the clerk suggested the chapel. So they opened the chapel (it was late at night), and brought in a light to look for him. . . And there, sure enough, he was, sitting in his confession-box in the dark, wide awake, and laughing like softly to himself. Then they knew something was wrong."

"God rest his soul!"

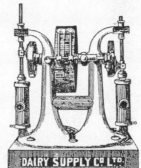

Two views of the Martello Tower at Sanycove, where Joyce lived with his friend Oliver St. John Gogarty in September 1904
(courtesy of Irish Tourist Board)

Nora Barnacle and a Life Abroad

Nora Barnacle met James Joyce on 10 June 1904, a few months after she arrived in Dublin from Galway. They went walking together at Ringsend, a Dublin suburb, on the sixteenth of that month, the date memorialized in Ulysses *and known throughout the world as Bloomsday. On 9 October, Nora eloped with Joyce for the Continent where the two lived in cities—Pola, Trieste, Rome, Zurich, and Paris—for the rest of their lives. The couple did not legally marry until 4 July 1931 because Joyce rejected marriage as a social institution; the only reason the couple did marry was to protect the inheritance rights of their children.*

Joyce and Nora first journeyed to Zurich, where he thought an English agent had secured a teaching position for him at the Berlitz Language School. When he found that no such position was available, the couple continued on first to the Berlitz School in Trieste and then to the one in Pola, where Joyce taught until the Austrian authorities expelled

Nora Barnacle Joyce (Croessmann Collection of James Joyce, Special Collections/Morris Library, Southern Illinois University Carbondale)

Joyce in 1904 (photograph by Constantine P. Curran). According to his biographer Richard Ellmann, Joyce later said that at that moment, "I was wondering would he lend me five shillings" (James Joyce Collection. General Collection, Beinecke Rare Book and Manuscript Library, Yale University).

aliens from the city in March 1905. Joyce then accepted a position at the Berlitz School in Trieste. With the exception of a seven-month stay in Rome from the end of July 1906 to the beginning of March 1907, Joyce and Nora for the next ten years lived in Trieste where their two children, George and Lucia, were born.

While in Trieste, Joyce published Chamber Music *in 1907 to positive reviews that often emphasized the musical quality of the poetry. Arthur Symons, who was instrumental in getting Elkin Mathews to publish the poems and who was their first reviewer, favorably wrote in the 22 June 1907 issue of* The Nation *that the verses "are all so singularly good, so firm and delicate and yet so full of music and suggestion that I can hardly choose among them." In 1907, Joyce also finished* Dubliners, *but publication of this collection of short stories was delayed until 1914 because of publishers' objections about certain passages considered offensive and about the use of real names.*

Agreement made this *twenty sixth* day of *February 1906* between

James A. Joyce. Esq.

of *Via Giovanni Boccaccio 1.º Trieste Austria*

(hereinafter called the AUTHOR) of the one part and E. GRANT RICHARDS of No. 7 Carlton Street S.W. Publisher (hereinafter called the PUBLISHER) of the other part each on behalf of themselves and their heirs executors administrators and assigns WHEREBY it is agreed as follows:

1. The PUBLISHER agrees to purchase and the AUTHOR agrees to sell the entire copyright without any reserve in the United Kingdom and all other parts of the world of a work entitled

Dubliners

the completed manuscript executed in a proper manner of which the AUTHOR has delivered ~~or hereby undertakes to deliver~~ to the PUBLISHER ~~within~~ ————————— in consideration of the following payments viz.:

A royalty of 10% on the published price of copies sold. no royalty being paid on the first five hundred copies of the English edition.

2. The PUBLISHER will according to her own judgment and in such manner as in her unfettered discretion she may consider advisable at her own cost print and publish a first edition of the said work and further editions if in her judgment further editions are required and in her absolute discretion advertise the same and shall determine all details and in her absolute discretion make all arrangements of and incidental to the printing publishing advertising sale price and reviewing of the said work.

3. Should the PUBLISHER sell exchange assign or otherwise dispose of any serial rights or any right of publication or of translation of the said work for the colonies or foreign countries or otherwise an amount equivalent to *50%* of the net profits realised and actually received by the PUBLISHER shall be paid to the AUTHOR.

The first page of the agreement between Joyce and Grant Richards to publish Dubliners. *This contract was not honored by the publisher. (Division of Rare and Manuscript Collections, Carl A. Kroch Library, Cornell University [Scholes 1396])*

Chamber Music

Recommended by Symons, Chamber Music, *Joyce's first book of poetry, was published by Mathews in London in May 1907. The work is a suite of thirty-six lyrical poems in which the speaker, a young man, captures the varied emotions of romantic and sexual love. Composed between 1901 and 1904, the poems reflect Joyce's own emotional state during this period and introduce several important themes found in his later writings, such as companionship, frustrated love, loneliness, betrayal, and the role of the poet. In his 21 August 1909 letter to Barnacle, who had stayed behind in Trieste while her husband was visiting Dublin, Joyce writes that he "was a strange lonely boy" when he composed* Chamber Music, *waiting for that day when "a girl would love" him. Joyce told his common-law wife that "the book of verses is for you. It holds the desire of my youth and you, darling, were the fulfilment of that desire"* (Letters II, pp. 236, 237).

On the Title *Chamber Music*

In an 18 October 1906 letter to Stanislaus, Joyce expressed dissatisfaction with the title: "The reason why I dislike Chamber Music *as a title is that it is too complacent. I should prefer a title which to a certain extent repudiated the book, without altogether disparaging it"* (Letters II, p. 182). *In general, Joyce's attitude toward* Chamber Music *seems to have been ambivalent.*

In James Joyce *Ellmann records an anecdote regarding the title of* Chamber Music:

Gogarty . . . had brought Joyce to visit Jenny, an easy-going widow, and while they all drank porter Joyce read out his poems, which he carried with him in a large packet, each written in his best hand in the middle of a large piece of parchment. The widow was pleased enough by this entertainment, but had to interrupt to withdraw behind a screen to a chamber pot. As the two young men listened, Gogarty cried out, "There's a critic for you!" Joyce had already accepted the title of *Chamber Music* which Stanislaus had suggested; and when Stanislaus heard the story from him, he remarked, "You can take it as a favorable omen."

In the Sirens *episode of* Ulysses, *Leopold Bloom momentarily muses upon the phrase "Chamber music" and thinks of his wife Molly:*

Chamber music. Could make a kind of pun on that. It is a kind of music I often thought when she. Acoustics that is. Tinkling. Empty vessels make most noise. Because the acoustics, the resonance changes according as the weight of the water is equal to the law of falling water. Like those rhapsodies of Liszt's, Hungarian, gipsyeyed. Pearls. Drops. Rain. Diddleiddle addleaddle ooddleooddle. Hissss.

In his 21 August 1909 letter Joyce told Nora that there was something higher in her than anything he had been able to realize in his verse, that he had written poems such as "Gentle lady" and "Thou leanest to the shell of night" for an imagined girl, one "fashioned into a curious grave beauty by the culture of generations before her" (Letters II, p. 237).

XXVI

Thou leanest to the shell of night,
    Dear lady, a divining ear.
In that soft choiring of delight
    What sound hath made thy heart to fear?
Seemed it of rivers rushing forth
From the grey deserts of the north?

    That mood of thine, O timorous,
Is his, if thou but scan it well,
    Who a mad tale bequeaths to us
At ghosting hour conjurable–
    And all for some strange name he read
    In Purchas or in Holinshed.

Title page for Joyce's first book (courtesy of C.W. Post Library of Long Island)

Reviews of *Chamber Music*

Chamber Music
Thomas Kettle
Freeman's Journal, 1 June 1907

Those who remember University College life of five years back will have many memories of Mr. Joyce. Wilful, fastidious, a lover of elfish paradoxes, he was to the men of his time the very voice and embodiment of the literary spirit. His work, never very voluminous, had from the first a rare and exquisite accent. One still goes back to the files of "St. Stephen's," to the "Saturday Review," the "Homestead," to various occasional magazines to find those lyrics and stories which, although at first reading so slight and frail, still hold one curiously by their integrity of form. "Chamber Music" is a collection of the best of these delicate verses, which have, each of them, the bright beauty of a crystal. The title of the book evokes that atmosphere of remoteness, restraint, accomplished execution characteristic of its whole contents. There is but one theme behind the music, a love, gracious, and, in its way, strangely intense, but fashioned by temperamental and literary moulds, too strict to permit it to pass over into the great tumult of passion. The inspiration of the book is almost entirely literate. There is no trace of the folk-lore, the folk-dialect, or even the National feeling that have coloured the work of practically every writer in contemporary Ireland. Neither is there any sense of that modern point of view which consumes all life in the languages of "problems." It is clear, delicate, distinguished playing, of the same kindred with harps, with wood-birds, and with Paul Verlaine. But the only possible criticism of poetry is quotation.

I

Strings in the earth and air
  Make music sweet;
Strings by the river where
  The willows meet.

There's music along the river
  For Love wanders there;
Pale flowers on his mantle,
  Dark leaves on his hair.

All softly playing,
  With head to the music bent,
And fingers straying
  Upon an instrument.

. . . .

Mr. Joyce's book is one that all his old friends will, with a curious pleasure, add to their shelves, and that will win him many new friends.
  —reprinted from James Joyce: The Critical Heritage

Arthur Symons (1865–1945) was a literary journalist, an early advocate of the French symbolist movement, and editor of Savoy. *Symons's book* The Symbolist Movement in Literature, *which Joyce read while a student at University College, Dublin, had significant influence on Joyce's writings.*

A Book of Songs
Arthur Symons
Nation, 1 (22 June 1907): 639

Chamber Music, by James Joyce, an Irishman, who was in no Irish movement, literary or national, has not anything obviously Celtic in its manner. The book is tiny, there are 37 pages, with a poem on each page. And they are all so singularly good, so firm and delicate, and yet so full of music and suggestion, that I can hardly choose between them; they are almost all of an equal merit. Here is one of the finest:

Gentle lady, do not sing
  Sad songs about the end of love;
Lay aside sadness and sing
  How love that passes is enough.

Sing about the long deep sleep
  Of lovers that are dead and how
In the grave all love shall sleep.
  Love is aweary now.

No one who has not tried can realize how difficult it is to do such tiny evanescent things as that; for it is to evoke, not only roses in mid-winter, but the very dew of the roses. Sometimes I am reminded of Elizabethan, but more often Jacobean, lyrics; there is more than sweetness, there is now and then the sharp prose touch, as in *Rochester,* which gives a kind of malice to sentiment:

For elegant and antique phrase,
  Dearest, my lips wax all too wise;
Nor have I known a love whose praise
  Our piping poets solemnise,
Neither is love where may not be
Ever so little falsity.

There is a rare kind of poetry to be made out of the kind or unkind insinuation of lovers, who are not always in a state of rapture, even when the mood comes for singing, and it may, like this love-poet, be turned to a new harmony.

And all for some strange name he read,
In Purchas or in Holinshed.

There is no substance at all in these songs, which hardly hint at a story; but they are like a whispering clavichord that someone plays in the evening, when it is getting dark. They are full of ghostly old tunes, that were never young, and will never be old, played on an old instrument. If poetry is to be a thing overheard, these songs, certainly, will justify the definition. They are so slight, as a drawing of Whistler is slight, that their entire beauty will not be discovered by those who go to poetry for anything but its perfume. But to those who care only for what is essentially poetry in a poem, they will seem to have so much the more value by all they omit. There is only just enough, but these instants are, in Browning's phrase, "made eternity."

Perhaps the rare quality of these songs might captivate certain readers. Such a song as *Bright Cap and Streamers* or *Silently She's Combing* ought to catch every fancy, and the graver poems ought to awaken every imagination. But if anything in art is small, and merely good, without anything but that fact to recommend it, it has usually to wait a long time for recognition. People are so afraid of following even an impulse, fearing that they may be mistaken. How unlikely it seems, does it not, that any new thing should come suddenly into the world and be beautiful?

In spring 1914 Joyce was reading proofs for his story collection Dubliners, *which was being published by Grant Richards. In an 8 May 1914 letter to Richards (Letters II, p. 332), Joyce mentioned that he was sending separately excerpts from reviews of* Chamber Music—*which he had selected himself and had printed—that he hoped would be useful in advertising his new book. The excerpts Joyce chose from the reviews of Symons and Kettle are not included.*

Chanel in the '*Leader*': Mr. Joyce has a wonderful mastery over the technique of poetry. It is not without supreme skill that he produces lines of such apparent ease and simplicity, every word in its right place, the whole beautiful in its unadorned charm with a faint subtle fragrance of earthly loveliness. . . . Mr. Joyce flows in a clear delicious stream that ripples. . . . Mr. Joyce complies will [sic] none of my critical principles: he is, in truth, entirely earthly, unthinking of the greater and the further, though let me say in justice that the casual reader will see nothing in his verses to object to, nothing incapable of an innocent explanation. But earthly as he is, he is so simple, so pretty, so alluring, I cannot bring myself to chide him.

. . . .

Daily News: Light and evanescent, pretty and fragile. . . . His poems are attempts at music: he has tried to express one art in terms of another. His aim has been to catch in his rhythms something of the music of pipe or lute as distinct from the verbal music of the great lyrical masters. . . . His poems have at once the music and the want of music of a harpstring played on by the winds in some forest of Broceliande.

Evening Standard: Pretty lyrics with a delusive title.

Manchester Guardian: A welcome contribution to contemporary poetry. Here are thirty-six lyrics of quite notable beauty. . . . Something of the spirit of Waller and Herrick . . . grace and simplicity . . . an elegance and delicacy that are as uncommon as they are perilous. At their best they reveal a rare musical quality. His muse is a gentle tender spirit that knows smiles and tears, the rain, the dew and the morning sun.

Nottingham Guardian: Lovers of verse will delight in many of the pieces for their simple unaffected merit. 'Chamber Music' has a tuneful ring befitting the title and both the rhythm and the smoothness of his lines are excellent.

Glasgow Herald: In verse which has an old-fashioned sweetness and flavour, Mr. Joyce sings of the coming and, apparently, inexplicable going of love. The most are but snatches of song and one has to be penetrated by the subtle music of them before their poetic value is perceived. Once that is felt their merit is beyond dispute though only lovers of poetry will be likely to see or acknowledge it. Verse such as this has its own charm but where will it find its audience.

Irish Daily Independent: . . . Music in verse, poems, sweet, reposeful and sublime; poems that lying in the shade amid the scent of new-mown hay one would read and dream on, forgetful of the workaday world.

Bookman: A little book of poetry which charms, provokes criticism and charms again. Mr. Joyce has a touch reminiscent of the sixteenth century poets, with here and there a break in his lines' smoothness which can only be smoothed by an oldtime stress on the syllable, such as Vaughan and Herbert demanded. . . . At times there are bold liberties taken with rhyme and rhythm but there is much of music and quaintness in this little volume.

Scotsman: A volume of graceful verse: it contains some little gems of real beauty.

Country Life: A very promising little volume.

Setting Joyce's Poems to Music

The English-born Irish composer, G. Molyneux Palmer (1882–1957), was one of the first to write musical settings for the poems in Chamber Music. In a 27 December 1937 letter to his son (Letters III), Joyce asserted that Palmer was the best of the thirty or forty composers who had set his poems to music. In all Palmer set to music thirty-two of the thirty-six poems in the collection. Myra Russel discusses Palmer's settings in James Joyce's Chamber Music: The Lost Settings (1993).

The opening lines of G. Molyneux Palmer's setting for poem XXXI from Chamber Music, "O, it was out by Donnycarney . . ." The only poem in the collection that makes a direct reference to Ireland, this poem was the first of three of Palmer's settings that Joyce listed as the ones he preferred in a 6 October 1913 letter to the composer; the other two favored settings were for "At that hour when all things have repose" and "Gentle lady, do not sing" (Croessmann Collection of James Joyce, Special Collections/Morris Library, Southern Illinois University Carbondale).

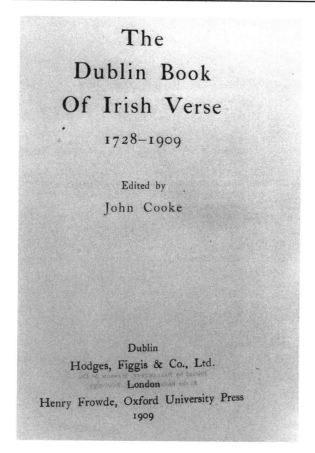

Title page for the book that first anthologized Joyce's writing; the collection included three poems from Chamber Music: I, "Strings in the earth and air"; XI, "Bid adieu, adieu, adieu"; and XII, "What counsel has the hooded moon."

Drawing of the cinematograph, the first in Dublin, that Joyce opened with the backing of Trieste businessmen on 20 December 1909. The theater was sold at a loss in the summer of 1910 (Croessmann Collection of James Joyce, Special Collections/Morris Library, Southern Illinois University Carbondale).

Publishing *Dubliners*

Dubliners *consists of fifteen short stories that Joyce wrote over a period of three years, from 1904 to 1907. Because of difficulties with publishers, however, the collection did not come out until 1914. Three of the stories—"The Sisters," "Eveline," and "After the Race"—were previously published in the* Irish Homestead *in 1904. Joyce revised "The Sisters" and "Eveline" but not "After the Race." Although he was not pleased with the story and intended to rewrite it, as he confided to his brother in a 19 August 1906 letter* (Letters II, *p. 151), he never got around to doing so; it was about this time that the long drawn-out delay in publishing* Dubliners *began with Grant Richards's 23 April 1906 letter to Joyce in which Richards voiced objections to certain passages in "Two Gallants," "Counterparts," and "Grace." Joyce's dissatisfaction with "After the Race" was again expressed in a November 1906 letter to his brother* (Letters II, *p. 189) in which he identifies it as one of "the two worst stories" in the collection; the other was "A Painful Case."*

The stories provide a realistic portrayal of the customs, thought, and behavior of Dubliners at the turn of the century. In an October 1905 letter to the British publisher Richards, who published Dublin-ers *nine years later, Joyce argues that in his judgment no "writer has yet presented Dublin to the world" though it is supposedly "the second city of the British Empire"* (Letters II, *p. 122). In a May 1906 letter to Richards, Joyce explains further his intent and the overall design of the stories:*

My intention was to write a chapter of the moral history of my country and I chose Dublin for the scene because that city seemed to me the centre of paralysis. I have tried to present it to the indifferent public under four of its aspects: childhood, adolescence, maturity and public life. The stories are arranged in this order. I have written it for the most part in a style of scrupulous meanness and with the conviction that he is a very bold man who dares to alter in the presentment, still more to deform, whatever he has seen or heard. (*Letters II*, p. 134)

In this same letter Joyce defends two stories in Dubliners, *"Two Gallants" and "Counterparts," against objections leveled by Richards's printer. These objections marked the beginning of an eight-year delay in the publication of* Dubliners.

Joyce chronicled the difficulties he encountered in getting Dubliners *published in "A Curious History," a collation of two letters that he sent to Ezra Pound in November 1913. With an introduction by Pound–*

The following statement having been received by me from an author of known and notable talents, and the state of the case being now, so far as I know, precisely what it was at the date of his last letter (November 30th), I have thought it more appropriate to print his communication entire rather than to indulge in my usual biweekly comment upon books published during the fortnight.

–it was published in the London-based periodical The Egoist *on 15 January 1914 and reprinted as a broadside by the New York publisher B. W. Huebsch in May 1917.*

A Curious History
James Joyce
Egotist, 1 (15 January 1914): 26–27

The following letter, which was the history of a book of stories, was sent by me to the Press of the United Kingdom two years ago. It was published by two newspapers so far as I know: *Sinn Fein* (Dublin) and the *Northern Whig* (Belfast).

Sir May I ask you to publish this letter which throws some light on the present conditions of authorship in England and Ireland?

Nearly six years ago Mr Grant Richards, publisher, of London signed a contract with me for the publication of a book of stories written by me, entitled *Dubliners.* Some ten months later he wrote asking me to omit one of the stories and passages in others which, as he said, his printer refused to set up. I declined to do either and a correspondence began between Mr Grant Richards and myself which lasted more than three months. I went to an international jurist in Rome (where I lived then) and was advised to omit. I declined to do so and the MS was returned to me, the publisher refusing to publish notwithstanding his pledged printed word, the contract remaining in my possession.

Six months afterwards a Mr Hone wrote to me from Marseilles to ask me to submit the MS to Messrs Maunsel, publishers, of Dublin. I did so: and after about a year, in July 1909, Messrs Maunsel signed a contract with me for the publication of the book on or before 1 September 1910. In December 1909 Messrs Maunsel's manager begged me to alter a passage in one of the stories, *Ivy Day in the Committee Room,* wherein some reference was made to Edward VII. I agreed to do so, much against my will, and altered one or two phrases. Messrs Maunsel continually postponed the date of publication and in the end wrote, asking me to omit the passage or to change it radically. I declined to do either, pointing out that Mr Grant Richards of London had raised no objection to the passage when Edward VII was alive and that I could not see why an Irish publisher should raise an objection to it when Edward VII had passed into history. I suggested arbitration or a deletion of the passage with a prefatory note of explanation by me but Messrs Maunsel would agree to neither. As Mr Hone (who had written to me in the first instance) disclaimed all responsibility in the matter and any connection with the firm I took the opinion of a solicitor in Dublin who advised me to omit the passage, informing me that as I had no domicile in the United Kingdom I could not sue Messrs Maunsel for breach of contract unless I paid £100 into court and that, even if I paid £100 into court and sued them, I should have no chance of getting a verdict in my favour from a Dublin jury if the passage in dispute could be taken as offensive in any way to the late king. I wrote then to the present king, George V, enclosing a printed proof of the story with the passage therein marked and begging him to inform me whether in his view the passage (certain allusions made by a person of the story in the idiom of his social class) should be withheld from publication as offensive to the memory of his father. His Majesty's private secretary sent me this reply:

Buckingham Palace

The private secretary is commanded to acknowledge the receipt of Mr James Joyce's letter of the 1 instant and to inform him that it is inconsistent with rule for His Majesty to express his opinion in such cases. The enclosures are returned herewith

11 August 1911

Here is the passage in dispute:

–But look here, John,–said Mr O'Connor.–Why should we welcome the king of England? Didn't Parnell himself . . . ?–

–Parnell,–said Mr Henchy,–is dead. Now, here's the way I look at it. Here's this chap come to the throne after his old mother keeping him out of it till the man was grey. He's a jolly fine decent fellow, if you ask me, and no damn nonsense about him. He just says to himself:–*The old one never went to see these wild Irish. By Christ, I'll go myself and see what they're like.*–And are we going to insult the man when he comes over here on a friendly visit? Eh? Isn't that right, Crofton?–

Mr Crofton nodded his head.

–But after all now,–said Mr Lyons, argumentatively,–King Edward's life, you know, is not the very . . .–

–Let bygones be bygones.–said Mr Henchy–I admire the man personally. He's just an ordinary knockabout like you and me. He's fond of his glass of grog and he's a bit of a rake, perhaps, and he's a good sportsman. Damn it, can't we Irish play fair?–

I wrote this book seven years ago and, as I cannot see in any quarter a chance that my rights will be protected, I hereby give Messrs Maunsel publicly permission to publish this story with what changes or deletions they may please to make and shall hope that what they may publish may resemble that to the writing of which I gave thought and time. Their attitude as an Irish publishing firm may be judged by Irish public opinion. I, as a writer, protest against the systems (legal, social and ceremonious) which have brought me to this pass. Thanking you for your courtesy, I am, Sir, Your obedient servant

JAMES JOYCE

I waited nine months after the publication of this letter. Then I went to Ireland and entered into negotiations with Messrs Maunsel. They asked me to omit from the collection the story 'An Encounter', passages in 'Two Gallants', 'The Boarding House', 'A Painful Case', and to change everywhere through the book the name of restaurants, cake-shops, railway stations, public houses, laundries, bars and other places of business. After having argued against their point of view day after day for six weeks and having laid the matter before two solicitors (who, while they informed me that the publishing firm had made a breach of contract, refused to take up my case or to allow their names to be associated with it

---

Symons responded to receiving a copy of Dubliners *from Joyce in a letter dated 29 June 1914.*

No, I have not forgotten you. I still have your verses here. I find a great deal to like in *Dubliners*– unequal as the short stories are, but original, Irish, a kind of French realism, of minute detail, sordid; single sentences tell: I like the kind of abrupt style in the book. 'Counterparts' is quite fine–grim humour–a sense of Dublin as I saw it– a lurid glare over it. It gave me a sensation of Fountain Court and the pubs. But the best is the last: the end imaginative.

Karl Beckson and John M. Munro,
"Letters from Arthur Symons
to James Joyce: 1904–1932,"
James Joyce Quarterly, iv, No. 2 (Winter 1967), p. 98

Publishing a Protest

John J. Slocum and Herbert Cahoon provide Joyce's explanation of how he came to write "Gas from a Burner" in A Bibliography of James Joyce, *quoting a handwritten note on the Esher-Randle-Keynes-Spoerri copy of the broadside:*

This pasquinade was written in the railway station waiting room at Flushing, Holland on the way to Trieste from Dublin after the malicious burning of the 1st edition of *Dubliners* (1000 copies less one in my possession) by the printer Messrs John Falconer. Upper Sackville Street Dublin in July 1912.

Joyce had an unknown number of copies of the broadside printed in Trieste soon after he arrived on 15 September 1912 and prevailed upon his brother Charles to distribute them in Dublin. He never returned to his native country.

---

in any way.) I consented in despair to all these changes on condition that the book were brought out without delay and the original text were restored in future editions, if such were called for. Then Messrs Maunsel asked me to pay into their bank £1000 as security, or to find two sureties of £500 each. I declined to do either; and they then wrote to me, informing me that they would not publish the book, altered or unaltered, and that if I did not make them an offer to cover their losses on printing it they would sue me to recover the same. I offered to pay sixty per cent of the cost of printing the first edition of one thousand copies if the edition were made over to my order. This offer was accepted, and I arranged with my brother in Dublin to publish and sell the book for me. On the morrow when the draft and agreement were to be signed the publishers informed me that the matter was at an end because the printer refused to hand over the copies. I then went to the printer. His foreman told me that the printer had decided to forego all claim to the money due to him. I asked whether the printer would hand over the complete edition to a London or continental firm or to my brother or to me if he were fully indemnified. He said that the copies would never leave his printing house, and that the type had been broken up and that the entire edition of one thousand copies would be burnt the next day. I left Ireland the next day, bringing with me a printed copy of the book which I had obtained from the publisher.

JAMES JOYCE

GAS FROM A BURNER.

Ladies and gents, you are here assembled
To hear why earth and heaven trembled
Because of the black and sinister arts
Of an Irish writer in foreign parts.
He sent me a book ten years ago
I read it a hundred times or so,
Backwards and forwards, down and up,
Through both the ends of a telescope.
I printed it all to the very last word
But by the mercy of the Lord
The darkness of my mind was rent
And I saw the writer's foul intent.
But I owe a duty to Ireland:
I hold her honour in my hand,
This lovely land that always sent
Her writers and artists to banishment
And in a spirit of Irish fun
Betrayed her own leaders, one by one.
'Twas Irish humour, wet and dry,
Flung quicklime into Parnell's eye;
'Tis Irish brains that save from doom
The leaky barge of the Bishop of Rome
For everyone knows the Pope can't belch
Without the consent of Billy Walsh.
O Ireland my first and only love
Where Christ and Caesar are hand and glove!
O lovely land where the shamrock grows!
(Allow me, ladies, to blow my nose)
To show you for strictures I don't care a button
I printed the poems of Mountainy Mutton
And a play he wrote (you've read it, I'm sure)
Where they talk of „bastard" „bugger" and „whore"
And a play on the Word and Holy Paul
And some woman's legs that I can't recall
Written by Moore, a genuine gent
That lives on his property's ten per cent:
I printed mystical books in dozens:
I printed the table book of Cousins
Though (asking your pardon) as for the verse
'Twould give you a heartburn on your arse:
I printed folklore from North and South
By Gregory of the Golden Mouth:
I printed poets, sad, silly and solemn:
I printed Patrick What - do - you - Colm:
I printed the great John Milicent Synge
Who soars above on an angel's wing
In the playboy shift that he pinched as swag
From Maunsel's manager's travelling - bag.
But I draw the line at that bloody fellow,
That was over here dressed in Austrian yellow,
Spouting Italian by the hour
To O' Leary Curtis and John Wyse Power
And writing of Dublin, dirty and dear,
In a manner no blackamoor printer could bear.

Poem Joyce had privately published as a broadside after being told that Dubliners *would be destroyed. This copy was inscribed by Sylvia Beach* (Important Modern First Editions, *N.Y.: Sotheby, 1977, item 170*).

Shite and onions! Do you think I' ll print
The name of the Wellington Monument,
Sydney Parade and the Sandymount tram,
Downes's cakeshop and Williams's jam?
I'm damned if I do — I'm damned to blazes!
Talk about *Irish Names of Places!*
Its a wonder to me, upon my soul,
He forgot to mention Curly's Hole.
No, ladies, my press shall have no share in
So gross a libel on Stepmother Erin.
I pity the poor — that's why I took
A red - headed Scotchman to keep my book.
Poor sister Scotland! Her doom is fell;
She cannot find any more Stuarts to sell.
My conscience is fine as Chinese silk:
My heart is as soft as buttermilk.
Colm can tell you I made a rebate
Of one hundred pounds on the estimate
I gave him for his Irish Review.
I love my country — by herrings I do!
I wish you could see what tears I weep
When I think of the emigrant train and ship.
That's why I publish far and wide
My quite illegible railway guide.
In the porch of my printing institute
The poor and deserving prostitute
Plays every night at catch - as - catch - can
With her tight - breeched British artilleryman
And the foreigner learns the gift of the gab
From the drunken draggletail Dublin drab.
Who was it said: Resist not evil?
I'll burn that book, so help me devil.
I'll sing a psalm as I watch it burn
And the ashes I'll keep in a one - handled urn.
I'll penance do with farts and groans
Kneeling upon my marrowbones.
This very next lent I will unbare
My penitent buttocks to the air
And sobbing beside my printing press
My awful sin I will confess.
My Irish foreman from Bannockburn
Shall dip his right hand in the urn
And sign crisscross with reverent thumb
Memento homo upon my bum.

                                        James Joyce.

Flushing, September 1912.

given to Cyril Connolly by Sylvia Beach

Agreement made this *twentieth* ·day of *March 1914* between

James A. Joyce Esq
of *Via Donato Bramante 4 II. Trieste*   *Limited*
(hereinafter called the AUTHOR) of the one part and GRANT RICHARDS of No. 7 Carlton Street S.W. Publisher (hereinafter called the PUBLISHER) of the other part each on behalf of himself or herself his or her heirs executors administrators and assigns WHEREBY it is agreed as follows :

1. The PUBLISHER agrees to purchase and the AUTHOR agrees to sell the entire copyright without any reserve in the United Kingdom and all other parts of the world of a work entitled

Dubliners

the completed manuscript executed in a proper manner of which the AUTHOR has delivered ~~or hereby undertakes~~ to deliver to the PUBLISHER ⸺ in consideration of the following payments viz :

A royalty of ten per cent on the published price of copies sold rising to fifteen per cent after the sale of eight thousand copies no royalty being paid on the first five hundred copies of the English edition

2. The PUBLISHER will according to his own judgment and in such manner as in his unfettered discretion he may consider advisable at his own cost print and publish a first edition of the said work and further editions if in his judgment further editions are required and in his absolute discretion advertise the same and shall determine all details and in his absolute discretion make all arrangements of and incidental to the printing publishing advertising sale price and reviewing of the said work.

3. The AUTHOR shall revise and return for press with all reasonable speed the proof sheets of the said work so that the same may be printed without interruption and shall also revise with all possible despatch any new edition of the said work and correct the proofs and otherwise assist as may be required by the PUBLISHER and if the Printer's charges for AUTHOR'S corrections of the first or any other edition of the said work exceed an average of *six shillings* per sheet of thirty-two pages the excess shall be repaid to the PUBLISHER by the AUTHOR and may be deducted from royalties due or to become due hereunder or from any moneys held by the PUBLISHER on account of the AUTHOR.

First page of the 1914 contract between Joyce and Richards that resulted in the publication of Dubliners *(Division of Rare and Manuscript Collections, Carl A. Kroch Library, Cornell University [Scholes 1396])*

Extracts from Press Notices

of

DUBLINERS

by

JAMES JOYCE

(Grant Richards: London: 1914)

Mr Ezra Pound in The Egoist: Mr Joyce writes a clear hard prose.... He presents his people swiftly and vividly.... He is a realist. He accepts an international standard of prose writing and lives up to it. He gives us things as they are, not only for Dublin, but for every city.... I think there is a new phase of Irish literature in the works of Mr Joyce. He writes as a contemporary of continental writers.... He is classic in that he deals with normal things and with normal people.... He excels most of the impressionist writers because of his more rigorous selection, because of his exclusion of all unnecessary detail.... These stories are such as to win for Mr Joyce a very definite place among English contemporary prose writers.

Mr Dixon Scott in the Liverpool Daily Courier: Nothing in his verse could have been held to augur work like this, so sunless, searching and relentless.... Some law to which we are strangers seems to guide the construction.... As the level sentences go on your will is gradually overpowered.... It is a horrible sensation but it is one well worth experiencing and it has its deep jusifications, human and artistic. There are few writers who could administer that shock.... Some obscure genius working in his brain gave the words which he used and the scenes which he chose a mesmeric quality that induces a kind of clairvoyance.... It is one of the most curious pieces of writing modern Ireland has given us. It has beauty, it has strangeness, it has power.

Times : Admirably written.... Mr. Joyce avoids exaggeration.... He leaves the conviction that his people are as he describes them.

Saturday Review : The trail of morbidity lies over the stories in this volume. Most of them are quite disgusting and ought not to have been written.... Mr Joyce seems bent on proving that there is a beast lurking behind even the mildest aspect of human nature.... In none of them is there lacking a strange unhealthiness. This is not the sort of cleverness that is to be encouraged. It is diseased art and poisons the springs of one's thoughts.

First of three pages of extracts published to advertise Joyce's only story collection (Division of Rare and Manuscript Collections, Carl A. Kroch Library, Cornell University [Scholes 1391])

Reviews of *Dubliners*

Reviewers of Dubliners, *even those objecting to certain passages and stories or to Joyce's subject, praised his style, precision, and keen observations on life.*

Review of *Dubliners*
Times Literary Supplement, 18 June 1914, p. 298

Dubliners is a collection of short stories, the scene of which is laid in Dublin. Too comprehensive for the theme, the title is nevertheless typical of a book which purports, we assume, to describe life as it is and yet regards it from one aspect only. The author, Mr. James Joyce, is not concerned with all Dubliners, but almost exclusively with those of them who would be submerged if the tide of material difficulties were to rise a little higher. It is not so much money they lack as the adaptability which attains some measure of success by accepting the world as it is. It is in so far that they are failures that his characters interest Mr. Joyce. One of them—a capable washerwoman—falls an easy prey to a rogue in a tramcar and is cozened out of the little present she was taking to her family. Another—a trusted cashier— has so ordered a blameless life that he drives to drink and suicide the only person in the world with whom he was in sympathy. A third—an amiable man of letters—learns at the moment he feels most drawn to his wife that her heart was given once and for all to a boy long dead.

Dubliners may be recommended to the large class of readers to whom the drab makes an appeal, for it is admirably written. Mr. Joyce avoids exaggeration. He leaves the conviction that his people are as he describes them. Shunning the emphatic, Mr. Joyce is less concerned with the episode than with the mood which it suggests. Perhaps for this reason he is more successful with his shorter stories. When he writes at greater length the issue seems trivial, and the connecting thread becomes so tenuous as to be scarcely perceptible. The reader's difficulty will be enhanced if he is ignorant of Dublin customs; if he does not know, for instance, that 'a curate' is a man who brings strong waters.

—reprinted from James Joyce: The Critical Heritage

Review of *Dubliners*
Athenæum, 20 June 1914, p. 875

Mr. George Moore says in his *Confessions,* if our memory does not deceive us, that when he and a certain French writer are dead no more 'naturalistic' novels will be written. Whether this is one of his characteristic outbursts of candour as to his and his friend's abilities, or merely a statement to the effect that novelists as a whole have no taste for such writing,

> The literary ability of the accomplished craftsman. . . . They are not pleasant tales but they show power. . . . He is an author of whom we shall hear more.
>
> *—Morning Post* (Dublin)

we need not discuss. But we can frankly say that Mr. Joyce's work affords a distinct contradiction of the saying.

The fifteen short stories here given under the collective title of *Dubliners* are nothing if not naturalistic. In some ways, indeed, they are unduly so: at least three would have been better buried in oblivion. Life has so much that is beautiful, interesting, educative, amusing, that we do not readily pardon those who insist upon its more sordid and baser aspects. The condemnation is the greater if their skill is of any high degree, since in that case they might use it to better purpose.

Mr. Joyce undoubtedly possesses great skill both of observation and of technique. He has humour, as is shown by the sketch of Mrs. Kearney and her views on religion, her faith 'bounded by her kitchen, but if she was put to it, she could believe also in the banshee and in the Holy Ghost.' He has also knowledge of the beauty of words, of mental landscapes (if we may use such a phrase): the last page of the final story is full evidence thereto. His characterization is exact: speaking with reserve as to the conditions of certain sides of the social life of Dublin, we should say that it is beyond criticism. All the personages are living realities.

But Mr. Joyce has his own specialized outlook on life—on that life in particular; and here we may, perhaps, find the explanation of much that displeases and that puzzles us. That outlook is evidently sombre: he is struck by certain types, certain scenes, by the dark shadows of a low street or the lurid flare of an ignoble tavern, and he reproduces these in crude, strong sketches scarcely relieved by the least touch of joy or repose. Again, his outlook is self-centred, absorbed in itself rather; he ends his sketch abruptly time after time, satisfied with what he has done, brushing aside any intention of explaining what is set down or supplementing what is omitted.

All the stories are worth reading for the work that is in them, for the pictures they present; the best are undoubtedly the last four, especially 'Ivy Day in the Committee Room.' The last of all, 'The Dead,' far longer than the rest, and tinged with a softer tone of pathos and sympathy, leads us to hope that Mr. Joyce may attempt larger and broader work, in which the necessity of asserting the proportions of life may compel him to enlarge his outlook and eliminate such scenes and details as can only shock, without in any useful way impressing or elevating, the reader.

—reprinted from James Joyce: The Critical Heritage

Review of *Dubliners*
Gerald Gould
The New Statesman, 27 June 1914, pp. 374–375

It is easy to say of Gorky that he is a man of genius. To say the same of Mr. James Joyce requires more courage, since his name is little known; but a man of genius is precisely what he is. He has an original outlook, a special method, a complete reliance on his own powers of delineation and presentment. Whether his powers will develop, his scope widen, his sympathies deepen, or not–whether, in short, his genius is a large one or only a little one, I cannot pretend to say. Maturity and self-confidence in a first book (and I believe that, in prose, this is Mr. Joyce's first book) contain a threat as well as a promise. They hint at a set mode of thought rather than a developing capacity. Certainly the maturity, the individual poise and force of these stories are astonishing. The only recent work with which they suggest comparison is *The House with the Green Shutters,* and even that was very different, for one heard in it the undertone of human complaint–its horrors were partly by way of expressing a personal unhappiness; while Mr. Joyce seems to regard this objective and dirty and crawling world with the cold detachment of an unamiable god.

He has plenty of humour, but it is always the humour of the fact, not of the comment. He dares to let people speak for themselves with the awkward meticulousness, the persistent incompetent repetition, of actual human intercourse. If you have never realised before how direly our daily conversation needs editing, you will realise it from Mr. Joyce's pages. One very powerful story, called *Grace,* consists chiefly of lengthy talk so banal, so true to life, that one can scarcely endure it– though one can still less leave off reading it. Here is one of the liveliest passages:

> "Pope Leo XIII.," said Mr. Cunningham, "was one of the lights of the age. His great idea, you know, was the union of the Latin and Greek churches. That was the aim of his life."
>
> "I often heard he was one of the most intellectual men in Europe," said Mr. Power. "I mean apart from his being Pope."
>
> "So he was," said Mr. Cunningham, "if not the most so. His motto, you know, as Pope was *Lux upon Lux – Light upon Light.*"
>
> "No, no," said Mr. Fogarty eagerly. "I think you're wrong there. It was *Lux in Tenebris,* I think–*Light in Darkness.*"
>
> "O yes," said Mr. M'Coy, "Tenebre."
>
> "Allow me," said Mr. Cunningham positively, "it was *Lux upon Lux.* And Plus IX. his predecessor's motto was *Crux upon Crux*– that is, *Cross upon Cross*–to show the difference between their two pontificates."
>
> The inference was allowed. Mr. Cunningham continued.

> "Pope Leo, you know, was a great scholar and a poet."
>
> "He had a strong face," said Mr. Kernan.
>
> "Yes," said Mr. Cunningham. "He wrote Latin poetry."
>
> "Is that so?" said Mr. Fogarty.

You see the method? It is not employed only in conversation. The description of mood, of atmosphere, is just as detailed and just as relentless. Horrible sordid realities, of which you are not spared one single pang, close in upon you like the four walls of a torture-chamber. It is all done quite calmly, quite dispassionately, quite competently. It never bores. You sometimes rather wish it did, as a relief.

The best things in the book are *Araby,* a wonderful magical study of boyish affection and wounded pride, and *The Dead,* a long story (placed at the end) in which we begin with a queer old-fashioned dance, where the principal anxiety is whether a certain guest will arrive "screwed," and are led on through all the queer breathless banalities of supper and conversation and leave-taking till we find ourselves back with a husband and wife in their hotel bedroom, the husband's emotion stirred, the wife queerly remote and sad, remembering the boy, Michael Furey, whom she had loved and who had died because of her. To quote the end without the innumerable preparatory touches that prepare for it seems unfair; yet it must be quoted for its mere melancholy beauty:

> A few light taps upon the pane made him turn to the window. It had begun to snow again. He watched sleepily the flakes, silver and dark, falling obliquely against the lamplight. The time had come for him to set out on his journey westward. Yes, the newspapers were right: snow was general all over Ireland. It was falling on every part of the dark central plain, on the treeless hills, falling softly upon the Bog of Allen and, farther westward, softly falling into the dark mutinous Shannon waves. It was falling, too, upon every part of the lonely churchyard on the hill where Michael Furey lay buried. It lay thickly drifted on the crooked crosses and headstones, on the spears of the little gate, on the barren thorns. His soul swooned slowly as he heard the snow falling faintly through the universe and faintly falling, like the descent of their last end, upon all the living and the dead.

Frankly, we think it a pity (perhaps we betray a narrow puritanism in so thinking) that a man who can write like this should insist as constantly as Mr. Joyce insists upon aspects of life which are ordinarily not mentioned. To do him justice, we do not think it is a pose with him: he simply includes the "unmentionable" in his persistent regard.

–reprinted from James Joyce: The Critical Heritage

Review of *Dubliners*

Everyman, 3 July 1914, xc, p. 380

Mr. James Joyce writes with a sense of style that makes his work distinctive. *Dubliners* is a collection of short stories dealing with undercurrents of Irish character. The author understands the technique of his craft to perfection, and uses words as a sculptor uses clay. Every phrase is pregnant with suggestion, but the suggestion for the most part is unpleasantly and curiously tinged with a pessimism that finds virility and purpose only in the power of evil. 'A Painful Case,' one of the best-written sketches in the volume, strips life of all hope of consolation and leaves the reader faced by a cold, cruel egotism that finds expression in perpetual self-exultation. 'Two Gallants' reveals the shuddering depths of human meanness. The men, villainous of soul and repugnant of aspect, trade on the affections of young servant-girls, and the story reproduces the hopes of the one who waits the results of the wiles of the other. Even for these outcasts some hope might remain. But the author, with a ruthless callousness, decides they shall be doomed and damned. The book may be styled the records of an inferno in which neither pity nor remorse can enter. Wonderfully written, the power of genius is in every line, but it is a genius that, blind to the blue of the heavens, seeks inspiration in the hell of despair.

—reprinted from James Joyce: The Critical Heritage

Review of *Dubliners*

Academy, 11 July 1914, p. 49

In the matter of literary expression these sketches—of which the book contains fifteen in all—are akin to the work of Mr. Cunningham Graham and of Mr. George Moore; there is a clarity of phrasing and a restraint such as characterises the work of these two authors, and in every sketch atmosphere is so subtly conveyed that, without mention of a street or of a jaunting car, we feel Dublin about us as we read. In one, 'Counterparts,' is power enough to make us wish for a novel from Mr. Joyce's pen, and in the earlier, schoolboy stories are all the dreaming and mystery of an imaginative boy's life. The book is morbid, to a certain extent, in its tone, but it is of such literary quality that we forgive the defect for the sake of the artistic value. The work is not all morbid however, for here and there are flashes of humour, rendered more forceful by their settings. Altogether, this is a book to recommend evidently written by a man of broad sympathies and much human understanding.

—reprinted from James Joyce: The Critical Heritage

Pound republished his essay on Dubliners *in* Pavannes and Divisions *(1918); it was also included in* The Literary Essays of Ezra Pound *(1954), edited by T. S. Eliot.*

'Dubliners' and Mr. James Joyce

Ezra Pound

Egoist, 1, no. 14 (15 July 1914), p. 267

Freedom from sloppiness is so rare in contemporary English prose that one might well say simply, 'Mr. Joyce's book of short stories is prose free from sloppiness,' and leave the intelligent reader ready to run from his study, immediately to spend three and sixpence on the volume.

Unfortunately one's credit as a critic is insufficient to produce this result.

The readers of *The Egoist,* having had Mr. Joyce under their eyes for some months, will scarcely need to have his qualities pointed out to them. Both they and the paper have been very fortunate in his collaboration.

Mr. Joyce writes a clear hard prose. He deals with subjective things, but he presents them with such clarity of outline that he might be dealing with locomotives or with builders' specifications. For that reason one can read Mr. Joyce without feeling that one is conferring a favour. I must put this thing my own way. I know about 168 authors. About once a year I read something contemporary without feeling that I am softening the path for poor Jones or poor Fulano de Tal.

I can lay down a good piece of French writing and pick up a piece of writing by Mr. Joyce without feeling as if my head were being stuffed through a cushion. There are still impressionists about and I dare say they claim Mr. Joyce. I admire impressionist writers. English prose writers who haven't got as far as impressionism (that is to say, 95 percent. of English writers of prose and verse) are a bore.

Impressionism has, however, two meanings, or perhaps I had better say, the word 'impressionism' gives two different 'impressions'.

There is a school of prose writers, and of verse writers for that matter, whose forerunner was Stendhal and whose founder was Flaubert. The followers of Flaubert deal in exact presentation. They are often so intent on exact presentation that they neglect intensity, selection, and concentration. They are perhaps the most clarifying and they have been perhaps the most beneficial force in modern writing.

There is another set, mostly of verse writers, who founded themselves not upon anybody's writing but upon the pictures of Monet. Every movement in painting picks up a few writers who try to imitate in words what someone has done in paint. Thus one writer saw a picture by Monet and talked of 'pink pigs blossoming on a hillside', and a later writer talked of 'slate-blue' hair and 'raspberry-coloured flanks'.

These 'impressionists' who write in imitation of Monet's softness, instead of writing in imitation of Flaubert's definiteness, are a bore, a grimy, or perhaps I should say, a rosy, floribund bore.

The spirit of a decade strikes properly upon all of the arts. There are 'parallel movements'. Their causes and their effects may not seem, superficially, similar.

This mimicking of painting ten or twenty years late, is not in the least the same as the 'literary movement' parallel to the painting movement imitated.

The force that leads a poet to leave out a moral reflection may lead a painter to leave out representation. The resultant poem may not suggest the resultant painting.

Mr. Joyce's merit, I will not say his chief merit but his most engaging merit, is that he carefully avoids telling you a lot that you don't want to know. He presents his people swiftly and vividly, he does not sentimentalise over them, he does not weave convolutions. He is a realist. He does not believe 'life' would be all right if we stopped vivisection or if we instituted a new sort of 'economics.' He gives the thing as it is. He is not bound by the tiresome convention that any part of life, to be interesting, must be shaped into the conventional form of a 'story.' Since De Maupassant we have had so many people trying to write 'stories' and so few people presenting life. Life for the most part does not happen in neat little diagrams and nothing is more tiresome than the continual pretence that it does.

Mr. Joyce's 'Araby,' for instance, is much better than a 'story,' it is a vivid writing.

It is surprising that Mr. Joyce is Irish. One is so tired of the Irish or 'Celtic' imagination (or 'phantasy' as I think they now call it) flopping about. Mr. Joyce does not flop about. He defines. He is not an institution for the promotion of Irish peasant industries. He accepts an international standard of prose writing and lives up to it.

He gives us Dublin as it presumably is. He does not descend to farce. He does not rely upon Dickensian caricature. He gives us things as they are, not only for Dublin, but for every city. Erase the local names and a few specifically local allusions, and a few historic events of the past, and substitute a few different local names, allusions and events, and these stories could be retold of any town.

That is to say, the author is quite capable of dealing with things about him, and dealing directly, yet these details do not engross him, he is capable of getting at the universal element beneath them.

The main situations of 'Madame Bovary' or of 'Doña Perfecta' do not depend on local colour or upon local detail, that is their strength. Good writing, good presentation can be specifically local, but it must not depend on locality. Mr. Joyce does not present 'types' but individuals. I mean he deals with common emotions which run through all races. He does not bank on 'Irish character.' Roughly speaking, Irish literature has gone through three phases in our time, the shamrock period, the dove-grey period, and the Kiltartan period. I think there is a new phase in the works of Mr. Joyce.

He writes as a contemporary of continental writers. I do not mean that he writes as a faddist, mad for the last note, he does not imitate Strindberg, for instance, or Bang. He is not ploughing the underworld for horror. He is not presenting a macabre subjectivity. He is classic in that he deals with normal things and with normal people. A committee room, Little Chandler, a nonentity, a boarding house full of clerks—these are his subjects and he treats them all in such a manner that they are worthy subjects of art.

Francis Jammes, Charles Vildrac and D. H. Lawrence have written short narratives in verse, trying, it would seem, to present situations as clearly as prose writers have done, yet more briefly. Mr. Joyce is engaged in a similar condensation. He has kept to prose not needing the privilege supposedly accorded to verse to justify his method.

I think that he excels most of the impressionist writers because of his more rigorous selection, because of his exclusion of all unnecessary detail.

There is a very clear demarcation between unnecessary detail and irrelevant detail. An impressionist friend of mine talks to me a good deal about 'preparing effects,' and on that score he justifies much unnecessary detail, which is not 'irrelevant,' but which ends by being wearisome and by putting one out of conceit with his narrative.

Mr. Joyce's more rigorous selection of the presented detail marks him, I think, as belonging to my own generation, that is, to the 'nineteen-tens,' not to the decade between 'the 'nineties' and today.

At any rate these stories and the novel now appearing in serial form are such as to win for Mr. Joyce a very definite place among English contemporary prose writers, not merely a place in the 'Novels of the Week' column, and our writers of good clear prose are so few that we cannot afford to confuse or to overlook them.

—*reprinted from* James Joyce: The Critical Heritage

Review of *Dubliners*
Irish Book Lover, 6, no. 4 (November 1914), pp. 60–61

Dublin, like other large cities, shelters many peculiar types of men and women, good, bad and indifferent; in fact some, whose knowledge of it is extensive and peculiar, would say more than its fair share. Of some of these Mr. Joyce here gives us pen portraits of great power, and although one naturally shrinks from such characters as are depicted in 'An Encounter' or 'Two Gallants,' and finds their descriptions not quite suited 'virginibus puerisque,' one cannot deny the existence of their prototypes, whilst wishing that the author had directed his undoubted talents in other and pleasanter directions. . . .

—*reprinted from* James Joyce: The Critical Heritage

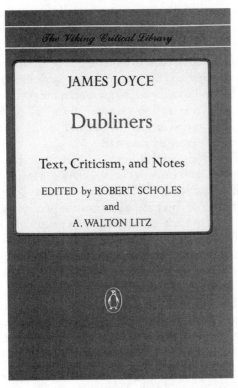

Cover for the 1996 revised critical edition of Joyce's only collection of short stories

Sir Edward Marsh, who at the time was secretary in charge of Civil List pensions, had written to George Moore for his opinion of Joyce's work. In his 3 August 1916 reply, Moore wrote in favor of Joyce receiving government support.

Now to answer your questions. The only book of Joyce's that I have read is a collection of stories called 'Dubliners,' some of them are trivial and disagreeable, but all are written by a clever man, and the book contains one story, the longest story in the book and the last story which seemed to me perfection whilst I read it: I regretted that I was not the author of it. But this story, which I am sure you would appreciate as much as I did, does not prove that Joyce will go on writing and will end by writing something like a masterpiece. A talent, musical, literary or pictorial, is a pale fluttering thing that a breath will extinguish. I will get 'Dubliners' from Heinemann to whom I lent the book and you will see for yourself. Of the novel I know nothing. Joyce left a disagreeable reputation behind him in Dublin, but he came back after some years a different man and everything I heard of him is to his credit.

Letters II, p. 380

The Gresham Hotel in Dublin, the setting of the final scene in "The Dead" (courtesy of Irish Tourist Board)

Director John Huston with his daughter Angelica, who plays Gretta Conroy, and Frank Patterson, who plays Bartell D'Arcy, on the set of the 1987 movie version of The Dead

Cover and cast page for the musical adaptation of "The Dead," which premiered at Playwrights Horizons in New York City on 1 October 1999 and ran until 14 November 1999

Establishing a Reputation: *A Portrait of the Artist as a Young Man* and *Exiles*

The genesis of A Portrait of the Artist as a Young Man *goes back to the prose sketch titled "A Portrait of the Artist" that Joyce completed in 1904 for the Dublin periodical* Dana. *When the essay was rejected by editors John Eglinton and Frederick Ryan, Joyce decided to expand it into a novel he called "Stephen Hero." By 1905, when Joyce was about halfway through that work, he put it aside until after he finished his last* Dubliners *short story, "The Dead," in 1907. Soon after Joyce began revising "Stephen Hero," in which he took a realistic and naturalistic approach to his material, into the prototypical modernist text* A Portrait of the Artist as a Young Man, *which was serialized in* The Egoist *from February 1914 through September 1915. Both William Butler Yeats and Ezra Pound praised the novel as it was being serialized, with Yeats calling Joyce "the most remarkable new talent in Ireland to-day"and Pound comparing him to Gustave Flaubert and Stendhal.*

While A Portrait of the Artist as a Young Man *was being serialized Joyce was working on his only extant play,* Exiles, *which he wrote in Trieste. The novel was first published in book form in the United States in late December 1916 by B.W. Huebsch*

and in England in February 1917 by The Egoist, Ltd. The publication of Exiles, *by Grant Richards in London and B. W. Huebsch in New York, was delayed until 1918. The play has not been frequently performed, but it, like* A Portrait of the Artist as a Young Man, *is a deeply personal work.* Exiles *is also interesting because it stands as a transitional work between Joyce's first novel and* Ulysses. *Together* A Portrait of the Artist as a Young Man *and* Exiles *brought Joyce recognition as one of the most innovative, daring, and promising writers of his time.*

Turning *Stephen Hero* into *A Portrait*

In this excerpt from "The Book of Himself," the third chapter of his book James Joyce *(1985), Bernard Benstock discusses the relationship between* Dubliners *and* A Portrait of the Artist as a Young Man *and how Joyce reorganized his* Stephen Hero *material for his revision of the novel.*

James Joyce
Bernard Benstock
(New York: Frederick Ungar, 1985), pp. 49–52

Almost all of the stories contained in *Dubliners* were written by the time James Joyce was twenty-three years old, and "The Dead," added when he was in his twenty-fifth year. The novella coda was the result of a bout of rheumatic fever at a crucial point in his life, and the decision to scrap the thousand or so manuscript pages of *Stephen Hero,* his first attempt at writing a novel, and begin again on the quasi-autobigraphical novel was made at the same time. *Stephen Hero* looked inward into a life, charting it meticulously and completely, and the titular hero, Stephen Daedalus, was to be viewed by a literary process that moved from first-person singular to the third, as in the ballad of "Turpin Hero." In the revised *Portrait of the Artist as a Young Man* Stephen explains his aesthetics by stating that

The simplest epical form is seen emerging out of lyrical literature when the artist prolongs and broods upon himself as the centre of an epical event and this form progresses till the centre of emotional gravity is equidistant from the art-

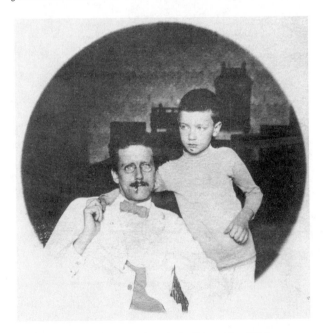

Joyce with his son, Georgio, in Trieste, circa 1915

ist himself and from others. The narrative is no longer purely personal. The personality of the artist passes into the narration itself, flowing round and round the persons and the action like a vital sea. This progress you will see easily in that old English ballad *Turpin Hero* which begins in the first person and ends in the third person.

During the preceding years Joyce had worked simultaneously on the personal narrative of the artist himself and on the book of the "Others," those Dubliners who gravitated in concentric circles around the consciousness of the artist. *Dubliners* and *A Portrait* are best read as superimposed upon each other, as facing narratives of the two facets of the artist's consciousness of "Self" and "Others." The boy in the opening triad of stories comes close to the Stephen of the first chapter of *A Portrait,* sensitive and aware, observing without revealing his thoughts. At the Christmas dinner which is the centerpiece of that first chapter, Stephen registers the impact of the disruptive quarrel but is stunned into silence, much like the boy listening to the two sisters gossip about the dead priest. A sensitivity to words is also characteristic of Stephen Dedalus (Joyce had momentarily toyed with demythologizing Daedalus to a simply Daly, but settled for dropping the digraph–he saved Daly as one of the aliases used by the Dedaluses in chapter 5 when pawning their possessions), as he considers homonyms ("That was a belt round his pocket. And belt was also to give a fellow a belt"), and onomatopoeia ("Suck was a queer word. . . . Once he had washed his hands in the lavatory of the Wicklow Hotel and his father pulled the stopper up by the chain after and the dirty water went down through the hole in the basin. And when it had all gone down slowly the hole in the basin had made a sound like that: suck"), and names ("God was God's name just as his name was Stephen. *Dieu* was the French for God"). The direction of young Stephen toward the vocation of the literary artist determines the structure of *A Portrait of the Artist as a Young Man.*

Stephen Hero had the potential shape and girth of a nineteenth-century novel; *A Portrait,* afflicted with the style of scrupulous meanness Joyce had employed in *Dubliners,* points toward the modernism of the twentieth. The extant pages from the earlier version (published after Joyce's death) contain fully developed incidents, some eliminated, some retained, others merely suggested in the succeeding *Portrait,* and the economy practiced by Joyce in his revision becomes all the more apparent in contrast to the remnants of *Stephen Hero.* As soon as he began the reconstitution of his material, Joyce envisioned a book in five long chapters, the first three of which he completed within a year. The rhythmic rise and fall within each of the five parts tightens the structure of *A Portrait of the Artist as a Young Man,* as Stephen undergoes

the traumatic instances of development and maturation between the infancy with which the book begins and the suspended conclusion at which the university graduate prepares to embark for Paris. Chapter 1 concludes with schoolboy Stephen in triumph, lauded by his schoolmates for having bravely defied authority by having sought redress from the rector when he had been unjustly punished by Father Dolan. Chapter 2 ends with the adolescent swooning in the arms of a prostitute for the first time, while chapter 3 ends with his return to piety, having confessed his sins and been absolved. At the end of chapter 4 the potential artist undergoes an equally spiritual conversion, having encountered his muse and embraced his vocation, rejecting the possibility of the priesthood, and at the conclusion of chapter 5 he sets out for his new career and a new life: "Welcome, O life! I go to encounter for the millionth time the reality of experience and to forge in the smithy of my soul the uncreated conscience of my race."

The heightened curve of Stephen's emotions are inevitably countered by the realities of his youthful experience, and each new chapter begins in sharp contrast to the exultations with which the previous one concludes. At the beginning of the second chapter Stephen is very much at loose ends: he has been withdrawn from the prestigious Jesuit boarding school because of the decline of his father's financial condition. As the third chapter opens ("The swift December dusk had come tumbling clownishly after its dull day and, as he stared through the dull square of the window of the schoolroom, he felt his belly crave for its food"), the ecstasy of sexual initiation has become a sordid commonplace, quickly developing into morbid guilt, and although his spiritual cleansing evokes "Another life! A life of grace and virtue and happiness!", that life as seen at the start of the fourth chapter is jejune, mechanical, and without spiritual enthusiasm: "Sunday was dedicated to the mystery of the Holy Trinity, Monday to the Holy Ghost, Tuesday to the Guardian Angels, Wednesday to Saint Joseph, Thursday to the Most Blessed Sacrament of the Altar, Friday to the Suffering Jesus, Saturday to the Blessed Virgin Mary". And although the élan of his decision to become an artist is expected to carry over through the entire last chapter, that chapter nonetheless commences in the most banal circumstances, as Stephen drags out his pathetic breakfast before going off late to his university classes, as his mother scrubs his dirty neck, resentful that he chose the university in lieu of the seminary, and his father gratuitously curses him. The aftermath of elation is invariably depression, and the triumph with which *A Portrait* concludes is undercut by the deflated opening of *Ulysses.*

Published the 1st and 15th of each month.

THE EGOIST

AN INDIVIDUALIST REVIEW.

Formerly the NEW FREEWOMAN.

No. 4.   Vol. I.   MONDAY, FEBRUARY 16th, 1914.   SIXPENCE.

Assistant ⎰ RICHARD ALDINGTON.   *Editor:* DORA MARSDEN, B.A.
Editors: ⎱ LEONARD A. COMPTON-RICKETT.

CONTENTS.

	Page		Page		Page
Mainly Anent the Decalogue.	61	Agni Konda. By Leonard A. Compton-Rickett.	72	Modern Writers on "Chastity." Quotations selected by Beeban and Noel Teulon Porter.	77
Two Books. By Richard Aldington.	66	Modern Dramatists. By Storm Jameson.	74		
The New Sculpture. By Ezra Pound.	67	Schönberg, Epstein, Chesterton, and Mass-Rhythm. By Huntly Carter.	75	Correspondence.	78
Poems. By Amy Lowell.	68				
Serial Story:— Portrait of the Artist as a Young Man. By James Joyce.	70	An Essay in Constructive Criticism. By Herrmann Karl Georg Jesus Maria.	76	Two Statues and a Drawing. By H. M. Gaudier-Brzeska.	80

MAINLY ANENT THE DECALOGUE.

FOR a period of eight months or more we have been explaining that "ideas" of the static kind commonly called "absolute," i.e., those which do not with more or less speed dissolve into ascertained fact, are delusions of intelligences too feeble to be quite aware of what they speak. It appears that a proportion of our readers, mindful of past benefits no doubt, have tolerated the broaching of this subject with only a very strained patience : and that now, at long length, with a pained realisation that the theme shows no sign of flagging, they are driven to ask whether we are not buffooning. "Are we in earnest? Have we *none* of the standard (i.e. absolute) ideas?" We therefore propose here to make a number of forthright statements on the absolute virtues which are associated with the injunctions promulgated in the decalogue. After that, we shall make no further comment on questions as to whether we are "earnest." Before dealing with the concepts bolstered up by the commandments it will serve us to notice an assumption relating to the "Search for Truth," for supported by "opinions" and "beliefs" merely a critic will only feel justified to the extent of advancing opposing arguments : but on the strength of his assumptions he will base reproaches. A reproachful one writes : "It is silly to be contemptuous of people who are *trying to get at Truth.*" The assumption is clear and it is very widely adopted. It is considered that the making of an earnest Search for Truth should of itself ensure immunity from scoffs and jeers : that the "Search for Truth" represents an activity the worth of which will be self-evident, and that not to be in earnest about it is the mark which separates the "frivolous-

minded" from the "serious" man : "Are you in earnest or are you buffooning?" means "Do you enter into the debate on Truth seriously?" Our answer of course is that we are as earnest in the inquiry into the nature of Truth as—but no more than—any one of our readers would be in debating the question "What is a Boojum : or a Snark : or the Jubjub Bird?" We are quite prepared to agree that in the hunt for the Bird of Truth (whereon see Miss Olive Schreiner) as in the Hunt for the Snark, all methods of search are equally worthy of respect, and equally admitted of, and that the choice should be left to individual preference.

"Do all that you know, and try all that you don't" is applicable in both cases.

"You may seek it with thimbles and seek it with care,
 You may seek it with forks and hope,
 Threaten its life with a railway-share
 Charm it with smiles and soap."

Or if you are a modern reformer—a rebel or a suffragist—you will go as well in the search and as far by vigorous clapping of hands, by a tract on venereal disease, or best of all by a throb and a whirl inside your head.

"For 'Truth' is a peculiar creature and won't
 Be caught in a commonplace way!"

but like the Snark, if and when discovered may be put to all manner of uses! One may

"Serve it with greens in shadowy scenes
 Or use it for striking a light."

Cover and first page of the serialization for the periodical that originally published Joyce's first novel
(courtesy of The Lilly Library, Indiana University)

70   *THE EGOIST*   February 16th, 1914.

A Portrait of the Artist as a Young Man.

By James Joyce.

Chapter I.—*continued.*

THE bell rang for night prayers and he filed out of the study hall after the others and down the staircase and along the corridors to the chapel. The corridors were darkly lit and the chapel was darkly lit. Soon all would be dark and sleeping. There was cold night air in the chapel and the marbles were the colour the sea was at night. The sea was cold day and night: but it was colder at night. It was cold and dark under the sea-wall beside his father's house. But the kettle would be on the hob to make punch.

The prefect of the chapel prayed above his head and his memory knew the responses:

> *O Lord, open our lips*
> *And our mouth shall announce Thy praise.*
> *Incline unto our aid, O God!*
> *O Lord, make haste to help us!*

There was a cold night smell in the chapel. But it was a holy smell. It was not like the smell of the old peasants who knelt at the back of the chapel at Sunday mass. That was a smell of air and rain and turf and corduroy. But they were very holy peasants. They breathed behind him on his neck and sighed as they prayed. They lived in Clane, a fellow said: there were little cottages there and he had seen a woman standing at the half-door of a cottage with a child in her arms, as the cars had come past from Sallins. It would be lovely to sleep for one night in that cottage before the fire of smoking turf, in the dark lit by the fire, in the warm dark, breathing the smell of the peasants, air and rain and turf and corduroy. But, O, the road there between the trees was dark! You would be lost in the dark. It made him afraid to think of how it was.

He heard the voice of the prefect of the chapel saying the last prayer. He prayed it too against the dark outside under the trees.

> *Visit, we beseech Thee, O Lord, this habitation and drive away from it all the snares of the enemy. May Thy holy angels dwell herein to preserve us in peace, and may Thy blessing be always upon us through Christ our Lord. Amen.*

His fingers trembled as he undressed himself in the dormitory. He told his fingers to hurry up. He had to undress and then kneel and say his own prayers and be in bed before the gas was lowered so that he might not go to hell when he died. He rolled his stockings off and put on his nightshirt quickly, and knelt trembling at his bedside and repeated his prayers quickly fearing that the gas would go down. He felt his shoulders shaking as he murmured:

> God bless my father and my mother and spare them to me!
> God bless my little brothers and sisters and spare them to me!
> God bless Dante and Uncle Charles and spare them to me!

He blessed himself and climbed quickly into bed and, tucking the end of the nightshirt under his feet, curled himself together under the cold white sheets, shaking and trembling. But he would not go to hell when he died; and the shaking would stop. A voice bade the boys in the dormitory good-night. He peered out for an instant over the coverlet and saw the yellow curtains round and before his bed that shut him off on all sides. The light was lowered quietly.

The prefect's shoes went away. Where? Down the staircase and along the corridors or to his room at the end? He saw the dark. Was it true about the black dog that walked there at night with eyes as big as carriage-lamps? They said it was the ghost of a murderer. A long shiver of fear flowed over his body. He saw the dark entrance hall of the castle. Old servants in old dress were in the ironing-room above the staircase. It was long ago. The old servants were quiet. There was a fire there but the hall was still dark. A figure came up the staircase from the hall. He wore the white cloak of a marshal; his face was pale and strange; he held his hand pressed to his side. He looked out of strange eyes at the old servants. They looked at him and saw their master's face and cloak and knew that he had received his death-wound. But only the dark was where they looked: only dark silent air. Their master had received his death-wound on the battlefield of Prague far away over the sea. He was standing on the field; his hand was pressed to his side; his face was pale and strange and he wore the white cloak of a marshal.

O how cold and strange it was to think of that! All the dark was cold and strange. There were pale strange faces there, great eyes like carriage-lamps. They were the ghosts of murderers, the figures of marshals who had received their death-wound on battlefields far away over the sea. What did they wish to say that their faces were so strange?

> *Visit, we beseech Thee, O Lord, this habitation and drive away from it all   . . .*

Going home for the holidays! That would be lovely: the fellows had told him. Getting up on the cars in the early wintry morning outside the door of the castle. The cars were rolling on the gravel. Cheers for the rector!

Hurray! Hurray! Hurray!

The cars drove past the chapel and all caps were raised. They drove merrily along the country roads. The drivers pointed with their whips to Bodenstown. The fellows cheered. They passed the farmhouse of the Jolly Farmer. Cheer after cheer after cheer. Through Clane they drove, cheering and cheered. The peasant women stood at the half-doors, the men stood here and there. The lovely smell there was in the wintry air: the smell of Clane: rain and wintry air and turf smouldering and corduroy.

The train was full of fellows: a long long chocolate train with cream facings. The guards went to and fro opening, closing, locking, unlocking the doors. They were men in dark blue and silver; they had silvery whistles and their keys made a quick music: click, click: click, click.

And the train raced on over the flat lands and past the Hill of Allen. The telegraph poles were passing, passing. The train went on and on. It knew. There were lanterns in the hall of his father's house and ropes of green branches. There were holly and ivy round the pier-glass and holly and ivy, green and red, twined round the chandeliers. There were red holly and green ivy round the old portraits on the walls. Holly and ivy for him and for Christmas.

Lovely   . . .

All the people. Welcome home, Stephen! Noises of welcome. His mother kissed him. Was that right? His father was a marshal now: higher than a magistrate. Welcome home, Stephen!

Noises   . ■ ■

There was a noise of curtain-rings running back along the rods, of water being splashed in the basins. There was a noise of rising and dressing and washing in the dormitory: a noise of clapping of hands as the prefect went up and down telling the fellows to look

Publication in *The Egoist*

The Egoist *was first called* The New Free-woman, *a little magazine founded by Dora Marsden in England in 1911. Pound and John Gould Fletcher convinced Marsden and the journal's shareholders to change the name to* The Egoist, *which they did in December 1913. With its new name, the journal broadened its scope and shifted from being a strictly feminist publication to one that became a voice for imagist poetry and criticism. Pound contributed essays to* The Egoist.

Four months before Dubliners *was published on 15 June 1914, the serialization of* A Portrait of the Artist as a Young Man *began in the magazine. The novel was published in twenty-five installments between 16 February 1914 and 1 September 1915.*

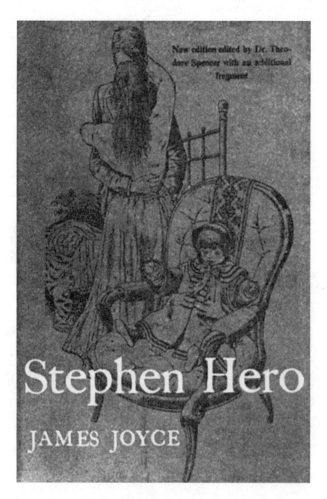

Dust jacket for the revised edition of Joyce's first novel, published in 1956. The first edition was published in 1944.

In his 1937 autobiography Wyndham Lewis compares his initial reaction to A *Portrait of the Artist as a Young Man with his settled opinion of the novel.*

. . . Some pages of the *Portrait* I had read, when it first appeared as a serial in the *Egoist*. . . . But I took very little interest. At that time, it was of far too tenuous an elegance for my taste. Its flavor was altogether too literary. And as to its emotional content, that I condemned at once as sentimental- Irish. Even now, for that matter, I feel much the same about the *Portrait of the Artist,* with the important difference that I have obliged myself to read a great many more books, in the meanwhile, many of which suffer from the same shortcomings, as I see it. So I do recognize the *Portrait of the Artist as a Young Man* to be one only of a large class, and of its kind a very excellent example.
– *Blasting and Bombardiering*, pp. 271–272

Ezra Pound wrote to Joyce in January 1914 to tell him The Egoist *would publish his novel.*

Dear Joyce I'm not supposed to know much about prose but I think your novel is damn fine stuff–I dare say you know it quite as well as I do–clear and direct like Merimee.

I'm sending it off at once to THE EGOIST, it seems a crime not to get paid for it but you recognize the difficulties and the rows any publisher would make.

I hope to got [God] THE EGOIST dont jibe at one or two of your phrases, but I shall try to keep the burden of argument from your shoulders.

Confound it, I cant usually read prose at all not anybody's in English except James and Hudson and a little Conrad.

I am writing this at once. have just finished the reading.
–*Letters II*, p. 327

Supporting Joyce

Pound, who knew of Joyce's financial difficulties during World War I while Joyce and his family were living in Zurich in 1915, planned with Yeats to help Joyce get assistance from the Royal Literary Fund. According to Ellmann in James Joyce, *Pound and Yeats agreed to have Edmund Gosse, an Englishman and an official with the Fund, request support for Joyce. Yeats corresponded with Gosse, who in turn wrote to the Secretary of the Royal Literary Fund on Joyce's behalf. Their efforts paid off, and Joyce was awarded a £75 grant over a period of nine months. At this time, Joyce also received a subsidy from Mrs. Edith Rockefeller McCormick. Supported by this combined income, Joyce completed* Exiles *and continued to write* Ulysses.

Pound wrote a long letter on 3 August 1915 to A. Llewe-lyn Roberts of the Royal Literary Fund in support of Joyce.

Dear Sir: Re/ your request for information regarding James Joyce. (B.A. R. Univ. Dublin).

He is a refugee from Trieste. He kept on teaching in that city until the last possible moment. He is now searching for work in Switzerland. He has a wife and children. Two–boy and girl, 10 and 8. He has, also, some eye trouble that is likely to incapacitate him for several weeks at a time.

He has degrees from Dublin and, I think, Padua, and various certificates from commercial training schools so he feels he may find work later. The schools are now shut for the summer, I believe.

I understand that he arrived in Zurich with clothing suitable for Trieste but not for the Swiss temperature. A relative of his wife's has advanced him a little money, now nearly or wholly gone. This relative is not a man of means and can scarcely be expected to advance or give more money. My own gross takings for the month of July were £2/17 so I am not in a position to help Mr Joyce directly, though I should be glad to do so. (I do not think he would accept assistance unless he were on the edge of necessity.) I do not imagine that my opinion of Mr Joyce's writing can have any weight with your committee, still it gives me a certain satisfaction to state that I consider Joyce a good poet, and *without exception* the best of the younger prose writers. (This is not an opinion influenced by personal friendship, for I was drawn to the man through his work.)

The book 'Dubliners' is uneven. It has been well received but I think he has received nothing yet from his publishers.

His novel 'The Portrait of the Artist as a Young Man' has not yet appeared in book form. It is a work of indubitable value, and permanence. It is appearing serially in a paper called 'The Egoist'. This paper is conducted by enthusiasts who can not afford to pay their contributors.

Your older magazines are so sunk in sloth and stupidity that it [is] impossible for anyone under ninety and unrelated to your detestable victorian rhetoricians to get published in them. Joyce was in Trieste and without friends of influence and I therefore induced him to print this novel in such an out of the way place rather than to leave it longer hidden awaiting the caprice of commerce. This move has been justified, since it has interested several well known authors in Mr Joyce's work. He has lived for ten years in obscurity and poverty, that he might perfect his writing and be uninfluenced by commercial demands and standards 'Ho sofferto fame tre anni a Lipsia, come magister, io non m'arrendi.'
His style has the hard clarity of a Stendhal or a Flaubert. (I am not using these comparisons in a fit of emotional excitement. I have said as much in print already and the opinion is one which has stayed with me for over a year without diminution.) He has also the richness of erudition which differentiates him from certain able and vigorous but rather overloaded impressionist writers. He is able, in the course of a novel, to introduce a serious conversation, or even a stray conversation on style or philosophy without being ridiculous. With the rest, or with most of your novelists, save Henry James and Thomas Hardy, any author who lets a flash of his own personality leak out through the chinks of his story is lost, utterly and hopelessly lost, and we know we can not possibly care a hang what such an author says, or invents for his characters.

If it might be permitted me, to exceed slightly the request you have made to me for information, and if as a foreigner, viewing as a spectator the glories and shames of your country, I might say that it seems to me ridiculous that your government pensions should go for the most part to saving wrecks rather than in the fostering of letters. Thus you give a pension to De la Mare (God knows I am thankful for any good fortune that may befall Walter de la Mare, he is a man who has written a few charming poems, who has been worried to death, who is practically at the end of his tether and who is unlikely to write anything more of any value. Pensioned and put to rest.

On the other hand you have a really great writer like Joyce, capable of producing lasting work if he had any chance of leisure, such chance of leisure as a small pension might give him.

I know it is not my place to make suggestions to your august committee, but I do very strongly make this suggestion. I assure you that England's thoughtfulness, in the midst of war, in stopping to pension De la Mare, has had a good effect on my country. America will have given England more credit for that small act than she will have given to Germany for a propaganda of Kultur. The effect on a foreign nation is perhaps irrelevant but it may be considered.

I do not know how these things are arranged, and I am, I believe, persona non grata to most of my elders but that fact might be overlooked for the moment in a matter so intimately concerning the welfare of English letters as I believe Mr. Joyce's welfare to be. I trust I have given the information that you desire. I shall be glad to supply any more data than [sic] I can. Joyce has two children aged 5 and 8. The eye trouble is the after effect of malarial fever. The school term begins in October, but there is of course no absolute certainty that he will be able to find a position. Respectfully yours,

Ezra Pound
–Letters II, pp. 358–360

Pound wrote to Joyce on 7 September 1915, six days after the last installment of A Portrait of the Artist as a Young Man *was published in* The Egoist. *He not only commented on Joyce's novel but also responded to reading* Exiles *for the first time*

Dear Joyce I have just read the splendid end of 'The Portrait of the Artist', and if I try to tell you how fine it is, I shall only break out into inane hyperbole.

I think the Chapter V. went straight to the Egoist, or came when I was away and had to be forwarded at once,,, anyhow I have been reading it *in* the paper. I have been doing nothing but write 15 page letters to New York about the new magazine and my head is a squeezed rag, so don't expect le mot juste in this letter.

However I read you[r] final instalment last night when I was calm enough to know what I was doing, and I might have written then with more lucidity.

Anyhow I think the book hard, perfect stuff. I doubt if you could have done it in 'the lap of luxury' or in the whirl of a metropolis with the attrition of endless small amusements and endless calls on one's time, and endless trivialities of enjoyment (or the reverse).

I think the book is permanent like Flaubert and Stendhal. Not so squarish as Stendhal, certainly not so varnished as Flaubert. In english I think you join on to Hardy and Henry James (I don't mean a resemblance, I mean that there's has [sic] been nothing of permanent value in prose in between. But I think you must soon, or at least sooner or later, get your recognition.

Hang it all, we dont get prose books that a man can *re*read. We don't get prose that gives us pleasure paragraph by paragraph. I know one man who occasionally burries a charming short chapter in a long ineffective novel . . . but that's another story.
It is the ten years spent on the book, the Dublin 1904, Trieste 1914, that counts. No man can dictate a novel, though there are a lot who try to. And for the other school. I am so damn sick of energetic stupidity. The 'strong' work . . . balls! And it is such a comfort to find an author who has read something and knows something. This deluge of work by subirban counter-jumpers on the one hand and gut-less Oxford graduates or flunktuates on the other . . . bah! And never any intensity, not in *any* of it.
The play has come, and I shall read it as soon as I can be sure of being uninterrupted.
I have just finished the play.
 Having begun it (cliche) I could not (cliche) leave off until (cliche)

Yes, it is interesting. It won't do for the stage. (No, it is unsuitable for the 'Abbey', as mebbe ye might kno'aw fer yourself, Mr. J'ice).

It is exciting. But even read it takes very close concentration of attention. I don't believe an audience could follow it or take it in, even if some damd impracticable manager were to stage it.

Not that I believe any manager would stage it in our chaste and castrated english speaking world.

Roughly speaking, it takes about all the brains I've got to take in thing, reading. And I suppose I've

In a 29 July 1915 letter W. B. Yeats responded to a request for information about Joyce from A. Llewelyn Roberts, the secretary of the Royal Literary Fund.

I have read in a paper called 'The Egoist' certain chapters of a new novel, a disguised autobiography, which increases my conviction that he is the most remarkable new talent in Ireland to-day.
–Letters II, p. 356

William Butler Yeats, circa 1905

more intellogence that [than] the normal theatre goer (god save us)

I may be wrong, the actual people moving on a stage might underline and emphasise the meaning and the changes of mood but . . .

. . . again count it the fact that I 'dont go to the thatre', that is to say I'm always enraged at any play (I don't know that I'm bored) I have cheap cinema amusement and that I get wroth at the assininity of the actors or the author etc. etc. I get a few moments pleasure and long stretches of annoyance. And now my wife dont care much about late hours . . . still I never did go much . . . it always cost money which I couldn't afford. At least I like comfortable seats, which I occasionally get free, and I'm not devotee enough to stand in a shilling line waiting for a board in the gallery.

My whole habit of thinking of the stage is: that it is a gross, coarse form of art. That a play speaks to a thousand fools huddled together, whereas a novel or a poem can lie about in a book and find the stray persons worth finding, one by one seriatim. (so here I am with a clavicord beside me, which I cant afford, and cant reasonably play on . . . here I am chucked out of the Quarterly Review for having contributed ithyphallic satirical verse to 'BLAST' . . . .

and if I had written this letter last night (2 a.m.) just after finishing the 'Portrait', I should have addressed you 'Cher Maitre'.

Now what would he want to write for the stage for ????? Can one appeal to mass with anything requiring thought? Is there anything but the common basis of a very few general emotions out of which to build a play that shall be at once

A. a stage play

B. not common, not a botch.

There is no union in intellect, when we think we diverge, we explore, we go away.

When we feel we unite.

Of course your play is emotional. It works up quite a whirl of emotion, and it hasm undoubtedly, form. I dont think it is nearly as intense as 'The Portrait', at least I dont feel it as much.

My resultant impression is one of a tired head. (Count that I have written out three thousand words of complicated business plan . . been down town and bought two modern pictures for another man . . . played a bit of tennis . . . well it's not more than any one in your theatre audience might have done. . . .

I

might have come to your mss. with a fresher mind . . . ma che . . .

All through the first act I kept doubting the fitness for the stage . . . for though I hate (oh well, not hate)

the theatre I cant help reading a play with constant thoughts about its fitness for the stage (habit contracted when I was supposed to be doing a doctor's thesis on 'The functions of the *gracioso* in the Plays of Lope de Vega')

Without re-reading, I should say that the first spot in the play where it would in any way gain by being staged is the exquisite picture of Robert squirting his perfume pump.

That is to say or to quote 'character' is comedy. Tragedy is emotion.

I may be wrong. The thing might carry. The Stage-Society might give it a try out.

I so loathe the Granville Barker tone . . . ma che . . .

Whether one would want to see those detestable people acting it. . . .

mind you . . . there's no telling what they mightn't do, or what they mightn't take to . . . (if it were castrated . . . the virginal Shaw would want it castrated . . . they're all vegetarians.

It will form an interesting 1/4 volume when you bring out your collected works. When you are a recognized classic people will read it because you wrote it and be duly interested and duly instructed . . . but until then I'm hang'd if I see what's to be done with it.

The prudery of my country (i.e. all of it that isn't lured by vulgarity.) The sheer numbers to which a play must appeal before it is any use to a manager.

Bed rooms scenes where the audience can be tittivated, eroticised . . . excited and NOT expected to think . . . balcony full . . . dress circle ditto . . . boxes ditto . . . .

Ibsen is no longer played. If there were an Ibsen theatre in full blast I dare say your play could go into it . . . ma che. . . .

I shall end this and send it by the midnight post.

I shall read the play again and see if I can think of anything.

Lane's manager writes ((with regard to Mr Joyce's novel, we are very glad to know about this, but Mr Lane will not deal with an agent. If, however, either you or Mr Joyce likes to send the MS. here we shall be very glad indeed to consider it)).

Don't botther to write to Pinker, I will get the ms. from him and take it round to Lane. Lane is publishing my memoir on Brzeska, so I am in touch with him.

(of course its pure bluff their talking about not dealing with an agent. They all do . . . at least I believe they do. . . . I must stop this if it is to go tonight. yours

EZRA POUND
– *Letters II,* pp. 364–367

Pound soon wrote an essay in which he used Joyce's play to raise questions about the future of serious theater.

Mr. James Joyce and the Modern Stage
Ezra Pound
The Drama, 6 (February 1916):122–125, 132

. . . Last week I received a play by Mr. James Joyce and that argumentative interest, which once led me to spend two years of my life reading almost nothing but plays, came back upon me, along with a set of questions 'from the bottom up': Is drama worth while? Is the drama of today, or the stage of today, a form or medium by which the best contemporary authors can express themselves in any satisfactory manner?

Mr. Joyce is undoubtedly one of our best contemporary authors. He has written a novel, and I am quite ready to stake anything I have in this world that that novel is permanent. It is permanent as are the works of Stendhal and Flaubert. Two silly publishers have just refused it in favor of froth, another declines to look at it because 'he will not deal through an agent'–yet Mr. Joyce lives on the continent and can scarcely be expected to look after his affairs in England save through a deputy. And Mr. Joyce is the best prose writer of my generation, in English. So far as I know, there is no one better in either Paris or Russia. In English we have Hardy and Henry James and, chronologically, we have Mr. James Joyce. The intervening novelists print books, it is true, but for me or for any man of my erudition, for any man living at my intensity, these books are things of no substance.

Therefore, when Mr. Joyce writes a play, I consider it a reasonable matter of interest. The English agent of the Oliver Morosco company has refused the play, and in so doing the agent has well served her employers, for the play would certainly be of no use to the syndicate that stars *Peg o' My Heart;* neither do I believe that any manager would stage it nor that it could succeed were it staged. Nevertheless, I read it through at a sitting, with intense interest. It is a long play, some one hundred and eighty pages.

It is not so good as a novel; nevertheless it is quite good enough to form a very solid basis for my arraignment of the contemporary theatre. It lays before me certain facts, certain questions; for instance, are the excellences of this play purely novelist's excellences? Perhaps most of them are; yet this play could not have been made as a novel. It is distinctly a play. It has the form of a play–I do not mean that it is written in dialogue with the names of the speakers put in front of their speeches. I mean that it has inner form; that the acts and speeches of one person work into the acts and speeches of another and make the play into an indivisible, integral whole. The action takes place in less than twenty-four hours, in two rooms, both near Dublin, so that even the classical unities are uninjured. The characters are drawn with that hardness of outline which we might compare to that of Durer's painting if we are permitted a comparison with effects of an art so different. There are only four main characters, two subsidiary characters, and a fishwoman who passes a window, so that the whole mechanics of the play have required great closeness of skill. I see no way in which the play could be improved by redoing it as a novel. It could not, in fact, be anything but a play. And yet it is absolutely unfit for the stage as we know it. It is dramatic. Strong, well-wrought sentences flash from the speech and give it 'dramatic-edge' such as we have in Ibsen, when some character comes out with, 'There is no mediator between God and man': I mean sentences dealing with fundamentals.

Ezra Pound

It is not unstageable because it deals with adultery; surely, we have plenty of plays, quite stageable plays, that deal with adultery. I have seen it in the nickel-plush theatre done with the last degree of sentimental bestiality. I admit that Mr. Joyce once mentions a garter, but it is done in such a way . . . it is done in the only way . . . it is the only possible means of presenting the exact social tone of at least two of the characters.

'Her place in life was rich and poor between,' as Crabbe says of his Clelia; it might have been done in a skit of a night club an no harm thought; but it is precisely because it occurs neither in fast nor in patrician circles, but in a milieu of Dublin genteelness, that it causes a certain feeling of constraint. Mr. Joyce gives his Dublin as Ibsen gave provincial Norway.

Of course, oh, of course, if, *if* there were an Ibsen stage in full blast, Mr. Joyce's play would go on at once.

But we get only trivialized Ibsen; we get Mr. Shaw, the intellectual cheese-mite.

The trouble with Mr. Joyce's play is precisely that he *is* at prise with reality. It is a "dangerous" play precisely because the author is portraying an intellectual- emotional struggle, because he is dealing with actual thought, actual questioning, not with clichés of thought and emotion.

It is untheatrical, or unstageable, precisely because the closeness and cogency of the process is, as I think, too great for an audience to be able to follow . . . under present conditions.

So Mr. Joyce's play is dangerous and unstageable because he is not *playing* with the subject of adultery, but because he is actually driving in the mind upon the age-long problem of the rights of personality and of the responsibility of the intelligent individual for the conduct of those about him, upon the age-long question of the relative rights of intellect, and emotion, and sensation, and sentiment.

And the question which I am trying to put and which I reform and reiterate is just this: Must our most intelligent writers do this sort of work in the novel, *solely in the novel,* or is it going to be, in our time, possible for them to do it in drama?

On your answer to that question the claims of modern drama must rest.

W. B. Yeats wrote to Joyce about Exiles *on 26 August 1917. The poem "about the sea" that Yeats admired is the last poem in* Chamber Music, *"I hear an army charging upon the land."*

Dear Joyce: I did not recommend your play to the Irish Theatre because it is a type of work we have never played well. It is too far from the folk drama; and just at present we do not play the folk drama very well, as a popular commercial play 'Peg of My Heart' has taken away four of our women and those the best. We have also had a dispute with certain players that lost us both men and women. In fact we are almost starting afresh. It is some time since I read your play and my memory is not very clear–I thought it sincere and interesting but I cannot give you the only criticism worth anything, detailed criticism of construction. I could at the time I read it, I have no doubt. I do not think it at all so good as 'A Portrait of the Artist' which I read with great excitement and recommended to may people. I think 'A Portrait' very new and very powerful. Ezra tells me that you have some new work of the kind on hand and that work I await with impatience. A poem of yours about the sea quoted by K Tynan in an anthology is always a delight to me for its substance and for its tecnical mastery Yrs sincry W B YEATS

I wish you better health

– *Letters II,* p. 405

With its vivid imagery of menacing forces, the poem Yeates admired stands in sharp contrast to the lyrical pieces preceding it. Pound was also struck by this poem; it prompted him in December 1913 to write and introduce himself to Joyce and ask permission to include the poem in Des Imagistes, *where it was reprinted in 1914.*

I hear an army charging upon the land,
  And the thunder of horses plunging, foam about
    their knees:
Arrogant, in black armour, behind them stand,
  Disdaining the reins, with fluttering whips, the
    charioteers.

They cry unto the night their battle-name:
  I moan in sleep when I hear afar their whirling
    laughter.
They cleave the gloom of dreams, a blinding flame,
  Clanging, clanging upon the heart as upon an
    anvil.

They come shaking in triumph their long, green
    hair:
  They come out of the sea and run shouting by
    the shore.
My heart, have you no wisdom thus to despair?
  My love, my love, my love, why have you left me
    alone?

An English Reader's Response

In a 26 January 1916 letter to James B. Pinker, Joyce's literary agent, Jonathan Cape (founder of Jonathan Cape, Ltd., publishers), included a reader's report by Edward Garnett of Duckworth & Company.

Dear Mr. Pinker, With reference to James Joyce's novel—A PORTRAIT OF THE ARTIST AS A YOUNG MAN—I am enclosing you 'copy' of a Reader's report. It is a little difficult to give exact chapter and verse for what we think ought to be done to the MS. as the MS. is not in front of us, but the report is sufficiently general for Mr. Joyce to judge of the value of the criticism and his ability to revise the MS. accordingly. Yours very truly,   HERBERT J. CAPE Encl.

Reader's report
[by EDWARD GARNETT]

Duckworth & Co., Publishers,
3 Henrietta Street,
Covent Garden, London, W.C.

James Joyce's 'Portrait of the Artist as a Young Man' wants going through carefully from start to finish. There are many 'longueurs'. Passages which, though the publisher's reader may find them entertaining, will be tedious to the ordinary man among the reading public. That public will call the book, as it stands at present, realistic, unprepossessing, unattractive. We call it ably written. The picture is 'curious', it arouses interest and attention. But the author must revise it and let us see it again. It is too discursive, formless, unrestrained, and ugly things, ugly words, are too prominent; indeed at times they seem to be shoved in one's face, on purpose, unnecessarily. The point of view will be voted 'a little sordid'. The picture of life is good; the period well brought to the reader's eye, and the types and characters are well drawn, but it is too 'unconventional'. This would stand against it in normal times. At the present time, though the old conventions are in the background, we can only see a chance for it if it is pulled into shape and made more definite.

In the earlier portion of the MS. as submitted to us, a good deal of pruning can be done. Unless the author will use restraint and proportion he will not gain readers. His pen and his thoughts seem to have run away with him sometimes.

And at the end of the book there is a complete falling to bits; the pieces of writing and the thoughts are all in pieces and they fall like damp, ineffective rockets.

The author shows us he has art, strength and originality, but this MS. wants time and trouble spent on it, to make it a more finished piece of work, to shape it more carefully as the product of the craftsmanship, mind and imagination of an artist.

Letters II, pp. 371–372

In his 30 January 1916 letter to Pinker, Pound took great offense to the reader's response, which had been forwarded to him.

Dear Mr Pinker I have read the effusion of Mr Duckworth's reader with no inconsiderable disgust. These vermin crawl over and be-slime our literature with their pulings, and nothing but the day of judgement can, I suppose, exterminate 'em. Thank god one need not, under ordinary circumstances, touch them.

Hark to his puling squeek. too 'unconventional'. What in hell do we want but some change from the unbearable monotony of the weekly six shilling pears soap annual novel. [and the George Robey–Gaby mixture] 'Carelessly written,' this of the sole, or almost sole piece of contemporary prose that one can enjoy sentence by sentence and reread with pleasure. (I except Fred. Mannings 'Scenes and Portraits' (pub. Murray, 1910.)

It is with difficulty that I manage to write to you at all on being presented with the . . . , the dungminded dung-beared, penny a line, please the mediocre-at-all-cost doctrine. You English will get no prose till you enterminate [sic] this breed. . . .

to say nothing of the abominable insolence of the tone.

I certainly will have nothing to do with the matter. The Egoist was willing to publish the volume, Lane would have read it a while ago.
I must repeat my former offer, if this louse will specify exactly what verbal changes he wants made I will approach Joyce in the matter. But I most emphatically will not forward the insults of an imbecile to one of the very few men for whom I have the faintest respect. Canting, supercilious, blockhead. . . . I always suposed from report that Duckworth was an educated man, but I can not reconcile this opinion with his retention of the author of the missive you send me.
If you have to spend your life in contact with such minds, God help you, and

do accept my good will and sympathy in spite of the tone of this note.

God! 'a more finished piece of work'.

Really, Mr Pinker, it is too insulting, even to be forwarded to Joyce's friend, let alone to Joyce.

And the end . . also found fault with . . . again, O God, O Montreal. . . .

Why can't you send the publishers readers to the serbian front, and get some good out of the war . .

Serious writers will certainly give up the use of english altogether unless you can improve the process of publication.

In conclusion, you have given me a very unpleasant quarter of an hour, my disgust flows over, though I suppose there is no use in spreading it over this paper. If there is any phrase or form of contempt that you care to convey from me to the reeking Malebolge of the Duckworthian slum, pray, consider yourself at liberty to draw on my account (unlimited credit) and transmit it.

Please, if you have occasion to write again, either in regard to this book or any other. Please do not enclose publisher's readers opinions.

sincerely yours   Ezra Pound

They pour out Elinor Glyn and pornography after pornography, but a piece of good writing they hate.

P.S.

I am reminded that Landor had equal difficulty in getting published–yet he is the best mind in your literature.

B. W. Huebsch, whose firm published the first American editions of Chamber Music *(1918),* Dubliners *(1916),* A Portrait of the Artist as a Young Man *(1916), and* Exiles *(1918)*

as for altering Joyce to suit Duckworth's readers–I would like trying to fit the Venus de Milo into a piss-pot.–. . a few changes required.

Letters II, pp. 372–373

The First Edition of *A Portrait*

Harriet Shaw Weaver (1876–1961), the editor of The Egoist, *became Joyce's longtime benefactor and friend. She was instrumental in getting* A Portrait of the Artist as a Young Man *published as a book, for she promised the American publisher B. W. Huebsch that she would take 750 copies of the American edition to publish as an English edition. The novel was first published in book form on 29 December 1916 in New York by Huebsch; the first English edition appeared under the imprint of* The Egoist *on 12 February 1917.*

In his letter dated 16 June 1916, Huebsch wrote to Weaver regarding rights to publish the novel.

Dear Sir: I am much impressed with Mr Joyce's *A Portrait of the Artist as a Young Man* and should be glad to publish it here giving it my best efforts, though I am inclined to believe that such success as it may attain will be artistic rather than popular. Nevertheless it will afford a foundation for Mr Joyce's other works on this side.

I should be willing to print absolutely in accordance with the author's wishes, without deletion, and would undertake to supply printed sheets with joint imprints for the English publisher and myself sharing the cost at such rate as may seem fair to you.

I would pay a 10% royalty on the published price but I should like to make the condition that I secure an option on the book which would normally succeed *A Portrait of the Artist as a Young Man*. Also that some arrangement be made by which I secure sheets of *Dubliners* concerning which I have had correspondence with Mr Richards and Mr Joyce.

After hearing from Mr Joyce, last year, about his book of poems published by Mr Mathews, I believe that I wrote to the latter without receiving any response. You will see that I am anxious, not only for my sake but for Mr Joyce's, to get all of his works so that by concentration of interest and economy of effort, he may be properly introduced on this side. Is Mr Joyce still in Switzerland? I am inclined to believe, from our correspondence, that he would favor an arrangement by which I become his publisher here.

Letters I, pp. 91–92

Reviews of *A Portrait of the Artist as a Young Man*

One of the first reviews of A Portrait of the Artist as a Young Man, *"A Study in Garbage" published in* Everyman, *compared the Irish Joyce to the Welsh Caradoc Evans in that they "have made it their business in life to portray the least estimable features of their respective countrymen." Joyce's novel, this unsigned review continues, "is an astonishingly powerful and extraordinary dirty study of the upbringing of a young man by Jesuits, which ends—so far as we have been at all able to unravel the meaning of the impressionist ending—with his insanity." The reviewer's unraveling, however, did not go far enough, for Stephen Dedalus does not end up insane. Writing in his diary in an almost prayerful meditation, Dedalus at the end of the novel is hopeful of a future and confident in his untested abilities as he invokes the mythic source of his surname, the cunning Daedalus: "Old father, old artificer, stand me now and ever in good stead."*

Whether or not H. G. Wells was right in suggesting that Joyce had "a cloacal obsession" in his review in the Nation, *he was surely correct in praising the novel as "by far the most living and convincing picture that exists of an Irish Catholic upbringing. It is a mosaic of jagged fragments that does altogether render with extreme completeness the growth of a rather secretive, imaginative boy in Dublin." What struck many early reviewers were the novel's stark realism and the striking characterization of the protagonist, which Joyce skillfully achieved through a dramatic exposition that demanded of the reader an attentiveness not necessarily required of direct narrative description.*

At Last the Novel Appears
Ezra Pound
The Egoist, 4, no. 2 (February 1917): 21–22

It is unlikely that I shall say anything new about Mr. Joyce's novel, *A Portrait of the Artist as a Young Man.* I have already stated that it is a book worth reading and that it is written in good prose. In using these terms I do not employ the looseness of the half-crown reviewer.

I am very glad that it is now possible for a few hundred people to read Mr. Joyce comfortably from a bound book, instead of from a much-handled file of EGOISTS or from a slippery bundle of typescript. After much difficulty THE EGOIST itself turns publisher and produces *A Portrait of the Artist* as a volume, for the hatred of ordinary English publishers for good prose is, like the hatred of the *Quarterly Review* for good poetry, deep-rooted, traditional.

Since Landor's *Imaginary Conversations* were bandied from pillar to post, I doubt if any manuscript has

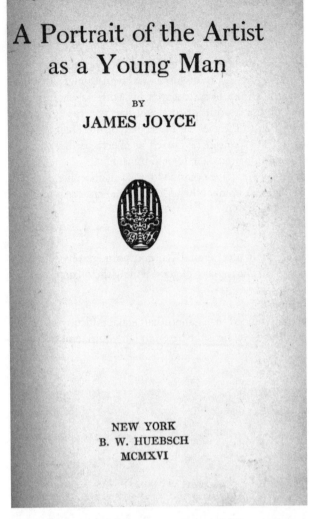

Title page for the first edition of Joyce's first novel (courtesy of Special Collections, Thomas Cooper Library, University of South Carolina)

met with so much opposition, and no manuscript has been more worth supporting.

Landor is still an unpopular author. He is still a terror to fools. He is still concealed from the young (not for any alleged indecency, but simply because he did not acquiesce in certain popular follies). He, Landor, still plays an inconspicuous role in university courses. The amount of light which he would shed on the undergraduate mind would make students inconvenient to the average run of professors. But Landor is permanent.

Members of the "Fly-Fishers" and "Royal Automobile" clubs, and of the "Isthmian," may not read him. They will not read Mr. Joyce. *E pur si muove.* Despite the printers and publishers the British Government has recognized Mr. Joyce's literary merit. That is a definite gain for the party of intelligence. A number of qualified judges have acquiesced in my statement of two

An Unknown and Generous Friend

Harriet Shaw Weaver first sent Joyce anonymous support on 22 February 1917, using a law firm to make a promise of four £50 checks to be delivered "on the 1st May, August, November and February next." Joyce at first incorrectly guessed the anonymous donor to be Lady Cunard. Only after a letter from Weaver, written, as Ellmann points out "to prevent embarrassment" rather than "to claim credit," did Joyce learn the true identity of his patron. In a 20 July 1919 letter to Weaver, Joyce apologetically explained that he misinterpreted the information he got from her solicitors (see Selected Letters, *p. 240). Weaver continued to help the writer throughout his life and even paid for his funeral; she also acted as Joyce's literary executor. According to the estimate of Robert Adams Day, Weaver's financial support would be equivalent to one million dollars in today's currency.*

Harriet Shaw Weaver in 1919

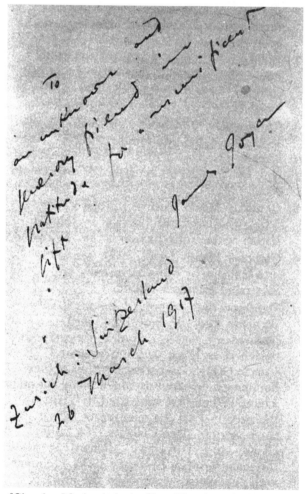

Joyce's inscription to Weaver in a copy of Chamber Music. *At the time Joyce did not know that Weaver was his benefactor (*James Joyce at 101: An Exhibition, *catalogue compiled by Charles Kemnitz, The University of Tulsa, McFarlin Library).*

Joyce in Zürich, circa 1917 (Croessmann Collection of James Joyce, Special Collections/Morris Library, Southern Illinois University at Carbondale)

years ago, that Mr. Joyce was an excellent and important writer of prose.

The last few years have seen the gradual shaping of a party of intelligence, a party not bound by any central doctrine or theory. We cannot accurately define new writers by applying to them tag-names from old authors, but as there is no adequate means of conveying the general impression of their characteristics one may at times employ such terminology, carefully stating that the terms are nothing more than approximation.

With that qualification, I would say that James Joyce produces the nearest thing to Flaubertian prose that we have now in English, just as Wyndham Lewis has written a novel which is more like, and more fitly compared with, Dostoievsky than is the work of any of his contemporaries. In like manner Mr. T. S. Eliot comes nearer to filling the place of Jules La Forgue in our generation. (Doing the "nearest thing" need not imply an approach to a standard, from a position inferior.)

Two of these writers have met with all sorts of opposition. If Mr. Eliot probably has not yet encountered very much opposition, it is only because his work is not yet very widely known.

My own income was considerably docked because I dared to say that Gaudier-Brzeska was a good sculptor and that Wyndham Lewis was a great master of design. It has, however, reached an almost irreducible minimum, and I am, perhaps, fairly safe in reasserting Joyce's ability as a writer. It will cost me no more than a few violent attacks from several sheltered, and therefore courageous, anonymities. When you tell the Irish that they are slow in recognizing their own men of genius they reply with street riots and politics.

Now, despite the jobbing of bigots and of their sectarian publishing houses, and despite the "Fly-Fishers" and the types which they represent, and despite the unwillingness of the print-packers (a word derived from pork-packers) and the initial objections of the Dublin publishers and the later unwillingness of the English publishers, Mr. Joyce's novel appears in book form, and intelligent readers gathering few by few will read it, and it will remain a permanent part of English literature—written by an Irishman in Trieste and first published in New York City. I doubt if a comparison of Mr. Joyce to other English writers or Irish writers would much help to define him. One can only say that he is rather unlike them. *The Portrait* is very different from *L'Education Sentimentale,* but it would be easier to compare it with that novel of Flaubert's than with anything else. Flaubert pointed out that if France had studied his work they might have been saved a good deal in 1870. If more people had read *The Portrait* and certain stories in Mr. Joyce's *Dubliners* there might have been less recent trouble in Ireland. A clear diagnosis is never without its value.

Apart from Mr. Joyce's realism—the school-life, the life in the University, the family dinner with the discussion of Parnell depicted in his novel—apart from, or of a piece with, all this is the style, the actual writing: hard, clear-cut, with no waste of words, no bundling up of useless phrases, no filling in with pages of slosh.

It is very important that there should be clear, unexaggerated, realistic literature. It is very important that there should be good prose. The hell of contemporary Europe is caused by the lack of representative government in Germany, *and* by the non-existence of decent prose in the German language. Clear thought and sanity depend on clear prose. They cannot live apart. The former produces the latter. The latter conserves and transmits the former.

EXTRACTS
FROM AMERICAN PRESS NOTICES

OF

A PORTRAIT
OF THE ARTIST AS A YOUNG MAN

BY

JAMES JOYCE

(B. W. HUEBSCH : NEW YORK : 1916)

Mr. JAMES HUNEKER in *The New York Sun* . . . . A realist of the Maupassant breed he envisages Dublin and the Dubliners with a cruel scrutinising gaze. He is as truthful as Tchekov and as gray . . . . as implacably naturalistic as the Russian in his vision and he sometimes suggests the Frenchman in his clear concise technical methods . . . . A veritable portrait . . . . Rather depressing . . . . We do not recall a book like this since the autobiography *En Route* of J. K. Huysmans. This Parisian of Dutch extraction is in the company of James Joyce. Neither writer stops at the halfway house of reticence . . . . With both men the love of Rabelaisian speech is marked . . . . The portrait is well nigh perfect. Mr. Joyce holds the scales evenly. He neither abuses nor praises . . . . The scene in the house of Stephen's parents simply blazes with verity . . . . The novel as a whole is hardly cheerful. Its grip on life, its intensity and unflinching acceptance of facts will make it disagreeable to the average reader . . . . It is too Irish to be liked by the Irish.

Mr. HENRY SELL in *The Chicago Daily News :* The firm delicate strokes with which he has drawn his portrait never link as outline . . . . Refreshingly unlike the traditional youthful genius of psychoanalytic narrative . . . . an oddly fascinating style . . . . Exquisite esthetic analysis.

Mr. JOHN QUINN in *Vanity Fair :* A new star has appeared in the firmament of Irish letters, a star of the first magnitude. All of a sudden everyone that one meets is reading and talking about this book . . . . A great novel . . . . the book is a distillation of bittersweet . . . . It stands out above anything that has been published in this country or in Great Britain in the last two years . . . . It will live . . . . His style is vital and has the radium that makes art live . . . . Bracing and hard and clean . . . . He has no thesis. His book is just life. Some of his phrases are as startling as many that could be culled from the bible. His is a new style. There is no ornament, no rhetoric, nothing declamatory, no compromise, complete realism and great sincerity . . . . the sincerity of genius . . . . a fine hard great piece of work. If the book had been translated from the Russian it would

The initial page of press notices published by Huebsch to advertise the novel (Division of Rare and Manuscript Collections, Carl A. Kroch Library, Cornell University [Scholes 1391])

The mush of the German sentence, the straddling of the verb out to the end, are just as much a part of the befoozlement of Kultur and the consequent hell, as was the rhetoric of later Rome the seed and the symptom of the Roman Empire's decadence and extinction. A nation that cannot write clearly cannot be trusted to govern, nor yet to think.

Germany has had two decent prose-writers, Frederick the Great and Heine—the one taught by Voltaire, and the other saturated with French and with Paris. Only a nation accustomed to muzzy writing could have been led by the nose and bamboozled as the Germans have been by their controllers.

The terror of clarity is not confined to any one people. The obstructionist and the provincial are everywhere, and in them alone is the permanent danger to civilization. Clear, hard prose is the safeguard and should be valued as such. The mind accustomed to it will not be cheated or stampeded by national phrases and public emotionalities.

These facts are true, even for the detesters of literature. For those who love good writing there is no need of argument. In the present instance it is enough to say to those who will believe one that Mr. Joyce's book is now procurable.

A Study in Garbage
Everyman, 23 February 1917, p. 398

Mr. James Joyce is an Irish edition of Mr. Caradoc Evans. These writers, that is to say, have made it their business in life to portray the least estimable features of their respective countrymen, Irish or Welsh. Mr. Joyce's new book, *A Portrait of an Artist as a Young Man* is an astonishingly powerful and extraordinary dirty study of the upbringing of a young man by Jesuits, which ends—so far as we have been at all able to unravel the meaning of the impressionist ending—with his insanity. The description of life in a Jesuit school, and later in a Dublin college, strikes one as being absolutely true to life—but what a life! Parts of the book are perhaps a little too allusive to be readily understood by the English reader. On pp. 265–6, there is an account of what happened at the Abbey Theatre, Dublin, when *The Countess Cathleen,* by Mr. W. B. Yeats, was put on, but the fact is darkly hidden. Mr. Joyce is a clever novelist, but we feel he would be really at his best in a treatise on drains. . . .

—reprinted from *James Joyce: The Critical Heritage*

H. G. Wells

The British novelist H. G. Wells's early review carried weight and was often quoted by later reviewers.

James Joyce
H. G. Wells
Nation, 20 (24 February 1917): 710, 712

. . . Even more considerable is *A Portrait of the Artist as a Young Man,* by James Joyce. It is a book to buy and read and lock up, but it is not a book to miss. Its claim to be literature is as good as the claim of the last book of *Gulliver's Travels.*

It is no good trying to minimize a characteristic that seems to be deliberately obtruded. Like Swift and another living Irish writer, Mr. Joyce has a cloacal obsession. He would bring back into the general picture of life aspects which modern drainage and modern decorum have taken out of ordinary intercourse and conversation. Coarse, unfamiliar words are scattered about the book unpleasantly, and it may seem to many, needlessly. If the reader is squeamish upon these matters, then there is nothing for it but to shun this book, but if he will pick his way, as one has to do at times on the outskirts of some picturesque Italian village with a view and a church and all sorts of things of that sort to tempt one, then it is quite worth while. And even upon this unsavory aspect of Swift and himself, Mr. Joyce is suddenly illuminating. He tells at several points how his hero Stephen is swayed and shocked and disgusted by harsh and loud *sounds,* and how he is stirred to

intense emotion by music and the rhythms of beautiful words. But no sort of smell offends him like that. He finds olfactory sensations interesting or aesthetically displeasing, but they do not make him sick or excited as sounds do. This is a quite understandable turn over from the more normal state of affairs. Long ago I remember pointing out in a review the difference in the sensory basis of the stories of Robert Louis Stevenson and Sir J. M. Barrie; the former visualized and saw his story primarily as picture, the latter mainly heard it. We shall do Mr. Joyce an injustice if we attribute a normal sensory basis to him and then accuse him of deliberate offense.

But that is by the way. The value of Mr. Joyce's book has little to do with its incidental insanitary condition. Like some of the best novels in the world it is the story of an education; it is by far the most living and convincing picture that exists of an Irish Catholic upbringing. It is a mosaic of jagged fragments that does altogether render with extreme completeness the growth of a rather secretive, imaginative boy in Dublin. The technique is startling, but on the whole it succeeds. Like so many Irish writers from Sterne to Shaw Mr. Joyce is a bold experimentalist with paragraph and punctuation. He breaks away from scene to scene without a hint of the change of time and place; at the end he passes suddenly from the third person to the first; he uses no inverted commas to mark off his speeches. The first trick I found sometimes tiresome here and here, but then my own disposition, perhaps acquired at the blackboard, is to mark off and underline rather fussily, and I do not know whether I was so much put off the thing myself as anxious, which after all is not my business, about its effect on those others; the second trick, I will admit, seems entirely justified in this particular instance by its success; the third reduces Mr. Joyce to a free use of dashes. One conversation in this book is a superb success, the one in which Mr. Dedalus carves the Christmas turkey; I write with all due deliberation that Sterne himself could not have done it better; but most of the talk flickers blindingly with these dashes, one has the same wincing feeling of being flicked at that one used to have in the early cinema shows. I think Mr. Joyce has failed to discredit the inverted comma.

The interest of the book depends entirely upon its quintessential and unfailing reality. One believes in Stephen Dedalus as one believes in few characters in fiction. And the peculiar lie of the interest for the intelligent reader is the convincing revelation it makes of the limitations of a great mass of Irishmen. Mr. Joyce tells us unsparingly of the adolescence of this youngster under conditions that have passed almost altogether out of English life. There is an immense shyness, a profound secrecy, about matters of sex, with its inevitable accompaniment of nightmare revelations and furtive scribblings in unpleasant places, and there is a living belief in a real hell. The description of Stephen listening without a doubt to two fiery sermons on that tremendous theme, his agonies of fear, not disgust at dirtiness such as unorthodox children feel but just fear, his terror-inspired confession of his sins of impurity to a strange priest in a distant part of the city, is like nothing in any boy's experience who has been trained under modern conditions. Compare its stuffy horror with Conrad's account of how under analogous circumstances Lord Jim wept. And a second thing of immense significance is the fact that everyone in this Dublin story, every human being, accepts as a matter of course, as a thing in nature like the sky and the sea, that the English are to be hated. There is no discrimination in that hatred, there is no gleam of recognition that a considerable number of Englishmen have displayed a very earnest disposition to

put matters right with Ireland, there is an absolute absence of any idea of a discussed settlement, any notion of helping the slow-witted Englishman in his three-cornered puzzle between North and South. It is just hate, a cant cultivated to the pitch of monomania, an ungenerous violent direction of the mind. That is the political atmosphere in which Stephen Dedalus grows up, and in which his essentially responsive mind orients itself. I am afraid it is only too true an account of the atmosphere in which a number of brilliant young Irishmen have grown up. What is the good of pretending that the extreme Irish 'patriot' is an equivalent and parallel of the English or American liberal? He is narrower and intenser than any English Tory. He will be the natural ally of the Tory in delaying British social and economic reconstruction after the war. He will play into the hands of the Tories by threatening an outbreak and providing the excuse for a militarist reaction in England. It is time the American observer faced the truth of that. No reason in that why England should not do justice to Ireland, but excellent reason for bearing in mind that these bright-green young people across the Channel are something quite different from the liberal English in training and tradition, and absolutely set against helping them. No single book has ever shown how different they are, as completely as this most memorable novel.

—reprinted from *James Joyce: The Critical Heritage*

First pointing out what he calls the "improprieties" of Joyce's novel, A. Clutton-Brock examines the mind of Stephen Dedalus and concludes that Joyce gives the reader something very worth having. One of the first reviewers to discern the lyricism in the novel, Clutton-Brock ends with the observation: "It is wild youth, as wild as Hamlet's, and full of wild music."

Wild Youth

A. Clutton-Brock

Times Literary Supplement, no. 789 (1 March 1917): 103–104

If we begin by some complaining of the title of this book, it is only because it may turn some people away from it. Others may be put off by occasional improprieties—there is one on the very first page; and it is useless to say that people ought not to be put off by such things. They are; and we should like the book to have as many readers as possible. It is not about the artist as a young man, but about a child, a boy, a youth. As one reads, one remembers oneself in it, at least one reader does; yet, like all good fiction, it is as particular as it is universal.

It is about a young Irishman, the son of a father whom he describes to a friend as 'a medical student, an

It has of late years been the custom to expect literary surprises from Ireland. This began with Sterne 150 years ago and that wonders have not ceased with Mr. Shaw this book of James Joyce plainly testifies. . . . From the first page to the last the reader feels himself in the hands of one who plainly knows what he means to do and how he is to do it.

— *Springfield Republican*

oarsman, a tenor, an amateur actor, a shouting politician, a small landlord, a small investor, a drinker, a good fellow, a story-teller, somebody's secretary, something in a distillery, a tax-gatherer, a bankrupt, and at present a praiser of his own past.' He seems neither to love nor to hate his father; he is educated by the Jesuits, and he neither hates nor loves them; he tries to love God. 'It seems now I failed,' he says. 'It is very difficult to unite my will with the will of God instant by instant. In that I did not always fail. I could perhaps do that still.' Told thus baldly, it sounds futile, but it is not. Mr. Joyce does not talk about futilities because he cannot make anything happen in his story. He can make anything happen that he chooses. He can present the external world excellently, as in the quarrel over Parnell at a Christmas dinner at the beginning of the book. No living writer is better at conversations. But his hero is one of those many Irishmen who cannot reconcile themselves to things; above all, he cannot reconcile himself to himself. He has at times a disgust for himself, a kind of mental queasiness, in which the whole universe seems nauseating as it is presented to him through the medium of his own disgusting self. That perhaps is the cause of those improprieties we have mentioned. What an angel he would like to be, and what a filthy creature, by comparison with that angel, he seems to himself! And so all men and women seem to him filthy creatures. So it was with Hamlet. There is nothing good or bad but thinking makes it so; and thoughts pass through his mind like good or bad smells. He has no control of them.

So it is with all youth; we can all look back on ourselves and remember how disgusting we were to ourselves sometimes. But now we are used to ourselves; and we have established some relation with reality outside us, and made a habit of it, so that we do not permit those self-disgusts. But this youth, Stephen Dedalus is his name, has formed no habits that he consents to. His mind is a mirror in which beauty and ugliness are merely intensified; but how they are intensified in Mr. Joyce's story! Perhaps he is called the artist because everything to him is beauty or ugliness; but that is often so with youths who never become artists. They have their period of passive experience, and suffer because they know it to be passive; and yet they cannot but despise those elders who will themselves out of all experience, to whom nothing happens, or is, except as they wish it to be. But what Mr. Joyce gives us is the unwilled intensity of this youth's experience. He makes it like the unwilled intensity of dreams. And we have the talk of his fellow-students intensified by his experience of it. It is more real than real talk; it is like our memories of youth, but more precise than they ever are to most of us. The students often do not talk nicely; but then they are students, not nice students. They remind us of Dosto-

evsky's Russians in the manner in which thoughts happen to them, thoughts, irritations, disgusts; and also in the manner in which they can vent these in mere talk without ever passing on to action. Hence their malease, which is strongest in the hero; and yet they have the Irish and Russian contempt for those in whom experience converts itself into action before it has ever been really experience. They cannot but laugh at the man of action; and their chief pleasure in life is in making their laughter articulate, in making a kind of music of it. The phrase satisfies them; yet it does not satisfy, because they want a world in which phrases will act.

The hero is distinguished from the rest of them by a deeper malease. His experience is so intense, such a conflict of beauty and disgust, that it must drive him to do something. For a time it drives him into an immoral life, in which also there is beauty and disgust; but the fear of hell drives him away from this into a period of rigid piety. That again, like his immorality, begins with beauty—in the wonderful scene of his confession—and ends in listlessness. There is always something in himself that laughs at him, and it translates itself into laughers outside him. That is a common experience of youth, but with Stephen Dedalus it is always happening.

> He remembered an evening when he had dismounted from a borrowed breaking bicycle to pray to God in a wood near Malahide. He had lifted up his arms and spoken in ecstasy to the solemn noise of the trees, knowing that he stood on holy ground and in a holy hour. And when two constabulary men had come into sight round a bend in the gloomy road he had broken off his prayer to whistle loudly an air from the last pantomime. That is always happening to him, from outside or inside. It happens about the lady whom he loves, or does not love.

> While he sang and she listened, or feigned to listen, his heart was at rest, but when the faint old songs had ended and he heard again the voices in the room he remembered his own sarcasm: the house where young men are called by their Christian names a little too soon.

That kind of sarcasm starts up in his mind about everything, like a whisper of Satan, and it destroys all his values. He has not enough egotism to have any values, and when the book ends suddenly he is setting out to find some. But for all that he is not futile, because of the drifting passion and the flushing and fading beauty of his mind. Mr. Joyce gives us that, and therefore gives us something that is worth having. It is wild youth, as wild as Hamlet's, and full of wild music.

Recognizing that Joyce's novel is the product of a man of genius and that its central character is a "sensitivist" who has not yet proved an artist, this reviewer for The Manchester Guardian *praises the author while at the same time criticizing him for the demands he makes on the reader.*

A Sensitivist
A.M.
The Manchester Guardian, 2 March 1917, p. 3

When one recognizes genius in a book one can perhaps best leave criticism alone . . . There are many pages, and not a few whole scenes, in Mr. Joyce's book which are undoubtedly the work of a man of genius, nevertheless, it leaves us combative. The reader—who is as much ignored, and as contemptuously, as it is possible for him to be in a printed work—revolts and asserts himself from time to time, and refuses to sit down passively under the writer's scorn. Once criticism is let loose, it finds range enough and many marks to hit.

Nor for its apparent formlessness should the book be condemned. A subtle sense of art has worked amidst the chaos, making this hither-and-thither record of a young mind and soul . . . a complete and ordered thing. There are ellipses, though, that go beyond the pardonable. A little too much is asked of the even eager reader in the way of understanding situations that have not been led up to, and obscure allusions. One has to be of the family, so to speak, to 'catch on.' This is part of one distinguishing feature of the book—its astounding bad manners. About this one must speak frankly at the start and have done with it. Not all the scenes are touched by genius. Some read like disagreeable phonographic records of the stupid conversations of ill-born and ill-bred youths, compact of futile obscenities, aimless outrages against reasonable decencies—not immoral, but non-moral in a bad-mannered fashion. Perhaps Mr. Joyce wants to show what may be, and often is, the ugly background of fairer things which consent astonishingly to grow in a sordid neighbourhood. Well, there is too much of this background. Also, an idiosyncrasy of Stephen, the central figure of the book—and some of his companions seem to share it—is a passion for foul-smelling things. A doctor could put a definite name to this disease, not an interesting one to the general reader, though Mr. Joyce by his insistence on it seems to think the contrary. One is driven to the conclusion that this gifted and very modern writer who rejects old theories so contemptuously is a slave to a new and particularly stupid one.

At the end Stephen has not yet proved his title to the name of artist, but is still looking for a formula to work by. He is a sensitivist. For heat and cold and discomfort, for the atmosphere of persons and companies, he has extra-subtle senses. For the pace of the world, for the things of the soul, too, he has a rare keenness of feel-

An unusual book for many reasons . . . a close and searching study of mental processes. . . . It is of surprising worth. . . . It is a man's life such as you know and the writer of these lines knows to be true. . . . Joyce is not only a writer of the first rank but an analyst of human character whose knife is dexterously handled.

– Medicine and Surgery

ing, and his interpreter gives these exquisite expression. Mr. Joyce's literary gift is beyond praise. At his best he is a master. His methods are hard to define. It is almost without narrative that he depicts inimitably the condition of the Dedalus family in its prosperity and the nameless squalor which it falls into when fortune fails. Lounging feebly among this squalor we find Stephen, helpless against the ruin, but with life in him, the life of the mind, keenly concerned for intellectual experience and for a faith his mind can live by. All this is true and pathetic. True also to this kind of youth is the half-expressed notion that mainly by sin he is to win his way to mental salvation. So convenient a theory for the lounger! Yet Stephen is better than his theory. Among the new-fangled heroes of the newest fiction devoted to the psychology of youth he is almost unique in having known at least once a genuine sense of sin and undergone a genuine struggle. There is drama in Stephen. The struggle might conceivably recur, and from the lounger emerges the man and the artist.

Francis Hackett was an associate editor of The New Republic *from 1914 through 1922 and many years later book critic for* The New Times. *Hackett attended Clongowes Wood College in Salins, County Kildare, where Joyce was a student between 1888 and 1891. In the following review Hackett speaks to the evocative power and striking candor of the novel.*

Green Sickness
Francis Hackett
The New Republic, 10 (3 March 1917): 138–139

There is a laconic unreasonableness about the ways of creators. It is quite true that the Irish literary revival was beginning to be recognized at precisely the period of Mr. Joyce's novel, and it is also true that his protagonist is a student in Dublin at the hour of the so-called renaissance, a writer and poet and dreamer of dreams. So perverse is life, however, there is scarcely one glimmer in this landscape of the flame which is supposed to have illuminated Dublin between 1890 and 1900. If

A book that would surely give distinction to any list of contemporary fiction in any country in Europe.

– *Land and Water*

Stephen Dedalus, the young man portrayed in this novel, had belonged to the Irish revival, it would be much easier for outsiders to "place" him. The essential fact is, he belonged to a more characteristic group which this novel alone has incarnated. One almost despairs of conveying it to the person who has conventionalized his idea of Ireland and modern Irish literature, yet there is a poignant Irish reality to be found in few existing plays and no pre-existent novel, presented here with extraordinary candor and beauty and power.

It is a pleasant assumption of national mythology that the southern Irish are a bright and witty people, effervescent on the sunny side and pugnacious on the other, but quick to act in any event, and frequently charming and carefree and impossible. It may be that the Irish exhibit this surface to outsiders and afford a case of street angel and house devil on a national scale, or it may be that the English landlord has chosen to see the Irishman as funny in the way the Southern gentleman chooses to see the Negro as funny, but, however the assumption got started it has been fortified by generations of story-tellers and has provided a fair number of popular writers with a living. It is only when a person with the invincible honesty of James Joyce comes to write of Dubliners as they are, a person who is said to be mordant largely because he isn't mushy, that the discrepancy between the people and the myth [the myth that the southern 'Irish are a bright and witty people'] is apparent. When one says Dubliners 'as they are', one of course is pronouncing a preference. One is simply insisting that the Irishmen of James Joyce are more nearly like one's own estimate of them than the Irishmen of an amiable fabulist like George Birmingham. But there is the whole of the exquisite "Portrait of the Artist as a Young Man" to substantiate the assertion that a proud, cold, critical, suspicious, meticulous human being is infinitely more to be expected among educated Catholic Irishmen than the sort of squireen whom Lever once glorified. If this is a new type in Ireland, come into existence with the recent higher education of Catholics, one can only say that it is now by far the most important type of recognize. Bernard Shaw suggested it in the London Irishman, Larry Doyle, who appeared in "John Bull's Other Island," but the main character of the present novel is much more subtly inflected and individualized than Larry Doyle, and is only said to belong to a type to intimate that his general mode is characteristic.

Mr. Joyce's power is not shown in any special inventiveness. A reader of novels will see at once that he has never even thought of 'plot' in the ordinary sense, or considered the advantage or importance of the thing he knows best, himself, himself at boarding school and university, and any radical variation on the actual terms of that piercing knowledge he has declined to attempt. He has sought above everything to reveal those circumstances of his life which had poignancy, and the firmest claim on him to being written was not that a thing should be amenable to his intentions as a sophisticated novelist, but that a thing should have complete personal validity. It did not weigh with him at any moment that certain phrases or certain incidents would be intensely repugnant to some readers. Was the phrase interwoven with experience? Was the incident part of the fabric of life? He asked this searchingly, and asked no more. It is not even likely that he made inquiry why, out of all that he could write, he selected particularly to reveal details that seldom find expression. Had he made inquiry he might well have answered that the mere consciousness of silence is an incitement to expression, that expression is the only vengeance a mortal can take on the restrictions to which he finds himself subject. If others submit to those restrictions it is their own affair. To have the truth one must have a man's revelation of that which was really significant to himself.

Considering that this portrait is concluded before its subject leaves college one may gather that the really significant relations are familiar and religious, and that the adjustment is between a critical spirit and its environment. What gives its intensity to the portrait is the art Mr. Joyce has mastered of communicating the incidents of Stephen's career through the emotions they excited in him. We do not perceive Stephen's father and mother by description. We get them by the ebb and flood of Stephen's feeling, and while there are many passages of singularly lifelike conversation—such, for example, as the wrangle about Parnell that ruined the Christmas dinner or the stale banter that enunciated the father's return to Cork—the viridity is in

A jerky spasmodic style which may please a certain class of readers. . . . Much talent is exhibited in this work but it is talent of a wild and uncultivated order. . . . He uses unnecessarily coarse language. . . . His psychology is crude. . . . He writes as if he did not know how or where to begin or end. . . . chaotic.

– *Rochester Post Express*

Stephen's soul. "Stephen watched the three glasses being raised from the counter as his father and his two cronies drank to the memory of their past. An abyss of fortune or of temperament sundered him from them. His mind seemed older than theirs: it shone coldly on their strifes and happiness and regrets like a moon upon a younger earth. No life or youth stirred in him as it had stirred in them. He had known neither the pleasures of companionship with others nor the vigor of rude male health nor filial piety. Nothing stirred within his soul but a cold and cruel and loveless lust. His childhood was dead or lost and with it his soul capable of simple joys and he was drifting amid life like the barren shell of the moon."

It is his mortal sin of masturbation that preys most terribly on this youth, and he suffers all the blasting isolation which is created by the sense of sin in connection with it. Eventually he makes a "retreat"—he is being educated by the Jesuits—and goes to confession and for a time knows religious happiness. The explicitness of this experience is more telling than the veiled account of sexual stupidity in Samuel Butler's "Way of All Flesh," and Mr. Joyce is more successful than Samuel Butler in making religious belief seem real. The efforts of a Jesuit father to suggest a religious vocation to Stephen are the beginning of the end of his religion. In "lucid, supple, periodic prose" Mr. Joyce describes the transition from devotional life and a private specializing in mortification to the acceptance of nature and the earth. "His soul had arisen from the grave of boyhood, spurning her grave-clothes. Yes! Yes! Yes! He would create proudly out of the freedom and power of his soul, as the great artificer whose name he bore, a living thing, new and soaring and beautiful, impalpable, imperishable." The "Yes! Yes! Yes!" gives that touch of intense youthfulness which haunts the entire book, even though Mr. Joyce can be so superb in flaunting Aristotle and Aquinas.

The last chapter of the portrait gives one the *esprit* of the Catholic nationalist students in University College. It is a marvelous version of scurrilous, supercilious, callow youth. Mr. Joyce's subject is not in sympathy with the buzzing internationalist any more than with the arcane Irishman whom he compares to Ireland, "a batlike soul waking to the consciousness of itself in darkness and secrecy and loneliness." Stephen walks by himself, disdainful and bitter, in love and not in love, a poet at dawn and sneerer at sunset, cold exile of "this stinking dunghill of a world."

A novel in which a sensitive, critical young man is completely expressed as he is can scarcely be expected to be pleasant. "A Portrait of the Artist as a Young Man" is not entirely pleasant. But it has such beauty, such love of beauty, such intensity of feeling, such pathos, such candor, it goes beyond anything in English

that reveals the inevitable malaise of serious youth. Mr. Joyce has a peculiar narrative method, and he would have made things clearer if he had adopted H. G. Wells's scheme of giving a paragraphed section to each episode. As the book is now arranged, it requires some imagination on the part of the reader. The Catholic "retreat" also demands attentiveness, it is reported with such acrimonious zeal. But no one who has any conception of the Russian-like frustrations and pessimisms of the thin-skinned and fine-grained Irishman, from early boarding school onward, can miss the tenacious fidelity of James Joyce. He has made a rare effort to transcend every literary convention as to his race and creed, and he has had high success. Many people will furiously resent his candor, whether about religion or nationalism or sex. But candor is a nobility in this instance.

The editors of The Little Review, *Jane Heap and Margaret Anderson, recognized the brilliance of Joyce's novel. They later serialized* Ulysses *in their magazine until its publication was halted when the co-editors were found guilty for publishing obscenity, fined, and prohibited from publishing any further episodes of the novel.*

James Joyce
Jane Heap
The Little Review, 3 (April 1917): 8–9

I suppose Mr. Joyce had some idea in mind when he gave his book the title of *A Portrait of the* ARTIST *as a Young Man.* But the critics seem to want it their own way and say, 'Mr Joyce paints the Irishman as he really is.' . . . Irishman, doctor, lawyer, merchant, chief, I suppose. Francis Hackett says it 'reveals the inevitable malaise of serious youth.' Why then doesn't this inevitable malaise of all our serious youth end inevitably like this: the call 'to create proudly out of the freedom and power of his soul, a living thing, new and soaring, and beautiful, impalpable, imperishable.'

H. G. Wells assures us that the youth of his country need not suffer such tortures of adolescence because of England's more common-sense treatment of the sex question. And all the time Mr. Joyce was talking about the artist of any land, not the youth of England or any other country. In this country there is only God to thank that the young artist does not go entirely mad over one and all of its institutions. In our country the young artists could suffer tortures far beyond anything suffered by Stephen, over the utter emptiness of the place. But he will always suffer. He will always be 'a naked runner lost in a storm of spears.'

There is too much geography of the body in this education of ours. You can talk about or write about or paint or sculp some parts of the body but others must be treated like the Bad Lands. You can write about what you see that you don't like, what you touch, taste, or hear; but you can't write abut what you smell; if you do you are accused of using nasty words. I could say a lot more about the geography of the body, and how its influence goes all the way through until the censor makes a geography for your mind and soul. But I want to talk abut nasty words. The result of this education is that we have all the nasty words in the world in our language. How often a European or an Oriental will say: 'Oh to us it is something very nice—beautiful; but to you it would not be nice; it is much different in English.' When they told James Joyce he had words like that in his book he must have been as surprised as a painter would be if he were told that some of his colors were immoral.

His story is told the way a person in a sick room sharply remembers all the over-felt impressions and experiences of a time of fever; until the story itself catches the fever and becomes a thing of more definite, closer-known, keener-felt consciousness—and of a restless oblivion of self-consciousness.

* * *

Note on Joyce and *A Portrait of the Artist as a Young Man*
Margaret Anderson
The Little Review, 3 (April 1917): 9–10

This James Joyce book is the most beautiful piece of writing and the most creative piece of prose anywhere to be seen on the horizon to-day. It is consciously a work of Art in a way that *Jean-Christophe* made no effort to be; it is such head and shoulders above *Jacob Stahl* or Gilbert Cannan's *Mendel* that one must realize those books as very good novels and this as something quite more than that. It can be spoken of in terms that apply to *Pelle the Conqueror,* but only in this way: each is a work of Art and therefore not to be talked of as lesser or greater; but while *Pelle* is made of language as it has been used the *Portrait* is made of language as it will come to be used. There is no doubt that we will have novels before long written without even as much of the conventional structure of language as Mr. Joyce has adhered to—a new kind of 'dimension in language' which is being felt in many places and which George Soule has illustrated beautifully in an article in *The New Republic*.

But that isn't the most important thing. The interest in *Pelle* is in the way its stories are told. The interest in the *Portrait* is in the way its aesthetic is presented. . . .

—reprinted from *James Joyce: The Critical Heritage*

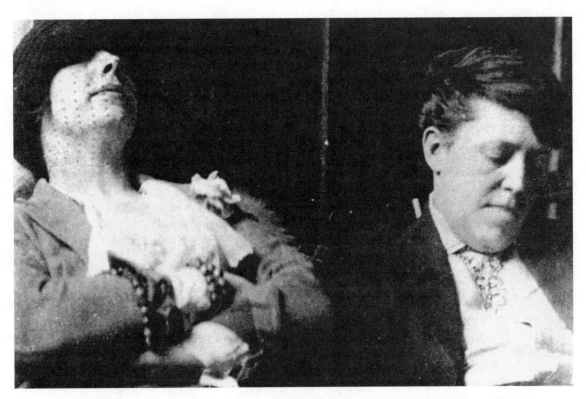

Margaret Anderson and Jane Heap in the early 1920s (Sylvia Beach Collection, Princeton University Library)

Some Irish critics took umbrage in particular at English reviews in which Joyce's novel was treated as a faithful depiction of Irish life; the last lines of this review are a rejoinder.

A Dyspeptic Portrait

Freeman's Journal, 7 April 1917, n.p.

If indignation makes verses literature—great literature that is to say—does not spring easily from the mood of satiety and disgust. Yet the mood is all too common amongst a certain section of modern novelists. Man delights them not nor woman neither; like Hamlet, "This brave o'erhanging firmament, this magestical roof fretted with golden fire," appears to them "a foul and pestilential congregation of vapours." The high priest of the school is Huysmans—the earlier Huysmans—who paraded before Europe, not as Byron did "The pageant of a bleeding heart," but of a tortured liver. With most of his disciples the pose has no reality; the blue devils dance in their pages merely to shock the bourgeois. Mr. Joyce, however, takes himself more seriously. The startling thing in his work is not the mimicry of Huysmans' methods—anybody with a deft pen can manage that—but the similarity of outlook; and the result is a book nearer to "En Ménage" than anything written in English. "A Portrait of the Artist" has notable positive merits. Mr. Joyce's prose is masterly in its terseness and force; even his most casual descriptions haunt the mind by their vividness and wonderful economy of line. What he sees he can reproduce in words with a precision as rare as it is subtle; the pity is, that in one of his own phrases the memory of these things has too often "coated his palate with the scum of disgust." Take, for instance, this vignette of a tea-table.

> He pushed open the latchless door of the porch and passed through the naked hallway into the kitchen. A group of his brothers and sisters was sitting round the table. Tea was nearly over, and only the last of the second watered tea remained in the bottom of the small glass jars and jampots which did service for tea-cups. Discarded crusts and lumps of sugared bread, turned brown by the tea which had been poured over them, lay scattered on the table, and little wells of tea lay here and there on a board, and a knife with a broken ivory handle was struck through the pith of a ravaged turnover.

Had it been a description of the desolation of No Man's Land on the Somme or the Yser, the horror could hardly have been laid on more thickly, and all through the book food is scarcely mentioned without the same shudder of disgust, which is more reminiscent of the pangs of dyspepsia than of the joy of art. Had the author confined himself to this particular form of ugliness it would not have been so bad, but, as Whistler

A hodge-podge. . . . in turn flagrantly coarse and muddled and uninteresting. . . . There is much in the book to offend . . . and little compensating beauty. . . . If many Irish took offence at the naif boastings of *The Playboy* it is a little terrifying to know what will be thought of this book. . . . an Irish stew. . . . it lacks fineness and good taste and a clear purpose.

– New York Globe

said of Oscar Wilde, that he could not keep out of the area, so Mr. Joyce plunges and drags his readers after him into the slime of foul sewers. He is not, indeed, like Mr. George Moore, who points to the iridiscence as a proof of the beauty of corruption. Mr. Joyce knows better, but despite his repulsion his pen, instead of pointing to the stars overhead, is degraded into a muck-rake. This is due in a measure to a false theory of aesthetics, but it springs even more from temperamental defects. Tennyson, in his salad days, wrote "The Confessions of a Second-rate Sensitive Mind," and the description would make an admirable sub-title for "A Portrait of the Artist as a Young Man." The great masters have not been blind to the aspects of life that Mr. Joyce exploits, but they see them in their true perspective and do not dwell on them to the exclusion of everything else. They know the value of proportion and the importance of sanity and clear judgment and realise that to see life steadily one must see it whole. It is an accident that Mr. Joyce's book should have Dublin as its background. A youth of the temperamental quality of his Stephen Dedalus was bound to react just as sharply against any other environment; had he been brought up in an English cathedral town or an American industrial centre he would have pilloried them in just as repellant a fashion. Yet English critics, with a complacency that makes one despair of their intelligence, are already hailing the author as a typical Irishman, and his book as a faithful picture of Irish life. It would be just as accurate to declare that De Quincey's "Opium Eater" embodied the experiences of the average English youth or that Carlyle's splenetic railings reflected the emotions of Victorian England.

The author of this curious book is clever and highly observant . . . A quite false presentment of perspective . . . So much pain to so little purpose!

– Manchester Weekly Times

The following review by the English critic J. C. Squire echoes a reaction to the novel that was the experience of many readers—on the one hand an admiration for Joyce's prose style and straightforward realism and on the other hand a disapproval of Joyce's material and what was seen as the formlessness of the work (a characteristic later to be identified with literary modernism).

Mr. James Joyce
J. C. Squire
The New Statesman, 9 (14 April 1917), p. 40

Mr. James Joyce is a curious phenomenon. He first appeared in literary Dublin about (I suppose) a dozen years ago: a strangely solitary and self-sufficient and obviously gifted man. He published a small book of verse with one or two good lyrics in it; and those who foresaw a future for him became certain they were right. He published nothing; but his reputation spread even amongst those who had never read a line he had written. He disappeared from Ireland and went to Austria, where he settled. The war came, and soon afterwards his second book—*Dubliners*—was issued and reviewed with a general deference, after wandering about for years among publishers who had been fighting shy of it because of its undoubted unpleasantness and a reference to Edward VII. Another interval and *A Portrait of the Artist as a Young Man* began to run serially in the *Egoist.* 'The Egoist, Ltd.' has now published this book, and nobody is surprised to find all writing London talking about it. Mr. Joyce has only done what was expected.

Whether this book is supposed to be a novel or an autobiography I do not know or care. Presumably some characters and episodes are fictitious, or the author would not even have bothered to employ fictitious names. But one is left with the impression that almost all the way one has been listening to sheer undecorated, unintensified truth. Mr. Joyce's title suggests, well enough, his plan. There is no 'plot.' The subsidiary characters appear and recede, and not one of them is involved throughout in the career of the hero. Stephen Dedalus is born; he goes to school; he goes to college. His struggles are mainly inward: there is nothing unusual in that. He has religious crises: heroes of fiction frequently do. He fights against, succumbs to, and again fights against sexual temptation: we have stories on those lines in hundreds. All the same, we have never had a novel in the least degree resembling this one; whether it is mainly success or mainly failure, it stands by itself.

You recognize its individuality in the very first paragraph. Mr. Joyce tries to put down the vivid and incoherent memories of childhood in a vivid and incoherent way: to show one Stephen Dedalus's memories precisely as one's own memories might appear if one ransacked one's mind. He opens:

> Once upon a time and a very good time it was there was a moocow coming down along the road and this moocow that was coming down along the road met a nicens little boy named baby tuckoo. . . .

'His mother had a nicer smell than his father,' he proceeds. There is verisimilitude in this; but a critic on the look-out for Mr. Joyce's idiosyncrasies would certainly fasten upon his preoccupation with the olfactory—which sometimes leads him to write things he might as well have left to be guessed at—as one of them. Still, it is a minor characteristic. His major characteristics are his intellectual integrity, his sharp eyes, and his ability to set down precisely what he wants to set down. He is a realist of the first order. You feel that he means to allow no personal prejudice or predilection to distort the record of what he sees. His perceptions may be naturally limited; but his honesty in registering their results is complete. It is even a little too complete. There are some things that we are all familiar with and that ordinary civilized manners (not pharisaism) prevent us from importing into general conversation. Mr. Joyce can never resist a dunghill. He is not, in fact, quite above the pleasure of being shocking. Generally speaking, however, he carries conviction. He is telling the truth about a type and about life as it presents itself to that type.

He is a genuine realist: that is to say, he puts in the exaltations as well as the depressions, the inner life as well as the outer. He is not morosely determined to paint everything drab. Spiritual passions are as powerful to him as physical passions; and as far as his own bias goes it may as well be in favour of Catholic asceticism as of sensual materialism. For his detachment as author is almost inhuman. If Stephen is himself, then he is a self who is expelled and impartially scrutinized, without pity or 'allowances,' directly Mr. Joyce the artist gets to work. And of the other characters one may say that they are always given their due, always drawn so as to evoke the sympathy they deserve, yet are never openly granted the sympathy of the author. He is the outsider, the observer, the faithful selector of significant traits, moral and physical; his judgments, if he forms them, are concealed. He never even shows by a quiver of the pen that anything distresses him.

His prose instrument is a remarkable one. Few contemporary writers are effective in such diverse ways; his method varies with the subject-matter and never fails him. His dialogue (as in the remarkable discussions at home about Parnell and Stephen's education) is as close to the dialogue of life as anything I have ever come across; though he does not make the gramophonic mistake of spinning it out as it is usually spun out in life and in novels that aim at a faithful reproduction of life and only succeed in sending one to sleep. And his descriptive and narrative passages include at one pole sounding periods of classical prose and at the other disjointed and almost futuristic sentences. The finest sustained pages in the book contain the sermon in which a dear, simple old priest expounds the unimaginable horrors of hell: the immeasurable solid stench as of a 'huge and rolling human fungus,' the helplessness of the damned, 'not even able to remove from the eye a worm that gnaws it,' the fierceness of the fire in which 'the blood seethes and boils in the veins, the brains are boiling in the skull, the heart in the breast glowing and bursting, the bowels a red-hot mass of burning pulp, the tender eyes flaming like molten balls.' Stephen, after listening to this, 'came down the aisle of the chapel, his legs shaking and the scalp of his head trembling as though it had been touched by ghostly fingers. He passed up the staircase and into the corridor along the walls of which the overcoats and waterproofs hung like gibbeted malefactors, headless and dripping and shapeless.'

No wonder. For myself, I had had an idea that this kind of exposition had died with Drexelius; but after I had read it I suddenly and involuntarily thought, 'Good Lord, suppose it is all true!' That is a sufficient testimony to the power of Mr. Joyce's writing.

This is not everybody's book. The later portion, consisting largely of rather dull student discussions, is dull; nobody could be inspired by the story, and it had better be neglected by any one who is easily disgusted. Its interest is mainly technical, using the word in its broadest sense; and its greatest appeal, consequently, is made to the practising artist in literature. What Mr. Joyce will do with his powers in the future it is impossible to conjecture. I conceive that he does not know himself: that, indeed, the discovery of a form is the greatest problem in front of him. It is doubtful if he will make a novelist.

> A book which has created already a sensation for its realism . . . I should class it with Huysmans and Zola . . . with its vagaries, its paradoxes and its intense sincerity it is undoubtedly a powerful book.
>
> – *Irish Life*

While repudiating A Portrait of the Artist as a Young Man *as art, the anonymous reviewer, nonetheless, finds Joyce's "pseudo autobiography" fascinating reading. At first many Irish readers judged the novel unfavorably, but nationalistic opinions ameliorated as Joyce's stature as a major international literary figure grew.*

Review of *A Portrait of the Artist as a Young Man*
Irish Book Lover, 8 (April–May 1917): 113

In spite of the serious drawbacks to be mentioned later, truth compels one to admit that this pseudo autobiography of Stephen Dedalus, a weakling and a dreamer, makes fascinating reading. We read it as a single sitting. The hero's schooldays at Clongowes Wood, and later at Belvedere, are graphically and doubtless, faithfully portrayed, as is the visit to Cork in company with his father, a clever ne'er-do-well, gradually sinking in the social scale. One of the strongest scenes in the book is the description of the Christmas dinner party during the black year of 1891, when Nationalist Ireland was riven to the centre over the Parnell 'split'. Mr. Joyce is unsparing in his realism, and his violent contrasts–the brothel, the confessional–jar on one's finer feelings. So do the quips and jeers of the students, in language unprinted in literature since the days of Swift and Sterne, following on some eloquent and orthodox sermons! That Mr. Joyce is a master of a brilliant description style and handles his dialogue as ably as any living writer is conceded on all hands, and, oh! the pity of it. In writing thus he is just to his fine gifts? Is it even wise, from a worldly point of view–mercenary, if you will–to dissipate one's talents on a book which can only attain a limited circulation?–for no clean-minded person could possibly allow it to remain within reach of his wife, his sons or daughters. Above all, is it Art? We doubt it.

James Joyce, A New Irish Novelist
John Quinn
Vanity Fair, 8 (May 1917): 48, 128

James Joyce has come to town, and he has come to stay. A new star has appeared in the firmament of Irish letters, a star of the first magnitude. The question that one is now asked is not have you *seen* a portrait, but "Have you *read* "The Portrait'?" All of a sudden everyone is reading and talking about "The Portrait." Everywhere one hears of it. In a recent review of the book an acute and subtle critic said that the question "Who is James Joyce?" is doubtless a question easier to answer in Dublin than in New York. I will give the answer. James

A Lawyer and Collector

The American attorney John Quinn (1870–1924) was an enthusiastic champion of Joyce's work. In 1921 Quinn unsuccessfully defended the co-editors of The Little Review *against obscenity charges for publishing in the magazine's July–August 1920 issue a section of the Nausicaa episode, chapter 13, of* Ulysses. *In October 1923, Joyce and Quinn met in Paris, for the first time. According to Ellmann in his biography of the author, Joyce commented to the writer and vorticist painter Wyndham Lewis that "with a person like Quinn you should never hint at any imperfection in your work; he wouldn't understand it."*

A benefactor of the arts and collector of manuscripts and works by artists such as Joyce, T. S. Eliot, Pablo Picasso, and Henri Matisse, Quinn owned the manuscripts of Joyce's play Exiles *(1918) and novel* Ulysses *(1922), the latter of which—a fair copy of the novel, that is, a clean handwritten copy ready to be typed or printed—Quinn had auctioned for $1,975 at the Anderson Galleries in New York six months before his death from cancer. Purchased by the American collector and dealer Dr. A. S. W. Rosenbach, it is now known as the Rosenbach manuscript and housed at the Rosenbach Library and Museum in Philadelphia. Quinn also owned the long lost eighth draft of the Circe episode, chapter 15, which was purchased in December 2000 by the National Library of Ireland for $1,546,000.*

John Quinn

Joyce is a Dubliner of about thirty-six. He was educated at the well-known Jesuit college, Clongowes, near Dublin. After leaving Clongowes, he attended University College, Dublin, for some years. The critic that I have referred to wrote that he had no news as to the reception of Joyce's book in Dublin, but added that "it must have aroused hostility." The fact is that it has not yet reached Dublin at all. When it does, a few Irish puritans and patriots may get hot under the collar, and it will be very amusing, as it was in the case of Synge. A pious Catholic here or there may call Joyce an Irish decadent. Good old phrase! It saves so much thought. Before the war he would have been called by the same sort of "patriot" a French decadent. But the war has killed that overworked phrase, and we are hearing no more, as we did in the case of Synge, of French decadence. The miracle of France's great gesture in arms has put an end to that cheap and ignorant cry.

James Joyce is the author of three books: (1) A book of poems called "Chamber Music" (Elkin Mathews, London, 1907)—a little volume of very perfect verse; (2) "Dubliners," containing fifteen stories (Grant Richards, London, 1914); (3) and his last book, "A Portrait of the Artist as a Young Man," just published (Huebsch, New York, 1916).

"Dubliners" was refused by a well-known Dublin publishing house because, it has been stated, pressure was brought to bear from high quarters against it. It also has just been published here by Mr. Huebsch. "Dubliners" is one of the most sincere and most realistic books ever written. Its great sincerity is one of its chief attractions. The book does not belong to the flashy school of literature. It is the work of a writer who was moved by what he felt and saw, but apparently remained as cold as stone. It is the reader who catches the infection. I am tempted to say it is the most powerful book of short stories in English published in the last ten years.

"A Portrait of the Artist as a Young Man" is dated at the end: "Dublin 1904–Trieste 1914." Those two dates, to one who knows, tell the story: Ten years of teaching in Trieste, so as to be able to write as he liked, so as to be independent, without having to listen to editors; ousted by the war, sick, subject to eye-rheumatism or something or other that makes him temporarily blind, or at least too blind to keep most jobs; given a few months ago a grant of one hundred pounds from the British government; his book refused by a half a dozen nincompoop London publishers who were afraid to touch it; its appearance in instalments in that too-little known monthly review, "The Egoist," published in London; and now its publication in book form in New York. No change from the text as it appeared in "The Egoist" is made in the story in book form. But the book has the addition of a vivid scene; so that the book is the real article. Ten or twenty years hence, collectors will buy "The Egoist" because it contains this great novel by James Joyce and Wyndham Lewis' novel, "Tarr," and poems and translations by Ezra Pound and others; just as collectors to-day buy "Once a Week" because it contains things by George Meredith, Swinburne, Rossetti, William Morris and Whistler published in it in the sixties. It is due to the enterprise and courage of an American publisher that Joyce's book has first seen the light of day. The publisher is receiving his reward. The book places James Joyce in the same rank with James Stephens and John M. Synge.

Partial blindness! No wonder the book is a distillation of bitter-sweet. It is not "unpleasant." No one could recall the Christmas dinner and the row over Parnell, the wonderful sermon, the confession, and the other episodes in the book, and complain that it lacked special inventiveness. The sermon itself is epical. There is no record of any "movement" or "revival" in it, for Joyce is too good an artist to mix propaganda with his art. He knows the vital distinction that poetry is never propaganda.

I received a letter from Joyce in October, 1916, from Zurich, Switzerland, telling me that he had received just a few days before a letter from the British Treasury informing him that on the recommendation of the Prime Minister a royal bounty of one hundred pounds had been granted to him. Joyce added: "I can now see my way ahead for a certain time and I hope that in the meantime I shall have no more trouble with my book."

This was a grant of one lump sum, not "a hardy annual" pension. I hope that the present regime in England will be as discerning and as generous and will renew the grant. But now that two of his books are out in this country, the start has been made.

One often hears in these days of war the remark that very little good literature is written or published. When I hear that, I often refer to the modern Irish writers and say that anything by Willam Butler Yeats, Lady Gregory, George Russell (A. E.), James Stephens, Padraic Colum, and now I shall add James Joyce, is literature and is always worth reading. Joyce's last book stands out above anything that has been published in this country or in Great Britain in the last two years. It will naturally be compared with the recollections of that other distinguished Irish poet and dramatist, William Butler Yeats, whose "Reveries Over Childhood and Youth" was published about a year ago. Yeats' book is like a series of tapestries depicting his youth and childhood in Sligo and in the art and literary world of London. Joyce's book is like a series of etchings. In some cases the acid has bit deep into the plate. To read Yeats' book might be compared to going into a finely proportioned room hung with noble paintings by Puvis de Chavannes. To read Joyce is like being in a room decorated with paintings by Daumier or Toulouse-Lautrec. "A Portrait of the Artist as a Young Man" is a great work of art. It will live. There is nothing abstract about Joyce. His style is vital and has the radium that makes art live. He writes with the frankness and freedom that is not uncommon in Ireland. That Irish frankness surprised and shocked a few in Synge's plays, notably in the "Playboy of the Western World." But Synge's writings have now taken their place as classics. If James Joyce can keep up the pace that this book sets, he is assured of an equally high place. Synge is perhaps the more Irish of the two; more Irish in the richness of his idiom and the color of his thought and the quality of his style, although the culture of both is European. Joyce has not so deep a talent. He has written a play which may be as great a success as "The Portrait" and "Dubliners," and one can never tell how far a first-rate man will go. I do not say that with two books of prose and a small volume of verse to his credit he is a great writer. But I do say that this last book is a great work of art. Conrad, a friend of mine, is a great creative artist. I do not compare him, a veteran writer, with Joyce, a young one. But Joyce's mind interests me greatly. I like his way of writing tremendously. After all, there is plenty of room for the work of artists like Joseph Conrad and George Moore, as well as for the work of James Joyce, just as in a live gallery there should be room for paintings by Manet and Cezanne and Picasso.

Ezra Pound in "The Drama" for February of 1916 had an article on "James Joyce and the Modern Stage." As a pure matter of literary history that article by a great poet and critic, our only real knight-errant of letters, will be remembered. I must quote one paragraph of what Mr. Pound there said:

"Mr. Joyce is undoubtedly one of our best contemporary authors. He has written a novel, and I am quite ready to stake anything I have in this world that that novel is permanent. It is permanent as are the works of Stendhal and Flaubert. Two silly publishers have just refused it in favor of froth, another declines to look at it because 'he

> A very comprehensive study . . . vivid pictures . . . a habit of plain speaking . . . The portrait is moulded of such small things that we are not always conscious until afterwards of how vitally important are these parts. The style is marvellously simple and the psychological insight and naturalism point to unusual literary power.
> – *Boston Advertiser*

will not deal through an agent'–yet Mr. Joyce lives on the continent and can scarcely be expected to look after his affairs in England save through a deputy. And Mr. Joyce is the best prose writer of my generation, in English. So far as I know, there is no one better in either Paris or Russia. In English we have Hardy and Henry James, and, chronologically, we have Mr. James Joyce. The intervening novelists print books, it is true, but for me or for any man of my erudition, for any man living at my intensity, these books are things of no substance."

"A Portrait of the Artist as a Young Man" was refused by publisher after publisher in London ostensibly because of the frankness with which certain episodes in the life of a young man were treated. It is perhaps not a book for all young women: *pas pour la jeune fille.* And yet no young man or young woman of the right fibre would be harmed by it. Compared to such a soft and false and dangerous book as "Ann Veronica," by H. G. Wells, for example, not to speak of similar American trash that reeks and smells of sex, Joyce's book is bracing and hard and clean. Neither is it a book for suffragettes, for Joyce never argues. He does not try to convince. He has no thesis. His book is just life. It is good, clean writing, even if some of his phrases are as startling as many that could be culled from the bible. His is a new style. There is no ornament, no rhetoric, nothing declamatory, no compromise, complete realism, and great sincerity. This way of writing is not easy. The book was not written on a typewriter, one may be sure; nor was it dictated to a stenographer between motor trips or while the author strolled about his room smoking a cigarette or puffing at his pipe.

He has the sincerity of genius. Let a man be ever so frank and plain-spoken, as Joyce is, if he is sincere, he is not vulgar or "unpleasant." In "The Portrait" we have a man at grips with himself and with his love of life. The book must not be read line by line as a pedant would read it, or as a conventional reviewer would read it, but as a whole, and then one will realize what a fine, hard, great piece of work it is.

If the book had been translated from the Russian, it would have instantly been hailed as a masterpiece. But it is a finer work of art than any Russian novel written in the last ten years that has been translated into English. The conversations of those young men will be most intelligible to Irish Catholics. Irish Ireland is in some respects a mediaeval country, and the talks of those young students, saturated with their religion in spite of their free-thinking, with the boy-Latin that they talk, is mediaeval and yet quite modern.

When "Dubliners" was published three years ago I handed a copy of it to an Irish friend of mine, an artist and a man of letters, and said to him that

Pound, who later arranged the publication of Ulysses *in* The Little Review, *believed that avant-garde magazines played an important role in the advancement of literature.*

. . . In so far as it is possible, I should like *The Little Review* to aid and abet *The Egoist* in its work. I do not think it can be too often pointed out that during the last four years *The Egoist* has published serially, in the face of no inconsiderable difficulties, the only translation of Remy de Gourmont's *Chevaux de Diomedes;* the best translation of *Le Comte de Gabalis,* Mr. Joyce's masterpiece *A Portrait of the Artist as a Young Man,* and is now publishing Mr. Lewis's novel *Tarr.* Even if they had published nothing else there would be no other current periodical which could challenge this record, but *The Egoist* has not stopped there; they have in a most spirited manner carried out the publication in book form of the *Portrait of the Artist,* and are in the act of publishing Mr. Eliot's poems, under the title *Mr. Prufrock and Observations.*

I see no reason for concealing my belief that the two novels, by Joyce and Lewis, and Mr. Eliot's poems are not only the most important contributions to English literature of the past three years, but that they are practically the only works of the time in which the creative element is present, which in any way show invention, or a progress beyond precedent work. The mass of our contemporaries, to say nothing of our debilitated elders, have gone on repeating themselves and each other.

– Editorial, *Little Review,* 4 (May 1917): 3–6

here was a new Irish writer that had the real stuff in him. My friend read the book and returning it to me said: "Good God, Quinn, that is a gray book! One always knew that there were such places in Dublin, but one never wanted to go near or to hear of them. But the man can write."

I have compared William Butler Yeats' "Reveries Over Childhood and Youth" with Joyce's "A Portrait of the Artist as a Young Man." Both Yeats and Joyce are poets. Yeats in his Reveries is a poet looking back to his youth fondly, and seeing things through mists of tenderness. Joyce writes his book about his youth in his youth. It has the bite and the harshness of strong youth, but what art! Yeats is a great poet at fifty writing of his youth. Joyce, the most gifted of all the young Irish writers, does the story of his youth at twenty-five. There we have the

> A novel that is being talked about . . . A story of originality and more besides.
>
> — *Daily Chronicle*

difference. The older poet has acquired the sense of life. The younger struggles with the stuff of life. Both are frank and very sincere. Some may think Joyce is bitter. But he is not. He is true to life. In one of his lyrics he speaks of

"A sage that is but kith and kin
With the comedian Capuchin."

But perhaps the truer key is found in Joyce's words toward the end of his book: "and I will try to express myself in some mode of life or art as freely as I can and as wholly as I can, using for my defense the only arms I allow myself to use, silence, exile and cunning."

Yeats read no bitterness into his "Reveries" for he wrote of his youth as he had lived it. Bitterness or regret may be found in a poem on his forbears that he wrote about the time that he was writing his "Reveries":

"Pardon that for a barren passion's sake,
Although I have come close on forty-nine,
I have no child, I have nothing but a book,
Nothing but that to prove your blood and mine."

Folk-lore is always in the making in Dublin. And Dublin has its folk-lore about James Joyce and his father. Here is one bit of Dublin folk-lore about the elder Joyce: He was living with a very pious Catholic friend. They were out going to mass one Sunday morning. It started to rain. The elder Joyce cursed. His pious friend remonstrated and said: "Don't curse, James, for you know our divine Lord has the power to flood the world again, and therefore we should be thankful if it only rains." "He could indeed flood the world again," replied the elder Joyce,—"if he was an auld fool."

One of the legends of the younger Joyce is that some ten years ago he parted from William Butler Yeats after a long talk on letters and art with the remark: "I am sorry that I met you too late in life influence you." Another legend is that Yeats introduced Joyce to Arthur Symons at about the same time and that Symons talked of Balzac. Joyce said: "Balzac! Who reads Balzac to-day?" While Joyce might have pretended to scorn Balzac then, it is quite evident that he has read Balzac many times. An Irish friend of mine says that the Irish are a harsh people like the Spaniards and do not care whether they do or do not offend and bewilder other people. Joyce is a master of the pungent phrase. It is partly his harshness. There is poetry in his book, plenty of a stormy sort of poetry, cloudy and wild, like the Irish skies in the winter months. He is great student. That often makes all the difference between the major and the minor writer. He is a thinker, a man looking for principles; his purpose is other than mere mischief. And thank God he is not a propagandist. His book is a picture of Dublin. Dublin has something of the charm of Athens. Belfast has no charm. For all its vitality, it is sterilized in business, sterilized so far as the joy and variety of life go. Dublin is rediscovered.

I have said that Joyce's first book was a little volume of very perfect verse. Could anything surpass the beauty and perfection of this, which might be one of Douglas Hyde's Love Songs of Connacht:

"O sweetheart, hear you
    Your lover's tale;
A man shall have sorrow
    When friends him fail.

For he shall know then
    Friends be untrue,
And a little ashes
    Their words come to.

But one unto him
    Will softly move
And softly woo him
    In ways of love.

His hand is under
    Her smooth round breast;
So he who has sorrow
    Shall have rest."

While Dublin folk-lore may give Joyce as saying to Yeats that they met too late for Joyce to influence Yeats, Joyce's poems show that he has been influenced by Yeats. But what young Irish writer has not been influenced or helped by him, the most helpful, the most disinterested, the most fastidious critic and appreciator of contemporary literature that we have!

> A relentless realist whose craftsmanship is undeniable.
>
> — *Birmingham Post*

Van Wyck Brooks, American biographer and literary critic

Van Wyck Brooks, who was early in his career when he wrote this review, was the author of The Wine of the Puritans *(1909) and* America's Coming-of-Age *(1915), in which he argued that the Puritan tradition had adversely affected American culture.*

Review of *A Portrait of the Artist as a Young Man*
Van Wyck Brooks
The Seven Arts, 2 (May 1917): 122

The seven veils are dropping from the face of Ireland and it is a strange reality that face presents, strange at least to those who know nothing of the harsh old Irish world of a past that has been perpetuated as hardly any other European past has been, strange to those who know nothing of the black chieftains and the subterranean sympathies of Catholic Ireland and Catholic Spain. You have to go back generations in any other Western country to find a spiritual equivalent of James Joyce, whose *Portrait of the Artist as a Young Man* (Huebsch) is altogether atavistic from the standpoint of English literature, full as it is of Shandyisms but Rabelaisian in a pure style that Sterne was born too late to compass. Yet it is a living society that Mr. Joyce pictures, one that conforms to the twentieth century in its worldly apparel but reveals in its table-talk and its more intimate educational and religious recesses a mediaevelism utterly untouched by that industrial experience which has made the rest of the world kin, for good or ill. Mr. Joyce's literary culture is of a piece with his theme; he stems from Cardinal Newman as other men stem from Goethe, and his pages bristle with Aristotle and Thomas Aquinas. . . . Do young men in other countries than Ireland still lift vermin from their collars and soliloquize over them, as Uncle Toby soliloquized over the fly, and as the goliards used to do at the Sorbonne eight hundred years ago? . . . Emotionally the book is direct, spare, and true in its flight as hardly any Anglo-Saxon books are, and its style goes to bear out Thomas MacDonagh's assertion that the English tongue possesses in Ireland and uncodified suggestiveness, a rich concreteness, that it has largely lost in its own country.

—reprinted from *James Joyce: The Critical Heritage*

American scholar John Macy, who argued for realism and the use of native material in The Spirit of American Literature *(1913), praises the originality and honesty of* A Portrait of the Artist as a Young Man *and* Dubliners, *both of which had been published by Huebsch in the United States in 1916.*

James Joyce

John Macy

The Dial, 62 (14 June 1917): 525–527

In the preface of "Pendennis" Thackeray says: "Since the author of 'Tom Jones' was buried, no writer of fiction among us has been permitted to depict to his utmost power a Man. We must drape him and give him a certain conventional simper. Society will not tolerate the Natural in our Art." If Thackeray felt that, why did he not take his reputation and his fortune in his hands and, defying the social restrictions which he deplored, paint us a true portrait of a young gentleman of his time? He might have done much for English art and English honesty. As it was, he did as much as any writer of his generation to fasten on English fiction the fetters of an inartistic reticence. It was only in the last generation that English and Irish novelists, under the influence of French literature, freed themselves from the cowardice of Victorian fiction and assumed that anything human under the sun is proper subject-matter for art. If they have not produced masterpieces (and I do not admit that they have not), they have made a brave beginning. Such a book as "A Portrait of the Artist as a Young Man" would have been impossible forty years ago. Far from looking back with regret at the good old novelists of the nineteenth century (whom, besides, we need never lose), I believe that our fiction is immensely freer and richer than the fiction of our immediate forefathers.

Joyce's work is outspoken, vigorous, original, beautiful. Whether it faithfully reflects Irish politics and the emotional conflicts of the Catholic religion one who is neither Irish nor Catholic cannot judge with certainty. It seems, however, that the noisy controversies over Parnell and the priests in which the boy's elders indulge have the sound of living Irish voices; and the distracted boy's wrestlings with his sins and his faith are so movingly human that they hold the sympathy even of one who is indifferent to the religious arguments. I am afraid that the religious questions and the political questions are too roughly handled to please the incurably devout and patriotic. If they ever put up a statue of Joyce in Dublin, it will not be during his life time. For he is no respecter of anything except art and human nature and language.

There are some who, to turn his own imaginative phrase, will fret in the shadow of his language. He makes boys talk as boys do, as they did in your school and mine, except that we lacked the Irish imagery and whimsicality. If the young hero is abnormal and precocious, that is because he is not an ordinary boy but an artist, gifted with thoughts and phrases above our common abilities. This is a portrait of an artist by an artist, a literary artist of the finest quality.

The style is a joy. "Cranly's speech," he writes, "had neither rare phrases of Elizabethan English nor quaintly turned versions of Irish idioms." In that Joyce has defined his own style. It is Elizabethan, yet thoroughly modern; it is racily Irish, yet universal English. It is unblushingly plain-spoken and richly fanciful, like Shakespeare and Ben Jonson. The effect of complete possession of the traditional resources of language is combined with an effect of complete indifference to traditional methods of fiction. Episodes, sensations, dreams, emotions trivial and tragic succeed each other neither coherently nor incoherently; each is developed vividly for a moment, then fades away into the next, with or without the mechanical devices of chapter divisions or rows of stars. Life is so; a fellow is pandied by the schoolmaster for no offense; the cricket bats strike the balls, pick, pock, puck; there is a girl to dream about: and Byron was a greater poet than Tennyson anyhow. . . .

The sufferings of the poor little sinner are told with perfect fidelity to his point of view. Since he is an artist his thoughts appropriately find expression in phrases of maturer beauty than the speech of ordinary boys. He is enamored of words, intrigued by their mystery and color; wherefore the biographer plays through the boy's thoughts with all manner of verbal loveliness.

> Did he then love the rhythmic rise and fall of words better than their associations of legend and colour? Or was it that, being as weak of sight as he was shy of mind, he drew less pleasure from the reflection of the glowing sensible world through the prism of a language many-coloured and richly storied than from the contemplation of an inner world of individual emotions mirrored perfectly in a lucid supple periodic prose?

From the fading splendor of an evening as beautifully described as any in English, he tumbles into the sordid day of a house rich in pawn tickets. That is life. "Welcome, O life!" he bids farewell to his young manhood. "I go to encounter for the millionth time the reality of experience and to forge in the smithy of my soul the uncreated conscience of my race. Old father, old artificer, stand me now and ever in good stead."

I know nothing of Mr. James Joyce, the man, and I have not yet tried to look up his history; it is pleasanter to read him first and find out about him afterward. "A Portrait of the Artist" bears the dates, "Dublin, 1904: Trieste, 1914." The first American edition was published last year. One book which I have not seen, "Chamber Music," is not yet printed in this country. The third book, a collection of sketches called "Dubliners," bears only the American dates, 1916, 1917. Is this a man who writes little and writes slowly? Or has he been buried and come to life again? The dates show a writing life of more than ten years, and the writing shows a trained artist, not a casual wanderer into literature.

The sketches in "Dubliners" are perfect, each in its own way, and all in one way: they imply a vast deal that is not said. They are small as the eye-glass of a telescope is small; you look through them to depths and distances. They are a kind of short story unknown to the American magazine if not to the American writer. An American editor might read them for his private pleasure, but from his professional point of view he would not see that there was any story there at all. The American short story is explicit and overdeveloped and thin as a moving-picture film; it takes nothing for granted, except in some of its rapid-fire farcical humor; it knows nothing of the art of the hintful, the suggestive, the selected single detail which lodges fertilely in the reader's mind begetting ideas and emotions. America is not the only offender (for patriotism is the fashion and bids criticism relent); there is much professional Irish humor which is funny enough but as subtle as a shillallah. And English short stories, such at least as we see in magazines, are obvious and "express" rather than expressive. Joyce's power to disentangle a single thread from the confusion of life and let you run briefly back upon it until you encounter the confusion and are left to think about it yourself—that is a power rare enough in any literature. I have an impression of having felt that power in some of Gissing's sketches, though that is only an impression which I should not care to formulate as a critical judgment until I had read Gissing again. (A good thing to do, by the way.)

Except one story, "A Painful Case," I could not tell the plot of any of these sketches. Because there is no plot going from beginning to end. The plot goes from the surface inward, from a near view away into a background. A person appears for a moment— a priest, or a girl, or a small boy, or a streetcorner tough, or a drunken salesman— and does and says things not extraordinary in themselves; and somehow you know all about these people and feel that you could think out their entire lives. Some are stupid, some are pathetic, some are funny in an unhilarious way. The dominant mood is reticent irony. The last story in the book, "The Dead," is a masterpiece which will never be popular, because it is all about living people; there is only one dead person in it and he is not mentioned until near the end. That's the kind of trick an Irishman like Synge or Joyce would play on us, and perhaps a Frenchman or a Russian would do it; but we would not stand it from one of our own writers.

—reprinted from *James Joyce: The Critical Heritage*

Most readers at the time A Portrait of the Artist as a Young Man *was published were accustomed to the narrative practices of the nineteenth-century novel. By judging the novel as fragmentary and lacking in coherence, the anonymous reviewer for* New Age *is unwittingly uncovering a characteristic of literary moderism.*

Review of *A Portrait of the Artist as a Young Man*
New Age, 21 (12 July 1917), p. 254

If this book had been written by Dostoieffsky, it would have been a masterpiece; and we invite Mr. Joyce to read that famous thirteenth chapter of Corinthians and apply to himself the teaching For his wilful cleverness, his determination to produce kinematographic effects instead of literary portrait, are due entirely to a lack of clarity. He fears to suffer, and will not, therefore, put himself in the place of his hero; he will record with wonderful fidelity, and frequently with remarkable dramatic skill, what happened around or to Stephen Dedalus, but as it is all objectively viewed and objectively rendered, the character has no continuum, no personality. Even the introspective passages have the same character of objectivity; Stephen only observes the thoughts that come to him, only suffers the impact of external emotions, but never do his experiences reveal him to himself or to the reader. There are passages in this book comparable with the best in English literature; the scene wherein Mr. Dedalus carves the Christmas turkey is perfectly rendered, the Jesuit sermons on Hell are vivid intellectual tortures, Stephen's first experience in a brothel, and the whole history of his sexual obsession are given with pitiless accuracy. But Mr. Joyce never answers the reader's: 'Why?': he keeps on the circumference of his hero's mind, and never dives to the center of his soul. So this portrait seems to be a mere catalogue of unrelated states; there is everything in it that becomes a man, but it never does become the man, Stephen Dedalus. Samuel hewed Agag to pieces, but the pieces were not Agag; and the fragments here offered of the experience of Stephen Dedalus are no substitute for a 'portrait of the artist as a young man.' It is a composition that does not hang together, a creation into which the creator has forgotten to breathe the breath of life, and, therefore, Stephen Dedalus never becomes a living soul. He never 'shows forth' anything but a furtive lust; his occasional exercises in theories of aesthetics have an interest that is not personal, his mind has no apparent relation to his experience. Yet if it fails as a personal portrait, the value of the book as a portrait of young Ireland, Catholic Ireland, cannot be over-estimated. Beware of the men who have no souls, is the warning conveyed to England by this book; they are not even consumed with a holy hatred of those who are opposed to them, contempt, even, is too violent for them, but they conceal an essential dissimilarity under a superficial resemblance of technical proficiency, and are incalculable in their divergence of purpose.

The enthusiastic review of the Italian novelist and critic of English literature Diego Angeli, "Un Romanzo di Gesuiti," was originally published in Il Marzocco *(Florence) on 12 August 1917; it was translated by Joyce at the request of Harriet Weaver.*

Review of *A Portrait of the Artist as a Young Man*
Diego Angeli
The Egoist, 5 (February 1918): 30

Mr. James Joyce is a young Irish novelist whose last book, *A Portrait of the Artist as a Young Man,* has raised a great tumult of discussion among English-speaking critics. It is easy to see why. An Irishman, he has found in himself the strength to proclaim himself a citizen of a wider world; a Catholic, he has had the courage to cast his religion from him and to proclaim himself an atheist; and a writer, inheriting the most traditionalist of all European literatures, he has found a way to break free from the tradition of the old English novel and to adopt a new style consonant with a new conception. In a word such an effort was bound to tilt against all the feelings and cherished beliefs of his fellow countrymen but, carried out, as it is here, with a fine and youthful boldness, it has won the day. His book is not alone an admirable work of art and thought; it is also a cry of revolt:

Extracts
from Continental Press Notices
of
A Portrait
of the Artist as a Young Man
by
JAMES JOYCE
[The Egoist, Ltd: London: 1916].

———

Mr Diego Angeli nel Marzocco: Scrittore della più tradizionalista fra tutte le letterature europee ha saputo rompere la tradizione del vecchio romanzo inglese e adottare uno stile nuovo per una nuova forma .... Non è solamente un bel libro d'arte e di pensiero ma è anche un grido di rivolta ....: Il suo romanzo segna una data nella cronistoria del romanzo inglese .... Il Joyce analizza con una meravigliosa sottigliezza. Nessuno scrittore, credo, è sceso tanto oltre nell'esame dell' influenza più sensuale che spirituale degli esercizi .... un magnifico processo di liberazione .... un' analisi schiettamente moderna, crudelmente e audacemente vera .... Il Joyce in questa evocazione della verità è veramente maestro .... Il verismo di Emilio Zola era un verismo romantico mentre questo di James Joyce è un verismo impressionista ... uno stile rapido e conciso, uno stile che rifugge da ogni effetto pittorico, da ogni amplificazione retorica, da ogni imagine, da ogni aggettivo. Ci dice quello che ci deve dire nel minor numero di parole .... mezza pagina di quella sua prosa secca, precisa, angolosa esprime molto più che non tutta l' affannosa ricerca d' immagini a cui

First page of extracts of European reviews published to advertise Joyce's first novel (Division of Rare and Manuscript Collections, Carl A. Kroch Library, Cornell University. (Scholes 1391)

it is the desire of a new artist to look upon the world with other eyes, to bring to the front his individual theories and to compel a listless public to reflect that there are another literature and another esthetic apprehension beyond those foisted upon us, with a bountifulness at times nauseating, by the general purveying of pseudo-romantic prose and by fashionable publishers, with their seriocomic booklists, and by the weekly and monthly magazines. And let us admit that such a cry of revolt has been uttered at the right moment and that it is in itself the promise of a fortunate renascence . . . in the midst of the great revolution of the European novel English writers continued to remain in their 'splendid isolation' and could not or would not open their eyes to what was going on around them. Literature, however, like all the other arts underwent a gradual transformation and Mr. Joyce's book marks its definite date in the chronology of English literature. I think it well to put so much on record here not only for that which it signifies actually but also for that which in time it may bring forth.

The phenomenon is all the more important in that Mr. Joyce's *Portrait* contains two separate elements, each of which is significant and worthy of analysis; its ethical content and the form wherewith this content is clothed. When one has read the book to the end one understands why most English and American critics have raised an outcry against both form and content, understanding, for the most part, neither one nor the other. Accustomed as they are to the usual novels, enclosed in a set framework, they found themselves in this case out of their depth and hence their talk of immorality, impiety, naturalism and exaggeration. They have not grasped the subtlety of psychological analysis nor the synthetic value of certain details and certain sudden arrests of movement. Possibly their own Protestant upbringing renders the moral development of the central character incomprehensible to them. For Mr. Joyce is a Catholic and, more than that, a Catholic brought up in a Jesuit college. One must have passed many years of one's own life in a seminary of the society of Jesus, one must have passed through the same experiences and undergone the same crises to understand the profound analysis, the keenness of observation shown in the character of Stephen Dedalus. No writer, so far as I know, has penetrated deeper in the examination of the influence, sensual rather than spiritual, of the society's exercises.

For this analysis so purely modern, so cruelly and boldly true, the writer needed a style which would break down the tradition of the six shilling novel: and this style Mr. Joyce has fashioned for himself. The brushwork of the novel reminds one of certain modern paintings in which the planes interpenetrate and the external vision seems to partake of the sensations of the onlooker. It is not so much the narrative of a life as its reminiscence but it is a reminiscence whole, complete and absolute, with all those incidents and details which tend to fix indelibly each feature of the whole. He does not lose time explaining the wherefore of these sensations of his nor even tell us their reason or origin: they leap up in his pages as do the memories of a life we ourselves have lived without apparent cause, without logical sequence. But it is exactly such a succession of past visions and memories which makes up the sum of every life. In this evocation of reality Mr. Joyce is truly a master. The majority of English critics remark, with easy superficiality, that he thinks himself a naturalist simply because he does not shrink from painting certain brutal episodes in words more brutal still. This is not so: his naturalism goes much deeper. Certainly there is a difference, formal no less than substantial, between his book and let us say, *La Terre* of Emile Zola. Zola's naturalism is romantic whereas the naturalism of Mr. Joyce is impressionist, the profound synthetic naturalism of some pictures of Cézanne or Maquet, the naturalism of the late impressionists who single out the characteristic elements of a landscape or a scene or a human face. And all this he expresses in a rapid and concise style, free from every picturesque effect, every rhetorical redundancy, every needless image or epithet. Mr. Joyce tells us what he must tell in the least number of words; his palette is limited to a few colours. But he knows what to choose for his end and therefore half a page of his dry precise angular prose expresses much more (and with much more telling effect) than all that wearisome research of images and colour of which we have lately heard and read so much.

And that is why Mr. Joyce's book has raised such a great clamour of discussion. He is a new writer in the glorious company of English literature, a new writer with a new form of his own and new aims, and he comes at a moment when the world is making a new constitution and a new social ordinance. We must welcome him with joy. He is one of those rude craftsmen who open up paths whereon many will yet follow. It is the first streaks of the dawn of a new art visible on the horizon. Let us hail it therefore as the herald of a new day.

–reprinted from *James Joyce: The Critical Heritage*

John F. Harris's review appeared two months after The Egoist, Ltd., published the first edition of A Portrait of the Artist as a Young Man *that was actually printed in England (March 1918). The edition originally published by The Egotist Ltd. in 1917 was produced with American sheets since at the time no English printer would accept the responsibility of printing the novel.*

A Note on James Joyce
John F. Harris
To-Day, 3 (May 1918): 88–92

There are some books written in English that come upon one with a certain surprise. They are so unlikely. One might have expected to find them in French or Russian literature; in English they seem a little uncomfortable like an unconventional son in a very respectable family. The general attitude towards them is hostility–the hostility which is always aroused by an artist who treats a subject from a new and original angle, whose discoveries do not immediately recommend themselves to ordinary people as smooth and satisfying.

Mr. James Joyce, the author of "A Portrait of the Artist as a Young Man," is an Irishman and one of the modern writers who has the courage of his convictions and of his own artistic methods. He was born in 1882 and is a native of Dublin, but since 1904 he has lived in Trieste, except for a stay of one year in Rome. He left Trieste in July 1915, when the Austrian authorities gave him and his family a permit to the Swiss frontier. Since that date he has lived in Zurich. His first publication was a pamphlet entitled "Parnell," written at the age of nine, which was printed and circulated in Dublin. Later he contributed verse to the *Saturday Review* and the *Speaker,* which was afterwards republished in his first book, "Chamber Music." In 1902 he was studying medicine in Paris when he met J. M. Synge, who showed him his *Riders to the Sea,* and after Synge's death he translated the play into Italian: he also undertook to translate Mr. Yeats's play, *The Countess Kathleen,* but the project fell through. Mr. Joyce's first attempt at fiction was the book of short stories published four years ago under the title "Dubliners." These stories, some of which were written in Ireland and some in Austria, are notable for their terse realism and craftsmanship. Since then, however, Mr. Joyce has written two novels, the second of which, "Ulysses"–a continuation of "A Portrait of the Artist"–is announced for serial publication in the *Egoist.* His three-act play, *Exiles,* the scene of which is laid in Dublin, is also to appear this spring.

A Portrait of the Artist as a Young Man is not only an original book; it strikes us as fundamentally true. It is not the kind of book of which the ordinary subscriber to Mudie's is likely to approve. Indeed, no publisher could be found for it in England, nor was there an English printer who would consent to print it. It was therefore set up in America and has been issued in England by the proprietors of the *Egoist.* We are aware, of course, that these facts do not in themselves necessarily establish any particular merit in Mr. Joyce's novel.

Yet it has taken a very definite place in modern fiction for its fearlessness of expression, its insight into the stress and turmoil of the artist's mind and soul, its exposure of the emotional shams of a certain type of religious upbringing, and its utter disregard of the ordinary customs of polite novel-writing. Mr. Joyce has no literary *gaucherie.* He may be classified as a realist: his realism is naked and unashamed. Yet his improprieties and *mesquineries,* his insistence on the material squalor and ugliness of his hero's surroundings, have their origin in an artistic purpose. And, we may add in parentheses, however much his characters may indulge in furtive nastiness, we are never in doubt about the sensitiveness of the author himself. Only a man with a mind and spirit painfully aware of the hideous brutality and cruelty that is in the world could have written this book.

Stephen Dedalus is the artist whose portrait Mr. Joyce has drawn so convincingly in these pages. "The interest of the book," says Mr. H. G. Wells, "depends entirely on its quintessential and unfailing reality. One believes in Stephen Dedalus as one believes in few characters in fiction." Here, then, is the story of an education. We meet Stephen first as a small boy in his own home, then as a schoolboy at Clongowes Wood College; later the scene shifts to a Jesuit School in Dublin. It is in this later phase of the book, which deals with a distinctively Irish and Catholic education, that the author writes with the most surprising intimacy. But before this point is reached there is a scene in a brothel–the central episode of the story–which better than any other gives the measure of Mr. Joyce's powers of artistic description. He passes with characteristic detachment to the most depressing passages in Stephen's development. Stephen, full of disturbing thoughts, is sitting at the schoolroom window staring into the twilight.

"It would be a gloomy secret night. After early nightfall the yellow lamps would light up, here and there, the squalid quarters of the brothels. He would follow a devious course up and down the streets, circling always nearer in a tremor of fear and joy, until his feet led him suddenly around a dark corner. . . ."

And in the chapter that follows Stephen is momentarily released from his temptations by the fierce denunciations of the Roman faith. He hears two revolting sermons on the terrors of Hell: he is driven shrinkingly to the confessional. So obsessed is he with a conviction of sin that he seems unaware of the materialism of a religion which interprets eternal damnation almost entirely in the language and ideas of the material world. But his restless thoughts jump away from the present to the place where

*A photo of Joyce taken in Zürich in December 1918 and inscribed
by the author (Collection of Paul Ruggiero)*

he is not: he sees himself in the past with complete mental detachment: "A little boy had been taught geography by an old woman who kept two brushes in her wardrobe. Then he had been sent away from home to a college, he had made his first communion . . . and watched the firelight leaping and dancing on the wall of a little bedroom in the infirmary and dreamed of being dead, of Mass being said for him by the rector in a black and gold cope. . . ."

At the conclusion of the narrative Stephen has made his revolt: the confusions of life still press in upon him; but he longs for a wider life. "Away! Away!" he exclaims in the chaotic diary which fills the last pages of the book. "The spell of arms and voices: the white arms of roads, their promise of close embraces and the black arms of tall ships that stand against the moon, their tale of distant nations. They are held out to say: We are alone—come. . . ."

We have little space left in which to speak of Mr. Joyce as a prose writer. He writes with a marked economy of words; his style is nervous and impressionistic, but it rises at times to a very definite beauty. It has about it some of that "superb and wild" quality of which Synge has spoken; it reflects the emotional longings and exaltations which from time to time stir men's spirit. It has in it the wild Irish beauty of rivers and clouds and changing seas. There is a passage full of this fierce beauty which pictures Stephen Dedalus, at a disheartened moment which is to change immediately to one of spiritual uplifting, as he gazes at the slow-drifting clouds. "They were voyaging high over Ireland, westward bound. The Europe they had come from lay out there beyond the Irish Sea, Europe of strange tongues and valleyed and woodbegirt and citadelled and of entrenched and marshalled races. He heard a confused music within him as of memories and names which he was almost conscious of but could not capture even for an instant. . . . Again! Again! Again! A voice from beyond the world was calling."

Nor is Mr. Joyce less successful in his management of dialogue. His dialogue has all the naturalness of conversations that we have heard and taken part in. Indeed, "A Portrait of the Artist" is a book of contrasts; it has its Rabelaisian moments and its moments of beauty. But over the whole of it is a deep sincerity, a painful searching for truth. It is the work of a genuine artist.

Padraic Colum

Contemporary Writers Respond

Associated with the Irish Literary Revival and one of the first members of the Irish National Theatre Society, Padraic Colum knew Joyce in Dublin, and he is one of the writers Joyce includes in his satiric broadsides, "The Holy Office" (1904) and "Gas from a Burner" (1912). At first, Joyce was envious of Colum for the attention Colum received from Yeats and other established writers, but the feeling waned once Joyce started to come into his own as a literary figure. Even after he immigrated to the United States in 1914, Colum and his Irish-American wife, the literary critic Mary Maguire Colum, were frequently with the Joyces during the 1920s and 1930s. In the following commentary, Colum introduces Joyce and his achievement to an American audience.

James Joyce
Padraic Colum
Pearson's Magazine (May 1918), pp. 38–42

People here who are interested in the subject, after talking for a while about the new literature of Ire-land, often say to me, "But who is James Joyce? What a curious book his 'Portrait of the Artist as a Young Man' is! And the stories in his 'Dubliners' are quite extraordinary! What else has he written? Is he well known in Ireland?"

Generally I reply, "Joyce is not well known in Ireland. He left the country several years ago and he has been living abroad in Europe. He is a young man–about thirty-five. Besides 'Portrait of the Artist' and 'Dubliners,' he has written a book of verse which has not been published here–'Chamber Music.' He has also published a play which I have not read. Do you not know that James Huneker has an essay upon him in his book, 'Unicorns'? Huneker asks the same questions and he says that Joyce is evidently a member of the new group of Irish writers who see their country and their countrymen in anything but a flattering light. He talks about Joyce's cruel and scrutinizing gaze. He says that Joyce is as truthful as Tchekov, compared to whose realism Maupassant's is romantic bric-a-brac gilded with a fine style. And Huneker goes on to compare 'Portrait of the Artist as a Young Man' with Huysmans' 'En Route.' He calls Joyce a younger brother of Huysmans."

I speak like this about him because it is so hard to get down a real impression of Joyce–to suggest what material his mind has worked in and what ideal in art and life he has been striving towards. What comes vividly to my mind when I think of James Joyce is some melody–some strain of song. Perhaps it is that Irish ballad that Gabriel Conroy's wife heard in the story called "The Dead":

O the rain falls on my heavy locks,
And the dew wets my skin,
My babe lies cold . . .

Or perhaps it is a lyric of Ben Jonson's that I hear repeated in Joyce's modulated voice:

Still to be neat, still to be drest
As you were going to a feast;
Still to be powdered, still perfumed:
Lady, it is to be presumed.
Though art's hid causes are not found,
All is not sweet, all is not sound.

Give me a look, give me a face
That makes simplicity a grace;
Robes loosely flowing, hair as free:
Such sweet neglect more taketh me:
Than all the adulteries of art;
These touch mine eyes but not my heart.

Or perhaps it is one of Joyce's own lyrics that, to me, are no less excellent than the Elizabethans':

What counsel hath the hooded moon
Put in your heart, my shyly sweet?
Of love in ancient plenilune,
Glory and stars beneath his feet?
A sage who is but kith and kin
To the comedian Capuchin.

Believe me rather that am wise
In disregard of the divine–
A glory lightens in your eyes,
Trembles to starlight . . . . Mine, O mine:
No more be tears in moon or mist
For thee, sweet sentimentalist.

These lyric things come to me not merely because I have heard him sing and heard him repeat verse beautifully, but because I know how much his mind dwells upon the melody and because I know that his ideal in literature is that which is simple and free–the liberation of a rhythm. His aesthetic is in that conversation which the hero of "Portrait of the Artist," Stephen Dedalus, has with the student Lynch. What Stephen says there is, word for word, what Joyce used to say to many of us who were with him in the early twenties:

"'Aristotle has not defined pity and terror. I have, I say . . .'"
" Lynch halted and said bluntly:
"'Stop! I won't listen. I was out last night on a yellow drunk with Horan and Goggins.'
"Stephen went on:
"'Pity is the feeling which arrests the mind in the presence of whatsoever is grave and constant in human sufferings and unites it with the human sufferer. Terror is the feeling that arrests the mind in the presence of whatsoever is grave and constant in human sufferings and unites it with the secret cause.'
"'Repeat,' said Lynch.
"Stephen repeated the definitions slowly:
"'To speak of these things and to try to understand their nature and, having understood it, to try slowly and humbly and constantly to express, to press out again, from the gross earth or what it brings forth, from sound and shape and color which are the prison gates of our soul, an image of the beauty we have come to understand–that is art–'"

Stephen then interprets for his student-friend a definition of Aquinas' "I translate it so: Three things are needed for beauty, wholeness, harmony and radiance." He goes on:

"When you have apprehended that basket as one thing and have then analyzed it according to its form and apprehended it as a thing, you make the only synthesis which is logically and esthetically permissible. You see that it is that thing which it is and no other thing. The radiance of which he speaks is the scholastic *quidditas*, the *whatness* of a thing. The supreme quality is

felt by the artist when the esthetic image is first conceived in his imagination. The mind in that mysterious instant Shelley likened beautifully to a fading coal. The instant wherein that supreme quality of beauty, the clear radiance of the esthetic image, is apprehended luminously by the mind which has been arrested by its wholeness and fascinated by its harmony is the luminous silent stasis of esthetic pleasure, a spiritual state very like that cardiac condition which the Italian physiologist, Luigi Galvani, using a phrase almost as beautiful as Shelley's, called the enchantment of the heart."

"Portrait of the Artist" is dated: "Dublin, 1904; Trieste, 1914."

Joyce was ten years writing the book. I saw him in Dublin when he was mid-way in it and he told me there were parts that gave him physical nausea to write. "Portrait of the Artist as a Young Man" is a biography in which all inessentials are suppressed and people and incidents only stand out as a background for the emergence of a soul. It is a confession in which there are things as ignominious as the things in Rousseau's "Confessions." But there is heroism in the book, and in spite of corruption and precocity there is youth in it also. Halfway in the life that is shown to us Stephen Dedalus comes to a spiritual morass. He wins through it by virtue of a power of spiritual vision backed by the discipline of the Catholic Church. Later he loses his faith in the sanctions of that Church and at the end of the story he is leaving his country. He is going to discover a mode of life or art whereby his spirit may express itself in unfettered freedom.

What really makes "Portrait of the Artist as a Young Man" strange to English and American people is that is gives a glimpse into a new life–into the life that has been shaped by Catholic culture and Catholic tradition. James Joyce's book is profoundly Catholic. I do not mean that it carries any doctrine or thesis: I mean that, more than any other modern book written in English, it comes out of Catholic culture and tradition–even that culture and tradition that may turn against itself. Even in the way the book is written there is something that makes us think of the Church–a sense of secrecy, of words being said in a mysterious language, of solidity breaking into vision. Stephen Dedalus is unable to analyze his ideas or to shape his life except in terms of the philosophy that the Catholic Church has evolved or adopted. His ideal of beauty is the ideal that has been attained to in the masterpieces of Catholic art. It is the speech of the Church that fills his soul with apprehension because of his secret sins, and it is the absolution of the Church that gives him peace and the way to a new life. Cranly, one of his student friends, pointed this out to Stephen. "It is a curious thing, do you know," Cranly said dispassionately, "how your mind is super-saturated with the religion which you say you disbelieve." He may have disbelieved in the religion, but he had formed his life on a philosophy of which a *synopsis Philosophiae Scholasticae ad mentem divi Thomae* had a place with Aristotle's Poetics and Psychology: "Their souls have not the strength that mine has, steeled in the school of old Aquinas." So Joyce wrote of himself in a satire (unpublished) in which he reviled certain of Dublin's intellectuals. "Steeled in the school of old Aquinas"! And where did he dwell, the youth who made this his boast? In Dublin, the suburb—or, if one wanted to speak bitterly, the slum of Catholic Europe—Dublin, wherein the people wear "the fetters of the reformed conscience"; Dublin, which is intellectually neither in Ireland nor in England or in Continental Europe.

And this city, so thwarted on the side of culture, is low in material circumstances. The misery that comes from low wages and few opportunities pervades the "Portrait of the Artist" as it pervades "Dubliners." Stephen's bread-and-butter life is not merely sordid, it is on the verge of being squalid. He attends the University, but when he comes to his home:

He pushed open the latchless door of the porch and passed through the naked hallway into the kitchen. A group of his brothers and sisters was sitting round the table. Tea was nearly over and only the last of the second watered tea remained in the bottoms of the small glass jars and jam-pots which did service for teacups. Discarded crusts and lumps of sugared bread, turned brown by the tea which had been poured over them, lay scattered on the table. Little wells of tea lay here and there on the board and a knife with a broken ivory handle was stuck through the pitch of a ravaged turnover.

"The sad, quiet, gray-blue glow of the dying day came through the window and the open door, covering over and allaying quietly a sudden instinct of remorse in Stephen's heart. All that had been denied them had been freely given him, the eldest; but the quiet glow of evening showed him in their faces no sign of rancor.

"He sat near them at the table and asked where his father and mother were. One answered:

"'Goneboro toboro lookboro atboro houseboro.'

"Still another removal. A boy named Fallon, in Belvidere, had often asked him with a silly laugh why they moved so often. A frown of scorn darkened quickly his forehead as he heard again the silly laugh of the questioner.

"He asked:

"'Why are we on the move again, if it's a fair question?'

"'Becauseboro theboro landboro lordboro willboro putboro usboro outboro.'

"The voice of his youngest brother, from the farther side of the fireplace, began to sing the air. 'Oft in the Stilly Night.' One by one the others took up the air

until a full choir of voices was singing. They would sing so for hours, melody after melody, glee after glee, till the last pale light died down on the horizon, till the first dark night-clouds came forth and night fell.

"He waited for some moments, listening, before he took up the air with them. He was listening with pain of spirit to the overtone of weariness behind their frail, fresh, innocent voices. Even before they set out on life's journey they seemed weary already of the way.

"He heard the choir of voices in the kitchen echoed and multiplied through an endless reverberation of the choirs of endless generations of children: and heard in all the echoes an echo also of the recurring note of weariness and pain. All seemed weary of life even before entering upon it. And he remembered that Newman had heard this note also in the broken lines of Virgil 'giving utterances, like the voice of Nature herself, to that pain and weariness yet hope of better things which has been the experience of her children in every time.'"

Stephen's father is a gentleman and has been a man of property, but he has come down in the world through his easiness, as one guesses, and his good fellowship. Stephen, it would seem, is able to attend the secondary school and the University through the interest of the Jesuits.

Against this background of economic decay and incomplete culture and of shut-in sin Stephen Dedalus makes his spiritual assertion. He will win toward freedom and the power to create. He will strive, too, to give a soul to this people. "He stared angrily back at the softly lit drawing-room of the hotel in which he imagined the sleek lives of the patricians of Ireland housed in calm. They thought of army commissions and land agents: peasants greeted them along the roads in the country: they knew the names of certain French dishes and gave orders to jarvies in high-pitched provincial voices which pierced through their skin-tight accents. How could he hit their conscience or how cast his shadow over the imaginations of their daughters, before their squires begat upon them, that they might breed a race less ignoble than their own?" But he would do it, and do it out of those scraps of monkish learning which, as he felt bitterly, were held no higher by the age he lived in than the subtle and curious jargons of heraldry and falconry.

And out of his squalor, his lack of companionship, his closed future, he created a proud soul. Liberation came to him through his poetry. Many squalid and vicious things are described in "Portrait of the Artist as a Young Man," but also the pure ecstasy of poetic creation has been rendered in it as in no other book that I know of:

"An enchantment of the heart! The night had been enchanted. In a dream or vision he had known the ecstasy of seraphic life. Was it an instant of enchantment only, or long hours and years and ages?

"The instant of inspiration seemed now to be reflected from all sides at once from a multitude of cloudy circumstances of what had happened or of what might have happened. The instant flashed forth like a point of light and now from cloud on cloud of vague circumstance confused form was veiling its afterglow. O! In the virgin womb of the imagination the word was made flesh. Gabriel the seraph had come to the virgin's chamber. An afterglow deepened within his spirit, whence the white flame had passed, deepening to a rose and ardent light. That rose and ardent light was her strange, wilful heart strange that no man had known or would know, wilful from before the beginning of the world: and lured by that ardent roselike glow the choirs of the seraphim were falling from heaven:

"Are you not weary of ardent ways,
Lure of the fallen seraphim?
Tell no more of enchanted days."

The verses passed from his mind to his lips, and, murmuring them over, he felt the rhythmic movement of a villanelle pass through them. The roselike glow sent forth its rays of rhyme: ways, days, blaze, praise, raise. Its rays burned up the world, consumed the hearts of men and angels: the rays from the rose that was her wilful heart.

The book does not end with Stephen Dedalus having won a love or made a career or achieved a fortune. It ends with a young man going into exile and saying to himself, "I will try to express myself in some mode of life or art as freely as I can and as wholly as I can, using for my defense the only arms I allow myself to use, silence, exile, and cunning."

James Joyce was very noticeable amongst the crowd of students who frequented the National Library or who sauntered along the streets between Nelson's Pillar and Stephen's Green. He was tall and

St. Stephen's Green, a twenty-seven-acre park in the center of Dublin that in Joyce's time faced University College.
Stephen Dedalus in A Portrait of the Artist as a Young Man *calls it "my green" (Irish Tourist Board).*

slender when I knew him first, with a Dantesque face and steely blue eyes. The costume I see him in includes a peaked cap and tennis shoes, more or less white. He used to swing along the street, carrying in his hand an ash-plant for a cane. Although he had a beautiful voice for singing or for repeating poetry, he spoke harshly in conversation, using many words of the purlieus. Stories were told about his arrogance. Did not this youth say to Yeats, "We have met too late: you are too old to be influenced by me"? And did he not laugh in derision when a celebrated critic spoke of Balzac as a great writer? He had taught himself whatever Scandinavian language Ibsen wrote in—he used to repeat Ibsen's lyrics in the original—and when "We Dead Awaken" was published in English, he wrote—he was then eighteen—the article for the "Fortnightly Review" on it. He took part in an amateur production of "Hedda Gabler," taking the part of Lovborg. I did not see the production, but I imagine that he did excellently in it.

He talked of Ibsen the night I first spoke to him. We met coming out of the National Library and we walked together toward his home in the north side of the city. For most of the way he listened, rather ironically, to what I had to say for myself. The Irish Revival had no allegiance from him—he distrusted all enthusiasm, he said. He discounted the prospect of creating a national theatre for Ireland. Already he had written a student pamphlet—"The Day of the Rabblement"—in which the project as it was now disclosed was belittled by him. In this pamphlet he had called upon the projectors of the National Theatre to avail themselves of the franchise Dublin had and produce the masterpieces of European drama—the drama that the foolish theatrical censorship exercised by the Chamberlain of the King's Household would not permit of being produced in London or in any English city. He talked of Ibsen with enthusiasm. "A Doll's House" had just been given by some amateur company, but Joyce in conversation dismissed this play. It was interesting, he said, just as a letter written by Ibsen would be interesting, but it had no relation to such great drama as "Hedda Gabler" or "The Wild Duck." I contrasted Joyce's tone with George Moore's, whom I had heard speak of the same production a night or two before. "Sophocles, Raphael, Shelley!" George Moore had cried, running his hands through his blond hair. "What have they done compared with 'A Doll's House'?"

Afterwards we came to be on friendly terms and we walked about together. He gave me his poems to read—they were in a beautiful manuscript. He used to speak very arrogantly about these poems of his, but I remember his saying something that made me know

how precious these beautifully wrought lyrics were to him—he talked about walking the streets of Paris, poor and tormented, and about what peace the repetition of his poems had brought him.

His poems were perfect in their form. But could one who expressed himself so perfectly at twenty really go far? Yeats had said to him, "I do not know whether you are a fountain or a cistern," and A. E. had remarked, "I do not see in your beginnings the chaos out of which a world is created."

He went to Paris for a while and returned to Dublin. It was then that he wrote the stories that are in "Dubliners" and began the writing of "Portrait of the Artist" (Dublin, 1904). After he had begun the book he went abroad to take a place as teacher of English in a Berlitz School. I saw him back in Dublin a few years later. He had married and had a little boy with him, of whom he was very proud. He was more mellow than ever I had known him before—happy about himself, his family and his work. It was then that he told me the name of the book he was writing—the book that was being referred to in Dublin as "Joyce's Meredithian novel"—it was "Portrait of the Artist as a Young Man." It was not "Meredithian" at all.

He was glad to be away from a place where "the reformed conscience" had left its fetter and away from the fog of Anglo-Saxon civilization. His boy went to all the operas in the Italian city where they lived and he would have him brought up neither as an Englishman nor a modern Irishman.

He was in Dublin then on business. The Cinematograph had come in and was already popular in Italy. An Italian company was opening "Electric Theatres" in various cities, and Joyce had been sent over to open one in Dublin. His "Volta Theatre" was opened, but I never heard that it was successful. This was the second of Joyce's business adventures that I remember. He had when I knew him first a project for a new daily newspaper in Dublin: it was to be unlike any newspaper in Europe, and already he had registered its title—"The Goblin." As far as I remember he had worked out the whole idea, even to the character of the book reviews, and he had actually undertaken the adventure of raising the necessary twenty-five thousand pounds. He didn't get it. Looking for twenty-five thousand pounds in Dublin would be like looking for a couple of million dollars in New York.

He was less happy when I saw him in Dublin again, a few years later. His stories, "Dubliners," were being brought out. But now the printer refused to let the sheets go out of his office. He had discovered scandal in the pages and had ordered all the sheets to be burned. Joyce had no redress. Printer and publisher claimed that there was libel in what he had written and that they would not make themselves responsible for it. Joyce saved a set of proofs and took them over to London. But in London he met with no better reception—they were all afraid of the scandal and the libel. But "Dubliners" won to the light at last and Mr. Huebsch has brought it out on this side with "Portrait of the Artist as a Young Man."

The last sentences in one of the stories in "Dubliners" seems to me to show the quality of Joyce's writing at its best. I refer to the story called "The Dead." It is after a party at which an old song, "The Maid of Aughrim," had been sung. Gabriel Conroy's wife had remained strangely abstracted after having heard it. Suddenly she lifts a veil by telling her husband that she had known in Galway a young man who used to sing that song, Michael Furey, and that he had died for love of her. Yes, he had come into her garden one night to speak to her before she went to the convent. It was raining bitterly and the chill he had taken, working on a weakened constitution, had brought him to his grave. She did not love him, but they had been friends. At first the husband is jealous of poor young Michael Furey, but then he is won to a mood of compassion:

"Generous tears filled Gabriel's eyes. He had never felt like that himself toward any woman, but he knew that such a feeling must be love. The tears gathered more thickly in his eyes, and in the partial darkness he imagined he saw the form of a young man standing under a dripping tree. Other forms were near. His soul had approached that region where dwell the vast hosts of the dead. He was conscious of, but could not apprehend, their wayward and flickering existence. His own identity was fading out into a gray, impalpable world: the solid world itself, which these dead had one time reared and lived in, was dissolving and dwindling.

"A few light taps upon the pane made him turn to the window. It had begun to snow again. He watched sleepily the flakes, silver and dark, falling obliquely against the lamplight. The time had come for him to set out on his journey westward. Yes, the newspapers were right: snow was general all over Ireland. It was falling on every part of the dark central plain, on the treeless hills, falling softly upon the Bog of Allen, and farther westward, falling softly into the dark, mutinous Shannon waves. It was falling, too, upon every part of the lonely churchyard on the hill where Michael Furey lay buried. It lay thickly drifted on the crooked crosses and headstones, on the spears of the little gate, on the barren thorns. His soul swooned slowly as he heard the snow falling faintly through the universe and faintly falling, like the descent of their last end, upon all the living and the dead."

Hart Crane

When one critic attacked A Portrait of the Artist as a Young Man *as an expression of decadence, the American poet Hart Crane, who considered that novel one of the two most spiritually inspiring books he had ever read, could not resist responding to the indictment.*

Joyce and Ethics
Hart Crane
The Little Review, 5 (July 1918): 65

The Los Angeles critic who commented on Joyce in the last issue was adequately answered, I realize,—but the temptation to emphasize such illiteracy, indiscrimination, and poverty still pulls a little too strongly for resistance.

I noticed that Wilde, Baudelaire and Swinburne are 'stacked up' beside Joyce as rivals in 'decadence' and 'intellect'. I am not yet aware that Swinburne ever possessed much beyond his 'art ears', although these were long enough, and adequate to all his beautiful, though often meaningless mouthings. His instability in criticism and every form of literature that did not depend almost exclusively on sound for effect, and his irrelevant metaphors are notorious. And as to Wilde,—after his bundle of paradoxes has been sorted and conned,—very little evidence of intellect remains. 'Decadence' is something much talked about, and sufficiently misconstrued to arouse interest in the works of any fool. Any change in form, viewpoint or mannerism can be so abused by the offending party. Sterility is the only 'decadence' I recognize. An abortion in art takes the same place as it does in society,—it deserves no recognition whatever,—it is simply outside. A piece of work is art, or it isn't: there is no neutral judgment.

However,—let Baudelaire and Joyce stand together, as much as any such thing in literary comparison will allow. The principal eccentricity evinced by both is a penetration into life common to only the greatest. If people resent a thrust which discovers some of their entrails to themselves, I can see no reason for resorting to indiscriminate comparisons, naming colours of the rainbow, or advertising the fact that they have recently been forced to recognize a few of their personal qualities. Those who are capable of being only mildly 'shocked' very naturally term the cost a penny, but were they capable of paying a few pounds for the same thinking, experience and realization by and in themselves, they could reserve their pennies for work minor to Joyce's.

The most nauseating complaint against his work is that of immorality and obscenity. The character of Stephen Dedalus is all too good for this world. It takes a little experience,—a few reactions on his part to understand it, and could this have been accomplished in a detached hermitage, high above the mud, he would no doubt have preferred that residence. *A Portrait of the Artist as a Young Man,* aside from Dante, is spiritually the most inspiring book I have ever read. It is Bunyan raised to art and then raised to the ninth power.

In her review of several novels, the English writer Virginia Woolf (1882–1941), an exact contemporary of Joyce, examines the apparent disconnectedness of A Portrait of the Artist as a Young Man.

Modern Novels
Virginia Woolf
Times Literary Supplement, no. 899 (10 April 1919): 189–190

. . . We are not pleading merely for courage and sincerity; but suggesting that the proper stuff for fiction is a little other than custom would have us believe it.

In some such fashion as this do we seek to define the element which distinguishes the work of several young writers, among whom Mr. James Joyce is the most notable, from that of their predecessors. It attempts to come closer to life, and to preserve more sincerely and exactly what

Virginia Woolf

interests and moves them by discarding most of the conventions which are commonly observed by the novelists. Let us record the atoms as they fall upon the mind in the order in which they fall, let us trace the pattern, however disconnected and incoherent in appearance, which each sight or incident scores upon the consciousness. Let us not take it for granted that life exists more in what is commonly thought big than in what is commonly thought small. Any one who has read *The Portrait of the Artist as a Young Man* or what promises to be a far more interesting work, *Ulysses,* now appearing in the *Little Review,* will have hazarded some theory of this nature as to Mr. Joyce's intention. On our part it is hazarded rather than affirmed; but whatever the exact intention there can be no question but that it is of the utmost sincerity and that the result, difficult or unpleasant as we may judge it, is undeniably distinct. In contrast to those [H. G. Wells, Arnold Bennett, John Galsworthy] whom we have called materialists Mr. Joyce is spiritual; concerned at all costs to reveal the flickerings of that innermost flame which flashes its myriad messages through the brain, he disregards with complete courage whatever seems to him adventitious, though it be probability or coherence or any other of the handrails to which we cling for support when we set our imaginations free. Faced, as in the Cemetery scene, by so much that, in its restless scintillations, in its irrelevance, its flashes of deep significance succeeded by incoherent inanities, seems to be life itself, we have to fumble rather awkwardly if we want to say what else we wish;

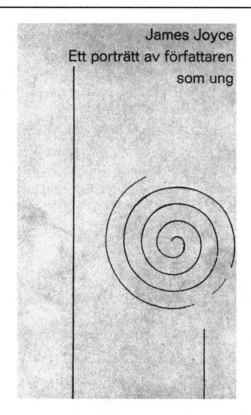

Dust jackets for Finnish and Swedish editions of Joyce's most accessible novel

and for what reason a work of such originality yet fails to compare, for we must take high examples, with *Youth* or *Jude the Obscure*. It fails, one might say simply because of the comparative poverty of the writer's mind. But it is possible to press a little further and wonder whether we may not refer our sense of being in a bright and yet somehow strictly confined apartment rather than at large beneath the sky to some limitation imposed by the method as well as by the mind. It is due to the method that we feel neither jovial nor magnanimous, but centred in a self which in spite of its tremor of susceptibility never reaches out or embraces or comprehends what is outside and beyond? Does the emphasis laid perhaps didactically upon indecency contribute to this effect of the angular and isolated? Or is it merely that in any effort of such courage the faults as well as the virtues are left naked to the view? In any case we need not attribute too much importance to the method. Any method is right, every method is right, that expresses what we wish to express. This one has the merit of giving closer shape to what we were prepared to call life itself; did not the reading of *Ulysses* suggest how much of life is excluded and ignored, and did it not come with a shock to open *Tristram Shandy* and even *Pendennis*, and be by them convinced that there are other aspects of life, and larger ones into the bargain? . . .

–reprinted from *James Joyce: The Critical Heritage*

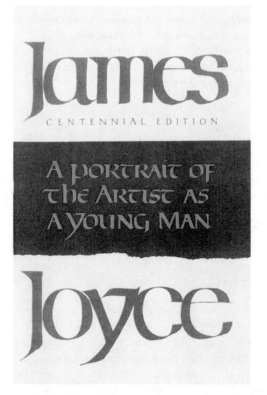

Dust jacket for the edition of Joyce's first novel published in 1982 by the Viking Press marking the centennial of the author's birth

Stills from the 1977 movie version of A Portrait of the Artist as a Young Man: *top, Luke Johnson (center) as the ten-year-old Stephen Dedalus; bottom, Rosaleen Linehan and Bosco Hogan as May and Stephen (Collection of Paul Talbot)*

Exiles

In his notes for Exiles, *which was first published in the 1951 Viking edition, Joyce referred to his play as "three cat-and-mouse acts," and in a 5 April 1915 letter to Richards, he characterized it as "a comedy in three acts"* (Letters I, *p. 78). In his notes, Joyce commented on the personalities of the four main characters of the drama—Richard Rowan, Bertha, Robert Hand, and Beatrice Justice—and their moral and spiritual states. He also explained the idea for the title. "Why the title Exiles? A nation," Joyce answered, "exacts a penance from those who dared to leave her payable on their return." His interest in the idea of exile was no doubt especially important to Joyce at this time in his life.* Exiles *takes place during the summer of 1912, the same summer of Joyce's last trip to Ireland.*

In James Joyce's Exiles: A Textual Companion *(1979), John MacNicholas identifies four sequences of events in Joyces' life as the most important sources for* Exiles:

1. Joyce's courtship of Nora Barnacle, which culminated in their elopement and exile to Europe (16 June–8 October 1904).

2. Joyce's subsequent visits to Ireland. During the first return (29 July–9 September 1909) he was severely jolted by Vincent Cosgrave's claim to have been intimate with Nora during the summer of 1904. Also during this visit his university friend Thomas Kettle urged Joyce to seek a university chair in Italian. Three years later, Joyce brought Nora and their children to Ireland (16 July–11 September 1912). He made a vain attempt to force the recalcitrant George Roberts at Maunsel and Co. to publish Dubliners.

3. His association with Roberto Prezioso, an Italian journalist who attempted sexual intimacy with Nora (1911–13).

4. His association with a young, well-born Italian Jewess, Amalia Popper, who was his language student (1912–14).

The themes of exile, love, freedom, friendship, doubt, and betrayal, themes found throughout Joyce's writings, are forthrightly treated in Exiles.

Reviews of *Exiles*

Although not performed until September 1919, when a translated version was staged at the Münchener Theater in Munich, Exiles *was published in book form on 25 May 1918 in both England and the United States. Reviewers of the play often compared it to Ibsen's dramas and questioned its stageability but also recognized its originality. Admitting at the outset of his review in* The New Statesman *that he could never undertake a production of the play unless Joyce were at his elbow, Desmond MacCarthy nevertheless regards* Exiles *as a remarkable work. "To be made to wonder and to think about characters in a play," he writes, "is a rare experience—outside the drama of Ibsen. . . . Exiles excited me for the same reason that the plays of Ibsen excite me—the people in it were so interesting." Although the play has had limited success on the stage, it is a significant work in the development of Joyce's writings and stands as a transitional piece between* A Portrait of the Artist as a Young Man *and* Ulysses.

EXILES
A PLAY IN THREE ACTS

BY
JAMES JOYCE

NEW YORK
B. W. HUEBSCH
MCMXVIII

Title page for Joyce's only extant play (courtesy of Special Collections, Thomas Cooper Library, University of South Carolina)

Two of the models for Robert Hand, a central character in Exiles: *Roberto Prezioso, the editor of the* Piccolo della Sera *who admired Nora Joyce, and Oliver St. John Gogarty in August 1917 (painting by Augustus John; collection of J. Robert Maguire)*

One of the first Irish reviews of Joyce's play, an unfavorable one, appeared in the Freeman's Journal, *a Dublin newspaper.*

Ibsen in Ireland
J.W.G.
Freeman's Journal (15 June 1918): 4

The obvious thing to say about Mr. James Joyce's *Exiles* is that though the scene is laid in Dublin, the spiritual home of the characters is less Ireland than Norway. This would not in itself detract from the value of the play as a work of art, except perhaps in the eyes of literary chauvinists who have schooled themselves to believe, in defiance of all precedents, that the merit of a writer depends not on how he uses influences for his own end, but on whether these influences are native or alien. One's quarrel with Mr. Joyce is not that he borrows from Ibsen, but that he borrows the wrong things. The cloudy enigmas of 'When the dead awaken' appeal to him, if we may judge from this play, as the high-water mark of Ibsen's achievement. But it is precisely this side of Ibsen's genius that shows the most signs of wear and tear. His greatness did not lie in the fact that his characters were adepts in the analysis of their emotions, but that this analysis was so presented as to strengthen the impression of dramatic personality. This is exactly what Mr. Joyce fails to do, and his failure is the more curious because it is due to no lack of

power. The appalling discussion at the dinner party, in the opening chapters of *Portrait of the Artist as Young Man*, crams into a single page more dramatic reality than is to be found in the three acts of *Exiles*. In his play, where one looks for men and women one finds instead states of mind loosely personified. Vital energy seems to have been drained out of the characters, and they impress one less as individuals than as Æolian harps vibrating to the waves of emotions they are powerless to direct or control. Subtlety is possible in the theatre, but to be effective it must be expressed in terms of the theatre. Mr. Joyce scarcely makes a pretence of attempting to hold the interest of his audience, and though he introduces, as Ibsen certainly would not have done, a suburban sitting-room equipped with no less than four doors, he disdains to conjure up a single dramatic situation in the real sense of the word. The plot of *Exiles* is not unlike that of *Candida*, with the humour left out. Betha Rowan is in much the same plight as Mr. Shaw's heroine was between Marchbanks and Morell, only in Mr. Joyce's play all the three principals see themselves and are presented by their author from the Marchbanks' point of view. Dramatically it is a case of great cry and little wool; and while *Exiles* contains, as one expects from Mr. Joyce, some dialogue that is wonderfully subtle and effective, good dialogue is the beginning, and not the end, of play-making.

Claud W. Sykes

Nora Joyce dressed for her role in John Millington Synge's
Riders to the Sea

PFAUEN-THEATER

Schauspielbühne des Stadt-Theaters

Monday, 17 June 1918, at 8 ᴘᴹ.

The English Players

present

The Twelve-Pound Look

by J. M. BARRIE.

Cast:

Sir Harry Sims	Claud. W. Sykes
Lady Sims	Evelyn Cotton
Kate	Daisy Race
Toombs, a butler	Charles Fleming

Scene: A room in Sir Harry Sims's house.

Riders to the Sea

by JOHN M. SYNGE.

Cast:

Maurya, an old woman	Daisy Race
Bartley, her son	Bernard Glenning
Catheleen, her daughter	Nora Joyce
Nora, a younger daughter	Mary Laney
Colum Shawn	Charles Fleming
A Woman	Ethel Turner

Scene: An island off the west of Ireland.

The Dark Lady of the Sonnets

by GEORGE BERNARD SHAW.

Cast:

The Dark Lady	Dorothy Bernton
Queen Elizabeth	Marguerite Matthews
Shakespeare	Tristan Rawson
A Beefeater	Claud. W. Sykes

Scene: The terrace of the palace at Whitehall.

*

The plays produced by Claud. W. Sykes.

An interval of 10 minutes after each piece.

*Advertisement for a production by the company for which Joyce
served as business manager*

The English Players

In spring 1918 Joyce joined Claud Sykes in founding a theater company to perform plays in English in Zurich. Sykes was the producer and director of the company while Joyce was its business manager. Joyce became involved in the venture in part because he hoped to see the company perform Exiles; indeed the play was listed as one of the plays in the group's repertoire. The company, however, was never able to find the right actor to play Richard Rowan, the central character of the play.

Clutton-Brock's call for Exiles *to be staged was not heeded. As Ellmann points out in* James Joyce, *Joyce's September 1919 letter to the Italian translator of* Exiles, *Carlo Linati, shows that he believed that George Bernard Shaw had vetoed the acceptance of his play by the Stage Society (p. 415n). For a discussion about this assumption, see William White's "G. B. S. on Joyce's* Exiles*" in the 4 December 1959 issue of* Times Literary Supplement; *Stephen Winsten's reply, "G. B. S. on Joyce's Exiles," in the 18 December 1959 issue; and White's reply to Winsten, "Irish Antithesis: Shaw and Joyce," in the February 1961 issue of* The Shavian.

The Mind to Suffer

A. Clutton-Brock

Times Literary Supplement, 25 July 1918, p. 346

Many men have written interesting books about their childhood and youth, and never succeeded again in the same degree. Not only was esteem for Mr. James Joyce's *Portrait of the Artist as a Young Man* subject to this discount, but it unfortunately raised both friends and enemies whose excitement about it was unconnected with its merits: here brilliant, there tedious, the book itself rendered the stream of opinion yet more turbid. An unacted problem play is not the book to clear the public mind. Yet this work does prove the author's imagination independent of stimulus from self-preoccupation; and, though a first play, roughly straining its means, it reveals resources of spiritual passion and constructive power which should greatly cheer the friends of his talent.

Richard Rowan, like so many gifted young men, has early rebelled against current compromises. He will not stoop either to seduce or to marry Bertha, yet of her own impulse she accompanies him to Rome, where they live in voluntary exile for nine years and bring up their little son. Meanwhile scholarly and brilliant work has won him the first fruits of renown, and by absorbing him has oppressed Bertha with the loneliness of the unequally mated. Her man is one who clings to the soul's absolute integrity as feverishly as others cling to material existence. He suffers agonies of shame and remorse when he finds himself less faithful to her than she has been to him; he confesses everything to her, and insists that she is equally free. When the play opens they are back in Dublin, Robert Hand, the great friend of his youth, a journalist, zealously prepares the University and the Press to ignore the fact that Richard and Bertha's happy union owes nothing to the law, but at the same time he undermines their domestic quietude by covertly courting Bertha. She, jealous of Richard's relations with an intellectual lady who is able to discuss his ideas in a way she cannot, and constantly indoctrinated as to her absolute freedom, receives Robert's addresses, yet relates every advance as it is made to Richard, partly in hopes of rousing his jealously, which her own prescribes as its proper antidote, partly because, like himself, she has never hidden anything. He perceives that his old friend is acting like 'a common thief' and precedes Bertha to the first assignation. But Robert, cynic and rake though he is, genuinely loves and admires his friend. His humility touches Richard, in whom, as he listens, dread wakes lest, like the ghost of his own passion, he may stand between Bertha and experiences which are her due. Like another Shelley, he decides that their rivalry must be open and unprejudiced by the past. Does he any longer really possess Bertha's heart? She arrives; he explains to her again her absolute freedom, and leaves her to meet his friend. The second curtain falls before that interview has ended. In the third act both Bertha and Robert, equally admiring and loving Richard, assure him that nothing has happened between them; but he has doubted both and cannot recover his faith—the torture of a night of suspense has been too great.

> I have wounded my soul for you—a deep wound of doubt which can never be healed. . . . I do not wish to know or to believe. . . . It is not in the darkness of belief that I desire you, but in restless living, wounding doubt.

and she can only answer:—

> Forget me and love me. . . . I want my lover . . . . You Dick. O, my strange, wild lover, come back to me again!

So the play ends—a situation after Browning's own heart, and seen more distinctly, less as a case put, than he would probably have seen it; only the machinery used is Ibsen's.

The second act transcends this machinery and is in outline and effect a poetical creation; the other two acts, in which minor characters figure, are less happy. On the stage custom shows people in such situations, light-heartedly, sentimentally, or cynically: to show them seriously and sympathetically alarms some folk as Jesus did when he persisted in dining with harlots and publicans. Intellectual charity is to-day as rare a virtue as human compassion was then. Those for whom certain themes and certain words constitute either a 'taboo' or a 'hall mark' are debarred from exercising it. Sympathy opens both the heart and the eye that discerns beauty; prejudice closes both. In the last act a doubt arises in the reader's mind whether Bertha and Robert are not lying to Richard; probably this is due to inadvertence on the author's part. Their falsehood by increasing their inferiority would deepen the grounds of his lonely suffering, but by proving their response to his lead superficial it would diminish the poignancy of his tragic doubt. Thus an outline is doubled, one intention cancelling the other: such ambiguity is merely distracting, and might easily be removed. But this is a detail, an accident; the whole is lifted and throbs, like *King Lear,* with a capacity for suffering more startling even than the situations in which it is manifested. Of course, work so young and in some ways crude is no match for the varied enchantments of *King Lear.* The woodenness of realism is made painfully apparent by the passion that contrasts to it the bone-structure and blood of a creation—of *Exiles.* Experience in the use of words and the management of scenes may supply what Mr. James Joyce lacks, though, of course, they may not, and a world that crushes and pampers authors with equal blindness may be trusted to make the finest success the most difficult and least likely. Will not the Stage Society or the Pioneers let us and the author see this play, so that its shortcomings may become apparent to him and its virtues be brought home to us with their full force?

—reprinted from *James Joyce: The Critical Heritage*

The wealthy Scofield Thayer, who at one time was the editor of The Dial *and its banker, commented on Joyce's works, notably* Exiles, *in the following article. Less than a year later, in June 1919, he cabled Joyce a sum of money when he learned of the author's financial problems from mutual friends, Padraic and Mary. In February 1921, Thayer was one of the defense witnesses whom attorney John Quinn called to testify at the obscenity trial of* The Little Review.

James Joyce

Scofield Thayer

The Dial, 65 (19 September 1918): 201–203

Stephen Dedalus, the hero of "A Portrait of the Artist as a Young Man," desires to try out all possible means of expression. Whether or not the somewhat scattered personality of this hero be a child wholly after his father's heart, at any rate Mr. Joyce himself is publicly trying out his own mettle in the short story, the novel, the Elizabethan lyric, and the Ibsenesque drama. The most recent of his publications in this country is "Exiles," a prose play in three acts. The scene is laid in the suburbs of Dublin and the important characters are of the upper class. The play appears to be intended to illustrate a problem and perhaps to throw light upon it; the question is so intricate that I for one am quite

George Bernard Shaw, who read Exiles *when it was submitted to the Stage Society. He denied responsibility for the rejection of the play, though he admitted suggesting that indecent passages be deleted if the play were to be performed by the society.*

unable to follow even the speeches of the characters, still less to fathom the author's own intention or conclusion. The problem is the seasoned one of marriage and freedom, but just what takes place and why and what the upshot of it all is does not emerge form the emotional scenes and the final disintegration of the protagonist. On the stage, which stops for no man, this drama would be an impregnable puzzle; and even when it is held fast on the printed page, hopelessly conflicting solutions vie with one another. Next time Mr. Joyce would do well to try his hand at exegesis and to take this play as his subject.

"Chamber Music" is—all but the intensely contemporary and distinguished final poem—a remarkable perfect echo of the best in early seventeenth century prosody. These little songs are so intimately alluring that no one but a schoolmaster would cavil at their harping upon one note, and that the secular one of courteous-mannered love.

> And I but render and confess
> The malice of thy tenderness

disarms all strictures that might be made upon the futility of repeating an already deviously explored manner. After all, when we see a beautiful face we do not savor it the less because we have loved one like it before. Indeed in the case of these lyrics our reminiscence of earlier pipings does but enhance our pleasure: It is good to know that a mind so crammed with the impertinences of modern city life as the creator of "Dubliners" can yet achieve the liquid grace of a less handicapped age.

This collection of short stories published under the title "Dubliners" is certainly Mr. Joyce's finest piece of work; indeed I should not know where to go for their betters. The title is a very appropriate one, for these stories are not so much narratives of events as they are evolvements of character. To be sure, these people of Joyce are not painted as standing still for our perusal of their complicated lineaments; they are caught, so to speak, on the wing, and the portrait is the more successful for this fact. In the changing light and shadow of their veering flight we are able to look them over pretty thoroughly, and Mr. Joyce sees to it that we look to the right place at the right time. Judged from Aristotle's point of view, the vague plots of these stories are so unsymmetrical as to be definite malformations: they are the hunchbacks of fiction. Yet the sparse incidents that make them up are casual only in their relations to each other and to the rest of incidental, practical life; they are uncannily indicative, even ratiocinative, when rightly taken for what they are—media for the expression of character.

There is therefore almost no plot tension; and however much we may sympathize with certain of the characters, curiosity as to the outcome of the predicament is scarcely awakened. As in some dreams, we ourselves are unaccountably detached not only from the incidents narrated but also from practical interest of every kind. With an hypnotic attention we perceive these characters evolve and our whole will is so strangely absorbed in their contemplation that otherwise we neither wonder nor desire. When Eveline, in sight of the boat that should bear her lover and herself to America, grips with both hands the iron railing of the pier, her soul at odds, unable to move, we do not question what the outcome will be, far less do we wish upon her the happiness of either going or staying; like her we are wholly passive. This does not mean that our emotions are unmoved. On the contrary, our hearts as well as our minds are roused to an unusual tense activity. Controlled by the genius of Mr. Joyce, the short story is an art not less pure than music: we do not ask how the piece will end, still less that it should end sunnily; that our emotions and our imaginations are so proudly stirred gives us a profound content.

The people of Mr. Joyce are for the most part not less casual than the tales in which they figure. More obviously flotsam even than the majority of mankind, they are yet almost at home on the shifting, contradictory currents of their life. Casual in soul, they are casual too in manners and in dress. They sidle through the stale streets, and they wear yachting caps, and those pushed far back. They are not markedly discontented in their element, and like fishes in the yellow waters of an ill-kept aquarium they gravely drift before us. They exhibit now one side, now the other, and with a sad shamelessness they keep back nothing. At the last we are reminded that they are not fishes: we are aware of their body smells.

The "Portrait of the Artist as a Young Man" is, paradoxically, less a portrait than these stories in "Dubliners." Ostensibly and successfully the biography of a young man of sensitive imagination bent upon the difficult career of letters, it is yet primarily a cross-section of contemporary Irish middle-class life. When the boy is at home, it is so overpoweringly an Irish one that we almost forget home and boy together in the glory of this immense gulp of Celtic domesticity. When fate submits poor Stephen to the smooth, disagreeable machinery of boarding-school, the pallid boy is easily lost sight of against the highly coloured Jesuitical background. Even in the latter half of the book, where the harsh insistence of sex replaces the home and school interest, we almost forget the patient, so intent are we upon this catastrophic disease of puberty. We who had first read "Dubliners" smiled at Mr. Huebsch's advertisement on the wrapper of the "Portrait": we looked for better things from James Joyce than an "account which would enable us to understand the forces—social, political, religious—that animate Ireland today." We said to ourselves, "There are some shopmen who would advertise Keats's 'Hyperion' as to be read for tips on real estate in a select vale." After we have read this book we feel the publisher was not without shreds of justification. Although it is the religious passages, rising in the middle of the book to so shrill a pitch, which convince us least and to which indeed we remain the cold students Mr. Huebsch addresses, nevertheless the preacher's exhortation is so well produced that, scoffers as we are, we yet do fall half in love with this brilliant hell, and feel once again that at any rate as an aesthetic phenomenon the concept is quite justifiable.

This particular passage is also interesting as an example of what good old pitchfork rhetoric Mr. Joyce can on occasion throw. For in his prose style the intelligent Irishman is not less protean than in his flittings among literary genres. Beside this God-given buncombe of the priest, there is the pre-prandial conversation in the Dedalus household, so delicately reminiscent of Thackeray, and most everywhere else in the novel, as in all of "Dubliners," that singular, spare, athletic phraseology which is perhaps the most distinguished achievement of this author. While the limber quality of Joyce's speech is most peculiarly apposite in dialogue, yet his clear, nervous language is not less well illustrated by a paragraph in which Dedalus, whom we may surely take at least here as the mouthpiece of our author, reflects to himself upon his enforced use of our Anglo-Saxon tongue:

> The language in which we are speaking is his before it is mine. How different are the words *home, Christ, ale, master,* on his lips and on mine! I cannot speak or write these words without unrest of spirit. His language, so familiar and so foreign, will always be for me an acquired speech. I have not made or accepted its words. My voice holds them at bay. My soul frets in the shadow of his language.

Reading these lithe sentences it is not easy to commiserate with so gifted an alien.

The last pages of the "Portrait" are in the form of a diary and written in a style jotty and spasmodic. If we look back we find something similar in the paragraphs picturing the sensations and thoughts of the boy Stephen ill in the school infirmary:

> The face and the voice went away. Sorry because he was afraid. Afraid that it was some disease. Canker was a disease of plants and cancer one of animals: or another different. That was a long time ago then out on the playgrounds in the evening light, creeping from point to point on the fringe of his line, a heavy bird flying low through the grey light. Leicester Abbey lit up. Wolsey died there. The abbots buried him themselves.

This style, suggestive fancifully at least of pointillist painting, is a perfect expression of the mood of the sick boy. But a novel written in this jerky way becomes very tiring, and that seems to be the case with Mr. Joyce's "Ulysses," now appearing in "The Little Review." It has something in common with not a few of Shakespeare's prose passages. But while the poet is inclined to employ this disconnected utterance only for brief intervals set off between the smooth periods of his verse, Joyce now makes of it a narrative style. This is not, however, perverse. For Shakespeare's characters are of course speaking aloud, and naturally, except in rare instances of madmen and women who keep inns, speak connectedly; while Joyce's novel is really a long inward soliloquy broken only by haphazard small talk.

After comparing Joyce to impressionist writers like Flaubert, Ezra Pound in his "Pavannes and Divisions" finds "that he excels most of the impressionist writers because of his more rigorous selection, because of his exclusion of all unnecessary detail." This is true of "Dubliners," where each story is an imaginative entity, but in "Ulysses" Joyce is no longer an impressionist in the same way as Flaubert. The great Frenchman did his best to depict things as he saw them, and that is all the word "impressionist," at least in literature, heretofore implied. Joyce has become impressionist in a much more subtle sense. He gives us, especially in "Ulysses," the streaming impressions, often only subconsciously cognate to one another, of our habitual life—that vague, tepid river of consciousness to which only our ephemeral moments of real will or appetite can give coherence. Joyce succeeds in this undertaking to a remarkable degree. The chief fault of this method is its jerkiness, peculiarly inapt to interpret the calm flow of our sensations merging so noiselessly one into another. Some of us feel it a pity that he who could write the strangely sinuous final pages of "The Dead" should now have adopted so different a medium. But there is a time for all things.

The Ireland of this "Dubliners" is a long shot from the land of legend and of poetry; for Joyce, despite his own verses, is persistently occupied with such muddy raptures as in this life we do attain. The creation of which he is author has gold in its teeth and walks not so much on feet as in decayed sport shoes. It is a world of battered derbies and bleared souls, where if there be gallants at all they are of the sort who wait outside areaways for the sovereigns of amorous housemaids. Mr. Joyce exhibits the cynicism of a fine nature habituated but not subdued to the sordidity of our industrial civilization, and his pictures are too acrid not to persuade us of their truth. In the end we come uncomfortably near feeling that human life itself may be insolvent.

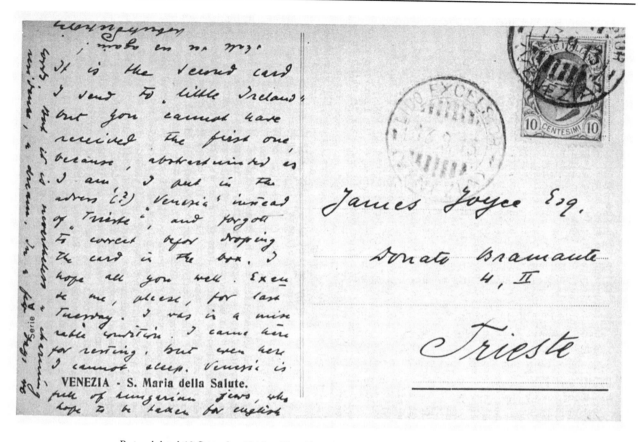

Postcard dated 13 September 1913 to Nora Joyce from Roberto Prezioso in which he refers to her as "little Ireland" (Cornell University Library)

Desmond MacCarthy (1878–1952) was a respected theater critic whose books include The Court Theatre, 1904–7 *(1907),* Drama *(1940), and* Shaw *(1951).*

Review of *Exiles*
Desmond MacCarthy
The New Statesman, 11 (21 September 1918): 492–493

Exiles is a remarkable play. I am more sure of this than of having understood it. I could never undertake to produce it unless the author were at my elbow; and when a critic feels like that about a play which has excited him it means he has not quite understood it. What I can do is to give an account of the play and show where I was puzzled. But first I must come to terms with a misgiving. It is a treat to be puzzled by a play. Perhaps I overrate this one because it has puzzled me? I do not think that is the case, but that possibility is the grain of salt with which what follows must be taken. To be made to wonder and to think about characters in a play is a rare experience—outside the drama of Ibsen. It is a pleasure far excelling the simple pleasure of delighted recognition which is all that the character-drawing in the ordinary respect-worthy play provides. On the stage

temptations to superficiality and exaggeration are so many, and the drama is a form which requires so much condensation of subject-matter and imposes so many limitations that, within those limits, all except duffers and men of genius are, alas! more or less on a level. Once a certain knack is learnt the happy proficient in play-writing finds he can produce a play with an expenditure of a fifth of the intellectual energy and emotion necessary to produce a novel of the same calibre. If he has more to give, it does not show; if he has not, it does not matter, for what he may still be able to produce may be on a par with the work of a far better intellect. Hence it is that there is so much truth in sayings like: "In the art of play-writing construction is everything"; "The idea of a good play should be capable of being written on half a sheet of notepaper," etc., etc. They are certainly true of the common run of respect-worthy plays, but only true of them.

Exiles excited me for the same reason that the plays of Ibsen excite me—the people in it were so interesting. Ibsen's characters have roots which tempt one to pull at them again and again. And they are so deeply embedded in the stuff of experience that tugging at them brings up incidentally every sort of moral, social and psychological question, upon which those who would understand themselves and mankind can go on meditating, feeling that they have still more to learn. The relations of his characters to each other are presented with a sureness and brevity which gives the impression of masterly definition, and yet the complexity and obscurity of intimate relations between living people at intense moments are there too. If one lays a finger on a spinning rainbow top one discovers that the effect has been produced by a few discs of different coloured paper (red, green, yellow, and blue) superimposed upon each other; but while it was spinning that changing iridescence had too many hues to be identified. The rainbow top will pass as an emblem of the manner in which the plays of Ibsen satisfy at once the two prime contemplative pleasures—the exercise of the analytical faculty and delight in watching the movement of life.

I do not take Ibsen's name in vain in connection with the work of Mr. Joyce. It is not (I beg you to believe) that habit so common in critics of chattering about anything but the subject in hand which persuades me to approach *Exiles* through the art of Ibsen. It is extraordinary, but the greatest of modern dramatists has as yet only had a destructive effect on the drama of this country. The plays of Ibsen have destroyed a certain amount of nonsense. Of late years his influence has been countered by the suggestion that he is a writer of problem plays, and "problems," it is explained, have nothing to do with art. Ibsen is supposed to be out of date! Of all the verdicts which are now passed on the writers of the last century, this is the one which maddens me most. That great contemplative mind . . . but here it would indeed be irrelevant to break out about him. The point I wish to make is that constructively Ibsen has had little influence. Most dramatists have not learnt much from his example. I hail Mr. Joyce as one of the few who have grasped the value of two principles in dramatic art of which Ibsen is the master exponent. The first is that on the stage, as in the novel, character (the individual) is the most interesting thing, the ultimate thing; for nothing *happens* at all unless it happens to a particular person, and action is dependent on character. The dramatist therefore must choose characters who illustrate his theme better and better the more he goes into them; so that the deeper he digs the clearer sounds in our ears the running water of his theme. He cannot dig too deep, if he has chosen them well. By what sign is he to know those characters? I do not know. His theme, intellectually stated, is certainly not the right clue. He usually finds them in himself—at least, a shaft which goes down any depth is nearly always, I think, opened from within, though afterwards sympathy and observation may continue the excavation and even control its direction; but that ground is not broken to any

depth except by an author who has an inner life of his own to explore is certain. Now what happens with most dramatists who are blessed with an idea is that they allow their theme to control their interest in character. In other words, either they have chosen characters which only illustrate superficially what they wish to show, or they only attempt to understand them in so far as they illustrate it. If they get really interested in human beings their theme becomes instead of clearer more obscure. I know no better test of a dramatist's imagination than observing if this happens. One of the qualities which delighted me in *Exiles* was that evidently nothing would induce Mr. Joyce to make his characters less complex and interesting than he saw them to be. He would rather obscure his theme than do that, and it is a fault on the right side—on the interesting side. The second respect in which he has learnt from the master is his practice of intensifying our interest in the present by dialogue which implies a past. What a little scrap of people's lives a dramatist can show us—just an hour or two! In life it is usually what has gone before that makes talk between two people significant. If we did not add the days and months and years together our relations would be as empty as those of children without being as delightful. The deduction is obvious; make people talk on the stage as though much had already passed between them. Dramatists are too afraid of mystifying their audience to use that obvious method of enriching their subject; for that there are not many people as quick and clever as themselves is a common delusion among them. Sometimes it may be no delusion; still, I am sure it is not necessary to temper their intelligence to the extent they commonly do. Besides, it is a writer's first point of honour not to write for people stupider than himself: let birds of a feather write for each other.

The merits of this play make it hard to tell its story. Summarised, that story would not distinguish it from many a play in which the love relations of two men and a woman wove the plot. Its distinction lies in the relations of the three points in that familiar triangle being complex and intense. Art is usually so superficial, life so profound. I admire Mr. Joyce for having tried to deepen our conventional simplification of such relations and bring them nearer to nature. Now and then I lost my way in his characters as in a wood, but that did not make me think they were not true; rather the contrary. When I put my finger on his spinning rainbow top, I do not see the coloured rings which produced that iridescence so definitely as in the case of Ibsen. The theme of *Exiles* is not so clear to me. I conjecture that I get nearest to it in saying that the play is a study in the emotional life of an artist. (I am sure, at any rate, that I am giving the reader a useful tip in bidding him keep one eye *always* upon Richard Rowan, whatever else may be interesting him besides.) And when I say that the play is a study in an artist's life, I mean that its theme is the complication which that endowment adds to emotional crises which are common to all men. It makes sincerity more difficult and at the same time more vitally important. Imagination opens the door to a hundred new subtleties and possibilities of action; it brings a man so near the feelings of others that he has never the excuse of blindness, and keeps him at a distance, so that at moments he can hardly believe he cares for anything but his own mind.

When he acts spontaneously, he knows he is acting spontaneously—if not at the moment, the moment after—much as some people, thought modest, have hardly a right to be considered so, because they invariably know when they are. *Exiles* is a play in which two men are struggling to preserve each his own essential integrity in a confusing situation where rules of thumb seem clumsy guides; and between them is a bewildered, passionate woman—generous, angry, tender, and lonely. To understand Bertha one need only remember that she has lived nine years with Richard Rowan in that intimacy of mind and feeling which admits of no disguises, merciful or treacherous; that she has known all the satisfactions and disappointments of such an intimacy. Her nature cries out for things to be simple as they once were for her; but she, too, has eaten of the tree of knowledge and knows that they are not.

If you ask how Richard Rowan and Robert Hand stood towards each other, the answer is they were friends. There was a touch of the disciple in Robert. Richard was the intenser, more creative, and also the more difficult nature. He was an exile in this world; Robert was at home in it. But the essence of their relation was that they were friends, and friends who from youth had made life's voyage of discovery together. One was a journalist, the other an artist; but in experience they were equals. Both had lived intensely enough, and had been intimate enough to reach together that pitch of mutual understanding at which consciousness that each is still at bottom solitary is, in a strange way, the tenderest bond between them. Am I over-subtle? I think what I mean is recognizable. After all, it is in friendships of the second order (Heaven forfend that they should be held cheap!) that men are least troubled about the value of what they give. It is between these two friends that competition for the same woman rises, bringing with it jealousy, suspicion, and making candour—the air in which alone such a friendship as theirs can live—almost impossible. Well, very hard. Both make a mighty effort to preserve it; Richard succeeds best; how far Robert Hand failed is not quite clear to me. At first Richard thought his friend a common vulgar thief; against such a one he would protect Bertha tooth and

nail. But he has misgivings which in different ways torture him more than natural jealousy. Perhaps Robert can give her something he cannot (O, he knows how unsatisfying and yet how much that has been!); something no human being has a right to prevent another having. This is the first thing he must find out. The scene in Act II. between the two men is wonderful in its gradually deepening sincerity. Hand is a coward at first, but he gets over that. Then Richard is tormented by misgivings about himself. Is not there something in him (for ties, however precious, are also chains) which is attracted by the idea that Bertha might now owe most to another—now, at any rate, that their own first love is over? How far is he sincere in leaving her her liberty? Is it his own that he is really thinking of? Bertha taunts him with that. And Bertha's relation to Robert—what is that? I think it is the attraction of peace. To be adored, to be loved in a simpler, more romantic, coarser way, what a rest! Besides, Robert is the sort of man a woman can easily make happy; Richard certainly is not. Yet, just as she decided between them years ago, in the end it is her strange, elusive lover who comes so close and is so far away whom she chooses. But was she Robert's mistress? The dramatist leaves that ambiguous. He does not mean us to bother much one way or another about that. Richard says at the end he will never know what they were to each other; but I do not think he is thinking of Divorce Court facts. He means how completely Bertha still belongs to him. Bertha tells Robert to tell Richard everything; but does he? She also tells him to think of what has passed between them as something like "a dream." That, I think, is the line on which one must fix one's attention to get the focus. Robert is happy; quite content with that. Perhaps because less hot for certainties in life than Richard, he thinks he has enjoyed a solid reality. I do not know.

I have left out much it would be a pleasure to mark. Richard's relation to Beatrice Justice (the other woman in the play)—I could write an article on that; but what I have written will be perhaps enough to persuade you that this is a remarkable play.

—reprinted from *James Joyce: The Critical Heritage*

As little characteristic of Irish family life as it well could be, the muckrake—in the handling of which this author is a past master—being largely relied upon to provide the stage effects.

—*Irish Daily Independent*

Hackett, an associate editor of The New Republic, *speaks to the evocative power and striking candor of the novel.*

Review of *Exiles*
Francis Hackett
The New Republic, 16 (12 October 1918): 318–319

So good are the fine qualities of Exiles that the defects seem to be an illusion, but the more the play is examined the more fundamental and inexplicable seem its defects. It is part of Mr. Joyce's gift that he appears intuitive and occult. It does not seem possible that all his intuition and penetration could go astray. But Exiles neither creates a perfect conviction of being like human experience nor quite recalls experience in terms anything like its own. On the contrary, Mr. Joyce seems definitely to force human beings to do and say unlikely things, and to jumble up the true perspective of their lives. He is exceedingly keen in making people talk like people. He has a genius for idiom and idiosyncrasy and no one could be better than he in the way he dovetails his conversations. His ear is sharp, also, for the click of one personality against another, and for the corroborative phrase. But when it comes to comprehending men and women in their skins and under them, he can hardly be said to be reliable. There is an unreality around certain passages in Exiles that suggests the literary alchemist vaguely striving to transmute pretty theories into honest flesh and blood. The flesh and blood of Exiles, so far as it is honest, does not fit the theories. They are imposed by their author on subjects unwilling and rebellious. The result is a disharmony that almost defies literary analysis. It condemns Exiles to a limbo outside the normal hell and heaven of appraisal.

So far as Richard and Bertha are concerned, the play is clear enough. Bertha is the simple woman who falls desperately in love with Richard, who is a writer, nine years before, and runs off with the "curious bird," regardless of everything else. Richard is the man of pride and scorn who does not deign to explain himself to his dying mother and who allows her to judge him hardly and savagely for his refusal to bind Bertha by marriage. The situation of Richard and Bertha, back in Dublin with their child nine years after the event, only becomes obscure and confusing by the introduction of Bertha's old suitor, the journalist Robert Hand.

In the old days, it is made clear, Robert Hand and Richard Rowan were extremely intimate. They rented a little cottage in the suburbs together, where they had "wild nights long ago—talks by the hour, plans, carouses, revelry. . . . It was not only a house of revelry, it was to be the hearth of a new life. And in that name all [their] sins were committed." In the new days of the play Robert, still intimate with Richard, is carrying on between thirty and forty

the experimental attitude of his youth. And it is with Bertha, the simple woman, that he is now experimenting. Bertha "is a young woman of graceful build. She has dark grey eyes, patient in expression, and soft features." It is this aspect of her that most arrests Robert. Robert loves what is beautiful, and desires what he loves. Under the eyes of his friend Richard, Robert actually woos Bertha, at the same time seeking to secure for the distinguished Richard a professorship in a Dublin university.

The intrusion of Robert into the scene is not in itself confusing. Bertha is somewhat attracted by Robert and her jealousy of a woman who admires Richard induces her to encourage Robert, though she keeps reporting to the mordant Richard every stage of the amour. What is hopelessly confusing is the spiritual seriousness that Richard seems to attach to Robert and Robert's views. At times it seems quite clear that the portrait of Robert is a delighted satire of the middle-aged philanderer. Robert is facile, facetious, hackneyed, uncritical, cheap. But just when one is ready to conclude that this is a most amusing version of the Irish gadfly, Richard begins to address solemn words to him with regard to Bertha. "Have you," says Richard, "have you the luminous certitude that yours is the brain in contact with which she must think and understand and that yours is the body in contact with which her body must feel? Have you this certitude in yourself?" The glib Robert retorts, "Have you?" Instead of an irony, Robert receives a solemn answer. "Once I had it, Robert: a certitude as luminous as that of my own existence—or an illusion as luminous." And then is reported the flippant comment of the journalist. "On the last day (if it ever comes)," he brightly suggests, "when we are all assembled together the Almighty will speak to us like this. . . . He will say to us: Fools! Who told you that you were to give yourselves to one being only? You were made to give yourselves to many freely. I wrote that with My finger on your heart." Yes, and on woman's heart, too. We think too much of bodily union, declares Robert. "We think too much of it because our minds are warped. For us today it is of no more consequence than any other form of contact—than a kiss."

If there were anything in Robert to give depth to his attitude on romantic love, it would be easy to suppose that Mr. Joyce was balancing it against Richard's attitude. But the triviality of Robert with Bertha, his second-hand epigrams, his stale pleasantries, his general imperviousness to "the spirit," make him utterly impossible as a protagonist. The excitement that he creates by making love to Bertha has no genuine significance. If Mr. Joyce had made him less frivolous he might have been supposed to disturb the fine assumptions of Richard's life. As it is he could but rumple their surface, provided Richard had any gravity. But Richard is strangely credulous for a man of insight. He is prepared, if necessary, to give up Bertha. Leaving Bertha to an assignation with Robert in the famous cottage of his own youthful revelries, he writes all night (and thinks) and before dawn goes walking on the strand, "hearing voices." He even "despairs." "I have wounded myself for you," he says to Bertha, "a deep wound of doubt that can never be healed." She protests that nothing happened with Robert during their evening together, she has remained faithful. "I can never know, never in this world," intones Richard. "I do not wish to know or to believe. I do not care. It is not in the darkness of belief that I desire you. But in restless living wondering doubt. To hold you by no bonds, even of love, to be united with you in body and soul in utter nakedness—for this I longed. And now I am tired for a while, Bertha. My wound tires me."

Had Richard possessed humor, his "wound" would not have tired him. He would have disposed of the debonair Robert more easily, or at least seen more readily the folly of discussing with Robert "the death of the spirit." Two such characters, in real life, could not have met in the same sexual plane.

But in spite of this curiously jarring supposition, with all Richard's cold dissection of Robert's kisses and his meticulous desire to release Bertha, there is a strong reality in the woman's love for him and her yearning for him and her jealousy. His desire to be betrayed by her is also intelligible. It is only his interchanges on the subject of love and freedom that seem so unimaginable.

To say "unimaginable" is merely to protest incredulity. Those who can imagine the proud and scornful Richard tolerating the discourse of Robert will take a different view of Exiles. To them it will be much more than an imperfect antithesis of sacred and profane love, much more than a glimpse of the finite munching away at the infinite. It will be a genuine drama with no false intimations, no cross-currents, no theorist frigidity at the core of its being.

What Strindberg might have written had he tried to do so in a year of absolute lucidity . . . *Exiles* pains dreadfully but like fire it sterilises and leaves one healthier . . . He can no more help being startling than he can prevent himself from tackling old problems and finding new answers for them . . . The glittering piercing lines of the play draw it on in a revelry of tense action almost without the aid of stage directions.

—Springfield Union

Colum later wrote an introduction to the 1951 edition of Exiles.

James Joyce as a Dramatist
Padraic Colum
The Nation, 107 (12 October 1918): 430–431

James Joyce's "Portrait of the Artist as a Young Man" is dated "Dublin 1904, Trieste 1914." The action of "Exiles" is indicated as passing in 1912. The play, therefore, succeeds the novel in time. But if "Exiles" be more recent than "Portrait of the Artist," it is far less modern. In the novel James Joyce created a form that was individual and distinctively modern, that suggested new horizons. The play is in Ibsen's form, without the symbolism that haunted Ibsen's plays and without his conclusiveness and his climaxes. Mr. Joyce may return to the drama and bring into it some of the discoveries that make his narrative so startling. Meantime, *Exiles* would make it appear that narrative is his peculiar domain.

The distinction of the play is in the characters presented. Richard Rowan, a writer newly returned to his native Dublin; Bertha, his young wife; and Robert Hand, a journalist, are unusual people. They are Catholic Irish, and two of them, Richard Rowan and Robert Hand, would pass beyond good and evil with words derived from Catholic philosophy on their lips. The play is a triangle, but we forget to name it so because of the oddness of the trio's relation. The characters in the triangle are Richard, Bertha, and Robert. In a way this triangle is duplicated by another, a shadowy one: Richard Rowan, Robert Hand, and Robert's cousin and supposed betrothed, Beatrice Justice. Richard Rowan is a man with a hurt soul. He is deeply in love with Bertha, a girl with whom he eloped some years before, but Bertha is not adequate to the whole of his personality. He corresponds with Beatrice Justice, and his new work is influenced by her. Moreover, he has been unfaithful to Bertha through many casual connections. He knows, too, that Robert Hand, his soul-friend of former days, is making love to Bertha. He will not deny her a particle of freedom, but he is tortured by a doubt as to her faithfulness. The play ends inconclusively–without Richard's having attained that liberation that he has been striving for with such agony. "I am wounded, Bertha," he says to her at the end.

> . . . I have wounded my soul for you–a deep wound of doubt which can never be healed. I can never know– never in this world. I do not wish to know or to believe. I do not care. It is not in the darkness of belief that I desire you. But in restless, living, wounding doubt. To hold you by no bonds even of love, to be united to you in body and soul in utter nakedness–for this I longed.

And now I am tired for a while, Bertha. My wound tires me.

Bertha, with her candid, forgiving nature, may cure Richard of his wound. But in the last scene he has hardly been frank with her. For in the second act he has told Robert Hand:

> Because at the very core of my ignoble heart I longed to be betrayed by you and her–in the dark, in the night, meanly, craftily . . . . She has spoken always of her innocence as I have spoken always of my guilt, humbling myself. . . . From pride and from ignoble longing . . . And from a deeper motive still.

So he accuses himself, and Robert tells him that the Church has lost a theologian in him. But Robert Hand is something of a theologian, too, and he can quote Duns Scotus with effect. Meanwhile, Beatrice Justice has faded out of the play.

Bertha is the first notable woman character that James Joyce has created. She is a subtle character. We get the suggestion that she has had little education, yet she carries herself with real simplicity and dignity. For all her contact with the super-subtle Richard she remains unspoiled, alluring, unconventional, faithful. She has her outbreaks and she knows where to strike at Richard. Her simplicity and her good sense are shown in her last dialogue with Beatrice Justice, the woman who is able to understand her husband's mind and work. When Beatrice says, "Do not let them humble you, Mrs. Rowan," Bertha answers:

> Humble me! I am very proud of myself, if you want to know. What have they ever done for him? I made him a man. What are they all in his life? No more than the dust under his boots. He can despise me too, like the rest of them–now. And you can despise me. But you will never humble me, any of you.

It is in passages such as this that James Joyce shows his power to draw a real and distinctive character.

An absorbing analysis of four human souls . . . A soulsearching work . . . Mr Joyce's insight into human motives is appallingly clear. He is wise–possibly a little too wise.

—New York Sun

The four contributors to this article in The Little Review *did not compare notes or talk over their differences of opinion. The last contributor, "jh," is Janet Heap, one of the editors of the magazine. The January 1919 issue of* The Little Review *included the eighth installment of* Ulysses, *the first part of the Lestrygonians episode, which was confiscated and burned by U.S. postal authorities. By January 1920, two other issues–May 1919 (containing the last part of the Scylla and Charybdis episode) and January 1920 (containing a portion of the Cyclops episode)–were confiscated and burned by the postal authorities. In a 25 February 1920 letter to Harriet Shaw Weaver, Joyce commented: "This is the second time I have had the pleasure of being burned while on earth so that I hope I shall pass through the fires of purgatory as quickly as my patron S. Aloysius" (*Selected Letters, *p. 249).*

Exiles: A Discussion of James Joyce's Plays
The Little Review, 5 (January 1919): 20–27

by John Rodker

Again in this play Mr. Joyce exploits that part of mind merging on the subconscious. The drama is one of will versus instinct, the protagonist Richard Rowan, a writer. This particular psychological triangle is one of barely comprehended instincts, desires for freedom (equally undefined), emotions that hardly crystallise before fading out. Inter-action of thought and will is carried so close to this borderline that the reader fears continually lest he miss any implication. Analysis digs continually deeper. At a certain moment it is lost. Mind will go no further.

People are built on no plan and since it is impossible at any moment to say that either will or instinct is dominant, the author lets the curtain fall finally on the hero's temporary surrender to both.

> RICHARD (*still gazing at her and speaking as if to an absent person*).
> "I have wounded my soul for you – a deep wound of doubt which can never be healed. I can never know, never in this world. I do not wish to know or to believe. I do not care. It is not in the darkness of belief that I desire you. But in restless living wounding doubt. To hold you by no bonds, even of love, to be united with you in body and soul, in utter nakedness–for this I longed. And now I am tired for a while Bertha. My wound tires me.

The play is particularly à propos. Everyone talks of individual freedom,–(Stirner is a name to conjure with, though unread),–identifying it in some obscure way with Women's Suffrage. But the issues are psychological and no spread of popular education will simplify them. In this case Rowan leaves his wife to do as she will. She naturally reviles him for leaving her without the prop of his decisions. After nine years of conjugal life she is unable to make up her mind as to whether she needs a lover. If in the end she does not sin, it is because she uses her virginity as he his profligacy; for pride and humiliation. I have read the play often but without arriving at whether it is an ultimate cowardice or love for her husband that keeps her faithful. To Rowan detail of what has happened does not matter. The atmosphere of their communion would make a more treacherous betrayal than any carnal sideslip. That he can never know.

His anguish at the possible withholding from his wife of any instant of experience which might make her life more full may be interpreted as moral strength or cowardice. Where it is his will demanding Bertha's freedom, he is diffident, but instinct in him speaks fiercely . . . . . "I told you that I wished you not to do anything false and secret against me – against our friendship, against her; not to steal her from me, craftily, secretly, meanly – in the dark, in the night – you, Robert, my friend . . . . ." (*Looks away again; in a lower voice*) "That is what I must tell you too. Because in the very core of my ignoble heart I longed to be betrayed by you and by her – in the dark, in the night – secretly, utterly, craftily. By you my best friend and by her. I longed for that passionately, crazily, ignobly, to be dishonoured for ever in love and in lust, to be . . . . . . To be forever a shameful creature and to build up my soul again out of the ruins of its shame."

The play is very romantic, poetical in a manner rare among plays. It is as fervent as the *Seagull* of Tchekhof. It was no small achievement of Mr. Joyce to have made dramatic such very pure cerebration, and that with a touch so delicate that no most intricate part of the mechanism has suffered by the inquisition. One sees Ibsen ruining such a situation with coarse fingers. Tchekhof got his purity of apprehension from taking people by their instincts. Joyce has done the same thing with a difference. Not that his people have necessarily more brains, but beyond instinct the brain ramifies into obscurer delicacies. The implication of *Exiles* are so numerous – each one subject for minute elucidation – that only with great familiarity would a total impression be possible. Tchekhof's subtleties are plain-sailing, instinctively apparent, so that for stage purposes he is the last word in effectiveness. *Exiles* will have however to become classical – a repertory play, seen often – before any audience can be familiar with it. It is a play which though perfect as literature, might easily lose significance on the stage: it is too full of meat. The most accustomed stomachs only will avoid indigestion.

Nevertheless a production should be full of interest. No manager will, I fancy, care to produce a play without a real suicide, even though it be a "death of the spirit" that drops the curtain; but a small theatre, of which there are many in America and one or two in this country, might easily gain a reputation for intelligence by its production.

by Israel Solon

Let me say at once that I was most painfully disappointed with James Joyce's *Exiles*. My disappointment was so keen because of what he might have achieved and came near achieving but failed to achieve. His merely good is not good enough where the great was so nearly within his reach. With that theme, the author of the *Portrait* and *Ulysses* should have achieved nothing short of the sublime. No poet since Sophocles has had so dramatic a vehicle. Indeed, I think Joyce's the more dramatic.

Sophocles took for his theme the fate of a man incompletely born and who was therefore bound to rejoin his mother. Sophocles held that man strictly to his inheritance. And so vividly did he present his argument that to this day those of us who are doomed to love our own mothers are forced to accept his terrible but valid judgment. We may fling a feeble fist at whatever gods we choose; escape our doom we can not. James Joyce in *Exiles* has taken for his dramatic vehicle the fate of two men who are in love with each other and who are at the same time excessively amenable to all social coercion. Bound by the letter of conventional morality more completely than most men, the disguises winked at by organised society and thereby made available to most men is not available to these two men. They will have nothing they may not have openly. Drawn to each other from within and held back from without, these two men are doomed to keep within sight of each other but beyond the reach of each other. The "eternal triangle" of our conventional comedy is repulsive to these men. Here is matter worthy of the very best that James Joyce has it within him to lend. Why, then, does James Joyce fail to achieve that measure of greatness we have every right to expect of him and the theme he has chosen?

I believe it is because he has failed to make his characters conscious of what fate has in store for them. Had he made these men fully aware of what their lives held for them, the rôles fate meant them to play, and he, furthermore, made them struggle valiantly against it, then if they had won in the end we should have had great comedy, and if they lost we should have had sublime tragedy. Consciousness would have made of them such responsible human beings as would have engaged our sympathies to the utmost; whereas unconsciousness has left them feeble victims blindly wallowing to no purpose. And since it is unthinkable to me that the author of the *Portrait* and *Ulysses* could be lacking in moral courage, I am forced to the conclusion that James Joyce was not himself aware of the matter of his play.

by Samuel A. Tannenbaum, M. D.

Exiles will in all probability prove to be cavaire to the general, not only because it is open to the obvious criticism that it is not true to life, but because its subject- matter is one that unconsciously stirs up the most passionate resistances of a reader unaccustomed to the most honest and deep-searching self-analysis. To the psychologist trained in psychoanalysis, on the contrary, the book will be agreeably welcome as an inspired contribution from the depths of an artist's soul to one of the most tabooed and falsified motives of human conduct, —we mean homosexuality. It is true that the reader unlearned in such matters, and perhaps the author too, may not be aware that this is the theme of the play and may look for it in vain. Of course, this is not all there is to the play: just as in a dream the main motive is overladen and disguised with other subsidiary motives and rationalizations, so is it in the drama before us.

The comparison of *Exiles* with a dream may be carried much further. Every work of fiction is its creator's dream; the more fictitious, the more dream-like, the more apparently absurd and unreal, the truer it is to the hidden forces in the maker's soul and the truer too to the generality of mankind for whose repressed springs of action the poet is the mouthpiece. *Exiles* very often reads like a dream and must be interpreted as such. As such it may be said to derive its motive power from the author's repressed but most urgent impulses, to emanate from the unconscious forces within him and to enable him to gratify in this "harmless" way his unacted and unactable longings. In all this, it need hardly be said, there is not the slightest reproach for or condemnation of the dramatist: every purely fictitious literary work is the self-revelation of a burdened soul that saves itself from a neurosis or from a perversion by the cathartic effect of the creative process.

Richard Rowan's, the protagonist's, homopsychism is never once referred to in the story but is clearly to be deduced from his character and conduct. He has no love for his dead mother and several times refers bitterly to her hardness of heart, at the same time crediting her with having been a remarkable woman; of his "handsome father", on the contrary, he always speaks with great affection. He is utterly incapable of making love to a woman or of loving one unless she is or has been in love with a man to whom he is attached; for this reason he connives at his life-long friend's, Robert Hand's wooing of his wife and urges her, nay, goads her on to be unfaithful to him. The author subtly and delicate leads us to infer that Richard and Bertha are living a life of abstinence ever since his betrayal of her nine years before and that he gives her full freedom only that they might thus be reunited. Speaking to Robert of the moment when he surprised him wooing Bertha, he says: "At that moment I felt our whole life together in the past, and I longed to put my arm around your neck". A little later he says to him: "In the very core of my ignoble heart I longed to be betrayed by you and by her – in the dark, in the night – secretly, meanly craftily. By you, my best friend, and by her. I longed for that passionately and ignobly". Being asked why he did so, he replies: "From pride and from ignoble longing. And from a deeper motive still". From a psychological point of view it is important, too, to note that before Richard's marriage he and Robert had for years shared a house in the country as a rendez-vous for erotic escapades. Of course Richard rationalizes his motives in his unconscious conflict with his latent passion ("I fear that I will reproach myself for having taken all for myself because I would not suffer her to give to another what was hers and not mine to give; because I accepted from her her loyalty and made her life poorer in love"), but even the few sentences we have quoted prove the correctness of our deduction concerning him. Fully to comprehend this splendid portrait of a type of artistic soul that one meets often enough in real life, though exiled, it is necessary not to overlook Richard's intensely masochistic and voyeur impulses. He delights in putting himself in situations that entail a great deal of anguish for him, and he compels his wife to give him the fullest details of his friend's assaults upon her honor. That he can be cruel too on occasion is not at all surprising; by virtue of the law of bi-polarity the masochist is also a sadist.

The portraits of the Wife, the Friend, the Other Woman and even the Child are interesting characterizations that will repay careful study. They are all intensely individualized and unquestionably human though not conventional. Archie, aged eight, is one of the few life-like children to be found in literature and is introduced into the play very effectively – perhaps because in portraying him the author was inspired by Shakespeare's Prince Mamillius to whom the little lad bears a strong resemblance. (Incidentally it may be remarked that *The Winter's Tale* is largely unintelligible if we fail to see the homopsychic conflict in it and do not recognize the erotic relationship between Leontes and Polixenes. Othello's fate too might have been different had it not been for his unconscious love for Cassius.

Many of the minute details of this play, such as Richard's slip of the tongue about his interest in Robert's cottage, Beatrice's forgetting to bring her music, Bertha's sudden attack of fear when Robert speaks to her from the bed-room, etc., prove Mr. Joyce to be a fine psychologist and a keen observer of human nature. But his courage to be true and unconventional, combined with the fact that his chief characters are neurotic, exiles, will we fear doom him to a small but select following.

by j h

I find it difficult to put any of my thoughts on *Exiles* into words. They are not used to words: they die. I feel that Joyce's play has died in words. I do not mean because of the words literally, — all Art is linguistic. But even Art must fail many times before it conquers those things whose nature it is to keep themselves a secret from us forever.

On the surface the play gives itself up to many interpretations. Propagandists declare it is a play on the freedom of the individual. Other reviewers talk of triangles and Ibsen and neurotics. All these things are easy and semi-intelligent things to say. But when it is unanimously agreed that Joyce hasn't "put over his idea clearly" or that he hasn't known just what he was trying to put over, I grow a bit nervous and wonder why it doesn't appear to them that perhaps Joyce couldn't reach their darkness. I also wonder why not read *Exiles* with Joyce in mind. The man who wrote *A Portrait of the Artist* and *Ulysses,* a highly-conscious, over-sensitized artist living at the vortex of modern psychology, would scarcely go back to dealing with material in a pre-Nietzsche manner. Joyce is not Galsworthy; on the other hand he is not D. H. Lawrence. And to discuss courage in connection with Joyce is ridiculous. Joyce outlived courage in some other incarnation.

There are people, a few, always the artist I should say, who inspire such strong love in all who know them that these in turn become inspired by love for one another. The truth of the matter is that such a person is neither loved nor lover but in some way seems to be an incarnation of love, possessing an eternal element and because of it a languor, a brooding, a clairvoyance of life and a disdain. In other people he breeds a longing akin to the longing for immortality. They do not love him: they become him. Richard is one of these.

There is much talk of freedom in the play. Everyone wanting everyone else to be free, it is shown that there is at no time any freedom for anyone. The discussion of the wife's decision when she went away with Richard — unasked by him — proves she has no freedom to make a decision. She may have been in love with Robert, but she had no choice: she was Richard. Robert is in love with Richard, has always been; but he is an unthinking, natural man. He follows nature with his brain and thinks he is in love with Richard's wife, a woman being the conventional symbol for a man's love. But when he has a meeting with her and they are left alone by Richard in perfect freedom they are foiled, they are both Richard, both trying to reach Richard, not each other. Richard's old conflict with his mother (just indicated) was based on her refusal to become him. The wife sees the child going the way of all of them.

There is no where in the world for Richard to turn for love. Sex as other men know it can be for him only a boring, distasteful need of the body. Love strikes back at him from every source. His becomes a Midas tragedy.

He is tormented by the commonplace "beaten path" love-making of Robert and his wife. He asks her infinite questions; he directs the love-making to save his sensibilities. He says to Robert: "Not like this — this is not for people like us." Yet he wishes darkly that they had dishonoured him in a common, sneaking way. Not that he cares for either of them, not that he cares for honour or for conventions, but then he might have been free of them. They would have acted for once without his spirit having been the moving force.

We see Richard wearily contemplating his despair. There is much of the child in Richard. He has a need to create some hold on life, some connection with the experiences of other men. He chooses the least uncomplimentary to himself of those in the play as the symbol through which he can make his connection with love. He sees himself less handicapped intellectually in the music teacher, so he loves love through her. When they taunt him with her he answers "No, not even she would understand." He writes all night endless pages at this image of himself, and in the morning walks on the beach maddened by emptiness and despair. At the last curtain he falls on to a couch, worn and helpless, in need only of a "great sweet mother": but he must be forever on the wheel: his wife kneels beside him babbling of her love.

Statue of William Smith O'Brien, possibly the model for the statue referred to in Exiles *who seems to be asking "How shall I get down?" (photograph by John van Voorhis)*

An American living in Brazil at the time of this review, Scott later published poetry, a play, short stories, and novels, including A Calendar of Sin *(1931) and* Breathe Upon These Slain *(1934).*

A Contemporary of the Future
Evelyn Scott
The Dial, 69 (October 1920): 353–367

STENDHAL, called the first realist, might better have been considered the first naturalist, though either epithet is over exact when applied to this figure of transition. Balzac, generalizing in motives rather than emotions, has most of the vulgarity of the romantic. His deficiencies of temperament alone save him from a grandiose fate. It was Flaubert who, with the consistency of intuition rather than logic, united the incidents of his moods so that they completed themselves in his audience—the true resolution of the creative act.

However, though he sought to translate to us, through suggestive means, the indefinable experience

---

The Statue Not Chosen

In Exiles *Robert Hand encrouages Richard Rowan to accept the "very warm invitation" of the vicechancelor.*

RICHARD

For what hour?

ROBERT

Eight. But. Like yourself, he is free and easy about time. Now, Richard, you must go there. That is all. I feel tonight will be the turningpoint in your life. You will live here and work here and think here and be honoured here—among our people.

RICHARD

[Smiling.] I can almost see two envoys starting for the United States to collect funds for my statue a hundred years hence.

ROBERT

[Agreeably.] Once I made a little epigram about statues. All statues are of two kinds. [He folds his arms across his chest.] The statue which says: How shall I get down? And the other kind [he unfolds his arms and extends his right arm, averting his head] the statue which says: In my time the dunghill was so high.

RICHARD

The second one for me, please.

In James Joyce Exiles, *John MacNichols suggests a parallel between Rowan and O'Brien, who like Parnell was "a protestant and an ardent Irish Nationist, was tried and convicted for treason by British authority, exiled, pardoned, and finally repatriated to Ireland." The statue of Charles Stuart Parnell whose arm is raised shoulder height (see "Early Life and Work:* Chamber Music *and* Dubliners*").*

---

of emotion, an attitude of philosophical skepticism influenced and limited his art, leading him to consider emotion only as the response to an elementary stimulus. Emotion as a quality of feeling forcing itself into expression, though it frequently follows as the direct result of a sensory stimulus, is not nearly always a mere subjective elongation of what the senses register, but is complicated again and again by the conflict of mentally stored impulses. Yet the naturalistic writers treat the brain of the civilized human, with its accumulated complexities, exactly as though it were the brain of a dog or a savage.

In Madame Bovary, for example, there does not result in Emma's mind that accumulation of perception, dim though it may be, which would serve to heighten the tragedy of the book and fortify the author's intention. The mental and emotional experiences of Flaubert's heroine remain apart. Except that her banal ideals are indicated in a general way, she suggests nothing complex to us or to herself. In the exquisite instant of feeling we are aware of the moment, radiant, impalpable, unduplicatable as a rainbow or a cloud. It passes over her futile soul as a reflection over a lake, leaving, contrary to all records of the psychology of even moderately self-aware beings, not even the intellectual residue of itself stored up in her soul to complicate the future with its thinly distilled direction.

Naturalism is sometimes described as the logical obverse of romanticism, but there is a difference. The romantic ideal of beauty and moral perfection was incorporate in romantic art as a soul in a body. Naturalism, on the other hand, took no ultimate shape, and was no more than a theory of limitations. As such it restrained rather than moulded individual expression, developing inhibitions which resulted in a kind of aborted realism.

To Flaubert, as to our modern George Moore, all moments are as one. They reflect their sense impressions with oriental lucidity and quiescence. No psychological interactions are possible in his atmosphere of timelessness. And as there is little conscious response to life in their work, there is little tragedy. Moore writes like a man in a trance. His voluptuous sentences carry us forward indefinitely, and their rhythm is the rhythm of waves in a tideless sea. No confused impulses strike like contrary rays of light on this huge surface. Pathos with its quality of obliviousness gives the character to Moore's writing. In Evelyn Innes, for example, there is no real struggle between the religious and the secular impulse. Emotional nuances, shed like dim rays from a hidden sun, tint the receptive yet negative personality of the heroine, and we acknowledge her the medium for this or that feeling, but it is the emotion living through her and not by her that we apprehend, and, when the emotion passes, the loss we sense is rather our loss than hers.

As the character of feeling displayed by Emma Bovary and Evelyn Innes is that of minds controlled in their operations by no experience of the past or anticipation of the future, it is the type of feeling which psychology has associated with the mentality of the child; and when James Joyce, in his Portrait of the Artist as a Young Man, gives us the early life of Stephen Dedalus in a similar vein we find exquisite appropriateness in the method so used. It is a mind which has not yet developed complexities that responds so simply yet so delicately to the obvious aspects of its surroundings.

Here is the whole pathos of the child's life. Strange yet familiar objects are grouped about the little boy and their newly acquired nomenclature suggests to him relations as yet clouded with the emotional obscurity of the first contact. The relative depth of the emotional values which illuminate Stephen's environment are proven, I should think, in the memory of almost any one's childhood. Thus Irish politics are nebulously conceived and only crystallize in Mrs Riordon's green and maroon backed brushes. The association of phrases from The Litany of the Blessed Virgin with the little girl of the cool hands have just that naïve and remote harmony with their inspiration which is born of feeling rather than thought. The little boy is as much a poet as the author of The Song of Solomon, and in the same manner. To heighten the heart-rending effect of Stephen's simplicity, we are given bits of childish humour often permeated with a grotesque and subconscious sensuality. When Jesus told his followers to become as little children he established in the minds of the narrower ascetics who came after him the convention of innocence as a kind of bomb-proof indestructible blankness of the senses. This misinterpretation, responsible for most of the tragedies of childhood and adolescence, has captured even the vision of art and made it, in this direction, quite generally myopic.

Occasionally some determinedly courageous writer like Miss May Sinclair, who, in her recent study of Mary Olivier, has shown us the evolution of an individuality from childhood to maturity, attempts to assert the irresponsibility of her senses as against what I should call, were I in ignorance of Miss Sinclair's liberal philosophy, her Presbyterian conviction of sin. In perusing Mary Olivier, however, we are never free from an impression that the author is doing her duty by the flesh. She is a conscientious spinster in the confessional and we blush with her, not that her sins are many, but that they are few. Miss Sinclair, it would seem, has an incurably virginal outlook and we dislike being forced to this mistaken emphasis of the weaker incidents of a personality which, on its intellectual side, so entirely commands our respect.

The consciousness of virtue exists to assert a consciousness of sin in the soul which requires a witness for its acts. As an artist Mr Joyce, unlike Miss Sinclair, is able to dispense with the moral audience–even with the self that sits in judgement before it can give absolution.

Stephen's home, family, and early associates pass from us distantly in a procession of fate. Poverty, a meaningless word to the child, becomes concrete in the repeated sight of moving vans, the thumbed and grease-marked pawn tickets, and the meagre disarray of ill-assorted china on a clothless board. It is effectively hinted to the reader by such trivial things as the wondering remark of an elderly aunt and the admiration of the small cousin who looks at the picture of the variety artist as at a lovely being of another life.

It is because Stephen has not catalogued these people that they live for us in his imagination. From his contact with Mr and Mrs Dedalus, Mrs Riordon, Uncle Charles, and Eileen is sprung the first spark of self-awareness. That part of our environment which lives is the part which makes emotional demands on us. When the figures of childhood fade from Stephen's emotional vision, they cease to exist, and the vitality of the father and mother and the priests and boys at Clongowes is transmuted into the vitality of the whore in the mean street.

One's childhood impressions have the significance of an occasion, but it is the impersonal nature of the first stirrings of sex which make the whole world live in the adolescent's spirit. Overpowered by the magnitude of this counter-self, the youth grasps at the defence of an ideal with which to hold his own turgid soul at bay. Clutching the easiest acceptable generality, he describes himself in its terms. So the power of the word gradually eliminates from his consciousness those inconvenient propensities which do not coincide with his definition.

The period of growing pains is the time in which the emotional capacities of the individual have reached their full and have not yet been brought under control of this sub-conscious hypnosis. In the case of the average man with an easy facility for self-deception, lingering uncataloguable traits are, in some manner only to be explained by the subtleties of sophist reasoning, soon made to appear a confirmation of his conception of a simplified self. If the machinery of a theory be logical, only the exceptional person will trouble about the premise on which it is built, and even this extraordinary being, without an ideal of himself would be forced to face a world of unrelated values, a reality of pure emotion, in fact, and so a kind of madness.

Art preserves itself through its conventions, but these conventions justify themselves only when the artist makes use of them paradoxically, so that they are a kind of negation of all they represent. To achieve a practical purpose one defines one's self positively. For the purposes of art there are only negative definitions. So in the manner of his denial, through the order of a sophisticated technique, he may assert that magnificent disorder that preceeds our small perfections.

When Stephen Dedalus casts off the thraldom of the religion which has dominated his childhood, he becomes a man, and probably a great man—certainly an artist—by asserting himself in this negative sense. In the freedom of denial which never belongs fully to any one but the artist, he is able to feel the life about him with exquisite and intimate detachment. For ever apart from him, the clouds, the sea, the young girl with the long white legs like a stork's, are intimate, perfect, and indivisible incidents of his being.

If only Mr Joyce had possessed the artistic courage to end his book with these most intense paragraphs of emotional realization, and had not diffused the effects of a priceless moment in some one hundred pages of brilliant but disintegrating comment! The aesthetic formulas which originate in Stephen's maturing mind articulate so small a part of the reality which is Stephen, a reality which we have not touched curiously from the outside but have entered into.

However, as extraneous as is Mr Joyce's exposition of art to the very effective impressionism of the creation which goes before, he gives us, on the lips of the maturing adolescent, more than one hint, from the critic standpoint, of a tendency which later fulfils itself in Ulysses, the first imaginative attempt at a complete history of consciousness.

Mr Joyce might be described as the only artist who has seen himself through. Even in his volume of poems, Chamber Music—made up of plaintive little Elizabethan numbers of irrelevant perfection—there is discernible that balance between sense and consideration which should characterize the seeker for reality. One imagines it impossible for Mr Joyce to intoxicate himself with the approximate expression; and the clarity of his vision, always so precise, is at the same time quietly and endlessly intense, like a continuous pain.

Mr Joyce is still a young writer, but even in Dubliners, one of his first published volumes, there is in his style an extreme lucidity and composure which give one the impression of fulfilment rather than promise. In this book he broke no new ground, but at least he showed us that the absence of spiritual nuance in most of the prose written in the English tongue was not due to any lack in the potentialities of the language, but was rather the result of a crassness of mentality in the people who used it.

To-day, when this author's technique has developed unique aspects that threaten to indicate a revolution of style for the future, the spirit of his work suggests the culmination of a long and slowly evolving line rather than the ebullition of a fresh impulse. Most of the Dubliners are presented to us statically through a quality of mind comparable only to the poetic quality in emotions. That is to say these are true sketches which escape the suggestion of direction; though occasionally one moves toward an irrevocable climax in the manner of the short story formula.

No man is wholly himself who is wholly aware of himself, and it is only through the delicacy of his method that the most exquisite ironist escapes a taint of complaisance. Mr Joyce, who in this single instance resembles Chekhov, is sometimes ironical, and on these occasions is, one might say, almost imperceptibly obvious. Some of the studies seem a bit opaque, like faithful transparencies which require the gilding of sense to throw them into relief. There is more than one hint of that submerged drama in which half of the human race is still-born–the drama of the incomplete act. The man without imagination is able to act entirely; but our past asserts itself through our refinements and chains us in a sterility of the emotions.

Mr Joyce's mentality is as complex as that of the Russian realist and expresses itself in paradox, so that one suggestion modifies another and subtly evades that polarity in idea in which the simple or romantic emotions have a tendency to concentrate. It is the intelligence which forces us to live alone, however, and the Irish writer's moods, even when most of the earth, are cloistral, so that he echoes himself as from an infinite distance.

In a Portrait of the Artist as a Young Man the material is broad and simple and the author's triumph, as in Dubliners, is in his superior application of a method already half established by precedent. When Mr Joyce set out to write a play, on the contrary, he initially distinguished his effort by his daring selection of a theme which is exquisitely complex. And in presenting his situation he dares to express himself through the medium of a *vis-à-vis* who is on a perfect equality–emotional and intellectual–with his creator. Very few dramatists can resist the advantage which comes through an intellectual simplification of their creatures, for the emotional reactions of a complex mentality are elusive almost beyond dramatization. For the sake of an emphasis which expressed his philosophy of life, Ibsen again and again embodied his dramatic conceptions in small-minded individuals.

Before reading Exiles, Mr Joyce's work, I looked upon Strindberg as the single instance in contemporary and nearly-contemporary drama, of the artist able to include the finest counter-currents of reaction in the general forward motion of the drama, without halting or impeding the culmination of this movement. Strindberg's effects were achieved through the instinct which made him cling to his very limitations–so to hold himself together against the dispersion of his personality in the temperamental winds of madness. Not once was he able to see through to the clear side of self-realization, nor were his characters.

When Mr Joyce drew Richard Rowan, however, he gave us a character highly self-perceptive and ruth-

lessly so, one whose experience of life is complete, each instant born of the senses dying a beautiful and perfect death in the mind. So clearly does Richard Rowan appreciate the value of moments detached from each other, as they must be in realization, that he is no longer capable of what might be termed the lie of action. Action is a simple and entire expression of the individual, and becomes possible only through a temporary obliviousness to complex values. The tendency of a high state of perception is to arrest the motive force which is behind the will.

Action is self-assertion. It gathers into one the forces of unresolved impressions, which then contribute to proclaim the actor. If a man be receptive, and take into himself a thousand moments which he can not express, he gradually becomes a disassociated personality. Overpowered by opportunities for selecting his assertion, he remains in such slavery to truth that he has not the heart to proclaim one reality over another.

When the Bible states that it is more blessed to give than to receive, the prophet might well be poetically announcing the superiority of the actor over the acted upon. But art has an advantage which is beyond philosophical professions, and even religions bound to the definitions of their creeds: it permits one to assert an infinite number of truths without forcing them into logical relationship.

Richard Rowan's is essentially the type of mind which must flee to art to save itself; and when we are told that he is an author, we are given another example of the accuracy of Mr. Joyce's instinct. Just as it seems most plausible that Richard should wield his pen according to his fancy, it is also in the nature of men that Robert Hand, his friend for many years, should have taken to the readier profession of journalism. Robert's inclinations are practical. Action for him is easy and spontaneous. Feeling no prudent obligation to truth, he ends, through all his trickery toward others, in being, of Joyce's group, most true to himself. Mr Joyce juxtaposes Robert Hand and Richard Rowan as the lie which creates and the truth which destroys. Richard's inhibitions first proclaim themselves in his aversion to moral responsibility, the subjective equivalent of action.

Nine years before the play begins Bertha has made an independent decision to cast her lot with Richard. He neither accepts nor refuses her gift of self; but after this time together, with the burden of the child she has borne him, he finds himself irked and intangibly bound to her and, through her unsolicited abandon, made responsible in spite of himself. The object of sacrifice is always a victim, and this is a drama on the motive of self-sacrifice modified by subtleties of sex feeling. Where Ibsen describes the accidental motive that incites to sacrifice and the irony of its particular result,

Joyce shows us what sacrifice is as a gesture of mind before it is translated in the conventions of religious or sexual vanity–the ego's attempt to elude restraint. As such it is the response to a deep but unconsidered psychological need.

Richard, to deny the bond imposed on his will and binding him to Bertha, carnally betrays her again and again, each time, by refusing to lie to her, denying his obligation to preserve their relationship. He gives her the frankest knowledge of what she has suffered through him, and so forces upon her the repeated resolution of their common attitude. Richard has not realized that on the moral plane passivity is as positive as action, and that in this sense there is no such thing as a negative decision.

Again Bertha entraps him by refusing to resent her burdens. The desire for irresponsibility can be entirely gratified only when one is acted upon in a manner against which volition has no defence. Richard encourages Bertha to accept the amorous attentions of Robert. If she accept Robert for her lover, then by her act against Richard she admits his freedom, having injected into their relationship an element over which he has not even potential control. Bertha, in her love affair, clutches the Christian's advantage. She will accept Robert if Richard wills it. Even in this triangular situation she will remain quiescent.

Again we have Richard on the defensive, obliged to initiate. At a crucial point he revolts and his nihilism is so complete that Bertha, without the courage to follow him, finds herself again bearing the burden which he has eschewed. She is bound by necessities inherent in her sex, while Richard, more superfluous in Nature's device, has liberated himself.

Further detaching himself from the circumstances he has evolved, Richard gives to Robert, also, freedom to decide his future with Bertha. Thus the parties to the contemplated liason are stripped even of the comfort of a sense of wrongdoing. Sin, inferring an assertion of some authority over the sinner, is the confirmation of the individual's dependence–and dependence is a relatively irresponsible condition. Richard leaves Robert and Bertha as free as the gods, and so reduces them, for the time being, to his own state of inanition.

With a fatalistic conviction of wrongdoing strong in her soul, Bertha might be imagined as yielding herself abandonedly to Robert's caresses; but shame has been taken away from her. Shame is an emotional resolution. Richard forces Bertha to intellectualize her surrender and so destroys its counterpart in her emotions. Her relation to Robert has, after all, never been more than an attempt to evaluate through another the quality of her devotion to Richard. Indeed, she and Richard have both used Robert to work out the theory of another love.

Richard, when he invited Bertha to betray him, flayed her vanity and forced her to recklessness. In the last act we see her so pained by the consciousness that he has destroyed her moral superiority, that, for the moment, she regards him with a defensive hatred. He, too, in his heart is resenting her docility, for she has yielded to his suggestion that she betray him. His self-love has invented a torture to prove itself through her, and she has failed. The recriminations and counter-recriminations of the two confirm the hopeless authenticity of all special pleading.

The woman's conserving instinct stirs in her an aversion to this fatal dalliance with truth, and she demands of man the lie that will make her whole. To him she looks to justify, by an exaggerated gratitude for what she is, her necessity to live even in the depths of her humiliation. This is what Richard refuses.

Bertha's profound doubt of herself impels her to heighten the obstacles between her and Richard in proportion as she aches to see them demolished. If he overthrows them, he will establish a faith which has the dimensions of her disbelief. Her tragedy becomes sordidly simple when she sees that Richard's yearning for escape is half the cloak of a perplexed desire for a woman as yet uncontaminated by his moral uncertainty–a woman whose virgin will shall force him to a contradiction of himself.

Of incidental defects, this play has a few. The character of Beatrice Justice is utterly without insistence. It is the projection of a passive personality which endures dramatization, but offers no interchange of life to the characters which surround it. The child, too, by very obvious, unindividual tricks of thought and speech, is recognizable as a member of the genus child. There are other things, more or less inconsequential, like Bertha's intimate postures with her son–trivial acts often repeated–which, with their permanent aspect and their ephemeral significance, leave a catch in the throat.

One after another Ibsen's characters, to continue our previous comparison, die or are resurrected to witness a lie of living–a lie toward themselves, made manifest in the falseness of an external relationship. Only in the Wild Duck is fidelity to truth given as the proof of failure. Yet The Wild Duck is illustrative only allegorically. In creating Richard Rowan, Joyce goes a step further and identifies the doubter with his doubt, in a literal psychological sense. The principal character of Exiles reveals to us that, not by his action but by his being, the truth-seeker destroys himself and those whom he would impregnate with his vanity.

Truth is a never-finished revelation. To be always aware of this unending thing, one must preserve a continuous detachment toward one's experience of self. There is the shadow or expression of what one is from moment to moment, and there is one's consciousness of the shadow. The consciousness is the ego. As long as the shadow falls, rejected, before or behind, one may perceive it; but at midday the shadow disappears, and one only feels the light, seeing no longer. The light of midday is the moment of acceptance–the highest moment of being–and all of the elucidation that follows is a lie, since it pretends to reflect an identical image of that vanished instant.

Richard Rowan perceived understanding to be an approximation of the thing understood. In his vanity he preferred to hold himself always apart from the realization that extinguishes the egoistic sense, and his gaze remained fixed on the shadow which assured him that he existed.

Mr Joyce approaches psychology, not as a study of the means through which life comes to us, but as a revelation of life itself, all inhering in the quality of mind. Our socially cultivated imagination revolts from the spectacle of human beings sacrificed to truth, and our sympathies often incline toward Bertha and Robert as the crasser attitude of these two provides Richard with the luxury of absolute integrity of feeling. If Richard had killed himself, we could have forgiven him in the sensation of release, for tragedy provides us with an expulsive channel for the emotions. But Mr Joyce writes a tragi-comedy and allows a tension to accumulate which he does not resolve. His last page leaves us as baffled as the characters themselves, weary even in understanding. In doing so he ignores orthodox requirements of audiences of the drama, but he completes consummately an extraordinary study.

At present his latest work, Ulysses, is available only in the first instalments of the serial form in which it has been brought out simultaneously by The Little Review in this country, and in England by the London Egoist. Just now one may consider no more than the effectiveness of its detail, for the scope of the whole can as yet be no more than a matter of conjecture.

Ulysses is a slice of life in a new sense, a cross section of the mind in action. This action might be diagramatically represented as wave-like, a fluid motion toward articulation which only momentarily achieves itself. The quality of minds intensely heated by feeling is thinly flowing, constantly mounting toward the crest of climax. If the emotional mind be intellectually subtle, it may preserve itself in immanence over long periods, and the final burst of escape in expression be shatteringly explosive. Mr Joyce's very wonderful technical feat in this book is the manner in which he is able to indicate to us the quality and tempo of many distinct streams of consciousness, while preserving the comparative immediacy of his effect.

Of authors who would inundate us in the current of a single being, there have been a few, and among these Miss Dorothy Richardson offers, in her method, the most consummate example. In Interim, which is representative of her usual style of approaching a subject, she holds us as if head downward in the ambiguous jelly of Miriam's mind, which flows over us almost as imperceptibly as a glacier, never reaching a point at which it might crystalize in permanent self-recognition.

The quality of an individual is best recognized by the type of idea in which his emotions culminate. In the purely sensuous soul the undulation of being is voluptuously monotonous, and only dim perceptions light the ebb and flow. But persons who exist entirely on the plane of sensation are infants or senile people, abortive or defective. There are indications that Miss Richardson's heroine is a rounded human and we resent somewhat being forced to regard her existence as if passed for ever under water. She is not once allowed to come up for air. Miss Richardson has admirably achieved the intimate impression; but she wilfully curtails the intellectual processes of her creatures in order to preserve indefinitely for her readers the moment of emotional intensification which preceeds realization.

To behold life for ever as if from the depths of the sea becomes fatiguing. Here the shapes about us are distorted in the swell of waters which bear us onward, waters which we can not see, waters that roar in our ears. And whether we are submerged in the consciousness of one heroine or another we come finally to the moment when we desire escape toward oxygen. Miss Richardson has a colour register of the emotions which she may call by a hundred different names, but it remains always recognizable through its limitations.

Mr Joyce, in Ulysses, preserves all the advantage which inheres in subjective immersion without suffocating us in the closeness of prolonged immediacy. The succession of rapidly dissolving climaxes which occur in the minds of Stephen and Mr Bloom affect us in a very direct manner, while we are at the same time permitted to preserve an exterior and critical consciousness of life. Stephen's subtle psychology allows him an attenuated awareness of self even when his senses are at white heat. Mr Bloom's mind suggests a fluid that is colder and thicker. It congeals readily in recognition of the concrete, and his massive senses are fired to slow intensity only by a fleshly contact. His mental processes are quick and simple, and he preserves, in his outlook on life, a kind of chastity of common sense.

In Stephen's finely strung being there is a continual turmoil, and a swell of confusion which carries the residue from one incomplete crisis to lift the crest of another, where he reaches the peak of an almost insupportably clear vision. For the most part hyper-responsiveness has frayed his sensations thin, so that the jargon of his unleashed thought rarely articulates sensation.

Yet this thinness of sense is only the fatigue of a too precious pain, as we feel through the poignant scene in Episode X, where he encounters his sister surreptitiously fondling the coverless French primer which she has purchased at a second hand booth. Through the mist of his brooding reflections Stephen echoes her poverty- stricken ambition, the counterpart of his aesthetic hunger. In her shamed eyes he reads their common conviction of a hopeless future.

Old Simon Dedalus swaggers again through this book, as crassly alive as he was in the first pages of the Portrait, a man with a happy obliviousness to subtleties which permits him successfully to assert himself over his spiritual betters. He is the type of male who has fostered in women their defensive deviousness–a handsome and benevolent skunk, ingratiatingly proud of its stink.

Through the haze of Stephen's mental suffering we see, looming large and menacing, as shapes in a field on a grey day, the sordid outlines of the Dedalus environment; and a few reflective phrases revive for us the horrid commonplace of Mrs Dedalus's death. Many minor characters in the pages of Ulysses appeared first in Dubliners, and in their reincarnation their lineaments are once more distinct. Mr Joyce's parsimony of method is in a sense the mark of his lavishness, for he uses the stuff of the whole world to prove one man.

In Ulysses there is the touch of a Rabelaisian humour, felt occasionally in the Portrait, but entirely missing from Exiles and Dubliners. It furnishes a base in permanent and simple requirements for the super-structure of refined perceptions; and contradicts the tendency of the sophisticated mind toward a sterile disassociation from essentials. In the literature of an average intelligence is the tradition of a humour which would be flavourless without the conventions, the humour of man's astonishment when Nature intrudes.

Mr Joyce's humour anticipates the conventions. It is the humour of dirt, of Nature herself as she regards man in his fastidiousness. This is the humour of the god and of the child. It does not discriminate in a secondary sense, and is not surprised by a disarrangement of particular conventions, but by the phenomena of convention as a single incongruity. This is expressed in the freshness of Bloom's curiosity as he examines his sensations, and, with an added sharpness, it is in Buck Mulligan's contemplation of himself and his friend. I do not know of any contemporary prose writer of specious gusto whose work shows a hardihood which could sustain it. Certainly the red-blooded *littérateurs* of America would faint with the odour of Mr Joyce's sanity.

After the first several episodes, Ulysses changes *tempo* and takes on a quality of intricacy which can be nei-

ther condemned nor justified until we are presented with the volume entire and are able to gauge the scope of its pretensions. In representing mass-consciousness by cross current impressions of individuals reacting almost simultaneously to a common stimulus, Mr Joyce sometimes arrives at a doubtful effect; but putting aside an end, which at this writing is still beyond us, there remain the means through which the Irish artist is recreating a portion of the English language.

By a compounding of nouns with adjectives and even of adjectives with adverbs–"Eglintoneyes, looked up shybrightly," and so forth–he conveys to us a simultaneous rather than a cumulative impression which has these components. The established conventions of the English tongue have hitherto permitted us to represent only in artificial sequence the composition of a single moment. Mr Joyce is developing a theory of harmonics in language, somewhat equivalent to the harmonics of musical form. By his agglutinative method of printing words we become aware, as in an actual occurrence in which the senses coöperate, of many qualities at once as if they were one, and the result is a reaction that is simple yet full of nuance.

In attributing quotations he also places the adverb of modification before rather than after the name of the person speaking, which is, except in the shock of meeting on a street corner, the true order of recognition. Again convention falsely lays the emphasis of our attention on a recognition of the speaker's identity.

There is no great courage that does not reflect a proportionate fear. The dauntless self-recognition of the great artist is the despairing protest of his egotism. Against the blankness of emotion with which one must regard annihilation, are thrown into relief the sharp details of existence. If James Joyce were not clear-thinking and deliberate in his pessimism, he could not register so exquisitely the delicate ramifications of living.

It is the defect of many a compelling and responsive personality that it intoxicates itself with life until it cannot longer make accurately the great distinction between this world and the next. This is the psychology of the martyr's triumph. James Joyce escapes the intoxication of self through the marvelous fineness of his psychological balance.

The human race accepts slowly its subconscious convictions, which then rise almost imperceptibly to the lips of its great artists and become articulate in their work. James Joyce, to my mind, expresses, more clearly than any other writer of English prose in this time, the conviction of modernity–a new and complex knowledge of self which has passed its period of racial gestation and is ready for birth in art.

Extracts from Press Notices

of

Exiles

by

JAMES JOYCE

(Grant Richards, London: 1918)
(B. W. Huebsch, New York: 1918)

———

Mr Ezra Pound in The Drama: Mr Joyce is the best prosewriter of my generation in English ... His play has inner form ... The characters are drawn with that hardness of outline which we might compare to that of Dürer's painting ... Strong wellwrought sentences flash from the speech and give it dramatic edge such as we have in Ibsen ... Mr Joyce gives his Dublin as Ibsen gave provincial Norway ... Mr Joyce's play is dangerous and unstageable because he is not playing with the subject of adultery but because he is actually driving in the mind upon the agelong problem of the rights of personality.

Mr Clutton Brock in The Times: The mind to suffer ... This work does prove the author's imagination independent of stimulus from self-preoccupation ... It reveals resources of spiritual passion and constructive power which should greatly cheer the friends of his talent ... A situation after Browning's own heart but seen more distinctly, less as a case put ... The second act transcends the machinery and is in outline and effect a poetical creation ... The whole is lifted and throbs like "King Lear" with a capacity for suffering more startling even than the situation in which it is manifested ... The bonestructure and blood of a creation.

Mr Ben Hecht in The Chicago News: The play has a furious unmistakable note in it, a note heightened by the dramatic rather than literary handling of the theme ... He manipulates his characters with a keen regard for human and dramatic values. Nevertheless the play is unconvincing. Here and there it dissipates into mist, its characters disappear hopelessly behind the furious generality which gave them birth. This generality is the sardonic cry of purity and idealism in their inevitable death beneath the leaden feet of life ... Exiles furthers Mr Joyce's claims to consideration as a thorough virileminded artist

Mr Kwan Yang Li in the Shanghai Kuo Min Pao (North China Press): We welcome „Exiles" as a new model of the modern European dramatic literature. It is true no problems are presented there as in Ibsen; nothing is lamented as in Andrieff; nothing is ridiculed as in Shaw; no particularly interesting characters are chosen as in Hauptmann. Like our Chinese dramatists, Mr Joyce is only interested in art and not in problems. He takes any part of the continuum of Life's procession and merely presents it to us in clear and concrete shape

First page of extracts of reviews published to advertise Joyce's only play (Division of Rare and Manuscript Collections, Carl A. Kroch Library, Cornell University [Scholes 1391])

Reassessing *Exiles*

The American drama critic Francis Fergusson examines Joyce's debt to Norwegian playwright Henrik Ibsen.

Exiles and Ibsen's Work
Francis Fergusson
Hound & Horn, 5 (April–June 1932): 345–353

In *A Portrait of the Artist as a Young Man* we read of Stephen that 'as he went by Baird's stonecutting works in Talbot Place the spirit of Ibsen would blow through him like a keen wind, a spirit of wayward boyish beauty.' This spirit blows through *Exiles* with a super-Ibsen keenness over a colder-than-Ibsen structure of cut stone. Professor Rubek, in *When We Dead Awaken,* asks Irene with weariness and bewilderment, 'Do you remember what you answered when I asked if you would go with me out into the wide world?'

Irene

I held up three fingers in the air and swore that I would go with you to the world's end and to the end of life. And that I would serve you in all things—
Professor Rubek

As the model for my art—
Irene

—In frank, utter nakedness—

But there is no such bewilderment in *Exiles,* and in the last scene Richard can tell Bertha, 'It is not in the darkness of belief that I desire you. But in restless, wounded, living doubt. To hold you by no bonds, even in love, to be united with you in body and soul in utter nakedness—for this I longed.' It is like the analogy between Stephen Dedalus on one side, a bird-man, unique, soaring straight toward the Sun, and on the other, Brand with his gloomy aspiration, and Peer Gynt with his irresponsible histrionics. In each case we gulp, we gape, we are astounded as though by a superb stunt. This 'stunt,' both in *Exiles* and in the Ibsen plays, is a feat of the author's mind, a presentation of new and startling simplifications. All drama depends on some sort of simplification. But, Sophocles and Shakespeare offer us theirs as distillments of common traditional human wisdom, and though their insights may be ever new, the newness, and the author's discovery of it, is never the point. In Ibsen and *Exiles* the newness *is* the point, and in *Exiles* the point is the finality also. . . . Joyce, faced with this problem [of presenting characters who debate, self-consciously, their rights and wrongs], manages differently. His characters all come clear in the mere presence of the compelling and inquisitorial Richard. He makes their halting apologias more credible, as he makes them more complete, once you grant him Richard, in the light of whose mind and under the influence of whose strenuous ethic everything is presented. . . . And the characters meet, if at all, on the basis of the barest facts of the inescapable human relations, those of parent to child and of man to woman. There is the lamp of the spirit with a vengeance, but with its flame not 'practically exposed,' but as near to 'utterly naked' as Rowan-Joyce can make it. Richard Rowan will not have it that the world and the flesh can make him a whit different from what he chooses to be. And the mind of this Rowan-Joyce being is far less provincial than James's own.

This is as much as to say that *Exiles* is by no means to be thought of as an Ibsen type of play in the sense in which Strindberg's, for instance, or Andreyev's or some of O'Neill's plays belong in that category. These writers have run the Ibsen prophetic or didactic tradition up several blind alleys, where it is expiring loudly but without vision, force or dignity. Ibsen had no Ibsen to study; and his followers, taking the direction he marked out, have failed to profit by his example. But the author of *Exiles* has precisely profited by Ibsen's example, taking what he needed of Ibsen's technique to state once and for all what is inescapable in Ibsen's story or theme. He finishes off the modern intellectual drama, the drama of 'individualism,' the drama which attempts to dispense with tradition. Yet at the same time he attains a static perfection of vision which carries him quite beyond that genre, and even amounts to destroying it. This may be shown in a number of ways.

Take, for instance, the perfection of Mr. Joyce's portraits in *Exiles* . . . Lacking a traditional theme like those of the Greeks or Elizabethans, Ibsen's actions remain like umbilical cords which he could never cut. But Mr. Joyce substitutes for action a motionless picture, and for a thesis a metaphysical vision of a kind of godless monadology or Pluralistic Universe, of a consistency and strictness which William James the liberal never dreamed of. So it serves the consistency of his vision to bring out all the qualities of his people which make them what they are 'and not another thing'; which distinguish them, above all, from Rowan-Joyce. Ibsen was interested in what people *do,* and in the effort to show their actions as significant sometimes seems to do violence to what they *are.* If Mr. Joyce falsifies his people, it is in the opposite way. However much he may sympathize with them, he *sees* them, much more than he invents them out of his own inner life–sees them as hopeless, 'looks and passes,' like Dante touring Hell; and cut them off, with the most sober and delicate exactitude, in their actual frivolity and darkness.

An analysis of this kind might be pursued indefinitely, as though along a thousand centripetal spirals leading ever more subtly up to the unity of the work. It leads beyond the play *as play,* as soon as we see that there is no action here as other dramas have taught us to understand action. A hasty reading of the play might lead one to believe that the action was Robert's unsuccessful attempt to seduce Richard's wife. Another reading will show that this is only part of a larger whole . . .

In the last speech of the play, a speech of extreme beauty, wherein a Joycean character comes very near the Ibsen trick of speaking with the author's voice, Bertha places Rowan-Joyce himself among the exiles: 'Forget me, Dick', she says. 'Forget me and love me again as you did the first time.' Which we see—if we remember that all is shown in the light of Richard's mind—as making the exile-vision absolute, removing it from the relativity or meaningfulness of action. For action is the *lingua franca* on which drama as an art among other arts depends; it is the common guide-line for actors and audience, and it gives the meaning of the play in terms of something outside itself. It is meaning in this sense which Mr. Joyce has been at great pains to eliminate.

Exiles is thus a 'drama to end dramas.' And it invokes to this end the authority of life 'caught in the fact'—an ultimate fact, we are supposed to feel, not the mere real circumstances, which is what Henry James had in mind when he applied this phrase to Ibsen . . . Mr. Joyce has been concerned to save the truth and authority of his image by removing every trace of radiance as symbolism, which amounts to predication, to meaning in relation to other images, whereby *Exiles* would take its place, as a play, not a metaphysical vision, in due relation to other images. Hence that unique glare, as of a spot of brilliant light in surrounding blackness, before which we are supposed to come to rest 'in the silent stasis of esthetic pleasure.'

If the authority of the exile-vision stops you 'cold,' you must come to rest indeed—like Beatrice, perhaps, 'with pride and scorn in your heart,' but like her caught in the fascination of what it claims as intelligibility in terms of itself. If not, you must explain it in terms of Rowan-Joyce as a human being. Nowhere outside *Exiles* will you find human isolation so finely rendered—that obstinate incommensurability of human longings which seems to be the cold little wisdom special to our time—both in its bracing fear and exaltation, and in its pity. Yet even while you mourn and thrill you may begin to feel, as in Ibsen, that the case is too special to be satisfying, and the simplification, however brilliant, somehow arbitrary. This is my experience. The 'silent stasis of esthetic pleasure' gives place, for me, at a certain point, to an obsessive circling of the mind around a fixed, compelling thought, which is the Stephen-Rowan-Joyce thought of himself. It is this being which is both the shadow and the idea

of *Exiles,* if we ask it to have a meaning, and it is this being we must question. This may only be done with the help of Mr. Joyce's other works.

The Joycean cycle will doubtless not be understandable till long after it is completed. But it may already help us to make the Richard-Stephen character conceivable. Surely the barren askesis of his life, as we are shown it in *Exiles,* is intolerable?—But *Exiles* shows us only the ethical side of that character, and only a moment in his relation to the other personages. Richard is evidently the continuation of Stephen; Robert seems to be another incarnation of Mulligan. Richard is also in some ways intermediate between the Stephen and the Bloom of *Ulysses.* Most important of all, the other works, which are more directly concerned with his consciousness, show us the perceptions he lives by and for fragments of beauty which are for him equivalents neither of the Dantesque *Esser beato nell' atto che vede* nor of Aristotelian contemplation.

With the aid of the larger Joycean testimony, too, we can get a more exact conception of the relation between *Exiles* and Ibsen . . . The work of Ibsen may speak to our need for a faith even if it leads nowhere, but *Exiles,* rightly understood, appeals only to the eye of the mind. It is a point in the heroic but necessarily unique living out of a 'heresy'; it is like a new geometry, based on the denial of a Euclidean axiom, and worked out, to the enrichment of mathematics, in accordance with mathematical laws.

Meanwhile there remains one's delight in *Exiles* as the most terrible and beautiful of modern plays. This delight, like one's admiration for the Joycean sanity and common sense, is the mark of a certain stage in the understanding of it; but in the same way it has its truth, it is there to return to, and it is to be preserved with the utmost care as a part of the experience of Mr. Joyce's work which consents to take its place alongside other experiences.

In the following discussion of Exiles, *Bandler analyzes Joyce's theme of exile as having its basis in a spurious understanding of the relation between the body and the soul.*

Joyce's *Exiles*
Bernard Bandler II
Hound & Horn, 6 (January–March 1933): 266–285

The note of exile recurs frequently in our age. It is the one constant among the voices which have most engaged contemporary attention in literature, dissimilar as those voices otherwise are as in Proust, Eliot, and Joyce. Yet the note is not new: it has been sounded in the occident from the time of the Orphic mysteries and the Pythagorean order and magnificently by the youthful Plato. Similar circumstances everywhere prompt it. When the conditions of life are difficult, treacherous, and unstable, the soul of man repudiates its natural relation to the body and seeks its true home elsewhere. In some way or other it seeks to detach itself from the foreign and inimical substance in which it finds itself mysteriously entangled and aspires to a better and more spiritual life. Its true life, it declares, is not realized through the gross material body which at best must be patronized, indulged, chastised, and bullied, but through a discipline and purification which will restore it to its native element. But not since the decline of Rome and the rise of Christianity has the note of exile been so general and emphatic, vague and desperate. Exile has ceased to be exceptional, a voice crying in the wilderness, and has become typical. Human isolation is taken for granted.

The attempts to escape from exile and to attain some sufficiency are various and bewildering. The sands of history are heaped with motley ideals; every person ranging through the past can pick up some discarded shell and make his life therein, or else adopt some form that is not yet wholly abandoned. Throughout there is uncertainty as to the character of each special exile. Is it the exile from some particular period in the past that one seeks to restore; or from some qualities of personality, feeling, and action that are neglected by recent generations; or from some institutions which sheltered these qualities? However diverse the expressions of exile seem to be, there is, I believe, one element common to them all. That element is the refusal to be a man before all else, and the substitution of other ideals in place of the human one. The desire to be an artist, mystic, angel, or God instead of a man often produces works of extraordinary beauty; but these desires are usually based on the denial of the true nature of man; they are distorted; and their ultimate fruit is exile.

A familiar solution to the problem of exile is not that the nature of man has been misrepresented but that God has been forgotten. Reintroduce the idea of God and faith in Him, one hears said, and the maladies of our age will depart. No solution could be more irrelevant. Man is exiled from man and that exile is not caused by disbelief in God. The ground of exile is always, I believe, a false interpretation of the relation between the body and the soul; an ignoring of the function of the body and hence an erroneous analysis of the soul; and as a result of this untrue conception of man an incomplete and often destructive ideal is striven for. This thesis cannot be demonstrated apart from multiple examples, but an analysis of *Exiles* by James Joyce,

where the problem is most clearly stated, will illustrate my argument.

What first strikes one upon consideration of *Exiles* is the irrelevance of God. There is simply no need for Him. The characters' exile and sorrow is the human one of incompatible desires and unrealized hopes, a sorrow suffered in a universe with God in all times as well as in a universe without Him. Their longing is not for God and their exile is not from Him. In such a world the only function left to God would be to render people's longings commensurate and satisfied, and to give them all complete happiness. But Joyce makes no such demands: he dispenses with God as the end and provider of human happiness. The picture which Joyce presents would not be materially affected by the addition of the various gods imagined or conceived by Jews, Greeks, and Christians; the existence of these gods, their attempted grace, even their omnipotence would not alter Joyce's vision of man. For Joyce's people are not only magnificently done, beautifully realized individuals of certain human types, but their dilemma is presented as true of all people, and hence inescapable. Exile as Joyce sees it, is necessarily our lot; it is the result of no accident, nor weakness, nor sin in human nature, the consequence of a fall from a Paradise to which a beneficent providence could restore us. Exile follows from the necessity of human nature itself, the incommensurability of our desires and goods, each man like the angels of St. Thomas being a separate species. Since each man's essence or soul tends to a unique and incommensurable perfection there is no parity of human goods and not even God could redeem us from exile. To save man, to harmonize one man's desires with his neighbor's, would be to destroy man as Joyce sees him: grace can but gives us the strength and fortitude to bear our exile. When Richard Rowen appeals for help, it is not the light of self-knowledge that he seeks, or the knowledge of others, for their goods or salvation, being intrinsically different from his, are unknowable: Richard seeks the strength to be immovably and unchangeably himself

"O, if you knew how I am suffering at this moment! For your case, too. But suffering most of all for my own (*with bitter force*) and how I pray that I may be granted again my dead mother's hardness of heart! For some help, within me or without, I must find and find it I will".

If *Exiles* were presented in its relative truth, as a play that distilled the sorrow of human isolation, the office of the critic would be limited to understanding and enjoyment. But *Exiles* goes further; the vision claims to be universal and as final and as irrevocable as the Last Judgment. From such a sentence there is no appeal; mercy has no lien on truth; and *Exiles* is held up as the Medusa head of truth. Hence it is the truth itself of *Exiles* that one must question, its absolute truth about human destiny. Why are Beatrice and Bertha, Robert and Richard, exiles? From what are they exiled? The formal statement that they have incommensurable goods can be answered by an equally formal dialectic. Since they are human and have bodies, senses, appetites, and reason, in a common world, their generic human identity would imply fundamentally similar goods. Individual differences would permit them to realize these goods in different ways and in different mediums, weakness and the failure of fortune might prevent their realization altogether, but the essence of man, as societies and communities achieved in the past witness, is social. Exile, like pain and all other evils, is interwoven with our human lot, but apart from the goods of which it is a privation, it is meaningless. But such a dialectic is general. Looked at individually and concretely, are each of the characters exiled for the same reason, necessarily, beyond redemption, because of the inmost demands of their nature, or is their exile accidental, arbitrary, and imposed from without? Would these characters naturally and under all conditions revolve in their hard isolation, would they fail of happiness because happiness is no real possibility for man, or are they thus solitary because they have gravitated into the orbit of an intense and powerful personality which then forsook them? If exile is imposed by the lure of a superior personality, what is the nature of that personality, what is his idea of himself and of others, and his demands from life? Does he regard himself as a rational animal, or a fallen angel, or a strange and untrammelled spirit? Is his exile less from mother and wife, friends, Ireland, and the Catholic Church, from their understanding, compassion, and love, as he would have us believe, than from the goods and limitations of human nature itself, society, and every form of order? Is the exile of Richard Rowen so hopeless and terrifying because he is in revolt against the conditions of life itself?

Certainly the exiles of Beatrice, Robert Hand and Bertha, while desperate and inevitable for them, are arbitrary. They are exiles because of their absorption in Richard, an absorption as involuntary as the moths in the flame. Once attracted by his luminous power, and consumed by his mind, they are indifferently cast forth, to wait until such time as his curiosity and art require them. Beatrice at the beginning of the play comes regularly to the Rowen house, ostensibly to give Archie piano lessons. She had been engaged to Robert, but after Richard's departure from Ireland, Robert seemed to change. After a year Richard wrote her, he sent her

chapters of his novel, and for eight years continued to write her. Since his return from Italy, a return never fully explained, he is working on a new book for which he uses Beatrice as material. In the first scene between them he explains the power that holds Beatrice's gaze, nine years before.

> RICHARD: (with some vehemence) Then that I expressed in those chapters and letters, and in my character and life as well, something in your soul which you could not—pride or scorn?
>
> BEATRICE: Could not?
>
> RICHARD: (leans toward her) Could not because you dared not. Is that why?
>
> BEATRICE: (bends her head) Yes.
>
> RICHARD: On account of others or for want of courage—which?
>
> BEATRICE: (softly) Courage.
>
> RICHARD: (slowly) And so you have followed me with pride and scorn also in you heart?
>
> BEATRICE: And loneliness.

In this first scene Richard accuses Beatrice of being unable to give herself freely and wholly. But what does Richard want from her, and what in return is he willing to give? Richard wanted her to follow him as did Bertha, and he resented her love for Robert and sulked for a year in silence. If Beatrice had followed him she would have enjoyed the beatitude similar to that extended by God to His saints, the beatitude of watching Richard be himself. Beatrice has not the courage to embrace such a fearsome privilege. For this reason together with her protestant reluctance to give, a quality she shares with Lady Chaterley's sister, Beatrice is in exile. The tragedy flows from a fault in her character, a defect true for her and many others, but nevertheless a defect, and not a quality necessarily inherent in human nature. Even this unyielding, cold, barren soul which could not part with its virginity to God, might in time have responded to the pagan warmth of Robert. Only when the brighter star of Richard, by its sheer intensity, pulled her away without map and compass, was she irrevocably damned to exile.

Beatrice's exile one feels is for life and without remedy, for no one will replace Richard in her mind's heart. Less hopeless, more like the purgatory of defeated desire than an everlasting sentence is Robert's exile. At the close of the play he leaves for a fortnight's visit to his cousin. The visit is a retreat, a chance to rest and heal his wounds, and when he returns to Dublin that particular exile will be over. He will necessarily suffer other disappointments, as fugitive as his ecstacies, but only death can exile him completely. For Robert is a pagan and a lover of life, a romantic pagan who narrows living to the lyrical immediacy of the moment. It is no accident of Robert's nature that while he awaits Bertha he is playing the first bars of Wolfram's song in the last act of *Tannhäuser,* nor is it an accident that after kissing Bertha he sighs

ROBERT: (sighs) My life is finished–over.

BERTHA: O don't speak like that now, Robert.

ROBERT: Over, over. I want to end it and have done with it.

BERTHA: (Concerned but lightly) You silly fellow!

ROBERT: (Presses her to him) To end it all–death. To fall from a great high cliff, down, right down into the sea.

BERTHA: Please, Robert. . . .

ROBERT: Listening to music and in the arms of the woman I love–the sea, music and death.

He cannot feel otherwise. As he says to Richard in the language Richard used in his youth "There was an eternity before we were born and another will come after we are dead. The blinding instant alone . . . passion, free, unashamed, irresistible, that is the only gate through which we can escape from the misery of what slaves call life."

But there is another side to Robert besides the pagan and the romantic, and that is the sentimental. He hopes and believes that passion will give not only life but eternal life. He refuses to accept mutability, and to learn from experience. Hence there is something ludicrous and pathetic in his passion. Like the roses he gives to Bertha it is overblown.

RICHARD: And that other law of nature, as you call it: change. How will it be when you turn against her and against me; when her beauty, or what seems so to you now, wearies you and my affection for you seems false and odious?

ROBERT: That will never be. Never.

One can easily see the attraction Richard exercises on Robert. It is the hold of master on disciple. In the past Richard professed and practiced the ideals

Robert now partially follows. Richard sought a new life, free from human laws and bonds, free from deceit and falsehood. Rather than compromise, Richard went into exile. His ideals, his genius, and his mode of life all proved him different from other men. Robert is even drawn to Bertha partly because she is Richard's work.

ROBERT: (With animation) You have that fierce indignation which lacerated the heart of Swift. You have fallen from a higher world, Richard, and you are filled with fierce indignation, when you find that life is cowardly and ignoble. While I . . . shall I tell you?

RICHARD: By all means.

ROBERT: (Archly) I have come up from a lower world and I am filled with astonishment when I find that people have any redeeming virtue at all.

The disciple never loses faith in his master's intellect. At the end of the play Robert can say to Bertha "Richard is always right." But Robert not only sees Richard, he finally sees through him. When Robert appeals to Richard for help he is refused. Richard will not free him to fight the spectre of friendship. Robert must free himself. Nor will Richard commit himself about Bertha's good. To Robert's request that he keep Bertha and forgive him, Richard replies "I will not live on your generosity. You have asked her to meet you here tonight and alone. Solve the question between you." Robert knows that Richard has left him in his hour of need. Hence in the future he will not place his hopes in Richard as Beatrice does, repeatedly to be disappointed. He is not predestined to exile by a life accessible to him alone, nor does he seek some supernatural good in which he no longer believes. His exile is the one his God, nature, imposes on the body when it contains a wayward, sentimental, and unripened heart.

More desperate and heartbreaking is Bertha's exile. It is simpler than Robert's because more natural and easier to remedy, more hopeless than Beatrice's because of its entire dependence on Richard. There is no need to analyze Bertha in order to understand her suffering. She gave up everything for Richard, "religion, family, and my own peace," yet finds herself in exile from him. "You are a stranger to me. You do not understand anything in me–not one thing in my heart or soul. A stranger! I am living with a stranger!" And with her last agonized cry the play closes. "Forget me Dick. Forget me and love me again as you did the first time. I want my lover. To meet him, to go to him, to give myself to him. You, Dick, O, my strange wild lover, come back to me again."

There is nothing to show that Bertha has changed from the day she accompanied Richard in exile. She followed him then voluntarily and by her own proposal. Why did you choose him—asks Robert.—Is that not love? she replies. She never pretended to understand or to enter into Richard's ideas: she had no interest in the complete liberty he allowed her; she did not understand nor want it; nor did it make her happy. The books he wrote were beyond her. Her jealousy of Beatrice, her belief that Richard allowed her liberty in order that he might love Beatrice could have arisen as easily before they left Ireland as after their return. She gave Richard her love and asked to be loved as he once had loved her, in return. As she drifted with Robert she appealed to Richard for help which he denied her.

> BERTHA: (almost passionately) Why do you not defend me then against him? Why do you go away from me now without a word? Dick, my God, tell me what you wish me to do?

> RICHARD: I cannot, dear. (Struggling with himself) Your own heart will tell you. (He seizes both her hands) I have a wild delight in my soul, Bertha, as I look at you. I see you as you are yourself. That I came first in your life or before him then—that may be nothing to you. You may be his more than mine.

> BERTHA: I am not. Only I feel for him, too.

> RICHARD: And I do too. You may be his and mine. I will trust you, Bertha, and him too. I must. I cannot hate him since his arms have been around you. You have drawn us near together. There is something wiser than wisdom in your heart. Who am I that I should call myself master of your heart or of any woman's? Bertha, love him, be his, give yourself to him if you desire—or if you can.

Bertha's exile is Penelope's. While she sorrowfully awaits her Ulysses she feels that the time of love "comes only once in a lifetime. The rest of life is good for nothing except to remember that time."

In an artist so conscious as Joyce each character has his full significance. Neither old Brigid nor Archie at eight are exiles. Their roles are secondary and aesthetic, to inform us of the natures and motives of the other characters. Brigid figures seriously only in the opening scene of the third act. She there appears as the mother substitute: even when Richard's mother lived he confided to Brigid his love for Bertha, talked of her letters and discussed his plans. Brigid's weight in the play rests on her material assurance to Bertha that "there's good times coming still." Archie plays a more important part. To Brigid he is master Richard's son; to Beatrice he is an excuse for coming to see Richard; to Bertha he is son and symbol of Richard's love; and to Robert he is lusty, buoyant, hopeful youth. Archie scrambles through windows, crawls out of piano lessons, and arranges to drive early mornings with the milkman.

> ARCHIE: Open the window, please, will you?

> ROBERT: Perhaps, there, Richard, is the freedom we seek—you in one way, I in another. In him and not in us. Perhaps . . .

> RICHARD: Perhaps . . . ?

> ROBERT: I said *perhaps.* I would say almost surely if.

> RICHARD: If what?

> ROBERT: (with a faint smile) If he were mine.

Richard's feeling for Archie is ambiguous. He takes pride in him as a son, but is this son child or angel. Richard is uncertain and one sees him hesitant, fearful to correct a higher, wiser spirit, watching with curiosity and in indulgence. To Bertha is left the responsibility of Archie's discipline.

> BERTHA: Whenever I tried to correct him for the least thing you went on with your folly, speaking to him as if he were a grownup man. Ruining the poor child, or trying to. Then of course, I was the cruel mother and only you loved him. (With growing excitement) But you did not turn him against me—against his own mother. Because why? Because the child has too much nature in him.

> RICHARD: I never tried to do such a thing, Bertha. You know I cannot be severe with a child.

> BERTHA: Because you never loved your own mother. A mother is always a mother, no matter what. I never heard of any human being that did not love the mother that brought him into the world, except you.

> RICHARD: (Approaching her quietly) Bertha, do not say things you will be sorry for. Are you not glad my son is fond of me?

> BERTHA: Who taught him to be? Who taught him to run to meet you? Who told him you would bring him home toys when you were out on your rambles in the rain, forgetting all about him—and me? I did. I taught him to love you.

Who then is this being Richard about whom the destinies of Bertha and Beatrice and Robert revolve? Without him their lives and personalities would have been different, they affect each other only as they are acted on by Richard. Like so many iron filings they are forced into a pattern of exile by the magnet of a single energizing personality. No formula can simplify Richard to a few elements: he has portrayed himself, like Rousseau, in all his strength and weaknesses. So complex is this man, so lucid and subtle and consistent is his mind, that we can hardly distinguish at first pride from humility. Judgment waivers between the exile of the Mount of Olives drinking in solitude and pain his cup of suffering, and the rebel exile cast from the hosts of heaven. "There is a faith still stranger than the faith of the disciple in his master", Richard says to Robert, . . . "And that is?–"–"The faith of a master in the disciple who will betray him".

The betrayal is attempted, the master is deserted.

RICHARD: Before dawn I went out and walked the strand from end to end.

ROBERT: (Shaking his head) Suffering. Torturing yourself.

RICHARD: Hearing voices about me. The voices of those who say they love me.

ROBERT: And what did they tell you?

RICHARD: They told me to despair.

Yet forseeing his fate, what counsels and examples of perfection does Richard not give so that one almost hears again: "he who seeks his life shall lose it, and he who loses his life for my sake shall find it."

RICHARD: Do you understand what it is to give a thing?

ARCHIE: To give? Yes.

RICHARD: While you have a thing it can be taken from you.

ARCHIE: By robbers? No?

RICHARD: But when you give it, you have given it. No robber can take it from you. It is yours then for ever when you have given it. It will be yours always. That is to give.

I say, one *almost* hears again for we have yet to see for whose sake Richard loses his life. Certainly, at first sight, it seems that Richard loses his life for the sake of those he loves. To love Bertha, to Richard, means "to wish her well". His only fear is that he will deprive her of one instant of the good that should be hers.

RICHARD: But that I will reproach myself then for having taken all for myself because I would not suffer her to give to another what was hers and not mine to give, because I accepted from her her loyalty and made her life poorer in love. That is my fear. That I stand between her and any moments of life that should be hers, between her and you, between her and anyone, between her and anything. I will not do it. I cannot and I will not. I dare not.

Hence Richard's indecision and inability to give help to Robert and Bertha. He does not know what is their good, and in default of knowledge cannot act.

RICHARD: Have you the luminous certitude that yours is the brain in contact with which she must think and understand and that yours is the body in contact with which her body must feel? Have you this certitude in yourself?

ROBERT: Have you?

RICHARD: (Moved) Once I had it, Robert: a certitude as luminous as that of my own existence–or an illusion as luminous.

ROBERT: (Cautiously) And now?

RICHARD: If you had it and I could feel that you had it–even now . . .

ROBERT: What would you do?

RICHARD: (Quietly) Go away. You, and not I, would be necessary to her. Alone as I was before I met her.

But is it really the humility of ignorance and the desire for Bertha's happiness that determines Richard? Is his the abasement that resigns itself to another's will and his the love that relieves and enlightens? Does he want those who are weary and heavy laden to come unto him? Or are his humility and love, sincere as they are but the semblance of humility and love, counterfeit virtues necessary to Richard in the consistency of his life? A passage in the *Portrait of an Artist As a Young Man* shows clearly the nature of his love.

"–Brother Hickey

Brother Quaid

Brother MacArdle

Brother Keogh.–

Their piety would be like their names, like their faces, like their clothes; and it was idle for him to tell himself that their humble and contrite hearts, it might be, paid a far richer tribute of devotion than his had ever been, a gift tenfold more acceptable than his elaborate adoration. It was idle for him to move himself to be generous towards them, to tell himself that if he ever came to their gates, stripped of his pride, beaten and in beggar's weeds, that they would be generous towards him, loving him as themselves. Idle and embittering, finally, to argue, against his own dispassionate certitude, that the commandment of love bade us not to love our neighbors as ourselves with the same amount and intensity of love but to love him as ourselves with the same kind of love."

Richard is no charlatan, he is without deceit and hypocrisy, and is moral in the sense that what he wants for himself he wants for others. He has conceived a new life. Since his youth, when he and Robert lived together, he has followed it, sought to give it to Bertha, and pursues it still. In his conception of that life he is unchanged; any changes of action, any rifts of friendship, and exiles are the consequences of that conception. Robert repeats Richard's declarations about the blinding instant of passion and asks if he has changed from the language of his youth. But the present opposition of their attitudes existed then—either has changed. Their house in the past was to Robert a house of revelry; to Richard it was to be the "hearth of a new life". To Robert a kiss is an act of homage as natural as any act possessing beauty; to Richard it is "an act of union between man and woman", and without contact of minds carnal intercourse is what Duns Scotus calls "the death of the spirit." Richard's desire was to hold "by no bonds, even of love, to be united with you in body and soul in utter nakedness." But it was Richard who wandered from Bertha, only in his absence did Penelope entertain her suitor. Why did he wander so that she found herself living with him as with an utter stranger? Why did he not desire to be held by the bonds of love and the spectre of fidelity? Why after nine years should he profess ignorance of Bertha's good, leaving her freer than Eve and with no commandments, when what she wanted was Richard, her lover? The answer lies in Richard's conception of himself and in the nature of the new life he proposed to follow. That life is the source of Richard's exile. Seeking it he led his world into exile. When Satan fell, a third of the Heavenly Hosts fell with him.

When Bertha accuses Richard of granting her complete liberty because he wants complete liberty for himself, she is right in her charge. But she is wrong in believing that he wants his freedom in order to love Beatrice. Richard wants to be free from all bonds in order to be himself. He must be himself and that self in all its courage and shame must be

understood by others. When for the first time he betrayed Bertha carnally, he came home, awakened her from her sleep, told her, cried beside her bed and pierced her heart. "O, Richard, why did you do that?" asks Robert. "She must know me as I am" he replies. Bertha reproaches Richard for having left her with Robert:

> BERTHA: Why, then, did you leave me last night?
>
> RICHARD: (Bitterly) In your hour of need.
>
> BERTHA: (Threateningly) You urged me to it. Not because you love me. If you loved me or if you knew what love was you would not have left me. For your own sake you urged me to it.

Richard does not answer because he loved her, because he wished her well, and because he feared to deprive her of a moment of life. These sentiments are but deductions and corollaries from the fundamental axiom of his nature, the definition of Himself God gave to Moses, "I am what I am". What that "I" is Richard reveals to Robert in absolute confession. "For you, too, must know me as I am—now."

> RICHARD: Because in the very core of my ignoble heart I longed to be betrayed by you and by her—in the dark, in the night—secretly, meanly, craftily. By you, my best friend, and by her. I longed for that passionately and ignobly, to be dishonoured for ever in love and in lust, to be . . .
>
> ROBERT: Enough. Enough. But no. Go on.
>
> RICHARD: To be for ever a shameful creature and to build up my soul again out of the ruins of its shame.

How similar the words are to those of Stephen Dedalus when, after having renounced his ambitions in the Jesuit order, he wanders up the rivulet in the strand and sees a girl of mortal beauty.

> "Her image had passed into his soul for ever and no word had broken the holy silence of his ecstasy. Her eyes had called him and his soul had leaped at the call. To live, to err, to fall, to triumph, to recreate life out of life! A wild angel had appeared to him, the angel of mortal youth and beauty, an envoy from the fair courts of life, to throw open before him in an instant of ecstasy the gates of all the ways of error and glory. On and on and on!"

Richard demands freedom, complete and absolute freedom from every possible and conceivable form life can assume if it is to emerge from chaos and from death. But this liberty is not purely negative. Opposed to it is the good, the new life that Richard embraces. It is no accident that he leaves Bertha and seeks to be betrayed. That destruction and exile are imposed ineluctably by the same new life that imposed Stephen Dedalus' decline from the priesthood and his lapse from the Catholic Church. Stephen did not refuse the Jesuit order because he thought it unaesthetic, though its ugliness revolted him; and he did not forsake the Church because he thought the dogmas of Christianity literally absurd. As Stephen pictured himself a Jesuit in the routine of his daily life he wondered

> "what, then had become, of that deep rooted shyness of his which had made him loath to eat and drink under a strange roof? What had come of the pride of his spirit which had always made him conceive himself as a being apart in every order?

> The Reverend Stephen Dedalus, S.J."

> No,

> "His destiny was to be elusive of social or religious orders. The wisdom of the priest's appeal did not touch him to the quick. He was destined to learn his own wisdom apart from others or to learn the wisdom of others himself wandering among the snares of the world.
> "The snares of the world were its ways of sin. He would fall. He had not yet fallen but he would fall silently, in an instant. Not to fall was too hard, too hard: and he felt the silent lapse of his soul, as it would be at some instant to come, falling, falling, but not yet fallen, still unfallen, but about to fall."

The new life that Richard-Stephen sought was that of artist-creator. The name he bore was "a prophecy of the end he had been born to serve and had been following through the mists of childhood and boyhood, symbol of the artist forging anew in his workshop out of the sluggish matter of the earth, a new soaring impalpable, imperishable being." It was in order to create that Richard demanded the freedom which would liberate him from every bond of life. Outside of his sacerdotal office of artist he wished for no real earthly existence. As a pure spirit, as an angel, as a Jesuit who aspired to sanctity he would have little intercourse with the world which was to nourish his imagination. Contemptuous of life and impatient of restrictions he must submit time and time again to the immediacy of experience in order to forage materials for his art. The higher world that according to Robert he had fallen from is the world of the creator-artist; but it is not absolute: to create,

the artist must refuse the Jesuit Order or any other, even of love, so that he may fall and be betrayed and build a soul again out of the ruins of its shame. When you have given a thing, Richard tells Archie, it is yours forever; it is his because the artist possesses the image and essence as the image of the girl in the inlet passed into Stephen's soul forever. But as the artist-creator must fall in order to meet with experience so he must first possess and attract in order to give. But how, without deliberate hurt to others is he to fall, be betrayed, and give? Superior being as he is he refuses to possess in body just as he refuses to be possessed, and gives complete freedom just as he demands it. His love for the creatures of the earth is sincere, he wishes them well, and would carry them aloft with him in his flight. But they must follow freely, he will exercise no compulsion and will make no proposals. He is what he is and will seem no other. He will attract in the only way open to him, by the sheer luminous power of his being, a sort of unmoved mover, which as Aristotle says, moves in the way a loved object moves a lover. But having shown himself, having looked, attracted, possessed, and renounced, he moves on, moves on to create. His exile is to be forced to fall and to be in life, but those in life who follow him are exiled first from life and then from him.

Robert's exile is partial since the ecstasy of the new life, that of the artist-creator, is interpreted by him as the ecstasy of the body: he has at least the joys of the sensualist. Beatrice's exile is greater; she is suspended between body and spirit, fearful to give herself to either. But Bertha does more than follow Richard with her eyes. "I will tell you what I will do and what I will not do" says Stephen Dedalus to Cranly "I will not serve that in which I no longer believe, whether it call itself my home, my fatherland or my Church: and I will try to express myself in some mode of life or art as freely as I can, using for my defense the only arms I allow myself to use, silent, exiled, and cunning." Bertha becomes Richard's "bride in exile", she gives up country, religion, and peace for him, her lover. Then he leaves her, alone in Italy, with Archie and her memories, leaves her to return from his exile to his true home of creator-artist. It was for the book he wrote that Richard left Bertha, just as it was for his book that he corresponded with Beatrice, and continued to see her, and it was for his future book that he longed to be betrayed. Richard's asceticism is the most severe ever imposed by man. All life including the personality of the artist must be crucified to gain the kingdom of art.

"The dramatic form is reached," says Stephen to Lynch, "when the vitality which has flowed and eddied round each person fills every person with such vital force that he or she assumes a proper and intangible esthetic life. The personality of the artist, at first a cry or a cadence or a mood and then a fluid and lambent narrative, finally refines itself out of existence, impersonalizes itself, so to speak. The esthetic image in the dramatic form is life purified in and reprojected from the human imagination. The mystery of esthetic like that of material creation is accomplished. The artist, like the God of the creation, remains within or behind or beyond or above his handiwork, invisible, refined out of existence, indifferent, paring his fingernails.–"

When the man is identified with the artist he is refined out of existence and perishes with him. Unless he has a separate individual personal existence he will necessarily divert and destroy every human relationship he enters into. For while pleasure and friendship and love are sufficient ends in themselves, they are to the artist only means, the indispensable sacrifices at the altar of art. Hence all life that comes into contact with him is exiled from nature and humanity. It is sucked up by the insatiable greed of the artist-creator, squeezed dry, and discarded. Acute as the suffering is which the artist-creator inflicts on others, greater still is his own agony. His life like that of the mystic demands unceasing discipline, obedience, and self-immolation for the object of his love. "I tried to unite my will with the will of God instant by instant", said Stephen to Crowley "in that I did not always fail. I could perhaps do that still. . . ." Instead he united his will to the will of the artist-creator and wished for his fellow man the same kind of good. The suffering of the mystic in the night of his soul appears to be greater than any form of human suffering, as his ecstacies transcend other forms of ecstasies. There is no reason to doubt the similarity of Stephen-Richard's suffering and joy. But there is an element in Stephen-Richard not found in the mystic and which is the cause of his exile. That element is not the belief that art is an end in itself. The contemplation that is the artist's is an end in itself, just as is the contemplation of the mystic, of the scientist, and of the philosopher. The greatest tragedy connected with the dying of Christianity and Judaism is the disappearance from the world of the knowledge that the contemplative life is superior to the practical life, and that in the activity of contemplation our restless motion finds its repose and finality. It is the glory of the artist in modern times to have kept alive some form of contemplation to refuse to be deceived by Mammon, by the snares of any group, social, political, or religious, who move and

act and would change the world without knowing for what good. Stephen-Richard's conception of the artist is no more the cause of his exile than the belief in art as an end in itself. The account of the relations between the maker and the material which he shapes is not a theory to be disputed but a description to be understood. The element that distinguishes Stephen-Richard from the mystic is that Stephen-Richard plays the role of a man without accepting the responsibilities of being a man. The mystic aims at a supernatural life and accepts its discipline, but he knows that a specifically human life has its discipline and bonds and obligations. Stephen-Richard in his concentration on himself as artist has neglected himself as man. His exile is caused by his refusal to submit to his nature as a man, to the patient perfecting of the body which forms the soul. Creation accomplished the artist returns to his body as to an alien substance.

> "I am very proud of myself, if you want to know" Bertha declares to Beatrice "What have they ever done for him? I made him a man."

Rather she made it possible for him to be a man and to end his exile. Restored to the body Richard can enter into human life. But to enter into life he must admit his common nature, the most difficult of all things for him who would be a being apart in every order. Bertha can make him a man and she can teach her son to love him. But one thing more is needed. Richard must want to be a man. As artist, so great is his genius, he can for a time attain angelic perfection, and so long as he can sustain himself as pure spirit he is at peace. But if in the body and with people in life he continues to deny his nature and to act as an immaterial being he is painfully in exile. And all who yield to his attraction are forced with him into an exile which no god could relieve. Out of that exile there is only one way, more difficult than art and sanctity which it includes, the destiny of being a man.

Introduction to *Exiles*
Padraic Colum
(New York: Viking, 1951), pp. 7–11

To BREAK DELIBERATELY with an order one has been brought up in, a social, moral, and spiritual order, and, out of one's own convictions, to endeavour to create a new order, is to embark on a lonely and hazardous enterprise. Stephen Daedalus at the end of *A Portrait of the Artist as a Young Man* contemplates doing this. Richard Rowan in *Exiles* has attempted it. Through secrecy and exile Stephen Daedalus would forge the uncreated conscience of his race. He would go into his exile alone. Richard Rowan, going into exile, brought Bertha with him, and on two he left behind, Beatrice Justice and Robert Hand, he left the impress of his personality. The struggle on Richard Rowan's side to free friendship and love from all their bonds makes the drama of *Exiles*.

Exiles is not a play about adultery, actual or suspected; the writer of *A Portrait of the Artist* is not going to lay before us anything so banal; it is not a duel between Richard Rowan and Robert Hand for the possession of Bertha. In the crucial scene one says to the other, "A battle of both our souls, different as they are, against all that is false in them and in the world. A battle of your soul against the spectre of fidelity, of mine against the spectre of friendship."

What has this to do with exile as a theme? The title of the play is no misnomer, although Richard Rowan is now back in his native city and is being received as well as might be expected. For Bertha, Beatrice Justice, Robert Hand have been taken, as Richard Rowan took himself, beyond the accepted moralities and to where they have to make choices for themselves.

Among Joyce's works his single play has never been given a fair show. *Exiles* comes after *Portrait of the Artist* and before *Ulysses,* and critics have recorded their feeling that it has not the enchantment of the first nor the richness of the second, and they have neglected to assess what quality is actually has. They have noted that *Exiles* has the shape of an Ibsen play and have discounted it as being the derivative work of a young admirer of the great Scandinavian dramatist. It has certain characteristics that suggest one of the later Ibsen plays. With clearly defined form it has sparseness and significance of dialogue. And at an important part it has an accidental resemblance to a well-known scene in an Ibsen play: when Robert Hand enters there is much about him to recall Judge Brack. And this resemblance, besides giving a sense of something reminiscent, also gives a wrong lead. But it should be noted that the attempt to set up a three-cornered establishment has no effect in Joyce's play. And in *Exiles* the situations, being motivated by a Catholic and not by a Protestant conscience, are different from the situations in an Ibsen play.

As he was working on it, Joyce made copious notes for *Exiles,* note that were directives for himself and which are being published with the present edition. The copy-book in which the notes were written was saved from Mr. Joyce's apartment, 17 rue des Vignes, Paris, in 1940 by his confidant, Paul L. Léon,

who consigned it with other documents to the care of a friend who, in April 1948, restored all of the material to Mr. Leon's widow.

In some of the notes there is a strain of youthfulness. There is youthfulness in the notion that, as the Scandinavian heroines of Ibsen have supplanted the Slav heroines of the Russian novelists, it may be that a Celtic heroine, his own Bertha, will supplant the Scandinavian. There is youthfulness, too, in the affinity he sees between Bertha and Isolde. In reading these notes–they have the revelation of a long soliloquy–we perceive that *Exiles* is a sort of watershed between the work James Joyce has done and the work he is to do. There is a comparison of Bertha with the earth made in the notes, a comparison that suggests she is facing toward Mollie Bloom. She is seen as the moon, too. In the play she is living near the beach on which Ulysses-Bloom is to see Nausicaa-Gertie. She has in her the virginal Gertie MacDowell. And there is a passage in the notes that lets us know that Joyce will treat his Bertha as Mollie Bloom: a modern writer, he tell us, Paul de Kock, writes a hesitating, painful story about cuckoldry, while his forefathers, Rabelais and Molière, were able to get salacity and humour into their accounts of the subject. He will go back to Rabelais and Molière.

If James Joyce had gone from *Portrait of the Artist* to *Ulysses* (according to the way most commentators discount *Exiles* he might as well have done this) we should not have known the drama that was implicit in Stephen Daedalus's resolve to forge the uncreated conscience of his race. The drama is poignant in *Exiles*. And we should not have known that Joyce was able to give an appealing presentation of a young woman. Bertha, it is true, is a development of Gretta, Gabriel Conroy's wife, in "The Dead." Gretta exists only through her grief for the young man who lies under the nettles in Rahoon. But Bertha exits through her tenderness, her pride, her capability of sorrow for a past, which is also the sorrow of exile, and her resentments which come out of her awareness of her own simplicity. She is a woman who can weep and with whose tears we can sympathize because they are for things that are irretrievably lost– an unspoiled youthful love. She is not really concerned with principles, and she looks on philosophical discourse as a game that engages men's wandering minds. She is neither shocked nor thrilled at Richard's break with the order she was brought up in and his dedication to the creation of a new order. Being a woman, she has in herself an immemorial and universal order.

It is the woman who cannot give anything freely, Beatrice Justice, who can understand Richard

Stills from the 1995 Liquid Theater production of Exiles *involving John Postley as Robert Hand*
and Megan Johnson as Bertha (courtesy of Heidi I. Siedlecki)

Rowan's mind, and she can understand it because it has a repressed part of herself, her pride and her scorn. Richard's exile has divided her life into halves. She has recovered from an illness that was the consequence of his departure, but her life will be the life of a convalescent. As a Protestant she is not dismayed by Richard Rowan's attempt to transvalue the values of his people. He had initiated a correspondence with her and had kept it up for nine years, and Bertha, lonely in her exile, had meditated on the person he gave so much of his mind to. She meets her and is jealous—not jealous, perhaps, but envious—of an intelligence and education that can attract Richard; then she loses her grievance and becomes friendly with her. And now it should be possible for Richard Rowan to retrain Beatrice Justice as a devoted friend. Richard may have wanted that. But his probings at the beginning of the play were directed to showing her that she is in love with him and so making it impossible for one with her kind of conscience to stay near him. Then Beatrice fades out of the play.

His relation with Beatrice Justice shows Richard Rowan as a moralist, and a narrow moralist at that. Not his gay father but his austere mother is the one he would bring into his life. It is Robert Hand who is the immoralist in *Exiles*—but only conventionally an immoralist. He is able to offer Bertha simplic-ities for Richard's subtleties. He might be one of the students Stephen Daedalus left behind when he chose secrecy and exiles as a means of forging the uncreated conscience of his race, one of the students who, mature now, has found his place in the world. And yet he says something that makes him extraordinary. "A battle of your soul against the spectre of fidelity, of mine against the spectre of friendship. All life is conquest, the victory of human passion over the commandment of cowardice." Yes, but Beatrice Justice had seen that her cousin had become a pale reflection of another. Is this a challenge from himself or from that part of him that images Richard Rowan? Richard knows him as a disciple who will betray his master. For Richard Rowan the struggle between them eventuates in the breaking of bonds, the bond between master and disciple, the bond of his security in his love for Bertha. In the end, the order that Bertha maintained in herself is shown to be more fundamental than the order Richard would destroy or the order he would create. It is Richard Rowan's sense of fatherhood and Bertha's tenderness for her man that are left as the means by which the transvaluer of accepted values will be healed of his self-inflicted wound. In its structure, *Exiles* is a series of confessions; the dialogue has the dryness of recitals in the confessional; its end is an act of contrition.

Ulysses

In mock-heroic style, James Joyce's epic novel Ulysses celebrates the events of a single day in the lives of three Dubliners: Leopold
Bloom, his wife, Molly, and Stephen Dedalus. That day, 16 June
1904, is now known throughout the world as Bloomsday. Joyce began
working on Ulysses in Trieste sometime in late 1914 or early 1915,
right before he and his family moved to Zurich, where he continued to
work on the novel for the next four years. Ulysses was completed in
Paris and published on Joyce's fortieth birthday, 2 February 1922.

Even prior to its publication in book form Ulysses had gained
international recognition through The Little Review, an American
magazine that serialized major portions of the novel between March
1918 and September 1920. An official complaint against the magazine, filed by the New York Society for the Suppression of Vice, led to
the trial and conviction of its co-editors, Margaret Anderson and Jane
Heap, for publishing obscenity, and the periodical was forced to cease
publication of the novel. An unexpurgated Ulysses could not be legally
published in the United States until Judge John M. Woolsey lifted the
ban on the novel on 6 December 1933.

Despite the attempts to dismiss it as obscene, Ulysses was
acclaimed by many for its revolutionary style and celebrated as an artistic
achievement of the first order. In his essay "Ulysses, Order and Myth"
T. S. Eliot wrote, "I hold this book to be the most important expression
which the present age has found; it is a book to which we are all
indebted, and from which none of us can escape." Joyce's masterpiece has
since been recognized as one of the most influential novels ever written.

*Portrait of James Joyce, inscribed to John Quinn (*The Library
of John Quinn, Part Three, *1924)*

The Making of *Ulysses*

Frank Budgen met Joyce in Zurich in 1918 and became a life-
long friend of the author. In 1934 he published an introduction to the
novel and its background.

I enquired about Ulysses. Was it progressing?

"I have been working hard on it all day," said Joyce.

"Does that mean that you have written a great deal?"
I said.

"Two sentences," said Joyce.

I looked sideways but Joyce was not smiling. I
thought of Flaubert.

"You have been seeking the *mot juste?*" I said.

"No," said Joyce. "I have the words already. What I
am seeking is the perfect order of words in the sentence.

There is an order in every way appropriate. I think I have
it."

"What are the words?" I asked.

"I believe I told you," said Joyce, "that my book is a
modern Odyssey. Every episode in it corresponds to an
adventure of Ulysses. I am now writing the *Lestrygonians* episode, which corresponds to the adventure of Ulysses with
the cannibals. My hero is going to lunch. But there is a
seduction motive in the Odyssey, the cannibal king's daugh-

ter. Seduction appears in my book as women's silk petticoats hanging in a shop window. The words through which I express the effect of it on my hungry hero are: 'Perfume of embraces all him assailed. With hungered flesh obscurely, he mutely craved to adore.' You can see for yourself in how many different ways they might be arranged."

A painter is, perhaps, more originality proof than any other artist, seeing that all recent experimental innovations in the arts have first been tried out on his own. And many a painter can labour for a day or for many days on one or two square inches of canvas so that labour expended on achieving precious material is not likely to surprise him. What impressed me, I remember, when Joyce repeated the words of Bloom's hungrily abject amorousness to me, was neither the originality of the words themselves nor the labour expended on composing them. It was the sense they gave me that a new province of material had been found. Where that province lay I could not guess, but as our talk proceeded Joyce spoke of it himself without question of mine. We were by this time sitting in the Astoria Café.

"Among other things," he said, "my book is the epic of the human body. The only man I know who has attempted the same thing is Phineas Fletcher. But then his *Purple Island* is purely descriptive, a kind of coloured anatomical chart of the human body. In my book the body lives in and moves through space and is the home of a full human personality. The words I write are adapted to express first one of its functions then another. In *Lestrygonians* the stomach dominates and the rhythm of the episode is that of the peristaltic movement."

"But the minds, the thoughts of the characters," I began.

"If they had no body they would have no mind," said Joyce. "It is all one. Walking towards his lunch my hero, Leopold Bloom, thinks of his wife, and says to himself, 'Molly's legs are out of plumb.' At another time of day he might have expressed the same thought without any underthought of food. But I want the reader to under-

Frank Budgen, the author of James Joyce and the Making of Ulysses, *first published in 1934; a revised edition, with three new essays, was published in 1972.*

stand always through suggestion rather than direct statement."

"That's the painter's form of leverage," I said. We talked of words again, and I mentioned one that had always pleased me in its shape and colour. It was Chatterton's "acale" for freeze.

"It is a good word," said Joyce. "I shall probably use it."

He does use it. The word occurs in *The Oxen of the Sun* episode of *Ulysses* in a passage written in early English, describing the death and burial of Bloom's son Rudolph: ". . . and he was minded of his good lady Marion that had borne him an only manchild which on his eleventh day on live had died and no man of art could save so dark is destiny and she was wondrous stricken of heart for that evil hap and for his burial did him on a corselet of lambswool the flower of the flock, lest he might perish utterly and lie akeled. . . ."

In leaving the café I asked Joyce how long he had been working on *Ulysses*.

"About five years," he said. "But in a sense all my life."

"Some of your contemporaries," I said, "think two books a year an average output."

"Yes," said Joyce. "But how do they do it? They talk them into a typewriter. I feel quite capable of doing that if I wanted to do it. But what's the use? It isn't worth doing."

– *James Joyce and the Making of* Ulysses, *pp. 19–22*

William Butler Yeats wrote of his admiration for Joyce and Ulysses *in a 23 July 1918 letter to John Quinn.*

. . . If I had had this tower of mine when Joyce began to write, I daresay I might have been of use to him, have got him to meet those who might have helped him. I think him a most remarkable man, and his new story in the *Little Review* looks like becoming the best work he has done. It is an entirely new thing–neither what the eye sees nor the ear hears, but what the rambling mind thinks and imagines from moment to moment. He has certainly surpassed in intensity any novelist of our time.

–*The Letters of W. B. Yeats,* p. 651

THE LITTLE REVIEW

THE MAGAZINE THAT IS READ BY THOSE
WHO WRITE THE OTHERS

MARCH, 1918

Ulysses, 1.   *James Joyce*

Imaginary Letters, VIII.   *Wyndham Lewis*

Matinee   *Jessie Dismorr*

The Classics "Escape"   *Ezra Pound*

Cantico del Sole

Women and Men, II.   *Ford Madox Hueffer*

Bertha   *Arthur Symons*

A List of Books   *Ezra Pound*

Wyndham Lewis's "Tarr"

Raymonde Collignon

The Reader Critic

Copyright, 1918, by Margaret Anderson

MARGARET ANDERSON, Editor
EZRA POUND, Foreign Editor

24 *West Sixteenth Street, New York*

Foreign office:

5 *Holland Place Chambers, London W. 8.*

25 cents a copy $2.50 a year

Entered as second-class matter at P. O., New York, N. Y.
Published monthly by Margaret Anderson

THE LITTLE REVIEW

Vol. V.   MARCH, 1918   No. 11

ULYSSES

JAMES JOYCE

Episode 1

STATELY, plump Buck Mulligan came from the stairhead, bearing a bowl of lather on which a mirror and a razor lay crossed. A yellow dressing gown, ungirdled, was sustained gently behind him on the mild morning air. He held the bowl aloft and intoned:

—*Introibo ad altare Dei.*

Halted, he peered down the dark winding stairs and called up coarsely:

—Come up, Kinch. Come up, you fearful jesuit.

Solemnly he came forward and mounted the round gunrest. He faced about and blessed gravely thrice the tower, the surrounding country and the awaking mountains. Then, catching sight of Stephen Dedalus, he bent towards him and made rapid crosses in the air, gurgling in his throat and shaking his head. Stephen Dedalus, displeased and sleepy, leaned his arms on the top of the staircase and looked coldly at the shaking gurgling face that blessed him, equine in its length, and at the light untonsured hair, grained and hued like pale oak.

Buck Mulligan peeped an instant under the mirror and then covered the bowl smartly.

—Back to barracks, he said sternly.

He added in a preacher's tone:

—For this, O dearly beloved, is the genuine christine: body and soul and blood and ouns. Slow music, please. Shut your eyes, gents. One moment. A little trouble about those white corpuscles. Silence, all.

Contents page and first page of the novel in the magazine that serialized Ulysses *until its publication was halted by the Court of Special Sessions in New York*

Ulysses in *The Little Review*

Pound, who acted as foreign correspondent for The Little Review, *brought* Ulysses *to the attention of editors Margaret Anderson and Jane Heap. As she recalls in her autobiography,* My Thirty Years' War *(1930), Anderson was so struck by the opening of the Proteus episode that she cried out, "This is the most beautiful thing we'll ever have. We'll print it if it's the last effort of our lives." In all, twenty-three installments of the novel—totaling thirteen episodes and part of the fourteenth—were serialized in* The Little Review *between March 1918 and December 1920. On four occasions issues were burned by the United States Post Office.*

When John S. Sumner, the secretary of the New York Society for the Suppression of Vice, brought suit against The Little Review, *John Quinn served as the attorney for the magazine before the three-judge panel of the Court of Special Sessions. His arguments were unavailing, and each editor was fined $50 for publishing obscenity. After the trial, Quinn warned his clients against publishing any more obscene literature. Anderson recalls that when she asked him how she was to know what was obscene, Quinn responded, "I'm sure I don't know, but don't do it."*

Ezra Pound compared Joyce's Ulysses *to Gustave Flaubert's* Bouvard et Pécuchet *(1881) in his 22 November 1918 letter to the author.*

Dear Joyce: Bloom is a great man, and you have almightily answered the critics who asked me whether having made Stephen, more or less autobiography, you could ever go on and create a second character. 'Second character is the test' etc. etc., jab jab jobberjabble.

. . . .

I looked back over Bouvard and Pecuchet last week. Bloom certainly does all Flaubert set out to do and does it in one tenth the space, and moreover there is the sense all the time that something might happen, in fact that anything might happen at any moment, while in Bouvard they are anchored in the mud and even when some thing does happen you keep on feeling that nothing can.

— Letters II, p. 423

It was like a burning at the stake as far as I was concerned. The care we had taken to preserve Joyce's text intact; the worry over the bills that accumulated when we had no advance funds; the technique I used on printer, bookbinders, paper houses—tears, prayers, hysterics or rages—to make them push ahead without a guarantee of money; the addressing, wrapping, stamping, mailing; the excitement of anticipating the world's response to the literary masterpiece of our generation ... and then a notice from the Post Office: BURNED.
—Margaret Anderson, *My Thirty Years' War*, p. 175

A Reaction to the Censorship of *Ulysses*

The call by R.H.C. (Alfred R. Orage) for the immediate publication of Ulysses *in England was not heeded. Because printers in the United Kingdom feared they would be held liable for publishing obscenity, no edition of the novel was published there until 1936, two years after* Ulysses *was published by Random House in the United States.*

Readers and Writers
R.H.C.
New Age, 28 (28 April 1921): 306–307

Just when we in Europe were beginning to envy America her promise, contrasting it with the winter of our own discontent, 'the authorities' (as one might say the furies, the parcae or the weird sisters) have descended upon our unfortunate but deserving friend, the *Little Review,* and suspended its mail service on account of its publication of a chapter of Mr. James Joyce's new novel, *Ulysses.* That such an absurd act of puritanic spleen should be possible after and before years of world-war is evidence that, after all, spiritual meanness is hard to transcend; and it confirms the justice or, at least, the apprehension expressed in Mr. Ezra Pound's bon mot that the U.S.A. should be renamed the Y.M.C.A. Not only is the *Little Review* perfectly harmless; would to heaven, indeed, that it were or could be otherwise, for never can any good be done by something incapable of doing harm; but the *Ulysses* of Mr. James Joyce is one of the most interesting literary symptoms in the whole literary world, and its publication is very nearly a public obligation. Such sincerity, such energy, such fearlessness as Mr. Joyce's are rare in any epoch, and most of all in our own; and on that very account they demand to be given at least the freedom of the Press. What the giant American can *fear* from Mr. Joyce or from his publication in the *Little Review* passes understanding. Abounding in every variety of crime and stupidity as America is, even if *Ulysses* were a literary crime committed in a journal of the largest circulation, one more or less could not make much difference to America. But

Robert McAlmon (Sylvia Beach Collection, Princeton University Library)

American writer Robert McAlmon became friends with Joyce in 1920. In his 1938 memoir he recalls his work as a typist on Ulysses.

The husband of the English typist who was typing his work had destroyed some forty pages of the original script of *Ulysses,* because it was obscene. Joyce was naturally scared about handing work out to typists, and most typists would insist upon putting in punctuation which he did not desire. He knew that I typed not well, but quickly, and spoke suggestively of the point as we were drinking. I thought then, fifty pages, that's nothing, sure I'll type it for you.

The next day he gave me the handwritten script, and his handwriting is minute and hen-scrawly; very difficult to decipher. With the script he gave me some four notebooks, and throughout the script were marks in red, yellow, blue, purple, and green, referring me to phrases which must be inserted from one of the notebook. For about three pages I was painstaking and actually re-typed one page to get the insertion in the right place. After I thought 'Molly might just as well think this or that a page or two later or not at all', and made the insertions wherever I happened to be typing. Years later upon asking Joyce if he'd noticed that I'd altered the mystic arrangement of Molly's thought he said that he had, but agreed with my viewpoint. Molly's thoughts were irregular in several ways at best.

—*Being Geniuses Together: An Autobiography*, pp. 90–91

Ulysses is, of course, no crime; but, on the contrary, a noble experiment; and its suppression will, in consequence, sadden the virtuous at the same time that it gratifies the base. America, we may say, is not going to 'get culture' by stamping upon every germ of new life. America's present degree of cultural toleration may ensure a herb-garden, but not a flower will grow upon the soil of Comstock. It only remains for some reputable English publisher to produce *Ulysses* to secure a notable triumph for the Empire over America.

* * *

Among the scores of interesting experiments in composition and style exhibited in *Ulysses,* not the least novel is Mr. Joyce's attempt to develop a theory of harmonies in language. By compounding nouns with adjectives or adjectives with adverbs, Mr. Joyce tries to convey to the reader a complex of qualities or ideas simultaneously instead of successively. "Eglingtoneyes looked up skybrightly." In such a sentence agglutination has been carried beyond the ordinary level of particles into the plane of words; and the effect is, as Miss Evelyn Scott points out in the *Dial,* to present a multitude of images as if they were one. Thus "a new and complex knowledge of self" finds its "appropriate medium of expression in terms of art." I am not so sure that Mr. Joyce has not carried the experiment too far; but this, again, is a virtue rather than a defect in a pioneer. Moreover, as I have often said, the world needs a few studio-magazines like the *Little Review* and a few studio-writers like Mr. James Joyce. What does it matter if, in his enthusiasm, Mr. Joyce travels beyond the limits of good taste, beyond, that is to say, the already cultivated? If only a single new literary convention is thereby brought into common use, his work will have been done. More than ever, in view of the example of experiment just mentioned, the immediate publication of *Ulysses* in England is imperative; and every literary craftsman in the country should make a point of insisting upon it.

In a 19 June 1920 letter to Quinn, Pound describes his impression of Joyce the man.

Joyce—pleasing, after the first shell of cantankerous Irishman, I got the impression that the real man is the author of *Chamber Music,* the sensitive. The rest is the genius; the registration of realities on the temperament, the delicate temperament of the early poems. A concentration and absorption passing Yeats'—Yeats has never taken on anything requiring the condensation of *Ulysses.*

— The Letters of Ezra Pound, p. 153

Schema for *Ulysses*

In September 1920, for the private use of a few early interpreters of the novel, Joyce prepared a schema, or diagrammatic plan, of Ulysses that outlined its structure and parallels to Homer's Odyssey. The first copy Joyce sent to Carlo Linati, the Italian translator of Exiles, and in late 1921, Joyce gave the French writer and translator, Valéry Larbaud, a slightly different version of the schema to help in the preparation of his 7 December lecture on the forthcoming novel. In a September 1920 letter to the American attorney John Quinn, Joyce divides Ulysses into three major divisions that parallel the three divisions of The Odyssey (Telemachia, Odyssey, and Nostos) and provides chapter titles for the novel's eighteen episodes (Letters I, pp. 145–146). These chapter titles, however, do not appear in the novel itself. Telemachia consists of the first three episodes: Telemachus, Nestor, and Proteus; Odyssey (or the Wanderings of Ulysses) consists of the next twelve episodes: Calypso, Lotus-Eaters, Hades, Aeolus, Lestrygonians, Scylla and Charybdis, The Wandering Rocks, Sirens, Cyclops, Nausikaa, Oxen of the Sun, and Circe; Nostos consists of the last three episodes: Eumaeus, Ithaca, and Penelope. In addition to chapter titles, the Ulysses schema also lists key ideas and correspondences in each episiode. Richard Ellmann includes a copy of the original Italian schema that Joyce sent to Linati followed by an English translation in the appendix to Ulysses on the Liffey (1972).

Shakespeare and Company

The daughter of a Presbyterian minister, Sylvia Beach opened her bookshop, Shakespeare and Company, at 8 rue Dupuytren in November 1919. Her bookstore became the meeting place of many American and English writers during the 1920s, including H.D., Sherwood Anderson, F. Scott Fitzgerald, and Ernest Hemingway. Beach met Joyce in July 1920 and that same year introduced him to Valéry Larbaud, a French novelist, translator, and critic who became an enthusiastic supporter of Joyce and his work. When The Little Review censorship case seemed to make the book publication of Ulysses even more unlikely, Beach offered to publish the novel through her Preis bookstore. Joyce was at the point of giving up publishing the novel when Beach suggested the idea. She was able to finance the project by diligently pursuing subscribers willing to buy a first edition. She also hired the Dijon printer, Maruice Darantiere, who willingly provided Joyce with multiple galley proofs so that he could continue to revise the novel until it was actually published on 2 February 1922, Joyce's fortieth birthday.

TITLE	SCENE	HOUR	ORGAN	ART	COLOUR	SYMBOL	TECHNIC	CORRESPONDENCES	
1. Telemachus	The Tower	8 a.m.		Theology	White, gold	Heir	Narrative (young)	*Stephen:* Telemachus, Hamlet. *Buck Mulligan:* Antinous. *Milkwoman:* Mentor.	226
2. Nestor	The School	10 a.m.		History	Brown	Horse	Catechism (personal	*Deasy:* Nestor. *Sargent:* Pisistratus. *Mrs. O'Shea:* Helen.	
3. Proteus	The Strand	11 a.m.		Philology	Green	Tide	Monologue (male)	*Proteus:* Primal Matter. *Kevin Egan:* Menelaus. *Cocklepicker:* Megapenthus.	
4. Calypso	The House	8 a.m.	Kidney	Economics	Orange	Nymph	Narrative (mature)	*Calypso:* The Nymph. *Dluglacz:* The Recall. *Zion:* Ithaca.	
5. Lotus-eaters	The Bath	10 a.m.	Genitals	Botany, Chemistry		Eucharist	Narcissism	*Lotuseaters:* the Cabhorses, Communicants, Soldiers, Eunuchs, Bather, Watchers of Cricket.	
6. Hades	The Graveyard	11 a.m.	Heart	Religion	White, black	Caretaker	Incubism	*Dodder, Grand, and Royal Canals, Liffey:* the 4 Rivers. *Cunningham:* Sisyphus. *Father Coffey:* Cerberus. *Caretaker:* Hades. *Daniel O'Connell:* Hercules. *Dignam:* Elpenor. *Parnell:* Agamemnon, Ajax.	
7. Aeolus	The Newspaper	12 noon	Lungs	Rhetoric	Red	Editor	Enthymemic	*Crawford:* Aeolus. *Incest:* Journalism. *Floating Island:* Press.	
8. Lestrygonians	The Lunch	1 p.m.	Esophagus	Architecture		Constables	Peristaltic	*Antiphates:* Hunger. *The Decoy:* Food. *Lestrygonians:* Teeth.	
9. Scylla & Charybdis	The Library	2 p.m.	Brain	Literature		Stratford, London	Dialectic	*The Rock:* Aristotle, Dogma, Stratford. *The Whirlpool:* Plato, Mysticism, London. *Ulysses:* Socrates, Jesus, Shakespeare.	227
10. Wandering Rocks	The Streets	3 p.m.	Blood	Mechanics		Citizens	Labyrinth	*Bosphorus:* Liffey. *European Bank:* Viceroy. *Asiatic Bank:* Conmee. *Symplegades:* Groups of Citizens.	
11. Sirens	The Concert Room	4 p.m.	Ear	Music		Barmaids	Fuga per Canonem	*Sirens:* Barmaids. *Isle:* Bar.	
12. Cyclops	The Tavern	5 p.m.	Muscle	Politics		Fenian	Gigantism	*Noman:* I. *Stake:* Cigar. *Challenge:* Apotheosis.	
13. Nausicaa	The Rocks	8 p.m.	Eye, Nose	Painting	Grey, blue	Virgin	Tumescence, detumescence	*Phaeacia:* Star of the Sea. *Gerty:* Nausicaa.	
14. Oxen of the Sun	The Hospital	10 p.m.	Womb	Medicine	White	Mothers	Embryonic development	*Hospital:* Trinacria. *Nurses:* Lampetie, Phaethusa. *Horne:* Helios. *Oxen:* Fertility. *Crime:* Fraud.	
15. Circe	The Brothel	12 midnight	Locomotor Apparatus	Magic		Whore	Hallucination	*Circe:* Bella.	
16. Eumaeus	The Shelter	1 a.m.	Nerves	Navigation		Sailors	Narrative (old)	*Skin the Goat:* Eumaeus. *Sailor:* Ulysses Pseudangelos. *Corley:* Melanthius.	
17. Ithaca	The House	2 a.m.	Skeleton	Science		Comets	Catechism (impersonal)	*Eurymachus:* Boylan. *Suitors:* Scruples. *Bow:* Reason.	
18. Penelope	The Bed		Flesh			Earth	Monologue (female)	*Penelope:* Earth. *Web:* Movement.	

ODYSSEUS

THE PLAN OF *ULYSSES*

Hugh Kenner's schema of Ulysses *from* Dublin's Joyce *(Reproduced by permission of Indiana University Press. Copyright 1956 © by Hugh Kenner)*

ULYSSES suppressed four times during serial publication in "The Little Review" will be published by "SHAKESPEARE AND COMPANY" complete as written.

This edition is private and will be limited to 1.000 copies :

100 copies signed on Dutch hand made paper . . . . **350** fr.
150 copies on vergé d'Arches. . . . . **250** fr.
750 copies on hand made paper. . . . . **150** fr.

The work will be a volume in-8° crown of 600 pages.

Subscribers will be notified when the volume appears, which will be sent to them by registered post immediately on receipt of payment.

All correspondence, cheques, money-orders should be addressed to :

Miss SYLVIA BEACH

"SHAKESPEARE AND COMPANY"

8, RUE DUPUYTREN, PARIS — VI°

Prospectus mailed in fall 1921 to announce the forthcoming publication of Ulysses. *An order form to be filled in by the subscriber was printed on the back of the announcement (Princeton University Library).*

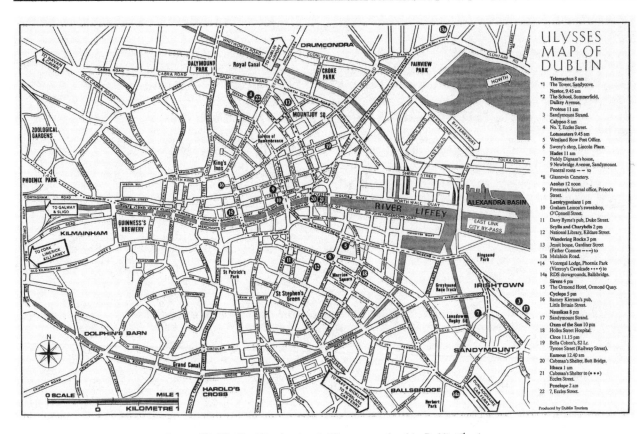

A map of Dublin identifying locations in Ulysses, *produced by Dublin Tourism*

Produced by Dublin Tourism

Although impressed by Ulysses, *George Bernard Shaw in his 10 October 1921 letter to Sylvia Beach declined to purchase a copy.*

Dear Madam, I have read several fragments of *Ulysses* in its serial form. It is a revolting record of a disgusting phase of civilisation; but it is a truthful one; and I should like to put a cordon round Dublin; round up every male person in it between the ages of 15 and 30; force them to read it; and ask them whether on reflection they could see anything amusing in all that foul mouthed, foul minded derision and obscenity. To you, possibly, it may appeal as art: you are probably (you see I don't know you) a young barbarian beglamoured by the excitements and enthusiasms that art stirs up in passionate material; but to me it is all hideously real: I have walked those streets and known those shops and have heard and taken part in those conversations. I escaped from them to England at the age of twenty; and forty years later have learnt from the books of Mr. Joyce that Dublin is still what it was, and young men are still drivelling in slackjawed blackguardism just as they were in 1870. It is, however, some con-

Sylvia Beach, the owner of Shakespeare and Company

Dust jacket for the book in which Beach describes her involvement in the publication of Ulysses

William Butler Yeats, one of the first subscribers to Ulysses *(courtesy of the Irish Tourist Board)*

SHAKESPEARE AND COMPANY

SYLVIA BEACH

12 RUE DE L'ODÉON — PARIS VIᵉ

BOOKSHOP

LENDING LIBRARY

MODERN ENGLISH AND AMERICAN LITERATURE

POETRY - PLAYS - NOVELS - ESSAYS
WORKS ON ART AND THE THEATRE
REVIEWS

Open every day from 9 to 12.30 and from 2 to 7
except Sundays

Tél. Littré 33-76   R. C. Seine N° 284.402

Advertising card for the publisher of Ulysses *(Collection of Matthew J. Bruccoli)*

solation to find that at last somebody has felt deeply enough about it to face the horror of writing it all down and using his literary genius to force people to face it. In Ireland they try to make a cat cleanly by rubbing its nose in its own filth. Mr. Joyce has tried the same treatment on the human subject. I hope it may prove successful.

I am aware that there are other qualities and other passages in *Ulysses:* but they do not call for any special comment from me.

I must add, as the prospectus implies an invitation to purchase, that I am an elderly Irish gentleman, and that if you imagine that any Irishman, much less an elderly one, would pay 150 francs for a book, you little know my countrymen. Faithfully,

G. Bernard Shaw
– Letters III, p. 50

An Early Affirmation

Larbaud's reading of Ulysses *prompted him to write to Joyce, who reported in a 1 March 1921 letter to Harriet Shaw Weaver that he had received "a most enthusiastic letter from Mr Valéry Larbaud," who "says that he has been unable to write or sleep since he read it" (Letters III, p. 39–40). With Joyce's approval, Larbaud gave the first public lecture on the novel, at Adrienne Monnier's bookshop, the Maison des Amis des Livres. Joyce aided Larbaud in his preparations for the lecture by giving him a schema for the novel outlining its Homeric parallels and techniques. In a 24 June 1921 letter to Weaver, Joyce again wrote of the critic: "The only person who knows anything worth mentioning about the book or did or tried to do anything about it is Mr Valéry Larbaud" (Selected Letters, p. 283). Larbaud also played a pivotal role in the 1929 French translation of the novel.*

Valéry Larbaud

Larbaud and Joyce

Sylvia Beach describes how she introduced Larbaud to Joyce and his work in her memoir.

Larbaud, when he visited the bookshop, always asked me what he should read in English, and one time when he came I asked him if he had seen any of the writings of the Irishman James Joyce. He said that he had not, so I gave him *A Portrait of the Artist as a Young Man*. He brought it back soon, saying that it interested him very much, and that he would like to meet the author.

I arranged a meeting between the two writers at Shakespeare and Company on Christmas Eve, 1920. They immediately became great friends. Perhaps I realize more than anyone what the friendship of Valéry Larbaud meant to Joyce. Such generosity and unselfishness toward a fellow writer as Larbaud showed to Joyce is indeed rare.

Larbaud had yet to make the acquaintance of *Ulysses*. Hearing that he was laid up with the grippe, I thought this was the right moment for Mr. Bloom to introduce himself. I bundled up all the numbers of the *Little Review* containing parts of *Ulysses*, and sent them to the invalid with some flowers.

The very next day I had a letter from Larbaud in which he said that he was "raving mad over *Ulysses*," and that since he had read Whitman, "when I was eighteen," he had not been so enthusiastic about any book. "It is wonderful! As great as Rabelais!"

—Shakespeare and Company, p. 57

LA MAISON DES AMIS DES LIVRES

7, rue de l'Odéon, Paris - VI* — Tél.: Fleurus 25-05

Mercredi 7 Décembre
à 9 h. précises du soir

SÉANCE CONSACRÉE A

L'ÉCRIVAIN IRLANDAIS

JAMES JOYCE

CONFÉRENCE PAR

M. VALERY LARBAUD

Lecture de fragments de ULYSSES
traduits pour la 1re fois en français

— *Nous tenons à prévenir le public que certaines des pages qu'on lira sont*
d'une hardiesse d'expression peu commune qui peut très légitimement choquer.—

Cette séance étant donnée au bénéfice de JAMES JOYCE,
le droit d'admission sera, exceptionnellement, de 20 francs par
personne. Nous serions particulièrement reconnaissants envers
les personnes qui voudraient bien dépasser la somme fixée.

Les places doivent être retenues à l'avance. Nous rappelons qu'elles sont limitées
à cent.

Announcement of Valéry Larbaud's lecture on Ulysses *(Division of Rare and Manuscript Collections, Carl A. Kroch Library, Cornell University. Scholes 1385)*

Larbaud's 7 December 1921 lecture, in which he discussed all of Joyce's works, was originally published in the Nouvelle Revue Française *in April 1922. The fourth section of the lecture, which was translated for the October 1922 issue of* Criterion, *is published below.*

The *Ulysses* of James Joyce
Valéry Larbaud

The reader who approaches this book without the *Odyssey* clearly in mind will be thrown into dismay. I refer, of course, to the cultivated reader who can fully appreciate such authors as Rabelais, Montaigne, and Descartes: for the uncultivated or half-cultivated reader will throw *Ulysses* aside after the first three pages. I say that the reader is at first dismayed: for he is plunged into the middle of a conversation which will seem to him incoherent, between people whom he cannot distinguish, in a place which is neither named nor described; and from this conversation he is to learn little by little where he is and who the interlocutors are. Furthermore, here is a book which is entitled *Ulysses,* and no character in it bears this name; the name of Ulysses only appears four times. But gradually the reader begins to see his way. Incidentally, he learns that he is in Dublin. He identifies the hero of the *Portrait of the Artist* Stephen Dedalus, returned from Paris and living among the intellectuals of the Irish capital. He follows Stephen Dedalus for three chapters, watches him and hears him think. From eight to eleven o'clock, in the morning, he follows Stephen Dedalus; in the fourth chapter he makes the acquaintance of a certain Leopold Bloom, whom he pursues step by step throughout the day and a part of the night–that is to say, through the fifteen chapters which, with the three first, compose the whole book of 732 pages. Accordingly this huge book chronicles a single day; or, to be exact, begins at eight o'clock in the morning and ends towards three in the next morning.

As we have indicated, the reader follows the course of Bloom through his long day; for even if much eludes him at the first reading, he will perceive enough to keep his curiosity and interest constantly awake. He remarks that, with the appearance of Bloom, the action begins again at eight o'clock, and that the three first chapters of Bloom's progress through his day are synchronous with the three first chapters of the book, in which he has followed Stephen Dedalus. For example, a cloud observed by Stephen from the top of the tower at a quarter to nine is seen sixty or eighty pages later by Leopold Bloom crossing a street.

I said that we follow Bloom step by step: in fact, we begin with him when he rises, we accompany him from the bedroom where he has just left his wife Molly half-asleep, to the kitchen, into the hall, to the earth-closet where he reads an old newspaper and lays his literary plans while he eases himself; then to the butcher's, where he buys kidneys for his breakfast; and on the way home he is excited by the form of a servant-girl. Again in his kitchen he puts the kidneys in a frying-pan and the pan on the fire; he goes upstairs to take his wife her breakfast; lingers to talk to her; a smell of burning meat; he redescends to the kitchen in haste; and so on. Again in the street; at the baths; at a funeral; in the editorial offices of a newspaper; at the restaurant where he lunches; in the public library; in the bar of a hotel where a concert is going on, on the beach; in a lying-in hospital where he goes for news of a friend and where he meets his comrades; in the red-light district and in a brothel, where he remains for a long time, loses the rest of his dignity, sinks into a dismal delirium induced by alcohol and fatigue, and finally leaves in the company of Stephen Dedalus, whom he has rejoined and with whom he passes the two last hours of his day– that is to say, the sixteenth and seventeenth chapters of the book: the last being devoted to a long train of thought of his wife, whom he has awakened in going to bed.

None of this, as I have already said, is told us in narrative form, and the book is a great deal more than the detailed history of Stephen's and Bloom's day in Dublin. It contains a vast number of other things, characters, incidents, descriptions, conversations, visions. But for us the readers, Bloom and Stephen are, so to speak, the vehicles in which we pass across the book. Stationed in the intimacy of their minds, and sometimes in the minds of the other characters, we see through their eyes and hear through their ears what happens and what is said around them. In this way, in this book, all the elements are constantly melting into each other,

and the illusion of life, of the thing in the act, is complete: the whole is movement.

But the cultivated reader whom I have postulated will not let himself be wholly carried along by this movement. With the habit of reading and a long experience of books, he looks for the method and the material of what he reads. He will analyse *Ulysses* as he reads. And this is what will certainly be the result of his analysis after a first reading. He will say: This is still the society of *Dubliners* and the eighteen parts of *Ulysses* can provisionally be considered as eighteen tales with different aspects of the life of the Irish capital as their subjects. Nevertheless, each of these eighteen parts differs from any of the fifteen tales of *Dubliners* on many points, and particularly by its scope, by its form, and by the distinction of the characters. Thus, the characters who take the principal roles in the tales of *Dubliners* would be in *Ulysses* only supers, minor characters, or–it comes to the same thing–people seen by the author from the outside. In *Ulysses* the protagonists are all (in a literary sense) princes, characters who emerge from the depths of the author's inner life, constructed with his experience and his sensibility, and endowed by him with his own emotion, his own intelligence, and his own lyricism. Here, the conversations are something more than typical of individuals of such and such social classes; some of them are genuine essays in philosophy, theology, literary criticism, political satire, history. Scientific theories are expounded or debated. These pieces, which we might treat as digressions, or rather as appendices, essays composed outside of the book and artificially interpolated into all of the "tales," are so exquisitely adapted to the plot, the movement, and the atmosphere of the different parts in which they appear that we are obliged to admit that they belong to the book, by the same rights as the characters in whose mouths or whose minds they are put. But already we can no longer consider these eighteen parts as detached tales: Bloom, Stephen, and a few other characters remain, sometimes together and sometimes apart, the principal figures; and the story, the drama, and the comedy of their day are enacted through them. It must be acknowledged that, although each of these eighteen parts differs from all of the others in form and language, the whole forms none the less an organism a book.

As we arrive at this conclusion, all sorts of coincidences, analogies, and correspondences between these different parts come to light; just as, in looking fixedly at the sky at night, we find that the number of stars appears to increase. We begin to discover and to anticipate symbols, a design, a plan, in what appeared to us at first a brilliant but confused mass of notations, phrases, data, profound thoughts, fantasticalities, splendid images, absurdities, comic or dramatic situations; and we realise that we are before a much more complicated book than we had supposed, that everything which appeared arbitrary and sometimes extravagant is really deliberate and premeditated; in short, that we are before a book which has a key.

Where then is the key? It is, I venture to say, in the door, or rather on the cover. It is the title: *Ulysses.*

Is it possible that this Leopold Bloom, this personage whom the author handles with so little consideration, whom he exhibits in all sorts of ridiculous or humiliating postures; is the son of Laertes, the subtle Ulysses?

We shall see. Meantime, I return to the uncultivated reader who was put off by the first pages of the book, too difficult for him; and I imagine that after reading him several passages taken from different episodes, we tell him: "You understand, that Stephen Dedalus is Telemachus, and Bloom is Ulysses. He will now think that he does understand: the work of Joyce will no longer seem to him disconcerting or shocking. He will say: "I see! it's a parody of the *Odyssey*!" For indeed, to such a reader the *Odyssey* is a great awe-inspiring machine, and Ulysses and Telemachus are *heroes,* men of marble invented by the chilly ancient world to serve as moral ensamples and subjects for scholastic theses. For him they are awe-inspiring and tedious personages, inhuman; he can be interested in them only by being made to laugh at them– that is, by having them shown to him with a little of that humanity which he genuinely believes them to lack.

It is quite likely that the cultivated reader's opinion will not be very different. The latter has preserved the impression that he received at school–an impression of boredom; and since he has forgotten his Greek (if he even knew it well enough to read fluently), he can hardly be expected to find out whether his first impression was correct. The only distinction between him and the uncultivated reader is that for him the *Odyssey* is not majestic and pompous, but simply uninteresting; and consequently he will not be so ingenuous as to laugh when he sees it burlesqued. The parody will bore him as much as the work itself. How many people of culture are in this position, even among those who could read the *Odyssey* in Greek! Others think of it as a study for a favoured few, a study of philology, history, and ethnology, a speciality, a very dignified hobby; and only by accident would the beauty of this or that passage strike them. As for the creators, the poets, they have not the time to examine the question, and prefer to consider it closed. The ancient world, the Athens of the intellect, is too far away; the voyage is too expensive; and they are too busy to take it. Besides, has not its civilisation been

Joyce with his son, George, his daughter, Lucia, and his wife, Nora, in Paris in the early 1920s (Croessmann Collection of James Joyce, Special Collections/Morris Library, Southern Illinois University, Carbondale)

passed on to them by inheritance, from poet to poet, down to their own day? And yet none but they could understand the worlds of their common ancestor. Some of them, in the end, make the voyage, but too late, at a period of life when their creative power is dead. They can do more than admire and speak to others of their admiration; some of them try to communicate it and to justify it; and so they employ their final years in making a translation, usually bad, and always inadequate, of the *Iliad* or of the *Odyssey.*

The great good fortune, the extraordinary luck of James Joyce is to have made the voyage at the age when the creative power began to stir within him.

While still a schoolboy, in the seminary, he was attracted toward Ulysses through a translation of the *Odyssey;* and one day, when the master proposed to the whole class this subject: "Who is your favourite hero?" and the other boys responded with the names of various national heroes of Ireland, or great men such as St. Francis of Assisi, Galileo, or Napoleon, Joyce replied, "Ulysses." It was a reply hardly satisfactory to the master, who, as a good humanist, and well acquainted with the Homeric hero, had to take an unfavourable view. But the choice of Ulysses as favourite hero was not a child's whim. Joyce remained faithful to the son of Laertes, and throughout his adolescence he read and reread the *Odyssey,* not from love of Greek or a particular admiration for the poetry of Homer, but for the love of Ulysses. The creative labour must have begun from that day. Joyce extricated Ulysses from the text, and still more from the mighty fortifications which criticism and learning have erected about the text; and instead of trying to return to Ulysses in time, to reascend the stream of history, he made Ulysses his own contemporary, his ideal companion, his spiritual father.

What, then, in the *Odyssey,* is the moral figure of Ulysses? I am incompetent to answer this question, but better qualified persons have studied the subject, and there are several works upon it. I take that of Emile Gebhart, which has the virtue of brevity and a definite conclusion. Here are the principal points: "Homo est"– he is a man; "Ithacæ, matris, nati, patris, sociorumque amans"–he loves his country, his wife, his son, his father, and his friends; "Misericordia benevolentiaque insignis"–he is highly benevolent, and sensitive to the sorrows of others. But, our author says, "Humanum fragilitatem non effugit"–he is not exempt from human foibles. No more is Leopold Bloom, as we have seen. "Mortem scilicet reformidat"–exactly, he fears death. "Acdiutius in insula Circes moratur"–and he remains too long in Circe's island: like Bloom in the brothel.

He is a man, and the most completely human of all the heroes of the epic cycle: it is this characteristic which first endeared him to the schoolboy. Then, little by little, always bringing Ulysses nearer to himself, the young poet recreated this humanity, this human, comic, and pathetic character of his hero. And recreating him, he has set him among the circumstances of life which the author had before his own eyes–in Dublin, in our time, in the complexity of modern life, and amidst the beliefs, the sciences, and problems of our time.

From the moment that he recreates Ulysses he must logically recreate all the characters who have, in the *Odyssey,* more or less to do with Ulysses. From this point, to recreate an Odyssey on the same plane, a modern Odyssey, was only a step to take.

Hence the plan of the poem. In the *Odyssey,* Ulysses only appears in Book V. In the first four he is concerned, but the character on the stage is Telemachus. That is the part of the *Odyssey* called the Telemachy: it depicts the almost desperate situation into which the pretenders put the heir of the King of Ithaca, and the departure of Telemachus for Lacedæmon, where he expects to have news of his father. Accordingly, in *Ulysses,* the three first episodes correspond to the Telemachy; Stephen Dedalus, the spiritual son and heir of Ulysses, is constantly on the scene.

From Book V to Book XIII are unfolded the adventures of Ulysses. Joyce distinguishes twelve chief adventures, to which correspond the twelve central chapters or episodes of his book. The last books of the *Odyssey* relate the return of Ulysses to Ithaca and all the detours which terminate in the massacre of the pretenders and the recognition by Penelope. To this part of the *Odyssey,* which is called the Return (*Nostos*), correspond, in *Ulysses,* the three last episodes, which there balance the three episodes of the Telemachy.

Such are the principal lines of the design, which could be represented graphically as follows: at the top three panels, the Telemachy; below, the Twelve Episodes; at the foot, the three episodes of the Return. Eighteen panels in all; the eighteen tales.

Upon this design, without wholly losing sight of the *Odyssey,* Joyce traces a particular design in each of his panels or episodes. In this way, each episode deals with a particular art or science, contains a particular symbol, represents a special organ of the human body, has its particular colour (as in the catholic liturgy), has its proper technique, and takes place at a particular hour of the day. But this is not all: in each of the panels, thus divided, the author inscribes more particular symbols and relations.

To make this clear, let us take an example, Episode V of the adventures. Its title is Æolus. It takes place in the offices of a newspaper. The hour is noon. The relative organ of the body: the lungs. The art of which it treats: rhetoric. Its colour: red. Its symbolic figure: the editor-in-chief. Its technique: the enthymeme. Its relations: a person who corresponds to the Æolus of Homer; incest compared with journalism: the floating isle of Æolus to the press; the person called Dignam, who died suddenly three days before, and whose funeral Leopold Bloom has just attended (the funeral composes the episode of the descent into Hades), corresponds to Elpenor.

Naturally, Joyce has traced for himself, and not for the reader, this minutely detailed scheme, these eighteen subdivided panels, this close web. There is no explanatory heading or sub-heading. It is for us to decipher, if we care to take the trouble. On this web, or rather in the compartments thus prepared, Joyce has arranged his text. It is a genuine example of the art of mosaic. I have seen the drafts. They are entirely composed of abbreviated phrases underlined in various-coloured pencil. These are annotations intended to recall to the author complete phrases; and the pencilmarks indicate according to their colour that the underlined phrase belongs to such or such an episode. It makes one think of the boxes of little coloured cubes of the mosaic workers.

This plan, which cannot be detached from the book, because it is the very web of it, constitutes one of its most curious and fascinating features. If one reads *Ulysses* with attention, one cannot fail to discover this plan in time. But when one considers its rigidity, and the discipline which the author imposed upon himself, one asks how it can be that out of such a formidable labour of manipulation so living and moving a work could issue.

The manifest reason is that the author has never lost sight of the humanity of his characters, of their whole composition of virtues and faults, turpitude, and greatness: man, the creature of flesh, living out his day. And this is what one finds in reading *Ulysses*.

Among all the points which I ought to deal with, and have not space to deal with here, there are two on which it is indispensable to say a few words. One is the supposedly licentious character of certain passages– passages which in America provoked the intervention of the Society for the Suppression of Vice. The word "licentious" is inappropriate; it is both vague and weak: it should be *obscene*. In *Ulysses* Joyce wished to display moral, intellectual, and physical man entire, and in order to do so he was forced to find a place, in the moral sphere, for the sexual instinct and its various manifestations and perversions; and, in the physiological sphere, for the reproductive organs and their functions. He does not hesitate to handle this subject any more than the great casuists do, and he handles it in English in the same way that they have handled it in Latin, without respect for the conventions and scruples of the laity. His intention is neither salacious nor lewd; he simply describes and represents; and in his book the manifestations of sexual instinct do not occupy more or less place, and have neither more nor less importance, than such emotions as pity or scientific curiosity. It is of course especially in the interior monologues, the trains of thought, of the characters, and not in their conversations, that sexual instinct and erotic revery emerge; for example, in the long interior monologue of Penelope– that is to say, Bloom's wife, who is also the symbol of Gæa, the Earth. The English language has a very great store of obscene words and expressions, and the author of *Ulysses* has enriched his book generously and boldly from this vocabulary.

The other point is this: Why is Bloom a Jew? There are symbolical, mystical, and ethnological reasons which limitations of space prevent me from examining here–but which should be quite clear to readers of the book. All that I can say is that if Joyce has made his chosen hero, the spiritual father of this Stephen Dedalus who is his second self, a Jew–it is not because of anti-Semitism.

Reviews of *Ulysses*

Ulysses generated both favorable and unfavorable reactions from the moment it began being serialized in The Little Review. Its serialization halted when the magazine was found guilty of publishing obscenity, Ulysses was banned in the United States until Judge John M. Woolsey's 6 December 1933 decision overturning the ban paved the way for Random House to publish the novel in January 1934. In England Ulysses was not published until The Bodley Head edition in 1936. Amid the detractors, many reviewers recognized the significance of Joyce's novel. Joseph Collins writing in The New York Times in May 1922 made the prophetic claim that Ulysses "is the most important contribution that had been made to fictional literature in the twentieth century" and "will immortalize its author."

Although Rehm expresses uncertainty as to the future status of Ulysses, *he does recognize what Joyce has achieved.*

Review of *Ulysses*
George Rehm
Chicago Tribune (European Edition), 13 February 1922, p. 2

Ulysses, long attended upon, waited for these several years with bated breath or hopeful curiosity has at last appeared.

What it will mean to the reader is a question. Too many are the possibilities of this human flesh when finally in contact with the crude, disgusting and unpalatable facts of our short existence. One thing to be thankful for is that the volume is in a limited edition, therefore suppressed to the stenographer or high school boy. But another thing to be thankful for is that it might be the precursor to a new understanding of the printed word, a new 'coup de grace' for the salacious prudishness of our present day conventions. Great harm can be done or great good will be done by *Ulysses*.

James Joyce, an Irishman, has been hailed as a genius by several of our truly capable cognoscenti. Generally, he has been condemned, both in Great Britain and the United States by the highly moral, but unperceiving element of Comstockery that reigns with iron hand, turning down an unkempt, sticky thumb on every gladiatorial attempt to break away from the suffocating restrictions laid down by its censorship.

Yet there are passages in *Ulysses* that force a murmur of approval from the most thoroughly ordered Christian–passages deep in their understanding, profound in their knowledge, sparkling in their expression. And then there are excerpts to cause the most ultra-modern brain to gasp and question the verity of eyesight.

All known borders encircling the hemisphere of literature have been traversed with a cynical grin tossed to worldly criticism. Religion, government, ideals, life and death, all are scathingly ridiculed. I am shocked, so will you be, but I am also disturbed to find I am so easily shocked. Bah! I know that Mrs. Bloom could only think within the narrow cycle depicted by Joyce. I know that Buck Mulligan with his blasphemy against religion and convention has existed for centuries and that Stephen, firmly seated on his erudite throne, will ever decry and curse the precepts and silly credo of this life and all that has been gleaned from its past. Then why be upset?

Actually it is the unaccustomed eye and not the calloused brain that takes exception to the crude black imprint of hitherto unknown type.

The theme of *Ulysses* might be outlined as the thoughts and reflections of a number of characters, some ordinary, some extraordinary, but all genuine. The rawness of expression, the employment of words chosen from the seamy, filthy side of our vocabulary, may seem without excuse, but it is true that the prized volumes of our latter-day geniuses are permitted to repose in honored manner on library shelves only by means of a subtler turning of word and phrase.

Similar thoughts, expressions and actions have long been placed before the public but in politer terms. Joyce has gone farther, raised these thoughts, expressions and actions to their true and sometimes nasty reality.

Where is the value? Better to wait a few generations. Give the Phillistine an opportunity to rise above his level or disappear. Allow worthy judges to pass sentence on such a work, be it masterpiece or rot, and so prevent the usual mauling and manhandling invariably accorded to a comparable production by our dearly beloved public.

In all events, it is fitting to extend congratulations to Shakespeare and company and Sylvia Beach for having finally published the book.

I suppose 'Circe' will stand as the most horrible thing in literature, unless you have something on your chest still worse than this 'Agony in the Kips'. [. . .] Everything dirty seems to have the same irresistable attraction for you that cow-dung has for flies.

Stanislaus Joyce, 26 February 1922
– *Letters III,* p. 58

In one of the first reveiws of Ulysses, *Huddleston points out that Joyce is "caviare" to the general reading public. Ellmann notes that Huddleston's review "brought in 136 orders in one day" (*James Joyce, *p. 531).*

Ulysses

Sisley Huddleston
Observer, No. 6823 (5 March 1922), p. 4

No book has never been more eagerly and curiously awaited by the strange little inner circle of book-lovers and littérateurs than James Joyce's *Ulysses.* It is folly to be afraid of uttering big words because big words are abused and have become almost empty of meaning in many mouths; and with all my courage I will repeat what a few folk in somewhat precious *cénacles* have been saying–that Mr. James Joyce is a man of genius. I believe the assertion to be strictly justified, though Mr. Joyce must remain, for special reasons, caviare to the general. I confess that I cannot see how the work upon which Mr. Joyce spent seven strenuous years, years of wrestling and of agony, can ever be given to the public.

What, it will be asked, is the good of a book which must be carefully locked up, which only a handful of people will read, and which will be found unspeakably shocking even by that little handful? But one must not talk about the utility, the wisdom, the necessity, of a work of art. It is enough to know that Mr. Joyce felt that he had to write *Ulysses,* and that accordingly he wrote *Ulysses.* Of his sincerity–the sincerity of an artist–there can be no doubt. I suppose he wants readers, but he is perfectly prepared to do without readers. An expurgated edition? Not if his labour were to be entirely lost would he consent to cancel half a line! He would rather that nothing were printed than that all were not printed. Personally I may consider him misguided; personally I might find much to write about the folly of a fixed idea. But one does not, one must not, argue with authors. Whatever virtue there is in Mr. Joyce, whatever value in his work, is there because he will listen to no advice and brook no impertinent discussions. You may like or you may dislike *Ulysses,* and you are entitled to express your opinion of its merits or demerits, but you are not entitled to demand that it should be other than it is; you are not entitled to dictate to Mr. Joyce what he should do. You have to take it or leave it. This is how he is. This is what he feels about the human comedy.

He makes the painter who plumes himself on putting in the warts exceedingly foolish and outmoded, for he paints not from the outside but from the inside. Obscenity? Yes. This is undoubtedly an obscene book; but that, says Mr. Joyce, is not his fault. If the thoughts of men and women are such as

ULYSSES

by

JAMES JOYCE

SHAKESPEARE AND COMPANY
12, Rue de l'Odéon. 12

PARIS

1922

Title page for Joyce's second novel, published on 2 February 1922, his fortieth birthday (Matthew J. and Arlyn Bruccoli Collection, University of South Carolina)

The First Inscribed *Ulysses*

Harriet Shaw Weaver, Joyce's long-time benefactor, received the first copy of *Ulysses,* which he inscribed "To/ Harriet Weaver/ in token of gratitude/ James Joyce/ Paris/ 13 February 1922." In 1952 Weaver gave this copy of the novel to the National Library of Ireland, with the inscription "I give this first copy of *Ulysses* to/ the National Library of Ireland/ after thirty years/ Harriet Weaver/ Oxford/ S. Patrick's Day 1952."

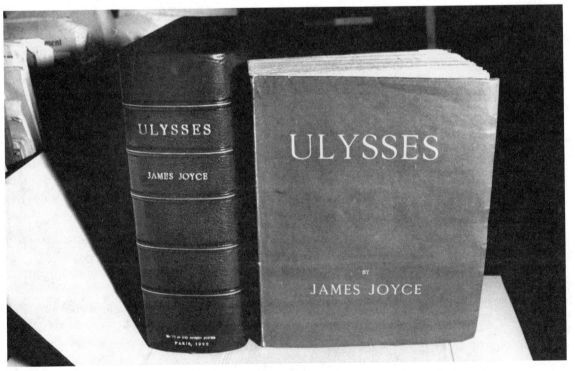

Slipcase and front wrapper for the first edition of Ulysses *(Philip Lyman, Gotham Book Mart)*

may be properly described as obscene then how can you show what life is unless you put in the obscenity? This may not be your view or mine, but if it is Mr. Joyce's he has no option but to fulfil his mission as a writer. If I understand him aright he sets out to depict not merely the fair show of things but the inner truth, and whether it is dubbed ugly or beautiful, or is a heart-wracking inextricable mixture and mystery of ugliness and beauty, has nothing to do with him as artist. He would be untrue to himself and to his subject were he to tone down and leave out. Surely it is not necessary to say that his purpose is not pornographic? The pornographic writer can always get his books published. If it is desirable he will employ the blue pencil. But Mr. Joyce, unable to obtain publication, would certainly have grown indignant at the idea of the blue pencil. The story of his difficulties has been told; the prosecution of the *Little Review* of America, which printed some chapters; the stony stare of commercial publishers; the largely accidental meeting with private persons willing to take the risk of having this gigantic volume of over 700 pages printed in France for uncertain subscribers.

The expectation that these difficulties and the belief in the exceptional genius of Mr. Joyce aroused in the restricted circles of literary craftsmen is, in my experience, unprecedented. Those who have read the earlier books of Mr. Joyce have realised that here is a man who can write. 'We are mighty fine fellows nowadays,' cried Stevenson, 'but we cannot write like Hazlitt!' and many of us have felt like that about Joyce. There are phrases in which the words are packed tightly, as trim, as taut, as perfect as these things can be. There are fine ellipses in which a great sweep of meaning is concentrated into a single just-right sentence. There is a spot of colour which sets the page aglow. There is a point of light which gives life to the world as the lamp-lighter gives sudden life to the street. Here is erudition transfigured by imagination. A piece of out-of-the-way book knowledge or two lines of a silly jingle which we heard when we were boys—they fall wonderfully into their place. I detect a certain slackness here and there, as is inevitable in a book of such length; but I think that the craftsman will, forgetful altogether of the ethics of this book, its amazing a- morality, and completely careless of the content, best appreciate the sheer power of craftsmanship.

As for the matter, I think I can best convey some idea of *Ulysses* by reminding the reader how odd is the association of ideas when one allows all kinds of what are called thoughts, but which have nothing to do with thinking, to pass in higgledy-piggledy procession through one's mind—one's subconscious mind, I suppose it is called in present-day jargon. Psycho-analysis is, I believe, very strong about this. . . . Now the purpose of Mr. Joyce is, of course, much larger than to jot down all the incongruous notions that rattle around the arena of the cranium; but,

Sandymount Strand, circa 1952, the setting of the Proteus and Nausikaa episodes, chapters 3 and 13 (Courtesy of the Irish Tourist Board)

Joyce in the 1920s after one of his eye operations. Joyce began having serious eye problems in August 1917 while living in Zürich after his first attack of glaucoma. Joyce wrote the poem "Bahnhofstrasse" (the place of the attack) in 1918, which was included in Pomes Penyeach *(James Joyce Collection, General Collection, Beinecke Rare Book and Manuscript Library, Yale University).*

described narrowly, that is what he does. Has anybody done it before? I do not know, but I am certain that no one ever did it at such length and with such thoroughness. It is obvious that if one tries to put down everything in the life of a man, a single day in that life will fill many volumes. The external events are really of little importance except as forming a starting-point for reflection. Mr. Joyce's style is such that it is sometimes difficult to distinguish between what is taking place externally and what is taking place internally. The internal action is put on the same plane as the external action. Mr. Joyce indicates both with infinite humour and with extraordinary precision. One feels that these things are essentially, ineluctably, true. These are exact notations of trivial but tremendous motions, and these are truly the inconsequential but significant things that one says to oneself. There is Mr. Bloom at the funeral wondering how he can discreetly shift the tablet of soap which he has purchased and put in his tail pocket. As he passes the gasworks in the mourning carriage he wonders whether it's true that to live near a gasworks prevents whooping-cough. A rat in

the cemetery inspires horrible and humorous speculations. There are comic and sublime contrasts. The irrelevance and irreverence of the attitude of mankind before the great facts are remorselessly laid bare. Gross animality and subtle spirituality intermingle. Blasphemy and beauty, poetry and piggishness, jostle each other. But, on the whole, one becomes tired of beastliness always breaking in. There is one chapter devoted to the reverie of a woman, and her *monologue intérieur* is, I imagine–and am bound in all honesty to say–the vilest, according to ordinary standards, in all literature, And yet its very obscenity is somehow beautiful and wrings the soul to pity. Is that not high art? I cannot, however, believe that sex plays such a preponderant part in life as Mr. Joyce represents. He may aim at putting everything in, but he has, of course, like everybody else, selected carefully what he puts in. Has he not exaggerated the vulgarity and magnified the madness of mankind and the mysterious materiality of the universe?

Although many readers thought Ulysses *obscene and vulgar, most recognized it as an exceptional accomplishment. In the penultimate paragraph of the following review, George Slocombe, who was later among the handful of reviewers of* Pomes Penyeach *(1927), concludes that "the book is a staggering feat which . . . may never be attempted again."*

Review of *Ulysses*

George Slocombe
Daily Herald (London), 17 March 1922, p. 4

An important event in Paris this week has been the appearance, long-heralded and joyfully acclaimed, of Mr. James Joyce's *Ulysses.* Mr. Joyce is a young Irishman who is better known in the United States than in his native country, and better known in Paris perhaps than in either. When the early portents of *Ulysses* broke upon a dazed and incredulous world of very wide-awake and credulous young men, in the pages of the defunct *Little Review,* there was one very occasional reader of that publication who read the first instalments of this astonishing work very carefully five times, and then pressed firmly on the button labelled 'Literary Censorship and Public Morals.'

Painting by Paul Joyce for chapter 3, the Proteus episode
(Courtesy of Paul Joyce)

Whereupon a squad of six large Irish policeman sprang up kinema-fashion from their porterhouse-steak breakfasts and sallied forth to suppress . . . .

And here it is at last, as large as a telephone directory or a family Bible, and with many of the literary and social characteristics of each. It took, I understand, nearly six years of Mr. Joyce's life to write, and it will take nearly six years of ours to read. And, after all, that is not much for the task, which apparently Mr. Joyce set himself, of writing the complete physical and spiritual life of a man during a day and a night. No other writer in the world, save perhaps an eighteenth-century clergyman writing Universal Treatises on forty pounds a year, has ever attempted anything so stupendous. And few writers have flung at the world Mr. Joyce's amazing precocity, untrammelled licence, prodigious patience, and shameless unreserve.

The real book begins with the uprising in the morning of a humble, though not obscure, man in the city of Dublin, and ends with his return home in the small hours of the following morning. During that interval the spiritual projection of Mr. Joyce, expressed in the interesting mind of Mr. Leopold Bloom, ranges like Moby Dick throughout the watery globe, and communes with incommunicable things under the stars.

Yet during that interval the body and the chained spirit of Mr. Bloom have merely partaken of, or assisted in, a bath at a public bathing establishment, a funeral, a luncheon in an odorous eating-house, an argument in the editorial offices of the *Freeman's Journal,* a discussion in a public-house, another meal and the song of a man at a piano, drinks with medical students in the common room of a lying-in hospital (with a woman three days in labour overhead), a discussion at the house of 'Æ,' a walk to the rocky shore at Howth, the return to town, a meeting with friends wandering drunkenly in a slum, a dispute with English soldiers, and a talk with a sailor in a cabmen's shelter.

And of these thin incidents Mr. Joyce makes a book that is a man's life; not every man's life, perhaps, but the life of Everyman. Among other things which we knew before, and some that we did not want to know, the book shows chiefly (1) that no man is an ordinary man, and (2) that all a man's thoughts do not make a book, though some of them may, as witness the incomparable Book of job.

Mr. Joyce would have us see the wide waters and the illimitable stars of this universe through the rather muddied if wondering eye of his introspective Jewish husband in Dublin. We do not see the universe, but we end by seeing the man, approaching him through scorn to pity. And approaching his wife through pity to scorn, we see her too, a shallower water running fast.

There is much in this book to be forgiven to Mr. Joyce. For hundreds of pages he will write desperately, erudite nonsense, that, unfortunately, is not nonsense to himself. Often he writes as if his pen were dipped in obscenity and there were a whole ink-bottle of it to be exhausted before his thoughts would run clear. And his pen is often a scratchy pen, and scratchiness worries us for chapter after chapter as if (it being Sunday and the shops closed) no other pen were available.

But all in all, and by and large, and reading the end first, and skipping the interminable and elaborate syntheses of the middle part, the book is a staggering feat which, once attempted and more than half achieved, may never be attempted again–the way of a cosmic atom under heaven during a day and a night.

S. P. B. Mais's unfavorable review of Ulysses *appeared in the same journal for which Joyce once wrote reviews.*

An Irish Revel: And Some Flappers
S. P. B. Mais
Daily Express, 25 March 1922, n. p.

A few days ago Mr. Gilbert Cannan warned us on this page that the modern novelist's function was to 'follow life to places and recesses in the human soul and heart inaccessible to the camera.'

Mr. James Joyce, an Irish novelist to whom no one would deny originality, has followed it in *Ulysses* . . . to recesses which few of us altogether care to probe. It is significant that most of the younger writers defy conventional reticences in so far as they describe all that most of us do and say. Mr. Joyce goes much further: from his pages there leap out at us all our most secret and most unsavoury private thoughts. Our first impression is that of sheer disgust, our second of irritability because we never know whether a character is speaking or merely thinking, our third of boredom at the continual harping on obscenities (nothing cloys a reader's appetite so quickly as dirt); our fourth, of real interest as watching the vagaries of a mind sensitive to all scents and sounds and colours. But art (if this is art) consists no longer in selection . . . Reading Mr. Joyce is like making an excursion into Bolshevist Russia: all standards go by the board: reading Mr. Coleridge's excellent selections [in *Letters to my Grandson on the*

Glory of English Prose, by Stephen Coleridge] is to be soothed into sanity again and to be made aware of the necessity for putting up a fight to preserve the noble qualities of balance, rhythm, harmony, and reverence for simple majesty that have been for three centuries the glory of our written tongue. . . .

Critic Alfred Noyes in his essay "Rottenness in Literature" (Sunday Chronicle, 29 October 1922) asserted that this review was the only "sound analysis of the book" that he had seen in England.

The Scandal of *Ulysses*
Aramis
Sporting Times, no. 34 (1 April 1922), p. 4

After a rather boresome perusal of James Joyce's *Ulysses,* published in Paris for private subscribers at the rate of three guineas in francs, I can realise one reason at least for Puritan America's Society for the Prevention of Vice, and can understand why the Yankee judges fined the publishers of *The Little Review* one hundred dollars for the original publication of a very rancid chapter of the Joyce stuff, which appears to have been written by a perverted lunatic who has made a speciality of the literature of the latrine.

As a readers of the *Pink' Un* know, I have dealt appreciatively with many unconventional books in these pages; but I have no stomach for *Ulysses,* and do not care to expose my editor to the imminent risk of appearance in court for countenancing the unprintable. James Joyce is a writer of talent, but in *Ulysses* he has ruled out all the elementary decencies of life and dwells appreciatively on things that sniggering louts of schoolboys guffaw about. In addition to this stupid glorification of mere filth, the book suffers from being written in the manner of a demented George Meredith. There are whole chapters of it without any punctuation or other guide to what the writer is really getting at. Two-thirds of it is incoherent, and the passages that are plainly written are devoid of wit, displaying only a coarse salacrity intended for humour.

. . . .

The main contents of the book are enough to make a Hottentot sick. *Ulysses* would have been boycotted in the palmiest days of Holywell Street. And yet there are quite a number of the New York intelligentsia who declare that Joyce has written the best book in the world, and that *Ulysses* is the topmost of them.

*Painting by Paul Joyce for chapter 4, the Calypso epsiode
(courtesy of Paul Joyce)*

Over the one supremely nauseous chapter that the publishers of *The Little Review* were indicted on, a great deal of highbrow nonsense was talked in court by the witness for the defence. Mr. Philip Moeller, in bland tones, said that the chapter was 'an unveiling of the subconscious mind in the Freudian manner, and that he saw no possibility of these revelations being aphrodisiac in their influence.'

The court gasped, and one of the judges protested: 'Here, here, you might as well talk Russian. Speak plain English if you want us to understand what you're saying.'

Moeller was then asked what he thought would be the effect of the objectionable chapter on the mind of the average reader. The suave and lofty littérateur replied: 'I think it would mystify him.'

I fancy that it would also have the very simple effect of an ordinary emetic. *Ulysses* is not alone sordidly pornographic, but it is intensely dull. As the volume is about the size of the *London Directory*, I do not envy anyone who reads it for pleasure.

—reprinted from *James Joyce: The Critical Heritage*

The English literary critic and journalist John Middleton Murry was married to the writer Katherine Mansfield; he was editor of Athenaeum *(1919–1921) and later the* Adelphi *(1923–1930). In his review of* Ulysses, *he sharply disagrees with the French critic and translator M. Valéry Larbaud's comment that with this novel Ireland re-enters European literature. For Murry, Joyce as a novelist is too much the individualist to have succeeded in such a feat.*

Mr. Joyce's *Ulysses*
J. Middleton Murry

The Nation & Athenæum, 31 (22 April 1922): 124–125

The cant phrase of judgment upon Mr. Joyce's *magnum opus*—700 quarto pages, 1,400 of ordinary novel size—has been launched by a French critic. 'With this book,' says M. Valéry Larbaud, 'Ireland makes a sensational re-entrance into high European literature.' Whether anyone, even M. Larbaud himself, knows what is meant by the last three words, we cannot tell. A phrase does not have to be intelligible in order to succeed, and we already hear echoes of this pronouncement. "Ulysses" somehow is European; everything else is not.

Well, well. "Ulysses" is many things: it is very big, it is hard to read, difficult to procure, unlike any other book that has been written, extraordinarily interesting to those who have patience (any they need it), the work of an intensely serious man. But European? That, we should have thought, is the last epithet to apply to it. Indeed, in trying to define it, we return again and again, no matter by what road we set out, to the conception that it is non-European. It is not the less important for that. "The Brothers Karamazov," for instance, is not European; and, precisely because of the non-European elements which it contains, it is a mighty work. And "Ulysses" is, perhaps, even less European than "Karamozov."

For what does the word "European," applied to a work of literature, mean? It means that the author, consciously or unconsciously, accepts the postulates of Western civilization. He accepts the principle of order, the social law (or convention) that certain things are good and certain other things are evil. He obeys the law because he feels himself to be a member of society, and an instinct warns him that deliberate and continual disobedience leads to the disintegration of the society which is Europe. It is not the morality (which is an individual affair) which makes the European, but the social morality. A Christian, for instance, may or may not be a European; if he is an extreme Christian, he will probably not be one. The Catholic Church represents the triumph of Europeanism over the anti-European principles of its founder–the submission of the individual to the social principle. And a writer who is

European not only makes this act of submission in himself, but regards his writing also as a social act. He respects the limitations which the essential social law of taste imposes; he acknowledges the social tradition of Europe.

Mr. Joyce does none of these things. He is the extreme individualist. He acknowledges no social morality, and he completely rejects the claim of social morality to determine what he shall, or shall not, write. He is the egocentric rebel in *excelsis,* the arch-esoteric. European! He is the man with the bomb who would blow what remains of Europe into the sky. But he is so individual that very few people will know when the bomb has exploded. His intention, so far as he has any social intention, is completely anarchic.

But in order to be a successful anarchist you must work within the comprehension of society. You have to use the time-tables and the language of ordinary men. By the excess of his anarchy, Mr. Joyce makes himself socially harmless. There is not the faintest need to be concerned about his influence. He will have some, no doubt; but it will be canalized and concentrated. The head that is strong enough to read "Ulysses" will not be turned by it.

Upon such a head, indeed, the influence of "Ulysses" may be wholly excellent. For the driving impulse of this remarkable book is an immense, an unprecedented, liberation of suppressions. Something utterly different from the childish and futile coprophily of the "Young Girl's Diary" and other Freudian confessions; the liberation of the suppressions of an adult man who has lived under the shadow of the Roman Catholic Church in a country where that Church is at its least European, and is merely an immense reinforcement of Puritanism. And not only is the effort at liberation much vaster and more significant than the corresponding efforts with which modern literature begins to be strewn, but the mind which undertakes it is indisputably the mind of an artist, abnormally sensitive to the secret individuality of emotions and things, abnormally sensitive also to spiritual beauty. A singular chapter of "The Brothers Karamazov" bears the title "Self-Lacerations." "Ulysses" is, fundamentally (though it is much besides), an immense, a prodigious self-laceration, the tearing-away from himself, by a half-demented man of genius, of inhibitions and limitations which have grown to be flesh of his flesh. And those who read it will profit by the vicarious sacrifice.

But limitations and inhibitions are necessary to the European. Not, indeed, the extraordinary ones which oppressed the author of "Ulysses," the explosiveness of whose anarchy is in direct proportion to the closeness of the constraint, but some. The best European is the one who bears his restrictions with the best grace, as recogniz-

ing their necessity. Mr. Joyce's book will possibly serve others as an indication of the limits they must not pass. It may help them to free themselves of inhibitions which are really destructive of vitality and, at the same time, make it easier for them to accept those which are the conditions of civilization, and perhaps of art itself. For just as Mr. Joyce is in rebellion against the lucidity and comprehensibility of civilized art. Esoteric masterpieces are all very well, and they may be potent esoteric influences, but they are not masterpieces simply because they are esoteric. The enthusiast who tries to bludgeon the *bourgeois* with "Ulysses," who tries to convict the age of intolerable crassness because it will not read it, is not only an enthusiast, he is a fool. A literary masterpiece lends itself to enjoyment at many angles of interpretation; "Ulysses" only at one and that one an angle which imposes a great deal of discomfort and fatigue on the person who tries to adjust himself to it.

Still, if we ask the essential question: Is "Ulysses" a refection of life through an individual consciousness! there can be no doubt of the reply. It is. It is a reflection of life through a singularly complex consciousness; and this existence of three human beings: Stephen Dedalus (the hero of "The Portrait of the Artist as a Young Man"), Leopold Bloom, a Hungarian Jew by descent, now an advertisement canvasser in Dublin, and Bloom's wife Marion. One might almost say that all the thoughts and all the experience of those beings, real or imaginary, from their waking to their sleeping on a spring day in Dublin in 1904, are somehow given by Mr. Joyce: and not only their conscious thoughts–and they are very differently conscious–but the very fringes of their sentience. More even than that, for in what seems to us to be indisputably the most masterly part of the book, a manifestation of a really rare creativeness, Mr. Joyce stages a kind of *Walpurgisnacht* of his chief characters. Bloom and Dedalus are revealed in a kingdom where the practical reactions of life are no more. They become human quintessentialities, realized potencies of the subconscious, metaphysical egos. How shall we describe them? Mr. Joyce wields a magic comparable to that of Goethe in the second part of "Faust," or of Dostoevsky in "Ivan's Dream." In this part of "Ulysses"–let us say it plainly, in order that we may have our share of the contempt or the glory a hundred years hence–a genius of the very highest order, strictly comparable to Goethe's or Dostoevsky's is evident. This transcendental buffoonery, this sudden uprush of the *vis comica* into a world wherein the tragic incompatibility of the practical and the instinctive is embodied, is a very great achievement. It is the vital centre of Mr. Joyce's book, and the intensity of life which it contains is sufficient to animate the whole if it.

And much of it needs animation. The curse of nimiety, of too-muchness, hangs over it as a whole. Mr.

In chapter 5, the Lotus-Eaters episode, Bloom buys a cake of lemon soap at F. W. Sweny, Chemist. He planned, but forgot to return later in the day, to pick up a refill of Molly's face lotion (courtesy of Lucretia Joyce Lyons).

Joyce has made a superhuman effort to empty the whole of his consciousness into it. He has poured into it his inhibitions, not only as a man and as an artist–these we have tried to explain–but also as a writer in the purely technical sense. In one of his sections he goes so far as to put his narrative in the form of successive parodies of English prose, from the Anglo-Saxon chronicles to the latest American slang. Every trick that a keen-witted man could conceivably play with the English language, and some that were inconceivable until Mr. Joyce arrived, is played somewhere in his book. Every thought that a super-subtle modern can think seems to be hidden somewhere in its inspissated obscurities. We have done our utmost during the best part of a fortnight to master "Ulysses," yet even now we should hesitate to say that we understand–in the sense of understanding not merely the thing said, but the motive of its being said–more than four-fifths of it.

It may, therefore, be said that our negative judgments are only provisional, and that fuller illumination would make the dark places clear. Possibly. But we cannot spend our life with "Ulysses." And there are many places in which both the thing said and the motive are plain to us, where the trouble seems to be simply that Mr. Joyce has been unable to hold his hand, where he

seems to have dropped the illusion of truth for the truth, the effect of truth for the fact, which is, in art, to drop the bone for the shadow. There is a vast difference between emptying a man's mind of all its possible thoughts during an hour on to paper, and producing the impression of an hour of a man's thinking. The thoughts of an imaginary half-minute may give us that far better than the thoughts of an actual hour. Again and again in "Ulysses" we lose the circumstance in the circumstantiality. Had it been half the size it might have been twice as big. But then Mr. Joyce might not have been able to give rein to all his inhibitions.

That purpose, we repeat, seems to have determined Mr. Joyce's creation. "Ulysses" has form, a subtle form, but the form is not strong enough to resist overloading, not sufficient to prevent Mr. Joyce from being the victim of his own anarchy. One cannot be too conservative in one's methods of proclaiming the *Weltvernichtungsidee.* Mr. Joyce should ride his genius like a hippogriff. If he bitted it with a chain-cable it would still be a tremendous steed–but not a European one. That, never!

Whether the day of the European is over is another question.

Although the English journalist, naturalistic novelist, and playwright Arnold Bennett had been bored by A Portrait of the Artist as a Young Man, *he thought* Ulysses *a masterpiece.*

James Joyce's *Ulysses*
Arnold Bennett
Outlook (London), (29 April 1922): 337–339

The fame of James Joyce was founded in this country mainly by H. G. Wells, whose praise of *A Portrait of the Artist as a Young Man* had very considerable influence upon the young. For although the severe young spend much time, seated upon the floor, in explaining to each other that H. G. Wells is and must be a back number, he can do almost what he likes with them. I read *A Portrait of the Artist as a Young Man* under the hypnotic influence of H. G. Wells. Indeed, he commanded me to read it and to admire it extremely. I did both. I said: "Yes, it is great stuff." But in the horrid inaccessible thickets of my mind I heard a voice saying: "On the whole, the book has bored you." And on the whole it had; and with the efflux of time I began to announce this truth. There are scenes of genius in the novel; from end to end it shows a sense of style; but large portions of it are dull, pompous, absurb, confused, and undirected. The author had not quite decided what he was after, and even if he had decided he would not have known how to get it. He had resources, but could not use them. He bungled the affair, and then threw his chin up and defied anyone to assert that he had not done what he did in the way he did solely because he wanted to do precisely that thing in precisely that way. A *post facto* pose with which all creative artists, and some others, are experientially acquainted.

A year or two later one of the intellectual young exhibited to me a copy of *The Little Review,* which monthly was then being mentioned in the best circles. I think this must have been in the period when even Mr. Middleton Murry was young. *The Little Review* contained an instalment of James Joyce's *Ulysses.* I obediently glanced through the instalment and concluded that it was an affected triviality which must have been planned in what the French so delicately call a *chalet de nécessité.* I expressed this view, and the intellectual young concurred therein; but I seemed to detect in the concurrence a note of mere politeness to the grey-haired. Hence, recalling the time when I laughed at Cézanne's pictures, I wondered whether there might not be something real in the pages after all.

And then the other day, opening *La Nouvelle Revue Française,* I beheld blazing on its brow an article by Valéry Larbaud entitled " James Joyce." I was shaken. *La Nouvelle Revue Française* is in my opinion the finest literary periodical in the world. Valéry Larbaud is a critic whom it is impossible to ignore. He is neither old nor young. He is immensely experienced in imaginative literature, and a novelist himself. He has taste. His knowledge of the English language and English literature is only less peculiar and profound than his knowledge of the French language and French literature. He is, indeed, a devil of a fellow. He probably knows more about Walter Savage Landor and Samuel Butler than anybody else on earth. He and Léon Paul Fargue are the only persons on earth who understand the verse of St. Léger Léger. He once amazed and delighted me by stating, quite on his own, that the most accomplished of all the younger British poets was Edith Sitwell: a true saying, though I had said it before him. And here was Valéry Larbaud producing a long article on James Joyce, and *La Nouvelle Revue Française* giving it the place of honour! At this point, if I was A. B. Walkley, I should interject that that *m'avait donné furieusement à penser,* and, if I were Mr. Clive Bell, that that had made me exclaim (in French) *Mon Dieu!* What I actually did say was something other.

Valéry Larbaud's article was, according to his wont, exhaustive. It contains a comprehensive account of James Joyce from the creation to the present day, and in particular a full analysis and final estimate of *Ulysses.* And the conclusion of it is that *Ulysses* is a masterpiece, considered, shapely, and thoroughly achieved. I was left with no alternative but to read the thing. I saw the book at the house of a friend and I said: "You have just got to lend me this." She lent it to me. It looks like a quarto, but it is an octavo: over two inches thick; 730 pages, each of a superficies of seventy square inches; over half a million words; and so precariously *broché* that when you begin to read it in bed it at once disintegrates into leaves, largely Sybilline. However, I read it. Perhaps some pages here and there I only inspected, but roughly speaking did I read it. And as I finished it I had the sensation of a general who has just put down an insurrection.

Much has been made of the fact that the author takes more than seven hundred big pages to describe the passage of less than twenty hours. But I see nothing very wonderful in this. Given sufficient time, paper, childish caprice, and obstinacy, one might easily write over seven thousand pages about twenty hours of life. A young French author once dreamed of a prose epic in many volumes, of which the first one was to be entirely devoted to the hero's journey in a cab from his home to the railway terminus. And why not? Certainly a book to a day need not be excessive. But it all depends on the day chosen. There is no clear proof that James Joyce chose for his theme any particular day. He is evidently of a sardonic temper, and I expect that he found malicious pleasure in picking up the first common day that came to hand. It happened to nearly the dailiest day possible. (If he had thought of it he would have chosen a day on which the hero was confined to his bed with a *colique sèche*.) The uninstructed reader can perceive no form, no artistic plan, no "organisation" (Henry James's excellent word) in the chosen day.

But the uninstructed reader is blind. According to Valéry Larbaud the day was very elaborately planned and organised. James Joyce loved the *Odyssey* in his youth, and the spirit of Homer presided over the shaping of the present work, which is alleged to be full of Homeric parallels. It may be so. Obviously Valéry Larbaud has discussed the work at length with the author. I should suspect the author of pulling Valéry Larbaud's leg, were it not that Larbaud has seen with his own eyes the author's drafts. They consist of notes of phrases meant to remind the author of complete phrases; the notes are crossed out by pencil marks of different colours; and the colour indicates the particular episode into which the phrase has been inserted. This method of composing a novel recalls Walter Pater's celebrated mosaics of bits of paper each holding a preciosity. It is weird, but it does demonstrate that the author laboured on some sort of an organised plan.

I therefore concede him a plan, successful or unsuccessful. And in doing so I must animadvert upon his lamentable lack of manners. For he gives absolutely no help to the reader. He behaves like a salesman in an old-fashioned, well-established small West-End shop, whose deameanour seems to say to you as you enter: "What! Here's another of 'em. I'll soon put him off. Now what in hell do *you* want, sir?" Nothing is easier than for an author to help his reader; to do so involves no sacrifice of principle, nor can it impair the value of the book. A writer writes not merely because he is interested, but also because he desires to interest. A sound book ought to be a fair compromise between author and reader. James Joyce, however, does not view the matter thus. He apparently thinks that there is something truly artistic and high-minded in playing the lout to the innocent and defenceless reader. As a matter of fact, there isn't. In playing the lout there is something low-minded and inartistic. *Ulysses* would have been a better book and a much better appreciated book, if the author had extended to his public the common courtesies of literature. After all, to comprehend *Ulysses* is not among the recognised learned professions, and nobody should give his entire existence to the job.

A more serious objection to the novel is its pervading difficult dullness. There is always a danger that short quotations may give a misleading and unfair impression of a work, or even of a chapter in a work; but I must risk the following extract, which I have conscientiously chosen as representative:

Making for the museum gate with long windy strides he lifted his eyes. Handsome building. Sir Thomas Deane designed. Not following me?

Didn't see me perhaps. Light in his eyes.

The flutter of his breath came forth in short sighs. Quick. Cold statues; quiet there. Safe in a minute.

No, he didn't see me. After two. Just at the gate.

My heart!

His eyes beating looked steadfastly at cream curves of stone. Sir Thomas Deane was the Greek architecture.

Looking for something I.

Scores and hundreds of pages are filled with this kind of composition. Of course, the author is trying to reproduce the thoughts of the personage, and his verbal method can be justified–does, indeed, richly justify itself here and there in the story. But upon the whole, though the reproduction is successful, the things reproduced appear too often to be trivial and perfectly futile in the narrative. I would not accuse him of what is absurdly called "photographic realism." But I would say that much of the book is more like an official short-hand-writer's "note" than a novel. In some of his moods the author is resolved at any price not to select, nor to make even the shortest leap from one point of interest to another. He has taken oath with himself to put it all down and be hanged to it. He would scorn the selective skill in such a masterpiece of narrative technique as *Esther Waters* (whose brilliance only experts can fully appreciate). He would probably defend himself, and find disciples to defend him. But unless the experience of creative artists since the recorded beginning of art is quite worthless, James Joyce is quite wrongheaded. Anyhow, with his wilfulness, he has made novel-reading into a fair imitation of penal servitude. It is not as if his rendering of life was exhaustive, or had the slightest pretension to be exhaustive. The rendering is extremely and ostentatiously partial. The author seems to have no geographical sense, little sense of environment, no sense of the general kindness of human nature, and not much poetical sense. Worse than all, he has positively no sense of perspective. But my criticism of the artist in him goes deeper. His vision of the world and its inhabitants is mean, hostile, and uncharitable. He has a colossal "down" on humanity. Now, Christ in his all-embracing charity might have written a supreme novel. Beelzebub could not.

Withal, James Joyce is a very astonishing phenomenon in letters. He is sometimes dazzlingly original. If he does not see life whole he sees it piercingly. His ingenuity is marvellous. He has wit. He has a prodigious humour. He is afraid of naught. And had heaven in its wisdom thought fit not to deprive him of that basic sagacity and that moral self-dominion which alone enable an artist to assemble and control and fully utilise his powers, he would have stood a chance of being one of the greatest novelists that ever lived.

The best portions of the novel (unfortunately they constitute only a fraction of the whole) are superb. I single out the long orgiastic scene, and the long unspoken monologue of Mrs. Bloom which closes the book.

The former will easily bear comparison with Rabelais at his fantastical finest; it leaves Petronius out of sight. It has plenary inspiration. It is the richest stuff, handled with a virtuosity to match the quality of the material. The latter (forty difficult pages, some twenty-five thousand words without any punctuation at all) might in its utterly convincing realism be an actual document, the magical record of inmost thoughts thought by a woman that existed. Talk about understanding "feminine psychology" . . . I have never read anything to surpass it, and I doubt if I have ever read anything to equal it. My blame may have seemed extravagant, and my praise may seem extravagant; but that is how I feel about James Joyce.

It would be unfair to the public not to refer to the indecency of *Ulysses*. The book is not pornographic, and can produce on nobody the effects of a pornographic book. But it is more indecent, obscene, scatological, and licentious than the majority of professedly pornographical books. James Joyce sticks at nothing, literally. He forbids himself no word. He says everything–everything. The code is smashed to bits. Many persons could not continue reading *Ulysses;* they would be obliged, by mere shock, to drop it. It is published in France, but not in French, and I imagine that if it had been published in French there would have been trouble about it even in Paris. It must cause reflection in the minds of all those of us who have hitherto held and preached that honest works of art ought to be exempt from police interference. Is the staggering indecency justified by results obtained? The great majority of Britons would say that nothing could justify it. For myself I think that in the main it is not justified by results obtained; but I must plainly add, at the risk of opprobrium, that in the finest passages it is in my opinion justified.

Joyce and Beach at Shakespeare and Company, with posters citing reviews of Ulysses *on the wall behind them (Princeton University Library)*

James Joyce's Amazing Chronicle
Joseph Collins
The New York Times Book Review (28 May 1922), pp. 6, 17

A few intuitive, sensitive visionaries may understand and comprehend *Ulysses*, James Joyce's new and mammoth volume, without going through a course of training or instruction, but the average intelligent reader will glean little or nothing from it–even from careful perusal, one might properly say study, of it– save bewilderment and a sense of disgust. It should be companioned with a key and a glossary like the Berlitz books. Then the attentive and diligent reader would eventually get some comprehension of Mr. Joyce's message.

That he has a message there can be no doubt. He seeks to tell the world of the people that he has encountered in the forty years of sentient existence; to describe their conduct and speech and to analyze their motives, and to relate the effect the 'world', sordid, turbulent, disorderly, with mephitic atmosphere engendered by alcohol and the dominant ecclesiasticism of his country, had upon him, an emotional Celt, an egocentric genius, whose chief diversion and keenest pleasure is self-analysis and whose lifelong important occupation has been keeping

*Painting by Paul Joyce for chapter 7, the Æolus episode
(courtesy of Paul Joyce)*

a notebook in which has been recorded incident encountered and speech heard with photographic accuracy and Boswellian fidelity. Moreover, he is determined to tell it in a new way. Not in straightforward, narrative fashion, with a certain sequentiality of idea, fact, occurrence, in sentence, phrase and paragraph that is comprehensible to a person of education and culture, but in parodies of classic prose and current slang, in perversions of sacred literature, in carefully metered prose with studied incoherence, in symbols so occult and mystic that only the initiated and profoundly versed can understand–in short, by means of every trick and illusion that a master artificer, or even magician, can play with the English language.

Before proceeding with a brief analysis of "Ulysses," and comment on its construction and its content. I wish to characterize it. "Ulysses" is the most important contribution that has been made to fictional literature in the twentieth century. It will immortalize its author with the same certainty that Gargantua and Pantagruel immortalized Rabelais, and "The Brothers Karamazof" Dostoyevsky. It is likely that there is no one writing English today that could parallel Mr. Joyce's feat, and it is also likely that few would care to do it were they capable. That statement requires that it be said at once that Mr. Joyce has seen fit to use words and phrases that the entire world has covenanted and people in general, cultured and uncultured, civilized and savage, believer and heathen, have agreed shall not to be used, and which are base, vulgar, vicious and depraved. Mr. Joyce's reply to this is: 'This race and this country and this life produced me–I shall express myself as I am.'

An endurance test should always be preceded by training. It requires real endurance to finish "Ulysses." The best training for it is careful perusal or reperusal of "The Portrait of the Artist as a Young Man," the volume published six or seven years ago, which revealed Mr. Joyce's capacity to externalize his consciousness, to set it down in words. It is the story of his own life before he exiled himself from his native land, told with uncommon candor and extraordinary revelation of thought, impulse and action, many an incident of a nature and texture which most persons do not feel free to reveal, or which they do not feel it is decent and proper to confide to the world. . . .

The salient facts of Mr. Joyce's life with which the reader who seeks to comprehend his writings should be familiar are as follows: He was one of many children of South Ireland Catholic parents. In his early childhood his father had not yet dissipated his small fortune and he was sent to Clongowes Woods, a renowned Jesuit college near Dublin, and remained there until it seemed to his teachers and his parents that he should decide whether or not he had a vocation; that is, whether he felt within himself, in his soul, a desire to join the order. After some religious experiences he lost his faith, then his patriotism, and held up those with whom he formerly worshipped to ridicule, and his country and her aspirations to contumely. He continued his studies in the University of Dublin notwithstanding the sordid poverty of his family. After graduation he decided to study medicine, and in fact he did pursue such studies for two or three years, one of them in the medical school of the University of Paris. Eventually he became convinced that medicine was not his vocation, even though funds were available for him to continue his studies, and he decided to take up singing as a profession, having a phenomenally beautiful tenor voice.

These three novitiates furnished him with all the material he has used in the four volumes that he has published. Matrimony, parentage, ill health and a number of other factors put an end to his musical ambitions and for several years previous to the outbreak of the war he gained his daily bread by teaching the Austrians of Trieste English and Italian, having a mastery of the latter language that would flatter a Padovian professor. The war drove him to the haven of the expatriate, Switzerland, and for four years he taught German, Italian, French, English to anyone in Berne who had time, ambition and money to acquire a new language. Since the armistice he has lived in Paris, finishing "Ulysses," his magnum opus, which he says and believes represents everything that he has to say and which ill advisedly he attempted to submit to the world through the columns of The Little Review. It is now published "privately for subscribers only."

As a boy Mr. Joyce's favorite hero was Odysseus. He approved of his subterfuge for evading military service, he envied him the companionship of Penelope, all his latent vengeance was vicariously satisfied by reading of the way in which he revenged himself on Palamedes, while the craftiness and resourcefulness of the final artificer of the siege of Troy made him permanently big with admiration and affection. But it was the ten years of his hero's life after he had eaten of the lotus plant that wholly seduced Mr. Joyce, child and man, and appeased his emotional soul. As years went by he identified many of his own experiences with those of the slayer of Polyphemus and the favorite of Pallas-Athene; so, after careful preparation and planning he decided to write a new Odyssey, to whose surge and thunder the whole world would listen. In early life Mr. Joyce had definitely identified himself as Dedalus, the Athenian architect, sculptor and magician. This probably took place about the time that he became convinced he was not the child of his parents but a person of distinction and they his foster parents. A very common occurrence in potential psychopaths and budding geniuses. It is as Stephen Dedalus that Mr. Joyce carries on in "Ulysses." Indeed, that book is the record of his thoughts, antics, vagaries, and more particularly his actions, and of Leopold Bloom, a Hungarian Jew, who has lost his name and religion, a sensuous rags and tatters Hamlet, and who took to wife one Marion Tweedy, the daughter of a noncommissioned officer stationed in Gibraltar.

Mr. Joyce is an alert, keen-witted, brilliant man who has made it a lifelong habit to jot down every thought that he has had, whether he is depressed or exalted, despairing or hopeful, hungry or satiated, and likewise to put down what he has seen or heard others do or say. It is not unlikely that every thought that Mr. Joyce has had, every experience he has ever encountered, every person he has ever met, one might almost say everything he has ever read in sacred or profane literature, is to be encountered in the obscurities and in the franknesses of "Ulysses." If personality is the sum total of all one's experiences, all one's thoughts and emotions, inhibitions and liberations, acquisitions and inheritances, then it may truthfully be said "Ulysses" comes nearer to being the perfect revelation of a personality than any book in existence. Rousseau's "Confessions," Amiel's "Diary," Bashkirtseff's vaporings and Cassanova's "Memoirs" are first readers compared with it.

He is the only individual that the writer has encountered outside of a madhouse who has let flow from his pen random and purposeful thoughts just as they are produced. He does not seek to give them orderliness, sequence or interdependence. His literary output would seem to substantiate some of Freud's contentions. The majority of writers, practically all, transfer their conscious, deliberate thought to paper. Mr. Joyce transfers the product of his unconscious mind to paper without submitting it to the conscious mind, or, if he submits it, it is to receive approval and encouragement, perhaps even praise. He holds with Freud that the unconscious mind represents the real man, the man of nature, and the conscious mind the artificed man, the man of convention, of expediency, the slave of Mrs. Grundy, the sycophant of the Church, the plastic puppet of society and State. For him the movements which work revolutions in the world are born out of the dreams and visions in a peasant's heart on the hillside. "Peasant's heart" psychologically is the unconscious mind. When a master technician of words and phrases sets himself the task of revealing the product of the unconscious mind of a moral monster, a pervert and an invert, an apostate to his race and his religion, the simulacrum of a man who has neither cultural background nor personal self-respect, who can neither be taught by experience nor lessoned by example, as Mr. Joyce has done in drawing the picture of Leopold Bloom, and giving a faithful reproduction of his thoughts, purposeful, vagrant and obsessive, he undoubtedly knew full well what he was undertaking, and how unacceptable the vile contents of that unconscious mind would be to ninety-nine men out of a hundred, and how incensed they would be at having the disgusting product thrown in their faces. But that has nothing to do with that with which I am here concerned, viz., has the job been done well and is it a work of art, to which there can be only an affirmative answer.

It is particularly in one of the strangest chapters of all literature, without title, that Mr. Joyce succeeds in displaying the high-water mark of his art. Dedalus and Bloom have passed in review on a mystic stage, all their intimates and enemies, all their detractors and sycophants, the scum of Dublin and the spawn of the devil. Mr. Joyce resurrects Saint Walpurga, galvanizes her into life after twelve centuries of death intimacy with Beelzebub and substituting a squalid section of Dublin for Brocken, proceeds to depict a festival, with the devil as host. The guests in the flesh and of the spirit have still many of their distinctive corporeal possessions, but the reactions of life no longer exist. The chapter is replete with wit, humor, philosophy, learning, knowledge of human frailties and human indulgences, especially with the brakes of morality off, and alcohol or congenital deficiency takes them off for most of the characters. It reeks of lust and of filth, but Mr. Joyce says that life does, and the morality that he depicts is the one he knows. In this chapter is compressed all of the author's experiences, all his determinations and unyieldingness, most of the incidents that have given a persecutory twist to his mind, made him an exile from his native land and deprived him of the courage to return to it. He does not hesitate to bring in the ghost of is mother whom

he had been accused of killing because he would not kneel down and pray for her when she was dying and to question her of the verity of the accusation. But he does not repent even when she returns from the spirit world. In fact, the capacity for repentance is left out of Mr. Joyce's make-up. It is just as impossible to convince Mr. Joyce that he is wrong about anything on which he has made up his mind as it is to convince a paranoiac of the unreality of his false beliefs, or a jealous woman of the groundlessness of her suspicions.

It may be said that this chapter does not represent life, but I venture to say that it represents life with photographic accuracy as Mr. Joyce has seen it and lived it, and that every scene has come within his gaze and that every speech has been heard or said, and every sentiment experienced or thrust upon him. It is a mirror held up to life, life which we could sincerely wish and devoutly pray that we were spared.

In another connection Mr. Joyce once said:

My ancestors threw off their language and took another. They allowed a handful of foreigners to subject them. Do you fancy I am going to pay in my own life and person debts they made? No honorable and sincere man has given up his life, his youth and his affections to Ireland from the days of Tome to those of Parnell but the Irish sold him to the enemy or failed him in need or reviled him and left him for another. Ireland is the old sow that eats her farrow.

In chapter 8, the Lestrygonians episode, Leopold Bloom passes by the Ballast Office clock (courtesy of the Irish Tourist Board)

He has been saying that for many years, and he tries to make his actions conform with his words. However, every day of his life, if the mails do not fail, he gets a Dublin newspaper and reads it with the dutifulness with which a priest reads his breviary.

Mr. Joyce had the good fortune to be born with a quality which the world calls genius. Nature exacts a penalty, a galling income tax from geniuses, and as a rule she co-endows them with unamenability to law and order. . . . Genius and reverence are antipodal, Galileo being the exception to the rule. Mr. Joyce has no reverence for organised religion, for conventional morality, for literary style or form. He has no conception of the word obedience, and he bends the knee neither to God nor man. It is very interesting, and most important to have the revelations of such a personality, to have them first-hand and not dressed up. Heretofore our only avenues of information of such personalities led through the asylums for the insane, for it was there that such revelations as those of Mr. Joyce were made without reserve. Lest any one should construe this statement to be a subterfuge on my part to impugn the sanity of Mr. Joyce, let me say at once that he is one of the sanest geniuses that I have ever known.

He had the profound misfortune to lose his faith and he cannot rid himself of the obsession that the Jesuits did it for him, and he is trying to get square with them by saying disagreeable things about them and holding their teachings up to scorn and obloquy. He was so unfortunate as to be born without a sense of duty, of service, of conformity to the State, to the community, to society, and he is convinced that he ought to tell about it, just as some who have experienced a surgical operation feel that they must relate minutely all the details of it, particularly at dinner parties and to casual acquaintances.

Finally, I venture a prophecy: Not ten men or women out of a hundred can read "Ulysses" through, and of the ten who succeed in doing so, five of them will do it as a tour de force. I am probably the only person, aside from the author, that has ever read it twice from beginning to end. I have learned more psychology and psychiatry from it than I did in ten years at the Neurological Institute. There are other angles at which "Ulysses" can be viewed profitably, but they are not many.

Stephen Dedalus in his Parisian tranquility (if the modern Minos has been given the lethal warm bath) will pretend indifference to the publication of a laudatory study of "Ulysses" a hundred years hence, but he is as sure to get it as Dostoyevsky, and surer than Mallarmé.

Best known for his book The Eighteen Nineties *(1913), editor and English literary critic Jackson considers* Ulysses *chaotic but also recognizes it as "the biggest event in the history of the English novel since* Jude.*"*

Review of *Ulysses*
Holbrook Jackson
To-Day, 9 (June 1922): 47–49

Mr. James Joyce's *Ulysses* is an affront and an achievement. It is not indecent. There is not a salacious line in it. It is simply naked: naked and unconscious of shame. Some of those who have read the novel either in the *Little Review* or in its present volume form have considered it immoral. They are wrong. It is neither moral nor immoral. Mr. Joyce writes, not as though morals had never existed, but as one who deliberately ignores moral codes and conventions. Such frankness as his would have been impossible if such frankness had not been forbidden. Everything that is never done or never mentioned is done and said by him. Compared with Joyce, Zola is respectable and George Moore merely mincing. He is the first unromantic writer of fiction, for, after all, the Realists, were only Romantics striving to free themselves from Medievalism. . . .

He is not even out to amuse, like George Moore and the storytellers, or to criticise, like Meredith, or satirise, like Swift. He simply records like Homer, or, indeed, Froissart.

The attitude has its dangers. Mr. Joyce has faced them, or, rather, ignored them. He has been perfectly logical. He has recorded everything–everything in a single day of the life of an uninteresting and, to me, unpleasant, and, if we forget the parable of the sparrows, negligible human being. This modern Ulysses is one Bloom, the Irish-Jewish advertisement canvasser of a Dublin newspaper. To read the novel is to spend a full day in the company of this person from the time he rises in the morning and gives his wife breakfast in bed to the time of retiring to his bed late at night, whither his wife has already preceded him. You spend no ordinary day in his company; it is a day of the most embarrassing intimacy. You live with him minute by minute; go with him everywhere, physically and mentally; you are made privy to his thoughts and emotions; you are introduced to his friends and enemies; you learn what he thinks of each, every action and reaction of his psychology is laid bare with Freudian nastiness until you know his whole life through and through; know him, in fact, better than you know any other being in art or life–and detest him heartily. The creation of Bloom is an achievement of genius. . . . You do not feel grateful to Mr. Joyce for the introduction [of Bloom]. It is not clear why he troubled to introduce him. At times I

The plaque commemorating the setting for the Sirens episode, chapter 11 of Ulysses *(courtesy of Giuliana and Joshua Chapman)*

Bloom at the Ormond

The Ormond Hotel is where Leopold Bloom has an early dinner with Richie Goulding, Stephen Dedalus's maternal uncle. Having been preoccupied the whole day with the thought of his wife Molly's impending infidelity, Bloom resigns himself at this moment, soothed partly by the music being played in the bar next to the dining room, to the assignation between Molly and Blazes Boylan that will soon be occurring. It is also here where Bloom, using the pen name Henry Flower, Esq., writes his letter to Martha Clifford.

Joyce drew his caricature of Bloom sometime around 1923 in the Paris studio of Myron Nutting, the American artist who was painting portraits of Joyce, his wife, Nora, and daughter, Lucia. (These portraits now hang in the McCormick Library of Special Collections at Northwestern University Library.) In James Joyce and the Making of Ulysses, *Budgen reports that Joyce told him, "I see [Bloom] from all sides, and therefore he is all-round. . . . But he is a complete man as well—a good man."*

---

could not help feeling that the object was not so objectless as I had believed. Is *Ulysses* a stone flung at humanity–is Bloom the Twentieth Century Yahoo? . . . an ungainly, loose-limbed book which falls to pieces as you read it– as, indeed, you do. The very format of the book is an affront. Bloom could have been drawn effectively in a quarter the words. There are the deadliest of Dead Seas in this ocean of prose. You get becalmed in them–bored, drowsed, bewildered. And there are gulfs and bays which are muddy and noisome with the sew-

age of civilisation. On the other hand there are wide stretches of magnificent prose even when it is made up of unsavoury ingredients. Mr. James Joyce can write.

But the greatest affront of all is the arrangement of the book, *Ulysses* is a chaos. All the conventions of organised prosed which have grown with our race and out of our racial consciousness which have been reverently handed on by the masters with such improvements as they have been able to make, have been cast aside as so much dross. Quotation marks for conversational passages are omitted; punctuation follows new and unknown rules; sentences begin and forget to end; chapters have no apparent relation to one another, and neither numbers nor titles; and one chapter, the last, runs to 42 pages (25,000 words) with not a single punctuation of any kind, and where the enormous stretches of type are condescendingly broken into occasional paragraphs, no capitals are used. Mr. Joyce evidently believes in making it difficult for his readers–but perhaps he wants to scare them away. I am bound to admit, however, that this chapter, perhaps the best in the book, and one of the most disgusting, is by no means so difficult to read as one might expect.

This absence of the ordinary guide-posts of literature injures author as well as reader, for one may fairly assume that the author has something to say to his reader or he would not go to the trouble of writing and printing his work. He knows also that he is saying it in a new way. It seems gratuitous to put unnecessary difficulties in the way of a proper understanding of his message, story or record. For instance, much of the action of *Ulysses* is sub-conscious. Innumerable passages, and often whole pages together, record inward mental impressions, reactions from some external happening–a word, a sight of thing or person, a smell, a sound,–no hint or guide is given as to where these interpolations begin or end. They run on without warning from the known and familiar to the unknown and strange, on the assumption that the reader is a well-informed on the subject as James Joyce. The result is that the reader is continually losing his way and having to retrace his steps. *Ulysses* is like a country without roads. But it is a novel and if it will not amuse the idle novel reader, or even attract the lewd by its unsavoury frankness, it must claim the attention of those who look upon fiction as something more than confectionery. With all its faults, it is the biggest event in the history of the English novel since *Jude*.

–reprinted from *James Joyce: The Critical Heritage*

In his book Axel's Castle: A Study of the Imaginative Literature of 1870–1930 *(1931), the American essayist, critic, and novelist Edmund Wilson wrote one of the first serious critiques of* Ulysses, *discussing the influence of symbolism and realism on the novel within the European literary traditon. Predating* Axel's Castle *by nine years, the following essay anticipates some of the ideas he discusses in the book.*

Review of *Ulysses*
Edmund Wilson
New Republic, 31 (5 July 1922), pp. 164–166

On the 16th of June, 1904, Stephen Dedalus and Leopold Bloom were both living in Dublin. Both differed from the people about them and walked in isolation among them because each was, according to his capacity, an intellectual adventurer—Dedalus, the poet and philosopher, with a mind full of beautiful images and abstruse speculations and Bloom, the advertisement canvasser, in a more rudimentary fashion. In the evening, Mr. Bloom and Dedalus became involved in the same drunken party and Dedalus was knocked unconscious in a quarrel with a British soldier. Then their kinship was made plain. Bloom felt wistfully that Stephen was all he would have had his own son be and Stephen, who despised his own father—an amiable wastrel—found a sort of spiritual father in this sympathetic Jew, who, mediocre as he was, had at least the

Edmund Wilson

dignity of intelligence. Where they not both outlaws to their environment by reason of the fact that they thought and imagined?

Stated in the baldest possible terms, this is the story of Ulysses—an ironic and amusing anecdote without philosophic moral. In describing the novel thus, I have the authority of the author himself, who said to Miss Djuna Barnes, in an interview published in Vanity Fair: "The pity is the public will demand and find a moral in my book–or worse they may take it in some more serious way, and on the honor of a gentleman, there is not one single line in it." The thing that makes Ulysses imposing is, in fact, not the theme but the scale upon which it is developed. It has taken Mr. Joyce seven years to write Ulysses and he has done it in seven hundred and thirty pages which are probably the most completely "written" pages to be seen in any novel since Flaubert. Not only is the anecdote expanded to its fullest possible bulk–there is an elaborate account of nearly everything done or thought by Mr. Bloom from morning to night of the day in question–but you have both the "psychological" method and the Flaubertian method of making the style suit the thing described carried several steps further than they have ever been before, so that, whereas in Flaubert you have merely the words and cadence carefully adapted to convey the specific mood or character without any attempt to identify the narrative with the stream of consciousness of the person described, and in Henry James merely the exploration of the stream of consciousness with only one vocabulary and cadence for the whole cast of moods and characters, in Joyce you have not only life from the outside described with Flaubertian virtuosity but also the consciousness of each of the characters and of each of the character's moods made to speak in the idiom proper to it, the language it uses to itself. If Flaubert taught de Maupassant to find the adjective which would distinguish a given hackney-cab from every other hackney-cab in the world, James Joyce has prescribed that one must find the dialect which would distinguish the thoughts of a given Dubliner from those of every other Dubliner. So we have the thoughts of Mr. Bloom presented in a rapid staccato notation continually jetting out in all directions in little ideas within ideas with the flexibility and complexity of an alert and nimble mind: Mrs. Bloom's in a long rhythmic brogue like the swell of some profound sea; Father Commee's in precise prose, perfectly colorless and orderly; Stephen Dedalus's in a kaleidoscope of bright images and fragments of things remembered from books; and Gerty-Nausicaa's half in school girl colloquialisms and half in the language of the cheap romances which have given their color to her mind. And these voices are used to record all the eddies and stagnancies of thought;

though exercising a severe selection which makes the book a technical triumph, Mr. Joyce manages to give the effect of unedited human minds, drifting aimlessly along from one triviality to another, confused and diverted by memory, by sensation and by inhibition. It is, in short, perhaps the most faithful X-ray ever taken of the ordinary human consciousness.

And as a result of this enormous scale and this microscopic fidelity the chief characters in Ulysses take on heroic proportions. Each one is a room, a house, a city in which the reader can move around. The inside of each one of them is a novel in itself. You stand within a world infinitely populated with the swarming life of experience. Stephen Dedalus, in his scornful pride, rears his brow as a sort of Lucifer; poor Bloom, with his generous impulses and his attempts to understand and master life, is the epic symbol of reasoning man, humiliated and ridiculous, yet extricating himself by cunning from the spirits which seek to destroy him; and Mrs. Bloom, with her terrific force of mingled amorous and maternal affection, with her roots in the dirt of the earth and her joyous flowering in beauty, is the gigantic image of the earth itself from which both Dedalus and Bloom have sprung and which sounds a deep foundation to the whole drama like the ground-tone at the beginning of The Rhine-Gold. I cannot agree with Mr. Arnold Bennett that James Joyce "has a colossal 'down' on humanity." I feel that Mr. Bennett has really been shocked because Mr. Joyce has told the whole truth. Fundamentally Ulysses is not at all like Bouvard et Pécuchet (as some people have tried to pretend). Flaubert says in effect that he will prove to you that humanity is mean by enumerating all the ignobilities of which it has ever been capable. But Joyce, including all the ignobilities, make his bourgeois figures command our sympathy and respect by letting us see in them the throes of the human mind straining always to perpetuate and perfect itself and of the body always laboring and throbbing to throw up some beauty from its darkness.

Nonetheless, there are some valid criticisms to be brought against Ulysses. It seems to me great rather for the things that are in it than for its success as a whole. It is almost as if in distending the story to ten times its natural size he had finally managed to burst it and leave it partially deflated. There must be something wrong with a design which involves so much that is dull–and I doubt whether anyone will defend parts of Ulysses against the charge of extreme dullness. In the first place, it is evidently not enough to have invented three tremendous characters (with any quantity of lesser ones); in order to produce an effective book they must be made to do something interesting. Now in precisely what is the interest of Ulysses supposed to consist? In

the spiritual relationship between Dedalus and Bloom? But too little is done with this. When it is finally realized there is one poignant moment, then a vast tract of anticlimax. This single situation in itself could hardly justify the previous presentation of everything else that has happened to Bloom before on the same day. No, the major theme of the book is to be found in its parallel with the Odyssey: Bloom is a sort of modern Ulysses–with Dedalus as Telemachus–and the scheme and proportions of the novel must be made to correspond to those of the epic. It is these and not the inherent necessities of the subject which have dictated the size and shape of Ulysses. You have, for example, the events of Mr. Bloom's day narrated at such unconscionable length and the account of Stephen's synchronous adventures confined almost entirely to the first three chapters because it is only the early books of the Odyssey which are concerned with Telemachus and thereafter the first half of the poem is devoted to the wanderings of Ulysses. You must have a Cyclops, a Nausicaa, an Aeolus, a Nestor and some Sirens and your justification for a full-length Penelope is the fact that there is one in the Odyssey. There is, of course, a point in this, because the adventures of Ulysses were fairly typical; they do represent the ordinary man in nearly every common relation. Yet I cannot but feel that Mr. Joyce made a mistake to have the whole plan of his story depend on the structure of the Odyssey rather than on the natural demands of the situation. I feel that though his taste for symbolism is closely allied with his extraordinary poetic faculty for investing particular incidents with universal significance, nevertheless–because it is the homeless symbolism of a Catholic who has renounced the faith–it sometimes overruns the bounds of art into an arid ingenuity which would make a mystic correspondence do duty for an artistic reason. The result is that one sometimes feels as if the brilliant succession of episodes were taking place on the periphery of a wheel which has no hub. The monologue of Mrs. Bloom, for example, tremendous as it is and though in Mrs. Bloom's mental rejection of Blazes Boylan in favor of Stephen Dedalus it contains the greatest moral climax of the story, seems to me to lose dramatic force by hanging loose at the end of the book. What we have is nothing less than the spectacle of the earth tending naturally to give birth to higher forms of life, the supreme vindication of Bloom and Dedalus against the brutality and ignorance which surround them, but after the sterilities and practical jokes of the chapters immediately preceding and the general diversion of interest which the Odyssean structure has involved the episode lacks the definite force which a closer integration would have provided for.

Barney Kiernan's pub is the setting for chapter 12, the Cyclops episode, in which Bloom encounters the jingoistic Citizen

These sterilities and practical jokes form my second theme of complaint. Not content with inventing new idioms to reproduce the minds of his characters, Mr. Joyce has hit upon the idea of pressing literary parody into service to create certain kinds of impressions. It is not so bad when in order to convey the atmosphere of a newspaper office he merely breaks up his chapter with newspaper heads, but when he insists upon describing a drinking party in an interminable series of imitations which progresses through English prose from the style of the Anglo-Soxon chronicles to that of Carlyle one begins to feel uncomfortable. What is wrong is that Mr. Joyce has attempted an impossible genre. You cannot be a realistic novelist in Mr. Joyce's particular vein and write burlesques at the same time. Max Beerbohm's *Christmas Garland* is successful because Mr. Beerbohm is telling the other man's story in the other man's words but Joyce's parodies are labored and irritating because he is trying to tell his own story in the other man's words. We are not interested in his skill at imitation but in finding out what happens to his characters and the parody interposes a heavy curtain between ourselves and them. Even if it were at all conceivable that this sort of thing could be done successfully, Mr. Joyce would be the last man to do it. He has been praised for being Rabelaisian but he is at the other end of the world form Rabelais. In the first place, he has not the style for it–he can never be reckless enough with words. His style is thin–by which I do not mean that it is not strong but that it is

like a thin metallic pipe through which the narrative is run–a pipe of which every joint has been fitted by a master plumber. You cannot inflate such a style or splash it about. Mr. Joyce's native temperament and the method which it has naturally chosen have no room for superabundance or extravagant fancy. It is the method of Flaubert–and of Turgenev and de Maupassant: you set down with the most careful accuracy and the most scrupulous economy of detail exactly what happened to your characters, and merely from the way in which the thing is told–not from any comment of the narrator–the reader draws his ironic inference. In this genre–which has probably brought novel-writing to its highest dignity as an art–Mr. Joyce has long proved himself master. And in *Ulysses* most of his finest scenes adhere strictly to this formula. Nothing, for example, could be better in this kind than the way in which the reader is made to find out, without any overt statement of the fact, that Bloom is different from his neighbors, or the scene in which we are made to feel that this difference has become a profound antagonism before it culminates in the open outburst against Bloom of the Cyclops-Sinn Feiner. The trouble is that this last episode is continually being held up by long parodies which break in upon the text like a kind of mocking commentary. It is as if *Boule de Suif* were padded out with sections from J. C. Squire–or rather from a parodist whose parodies are even more boring than Mr. Squire's. No: surely Mr. Joyce has done ill in attempting to graft burlesque upon realism; he has written some of the most unreadable chapters in the whole history of fiction. – (If it be urged that Joyce's gift for fantasy is attested by the superb drunken scene, I reply that this scene is successful, not because it is reckless nonsense but because it is an accurate record of drunken states of mind. The visions that bemuse Bloom and Dedalus are not like the visions of Alice in Wonderland but merely the repressed fears and desires of these two specific consciousnesses externalized and made visible. What the reader sees is not a new fantastic world with new and more wonderful beings but two perfectly recognizable drunken men in a squalid and dingy brothel no harsh detail of which is allowed to escape by the great realist who describes it.)

Yet, for all its appalling longueurs, Ulysses is a work of high genius. Its importance seems to me to lie, not so much in its opening new doors to knowledge–unless in setting an example to Anglo-Saxon writers of putting down everything without compunction–or in inventing new literary forms–Joyce's formula is really, as I have indicated, nearly seventy-five years old–as in its once more setting the standard of the novel so high that it need not be ashamed to take its place beside poetry and drama. Ulysses has the effect at once of making everything else look brassy. Since I have read it, the texture of other novelists seems intolerably loose and careless; when I come suddenly unawares upon a page that I have written myself I quake like a guilty thing surprised. The only question now is whether Joyce will ever write a tragic masterpiece to set beside this comic one. There is a rumor that he will write no more–that he claims to have nothing left to say–an it is true that there is a paleness about parts of his work which suggests a rather limited emotional experience. His imagination is all intensive; he has but little vitality to give away. His minor characters, though carefully differentiated, are sometimes too drily differentiated, insufficiently animated with life, and he sometimes gives the impression of eking out his picture with the data of a too laborious note-taking. At his worst he recalls Flaubert at his worst–in L'Education Sentimentale. But if he repeats Flaubert's vices–as not a few have done–he also repeats his triumphs–which almost nobody has done. Who else has had the supreme devotion and accomplished the definitive beauty? If he has really laid down his pen never to take it up again he must know that the hand which laid it down upon the great affirmative of Mrs. Bloom, though it never write another word, is already the hand of a master.

With her husband, the Irish playwright and poet Padraic Colum, Mary Colum wrote Our Friend James Joyce (1958), *a reminiscence of their time with Joyce in Dublin and Paris. In addition to the essays and criticism that appeared in* The New Republic *and* Saturday Review, *Mary Colum published* Life and the Dream, *recollections of the literary circles she encountered.*

The Confessions of James Joyce

Mary Colum

Freeman, 5 (19 July 1922): 450–452

Mr. James Joyce's *Ulysses* belongs to that class of literature which has always aroused more interest than any other. Although *Ulysses* is new and original in its form, it is old in its class or type: it actually, if not obviously, belongs to the Confession class of literature, and although everything in it takes place in less than twenty-four hours, it really contains the life of a man. It is the Confessions of James Joyce, a most sincere and cunningly-wrought autobiographical book; it is as if he had said, 'Here I am; here is what country and race have bred me, what religion and life and literature have done to me.' Not only his previous book, *Portrait of the Artist,* but all of Joyce's work, gives the impression of being literally derived from experience; and from internal evidence in *Ulysses,* notably the conversation of Stephen Dedalus on Shakespeare in the National Library, one suspects that Joyce believes only in the autobiographical in art.

Such being the nature of the book, it is clear that the difficulty of comprehending it will not be allowed to stand in the way by anybody who can get possession of it. Joyce has so many strange things to say that people would struggle to understand him, no matter in what form or tongue he wrote. Yet the difficulties in the way are very real; "Ulysses" is one of the most racial books ever written, and one of the most Catholic books ever written; this in spite of the fact that one would not be surprised to hear that some official of the Irish Government or of the Church had ordered it to be publicly burned. It hardly seems possible that it can be really understood by anybody not brought up in the half-secret tradition of the heroism, tragedy, folly and anger of Irish nationalism, or unfamiliar with the philosophy, history and rubrics of the Roman Catholic Church; or by one who does not know Dublin and certain conspicuous Dubliners. The author himself takes no pains at all to make it easy of comprehension. Then, too, the book presupposes a knowledge of many literatures; a knowledge which for some reason, perhaps the cheapness of leisure, is not uncommon in Dublin, and, for whatever reason, perhaps the dearness of leisure, is rather uncommon

The Holles Street Maternity Hospital, Dublin, the setting for chapter 14, the Oxen of the Sun episode (courtesy of the Irish Tourist Board)

in New York. In addition, it is almost an encyclopedia of odd bits and forms of knowledge; for the author has a mind of the most restless curiosity, and no sort of knowledge is alien to him.

"Ulysses" is a kind of epic of Dublin. Never was a city so involved in the workings of any writer's mind as Dublin is in Joyce's; he can think only in terms of it. In his views of newspaper-offices, public houses, the National Library, the streets, the cemetery, he has got the psychology of that battered, beautiful eighteenth-century city in its last years of servitude, when, as Padraic Pearse said, using Geoffrey Keating's words, Ireland was "the harlot of England." "Ulysses" is a record of a certain number of hours–fewer than twenty four–in the lives of Stephen Dedalus, the hero of "Portrait of the Artist," and Leopold Bloom, and of a shorter space of time in the lives of certain other Dubliners, nearly all of whom are called by their real names. The day opens in a disused Government tower by the sea a few miles outside Dublin, occupied for the summer by a few young men as their bathing-quarters. In this first brilliant, blasphemous section, we have Stephen, Malachi Mulligan, and an Englishman called Haines. The key to the life and mind of Stephen is in these first pages.

Stephen, an elbow raised against the jagged granite, leaned his palm against his brow . . . pain that was not yet the pain of love fretted his heart. Silently as in a dream she had to come to him after her death, her wasted body within its loose brown grave-clothes, giving off an odour of wax and rosewood, her breath that had bent upon him, mute, reproachful . . . a faint odour of wetted ashes. Across his threadbare cuff-edge he saw the sea, hailed as a great sweet mother by the well-fed voice beside him.

Wherever Stephen comes in, we have the vision of his dying mother; her death was the great episode of his life. True to his race, death is the one thing that rocks him to the foundations of his being; *la gloire* may be the great emotional interest of the French, love of the English, but death is that of the Celt. Stephen further reveals himself in the conversation with Haines the Englishman. "I am the servant of two masters . . . an English and an Italian . . . the imperial British State and the Holy Roman Catholic and Apostolic Church."

He is the servant of these two; and where has the peculiar spiritual humilation that the English occupation of Ireland inflicted on sensitive and brilliant Irishmen ever been expressed as in this book? Where has the æsthetic and intellectual fascination of the Roman

Catholic Church ever found subtler fascination? "The proud, potent titles clanged over Stephen's memory the triumph of their brazen bells . . . *et unam sanctam catholicam et apostolicam ecclesiain!* The slow growth and change of rite and dogma like his own rare thoughts." Has the Catholic Church ever been described with such eloquence as in the paragraph that has that beginning?

The slender portrait of Haines, the Englishman friendly to Ireland, given in this section, is done with a subtlety beside which Shaw's Broadbent is a crude daub. Stephen regards him with a suspicion and contempt that in their sinousities never once become either hatred or tolerance. The lines with which he is drawn are barely visible–a rambling conversation, some words of description, a few jagged phrases in Stephen's subconsciousness, some of which must be cryptic to non-Irish readers, like those in which his mind takes farewell of him. "Horn of a bull . . . hoof of a horse . . . smile of a Saxon" – a variant of that old Irish proverb muttered by nurses in the ears of their sleeping charges: "Of three things beware; the teeth of a dog, the horns of a bull, the word of an Englishman."

Stephen leaves the tower to go to his task of giving lessons in a Unionist school. As he leaves after a conversation with the head master on many things, including Jews, the head master runs after him to inform him that the reason Ireland has the reputation of being the only country which never persecuted Jews, is that she never let them in. Then with delicate irony, we are given, in a few sections later, almost the whole history of modern Ireland and of Dublin, as it passes through the subconsciousness of a Jew, Leopold Bloom, a typical and perfect Dubliner in spite of the sex-obsession with which Joyce endows him in common with all his other characters. Bloom and Stephen, like good Dubliners, parade over the whole city in the course of the day; Bloom's itinerary brings him from the north side. Stephen's from the south side. They almost meet at various places, are actually in the newspaper-office and in the library at the same time; finally, at night, they do meet in a brothel in a low part of the city. There Stephen has a fight with two English soldiers, and is rescued from the hands of the police by the tact of Bloom. He and Bloom then stroll around the north side of the city, and have coffee in a cabman's shelter which is supposed to be run by "Skin-the-Goat," that mysterious character in the history of Irish attacks upon English authority. Bloom then takes Stephen to his own home for a cup of cocoa, and the episodes of the book end at about three in the morning, some twenty hours from the time when the story begins.

There is little in the way of incident, but everything in the way of revelation of life and character. Joyce gives us the characters of Stephen and Bloom as they appear externally and in their own subconsciousnesses. One of the remarkable feats of the book is the manner in which the separate subconsciousness of Stephen and Bloom are revealed, with every aimless thought, every half-formed idea and every unformed phrase indicative of their separate character and personality, and of the influences that have gone into their making. This is most marked when they think of the same things. Stephen's mind, young, sad, visionary, is held in a fast grip by the books he has read; his emotions . . . pass through his consciousness in vivid imaginative pictures; his whole temper is coloured by the humiliations he has undergone; his mind is so sensitive that everything is impressed upon it as with a branding-iron. Bloom's mind is bright, jerky, limited; unformed by literature, but strongly affected by music, and concerned mostly with concrete things. Bloom is drawn with the most careful solicitude for every shade of his character and with a humour that is all-embracing, and yet never approaching the extravagant. He is so real that no Dubliner can fail to recognize in him a father or an uncle–with his plans for improving the city, the extreme political views of his youth when he was more advanced than Michael Davitt, the milder ones of his middle-age (though his wife speaks resentfully of his taking up with Sinn Feiners), his attempts to be fair to the English, as becomes a sensible man, his conviction that he can invent something, or anyhow compose a song for the pantomime, his dash of artistry, his sketchy occupation, his industrious idleness, his anxiety over getting a free pass for something or other–a railway journey, a concert, or a voyage to England. There is also a subtly suggested foreignness about Bloom, particularly in the sections where he goes to drink in public houses with other middle-aged Dubliners; and there is a striking passage where Bloom, remembering the other race to which he belongs, comes out with a quite impressive philosophy of life. He is the one character whom Joyce really loves and whom he endows with kindliness: and we remember his terrible concern for Mrs. Beaufoy who has spent three days in childbirth, and his buying biscuits to feed wild birds, and his care for the blind boy whom he meets in the street.

Almost every section of the book has a different form and manner. The account of events in Barney Kiernan's public house is given by one of the bar-haunters in the vivid and circumstantial parlance of a public-house idler, interlarded with mock-epical narrative. There is a point where the rage against Bloom for not treating mounts up to a quarrel, and a peacemaker gets them all off on a jaunting car, followed by the citizen's barking mongrel, "and all the ragamuffins and sluts of the nation around the door, and Martin telling the jarvey to drive ahead, and the citizen bawling, and Alf and Joe at him to whisht."

The scene in the hospital where Bloom goes to see Mrs. Beaufoy is described in parodies of almost every style of narrative in English, from Latin and Anglo-Saxon to the method of the Irish provincial reporter; an accomplishment in itself possible only to a man with a minutely technical knowledge of the development of the language. From this half-way chapter to the end, "Ulysses" ceases to be of paramount literary interest; to what extent a writer can parody different styles in the historic development of English is not of literary interest, it is of scientific interest. The catechism relating to Bloom and Stephen, being merely informing, is not of literary interest. The revelation of the mind of Marion Bloom in the last section would doubtless interest the laboratory, but to normal people it would seem an exhibition of the mind of a female gorilla who has been corrupted by contact with humans. The Walpurgis night scene (not called by that name) is too long and too incomprehensible; one feels that Joyce has here driven his mind too far beyond the boundary-line that separates fantasy and grotesquerie from pure madness. . . . There is a salient abutting on the real and the fantastical, where they all meet, jumble in and out of each other's consciousness and subconsciousness, and disappear. For Stephen there appears inevitably the vision of his mother, as well as Shakespeare and old Gummy Granny (a satirical impersonation of Kathleen-ni-Houlihan). It is in parts wonderful, terribly impressive and revealing, but the prolonged scene gives too much the impression of a feat of intellectual and psychological gymnastics.

One of the chief occupations of critics of this book is making parallels between the sections and characters of "Ulysses," and the Odyssey. The chief reason for this performance is that the author exhibits a notebook with all these parallels and many other symbolical explanations. When it comes to symbolizing, authors have from all time talked the greatest nonsense; think of the nonsense that Goethe achieved when explaining the second part of "Faust" and "Ulysses" as between the Odyssey and "Ulysses."

What actually has James Joyce accomplished in this monumental work? He has achieved what comes pretty near to being a satire on all literature. He has written down a page of his country's history. He has given the minds of a couple of men with a kind of actuality not hitherto found in literature. He has given us an impression of his own life and mind such as no other writer has given before; not even Rousseau, whom he resembles.

The Confession-mind in literature is of two classes. We have the Saint Augustine-Tolstoy type and the Rousseau-Strindberg-Joyce type. The difference between Rousseau and Joyce is, of course, extraordinary, but the resemblances are also extraordinary–a psychoanalyst would say they had the same complexes. Like Rousseau, Joyce derives everything from his own ego; he lives in a narrow world in which he himself is not only the poles, but the equator and the parallels of latitude and longitude; like Rousseau, he has a passion not only for revealing himself, but for betraying himself; like him also, he deforms everything he touches. Joyce's method of deforming is chiefly with a sexual smear; where Rousseau romanticizes, Joyce de-romanticizes. In Joyce, as in Rousseau, we find at its highest a quality which in lesser men is the peculiar fault of the literature of their time; in Rousseau this was sentimentalism, in Joyce it is intellectualism. In the quality of pure intellect, whilst one remembers that a man can be a great writer with little intellect, Joyce is probably unsurpassed by any living writer. Some attempt is being made by admirers to absolve Joyce from accusations of obscenity in this book. Why attempt to absolve him? It is obscene, bawdy, corrupt. But it is doubtful that obscenity in literature ever really corrupted anybody. The alarming thing about "Ulysses" is very different; it is that it shows the amazing inroads that science is making on literature. Mr. Joyce's book is of as much interest as science as it is as literature; in some parts it is of purely scientific and non-artistic interest. It seems to me a real and not a fantastic fear that science will oust literature altogether as a part of human expression; and from that point of view "Ulysses" is a dangerous indication. From that point of view, also, I do not consider it as important to literature as "Portrait of the Artist." After "Ulysses," I cannot see how anyone can go on calling books written in the subconscious method, novels. It is as plain as day that a new literary form has appeared, from which the accepted form of the novel has nothing to fear; the novel is as distinct from this form as in his day Samuel Richardson's invention was from the drama.

Gilbert Seldes, American journalist and critic whose books include The Seven Lively Arts *(1924), a study of popular art forms*

Gilbert Seldes was one of the critics quoted in Morris Ernst's brief when the latter in December 1933 argued before Judge John M. Woolsey against the ban on Ulysses *in the United States. In his review Seldes rightly speculated that* Ulysses *would have an immeasurable effect on future writers.*

Ulysses
Gilbert Seldes
Nation, 115 (30 August 1922): 211–212

"WELCOME, O life! I go to encounter for the millionth time the reality of experience and to forge in the smithy of my soul the uncreated conscience of my race . . . Old Father, old artificer, stand me now and ever in good stead." With this invocation ended James Joyce's first novel, "A Portrait of the Artist as a Young Man." It has stood for eight years as the pledge of Joyce's further achievement; today he has brought forth "Ulysses" a monstrous and magnificent travesty, which makes him possibly the most interesting and the most formidable writer of our time.

James Joyce is forty years old and these two novels represent his major work; there are in addition "Chamber Music," a book of exquisite lyrics; "Exiles," a play; and "Dubliners," a collection of eighteen superb short stories. As some of these antedate the "Portrait" it is fair to say that Joyce has devoted eighteen years of his life to composing the two novels. Except that he is Irish, was educated at a Jesuit school, studied medicine, scholastic philosophy, and mathematics on the Continent, where he has lived for many years, nothing else in his biography need to be mentioned. Among the very great writers of novels only two can be named with him for the long devotion to their work and for the triumphant conclusion–Flaubert and Henry James. It is the novel as they created it which Joyce has brought to its culmination; he has, it seems likely, indicated the turn the novel will take into a new form. "Ulysses" is at the same time the culmination of many other things: of an epoch in the life of Stephen Dedalus, the protagonist of the "Portrait"; of an epoch in the artistic life of Joyce himself; and, if I am not mistaken, of a period in the intellectual life of our generation.

"A Portrait of the Artist" is the story of the interior life of Stephen Dedalus, from his earliest memories to the time of his leaving home with the invocation quoted above. It is easy to distinguish it from contemporary autobiographical novels, for they resemble it only in what they have borrowed from it. It is a work of the creative imagination more than of the memory; it is marked by a dignity and a lyric beauty almost without equal in prose fiction; the concern is the soul of a young man destined by circumstances to be a priest and by his nature to be a poet. He struggles against the forces which urge him to repair the family fortunes, to be loyal to the faith, to fight for Ireland. "He wanted to meet in the real world the unsubstantial image which his soul so constantly beheld." Against the sense of sin excited at the school was his ecstasy: "He closed his eyes, surrendering himself to her, body and mind, conscious of nothing in the world but the dark pressure of her softly parting lips. They pressed upon his brain as upon his lips as though they were the vehicle of a vague speech; and between them he felt an unknown and timid pressure, darker than the swoon of sin, softer than sound or odor." And his joy: "A girl stood before him in midstream; alone and still, gazing out to sea. . . . Her long slender bare legs were delicate as a crane's and pure save where an emerald trail of seaweed had fashioned itself as a sign upon the flesh. Her thighs, fuller and soft-hued as ivory, were bared almost to the hips where the white fringes of her drawers were like feathering of white down. . . . Her bosom was soft as a bird's, soft and slight, slight and soft as the breast of some dark-plumaged dove. But her long fair hair was girlish; and girlish, and touched with the wonder of mortal beauty, her face." There was also his clear proud mind.

"Ulysses" is, among other things, a day in the life of this same Stephen Dedalus, an average day after his return to Dublin from Paris. As an average day it marks the defeat of the poet; he has encountered and been overcome by the reality of experience; the ecstasy and lyric beauty are no more; instead of it we have a gigantic travesty. That is, as I see it, the spiritual plot of "Ulysses." And as Stephen, in addition to being a created character, is both " the artist" generically and specifically James Joyce, "Ulysses" naturally takes on the proportions of a burlesque epic of this same defeat. It is not surprising that, built on the framework of the "Odyssey" it burlesques the structure of the original as a satyr-play burlesqued the tragic cycle to which it was appended; nor that a travesty of the whole of English prose should form part of the method of its presentation. Whether a master piece can be written in caricature has ceased to be an academic question.

The narrative of "Ulysses" is simple. The portions corresponding to the story of Telemachus tell of a few hours spent by Stephen Dedalus on the morning of June 16, 1904: he visits the Nestorian head of the school where he teaches, goes to the modern cave of the winds in a newspaper office, tests the "ineluctable modality of the visible." It is in the newspaper office that he first sees one Leopold Bloom, *né* Virag, an advertising solicitor whose early day has already been recounted. Him we see in all the small details of his morning, preparing his wife's breakfast, going to a funeral, trying to get a reading notice for an advertiser, gazing a bit wistfully at the intellectual life of Dublin, under the name of Flower carrying on amorous correspondence with young girls, to the first climax of his day when he gets into a quarrel in a public house and is stoned as he drives off because he reminded a Cyclopean citizen there that Christ was a Jew. From this he goes to his second climax an erotic one caused by observing a young girl on the rocks near Sandymount–an episode which officially corresponds to that of Nausicaa, but more interestingly to the scene in the "Portrait" I have quoted. Bloom sees Stephen a second time at a lying-in hospital where he goes to inquire the issue of an accouchement. Much later that evening Stephen and Bloom encounter each other in a brothel in the nighttown of Dublin. Bloom protects Stephen from an assault by a drunken soldier and takes him to his home where they talk until nearly daybreak. After Stephen leaves, Bloom goes to bed, and the catamenial night thoughts of his wife, thoughts of her first lovers and of her adulteries, complete the book. Bloom being Ulysses, his wife is Penelope. The authoritative version makes her also Gea, the earth-mother.

This is what is technically known as a slender plot for a book which is the length of five ordinary novels. But the narrative is only the thread in the labyrinth. Around and about it is the real material of the

Flora H. Mitchell's painting of 7 Eccles Street, located off Dorset Street in northwest Dublin, the address of Leopold and Molly Bloom. Joyce's fellow student and friend, John Francis Byrne, once lived at the address (Croessmann Collection of James Joyce, Special Collections/Morris Library, Southern Illinois University, Carbondale).

psychological story, presented largely in the form of interior monologues–the unspoken thoughts of the three principal characters and at times of some of the others, separately or, in one case, simultaneously. In a few words, at most a few pages, the essential setting is objectively presented; thereafter we are actually in the consciousness of a specified or suggested individual; and the stream of consciousness, the rendered thoughts and feelings of that individual, are actually the subject matter of the book. There is no "telling about" things by an outsider, nor even the looking over the hero's shoulder which Henry James so beautifully managed; there is virtually complete identification. The links in the chain of association are tempered by the nature and circumstances of the individual; there is no mistaking the meditations of Stephen for those of Bloom, those of either for the dark flood of Marion's consciousness. I quote a specimen moment from this specimen day: "Reading two pages apiece of seven books every night, eh? I was young. You bowed to yourself in the mirror, stepping forward to applause earnestly, striking face. Hurray for the Goddamned idiot! Hray! No, one saw: tell no one. Books you were going to write with letters for titles. Have you read his F? O yes, but I prefer Q. Yes, but W is wonderful. O yes, W. Remember your epiphanies on green oval leaves, deeply deep, copies to be sent if you died to all the great libraries of the world, including Alexandria? Someone was to read them there after a few thousand years, a mahamanvantara. Pico della Mirandola like. Ay, very like a whale. When one reads these strange pages of one long gone one feels that one is at one with one who once. . . ."

The swift destructive parody in the last sentence is a foretaste of what arrives later in the book. In the episode at the *Freeman's Journal* Joyce has sown headlines through the narrative, the headlines themselves being a history by implication of the vulgarization of the press. In the public house a variety of bombastic styles sets off the flatness of the actual conversation; on the beach the greater part of the episode is conveyed through a merciless parody of the sentimental serial story: "Strength of character had never been Reggy Wylie's strong point and he who would woo and win Gerty MacDowell must be a man among men" and so on. Here the parody creates itself not in the mind of Bloom but in that of the object in his mind, and renders the young-girlish sentimentality of Gerty with exceptional immediacy and directness. The burlesque of English prose, historically given, against which great complaint has been made, is actually one some sixty pages long; the parodies themselves I find brilliant, but their function is more important than their merit. They create with rapidity and as rapidly destroy the whole series of noble aspirations, hopes, and illusions of which the centuries have left their record in prose. And they lead naturally, therefore, to the scene in the brothel where hell opens.

This is the scene which, by common consent, is called a masterpiece. The method is a variation from that of the preceding; the apparent form is that of a play with spoken dialogue and italicized stage directions. The characters at the beginning are the inhabitants of nighttown; they and the soldiers and Bloom and Stephen have this real existence. But the play is populated by the phantasms and nightmares of their brains. Bloom's dead parents appear and converse with him; later his inflamed imagination projects him successively in all the roles he has played or dreamed of playing, from seducer of serving wenches to Lord Mayor of Dublin; he is accused of his actual or potential perversions; the furies descend upon him; he is changed into a woman, into a pig. Stephen's

mother, at whose death-bed he refused to pray and who literally haunts his conscious thought, appears to him. In the Witches' Sabbath brute creation and inanimate things give voice; the End of the World appears and dances on an invisible tight-rope; and the Walpurgisnacht ends in a hanging of totally unnamable horror. It is here that Bloom recognizes Stephen as his spiritual kin.

The galvanic fury in which this episode is played is, one feels certain, not equalled in literature; it is a transcription of drunken delirium, with all the elements of thought and imagination broken, spasmodic, tortured out of shape, twitching with electric energy. The soft catlike languor of the whores, the foulness of the soldiers, the whole revel of drink and lust, are of Stephen and Bloom. At the end of it Bloom accepts Stephen as the man his own son, and so himself, might have been; Stephen, more vaguely, seems to see in Bloom the man he himself may become. The orgy dies out in a cabman's shelter, in dreary listlessness, and after a description of their affinities and differences, given in the form of an examination paper, the two men part. The poet defeated by his self-scorn and introspection, the sensualist, with his endless curiosity, defeated by weakness, disappear; and in the thoughts of Mrs. Bloom something coarse and healthy and coarsely beautiful and healthily foul asserts itself. Like the Wife of Bath, she can thank God that she has had her world, as in her time.

Although her last words are an affirmation that her body is a flower, although she morally rejects her brutal lovers in favor of Stephen and ends with a memory of her first surrender to Bloom, there is no moral triumph here. For Mrs. Bloom there can be no defeat similar to that of the others, since there has been no struggle. Their impotence is contrasted with her wanton fornication; she occurs, a mockery of the faithful Penelope, to mark their frustration. In their several ways Bloom and Stephen have been seekers, one for experience and the other for the reality of experience; and finding it they have been crushed and made sterile by it.

If it is true, as Mr. Yeats has said, that the poet creates the mask of his opposite, we have in "Ulysses" the dual mask–Bloom and Stephen–of James Joyce, and in it we have, if I am not mistaken, the mask of a generation: the broken poet turning to sympathy with the outward-going scientific mind. (Bloom is completely rendered by Joyce, with infinite humor and kindness and irony, to give point to this turning.) Conscious despair turns to unconscious futility; in the end, to be sure, Stephen leaves the house of Bloom, to be homeless the last few hours of the night. And this homelessness, beside which is the homelessness of Joyce himself, strikes us as a joyful tragedy in Stephen's freedom and solitude and exaltation. The one thing one does not find in "Ulysses" is dismal pessimism; there is no "down" on humanity. Lust and superstition, Mr. Santayana has told us, are canceled by the high breathlessness of beauty; in this book love and hate seem equally forgotten in an enormous absorption in things, by an enormous relish and savoring of palpable actuality. I think that Nietzsche would have cared for the tragic gaiety of "Ulysses."

I have not the space to discuss the aesthetic questions which the book brings up nor to indicate what its effect upon the novel may be. I have called Joyce formidable because it is already clear that the innovations in method and the developments in structure which he has used with a skill approaching perfection are going to have an incalculable effect upon the writers of the future; he is formidable because his imitators will make use of his freedom without imposing upon themselves the duties and disciplines he has suffered; I cannot see how any novelist will be able (nor why he should altogether want) entirely to escape his influence. The book has literally hundreds of points of interest not even suggested here. One must take for granted the ordinary equipment of the novelist; one must assume also that there are faults, idiosyncrasies, difficulties. More important still are the interests associated with "the uncreated conscience of my race"–the Catholic and Irish. I have written this analysis of "Ulysses" as one not too familiar with either–as an indication that the book can have absolute validity and interest, in the sense that all which is local and private in the "Divine Comedy" does not detract from its interest and validity. But these and other points have been made in the brilliant reviews which "Ulysses" has already evoked. One cannot leave it without noting again that in the change of Stephen Dedalus from his affinity with the old artificer to his kinship with Ulysses-Bloom, Joyce has created an image of contemporary life; nor without testifying that this epic of defeat, in which there is not a scamped page nor a moment of weakness, in which whole chapters are monuments to the power and the glory of the written word, is in itself a victory of the creative intelligence over the chaos of uncreated things and a triumph of devotion, to my mind one of the most significant and beautiful of our time.

Shane Leslie's reason for writing this review under a pseudonym is unknown. The phrase domini canis, *a Latin play on words, was used as an insult to identify a member of the Dominican religious order–a dog of the Lord. He reviewed the novel under his own name a month later.*

Ulysses
Domini Canis
Dublin Review, 171 (July–September 1922): 112–119

Since a leading French critic has announced that with Mr. James Joyce's *Ulysses* "Ireland makes a sensational re-entrance into high European literature," and since reputable English guides like Mr. Middleton Murry and Mr. Arnold Bennett seem to be wandering in his track, and since the entire setting of this book is Catholic Dublin, and since the seven hundred pages contain a fearful travesty on persons, happenings and intimate life of the most morbid and sickening description, we say not only for the *Dublin Review* but for Dublin *écrasez l'infâme!*

The Irish literary movement may have arisen in the bogs of Aran and Mayo, but it is not going to find its stifling climax in a French sink. The vain folk who speak of this book as the greatest English writing since Shakespeare may take what attitude they like concerning English literature, but as for *Ulysses* being a great creation of the Irish Celt, a Cuchulain of the sewer even, or an Ossian of obscenity, it may safely be repudiated, before reading, by the Irish people, who certainly do not get either the rulers or writers they deserve. The bulk of this enormous book is quite unquotable and we hope that, as the edition is limited and the price is rapidly ascending in the "curious" market, it will remain out of the reach of the bulk of the author's fellow-countrymen. We are prepared to do justice to the power and litheness of the style, when intelligible, to the occasional beauty of a paragraph and to the adventurous headlong experiments in new literary form, but as whole we regard it as the screed of one possessed; a commoner complaint than is generally realized in these days, but one seldom taking a literary channel of expression. Samuel Butler bitterly, but truly, said that God had written all the books, meaning no doubt that he would like to see what the devil had to say for himself. That opportunity has been now afforded, and we must say that Mr. Joyce has rather added than otherwise to the sorrows of Satan.

The official Inquisition has always distinguished between what is filthy in books and what is blasphemous, according different warnings and condemnations as the faithful were liable to be affected by either. With the mass of underground Priapic literature the Holy

Church has not let the hem of her vesture be soiled, but to those who have reason to read the whole of the Classics or to study the bypaths of ethnology or psychology she has lifted no prohibitive finger. She is a lady, not a prude. Her inquisitions, her safeguards and indexes all aim at the avoidance of the scriptural millstone, which is so richly deserved by those who offend one of her little ones. But to those who can take care of themselves she leaves her guarded permission, and she never forgets the simple truth of better human nature that *puris omnia pura.* The converse, that to some minds nothing remains pure or sacred, is shown in this lamentable work of which we trust no copy will ever be added to the National Library of Ireland. In this work the spiritually offensive and the physically unclean are united. We speak advisedly when we say that though no formal condemnation has been pronounced, the Inquisition can only require its destruction or, at least, its removal from Catholic houses. Without grave reason or indeed the knowledge of the Ordinary no Catholic publicist can even afford to be possessed of a copy of this book, for in its reading lies not only the description but the commission of sin against the Holy Ghost. Having tasted and rejected the devilish drench, we most earnestly hope that this book be not only placed on the *Index Expurgatorius,* but that its reading and communication be made a reserved case.

So much literary curiosity has been aroused by the surreptitious printing and distribution of this vile volume that we recognize the legitimate desire to know whether new forms really have been added to modern writing or a new elixir wrung out of the exhausted English speech. The theme of the book may be stated, ridiculous as it is. It covers to the extent of half a million of words the experiences and current thoughts, acts, idiocies and natural intimacies of a pupil of Clongowes School during twenty-four hours of mortal life in Dublin. The day consists of the preparation for breakfast, the bath, attendance at a Glasnevin funeral, some hours in the advertising department of the *Freeman's Journal,* lunch in a Dublin eating-house, a visit to the National Library with an interesting Shakespearean discussion, a concert in the Ormond Hotel, an altercation in a public house, a car-drive, a scene in the Women's Hospital and the birth of a child, a visit to a house of ill-fame in Tyrone Street, followed by a brawl, a visit to a cabman's shelter, and finally a very horrible dissection of a very horrible woman's thought. There is also an account of the Black Mass to which the *vis comica* and the *vis diabolica* have contributed in equal quantities.

As for the vaunted new experimentation in literary forms, we doubt if the present generation is likely to adopt them by writing, for instance, forty-two pages without a capital or a stop, or by abandoning all reasoned sequence of thought and throwing the flash and flow of every discordant, flippant, allusive or crazy suggestiveness upon paper without grammar and generally without sense. Of course, when the allusion can be caught, and the language is restrained, the effect can be striking and even beautiful, but how few of such passages can be meshed in the dreary muck-ridden tide. We will give the devil his due and appreciate the idyll of Father Conmee, S. J., who, with most people mentioned in the course of the book, is really a Dubliner. Many pages are saturated with Catholic lore and citation, which must tend to make the book more or less unintelligible to critics, who are neither of Catholic or Dublin origin. Nothing could be more ridiculous than the youthful dilettantes in Paris or London who profess knowledge and understanding of a work which is often mercifully obscure even to the Dublin-bred. For instance, who but a Catholic could interpret this rush of allusion loosed by the chanting of the creed?

> The proud potent titles clanged over Stephen's memory the triumph of their brazen bells: *et unam sanctam catholicam et apostolicam ecclesiam;* the slow growth and change of rite and dogma like his own rare thoughts, a chemistry of stars. Symbol of the Apostles in the Mass for Pope Marcellus, the voices blended, singing alone aloud in affirmation: and behind their chant the vigilant angel of the church militant disarmed and menaced her heresiarchs. A horde of heresies fleeing with mitres awry: Photius and the brood of mockers and Arius, warring his life long upon the consubstantiality of the Son with the Father and Valentine spurning Christ's terrene body and the subtle heresiarch Sabellius who held that the Father was Himself His own Son . . . idle mockery. The void awaits surely all them that weave the wind: a menace, a disarming and a worsting from those embattled angels of the Church, Michael's host who defend her ever in the hour of conflict with their lances and their shields.

If there were only more such, but it is a case of *corruptio optimi pessima,* and a great Jesuit-trained talent has gone over malignantly and mockingly to the powers of evil. Parodies of Society-clippings in the Press or of honest Irish chauvinism are well in their way; but the Apostles Creed and the Litany of the Saints must remain untouchable as they are intangible, and the effort luckily only brings the parodist squeaking feebly to earth. Perhaps he overshoots his mark when he includes, "Saint Anonymous, Saint Eponymous, Saint Pseudonymous, Saint Homonymous, Saint Synonymous, etc.," for some of the choicest saints are unknown and unnamed. There follows one of his Rabelaisian lists of a kind that also reads like an imitation of Huysmans– "and all came with nimbi and aureoles and gloriae, bearing palms and harps and swords and olive crowns, in robes whereon were woven the blessed symbols of their efficacies, inkhorns, arrows, loaves, cruses, fetters, axes, trees, bridges, babes in a bathtub, shells, wallets, shears, keys, dragons, lilies, buckshot, beards, lamps, bellows, beehives, soupladles, stars, snakes, anvils, bells, crutches, forceps, stagshorns, millstones, eyes on a dish, aspergills, unicorns."

Reading a textbook and boiling it down into lists is no new device and depends for its success on the eliminating touch with which Mr. Joyce is most inartistically unendowed. In fact, the reader in struggling from oasis to oasis will find himself caught in a Sahara that is as dry as it is stinking. It is only when he varies his cataloguing with rare or new words that he is endurable, as of the Dublin vegetable market:

> Thither the extremely large wains bring foison of the fields, flaskets of cauliflowers, floats of spinach, pineapple chunks, Rangoon beans, strikes of tomatoes, drums of figs, drills of swedes, spherical potatoes, and tallies of irridescent kale, York and Savoy, and trays of onions, pearls of the earth, and pumets of mushrooms and custard marrows and fat vetches and bere and rape, red green yellow brown russet sweet big bitter ripe pomellated apples and chips of strawberries and sieves of gooseberries, pulpy and pelorious . . .

This may, or may not, be literature. It is certainly good cataloguing, but fifty pages have to be squeezed to find a like passage, so that the reader need not expect to be sustained by a genuine spate of words, wherever he dips. He is far more likely to encounter a bad smell, and find himself in a drain. One of the few passages we could overlook is a comic skit on the style of the Dublin patriotic Press, if the writer had not taken the inhuman subject of an Irish execution as the subject of his unsparing satire. The parody of a Celtic Saga is pleasanter, and winds up with an amusing caricature of the national facility for tracing Irish blood in so many of the great ones of the world. The hero is thus approximated in Ossianic style:

> The wide-winged nostrils, from which bristles of the same tawny hue projected, were of such capaciousness that within their cavernous obscurity the field lark might easily have lodged her nest. The eye in which a tear and a smile strove ever for mastery was of the dimensions of a good-sized cauliflower . . . his girdle was engraved with the tribal images of Irish heroes including Goliath, Cuchulain, Captain Moonlight, Captain Boycott, the Mother of the Macabees, the Last of the Mohicans, the Man for Galway . . . Peter the Hermit, Peter the Packer, Patrick W. Shakespeare, Brian Confucius, Murtagh Gutenburg, Partricio Velasquez . . .

His method of allusion is something between Pelmanism and morbid psycho-analysis. Outside the obsession of sex it is sometimes intelligible, for instance the phrases recalling Algebra at school; "Across the page the symbols moved in grave morrice, in the mummery of their letters, wearing quaint caps of squares and cubes. Give hands, traverse bow to partner: so: imps of fancy of the Moors." Or again, of the Orange toast, "Glorious pious and immortal memory. The lodge of Diamond in Armagh the splendid behung with corpses of papishes. Hoarse, masked and armed the planters covenant. The black north and true blue bible. Croppies lie down." This conveys something and there is a corresponding account of the *Raimeis* of the patriot in his pathetic pleading for recognition of Ireland's greatness:

> Where are our missing twenty millions of Irish should be here to-day instead of four, our lost tribes? And our potteries and textiles the finest in the whole world! And our wool that was sold in Rome in the time of Juvenal and our flax and our damask from the looms of Antrim and our Limerick lace, our tanneries and our white flint glass down there by Ballybough and our Huguenot poplin, that we have since Jacquard de Lyon, and our woven silk and Foxford tweeds and ivory raised point from the Carmelite convent in New Ross, nothing like it in the whole wide world. Where are the Greek merchants that came through the pillars of Hercules, the Gibraltar now grabbed by the enemy of mankind, with gold and Tyrian purple to sell in Wexford at the fair of Carmen? Read Tacitus and Ptolemy, even Giraldus Cambrensis, Wine, peltries, Connemara marble, silver from Tipperary, second to none, our far-famed horses even to-day, the Irish hobbies with King Philip of Spain offering to pay customs duties for the right to fish in our waters. What do the yellow-johns of Anglia owe us for our ruined trade and our ruined hearths?

The Dublin causerie about Shakespeare, "the chap that writes like Synge," is a real reflection of the best in Irish circles, especially when John Eglinton commands the floor:

> All events brought grist to his mill. Shylock chimes with the jew-baiting that followed the hanging and quartering of the queen's leech Lopez, his jew's heart being plucked forth while the sheeny was yet alive: Hamlet and Macbeth with the coming to the throne of a Scotch philosophaster with a turn for witch roasting. The lost Armada is his jeer in Love's Labour Lost. His pageants, his histories sail full-bellied on a tide of Mafeking enthusiasm. Warwickshire jesuits are tried and we have a porter's theory of equivocation. The Sea Venture comes home from Bermudas and the play Renan admired is written with Patsy Caliban, our American cousin. The sugared sonnets follow Sydney's. As for fay Elizabeth otherwise carotty Bess the gross virgin, who inspired the Merry Wives of Windsor, let some meinherr from Almany grope his lifelong for deephid meanings. . . .

"Why is the underplot of King Lear lifted out of Sidney's Arcadia and spatchcocked on to a Celtic legend older than history?" That was Will's way Eglinton defended. We should not now combine a Norse Saga with an excerpt from a novel by George Meredith . . ."

And the seaweed in Dublin Bay brings a reminiscence from the Fathers so perfect that we lament the ocean of inferior writing which surrounds it all the more:

"Under the upswelling tide he saw the writhing weeds lift languidly and sway reluctant arms, in whispering water swaying and upturning coy silver fronds. Day by day: night by night; lifted, flooded and let fall. Lord they are weary: and whispered to they sigh. St. Ambrose heard it, sigh of leaves and waves, waiting, awaiting the fullness of their times, *diebus ac noctibus injurias patiens ingemiscit.* To no end gathered: vainly then released, forth flowing, wending back: loom of the moon . . ."

And take the curious mosaic of human life like a passage of Sir Thomas Browne:

We wail, batten, sport, clip, clasp, sunder, dwindle, die: over us dead they bend. First saved from water of old Nile among bulrushes, a bed of fascinated wattles: at last the cavity of a mountain, an occulted sepulchre amid the conclamation of the hillcat and the ossifrage. And as no man knows the ubicity of his tumulus nor to what processes we shall thereby be ushered nor whether to Tophet or to Edenville in the like way is all hidden when we would backward see from what region of remoteness the Whatness of our Whoness hath fetched his Whenceness.

And these last words rather describe the bewildering impression left by the book. We have made these quotations to save anyone the trouble of poring over a volume in which such are scarce rarities. We do not think it worth while to bolt the mud in the sieve to find an occasional phrase like "Angenbite of inwit" for conscience, "turlehide whales," "dykedropt," "antelucan hour," "chryselephantine papal standard." Our search was cursory and we have tried to do justice to this abomination of desolation. By doing so we hope we have quenched the curiosity of the *literati* and *dilettanti.* As for the general reader, it is, as it were, so much rotten caviare, and the public is in no particular danger of understanding or being corrupted thereby. Doubtless this book was intended to make angels weep and to amuse fiends, but we are not sure that "those embattled angels of the Church, Michael's host," will not laugh aloud to see the failure of this frustrated Titan as he revolves and splutters hopelessly under the flood of his own vomit.

Ulysses

C. C. Martindale, S. J.
Dublin Review, 171 (October–December 1922): 273–276

When we read *Ulysses,* reviewed in the last issue of the *Dublin,* we were haunted by a puzzle on which the reviewer did not touch. Why, we asked ourselves, is the whole method of this book wrong? What is its interior untruth which vitiates its art far more radically than the surface faults so easy to discern? At last an early Futurist exhibition occurred to us, and the reason why we had disapproved it. Those artists did not, of course, claim to reproduce what they knew their subject to be, but all that in any way it set stirring in their mind.

. . . .

But in the Futurist painting you had no idea of what the next ripple in the painter's impressions might be or not be; not only in the picture there was no 'whole,' but you were quite unable to surmise a future Whole, and so you felt as mad as the picture looked.

Mr. Joyce is guilty of both these atrocities, in words instead of paint. He goes down to that level where seething instinct is not yet illuminated by intellect, or only just enough to be not quite invisible . . . Great tracts of his enormous book consist of a man's stuff-for-thought—not thoughts—blindly plunging forward through the space of a day. Hence the elimination of stops—the unfinished sentences—the sentences with half of the next sentence inserted in the midst; the mixture of styles, of languages. Hence the refusal to reject anything that instinct, by action or reaction, may supply. He has plunged below the level where ideas shine, energize, select, construct . . . Well, Mr Joyce gets as far down as he can to this level of animality which exists, of course, as an ultimate in every man, and then, consciously and by art, tries to reproduce it. And this requires the most strong mental effort. For he has to *hold together* what yet must somehow *remain* incoherent; never to forget what the conscious memory has never been in possession of; to put into the impressions of the evening all that the morning held but was never known to hold, and to put it there, not in the shape in which morning offered it, but in the shape into which noon and all the hours between have distorted it. Thus the author, by a visibly violent effort of memory and intelligence, had to show us what essentially was never consciously known, still less remembered. Hence an angry sense of contradiction in the reader. Mr. Joyce is trying to think as *if* he were insane.

Again, since he introduces several characters and seeks to show the sort of instinctive reaction they severally experience on the same event, he has to present the simultaneous consecutively. But neither paint nor words can thus convey, by means of a series, the simultaneous. We do not even float equably down the dim disgusting sewer, but continually find ourselves hitched back, with a jerk, to where we started from. Hence a new impression of desperate nightmare.

Mr. Joyce would therefore seem not only to have tried to achieve a psychological impossibility but to have tried to do so in what would, anyhow, have been the wrong medium. He would most nearly have succeeded by using music, and counterpoint. . . .

However, we did, in reading, collect one impression: that is, that in calling his book, and in a sense his hero, *Ulysses,* Mr. Joyce meant to portray in him that 'No Man' who yet is 'Everyman,' just because Mr. Joyce considers he has got down to the universal substratum in man which yet cannot be identified with any man in particular. We surmise, too, that there is a deal of Ulysses-symbolism running through the book; but we were not nearly interested enough to try to work it out. But what we object to is this: if that 'ultimate,' that human Abyss, is to be seen at all, described at all, *some* light some intellectual energy, must have played upon it. But here it is most certainly not the Spirit of the Creator that has so played. What black fires may not the Ape of God light up? Into what insane caricatures of humanity may not the Unholy Ghost, plunging gustily upon animal instinct, fashion it? This book suggests an answer. At best the author's eyes are like the slit eyes of Ibsen's Trolls. They see, but they omit what is best worth seeing; they see, but they see all things crooked. Take a concrete instance: Mr. Joyce has, in this book too, the offensive habit of introducing real people by name. We know some of them. One such person (now dead, it is true) we knew well enough to see that Mr. Joyce, who describes him in no unfriendly way, yet cannot *see.* We absolve him of wilful calumny.

But we realize that he is at least more likely than not to have a mis-seen not only one person, but whole places, like Dublin, or Clongowes; whole categories, like students; whole literatures, like the Irish, or the Latin.

Alas, then, that a man who can write such exquisite prose-music when he chooses, who has so much erudition, such power of original criticism, such subtlety of intuition, and of construction, and the possibility of mental energy so long-continued, should either by preference or because by now he cannot help it, immerse his mind into the hateful dreams of drunkenness, the phantom-world of the neuropath; should be best when he portrays collapse; should be at his most convincing in his chosen line when murmuring through half a hundred pages the dream-memories of an uneducated woman.

—reprinted from *James Joyce: The Critical Heritage*

Anglo-Irish man of letters Shane Leslie

Ulysses

Shane Leslie
Quarterly Review, 238 (October 1922), pp. 219–234

When a massive volume, whose resemblance in size and colour to the London Telephone Book must make it a danger to the unsuspecting, is written by a well-known Dublin author, printed at Dijon, and published in Paris at an excessive price, it is liable to escape the dignity of general notice unless for particular reasons. 'Ulysses,' however, has achieved the success of a scandal behind the scenes. In the first place, it has been brought out in a limited edition, and in the second the author has passed all limits of restraints or convention. It is not the kind of book readily to be met with on Messrs. W. H. Smith's ubiquitous stalls or obtained from the most obliging of lending libraries. It is doubtful if the British Museum possesses a copy, as the book apparently could not be printed in England, and no copy could fall by law to the great national collection. Whether a copy will ever be procured by purchase may be left to the taste of the Trustees of the future. The rulers of the National Library of Ireland will have the more difficult task of deciding whether to house the largest book composed by an Irish author since the publication of the 'Annals of the Four Masters,' a book, moreover, which is most intimately bound up with the daily life of Dublin twenty years ago. For while it contains some gruesome and realistic pictures of low life in Dublin, which would duly form part of the sociological history of the Irish capital, it also contains passages fantastically opposed to all ideas of good taste and morality.

As a whole, the book must remain impossible to read; and in general undesirable to quote. It is possible for the fairly intelligent to fail to obtain any intelligible glimmer even from a prolonged perusal It is an Odyssey no doubt; but divided into twenty-four hours instead of books. Apparently anything that can happen, every thought that might occur to the mind, and anything that could be said in conversation during a twenty-four hours of Dublin life, has been crowded upon this colossal canvas; and yet the conscious conscientiousness required in trying to secure and enscroll for ever a day out of the past, down to its lowest detail and most remote allusion, has failed, as the Tower of Babel failed, of very opheaviness as well as of antitheistic endeavour, and the writer ceases to be comprehensible, possibly even to himself. Of whole passages he can only feel as Browning did of some of his verses that however well God may have known their meaning the writer, at least, had forgotten. To a fair bulk of 'Ulysses' no adequate meaning can be attached at first reading, and for this reason the book, which is an assault upon Divine Decency as well as on human intelligence, will fail of its purpose, if purpose it has to grip and corrupt either the reading public or the impressionable race of contemporary scribes.

Our own opinion is that a gigantic effort has been made to fool the world of readers and even the Pretorian guard of critics. Of the latter a number have fallen both in France and England, and the greatness of their fall has been in proportion to their inability to understand what perhaps they cannot have been intended to understand. For the well-meaning but open-mouthed critics in France, who have seriously accepted 'Ulysses' as a pendant to Shakespeare and as Ireland's contribution to the modern world's reading, we can only feel sympathy. It is vain to say that in 'Ulysses' *maius nascitur Iliade.* The great name of Ulysses is horribly profaned. We have only an Odyssey of the sewer. Those critics have been colossally deceived, in the same way that some folk were persuaded that Cubist pictures were great works of art, or as the unfortunate Russian people were deceived by the spurious and God-defying claims of Bolshevism. Here we shall not be far wrong if we describe Mr Joyce's work as literary Bolshevism. It is experimental, anti-conventional, anti-Christian, chaotic, totally unmoral. And it is no less liable to prove the entangling shroud of its author. From it he can never escape. We can well believe that Mr Joyce has put the best years of his life into its pages, toiling during the world's toil and refusing to collapse with the col-

lapse of civilisation. The genius and literary ability of the author of the 'Portrait of the Artist as a Young Man' have always been apparent. They have since been remorselessly pressed and driven into the soul-destroying work of writing entire pages, which alienists might only attribute to one cause. Over half of million words crowd the disconcerting paginal result, for the form and scale of which 'Balzacian' and 'Zolaesque' would be appropriate but insufficient epithets. But in the matter of psychology or realism Balzac is beggared and Zola bankrupted. It may sound amazing to say so, but neither of those remorseless and unflinching writers, one the revealer of the human mind, the other the painter of sordidness, ever dared to go to the lengths that this alumnus of an Irish College has carelessly and floridly gone. And all this effort has been made, not to make any profound revelation or to deliver a literary message, but to bless the wondering world with an accurate account of one day and one night passed by the author in Dublin's fair City, Lord Dudley being Viceroy (the account of his driving through the streets of Dublin is probably one of the few passages intelligible to the ordinary English reader). The selected day and night are divided into the following series of episodes, if we may quote what appears to be a summary given towards the close of the book:

> 'the preparation of breakfast, intestinal congestion, the bath, the funeral, the advertisement of Alexander Keyes, the unsubstantial lunch, the visit to Museum and National Library, the book-hunt along Bedford Row, Merchants' Arch, Wellington Quay, the music in the Ormond Hotel, the altercation with a truculent troglodyte in Bernard Kieran's premises, a blank period of time including a car-drive, a visit to a house of mourning, a leave-taking, . . . the prolonged delivery of Mrs. Nina Purefoy, the visit to a disorderly house . . . and subsequent brawl and chance medley in Beaver Street, nocturnal perambulation to and from the cabman's shelter, Butt Bridge.'

The advertisement of Alexander Keyes covers a chapter, tedious beyond recapitulation, in the office of the 'Freeman's Journal.' The visit to the National Library expands into a Shakespearean discussion.

The thesis reads like that of a novel from the Mud and Purple school of Dublin novelists, who prefer to lay emphasis on the second adjective in the familiar phrase 'dear dirty Dublin.' Of all literary movements the semi- Gaelic Renaissance, or Anglo-Irish outburst, has had the most varied and chequered existence. Whether it began with surreptitious keening for Parnell, or with the love songs and ballads which Douglas Hyde rescued from the lips of the last rhymers and gleemen, its literature always offered the first promise of a channel of escape from the tremendous political and theological conventions which bind all Irish life, whether Catholic or Protestant. Though the Catholic strand ran through what was most Irish in remimiscence and expression, the movement was never guided by religious influences or decoyed into political uses. There were plays which raised both Protestant and Catholic points of interest like Yeats' 'The Countess Kathleen' or St John Ervine's 'Mixed Marriage.' But as the movement became less antiquarian and Celtic, and more modernised and Europeanised, the names of George Moore and Synge alone attained a first rank and stood in London or Paris for the Irish literary movement. Enough may be said in asserting that each wrote a tolerable masterpiece, and that their minor works made the rest of the Irish writers look small fry. George Moore wrote French novels in English on Ireland. Synge wrote Shakespearean-looking stuff, which proved to be a fancy kind of Anglo-Irish rhodomontade. In 'Ulysses' he is amusingly alluded to as 'the fellow that Shakespeare wrote like!' There was no other writer except James Stephens near them. Then James Joyce, with Patrick MacGill for his modest Mercury, joined the group. There can be no doubt that Moore and Synge have been two main influences on his writing. But he has certainly outdone them and incidentally outdone himself. George Moore is the easiest of the Irish novelists to read. The suave, writhing well-chopped sentences follow each other, leaving a sense of perfect English and stylish grammar (though Susan Mitchell has written strongly in the other sense). Every now and again, the gentle current of his prose is rippled or broken by an unpleasant word or by a suggestive phrase. It is his chief artifice. His second artifice was to introduce people, still living, by name into his novels. This secured him the double audience of his victims' enemies and friends. In any case, enough has been written about him. Synge, his co-star, set the Irish school something very different from the Parisian models and the boulevard touch. He took Elizabethan English and County Wicklow grammar with the slang of the Irish cross-roads, and deftly put together a lingo which made the everlasting richness and originality of the 'Playboy.' Its theme, which distressed the patriotic pious and interested the alien problem-play-goer, was beside the point. It was real literature. It was pseudo-Shakespearean in parts, but the critic could not be certain that he was not making game of Irish audiences and English readers. But it was great game. To him came no dramatic successors. A hundred plays have been written in Ireland since, but the genre and school of Synge died with him. Not so his influence, which can be detected in 'Ulysses.' One whole chapter describing a Lying-in Hospital in Dublin and the birth

of a child is written not in mock-Elizabethan, but in the pseudo-style of English and Norse Saga which William Morris affected. What is the following, then?

'Her he asked if O'Hare Doctor tidings sent from far coast and she with grameful sigh him answered that O'Hare Doctor in heaven was. Sad was the man that word to hear, that him so heavied in bowels ruthful. All she there told him, ruing death for friend so young, algate sore unwilling God's rightwiseness to withsay. She said that he had a fair sweet death through God His goodness with masspriest to be shriven, holy housel and sick men's oil to his limbs. The man then right earnest asked the nun of which death the dead man was died and the nun answered him and said that he was died in Mona island through bellycrab three year agone come Childermas and she prayed to God the Allruthful to have his dear soul in his undeathliness. He heard her sad words, in held hat sad staring. So stood they there both awhile in wanhope sorrowing one with another.'

Reams of such-like follow, to ring even falser when the Dublin medical students eat sardines and drink whisky thus,

'. . . strange fishes withouten heads though misbelieving man nie that this be possible thing without they see it, natheless they are so. And these fishes lie in an oily water brought there from Portugal land because of the fatness that therein is like to the juices of the olive press. And also it was a marvel to see in that castle how by magic they make a compost out of fecund wheat kidneys out of Chaldee. . . .'

In this curious jargon the most modern questions in medico-eugenics are discussed. The mediæval view against restriction of the race finds mediæval expression and almost beautiful form in the words,

'Murmur, Sirs, is eke oft among layfolk. Both babe and parent now glorify their Maker, the one in limb gloom the other in purge fire. But, gramercy, what of those God-possibled souls that we nightly impossibilise, which is the sin against the Holy Ghost, Very God, Lord and Giver of Life.'

The language becomes interesting as the chart of Astrology is set in the heavens.

. . . 'on the highway of the clouds they come muttering thunder of rebellion, the ghosts of beasts . . . Elk and Yak, the bulls of Bashan and Babylon, mammoth and mastodon, they come trooping to the sunken sea *Lacus Mortis*. Ominous revengeful zodaical host! They moan, passing upon the clouds, horned and capricorned, the trumpeted with the tusked, the lion maned, the giant antlered, snouter and crawler, rodent, ruminant and pachyderm, all their moving moaning multitude, murderers of the sun. Onward to the Dead sea they tramp to drink, unslaked and with horrible gulpings, the salt somonlent inexhaustible flood. And the equine portent grows again, magnified in the deserted heavens, may to heaven's own magnitude till it looms vast over the House of Virgo. . . . How serene does she now arise a queen among the Pleiades, in the penultimate antelucan hour, shod in sandals of bright gold, coifed with a veil of what do you call it gossamer! It floats, it flows about her starborn flesh and loose it streams emerald, sapphire, mauve, and heliotrope sustained on currents of cold interstellar wind, winding, coiling, simply swirling, writhing in the skies a mysterious writing, till after a myriad metamorphoses of symbol, it blazes, Alpha, a ruby and triangled sign upon the forehead of Taurus.'

But on the next page, money is being lost in backing Sceptre, a once-famous racehorse, and the tale winds up with a visit of Mr Dowie to Merrion Square and a parody of American Revivalism, which seems taken literally from one of Mr Billy Sunday's sermons,

'Come on you wine-fizzling, gin-sizzling, boose-guzzling existences! Come on you dog-gone, bull-necked, beetle-browed, hog-jowled, peanut-brained, weasel-eyed, four-flushers, false alarms and excess baggage! Come on you triple extract of infamy. Alexander J. Christ Dowie that's yanked to glory most half this planet . . .' etc.

Parody is so discernible in the book that of itself should convince the reader that a gigantic joke has been played on the French, English and Irish public, and except for the last-named, with fair success. The French and many of the English have taken it seriously. From Dublin as yet we have only heard jocular contempt. Dublin has had a way, however, of rejecting her best writers as well as her politicians; her prophets and her procurers.

The Catholic reader will close the volume at the parodies of the Creed and of the Litany of the Virgin; the Puritan will resent even an adaptation of the 'Pilgrim's Progress,' though outside the book it does not read too ill,

'then wotted he nought of that other land which is called Believe-on-me, that is the land of promise which behoves to the King Delightful and shall be for ever where there is no death and no birth, neither wiving nor mothering at which all shall come as many as believe on it. Yes Pious had told him of that land and Chaste had pointed him to the way, but the reason was that in the way he fell in with a certain—whose name is Bird-in-the-Hand . . .'

The writer has little care for the *sacra* of Catholic or Protestant Christianity. He writes to vilify and ridicule them both, and does not hesitate to introduce the

venerable names of Archbishop Alexander and Cardinal Logue into one of his witches' Sabbaths. The practice of introducing the names of real people into circumstances of monstrous and ludicrous fiction seems to us to touch the lowest depth of Rabelaisian realism. When we are given the details of the skin disease of an Irish peer, famous for his benefactions, we feel a genuine dislike of the writer. There are some things which cannot and, we should like to be able to say, shall not be done.

From any Christian point of view this book must be proclaimed anathema, simply because it tries to pour ridicule on the most sacred themes and characters in what has been the religion of Europe for nearly two thousand years. And this is the book which ignorant French critics hail as the proof of Ireland's re-entry into European literature! It contains the literary germs of that fell movement which politically has destroyed the greater part of Slavic Europe. If it is a summons or inspiration to the Celtic end of Europe to do likewise, it would be better for Ireland to sink under the seas and join Atlantis, rather than allow her life of letters to affect the least reconciliation with a book which, owing to accidents of circumstance, probably only Dubliners can really understand in detail. Certainly, it takes a Dubliner to pick out the familiar names and allusions of twenty years ago, though the references to men who have become as important as Arthur Griffith assume a more universal hearing. And we are sorry to say that it would take a theologian, even Jesuit, to understand all the theological references. At the same time, nobody in his senses would hold Clongowes School responsible for this portent. It was its ill fortune to breed without being able to harness a striking literary genius, who has since yoked himself to the steeds of Comedy and Blasphemy and taken headlong flight, shall we say like the Gadarene swine, into a choking sea of impropriety. If George Moore is right in saying that 'blasphemy is the literature of Catholic countries,' this is verily literature!

Mr Joyce spares nobody if he can help it. It was said of a cold-blooded botanist that he would not hesitate to collect specimens on his mother's grave. Mr Joyce's Stephen Dedalus is represented as refusing to pray with his dying mother. 'He kills his mother but he can't wear grey trousers,' is the criticism of Mr Buck Mulligan. The most ghastly detail is given of her deathbed and no one can be surprised if she haunts his prose, if not his life,

'Silently in a dream she had come to him after her death, her wasted body within its loose brown grave-clothes giving off an odour of wax and rosewood, her breath that had bent upon him, mute, reproachful, a faint odour of wetted ashes . . .

And again he recalls–

'her secrets; old feathers fans, tassled dance cards, powdered with musk . . . her glass of water from the kitchen tap when she had approached the sacrament. Her shapely fingernails reddened by the blood of squashed lice from the children's shirts . . . her glazing eyes staring out of death to shake and bend my soul.'

Mr Joyce's method of allusion, cross-reminiscence and thought-sequence makes most of the book tediously obscure and irrelevantly trivial. He simply dots down whatever succession of thoughts might occur to his mind in certain circumstances. Sometimes the reader catches a flash as in the allusion . . . 'white teeth with gold points. Chrysostomos' . . . The account of the old servant pouring out the milk in Dublin raises a host of Gaelic imagery.

'She praised the goodness of the milk pouring it out. Crouching by a patient cow at daybreak in the lush field, a witch on her toadstool, her wrinkled fingers quick at squirting dugs. They lowed about her whom they knew, dew silky cattle. *Silk of the kine* and *poor old woman,* names given her [Ireland] in old times. A wandering crone, lowly form of an immortal, serving her conqueror and her gay betrayer, their common cuckquean, a messenger from the secret morning. To serve or to upraid whether, he could not tell: but scorned to beg her favour.'– [*Our italics*].

A discussion about the Jews leads to the corollary that the reason why Ireland never persecuted them was because she never let them in; but a curious vision in words is vouchsafed the reader of

'goldskinned men quoting prices on their gemmed fingers. Gabble of geese. They swarmed loud, uncouth about the temple, their heads thick-plotted under maladroit silk hats. Not theirs: these clothes, this speech, these gestures. Their full slow eyes belied the words, the gestures eager and unoffending, but knew the rancours massed about them and knew their zeal was vain. Vain patience to heap and hoard. Time would surely scatter all. A hoard heaped by the roadside: plundered and passing on. Their eyes knew the years of wandering.'

Such pictures as can be rescued from the *cloaca* are distinct and sometimes unforgettable. When the style is lucid and restrained, literature is the result in patches; but who can wade through the spate in order to pick out what little is at the same time intelligible and not unquotable? We can catch in our sieve some account of a refugee Fenian in the Latin Quarter of Paris:

. . . 'Paris rawly waking, crude sunlight on her lemon streets. Moist pith of farls of bread, the frog-green wormwood, her matin incense, court the air. Belluomo rises from the bed of wife's lover's wife. . . . Noon slumbers. Kevin Egan rolls gunpowder cigarettes through fingers smeared with printer's ink . . . About us gobblers fork spiced beans down their gullets . . . Well *slainte*! Around the slabbed tables the tangle of wined breaths and grumbling gorges . . . Of Ireland, the Dalcassians, of hopes, conspiracies, of Arthur Griffith now . . . a flame and acrid smoke light our corner. Raw facebones under his peep-of-day boy's hat. How the Head Centre got away, authentic version. Got up as a young brideman, veil orange-blossoms, drove out the road to Malahide . . . he prowled with Colonel Richard Burk, tanist of his sept, under the walls of Clerkenwell and crouching saw a flame of vengeance hurl them upward in the fog. Shattered glass and toppling masonry. In gay Paree he hides, Egan of Paris, unsought by any save by me. Making his day's stations, the dingy printing case, his three taverns, the Montmartre lair he sleeps short night in, *rue de la Goutte d'Or,* damascened with flyblown faces of the gone.'

The novel of Fenianism was never written, but these words seem to outline it in a nutshell.

We are led to make quotations because the confusion of the book is so great that there is not circumventing its clumsiness and unwinding its deliberate bamboozlement of the reader. With an occasional lucid bait the attention is gripped, and then the expectant eye is lost in incoherent fantasies. For sheer realism we have never read such a passage as the paragraphs describing the drowned man in Dublin Bay, and we add that they are unequalled elsewhere in the book.

'Five fathoms out there. Full fathom five thy father lies. At one he said. Found drowned. High water at Dublin Bar. Driving before it a loose drift of rubble, fanshoals of fishes, sills shells. A corpse rising salt-white from the undertow, bobbing landward, a pace a pace a porpoise. There he is. Hook it quick. Sunk though he be beneath the watery floor. We have him. Easy now. Bag of corpse gas sopping in foul brine. . . . Dead breaths I living breathe, tread dead dust. . . . Hauled stark over the gunwale he breathes upward the stench of his green grave, his leprous nosehole snoring to the sun.'

We need not quote the account of underground chemistry in Glasnevin cemetery except to observe that in letters as in cuisine some gourmands prefer their meat high. The morbid train of thought in Mr Joyce is expressed sufficiently by one sentence–'a corpse is meat gone bad. Well, and what's cheese? Corpse of milk!'

Mr Joyce is apparently as fond of rats as Chinese ladies of their Pekinese. His affection seems divided between churchyard and brewery rats. Of Guinness' Brewery he has a peculiar statistic: 'Regular world in itself. Vats of porter wonderful. Rats get in too. Drink themselves bloated as big as a collie floating. Dead drunk on the porter.' His snapshot of a butcher's shop should encourage vegetarianism, though the scene is common enough and only striking when put into words.

Through the mist of sexual analysis and psycho-unravelment we can only pass quickly for good. We are sorry that such stuff should have ever reached the dignity even of surreptitious print, and are glad that the limited copies and their exaggerated cost will continue to prevent the vast majority of the reading public from sampling even faintly such unpleasant ware. It will suffice for those who are interested, to know whether Mr Joyce has invented new styles of literature or written a book to be classed as a literary milestone with 'Madame Bovary' or 'Crime and Punishment,' to take a few more insights into Dublin life, the favoured subject of Mr Joyce's scalpel.

A jeweller's shop, the vegetable market, and the entrance to a Dublin slum are thus severally dealt with:

'Stephen Dedalus watched through the webbed window the lapidary's fingers prove a time-dulled chain. Dust webbed the window and the show trays. Dust darkened the toiling fingers with their vulture nails. Dust slept on dull coils of bronze and silver, lozenges of cinnabar, on rubies, leprous and winedark stones. Born all in the dark wormy earth, cold specks of fire, evil lights shining in the darkness. Where fallen archangels flung the stars of their brows. Muddy swinesnouts, hands, root and root, gripe and wrest them.'

If that is the feeling evoked by a cheap jeweller one need not be surprised by the portentous account of market gardening in the same city:

'thither the extremely large wains bring foison of the field, flaskets of cauliflowers, floats of spinach, pineapple chunks, Rangoon beans, strikes of tomatoes, drums of figs, drills of Swedes, spherical potatoes and tallies of iridiscent kale, York and Savoy, and trays of onions, pearls of the earth and pumets of mushrooms and custard marrows and fat vetches and bere and rape and red green yellow brown russet sweet big bitter ripe pomellated apples and chips of strawberries and sieves of gooseberries, pulpy and pelurious, and strawberries fit for princes and raspberries from their canes.'

One wonders if the writer had been reading Charles Kingsley's 'Poetry of a root-crop,' with its unforgettable

'Underneath their eider-robe
Russet swede and golden globe,
Feathered carrot burrowing deep.'

A large part of this stupendous volume is in the form of drama with the most intricate and vivid stage directions. The opening scene of a Dublin purlieu is set thus:

'The Mabbot Street entrance of night town, before which stretches an uncobbled tramsiding set with skeleton tracks red and green will o'the wisps and danger signals. Rows of flimsy houses with gaping doors. Rare lamps with faint rainbow fans. Round Rabaiotti's halted ice gondola stunted men and women squabble. They grab wafers between which are wedged lumps of coal and copper snow. Sucking they scatter slowly. Children. The swancomb of the gondola highreared forges on through the murk, white and blue under a lighthouse. Whistles call and answer . . .'

In the same desiccated rare-worded style he can sketch an Irish type in thirty words; 'enter Magee Mor Mathew a rugged rough rug-headed kern, in strossers with a buttoned codpiece, his nether stocks bemired with clauber of ten forests, a wand of wilding in his hand.'

Mr Magee's son is apparently the well-known 'John Eglinton,' who is the principal speaker in the Shakespearean discussion, a brilliant chapter of Dublin causerie and criticism, which might well be reprinted apart from the rest of the book. Playing on Miss Susan Mitchell's celebrated joke that George Moore was Edward Martyn's wild oats, Mr Joyce chimes; 'Good Bacon: gone musty. Shakespeare Bacon's wild oats. Cypher-jugglers going the highroads. Seekers on the great quest. What town good masters? Mummed in names: A. E., eon: Magee, John Eglinton. East of the sun, west of the moon: *Tir na nog.*'

One wonders what the French critics made of that! Yet it has a connected meaning. A.E. and John Eglinton are the literary names of distinguished Irishmen, and we almost see the latter 'glitter-eyed, his rufous skull close to his green-capped desk lamp . . . bearded amid dark-greener shadow, an ollav, holyeyed. He laughed low: a sizar's laugh of Trinity: unanswered.' And then

'all these questions are purely academic, Russell oracled out of his shadow. I mean whether Hamlet is Shakespeare or James I or Essex. Clergymen's discussions of the historicity of Jesus. Art has to reveal to us ideas, formless spiritual essences. The supreme question about a work of art is out of how deep a life does it spring. The painting of Gustave Moreau is the painting of ideas. The deepest poetry of Shelley, the words of Hamlet bring out mind into contact with the eternal wisdom. Plato's world of ideas. All the rest is the speculation of schoolboys for schoolboys. The schoolmen were schoolboys first, Stephen said superpolitely, Aristotle was once Plato's schoolboy—and has remained so one should hope, John Eglinton sedately said. One can see him a model schoolboy with his diploma under his arm.'

Whether it is English literature or not, as Dublin table talk it is living enough, and those parodied or reported have no real cause of complaint. Nor need the ladies of the Cuala Press resent the neat skit on one of their products, 'Five lines of text and ten pages of notes about the folk and the fishgods of Dundrum. Printed by the weird sisters in the year of the big wind!'

Mr Joyce's turn for epigram is keen. He probably looks upon it as an elephant-killer regards the pursuit of sparrows with peas. Here and there stray sayings reveal an ancient sense of humour quite apart from the terrible Comic Force which is his strongest weapon. We smile languidly when we hear that 'the Irishman's house is his coffin,' or that 'we haven't the chance of a snowball in hell,' unless maybe we go 'out of the frying pan of life into the fire of purgatory'. But these may all be second hand, and indeed epigrams can always be picked like blackberries in Dublin. Two of Arthur Griffith's grim sallies are recorded when he referred to the 'overseas or half-seas-over Empire,' and when he twitted the 'Freeman's Journal' with the woodcut printed over all their leaders as really 'a sunrise to the North West over Parliament building on College Green.' Occasionally we cull a real philosophical fragment, such as the truth that 'it is as painful perhaps to be awakened from a vision as to be born,' or the insight into Irish feelings that 'people could put up with being bitten by a wolf, but what properly riled them was a bite from a sheep.' There is a real feudalism in that. The Irish peasants never minded paying rent to wicked Earls and Rapparee Chiefs; but they fought shy of the counting-house agent and the bourgeois planter. We wish there were more texts and phrases of this quality. The huge bulk of the book rushes sewerward but in the great Rabelaisian way and its reading can only be summed in a sentence from the book itself,

---

Gertrude Stein's comment about Joyce, made in 1922, was recorded by Samuel Putnam in his 1947 memoir.

'Joyce,' she admitted, 'is *good*.' (The italics were in her voice.) 'He is a *good* writer. People like him because he is incomprehensible and anybody can understand him. But who came first, Gertrude Stein or James Joyce? Do not forget that my first great book, *Three Lives,* was published in 1908. That was long before *Ulysses*. But Joyce *has* done *something*. His influence, however, is local. Like Synge, another Irish writer, he has had his day. . . .'

– *Paris Was Our Mistress*, p. 138

---

drawn from the best theology; 'morose delectation Aquinas tunbelly calls this.'

We come back to our complaint that without form there cannot be art. Art must be logical, almost mathematical. Its material, its conditions, its effects must be calculable. Windiness, inconsequence and confusion argue the riot of Nature. We will make one more effort to understand the drift of James Joyce, and quote whole his outburst concerning water, whichis a presumed parody of Whitman (and there must be two score other authors parodied in different parts of the book). Of water this apparently may be considered:

'Its universality: its democratic equality and constancy to its nature in seeking its own level: its vastness in the ocean of Mercator's projection: its unplumbed profundity in the Sundam trench of the Pacific exceeding 8000 fathoms: the restlessness of its waves and surface particles visiting in turn all points of its seaboard: the independence of its units: the variability of states of sea: its hydrostatic quiescence in calm: its hydrokinetic turgidity in neap and spring tides: its subsidence after devastation: its sterility in the circumpolar icecaps, arctic and antarctic: its climatic and commercial significance: its preponderance of three to one over the dry land of the globe: its indisputable hegemony extending in square leagues over all the region below the subequatorial tropic of Capricorn: the multisecular stability of its primæval basin: its luteosfulvous bed; its capacity to dissolve and hold in solution all soluble substances including millions of tons of the most precious metals: its slow erosions of peninsulas and downward tending in promontories: its alluvial deposits: its weight and volume and density: its imperturbability in lagoons and highland tarns: its gradation of colours in the torrid and temperate and frigid zones: its vehicular ramifications in continental lake-contained streams and confluent ocean-flowing rivers with their tributaries and trans-oceanic currents, gulfstream, north and south, equatorial courses: its violence in seaquakes, waterspouts, Artesian wells, eruptions, torrents, eddies, freshets, spates, groundswells, watersheds, water-partings, geysers, cataracts, whirlpools, maelstroms, inundations, deluges, cloudbursts: its vast circumterrestrial horizontal curve: its secrecy in springs and latent humidity, revealed by rhabdomantic or hygrometric instruments and exemplified by the hole in the wall at Ashtown gate, saturation of air; distillation of dew: the simplicity of its composition, two constituent parts of hydrogen with one constituent part of oxygen: its healing virtues: its buoyancy in the waters of the Dead Sea: its persevering penetrativeness in runnels, gullies, inadequate dams, leaks on shipboard: its properties for cleansing, quenching thirst and fire, nourishing vegetation: its infallibility as paradigm and paragon: its metamorphoses as vapour, mist, cloud, rain, sleet, snow, hail: its strength in rigid hydrants: its variety of forms in loughs and bays and gulfs and bights and guts and lagoons and atolls and archipelagos and sounds and fjords and minches and tidal estuaries and arms of sea: its solidity in glaciers,, icebergs, iceflows: its docility in working hydraulic millwheels, turbines, dynamos, electric power stations, bleach-works, tanneries, scutchmills: its utility in canals, rivers if navigable, floating and graving docks: its potentiality derivable from harnessed tides or water courses falling from level to level: its submarine fauna and flora (anacoustic, photophobe) numerically if not literally the inhabitants of the globe: its ubiquity as constituting 90 per cent. of the human body: the noxiousness of its effluvia in lacustrine marshes, pestilential fens, faded flower-water, stagnant pools in the waning moon.'

Well, that is that, one feels. Such is water, and there is enough and satisfyingly enough said. Time will show what place and influence "Ulysses" will take in the thought and script of men. In spite of a thin parallelism with the movement of the Odyssey, for the episodes of Circe, Æolus, Nausikaa, are visible amongst others less easily traceable, there has been an abandonment of form and a mad Shelleyan effort to extend the known confines of the English language. Pages without punctuation or paragraph show an attempt to beat up a sustained and overwhelming orchestral effect. French and possibly American critics will utter their chorus of praise in proportion to their failure to understand. English critics will be divided and remain in amicable but squabbling disagreement. Ireland's writers, whose own language was legislatively and slowly destroyed by England, will cynically contemplate an attempted Clerkenwell explosion in the well-guarded, well-built, classical prison of English literature. The bomb has exploded, and creeping round Grub Street we have picked up a few fragments by way of curiosity.

We have had some hesitation (bewilderment almost) in noticing 'Ulysses' in the pages of the 'Quarterly Review,' and would not have done so, had we thought that such notice would lead the prurient-minded to read the book. Coarseness and Vice, it is true, have been introduced into books which have taken their place among the world's classics—from Aristophanes to Swift; but they have been presented with such literary skill, or humour, or reprobation, as to condone if not excuse their portrayal—for example, the 'Lysistrata' of Aristophanes. The question before the critic of 'Ulysses' is whether the literary power is a sufficiently extenuating circumstance. All that is unmentionable according to civilised standards has been brought to the light of day without any veil of decency. Our quotations, being chosen for their interest and decency, are intended to give a possible view of the author's literary ability, concerning which there may be as many views as critics. We believe that the cumbrousness of the style in which these things are revealed may prove their most effective screen from prying eyes, for the author has done his best to make his book unreadable and unquotable, and, we must add, unreviewable.

Commentary on Joyce and *Ulysses* in the 1920s and 1930s

The publication history of Ulysses, *from its first appearance in* The Little Review *in March 1918 to the 1997 edition of the novel edited by Denis Rose, has been surrounded by controversy. Since its first publication, readers, reviewers, and scholars have disputed not only interpretative views and aesthetic values but also the editorial integrity of the various editions of the text. In addition to being banned in the United States in the 1920s and early 1930s,* Ulysses *was also being pirated in 1926 by Samuel Roth in his American journal* Two Worlds Monthly. *The pirated version of the novel sparked another controversy that prompted two of Joyce's American friends, Ludwig Lewisohn and Archibald MacLeish, to draw up a letter of international protest that condemned the undertaking. Although Roth stopped publishing the unauthorized version of* Ulysses *in 1927, Justice Richard H. Mitchell of the New York State Supreme Court ordered an injunction in late 1928 that prohibited Roth from publishing anything by Joyce without his consent. Meanwhile in March 1932 Bennet Cerf, who with Donald S. Klopfer founded Random House in 1927, hired the American attorney Morris Ernst to argue against the ban on* Ulysses *in the United States. The lifting of the ban allowed the novel to be published by Random House in January 1934.*

Ezra Pound's essay "James Joyce et Pécuchet" was originally published in the June 1922 issue of Mercure de France. *The text was translated by Fred Bornhauser in the Autumn 1952* Shenandoah.

James Joyce et Pécuchet
Ezra Pound
Mercure de France, 156 (June 1922): 307–320

. . . The Flaubert centenary year, first of a new era, also sees the publication of a new book by Joyce, *Ulysses,* which from certain points of view can be considered as the first work that, descending from Flaubert, continues the development of the Flaubertian art from where he left it off in his last, unfinished book.

Although *Bouvard et Pécuchet* does not pass for the master's best thing,' it can be maintained that *Bovary* and *l'Education* are but the apogee of an earlier form; and that the *Trois Contes* give a kind of summary of everything Flaubert had accomplished in writing his other novels, *Salammbo, Bovary, l'Education,* and the first versions of *Saint Antoine.* The three tableaux—pagan, medieval, and modern—form a whole revolving around the sentence: 'And the idea came to him to devote his life to the service of others,' which is in the middle of *Saint Julien,* the first of the three tales to be written.

Bouvard et Pécuchet continues the Flaubertian art and thought, but does not continue this tradition of the novel or the short story. 'Encyclopedia in the form of farce,' which carries as a subtitle, 'Failings of method in the sciences,' can be regarded as the inauguration of a new form, a form which had no precedent. Neither *Gargantua,* nor *Don Quixote,* nor Sterne's *Tristram Shandy* had furnished the archetype. . . .

What is James Joyce's *Ulysses?* This novel belongs to that large class of novels in sonata form, that is to say, in the form: theme, counter-theme, recapitulation, development, finale. And in the sub-division: father and son novel. It follows in the great line of the *Odyssey,* and offers many points of more or less exact correspondence with the mercy, and drink-sodden, useless men, the same forces will surely push another into open defiance of the religion on which that life is presumed to rest. That is the revolt which you find in Mr. Joyce. I do not know that he detests the life of Dublin in particular with the same intensity as Mr. [Brinsley] Macnamara loathes his valley. But through Mr. Macnamara's book runs a suggestion of freer regions, in which all the windows do not squint and pry. For Mr. Joyce, as I take it, Dublin is life, life is Dublin, and he, being alive, is bound to the body of this death. In *Dubliners,* his first book, you find him making his hand; establishing a

miraculous power to reproduce a scene so that not the pettiest detail appears to be left out. For the most part, the people whom he depicts are as futile and as drunken as Mr. Macnamara's, but they have a kind of slack-twisted good nature instead of a slow-blooded spite. Next came his *Portrait of the Artist as a Young Man,* and the art is no longer detached and impersonal; there is declared revolt, suggestion that the detailed control over life exercised through the confessional turns sex into an obsession.

I do not pretend to like Mr. Joyce's work, and, admitting its power, it seems to me, even in this second book, that his preoccupation with images of nastiness borders on the insane. But the power of the writing is astonishing. In *Ulysses* it comes to the full. He uses language rather like an orchestra than an instrument. Half a dozen voices speak at once, inner voices and outer voices; he will plunge into mimicry and from mimicry pass to stark dramatisation. Of course *Ulysses* recalls Sterne–who also was of Irish race. But Sterne stayed in the Church; eighteenth century consciences had a robust digestion; there is nothing behind Sterne except a sometimes uneasy laughter. What gives value to *Ulysses* is passion; all through it runs the cry of a tortured soul. Mr. Joyce's Stephen Dedalus is the Catholic by nature and by tradition, who must revolt under the stress of an intellectual compulsion, to whom truth–the thing which he sees as true–speaks inexorably. Yet what he would shake off clings to his flesh like the poisoned shirt of

Joyce, Ezra Pound, John Quinn, and Ford Madox Ford in Paris

> *Hart Crane wrote of his enthusiasm for* Ulysses *in a 27 July 1922 letter to Wilbur Underwood.*
>
> I feel like shouting E U R E K A! When [Gorham] Munson went yesterday after a two weeks visit, he left my copy of *Ulysses*, a huge tome printed on Verge d'arche paper. But do you know–since reading it partially, I do not think I will care to trust it to any bookbinder I know of. It sounds ridiculous, but the book is so strong in its marvelous oaths and blasphemies, that I wouldn't have an easy moment while it was out of the house. You will pardon my strength of opinion on the thing, but it appears to me easily the epic of the age. It is as great a thing as Goethe's *Faust* to which it has a distinct resemblance in many ways. The sharp beauty and sensitivity of the thing! The matchless details! I DO HOPE you get a copy, but from what Munson says there is little hope unless you can get some friend of yours in Europe to smuggle it in his trunk. It has been barred from England. It is quite likely I have one of two or three copies west of New York. . . . His book is steeped in the Elizabethans, his early love, and Latin Church, and some Greek. . . .
>
> Joyce is still very poor. Recently some French writers headed by Valéry Larbaud, gave a dinner and reading for his benefit. It is my opinion that some fanatic will kill Joyce sometime soon for the wonderful things said in *Ulysses*. Joyce is too big for chit-chat, so I hope I haven't offended you with the above details about him. He is the one above all others I should like to talk to. . . .
>
> — *The Letters of Hart Crane*, pp. 94–95

Hercules. He wallows, it burns the more, but revolt persists. He can touch, taste, and handle every abomination; only one thing is impossible, to profess a belief that he rejects. Ancient pieties hold him to it, ties of his nearest life: his mother dying of cancer, dumbly prays of him to pray with her, and she dies without that solace; years pass, her thought, haunting him everywhere and always, only urges him to spit again on whatever she and her like thought holiest. It is revolt the more desperate because it sees no chance of deliverance; and against this fool, this Dedalus, with the stored complex of his brain oversubtilised and overcharged by the very training of that scholastic philosophy from which he breaks away, Mr. Joyce sets his wise man Ulysses, the fortunately happy, whom life cannot injure, lacerate, or bruise, because he has no shame; who must enjoy, so full is his sensuous development; who can enjoy, being without conscience. He likes music almost as genuinely as the nastinesses through which, with every elaboration of their detail, you are privileged to follow him. Seven hundred pages of a tome like a Blue-book are occupied with the events and sensations in one day of a renegade Jew, whose trade is touting for advertisements, but whose subsistence comes through marriage; I need not be more precise. . . .

Maitland argues that Joyce's failure as a novelist is due not to any defect in his creative imagination but to the ultimate failure of his Catholic upbringing and education.

Mr. Joyce and the Catholic Tradition
Cecil Maitland
New Witness, 20 (4 August 1922): 70–71

. . . It would be absurd to try to make a thorough analysis of *Ulysses* in a short article, and I shall not attempt to do so here. For the convenience of readers unacquainted with Mr. Joyce's early work, I shall try briefly to indicate his place in the modern movement of literature and then to make an analysis of one particular aspect of the book . . . This gap between literature and reality Mr. Joyce has tried to fill. An effort of this sort would have been interesting in any case, but Mr. Joyce succeeded in making works of art of his experiments. His first novel tells the story of the infancy, childhood and youth of Stephen Dedalus, an Irish writer, in a style that admits of the presentation of half-thoughts, broken images, emotions, vivid or obscure, and each dirty, profound, trivial or obscene thought that passes through his mind. This book is, however, only a prelude to *Ulysses*. Masterpiece of compression though it is, the *Portrait* was experimental. *Ulysses* shows the author in absolute control of his medium, and with this book he has definitely produced a new form of novel that owes nothing to tradition. A superficial critic might assert that Mr. Joyce owes something of the elasticity of his prose to Sterne. Personally I should not be surprised if he had never read *Tristram Shandy*. The resemblance between the two writers is more apparent than real, for while Sterne's style is an affectation, designed to display his wit and conceal his superficiality, Mr. Joyce elicits the subtlest processes of the mind, so that they are actually present to the reader and not merely recorded.

Ulysses is the *Odyssey* retold, episode by episode, as the story of a day's life in the streets, pubs and brothels of Dublin, and is an attempt to give a complete account of the nature of man. It is apparently almost miraculously successful, for he has reproduced the minds and impressions of his characters so vividly that the reader finds difficulty in separating his consciousness from theirs; and thus his conception of humanity from the author's, the boundaries of whose imagination become his own. These boundaries are very wide; at times Mr. Joyce gathers the thoughts of his characters into a whole that represents the consciousness of Dublin; but though municipal they are not cosmic. Indeed, these frontiers of the imagination are very rigid, for though there is in this book enough fun to make the reputation of a dozen humorous writers, there is no hint of a conception of the human body as anything but dirty, of any pride of life, or of any nobility but that of a pride of intellect. This vision of human beings as walking drain-pipes, this focussing of life exclusively round the excremental and sexual mechanism, appears on the surface inexplicable in so profoundly imaginative and observant a student of humanity as Mr. Joyce. He has, in fact, outdone the psycho-analysts, who admit 'sublimation,' and returned to the ecclesiastical view of man . . . No one who is acquainted with Catholic education in Catholic countries could fail to recognise the source of Mr. Joyce's 'Weltanschauung'. He sees the world as theologians showed it to him. His humour is the cloacal humour of the refectory; his contempt the priests' denigration of the body, and his view of sex has the obscenity of a confessor's manual, reinforced by the profound perception and consequent disgust of a great imaginative writer.

If we consider Mr. Joyce's work from this point of view, it becomes clear that while his study of humanity remains incomplete, the defect is not due to any inherent lack of imagination on his part. Rather it arises from the fact that to a Catholic who no longer believes that he has an immortal soul, fashioned in the image of God, a human being becomes merely a specially cunning animal. I suggest then that Mr. Joyce's failure is not his own, but that of the Catholic system, which has not had the strength to hold him to its transcendentalism, and from whose errors he has not been able to set himself free.

—reprinted from *James Joyce: The Critical Heritage*

A prolific English author, Alfred Noyes (1880–1958) was a popular poet who also wrote criticism, short stories, novels, biographies, and plays. He was decidedly traditional in his tastes and objected especially to the modernism of Joyce and T. S. Eliot. In his autobiography Two Worlds for Memory *(1953) he tells of throwing Hugh Walpole out of his house for trying to entice one of his children to read* Ulysses. *In the following commentary he calls Joyce's masterpiece the "foulest book" ever published and questions the validity of Joyce's genius.*

Rottenness in Literature
Alfred Noyes
Sunday Chronicle, 29 October 1922, p. 2

I have picked out *Ulysses* because it brings to a head all the different questions that have been perplexing literary criticism for some time past. There is no answer possible in this case. It is simply the foulest book that has ever found its way into print. It has received columns of attention from many of our leading journals, and its author has been proclaimed a slightly mad genius perhaps, but still a genius.

The writing of the book is bad simply as writing, and much of it is obscure through sheer disorder of the syntax. But—there is no foulness conceivable to the mind of madman or ape that has not been poured into its imbecile pages.

This is not a question of Puritanism. If it were not so serious a matter there would be considerable irony in the fact that the only sound analysis of the book in this country was made by the *Sporting Times,* which described it as 'the work of a madman,' and said that it was 'couched in language that would make a Hottentot sick' [No. 96].

Yet some of the 'intellectuals,' including one of our leading novelists, have been stating that its author comes within measurable distance of having written the best book in the world. An important review devoted eight columns to this book, and a more or less important novelist announced that Mr. Joyce had only just missed being the most superb member of his own craft, not only in his own times but in any other.

The *Quarterly Review* is perhaps justified in printing its exposure of the critics who proclaimed this insane product, but even the *Quarterly* was unable to tell the whole truth about it [No. 102]. Nobody can tell the whole truth about it; for, to put it plainly, if the book were submitted to the judges of any criminal court in this country, it would be pronounced to be simply a corrupt mass of indescribable degradation.

No word or thought conceivable in the gutters of Dublin or the New York Bowery is omitted, and the foulest references are made to real persons in this country, attributing vile diseases to them, amongst other equally disgusting suggestions.

I have recited the case of this book because it is the extreme case of complete reduction to absurdity of what I have called the 'literary Bolshevism of the Hour.' It can do little harm, however, because the police are, on the whole, circumventing our pseudo-intellectuals. It still remains that copies of Mr. Joyce's book are being smuggled into the country to find purchasers at five guineas apiece.

But what concerns us all, and most urgently demands consideration, is the appalling fact that our Metropolitan criticism should have been treating such works as those of Mr. Joyce seriously as works of genius at the very moment when journal after journal is helping to depreciate the value of some of the noblest pages in our literary history.

The battle that is being waged round the works of Tennyson, for instance, the assault that has been made upon all the great Victorian writers–and it is interesting to note that Bolshevik Russia has recently been declaring that Dickens is more dangerous than Denikin–are indications of a destructive spirit which may lead us far along the road to barbarism. . . .

—reprinted from *James Joyce: The Critical Heritage*

Born Ford Hermann Hueffer, Ford Madox Hueffer, who later changed his name to Ford Madox Ford, was a novelist and critic, the author of more than eighty books of fiction and nonfiction, including the novel The Good Soldier *(1915). As an editor, he was influential in promoting modernism. Under his editorship in April 1924, the* transatlantic review *was the first journal to publish an excerpt from Joyce's last work,* Finnegans Wake, *known then under its provisional title as* Work in Progress. *Hueffer here confidently claims that* Ulysses *will play a pivotal role in the consciousness of later writers.*

Ulysses and the Handling of Indecencies

Ford Madox Hueffer
English Review, 35 (December 1922): 538–548

I have been pressed to write for the English public something about the immense book of Mr. Joyce. I do not wish to do so; I do not wish to do so at all for four or five–or twenty–years, since a work of such importance cannot properly be approached without several readings and without a great deal of thought. To write, therefore, of all aspects of *Ulysses,* rushing into print and jotting down ideas before a hostile audience is a course of action to which I do not choose to commit myself. The same imperious correspondents as force me to write at all forward me a set of Press-cuttings, the tributes of my distinguished brothers of the pen to this huge statue in the mists.

One may make a few notes, nevertheless, in token of good will and as a witness of admiration that is almost reverence for the incredible labours of this incredible genius. For indeed, holding *Ulysses* in one's hand, the last thing one can do about it is to believe in it.

Let us, if you will, postulate that it is a failure–just to placate anybody that wants placating in that special way. For it does not in the least matter whether *Ulysses* is a success or a failure. *We* shall never know and the verdict will be out of our hands: it is no question of flying from London to Manchester under the hour. That we *could* judge. It fails then.

Other things remain. It is, for instance, obvious that the public–the lay, non-writing public of to-day–will not read *Ulysses* even in the meagre measure with which it reads anything at all, the best or the worst that is put before it. Perhaps no lay, non-writing public will ever read it even in the measure with which it reads Rabelais, Montaigne, or the *Imaginary Conversations* of Walter Savage Landor. (I am not comparing Mr. Joyce with these writers.) That perhaps would be failure.

Or perhaps it would not. For myself, I care nothing about readers for writers . . .

And yet, even though the great uninstructed public should never read *Ulysses,* we need not call it a failure. There are other worlds. It is, for instance, perfectly

safe to say that no writer after to-day will be able to neglect *Ulysses.* Writers may dislike the book, or may be for it as enthusiastic as you will; ignore it they cannot, any more than passengers after the 'forties of last century could ignore the railway as a means of transit.

I have called attention in another place to the writers' technical revolution that in *Ulysses* Mr. Joyce initiates. The literary interest of this work, then, arises from the fact that, for the first time in literature on an extended scale, a writer has attempted to treat man as the complex creature that man–every man!–is. The novelist, poet, and playwright hitherto, and upon the whole, have contented themselves with rendering their characters on single planes. A man making a career is rendered simply in terms of that career, a woman in love as simply a woman in love, and so on. But it does not take a novelist to see that renderings of such unilateral beings are not renderings of life as we live it. Of that every human being is aware! You conduct a momentous business interview that will influence your whole future; all the while you are aware that your interlocutor has a bulbous, veined nose; that someone in the street has a drink-roughened voice and is proclaiming that someone has murdered someone; that your physical processes are continuing; that you have a headache; you have, even as a major motive, the worry that your wife is waiting for you at the railway terminus and that you may miss your train to your country home. Your mind makes a psychological analysis of the mind of your wife as she looks at the great clock in the station; you see that great clock; superimposed over the almanack behind the head of the bulbous-nosed man, you see the enormous hands jumping the minutes.

And that is a rendering of a very uncomplex moment in the life of the most commonplace of men; for many, such a scene will be further complicated by associations from melodies humming in the ear; by associations sweeping across them with scents or conveyed through the eye by the colours and forms of wainscotings. . . . Or merely by pictures of estates that you may buy or lands that you may travel in if the deal on which you are engaged goes through.

Of this complexity man has for long been aware, nevertheless in Anglo-Saxondom until quite lately no attempt has been made by writers to approach this problem. For that reason in Anglo-Saxondom the written arts are taken with no seriousness as guides to life. In Dago-lands it is different. There for the hundred years that have succeeded the birth of Flaubert huge, earnest works distinguished by at least mixed motives in psychological passages or consisting almost solely of psychological passages that shiver with tenuously mixed motives–such works have been the main feature of European literature, from *Education Sentimentale* to the *Frères Karamazoff.*

To this literature Anglo-Saxondom, or at any rate England, has contributed nothing at all, or nothing of any importance,* and because of that Anglo-Saxondom remains outside the comity of civilised nations. So the publication of *Ulysses,* success or failure, is an event singularly important. It gives us at least our chance to rank as Europeans.

No doubt we shall take it—for I do not believe that it is the Anglo-Saxon publics that are at fault in the matter of civilisation. *Ulysses* will go on being miscalled or ignored by our official critics and will go on being officially disliked by our writers with livings to get. But the latter will have to take peeps at it so as not to let the always threatening "other fellow" get ahead; and gradually across our literature there will steal the Ulyssean complexion. That, I think, will be so obvious to any student of past literature that it hardly needs elaborating. Then our publics, learning to find their ways amongst complexities, will approach at least nearer to the fountain-head. This sounds improbable. But it should be remembered that there was once a time when the works of Alfred Tennyson were hailed as incomprehensible and when Charles Dickens clamoured for the imprisonment of Holman Hunt, painter of *The Light of the World,* as a portrayer of the obscene! Such strange revolutions have taken place; but they are conveniently ignored, as a rule.

I know that a thousand readers of THE ENGLISH REVIEW—or is it twenty thousand?—are waiting to tell me that Mr. Joyce is not Tennyson. But indeed I am aware of the fact and glad of it, since one more figure such as that must push English literature a thousand—or is it twenty thousand?—years back. And this is not to attack Tennyson!

It is to say that in matters of literature at least we have an ineffable complacency to which another such a Figure as that of the Bard of Haslemere could only immeasurably add: on the principle that "it is certain that my conviction gains immensely as soon as another soul can be found to" . . . put it into rhyme. Let that be how it may, it is certain that in Mr. Joyce we have at last, after one hundred and fifty-one years—I leave the date 1771 for the unriddlement of the literary learned—a writer who forms not only a bridge between the Anglo-Saxon writers and grown men,** but a bridge between Anglo-Saxondom and the Continent of Europe.

Ulysses, then, is an "adult," a European, work. That is why we fittingly call it incredible. For who, a year or so ago, would have believed it possible that any work having either characteristic would have been printed in the English language?

The question of the expression of what are called indecencies in the arts is one that sadly needs approaching with composure. I will claim to approach it with more composure than can most people. On the whole I dislike pornographic, or even merely "frank" writing in English—not on moral, but on purely artistic grounds, since so rare are franknesses in this language that frank words swear out of a page and frankly depicted incidents of a sexual nature destroy the proportions of a book. The reader is apt to read the book for nothing else.

On the question of whether the Young Person should be "told" truths about sexual matters I keep a quite open mind. If she should, well and good—as long as subtle-souled psychologists can be found at first to know and then to reveal that truth! If she shouldn't, there are locked book-cases and Acts of Parliament such as prevent the supply of cigarettes and racing circulars to the adolescent. But it is probably impossible to keep sexual knowledge from the Young Person who is determined to obtain it. Personally, I never had a book-case locked against me in my childhood; my father expressed to one of my schoolmasters the mild wish that I should not be encouraged to read "Byron," and naturally, as soon as I heard that I read three or four lines of *Manfred.* But I cannot remember a single indecent passage in any literature that I read before I was twenty, unless four lines of Milton that used to make one of my classes at school shiver with delight can be called indecent. My schoolfellows—at a great public school!—used to approach me, sometimes in bodies, I being reputed bookish, with requests that I would point out to them the "smutty" passages in the Bible and *Tom Jones.* But I did not know these, and I remember being severely man-handled on at least one occasion by ten or a dozen older boys, because I refused. I formed even then the opinion that the appetite in humanity for sexually-exciting written details was an instinct of great strength, and nothing that I have since experienced has caused me to change that opinion.

My own "suppressions"—three in number—have been merely funny, and yet, reflectively considered, they are nearly as revelatory as any others.

Thus: A great many years ago an American publisher who afterwards became United States Ambassador to Great Britain, proposed to publish one of my works in his country. It was a novel, Tudor in tone. He sent for me one day and protested: "You know, we could not print this speech in the United States!" . . . To indicate something of great rarity one of my characters said: "You will find a chaste whore as soon as that!" I suggested mildly that he should print it: "You will find a chaste—as soon as that!" But, "Oh!" exclaimed that publisher-diplomat, "we could never print the word 'chaste'; it is so suggestive!" And my book was never published in the United States.

Again: One of my colonels, formally using his powers under King's Regs., prohibited the publication of one of my books. He was of opinion that it was obscene; besides, he thought that "all this printing of books" ought to be stopped. He was a good fellow: he is dead now. My book he had not read. It was published by H. M. Ministry of Information over that officer's head—as British Governmental Propaganda, for recitation to French Tommies!

Again: Years ago I had a contract with a very respectable Liberal journal to supply once a week a critical article. Being in those days a "stylist," I had inserted in my contract a clause to the effect that the paper must publish what I wrote and must publish it without the alteration of a word. I had occasion then to write of two of the characters of some novel: "The young man could have seduced her for the price of a box of chocolates."

Late, late one night the editor of that journal rang me up on the telephone to beg me not to insist on his publishing those words; his readers, he said, were not so much strait-laced as particular. After I had gloated over his predicament a little I told him that he might alter the words to suit his readers.

He altered them to: "The young man could have taken advantage of her at small cost!"

Now I hope I may be acquitted of personal resentment if I say that that publisher-ambassador and that editor—we may leave the colonel out of it, since he was purely irresponsible, desiring to suppress all books and authors on principle—that publisher and that editor credited their respective readers with minds extremely objectionable. For the person who prefers the phrase "take advantage of" to the word "seduce," like the person who cannot read the word "caste" without experiencing indecent suggestions, must have the mind of a satyr. It would be better not to write, to publish, or to edit for him at all.

It is, of course, a fact that the serious artist is invariably persecuted when he trenches on matters that are open to the public handling of any pimp as long as he grins. It seems impossible to change that amiable *trait* in Anglo-Saxon officialdom. But that is not the same thing as saying that a change would not be a good thing. Before the war, when I was less of a hermit but much more ingenuous, I used to be shocked by the fact that a great many ladies whom I respected and liked possessed copies of, and gloated as it appeared over, a volume of dream-interpretations by a writer called Freud—a volume that seemed to me to be infinitely more objectionable in the fullest sense of the term, than *Ulysses* at its coarsest now seems to me. For I can hardly picture to myself the woman who will be 'taught to be immodest' by the novel; I could hardly in those days imagine anyone who could escape that fate when reading that–real or pseudo!–work of science. Yet I find to-day that the very persons who then *schwaermed* over Freud now advocate the harshest of martyrdoms for Mr. Joyce.

That is obviously because Mr. Joyce is composed, whilst Mr. Freud has all the want of balance of a scientist on the track of a new theory.

Composure, in fact, is the last thing that our ruling classes will stand in anything but games; that is to say that it is permitted to you to be earnest in frivolities, whereas to be in earnest about serious matters is a sort of sin against the Holy Ghost and the Common Law. That will have to be changed—or we as a race shall have to go under. And we shall have to go under because of the quality of our minds; and the quality of our minds is what it is— because we cannot *stand* the composure of Mr. Joyce!

I cannot help these things; but I expect to be severely censured for making the constatation. As Matthew Arnold pointed out, we were in his day the laughing-stock of the world; to-day we are the laughing-stock and the great danger to civilisation. That is largely due to the nature of our present rulers—but only partly! Other nations have bad Governments and are yet not so universally distrusted. We are distrusted, lock, stock, and barrel, and every man jack of us because we are regarded not merely as a nation of shopkeepers, but as personally and every one of us hypocrites to boot.

Here is a passage which, I suppose, Mr. Joyce risks—possibly quite justifiably, who knows?–a long sentence for writing. I comes from the very height of his *Walpurgisnacht:*

PRIVATE COMPTON (*waves the crowd back*). Fair play here. Make a b . . . . . g butcher's shop of the . . . . . .

(*Massed bands blare "Garryowen"* and *"God Save the King."*)

CISSY CAFFREY. They're going to fight. For me! . . .

STEPHEN. The Harlot's cry from street to street Shall weave old Ireland's winding-sheet.

PRIVATE CARR (*loosening his belt, shouts*). I'll wring the neck of any . . . . b . . . . . d says a word against my . . . . . . King.

BLOOM (*shakes* CISSY CAFFREY'S *shoulders*). Speak, you! Are you struck dumb? You are the link between nations and generations. Speak, woman, sacred life-giver!

CISSY CAFFREY (*alarmed, seizes* PRIVATE CARR'S *sleeve*). Amn't I with you? Amn't I your girl? Cissy's your girl. (*She cries*) Police!

VOICES. Police!

DISTANT VOICES. Dublin's burning! Dublin's burning! On fire! On fire!

(Brimstone fires spring up. Dense clouds roll past. Heavy Gatling guns boom. Troops deploy. Gallops of hoofs. Artillery. Hoarse commands. Bells clang. Backers shout. Drunkards bawl. W . . . . . s screech. Foghorns hoot. . . .

In strident discord peasants and townsmen of Orange and Green factions sing "Kick the Pope" and "Daily, Daily, Sing to Mary.")

PRIVATE CARR *(with ferocious articulation)*. I'll do him in, so help me . . . . . Christ! I'll wring the b . . . . d . . . . .'s . . . . d . . . . . g windpipe!

OLD GUMMY GRANNY *(thrusts a dagger towards* STEPHEN'S *hand)*. Remove him, acushla. At 8.35 a.m. you will be in heaven and Ireland will be free. *(She prays.)* O good God! Take him!

BLOOM. Can't you get him away? . . .

STEPHEN. *Exit Judas! Et laqueo se suspendit!*

BLOOM *(runs to* STEPHEN*)*. Come along with me now before worse happens. Here's your stick. . . .

CISSY CAFFREY *(pulling* PRIVATE CARR*)*. Come on. You're boosed. He insulted me, but I forgive him *(Shouting in his ear)*. I forgive him for insulting me. . . .

PRIVATE CARR *(breaks loose)*. I'll insult him!

(He rushes towards STEPHEN*, fists outstretched, and strikes him in the face.* STEPHEN *totters, collapses, falls stunned. He lies prone, his face to the sky, his hat rolling to the wall.* BLOOM *follows and picks it up.)*

That appears to have been an ordinary Dublin Night's Entertainment; the English reader may find it disagreeable to peruse. But I do not see that the adoption of a suppressive policy towards such matters does anyone much good. I ought to say that in Mr. Joyce's pages the epithets that my more coy pen has indicated with dots are written out in full. I don't see why they should not be: that is the English language as we have made it and as we use it–all except a very thin fringe of our More Select Classes. And that, in effect, is our civilisation of to-day–after a hundred years of efforts at repression on the part of those with Refined Poetic Imaginations.

For that, looking at the matter with the complete impartiality, and indeed the supreme indifference, of one who breeds animals, seems to me to be the main point about the whole matter. We have for just about a hundred years had, in Anglo-Saxondom, firstly repressive tendencies in the literary pundit, and then repressive legislation; at the present moment we are a race hysterical to the point of degeneracy in the pursuit of

the salacious; our theatres cannot pay their way without bedrooms on the stage; our newspapers cannot exist without divorce-court and prostitute-murder cases, and the lubricities of the Freudian *idéesfixes* creep subterraneous–"creeping-rootstocks," to use a botanical term–in the under-minds of our More Select.

The language of our whole nation, except for a tiny and disappearing class, is of an aching filthiness that would add to the agonies of the damned in hell! Those *are* the facts: no one who has lived with men during the last eight years will deny them.

Then, a hundred years of repression having brought us to that pass, it would seem to be better to drop repressions! The promotion of them is an excellent way of making a career–as the late Mr. Comstock found it; an excellent way of extorting boodle; inflicting pain on the defenceless; of attaining to haloes whilst perusing scabrous matter. All these ambitions, God knows, are human. Whether they are commendable would seem to be a matter of doubt. That they are extremely bad for a people is obvious to the composed in spirit. For if you expel Nature with handcuffs and the Tombs, it will burst forth on Broadway in pandemonium. Mr. Mencken in a *Book of Prefaces* presents us with evidence enough of that.

There is not very much about Mr. Joyce in all this –*et pour cause!* Mr. Joyce stands apart from this particular world of ambassador-publishers, lay and ecclesiastical editors, intelligentsia, and Comstockian orgies. To call a work that deals with city life in all its aspects "serene" would probably be to use the wrong word. And yet a great deal of *Ulysses* is serene, and possibly, except to our Anglo-Saxon minds, even the "disgusting passages" would not really prove disgusting. That is what one means when one calls *Ulysses* at last a European work written in English.

For indeed a book purporting to investigate and to render the whole of a human life cannot but contain "disgusting" passages; we come, every one of us, into a world as the result of an action that the Church–and no doubt very properly!–declares to be mortal sin; the great proportion of the food we eat and of the food eaten by the beasts that we eat is dung; we are resolved eventually into festering masses of pollution for the delectation of worms.

And it is probably better that from time to time we should contemplate these facts, hidden though they be from the usual contemplation of urban peoples. Otherwise, when, as inevitably we must, we come up against them we are apt to become overwhelmed to an unmanly degree. As against this weakness it would probably be good to read *Ulysses*. But I am not prescribing the reading of *Ulysses* as a remedy to a sick commonwealth.

Nor indeed do I recommend *Ulysses* to any human being. In the matter of readers my indifference is of the deepest. It is sufficient that *Ulysses,* a book of profound knowledge and of profound renderings of humanity, should exist– in the most locked of book-cases. Only . . . my respect that goes out to the human being that will read this book without much noticing its obscenities will be absolute; and I do not know that I can much respect any human being that cannot do as much as that. But I daresay no human being desires my respect!

Let us copy out a random page from this book: this is Mr. Bloom, the advertisement canvasser of a Dublin paper, coming out from Mass and, on his way to a funeral, entering a chemist's to get a lotion made up for Mrs. Bloom:

He passed, discreetly buttoning, down the aisle and out through the main door into the light. He stood a moment, unseeing, by the cold black marble bowl, while before him and behind two worshippers dipped furtive hands in the low tide of the holy water. Trams; a car of Prescott's dyeworks; a widow in her weeds. Notice because I'm in mourning myself. He covered himself. How goes the time? Quarter past. Time enough yet. Better get that lotion made up. Where is this? Ah, yes, the last time Sweny's in Lincoln Place. Chemists rarely move. Their green and gold beaconjars too heavy to stir. Hamilton Long's founded in the year of the flood. Huguenot church near there. Visit some day.

He walked southwards along Westland Row. But the recipe is in the other trousers. O, and I forgot the latchkey too. Bore this funeral affair. O well poor fellow it's not his fault. When was it I got it made up last? Wait. I changed a sovereign, I remember. First of the month it must have been or second. O he can look it up in the prescription book.

The chemist turned back page after page. Sandy shrivelled smell he seems to have. Shrunken skull. And old. Quest for the philosopher's stone. The alchemists. Drugs age you after mental excitement. Lethargy then. Why? Reaction. A lifetime in a night. Gradually changes your character. Living all the day among herbs, ointments, disinfectants. All his alabaster lily-pots. Mortar and pestle. Aq. Dist. Fol. Laur. Te Virid. Smell almost cure you like a dentist's door bell. Doctor whack. He ought to physic himself a bit. Electuary or emulsion. The first fellow that picked an herb to cure himself had a bit of pluck. Simples. Want to be careful. Enough stuff here to chloroform you. Test: turns blue litmus paper red. Chloroform. Overdose of laudanum. Sleeping draughts. Love philtres. Paregoric poppysup bad for cough. Clogs the pores or the phlegm. Poisons the only cure. Remedy where you least expect it. Clever of nature.

–About a fortnight ago, sir?

–Yes, Mr. Bloom said.

He waited by the counter, inhaling the keen reek of drugs, the dusty dry smell of sponges and loofahs. Lot of time taken up telling your aches and pains.

–Sweet almond oil and tincture of benzoin, Mr. Bloom said, and then orangeflower water. . . .

It certainly made her skin so delicate white like wax.

–And white wax also, he said.

Brings out the darkness of her eyes. Looking at me, the sheet up to her eyes, smelling herself, Spanish, when I was fixing the links in my cuffs. Those homely remedies are often the best: strawberries for the teeth: nettles and rainwater: oatmeal they say steeped in buttermilk. . . .

That is a page of *Ulysses,* selected at random and exactly measured. There are in this book 732 such pages; they were written in Trieste, Zurich, and Paris during the years 1914 to 1921. The reader will say they are not exhilarating: they are not meant to be. And yet . . . how exhilarating they are!

* I may as well say that I am not unaware of the *Tarr* of Mr. Wyndham Lewis; of the works of Miss Dorothy Richardson; *Nocturne* of Mr. Swinnerton, or even of *Legend* by Miss Clemence Dane, each of which three last attacks one or other corner of Mr. Joyce's problem, whilst *Tarr* makes a shot, unrealistically, at the whole of it. I am, however, writing notes on *Ulysses,* not a history of a whole movement.

**"I should be said to insist absurdly on the power of my own confraternity" (that of the novelists) "if I were to declare that the bulk of the young people in the upper and middle classes receive their moral teaching chiefly from the novels that they read. Mothers would no doubt think of their own sweet teaching; fathers of the examples which they set; and schoolmasters of the excellence of their instructions. Happy is the country that has such mothers, fathers, and schoolmasters! But the novelist creeps in closer than the father, closer than the schoolmaster, closer almost than the mother. He is the chosen guide, the tutor whom the young pupil chooses for herself. She retires with him, suspecting no lesson . . . and there she is taught how she shall learn to love; how she shall receive the lover when he comes; how far she should advance to meet the joy; why she should be reticent and now throw herself at once into this new delight. . . ."

I leave it to the reader to guess what–very great–novelist wrote that in the year 1880.

Ernest Boyd's Ireland's Literary Renaissance *was first published in 1916, two years before* Ulysses *began to be serialized in* The Little Review. *In the following excerpt from the 1923 revised edition of his book, Boyd considers* Ulysses, *which he regards as a masterpiece of realism and originality.*

Ireland's Literary Renaissance
Ernest Boyd
(London: Grant Richards, revised edition, 1923), pp. 402–412

While the tranquil power and subtle qualities of *The Threshold of Quiet* have been recognised by discerning critics here and there, the book has had neither the popular suffrage of the general public nor the ardent championship of a coterie. The work of James Joyce, on the other hand, has enjoyed both in turn, and is now in danger of those antagonisms invariably aroused by extravagant enthusiasts and uncritical imitators. When he published his little booklet of Elizabethan songs, *Chamber Music,* in 1907, his name was unknown outside Ireland, and his first prose work, *Dubliners,* was actually accepted for publication about the same time by a Dublin publisher. Owing to a variety of peculiar circumstances, partly explained by the disadvantages under which the press always suffers when controlled by an alien administration, that first Irish edition of *Dubliners* was all destroyed except one copy delivered to the author, and the book did not appear until 1914, when it was published in London. Two years later a similar experience befell *A Portrait of the Artist as a Young Man,* which could not find a London publisher and was issued in New York. Finally neither London nor New York could meet the responsibility imposed by this daring and extraordinary genius, and his great experiment, *Ulysses* (1922), was issued in a limited edition for subscribers in Paris, but not until after *The Little Review* of New York had been rewarded with a fine for its praiseworthy attempt to publish portions of the work serially. With the exception of *Chamber Music* and his one play, *Exiles* (1918), the publication of Joyce's books has failed to answer to that definition of happiness which consists in having no history.

Charming as his little poems are they would no more have established James Joyce as one of the most original figures in the whole world of contemporary letters than would his remarkable psychological drama in three acts, which is undoubtedly the only Irish play to realise the first intentions of Edward Martyn in helping to launch the Dramatic Movement. In its morbid and profound dissection of the soul, *Exiles* suggests the social analysis of Ibsen combined with the acute sexual perceptions of Strindberg. The originality of Joyce and the justification of the high esteem in which he is held must be sought in those three volumes of fiction, *Dubliners, A Portrait of the Artist as a Young Man* and *Ulysses,* which have rightly aroused the attention of the intelligent public in Europe and America, even though a French critic has rashly declared that with them "Ireland makes a sensational re-entry into European literature." Apart from its affecting and ingenuous belief in the myth of a "European" literature, this statement of M. Valéry Larbaud's has the obvious defect of resting upon two false assumptions. It is natural, perhaps, that he should know nothing whatever about Irish literature, and prove it by comparing the living Irish language to Old French. But a Continental writer might, at least, have remembered the vogue of Thomas Moore, who shared with Byron the curious distinction of a peculiarly "European" reputation due apparently to the enchantment which distance lends to the view of a foreign literature. In other words, to the Irish mind no lack of appreciation of James Joyce is involved by some slight consideration for the facts of Ireland's literary and intellectual evolution, and the effort now being made to cut him off from the stream of which he is a tributary is singularly futile. The logical outcome of this doctrinaire zeal of the coterie is to leave this profoundly Irish genius in the possession of a prematurely cosmopolitan reputation, the unkind fate which has always overtaken writers isolated from the conditions of which they are a part, and presented to the world without any perspective.

Fortunately, the work of James Joyce stands to refute most of the theories for which it has furnished a pretext, notably the theory that it is an unanswerable challenge to the separate existence of Anglo-Irish literature. The fact is, no Irish writer is more Irish than Joyce; none shows more unmistakably the imprint of his race and traditions. Those who have with some difficulty weaned themselves from the notion that the harum-scarum sportsmen and serio-comic peasants of the Lever school represent Ireland, only to adopt the more recent superstition of a land filled with leprechauns, heroes out of Gaelic legend, and Celtic twilight, naturally find James Joyce disconcerting. Accordingly, they either repudiate him altogether, or attempt to explain him at the expense of all his Irish contemporaries. The syllogism seems to be: J. M. Synge and James Stephens and W. B. Yeats are Irish, therefore James Joyce is not. Whereas the simple truth is that *A Portrait of the Artist as a Young Man* is to the Irish novel what *The Wanderings of Oisin* was to Irish poetry and *The Playboy of the Western World* to Irish drama, the unique and significant work which lifts the *genre* out of the commonplace into the national literature. Like most of his fellow-craftsmen in Ireland, as we have seen, Joyce began characteristically with a volume of short stories. *Dublin-*

ers differed from the others, not in technique, but in quality, and above all, in its affinity with the best work of the French Naturalists, from whom Joyce learned his craft as George Moore did before him. It is not mere coincidence that the greatest novels of contemporary Irish life should come from the only two writers who submitted to that French influence, until they had mastered it and created out of it something of their own. The genesis of all that the author has since published is in that superb collection of studies of middle-class Dublin life.

Dublin is the frescoe upon which James Joyce has woven all the amazing patterns designed by an imagination which is at once romantic and realistic, brilliant and petty, full of powerful fantasy, yet preserving an almost incredible faculty of detailed material observation. He is governed by a horror and detestation of the circumstances which moulded the life of his Stephen Dedalus, in that city which he has carried away with him during the long years of his expatriation, and whose record he has consigned to the pages of *A Portrait of the Artist* and *Ulysses*. With a frankness and veracity as impressive as they are appalling Joyce sets forth the relentless chronicle of a soul stifled by material and intellectual squalor. Stephen Dedalus, the son of a well-to-do Catholic family, passes through the various educational and social experiences of his class in Ireland. He is sent from school and college to the university, and these institutions, their pupils and staff are described with a candour which might have been considered more sensational had the victims moved in a more prominent world. The autobiographical and realistic character of the history of Stephen Dedalus is dismissed by certain critics as of no importance, but except for some disguises of name, the two volumes of his adventures are as effectively indiscreet as *Hail and Farewell*.

The gradual downfall of the Dedalus family provides the framework of the first book. A deep undertone of filth and sordid shiftlessness is the fitting accompaniment to the disintegration of Stephen's life. The atmosphere in which he is expected to respond to the stimulus of higher education is sardonically suggested in the chapter where he is shown preparing to attend his lectures:

"He drained his third cup of watery tea to the dregs and set to chewing the crusts of fried bread that were scattered near him, staring into the dark pool of the jar. The yellow dripping has been scooped out like a bog-hole, and the pool under it brought back to his memory the dark turf-coloured water of the bath in Clongowes. The box of pawn tickets at his elbow had just been rifled and he took up idly one after another in his greasy fingers the blue and white dockets, scrawled and

sanded and creased, and bearing the name of the pledger as Daly or MacEvoy. . . .

"Then he put them aside and gazed thoughtfully at the lid of the box, speckled with louse marks, and asked vaguely:

"How much is the clock fast now?"

This hideous interior is typical of the material surroundings in which Stephen Dedalus lives. When he leaves the house we are told:

"The lane behind the terrace was waterlogged, and as he went down it slowly, choosing his steps amid heaps of wet rubbish, he heard a mad nun screeching in the nuns' madhouse beyond the wall:

"'Jesus! O Jesus! Jesus!'

"He shook the sound out of his ears by an angry toss of his head and hurried on, stumbling through the mouldering offal, his heart already bitten by an ache of loathing and bitterness. His father's whistle, his mother's mutterings, the screech of an unseen maniac were to him now so many voices offending and threatening to humble the pride of his youth."

It is not an escape, however, which the university provides, for he simply exchanges physical ugliness for intellectual ugliness, so far as Joyce reports his life there. The only ray of idealism which penetrates the gloom of his existence is the influence of religion, which comes upon him in college, when he recoils in terrified horror before the prospects of a hell, described with a wealth of dreadful detail which seems to be suggested by an elaboration of the filthiness of Stephen's moral and physical habits. It is apparently the author's purpose to empty Catholicism of all its spiritual content, in order to provide his hero with a congruous religion background. Similarly he is tempted to depart from the strictly horrible veracity of his picture in order to romanticise the unclean initiation of Stephen into the adventure of love. It is, of course, possible, that the amourous and religious experiences of such a man should be on a level corresponding to the low quality of his own personality. But the redeeming feature of Stephen Dedalus is his sincerity, which enables him at all times to realise the significance of what he sees, and we find it hard to reconcile his realistic temperament with the preposterous idealisation of prostitution, in a city where it has not even a remote semblance of that disguise of joy, which is supposed to make it dangerous in more sophisticated places. So long as he describes the exterior of Dublin's underworld, Joyce is too good an observer to suggest anything more than its repulsiveness. It is the supreme irony of his portrait that the artist proceeds to Swinburnian romantics based upon material so unspeakably frowsy. The romance in Stephen's life is designedly of this degrading and degraded quality. For James Joyce shows himself throughout preoccupied with all that is mean and furtive in Dublin society, and so far as he permits his own views to emerge, he professes the greatest contempt for a social organisation which permits so much vileness to flourish squalidly, beneath, a rigid formality of conduct. The pages of this book are redolent of the ooze of our shabby respectability, with its intolerable tolerance of most shameful social barbarism. Joyce shows how we breed and develop our Stephen Dedaluses, providing them with everything they crave, except the means of escape from the slime which envelops them. Culture for Dedalus is represented by the pedantries of medieval metaphysics, religion by the dread of hell. Left to drift abjectly between these extremes, the young artist disintegrates in a process whose analysis becomes a remarkable piece of personal and social dissection.

In *Ulysses* the analysis of Stephen Dedalus in particular, and of Dublin in general, is carried a step further, how much further may be imagined from the fact that this vast work, of more than seven hundred and twenty-five quarto pages, covers the events of less than twenty-four hours. It recounts a day in the life of Stephen Dedalus and Leopold Bloom, and shows in a marvellous microcosm the movement of the city's existence, in ever spreading circles and ripples of activity, correlated by a method which recalls that of Jules Romains and the *Unanimistes*. But its form is more akin to that of the German Expressionists. The technical innovations which began to show in *A Portrait of the Artist as a Young Man* are here advanced to the point of a deliberate stylistic method, whose cumulative effect is wonderful. The occassional use of monologue, the notation of random and unspoken thoughts as they pass through the mind of each character, the introduction without warning of snatches of conversation, of prolonged dialogues, now almost entirely takes the place of narrative The final chapter, for instance, is a reverie of forty-two pages, without any kind of punctuation except the break of paragraphs, in which the whole sexual life of Leopold Bloom's wife rushes pell-mell into her consciousness. It is almost always in these passages of introspection that the author reveals the sex interests and experiences of his people, and in the emptying out of their minds naturally a great deal is uncovered to the discomfiture of convention. The charges of "immorality" which Joyce has had to face have been based as a rule upon such passages.

Yet, rarely in literature has eroticism appeared in such harsh and disillusioned guise as in the work of James Joyce, where it oscillates between contemptuous, Rabelaisian ribaldry, and the crude horror and fascination of the body as seen by the great Catholic ascetics. The glamour of love is absent, and there remains such an analysis of repressed and stunted instincts as only an Irishman could have made to explain the curious conditions of Irish puritanism. But the analysis is not put forward in any intention of criticism; didacticism is alien to all that Joyce has written. He has simply compiled the record, reconstructed a period in his life, and left us to draw conclusions. *Ulysses* is simultaneously a masterpiece of realism, of documentation, and a most original dissection of the Irish mind in certain of its phases usually hitherto ignored, except for the hints of George Moore. Dedalus and Bloom are two types of Dubliner such as were studied in Joyce's first book of stories, remarkable pieces of national and human portraiture. At the same time they serve as the medium between the reader and the *vie unanime* of a whole community, whose existence is unrolled before their eyes, through which we see, and reaches our consciousness as it filters into their souls. As an experiment in form *Ulysses* more effectively accomplishes its purpose than Jules Romains did in *La Mort de Quelqu'un,* for out of the innumerable fragments of which this mosaic is composed Joyce has created a living whole, the complete representation of life. The book might have been called *La Vie de Quelqu'un,* for it not the personal existence of Dedalus and Bloom that matters so much as the social organism of which they are a part.

Hermann Bahr, in his *Expressionismus* (1916), describes the advent of Expressionism in terms which summarise appropriately the evolution of Joyce. "The eye of the body is passive to everything; it receives, and whatever is impressed upon it by outward charm is more powerful than the activity of the eye itself, more powerful that what it seizes of that outward charm. On the other hand, the eye of the mind is active and merely uses as the material of its own power the reflections of reality . . . Now it seems that in the rising generation the mind is strongly asserting itself. It is turning away from exterior to interior life, and listening to the voices of its own secrets . . . Such a generation will repudiate Impressionism and demand an art which sees with the eyes of the mind: Expressionism is the natural successor of Impressionism."

Much has been written about the symbolic intention of this work, of its relation to the Odyssey, to which the plan of the three first and last chapters, with the twelve cantos of the adventures of Ulysses in the middle, is supposed to correspond. Irish criticism can hardly be impressed by this aspect of a work which, in its meticulous detailed documentation of Dublin, rivals Zola in photographic realism. In its bewildering juxtaposition of the real and the imaginary, of the commonplace and the fantastic, Joyce's work obviously declares its kinship with the Expressionists, with Walter Hasenclever or Georg Kaiser.

With *Ulysses* James Joyce has made a daring and valuable experiment, breaking new ground in English for the future development of prose narrative. But the "European" interest of the work must of necessity be largely technical, for the matter is as local as the form is universal. In fact, so local is it that many pages remind the Irish reader of *Hail and Farewell*, except that the allusions are to matters and personalities more obscure. To claim for this book a European significance simultaneously denied to J. M. Synge and James Stephens is to confess complete ignorance of its genesis, and to invest its content with a mysterious import which the actuality of references would seem to deny. While James Joyce is endowed with the wonderful fantastic imagination which conceived the fantasmagoria of the fifteenth chapter of *Ulysses*, a vision of a Dublin Brocken, whose scene is the underworld, he also has the defects and qualities of Naturalism, which prompts him to catalogue the Dublin tramways, and to explain with the precision of a guide-book how the city obtains its water supply. In fine, Joyce is essentially a realist as Flaubert was, but, just as the author of *Madame Bovary* never was bound by the formula subsequently erected into the dogma of realism, the creator of Stephen Dedalus has escaped from the same bondage. Flaubert's escape was by way of the Romanticism from which he started, Joyce's is by way of Expressionism, to which he has advanced.

T. S. Eliot

One of the most important modernist writers of the twentieth century, T. S. Eliot first met Joyce in August 1920 when Ulysses *was still being serialized in* The Little Review. *His highly influential essay "Ulysses, Order, and Myth" appeared almost two years after the novel was published in book form. Eliot comments on Joyce's parallel use of the* Odyssey *and Homeric myth: "In using myth, in manipulating a continuous parallel between contemporaneity and antiquity, Mr. Joyce is pursuing a method which others must pursue after him." An early supporter of* Finnegans Wake, *Eliot published a section of that work in* The Criterion, *a magazine which he helped found and which he edited between 1922 and 1939. As an editor at Faber and Faber, Eliot assisted Joyce in getting* Finnegans Wake *published by that firm in 1939. He also signed the 1928 letter protesting Samuel Roth's pirated serialization of* Ulysses *in* Two Worlds Monthly.*

Ulysses, Order and Myth
T. S. Eliot
The Dial, 75 (November 1923): 480–483

MR. JOYCE'S book has been out long enough for no more general expression of praise, or expostulation with its detractors, to be necessary; and it has not been out long enough for any attempt at a complete measurement of its place and significance to be possible. All that one can usefully do at this time, and it is a great deal to do, for such a book, is to elucidate any aspect of the book—and the number of aspects is indefinite—which has not yet been fixed. I hold this book to be the most important expression which the present age has found; it is a book to which we are all indebted, and from which none of us can escape. These are postulates for anything that I have to say about it, and I have no wish to waste the reader's time by elaborating my eulogies; it has given me all the surprise, delight, and terror that I can require, and I will leave it at that.

Among all the criticisms I have seen of the book, I have seen nothing—unless we except, in its way, M. Valéry Larbaud's valuable paper which is rather an Introduction than a criticism—which seemed to me to appreciate the significance of the method employed—the parallel to the *Odyssey,* and the use of appropriate styles and symbols to each division. Yet one might expect this to be the first peculiarity to attract attention; but it has been treated as an amusing dodge, or scaffolding erected by the author for the purpose of disposing his realistic tale, of no interest in the completed structure. The criticism which Mr. Aldington directed upon *Ulysses* several years ago seems to me to fail by this oversight—but, as Mr. Aldington wrote before the complete work had appeared, fails more honorably than the attempts of those who had the whole book before them. Mr. Aldington treated Mr. Joyce as a prophet of chaos;

and wailed at the flood of Dadaism which his prescient eye saw bursting forth at the tap of the magician's rod. Of course, the influence which Mr. Joyce's book may have is from my point of view an irrelevance. A very great book may have a very bad influence indeed; and a mediocre book may be in the event most salutary. The next generation is responsible for its own soul; a man of genius is responsible to his peers, not to a studio full of uneducated and undisciplined coxcombs. Still, Mr. Aldington's pathetic solicitude for the half-witted seems to me to carry certain implications about the nature of the book itself to which I cannot assent; and this is the important issue. He finds the book, if I understand him, to be an invitation to chaos, and an expression of feelings which are perverse, partial, and a distortion of reality. But unless I quote Mr. Aldington's words I am likely to falsify. "I say, moreover," he says [in the *English Review* (April 1921)], "that when Mr. Joyce, with his marvellous gifts, uses them to disgust us with mankind, he is doing something which is false and a libel on humanity." It is somewhat similar to the opinion of the urbane Thackeray upon Swift. "As for the moral, I think it horrible, shameful, unmanly, blasphemous: and giant and great as this Dean is, I say we should hoot him." (This, of the conclusion of the Voyage to the Houyhnhnms—which seems to me one of the greatest triumphs that the human soul has ever achieved.—It is true that Thackeray later pays Swift one of the finest tributes that a man has ever given or received: "So great a man he seems to me that thinking of him is like thinking of an empire falling." And Mr. Aldington, in his time, is almost equally generous.)

Whether it is possible to libel humanity (in distinction to libel in the usual sense, which is libelling an individual or a group in contrast with the rest of humanity) is a question for philosophical societies to discuss; but of course if *Ulysses* were a 'libel' it would simply be a forged document, a powerless fraud, which would never have extracted from Mr Aldington a moment's attention. I do not wish to linger over this point: the interesting question is that begged by Mr Aldington when he refers to Mr Joyce's 'great *undisciplined* talent.'

I think that Mr Aldington and I are more or less agreed as to what we want in principle, and agreed to call it classicism. It is because of this agreement that I have chosen Mr Aldington to attack on the present issue. We are agreed as to what we want, but not as to how to get it, or as to what contemporary writing exhibits a tendency in that direction. We agree, I hope, that 'classicism' is not an alternative to 'romanticism,' as of political parties, Conservative and Liberal, Republican and Democrat, on a 'turn-the-rascals-out' platform. It is a goal toward which all good literature strives, so far as it is good, according to the possibilities of its place and time. One can be 'classical,' in a sense, by turning away from nine-tenths of the material which lies at hand, and selecting only mummified stuff from a museum—like some contemporary writers, about whom one could say some nasty things in this connexion, if it were worth while (Mr Aldington is not one of them). Or one can be classical in tendency by doing the best one can with the material at hand. The confusion springs from the fact that the term is applied to literature and to the whole complex of interests and modes of behaviour and society of which literature is a part; and it has not the same bearing in both applications. It is much easier to be a classicist in literary criticism than in creative art—because in criticism you are responsible only for what you want, and in creation you are responsible for what you can do with material which you must simply accept. And in this material I include the emotions and feelings of the writer himself, which, for what writer, are simply material which he must accept—not virtues to be enlarged or vices to be diminished. The question, then, about Mr Joyce, is: how much living material does he deal with, and, how does he deal with it: deal with, not as a legislator or exhorter, but as an artist?

It is here that Mr Joyce's parallel use of the *Odyssey* has a great importance. It has the importance of a scientific discovery. No one else has built a novel upon such a foundation before: it has never before been necessary. I am not begging the question in calling *Ulysses* a 'novel'; and if you call it an epic it will not matter. If it is not a novel, that is simply because the novel is a form which will no longer serve; it is because the novel, instead of being a form, was simply the expression of an age which had not sufficiently lost all form to feel the need of something stricter. Mr Joyce has written one novel—the *Portrait;* Mr Wyndham Lewis has written one novel—*Tarr.* I do not suppose that either of them will ever write another 'novel.' The novel ended with Flaubert and with James. It is, I think, because Mr Joyce and Mr Lewis, being 'in advance' of their time, felt a conscious or probably unconscious dissatisfaction with the form, that their novels are more formless than those of a dozen clever writers who are unaware of its obsolescence.

In using the myth, in manipulating a continuous parallel between contemporaneity and antiquity, Mr Joyce is pursuing a method which others must pursue after him. They will not be imitators, any more than the scientist who uses the discoveries of an Einstein in pursuing his own, independent, further investigations. It is simply a way of controlling, of ordering, of giving a shape and a significance to the immense panorama of futility and anarchy which is contemporary history. It is a method already adumbrated by Mr Yeats, and of the need for which I believe Mr Yeats to have been the first contemporary to be conscious. It is a method for which the horoscope is auspi-

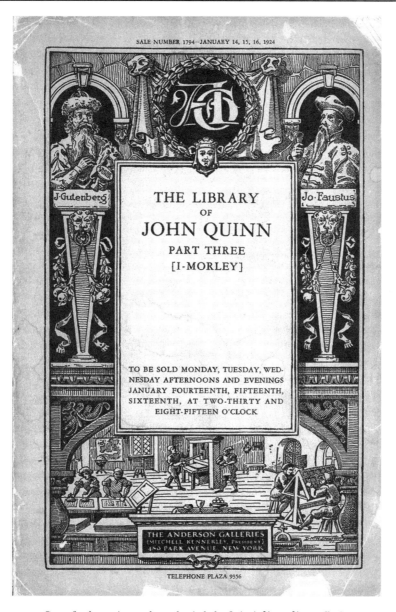

SALE NUMBER 1794—JANUARY 14, 15, 16, 1924

J·Gutenberg

Jo·Faustus

THE LIBRARY
OF
JOHN QUINN
PART THREE
[I-MORLEY]

TO BE SOLD MONDAY, TUESDAY, WED-
NESDAY AFTERNOONS AND EVENINGS
JANUARY FOURTEENTH, FIFTEENTH,
SIXTEENTH, AT TWO-THIRTY AND
EIGHT-FIFTEEN O'CLOCK

THE ANDERSON GALLERIES
(MITCHELL KENNERLEY, President)
489 PARK AVENUE, NEW YORK

TELEPHONE PLAZA 9556

Cover for the auction catalogue that includes Quinn's James Joyce collection

Joyce noted Larbaud's coining of a phrase to describe his technique in a 19 November 1923 letter to Harriet Shaw Weaver.

Mr Larbaud gave the reading public about six months ago the phrase "interior monologue" (that is, in *Ulysses*).

— *Letters III,* p. 83

cious. Psychology (such as it is, and whether our reaction to it be comic or serious), ethnology, and *The Golden Bough* have concurred to make possible what was impossible even a few years ago. Instead of narrative method, we may now use the mythical method. It is, I seriously believe, a step toward making the modern world possible for art, toward that order and form which Mr Aldington so earnestly desires. And only those who have won their own discipline in secret and without aid, in a world which offers very little assistance to that end, can be of any use in furthering this advance.

4917 JOURNAL OF THE SOCIETY OF ARTS (THE). Vol. XXIII, from November 20, 1874, to November 12, 1875. *Illustrated.* Thick 8vo, half brown morocco, gilt top. [London, 1874-5]

1.50

4918 JOWETT (BENJAMIN). Thucydides. Translated into English. To Which is Prefixed an Essay on Inscriptions and a Note on the Geography of Thucydides. 2 vols., 8vo, cloth, uncut. Oxford, 1900 Revised Edition.

5.50

4919 JOY (MAURICE). The Irish Rebellion of 1916 and its Martyrs: Erin's Tragic Easter. By Padraic Colum, Maurice Joy, T. Gavan Duffy, and others. Edited by Joy. *Illustrated.* 8vo, cloth. New York, [1916] *First Edition.*

6-

JAMES JOYCE

[*The author of "Ulysses" and other works which his colossal tour-de-force has somewhat obscured, was born in Dublin, February 1882. He was educated at Clongowes Wood College and Belvedere College, and at the Royal University, Dublin. He has lived in Paris, Rome and Trieste; teaches, writes, and thinks. He has enormous patience—it took eight years to write "Ulysses." He is almost painfully industrious—his modern Odyssey contains some 300,000 words (many of which are peculiar). He has originality, because he has ventured to attempt something new; courage, because he challenged the conventions and criticism of the world; faith, or otherwise his book could never have been published. It was suppressed four times during the course of serial publication, and was finally issued in a limited edition of 1000 copies by Shakespeare & Co.—that is to say, Miss Sylvia Beach, of the very unusual bookshop at 12 Rue de l'Odéon, Paris. Miss Beach, by the way, is the daughter of a pastor in Princeton, N. J. James Joyce's exceptional book has had an exceptional publisher. The venture has been completely successful. Almost every copy had been subscribed for before the date of publication in February 1922. Since then there has been a large demand for copies that could not possibly be supplied; and James Joyce and his work have attracted world-wide attention and provoked world-wide discussion.*

It is strange work for a man trained by Jesuits, and a student of scholastic philosophy. Mr. Joyce has also studied medicine, a point of interest, for there is something decidedly anatomical about "Ulysses." But to discuss the book here, or give any adequate idea of its scope and symbolism, beauty and squalidity, strength and weakness, is impossible. The outpouring of the stream of consciousness, turbid or clear, placid or seething (it is rarely placid) conveys a remarkable effect, mitigated occasionally by a sense of monotony. But the work is an epic. That anyone should want, or have wanted, to suppress it, only shows the large prevalence of little logic. One does not suppress natural phenomena: they are neither moral nor immoral. "Ulysses" is a phenomenon that is not entirely natural, perhaps: but its most scatological moments would scarcely impair the morals of a literary infant. Such infants could not possibly read the book: it is entirely too big for them, and they would be bored to death.

Mr. Arnold Bennett writes: "The best portions of the novel . . . are superb. I single out the long orgiastic scene, and the long unspoken monologue of Mrs. Bloom which closes the book. The former will easily bear comparison with Rabelais at his fantastical finest; it leaves Petronius out of sight. It has plenary inspiration. It is the

485

The Joyce pages from the catalogue for the Quinn sale held on 14–16 January 1924 in New York. Prices brought by the items are noted in the margins (Mathew J. Bruccoli Collection).

richest stuff, handled with a virtuosity to match the quality of the material. The latter (forty difficult pages, some 25,000 words without any punctuation at all) might in its utterly convincing realism be an actual document, the magical record of inmost thoughts thought by a woman that existed. Talk about understanding 'feminine psychology' . . . I have never read anything to surpass it, and I doubt if I have ever read anything to equal it . . ." (Mr. Bennett is right about the psychology, but wrong about the punctuation. There is a final period, and Mr. Joyce must have inserted it with a profound sense of satiety.)

"A Portrait of the Artist as a Young Man"—the first novel of this great Irishman —is a work of creative imagination more than of memory, and is marked by a dignity and a lyric beauty almost unequalled in prose fiction. Joyce is now forty-one, and his two novels have occupied the greater part of eighteen years of his life. In addition he has written "Exiles," a play; "Chamber Music," a book of fine and sometimes exquisite lyrics; and "Dubliners," a collection of eighteen superb short stories.]

4920 DUBLINERS. 12mo, cloth. London, [1914]
  First Edition.

4921 ORIGINAL AUTOGRAPH MANUSCRIPT of Corrections to be made in the Proof of "A Portrait of a Young Man," written on 7 pages, folio; also, Manuscript of Corrections for "Dubliners," written on 1 page, folio. In a cloth slip case.
  The autograph of Joyce appears in two places on the Manuscript, together with his Zurich address.

4922 A PORTRAIT OF THE ARTIST as a Young Man, extracted from the *Egoist*, where it appeared from February 1914 to September 1915. In a half blue morocco slip case.
  There are three copies of these excerpted sheets, each set containing manuscript corrections by the author and Miss Weaver. With one of the sets is a page of Manuscript entirely in Joyce's hand.
  The First Edition of this work was printed in America in 1916, as no English printer would undertake it. The following year a separate English edition was printed, as well as a second American edition.

4923 DUBLINERS. 12mo, cloth. New York, 1916
  First Edition, with American title-page.

4924 MR. JAMES JOYCE and the Modern Stage. A Play and Some Considerations. By Ezra Pound. In the *Drama* for February 1916. 8vo, half blue morocco, gilt top, uncut, wrappers bound in. [London], 1916

4925 DUBLINERS. 12mo, cloth. New York, 1917
  Second American Edition.

4926 A PORTRAIT OF THE ARTIST as a Young Man. 12mo, cloth.
  First English Edition. London, [1917]

4927 A PORTRAIT OF THE ARTIST as a Young Man. 12mo, cloth.
  Second American Edition. New York, 1917

4928 JAMES JOYCE, A New Irish Novelist. By John Quinn. In *Vanity Fair* for May 1917. Imp. 8vo, half blue morocco, gilt top, wrappers bound in. [New York, 1917]

486

4929 ORIGINAL AUTOGRAPH MANUSCRIPT of ''Exiles,'' written on 164 pages, quarto, together with title-pages and page of characters, 169 pages in all. In a crushed blue levant morocco solander case.

THE COMPLETE MANUSCRIPT, beautifully written in the author's unusually legible hand. Each of the title-pages is inscribed: ''*Exiles: a play in three acts. By James Joyce*,'' and at the foot of each of these title-pages Joyce has written: ''*Present address: Seefeldstrasse F 3*ⁱⁱⁱ, *Zurich: Switzerland.*''

Laid in with this Manuscript is an A.L.s. from Ezra Pound to Mr. Quinn, written on a wrapper for the Manuscript: ''*Dear Mr. Quinn. Here at last are the two remaining acts of Joyce's Play.*'' The mailing wrappers to Mr. Quinn in Ezra Pound's hand are also laid in.

195.

4930 EXILES. A Play in Three Acts. 12mo, boards, cloth back.   London, 1918
First Edition.

4⁵⁰

4931 EXILES. A Play in Three Acts. 12mo, boards, cloth back.
First American Edition.   New York, 1918

.5⁰

4932 CHAMBER MUSIC. 16mo, cloth, uncut.   London, n.d. [1918]
First Edition.

9⁵⁰

4933 CHAMBER MUSIC. 12mo, boards, uncut.   New York, 1918
First Authorized American Edition.

1.

4934 EXILES. A Play in Three Acts. 12mo, cloth.   London, [1921]
Second Edition.

..2⁵.

4935 DUBLINERS. 12mo, cloth.   London, [1922]
Second Edition.

1⁵⁰

4936 ORIGINAL AUTOGRAPH MANUSCRIPT OF ''ULYSSES,'' written on over 1200 pages. In four blue morocco slip cases.

THE COMPLETE MANUSCRIPT of this remarkable work, one of the most extraordinary produced in modern times and hailed by critics as epoch-making in modern literature.

The first slip case contains: Part I: Telemachus, Proteus, Nestor. Part II: Calypso, Lotus Eaters, Hades, Eolus, Lestrygonians, Scylla and Charybdis.

The second slip case contains Part II continued, made up of the following: Wandering Rocks, Sirens, Cyclops, Nausikaa, Oxen of the Sun.

The third slip case continues Part II and contains: Penelope, Ithaca, and Part III down to page 618 of the book.

The fourth slip case contains from page 618 to the end of the work.

In a recent review of Ulysses by Mr. T. S. Eliot he refers to Mr. Aldington's attack upon Mr. Joyce as ''a libel on humanity'' and quotes Thackeray's shameful attack upon Swift, Thackeray having damned Swift for the conclusion of the Voyage to the Houyhnhnms, which Mr. Eliot writes ''seems to me one of the greatest triumphs that the human soul has ever achieved.'' Referring to the form as well as the content of Ulysses, Mr. Eliot writes: ''Psychology (such as it is, and whether our reaction to it be comic or serious), ethnology, and The Golden Bough

1975.

487

have concurred to make possible what was impossible even a few years ago. Instead of narrative method, we may now use the mythical method. It is, I seriously believe, a step toward making the modern world possible for art . . . And only those who have won their own discipline in secret and without aid, in a world which offers very little assistance to that end, can be of any use in furthering this advance."

[SEE ILLUSTRATION, PAGE 489]

4937 ULYSSES. Thick small 4to, original wrappers, uncut.　　　Paris, 1922
First Edition. One of 100 copies on Dutch hand-made paper, signed by the author.

4938 CHAMBER MUSIC. 16mo, cloth.　　Boston: The Cornhill Company, n.d.
First American Edition. Pirated.

4939 AUTOGRAPH MANUSCRIPT of his translation of Gerhart Hauptmann's "Before Sunrise," written on pages numbered 1-198, inclusive, in a small quarto black oilcloth-covered notebook, dated Summer, 1901. In a cloth slip case.
THE COMPLETE MANUSCRIPT, entirely in the handwriting of Joyce, without corrections, and with portions scored in red ink. It is initialled by Joyce at the end. This translation has never been published.

P. W. JOYCE

[*M.A., LL.D., Trinity College, Dublin. Born at Limerick in 1827, and educated at private schools and at home. In 1845 he entered the service of the Commissioners of National Education, Ireland, and held successive posts until 1874, when he was appointed Professor, and subsequently Principal of the Commissioners' Training College, Dublin. He retired in 1893. He was one of the Commissioners for the publication of the ancient laws of Ireland.*]

4940 KEATING'S HISTORY OF IRELAND. Book I, Part I. Edited with Text, Translation, and Vocabulary. 12mo, cloth (stained).　　　Dublin, 1880
First Edition. With pencilled annotations throughout, and two pages of Gaelic manuscript laid in.

4941 A SHORT HISTORY of Ireland from the Earliest Times to 1608. *Map*. 12mo, cloth, uncut.　　　London, 1893
First Edition.

4942 IRISH LOCAL NAMES EXPLAINED. 12mo, cloth.　　　Dublin, 1898
First Edition.

4943 ANCIENT IRISH MUSIC. 4to, cloth.　　　Dublin, 1901

4944 OLD CELTIC ROMANCES. Translated from the Gaelic. 12mo, cloth. Revised and Enlarged Edition.　　　London, 1901

4945 THE ORIGIN and History of Irish Names of Places. 2 vols., 12mo, cloth.
　　　London and Dublin, 1901-1893

According to Richard Ellmann, Lawrence K. Emery was the pen name of A. J. Leventhal, an Irish writer and lecturer in French at Trinity College. "Joyce was gratified to be favourably noticed in Ireland" (Letters III, p. 88, n.3).

The *Ulysses* of Mr. James Joyce

Lawrence K. Emery

Claxon (Winter 1923–1924): 14–20

The phenomenon of James Joyce seems to most people inexplicable. Why seek the scabrous for a subject when the sweet and pure can be so beautifully expressed? Why walk on dungheaped roads when a rose-walk can be had for a twopenny tram drive? Irishmen, together with Englishmen and Americans, or rather the Irish, English, and American *public,* asked these pointed questions and ostracised Mr. Joyce without staying for an answer. Fortunately, however, it is not necessary for an artist to develop on his native soil to produce his best work. M. Barrè may theorise about *la terre et ses morts* till he is as blue in the face as his own Alsatian sky; all the evidences of literary history demonstrate that an artist is just as likely to flourish under an alien sun as in the shade of the bosky tradition of his fathers.

A slow and careful worker, Mr. Joyce worked for ten years on the *Portrait of the Artist as a Young Man.* It is usually described as an autobiography, a series of confessions *à la mode,* dressed in the form of a novel. These may be confessions, but Mr. Joyce is too much of an artist faithfully to record his own life. There is in all his work a cold objectivity. He has an uncanny keenness of perception which he does not let his ego influence. This perception he must have applied to himself, and he can synthesise a character from details observed in his own person.

The result can never be self-revelatory, for, like a true artist, this synthesis is coupled with the unusual touch that Shakespeare gives to Hamlet or Balzac to Pons.

Ulysses continues where the *Portrait* left off. At the end of the latter novel Stephen Dedalus left for Paris, and *Ulysses* begins at the point of his return from that city. Chronologically we only advance one day from page 1 to page 732. But actually there is such a world of learning, scientific, metaphysic, aesthetic, of life real and imagined, of force comic and tragic, of description, of lyricism, patter and rhetoric, heroics and eloquence, as to make the day longer than any conceived on this planet.

The incidents round which this immensity hangs are ordinary enough, are quite within the compass of twenty-four hours and are credible without Einstein.

. . . .

On this skeleton hangs the variegated fabric of *Ulysses*. I could not, tried I ever so hard, give an adequate notion of the vast number of characters, descriptions, parodies and visions that crowd so comfortably into the 800 pages without actually quoting the whole book, which is manifestly impossible.

. . . .

Ulysses cannot be termed pornographic. One might as well label the Venus de Milo indecent, and just as that piece of sculpture has been the urge to centuries of artists, so *Ulysses,* with its strange modernity, will carry away young writers on its irrepressible tide. But I do wrong to talk about a classic nude in relation to *Ulysses*. It has no more in common with the idealised naked beauties of a Cabanel or a Solomon J Solomon, or the holy etherealisations of the Pre-Raphaelites, than Ibsen with St. Francis of Assisi. Mr. Joyce is essentially the product of his age, or perhaps, as with all genius, a little ahead of it. In him we find collected all the strivings of the modern world. That which stands out most is the kinship between him and modern painters. This year's pictures at the Salon d'Automne have precisely the same effect as *Ulysses* on the conventional mind. It calls the true ugly, because truth comes in the shape of a squatting lady with an abundance of fat. If convention permits the regarding of nudes, then let them be as remote from reality as possible. But the revolution had to come. Artists could not be content to live in a world of inhibitions. Freud had begun to look at psychology in his own particular way. Psycho-analysts began to pursue their studies. The world learned new words and phrases—complexes, inhibitions, and all the jargon of the new psychology. Naturally the mob of followers abused the new learning just as they abused Christianity, using Freud to explain their own over-sexedness and booming psycho-analysis as a parlour game. Mr. Joyce, however, does not rush with the crowd, and has made skilful use of what the psychologists have taught him. He can open up a thought as a surgeon does a body.

There are so many aspects of Joyce's work that one does not know where to begin. It is comparable to the Bible, with which it has much in common, in the respect that one part differs so much from the other. One might argue, some hundreds of years later, that *Ulysses* was the work of many hands, were it not for the fact that in the seeming medley of chapters and styles there is a form as rigid as that of a sonnet. Here we come to an aspect of *Ulysses* which is not generally noticed. The name of the work is taken from the title of the Homeric hero, and the chapters follow the scenes of the earlier epic. I shall not here attempt to trace the parallelism between the modern and the classic work, save only to mention that Bloom is undoubtedly a humanised conception of Ulysses conceived in a modern vein, and tempered with a modern humour—and Stephen, an artistic Telemachus, aloof and serene, curious commentator on passing life. Nor shall I dwell long on the symbolism that lies hidden in each chapter, and which would have been as unsuspected by me as the mysteries underlying the marble verses of Mallarmé for his first readers, were it not that they were communicated to me by Mr. Joyce himself. It matters not one fiddlestick, however, whether Mr. Joyce's epic sonata sings its new word-music in the borrowed tones of Homer, or whether every chapter hangs on the symbol of some organ of the human body, as in the 17th century *Purple Island* of Phineas Fletcher, or whether the brothel in Dublin's under-world is the parallel of Ulysses' descent into hell: the whole has sufficient significance in itself to make it a work in immortality and in the best traditions of classic form.

Mr. Joyce might have been the comrade of Boccacio and supped at the table of Petronius. As a humorist he is a direct descendant of these men. He is akin to Rabelais and the Balzac of the *Contes Drolatiques*. But his uncanny aloofness distinguishes him from these.

His digressions, despite their apparent remoteness, belong to the action. They are either commentaries, a prose comic chorus, or the full-winged flight of a character's thought. Often scientific theories are discussed or literature. There is a scene in the National Library where Joyce, now clad in the garb of George Moore (I do not know whether it is intentional or not) makes the well-known librarians, whom he mentions by name, and Æ discuss a curious theory of the influence on Shakespeare of his wife, Anne Hathaway. And this Stephen expounds with rare critical acumen and style, fortified with Elizabethan anecdotes and a healthy disregard of the usual authorities.

The chapter, written in the manner of a lower middle-class Dubliner, which begins with a parody of a legal summons and ends in a public-house with the escape of Bloom on a hackney car, secure from the tin box which the angered and alcoholed citizen hurls at him, is a miracle of natural prose conversation illumined by humorous parody digressions. The seismic shock occasioned by the hurling of this missile, which destroys the whole of Dublin and scatters bits of Sir George Fottrell's umbrella to the Giant's Causeway, brings a message of condolence from the Sovereign Pontiff, and eventually carries Bloom along to Adonai, a new Elijah—in a jaunting-car-chariot-of-fire—is a supreme piece of buffoonery.

The form of burlesque which runs through the whole of *Ulysses* is a point of contact with the writings of some young Frenchmen known as Dadaists. Max Jacob in a curious prose poem has a titanic battle in the stalls of a theatre, where thousands are numbered amongst the slain, and the current Dada weeklies warm with this type of gigantic hyperbole. Mr. Joyce has a little more in common with the Dadaists: his inventions of onamatopaeic words and the mixing of science with literature. Joyce and the Dadaist arrived independently, of course, at the similarities. They merely prove how true a son of his age is the author of *Ulysses*. Laurence Sterne I have always considered the first Dadaist. He might almost be considered the christener before its birth of the movement. Every man has his hobby-horse and *de gustibus non est disputandum*. Tristram himself happens at certain intervals and changes of the moon to be both fiddler and painter according as the fly stings. Sterne is an eighteenth century Joyce. They both go to antiquity for quips and quibbles, and have the same taste for salaciousness and the use of names for comic effect. Sterne, however, is the more homely, and enjoys himself what Joyce would have us enjoy. The relationship of Joyce to modernism is a vast subject which I have only barely touched here, but which holds great scope for the critic. He has in him points of similarity with the painter Picasso; the early follower of tradition breaking into new modes and expressing life from a new angle with a changed vision.

Perhaps the most curious chapter in *Ulysses* is the night in the brothel, which most newspapers, for some superficial reason, have agreed to call the *Walpurgisnacht*. The only resemblance between it and Faust's adventures on the Brocken is the disregard of ordinary sequence of time. There are no witches with brooms in Joyce's night-town, but there are some very bawdy hags. Perhaps, too, the symbolism in Goethe in the introduction of contemporaries in strange guise may justify the comparison. But the whole tenor, the zig-zag movement, the supreme obscenity, the exposure of sexual repressions, is characteristically Joycean. It may be, however, from a desire to give some impression of this cinematographical, orthographical, physiological, erotic, psychological, scatological fantasy in play form that the *Walpurgisnacht* was invoked. It must, however, be read, and, of course, in conjunction with what has gone before, to be appreciated.

. . . .

When we come finally to the Penelope monologue, or the exhibition of what clergymen call the 'true inwardness' of Mrs. Bloom, we are amazed at the concentration of the author on female psychology. I do not know whether the psychology is true. The author of *The Pretty Lady* picks this out as the finest part of the book. I have no great admiration for Mr. Bennett, and believe that he yields too often to temptation, and keeps his literary pot too long on the boil, but he should be qualified to judge on so delicate a subject. For myself, who can only speak instinctively, and hence tentatively, on such matters, and am of necessity swayed by the conflicting views of male psychologists, I am in a state of uncertainty. Molly Bloom, however, sounds real. What Croce affirms of Ibsen's characters is truer still of Mrs. Bloom. She says aloud, or rather thinks aloud, what we hardly ever dare whisper to ourselves and never bend an ear to listen.

Ulysses is essentially a book for the male. It is impossible for a woman to stomach the egregious grossness. Through the book one hears the coarse oaths and rude jests of the corner-boy and the subtle salaciousness of the cultured. There is a tradition in these things. And as the Oriental shuts off his women from contact with the world with a yashmak and a harem, so we have cut off our womenfolk from our smoking-room hinterlands. It is not woman but man who has a secret, and Mr. Joyce is guilty of a breach of the male freemasonry in publishing the signs by which one man recognises a healthy living brother.

. . . .

It is impossible for any discerning mind to deny genius to Mr. Joyce, and that of a very high order. His work will persist in spite of the efforts to suppress it of such literary critics as the Society for the Suppression of Vice in America and the reviewer of the *Pink 'Un*. The style alone is sufficient to attract readers. The quaint Greek compounds, the melodious words, the rare vocabulary, apart altogether from the profundities and indecencies, will keep *Ulysses* alive for posterity. M. Valéry Larbaud believes Mr. Joyce to be as great as Rabelais. Naturally his reception in Paris was more cordial, for all the greatest French writers look upon life with their eyes open In these parts we are in the position of the pupil of Carrière who asked his teacher how he could attain excellence in painting. *Choose your subject,* said Carrière, *close your eyes, and paint what you see.*

On the Continent, however, there are artists who find that writing in the dark is not nearly so exciting as writing with ones eyes and ears open. In Austria, Schnitzler writes *Reigen,* the great Guillaume Appolinaire finds no subject that he dare not touch upon, the Dadaists make their humour out of the most intimate things. Even George Moore was too much for these isles, but you can find traces of fearlessness in Wyndham Lewis and D. H. Lawrence. So there is hope yet. I say this, however, that only an artist could handle his material as Mr. Joyce has done. In other hands there would really be a grave risk of a descent into the morbid and the pornographic. He will have influence, but I doubt if there will be imitators. In the Dorothy Richardsons and May Sinclairs I see already the influence of the Joyce literary style.

In truth, there is no real parallel to Mr. Joyce in literature. He has that touch of individuality that puts

genius on a peak. Rabelaisian, he hasn't the *joie de vivre* of the French priest; Sternesque, he is devoid of the personal touch of the Irish clergyman. Trained by the Jesuits, he can't guffaw like Balzac when he tells a good story. He is a scientist in his detachedness, but *Ulysses* is nevertheless, a human book, filled with pity as with the sexual instinct, and the latter in no greater proportion and of no greater importance in the book than any of the other fundamental human attributes.

Literary Causeries: vii: So She Went into the Garden
Ford Madox Ford
Chicago Tribune Sunday Magazine, 6 April 1924, pp. 3, 11

The other day a critic, a Frenchman and therefore a man of some intelligence and politeness, varied the form of the enquiry and asked: 'How is it possible that you take pleasure in the work of Mr. Joyce? You, a Classic?' . . . And you observe that he conceded without question the fact of my pleasure in the Advanced.

And indeed I do take that pleasure. And I am not paid to do it and to do so does not pay. . . .

I am driven into these speculations by being asked by my editor to explain to his readers, precisely the pleasure that I take in the work of Mr. Joyce . . .

For myself then, the pleasure–the very great pleasure– that I get from going through the sentences of Mr. Joyce is that given me simply by cadence of his prose, and I fancy that the greatest and highest enjoyment that can be got from any writing is simply that given by the cadence of the prose. . . .

Now I must not be taken as saying that there is any kinship or resemblance between the writings of Mr. Joyce, the Scriptures or the prose of Mr. Conrad. All that I am saying is that immense pleasure *can* be obtained from letting the cadences of Mr. Joyce pass through the mind. . . .

The reader will by now be saying: 'Well, but this fellow says nothing about what we want to hear of. There is not a single word about the obscenities, the blasphemies, the Bolshevism of which we have heard so much.' And there is not, simply because I have been asked to explain what makes me take pleasure in the work of Mr. Joyce, and I take no pleasure in obscenities, blasphemies or the propaganda of the Soviets. And indeed, of this last there is not a word in the works of Mr. Joyce. There are obviously passages that, in the ordinary vernacular, would pass for obscenities and blasphemies . . . And the reader who prefers to ignore the existence of these things in the world has one very simple remedy, as far as *Ulysses* is concerned. He can refrain from reading the book. I am not asking him to do otherwise. . . .

–reprinted from *James Joyce: The Critical Heritage*

Alec Waugh was the pen name of the English writer Alexander Raban Waugh, the brother of the famous novelist, Evelyn Waugh. In the excerpt below Waugh admits the value of Joyce's new technique.

The Neo-Georgians
Alec Waugh
Fortnightly, 115 (January 1924): 126–137

. . . *Ulysses* has been described, not unwarrantably, as the greatest outrage that has been ever committed on the English language, but few writers have been possessed of a more clear, a more rhythmed style than James Joyce has at his disposal on those rare occasions when he chooses to employ it. . . . It was from the strictly technical point of view that *Ulysses* was, in the majority of cases, discussed; in its realism, in its crudity, in its obscenity it is perhaps the most startling document that has ever been presented as a serious piece of literature to a civilised community. But it aroused none of the controversy that is regarded as inseparable from such productions. People did not sit in circles and discuss James Joyce's message, or wonder whether men and women 'really were like that.' A new way of writing had been invented; the question to be decided was: was it a good way or was it not? Its notoriety is due undoubtedly in a large measure to its realism. But had there not been in *Ulysses* a single indecent phrase, or scene, or sentence, the extent and quality of its interest to those interested primarily in letters would not have been diminished. No sensational book ever owed less to its sensationalism. It is an exercise in a new technique; that is its value, that is its significance. It could not have achieved such a success in a period that was not passionately concerned with the carpentry of writing. . . .

—reprinted from *James Joyce: The Critical Heritage*

The Scottish literary critic and poet Edwin Muir sees Joyce's earlier works as leading to his masterful use of language in Ulysses.

James Joyce: The Meaning of "Ulysses"
Edwin Muir
Calendar of Modern Letters, 1 (July 1925): 347–355

No other novelist who has written in English has had a greater mastery than Mr. Joyce of language as an instrument of literary expression, and no one else, probably, has striven so consciously to attain it. "Dubliners" was an ideal apprentice piece for an artist; in it Mr. Joyce set himself to describe accurately the things he saw, attempting at the beginning what most writers achieve

Urged by W. B. Yeats, Edmund Gosse in 1915 had been instrumental in securing a grant from the Royal Literary Fund for Joyce, who at the time was living in Zurich and in need of financial support. Gosse wrote to Louis Gillet on 7 June 1924.

I should very much regret you paying Mr. J. Joyce the compliment of an article in the *Revue des Deux Mondes.* You could only expose the worthlessness and impudence of his writings, and surely it would be a mistake to give him this prominence. I have difficulty in describing to you, *in writing,* the character of Mr. Joyce's notoriety . . . It is partly political; it is partly a perfectly cynical appeal to sheer indecency. He is of course not entirely without talent, but he is a literary charlatan of the extremest order. His principal book, *Ulysses,* has not parallel that I know of in French. It is an anarchical production, infamous in taste, in style, in everything.

Mr. Joyce is unable to publish or sell his books in England, on account of their obscenity. He therefore issues a 'private' edition in Paris and charges a huge price for each copy. He is a sort of Marquis de Sade, but does not write so well. He is the perfect type of the Irish *fumiste,* a hater of England, more than suspected of partiality for Germany, where he lived before the war (and at Zürich during the war).

There are no English critics of weight or judgement who consider Mr. Joyce an author of any importance. If, as you tell me, 'on fait grand bruit du nommé J. J. . . . à Paris,' it must be among persons whose knowledge of English literature and language is scanty. He is not, as I say, without talent, but he has prostituted it to the most vulgar uses. . .

Do not think that I have any *personal* prejudice. I have never seen Mr. Joyce and before the war I contributed to his needs. I speak in an exclusively literary sense.

—reprinted from *James Joyce: The Critical Heritage*

towards the end. "The Portrait of the Artist as a Young Man," marked a further stage. That book was as much a recreation of language as a record of experience. The marvellous dialogue which appeared first in it was not like the transcriptions of ordinary talk in "Dubliners"; it was a second language which was used consciously to vary and complete the lingual pattern of the work. That pattern of speech seemed complete in itself, a thing of different nature from, but as real as, the events and experiences, many of them sordid, which it described. There were thus two values in the novel, separate, yet necessary to each other: the value of language and that of life, the value of art and that of experience. To Mr.

Joyce the first of these is pure, the second mixed. Art must descend into life, the word must seek out all it can and enter into it; yet, having entered into it, it returns and remains pure in the consciousness of the artist. Life cannot soil it, but only a disobedience of its own laws.

In the "Portrait of the Artist as a Young Man" Mr. Joyce acquired the mastery of language, the knowledge of and reverence for its mysteries, which prepared him for "Ulysses." He learnt, too, for the second time, the strict realism which, because it demands perfect exactitude in the rendering, is valuable as a discipline, makes an intensive demand on the artists' powers of expression, and by putting a strain on them enhances them. In embracing this realism he discarded the facile sensibility of his time, which was occupied only with the secondary phenomena of consciousness—with the psychological effect of the object rather than the object, with distinctions rather than with things—and which in that preoccupation while seizing the shadow lost the substance. "The Portrait of the Artist as a Young Man" not only left Mr. Joyce with a greater command over English than any other novelist had possessed; it was as well a sort of self-inoculation against a sensibility grown burdensome. Without either of these "Ulysses" could never have been written. For in "Ulysses" the dual values of "The Portrait," the values of life and art, of reality and imagination, are developed side by side until each attains its maximum of expression, and the discrepancy between them issues in a form of humour which through its intellectual profundity becomes universal. It is a humour not of fashion, nor of character, but of the processes of life, those processes which create history and produce religions and civilisations while leaving the great part of the human race, the average sensual man outside us and within us, spiritually unchanged and apparently spiritually unchangeable. It sets forth the dreams of religion, the magic of language, the splendours of the intellect, the revolutions of history, over against the simple facts: the naïvety of physical desire, the functions of the body, the triviality of the floating thoughts the body sends up into our minds. A theme so tremendous could only be expressed in great tragedy or great comedy, could only in one of these two ways be lifted into a plane where it no longer overwhelms us, and where having passed through it we are freed from its worst oppression. Had Mr. Joyce not inoculated himself against sensibility by an overdose of realism he could never have attained this emancipating comic vision of the entire modern world. Had he not been so sensitive that he suffered monstrously from his sensibility his comedy would have had no driving power behind it. One feels again and again in "Ulysses" that the uproariousness of the farce, the recklessness of the blasphemy, is wildest where the suffering of the artist has been most intense. A writer whose sufferings were so great and so conscious needed a more elaborate technique than most writers do, as much to put a distance between himself and his sufferings as to express them.

"Dubliners" and "The Portrait" were a necessary preparation, an apprenticeship strengthening the artist against life. They were exercises working out a part of Mr. Joyce's problem; but in "Ulysses" the whole problem is faced and to the extent of Mr. Joyce's present powers resolved. That problem must needs have been the problem of all the things from which he suffered, for the sincere artist is distinguished from the rest by the fact that his essential concern is with the things which make him suffer, the things, in other words, which stand between him and freedom. There is thus a necessary and an organic relation between him and his work, to create being, as Ibsen said, an act of emancipation. But when, as in "Ulysses," the creation is encyclopædic, when it attempts to gain freedom not from one but all the bonds, all the suffering, of the artist's soul, the impulse from which it started becomes a part of the autobiography of the book as well as of the writer. What Mr. Joyce suffered from in writing "Ulysses" was obviously in its completeness the life he had known; our modern world in all its intellectual manifestations as well as in its full banality; in its beliefs, its hopes, its charities, its reverences; its religion, patriotism, humanitarianism, science, literature, politics; its illusions as well as its realities. How could the full volume of all these burdensome hopes, theories, sensibilities, banalities, cruelties, meannesses, sensualities, be rendered in a work of art? Obviously not in a story, an action having a beginning, a development, a climax and an end, but rather in a record of the most obvious unit of time in which all these could manifest themselves, in that unit of time which begins with something recalling birth and ends in something resembling death: in a day. "Ulysses" is a complete course, a set banquet, of the modern consciousness. And being that no other unit could have served; the author could not have got into the record of a year what he has got into the record of a day.

But this banquet of the modern consciousness was to be a comic summing up as well as a banquet; it was to be not only abundant, but so burdensomely, absurdly abundant that all the courses would be made to appear ridiculous, as Rabelais made the courses of the medieval banquet ridiculous. And as Mr. Joyce's encyclopædic plan justified the time unit of his chronicle, so his comic intention justified the minuteness of his portrayal, his huge accumulation of imaginative material. His humour is one on side, like that of Rabelais, a piling up of one burden on the mind after another until the breaking point is reached—the breaking point of laughter. It operates by oppressing us consciously with all the things which oppress us unconsciously, and by exaggerating all this until it seems ridiculous that we should bear it, or more exactly that it should exist at all. A sense of this or that anomaly in social relations, the sense which finds expression in polite comedy, is far too light to shift this immense weight. To do that comedy must include as many factors as the greatest tragedy; it must embrace not only man, but all that he believes in, the whole anthropomorphic cosmos. But even when the absurdities of the spirit are piled up in this way they are still not in the realm of universal comedy: the last touch is still wanting. That is given by a running contrast between the vast symbols invented by man and his simple earthy reactions, between the extravagance of belief and the simplicity of fact, the decency of civilised life and the unseemliness of instinct. That was the mainspring of Rabelais' humour, and it is also that of Mr. Joyce's. The more absurd and minute the description of physiological reactions, the greater obviously the effect. On the one hand an infinite immensity, on the other an infinitesimal smallness; the intellectual dreams and spiritual struggles of Stephen Dedalus in the one balance, the vagaries of Leopold Bloom's instincts in the other; around us the phantoms our minds have created, and within us the utilitarian functions of our bodies. And as the intellectual shapes which man has conceived to be first a release and then a burden are exaggerated, so his physical idiosyncrasies, his trifling thoughts, are refined upon. There is in Mr. Joyce's obscenity as in that of Rabelais an intellectual quality, as if in searching the recondite secrets of the natural processes of the body he were trying to penetrate to an unconscious humour of the cells, of those elementary principles of life which have built up not only the body but all this phantasmal structure which we call thought, religion and civilisation. His emphasis on the unseemly, on what, in other words, we have surpassed, depend upon, and wish to forget, is, at any rate, a necessary element in this kind of humour and an essential part of the plan of "Ulysses." It is perverse, that is to say, intellectualised deliberately, but so it had to be to achieve its purpose.

The vision of the world whose mainspring is in this radical sense of contrast is one which, if it did not issue in humour, would be nightmare. In "Ulysses" it does not always issue in humour. The brothel scene is horrible partly because it is a mis-shapen birth, because, conceived as a grand example of the humour of horror, it attains, through its failure, an atmosphere of horror which because it is unintentional is strictly monstrous, and incapable of being resolved either into art or into human experience. This scene is a work of genius; it is more astonishing than anything else Mr. Joyce has written; but it has the portentous appearance of something torn from the womb of imagination, not the completeness of something born of it. We derive from it a vivid notion of the monstrous suffering through which the artist is passing; but here he has not passed beyond it; and we suffer equally as participators in the horrors of a raw experience and as spectators of a heroic but unavailing attempt to escape from it and set it in the realm of freedom. Had Mr. Joyce succeeded with this gigantic scene he would have produced something supreme in literature and not merely something supremely astounding and terrifying. It was obviously designed to be the climax of the work; in it the last resources of the theme were to be brought on the stage; the unconscious desires which up to now had been allowed only a chance or oblique expression were to come nakedly to the surface and attain freedom. They do not attain freedom. This brothel scene is not a release of all the oppressions and inhibitions of life in our time; it is rather a gigantic attempt to attain release.

But if we grant this crucial failure in the book, and a number of minor failures, there remains more comedy in the grand style than has appeared in our literature since the Elizabethan age. The last chapter has been much praised, but there are others only less admirable. The scene in the pub. where Bloom is routed by the Citizen produces by an openly mechanical technique Mr. Joyce's sense of contrast between an ordinary happening in all its banality and richness, and the fantastic and etiolated symbols which the desires of men and the conventions of literature discover for it. Here it is the obviousness of the means, the mechanical ease with which the simple event assumes conventional or lofty forms in the fancy that is at the root of the humour. We seem to see the illusions at their normal work. The banal fact and the fantastic interpretation are both present before our eyes, are both obvious and credible, the one arising spontaneously from the other, and are both ridiculous. The chapter of parodies, which has been so much criticised, is still more remarkable. There we see the figure of Mr. Bloom passing, as it were, through a comic pageant of the English spirit. In his progression he assumes a sort of absurd universality; he is a man "of Israel's folk . . . that on earth wandering far had fared"; he is "childe Leopold" and "sir Leopold that had for his cognisance the flower of quiet," and "Master Calmer," and "Leop. Bloom of Crawford's journal sitting snug with a covey of wags," and "Mr. L. Bloom (Pubb. Canv.)." He is a type, and a succession of types through history, and a multiplication of types in space; one person in himself and many persons in time and in the minds of men. In this scene

Mr. Joyce's comic imagination is at its height; it raises Mr. Bloom into a lengendary figure and gives him history and the world for his stage. But in doing that it fulfils once more the requirements of Mr. Joyce's humour, for to squat Mr. Bloom on the centre of that stage was to attain a comic vision of the world and of history.

What is it that through this use of contrast, this breaking of our resistances by accumulation, Mr. Joyce tries to set in the plane of low comedy? First of all, professional seriousness of all kinds, and secondly the objects about which people are serious in this way: religion, to which the comic reaction is blasphemy; patriotism, to which it is little less; literature, to which it is parody; the claims of science, to which it is an application of anti-climax; sex, to which it is obscenity. When comedy attempts to become universal it has perforce to include blasphemy and obscenity, for these are the two poles of this comedy just as the soul and the body are the two poles of human existence. To see religion with the eyes of comedy is not, of course, to laugh it out of existence, any more than to see sex comically is to destroy it. All that comedy can destroy is strictly the second-rate, everything that is not in its mode the best, everything less genuine than the genuine—a class of thoughts and emotions which make up the preponderating part of the experience of most people and of all ages, and is a permanent burden which at times may become unbearable. Books such as "Ulysses" and "Gargantua" can only be written out of an almost insupportable feeling of oppression; for humour on this scale the sense of oppression is needed as a driving power. The load of oppression which Rabelais cleared away we can see now clearly enough; it is more difficult to realise, although it is easy to feel, what it is that oppresses in our age a creative writer like Mr. Joyce. But when the reverences of any time are taken very seriously and not very intensely, when a belief in enlightenment, progress and humanity becomes habitual, and men act and think with a fearful eye on it and on the most mediocre of its priests, it has already become as injurious to the creative impulse as the strictest obscurantism could be. It is a weight of second-rate sentiment and thought, and the time comes when the only thing to be done is to clear it away.

To destroy so completely as Mr. Joyce does in "Ulysses" is to make a new start. Or more exactly, the new start must have been made before the destruction began, for the new thing destroys only that it may have room to grow in freedom. But what is new in this sense in "Ulysses" it is hazardous to attempt to say yet; for the things which are most new in it have a breath of an antiquity which seems to antedate the antiquity of classical literature, and to come out of a folk rather than a literary inspiration. Mr. Joyce's prostitutes in the brothel scene exist neither in the world of literature, as that world has been conceived almost since its beginning, nor in the world of fact. They are rather figures in a folk-lore which mankind continually creates, or rather carries with it, creations and types in the dream in which sensual humanity lives, and which to humanity is the visible world. This folklore, which is the aesthetic utterance of the illiterate classes, and of the illiterate parts of our nature, which co-exists with literature, but in a separate world, is not inarticulate; but it expresses itself anonymously, and is such a constant attribute of human life that it rarely feels the need of the more permanent, the more specialised, expression of art. It attains its perfection from day to day by means which are as suited to its purposes as the means of literature are to the purposes of literature. Yet from it literature arose, for like literature, it is aesthetic, and has the freedom of perception which can only come when men are delivered from their utilitarian prejudices. And to it accordingly literature must periodically come back, as much to test as to renew itself. This is the world to which Mr. Joyce has in part returned, in part striven to return, in "Ulysses." He has seen, as only a profound theorist on art could have seen, that the sources of art lie here, that here is the primary division in our consciousness from which flow on the one hand the laws of art, and on the other the laws of the practical world in which we live. The great categories of literature, such as the pathetic, the tragic, and the comic, which with the interior development of literature tend ever to become more pure, more formal, Mr. Joyce has related to the loose and undifferentiated categories of popular imagination, and, starting from these, has set out to attain a more essential pathos, a more complete comedy, than the conventions of modern literature could have given him. He has not escaped the dangers of such an ambitious attempt. In "Ulysses" there are passages of unassimilated folk-lore which we feel do not belong to literature—diurnal phrases of Dublin talk which should not have survived the day, which, perfect in their time and place, get a false emphasis when set deliberately into the frame of a work of imagination. But where the attempt is successful, Mr. Joyce's imagination has a unique immediacy, a unique originality. In one glance we seem to see the life which he describes immediately before and immediately after he has set his seal upon it, and the transformation of reality into art takes place, as it were, under our eyes. Then we feel sometimes that in sweeping aside the aesthetic sense of three centuries, Mr. Joyce has penetrated to the aesthetic consciousness in itself, the aesthetic consciousness, that is to say, before it has become selective and exclusive, as the more it is developed and refined it tends to become, and still includes everything. It is, of course, obvious that the totality of the responses of that consciousness cannot be rendered in literature, of which selection is not merely a virtue, but also the condition. Yet in the history of literature, as has often been shown, the principle of selection sometimes becomes a conventional, an arbitrary one, and, indeed, continually tends to do so; and, therefore, it is at rare times necessary for the artist to put himself in a position where a fundamental act of selection becomes compulsory, and where he feels that every decision, whether to include or to reject, is significant not only on traditional grounds, but is made by his own unconditional volition and as if for the first time. "Ulysses" not only raises the problem of selection again; in part, it answers it by bringing into literature things banished from it, as we now see more clearly, on moral and conventional rather than essential grounds. In doing that, Mr. Joyce has both enriched literature and potentially widened its scope.

James Joyce as a Poet
Edmund Wilson
The New Republic, 44 (November 1925): 279–280

MR. R. C. TREVELYAN, the author of an interesting little book called Thamyris, or Is There a Future for Poetry? in the Today and Tomorrow Series, seems troubled by the lack of seriousness and ambition in contemporary English poetry. His discussion of the future possibilities of comic, philosophic, satiric, didactic and narrative poetry only serves to call attention to the fact that there is nobody of any importance attempting any of them. Mr. Masefield's long narrative poems have fallen progressively further below the success of The Everlasting Mercy; and Mr. Yeats, without doubt a great poet, has seldom passed beyond his personal lyrics, to write anything but short plays which still remain lyric rather than dramatic. It might, however, be worth while, in connection with the apparently rather discouraging condition of English poetry, to consider a prose writer who is perhaps as closely related to the poets as to the writer of prose fiction.

Mr. James Joyce, whose first book was a volume of lyrics, has from the beginning shown himself possessed of some of the peculiar genius of the poet at the same time that he has evidently lacked some of the gifts of the novelist. This appears very plainly in his language: few novelists have brought the language of prose fiction so close to the language of verse–"her long fair hair was girlish: and girlish, and touched with the wonder of mortal beauty, her face." "Kind air defined the coigns of houses in Kildare street. No birds. Frail from the housetops two plumes of smoke ascended, pluming, and in a flaw of softness softly were blown." But it is not merely in his language but in the whole

effect at which he aims that Mr. Joyce is akin to the poets as much as to the novelists. Perhaps the most remarkable and characteristic of the pieces in his first book of fiction, Dubliners, is the long story called the Dead, which, however, performs none of the functions which we ordinarily expect of a story: it is scarcely an anecdote and not even a character study; if it represents a situation, it is a situation which does not come to anything. It is simply an exquisite and complex presentation of the sensations of a single person on a particular evening; and it thus sets the type of everything that Joyce is afterwards to do. A Portrait of the Artist as a Young Man is merely a succession of such presentations; and Ulysses the same thing again on a larger scale and with a greater degree of complexity. Less than any other novelist is Joyce interested in staging a drama or telling a story. When he has put before us a particular nexus of thoughts, emotions, perceptions and sensations as they are found in combination at a particular moment, he is satisfied. All his sweep is in the areas of society and of the human consciousness which he makes these moments imply. Ulysses, vast as it is, has no action and scarcely any movement: it ends with the characters' falling asleep, as they do at the end of The Dead, after a day which, like most of the days which we know, takes no definite new direction from its predecessors. The parallel with the Odyssey does duty for a story and serves Joyce as a device for indicating the significance and relations of his characters, which his rigorously objective method makes it impossible for him to explain in his own person and which, as they do not realize them, they cannot of course reveal themselves.

Ulysses, therefore, has this in common with some of the greatest of long poems: that though the effect is cumulative and the parts necessary to each other, we read it as a series of episodes rather than a story which carries us straight through. We appreciate it best indeed when we have already read it once and have found out what it is about, and return to it from time to time to read the sections separately. It is only then that we are able properly to realize what a satisfactory artistic unit each episode makes in itself and at the same time what it contributes to the whole. For this reason Ulysses has perhaps been more readily understood by people who are used to reading poetry, that is, poetry on the great scale, than by people who read principally novels. The latter became bored and eventually baffled when they discovered they could not get through it in an evening, like a novel by Mr. Joseph Hergesheimer, or even in a week–though they would certainly never have tried the same thing with the Aeneid or the Divine Comedy, or even with Leaves of Grass or The Ring and the Book.

And there is a further particular reason why Ulysses is more likely to be understood by the reader of

In *Aspects of the Novel* (1927) E. M. Forster argued that *Ulysses* "is a dogged attempt to cover the universe with mud, it is an inverted Victorianism, an attempt to make crossness and dirt succeed where sweetness and light failed, a simplification of the human character in the interests of Hell."

poetry than by the reader of fiction. Mr. Joyce has been preoccupied with a problem to which Virgil and Dante most anxiously applied themselves and which has obviously been one of the principal concerns of poets in all civilized ages but to which novelists, with the exception of Flaubert, have not paid very much attention–the problem of varying the style to fit the subject. The kind of definitive propriety, intensity and economy of language which the great poets have attained and which Flaubert and Joyce aim at, has indeed remained so alien to the novel that many readers, accustomed to prose fiction, have not hesitated to declare Ulysses unintelligible–though its language departs nowhere more widely, I believe, from the language of ordinary prose than the language of much familiar poetry does. But one of the things which makes Ulysses formidable not merely to the modern novel but to the whole achievement of prose fiction is precisely its spectacular reintroduction of this problem and its appeal to standards which we long ago formed the habit of forgetting with the epic and dramatic poets who first set them–and whose race, like Mr. Trevelyan, we have come gradually no longer to count on.

For it may be said of novels in general that they have usually been written throughout in the same sort of prose–if a novelist has a literary sense sufficiently highly developed to vary his sentences from long to short in a passage presenting rapid action as distinguished from a passage of static description, we may consider ourselves very lucky; if he gets to the point of a little onomatopœia, we are astonished by his brilliance. Henry James did not concern himself with these matters; neither did Thomas Hardy; neither did Thackeray nor Jane Austen nor Fielding. Take the description of the concert from Sinister Street, a typical English modern novel, by no means badly written: "It seemed to go on for ever in a most barbaric and amorphous din; with corybantic crashings, with brazen fanfares and stinging cymbals it flung itself against the audience, while the wood-wind howled and the violins were harsh as cats. Michael brooded unreceptive; he had a sense of monstrous loneliness; he could think of nothing. The noise overpowered his beating heart, and he began to

count absurdly, while he bit his nails or shivered in alternations of fire and snow . . . Near him were lovers who in this symphony were fast imparadised; their hands were interlaced; visibly they swayed nearer to each other on the waves of melody. Old men were near him, solitary old men, listening, listening . . . At one point the bassoons became very active, and he was somehow reminded of Mr. Neech. He was puzzled for a while to account for this association of an old form-master with the noise of bassoons. *For he heard the loud bassoon.* Out of the past came the vision of old Neech, etc." Compare this with the episode in Ulysses in which Bloom listens to the song in the bar. Here Mr. Joyce tries to put directly and precisely before us the music, the talk in the bar and the sounds coming in from the street as they appear to the dreaming relaxation of the late afternoon. "A doudene of birdnotes chirruped bright treble answer under sensitive hands. Brightly the keys, all twinkling, linked, all harpsichording, called to a voice to sing the strain of dewy morn, youth, of love's leavetaking, life's, love's morn." Bloom watches the barmaids as they respond to the singing of the pathetic ballad: "Thrill now. Pity they feel. To wipe away a tear for martyrs. For all things dying, want to, dying to, die. For that all things born. Poor Mrs. Purefoy. Hope she's over. Because their wombs–A liquid of womb of woman eyeball gazed under a fence of lashes, calmly, hearing. See real beauty of the eye when she not speaks. On yonder river. At each slow satiny heaving bosom's wave. (her heaving embon) red rose rose slowly, sank red rose. Heartbeats her breath: breath that is life. And all the tiny tiny fernfoils trembled of maidenhair.

The poetic genius of Mr. Joyce appears particularly plainly in a part of the opening of his new novel which has been published in a French magazine, Le Navire d'Argent. This book is to begin, I am told, with a description of the river Liffey chattering over its stones–which are presently heard to speak with the voices of gossiping washwomen: they are babbling an indistinct rigmarole story, half unearthly, half vulgarly human, of some semi-legendary heroine; and Joyce's rendering of the voices of the river, light, rapid, half metrical but always changing, now running monotonously on one note, now for a moment syncopated, but bickering interminably on, is surely one of his most remarkable successes; "O tell me all about Anna Livia! I want to hear about Anna Livia. Well, you know Anna Livia? Yes, of course, we all know Anna Livia. Tell me all. Tell me now. You'll die when you hear . . . Tell me, tell me, how could she cam through all her fellows, the daredevil? Linking one and knocking the next and polling in and petering out and clyding by in the eastway. Who was the first that ever burst? Someone it was, whoever you are. Tinker, tailor, soldier, sailor, Paul Pry or polishman. That's the thing I always want to know. She can't put her hand on him for the moment. It's a long long way, walking weary! Such a long way backwards to row! She was herself she hardly knows who her graveller was or what he did or how young she played or when or where or how often he jumped her. She was just a young thin pale soft shy slim slip of a thing then, sauntering, and he was a heavy trudging lurching lie-abroad of a Curraghman, making his hay for the sun to shine on, as tough as the oaktrees (peats be with them!) used to rustle that time down by the dykes of killing Kildare, that forestfellfoss with a plash across her. She thought she'd sink under the ground with shame when he gave her the tiger's eye!"–As darkness falls, the voices seem to grow husky and vague: "Can't hear with the waters of. The chittering waters of. Flittering bats, fieldmice bawk talk. Ho! Are you not gone ahome? What Tom Malone? Can't hear with bawk of bats, all the liffeying waters of. Ho, talk save us! My foos won't moos. I feel as old as yonder elm. A tale told of Shaun or Shem? All Livia's daughtersons. Dark hawks hear us. Night! Night! My ho head halls. I feel as heavy as yonder stone. Tell me of John or Shaun? Who were Shem and Shaun the living sons or daughters of? Night now! Tell me, tell me, tell me, elm! Night night! Tell me tale of stem or stone. Beside the rivering waters of, hitherandthithering waters of. Night!"

Wyndham Lewis at one time had planned to publish portions of Joyce's Work in Progress *in* The Enemy, *a short-lived review he began in January 1927. Instead, in the initial issue of* The Enemy *he attacked* Ulysses *as formless and Joyce as virtually nothing more than a craftsman. "An Analysis of the Mind of James Joyce" in* Time and Western Man *is an expansion of an earlier essay, "The Revolutionary Simpleton," that was published in* The Enemy. *Joyce responded to Lewis's criticism in "The Ondt and the Gracehoper" (*Finnegans Wake, *pp. 414–419), published in the March 1928 issue of* transition, *defending his work and satirizing Lewis as the humorless Ondt (a Norwegian word for angry).*

An Analysis of the Mind of James Joyce
Wyndham Lewis
Time and Western Man (London: Chatto & Windus, 1927), pp. 91–130

1. The work of Mr. Joyce enters in various ways as a specimen into the critical scheme I am outlining. What I have to say will not aim at estimating his general contribution to contemporary letters. I prefer his writing to that of Miss Stein, that may as well be set down at once. It does not suffer from the obsessional afflatus that I

have noticed in the latter. It has more elasticity and freedom; it is much less psychological, it is more physical. His vices of style, as I understand it, are due rather to his unorganized susceptibility to influences, and especially from the quarter I have been discussing (Miss Stein has influenced him, for instance), than to a native shortcoming.

I cannot see that any work of Joyce–except *Ulysses*–is very significant. It was about six or seven years ago that I first became acquainted with his writing. The *Portrait of the Artist* seemed to me a rather cold and priggish book. It was well done, like the *Dubliners*, which I have just read; and that was all, that I could discover. *Chamber Music* would certainly not have secured its author a place 'among the english poets,'–it would hardly even have set the Liffey on fire for five minutes. No writing of his before *Ulysses* would have given him anything but an honourable position as the inevitable naturalist-french-influenced member of the romantic Irish Revival–a Maupassant of Dublin, but without the sinister force of Flaubert's disciple.

Ulysses was in a sense a different thing altogether. How far that is an effect of a merely technical order, resulting from stylistic complications and intensified display, with a *Dubliners* basis unchanged, or, further, a

Wyndham Lewis, circa 1912

question of scale, and mechanical heaping up of detail, I should have only partly to decide here. But it places him—on that point every one is in agreement– very high in contemporary letters.

Its evident importance, its success, induced people to go outside the contemporary field for their analogies; and, to start with, it may be as well to remove from our path a few of the unnecessary names at that time, in the first generous flush of praise, injudiciously imported. Ireland, of course, furnished the most obvious comparisons.

So, to start with, Joyce is not a homologue of Swift. That is a strange mistake. There is very little of the specific power of that terrible personage, that *terribilità,* in the amiable author of *Ulysses.* Another writer with whom he has been compared, and whom he is peculiarly unlike, is Flaubert. But to mention all the authors with whom Joyce has been matched would take an appreciable time. So I will rather attempt to find his true affinities. The choice would lie, to my mind, somewhere between Robert Louis Stevenson and Laurence Sterne, if you imagine those writers transplanted into a heavily-freudianized milieu, and subjected to all the influences resulting in the rich, confused ferment of *Ulysses.*

Contact with any of his writing must, to begin with, show that we are not in the presence of a tragic writer, of the description of Dostoievsky or of Flaubert. He is genial and comic; a humorous writer of the traditional English School–in temper, at his best, very like Sterne. But he has the technical itch of the 'sedulous ape'–the figure under which Stevenson (with peculiar modesty, it is true) revealed himself to his readers. The impression produced by his earlier books, merely as writing, is very like that of a page of Stevenson–not of Stevenson 'apeing' but of the finished, a little too finished, article.

Ulysses, on the technical side, is an immense exercise in style, an orgy of 'apeishness,' decidedly 'sedulous.' It is an encyclopaedia of english literary technique, as well as a general-knowledge paper. The schoolmaster in Joyce is in great evidence throughout its pages.

Next, as to his position among the celebrated group of Irishmen contemporary with himself, or his immediate predecessors, that is now fairly well defined. What has distinguished all the famous irish literary figures of recent years, whether Wilde, Shaw or Yeats, has been the possession of what we call 'personality.' This really amounts to a vein of picturesqueness, an instinct for the value of the *person* in the picture, which dominates them, externally at all events. And they have probably always been led into making a freer use of this than would a Frenchman, for instance, of the same cali-

bre, owing to the self-effacing, unassuming, over-plain habits of the english background, against which they have had to perform. Or it may have been that, as isolated adventures–when they had passed from Ireland and descended into Piccadilly Circus, thenceforth watched by an Empire on which the sun never sets– they were as a matter of course mere *persons,* as contrasted with the new alien *crowds* they were amongst. This florid personal aplomb is, however, now expected of the Irishman by his english audience–although, owing to the political separation of the two countries, probably those times of genial interplay are passed.

Mr. Joyce is by no means without the 'personal touch.' But in a sense he is not the 'personality' that Shaw or Yeats is, or that Wilde was. But that is in conformity with his rôle, which is a very different one from theirs. Joyce is the poet of the shabby-genteel, impoverished intellectualism of Dublin. His world is the small middle-class one, decorated with a little futile 'culture,' of the supper and dance-party in *The Dead.* Wilde, more brilliantly situated, was an extremely metropolitan personage, a man of the great social world, a great lion of the London drawing-room. Joyce is steeped in the sadness and the shabbiness of the pathetic gentility of the upper shopkeeping class, slumbering at the bottom of a neglected province; never far, in its snobbishly circumscribed despair, from the pawn-shop and the 'pub.'

Shaw, again, escaped early from his provincial surroundings. Joyce resembles him in some striking particulars; but the more recent figure, this quiet, very positive, self-collected irish schoolmaster, with that well-known air of genteel decorum and *bienséance* of the irish middle-class, with his 'if you pleases' and 'no thank-yous,' his ceremonious Mister-this and Mister-that, is remote from what must have been the strapping, dashing George Bernard Shaw of the shavian heyday. He is also quite unlike the romantic, aristocratical, magic-loving William Butler Yeats.

Shaw is much more a world-figure; but Joyce and Yeats are the prose and poetry respectively of the Ireland that culminated in the Rebellion. Yeats is the chivalrous embodiment of 'celtic' romance, more of St. Brandon than of Ossian, with all the grant manners of a spiritual Past that cannot be obliterated, though it wear thin, and of a dispossessed and persecuted people. Joyce is the cold and stagnant reality at which that people had at last arrived in its civilized Reservation, with all the snobbish pathos of such a condition, the intense desire to keep-up-appearances at all costs, to be ladylike and gentlemanly, in spite of a beggared position–above which that yeatsian emanation floats.

But on the purely personal side, Joyce possesses a good deal of the intolerant arrogance of the dominie, veiled with an elaborate decency beneath the formal calm of the jesuit, left over as a handy property from his early years of catholic romance–of that irish variety that is so english that it seems stranger to a continental almost than its english protestant counterpart.

The Ireland that culminated in the Rebellion reached that event, however, in a very divided state. There was an artificial, pseudo-historical air about the Rebellion, as there was inevitably about the movement of 'celtic' revival; it seemed to be forced and vamped up long after its poignant occasion had passed. As elsewhere in Europe, the fanatical 'nationalist' consciousness invoked, seemed belated and unreal. Joyce was, I understand, against Sinn Fein. In his autobiographical books you obtain an unambiguous expression of his attitude in the matter. In the *Portrait of the Artist,* where the nationalist, Davin, is talking to him, Stephen (the author, of whom that is a self-portrait as a young man) says:–

'My ancestors threw off their language and took another. They allowed a handful of foreigners to subject them. Do you fancy I am going to pay in my own life and person debts they made? What for?'

'For our freedom,' said Davin.

'No honourable and sincere man,' said Stephen, 'has given up to you his life and his affections from the days of Tone to those of Parnell but you sold him to the enemy or failed him in need or reviled him and left him for another. And you invite me to be one of you. I'd see you damned first.'

A little later Stephen remarks: 'You talk to me of nationality, language, religion. I shall try to fly by those nets.' So from the start the answer of Joyce to the militant nationalist was plain enough. And he showed himself in that a very shrewd realist indeed, beset as Irishmen have been for so long with every romantic temptation, always being invited by this interested party or that, to jump back into 'history.' So Joyce is neither of the militant 'patriot' type, nor yet a historical romancer. In spite of that he is very 'irish.' He is ready enough, as a literary artist, to stand for Ireland, and has wrapped himself up in a gigantic cocoon of local colour in *Ulysses.*

It is at this point that we reach one of the fundamental questions of value brought out by his work. Although entertaining the most studied contempt for his compatriots–individually and in the mass–whom he did not regard at all as exceptionally brilliant and sympathetic creatures (in a green historical costume, with a fairy hovering near), but as average human cattle with an irish accent instead of a scotch or welsh, it will yet be insisted on that his irishness is an important feature of his talent; and he certainly also does exploit his irishness and theirs.

The appreciation of any author is, of course, largely composed of adventitious sentiment. For his vogue to last, or ever to be a serious one, he must have some unusual literary gift. With that he reaches a considerable renown. But then people proceed to admire him for something equally possessed by a quantity of other people, or for reasons that have nothing to do with, or which even contradict, his gifts. So Englishmen or Frenchmen who are inclined to virulent 'nationalism,' and disposed to sentiment where local colour is concerned, will admire Joyce for his alleged identity with what he detached himself from and even repudiated, when it took the militant, Sinn Fein form. And Joyce, like a shrewd sensible man, will no doubt encourage them. That, however, will not at all help us to be clear about this very confused issue. Nor should we be very certain, if we left the matter in that state, in our valuation of Joyce. We should find ourselves substituting orthodox political reactions to the idea of fanatical 'nationalism' (which it is quite evident holds little reality for Joyce) for direct reactions to what is in his work a considerable achievement of art.

2. Here, then, we reach one of the most obvious critical traps, and at the same time one of the main things requiring a decisive reply, in his work. What makes the question of capital importance is the problem set throughout the world to-day by the contradiction involved in (1) a universal promotion of 'nationalism,' which seems to take, even in great cosmopolitan states, an ever more intolerant form, and (2) the disappearance of national characteristics altogether as a consequence of technical progress.

Everywhere the peoples become more and more alike. Local colours, which have endured in many places for two thousand years, fade so quickly that already one uniform grey tint has supervened. The astonishing advances in applied science and in industrial technique made this inevitable. Simultaneously, and in frenzied contradiction, is the artificially fostered nationalism rampant throughout the world since the War. So while *in reality* people become increasingly one nation (for the fact that they are fanatically 'nationalist' does not prevent them from approximating more and more closely to the neighbours against whom, in their abstract rage, they turn), they *ideologically* grow more aggressively separatist, and conscious of 'nationality.'

The same process, of course, may be observed in 'class-war.' A Restoration courtier was very unlike the Restoration workman, as men go; whereas the contemporary magnate, in appearance, culture, manners and general tastes, is hardly to be distinguished from the average workman on his estate or in his factory. But the more social distinctions of a real order disappear, the more artificial 'class-consciousness' asserts itself.

That sort of contradiction is paralleled throughout our life. There is no department that is exempt from the confusions of this strategy–which consists essentially in removing something necessary to life and putting an ideologic simulacrum where it was able to deceive the poor animal, who notices it in its usual place and feels that all is well, but which yet perplexes and does not satisfy him. The 'sex-war' illustrates this as plainly as the 'class-war.' For example, the Y.M.C.A. meeting at Helsingfors (November 1926) starts a discussion on that stock subject with all religious bodies–the naughty thrill of which never diminishes–the 'modern woman.' So 'short hair and short skirts were attacked,' the *New York Herald* reports. But the objectors were overruled, it being decided, in the end, that 'women are asserting their right to develop personality unhampered,' by these means.

Leaving aside the comedy implicit in the mischievous journalese of the statement (namely, the highly-specialized nature of the 'personality' to be 'developed' by those methods), we can state the facts at stake in this way: according to the laws of specialization, the more a woman complicates her attire, the more she 'develops her personality.' The nude is a platonic abstraction. A thousand naked women on a beach, such as Borrow once saw, in Spain, would be a thousand abstractions, or one great palpitating abstraction, compared with the same number dressed in a 'personal' way, and so more and more differentiated from each other. 'Personality,' therefore, is clearly the wrong word. Its sentimental use falsifies what is happening.

But it is the *abstraction,* of course, that is required, to-day, of every human being. To 'develop the personality' is an alluring invitation, but it invariably covers some process that is guaranteed to strip a person bare of all 'personality' in a fortnight. This does not seem to me necessarily a bad thing. I am only pointing out that this excellent result is obtained by fraud. So we must not take that fraud too seriously, however much we may applaud its aims.

But in the general arrangements made for our sex-life, there is this little contradiction also to be noted–that the otherwise popular notion of specialization of function (the key to the syndicalist doctrine) is taboo. The rationale of that taboo is that it is desired to turn people's minds away from sex altogether eventually. They are insidiously urged in a neuter direction. William Blake foresaw that development, with his prophet's eye, with a laudable equanimity. The anaesthetizing of the cruder desires and ambitions by closer disciplines is, after all, the only alternative to a rationalizing of impulses not excised. However that may be,

'sex' is in the same category as that of the family; it can hardly survive as it is. The family costs too much; and 'sex' is a very costly luxury, too. Its expensive ecstasies and personal adornments must go in the end. The supposed encouragement of them to-day is illusory.

The savage with only a loin-cloth is notoriously chaste, and even prudish, strange as at first that sounds. From every quarter of the world evidence of this is forthcoming. Havelock Ellis has collected its evidence in a pamphlet, with *Modesty among primitive people,* or some such title. The more clothes people have, and the colder the climate, the more 'immoral' they become; that is now generally established, but not widely enough known to have an enlightening effect where what we are discussing is concerned: so attracted by the lure of the 'immoral,' everybody in the end will be induced to become more moral, simply-clothed, well-behaved and inexpensive.

So you obtain, up to date, in our feminized world, the following result: every woman is conscious of being a very daring and novel being, and 'sex,' and even sexishness, it is universally believed, is more prominent than ever before, because of the 'short skirts,' etc., discussed so acrimoniously at the Y.M.C.A meeting, and which are thundered at by a thousand idiots to empty pews throughout the puritan world; and even the Pope chases 'short skirts' from St. Peter's. Few people have yet perceived that not only is the present fashion in its effect more chaste (that a 'comrade' or 'chum' is hardly as intense a thing on principle as a 'lover,' to arrive at it by way of popular catchwords), but that the *intention* behind the fiats of fashion, leading to 'short skirts,' etc., is hardly to debauch the world. It is much rather intended to uniform and discipline it, to teach it to be neat and handy, *to induce it to dispense with that costly luxury, 'personality,' instead of to 'develop' it, as it pretends;* to train people to be satisfied to be just like their neighbours, hat for hat, and button for button, and finally to be *active,* so that they can *work.* Skirts are short for work, not love. That is the principle to grasp beneath all the concentrated flattery directed upon the revolutionary amazon leading her sex to victory in a glorious 'war' or social revolution. So the fashion is much more sensible than it affects to be, but also much less romantic.

This long excursion into the province of sex-politics has been justified, I think, by the light it throws upon the other questions belonging to the main stream of our present argument. I will now return to the contradiction subsisting between doctrinaire 'nationalism,' and the conditions of international uniformity created by scientific advance.

The adventitious stimulus given to the historic sense, the imposition of this little picturesque flourish or that, a patina like that manufactured for the faking of 'antiques' (a good example is the 'roman' veneer in fascist Italy), goes hand in hand and side by side with a world-hegemony, externally uniform and producing more every day a common culture.

It is headlong into this sheer delusion, which makes a nonsense of our continued civilized advance (unless you repudiate the idea of *advance,* and substitute that of mere fashionable *change*), that we are running, every time that we essay to found our view of things upon some harmonious and precise picture. We fall immediately into that trap of an abstraction coloured to look concrete, and placed where once there was something but where now there is nothing.

The romantic persons who go picking about in the Arran Islands, Shetlands, the Basque Provinces, or elsewhere, for genuine human 'antiques,' are to-day on a wild-goose chase; because the sphinx of the Past, in the person of some elder dug out of such remote neighbourhoods, will at length, when he has found his tongue, probably commence addressing them in the vernacular of the *Daily Mail.* For better or for worse, local colour is now a thin mixture; it does not inhere in what it embellishes, but is painted on, often with a clumsy insolence. It suits the political intelligence with its immemorial device, *divide et impera,* to encourage it, but its application to the conditions of mind and to the external nature of the machine-age becomes more and more fantastic.

There is nothing for it to-day, if you have an appetite for the beautiful, but *to create new beauty.* You can no longer nourish yourself upon the Past; its stock is exhausted, the Past is nowhere a reality. The only place where it is a reality is in *time,* not certainly in space. So the mental world of time offers a solution. More and more it is used as a compensating principle.

From this devastating alternative–the creation of new beauty–most people shrink in horror. 'Create!' they exclaim. 'As though it were not already difficult enough to live'!–But it is questionable if even bare life is possible, denuded of all meaning. And the meaning put into it by millennial politics of the current type is as unsubstantial as a mist on a Never-Never landscape.

How these remarks apply to what we are discussing will be obscured for some readers at first by the fact of the challenging novelty of the work in question. But the local colour, or locally-coloured material, that was scraped together into a big variegated heap to make *Ulysses,* is–doctrinally even more than in fact–the material of the past. It is consciously the decay of a mournful province, with in addition the label of a twenty-year-old vintage, of a 'lost time,' to recommend it. The diffraction of this lump of local colour for the purposes of analysis will in the end isolate the time-quality, revealing the main motive of its collection.

3. Before turning to the more personal factors in the composition of *Ulysses,* I will briefly state what I have been approaching in the first phase of my analysis.

I regard *Ulysses* as a *time-book;* and by that I mean that it lays its emphasis upon, for choice manipulates, and in a doctrinaire manner, the self-conscious time-sense, that has now been erected into a universal philosophy. This it does beneath the spell of a similar creative impulse to that by which Proust worked. The classical unities of time and place are buried beneath its scale, however, and in this All-life-in-a-day scheme there is small place for them. Yet at the outset they are solemnly insisted on as a guiding principle to be fanatically observed. And certainly some barbarous version of the classical formula is at work throughout, like a conserted *daimon* attending the author, to keep him obsessionally faithful to the time-place, or space-time, programme.

The genteel-demotic, native subject-matter of Mr. Joyce assists him to a great deal of intense, sad, insipid, local colour. An early life-experience that had removed him from the small middle-class milieu would also have removed him from his local colour, and to a less extent from his time-factor. To this he adds the legendary clatter and bustle of Donnybrook Fair. Beyond that he is not above stealing a few fairies from Mr. Yeats, and then sending them in the company of Dr. Freud to ride a broomstick on the Brocken. Adventures of that order, in the middle of the book, take us still further from the ideal of the Unities, and both Space and Time temporarily evaporate. But on the whole the reader is conscious that he is beneath the intensive dictatorship of Space-time–the god of Professor Alexander and such a great number of people, in fact, that we can almost be said to be treading on holy ground when we compose ourselves to read a work dedicated to that deity, either in philosophy or fiction.

That Joyce and Proust are both dedicated to Time is generally appreciated, of course; Joyce is often compared to Proust on that score. Both Proust and Joyce exhibit, it is said, the exasperated time-sense of the contemporary man of the industrial age; which is undeniable, if the outward form of their respective work is alone considered. The ardent recapitulation of a dead thing–though so recently dead, and not on its own merits a very significant one–and as much the 'local colour' as what may be called the *local time,* ally them. But having got so far, I should put in a qualification which would, I think, unexpectedly discriminate these two methods.

4. I will interject at this point a note on the subject of the temporal equivalent of 'local colour,' since I have had occasion to refer to it once or twice. I will not enter into the confusing discussion of which is space and which time in any given complex. I will suppose that there is some partly discrete quality which can come under the separate head of 'time', and so for certain purposes be something else than the 'local colour.'

This psychological time, or duration, this mood that is as fixed as the matter accompanying it, is as romantic and picturesque as is 'local colour,' and usually as shallow a thing as that. Some realization of this is essential. *We can posit a time-district, as it were, just as much as we can a place with its individual physical properties.* And neither the local colour, nor the local time of the *time-district,* is what is recorded *sub specie aeternitatis,* it is unnecessary to say.

Both may, however, become obsessions, and are so, I believe, to-day. But that is merely–that is my argument–because people are in process of being locked into both places *and* times. (This can be illustrated, where place is concerned, in the way that Signor Mussolini is locking the Italians into Italy, and refusing them passports for abroad.)

We are now sufficiently prepared and can educe the heart of this obscure organism that so overshadows contemporary thought, by showing its analogies. That the time-fanaticism is in some way connected with the nationalisms and the regionalisms which are politically so much in evidence, and so intensively cultivated, seems certain–since 'time' is also to some extent a region, or it can be regarded in that light. We have spoken of a *time-district,* and that is exact. Professor Whitehead uses the significant phrase 'mental climate.' This is by no means a fanciful affiliation; for *time* and *place* are the closest neighbours, and what happens to one is likely to be shared by the other. And if that is so, the *time-mind* would be much the same as the geographic one, fanatically circumscribing this or that territorial unit with a superstitious exclusiveness, an aggressive nationalist romance. Has not time-romance, or a fierce partisanship on behalf of a *time,* a family likeness, at least, with similar partisanship on behalf of a *place?*

And then, too, the so much mocked and detested non-nationalist, universal mind (whose politics would be goëthean, we can say, to place them, and whose highest tolerance would approximate to that best seen in the classical chinese intelligence) would have to be reckoned with–once the *time-mind* had been isolated by a thorough analysis, and its essential antagonisms exposed. These two types of mind would be found confronted, eternally hostile to each other, or at least eternally different–for the hostility would be more noticeable on the side of the partisan, the 'time' mind, than on the side of the other. This is all that I shall say on this very interesting point, for the moment.

The philosophy of the space-timeist is identical with the old, and as many people had hoped, exploded, bergsonian philosophy of *psychological time* (or *durée,* as he called it). It is essential to grasp this continuity between the earlier flux of Bergson, with its Time-god, and the einsteinian flux, with its god, Space-time. Alexander, and his pupil Whitehead, are the best-known exponents, of philosophers writing in English, of these doctrines. It will not require a very close scrutiny of *Space Time and Deity,* for instance, and then of some characteristic book of Bergson's, to assure yourself that you are dealing with minds of the same stamp.

Temperamentally–emotionally, that is, and emotion is as important in philosophy as in other things–the earlier bergsonian, such as Péguy, for instance, and the relativist or space-timeist, are identical. The best testimony of this is the enthusiastic reception given by Bergson, the old time-philosopher, to Einstein, the later space-timeist. He recognized his god, Duration, cast into the imposing material of a physical theory, improved and amalgamated with Space, in a more insidious unity that he had been able to give to his paramount philosophic principle. Similarly the attitude of Whitehead, Alexander and so forth, where Bergson is concerned, is noticeably one of a considered respect, very different from the atmosphere of disrepute into which Bergson had fallen prior to the triumph of Relativity Theory. The so-called "Emergent' principle of Lloyd Morgan, adopted by Alexander and the rest, is our old friend 'Creative Evolution,' under another name, and with a few additional attributes. "Emergent Evolution' can for all practical purposes be regarded as synonymous with 'Creative Evolution.'

So from, say, the birth of Bergson to the present day, one vast orthodoxy has been in process of maturing in the world of science and philosophy. The material had already collected into a considerable patrimony by the time Bergson was ready to give it a philosophic form. The Darwinian Theory and all the background of nineteenth-century materialistic thought was already behind it. Under the characteristic headings Duration and Relativity the nineteenth-century mechanistic belief has now assumed a final form. It is there for any one to study at his leisure, and to take or leave. It will assume, from time to time, many new shapes, but it will certainly not change its essential nature again till its doomsday; for I believe that in it we have reached one of the poles of the human intelligence, the negative, as it were. So it is deeply rooted, very ancient, and quite defined.

In this part of my essay I am not developing my purely philosophic argument more fully than is necessary for the purposes of the literary criticism. I leave my attitude in the 'time' discussion as an announcement of principle, merely. Students of the philosophies cited will be able at once to supply the outline of the position such an announcement involves. And the reader who is not conversant with those theories would not be much the wiser at the end of such brief analysis as I should be able to supply in this place. The plan I am following is to help the reader to an inductive understanding of the principle involved, in the course of this analysis of its literary and artistic expression. With Spengler the more technical region is reached. And after that the philosophical analysis is begun. I hope to have interested the reader sufficiently in the questions involved to take him with me into that.

5. The psychological history of the triumph of an idea is interesting to follow; and it is necessary to acquire some knowledge of those processes. To understand how ideas succeed you must first consider what that 'success' implies, especially with reference to this particular age. You would have to ask yourself who those men are who profess them, the manner in which they get advertised, the degree of orthodoxy imposed, and by what means, at the moment. Then, behind that professional and immediate ring of supporters, the mass of people who blindly receive them on faith–as helpless, confronted with the imposing machinery of their popularization, as new-born children–they, too, would have to be studied, and their reactions registered.

Some such analysis of the domination achieved by an idea and how it ceases to be an idea, and becomes an *ideology,* as Napoleon called it, an instrument of popular government, has to be undertaken before you can hope to be in a position to meet on equal terms, without superstition, such prevalent intellectual fashions. If you are of that great majority who ask nothing better than to have intellectual fashions provided for them–with little handbooks describing which way up the idea (if a 'difficult' one) should be worn, whether it should be worn with a flourish or a languish, with a simper or a pout, with fanatical intensity or an easy catholic grace–then you will have no use, it is needless to say, for such an arduous analytical discipline. It is only if you belong to that minority who care for ideas for their own sake, if you are philosophic in the truest sense, possessing a personal life that is not satisfied with the old-clothes shop, or its companion, the vast ready-made emporium, that this procedure will have any meaning for you.

The physical or philosophical theory in the ascendant at any moment is humbly and reverently picked up, in an abridged, and usually meaningless, form, by the majority of people. So it was with Darwin, so it is with Einstein. Apart from questions of expert qualification, few people are able to appreciate all that is involved in such theories. There is certainly never a question in their mind of 'doubting' it. It is not a thing to doubt, but one that is either easy or impossible to understand, as the case may be. To repudiate it would be a still wilder presumption. It has be 'studied' in the few spare minutes that most people consider may be saved for such things from parties, golf, motoring and bridge, or the Russian Ballet. Then they will say in conversation, 'It appears that there is no such thing as time'; or 'Everything is relative, Einstein says. I always thought it was.' (Relativity seldom involves much more than that to people.) More often than not the professors, who adopt and expound whatever theory has just succeeded, examine it as little. It *amuses* them; professors, like other people, have their amusements–their work is theirs. It is uncomfortable to be unorthodox, life is short, science is long, much longer than art; that is sufficient.

When such a dominant theory is *applied* in literature or in art, then, certainly, even less does any one grasp the steps by which that theory has entered the mind of the author or artist; has either been welcomed at once as a friend and a brother, has taken up its abode there as a conqueror by main force, or else has seduced the sensitive little intelligence from the outside, from beneath the prudent casement from which the peeping-mind inside has watched, fascinated, the big romantic notion swelling invitingly; or has, on the other hand, as a matter of traffic and mutual profit, come to terms with a possible assistant or colleague. In short, any of the hundred ways and degrees in which assent is arrived at, and an intellectual monopoly or hegemony consummated, is even more arcane to the majority than is the theory itself.

Bergson and his time-philosophy exactly corresponds to Proust, the abstract for the other's concrete. There is so far no outstanding exponent in literature or art of einsteinian physics, for necessarily there is a certain interval, as things are, between the idea and the representation. But such a figure will no doubt occur; and further theorists of this great school will be accompanied by yet further artists, applying its philosophy to life. Or perhaps, since now the general outline of the cult is settled, and the changes within it will be incidental, largely, they may crop up simultaneously. Indeed, Proust and Joyce are examples to hand of how already it does not matter very much to what phase of the one great movement the interpreter belongs.

Without all the uniform pervasive growth of the time-philosophy starting from the little seed planted by

Bergson, discredited, and now spreading more vigorously than ever, there would be no *Ulysses,* or there would be no *A La Recherche du Temps Perdu.* There would be no 'time-composition' of Miss Stein; no fugues in words. In short, Mr. Joyce is very strictly of the school of Bergson-Einstein, Stein-Proust. He is of the great time-school they represent. His book is a *time book,* as I have said, in that sense. He has embraced the time-doctrine very completely. And it is as the critic of that doctrine and of that school that I have approached the analysis of his writings up to date. (I insert this last time-clause because there is no reason at all to suppose that he may not be influenced in turn by my criticism; and, indeed, I hope it may be so, for he would be a very valuable adherent.)

Yet that the time-sense is really exasperated in Joyce in the fashion that it is in Proust, Dada, Pound or Miss Stein, may be doubted. He has a very keen preoccupation with the Past, it is certain; he does lay things down side by side, carefully dated; and added to that, he has some rather loosely and romantically held notion of periodicity. But I believe that all these things amount to with him is this: as a careful, even meticulous, craftsman, with a long training of doctrinaire naturalism, the detail—the time-detail as much as anything else—assumes an exaggerated importance for him. And I am sure that he would be put to his trumps to say how he came by much of the time-machinery that he possesses. Until he was told, I dare say that he did not know he had it, even; for he is 'an instinctive,' like Pound, in that respect; there is not very much reflection going on at any time inside the head of Mr. James Joyce. That is indeed the characteristic condition of the *craftsman,* pure and simple.

And that is what Joyce is above all things, essentially the craftsman. It is a thing more common, perhaps, in painting or the plastic arts than in literature. I do not mean by this that he works harder or more thoroughly than other people, but that he is not so much an inventive intelligence as an executant. He is certainly very 'shoppy,' and professional to a fault, though in the midst of the amateurism of the day it is a fault that can easily be forgiven.

What stimulates him is *ways of doing things,* and technical processes, and not *things to be done.* Between the various things to be done he shows a true craftsman's impartiality. He is become so much a writing-specialist that it matters very little to him *what* he writes, or what idea or world-view he expresses, so long as he is trying his hand at this manner and that, and displaying his enjoyable virtuosity. Strictly speaking, he has none at all, no special point of view, or none worth mentioning. It is such people that the creative intelligence fecundates and uses; and at present that intelligence is

political, and its stimuli are masked ideologies. He is only a tool, an instrument, in short. That is why such a sensitive medium as Joyce, working in such a period, requires the attention of the independent critic.

So perhaps it is easy to see how, without much realizing what was happening, Joyce arrived where he did. We can regard it as a diathetic phenomenon partly—the craftsman is susceptible and unprotected. There are even slight, though not very grave, symptoms of disorder in his art. The painful preoccupation with the *exact* place of things in a room, for instance, could be mildly matched in his writing. The *things themselves* by which he is surrounded lose, for the hysterical subject, their importance, or even meaning. Their *position* absorbs all the attention of his mind. Some such uneasy pedantry, in a mild form, is likely to assail any conscientious craftsman—especially in an intensive 'space-time' atmosphere, surrounded by fanatical space-timeists. The poor craftsman has never been in such peril as to-day, for it is a frantic hornpipe indeed that his obedient legs are compelled to execute. But otherwise Joyce, with his highly-developed *physical* basis, is essentially sane.

The method that underlies *Ulysses* is known as the 'telling from the inside.' As that description denotes, it is psychological. Carried out in the particular manner used in *Ulysses,* it lands the reader inside an Aladdin's cave of incredible bric-à-brac in which a dense mass of dead stuff is collected, from 1901 toothpaste, a bar or two of Sweet Rosie O'Grady, to pre-nordic architecture. An immense *nature-morte is the result.* This ensues from the method of confining the reader in a circumscribed psychological space into which several encyclopaedias have been emptied. It results from the constipation induced in the movement of the narrative.

The amount of *stuff*—unorganized brute material—that the more active principle of drama has to wade through, under the circumstances, slows it down to the pace at which, inevitably, the sluggish tide of the author's bric-à-brac passes the observer, at the saluting post, or in this case, the reader. It is a suffocating, mœotic expanse of objects, all of them lifeless, the sewage of a Past twenty years old, all neatly arranged in a meticulous sequence. The newspaper in which Mr. Bloom's bloater is wrapped up, say, must press on to the cold body of the fish, reversed, the account of the bicycle accident that was reported on the fated day chosen for this Odyssey; or that at least is the idea.

At the end of a long reading of *Ulysses* you feel that it is the very nightmare of the naturalistic method that you have been experiencing. Much as you may cherish the merely physical enthusiasm that expresses itself in this stupendous outpouring of *matter,* or *stuff,* you wish, on the spot, to be transported to some more

F. Scott Fitzgerald's cartoon that he drew in Sylvia Beach's copy of The Great Gatsby: *(left to right) Adrienne Monnier, Lucie Chamson, Andre Chamson, Zelda Fitzgerald, F. Scott Fitzgerald, James Joyce, and Sylvia Beach. Beach had invited Fitzgerald to the dinner party so that he could meet Joyce (Sylvia Beach Collection, Princeton University Library).*

abstract region for a time, where the dates of the various toothpastes, the brewery and laundry receipts, the growing pile of punched 'bus-tickets, the growing holes in the baby's socks and the darn that repairs them, assume less importance. It is your impulse perhaps quickly to get your mind where there is nothing but air and rock, however inhospitable and featureless, and a little timeless, too. You will have had a glut, for the moment (if you have really persevered), of *matter,* procured you by the turning on of all this river of what now is rubbish, but which was not *then,* by the obsessional application of the naturalistic method associated with the exacerbated time-sense. And the fact that you were not in the open air, but closed up inside somebody else's head, will not make things any better. It will have been your catharsis of the objective accumulations that obstinately collect in even the most active mind.

Now in the graphic and plastic arts that stage of fanatic naturalism long ago has been passed. All the machinery appropriate to its production has long since been discarded, luckily for the pure creative impulse of the artist. The nineteenth-century naturalism of that obsessional, fanatical order is what you find on the one hand in *Ulysses.* On the other, you have a great variety of recent influences enabling Mr. Joyce to use it in the way that he did.

The effect of this rather fortunate confusion was highly stimulating to Joyce, who really got the maximum out of it, with an appetite that certainly will never be matched again for the actual *matter* revealed in his composition, or proved to have been lengthily secreted there. It is like a gigantic victorian quilt or antimacassar. Or it is the voluminous curtain that fell, belated (with the alarming momentum of a ton or two of personally organized rubbish), upon the victorian scene. So rich was its delivery, its pent-up outpouring so vehement, that it will remain, eternally cathartic, a monument like a record diarrhœa. No one who looks *at* it will ever want to look *behind* it. It is the sardonic catafalque of the victorian world.

Two opposite things were required for this result. Mr. Joyce could never have performed this particular feat if he had not been, in his make-up, extremely immobile; and yet, in contradiction to that, very open to new technical influences. It is the *craftsman* in Joyce that is progressive; but the *man* has not moved since his early days in Dublin. He is on that side a 'young man' in some way embalmed. His technical adventures do not, apparently, stimulate him to think. On the contrary, what he thinks seems to be of a conventional and fixed order, as though perhaps not to embarrass the neighbouring evolution of his highly progressive and eclectic craftsmanship.

So he collected like a cistern in his youth the last stagnant pumpings of victorian anglo-irish life. This he held steadfastly intact for fifteen years or more–then when he was ripe, as it were, he discharged it, in a dense mass, to his eternal glory. That was *Ulysses.* Had the twenty-year-old Joyce of the *Dubliners* not remained almost miraculously intact, we should never have witnessed this peculiar spectacle.

That is, I believe, the true account of how this creative event occurred with Joyce; and, if that is so, it will be evident that we are in the presence of a very different phenomenon from Proust. Proust *returned* to the *temps perdu.* Joyce never left them. He discharged it as freshly as though the time he wrote about were still present, because it was *his* present. It rolled out with all the aplomb and vivacity of a contemporary experience, assisted in its slick discharge by the latest technical devices.

6. So though Joyce has written a time-book, he has done it, I believe, to some extent, by accident. Proust, on the contrary, was stimulated to all his efforts precisely by the thought of compassing a specifically time-creation–the *Recherche du Temps Perdu.* The unconscious artist has, in this case, the best of it, to my mind. Proust, on the other hand, romanticizes his Past, where Joyce (whose Present it is) does not.

To create new beauty, and to supply a new material, is the obvious affair of art of any kind to-day. But that is a statement that by itself would convey very little. Without stopping to unfold that now, I will summarize what I understand by its opposite. Its opposite is that that thrives upon the *time-philosophy* that it has invented for itself, or which has been imposed upon it or provided for it.

The inner meaning of the *time-philosophy,* from whatever standpoint you approach it, and however much you paste it over with confusing advertisements of 'life,' of 'organism,' is the doctrine of a mechanistic universe; periodic; timeless, or nothing but 'time,' whichever you prefer; and, above all, essentially *dead.* A certain *deadness,* a lack of nervous power, an aversion to anything suggesting animal vigour, characterizes all the art, as has already been pointed out, issuing from this philosophy. Or in the exact mixing in the space-timeist scheme of all the 'matter' and all the 'organism' together, you get to a sort of vegetable or vermiform *average.* It is very mechanical; and according to our human, aristocratic standards of highly-organized life, it is very dead.

The theoretic truth that the time-philosophy affirms is a mechanistic one. It is the conception of an aged intelligence, grown mechanical and living upon routine and memory, essentially; its tendency, in its characteristic working, is infallibly to transform the living into the machine, with a small, unascertained, but uninteresting margin of freedom. It is the fruit, of course, of the puritan mind, born in the nineteenth century upon the desolate principles promoted by the too-rapidly mechanized life of the European.

I will now turn to the scandalous element in *Ulysses,* its supposed obscenity. Actually it appears to me that the mind of Joyce is more chaste than most. Once you admit the license that, at the start, Joyce set out to profit by, it is surprising how very little 'sex' matter there is in his pages. What is there is largely either freudian echoes (they had to enter into it), or else it is horse-play of a schoolboy or public-house order. The motif of the house-drain is once and for all put in its place, and not mentioned again. It is the fault of the reader if that page or two dealing with it assume, in retrospect, proportions it has not, as a fact, in Joyce's pages. That passage can be regarded in the light of the reply of Antigonus to the poet Hermodorus, when the latter had described him as the son of the Sun.

I will next take up in turn a few further items of importance, expiscating them one by one. Joyce is not a moralist, but he has a great relish, on the other hand, for politics. Indeed, Lady Bolingbroke's remark about Pope, that he 'played the politician about cabbages and turnips' (or as somebody else remarked, 'he hardly drank tea without a stratagem'), could be applied to the author of *Ulysses*–the mere name suggests a romantic predilection for guile.

He could claim another affinity with Pope– namely, that although a witty writer, he is, as far as his private and personal legend is concerned, a man of one story. 'One apothegm only stands upon record,' Johnson writes of Pope; it was directed at Patrick. Joyce has one story to his credit, and it is at the expense of Yeats. As it is the general custom, even in the briefest account of Joyce, to tell this story, lest I should be regarded as imperfectly documented, I will give it here. When Joyce was about twenty years old he was very hard up, we are told, and he decided to go to Yeats and see if that gentleman would do anything to help him. He seems to have foreboded the result, and provided himself with a plan of action in the event of a rebuff. The appointed time arrived. As he entered the room, sure enough he read on the face of Mr. Yeats the determination *not* to help him. Thereupon he bore down on Yeats, bade him good morning, and immediately inquired how old he was. On learning the extent of Yeats' seniority, with a start of shocked surprise, he mournfully shook his head, exclaimed, 'I fear I have come too late! I can do nothing to help you!' and, turning on his heel, left the apartment, the tables neatly turned.

There is perhaps a sequel to that story, and, if so, it is to be sought in the fact that Joyce himself has shown recently the baselessness of its major implication. He has whitewashed, I think, in one important respect that 'scoundrel' that Mr. Shaw has affirmed 'every man over forty' to be, by displaying in his own person, to this day, an undiminished ability to be influenced by all sorts of people and things, from the jaunty epistolary style of Ezra Pound to the 'compositional' stammerings of Miss Stein. Actually the further he advances the more susceptible to new influences, of a technical order, he becomes. What gives *Ulysses* the appearance of a merging of analects is a record of this. He was rather unenterprising and stationary in his early years. The *Dubliners* is written in one style, *Ulysses* in a hundred or so.

7. There are several other things that have to be noted as characteristic of Joyce for a full understanding of a technique that has grown into a very complex, overcharged façade. The craftsman, pure and simple, is at the bottom of his work. I have already insisted upon that; and in that connection it almost appears, I have said, that he has practised sabotage where his intellect was concerned, in order to leave his craftsman's hand freer for its stylistic exercises. That is a phenomenon very commonly met with in the painter's craft. Daring or unusual speculation, or an unwonted intensity of outlook, is not good for technical display, that is certain, and they are seldom found together. The intellect is in one sense the rival of the hand, and is apt to hamper rather than assist it. It interferes, at all events, with its showing-off, and affords no encouragements to the hand's 'sedulous apeishness'; or so would say the hand.

The extreme conventionality of Joyce's mind and outlook is perhaps due to this. In *Ulysses,* if you strip away the technical complexities that envelop it, the surprises of style and unconventional attitudes that prevail in it, the figures underneath are of a remarkable simplicity, and of the most orthodoxly comic outline. Indeed, it is not too much to say that they are, most of them, walking clichés. So much is this the case, that your attention is inevitably drawn to the evident paradox that ensues; namely, that of an intelligence so alive to purely verbal clichés that it hunts them like fleas, with remarkable success, and yet that leaves the most gigantic ready-made and well-worn dummies enthroned everywhere, in the form of the actual personnel of the book.

A susceptibility to verbal clichés is, however, not at all the same thing as a susceptibility to such a cliché as is represented by a stage Jew (Bloom), a stage Irishman (Mulligan), or a stage Anglo-Saxon (Haines). Clichés of that description thrive in the soil of *Ulysses*. This paradox is an effect of the craftsman-mind which has been described above; that is my reading of the riddle. You could, if you wanted to, reverse the analytical process. The virtuosity would then be deduced from the fact of the resourceful presence of a highly critical intellect, but without much inventiveness, nor the gift of first-hand observation–thriving vicariously, in its critical exercises, upon the masters of the Past. That would be a description of what, in music, is a common phenomenon, namely, the interpretative artist, the supreme instrumentalist.

If you examine for a moment the figures presented to you in the opening of *Ulysses,* you will at once see what is meant by these remarks. The admirable writing will seduce you, perhaps, from attending too closely, at first, to the characterization. But what in fact you are given there, in the way of character, is the most conventional stuff in the world; and the dramatic situation for which they are provided is not even an original one, for it is the situation of *John Bull's Other Island,* picturesquely staged in a Martello-tower, with the author in the principal role.

Haines, the romantic Englishman, or 'Sassenach,' with the 'pale eyes like the ocean wave that he rules,' his extreme woodenness and deep sentimental, callous imbecility, his amateur-anthropologist note-gathering among the interesting irish natives; and in lively contrast to this dreary, finished 'Saxon' butt (who always says what is expected of him), the jolly, attractive, Wild Irishman (Mulligan), who sees through, makes rings round, the ideally slow and stupid 'creeping Saxon,' while yet remaining 'the servant' with 'the cracked looking-glass' of Stephan's epigram–that is all pure *John Bull's Other Island.* Haines is a stage-"Saxon," Mulligan is a stage-Irishman; that on one side and the other of the Irish Channel such figures could be found is certain enough; but they are the material of broad comedy; not that of a subtle or average reality at all. They are the conventional reality of one satisfied with the excessive, unusual and ready-made; and they are juxtaposed here on the time-honoured shavian model.

But if they are clichés, Stephan Dedalus is a worse or a far more glaring one. He is the really wooden figure. He is 'the poet' to an uncomfortable, a dismal, a ridiculous, even a pulverizing degree. His movements in the Martello-tower, his theatrical 'bitterness,' his cheerless, priggish stateliness, his gazings into the blue distance, his Irish Accent, his exquisite sensitiveness, his 'pride' that is so crude as to be almost indecent, the incredible slowness with which he gets about from place to place, up the stairs, down the stairs, like a funereal stage-king; the time required for him to move his neck, how he raises his hand, passes it over his aching eyes, or his damp brow, even more wearily drops it,

closes his dismal little shutters against his rollicking irish-type of a friend (in his capacity of a type-poet), and remains sententiously secluded, shut up in his own personal Martello- tower–a Martello-tower within a Martello-tower–until he consents to issue out, tempted by the opportunity of making a 'bitter'–a very 'bitter'–jest, to show up against the ideally idiotic background provided by Haines; all this has to be read to be believed–but read, of course, with a deaf ear to the really charming workmanship with which it is presented. *Written* on a level with its conception, and it would be as dull stuff as you could easily find.

The stage-directions with which the novelist in general pursues his craft are usually tell-tale, and *Ulysses* is no exception to that rule. The stage-directions for getting Stephan Dedalus, the irritating hero, about, sitting him down, giving accent to his voice, are all painfully enlightening.

This is how the hero of *Ulysses* first appears on page 2 of the book:–

> Stephan Dedalus stepped up, followed him (Mulligan) *wearily* halfway and sat down. . . .'

He does almost everything 'wearily.' He 'sits down' always before he has got far. He moves with such dignified and 'weary' slowness, that he never gets further than *half-way* under any circumstances as compared with any other less dignified, less 'weary,' figure in the book– that is to say, any of the many figures introduced to show off his dismal supremacy. This is where (page 2) Stephan Dedalus first speaks:–

> '. . . Tell me, Mulligan,' Stephan said quietly.

In this *quiet* 'Tell me, Mulligan'–(irish accent, please)–you have the soul of this small, pointless, oppressive character in its entirety. You wonder for some pages what can be the cause of this weighty inanition. There is perhaps some plausible reason for it, which will be revealed in the sequel. That would make things a little better. But nothing happens of that sort. You slowly find out what it is. *The hero is trying to be a gentleman!* That is the secret–nothing less, nothing more. The 'artist as a young man' has 'the real Oxford manner,' you are informed; and you eventually realize that his oppressive mannerisms have been due in the first instance to an attempt to produce the impression of an 'Oxford manner.'

Let us, starting from the top of page 3, take a few of the clichés having a bearing on the point under consideration:–

(1) Mulligan asks the hero for his handkerchief. 'Stephan *suffered* him to pull out' the handkerchief, etc.

The word *suffered* and the bathos of the gesture involved in the offering of the pocket, are characteristic.

(2) Buck Mulligan 'turned abruptly *his great searching* eyes from the sea,' etc. Great searching eyes! Oh, where were the great searching eyes of the author, from whom no verbal cliché may escape, when he wrote that?

(3) Mulligan to Stephan: 'He (Haines) thinks you're not a gentleman.' That is what Stephan Dedalus is pursued and obsessed by, the notion of 'being a gentleman'; that is the secret, as has already been said, of most of the tiresome mannerisms that oppress a reader of *Ulysses* wherever Dedalus appears. (Compare 'the Oxford manner,' etc., above.)

(4) ' "Then what is it?" Buck Mulligan asked impatiently. "Cough it up." Stephan freed his arm quietly' (page 7). Stephan does everything 'quietly,' whether he 'quietly' touches Mulligan on the arm or 'quietly' frees his own. He is a very quiet man indeed.

(5) On page 19 Mulligan has chanted a popular theological ditty. Haines says to Stephan: 'We oughtn't to laugh, I suppose. He's rather blasphemous. I'm not a believer myself, that is to say. Still his gaiety takes the harm out of it, somehow, doesn't it? What did he call it? Joseph the Joiner?'

This is a good example of the Saxon (*John Bull's Other Island* model) talking. Provided with a such a foil, Stephan goes on replying 'dryly,' 'quietly,' or with 'pained' superiority, to the end of the chapter. Such is your introduction in *Ulysses* to some of the principal characters.

It is unnecessary to quote any further; the reader by referring to the opening of *Ulysses,* can provide himself with as much more as he requires; these few extracts will enable anybody to get a more concrete idea of what is under discussion. It would be difficult, I think, to find a more lifeless, irritating, principal figure than the deplorable hero of the *Portrait of the Artist* and of *Ulysses.*

The method of the growth of these books may be partly responsible for it, the imperfect assimilation of the matter of fact naturalism of the *Dubliners* to the more complex *Ulysses.* But the fact remains that in the centre of the picture, this mean and ridiculous figure remains–attitudinizing, drooping, stalking slowly, 'quietly' and 'bitterly' from spot to spot, mouthing a little Latin, 'bitterly' scoring off a regiment of conventional supers.

All you have got to do is to compare the frigid prig–hoping that his detestable affectations will be mistaken for 'an Oxford manner,' trusting that the 'quiet' distinction of his deportment will reassure strangers on the burning question of whether he is a *gentleman* or not–with one of the principal heroes of the russian novels, and a spiritual gulf of some sort will become apparent between the ardent, simple and in some cases truly heroical figures on the one side, and the drooping, simpering, leering, 'bitter' and misunderstood, spoilt-child conscious of its meanness and lack of energy, on the other, on that of Joyce.

The russian scene, which stood as a background for the great group of nineteenth-century russian writers, was mediaeval, it is true, and cast on more elemental lines than anything that has existed in the West since the days of Elizabeth. But the author of the *Dubliners* was alimenting himself from the French as much as were the last of the Russians, and Dublin as much as Moscow would be for a french contemporary of Flaubert a savage place. Historically the work of Joyce will probably be classed with books dealing with that last burst of heroical, pre-communist, european life.

What induced Joyce to place in the centre of his very large canvas this grotesque figure, Stephan Dedalus? Or having done so, to make it worse by contrasting it the whole time (as typifying 'the ideal') with the gross 'materialism' of the Jew, Bloom? Again, the answer to that, I believe, is that things *grew* in that way, quite outside of Joyce's control; and it is an effect, merely, of a confusion of method.

Joyce is fundamentally autobiographical, it must be recalled; not in the way that most writers to some extent are, but scrupulously and naturalistically so. Or at least that is how he started. The *Portrait of the Artist as a Young Man* was supposed to give you a neat, carefully-drawn picture of Joyce from babyhood upwards, in the result like an enlarged figure from the *Dubliners.* You get an accurate enough account, thereupon, of a physically-feeble, timid, pompous, ill-tempered, very conceited little boy. It is interesting, honest, even sometimes to naïveté–though not often that; but it is not promising material for anything but the small, neat naturalism of *Dubliners.* It seems as unlikely, in short, that this little fellow will grow into the protagonist of a battle between the mighty principles of Spirit and Matter, Good and Evil, or White and Black, as that the author of the little, neat, reasonable, unadventurous *Dubliners* would one day become the author of the big blustering *Ulysses.*

The effort to show Stephan Dedalus in a favourable, heightened light throughout, destroys the naturalism, and at the same time certainly fails to achieve the heroic. Yet the temper of *Ulysses* is to some extent an heroical one. So you are left with a neat little naturalist 'hero,' of the sort that swarms humorously in Chekov, tiptoeing to play his part in the fluid canvas of an ambitious *Ulysses,* unexpectedly expanding beneath his feet; urged by his author to rise to the occasion and live up to the rôle of the incarnation of the immaterial, and so be top-dog to Poldy Bloom. As it is, of course, the author, thinly disguised as a middle-aged Jew tout (Mr.

Leopold Bloom), wins the reader's sympathy every time he appears; and he never is confronted with the less and less satisfactory Dedalus (in the beau rôle) without the latter losing trick after trick to his disreputable rival; and so, to the dismay of the conscientious reader, betraying the principles he represents. It is a sad affair, altogether, on that side.

Turning to Mr. Bloom, we find an unsatisfactory figure, too, but of an opposite sort and in a very different degree. He possesses all the recognized theatrical properties of 'the Jew' up-to-date–he is more feminine than *la femme,* shares her couvade, the periodicity of her intimate existence is repeated mildly in his own; he counts the beer bottles stacked in a yard he is passing, computing with glee the profit to be extracted from that commerce; but such a Jew a Bloom, taken altogether, has never been seen outside the pages of Mr. Joyce's book. And he is not even a Jew most of the time, but his talented irish author.

In reality there is no Mr. Bloom at all, of course, except at certain moments. Usually the author, carelessly disguised beneath what other people have observed about Jews, or yet other people have believed that they have seen, is alone performing before us. There is no sign throughout the book that he has ever directly and intelligently observed any *individual* Jew. He has merely out of books and conversations collected facts, witticisms and generalizations about Jews, and wrapped up his own kindly person with these, till he has bloated himself into a thousand pages of heterogeneous, peculiarly unjewish, matter. So he has certainly contributed nothing to the literature of the Jew, for which task he is in any case quite unsuited.

This inability to observe directly, a habit of always looking at people through other people's eyes and not through his own, is deeply rooted with Joyce. Where a multitude of little details or some obvious idiosyncrasy are concerned, he may be said to be observant; but the secret of an *entire* organism escapes him. Not being observant where entire people (that is, people at all) are concerned, he depicts them conventionally always, under some general label. For it is in the fragmentation of a personality–by isolating some characteristic weakness, mood, or time-self–that you arrive at the mechanical and abstract, the opposite of the living. This, however, leaves him free to achieve with a mass of detail a superficial appearance of life; and also to exercise his imitative talents without check where the technical problem is concerned.

8. In the above account of the value of the figures to which the opening of *Ulysses* introduces us, I have given the direct impression received upon a fresh reading of it for the purposes of this essay. Had I undertaken to write a general criticism of the work of Joyce I should not have passed on this impression uncensored–in its native sensational strength–but have modified it, by associating it with other impressions more favourable to the author. As it is, however, it is my object to obtain the necessary salience for an aspect of Joyce's mind that is of capital importance to what I have to say on the subject of the time-mind, as I have called it.

The radical conventionality of outlook implied throughout *Ulysses,* and exhibited in the treatment of the characters, isolated from their technical wrapping, has the following bearing upon what I have said elsewhere. This conventionality (which leaves, as it were, lay-figures underneath, upon which the technical trappings can be accumulated at leisure with complete disregard for the laws of life) is the sign that we are in the presence of a craftsman rather than a creator. That sort of effect is invariably the sign of simple craftsman–an absence of meaning, an emptiness of philosophic content, a poverty of new and disturbing observation. The school of *nature-morte* painters in Paris, who made a fetish of Cezanne's apples; and indeed the *deadness* that has crept into all painting (so that whether it is people or things that are depicted, they all equally have the appearance of dead things or of dolls), is the phenomenon to which this other conventional deadness must be assimilated.

In *Ulysses* you have a deliberate display, on the grand scale, of technical virtuosity and literary scholarship. What is underneath this overcharged surface, few people, so far, have seriously inquired. In reality it is rather an apologuical than a real landscape; and the two main characters, Bloom and Dedalus, are lay-figures (the latter a sadly ill-chosen one) on which such a mass of dead stuff is hung, that if ever they had any organic life of their own, it would speedily have been overwhelmed in this torrent of matter, of *nature-morte.*

This torrent of matter is the einsteinian flux. Or (equally well) it is the duration-flux of Bergson–that is its philosophic character, at all events. (How the specifically 'organic' and mental doctrine of the time-philosophy can result in a mechanism that is more mechanical than any other, I shall be considering later.) The method of doctrinaire naturalism, interpreted in that way, results in such a flux as you have in *Ulysses,* fatally. And into that flux it is you, the reader, that are plunged, or magnetically drawn by the attraction of so much matter as is represented by its thousand pages. That is also the strategy implied by its scale.

But the author, of course, plunges with you. He takes you inside his head, or, as it were, into a roomy diving-suit, and, once down in the middle of the stream, you remain the author, naturally, inside whose head you are, though you are sometimes supposed to be aware of one person, sometimes of another. Most of the time you are being Bloom or Dedalus, from the inside, and that is Joyce. Some figures for a moment bump against you, and you certainly perceive them with great distinctness–or rather some fragment of their dress or some mannerism; then they are gone. But, generally speaking, it is *you* who descend into the flux of *Ulysses*, and it is the author who absorbs you momentarily into himself for that experience. That is all that the 'telling from the inside' amounts to. All the rest is literature, and dogma; or the dogma of time-literature.

I say, 'naturalism interpreted in this way' has that result, because there are so many varieties of naturalism. Some scientific naturalism does deal with things from the outside, indeed, and so achieves a very different effect–one of hardness, not of softness. But the method of *Ulysses* imposes a softness, flabbiness and vagueness everywhere in its bergsonian fluidity. It was in the company of that old magician, Sigmund Freud, that Joyce learnt the way into the Aladdin's cave where he manufactured his *Ulysses;* and the philosophic flux-stream has its source, too, in that magical cavern.

The claim to be employing the 'impersonal' method of science in the presentment of the personal of *Ulysses* can be entirely disregarded. If there were any definite and carefully demarcated personality–except in the case of Dedalus, or here and there where we see a casual person for a moment–it would be worth while examining that claim. But as there are no persons to speak of for the author to be 'impersonal' about, that can at once be dismissed. *Ulysses* is a highly romantic self-portrait of the mature Joyce (disguised as a Jew) and of his adolescent self–of Bloom and Dedalus. Poldy Joyce, luckily for him, is a more genial fellow than Stephan Joyce–else the *Portrait of the Artist* stage would never have been passed by James.

Another thing that can be dismissed even more summarily is the claim that Bloom is a creation, a great *homme moyen sensuel* of fiction. That side of Bloom would never have existed had it not been for the Bouvard and Pécuchet of Flaubert, which very intense creation Joyce merely takes over, spins out, and translates into the relaxed medium of anglo-irish humour. Where Bloom is being Bouvard and Pécuchet, it is a translation, nothing more.

Nor really can the admirable Goya-like fantasia in the middle of the book, in which all the characters enjoy a free metaphysical existence (released from the last remnants of the nineteenth-century restraint of the doctrine of naturalism), be compared for original power of conception with the *Tentation.* As to the homeric framework, that is only an entertaining structural device or conceit.

9. In *The Art of Being Ruled* (chap. vi. part xii.), I have analysed in passing one aspect of the 'telling from the inside' method, where that method is based upon a flaubertian naturalism, and used by an english writer

brought up in the anglo-saxon humorous tradition. There my remarks were called forth by the nature of the more general analysis I was at the time engaged upon, which included what I described as the 'sort of gargantuan mental stutter' employed by Miss Stein, in the course of her exploitation of the processes of the demented. I shall now quote what is essential to my present purpose from that chapter relative to Mr. Joyce:–

> . . . the repetition (used by Miss Stein) is also in the nature of a photograph of the unorganized word-dreaming of the mind when not concentrated for some logical functional purpose. Mr. Joyce employed this method with success (not so radically and rather differently) in *Ulysses*. The thought-stream or word-stream of his hero's mind was supposed to be photographed. The effect was not unlike the conversation of Mr. Jingle in *Pickwick*.
>
> The reason why you get this Mr. Jingle effect is that, in *Ulysses,* a considerable degree of naturalism being aimed at, Mr. Joyce had not the freedom of movement possessed by the more ostensibly personal, semi-lyrical utterances of Miss Stein. He had to pretend that we were really surprising the private thought of a real and average human creature, Mr. Bloom. But the fact is that Mr. Bloom was abnormally *wordy.* He *thought in words,* not images, for our benefit, in a fashion as unreal, from the point of view of the strictest naturalist dogma, as a Hamlet soliloquy. And yet the *pretence* of naturalism involved Mr. Joyce in something less satisfying than Miss Stein's more direct and arbitrary arrangements.

For Mr. Joyce's use of Miss Stein's method the following passage will suffice (it is of the more genial, Mr. Jingle, order):

> 'Provost's house. The reverend Dr. Salmon: tinned salmon. Well tinned in there. Wouldn't live in it if they paid me. Hope they have liver and bacon to-day. Nature abhors a vacuum. There he is: the brother. Image of him. Haunting face. Now that's a coincidence. Course hundreds of times you think of a person, etc.
>
> 'Feel better. Burgundy. Good pick-me up. Who distilled first. Some chap in the blues. Dutch courage. That *Kilkenny People* in the national library: now I must.'

Here is Mr. Jingle, from *Pickwick*:–

> 'Rather short in the waist, ain't it? Like a general postman's coat–queer coats those–made by contract–no measuring–mysterious dispensations of Providence– all the short men get the long coats–all the long men short ones.
>
> 'Come–stopping at Crown–Crown at Muggleton–met a party–flannel jackets–white trousers–anchovy sandwiches–devilled kidneys–splendid fellows–glorious.'
>
> So by the devious route of a fashionable naturalist

device–that usually described as 'presenting the character from the *inside*'–and the influence exercised on him by Miss Stein's technique of picturesque dementia– Mr. Joyce reaches the half-demented *crank* figure of traditional english humour.

The clowning and horseplay of english humour play a very important part in the later work of Joyce. In *Ulysses* Rabelais is also put under contribution to reinforce this vein, though it is the manner of Rabelais that is parodied, and the matter of that unusually profound writer is not very much disturbed. Since *Ulysses* (but still in the manner of that book) Mr. Joyce has written a certain amount–the gathering material of a new book, which, altogether almost, employs the manner of Nash–though again somewhat varied with echoes of Urquhart's translations. He has fallen almost entirely into a literary horseplay on the one side, and Steinesque child-play on the other.

As to the Nash factor, when read in the original, the brilliant rattle of that Elizabethan's high-spirited ingenuity can in time grow tiresome, and is of a stupefying monotony. What Nash says, from start to finish, is nothing. The mind demands some special substance from a writer, for words open into the region of ideas; and the requirements of that region, where it is words you are using, must somehow be met. Chapman, Donne or Shakespeare, with as splendid a mastery of language, supply this demand, whereas Nash does not.

But Nash is a great prose-writer, one of the greatest as far as sheer execution is concerned, and in that over-ornate bustling field. Yet his emptiness has resulted in his work falling into neglect, which, if you read much of him, is not difficult to understand. His great appetite for words, their punning potentialities, along with a power of compressing them into pungent arabesques, is admirable enough to have made him more remembered than he is. But certainly some instinct in Posterity turned it away from this *too* physical, too merely high-spirited and muscular, verbal performer. He tired it like a child with his empty energy, I suppose.

Nash appears to be at present the chief source of Joyce's inspiration– associated with his old friend Rabelais, and some of the mannerisms of Miss Stein, those easiest assimilated without its showing. There is a further source now, it appears; he has evidently concluded that the epistolary style of Ezra Pound should not be born to blush unseen, but should be made a more public use of than Pound has done. So in it has gone with the rest.

I am not able to give parallel examples of Pound's epistolary style of those parts of Joyce's recent prose

that derive from it; but a passage from Nash and one from a recent piece by Joyce I can. Here is Nash:–

> There was a herring, or there was not, for it was but a cropshin, one of the refuse sort of herrings, and this herring, or this cropshin, was sensed and thurified in the smoke, and had got him a suit of durance, that would last longer than one of Erra Pater's almanacks, or a constable's brown bill: only his head was in his tail, and that made his breath so strong, that no man could abide him. Well, he was a Triton of his time, and a sweet-singing calendar to the state, yet not beloved of the showery Pleiades or the Colossus of the sun: however, he thought himself another *Tumidus Antimachus,* as complete an Adelantado as he that is known by wearing a cloak of tuffed taffety eighteen years . . . etc.

Here is another piece from Nash, where Joyce and Nash meet on the common ground of Rabelais:–

> The posterior Italian and German cornugraphers stick not to applaud and canonize unnatural sodomitry, the strumpet errant, the gout, the ague, the dropsy, the sciatica, folly, drunkenness, and slovenry. The *galli gallinacei,* or cocking French, swarm every pissing while in their primmer editions, *imprimeda jour duy,* of the unspeakable healthful conducibleness of the *gomorrihan* great *poco,* a *poco,* their true countryman every inch of him, the prescript laws of tennis or balonne . . . the commodity of hoarseness, blear-eyes, scabbed-hams, thread-bare clokes, poached-eggs and panados.

Here is the opening of an *Extract from Work in Progress,* by James Joyce:–

> Shem is as short for Shemus as Jem is joky for Jacob. A few toughnecks are still getatable who pretend that aboriginally he was of respectable stemming (an inlaw to Mr. Bbyrdwood de Trop Blogg was among his most distant connections) but every honest to goodness man in the land to-day knows that his back life will not stand being written about in black and white.

Again:–

> . . . a ladies tryon hosiery raffle at liberty, a sewerful of guineagold wine and sickcylinder oysters worth a billion a bite, an entire operahouse of enthusiastic noble-women flinging every coronetcrimsoned stitch they had off at his probscenium, one after the others, when, egad, sir, he sang the topsquall in Deal Lil Shemlockup Yellin (geewhiz, jew ear that far! soap ewer! juice like a boyd!) for fully five minutes infinitely better than Barton Mc. Guckin with a scrumptious cocked hat and three green trinity plumes on his head and a dean's crozier that he won for falling first over the hurdles, madam, in the odder hand, but what with the murky light, the botchy print, the tattered cover, the jigjagged page, the fumbling fingers, the foxtrotting fleas, the liea-

bed lice, the scum on his tongue, the drop in his eye, the lump in his throat, the drink in his pottle, the itch in his palm, the wail of his wind, the grief from his breath, the fog of his brainfag, the tic of his conscience, the height of his rage, the gush of his fundament, the fire in his gorge, the tickle of his tail, the rats in his garret, the hullabaloo and the dust in his ears since it took him a month to steal a march, he was hardset to memorize more than a word a week.

The close similarity in every way of those characteristic passages that I have quoted will be evident. In the first of the extracts from Joyce, curiously enough, he reveals one of the main preoccupations of the hero of *Ulysses,* namely, that arising from the ravages of the gentleman-complex–the Is he or isn't he a gentleman?–the phantom index-finger of the old shabby-genteel typical query pursuing the author. In this instance, as he is not writing about himself, we are given to understand that the figure in question is *not.* His gargantuan villain-of-the-piece is not even allowed to be very closely connected with the noble *de trop Bloggs.* But the implicit theme of the entire piece, what moves Joyce to churn up the english tongue in a mock-elizabethan frenzy, is the burning question still of his shabby-genteel boyhood, namely, To be a 'toff,' or not to be a 'toff.'

In the respectable, more secluded corners of the anglo-saxon world, every one has at some time met keepers of tiny general-shops in provincial towns, char-ladies, faded old women in lodging-houses and so on, whose main hold upon life appears to be the belief that they have seen better days; and that really, if every one had their due, they, like their distant relatives, the *de Bloggs,* would be rolling in their Royces, and Ritzing it with the best. Because we do not usually associate this strange delusion with eminent authors, that is not a reason why, nevertheless, they should not be secretly haunted by it; especially if, as with Joyce, they issue from a similar shabby-gentility and provincial snobbishness. In spite of this necessary reflection it is always with a fresh astonishment that you come upon this faded, cheerless subject-matter.

But there is one thing that it will be well to note abut this type of preoccupation, namely, that it is essentially the victorian poor or the country people or provincials, still victorian, who display that obsession, not the metropolitan poor of to-day, certainly. It was Thackeray's world, or the denizens of the books of Dickens, who felt in that manner; and whether for better or worse, no such intense and maundering shabby-genteel snobs are any more manufactured in urban England, and I doubt if they are even in Ireland. So in the emotive psychology of these burlesques, even, Joyce is strangely of another day or, on the principle of the time-philosophy, provincial. To read him where

that emotion is in the ascendant is like listening to a contemporary of Meredith or Dickens (capering to the elizabethan hornpipe of Nash perhaps–as interpreted by Miss Stein).

10. The *Portrait of the Artist* is an extremely carefully written book; but it is not technically swept and tidied to the extent that is *Ulysses.* For instance, this passage from the opening of chapter ii. would not have remained in the later book:–

> Every morning, therefore, uncle Charles *repaired* to his outhouse, but not before he had greased and *brushed scrupulously* his back hair, etc.

People *repair* to places in works of fiction of the humblest order or in newspaper articles; and *brushed scrupulously,* though harmless certainly, is a conjunction that the fastidious eye would reject, provided it had time to exercise its function. But elsewhere in the *Portrait of the Artist,* in the scene on the seashore with the bird-girl, for instance, the conventional emotion calls to itself and clothes itself with a conventional expression; which however merely technically pruned, leaves a taste of well-used sentiment in the mind, definitely of the cliché order. The more full-blooded humour of *Ulysses* prevents that from happening so often.

It is in tracking this other sort of cliché–the cliché of feeling, of thought, and in a less detailed sense, of expression–that you will find everywhere beneath the surface in Joyce a conventional basis or framework. And until you get down to that framework or bed, you will not understand what is built over it, nor realize why, in a sense, it is so dead.

From this charge Joyce would probably attempt to escape by saying that with Dedalus he was dealing with a sentimental young man. But that unfortunately does not explain his strange fondness for his company, nor his groundless assumption that he will be liked by us. We do not find such a young man in Flaubert's *Education Sentimentale,* nor in any of the other modern masters of fiction. That is probably because they were in the truest sense less personal.

Into *Ulysses* a great many things have been mixed, however. You will find many traces in it of the influence of T. S. Eliot and of Pound's classical, romance, and anglo-saxon scholarly enthusiasms, not to be met with in earlier books. *The Enemy of the Stars,* a play written and published by me in 1914, obliterated by the War, turned up, I suspect, in Zurich, and was responsible for the manner here and there of Joyce's book. Then the viennese school of psychology made Molly Bloom mutter, 'What are they always rooting about up there for, to see where they come from, I wonder?' or words to that effect. No Irish Molly–however much of an 'eternal feminine' abstraction–would ever have soliloquized in that manner but for Sigmund Freud. Miss Stein can only be used–owing to the restrictions imposed by the naturalist method–when a character is half asleep, day-dreaming, its mind wandering, or, in short, in such circumstances as justify, naturalistically, the use of Miss Stein's technique. *Ulysses* is, however, able to come to an end as follows:–

> the jessamine and geraniums and cactuses and Gibraltar as a girl when I was a Flower girl of the mountain yes when I put the rose in my hair like the Andalusian girls used or shall I wear a red yes and how he kissed me under the Moorish wall and I thought well and as well his as another and then I asked him with my eyes to ask again yes and then he asked me would I yes to say yes my mountain flower and first I put my arms around him yes and drew him down to me so he could feel my breasts all perfume yes and his heart was going like mad and yes I said yes I will Yes.

That is the conclusion of *Ulysses*. This is Miss Stein (from *Saints in Seven*):–

> He comes again. Yes he comes again and what does he say he says do you know this do you refuse no more than you give. That is the way to spell it do you refuse no more than you give.

I have been gathering together all those factors in the mind of Joyce which make it, I am able to show, a good material for a predatory *time-philosophy*, bearing down upon it and claiming his pen as its natural servant. Social snobbery (for instance) suggests that he will probably be susceptible to merely fashionable hypnotisms; for more than any other thing it is the sign of the herd-mind. What Schopenhauer said of the jingo, that 'if a man is proud of being "a German," "a Frenchman," or "a Jew," he must have very little else to be proud of,' can equally well be applied to class. For one man that is proud of being a person, there are a hundred thousand who are compelled to content themselves with being vain about being somebody else, or a whole dense abstract mass of somebody elses–their nation, their class.

Joyce expresses the same idea as Pound in the quotation I have given (beginning, 'It is dawn at Jerusalem') in the *Portrait of the Artist*:–

> Stephanos Dedalos! Bous Stephanoumenos! Bous Stephaneforos!
> Their banter was not new to him. . . . Now, as never before, his strange name seemed to him a prophecy. So timeless seemed the grey warm air, so fluid and impersonal his own mood, that all ages were as one to him.

So we arrive at the concrete illustrations of that strange fact already noted–that an intense preoccupation with *time* or 'duration' (the psychological aspect of time that is) is wedded to the theory of 'timelessness.' It is, as it were, in its innate confusion in the heart of the reality, the substance and original of that peculiar paradox–that so long as *time* is the capital truth of your world it matters very little if you deny time's existence, like the einsteinian, or say there is nothing else at all, like Bergson; or whether space-time (with the accent on the time) is your god, like Alexander. For all practical purposes you are committed to the same world-view. *Practically* it will impose on you the same psychology; but further than that, if you wished to pursue it, you would find that the purely physical theory of Einstein is of such an order that, though it sets out to banish the mental factor altogether and to arrive at a purely physical truth, it nevertheless cannot prevent itself turning into a psychological or spiritual account of things, like Bergson's. For the mind of Einstein, like that of Bergson, or like that of Proust, is not a *physical* mind, as it could be called. It is psychologic; it is mental.

Beyond this rough preliminary statement it is not possible to go without much more elaboration, which I wish to avoid in this part of my essay. But a few further observations may be added to the foregoing, further to elucidate, upon this plane of discussion, the direction of my analysis, and its object as applied to the art-forms I have chosen to consider.

Most people have seen spirit-drawings–or drawings done, says the subject, under the influence of supernatural agencies. Whatever they may be like otherwise, they are generally characterized by a certain cloudiness, a misty uncertainty.

The processes of creative genius, however, are not so dissimilar to those of the spirit-draughtsman. A great artist falls into a trance of sorts when he creates, about that there is little doubt. The act of artistic creation is a trance or dream-state, but very different from that experienced by the entranced medium. A world of the most extreme and logically exacting physical definition is built up out of this susceptible condition in the case of the greatest art, in contrast to the cloudy phantasies of the spiritist.

It is a good deal as a pictorial and graphic artist that I approach these problems; and a method that does not secure that definition and logical integrity that, as a graphic artist, I require, I am, I admit, hostile to from the start. But no doubt what made me, to begin with, a painter, was some propensity for the exactly-defined and also, fanatically it may be, the physical or the concrete. And I do not think that you have to be a painter to possess such inclinations.

Many painters, indeed, have no repugnance, it would appear, for the surging ecstatic featureless chaos which is being set up as an ideal, in place of the noble exactitude and harmonious proportion of the european, scientific, ideal–the specifically Western heaven.

What I am concerned with here, first of all, is not whether the great *time-philosophy* that overshadows all contemporary thought is viable as a system of abstract truth, but if in its application it helps or destroys our human arts. With that is involved, of course, the very fundamental question of whether we should set out to transcend our human condition (as formerly Nietzsche and then Bergson claimed that we should); or whether we should translate into human terms the whole of our datum. My standpoint is that we are creatures of a certain kind, with no indication that a radical change is imminent; and that the most pretentious of our present prophets is unable to do more than promise 'an eternity of intoxication' to those who follow him into less physical, more 'cosmic,' regions; proposals made with at least equal eloquence by the contemporaries of Plato. On the other hand, politically it is urged that a-thousand-men is a better man than one, because he is less 'conscious' and is bigger. It seems to me, on the contrary, that the smaller you are, the more remarkable. So as far as all that side of the argument is concerned–of ecstatic propaganda, of plunges into cosmic streams of flux or time, of miraculous baptisms, of the ritual of time-gods, and of breathless transformations–I have other views on the subject of attaining perfection. I prefer the chaste wisdom of the Chinese or the Greek, to that hot, tawny brand of superlative fanaticism coming from the parched deserts of the Ancient East, with its ineradicable abstractness. I am for the physical world.

Stuart Gilbert discusses Joyce's style in his introduction to the first volume of Letters of James Joyce.

An interesting feature of *Ulysses* is the way in which, episode by episode, the style changes in harmony with the theme; one might almost say that the eighteen episodes give the impression of having been written by eighteen different people. . . . [T]here is no question that as a stylist Joyce was capable of chameleon-like changes and one would be hard put to it to decide which style was 'naturally' Joyce's.

—Letters I, p. 31

JAMES JOYCE'S
ULYSSES

A STUDY
BY
STUART GILBERT

LONDON
FABER & FABER LIMITED
24 RUSSELL SQUARE

Title page for an early study of Joyce's novel that stressed its formal design and Homeric parallels. Originally published in 1930, Gilbert's book remains in print.

W. K. Magee, who wrote under the pseudonym John Eglinton, knew Joyce in Dublin in the early 1890s. In this essay he views the author's career retrospectively through the lens of Ulysses, *which he regards as Joyce's singular masterpiece. Joyce, he concludes, "is a man of one book, as perhaps the ideal author always is."*

The Beginnings of Joyce
John Eglinton
Life and Letters, 8 (December 1932): 400–414

As I think of Joyce an extraordinary figure rises up in my memory. A Pair of burning dark-blue eyes, serious and questioning, is fixed on me from under the peak of a yachting cap; the face is long, with a slight flush suggestive of dissipation, and an incipient beard is permitted to straggle over a very pronounced chin, under which the open shirt collar leaves bare a full womanish throat. The figure is fairly tall and very erect, and gives a general impression of a kind of seedy hauteur; and very passer-by glances with a smile at the white tennis shoes (borrowed, as I gather from a mention of them in *Ulysses*). It was while walking homeward one night across Dublin that I was joined by this young man, whose appearance was already familiar to me; and although I cannot remember any of the strange sententious talk in which he instantly engaged, I have only to open the *Portrait of the Artist as a Young Man* to hear it again. "When we come to the phenomena of artistic conception, artistic gestation and artistic reproduction, I require a new terminology and a new personal experience.' I have never felt much interest in literary aesthetics, and he seemed to set a good deal of store by his system, referring, I recollect, to some remark made to him by 'one of his disciples', but I liked listening to his careful intonation and full vowel sounds, and as he recited some of his verses, 'My love is in a light attire', I kept glancing at the apple in the throat, the throat of a singer; for Mr. Joyce has turned out to be an exception to a sweeping rule laid down by the late Sir J. P. Mahaffy, who used to say that he had never known a young man with a good tenor voice who did go to the devil. Some ladies of the pavement shrieked at us as we crossed over O'Connell Bridge. I remember that we talked of serious matters, and at one point he impressed my by saying: 'If I knew I were to drop dead before I reached that lamp-post, it would mean no more to me than it will mean to walk past it.' Why did this young man seek out my acquaintance? Well, writing folk are interested in one another, and there were peculiarities in the occasion of the present writer's inglorious attempts at authorship about which it may be well to say something, as the relation may help indirectly to define the nature of Joyce's own portentous contribution to Irish literature.

James Joyce was one of a group of lively and eager-minded young men in the National University, amongst whom he had attained a sudden ascendancy by the publication in the *Fortnightly Review,* when he was only nineteen, of an article on Ibsen's play, *When We Dead Awaken.* The talk of these young men, their ribald wit and reckless manner of life, their interest in everything new in literature and philosophy (in this respect they far surpassed the students of Trinity College), are all reproduced in Joyce's writings; for his art seems to have found in this period the materials with which it was henceforth to work. Dublin was certainly at this moment a centre of vigorous potentialities. The older culture was still represented with dignity by Dowden, Mahaffy and others; political agitation was holding back its energies for a favourable opportunity, while the organization of Sinn Fein was secretly ramifying throughout the country; the language movement was arrogant in its claims; the Irish Literary Theatre was already famous; and besides Yeats and Synge, A. E.

and George Moore, there were numerous young writers, and even more numerous talkers, of incalculable individuality. There was hardly anyone at that time who did not believe that Ireland was on the point of some decisive transformation. What, then, was wanting to this movement, for it has passed away, leaving Ireland more intensely what it has always been, a more or less disaffected member of the British Commonwealth of Nations? That Ireland should achieve political greatness appeared then to most of us to be an idle dream; but in the things of the mind and of the spirit it seemed not a folly to think that Ireland might turn its necessity of political eclipse to glorious gains. A regenerate and thoughtful Ireland, an Ireland turned inwards upon itself in reverie, might recover inexhaustible sources of happiness and energy in its own beauty and aloofness, through a generous uprush of wisdom in its poets and thinkers. It was not in the interest of the constituted spiritual authorities in Ireland that such a dream should ever be realized: a new movement of the human mind in Ireland was indeed precisely what was feared; the noisy language movement, the recrudescence of political agitation, outrage, assassination—anything was preferable to that! There was a moment, nevertheless, when it seemed possible that this might be the turn events would take. A little magazine was started, under the editorship of the present writer, and A. E. boldly recommended *The Heretic* for a title, but the somewhat less comprising name, '*Dana:* a magazine of independent thought', was chosen. The fruitfulness of the moment was revealed in the number of eminent writers who contributed freely to its pages: Joyce, who chortled as he pocketed half a sovereign for a poem, was the only one to receive remuneration. Yeats held aloof, talking cuttingly of 'Fleet Street atheism'.

Joyce is, as all his writings show, Roman in mind and soul; for, generally speaking, to the Romanized mind the quest of truth, when it is not impious, is witless. What he seemed at this period I have attempted to describe, but what he really was is revealed in his *Portrait of the Artist as a Young Man,* a work completed in Trieste just ten years later. Religion had been with him a profound adolescent experience, torturing the sensitiveness which it awakened: all its floods had gone over him. He had now recovered, and had no objection to 'Fleet Street atheism'; but 'independent thought' appeared to him an amusing disguise of the proselytizing spirit, and one night as we walked across town he endeavoured, with a certain earnestness, to bring home to me the extreme futility of the ideals represented in *Dana,* by describing to me the solemn ceremonial of High Mass. (Dost thou remember these things, O Joyce, thou man of meticulous remembrance?) The little magazine laboured through a year, and the chief interest of the volume formed by its twelve numbers is now, no doubt, that it contains the series of sketches by George Moore, 'Moods and Memories', afterwards embodied in *Memoirs of My Dead Life*. It might have had a rare value now in the book market if I had been better advised one evening in the National Library, when Joyce came in with the manuscript of a serial story which he offered for publication. He observed me silently as I read, and when I handed it back to him with the timid observation that I did not care to publish what was to myself incomprehensible he replaced it silently in his pocket.

I imagine that what he showed me was some early attempt in fiction, and that I was not really guilty of rejecting any work of his which has become famous. Joyce at this time was in the making, as is shown by the fact that the friends and incidents of this period have remained his principal subject-matter. Chief among these friends was the incomparable 'Buck Mulligan', Joyce's name for a now famous Dublin doctor–wit, poet, mocker, enthusiast, and, unlike most of his companions, blest with means to gratify his romantic caprices. He had a fancy for living in towers, and when I first heard of him had the notion of establishing himself at the top of the Round Tower at Clondalkin; afterwards he rented from the Admiralty the Martello Tower at Sandycove, which presently became the resort of poets and revolutionaries, something between one of the 'Hell Fire Clubs' of the eighteenth century and the Mermaid Tavern. Joyce was certainly very unhappy, proud and impecunious: no one took him at his own valuation, yet he held his own by his unfailing 'recollectedness' and by his sententious and pedantic wit, shown especially in the limericks on the various figures in the literary movement, with which from time to time he regaled that company of roysterers and midnight bathers. Buck Mulligan's conversation, or, rather, his vehement and whimsical oratory, is reproduced with such exactness in *Ulysses* that one is driven to conclude that Joyce even then was 'taking notes'; as to Joyce himself, he was exactly like his own hero, Stephen Dedalus, who anounced to his delighted admirers that 'Ireland was of importance because it belonged to him'. He had made up his mind at this period, no doubt with vast undisclosed purposes of authorship, to make the personal acquaintance of everyone in Dublin of repute in literature. With Yeats he amused himself by delivering the sentence of the new generation, and 'Never', said Yeats, 'have I encountered so much pretension with so little to show for it.' When he mentioned his intention of breaking in on Dowden, Buck Mulligan pulled a wry face. 'Who, then, is Dowden?' asked Joyce. 'A little professor! I am a poet!' He was told that Lady Gregory, who was giving a literary party at her hotel, had refused to invite himself, and he vowed he would be there. We were all a little uneasy, and I can still see Joyce, with his white shoes and his air of half-timid effrontery, advancing towards his unwilling hostess and turning away from her to watch the company. Withal, there was something lovable in Joyce, as there is in every man of genius: I was sensible of the mute appeal of his liquid-burning gaze, though it was long afterwards that I was constrained to recognize his genius.

As already noted, nature had endowed him with one remarkable advantage, an excellent tenor voice, and there is still in existence at least one copy of the programme of a Dublin concert, in which the names of the singers appear thus, perhaps only in alphabetical order:

1. Mr. James A. Joyce
2. Mr. John McCormack.

He had almost persuaded himself to enter as a competitor in the Irish Musical Festival, the Feis Ceoil, but withdrew at the last moment because of the indignity of the preliminary test. Who but Joyce himself could have surmised in this the inhibition of his dæmon, or the struggle that may have been enacted in his dauntless and resourceful spirit? Perhaps at this very moment he slipped past the Sirens' Rock on the road to his destiny. Our dæmon, as Socrates pointed out, will only tell us what *not* to do, and if Joyce's dæmon had made the mistake of saying to him in so many words, 'Thou shalt be the Dante of Dubin, a Dante with a difference, it is true, as the Liffey is a more prosaic stream than the Arno: still, Dublin's Dante!' he might quite likely (for who is altogether satisfied with the destiny meted out to him?) have drawn back and 'gone to the devil' with his fine tenor voice. He chose, what was for him no doubt the better part, his old vagabond impecunious life. One morning, just as the National Library opened, Joyce was announced; he seemed to wish for somebody to talk to, and related quite ingenuously how in the early hours of the morning he had been thrown out of the tower, and had walked into town from Sandycove. In reading the early chapters of *Ulysses* I was reminded of this incident, for this day, at least in its early portion, must have been for Joyce very like the day celebrated in that work, and I could not help wondering whether the idea of it may not have dawned upon him as he walked along the sands that morning.

Certain it is that he had now had his draught of experience: all the life which he describes in his writings now lay behind him. Suddenly we heard that he had married, was a father, and had gone off to Trieste to become a teacher in the Berlitz School there. It must have been two or three years later that he looked into the National Library for a few minutes, marvellously smartened up and with a short, trim beard. The business which had brought him back had some connection, curiously enough, with the first introduction into Dublin of the cinema. The mission was a failure, and he was also much disgusted by the scruples of a Dublin publisher in reprinting a volume of short stories, of which all the copies had been destroyed in a fire. (It was not until 1914 that *Dubliners* was published in London.) 'I am going back to civilization', were the last words I heard from him. He has not, I believe, been in Dublin since.

From this point Joyce becomes for me, in retrospect, an heroic figure. He had 'stooped under a dark tremendous sea of cloud', confident that he would 'emerge some day,' 'using for my defence the only weapons I allow myself to use, silence, exile and cunning'. Pause on that word 'exile', a favourite one with Joyce. Why was it necessary for him to conjure up the grandiose image of his rejection by his countrymen? Ireland, though famous for flights of wild geese, banishes nobody, and Dublin had no quarrel with her Dante; and we have seen what he thought of the little group of those who were intent on blowing into flame the spark of a new spiritual initiative: the only people, be it said, of whom Catholic Ireland could be conceived of as anxious to rid herself. Still, a sensitive artist, reduced to impecunious despair as Joyce was at this period, might feel, in the very obscurity in which he was suffered to steal away out of Dublin, a sentence of banishment no less stern in its indifference than Florence's fiery sentence on her Dante. 'I go to encounter for the millionth time the reality of experience and to forge in the smithy of my soul the uncreated consciousness of my race.' He must have met with many curious adventures and suffered many a grief in the winning of his soul; but the strange thing is that in all his experience of the cities of men and of their minds and manners; while a new life claimed him and the desire of return departed from him; while his intellect consolidated itself through study and the acquisition of many lanuages; the city he had abandoned remained the home and subject-matter of all his awakening invention. Dublin was of importance because it belonged to him. Demonstrably, he must have carried with him into exile a mass of written material, but it was long before he learned how to deal with it, or to recognize, probably with some reluctance, in the merry imp of mockery which stirred within him, the spirit which was at length to take him by the hand and lead him out into the large spaces of literary creation.

His mind meanwhile retained some illusions: for example, that he was a poet. He has, in fact, published more than one volume of poems; but I will take A. E.'s word for it that most of them 'might have been written by almost any young versifying sentimentalist'. Another illusion was that he could write, in the ordinary sense, a novel; for *A Portrait of the Artist as a Young Man,* which took him ten years to write, is no more a novel than is Moore's *Confessions of a Young Man.* In style it is, for the most part, pompous and self-conscious, and in general we may say of it that it is one of those works which becomes important only when the author has done or written something else. That Joyce should have been able to make *Ulysses* out of much the same material gives the book now an extraordinary interest. It tells us a great deal about Joyce himself which we had hardly suspected, and both its squalor and its assumption wear quite a different complexion when we know that the author eventually triumphed over the one and vindicated the other. Genius is not always what it is supposed to be, self-realization: it is often a spirit to which the artist has to sacrifice himself; and until Joyce surrendered himself to his genius, until he died and came to life in his Mephistopheles of mockery, he remained what Goethe called 'ein trüber Gast auf der dunklen Erden'.

I confess that when I read *Ulysses* I took Stephen Dedalus (Joyce himself) for the hero, and the impression seemed justified by the phrase at the end of the book when Stephen falls asleep: 'at rest, he has travelled'. The commentators, however, all appear to be agreed that Mr. Leopold Bloom is Ulysses, and they refer to the various episodes, 'Nausicaa', 'The Oxen of the Sun', 'The Nekuia', and so forth, with an understanding which I envy them. All the same, I am convinced that the only person concerned in the narrative who comes out as a real hero is the author himself. What kind of hero, after all, is brought to mind by the name Ulysses if not a hero long absent from his kingdom, returning, after being the sport of the gods for ten years, in triumph and vengeance? And it was after nearly as many years of absence as Ulysses from the country 'which belonged to him,' that Joyce turned up again for us in Dublin, with a vengeance! Certain it is that when he decided to scrap the scholastic habiliments of his mind, the poor disguise of a seedy snobbishness, and in lieu thereof endued himself with the elemental diabolism of *Ulysses,* he was transfigured. A thousand unexpected faculties and gay devices were liberated in his soul. The discovery of a new method in literary art, in which the pen is no longer the slave of logic and rhetoric, made of this Berlitz School teacher a kind of public danger, threatening to the corporate existence of 'literature' as established in the minds and affections of the new generation.

He found this method, as the concluding pages of the *Portrait* suggest to us, in his Diary: a swift notation, in the first place, at their point of origination, of feelings and perceptions. In one way Joyce is no less concerned with style than was R. L. Stevenson: yet we mark in this pupil of the Irish Jesuits a spirit very different from the goodwill of the Scottish Protestant towards English literature. He is aware, like Stevenson, of every shade of style in English, and there is a chapter in *Ulysses* which presents an historic conspectus of English prose from its Anglo-Saxon beginnings down to the personal oddities of Carlyle, Henry James and others, and modern slang. But whereas, with Stevenson, English prose style, according to his own cheerful comparison, is a torch lit from one generation to another, our Romano-Celtic Joyce nurses an ironic detachment from the whole of the English tradition. Indeed, he is its enemy. Holding his ear to the subconscious, he catches his meanings unceremoniously as they rise, in hit-or-miss vocables. English is only one of the languages which he knows: they say he speaks Italian like a native, German, Spanish, Portuguese, and various other idioms; and he knows these lanugages not through books but as living organisms, their shop-talk and slang rather than their poets; they are companions to him, powerful agents, genii who bear him into the caverns whence they originated. And at the end of it all it must have seemed to him that he held English, his country's spiritual enemy, in the hollow of his hand, for the English language too came at his call to do his bidding. George Moore used to talk with envy of those English writers who could use 'the whole of the language', and I really think that Joyce must be added to Moore's examples of this power–Shakespeare, Whitman, Kipling. This language found itself constrained by its new master to perform tasks to which it was unaccustomed in the service of pure literature; against the grain it was forced to reproduce Joyce's fantasies in all kinds of juxtapositions, neologisms, amalgamations, truncations, words that are only found scrawled up in public lavatories, obsolete words, words in limbo or belike in the womb of time. It assumed every intonation and locution of Dublin, London, Glasgow, New York, Johannesburg. Like a devil taking pleasure in forcing a virgin to speak obscenely, so Joyce rejoiced darkly in causing the language of Milton and Wordsworth to utter all but unimaginable filth and treason.

Such is Joyce's Celtic revenge, and it must be owned that he has succeeded in making logic and rhetoric less sure of themselves among our younger writers. As an innovator in the art of fiction I conceive him to be less formidable. Mankind has never failed to recognize a good story-teller, and never will. They say that Joyce, when he is in good humour among his disciples, can be induced to allow them to examine a key to the elaborate symbolism of the different episodes, all pointing inward to a central mystery, undivulged, I fancy. *Ulysses*, in fact, is a mock-heroic, and at the heart of it is that which lies at the heart of all mockery, an awful inner void. None but Joyce and

his dæmon know that void: the consciousness of it is perhaps the 'tragic sense' which his disciples claim that he has introduced into English literature. But is there, then, no serious intention in *Ulysses?* As Joyce's most devout interpreters are at variance with respect to the leading motive we may, perhaps without much loss, assume its seriousness to be nothing but the diabolic gravity with which the whole work is conducted throughout its mystifications. Yet the original motive may have been quite a simple one. Near the centre of the book, in that chapter known as 'The Oxen of the Sun', which, in Mr. Stuart Gilbert's words, 'ascends in orderly march the gamut of English styles', 'culminating in a futurist cacophony of syncopated slang', there is a passage over which the reader may pause:

> There are sins or (let us call them as the world calls them) evil memories which are hidden away by man in the darkest places of the heart, but they abide there and wait. He may suffer their memory to grow dim, let them be as though they had not been and all but persuade himself that they were not, or at least were otherwise. Yet a chance word will call them forth suddenly and they will rise up to confront him in the most various circumstances, a vision or a dream, or while timbrel and harp soothe his senses, or amid the cool silver tranquillity of the evening, or at the feast at midnight when he is new filled with wine. Not to insult over him will the vision come as over one that lies under her wrath, not for vengeance to cut him off from the living, but shrouded in the piteous vesture of the past, silent, remote, reproachful.

The 'timbrel and harp' make me a little wary, but though some writer is doubtless parodied (Newman?), does there not seem here for once to be a relaxation of some significance, in the strain of mockery?

The conception of the Irish Jew, Leopold Bloom, within whose mind we move through a day of Dublin life, is somewhat of a puzzle. Buck Mulligan we know, and the various minor characters; and in the interview of the much-enduring Stephen with the officials of the National Library the present writer experiences a twinge of recollection of things actually said. But Bloom, if he be a real character, belongs to a province of Joyce's experience of which I have no knowledge. He is, I suppose, the jumble of ordinary human consciousness in the city, in any city, with which the author's experience of men and cities had deepened his familiarity: a slowly progressing host of instincts, appetites, adaptations, questions, curiosities, held at short tether by ignorance and vulgarity; and the rapid notation which I conceive Joyce to have discovered originally in his Diary served admirably well to record these mental or psychic processes. Bloom's mind is the mind of the crowd, swayed by every vicissitude, but he is distinguished through race-endowment by a detachment from the special crowd-consciousness of the Irish, while his familiarity with the latter makes him the fitting instrument of the author's encyclopædic humour. Bloom, therefore, is an impersonation rather than a type: not a character, for a character manifests itself in action, and in *Ulysses* there is no action. There is only the rescue of Stephen from a row in a brothel, in which some have discovered a symbolism which might have appealed to G. F. Watts, the Delivery of Art by Science and Common Sense. But the humour is vast and genial. There are incomparable flights in *Ulysses:* the debate, for instance, in the Maternity Hospital on the mystery of birth; and above all, I think, the scene near the end of the book in the cabmen's shelter, kept by none other than Skin-the-Goat, the famous jarvey of the Phoenix Park murders. Here the author proves himself one of the world's great humorists. The humour, as always, is pitiless, but where we laugh we love, and after his portrait of the sailor in this chapter I reckon Joyce, after all, a lover of men.

When Joyce produced *Ulysses* he had shot his bolt. Let us put it without any invidiousness. He is a man of one book, as perhaps the ideal author always is. Besides, he is not specially interested in 'literature', not, at all events, as well-wisher. A man who adds something new to literature often hates the word, as the poet shrinks from the tomb, even though it be in Westminster Abbey. Usually he is interested in something quite apart from literature, added unto it by him. As for Joyce, his interest is in language and the mystery of words. He appears, at all events, to have done with 'literature', and we leave him with the plea for literature that it exists mainly to confer upon mankind a deeper and more general insight and corresponding powers of expression. Language is only ready to become the instrument of the modern mind when its development is complete, and it is when words are invested with all kinds of associations that they are the more or less adequate vehicles of thought and knowledge. And after 'literature', perhaps, comes something else.

In his 1967 study Surface and Symbol: The Consistency of James Joyce's Ulysses, *Robert Martin Adams examined Joyce's use of factual materials.*

Ulysses is literature but it is not just literature; it is a visionary book, like those of Blake, intricate in many of its strategies but surpassingly direct in its impact. Few books, of our time or any other, respond more generously to the formulas of criticism, or encourage one more persistently to transcend them.

— Surface and Symbol, p. 256

The Pirating of *Ulysses*

In July 1926, without Joyce's authorization, the Austrian-born American editor and publisher Samuel Roth began publishing portions of Ulysses *in his inaugural issue of* Two Worlds Monthly. *At Joyce's request, Ludwig Lewisohn and Archibald MacLeish composed and circulated a protest statement, dated 2 February 1927. The statement was signed by more than 160 prominent writers.*

It is a matter of common knowledge that the ULYSSES of Mr. James Joyce is being republished in the United States, in a magazine edited by Samuel Roth, and that this republication is being made without authorization by Mr. Joyce; without payment to Mr. Joyce and with alterations which seriously corrupt the text. This appropriation and mutilation of Mr. Joyce's property is made under colour of legal protection in that the ULYSSES which is published in France and which has been excluded from the mails in the United States is not protected by copyright in the United States. The question of justification of that exclusion is not now in issue; similar decisions have been made by government officials with reference to works of art before this. The question in issue is whether the public (including the editors and publishers to whom his advertisements are offered) will encourage Mr. Samuel Roth to take advantage of the resultant legal difficulty of the author to deprive him of his property and to mutilate the creation of his art. The undersigned protest against Mr. Roth's conduct in republishing ULYSSES and appeal to the American public in the name of that security of works of the intellect and the imagination without which art cannot live, to oppose to Mr. Roth's enterprise the full power of honorable and fair opinion.

(signed)

Lascelles Abercrombie	Bryher	Edward Garnett
Richard Aldington	Olaf Bull	Giovanni Gentille
Sherwood Anderson	Mary Butts	André Gide
René Arcos	Louis Cazamian	Bernard Gilbert
M. Arcybacheff	Jacques Chenevière	Ivan Goll
Ebba Atterbom	Abel Chevalley	Ramon Gomez de la Serna
Azorin, *Président de l'Académie Espagnole*	Maurice Constantin-Wéyer	Cora Gordon
	Albert Crémieux	Jan Gordon
C. du Baissauray	Benjamin Crémieux	Georg Goyert
Léon Bazalgette	Benedetto Croce	Alice S. Green
Jacinto Benavente	Ernst Robert Curtius	Julian Green
Silvio Benco	Francis Dickie	Augusta Gregory
Julien Benda	H.D.	Daniel Halévy
Arnold Bennett	Norman Douglas	Knut Hamsun
Jacques Benoist-Méchin	Charles Du Bos	Jane Harrison
	Georges Duhamel	H. Livingston Hartley
	Edouard Dujardin	Ernest Hemingway

Konrad Bercovici
J. D. Beresford
Rudolf Binding
Massimo Bontempelli
Jean de Bosschère
Ivan Bounine, *de*
  l'Académie Russe
Robert Bridges
Eugène Brieux, *de*
  l'Académie
  Française
Juan Ramon Jimenez
Eugene Jolas
Henry Festing Jones
George Kaiser
Herman Keyserling
Manual Komroff
A. Kouprine
René Lalou
Pierre de Lanux
Valéry Larbaud
D. H. Lawrence
Emile Legouis
Wyndham Lewis
Ludwing Lewisohn
Victor Llona
Mina Loy
Archibald MacLeish
Brinsley Macnamara
Maurice Maeterlinck
Thomas Mann
Antonio Marichalar
Maurice Martin du
  Gard
Dora Marsden
John Masefield
W. Somerset
  Maugham
André Maurois
D. Merejkowsky
Régis Michaud
Gabriel Miró
Hope Mirrlees

Luc Durtain
Albert Einstein
T. S. Eliot
Havelock Ellis
Edouard Estaunié
  de l'Académie
  Française
Léon-Paul Fargue
E. M. Forster
François Fosca
Gaston Gallimard
T. Sturge Moore
Paul Morand
Auguste Morel
Arthur Moss
J. Middleton Murry
Sean O'Casey
Liam O'Flaherty
Jose Ortega y Gasset
Seumas O'Sullivan
Elliot H. Paul
Jean Paulhan
Arthur Pinero
Luigi Pirandello
Jean Prévost, *de*
  l'Académie
  Française
C. F. Ramuz
Alfonso Reyes
Ernest Rhys
Elmer E. Rice
Dorothy Richardson
Jacques Robertfrance
Lennox Robinson
John Rodker
Romain Rolland
Jules Romains
Bertrand Russell
George W. Russell
  'A. E.'
Ludmila Savitsky
Jean Schlumberger
May Sinclair

Yrjo Hirn
Hugo von
  Hofmannsthal
Sisley Huddleston
Stephen Hudson
George F. Hummel
Bampton Hunt
Bravig Imbs
Holbrook Jackson
Edmond Jaloux.
Storm Jameson
W. L. Smyser
E. Œ. Somerville
Philippe Soupault
André Spire
Th. Stephanides
James Stephens
André Suarès
Italo Svevo
Frank Swinnerton
Arthur Symons
Marcel Thiébaut
Virgil Thomson
Robert de Traz
R. C. Trevelyan
Miguel de Unamuno
Paul Valéry, *de*
  l'Académie
  Française
Fernand Vandérem
Fritz Vanderpyl
Francis Viélé-Griffin
Hugh Walpole
Jacob Wassermann
H. G. Wells
Rebecca West
Anna Wickham
Thornton Wilder
Robert Wolf
Virginia Woolf
W. B. Yeats

— Letters III, pp. 151–153

Professor William York Tindall (1903–1981) taught at New York University from 1926 to 1931. He was reputedly the first college teacher to make *Ulysses* required reading for his students, a bold assignment considering that the novel was banned in the United States at the time.

— James Joyce A to Z, p. 216

On 27 December 1928, the New York Supreme Court issued an injunction against Samuel Roth and his company.

INJUNCTION

At a Special Term, Part II, of the Supreme Court, held in and for the County of New York, at the Court House thereof in the Borough of Manhattan, New York City, on the 27th day of December 1928.

PRESENT:
  HON. RICHARD H. MITCHELL
    JUSTICE.

JAMES JOYCE
  Plaintiff,
  —against—
SAMUEL ROTH AND TWO WORLDS
  PUBLISHING COMPANY INC.,
  Defendants.

Upon the summons, amended complaint and the answers thereto, the deposition of Samuel Roth, subscribed January 10, 1928, the deposition of James Joyce, taken March 8, 1928, the stipulation between the attorneys for the respective parties and consent of defendants thereto, both dated December 19, 1928, and all other proceedings heretofore had herein:

Now, on motion of Chadbourne, Stanchfield & Levy, plaintiff's attorneys, it is

ADJUDGED AND DECREED that the above-named defendants Samuel Roth and Two Worlds Publishing Company Inc., and each of them, their officers, assistants, agents and servants are hereby enjoined, under the penalty by Law prescribed, from using the name of the plaintiff for advertising purposes or for purposes of trade by

(a) Publishing, printing, stating or advertising the name of the plaintiff in connection with any magazine, periodical or other publication published by defendants or either of them;

(b) Publishing, printing, stating or advertising the name of the plaintiff in connection with any book, writing, manuscript or other work of the plaintiff;

(c) Publishing, printing, stating or advertising, or otherwise disseminating the name of the plaintiff in connection with any book, writing, manuscript or other work of the plaintiff, including the book 'ULYSSES', in any issue of Two Worlds Monthly, Two Worlds Quarterly, or any other magazine, periodical or other publication, heretofore or hereafter published by defendants. Enter,

RICHARD H. MITCHELL
Justice of the Supreme Court
THOMAS F. FARLEY.
Clerk.

Jung and Joyce

In his September 1932 letter to Joyce, C. G. Jung refers to his essay, "'Ulysses': A Monologue," which that month first appeared in Europäische Revue *(Berlin). The essay is reprinted in the fifteenth volume of* The Collected Works of C. G. Jung.

Dear Sir, Your Ulysses has presented the world such an upsetting psychological problem, that repeatedly I have been called in as a supposed authority on psychological matters.

Ulysses proved to be an exceedingly hard nut and it has forced my mind not only to most unusual efforts, but also to rather extravagant peregrinations (speaking from the standpoint of a scientist). Your book as a whole has given me no end of trouble and I was brooding over it for about three years until I succeeded to put myself into it. But I must tell you that I'm profoundly grateful to yourself as well as to your gigantic opus, because I learned a great deal from it. I shall probably never be quite sure whether I did enjoy it, because it meant too much grinding of nerves and of grey matter. I also don't know whether you will enjoy what I have written about Ulysses because I couldn't help telling the world how much I was bored, how I grumbled, how I cursed and how I admired. The 40 pages of non stop run in the end is a string of veritable psychological peaches. I suppose the devil's grandmother knows so much about the real psychology of a woman. I didn't.

Well I just try to recommend my little essay to you, as an amusing attempt of a perfect stranger that went astray in the labyrinth of your Ulysses and happened to get out of it again by sheer good luck. At all events you may gather from my article what Ulysses has done to a supposedly balanced psychologist.

With the expression of my deepest appreciation, I remain, dear Sir,
Yours faithfully

C. G. JUNG
– Letters III, pp. 253–254

In his October 1932 letter to Georg Goyert, Joyce wrote that Jung seems to have gone through the novel from beginning to end "without one smile" and suggests that the "only thing to do in such a case is to change one's drink!" Joyce then wrote "v. Ulysses–episode Eolus" (Letters III, p. 262), alluding to an exchange in which Stephen Dedalus responds in a similar fashion to a florid passage in Dan Dawson's latest speech read by Ned Lambert.

The Circulation of *Ulysses* in England

On Joyce's behalf, Paul Léon wrote to F. V. Morley on 19 November 1933 to argue for the publication of the novel in Great Britain. Ulysses *was not published in England until The Bodley Head edition in 1936.*

Dear Mr Morley, Please find enclosed the several points concerning the circulation of ULYSSES in Great Britain which seem to me to have some bearing on a possible publication of this work in England. There are of course several others to be added, that of cases of Ulysses being sold under the mantel in fact at all booksellers in England. But the principals are mentioned in the appended notes. Naturally I am constantly following the matter up and as soon as anything new turns up I will let you know.

I cannot refrain from thinking that it would be time to do something about bringing out ULYSSES in England. I am sure (and I am not talking without reasons) that should the H.O. be approached you will find the authorities (though naturally unwilling to commit themselves or promise anything) less difficult to be talked to on the matter than they ever have been. In fact I think that unofficially they would hint that personally they will not start a case and ban the book. Of course the Director of Public Prosecution is at the mercy of letters from private persons who will complain

Paul Léon, a close friend of Joyce who supervised the author's business and financial affairs in the 1930s

but I am sure that he will think twice before starting a case himself.

Obviously the winning of the case in America will constitute a strong card in our game but I do not think that even independently of this something should be done in England. From the cuttings concerning L. Golding's book you will see how public opinion is being prepared independently from us. Unless something is actually started right away it will mean a terrible amount of time wasted, fro you must not forget that there is a constant stream of copies going to England which take away the readers of the eventual British publication.

I hope you will find your way in devising some scheme; it will not mean great investment of capital since a case can be provoked following the American precedent of having a copy of the current edition seized by the Customs authorities.

Please remember me to Mrs Morley and believe me sincerely yours,

PAUL LÉON

Mr Joyce, whom I have just seen, wishes me to tell you that in view of the lack of courage which he has met with up to now, he is strongly advised to undertake the publication of Ulysses in G. B. himself–

Notes on the circulation of the English edition of ULYSSES in England.

1.) In the last week of April or in the first week of May 1932 there appeared in the Evening Standard an interview with one of the keepers of the British Museum. This gentleman is quoted as saying (the question he was interviewed on was 'banned books') and emphasizing that ULYSSES was not a banned book that they took it off their catalogue at their own discretion and that they never made any difficulty in giving it to the reading public in fact to any person who had a valid reason to alledge for reading it. In fact Ulysses had been read so much that they had to acquire several copies and had them bound. Their proceedings would naturally had been different if ULYSSES had been under a ban of a decision taken by a Court.

2.) I do not know the details of the seizure of the 499 copies of the second edition of Ulysses by the Custom Authorities at Folkestone (The entire edition was of 500 copies). You may obtain the entire correspondence exchanged between the customs and the then editor of ULYSSES Mr John Rodker from this gentleman (whose address can be found in the P.O. Directory). The Customs at the time refused to send the copies back to France and the Chief of the Folkestone Customs Office is supposed to have destroyed them all. As a matter of fact, there are strong reasons (among which words said by the Custom Officers themselves) showing that this was not done and a copy of this edition can, I am sure be found on sale in London. It is an open secret that Ulysses is sold in London. Mr Stuart Gilbert at the time in India had a copy sent to him from Oxford from Messrs Blackwell to Burma–This copies bears the imprint: Printed for the Egoist Press by John Rodker, Paris.

3) Finally last year ULYSSES was placed as a text book in Cambridge on the list of a young professor's lectures on Modern English Litterature. The course took actually place and it is an open secret that a copy of Ulysses is easily obtainable (though expensively) at any bookseller of the University cities. In fact the course would have passed unnoticed had not this young lecturer applied to the Home Office to obtain a copy officially. As a result his course and his private life were investigated by H.O. authorities and the Director of Public Prosecution went so far as to warn the Vice-Chancellor of the unheard of thing that was going on in the Cambridge University. The Vice-Chancellor showed this letter to several persons including the incriminated professor. It contained amidst vehement protests about the indecency of Ulysses the humourous offer to forward a copy of ULYSSES for the Vice-Chancellor's private and personal edification.

4) The B.B.C. censor refused to allow Mr Harold Nicholoson's lecture discussing ULYSSES over the Radio. Only after three weeks of continual tergiversation and under the threat of Mr Nicholson's resignation did he finally give way with the condition that the title of Ulysses would not be mentioned.

– *Letters III*, pp. 289–291

Judge Woolsey's Decision

At the instigation of Bennett A. Cerf of Random House, a copy of Ulysses *was openly imported into the United States. Its seizure by customs officials led to a test case that was decided on 6 December 1933 by Judge John M. Woolsey of the United States District Court of the Southern District of New York, who lifted the ban on the novel.*

In At Random: The Reminiscenes of Bennett Cerf, *Cerf explains the pretrial strategy that his attorney Morris Ernst used before he argued the case against the ban on Ulysses: "We hoped to get a judge who we though would be favorably disposed to our cause. This is where Ernst's experience was invaluable. He knew that Judge John M. Woolsey was a man of eruditon who had already established a reputation for liberal literary opinions, so he timed our case to come up when Woolsey was sitting in New York." The trial was without a jury, lasted only two days, and left the defendants confidant that Judge Woolsey would rule in their favor.*

UNITED STATES DISTRICT COURT
SOUTHERN DISTRICT OF NEW YORK
United States of America,
Libelant

V.   OPINION

One Book called "Ulysses" A. 110–59
Random House, Inc.,
Claimant

On cross motions for a decree in a libel of confiscation, supplemented by a stipulation–hereinafter described–brought by the United States against the book "Ulysses" by James Joyce, under Section 305 of the Tariff Act of 1930, Title 19 United States Code, Section 1305, on the ground that the book is obscene within the meaning of that Section, and, hence, is not importable into the United States, but is subject to seizure, forfeiture and confiscation and destruction.

United States Attorney–by Samuel C. Coleman, Esq., and Nicholas Atlas, Esq., of counsel–for the United States, in support of motion for a decree dismissing the libel.

Messrs. Greenbaum, Wolff & Ernst,–by Morris L. Ernst, Esq., and Alexander Lindey, Esq., of counsel–attorneys for claimant Random House, Inc., in support of motion for a decree dismissing the libel, and in opposition to motion for a decree of forfeiture.

WOOLSEY, J.:

The motion for a decree dismissing the libel herein is granted, and, consequently, of course, the Government's motion for a decree of forfeiture and destruction is denied.

Accordingly a decree dismissing the libel without costs may be entered herein.

I. The practice followed in this case is in accordance with the suggestion made by me in the case of *United States* v. *One Book Entitled "Contraception"*, 51 F. (2d) 525, and is as follows:

After issue was joined by the filing of the claimant's answer to the libel for forfeiture against "Ulysses", a stipulation was made between the United States Attorney's office and the attorneys for the claimant providing:

1. That the book "Ulysses" should be deemed to have been annexed to and to have become part of the libel just as if it had been incorporated in its entirely therein.

2. That the parties waived their right to a trial by jury.

3. That each party agreed to move for decree in its favor.

4. That on such cross motions the Court might decide all the questions of law involved and render a general finding thereon.

5. That on the decision of such motions the decree of the Court might be entered as if it were a decree after trial.

It seems to me that a procedure of this kind is highly appropriate in libels for the confiscation of books such as this. It is an especially advantageous procedure in the instant case because on account of the length of "Ulysses" and the difficulty of reading it, a jury trial would have been an extremely unsatisfactory, if not an almost impossible, method of dealing with it.

II. I have read "Ulysses" once in its entirely and I have read those passages of which the Government particularly complains several times. In fact, for many weeks, my spare time has been devoted to the consideration of the decision which my duty would require me to make in this matter.

"Ulysses" is not an easy book to read or to understand. But there has been much written about it, and in order properly to approach the consideration of it, it is advisable to read a number of other books which have now become its satellites. The study of "Ulysses" is, therefore, a heavy task.

III. The reputation of "Ulysses" in the literary world, however, warranted my taking such time as was necessary to enable me to satisfy myself as to the intent with which the book was written, for, of course, in any case where a book is claimed to be obscene it must first be determined, whether the intent with which it was written was what is called, according to the usual phrase, pornographic,–that is, written for the purpose of exploiting obscenity.

If the conclusion is that the book is pornographic that is the end of the inquiry and forfeiture must follow.

But in "Ulysses", in spite of its unusual frankness, I do not detect anywhere the leer of the sensualist. I hold, therefore, that it is not pornographic.

IV. In writing "Ulysses", Joyce sought to make a serious experiment in a new, if not wholly novel, literary genre. He takes persons of the lower middle class living in Dublin in 1904 and seeks not only to describe what they did on a certain day early in June of that year as they went about the City bent on their usual occupations, but also to tell what many of them thought about the while.

Joyce has attempted–it seems to me, with astonishing success–to show how the screen of consciousness with its ever-shifting kaleidoscopic impressions carries, as it were on a plastic palimpsest, not only what is in the focus of each man's observation of the actual things about him, but also in a penumbral zone residua of past impressions, some recent and some drawn up by association from the domain of the subsconscious. He shows how each of these impressions affects the life and behavior of the character which he is describing.

What he seeks to get is not unlike the results of a double or, if that is possible, a multiple exposure on a cinema film which would give a clear foreground with a background visible but somewhat blurred and out of focus in varying degrees.

To convey by words an effect which obviously lends itself more appropriately to a graphic technique, accounts, it seems to me, for much of the obscurity which meets a reader of "Ulysses". And it also explains another aspect of the book, which I have further to consider, namely, Joyce's sincerity and his honest effort to show exactly how the minds of his characters operate.

If Joyce did not attempts to be honest in developing the technique which he has adopted in "Ulysses" the result would be psychologically misleading and thus unfaithful to his chosen technique. Such an attitude would be artistically inexcusable.

It is because Joyce has been loyal to his technique and has not funked its necessary implications, but has honestly attempted to tell fully what his characters think about, that he has been the subject of so many attacks and that his purpose has been so often misunderstood and misrepresented. For his attempt sincerely and honestly to realize his objective has required him incidentally to use certain words which are generally considered dirty words and has led at times to what many think is a too poignant preoccupation with sex in the thoughts of his characters.

The words which are criticized as dirty are old Saxon words known to almost all men and, I venture, to many women, and are such words as would be naturally and habitually used, I believe, by the types of folk whose life. physical and mental, Joyce is seeking to describe. In respect of the recurrent emergence of the theme of sex in the minds of his characters, it must always be remembered that his locale was Celtic and his season Spring.

Whether or not one enjoys such a technique as Joyce uses is a matter of taste on which disagreement or argument is futile, but to subject that technique to the standards of some other technique seems to me to be little short of absurd.

Accordingly, I hold that "Ulysses" is a sincere and honest book and I think that the criticism of it are entirely disposed of by its rationale.

V. Furthermore, "Ulysses" is an amazing *tour de force* when one considers the success which has been in the main achieved with such a difficult objective as Joyce set for himself. As I have stated, "Ulysses" is not an easy book

to read. It is brilliant and dull, intelligible and obscure by turns. In many places it seems to me to be disgusting, but although it contains, as I have mentioned above, many words usually considered dirty, I have not found anything that I consider to be dirt for dirt's sake. Each word of the book contributes like a bit of mosaic to the detail of the picture which Joyce is seeking to construct for his readers.

If one does not wish to associate with such folk as Joyce describes, that is one's own choice. In order to avoid indirect contact with them one may not wish to read "Ulysses"; that is quite understandable. But when such a real artist in words, as Joyce undoubtedly is, seeks to draw a true picture of the lower middle class in a European city, ought it to be impossible for the American public legally to see that picture?

To answer this question it is not sufficient merely to find, as I have found above, that Joyce did not write "Ulysses" with what is commonly called pornographic intent, I must endeavor to apply a more objective standard to his book in order to determine its effect in the result, irrespective of the intent with which it was written.

VI. The statute under which the libel is filed only denounces, in so far as we are here concerned the importation into the United States from any foreign country of "any obscene book". Section 305 of the Tariff Act of 1930, Title 19 United States Code, Section 1305. It does not marshal against books the spectrum of condemnatory adjectives found, commonly, in laws dealing with matters of this kind. I am, therefore, only required to determine whether "Ulysses" is obscene within the legal definition of that word.

The meaning of the word "obscene" as legally defined by the Courts is: tending to stir the sex impulses or to lead to sexually impure and lustful thoughts. *Dunlop v. United States,* 165, U.S. 486, 501; *United States v. One Book Entitled "Married Love",* 48 F. (2d) 821, 824; *United States v. One Book Entitled "Contraception",* 51 F. (2d) 525, 528; and compare *Dysart v. United States,* 272 U.S. 655, 657; *Swearingen v. United States,* 161 U.S. 446, 450; *United States v. Dennett,* 39 F. (2d) 564, 568 (C.C.A. 2); *People v. Wendling,* 258 N.Y. 451, 453.

Whether a particular book would tend to excite such impulses and thoughts must be tested by the Court's opinion as to its effect on a person with average sex instincts—what the French would call *l'homme moyen sensuel*—who plays, in this branch of legal inquiry, the same role of hypothetical reagent as does the "reasonable man" in the law of torts and "the man learned in the art" on questions of invention in patent law.

The risk involved in the use of such a reagent arises from the inherent tendency of the trier of facts, however fair he may intend to be, to make his reagent too much subservient to his own idiosyncrasies. Here, I have attempted to avoid this, if possible, and to make my reagent herein more objective than he might otherwise be, by adopting the following course:

After I had made my decision in regard to the aspect of "Ulysses", now under consideration, I checked my impressions with two friends of mine who in my opinion answered to the above stated requirement for my reagent.

These literary assessors—as I might properly describe them—were called on separately, and neither knew that I was consulting the other. They are men whose opinion on literature and on life I value most highly. They had both read "Ulysses", and, of course, were wholly unconnected with this cause.

Without letting either of my assessors know what my decision was, I gave to each of them the legal definition of obscene and asked each whether in his opinion "Ulysses" was obscene within that definition.

I was interested to find that they both agreed with my opinion: that reading "Ulysses" in its entirety, as a book must be read on such a test as this, did not tend to excite sexual impulses or lustful thoughts but that its net effect on them was only that of a somewhat tragic and very powerful commentary on the inner lives of men and women.

It is only with the normal person that the law is concerned. Such a test as I have described, therefore, is the only proper test of obscenity in the case of a book like "Ulysses" which is a sincere and serious attempt to devise a new literary method for the observation and description of mankind.

I am quite aware that owning to some of its scenes "Ulysses" is a rather strong draught to ask some sensitive, though normal, persons to take. But my considered opinion, after long reflection, is that whilst in many places the effect of "Ulysses" on the reader undoubtedly is somewhat emetic, nowhere does it tend to be an aphrodisiac.

"Ulysses" may, therefore, be admitted into the United States.

JOHN M. WOOLSEY
UNITED STATES DISTRICT JUDGE
December 6, 1933

No reasonable man applying the proper rule of law would come to any conclusion other than that *Ulysses* is obscene. Taking the test of obscenity which has been established in the Federal Courts and applying it to the numerous passages of grossly obscene matter with which this book fairly reeks, there can be no doubt that the District Court erred in its determination that *Ulysses* is not obscene.

– Martin Conboy, U.S. Attorney

Judge Woolsey's decision gave immediate impetus to efforts to publish Ulysses *in England, as is shown by publisher Geoffrey Faber's 5 January 1934 letter to solicitor-general Donald Somervell. Although Faber and Faber did not arrange to publish* Ulysses, *the firm did bring out* Finnegans Wake.

My dear Donald, I want your advice–if possible your help–in an obscure matter, not without its importance for English letters. I don't really know if it falls within the Solicitor-General's province; if it doesn't I feel sure you will tell me what authority we ought to approach, and perhaps even give us a line of introduction.

The question I am raising is that of the publication of James Joyce's ULYSSES in England. As I expect you know, this book was originally published–and is still published–in Paris. Arrangements were made for a part of the original Paris edition to be published in London by a small firm called THE EGOIST PRESS (whose publications we took over some time ago, but after the ULYSSES affair). Practically the whole of the consignment from Paris to the London publishers was seized by the Customs–I suppose by instructions from the Home Office–as 'obscene'. Copies imported from Paris are still liable to be seized, though they have always been obtainable quite easily from London booksellers. They can, in fact, now be brought at little more than one would have to pay in Paris.

Whatever the legal definition of obscenity may be, it has always been felt by most competent English critics that the term could not intelligently be applied to ULYSSES, which is certainly a work of genius and, in the opinion of many, much the most important literary work of art produced in English during the present century. The fact that it should have been classed by the police or the Home Office or the Customs authorities with pornographic literature has seemed, to those who hold the opinion I have suggested, to constitute a considerable slur on the intelligence of the authorities. Sooner or later the publication of ULYSSES In England is inevitable; and the question has now been raised in an acute form by its open publication in the U. S. A.

The position in the U. S. A. has been not dissimilar from that in this country. That is, the Customs seized all copies which came into their hands. Their action in doing so has recently been made the subject of a test case, heard by Judge Woolsey. The Judge gave a remarkable, and extremely intelligent judgement, to the effect that ULYSSES was not an obscene book and might be admitted into the United States. As the result of this judgement, the book will shortly be published in the U. S. A.

Naturally this decision has encouraged Mr. Joyce and his advisers to hope for English as well as American publication. My firm is particularly interested in this situation, because we are now Mr. Joyce's official publishers in England–we have issued parts of his unfinished book WORK IN PROGRESS and shall publish the book when it is finished. For some time Mr. Joyce has been pressing us to publish ULYSSES, and matters have now come to a head because (as we have just heard) another London firm has made him an offer to publish ULYSSES in the form of a six months' option.

I had intended to sound out official opinion in this country before long, but this communication obliges me to act more quickly than I had intended. We are, in fact, asked for an immediate reply in the form of a definite offer. That is, of course, of no interest to the English authorities, but it will explain to you why I am writing to you personally and informally in the matter. For any opinion or assistance you can give us I should be exceedingly grateful.

I have to go down to Wales this afternoon, and shall be away for ten days or so– whereas our answer to Joyce's agent cannot be delayed for more than two or three days. But in my absence the matter will be handled here by two of my directors–Mr. T. S. Eliot (of whom you know) and Mr. F. V. Morley. Is it asking too much of you to say that I should be very grateful if you could give Eliot and Morley an opportunity to see you for a quarter of an hour? They know the contents of this letter, and are–if anything–more familiar with the facts than I am myself. Either of them can be got on the telephone here on Monday morning.

–*Letters III,* pp. 296–298

T. S. Eliot wrote to Joyce on 9 January 1934 to explain the reluctance of Faber and Faber to push too hard for the publication of Ulysses.

It is impossible to get any positive statement form the Home Office, and nobody else will have any more success in that than we; but what can be done, and is a slow and delicate business, is to take the official temperature.

. . . .

My impressions are that the general atmosphere is steadily becoming more favourable. Now, if there were *no* symptoms of change, I should say: as well try the book now as any time. But I believe that there will be much better chances of success in six months or a years' time. What I have in mind is, that public opinion can change and is changing; but a decision of a high court is a different matter; and I am afraid that premature attempts might actually delay the general availability of the book. I say a *high* court, because it would be bad for both publisher and book, if a publisher undertook to publish it without being ready to go on fighting for it. If it were published, and the publisher then lay down tamely under a mere magistrate's decision, the effect would be bad. But if on the other hand the magistrate's decision were sustained, there would be a legal precedent difficult to break for a long time.

–*Letters III,* pp. 300–301

Martin Conboy, United States Attorney for the Southern District of New York, filed an appeal against Judge Woolsey's decision on 16 March 1934. On 7 August 1934 the United States Circuit Court of Appeals upheld Woolsey's decree.

Ulysses Pure; Customs "Goofy"
The Nice Little Tome Isn't Even Obscene, U.S. Circuit Court Rules
New York Evening Post, 7 August 1934

Ulysses wins. It's neither lewd, immoral nor obscene. Customs men who held otherwise were goofy or something.

So ruled the United States Circuit Court of Appeals today, with one of the three judges dissenting.

The ruling was pleasing to both James Joyce, the author of *Ulysses,* and to Random House, Inc., to which concern a copy of the book imported from Europe must be turned over by the customs without further let or hindrance.

Judge Is Pleased

It was pleasing to Federal District Judge John M. Woolsey, too, for the verdict was on appeal from a Woolsey finding of December 6, 1933, that though *Ulysses* perhaps was "somewhat emetic" to some readers, it nowhere tended to be an aphrodisiac.

The book, story of the thoughts and doings of Dublin folk on a certain June day of 1904, had been bootlegged throughout the United States for years prior to the court test.

Judge Woolsey spoke of modern frankness in discussions of sex and such. He spoke of *Ulysses* as an "amazing tour de force"; spoke of "the screen of consciousness with its ever-shifting kaleidoscopic impressions," of "plastic palimpsest," of "penumbral zone residua of past impressions" and a lot of other things.

He summed up by calling *Ulysses* a "sincere and honest book."

Said the Circuit Court of Appeals today, in an opinion written by Judge Augustus N. Hand and concurred in by Judge Learned Hand, with Presiding Judge Martin T. Manton disagreeing:

"Art certainly cannot advance under compulsion to the traditional forms, and nothing in such a field is more stifling to progress than limitation of the right to experiment with a new technique."

Judge Manton, dissenting, retorted that characterization of *Ulysses* as obscene "should be quite unanimous."

Higher Court Holds *Ulysses* Is Not Obscene
New York Herald-Tribune, 8 August 1934

Judges Augustus Noble Hand and Learned Hand, of the United States Circuit Court of Appeals, decided yesterday that James Joyce's *Ulysses,* taken on the whole of its 768 pages, was not obscene, thereby sustaining the ruling of Judge John M. Woolsey in District Court that importation of the book into the United States was permissible. Presiding Judge Martin T. Manton filed a dissenting opinion.

The majority opinion, written by Judge Augustus Noble Hand and concurred in by his cousin, held *Ulysses* to be a work of originality and sincerity of treatment, and without "the effect of promoting lust," thus making it admissible to the United States "even though it justly may offend many." Random House, Inc., publishers, first brought the case to a test by importing a copy of the work, which was promptly seized by customs authorities and impounded under section 305(a) of the Tariff Act.

Conboy May Appeal Again

Martin Conboy, United States Attorney, who argued the government's case before the Circuit Court of Appeals in May, mainly by reading aloud the more robust passages in the book and branding each one in turn as obscene, had not decided yesterday whether to make a recommendation to the Solicitor General that a petition of certiorari be filed with the United States Supreme Court in a final effort to obtain a reversal. When pressed for a statement, Mr. Conboy merely said he had read the opinions and "might" carry the case further.

"James Joyce," the prevailing opinion said, "may be regarded as a pioneer among those writers who have adopted the so-called stream of consciousness method of presentation which has attracted considerable attention in academic and literary circles. In this field *Ulysses* is rates as a book of considerable power by persons whose opinions are entitled to weight. It has become a sort of contemporary classic dealing with new subject matter.

"It attempts to depict the thoughts and lay bare the souls of a number of people, some of them intellectuals, some social outcasts and nothing more, with a literalism that leaves nothing unsaid.

"Certain passages are of beauty and of undoubted distinction, while others are of a vulgarity that is extreme, and the book as a whole has a realism characteristic of the present age."

"Sincere, Truthful and Real Art"

It was the feeling of Judges Hand that Joyce's depiction of character is "sincere and truthful and executed with real art." They felt that the author dealt with

"things that very likely might better have remained unattempted," but that his book was "a work of symmetry and excellent craftmanship of a sort."

. . . .

Ulysses contains many long passages that are obscene, but they are relevant to the author's purpose of depicting the thoughts of his characters and are introduced to give meaning to the whole, "rather than promote lust or portray filth for its own sake." The net effect of certain sections most open to attack, Judge Hand said, citing and famous soliloquey of the character Mrs. Bloom as an example, "is pitiful and tragic, rather than lustful."

"The book depicts the souls of men and women by turns bewildered and keenly apprehensive, sordid and aspiring, ugly and beautiful, hateful and loving," the opinion said. "In the end, one feels pity and sorrow for the confusion, misery and degradation of humanity."

It was conceded that page after page of the book was incomprehensible, but "many passages show the trained hand of an artist who can at one moment adapt to perfection the style of an ancient chronicler and at another become the veritable personification of Thomas Carlyle."

The book was not pornographic as a whole, the court held, "although in not a few spots is it coarse, blasphemous and obscene." However, the erotic passages were submerged in the complete book, the court ruled.

How About *Hamlet* Then?

"If those are to make the book subject to confiscation, Judge Hand remarked, "by the same test *Venus and Adonis, Hamlet, Romeo and Juliet,* and the story in the eighth book of *The Odyssey,* of the entrapment of Ares and Aphrodite in a net spread by the outraged Hephaestus, amid the laughter of the immoral gods, as well as many other classics, would have to be suppressed."

Doubting the ultimate durability of *Ulysses,* the opinion further set forth that "it may be the book will not last as a substantial contribution to literature and it is certainly easy to believe that in spite of the opinion of Joyce's laudators, the immortals will still reign; but the same may be said of the current works of art and music and of many other serious efforts of the mind."

"Art certainly cannot advance under compulsion to the traditional forms," it said, "and nothing in such a field is more stifling to progress than limitation of the right to experiment with a new technique. The foolish judgments of Lord Eldon about 100 years ago proscribing the works of Byron, Shelley and Southey are a warning to all who have to determine the limits of the field within which authors may exercise themselves."

Manton Insists It's Obscene

In his dissenting opinion Judge Manton said he could find no conflicting evidence and cited several authorities in support of his contention that *Ulysses* was obscene. He included in his opinion the numbers of pages on which the allegedly lewd passages might be found as pointed out by Mr. Conboy in his argument.

"Who can doubt the obscenity of this book after reading the pages referred to, which are too indecent to add as a footnote to this opinion?" the jurist wrote. "Its characterization as obscene should be quite unanimous."

Because *Ulysses* is a work of fiction, Judge Manton said, it may not be compared with books involving medical subjects or describing certain physical or biological facts. He maintained it was written for the alleged amusement of the reader only.

"The characters described in the thoughts of the author may in some instances be true," he said, "but, be it truthful or otherwise, a book that is obscene is not rendered less so by a statement of truthful fact.

"If we disregard the protection of the morals of the susceptible are we to consider merely the benefits and pleasures derived from letters by those who pose as more highly developed and intelligent? The court cannot indulge any instinct it may have to foster letters."

Defines Purpose of Literature

"The people do not exist for the sake of prevailing literature, or to give the author fame, the publisher wealth, and the book a market. On the contrary, literature exists for the sake of the people; to refresh the weary, console the sad, hearten the dull and downcast, to increase man's interest in the world, his joy of living and his sympathy in all sorts and conditions of men.

"Art for art's sake is heartless and soon grows artless; art for the public market is not art at all, but commerce; art for the people's service is noble, vital and a permanent element of human life. The people need and deserve a moral standard and it should be a point of honor among men of letters to maintain it.

"A refusal to imitate obscenity or to load a book with it is an author's professional chastity."

Morris L. Ernst and Alexander Lindey argued the case for Random House, Inc., and Mr. Conboy was aided by Francis H. Horan and John F. Davidson, Assistant United States Attorneys. To be valid, a recommendation to the Solicitor General must be made within ninety days from the entry of the Appellate Court's order.

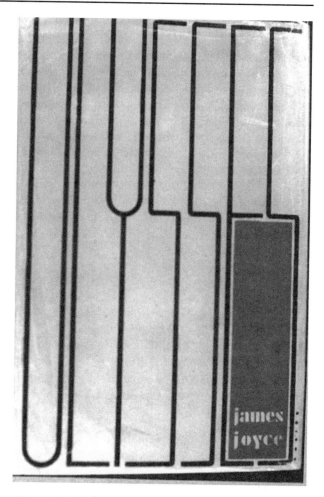

Dust jacket for the first authorized American edition of Ulysses, *published by Random House on 25 January 1934, a little more than a month and a half after Judge Woolsey lifted the ban on the importation of the novel into the United States*

Reviews of the first American edition of *Ulysses*

Judge Woolsey's landmark decision to lift the ban on Ulysses *was often cited or quoted in the reviews of the Random House edition of the novel, including this review by American critic and poet Horace Gregory.*

Review of Ulysses
Horace Gregory
New York Herald Tribune Books, 21 January 1934, Book Section, pp. 1–2

On Thursday, January 25, 1934, Joyce's "Ulysses," freshly cut and bound, will appear freely among us. Thanks to Judge John M. Woolsey, it is no longer a banned book in the company of red-backed, forbidden "classics." The misadventures of Molly

Bloom are no longer thrust into prominence by the lean hand of the censor, and we are allowed to relax in her presence. As for the esoteric mysteries of Stephen Dedalus and his companions of a memorable sixteen hours, even these have been cleared away within twelve long years of commentary. We can now approach the large, sparsely punctuated pages of this Homeric idyll in the same spirit that we read *Tristram Shandy,* and from them a curious experience emerges. In these days when newspaper headlines make nervous literature, the trip upstairs to Kinch's tower on a spring day in 1904 is an escape from the alarms of our present world that send us forth upon Odysseys of a later day.

Before we re-enter that room in Dublin where Buck Mulligan stands forever shouting, singing, as he blasphemously rubs fresh shaving lather into his cheek bones, it would be well to review briefly the history of "Ulysses" on this side of the Atlantic. In the year of the Armistice early chapters of the book appeared in Margaret Anderson's "Little Review." I remember one installment set alongside of W. B. Yeats's song of Solomon and Sheba. Here Mr. Bloom was in a newspaper office, very busy with his notice of poor Dignam's funeral, but I had little patience in following his adventures, for his progress onward through the day and through succeeding copies of the "Little Review" was blocked by great smudges of black ink across the page, blotting out full paragraphs by orders (I supposed) from Postoffice officials or Mr. Sumner. Finally, the adventurous Mr. Bloom, having seen his Nausicaa in the innocent person of Gerty McDowell, caused Mr. Sumner to haul the "Little Review" and its editors into court. The fight in the New York courtrooms was like a fragment of Dublin transported to a new land, the flaming Puritan John Quinn defending Joyce against a Tammany Irish influence on the bench. Unfortunately for Margaret Anderson, Jane Heap and Joyce, a young Norwegian jurist in the room grew bored and fell asleep. The day was won and lost by Irishmen.

Meanwhile, the "Ulysses" legend prospered. In 1922, 500 copies of the second edition, printed in London, were burned by New York Postoffice authorities. In 1923, 499 copies were seized by customs officials at Folkestone on the British coast. In 1927 chapters from "Ulysses" appeared more or less subterraneously in a magazine published in the United States, without Joyce's authorization and with no compensation to him. Behind smoked glasses sheets of "Ulysses" were offered with an obscene leer. Then came a protest signed by virtually every reputable name in contemporary literature, and the unathorized publisher made a stage offer of $2,500 to Joyce if he would come to America, knowing well that he (already in the care of a physician) could not accept the terms. At this moment, however,

the book was in its ninth printing, and tourist Americans, then overrunning Paris, found souvenir collecting incomplete without a copy of the thick paper-bound volume. Like the Bible, the perennial best seller of all time, the book was bought for added weight to one's library; and there, unread sat impressively on a shelf, or, in the company of Bohemian friends, sat, smoldering, upon the living-room table. Under these conditions the book made ready conversation, and it was not until Stuart Gilbert's analysis was published that free-lance interpretation simmered down to a recital of Valéry Larbaud's dispassionate facts about "Ulysses," which were disclosed by way of a short review in "The Criterion" for November, 1922.

Young writers, however, digested and redigested whole sections of what was now an "expatriate" Bible for artists. Dull passages were read with the same reverence that welcomed the livelier sections of the novel and from the body of the text came a new technic in the writing of English literature. To young Americans of this generation Joyce profoundly reiterated the lesson that the *manner* of saying a thing bore an important relationship to what was being said, and on this premise young men writing novels in Paris announced a revolution of the word. Today there is scarcely a novelist under thirty-five who has not seen (though possibly reflected by mirrors at fourth or even fifth hand) the shadow of "Ulysses" across the page of his typewriter.

II

As we reread the first page of "Ulysses," coarse, stately, plump Buck Mulligan points the way backward for us, and we return through the years of the war in which the book was written to the morning of June 16, 1904. This was one of the days that Joyce (here, Stephen Dedalus) wandered, a book of poems in his head, through the familiar streets of Dublin. He was a poet only by the courtesy of a few friends from whom he received but little recognition. We have a further index as to how he felt in reading the story of the submerged, ambitious clerk in "Dubliners"; here he merely recoils from Buck Mulligan's brutal gayety, remembers that an ancient Greek world held more security than his own, recalls his ever-present poverty and the image of his dead mother.

It is important, I think, at this point to remember that Dublin is an outpost of the European Continent; that one could lean from a tower over the Liffey and gaze out at the prospect of a dying culture on the mainland, a spectacle which gave Joyce the dramatic contrast to the ideal of Greek serenity he held in mind. We are accustomed to thinking of the World War as the moment of disaster, but the dissolution that Joyce witnessed had already sent out danger signals a decade earlier. Actual changes on the earth's surface are seldom spectacular; they are proverbially slow in making their appearance, and what seems to be the climax of an action is, more often than not, a spontaneous result of what had already passed, an echo of accumulated sound ending in a loud report, this time the literal impact of Big Berthas and machine-gun fire.

Faced with this obvious contrast to a dream of perfection which the exterior design of "Ulysses" implies, Joyce felt a deep sense of personal loss; yet he would be the last man living today who would care to credit himself with the role of prophet. Even less so than Thomas Mann, whose "Magic Mountain" suggests something of the same dissolution of European society that has its premise in "Ulysses." We have but to turn the pages of Joyce's "Chamber Music," the slight book of poems that waited until 1917 for publication, for knowledge of the emotion that stirred young Dedalus. Here he bade adieu to a time of innocence to which the eighteenth century doorways of Dublin promised an entrance, but where, once within, one found only shreds of last week's "Freeman's Journal" and moldy refuse. This mood, shared by modern poets, from E. A. Robinson to T. S. Eliot, finds its most detailed expression in "Ulysses." Just why Joyce should feel a mistrust of a commercialized democracy with greater depth than his fellows lies, I think, in two main sources. One, as "Dubliners" and "Portrait of the Artist" have already shown, may be found in his uneasy relationship to the world that surrounded him, his training in a medieval church, and the sensitive balance of his emotions and intellect which demanded that security which could be his only through mastery of an art. The other source may be revealed through the general condition of Ireland after Parnell's extraordinary failure. After a period of hope in which Parnell emerged as a hero came the reaction of defeat and concentrated disillusionment—but before we progress from this more general background let us return to Stephen Dedalus.

By reference to "The Portrait of the Artist" we know that Stephen was predestined for the church and why that predestination was not fulfilled. Failing the priesthood, he was subject to a poverty that he had known too well in childhood, and with this difference, that he was now declassed into an ill-paid schoolmaster. Like most sensitive men who had been born into the Church and broken with it, he felt no need for reconversion into another religion. Blasphemy and sin were the courses he had taken. In the opening pages of "Ulysses" we learn how Stephen Dedalus committed matricide; not in act, but by denial of the Church, and his sense of guilt was always to return, "because," as

Buck Mulligan said, "you have the cursed Jesuit strain in you, only it's injected the wrong way."

If we are to understand the mood of "Ulysses," it is significant, I think, that young Stephen carries with him an aura of failure and that a passing Dublin citizen would judge him by the company he keeps, look down upon him as the patronized friend of Mulligan or the chance companion of Bloom. He may have the airs of a gentleman, but Mulligan reminds him that his handkerchief is dirty and that the trousers he wears are secondhand. To place Stephen in dramatic juxtaposition with the real world, Joyce converts him into a ghost of Telemachus in search of a father, and once that identity is recognized, the complexion of Dublin's Inferno is given the surface of comedy, the kind of comedy that T. S. Eliot demands in poetry where one may look beneath to see "both beauty and ugliness; to see the boredom, and the horror and the glory." The funeral service for Dignam becomes a tribute for Elpenor, Bloom is Ulysses and this gall-tinctured analogy is extended until we arrive at last at Penelope, deliberately miscast as Molly Bloom.

Recently there has been some talk of Joyce's self-isolation from the cause of revolution in Ireland, but I think the sources of that isolation are more important than the result. I wish to suggest that Parnell's career, ending as it did in scandal and defeat, was of double significance to Joyce, who had chosen Stephen as his alter-ego. It is obvious that such a person as Stephen could not assume the ready-made patriotism that distinguished the later Parnellites; he would find little in common with the maudlin sentiments that motivated the Irish citizen in throwing a biscuit box at Bloom; such nationalism was meaningless to him. Yet Parnell's aristocratic bearing, his tightrope walking between, through and beyond party politics, his artful Hamlet-like deliberation made him an attractive figure to literary men whose families originated, as his had done, among the landed gentry. He represented an exaggerated ideal of nineteenth-century individualism, and his integrity, though rendered ineffectual through scandal, justified his memory as a martyr to a cause. Is it any wonder, then, that Stephen would regard political activity as a futile business for any honest man and that a symptom of deeper futility should appear in "Ulysses?" And that anywhere out of Ireland was a better place to live? Telemachus Stephen Dedalus talking to Ulysses Bloom in the cabmen's shelter will have none of Bloom's newspaper patriotism:

> . . . But I suspect, Stephen retorted with a sort of half laugh, that Ireland must be important because it belongs to me. . . . We can't change the country. Let us change the subject.

Stephen–Joyce–is ripe for exile; he is never to forget a detail of the impression that Dublin left upon his consciousness, for every word, every scene recalled in memory *belongs to him;* yet he is never to find peace at home, and here his position is analogous to the rootless Americans of the brief postwar era who hailed him as their leader, the perfect artist and the greatest expatriate of them all.

III

As Stuart Gilbert has very nearly proved, it would take a book twice the size of "Ulysses" to explain the great variety of its references, to unravel with exact notation the thought processes of Leopold and Molly Bloom, of Stephen Dedalus and Gerty McDowell. Joyce, the exile in Switzerland, with Europe in the flames of war around him, was writing down a universal history of the dead. Before he had finished, the entire world of 1904 had stepped into his Dublin canvas. The events of the daily newspaper, from obituaries to the sporting page, had crept into the large design, all parodied, all transfixed under a glaze of amber-tinted irony. And after this came the body of English prose, with Joyce, the smiling, deferential coroner, bat on knees, deliberately sitting on the corpse. No poet has ever executed a more subtle revenge for a final inversion of his lyric gifts; it was a revenge that involved great sacrifices as well as great awards. Now that his pedantry (which was in evidence in the writing of "Ulysses") has led him into the obscure channels of a "Work in Progress," now that his semi-blindness, as Alan Porter has remarked, may be responsible for an art that telescopes meaning and the sound of several words in one, the sacrifices Joyce has made are only too apparent. Only the artistry and a deep vein of humor remain. The "work" is a night world of dreams indeed, and if we accept the fragment, "Anna Livia Plurabelle," our terms are those accepting personal charm, an ear that is sensitive to each refinement of Dublin speech and a use of words that is so beautifully controlled that we cannot deny Joyce's right to be considered as one of the most expert poets of our time.

As I have already suggested, we are now moving away from the direct influence of Joyce's *Odyssey,* and as we drop discussion of its technical values, we will find a fresh enjoyment of its comedy and then accept the figure of Leopold Bloom as one of the great comic characters of all literature. It will then be natural to regard him as the peer of Uncle Toby or Falstaff or Mr. Micawber and the creation of his world is quite as complete as theirs. Once we are in it, there is no release from its singular atmosphere; we admit dull passages but what great novel is entirely free of this defect? Surely not "Don Quixote" or "Tristam Shandy" or "Gil Blas." I wish to make this prophecy: As Joyce's influence wanes and as the history of "Ulysses" becomes merely another chapter in an encyclopedia of English literature, our enjoyment of the book as major fiction will increase. As we read onward through that June day in 1904, Leopold Bloom's "stream of consciousness" will again enter our blood and lacking the need to consider Joyce's method in bringing him to life, we shall discover him as part of our heritage and he will be of greater vitality than the friend we boast of knowing all too well. Again we shall see him relish a breakfast of kidneys, feed the cat and follow his wife's directions in brewing a pot of tea, and we shall know by these signs that his day has begun. We shall be less aware, perhaps, of his author's purpose in creating him, but no matter, Bloom will outlive us all and will remain (as Uncle Toby has survived) as the arch symbol of humanity in a transient world.

The Random House edition of Ulysses *provided the occasion for Seldes to reflect on his original review of the novel written nearly twelve years before.*

Review of Ulysses
Gilbert Seldes
New York Evening Journal, 27 January 1934, p. 11

Although the new book by Sinclair Lewis is the event of the week, the free publication of James Joyce's *Ulysses* in America has to be noted as the event of the year. I have written perhaps too much about this book; there is certainly no need for me to review it now. But I am appalled to see that on the jacket of the very handsome volume, beautifully designed and printed and bound (Random House), I am quoted–from a review written about ten years ago. I am not appalled by an excuse of enthusiasm expressed at the time; the reverse. Like Warren Hastings, I am astonished at my own moderation. 'To my mind,' I wrote, *Ulysses* is one of the most significant and beautiful works of our time.' Mealymouthed words, weasel words, little, timid words introduced by an apologetic 'to my mind.' I am sure I said other, better, bolder things about *Ulysses.* I must have given the impression at least that for weeks I had lived in that book as I had lived in no other since I read *War and Peace;* I remember definitely saying that every page in the book is a tribute to the grandeur and beauty of the language in which all of our deepest thoughts and highest aspirations had been recorded. I denied that the book was ugly or black pessimism. I felt it to be a great affirmation to everything in life–the good and the evil. I still feel so. . . .

–reprinted from *James Joyce: The Critical Heritage*

Joyce portrait by Marcel Maurel on the cover of the leading newsweekly in the United States, 29 January 1934, after the novel had been published by Random House. The article concluded, "Enthusiasts have hailed James Joyce as an invigorator and inventor of language. But perhaps he will be longest remembered as the man who made 'unprintable' archaic" (Timepix).

A Stableboy's Book
Samuel Harden Church
Carnegie Magazine, VII (February 1934): 279–281

If this book had crept stealthily into the United States from Paris, the home of its author, it would have been handled by the literary bootleggers, as other meretricious books are handled; and no decent journal would ever have permitted it to be mentioned in review or advertisement. But an ambitious publisher challenged the right of the Government to burn or suppress it; and after a prolonged trial in the Federal court at New York Judge John Monro Woolsey decreed that it did not technically violate the statute against obscene literature, and that it was therefore free to be admitted, republished, and sold in this country. The notoriety thus given to the book and the almost immediate issue of a new edition by Random House, together with the attention it is receiving from the reviewers, make it a legitimate subject for discussion.

We are glad that Judge Woolsey took an advanced liberal ground in rendering this epochal decision. The official censors who stand on the steamship docks have too long exercised their prohibitory functions in the field of let-

ters; and they have consigned so many books of classical fame and merit to the flames that a final test of their standard of study might soon have reached Shakespeare. Judge Woolsey perceived the danger of this situation; and under his opinion all books which are not "pornographic" within the definition of the United States statute may henceforth be free from official censure. The age of prohibition by law of the things which an American may eat, drink, read, and do is dying away, and this judgment will contribute enormously to its demise.

We recall at this moment a pleasant visit at the residence of Myron T. Herrick at Paris, while he was ambassador to France. During the dinner that charming, amiable, accomplished gentleman had spoken of the harm done to art and letters in the United States by Anthony Comstock and his followers; and he asked:

"Do you remember a painting called 'September Morn' which was exhibited in the window of an art shop in New York, and which caused Comstock to arrest and imprison the art dealer?"

And when the dinner was over, Herrick said, "Come in here with me"; and he led the way into the drawing room, and there on the wall was "September Morn"–the original painting in oil of a young girl in the glorious beauty of youth, unclothed, standing in the sea, and shivering with a delicious innocence as the cold waves lapped her ankles.

"Think of a man," said Herrick; "think of a man's going to jail for showing that picture in his window, and think of our people's permitting it to be done!"

Well, Judge Woolsey's decision will prevent that thing from being done in this country again. And we sincerely hail him as a Daniel come to judgment.

And now what is this book that has brought about a striking of the shackles from the world's literary expression? We have read the book, and after reading it we declare our opinion that it is unreadable—not so much because it is so deadly dull that no mind can go through the mazes of its barbaric style and the length of its interminable pages except when moved by a sense of justice to read it before judging it.

The book comprises nearly eight hundred pages, set in small type. It tells the conversations and the thoughts of its characters, with an intimation of what they are doing, in their homes and haunts in Dublin during a day and a night in June, 1904. There is no story, no plot, no narrative; there is no conflict of motive; and the persons named appear from time to time in the book only to be lost in a sea of words. And the words are without form, and void. The author, consciously or unconsciously, follows the style of Thomas Carlyle in breaking up his incidents for the introduction of rhapsody; but while Carlyle uses his pages for rhapsodies which illuminate life in a flood of brilliant interpretations, the author here rambles into confused soliloquies which are without meaning in themselves and are inexplicable, having neither beauty of thought nor charm of diction and no relation to the things that have gone before or that are to come after.

We make the statement in good faith that it would be possible to tear out one hundred pages from this book near its opening words, another hundred at the middle, and a third hundred near the end, even including half the pages of the closing soliloquy, and that then the remaining five hundred pages could be read without any loss of sequence; furthermore, that the destroyed pages would contain no paragraph that is lucid, informative, or comprehensible under the rule of directness and force.

Here is his style at its clearest:

"Ineluctable modality of the visible: At least that if no more, thought through my eyes. Signatures of all things I am here to read, seaspawn and seawrack, the nearing tide, that rusty boot . . . [Necessary omission] Limits of the diaphane. But he adds: in bodies. Then he was aware of them against them, sure. Go easy. Bald he was and a millionaire. Limit of the diaphane in. Why in? Diaphane, adiaphane. If you can put your five fingers through it, it is a gate, if not a door. Shut your eyes and see."

Nearly eight hundred pages of trash like this, and Americans buying the book, according to the publisher's announcement, at five thousand a week.

The chief morsel for those who will stagger through hundreds of skipped pages will be found in the last forty-five pages, in which a prostitute closes this work with what might be called her famed, but not famous, soliloquy. In this final portion she introduces all the words that are known to the lowest followers of her trade. The author has not dared to present this piece of his work with the usual accompaniment of paragraphs and punctuation marks. There are no capitals, commas, semi-colons, periods, interrogation or exclamation points. The whole thing is a hodgepodge of type, closely run together, mostly without sense, difficult to read, and following on to the end of the book, like a sewer that had burst loose and overwhelmed a city with foul and pestilential vapors. If he or his publishers had had the hardihood to print these passages with the usual set-off of paragraphs, punctuation, and divided sentences we greatly doubt whether the book would have passed its judicial ordeal.

Judge Woolsey says that the book provokes disgust to the point of nausea. He is right. The book seems to us to be the output of the mind of a stableboy, trained amid the lowest habits of speech and conduct, who has then read with extraordinary attention a large collection of literature, ancient and modern, and who undertakes to write a book based upon this study and observation, and goes through his task with a stableboy's mind interpreting every part of the work. It is kaleidoscopic in a sense—that is, if we could imagine a kaleidoscope presenting foul and ugly pictures, instead of beautiful objects, if would be kaleidoscopic; for there is no continuity of purpose or connected expression in the entire volume. The people here introduced discuss various topics—at one point Shakespeare. But after fifty pages of rambling and licentious talk the only point from Shakespeare that is covered by them is the query as to whether Hamlet was Shakespeare's father or Shakespeare was Hamlet's father. He uses a hundred pages in the night-club scene—we call the place a night club in deference to our readers—to present his characters in a sort of Greek play; but there is no objective—it is insane in its picturization, full of fustian, wearisome to exhaustion, and violates throughout the inexorable Greek rule that a play must have a beginning, a middle, and an end. And no matter what his topic may be—opera, play, society, morals, or the Bible—there is scarcely a page in this bewildering wilderness of words which does not reek with this stableboy's abominable mind.

How absurd then is it to say, as some of the reviewers are extravagantly saying, and as the author himself encourages them in saying, that this book is a tour de force in literature, a profound study in philosophy, a presentation of life that is mysterious and recondite, an achievement that reaches up into the very stratosphere of thought, a transcendental portraiture that goes beyond the average limit of human understanding and, like a new Einstein Theory, can be comprehended by only twelve men in the world! There is nothing at all of any of these qualities about it. As a work of art we can compare it with nothing but that picture which provoked laughter in the galleries a few years ago, "Nude Descending a Staircase," in which there was neither nude nor staircase and where art was the only thing that was descending. The book has no more relation to Ulysses than it has to Oliver Cromwell or Lord Byron. Any novel of George Eliot's or Thackeray's could be named "Ulysses" more fittingly in its picture of life. The printed "key" which promises to unlock this esoteric achievement is not needed. We do not have to read far until we get the key for ourselves: the stableboy's words blaze themselves so shamelessly on every page that we soon choose the only key that will unlock the mystery, and that is the word–neurosis–a diseased mind that sees and feels life only in its deformed relationship to sex.

American writer Robert Cantwell, best known for his two novels, Laugh and Lie Down *(1931) and* The Land of Plenty *(1934), listed Joyce as his most important influence.*

Review of *Ulysses*

Robert Cantwell

New Outlook, 163 (March 1934): 57–58

There have been a number of good novels offered on the spring lists, beginning, of course, with *Ulysses* (Random House), now released from its shameful twelve-year censorship. Nothing need to be said about it, except that of all the literature produced in our time, it seems the surest of a place with the best of English writing–of writing in English; that it towers so high it has already cast its shadow on the important writing done since it appeared. Perhaps its tremendous influence will be clarified now that the book is widely available, for writers have usually had to form their opinions of it from borrowed copies (few writers having money enough to buy the illegal editions) and writers are seldom deeply influenced by that sort of hasty reading. They really respond, a real dent is made in their imaginations, when they grow troubled and uncertain about their own small efforts and turn automatically to study the great works of their time. . . .

–reprinted from *James Joyce: The Critical Heritage*

Review of *Ulysses*

Edwin Baird

Real America, 3 (April 1934), p. 44

Probably no book of the last decade has been so widely discussed, and none so misunderstood, as James Joyce's *Ulysses*. Certainly I know of none that has provoked so much bilge and blather. Solemn asses have written learned treatises on it; others have written 'interpretations.' Literary societies have used it for debate; reading circles for whispered innuendo. It has been hailed as 'the greatest novel in English.' It has been condemned as 'a filthy book, unfit for print.' And I have an idea that all the while Joyce was secretly laughing at all of them.

Of course, as every author and publisher knows, the best way to get publicity for a book is to have it banned as an obscene work. *Ulysses* was banned as obscene, though I have never been able to understand why. Except for half a dozen words rarely if ever encountered in print, I find nothing in its 767 pages that would shock the most sensitive reader. Indeed, such a reader would probably be less shocked than bored. And I venture to say that not one person in twenty who reads it will know what the devil it's all about.

Well, the ban has finally been lifted–by Federal Judge John M. Woolsey of the U S District Court of New York–and now you no longer need pay a fancy price for a booklegger's copy. You can purchase it in any book store, just as you would purchase *Alice in Wonderland* or *Little Women*. And Joyce, for the first time, will start drawing some royalties. (He never received a cent from any of the copies sold in America at exorbitant figures.)

But the smut hounds are in for the biggest surprise of their lives when they start sniffing for the dirt in this book. They will be as bewildered as a school boy trying to read Chinese. Even the most intelligent reader finds the going pretty hard in spots. Some parts are wholly unintelligible. Others are downright nasty. None arouse lasciviousness. . . .

Don't think, however, that Joyce can't write plain English. His letter to Bennett A. Cerf, his American publisher, is as clear and practical as a note from your landlord about the rent.

Ulysses, in my opinion, is not 'the greatest novel in English.' Nor is it 'a filthy book.' It's a literary curiosity. As such I recommend it. . . .

–reprinted from *James Joyce: The Critical Heritage*

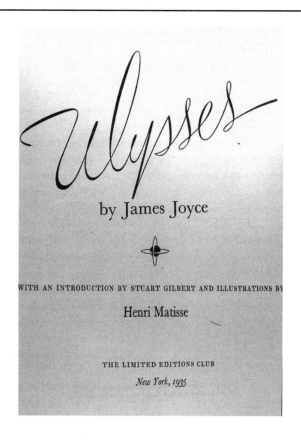
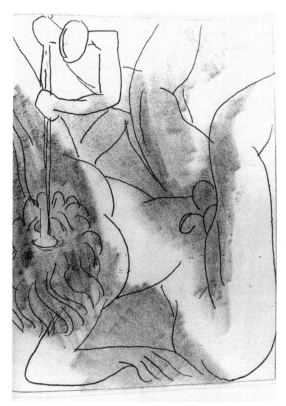
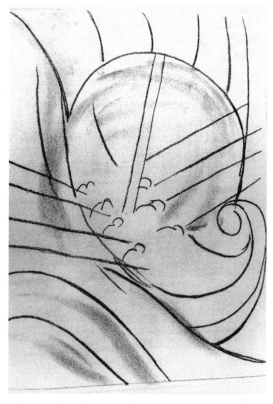

Title page and three Matisse etchings for the Aeolus (top right), Cyclops (bottom left), and Nausicaa (bottom right) episodes for an edition of 1,500 copies. Matisse's work was based more on Homer's Odyssey *than on Joyce's* Ulysses, *which he had not read (courtesy of Sid Shiff, The Limited Editions Club, New York, and the C. W. Post Library of Long Island).*

ULYSSES

James Joyce

JOHN LANE THE BODLEY HEAD

BURY STREET WCI

LONDON

THIS EDITION PUBLISHED 1936

Limited to 1,000 copies,
divided as follows:

100 COPIES ON MOULD-MADE PAPER BOUND IN
CALF VELLUM AND SIGNED BY THE AUTHOR

900 COPIES ON JAPON VELLUM PAPER BOUND IN
LINEN BUCKRAM, UNSIGNED

Presentation Copy

Title page and statement of limitation for the first edition of Ulysses *printed in England (courtesy of the C. W. Post Library of Long Island)*

Publication of *Ulysses* in England

Ulysses *was finally published in England in a limited edition in October 1936; a trade edition was published in September 1937. Allen Lane's 29 August 1934 letter to Ralph Pinker indicates the problems that beset potential English publishers of Joyce's masterpiece. Allen Lane was the nephew of the British publisher John Lane, who with The Bodley Head in 1936 published the first British edition of* Ulysses *printed in England.*

Dear Pinker In reply to your letter of August 28th and, as promised on the telephone to-day, I am writing to put the exact position with regard to this proposed first publication of Joyce's ULYSSES here before you.

We have, as you know, taken several opinions from barristers and others in authority on the probable result of publication here. This has, in addition to the time involved, cost us a not inconsiderable sum of money. Having decided that there was no possibility of getting a definite opinion as to whether there would be a prosecution or not, we then attempted to find a printer who would undertake the work.

We were unsuccessful and, in order to get around this, we have had to form a separate company to undertake the printing. This, in order to make it strictly legal, has necessitated preparing Articles of Association and I should think that our fees on this alone will certainly not be less than thirty guineas.

Then we feel that for safety's sake the only way in which we can produce the book in the first instance will be in a strictly limited edition at not too low a price. As I explained to you on the phone to-day, the number we print will have to be large enough to be able to refer to it at a future date should an objection be raised to a subsequent larger edition and small enough to ensure that there would not be many copies lying around in booksellers' shops for any length of time after publication. We feel that the number to be aimed at is between 1000 and 1500 copies and the length of the work, together with the words of appreciation from prominent literary figures and the report of the two American cases, will not be far short of 1000 pages. This being the case, I cannot think that it is conceivably possible for us to show a profit on this first publication taking into consideration:

    (a) our legal expenses.

    (b) the expenses of formation of the new printing company

    (c) the very large composition bill we shall have to face

    (d) the author's advance of £200 which will have to be, for the purpose of our accounting, worked out over this first printing.

In addition to this, as we will not be able to bring out another edition for 12 months from the original date of publication, we shall have either to make stereos from the standing type or pay rent on it for that period. This, as you will realise on a book of this length, will mount up to a considerable sum.

    In these circumstances I do think that we should let the present royalty, as stipulated in our contract, stand, the only alternative being that we should have to issue it in the first instance in an unlimited edition which, in my opinion, would be fatal to the prospects of the book in this country.

                  Yours sincerely, ALLEN LANE
                             Letters III, pp. 322–323

Leviathan

G. W. Stonier

The New Statesman and Nation, 12 (10 October 1936): 551–552

    Ulysses was originally published by Shakespeare and Company, of Paris, in 1922. Since then it has run through many editions; it has been confiscated, banned, burnt, read and re-read, translated into half a dozen languages. The first English edition appeared rather suddenly last week. It is a handsome volume, bound in buckram and printed on vellum paper, which those who can afford it will prefer to the old pale-blue directory smuggled through the Customs. The list of misprints has disappeared from the end; instead, there is an appendix giving the legal history of *Ulysses* in America. These documents are extraordinarily interesting, for they reveal the rare case of a book condemned for its obscenity being afterwards reclaimed by the weight of literary opinion. (Remember that in a similar case tried recently in an English court the magistrate refused to hear expert critical evidence for the defence.) Sooner or later, of course, unless the book dies naturally, this is bound to happen; but it may take a long time. The rehabilitation of *Ulysses* in 1933, thirteen years after the

original ban, must have come as a surprise to many who have read Joyce's novel and who know the attitude of the law, English and American, on the subject. Any book, in the words of Lord Campbell's Act, is obscene which "tends to corrupt those who are open to corruption"; and that means, literally, any book at all. The Bible and the dictionary are prime corrupters of youth. *Idylls of the King, Sartor Resartus and Sesame and Lilies* are cited by the author of a recent work on medical psychology as books which his patients mentioned for their erotic appeal. The *intention* of a writer is regarded by the law as unimportant. It may seem incredible to-day that *Madame Bovary* was attacked as an offence against public decency, and described by the public prosecutor as a "lascivious" book written in order to "glorify adultery"; but all such cases are brought in an atmosphere of distortion and panic. Flaubert was lucky in his judges and won his case. Mr. Joyce has been even more lucky. The decision of the New York Court by Judge Woolsey, reprinted here, is remarkable for its detachment and critical intelligence.

    I have read *Ulysses* once in its entirety and I have read those passages of which the Government particularly complains several times. In fact, for many weeks, my spare time has been devoted to the consideration of the decision which my duty would require me to make in this matter. *Ulysses* is not an easy book to read or to understand. But there has been much written about it, and in order properly to approach the consideration of it it is advisable to read a number of other books which have now become its satellites. The study of *Ulysses* is, therefore, a heavy task. The reputation of *Ulysses* in the literary world, however, warranted my taking such time as was necessary to satisfy myself as to the intent with which the book was written. . . .

What judge or magistrate has ever before admitted the necessity of understanding the work of art on which he is to pass judgment? (It was a trial without jury, of course.) Judge Woolsey goes on to say that he does not detect anywhere in *Ulysses* "the leer of the sensualist," in spite of its unusual frankness, and therefore it is not pornographic. He reviews the book at some length, commenting on its originality, on the "astonishing success" of its method, and the integrity of the author. To test the value of his own impressions he consulted separately two friends who had read *Ulysses* and whose "opinion on life and literature" he valued highly: note again the insistence on an aesthetic as well as a moral valuation.

    I was interested to find that they both agreed with my opinion: that reading *Ulysses* in its entirely, as a book must be read on such a test as this, did not tend to excite sexual impulses or lustful thoughts but that its net effect on them was only that of a somewhat tragic and very powerful commentary on the inner lives of men and women. It is only with the normal person that the law is concerned. Such a test as I have described, therefore, is the only proper test of obscenity in the case of a book like *Ulysses,* which is a sincere and serious attempt to devise a new literary method for the observation and description of mankind. I am quite aware that owing to some of its scenes *Ulysses* is a rather strong draught to ask some sensitive, though normal, persons to take. But my considered opinion, after long reflection, is that whilst in many places the effect of *Ulysses* on the reader undoubtedly is somewhat emetic, nowhere does it tend to be an aphrodisiac. *Ulysses* may therefore be admitted to the United States.

It is the tone we might expect from a critic writing a review, or from an intelligent man in conversation, but in a court of law it is unexpected. Since the decision was upheld on appeal. I assume that it interprets the law correctly, though the reference to "normal persons" makes me wonder what twelve normal rate-payers would have made of *Ulysses* if it had been flourished under their noses in a jury box and shot at them in snippets by indignant counsel. The importance of Judge Woolsey's decision, if we compare it with similar judgments in the past, is tremendous. It sets a new standard of dignity in cases of prosecution for literary obscenity. The only sentence which might possibly excite a smile from posterity is the statement that "in respect of the recurrent emergence of the theme of sex in the minds of Joyce's characters, it must be remembered that his locale was Celtic and his season Spring."

Ulysses itself remains a monstrous and fascinating book. What has surprised me most, re-reading it, is that the word "classical" should ever have been brought up by Joyce's more fervent admirers. No book for centuries has been so wildly, so elaborately and grotesquely twirled. Having been given the classical key to *Ulysses,* we may as well throw it away. Or–to vary the metaphor–it is as though we were asked to look at a building and to notice particularly the criss-cross of a builder's framework which years ago has been taken down. That is all, so far as I can see, that the Homeric structure, elaborately expounded by Messrs. Larbaud and Gilbert, amounts to. Joyce himself is well aware that the classical obsession, though necessary for writing the book, is not part of it. This passage is obviously autobiographical:

Buck Mulligan bent across the table gravely.
They drove his wits away, he said, by visions of hell. He will never capture the Attic note. The note of Swinburne, of all poets, the white death and the ruddy birth. That is his tragedy. He can never be a poet.

We may take *Chamber Music and Pomes Pennyeach* as the attempt at "the Attic note," by way of the English classicists, Jonson and Dryden. They are curiously perfect, dead little poems. *Ulysses* is the repository of a whole corpus of unwritten poetry, doggerel as it bobs to the surface of the mind, soliloquies of modern Hamlet, phrases and fag-ends of lines, the brooding commentary of Stephen Daedalus and the Bouvard-like reveries of Bloom. In the opening pages there are more passages of blank verse than in any other English prose-writer except Dickens. The effect of a pensive melancholy, overflowing the pointillist detail of the style, is curious, new, and perhaps the most original of the many original contributions of *Ulysses* to literature. Old Mother Grogan, who brings the milk in the morning:

He watched her pour into the measure and thence into the jug rich white milk, not hers. Old shrunken paps. She poured again a measureful and a tilly. Old and secret she had entered from a morning world, maybe a messenger. She praised the goodness of the milk, pouring it out. Crouching by a patient cow at daybreak in the lush field, a witch on her toadstool, her wrinkled fingers quick at the squirting dugs. They lowed about her whom they knew, dewsilky cattle. Silk of the kine and poor old woman, names given her in old times. A wandering crone, lowly form of an immortal serving her conqueror and her gay betrayor, their common cuckquean, a messenger from the secret morning. To serve or to upbraid, whether he could not tell: but scorned to beg her favour.

That is a very fair specimen of the prose in the early part of the book. It interrupts a boisterous conversation. Note even in this short passage how Joyce mixes his effects. The sixth sentence ("Crouching by a patient cow, etc."), so packed and pictorial, might have been written by Flaubert. It is situated surprisingly in the middle of slow musical sentences, almost metrical in their lull, which end in fact with several lines of blank verse. The whole passage communicates, as well as its picture of the old woman, the brooding temper of Stephen Daedalus. There are Hellenisms, but the note is not Attic.

Poetry, then, in all its forms, from the embryonic to the purple, is what strikes one first on a re-reading. Next, the amazing use of parody. Joyce uses a mixture of parody and pastiche in order to achieve effects of his own, and not only the Oxford Book of English prose, but newspapers, novelettes, scientific reports, advertisements are echoed ironically to suit the scene. The famous chapter of parodies ("The Oxen of the Sun") I have read for the first time straight through. It is an extraordinary fantasia, beginning with Beowulf and ending with polyglot slang, in which the language at times obliterates the characters and their setting. A group of medicos are carousing in the room of a hospital while upstairs a woman gives birth to a child. To express the idea of growth, the style moves up the centuries: a typically Joycean idea of "correspondences," the only value of which here is that it provides with an excellent chance for virtuoso writing. Some of it is extremely funny (Lamb and Carlyle), some of it funny and beautiful at the same time (Bunyan), and hardly a page is without some interest above mere virtuosity. The echo of De Quincey (recognisable but strangely unlike its original) has a terrifying grandeur.

> . . . Elk and yak, the Bulls of Bashan and of Babylon, mammoth and mastodon, they come trooping to the sunken sea. *Lucus Mortis.* Ominous, revengeful, zodiacal hosts! They moan, passing upon the clouds, horned and capricorned, the trumpeted and the tusked, the lionmaned the giantantlered, snouter and crawler, rodent, ruminant and pachyderm, and their moving, moaning multitude, murderers of the sun.

Joyce is a master of all styles, but he is not a stylist. His disgust with life extends also to literature; and in a sense *Ulysses* is a bonfire of literature, a glowing revenge. The process is carried still further in *Work in Progress,* where no one but the author finally can enter.

Yet along with the gigantic literary preoccupation of *Ulysses,* and saving it from Euphuism, there is Joyce's encyclopaedic love of fact. About some of the characters– Bloom, for example–we are told everything, from their thoughts to the tram tickets in their pockets. And as the two hundred or so characters file across the pages, the whole of Dublin with its narrow smoky streets seems to rise. Mr. Frank Budgen relates that when he was walking once with Joyce in Trieste, and they reached the university terrace overlooking the town, Joyce turned to him and said "I want to give a picture of Dublin so complete that if the city one day suddenly disappeared from the earth it could be reconstructed out of my book." Like most of his quoted remarks this one is intensely egotistic. Yes, Joyce has the egotism, without the charm, of Sterne; *Ulysses* is *Tristram Shandy* written by Brobdingnagian.

Interpretations of 'Ulysses'
The Times Literary Supplement, 23 January 1937

Mr. Joyce's major work is at any rate obscure enough to have invited several interpretations, and its structure is sufficiently unlike that of the ordinary novel to have suggested hidden messages and meanings. It has, for example, been supposed to have a pattern analogous to that of the *Odyssey,* to give an accurate and realistic account of the 'stream of consciousness' in the human mind, and by a new technique of writing to have expressed the nature of the characters' thoughts without the usual distortion of common sense and literary forms. But such explanations commonly arise when a new artistic method is invented; when the post-impressionists first startled the world with their pictures it was commonly believed that in some mysterious fashion they described essential as opposed to accidental properties of natural appearances. Later the artistic purpose of the new method emerges, and there is no longer any need to justify it either by supposing that it conceals as in a cryptogram an intelligible plan like that of previous and familiar works, or as a mode of scientific investigation.

There is, of course, a deliberate attempt to impose order on the incoherence of *Ulysses* by making all its events belong to a single day and by making the same episodes and characters appear and reappear in the kaleidoscope. But when one chapter contains a succession of masterly parodies of English prose in chronological order, from *Beowulf* to modern slang, when another is an amusing and satirical excursion on the Irish literary movement, another an irresistibly funny transcription of a young girl's day-dream in terms of the novelettes she has been reading, then the use of the same characters and episodes has the appearance of a merely conventional link between all the sections of the book. No doubt the link has a certain use in helping the reader along, but there is no reason to suppose that it makes the book a coherent whole from which no part can be removed without disaster. It is of no use to look for secret connexions, for in a work of art if the relations of the parts are not apparent enough to be felt, then the parts are not artistically related. Mr. Joyce's unit, in fact, is not the book as a whole but the chapter, often the paragraph, and sometimes, one might almost say, the phrase, or even the word. *Ulysses* is evidently the production of a man fascinated by language rather than by thought or observation; the progress of his style towards the final word-making and word-taking of the unintelligible *Work in Progress* has always been away from observation of life and towards the word as a complete substitute for the flesh. Like the lunatic whose speech degrades into a set of arbitrary sounds more and more remotely connected with his interior preoccupations, Mr. Joyce has played with language–it is perhaps the last development of the Irishman's habit of inventing new languages which shall not be English–until it has become his private construction. This is not, because he is content, like the lunatic, with any private or delusory world; but it is a curious fact, which several writers have noticed, that there is a remarkable similarity between Mr. Joyce's compositions and the prose style of certain lunatics. In the two instances the ordinary structure of the language is broken down for quite different reasons, but the results are oddly alike. And with the lunatic it may be worthwhile looking for the hidden connexion and meaning of apparently disorderly phrases; but with Mr. Joyce we are not to analyse the latent content of his verbal constructions, we are only concerned with the artistic and therefore immediate effect of his language.

But *Ulysses* only marks a stage in this progress, and his release from the ordinary linguistic conventions only enables Mr. Joyce to exercise all his talent, his almost incredible virtuosity, to the full. Passages that are genuine poetry alternate with the harshest and most deliberately contemptuous parodies, uproarious burlesque with subtle indications of character in a phrase. It is still a work of much observation, and of observation sharpened by disgust; but it is above all the profusion and fertility of language that will fascinate the reader. In this, the first edition published in England, there is an appendix giving, among other details of controversy, the decisions of the United States District Court and of the United States Court of Appeals which allowed *Ulysses* to be published in that country.

George Bernard Shaw wrote to the editor of Picture Post *on 3 June 1939 to clarify his opinion of* Ulysses.

In your issue of the 13th, Mr. Geoffrey Grigson, in an interesting article on James Joyce, states that I was "disgusted by the unsqueamish realism of *Ulysses,* and burnt my copy in the grate."

Somebody has humbugged Mr. Grigson. The story is not true. I picked up *Ulysses* in scraps from the American *Little Review,* and for years did not know that it was the history of a single day in Dublin. But having passed between seven and eight thousand single days in Dublin I missed neither the realism of the book nor its poetry. I did not burn it; and I was not disgusted. If Mr. Joyce should ever desire a testimonial as the author of a literary masterpiece from me, it shall be given with all possible emphasis and with sincere enthusiasm.

– *Letters III,* pp. 444–445

Cover for David Lasky's pocket-sized ten-page comic book version of Joyce's classic novel

Ulysses
as a
Movie

Joyce was approached by Warner Bros. about making a movie based on Ulysses *and at first did not give a definitive answer. He was disturbed, however, when he heard of reports that a movie project was going forward. In a 26 October 1932 letter to Ralph Pinker, Paul Léon explained Joyce's attitude.*

I have taken the matter up with Mr Joyce who in fact tells me that he is in principle opposed to the filming of Ulysses and would like the news in the paper to be denied. I must also add that I had warned Mr Cerf of the proposal in case there was some idea of pirating Ulysses. Mr Cerf replied to me that he considered the firm so first class that there could not be any piracy in it and that on the contrary he considered the filming of Ulysses as very beneficial for the circulation of the book. He naturally takes the material point of view, Mr Joyce on the contrary takes the literary point of view and is therefore opposed to the filming as irrealisable. Before however giving this answer which is an absolute and flat refusal I have advised him first to find out what our position is as regards the filming rights. Should the filming rights in the States also not belong to him then naturally there is no use refusing and it would be better to come to some arrangement. Should however the film rights belong to Mr Joyce then he would absolutely refuse.

– *Letters III*, pp. 262–263

No movie was made during Joyce's lifetime; the only movie version of the novel produced is a 1967 version produced and directed in the U.K. by Joseph Strick, who collaborated on the screenplay with Fred Hines.

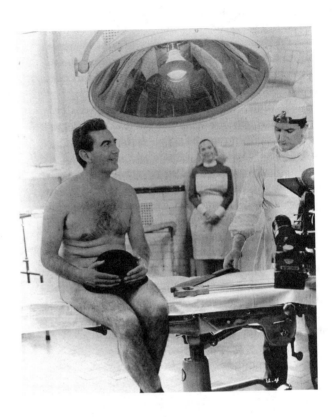

Scenes from the 1967 movie Ulysses, *starring Milo O'Shea and Barbara Jefford as Leopold and Molly Bloom (The Everett Collection)*

Volume One
EPISODES 1 THROUGH 11

U L Y S S E S

A Critical and Synoptic Edition

Prepared by HANS WALTER GABLER

with WOLFHARD STEPPE AND CLAUS MELCHIOR

Academic Advisory Committee
RICHARD ELLMANN • PHILIP GASKELL • CLIVE HART
assisted by A. WALTON LITZ AND MICHAEL GRODEN

Additional editorial assistance provided by HARALD BECK,
WALTER HETTCHE, JOHN O'HANLON, DANIS ROSE,
CHARITY SCOTT STOKES, AND KINGA THOMAS

James Joyce

Garland Publishing, Inc. • New York & London • 1984

Title page for the three-volume critical edition of Ulysses *that generated controversy*

Modern Editions

The Random House edition of Ulysses *was the accepted standard text of the novel until Hans Walter Gabler's revised critical edition,* Ulysses: A Critical and Synoptic Edition, *was published in 1984 by Garland Publishing. This edition includes textual notes, an historical collation list, and an afterword in which are discussed the composition history of the novel and the editorial procedures for the edition.*

On 16 June (Bloomsday) 1997, Danis Rose's *edition of* Ulysses *was published in Ireland by The Lilliput Press and in England by Picador. Rose's intent was to make Joyce's work more readable, in part by eliminating textual faults and restoring the novel to what Joyce wrote. Many critics, however, claimed that he was too intrusive, sometimes substituting his own aesthetic judgment for that of the author. Stephen Joyce, the grandson of the novelist, was adamant in his letter published in the 27 June 1997 issue of* Times Literary Supplement: *"If this book is to continue to be sold, the name James Joyce must be eliminated, stricken from the dustjacket, cover and inside title-pages of this edition." For a discussion of the critical reception of Rose's edition of* Ulysses, *see the "Reader's Ulysses Symposium" in* Dictionary of Literary Biography Yearbook 1997.

Dust jacket for the one-volume 1986 edition of the Gabler-edited text without the critical apparatus. The claim at the top of the jacket, "The Corrected Text," was removed from later printings.

Dust jacket for the heavily edited 1997 edition of Joyce's novel that Stephen Joyce argued should not bear his grandfather's name

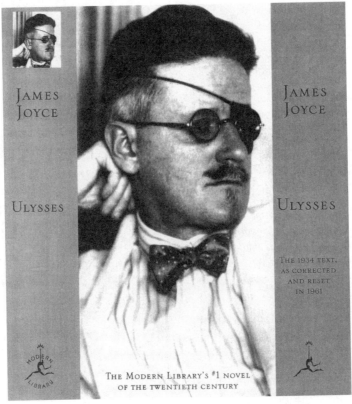

Dust jacket of The Modern Library edition announcing Ulysses *as the publisher's choice as the most significant novel of the twentieth century. Third on The Modern Library's list of the one hundred best novels is* A Portrait of the Artist as a Young Man; Finnegans Wake *was listed*

Lot 197

THE LOST 'EUMAEUS' NOTEBOOK

Joyce, James. Autograph manuscript of the 'Eumaeus' episode of 'Ulysses'

A heavily revised and substantially complete early working draft of the "Eumaeus" chapter, a largely continuous and fluent text written in Joyce's cursive and 'personal' hand in black ink (the earliest hand), with extensive revisions, insertions and additional passages, some interlinear, but the majority drafted in the margin or on facing (previously blank) pages, sometimes lengthwise, in (chiefly later hands of) red, black and green ink and pencil, every page heavily "deleted" by the author in characteristic fashion with large crosses in red or blue crayon or pencil; written in a small lined exercise book, a pencil inscription (possibly in Joyce's hand) on the first page: "Miss Collins, 18 r. Michodière, 18 de la Sourdière (rue S Honoré,–" [possibly the name and address of the typist used to type up the subsequent 'fair copy']

48 pages, text written on 44 pages, 4 pages blank, 24 leaves, 8vo (c.210 x 153mm.), with narrow white silk bookmark, purple paper wrappers with label lettered "EUMEO", modern white vellum folder lettered in gilt, in slipcase, [some portions possibly Trieste, between 1916 and 3 July 1920; other portions and many revisions and markings, Paris, summer and autumn of 1920]

each leaf with a single vertical fold, central staples rusted and with marks in margin, small tear up to 15mm. at foot of some pages in margin, minor staining to edges of upper margin of outer leaves, central eight-page section detached from staples, small holes or tears in four leaves with no loss of text, minor soiling or fingermarks (probably from authorial use)

AN EARLY DRAFT OF THIS EPISODE—WHICH HUGH KENNER HAS DESCRIBED AS "THE BOOK'S MOST PROFOUND TRIBUTE TO ITS HERO, ULYSSES"—WRITTEN BEFORE THE EXTENSIVE IMPLEMENTATION OF ITS RHETORICAL AND STYLISTIC STRUCTURE.

A PREVIOUSLY UNKNOWN AUTOGRAPH DRAFT OF ONE OF THE CLOSING EPISODES OF 'ULYSSES'. This is an extraordinary and highly important literary discovery, constituting the prolific re-working of an early state of the text, with extensive and substantive differences compared to the later Rosenbach "fair copy" manuscript (which was probably composed from the present draft, MS V.A.21 and possibly others) and subsequent published editions. IT IS ALSO THE ONLY KNOWN COMPLETE EARLY DRAFT OF 'EUMAEUS' TO HAVE COME TO LIGHT AND IS ONE OF THE EARLIEST COMPLETE WORKING DRAFTS OF *ANY* 'ULYSSES' EPISODE.

The textual history of *Ulysses* has been the subject of the most intense scrutiny and heated debate—generating a huge number of works of criticism and scholarship—ever since it was first published in Paris on 2nd February 1922 (Joyce's birthday).

The unusual format of the notebook and its revisions may lead to a revised understanding of the transition between *Ulysses* and *Finnegans Wake*.

Pages from the Sotheby's (London) catalogue, 10 July 2001

James Joyce, Paris, 1937

THE SIGNIFICANCE OF THE DISCOVERY OF THE PRESENT MANUSCRIPT

The previous configuration of texts for *Eumaeus* can be represented by the following table, assembled from the information provided in Hans Walter Gabler's edition of *Ulysses: A Critical and Synoptic Edition* (with Wolfhard Steppe and Claus Melchior, 1984), using his chapter line numbers:

Map of area of Dublin in which Eumaeus *takes place*

TABLE 2.	PREVIOUS CONFIGURATION OF TEXT	
LINES	DRAFT	FAIR COPY
1-489	no antecedent extant	R[osenbach]*, I, fols 1-12
490-1290	V.A. 21, rectos 1-19	R, II, fols 13-35
1290-1453	no antecedent extant	R,III, fols 35-39
1454-1894	V.A. 21, rectos 19-23 and in reverse order of the leaves, versos 24-20	R, IV, fols 40-54

* see *"Ulysses", the Manuscript and First Printings Compared*, (3 volumes, London, New York and Philadelphia, 1975)

Until the discovery of the present 'lost' notebook therefore, ALMOST 30% OF THE TEXT WAS UNKNOWN IN DRAFT FORM. It now restores draft text for two important sections of the narrative of this episode, and supplies one of the missing links in the evolution of the *Ulysses* text, previously hypothesised by Gabler and others. In his discussion of the composition of the *Eumaeus* episode Gabler asserts that

"In R [the Rosenbach "fair copy"] Joyce joined together the continuous chapter text from this [Buffalo draft V.A. 21] and another (or more than one other) draft source in alternation...The inferable loss at draft level for [*Eumaeus*] is of manuscripts reaching back to the phase of composition between 1914 and 1917. Joyce repeatedly indicates in his letters that he had preserved such manuscripts as a basis for the final composition of the book's end..." (Hans Walter Gabler (ed.), *Ulysses. A Critical and Synoptic Edition*, 1984, p.1863)"

Last Works: *Pomes Penyeach* and *Finnegans Wake*

Joyce began writing Finnegans Wake, *his last work, in March 1923 and continued during the next sixteen years until its publication in book form in May 1939. Fragments of the work started to appear under the title "Work in Progress" as early as April 1924. This provisional title was suggested by Ford Madox Ford, the English novelist and editor of the* transatlantic review, *where parts of Joyce's new work first appeared.*

Finnegans Wake *transcends the traditional boundaries of prose narrative. It is Joyce's most innovative work and one of the twentieth century's most perplexing. Written in a revolutionary linguistic style evoking a dreamworld abounding with mythic, cultural, and musical allusions, the novel tells the story of the Earwickers, a family residing in the western suburb of Dublin called Chapelizod. Humphrey Chimpden Earwicker (H C E) is a husband and father who with his wife, Anna Livia Plurabelle (A L P), has twin sons, Shem and Shaun, and a daughter, Issy. As in the transmutations that freely occur in dreams, these characters throughout* Finnegans Wake *appear in multiple forms and sometimes appear as mythological figures or as features of the landscape.*

Finnegans Wake *is not an easy book to read and many, including Joyce's brother Stanislaus, his benefactor Harriet Shaw Weaver, and his friend Ezra Pound, found this new work incomprehensible and thought Joyce to be squandering his talent. In a 7 August 1924 letter to Joyce, Stanislaus, who had read the installment of the new novel (*Finnegans Wake, *pp. 383–399) in the April 1924 issue of the* transatlantic review, *questions whether "the drivelling rigmarole about half a tall hat and ladies's modern toilet chambers . . . is written with the deliberate intention of pulling the reader's leg or not" (*Letters III, *p. 102). More than a year later, in an October 1925 letter to Weaver, Joyce sent a few advance opinions of the Anna Livia Plurabelle section of* Finnegans Wake *(pp. 196–216), among them his father's droll remark: "He has gone off his head" (*Letters I, *p. 235). The lack of enthusiasm by some of those closest to him caused Joyce to defend himself against their skepticism and admit his discouragement and need for emotional support.*

*Joyce, however, continued writing and at times in his correspondence to Weaver and others clarified the meaning behind certain passages. In a 15 November 1926 letter to Weaver (*Selected Letters, *pp. 315–317) he discusses the opening passage of* Finnegans Wake; *in a May 1927 letter (*Selected Letters, *pp. 321–323) he explains a section of p. 23; in a March 1928 letter (*Selected Letters, *pp. 329–332) he clarifies much of the fable of the Ondt and the Gracehoper (*Finnegans Wake, *pp. 414–418); in an August 1928 letter (see* Letters I, *pp. 263–264) he explains pp. 470–471; and in a November 1930 letter to her that Joyce dictated to his daughter, Lucia, (*Letters I, *p. 295) he explains the design of book II, chapter 1, of* Finnegans Wake. *Under Joyce's direction, Lucia, in a September 1933 letter to Frank Budgen (*Letters III, *pp. 284–285) elucidates the Mookse and the Gripes (*Finnegans Wake, *pp. 152–159). Joyce also explained that in his notes he used* sigla *(signs) for the main characters (see his 24 March 1924 letter to Weaver in* Letters I, *p. 213). For example, H C E became* ⊓, *his wife, Anna Livia,* △, *Shaun,* ∧, *and the siglum for the title of the book was* □. *Some of these sigla found their way into* Finnegans Wake *(see p. 6, 299). To help explain his new work and the techniques he was employing, Joyce enlisted the support of friends by orchestrating a collection of essays titled* Our Exagmination Round His Factification for Incamination of Work in Progress, *which was published in 1929, a full decade before* Finnegans Wake *appeared in book form. During the period of writing* Finnegans Wake, *Joyce also faced severe medical and family problems, as his biographer Richard Ellmann outlines.*

Life and Work, 1923–1939

In his introduction to the third volume of Letters of James Joyce *(1966), Richard Ellmann provides a brief summary of Joyce's work and life during the period in which he wrote* Pomes Penyeach *and* Finnegans Wake.

The subject of the book that was to follow *Ulysses* had probably begun to grow in Joyce's mind before *Ulysses* was finished, since one of the first things he did was to sort out unused notes left from the earlier book. On 10 March 1923, a month after he had done this, he began to write *Finnegans Wake.* The title was confided to his wife and to no one else; it referred both to the hod carrier of the ballad, who was miraculously resurrected by the whisky at his wake, and to the tough, vegetable recurrence of human life and mis-

Joyce's title for his new work was taken from an Irish ballad. The author did not divulge the title to anyone except Nora. Although he encouraged others to guess it, he was astonished when in 1938 his friend Eugene Jolas did so correctly and won the 1,000-franc wager Joyce offered. Joyce relates losing the bet in a 24 August 1938 letter to Maurice James Craig (Letters III, p. 427).

Finnegan's Wake

Tim Finnegan lived in Walkin Street,
   A gentleman Irish mighty odd.
He had a tongue both rich and sweet,
   An' to rise in the world he carried a hod.
Now Tim had a sort of a tipplin' way,
   With the love of the liquor he was born,
An' to help him on with his work each day,
   He'd a drop of the craythur every morn.

Chorus

Whack folthe dah, dance to your partner,
   Welt the flure, yer trotters shake,
Wasn't it the truth I told you,
   Lots of fun at Finnegan's Wake.

One morning Tim was rather full,
   His head felt heavy which made him shake,
He fell from the ladder and broke his skull,
   So they carried him home his corpse to wake,
They rolled him up in a nice clean sheet,
   And laid him out upon the bed,
With a gallon of whiskey at his feet,
   And a barrel of porter at his head.

His friends assembled at the wake,
   And Mrs. Finnegan called for lunch,
First they brought in tay and cake,
   Then pipes, tobacco, and whiskey punch.
Miss Biddy O'Brien began to cry,
   'Such a neat clean corpse, did you ever see,
Arrah, Tim avourneen, why did you die?'
   'Ah, hould your gab,' said Paddy McGee.

Then Biddy O'Connor took up the job,
   'Biddy,' says she, 'you're wrong, I'm sure,'
But Biddy gave her a belt in the gob,
   And left her sprawling on the floor;
Oh; then the war did soon enrage;
   'Twas woman to woman and man to man,
Shillelagh law did all engage,
   And a row and a ruction soon began.

Then Micky Maloney raised his head,
   When a noggin of whiskey flew at him,
It missed and falling on the bed,
   The liquor scattered over Tim;
Bedad he revives, see how he rises,
   And Timothy rising from the bed,
Says, 'Whirl your liquor round like blazes,
   Thanam o'n dhoul, do ye think I'm dead?'

behaviour. The book was to combine the affirmation of life, which he had always defined as the central function of literature, with the scepticism about particular living beings which had always been natural to him. It was to be alternately lyrical and combative or satirical, and always comic. To avoid and transcend a 'goahead plot', it was to be based upon a theory of cyclical recurrence which insisted on the typical character of every particular, whether person or incident.

Joyce must have known from the start that his new book would not be easy to read, for he intended it to be a night view of man's life, as *Ulysses* had been a day view. He would use the techniques of the dream, since in dreams all ages become one, attempts at concealment fail to convince, social and conventional barriers disappear. 'Wideawake language' and 'cutandry' grammar would not serve him; to represent night accurately Joyce thought he must descend to the makinghouse of language below the conscious choice of settled words. He determined upon the pun, often multilingual, as a linguistic mixture which could suggest the nighttime merging of the particular and the typical, of the struggle for expression and the forms of speech. As in his other books, the immediate focus would be on a family as the basic human group, and the flux of history would coalesce momentarily in the lives of the Earwicker family at Chapelizod near Dublin.

The composition of *Finnegans Wake* was harassed by two major impediments. The first was Joyce's eye trouble, which began again on his arrival in Paris. He suffered from a painful inflammation of the iris, and his vision was blurred by the formation of successive cataracts. The result was that he submitted to a series of ten operations in addition to the one he had already undergone in Zurich. These took place on 3, 15?, and 28 April 1923, 10 June 1924, 29 November 1924, 15? April 1925, 8 December 1925, 12 December 1925, June 1926, and 15 May 1930. The last of these, the only one performed by Professor Alfred Vogt of Zurich, proved fairly successful; but Joyce continued to have severe eye attacks and was never free of anxiety on the score of possible future operations.

The second major trouble was the response of his friends to *Finnegans Wake*. Some parts of the book came into existence easily and were published in preliminary form in magazines: in Ford Madox Ford's *transatlantic review* (April 1924), T. S. Eliot's *Criterion* (July 1925), Adrienne Monnier's *Navire d'argent* (October 1925), Ernest Walsh's *This Quarter* (Autumn–Winter 1925-1926), and then in Eugene and Maria Jolas's *transition* (April 1927–April–May 1938). As the first of these appeared, Joyce's friends waited indulgently for the clarity to come. But when

Lucia Joyce, whose mental illness in the 1930s became a terrible burden for Joyce

the book gave evidence of being written throughout in 'no language', they exchanged questioning looks and slowly began to express their doubts to Joyce himself. His brother denounced the 'drivelling rigmarole' as early as 1924, Ezra Pound wrote on 1 November 1926 that he could make nothing of the new work, Miss Weaver wondered on 4 February 1927 if he were not wasting his genius, Wyndham Lewis published an attack on all Joyce's writings later in this year.

Joyce was not so indifferent as might be supposed; he wrote hurt letters asking for encouragement and, with more vigour, sought new supporters. He worked into his fable, 'The Ondt and the Gracehoper', afterwards pp. 414–19 of *Finnegans Wake,* a defence of his book against Lewis; he sampled Pound's judgment in other literary matters in order to point out several obvious lapses of taste; he instructed Miss Weaver both by letter and personally in his method and purpose; he published, on 7 July 1927, *Pomes Penyeach,* a collection of his later verse, as evidence that he could be grammatically sane if he chose. In May 1929 a group of his friends, marshalled by him, published a defence of his book entitled, with mock modesty that was like pretentiousness, *Our Exagmination round his Factification for Incamination of Work in Progress.* In July of this year he formally proposed to James Stephens, his fellow Dubliner, that Stephens complete the book for him, but Stephens conceived the tactful reply that, though he was willing to try, he was sure Joyce would finish it himself. He added that *Anna Livia Plurabelle,* which had been published in book form in 1928, was 'the greatest prose ever written by a man'.

The result of these tearings and mendings was a realignment of Joyce's acquaintance. His relationship with Miss Weaver was the least strained; but that with Pound became merely polite, and that with Lewis was now mutually distrustful. Even Sylvia Beach seems to have secretly flagged in her literary loyalty. A group of new friends, readier for innovation, offered a more unqualified allegiance; these were Eugene and Maria Jolas, Paul and Lucy Léon, Stuart and Moune Gilbert, Samuel Beckett, Louis Gillet, Nino Frank, and others for short periods.

In a mood of self-commiseration, Joyce fled his own affairs to embrace the cause of an Irish-French opera singer, John Sullivan, whose immense tenor voice astounded him and whose failure to secure engagements worthy of his talent seemed a parallel of his own plight. He was convinced that established cliques were working against Sullivan as against himself, and threw himself fanatically into securing Sulli-van adequate recognition. This campaign began in November 1929, and did not taper off until after 1931. It gradually became clear to Joyce, as it was already to Sullivan, that the voice was losing some of its quality, but Joyce obstinately continued to work up interest in his friend.

He was recalled from his 'Sullivanizing' of the early 'thirties by some unexpected incidents in his family. The first was the marriage of his son George, on 10 December 1931, to Helen Kastor Fleischman. Next came his father's death in Dublin on 29 December 1931, a great grief which however was lightened somewhat for Joyce by the birth of his grandson, Stephen James Joyce, on 15 February 1932. But the principal family trouble came from his daughter, Lucia, who in 1932 showed signs of the schizophrenia which had presumably begun during her girlhood, but had been dismissed by her parents as childish eccentricity. The next seven years of Joyce's life were pervaded by a frantic and unhappily futile effort to cure her by every means known to medicine as well as by simples of his own devising. He felt in some sense responsible for her condition, and refused to accept any diagnosis which did not promise hope. It seemed to him that her mind was like his own, and he tried to find evidence in her writing and in her drawing of unrecognised talent. Lucia spent long and short periods in sanitariums and mental hospitals, between which she would return to stay with her parents until some incident occurred which made it necessary she be sent away again. Joyce found doctors to give her glandular treatments, others to inject sea water, others to try psychotherapy; he sent her on visits to friends in Switzerland, England, and even Ireland. The last in 1935 was disastrous: she grew worse rather than better. He placed her next in the care of Miss Weaver and a nurse in England, with a doctor attempting a new cure; when this failed, he brought her to France, where she stayed with Mrs Jolas; ultimately even Joyce conceded she must be put into a *maison de santé* near Paris. There he continued to visit her, he wrote letters to her, he refused to give up hope that she was getting better. Some of his friends felt he was too zealous in her behalf, but his family feeling had always been intense and now found full and open expression.

During the nineteen-thirties Joyce moved forward by fits and starts with *Finnegans Wake*. The outlines of the book were clear to him, but the interconnections had to be worded, the new linguistic medium had to be consistent and of one piece, and a few chapters were still to be written. At last after sixteen years he completed the book in 1938, and it was published on 4 May 1939.

The response to *Finnegans Wake* discontented him, and when war was declared in September he saw it as a force which might push his book into oblivion. A fresher anxiety was for Lucia, who had to be moved with the other occupants of her *maison de santé* to safer quarters at Pornichet near La Baule. Joyce and his wife made sure of her transfer by going there in September 1939. They returned to Paris in October, to find that George's wife had suffered a breakdown. They felt compelled to take charge of Stephen Joyce by sending him to Mrs Jolas's Ecole Bilingue, which had been moved from Neuilly to a village near Vichy called Saint-Gérand-le-Puy in what was later Unoccupied France. Joyce and his wife decided to follow their grandson there. After nineteen years in Paris they left the city and reached St Gérand on 24 December 1939. Their affairs were in dismal confusion.

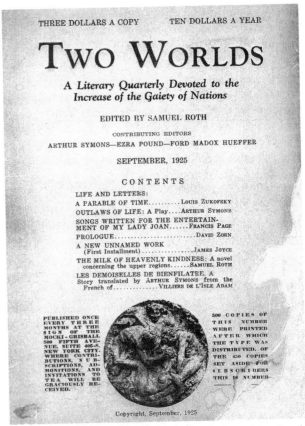

Cover for the journal that published a fragment of an early version of book I, chapter 5, of Finnegans Wake. *The quarterly was edited by Samuel Roth, who in July 1926, against Joyce's wishes, began to publish portions of* Ulysses *in a second journal,* Two Worlds Monthly. *By October 1927 these unauthorized publications ceased.*

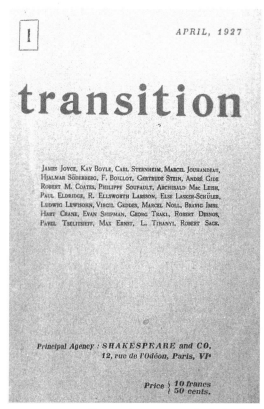

Cover and contents page for the first issue of transition, *in which Joyce's work appeared*

OPENING PAGES OF A WORK
IN PROGRESS

by JAMES JOYCE

riverrun brings us back to Howth Castle & Environs. Sir Tristram, violer d'amores, fr' over the short sea, had passencore rearrived from North Armorica on this side the scraggy isthmus of Europe Minor to wielderfight his penisolate war: nor had topsawyer's rocks by the stream Oconee exaggerated themselse to Laurens County's gorgios, while they went doublin their mumper all the time; nor avoice from afire bellowsed mishe mishe to tauftauf thuartpeatrick: not yet, though venissoon after, had a kidscad buttended a bland old isaac; not yet, though all's fair in vanessy, were sosie sesthers wroth with twone nathandjoe. Rot a peck of pa's malt had Jhem or Shen brewed by arclight and rory end to the regginbrow was to be seen ringsome on the waterface.

The fall (badalgharaghtakamminarronnkonnbronntonnerronntuonnthunntrovarrhounawnskawntoohoohoordenenthurnuck!) of a once wallstrait oldparr is retaled early in bed and later on life down through all christian minstrelsy. The great fall of the offwall entailed at such short notice the schute of Finnigan, erse solid man, that the humptyhillhead of humself promptly sends an unquiring one well to the west in quest of his tumptytumtoes: and their upturnpikepointandplace is at the knock out in the park where oranges have been

— 9 —

The first page of a fragment of Work in Progress *as published in the April 1927 issue of* transition

The Opening of *Finnegans Wake*

Most of Joyce's new work, known as Work in Progress, *was published in* transition, *an avant-garde literary magazine founded in 1927 by Eugene and Maria Jolas and Elliot Paul. In seventeen installments between April 1927 and May 1938,* transition *published the bulk of* Work in Progress (Finnegans Wake, *pp. 3–275, 282–331, 338–355 and 403–590).*

In the opening lines of Finnegans Wake, *the initial letters in the reference to "Howth Castle and Environs" provide the first allusion to the book's hero, Humphrey Chimpden Earwicker (H C E). The reference alludes to an identification between Earwicker and the Dublin landscape and also between Earwicker and the sleeping giant, Finn MacCool, whose head is said to form the Ben of Howth. The castle is also the setting for the episode concerning the Prankquean and Jarl van Hoother (*Finnegans Wake, *pp. 21–23).*

The peninsula Howth is on the northern part of Dublin Bay and is the site of Howth Castle and the Ben (or the hill) of Howth. Pronounced hoaeth, *the word is from the Danish* hoved, *which means* head *(Letters I, p. 247). Howth is also significant in* Ulysses; *it is where Molly and Leopold Bloom first kissed and where Bloom proposed to her.*

Howth Peninsula and Castle, which are referenced in the opening sentence of Finnegans Wake *(courtesy of the Irish Tourist Board)*

POMES PENYEACH

by
JAMES JOYCE

BY THE SAME WRITER

CHAMBER MUSIC.

DUBLINERS.

A PORTRAIT OF THE ARTIST
AS A YOUNG MAN.

EXILES.

ULYSSES.

POMES PENYEACH
BY
JAMES JOYCE

SHAKESPEARE AND COMPANY
PARIS
1927

Cover, card page, and title page for Joyce's second volume of poetry (courtesy of C.W. Post Library of Long Island)

Pomes Penyeach

First published by Shakespeare and Company on 5 July 1927, Pomes Penyeach *consists of thirteen short poems on a variety of topics, mostly personal in nature; eleven of the poems had been previously published. In a February 1927 letter to his benefactor, Harriet Shaw Weaver, Joyce mentioned Ezra Pound's earlier judgment that the poems "belong in the bible or the family album with the portraits" (*Letters III, *p. 155). The collection, however, was well-received.*

Writing here as Y. O., the Irish writer, intellectual, and theosophist George Russell (1867–1935) is often identified by his pen name Æ, which he derived from the Latin word aeon, *a transliteration of the Greek,* aion, *meaning "age" or "lifetime." When he was the editor of the weekly Dublin newspaper* The Irish Homestead, *Russell published "The Sisters," "Eveline," and "After the Race."*

Review of *Pomes Penyeach*
Y. O.
Irish Statesman (23 July 1927): 478

It is many years now since James Joyce wrote the verses which were published as *Chamber Music,* verses which had a deliberate, carved, delicate beauty in which the most subtle critic could not have discovered one single phrase suggestive of the terrible realism of *Ulysses.* The lyrics were so restrained, so delicately fashioned, one felt that the poet would not trust his heart into his poetry. He seemed rather to wish to create images like the finest porcelain and two or three of the lyrics had a light carven beauty as if the transcience of some lovely motion had been stayed so that it might be enjoyed for ever. There is nothing in the new book quite so exquisite as the best lyrics in *Chamber Music.* The poet seems to have been aware that in his youth he had created something which perhaps became more beautiful in retrospect in his imagination because the full strength of his intellect had since been devoted to writing the most realistic novels of our generation, and his early verse may have glittered in memory with the irridescence of a shell if a thought of it had come up when he was writing the meditations of Mrs. Bloom. Nobody likes losing a gift which one was theirs and Joyce seems every now and then to have tried whether he had lost the ancient art and the verses, all but one written between 1912 and 1924 are gathered up in this little volume. It is curious to find in this writer, the most resolute and unabashed explorer of the crypts and sewers of the soul a strain almost of sentimentality every now and then. This might have been written by almost any young versifying sentimentalist.

Rain on Rahoon falls softly, softly falling,
Where my dark lover lies.
Sad is his voice that calls me, sadly calling
At grey moonrise.

Love hear thou
How soft, how sad his voice is ever calling,
Ever unanswered, and the dark rain falling
Then as now.

Dark too our hearts, O love, shall lie and cold
As his sad heart has lain
Under the moongrey nettles, the black mould
And muttering rain.

I quote this, not because it is the best, but because it has a psychological interest suggesting that somewhere in the realist a submerged sentimentalist was sighing and in other lyrics also there are traces of this submerged mentality. The strongest poems are those in which he is further from the old mood, poems like *A Memory of the Players* or *A Prayer,* in which he seems to have deserted his old ideal of a carved, exquisite beauty and to have expressed a personal feeling or experience with passion and intensity. The book will have for many readers perhaps a greater psychological than poetic interest though I would be the last to deny the charm and precise beauty of some of the lyrics in *Pomes Penyeach.* They will be read by many who know Joyce only as the author of the *Portrait of the Artist* or of *Ulysses* with a surprise like that one feels discovering on a grey mountain height near the snows some tiny and exquisite flowers blossoming in some crevice amid the monstrous rocks.

American critic Wilson, who wrote one of the first critiques of Ulysses, *finds the lyrics in* Pomes Penyeach *more colorful and complex than those in* Chamber Music.

New Poems by Joyce
Edmund Wilson
The New Republic, 52 (26 October 1927): 268

This little book, hardly four inches by five, contains thirteen new poems by James Joyce. Like the poems in "Chamber Music," they are all brief lyrics, but they are much better than any but one or two in the earlier book. The pieces in "Chamber Music" aimed at the music, the lightness and the perfection of Elizabethan songs, and they derived somewhat, at the same, from the contemporary Irish poetry of A. E. and Yeats. I have been told by another Irish poet who knew Joyce in his Dublin days that two of Joyce's favorite poems—poems which he loved to repeat—are:

Have you seen but a bright lily grow
Before rude hands have touched it?

and the song from Shelley's "Cenci" which begins,

False friend, wilt thou smile or weep
when my life is laid to sleep?

And Yeats's song, "Who will drive with Fergus now"—
which figures as one of the themes of the opening episode of "Ulysses," is in the same way characteristic of his
taste.

These liquid snatches of song in two or three fleeting stanzas seem all that Joyce has ever cared to write in
verse; and, as a result, his range is not wide: he has only

one or two notes. It is interesting to see that, among these
later poems, there is one—"Watching the Needleboats at
San Sabba"—which still seems unmistakably haunted by
the lovely plaintive echo of Shelley's "O World! O Life!
O Time!" Joyce thus, however, attempts something
which is difficult and rare and, if he publishes but little
verse, it is because he knows that it is so. A success in this
field, where the short lyric, with something of the completeness of epigram, must border on the vagueness of
music and carry some poignant feeling, always has somewhat the air of a miracle. Only the Shelleys and the
Yeatses can do it—and they not often. In these thirteen
new poems, Joyce has outgrown the imitation of his early
masters and caused their influences to contribute to a
kind of lyric unmistakably original and with far more
color and complexity than the songs in "Chamber
Music." There is not much of it, but it is real poetry—perhaps some of the purest of our time—and a single strain
of its music is enough to strike dumb whole volumes
which we may previously have pretended to take seriously. . . .

---

*In his review of poetry Robert Hillyer asserted that
some of the lyrics of* Pomes Penyeach *were "among the
most memorable" he had encountered and cited "Bahnhofstrasse," a poem Joyce wrote after his first attack of glaucoma on Zurich's Bahnhofstrasse in August 1917.*

The eyes that mock me sign the way
Whereto I pass at eve of day,

Grey way whose violet signals are
The trysting and the twining star.

Ah star of evil! star of pain!
Highhearted youth comes not again,

Nor old heart's wisdom yet to know
The signs that mock me as I go.

The exquisite vowel sounds, the half-heard echo
from the carol, and the music of the whole poem
show an unconscious power that artistry alone
can never achieve. And we wonder at these qualities until we notice that the poems were written
some years ago, before Mr. Joyce had embarked
on his Odyssey, before pedantry had conquered
his talents. One critic in America, slavishly
devoted to the cult of the later Joyce, praised these
lyrics extravagantly, far, far beyond their actual
merits which are, indeed, high enough. This is a
curious inconsistency explained only by the fact
that anything signed by Mr. Joyce is sacrosanct to
some. The truth is that one cannot sincerely
admire both these simple lyrics and *Ulysses*: they
were written by two opposed personalities, one
the sensitive youth who composed the poems, the
other, the weary man who bestowed on them the
title *Pomes Penyeach*.

—*New Adelphi*, 1 (March 1928): 264

Responses to *Work in Progress* in the 1920s

*McCarthy, a respected theatrical critic who described himself
as a "literary journalist," responds to the section of* Work in
Progress *that appeared in the April 1927 issue of* transition.

Affable Hawk
Desmond McCarthy
The New Statesmen, 29 (14 May 1927), p. 151

'Here say figurines billycoose arming and mounting.
Mounting and arming bellicose figurines see here.
Futhorc, this liffle effingee is for a firefling called flintfor-
fall. Face at the eased! O I fay! Face at the Waist! Ho, you
fie! Upwap and dump em, Face to Face. When a part so
ptee does duty for the holos we soon grow to use of an
allforabit.'

In the case of the above passage, however, we need
not feel any sympathetic pain; for the writer, so far from
being an aphasiac, is a man remarkable for a command
of words. It is a passage from Mr. James Joyce's new
work now in progress; and so far from standing out from
the first thirty pages printed in the April number of *Transition*, published by the Shakespeare Co., it is characteristic of their texture. But though every deformation of
word and sentence in this passage is intentional and
deliberate, it should no more provoke laughter than the
attempt of the unfortunate sick man to state that he took
his dog out in the morning. It should disgust. The taste
which inspired it is taste for cretinism of speech, akin to

finding exhilaration in the slobberings and mouthings of an idiot. It is always possible that a dash of the Thersites mood may contribute to a work of art, to which mood, so deep its envious loathing of all that is human, gibberish and worse may become sympathetic. But although only a fragment of the work in question is before us, it is clear that this element will be out of all proportion. How poor, too, the sense of fun, if fun it can be called, which sustains the author through the labour of composing page after page of distorted rubbish! No low-water-mark comedian of the halls, smirking and strutting before the indifferent audience, ever sank lower in search of fun that to pronounce 'little,' 'liffle,' or exclaim 'O, I fay!' 'Ho, you, fie!' One of Mr. Joyce's muses, too, is that dreary lady Mrs. Malaprop. The eye, of course, cannot follow for more than a line or two this manufactured language. When will it strike Mr. Joyce that to write what it is a *physical* impossibility to read is possibly even sillier than to write what is mentally impossible to follow?

American poet Williams, who knew Joyce in Paris in the 1920s, was a great admirer of his work and one of the early defenders of Work in Progress. *He contributed to* Our Examination Round His Factification for Incamination of Work in Progress. *Williams reprinted the following essay in* Selected Essays *(1954).*

A Note on the Recent Work of James Joyce
William Carlos Williams
transition, No. 8 (November 1927), pp. 149–154

A subtitle to any thesis on contemporary reputations might well be: How truth fares among us today. I see no other approach, at least, to the difficulties on modern literary styles than to endeavor to find what truth lies in them. Not in the matter of the writing but in the style. For style is the substance of writing which gives it its worth as literature.

But how is truth concerned in a thing seemingly so ghostlike over words as style? We may at least attempt to say what we have found untrue of it. To a style is often applied the word "beautiful"; and "Beauty is truth, truth beauty," said Keats; "that is all ye know and all ye need to know." By saying this Keats showed what I take to have been a typical conviction of his time consonant with Byron's intentions toward life and Goethe's praise of Byron. But today we have reinspected that premise and rejected it by saying that if beauty is truth and since we cannot get along without truth, then beauty is a useless term and one to be dispensed with. Here is a location for our attack; we have discarded beauty; at its best it seems

truth incompletely realized. Styles can no longer be described as beautiful.

In fact it would not be stretching the point to describe all modern styles in their grand limits as ways through a staleness of beauty to tell the truth anew. The beauty that clings to any really new work is beauty only in the minds of those who do not fully realize the significance. Thus tentatively, James Joyce's style may be described, I think, as truth through the breakup of beautiful words.

If to achieve truth we work with words purely, as a writer must, and all the words are dead or beautiful, how then shall we succeed any better than might a philosopher with dead abstractions? or their configurations? One may sense something of the difficulties by reading a page of Gertrude Stein where none of the words is beautiful. There must be something new done with the words. Leave beauty out or, conceivably, one might begin again, one might break them up to let the staleness out of them as Joyce, I think, has done. This is, of course, not all that he does nor even a major part of what he does, but it is nevertheless important.

In Joyce it began not without malice I imagine. And continued, no doubt, with a private end in view, as might be the case with any of us. Joyce, the catholic Irishman, began with english, a full-dressed english which it must have been his delight to unenglish until it should be humanely catholic, never at least sentimental. This is purely my imagination of a possible animus. And again a broken language cannot have been less than affectionately fostered since it affords him a relief from blockheaded tormentors. Admirably, of course, Joyce has written his words to face neither customs officials nor church dignitaries, catholic or protestant, but the clean features of the intelligence. Having so suffered from the dirtiness of men's minds—their mixed ideas, that is—suffered to the point of a possible suppression of all he puts upon paper, there is a humane, even a divine truth in his appeal to us through a style such as his present one which leaves nothing out. Much that he must say and cannot get said without his brokenness he gets down fully with it. But this is, again, merely a fancy. It is nothing and I put it down to show that it is nothing, things that have very little general value.

We are confronted not by reasons for its occurrence in Joyce's writings but by his style. Not by its accidental or sentimental reasons but its truth. What does it signify? Has he gone backward since *Ulysses*? Hish-hash all of it?

To my taste Joyce has not gone back but forward since *Ulysses*. I find his style richer, more able in its function of unabridged commentary upon the human soul, the function surely of all styles. But within this function what we are after will be that certain bent which is peculiar to Joyce and which gives him his value. It is not that the world is round nor even flat, but that it might well today be catholic; and as a corollary, that Joyce himself is today the ablest protagonist before the intelligence of that way of thinking. Such to my mind is the truth of his style. It is a priestly style and Joyce is himself a priest. If this be true to find out just what a priest of best intelligence intends would be what Joyce by his style intends. Joyce is obviously a catholic Irishman writing english, his style shows it and that is, less obviously, its virtue.

A profitable beginning to going further is to note the kinship between Joyce and Rabelais. Every day Joyce's style more and more resembles that of the old master, the old catholic and the old priest. It would be rash to accuse Joyce of copying Rabelais. Much more likely is it that the styles are similar because they have been similarly fathered.

Take what is most obviously on the surface in both of them, their obscenity. Shall we object to Joyce's filth? Very well, but first answer how else will you have him tell the truth. From my own experience I am perfectly willing to venture that Joyce's style has been forced upon him, in this respect at least, by the facts, and that here he has understated rather than overstated the realistic conditions which compel him. One might even go on to say that in this respect of obscenity all other present styles seem lying beside his. Let his words be men and women; in no other way could so much humanity walk the streets save in such hiding clothes. Or put it the other way: in no other way could the naked truth hidden from us upon the streets in clothes be disclosed to us in a way that we could bear or even recognize save as Joyce by his style discloses it. We should praise his humanity and not object feebly to his fullness, liars that we are. It would be impossible for Joyce to be truthful and accurate to his understanding by any other style.

This it is, let us presume, to be a catholic of the world, or so Joyce has impressed me by his style. They say Joyce fears that were he to return to Ireland it would be seen to that they excommunicate him. I cannot believe such foolishness. They are wiser than that in the church today. Joyce writes and holds his place, I would assure them, solely by the extreme brilliance of his catholicism.

And all this is no more than a reflection of the truth about Rabelais now common property. He was not all the fatheaded debauchee we used to think him, gross, guffawing vulgarly, but a priest "sensitized" to all such grossness. Else his style would not have assured his lasting out a year.

Joyce is to be discovered a catholic in his style then in something because of its divine humanity. Down, down it goes from priesthood into the slime as the church goes. The Catholic Church has always been unclean in its fingers and aloof in the head. Joyce's style consonant with this has nowhere the inhumanity of the scientific or protestant or pagan essayist. There is nowhere the coldly dressed formal language, the correct collar of such gentlemen seeking perhaps an english reputation.

Joyce discloses the X-ray eyes of the confessional, we see among the clothes, witnessing the stripped back and loins, the naked soul. Thoughtfully the priest under the constant eyes of God looks in. He, jowl to jowl with the sinner, is seen by God in all his ways. This is Joyce. To please God it is that he must look through the clothes. And therefore the privacy of the confessional; he must, so to speak, cover the ache and the sores from the world's desecrating eye with a kindly bandage. Yet he must tell the truth, before God.

Joyce has carried his writings this far: he has compared us his reader with God. He has laid it out clean for us, the filth, the diseased parts as a priest might do before the Maker. I I am speaking of his style. I am referring to his broken words, the universality of his growing language which is no longer english. His language, much like parts of Rabelais, has no faculties of place. Joyce uses German, French, Italian, Latin, Irish, anything. Time and space do not exist, it is all one in the eyes of God–and man.

Being catholic in mind, to blatantly espouse the church, that is the superficial thing to do. The sensible thing is to risk excommunication by stupidity if it come to that in order to tell the truth. Therefore I rate Joyce far above such men as G. K Chesterton, that tailor, or even Cocteau, if he has turned catholic as I have heard, though in the case of the latter it chimes well with his acknowledged cleverness to be anachronistic.

And why should we fear, as do so many protestants, that all the world turn Romanist? What in that conglomerate is out of date would even there be finally corrected by the sovereign power of the intelligence than which nothing is greater including as it must at work the instincts and emotions, that is the round brain and not the flat one. And this is once more Joyce's style.

To sum up, to me the writings of James Joyce, the new work appearing in *transition,* are perfectly clear and full of great interest in form and content. It even seems odd to me now that anyone used to seeing men and women dressed on the street and in rooms as we all do should find his style anything but obvious. If there is a difficulty it is this: whether he is writing to give us (of men and women) the aspect we are most used to or whether he is stripping from them the "military and civil dress" to give them to us in their unholy (or holy) and disreputable skins. I am inclined to think he leans more to the humaner way.

MARCH, 1928

transition

JAMES JOYCE, GIORGIO DE CHIRICO, ANDRÉ BRETON,
JACQUES BARON, LAURA RIDING, RAYMOND ROUSSEL,
SYD. S. SALT, GERTRUDE STEIN, PETER NEAGOE,
PIERRE UNIK, M. G. SHELLEY, MORLEY CALLAGHAN,
ELLIOT PAUL, ROGER VITRAC, WALTER LOWENFELS,
RENÉ LAPORTE, GEORGETTE CAMILLE, MAN RAY,
EUGENE JOLAS, PAUL BOWLES, BENJAMIN PÉRET,
ANDRÉ MASSON, PAUL ELUARD, FRANCIS PICABIA,
JAMES DALY, STANLEY BURNSHAW, JOHN HERRMANN,
MARCEL NOLL, ALLEN TATE, ABRAHAM L. GILLESPIE,
MARCEL BRION, CHARLES NORMAN, ESTHER KAUFMAN,
EDWARD ROBBIN, CARL RAKOSI, KATHLEEN CANNELL,
EVAN SHIPMAN.

*Editorial and Business Offices
40, rue Fabert, Paris VII*.*

Principal Agency : SHAKESPEARE and CO.,
12, rue de l'Odéon, Paris, VI.*

Price { 10 francs
{ 60 cents.

CONTINUATION OF A WORK IN PROGRESS (1)

by JAMES JOYCE

Hark !
Tolv two elf kater ten (it can't be) sax.
Hork !
Pedwar pemp foify tray, (it must be) twelve.
And low stole o'er the stillness the heartbeats of sleep.
White fogbow spans. The arch embattled. Mark as capsules. The nose of the man who was nought like the nasoes. It is selftinted, wrinkling, ruddled. His kep is a gorsecone. He am Gascon Titubante of Tegmine — sub — Fagi whose fixtures are mobiling so wobiling befear my remembrandts. She, exhibit next, his Anastashie. She has prayings in lowdelph. Zeehere green eggbrooms. What named blautoothdmand is you who stares ? Gugurtha ! Gugurtha ! He has becco of wild hindigan. Ho, he hath hornhide ! And hvis now is for you. Pensée ! The most beautiful of woman of the veilch veilchen veilde. She would Kidds to my voult of my

(1) This commences Book III of Mr. Joyce's new work. Book I appeared consecutively in *transition* nos 1 to 8 and a fragment of Book II was published last month in *transition* number 11. Book III will continue to appear consecutively with each number of *transition*.

— 7 —

Cover for and opening page from the issue that included what became the first chapter of book III of Finnegans Wake
(courtesy of C. W. Post Library of Long Island)

Irish poet and playwright Colum's Dial *essay was reprinted as a preface to* Anna Livia Plurabelle, *a fragment of* Work in Progress (Finnegans Wake *pp. 196–216) that was published separately in 1928.*

The River Episode from James Joyce's Uncompleted Work
Padraic Colum
The Dial, 84 (April 1928): 318–322

Anna Livia Plurabelle is concerned with the flowing of a River. There have gone into it the things that make a people's inheritance: landscape, myth, and history; there have gone into it, too, what is characteristic of a people: jests and fables. It is epical in its largeness of meaning and its multiplicity of interest. And, to my mind, James Joyce's inventions and discoveries as an innovator in literary form are more beautifully shown in it than in any other part of his work.

But although it is epical it is an episode, a part and not a whole. It makes the conclusion of the first part of a work that has not yet been completed. The episode was first published in Le Navire d'Argent in September 1925. It was expanded and published in Transition in November 1927. Again expanded, a title has been given it: Anna Livia Plurabelle.

And so, like a river, it has gone on, and expanded, and gathered volume. . . . It is the same River that Stephen Dedalus of The Portrait of an Artist as a Young Man looked upon. "In the distance along the course of the slowflowing Liffey slender masts flecked the sky, and, more distant still, the dim fabric of the city lay prone in haze. Like a scene on some vague arras, old as man's weariness, the image of the seventh city of Christendom was visible to him across the timeless air, no older nor more weary nor less patient of subjection than in the days of the thingmote." . . . "O tell me all about Anna Livia! I want to hear all about Anna Livia. Well, you know

Anna Livia? Yes, of course, we all know Anna Livia. Tell me all. Tell me now." So the later prose begins, and at once we are in the water as it bubbles and hurries at its source. The first passage gives us the sight of the River, the second gives us the River as it is seen and heard and felt. The whole of the episode gives us something besides the sight and sound and feeling of water. . . . There are moments in our lifetime when, even although inarticulate, we are all poets, moments that are probably very frequent in childhood, moments when a bird hopping on the grass or a bush in blossom is something we could look upon for hours with a mind constantly stirred and forming images and thoughts that range through the visible world, through history, and through the experiences of one's own lifetime. Such moments might come to us in any place. They would come most appropriately whilst watching the flow of water. It is this range we get in this episode: over and above the sight and sound and feeling of water there is in Anna Livia Plurabelle that range of images and thoughts, those free combinations of words and ideas, that might arise in us, if with a mind inordinately full and on a day singularly happy we watched a river and thought upon a river and travelled along a river from its source to its mouth.

But in this episode the mind's range has its boundary: the range is never beyond the river banks nor away from the city towards which the river is making its slow-moving, sometimes hurrying way. Dublin, the city once seventh in Christendom, Dublin that was founded by sea-rovers, Dublin with its worthies, its sojourners, its odd characters, not as they are known to the readers of history-books, but as they live in the minds of some dwellers by the Liffey, is in this episode; Dublin, the Ford of Hurdles, the entrance into the plain of Ireland, the city so easily taken, so uneasily held. And the River itself, less in magnitude than the tributary of a tributary of one of the important rivers, becomes enlarged until it includes hundreds of the world's rivers. How many have their names woven into the tale of Anna Livia Plurabelle? More than five hundred, I believe. "She thought she'd sankh neathe the ground with nymphant shame when he gave her the tigris eye." In that sentence three of the world's great rivers are mentioned. How beautifully the sentence that goes before it gives the flow of water!

"She says herself that she hardly knows whon the annals her graveller was, a dynast of Leinster, a wolf of the sea, or what he did or how blyth she played or when or where and how often he jumped her. She was just a young thin pale soft shy slim slip of a thing then, sauntering, and he was a heavy

trudging lieabroad of a Curraghman, making his hay for the sun to shine on, as tough as the oaktrees (peats be with them!) used to rustle that time down the dykes of killing Kildare, that firstfellfoss with a plash across her."

There will be many interpretations of Anna Livia Plurabelle—as many as the ideas that might come to one who watched the flowing of the actual river. . . . To myself there comes the recollection of a feeling I had when, as a child, the first time in Dublin I crossed a bridge with an elder of mine beside me. I imagine other children's minds would have been occupied with such thoughts as occupied mine then. The city—who named it? The pavements—who laid them down? The statues—what had the men done that they should claim that men should look upon them now and that men should have looked upon them in one's father's and one's father's father's time? The River—who named it? Why that name and no other? And from what place did the River come? The mystery of beginnings filled the mind. And, combining with the questions that came, there were things that had to be noted—the elder one walked beside, now, strangely enough, become a man of the city, knowing its lore, being saluted by its inhabitants, the apple one bought and ate and the penny one paid for it, the beggar-woman on the bridge with her blinded eyes and her doleful voice . . . . I feel in this tale of Anna Livia Plurabelle the mystery of beginnings as it is felt through, as it combines with, a hundred stray, significant, trifling things.

Its author, the most daring of innovators, has decided to be as local as a hedge-poet. James Joyce writes as if it might be taken for granted that his readers know, not only the city he writes about, but its little shops and its little shows, the nick-names that have been given to its near-great, the cant-phrases that have been used on its side-streets. "The ghost-white horse of the Peppers," he writes, and some of us remember that there was an act in a circus called Pepper's Ghost, and that there is an Irish play called The White Horse of the Peppers—a play in which ancestral acres are recovered through the speed of a horse. Through these memories a mythical shape appears on the banks of the River. This localness belongs to James Joyce's innovations: all his innovations are towards giving us what he writes about in its own atmosphere and with its own proper motion. And only those things which have been encountered day after day in some definite place can be given with their own atmosphere, their own motion.

Much should be said, and some time much will have to be said, about the de-formations and the re-formations of words in James Joyce's later work. Some of these de-formations and re-formations will not be questioned by readers who have an understanding of language: they will know that they succeed clearly in giving what the writer wants to give us.

"Can't hear with the waters of. The chittering waters of. Flittering bats, fieldmice bawk talk. Ho! Are you not gone ahome? What Tom Malone? Can't hear with bawk of bats, all the liffeying waters of. Ho, talk save us! My foos won't moos. I feel as old as yonder elm. A tale told of Shaun or Shem? All Livia's daughtersons. Dark hawks hear us. Night! Night! My ho head halls. I feel as heavy as yonder stone. Tell me of John or Shaun? Who were Shem and Shaun the living sons or daughters of? Night now! Tell me, tell me, tell me, elm! Night night! Tell me tale of stem or stone. Beside the rivering waters of, hitherandthithering waters of. Night!"

Everything that belongs to the dusk and the gathering of the clouds of evening is in this passage: the de-formations and the re-formations of the

words give us the murk of the evening. There are other innovations in the language that are really difficult to explain. Or, rather, that would require the exposition of a theory to be properly explanatory. Let us say that words are always taking on new meanings, that they take on new meanings more quickly than we realize, and that, in the case of English, as the language becomes more and more wide-spread, the change is being accelerated. Take the word "girl," for instance. Contrast the meaning of the word as a mother uses it of her growing child with the meaning it has when Miss Loos talkes of "we girls," and, further, the meaning it has in those score of stories that tell us what "the girl," said, and the point of which is that one does not know whether the person who makes the remark is very simple-minded or very experienced. And remember that Chaucer, in one instance, uses the word as meaning a boy. Remember, too, that in "queen" and

 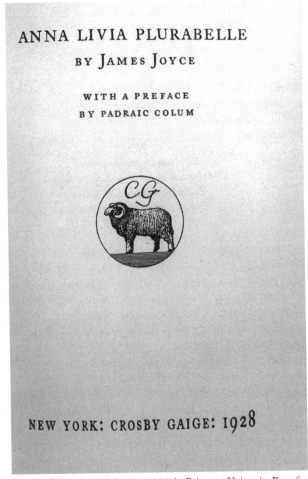

Cover and title page for the episode from Work in Progress, *of which 850 copies were printed on 20 October 1928 by Princeton University Press for the publisher Crosby Gaige (courtesy of C. W. Post Library of Long Island)*

"quean" the same word has been given opposite meanings; the form of the word that held dignity is now losing it as any one knows who has listened to talk about "movie-queens." James Joyce treats words as having shifting meanings: he lets us read a score of meanings into the words he sets down in his later work.

Anna Livia Plurabelle—two washerwomen tell her story. As it begins, the sun, we fancy, is dabbling the water; as it closes night is closing in. Voices become remote. Metamorphosis comes upon all that has been looked upon and talked about. The women, when we look to see them again, have been changed, one into a stone, and the other into an elm-tree. It is any story that might have been babbled about anywhere . . . a tale told of Shaun and Shem. . . .

Anna Livia

In his notes, Joyce used a delta siglum (Δ) to refer to Anna Livia, the matriarchal figure of Finnegans Wake. *He evokes her siglum in the typography at the beginning of the eighth chapter of book I, which begins with a single, centered letter, the top point of the delta.*

O
tell me all about
Anna Livia! I want to hear all
about Anna Livia. Well, you know Anna Livia? Yes, of course, we all know Anna Livia. Tell me all. Tell me now. . . .

—*Finnegans Wake,* p. 196

Although The Times Literary Supplement *reviewer of* Anna Livia Plurabelle *saw value in Joyce's experiments with language, he foresaw little chance that his work would influence literary language.*

Mr. Joyce's Experiment
The Times Literary Supplement, 20 December 1928, p. 1008

The dissatisfaction of the Irish with the English language and their efforts to change and revivify it make one of the most curious chapters in the history of English letters, but none has ever gone so far and made so many changes as Mr. Joyce. He is not content with an Irish dialect or with the simpler primi-

tive tendencies of Irish writers, but he has attempted to change the whole face of the English language. "Anna Livia Plurabelle" is a fragment of a work on which he is now engaged, and here, as Mr. Colum explains in an appreciative preface, he is still writing about Dublin. But while his subject is akin to that of "The Dubliners" and of "Portrait of the Artist as a Young Man," the treatment is altered out of all knowledge, though doubtless it is a development out of Mr. Joyce's intervening work. There is the same kind of poetry in prose, but it would seem that this has needed the stimulus of new language and new technical devices to prevent its exhaustion. "Anna Livia Plurabelle" is written in an outlandish dialect; the roots of English words can be recognized, sometimes after thought, but often the endings and the spelling are much changed. One is at times reminded of the devices of manufacturers in their trade names, when they spell words phonetically or change "f" into "ph." Undoubtedly, though inexplicably, this has a value in advertising, but it needs great boldness to find in it something of value for poetry or for poetical prose. "Frostivying tresses dasht with vireflies' is a good example of this device in Mr. Joyce's work. In addition to this there is every kind of euphuism, foreign words are used, and much alliteration and rhyme.

Certainly this is a new literary dialect, and it is possible to read it, though with more trouble than Chaucer demands; and one can see that if Mr. Joyce's real gifts of fantasy and poetry were in danger of exhaustion the invention of a new dialect is a conceivable means of restoring them. Mr. Joyce is, in fact, desperately and with remarkable courage trying to bring back the English language to a period like the Elizabethan, when each neologism was a happy discovery and the spout of words flowed freshly and with exuberance. . At the same time he avoids the obvious and never satisfactory method of definite archaism, though he does use at times archaic words, just as, lest any change should be neglected, he quite often uses the Irish poetical dialect of writers like Mr. Synge. It is an extraordinary attempt, perhaps to be matched with the attempt to revive the Irish language for a new Irish literature. It is probable enough that Mr. Joyce would be much happier with a language as triumphantly exuberant as that of the Elizabethan age, and that he could not excel in the polishing of Augustan lines when language (as perhaps now) needed the most scrupulous and careful handling. No one knows why a language should receive at moments a sudden stimulation and plunge into rapid growth, but it seems unlikely that this has ever happened as the result of a deliberate and conscious effort like that of Mr. Joyce. We may be fairly sure that such an effort will not change the literary language outside Mr. Joyce's books, but inside them there is little harm and great interest in the change. It cannot be denied that Mr. Joyce does at moments achieve an astonishingly vigorous diction, and there is sometimes beauty in his writing; though it is a beauty which can only be guessed at, like that of a poem in a language which we only half know.

Vladimir Dixon's Letter

Vladimir Dixon's 9 February 1929 letter to Joyce was written in the style of Finnegans Wake. *At one time it was thought that the letter was composed by Joyce, who suggested that Dixon's letter be included as the final word in* Our Exagmination Round His Factification for Incamination of Work in Progress, *a collection of twelve essays and two letters of protest first published by Shakespeare and Company in May 1929. In her memoir* Shakespeare and Company, *Sylvia Beach*

Sylvia Beach (portrait by Stephen Longstreet; Collection of Arlyn Bruccoli)

writes, "I never, as far as I know, had the pleasure of meeting Mr. Dixon, but I suspect him of being no other than 'The Germ's Choice' himself. It seemed to me that the handwriting of Dixon had one or two little Joycean characteristics." Richard Ellmann, who was probably influenced by Beach's supposition, comments in a footnote in Letters III, *"This letter, obviously composed if not written by Joyce himself but never acknowledged by him, was delivered by an unknown hand to Sylvia Beach's bookshop" (p. 187).*

Dixon, however, was a real person, an American citizen born in 1900 in Sormovo, Russia, of an English father, who had become an American in 1896, and a Russian mother. After serving in the United States Army as a translator (Dixon knew several languages), he graduated from M.I.T. in 1921 with a B.S. degree before going on to Harvard for a master's degree. From 1923 until his death on 17 December 1929, Dixon lived in Paris.

Vladimir Dixon

English critic, essayist, and novelist Connolly uses the occasion of the publication of Anna Livia Plurabelle *as a starting point for his commentary in which he examines the importance of Joyce as a cultural figure.*

The Position of Joyce
Cyril Connolly
Life and Letters, 2 (April 1929), 273–290

James Joyce has brought out a new book. It is a fragment of a longer one, and is called *Anna Livia Plurabelle.* We are used to the reputations of authors fluctuating from year to year, but Mr. Joyce's also fluctuates from place to place. He is resented in Ireland, neglected in England, admired by a set in America, and idolized by another in France. In every nation there is a general public and a literary public. In Ireland the general public is provincial and priest-ridden. It cannot forgive Joyce his blasphemy nor his contemptuous parodies of Irish jingoism. The other, the smaller public, has chosen escape in a romantic return to the past, characterized by a special lyric note of easy and indefinable melancholy born of self-pity. Joyce is a realist, and out of touch intellectually with that generation. 'Michael Roberts remembers forgotten beauty. He presses in his arms the loveliness which has long faded from the world. I desire to press in my arms the loveliness which has not yet come into the world.' Thus Joyce's only disciples in Ireland are the young realists of the post-rebellion period. In England the literary public is governed by good taste. Cautious as the cenotaph, the critics decide the value of a book in terms of 'delicious' and 'charming'. The general public is equally conservative, and the fate of a book like *Ulysses,* so hopelessly unpresentable when submitted to the Chelsea canon, is decided in advance. It is in America, where there is a large and less sophisticated general public, and in Paris, where there are a great many young writers anxious to experiment in literary form, that the 'Ulysses generation' has grown up.

Mr. Forster, in his lectures on the novel, states perfectly the English attitude to Joyce, the bad bogey-man of letters. '*Ulysses,*' he writes, 'is a dogged attempt to cover the universe with mud, an inverted Victorianism, an attempt to make coarseness and dirt succeed where sweetness and light failed, a simplification of the human character in the interests of Hell.' It is also an 'epic of grubbiness and disillusion . . . a superfetation of fantasies, a monstrous coupling of reminiscences . . . in which smaller mythologies swarm and pullulate, like vermin between the scales of a poisonous snake.' 'Indignation in literature,' adds Mr. Forster, 'never quite comes off,' and the passage I have quoted does little except to express the general attitude of English culture towards novelty, and to prove that the vocabulary of

A LITTER TO MR. JAMES JOYCE 14

27 Avenue de l'Opéra
Paris I

Dear Mister Germ's Choice,

in gutter dispear I am
taking my pen toilet you know
that, being Leyde up in bad with
the prewailent distemper (I opened
the window and in flew Enza), I
have been reeding one half ter
one other the numboars of „transition" in witch are printed the
severeall instorments of your
„Work in Progress".
you must not stink I

Dixon's letter on Work in Progress *that was being published in* transition *(courtesy of John Dixon)*

- 2 -

um attempting to ridicul (de sac!)
you or to be smart, but I am so
disturd by my inhumility to onthor-
stand most of the impslocations
constrained in your work that
(although I am by nominals dump
and in fact I consider myself
not brilliantly ejewcatered but still
of above Hverroëge men's tality and
having maid the most of the oport₀
unities I Kismet) I am writing
you, dear mysterre Shame's Voice,
to let you no how bed I fecloxe-
rab out it all.

-3.

I am überzeugt that the labour involved in the compostition of your work must be almost supper humane and that so much trarail from a man of your intellacked must ryeseult in somethinx rery signicophant.   I would only like to know have I been so strichnine by my illnest while wresting under my warm Coverlyette that I am as they say in my neightive land „out of the mind gone out" and unable to comb-pre-hen that which is clear or

4

is there really in your work
some ass pecked which is
Uncle Lear?

Please froggive my t'Emeritus
and any inconvince that may have
been caused by this litter.

Yours veri tass

Vladimir Dixon

9.2.29.

scandalized vituperation is drawn from the reptile-house in every age.

'Indignation' is not a quality of Joyce's work, but 'the raging of Joyce seems essentially fantastic, and lacks the note for which we shall be listening soon,' continues Mr. Forster, who proceeds to classify *Ulysses* as belonging to the period of *Zuleika Dobson*. Let us get a clear idea of *Ulysses* before we try to estimate the later work of its author. James Joyce is, by temperament, a mediaevalist. He has always been in revolt against his two greatest limitations, his Jesuit education and his Celtic romanticism. Each of his books reveals a growing fear of beauty; not because life is not beautiful, but because there is something essentially false and luxurious in the 'Celtic Twilight' approach to it. This tinsel element is very strong in Joyce's early poems, and is contrasted with an equally pronounced repulsion from it in "The Portrait of the Artist." In *Ulysses* he has got it in hand, and is experimenting in other approaches to beauty, the pagan simplicity of Mrs. Bloom's reverie, the mathematical austerity of the catechism which precedes it. Only Stephen Dedalus, the Hamlet young man, thinks automatically in the diction of the Celtic Twilight; but in him the remorse, the guilty sense of loneliness which attacks brave but weak men who destroy the religious framework of their youth, has fused with his minor poet melancholy, and gives to his reverie the quality of a Greek chorus. Stephen Dedalus, in fact, equips the Ulysses generation with a fatalism, a dramatization of their own forebodings, and with the mediaeval quality so rare in America, so reduced in England, so rife in Europe—the Tragic Sense of life. This is the great link between Joyce and Proust, otherwise so misleadingly compared. Both, one an Irishman and one a Jew, possess the tragic intelligence, the idea that life can only be appreciated, can only be lived even, if the intelligence is used to register all the beauty and all the intimacy that exists in ironic contrast to the unrelieved gloom of squalor and emptiness, mediocrity, disease and death. 'For all our wit and reading do but bring us to a truer sense of sorrow,' the whole climax of *Ulysses* is a single moment of intimacy, when Bloom, the comic character, rescues Stephen in a drunken brawl. Bloom had a son who died, Stephen a father who is alive; but for this instant of spiritual paternity all the swelter of that urban summer, all the mesembrian pub-crawls of Bloom and Stephen, the vermin and the scales and the serpents move into place. The central emotion of *Ulysses* is not indignation, but remorse; and remorse, though perhaps second-rate in life, is an emotion which entirely comes off in literature. Expiation and the sense of doom, which the essence of Greek tragedy, are only a variation of this feeling; and though remorse seems so feebly static in real people, the very tranquillity and remoteness from acts lend it a glassy literary beauty. In *Ulysses* Stephen goes in the consciousness of having hastened his mother's death by his atheism, Bloom feels obscurely his father's suicide and the troubled history of his people, while all Ireland seems listlessly aware of its destiny. Perhaps the most typical scene in *Ulysses* is that in which Stephen, who has run away from the squalor of his father's house, comes across his young sister also trying to escape her environment without the help he might have given:

He turned and halted by the slanted book cart.
Twopence each, the huckster said, four for sixpence.
Tattered pages. *The Irish Beekeeper. Life and miracles of the Curé of Ars. Pocket Guide to Killarney.*
'I might find there one of my pawned school prizes.'
'What are you doing here, Stephen?'
Dilly's high shoulders and shabby dress.
Shut the book quick. Don't let see.
'What are you doing,' Stephen said.
A Stuart face of nonsuch Charles, lank locks falling at its sides. It glowed as she crouched feeding the fire with broken boots. I told her of Paris. Late lieabed under a quilt of old overcoats, fingering a pinchbeck bracelet; Dan Kelly's token.
'What have you there?' Stephen asked.
'I bought it from the other cart for a penny,' Dilly said, laughing nervously. 'Is it any good?'
My eyes they say she has. Do others see me so? Quick, far and daring, shadows of my mind.
He took the coverless book from her hand. Chardenal's *French Primer.*
'What did you buy that for?' he asked. 'To learn French?'
She nodded, reddening and closing tight her lips.
Show no surprise, quite natural.
"Here,' Stephen said, 'it's all right. Mind Maggie doesn't pawn it on you. I suppose all my books are gone.'
"Some,' said Dilly, 'we had to.'
She is drowning. Agenbite. Save her, Agenbite. All against us. She will drown me with her, eyes and hair. Lank coils of seaweed hair around me, my heart, my soul. Salt green death.
We.
Agenbite of Inwit. Inwit's Agenbite.
Misery.

This quotation reveals many other aspects of the book; the old words for remorse, for instance, become one of those snowball phrases with which *Ulysses* is packed. Appearing continually in the characters' day-dreams, they gather momentum from each association, echoing through the chapters till they are charged by the end with as much personality as the thinkers themselves. Then the drabness of the scene, the halting, trite dialogue illustrate the other side of *Ulysses:* the attempt to create beauty out of city life, and style out of the demotic English which is spoken in them. Every year more people's lives are passed in towns than in the country; but while there is a whole vocabulary of rural beauty, there is so far only the slenderest aesthetic of cities, the roughest technique in appreciating them. What Baudelaire and Laforgue did for Paris, or Mr. T. S. Eliot for modern London, Joyce has done for Dublin: and at a time when Yeats and Synge had monopolized the Gaelic side of the Irish, he was able to create a language out of the demotic commercial speech of the anglicised burgers of Dublin itself. Literary English has become very hackneyed, as a glance at any book of essays or a preface to an anthology at once will show, and Joyce in *Ulysses* set out to revive it by introducing the popular colloquial idiom of his own city, by forming new words in the Greek fashion of compound epithets, by telescoping grammar, by using the fresh vocabulary of science manuals, public-houses, or Elizabethan slang. Here, for instance, are two quotations, one to illustrate the city aesthetic, the note of Celtic melancholy introduced into the descriptions of an urban summer sunset by the hill of Howth, where Bloom had once made love; the other, an example of Joyce's highly latinised English, which produces an effect of austere rhetoric and elaborate original rhythm.

A long lost candle wandered up the sky from Myrus' bazaar in search of funds for Mercer's hospital and broke, drooping, and shed a cluster of violet but one white stars. They floated, fell: they faded. The shepherd's hour: the hour of holding: hour of tryst. From house to house, giving his everwelcome double knock, went the nine o'clock postman, the glowworm's lamp at his belt gleaming here and there through the laurel hedges. And among the fine young trees a hoisted linstock lit the lamp at Leahy's Terrace. By screens of lighted windows, by equal gardens, a shrill voice went crying, wailing, *Evening Telegraph*—stop press edition! Result of the Gold Cup races!' And from the door of Dignam's house a boy ran out and called. Twittering the bat flew here, flew there. Far out over the sands the coming surf crept, gray. Howth settled for slumber, tired of long days, of yumyum rhododendrons (he was old) and felt gladly the night breeze lift, ruffle his fell of ferns. He lay but opened a red eye unsleeping, deep and slowly breathing, slumberous but awake. And far on Kish bank the anchored lightship twinkled, winked, at Mr. Bloom.

* * *

What play of forces, inducing inertia, rendered departure undesirable?

The lateness of the hour, rendering procrastinatory: the obscurity of the night, rendering invisible: the uncertainty of Thoroughfares rendering perilous: the

necessity for repose, obviating movement: the proximity of an occupied bed, obviating research: the anticipation of warmth [human] tempered with coolness [linen] obviating desire and rendering desirable: the statue of Narcissus, sound without echo, desired desire.

Besides this he directed a stream of parody against all the whimsy and archaism latent in English prose style. It is indeed as an enemy of 'literature' that Joyce really might appear to Mr. Forster as working 'in the interests of Hell'. Though he did not originate the 'stream of consciousness' as a form of writing, he saw that by recording the thoughts of each character he could take shorthand liberties with their syntax as well as get nearer to their selves. He too, among those who have used this method, is the only one who has realized that people, besides thinking differently, think at a different pace. Mrs. Woolf, whose *Mrs. Dalloway* is in many ways a feminine adaptation of one idea of *Ulysses* to English good taste, tends to make all her characters think in the same tempo. She gives us anatomical slices, not human beings, but sections of them, which portray the doubts, the tendernesses, the half-hopes and half-fears of the human mind conceived all in the same mood of genteel despair. Bloom, Mrs. Bloom, Stephen, however, and the nameless narrator of one chapter, all have mental processes which are quite incomparable with each other—Bloom's mean, good-tempered, second-rate, scientific curiosity colours all his commonplace meditations. Stephen's bitterness, imagination, and petulant intellect quicken feverishly the pulse of his thought. The racy, cynical and shamelessly prejudiced gusto of the Nameless One transforms his narrative into the whirl of the winds of Aeolus that it is meant to symbolize, while elaborate journalese retards the speed of the book for those chapters when the action is at a standstill. Lastly the even breathing of Mrs. Bloom times with her steady physical reverie, her pagan meditation so free of Stephen's mediaeval anguish, Bloom's scepticism, or all the problems which faced the morning of the one, the evening of the other, and their common night.

The link between the new work of Joyce and *Ulysses* is chiefly one of language; though both are united by the same preoccupation with the aesthetic of cities, with the absurdity of our Jewish-American democracy, and with the capacity for being beautiful which this democracy yet retains.

Here are two quotations, one showing the Hill of Howth treated again in a symbolic manner, the other the praise of Dublin, rhetorical as cities are—Earwicker (the Danish castle) is bragging to his wife, the Liffey, of all he has done for her. I have noted it in the text so that the complexity of the portmanteau language may be gauged:

'Old Whitehowth is speaking again. Pity poor White-oath! Deargone mummeries, goby. Tell the woyld I have lived true thousand hells. Pity please, lady, for poor O.W. in this profoundest snobbing I have caught. Nine dirty years mine age, hairs white, mummery failing, dear as Adder. I askt you, dear lady, to judge on my tree by our fruits. I gave you of the tree. I gave two smells, two eats: my happy blossoms, my all falling fruits of my boom. Pity poor Haveth Children Everywhere with Mudder. That was Communicator a former Colonel.'

'. . . And I built in Urbs in Rure for mine elskede, my shiny brows, an earth closet wherewithin to be quit in most convenience from her sabbath needs: did not I fest-fix my unniverseries, wholly rational and got alike; [three Dublin universities national and godlike with Trinity to suggest the holy] was not I rosetted on two stelas of little Egypt, had not (I) rockcut readers, hieros, gregos, and democriticos; [the Rosetta stone] and by my syvendialed changing charties Hibernska ulitzas made not I [allusion to superimposing a street map on an older one and rotating it to find what streets lie along a Roman road. Ulitza is the Slav for a street, but in this case is also a prophecy of Ulysses and his labours] to pass through 12 Threadneedles and Newgade and Vicus Veneris to cooinsight. [Allusions to Ulysses, to Newgate prison on the Roman Road.] Oi polled ye many, but my fews were chosen: and I set up twinminsters, the pro and the con [Christchurch and the pro-Cathedral] woven of peeled wands and attachattouchy floodmud [Italian root, 'sticky'] arched for the convenanters and shinner's rifuge; all truant trulls made I comepull, all rubbeling gnomes I pushed, go go; and thirdly for ewigs I did reform and restore for my smuggy piggiesknees her paddy palace on the crossknoll [St. Patrick's restored] and added there unto a shallow laver to put out her hell fire and posied windows for her oriel house and she sass her nach, chillybombom and 40 bonnets, upon the altarstane, may all have mossyhonours!

'I hung up at the Yule my pigmy suns helphelped of Kettil Flashnose [electric lights introduced in Dublin under Kettle, the chief of the electricians and descendant of Kettle Flatnose, an original Dane settler] for the supper hour of my frigid one, coulomba mea, frimosa mia, through all Livania's volted ampire from anods to cathods, and from the topazolites of Mourne by Arklow's sapphire seamanslure and Waterford's hook and crook lights to the polders of Hy Kinsella [old Danish beacons].'

The ordinary man of letters, when faced with modern civilization, plays the ostrich with its head in the sand. A very whimsical, arch, mock apologetic and well-subsidized ostrich too. In fact, they are the paid entertainers of democracy, the jesters who are allowed the licence of bewailing the rattle of hansom cabs, of beginning every sentence with 'I must needs avow that I have never seen eye to eye with those who', and ending 'nevertheless, to my thinking, when all is said and done. . . .' Of course, there is no law compelling any one to belong to his period; but not to belong to it, is to take sanctuary, to eke out a whimsical existence and an archaic style in a halftimbered Utopia, visited, like an Elizabethan teashop, by the most insipid of the public you would like to avoid. If *Ulysses* is largely a parody of literary manners, a dissatisfaction with style, the new work of Joyce is a parody of language, an attempt to create a new vocabulary for literature itself. And both, which readers are unwilling to see, are meant to be funny. After all, the ballad of the Jabberwock has passed into the accepted treasury of English humour; yet when the method Carroll used to reinforce words with double meanings is applied to contemporary prose, which surely needs it, the result is that we label the originator mad.

Literary language in England has become very far removed from conversation, nor is it able to profit, like American, from a rich background of polyglot slang. All literary words in addition tend to be used, especially by Georgian poets, without a due conviction of their meaning, and this depreciates the currency so that most epithets become like the dumb notes on an old piano, which go down when they are sounded, but never come up. The best instance of this is the penultimate passage of *The Oxford Book of English Prose*. The new language of Joyce is only a kind of piano-tuning, tightening up certain words by grafting fresher foreign equivalent on to them, approximating them to other words to strengthen their own vigour, above all by punning them freely, it gives words a synthetic meaning, either to express life, or simply to make a series of academic jokes with. The experiment may be a failure, just as Esperanto or phonetic spelling may be a failure, but there is nothing really contrary to reason in the idea itself. The chief defect of Mr. Joyce's new language is that, so far, it has swamped the lyrical quality of his other prose writings; he has not attempted purple patches in it so much as rhetorical imitations of them. Here is the close of a fable called 'The Mookse and the Gripes', which can be compared with Bloom's city sunset, quoted above:

> The shades began to glidder along the banks, dusk unto dusk, and it was as glooming as gloaming could be in the waste of peaceable wolds. The mookse had a sound eyes right but he could not all hear. The Gripes had light ears left yet he could but ill see. He ceased. And he ceased and it was so dusk of both of them. But still one thought of the deeps he would profound on the morrow and still the other thought of the scrapes he would escape if he had luck enough.

The new book is full of fables, because the whole of the first part is really a *surréaliste* to the prehistory of Dublin, the myths and legends of its origin, Duke Humphrey and Anna Livia, the mountain and the river, from

Samuel Beckett, who first met Joyce in Paris in October 1928. Beckett aided Joyce with Work in Progress *between 1928 and 1930 when Joyce's eyesight was failing*

a black reach of which the city took its name. The first words 'riverrun brings us back to Howth Castle and Environs' suggest the melodies to follow. All the urban culture of Ireland is by origin Scandinavian; and, to emphasize this, Joyce has introduced the greatest possible amount of Norse words into his description of it. There are four parts to the new work of Joyce, the first is a kind of air photograph of Irish history, a celebration of the dim past of Dublin, as was *Ulysses* of its grimy present; the second is an interlude in a barn near Chapelizod; some children are playing, and react unconsciously the old stories of the first (Iseult of Ireland linking in the suburb's name); and the third part, jumping from the 'past events leave their shadows behind' of the first, to 'coming events cast their shadows before', deals in four sections with the four watches of one night. As this is literary criticism, I cannot go into the metaphysics of Joyce's new book, which are based on the history of Vico and on a new philosophy of Time and Space; but two other things emerge, the same preoccupation of the author with his

native town, his desire to see all the universe through that small lense, and his poetic feeling for the phases of the dusk, for that twilight which originally got the Celtic revival its name.

. . . .

Anna Livia is an episode from this book describing the legend of the Liffey. Two old washerwomen stand on each side of the stripling river and gossip away as they pound the clothes. ('O tell me all about Anna Livia.') They talk of Earwicker's affair with her under his other identity, of Duke Humphrey, and gradually their language breaks into a melody of water music, a kind of paean like the praise of the brook Kishon into which the names of every conceivable river is brought as an onomatopaeic trainbearer:

> . . . . She sideslipped out by a gap in the devil's glen while Sally her nurse was sound asleep in a shoot, and fell over a spillway before she found her stride and lay and wriggled in all the stagnant black pools of rain under a fallow coo and she laughed with her limbs all aloft and a whole grove of maiden hawthorns blushing and looking askance upon her. . . . And after that she wore a garland for her hair. She pleated it. She plaited it. Of meadow grass and riverflags, the bulrush and the water weed, and of fallen griefs of weeping-willow.

Occasionally the charwomen break in with their own troubles:

> 'O my bach! my back! my back! I'd want to go to Aches-les-Pains . . . spread on your bank and I'll spread on mine. It's wat I'm doing. Spread! It's turning chill. Der went is rising.'

Gradually the growing stream carries them apart as the night falls, for they are standing on the two banks of the infant river like a moving stairway, and the gap between them has widened as the Liffey leaps, in the words of her song, 'to the slobs of the Tolka and the shores of Clontarf to hear the gay aire of my salt troublin' bay and the race of the saywint up my ambushure'. When night falls, the old women shouting across in the dark cannot understand each other; still gossiping, they are transformed into an elm and a stone, the strange obscurity is about them of the old myths from which they have emerged, and the *motiv* of the past of Ireland is re-echoed in their dumb blocklike language; for the Mookse and the Gripes had suffered the same fate, mortal beside the immortal river:

> '. . . and it was never so thoughtful of either of them. And there were left now only an elm tree and but a stone. O! Yes! and Nuvoletta, a lass.'

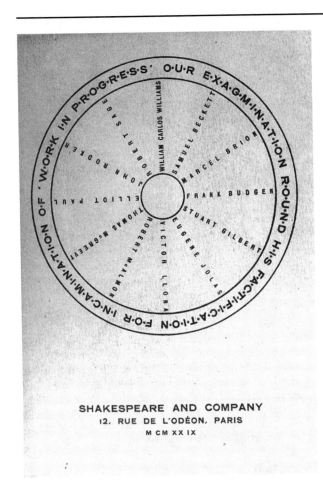

TABLE OF CONTENTS

	Pages.
DANTE... BRUNO. VICO.. JOYCE, by Samuel Beckett.	1
THE IDEA OF TIME IN THE WORK OF JAMES JOYCE, by Marcel Brion.	23
JAMES JOYCE'S *Work in Progress* AND OLD NORSE POETRY, by Frank Budgen.	35
PROLEGOMENA TO *Work in Progress*, by Stuart Gilbert.	47
THE REVOLUTION OF LANGUAGE AND JAMES JOYCE, by Eugene Jolas.	77
I DONT KNOW WHAT TO CALL IT BUT ITS MIGHTY UNLIKE PROSE, by Victor Llona.	93
MR. JOYCE DIRECTS AN IRISH WORD BALLET, by Robert McAlmon.	103
THE CATHOLIC ELEMENT IN *Work in Progress*, by Thomas McGreevy.	117
MR. JOYCE'S TREATMENT OF PLOT, by Elliot Paul.	129
JOYCE AND HIS DYNAMIC, by John Rodker.	139
BEFORE *Ulysses* — AND AFTER, by Robert Sage.	147
A POINT FOR AMERICAN CRITICISM, by William Carlos Williams.	171
WRITES A COMMON READER, by G. V. L. Slingsby.	189
A LITTER TO MR. JAMES JOYCE, by Vladimir Dixon.	193

Cover, title page, and table of contents for book of criticism by supporters of Joyce's work (courtesy of C. W. Post Library of Long Island)

The end of the *Anna Livia* marks another of Joyce's extraordinary descriptions of dusk:

'Whawk? Can't hear with the waters of. The chittering waters of. Flittering bats, fieldmice bawk talk. Ho! Are you not gone ahome? What Tom Malone? Can't hear with the bawk of bats, all the liffeying waters of. Ho, talk save us! My foos wont moos. I feel as old as yonder elm. A tale told of Shaun or Shem? All Livia's daughtersons. Dark hawks hear us. Night! Night! My ho head halls. I feel as heavy as yonder stone. Tell me of John or Shem? Who were Shem and Shaun the living sons and daughters of? Night now! Tell me, tell me, tell me, elm! Night night! Tell me tale of stem or stone. Beside the rivering waters of, mother and mithering waters of hither and thithering Night!' [All this has to be read as carefully as it has been written.]

The best way to read Joyce's new book, apart from this rare reprint of *Anna Livia,* is in a quarterly called *Transition,* edited by Americans living in Paris. The contents are often as grotesque as the idea is enterprising. But we have no paper for literary experiment in England, and literature is, after all, as technical a business as medicine or engineering. *Transition* is sometimes a very silly paper, and sometimes intensely amusing for, like most rebel journals, its satire is surer than its originality; but it is the only one which publishes the honest, sometimes fascinating, often incoherent research of those who take new literature seriously in every country. Of course, it is not possible to pronounce a verdict on Joyce's work when it is so fragmentary. The best that this article can hope to prove is that the new work of Joyce is respect-worthy and readable. There is nothing insane in its conception nor bogus in its execution. Though to many a spinster fancy it probably will continue to lack the 'note for which we will be listening soon', to others, it promises amusement and a very interesting and strange approach to life and beauty. After all, it is an experiment; we are content to accord the wildest tolerance to the latest unintelligible—even uncommercial—pamphlet of Einstein—can we not admit a little of the same tolerance to something in writing we do not understand? It must be remembered that Joyce, besides being a lover of words, is an Irishman under no obligation whatever to rest content with the English language, and also that, while our literature, unaware of a decline of the West or a defence of it, grows daily more bucolic and conservative, Continental Letters are nourished on an exhilarating sense of an uncertain future which makes the liberties of their volcano dwellers permissible—and which we are entirely without. Literature is in essence a series of new universes enforced on a tardy public by their creators. This one may be a fake, but it is not from a writer who has previously given us fakes; it may be a failure, but it is surely an absorbing one, and more important than any contemporary successes. I, personally, am biased as a critic by nationality, and by the same feeling for geography and Dublin, but still more by the enthusiasm which comes to everyone when they discover themselves through a book—a service which Joyce, Proust, and Gide have rendered generally to almost all our thinking generation; for me any criticism of *Ulysses* will be affected by a wet morning in Florence, when in the empty library of a villa with the smell of woodsmoke, the faint eavesdrip, I held the uncouth volume dazedly open in the big armchair—Narcissus with his pool before him.

The New York Times *was evidently bemused by Joyce's work, as is apparent in this editorial that appeared soon after the 9 August 1929 publication of* Tales Told of Shem and Shaun. *The new book was comprised of three fragments from* Work in Progress: *"The Mookse and the Gripes"* (Finnegans Wake, *pp. 152–159), "The Muddest Thick That Was Ever Heard Dump" (pp. 282–304), and "The Ondt and the Gracehoper" (pp. 414–419).*

Triumph of Jabberwocky
The New York Times, 23 August 1929, p. 20

Some fragments of another work of genius which Mr. James Joyce is slowly perfecting have been published in London. They show him as a fashioner or creator and transformer of language. He continues on a great scale the method of LEWIS CARROLL. Not infrequently he employs the metathesis system which the Oxford undergraduates so long and affectionately attributed to Dr. SPOONER. But his new strange tongue is not the perfume and suppliance of a moment. It is constant, elaborate, voluminous. The beginner has no trouble with such simplicities as "weight a momentum"; but there must be at least 160 seconds in a minute before we can read at sight a passage like this, cited by *The Spectator* and apparently relating to the operation of describing "an aquillitoral dryangle on a given strayed line." The theme is easy, but some of the language surprises by himself:

My faceage kink and kurkle trying to make keek peep. Are you right there, Michael, are you right? Ay, I'm right here, Nickel, and I'll write. But it's the muddest thick that was ever heard dump. Now join alfa pea and pull loose by dotties and, to be more sparematically logical, eelpie and paleale by trunkles.

Tales Told of
Shem and Shaun

Three Fragments from
Work in Progress

by

JAMES JOYCE

THE BLACK SUN PRESS
RUE CARDINALE
PARIS
MCMXXIX

CONTENTS

Portrait of the Author by C. Brancusi

Preface by C. K. Ogden

The Mookse and the Gripes

The Muddest Thick That Was Ever Heard Dump

The Ondt and the Gracehoper

Cover and table of the contents for the fragments published on 9 August 1929 (courtesy of C. W. Post Library of Long Island)

If we may say so without irreverence, this looks sleazy, broken, interrupted by surrenders to intelligibility. Compare it with the first stanza of "Jabberwocky":

'Twas brillig, and the slithy toves
 Did gyre and gimble in the wabe:
All mimsey were the borogoves,
 And the mome raths outgrabe.

Under so worthy a master, Mr. JOYCE'S studies ought to be as fruitful as his terminology is satisfactory. If he could but combine with that the mystic and mighty thought which Miss GERTRUDE STEIN has manifested in such a classic as "Certainly the union of oxygen with ostriches is not that of a taught tracer," the ultimate form would be married to the ultimate content. Then nothing but conservatism and decline could be expected of "revolutionary" literature. Mr. JOYCE'S purpose is not humor. His is the deep melancholy common to inveterate readers and writers. All words look shabby or sick to him. He hates them. He must have a new lot. To weary word-"slingers" the product of his Paris factory may bring encouragement and hope.

The Congressional Record, translated into Jabberwocky-Joycese, would double its circulation in a week.

English journalist and playwright Bennett had reviewed Ulysses *as a masterpiece.*

Comment on *Anna Livia Plurabelle*
Arnold Bennett
London Evening Standard, 19 September 1929, p. 7

The last of my rebels is James Joyce, a man who has done great stuff. I have referred before in these columns to his 'unfinished work,' and to the fragment of it entitled *Anna Livia Plurabelle*. This fragment has been published by Crosby Gaige, of New York, in a beautifully printed and produced volume as thin as a biscuit. Edition of 800 signed copies. A collector's morsel. A genuine curiosity. I am charmed to have it. But I cannot comprehend a page of it. For it is written in James Joyce's new language, invented by himself. Here are a few words from one page: limpopo, sar, icis, seints, zezere, hamble, blackburry, dwyergray, meanam, meyne, draves, pharphar, uyar. It ought to be published with a Joyce dictionary.

Someone (I read somewhere) said to Joyce: 'I don't understand it.' Joyce replied: 'But you will.' Joyce is an optimist. Human language cannot be successfully handled with such violence as he has here used to English. And *Anna Livia Plurabelle* will never be anything but the wild caprice of a wonderful creative artist who has lost his way.

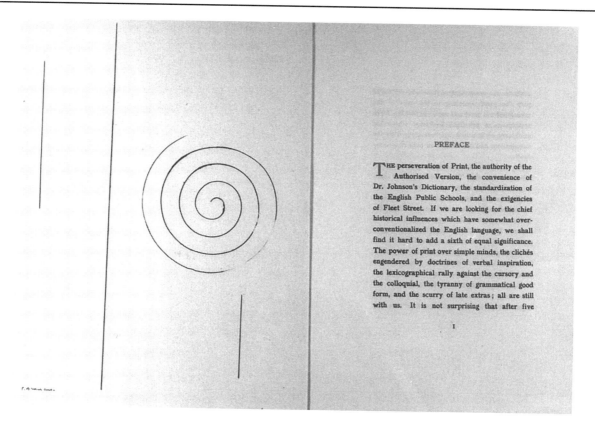

Portrait of Joyce by the Romanian sculptor Constantin Brancusi opposite the first page of the mathematician C. K. Ogden's Preface to Tales Told
*of Shem and Shaun. According to Richard Ellmann, Brancusi explained that the drawing "was a curleycue intended . . . to express the
'sens du pousser' which [Brancusi] found in Joyce; the sense of enigmatic involution is also conveyed"*
(courtesy of C. W. Post Library of Long Island).

Michael Stuart reviewed Tales Told of Shem and Shaun: Three Fragments from Work in Progress.

The Dubliner and His Dowdili
(A Note on the Sublime)
Michael Stuart
transition, No. 18 (November 1929), pp. 152–161

"But the sublime when uttered in good season, with the lightning's force scatters all before it in an instant, and shows at once the might of genius in a stroke."

"Work in Progress" is the ultimate pole in that tendency to objectivity in European letters which seeks to approach the condition of an element of nature recording like the winds upon the rocks and the trees the history of the human soul in its progress through the world. To establish a field of reference between the Dubliner's creation and that broader field of literature which influenced it and which in turn must suffer to be influenced by that revaluation of values which every new work of art imposes upon the past it is vital to note its limitations, if the

"graph" is to be considered for something more than another "Ayenbite of Inwit." The critic's office, the truism may be repeated by arrangement with the publishers, is to bring into play those ideas which will aid the "common reader" to a comprehension of the work itself, its relation to literature as a whole of which it is both the child and the parent, and perhaps, also, to consider the work in the light of general ideas to which literature more nearly than other arts must always be related.

If we are not overawed by the majesty of words and apply to "Work in Progress" the critical canon contained in the mock Joycian Latinity of the Geometrical Fragment which echoes in part Bruno's belief "that everything can only come to a knowledge of itself through a contrast with its opposite"– "quodlibet sese ipsum per aliudpiam agnoscere contrarium", we shall but follow the author's own guiding principle for the illumination of his dream-world, a principle holding true as well in other categories than literature. This criticism by contrast will justify itself largely on the ground of aiding us to understand what the work is by showing us first what it is

Carola Giedion-Welcker discussed Joyce's achievement in "Ein Sprachliches Experiment von James Joyce" (A Linguistic Experiment by James Joyce), an essay that originally appeared in the September 1929 issue of Neue Schweizer Rundschau *and was translated by Eugène Jolas for* transition.

Work in Progress is—as the title indicates—not a closed solution, but an evolutionary process. But here positively tangible: the productive controversy with the basic elements of the poetic material: language, today still a petrified and exhausted form. Through free association of word and thought, Joyce changes it from a carrier of mental content, become more or less passive, into an actively functioning mediator of the ideological.

—*transition,* Nos. 19–20 (June 1930), p. 174

not. . . It is wrong to suppose that such an estimate of the book as a whole is premature, because the work is not yet "finished". The author may not change the framework, the method of word-creation, the tone or the character-structure, nothing fundamental; the radius of the *quasi*-circle may be lengthened *ad infinitum* and the "story" continue to be told till the end of time, but the mystery is already revealed and the work may not be improperly be considered as "finished". And remembering Coleridge's dictum that there is no great poet who is not also a great philosopher we may feel certain that the Dubliner's method of illumination of his dream-world employed for critical purposes shall but enlighten and strengthen the understanding of his curious work. "In matters of philosophy, at least," writes Bruno, "by whose free altars I have taken refuge from the threatening waves, I shall listen only to those doctors who bid us not close the eyes but open them as widely as we may."

Something of a strange, out of the world sense is communicated by the work as a whole, "Metamnisia was all soon one coloroform bruen," the effect of a humanity abiding in a familiar planet, and yet, in some respects, if we but look at these shades attentively, so unlike anything found among other living or imaginary creatures. Shall we take note, of the passing procession in this "history" of the world? Mark as they pass you King Olaf, the founder of the city of Dublin, Sitric or the King of the silken beard, Wellington, a military genius, Daniel O'Connell, a religious statesman, Bartholomew Vanhomrigh, a Dutch Lord Mayor of Dublin and the father of Vanessa, Swift's "flame", Dunlop, an inventor of pneu-

matic tires, Jacobs, a cream-cracker manufacturer, the late Lord Northcliffe, Parnell, almost every Dubliner of note, and nearly everyone familiar to us in contemporary or ancient chronicles, Romulus and Remus, Adam and Eve, Mutt and Jeff, Old Father Knickerbocker, Tristan and Isolde. . . But these Dubliners and aliens, avatars obeying the poet's will, suffering a metamorphosis from beings of flesh and blood to objects, localities, events and elements of nature are here revealed *most characteristically,* as non-ethical creatures, not, indeed, as conscienceless beings, but as a race unaware of the existence of conscience as a vital element in the spiritual composition of mankind, (the soul without conscience bearing but partially, as it were, the robes of humanity). Here, one feels, the Great War has never been fought, the confusion, the clashing of arms, the tears, the songs of hatred, the struggle between the new and the old in our day, in the longer, more crowded day of our racial life, has found no voice, no echo . . .

. . . .

To the readers of "*Vera Historia,*" the Latin lyricists, Boccacio, yes, and the juvenile masterpiece "Alice in Wonderland" the non-ethical world of "Work in Progress", ringing with laughter, may prove a welcome refuge from the too facile literature of a restless age brimful with the struggles, complexes, conflicts of a low order. And the lovers of the sublime in literature may find there something to their taste also. . .

"Sublimity is an echo of the inward greatness of the soul." Attentive readers of the "Mookse and the Gripes" will realize something of the great-heartedness of the author who notwithstanding the spurns of the unworthy seeks to reconcile the warring elements in human nature in his fable. The artist's creed which laughs both at dogma and at heresy may prove, after all, the highest form of wisdom, since it is founded at the basis upon sentiment. And perhaps in that millenium where the "political man" and the "economic man" shall be regarded in the same light as our shadowy ancestors of the paleolithic or Magdalenian periods, and Dublin discovers something or someone of Dublin greater than Phœnix Park, Wellington Monument, or Guiness's Brewery, and literature and the arts achieve in the eyes of "homo Vulgaris" to the dignity of "politics" or "business" Joyce's "joyicity" like Oberon's midsummer madness shall be known at something of its true worth.

Joyce's Poetry and *The Joyce Book*

As Joyce continued to publish fragments of his novel, some critics chose to examine other aspects of his work. Zabel, who was then the associate editor of Poetry, *wrote one of the first lengthy treatments of Joyce's poetry.*

The Lyrics of James Joyce
Morton D. Zabel
Poetry, 36 (July 1930): 206–213

The interest aroused by the ever-expanding design of the *Work in Progress,* as it appears in quarterly installments in *transition,* as well as by the inclusion of three segments of this prose epic among the poems which the Messrs. Ford and Aldington have gathered in their recent *Imagist Anthology, 1930,* is probably sufficient reason for recalling that among Joyce's achievements is a small group of lyrics which certain readers still claim as his most beautiful work. Throughout his career Joyce has been regarded in many quarters as fundamentally a pet. When *Ulysses* appeared in 1922, its first readers and critics, encountering problems for which their earlier experiences with revolutionary forms of art had not prepared them, at once sought refuge behind the large assumptions that go disguised under the name of poetry. Most of the early notices called it "essentially a poem," "a poet's concept," etc., and thus gave support to a view of Joyce's genius which the autobiographical evidence in his stories, as well as the anecdotes of friends like Æ and Colum who picture him as a typical visionary of the Irish revival in the nineties, had already encouraged. His first published book was the collection of lyrics, *Chamber Music* (1907), and in earlier poems like *Tilly* (1904) he had sketched in himself the familiar traits of poetic adolescence, enraged at the stupidity of life:

Boor, bond of the herd,
Tonight stretch full by the fire!
I bleed by the black stream
For my torn bough.

The reportorial naturalism in *Dubliners* was illuminated by a lyric clairvoyance and sympathy, the story *Araby* first describing the restless creative temper which victimized Joyce's undecided youth. Ultimately, when Stephen Dedalus took shape as Joyce's fictional counterpart, he was a poet charmed by liturgical cadences, by the creative vitality of words, and by the treasury of coined phrases stored in his mind, any one of which—

A day of dappled seaborne clouds—

could set the train of creative enthusiasm running.

In spite of this testimony, we have little evidence that Joyce is not fundamentally a genius in prose. *Ulysses* may rely on Homeric symbolism, and, if we are to follow Foster Damon, on "the spiritual planes of the *Divine Comedy,* and the psychological problem of *Hamlet,*" together with a somewhat less convincing use of Blake's mechanism of the epic. The *Work in Progress* may require its exegetes to make use of far-scattered verse analogies. But, conventional definitions apart, his novels lack specific poetic elements, as well as poetry's absolute sublimation of experience. It is equally apparent that his lyrics are the marginal fragments of his art, minor in theme and too often, for all their precise and orderly felicities, undecided in quality. To the thirty-six poems in *Chamber Music* he added the thirteen which in 1927 came from the press of Shakespeare & Co., Paris, under the title *Pomes Penyeach,* eight having originally appeared in 1917 in POETRY. Though an extremely small part of his entire production, this body of lyrics is large enough to disclose changes and adjustments through which Joyce's mind has passed, as well as the creative impulses by which it has been guided.

The verse in *Chamber Music* has not the finality of single intention. Its deficiencies have been ascribed to the fact that, where it does not reflect the vaporous mysticism of the early Yeats, Æ, and the other Irish revivalists, it is a patent imitation of the Elizabethan song-books. Examination reveals in these poems little more than a superficial verbal similarity to the poetry of the Celtic twilight whose obvious accents appear only in *XXXVI,* "Oh, it was out by Donnycarney." Whatever Joyce retained from the bardic songs (or their modern translations) in the way of simplified expression and elegiac motives, was overlaid with the formal decorum, yet enlivened by the lucid sensibility, of Jonson and Herrick, or of those poems by Byrd, Dowland, and Campion which he knew from boyhood. To read *Chamber Music* with its familiar refrains is to revive sensations first gained from the *Book of Airs* or *A Paradise of Dainty Devices.* Yet the overlay of artificial elegance never conceals wholly a nerve of sharp lyric refinement. Little more than elegance is present in *VI:*

I would in that sweet bosom be
  (O sweet it is and fair it is!)
Where no rude wind might visit me.
  Because of sad austerities
I would in that sweet bosom be.

Adjusted to the courtly tone of Suckling and the Cavaliers, it reappears in *XII:*

What counsel has the hooded moon
  Put in thy heart, my shyly sweet,
Of love in ancient plenilune,

Glory and stars beneath his feet—
A sage that is but kith and kin
    With the comedian capuchin?

It is clear that in such poems one has, instead of direct and unequivocal poetic compulsion, a deliberate archaism and a kind of fawning studiousness which attempt to disguise the absence of profounder elements. Yet the archaism which exists at its extreme level in *X* and *XI*, or, phrased as *vers de société*, in *VII*, was converted into Joyce's own material in two or three lyrics which, for spiritual suavity and logic, approach the minor work of Crashaw, or at least of Crashaw's descendants in the nineteenth century, Thompson and Lionel Johnson. One of them is *XXVI:*

Thou leanest to the shell of night,
    Dear lady, a divining ear.
In that soft choiring of delight
    What sound hath made thy heart to fear?
Seemed it of rivers rushing forth
From the grey deserts of the north?

That mood of thine, O timorous,
    Is his, if thou but scan it well,
Who a mad tale bequeaths to us
    At ghosting hour conjurable—
And all for some strange name he read
In Purchas or in Holinshed.

It has been remarked before, by Edmund Wilson, that Joyce was closer to continental literature during his apprenticeship than to current English and Irish. In a writer so intentionally derivative, affiliations are natural. They can probably be traced here to the kind of lyric impressionism that grew, by a curious process of inversion, out of Dehmel and Liliencron toward the broken accent of expressionism as one finds it in Werfel, Joyce's closest ally among the figures of later German poetry. Through his lively contemporaneity and his curious sympathy with modern French art, Joyce was undoubtedly attracted by the inferential subtlety of the Symbolists. But his lyricism, like Dowson's or Rilke's, betrays too much diffusion to enable him to approach Mallarmé's faultless penetration or Rimbaud's intense discipline. It was more readily or Rimbaud's intense discipline. It was more readily susceptible to the colors and moods of Verlaine's songs.

All day I hear the noise of waters
    Making moan,
Sad as the seabird is when going
    Forth alone
He hears the winds cry to the waters'
    Monotone.

This is very nearly a tonal and metrical equivalent of the *Chanson d'automne,* whose lyric values, and those on other pages of the *Poèmes Saturniens* or *Fadis et Naguère,* are present in *Chamber Music.* But Joyce was testing his lyric gift by a stricter training, by a reading of Rimbaud and Samain perhaps, or of Meredith. The latter's homelier phrases in *Love in a Valley* are echoed in *XXIV,* and his unexpected power to order the material of allegory lies behind the last poem in *Chamber Music,* the magnificent lyric whose Yeatsian tendency has yielded to the vigor of Meredithian symbolism as one finds it in *Lucifer in Starlight* or *The Promise in Disturbance:*

I hear an army charging upon the land
    And the thunder of the horses plunging, foam about
    their knees.
Arrogant, in black armor, behind them stand,
    Disdaining the reins, with fluttering whips, the charioteers.

The later lyrics in *Pomes Penyeach* go so far in intergrating these disparate elements that Joyce achieved in the little booklet his own poetic character for the first time. The sedulous understudy which kept him from attaining intimacy or a unifying personality in his earlier work is largely avoided. The style may be defined by devices. It consists in the marked alliteration of *On the Beach at Fontana* and *Tutto e sciolto;* in the persistent periphasis of words like *rockvine, greygolden, slimesilvered, moongrey, loveward,* and *loveblown* (all suggestive of *Ulysses*); and in the transparent choral tonality of *She Weeps over Rahoon* and *Watching the Needleboats at San Sabra.* Archaisms are still present, and the humid emotionalism of impressionist verse still prevails in *Alone* and *Bahnhofstrasse.* But the pattern is constricted by severer form, the lyric accent gains edge, and the emotional content is more secure in its power. Ultimately the tragic surge and wrath of *Ulysses* finds voice in *A Prayer* and in *A Memory of the Players in a Mirror at Midnight:*

This grey that stares
Lies not, stark skin and bone.
Leave greasy lips their kissing. None
Will choose her what you see to mouth upon.
Dire hunger holds his hour.
Pluck forth your heart, saltblood, a fruit of tears,
Pluck and devour.

Even within this narrow range, Joyce's eclecticism, the long reach of his artistic interests, is revealed. Yet one sees likewise the limitations which have kept his lyric output small. The real functions of free-verse have escaped him, and his lyric ideas must otherwise submit to conventional stanzaic formalities. Diffusion mars the outline of many poems, and unnatural sobri-

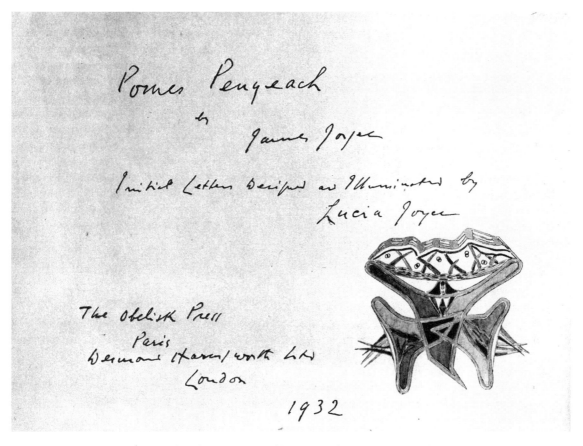

Title page for a facsimile edition in Joyce's hand of his second collection of poetry

ety and caution hinder the spontaneity of others. But in four or five pages he has achieved a complete fusion of rapture and lucidity, and written with mastery. *Simples* must rank as one of the purest lyrics of our time:

Of cool sweet dew and radiance mild
The moon a web of silence weaves
In the still garden where a child
Gathers the simple salad leaves.

A moondew stars her hanging hair
And moonlight kisses her young brow,
And gathering, she sings an air:
Fair as the wave is, fair art thou!

Be mine, I pray, a waxen ear
To shield me from her childish croon,
And mine a shielded heart for her
Who gathers simples of the moon.

The lyric motive and discipline have not been forgotten by Joyce among the problems and ingenuities of his prose epics. Wherever *Ulysses* avoids parody or satire, it is likely to soar in a lyric utterance; the river symphony at the beginning of the *Work in Progress* is one of the brilliant phonetic evocations in modern literature. His power to synthesize and formulate the swarming resources of his mind has demanded prose for its proper extension. Yet the poetic temper which has played an indubitable part in his career has given us, by the way, a small offering of exquisite poems, valuable both as diversions of one of the first literary geniuses of our day, and as lyrics which at their best have the mark of classic beauty upon them.

Six years after the publication of Pomes Penyeach, *musical settings for the poems were published in* The Joyce Book *(1933), edited by Herbert Hughes. Thirteen composers contributed work: E. J. Moeran, Arnold Bax, Albert Roussel, Hughes, John Ireland, Roger Sessions, Arthur Bliss, Herbert Howells, George Antheil, Edgardo Carducci, Eugene Goossens, C. W. Orr, and Bernard Ban Dieren. In 1932 the first English edition of* Pomes Penyeach *with letters designed and illuminated by Joyce's daughter, Lucia, was published by The Obelisk Press, Paris, and Desmond Harmsworth, London.*

James Joyce as Poet

Padraic Colum

The Joyce Book (London: The Sylvan Press, 1933), pp. 13–15

The poems *Chamber Music* have all that a musician looks for in a poet's arrangement of words–syllables that can be articulated, range of expression within little compass, situation, contrast; and, above all, the charm that is in a spontaneous rendering of some stirring mood–a charm which, being akin to melody, musicians readily feel. This book, written when James Joyce was nineteen, seems to be out of a young musicians's rather than out of a young writer's world. In the first of the sequence Love is seen as a musician 'with head to the music bent', in the second 'she bends upon the yellow keys', in the third one awakes 'to hear the sweet harps play to Love before him on his way', in the fourth there is 'one who is singing at your gate', in the fifth she is 'singing and singing a merry air'. The poet hears 'the noise of waters', he hears 'an army charging upon the land and the thunder of horses plunging', she leans 'to the shell of night', and harkens to sounds. It is no wonder musicians have been attracted to the volume named *Chamber Music*. One of the pieces, 'O it was out by Donneycarney', has been put to music a dozen times, and no less than twenty-six of the poems have been given musical settings.

These poems were not the first written by James Joyce: the villanelle which Stephen Delalus in *A Portrait of the Artist* labours to perfect is out of a group of poems earlier than *Chamber Music,* and there was another group even earlier. Both are lost; they were of 'villanelle and roundelay', we may imagine. The young poet had definite musical interests at the time he was making these early poems: he had made settings for one of Mangan's and for several of Yeats's lyrics–unprofessional settings. Probably it was through his impulse towards musical creation that he attained the distinctiveness that is in the lyrics in *Chamber Music*. He moulded his poetry on a tradition that was literary only in part and that was in part a musical tradition–the tradition of Elizabethan song. I recall how James Joyce in his early twenties would play and sing English songs. 'They are ample', he would say, contrasting their full- blooded gaiety with the mournfulness of Irish melodies. Perhaps it was because he was so completely possessed by this musical tradition that he wrote poems that are without a trace of Irish influence–except, perhaps, on the poem that is the last in the collection–and this at a time when a literary movement based upon Irish tradition had real influence in Dublin.

And yet I feel that I am not altogether exact in saying that there is no Irish influence on these poems. After all, they could not have been written in any other place than Dublin, which so belatedly receives, so lingeringly lets go of, a tradition-Dublin in which there is so little pressure of present day intellectual interests that a student could project himself into another period. As I read *Chamber Music* I feel close to the old squares with their high houses, I see twilit roads that lead out of the town and along which sweethearts walk; I hear the piano being played in an old-fashioned drawing-room–such a one as is shown in the last story in *Dubliners*. I feel Dublin as a background to these lyrics. And I cannot insist that they are really a re-creation of Elizabethan song. They are that, but their sequence gives a drama that is repeated in *A Portrait of the Artist as a Young Man*–they deal with youthful love, and they deal also with betrayal in friendship and with exile. The sequence of the poems ends like the novel with exile:

> The grey winds, the cold winds are blowing
>　　Where I go.
> I hear the noise of many waters
>　　Far below.
> All day, all night, I hear them flowing
>　　To and fro.

The themes of disappointment and betrayal are stated with tenderness and dignity in the XIX and XXI of the sequence. *Chamber Music,* indeed, goes parallel with *A Portrait of the Artist as a Young Man*. And as in the novel a detached intellectuality comes into the narrative, so in this lyrical book there are 'Thou leanest to the shell of night' and 'Though I thy Mithridates were', mordant pieces that contrast with the youthful fervours of the love-songs.

The exile which the end of *Chamber Music* prefigures has been realized in *Pomes Penyeach;* they bear the imprint of various cities– Dublin, Trieste, Zurich, Paris. They are intrinsically of exile for their burthen is memories. This brief collection was the *successor to Ulysses*–a flying fish coming after a whale– and so something as wide as a complete epoch in literature is between it and *Chamber Music,* James Joyce's first publication. The poet, it is evident, intended to give a dozen 'pomes' at a penny each (the 'pomes' which he offers are the 'pomes' of Chaucer or one of his contemporaries, and are nothing more nor less than 'apples'). He gives us thirteen. Now in Dublin when the milkman left in the pitcher at the door the measure rquired he added a little measure to it which was called a 'tilly'. James Joyce gives us 'Tilly' and he puts it first in the collection. There is another Irish mark. The boats he watches at San Sabba have pointed prows, and remembering similarly shaped boats on Irish waters he names them 'needleboats', using a Galway term.

The music of these poems is very different from the clear lilt of *Chamber Music,* for it is tragic, resigned, and very moving. I am thinking of 'She Weeps Over Rahoon', 'On the Beach at Fontana', 'Alone', 'A Memory of the Players in a Mirror at Midnight', 'A Prayer'. If one places them beside the poems in the first collection one perceives they are all night pieces– some have the blackness and oppression of the night, and some, as 'Simples', have night's quietude. And all of them render unforgettable some place– a beach, a garden at dewfall, an avenue leading to a railway-station, an empty theatre, a lakeside, a nettle-covered Irish graveyard. They are poems that have the tremulousness of night-blooming flowers.

Now when I read *Chamber Music* I can hear the verses as the young poet repeated them to a few of us as we walked along Dublin streets or on the strand at Sandymount. Remembering such hearing, I realize how much a few of his contemporaries owe to these poems which were so remote from the interests of that day– how much they owe to the lucidness of–

And where the sky's a pale blue cup
  Over the laughing land,
My love goes lightly, holding up
  Her dress with dainty hand.

and how much to the proud rhythm of –

He who hath glory lost nor hath
  Found any soul to fellow his,
Among his foes in scorn and wrath
  Holding to ancient nobleness,
That high unconsortable one–
  His love is his companion.

This lucidness, this proud movement, have been to the benefit of some Irish poets who belong to Joyce's day. I have not heard *Pomes Penyeach* repeated in that voice that has such singing quality. These poems are for singing more than for speaking, I think. Three of them are embodiments of feelings coming from hearing songs: 'Watching the Needleboats' arises out of the boat-song heard, 'Simples' is inspired by a child singing an Italian popular song, and 'Tutto e Sciolto' recalls that song in *La Sonnambula* which is hummed by one of the characters in *Ulysses*– 'All is lost now'. This collection appears to have the same relation to *Chamber Music* as *Work in Progress* has to *Ulysses: Ulysses* is of the day, *Work in Progress* belongs to the night. Before he planned *Ulysses* and *Work in Progress* James Joyce had made a book of the day and a book of the night– *Chamber Music* and *Pomes Penyeach.*

The English poet and critic Arthur Symons was instrumental in finding a publisher for Chamber Music. *He included his review of Joyce's first book, "A Book of Songs," originally published in the 22 June 1907 issue of* Nation, *in an epilogue he wrote for* The Joyce Book.

Epilogue
Arthur Symons
The Joyce Book (London: Sylvan Press, 1933), pp. 79–84

JAMES AUGUSTINE JOYCE, whenever I met him in Paris, seemed to me a curious mixture of sinister genius and uncertain talent. Refined, reserved, not without a touch of humour, speaking with a slight Irish accent, he has a fascination which is purely his own: at times, I must confess, diabolical. His *Chamber Music,* a book of verses, was published in 1907; and this is what I wrote on it:

. . . .

In his earlier essay, included in "Early Life and Work," Symons praised especially the poems "Bright Cap and Streamers" and "Silently She's Combing" and concluded with a question: "How unlikely it seems, does it not, that any new thing should come suddenly into the world and be beautiful?"

Not long ago I received a delightful letter from Joyce written in Paris in which he says (and I venture to give his own words): 'As for *Pomes Penyeach* I don't think they would have been published but for Mrs Symons's suggestion when she was with me'. She was right. There is in these poems a rare lyrical quality, with touches of pure magic, and some give me the effect of a warm wind wafting the scent of heather over me when on the cost of Cornwall I used to lie near the edge of a cliff, basking in the intense heat of the sun. There I could watch the sea, where, when the wind urges it, it heaves into great billows, that rise up green and tilt over, and, as the waves roll up to the shore, they leap suddenly at the rocks, and hammer at them with a loud voluminous softness, and fall back like a blown cataract, every drop distinct in the sunlight. And at times the sea was the colour of lilac deepening into rose, and it lay like a field of heather washed by the rain.

Wisdom, it has been said, is justified in her children: and why not Joyce? Words and cadences must have an intoxication for him, the intoxication of the scholar; and in his own wandering way he has been a wild vagabond, a vagabond of the mind and of the imagination. He knows that words are living things, which we have not created, and which go their way without demanding from us the right to live. He knows that words are suspicious, not without malice, and that they resist mere force with the impalpable resistance of fire or

First pages of Arthur Bliss's musical adaptation of the first stanza of "Simples," a musical setting of
his poem included in The Joyce Book *that especially pleased the author*

water. They are to be caught only with guile or trust. And his voice can be heard like a wandering music, which comes troublingly into the mind, bringing with it the solace of its old and recaptured melodies. And I am haunted by the strange wild beauty of two of his poems, *Flood* and *Nightpiece.* Take, for instance, this stanza:

> Seraphim,
> The lost host awaken
> To service till
> In moonless gloom as each lapses muted, dim,

> Raised when she has and shaken
> Her thurible.

What recur to me are the nights when I wandered to and fro in Cordova, hearing, when the muleteers went beside the mules, not so much their tinkling bells, but those male voices, so mysterious, and so full of pride and passion, whose songs made surge up before me the dramatic moment, the situation, the Crisis. Only, let this be my Epilogue. 'But the feast he spreads for us is a very Trimalcio feast;

the heaped profusion, the vaunting prodigality, which brings no surfeit. *Ita, inquit Quartilla, minor est ista, quam ego fui, cum primum virum passa sum? Funonem meam iratam habeam, si unquam me meminerim virginem fuisse.'*

Dubliners was published in 1914; *A Portrait of the Artist as a Young Man* in 1916; *Exiles, a Prose Play in Three Acts* in 1918. He wrote *Ulysses* (a book of 732 pages) in Trieste, Zurich, and Paris, between 1914 and 1921—an incredible achievement when one considers the difficulties he experienced during its composition. The novel was printed at Dijon in 1922 by Maurice Darantière, and for the simple reason that the printers in Paris who began to set up the type refused to go on with it on account of what seemed to them masses of indecencies. Some of our modern

craftsmen are aghast at passion, afraid of emotion, only anxious that the phrase and the sentiment should be right. Joyce is totally exempt from such fears as these: he is afraid of nothing; no more than his Stephen Dedalus, who said–and the words are the writer's own words and all the more significant for that: 'I will not serve that which I no longer believe, whether it call itself my home, my fatherland, or my church: and I will try to express myself in my art as freely as I can and as wholly as I can, using for my defence the only arms I allow myself to use, silence, exile, and cunning'. The man and his most creative work are an unholy mixture of these three singular qualities. Without cunning he could never have written *Ulysses*. Without exile he might never have created what he has created–nor in fact could Byron or Shelley or Landor. Byron was an exile from his country, equally condemned and admired, credited with abnormal genius and abnormal wickedness, confessing himself defiantly to the world, living with ostentatious wildness at Venice.

> We live and die,
> And which is best, you know no more than I.

All the wisdom (experience, love of nature, passion, tenderness, pride, the thirst for knowledge) comes to that in the end, not even a negation. He also suffered, as Pater and Joyce and myself have suffered, from that too vivid sense of humanity which is like a disease, that obsession to which every face is a challenge and every look an acceptance or a rebuff. How is content in life possible to those condemned to go about like magnets, attracting or repelling every animate thing, and tormented by restlessness which their own presence communicates to the air around them? This magnetic nature is not given to man for his happiness. It leaves him at the crowd's mercy, as he ceaselessly feels the shock of every disturbance which he causes them. Driving him into solitude for an escape, it will not let him even then escape the thought of what in himself is so much of an epitome of humanity, for 'quiet to quick bosoms is a hell'.

Joyce's vocabulary is unusually large and it is used too recklessly, but in a surprisingly novel, personal manner; and as for the craftsman, he has never curbed himself to a restraint in the debauch of words, still sufficiently coloured and sounding for an equally personal and novel effect; and with this a daring straightforwardness and pungency of epithet which refreshes one's thirst. Take for instance *A Portrait of the Artist as a Young Man.* 'In hell one torment instead of counteracting another lends it still greater force; and, moreover, as the internal faculties are more perfect than the external senses, so are they more capable of suffering. Just as every sense is afflicted with a fitting torment so is every spiritual faculty; the fancy with horrible images, the sensitive faculty with alternate longing and rage, the mind and understanding with an interior darkness more terrible even than the exterior darkness which reigns in that dreadful prison. The malice, impotent though it be, which possesses these demon souls is an evil of boundless extension, of limitless duration, a frightful state of wickedness which we can scarcely realize unless we bear in mind the enormity of sin and the hatred God bears it.' This prose is medieval. Compare it with my translation from the Spanish of San Juan de la Cruz. 'And so in this soul, in which now no appetite abides, nor other imaginings, nor forms of other created things; most secretly it abides in so much the mere inner interior and more straitly embraced, and is itself the more pure and single of all things but God.' This rapture of negation becomes poetry because it is part of a nature to which, if God is a deep but dazzling darkness, He is also the supreme love, to be apprehended humanly by this quality, for which, and in which, He put on Humanity. Valéry Larbaud rightly says that anyone who reads *Ulysses* will be thrown into dismay. 'For he is plunged into the middle of a conversation which will seem to him incoherent between people whom he cannot distinguish, in a place which is neither named nor described: and from this conversation he is to learn little by little where he is and where the interlocutors are.' The scene is Dublin and Stephen Dedalus has returned from Paris to live among the intellectuals of the Irish capital: the book chronicles an entire day: it begins at eight o'clock in the morning and ends towards three the next morning. The writer of this book deals with the sexual instinct and its infinite manifestations and perversions, with the animal's natural functions. 'He does not hesitate to touch this subject any more than the great Casuists do, and he handles it in English in the same way that they handle it in Latin, without respect for the conventions and scuples of the laity.' Joyce's prose is in a sense fascinating; there is no doubt that he has been and that he will be considered the most complex literary problem of this generation; and, apart from his intricate and elaborate subtleties, it seems to me that he has made such gigantic steps that the only possible comparison which has been hazarded is with Flaubert's *Bouvard et Pecuchet,* itself a satire of so tremendous a nature, and yet withal an unfinished satire, that, when I look backward, I turn to the greatest satire ever written, the *Gargantua* of Rabelais.

How few writers have aspired, as Mallarmé did, after an impossible liberation of the soul of literature from what is fretting and constraining in 'the body of that death', which is the mere literature of words! To search after the virginity of language is just as vain as if half one's life were spent in following after one's escaping chimera. I can imagine Proust, whose obscurity can become dense, reading with a mixture of surprise and delight this curious sentence of Mallarmé: 'Abolished the pretension, æsthetically an error, despite its dominion over almost all the masterpieces, to enclose within the subtle paper other than, for example, the horror of the forest, or the silent thunder afloat in the leaves; not the intrinsic dense wood of the trees'. This is one of the most amazing of his theories: 'I say: a flower! and out of the oblivion to which my voice consigns every contour, so far as anything save the known calyx, musically writes, idea, and exquisite, the

The musical setting for the opening lines of Joyce's poem "Ecce Puer," composed by novelist and Joyce scholar Anthony Burgess. First published in the January 1933 issue of Criterion *and later in* Collected Poems, *"Ecce Puer" celebrates the birth of Joyce's grandson Stephen James Joyce on 15 February 1932 and mourns the death of Joyce's father on 29 December 1931 (courtesy of Myra Russel).*

one flower absent from all bouquets'. Always, literature, in every generation, might at any moment endure a fundamental and exquisite crisis; such, for example, as when Hamlet—Shakespeare's—escapes from the antagonism of the dreams which in such souls as his are united with fatalities, 'dans sa traditionnel prèsque nudité sombre un peu à la Goya'. Another crisis might occur when Degas stood in the wings watching the ballet-dancers at the Eden. 'Comme l'éclair qui enveloppe une danseuse, fon-

dant une crudité électrique à des blancheurs extracharnelles de fards, et en fait bien l'étre prestigieux reculé au delà de toute vie possible.'

The forces which mould the thoughts of men change, or men's resistance to them slackens; with the changes of men's thought comes a change of literature, alike in its inmost essence and its outward form: after the world has starved its soul long enough in the contemplation and the rearrangement of material things, comes the turn of the soul. To Baudelaire the soul was always an uneasy guest at life's feast; to Flaubert the soul was of use mainly as the agent of fine literature; to Leconte de Lisle it was Nirvana. The whole soul of Huysmans characterizes itself in the turn of a single phrase: that 'art is the only clean thing on earth, except holiness'. Poetry can no longer represent more than the soul of things; it had taken refuge from the terrible improvements of civilization in a divine seclusion, where it sings, disregarding the many voices of the street. Then comes prose, and it is by the infinity of its detail that the novel, as Balzac conceived it, has become the modern epic. And yet, centuries before Balzac was born, no sooner had human life become by all its developments infinitely interesting, intensely amusing, than the novel came into existence. These novels began by giving prominence to one individual, whether he were Eumolpus, Pantagruel, Don Quixote, Gil Blas, or Tom Jones. Since then, in the more modern novels, the individuals, with certain exceptions, begin to decrease; the most wonderful exception is *Le Pere Goriot:*—Goriot is a Lear at heart, he grows downward into the earth and takes root there; he knows well enough the value of every banknote that his ungrateful daughters rob him of. In those of Huysmans's novels where Durtal has much of himself, Durtal is often forgotten. Still, in *En Route,* which is a confession, a self-ausculation of the soul, purged finely, by some divine revelation, of the distraction of the soul, liberated through some force of vision from the burden of a too realistic conversation, and from certain conventions, in which the very aim had been to convey the absolute failure of breathing life, internalized to an entire liberty, in which, simply because it is so utterly free, art is able to accept, without limiting itself, the expressive medium of a convention, we have the new form of a novel, which, as I said, may be at once the soul and a pattern, a decoration and a confession.

Worshipping colour, sound, perfume, for their own sakes, and not for their ministrations to a more divine beauty, Joyes stupefies himself on the threshold of ecstasy. And Joyce, we can scarcely doubt, has passed through the particular kind of haschisch dream which this experience really is. He has realized that the great choice, the choice between the world and something which is not visible in the world, but out of which the visible world has been made, does not lie in the mere contrast of the subtler and grosser senses. He has come to realize what the choice really is, and he has chosen. In his escape from the world, one man chooses religion, and seems to find himself; another, choosing love, may seem also to find himself; and may not another, coming to art as to a religion and as to a woman, seem to find himself not less effectually? The one certainty is, that

society is the enemy of man, and that formal art is the enemy of the artist. We shall not find ourselves in drawing-rooms or in museums. A man who goes through a day without some fine emotion has wasted his day, whatever he has gained in it. And it is so easy to go through day after day, busily and agreeably, without ever really living for a single instant. Art begins when a man wishes to immortalize the most vivid moment he has ever lived. Life has already, to one not an artist, become art in that moment. And the making of one's life into art is after all the first duty and privilege of every man. It is to escape from material reality into whatever form of ecstasy is our own form of spiritual existence. There is the choice; and our happiness, our 'success in life', will depend on our choosing rightly, each for himself, among the forms in which that choice will come to us.

Work in Progress in the 1930s

Rebecca West was the pen name of Cecily Isabel Fairfield. A critic, novelist, and feminist, West is best known for The Return of the Soldier *(1918) and* The Thinking Reed *(1936). In his essay, "A Point for American Criticism," published in* Our Exagmination Round His Factification for Incamination of Work in Progress, *William Carlos Williams directly responds to West's criticism.*

In the first part of her essay West argues that, unlike Virginia Woolf and D. H. Lawrence, Joyce has inspired an important following: "For if one looks round for the group that is cohering before the peril of the age in a formation that seems most likely to procure survival, one will probably find it in the group that, largely to his honor and glory, runs the magazine 'Transition.'"

James Joyce and His Followers
Rebecca West
New York Herald Tribune Books, 12 January 1930, pp. 1, 6

. . . They are engaged in transactions on such a large scale that, where they make losses, these seem pretty heavy; but the losses are counterbalanced by the gains, which also are true to the scale. This is so, too, in relation to the creative process in which they are most interested; that is, the workings of Mr. James Joyce's genius.

At present there might be suspected to be a heavy loss sustained in the quarter, because it appears more than possible that in "Work in Progress" he is following—if not a blind alley—for no path along which a genius travels can remain that for long—but an avenue hardly wide enough for the army of his powers. One cannot come to any final opinion on the subject until the whole of the book has been published.

It must be remembered how when only half of "A la Recherche du Temps Perdu" was published the complaint against Proust was that his book had no order and no design; whereas the completed work showed that if he had a fault it was that he had pledged himself from the first to symmetry almost too absolute, and controlled his characters too rigidly to maintain it. (Those who are reading it in English will find that the volume published under the name "The Prisoner," the recital of the author's tyrannous relationship with Albertine, which seems like a long and rather tiresome fugue, produces quite a different effect when one has read the succeeding volume, in which the author, distraught with grief over Albertine's death, is reduced to panic by a telegram that seems to announce that she is not dead after all. When one has reached this climax of ambivalence one sees that all the cunning twists and turns of his relationship with the girl, his sharp alternations of love and hate, have been designed to tighten up one's nerves for this explosion).

Quite possibly some features will appear in "Work in Progress" in its completed form, which will remove all the objections that at present rise up against it in the mind of any reader outside the cult. But since his own followers insist on discussing it at the present stage, and since if he does remove these objections, he will practically stand everything that is known about the human mind upside down, it is worth while stating them.

The distinctive attribute of "Work in Progress" is that is not written in English, or in any other language. Most of the words that James Joyce uses are *patés de langue gras.* Each is a paste of words that have been superimposed one on another and worked into a new word that shall be the lowest common multiple of them all. These words have been chosen out of innumerable languages, living and dead, either because of some association of ideas or of sound. They are "portmanteau" words such as Lewis Carroll invented when he wrote "Jabberwocky": "Twas brillig and the slithy toves Did gyre and gimble in the wabe." They are chosen, often but not always, in the sly, punning spirit that looks for disguises by which forbidden things may leer and sidle past the censor; so that very frequently by their grossness they recall Leopold Bloom out of "Ulysses," great embodiment of the repressed side of man. They are sometimes strung together in sequences that do not obey the ordinary laws of syntax.

The common accusation against the result of these processes is that it is incomprehensible. It is nothing of the sort. Unless one's parents brought one up in an unusual state of seclusion from contacts with the classics and the Teutonic and Latin languages, it is hard to avoid finding one's way through it. There emerges from the text clearly enough not only a superficial pattern of verbal suggestion which is intricate and amusing and occasionally poetically beautiful, but a phantasmagoria of types that represent the main forms thrown up by history. It cannot be read as quickly as ordinary English, just as a cross-word puzzle cannot be read as quickly as the words it contains set up in ordinary form. But that is the only thing against it from the reader's point of view. Granted it will take him ten times as long to read as an equal number of words put into ordinary Anglo-American realist novels, he will get ten times as much entertainment.

The main objections that make one, in spite of the fact that one is entertained, wonder whether James Joyce is not misapplying his genius in using this new form are three, and one of them involves this very question of effort and time. Even the youngest child in the nursery who hears the rhyme about the general who marched his troops up a hill and then marched them down again and went home to his tea is conscious that the chances are that this was not a very good general. The movements that sanction those who move in this universe are those that have results. Those that do not are taken as mere dithering spendthrifts of time and therefore discreditable to the doers. But if Mr. James Joyce is to take ten, or twenty, or thirty years packing allusions into portmanteau words; and if his readers are to take twelve (since a cipher takes longer for a stranger to read than for its inventor to write) or twenty-five, or forty years unpacking these allusions out of the portmanteau words, it is impossible to avoid the suspicion that troops have been marched up a hill and then down again. A work of art planned in a medium and then executed in a second medium, which cannot be comprehended by any audience unless they can transport it by mental effort back into the first medium, is a crazy conception, and even Mr. Joyce's most devoted followers do regard it as essential that they should unmake his words into the constituents of which he made them, and should acquaint themselves with his subject matter as it appeared to him before he clothed it in these words.

Another objection, which certainly cannot be resolved until "Work in Progress" is complete, is esthetic. We are all of us familiar with Croce's statement that an allegory from which we have to detach the secondary meaning by a purely intellectual process cannot give complete esthetic pleasure. The diffusion of interest, or rather the difference of value between the drama enacted by the symbols and the relationship between the abstractions they symbolize splits up the attention of the mind, is not in the right state of unity for esthetic perception. It would seem that the intellectual effort required to unmake James Joyce's words into their constituent parts would perpetually be splitting up the attention and breaking up the state of unity in which the mind must be to accept, say, his personification of the life of a river, the stream of creation. One remembers that there was in "Ulysses" a curious demonstration of Mr. Joyce's failure to appreciate the effect on the mind of simultaneous presentation of objects on different planes. The parallelism between "Ulysses" and the odyssey which James Joyce carefully contrives by sending Stephen Dedalus through incidents that correspond with the Odyssean wanderings is justified by him and his followers as being designed to afford a contrast between the Manichean spirit manifested by Joyce and the Greek spirit manifested in Homer. But it does nothing of the sort, because there can be no real contrast between its esthetic rendering of the Manichean spirit and its purely factual references (through these correspondences) to the Greek spirit, of which the intellect is invited to remember as much as it can, but which is never esthetically recreated. The two are almost as widely divided in their appeal to the attention as the printing on the page and the page numbers. At present "Work in Progress" seems to be invalidated by more diffused addiction to the same error; but we shall see.

There are two other objections, which both have reference to psychology. It is impossible to discuss James Joyce without frequent references to psychology, since nearly all of his recent subject matter and much of his technique he derives from his knowledge of Freud and Jung. The first point on which one would like to be satisfied is whether the main function he is trying to make the work perform is not one which is properly performed by the image in the mind for which the word is only a counter. "Work in Progress" is largely founded on the philosophy of Giambattista Vico, a late seventeenth-century early eighteenth-century Neapolitan who was popularized by Croce in one of his most charming books, and is a pet of the psychoanalysts because his philosophy of history accords with their conclusions. To condense his teaching, he saw that humanity invents its myths and advances through the world of action making life square with those myths, and therefore creates itself. This reciprocal movement between humanity and nature, the rhythm by which alternately the necessities of birth and maturity and death control man and man controls birth and maturity and death, give Vico his doctrine of reflux. Man was always freeing his will, and then being thrust down to helpless sensation again, and then rising again to a state of free will; and so on. It is Joyce's theory that if words are so handled as to recall meanings they had in the past we will go back into the

experience of the race in these bygone phases, and revitalize the words and ourselves by knowledge of these eternal and recurrent processes. But this does not seem to be necessary, if, as Freud and Jung hold in their different ways and to different degrees, the mind of man inherits in his unconscious the collective mythos of mankind and is perpetually in touch with it. That view cannot be considered irrelevant in this connection, because James Joyce has himself accepted it. The aim of this book is to make the unconscious conscious; and it represents the unconscious as a storehouse of primitive myths. It appears clumsy and uneconomical, then, to use obsolete words in order to bring the past to the present when an image spontaneously springing up from the unconscious will do the same thing with much more dynamic force.

The other objection to "Work in Progress" concerning the word has also to do with James Joyce's psychological sources. Obviously, he got this idea of the word-paste from the Freudian and Jungian analyses of the puns people make in dreams. These are resolved into their constituents when the dreamer practices free association on them. For example, a woman will dream that her hair has grown very long and that some one comes into the room and says: "This is the criminolation form of wearing one's hair." The patient, talking at random round the word, will be reminded of the words "crinis," Latin for hair, and crinkly, the fact being that there is an ancient rumor of black blood in the family, which would "incriminate" her if it were known. The word "crinoline" also comes to her, and she remembers that that garment was invented by the Empress Eugenie to conceal the arrival of the Prince Imperial; and since she has a strong sense of guilt about sex, motherhood seems as "incriminating" as black blood. So on the detective work goes, until it uncovers some complex in the unconscious. Now, why does James Joyce invent these words? Has he a naive faith that since free association shows the direct connection between such a word and the unconscious the invention of such a word by reversing the process of free association will automatically drive a connection down into the unconscious? Surely not. He must have entirely created the psyche which he is expressing; he must have before him its conscious and its unconscious and be completely aware of its contents and their relationship. Every portmanteau word he invents must have its causal connection in one of the mythological figures he describes. Then why is there no sense of clarity, of the gratification that comes from comprehension, such as pervades an analysis that is successful in coping with its subject matter in the same way and any work of art, such as "King Lear" or "The Divine Comedy" that has resolved the matter in the terms of its age? Is it because James Joyce feels a disposition, when in doubt, to create an effect of disinte-gration because the most satisfactory creation of his genius up to this date has been Leopold Bloom, the dis-integrator? Or is there some new sort of clarity that will appear in the completion of "Work in Progress?"

I would not myself stake a penny on any of my objections. I state them only because it seems to me of interest to consider what points James Joyce will have to make if he is to quell all resistance in the minds of his age who are looking for the inheritor of art and would like to find it in him. Can one think of any other writer concerning whose work such interesting considerations arise? Do they not make the ordinary naturalist novel by Arnold Bennett or John Galsworthy seem like the very body of death? And his followers, too, in their robust faith in him, are in the right frame of mind. They realize that though the intellect is to be distrusted, there is something else that transacts the holy business of the artist. Theirs, almost alone today, is a religious attitude to art.

---

*An American critic and biographer, Edel refers to Joyce's recording of the end of the Anna Livia chapter (*Finnegans Wake, *pp. 213–216); the recording is available through Caedmon.*

The New Writers
J. Leon Edel
Canadian Forum, 10 (June 1930): 329–330

James Joyce is the author of three books of prose fiction, two books of poems, one play, and a half-finished vol-ume. It is a meagre produciton in these days of copious-ness; but it has a profound influence on contemporary English literature. *Ulysses,* the story of a day in the lives of two Dubliners, and hence the story of one day in Dublin, and in turn of one day in the history of the world; the *Portrait of the Artist as a Young Man,* a study of the expanding consciousness of a young artist facing a conflict between religion and art: *Dubliners,* a book of short stories of Dublin life told with Flaubertian preci-sion—these are the products of a brain sensitive to the beauty of language and to the individual meanings, the philological values latent in words; and at the same time a brain bearing the imprint of scholasticism, the Jesuit strain which Stephen Dedalus possesses—injected the wrong way, as he is told in *Ulysses.* 'To live, to err, to fall, to triumph, to recreate life out of life.' This is the cry that comes to the artist's lips in the *Portrait* in an out-burst of profane joy. And this, I think, can be taken to be James Joyce's credo.

Mr. Joyce was recently persuaded to record a reading from his *Work in Progress,* which has been appearing at various intervals in *transition,* a journal of American expatriates and others, published in Paris. Listening to the record, in which Joyce's beautiful tenor voice has been reproduced with amazing clarity, the work for the first time took on, for me, a profound and poignant meaning: what had seemed before merely lit-erary and linguistic virtuosity assumed form and shape and evoked a thousand suggestions.

Work in Progress is approximately half-completed: the remainder will not be written for a long time, if ever, since Mr. Joyce is suffering from serious eye-trouble, and since it is not a type of work that lends itself to dictation. Joyce, it is told, recently suggested to James Stephens (when the two, who happen to have been born on the same day and in the same year, cele-brated their birthdays together in Paris) that he finish it; and it is interesting to reflect what the author of *The Crock of Gold* would have done with it had he taken Mr. Joyce's apparent jest seriously and added to the Joycean realism his land of philosophers and leprechauns. Fortu-nately we do not require the second half to arrive at some general estimate of what has been written. It has appeared thus far in periodicals: in the French journal *Le Navire d'Argent,* in *This Quarter,* in *transition.* The last section of the first part was published in a limited edi-tion in 1928 under the title *Anna Livia Plurabelle* with a preface by Padraic Colum, and three other fragments from the work appeared last year at the Black Sun Press in Paris, published by Harry and Caresse Crosby, also in a limited edition. We have, obviously, adequate mate-rial to work upon.

But most valuable of all, it seems to me, as a study of how the work developed, is the original ver-sion of the Anna Livia section published in Adrienne Monnier's journal, *Le Navire d'Argent,* in September 1925, when *The Calendar* for which it was destined had refused to bring it out in England unless Joyce modified the text. This version was revised and expanded for *transition* of November 1927, and further revised and expanded when it was published by Crosby Gaige in New York in 1928 under the title *Anna Livia Plurabelle.* A careful comparison of the first and last versions throws interesting light upon Joyce's aims and particularly upon his method.

In its broad outlines the section known as *Anna Livia Plurabelle* is merely the conversation of two washer-women by the river bank; it is growing dark; the air is filled with evening sounds; occasionally the flip-flap of the wet clothes on the wet stones breaks the talk; their backs bent and limbs stiff with the damp and the strain, the women work, and as they work their lively chatter becomes rapid, voluble. Night comes—night which is to be the domain of the whole work, even as *Ulysses* occupied itself principally with day:–

> Can't hear with the waters of. The chittering waters of. Flittering bats, field-mice bawk talk. Ho! Are you not gone ahome? What Tom Malone? Can't hear with bawk of bats, all the liffeying waters of. Ho, talk save us! My foos won't moos. I feel as old as yonder elm. A tale told of Shaun or Shem? All Livia's daughtersons. Dark hawks hear us. Night! Night! My ho head halls. I feel as heavy as yonder stone. Tell me of John or Shaun? Who were Shem and Shaun the living sons or daughters of? Night now! Tell me, tell me, tell me, elm! Night, night! Tell me tale of stem or stone. Beside the rivering waters of, hitherandthithering waters of. Night!

To hear Joyce read this passage is to hear the evening sounds fused, the movement of the water, the staccato phrases of the women . . . . . . far from meaningless it takes on the beauty of poetry and in the deformed words there is considerable suggestive power.

The first difference which we notice between the original version and the final form is the comparative simplicity of the first and the definite complexity of the second. In the original version Joyce has written the conversation of the Irish washerwomen for the most part in current English, in the revised version he attempts to write the language as it is spoken. 'Safety pin' in the first, becomes 'seifty pin' in the second: 'tailor' becomes 'tyler': 'week' becomes 'wik'. It is another important change, however, which renders the new version complex, but which gives it a peculiar richness. Joyce begins to combine words, to deform them, and to utilize other languages. He does not introduce these haphazardly. Quite often foreign words are closely related to English. 'I know by heart the places he likes to soil' remarks one of the washerwomen as she throws a garment into the water. In the second version this becomes 'I know by heart the places he likes to saale, duddurty devil!' The proximity of the deformed 'saale' to the English 'soil' and the French 'sale' is to be remarked. The same is true when Mr. Joyce expands this changing of the language from the simplicity of 'Wait till the rising of the moon' in the first, to 'Wait till the honeying of the lune, love!' Here he substitutes the French word for the English and gives the whole phrase an additional two-fold association, on the one hand with the English 'honeymoon' and on the other with the French equivalent 'lune de miel.' He substitutes Italian quite as readily . . . . . . 'poor little Petite MacFarlane' becomes 'poor Piccolina Petite MacFarlane': and in the same way the word 'mother' in the first version is changed to 'madre' in the second.

Notice, then, the change effected in these two passages and how the first is transmuted to the more intricate form:

> chipping her and raising a bit of a jeer or cheer every time she'd neb in her culdee sack of rubbish she robbed and reach out her maundry merchandise

which becomes

> chipping her and raising a bit of a chair or jary every dive she'd neb in her culdee sacco of wabash she raabed and reach out her maundy meerschaundize

And he changes 'She thought she'd sink under the ground with shame when he gave her the tigris eye!' to 'She thought she'd sankh neathe the ground with nymphant shame when he gave her the tigris eye!' In indicating that to emphasize the river motif Joyce used the names of more than five hundred rivers in this work Padraic Colum observes that in the latter sentence four rivers are mentioned, and the associations with 'nymph' and 'underground' are two more river references. More complex perhaps is the sentence inserted in the second version 'Reeve Gootch was right and Reeve Drughad was sinistrous,'–to the Parisian this comment on *rive gauche* and *rive droite* and the antithesis between 'right' and 'sinistrous' is of peculiar interest.

The work of necessity will lead to many interpretations. A whole book of criticism has already been compiled, and was recently published by Miss Sylvia Beach, in Paris. Mr. Joyce is giving us an important experiment; what will be its later value we cannot now estimate. But that it is worthy of consideration I am certain: on its evocative side, away from the particularized meaning, as Robert McAlmon has pointed out it is of the greatest interest. 'To him,' Mr. McAlmon says of Joyce, 'language does not mean the English language, it means a medium capable of suggestion, implication, and evocation; a medium as free as any art medium should be.' And he adds 'It is unlikely that Joyce himself understands from a re-reading of his present writing all that he thought it has in the way of implication.' There is latent in this, perhaps, a confusion of the arts, a mélange of too many things: something akin to Father Castel's *clavecin des couleurs*. It is quite possible that Mr. Joyce is trying to do too much: that there is a limit to the suggestive power of literature. But this thing brings us to the realm of aesthetics. What concerns us at the moment is method in *Work in Progress;* there is sufficient in it, I feel, to warrant a close scrutiny rather than a careless dismissal.

G. W. Stonier reviews Anna Livia Plurabelle *as well as* Haveth Childers Everywhere *(the last section of chapter 3 in Book III in* Finnegans Wake, *pp. 532–554).* Haveth Childers Everywhere, *one of several variations of H. C. E.'s name, mainly concerns Humphrey Chimpden Earwicker.*

Mr. James Joyce in Progress
G. W. Stonier
The New Statesman, 35 (28 June 1930): 372, 374

Mr. James Joyce's *Work in Progress* has been appearing in numbers of the Paris-American quarterly *Transition* during the last two and a half years. *Transition* has now ceased publication, but Mr. Joyce's work is still in progress; though what chance we shall have of seeing it, now that Mr. Joyce's one shop-window has gone, is uncertain. Mr. Joyce, apart from his achievement as a writer, demands not a little admiration, because he is one of the very few great writers of our time who have never cheapened or advertised themselves in any way. He has kept himself to himself, as the saying goes; and

that alone, in an age of self-advertisers, entitles him to our respect.

But Mr. Joyce's privacy has another side. True, it means that he has taken himself seriously as an artist and has always written at his best, but at the same time he has withdrawn himself altogether from any readers except a little coterie of initiates. *Ulysses* may sooner or later be available in England without the necessity of cheating the Customs, but I doubt if it will find as many readers as a book of its scope and imagination deserves. *Work in Progress* (to judge from extracts published from time to time) is even more withdrawn. *Ulysses,* with all its patter of advertisements and topical catchwords, is as solid as earth: Bloom, though a colossus, is recognisably each one of us, however buried; and the other characters in the book are as distinct and recognisable as their Dublin surroundings. In *Work in Progress* Mr. Joyce seems to have set out to make his characters even more universal. The protagonists are Anna Livia (the River Liffey) and Everyman, who appears as Here Comes Everybody, Haveth Childers Everywhere and H. C. E. *ad infinitum.* Here

HAVETH CHILDERS
EVERYWHERE

FRAGMENT FROM
WORK IN PROGRESS
by
JAMES JOYCE

HENRY BABOU AND JACK KAHANE
PARIS
THE FOUNTAIN PRESS. - NEW YORK
1930

Amtsadam, sir, to you! Eternest cittas, heil! Here we are again. I am bubub brought up under a camel act of dynasties long out of print, the first of Shitric Shilkanbeard (or is it Owllaugh MacAuscullpth the Thord?), but, in pontofacts massimust, I am known throughout the world wherever my good Allenglisches Angleslachsen is spo-

7

Title page and first page of a fragment first published in June 1930 (courtesy of C. W. Post Library of Long Island)

you have Bloom and his cronies without their physical symbols— they are wind and air and stream, a cosmic muttering, still savouring strongly of the bodies which now are only ghosts. This tremendous disproportion between the mass of allusions to every typical phase of contemporary life and the thin disembodied chant into which they are poured is the most striking fact about *Work in Progress*. It is possible to regard this book as a proof that Mr. Joyce, recoiling further and further from the underworld of Mr. Bloom and Dublin, has at last really shut himself up in his own snail's-house, leaving for the exasperated reader only a track. It is an extraordinary fact that before Mr. Joyce's latest book has been published at all, or even completed by its author, a volume criticising it has already appeared in France. What a hurry Mr. Joyce's disciples are in! With what explanations and implications and examinations have they trumpeted the dawn—before even the first grey streak is visible!

Haveth Childers Everywhere and *Anna Livia Plurabelle* are the first bits of Mr. Joyce's new book to reach England: neither is more than forty pages long. The first is a collector's piece, beautifully printed and bound, but, to me at least, almost completely unintelligible. *Anna Livia Plurabelle* is sold very cheaply, and no doubt Mr. Joyce has chosen this particular section as one likely to attract a wider public or, at any rate serve as sample of the book as a whole. I think that anyone reading it carefully for the first time should be able to follow most of the implications of Mr. Joyce's new speech. But it demands a little effort, and if our attitude is simply, "Here is another good writer gone wrong," we are not likely to get far. With most books it is possible to go on reading in a steady drowse without missing much, because the author puts his words together familiarly, and a cadence at the beginning of a sentence automatically predicts its close. With Mr. Joyce the cadences, the juxtaposition of words, the words themselves, are different. In reading him you begin reading again—or you leave off.

Work in Progress contains a very large number of invented words, of words spelt in unusual ways and compounded from almost every European language. The idiom shifts from mediæval doggerel to negro slang in the same sentence, perhaps even in the same word. Mr. Joyce takes any liberty with language which will enrich the music or the sense of his prose. His preoccupation with words is shown in a passage from *Portrait of the Artist as a Young Man,* published in 1916:

> He drew forth a phrase from his treasure and spoke it softly to himself:
> —A day of dappled seaborne clouds.

The phrase and the day and the scene harmonised in a chord. Words. Was it their colour? He allowed them to glow and fade, hue after hue; sunrise gold, the russet and green of apple orchards, azure of waves, the grey-fringed fleece of clouds. No, it was not their colours: it was the poise and balance of the period itself. Did he then love the rhythmic rise and fall of words better than their associations of legend and colour? Or was it that, being as weak of sight as he was shy of mind, he drew less pleasure from the contemplation of the glowing sensible world through the prism of a language many-coloured and richly storied than from the contemplation of individual emotions mirrored perfectly in a lucid supple periodic prose?

Two phrases there will be found useful in considering the method of *Work in Progress*. "The phrase and the day and the scene harmonised in a chord"—that is what Mr. Joyce is trying all the time to do; not so much to describe things in phrases as to harmonise the thing described and the phrase in one chord— hence the need for discarding familiar words and for creating new words *which shall include the old words with a new suggestion of what those words describe*. Thus, describing a girl singing, he gives her a voice "like water-glucks," and by substituting "Gluck" for "duck" and introducing several other names in this way for the sake of their musical suggestion he heightens the description of the girl's song. The second phrase in the passage quoted above, which helps, I think, to explain further Mr. Joyce's intention, is the distinction between two kinds of prose, one "mirroring perfectly," the other bunching and distorting objects as in a prism. Mr. Joyce has finally chosen this second kind of prose. His sentences reflect a number of images like a decanter-stopper held up to the light. The effect is never single: it is new and varied and often disturbing.

Most of the failures in Mr. Joyce's new prose come from too much distortion and the introduction of patterns and allusions which merely bewilder the reader with irrelevant deftness. I cannot see that the introduction of "catalogues"—a list of the names of rivers, for example, inlaid in the words of a passage like silver wire in wood—gives it any greater literary value than a poem written in the form of an acrostic. *Work in Progress* is said to contain the names of all the largest rivers in the world—the excuse being that the river Liffey is the chief character in the book and that these geographical allusions are all parts of the ground-plan. This seems to me even more fantastic than the Homeric pattern of *Ulysses*. Mr. Joyce is capable of an almost incredible childishness in his word-trickery. "The lunchlight in her eyes" is amusing parody, but what on earth can one say to this, Mr. Joyce's version of "a man with a pipe"?

with his g.b.d. in his f.a.c.e.

A commentator solemnly points out that a "g.b.d." is a well-known brand of pipe and that the letters exactly fit the spaces of "f.a.c.e." Well, what if they do? "God" read backwards spells "dog," but, having noted that, what more can we say? Mr. Joyce's obsession with the elementary processes of words, with their nurture and functioning (one feels that he nursemaids his prose, and takes a nagging interest in all the words to which he gives individuality), suggests again that it is the *privacy* of his writing which is its chief fault, quite apart from its unintelligibility. In time, when more of the words are current ("lemoncholy" and others will probably slip into general use), and when a shelf-full of commentaries has explained all the allusions of a complicated text, even then it will be possible for Mr. James Joyce alone to appreciate these difficult and pointless tricks. A ventriloquist, I believe, must be very skilful to pronounce a "w" properly, but it is he and not the audience that is amazed when he succeeds.

But it is advisable to approach this new book warily, as one would listen for the first time to a new and astonishing piece of music which at times jars on the ear. Whether language is capable of the musical extension to which Mr. Joyce attempts to push it (some of it is almost contrapuntal), I do not intend to discuss. We must have the whole of his book before it will be possible to venture judgment. Occasional passages in *Work in Progress* have amazed me by their beauty and complete originality; and these passages improve on being read a number of times. Phrases from the section published by Messrs. Faber and Faber jump to the memory: "a sugarloaf hat with a gaudyquivery peak," "owlglassy bicycles boggled her eyes," "she let her hair fall and down it flussed to her feet." It contains two passages which have been more than once quoted by Mr. Joyce's admirers: the one beginning, "She was just a young thin pale soft s hy slim slip of a thing," and the concluding paragraph, which I will quote because it shows how effective can be the recurrence of a few simple themes working up to a quiet climax. The allusions in these lines are plain to anyone who has read the pages leading up to them, but would need too much explanation here. The washerwomen by the side of the Liffey have packed up their tubs and linen for the day, and their last straggle of talk comes through the dusk:

Wait till the honeying of the lune, love! Die eve, little eve, die! . . .
My sights are swimming thicker on me by the shadows to this place. . . .

Can't hear with the waters of. The chittering waters of. Flittering bats, fieldmice bawk talk. Ho! Are you not gone ahome? What Tom Malone? Can't hear with bawk of bats, all the liffeying waters of. Ho, talk save us! My foos won't moos. I feel as old as yonder elm. A tale told of Shaun or Shem? All Livia's daughtersons. Dark hawks hear us. Night! Night! My ho head halls. I feel as heavy as yonder stone. Tell me of John or Shaun? Who were Shem and Shaun the living sons or daughters of? Night now! Tell me, tell me, tell me, elm! Night night! Telmetale of stem or stone. Beside the rivering waters of, hitherandthithering waters of. Night!

The echo ("Are you not gone ahome? What Tom Malone?"), the drowsy lisp of "my foos won't moos" (my foot won't move), the yawning "my ho head halls" (my head falls) suggest the evening and the deserted river-bank and the accents of the woman better than many lines of intruding description. This is an extraordinarily successful example, I think, of "the phrase and the day and the scene harmonised in a chord" or, rather, in a sequence of chords moving to a climax. Passages as finished and distinct as this are rare in *Work in Progress*. For the most part you are swept along in a gurgling stream of consciousness, in which Bloom and the Liffey and a Cro-Magnon chorus and the babble o'green fields seem all to be comically muttering together, and all to be one. Whether, after one glimpse into that green murky swirl, most readers will care to take the plunge is extremely doubtful.

A reviewer for The Times Literary Supplement *contrasted* Anna Livia Plurabelle, *which had previously been reviewed in the supplement (20 December 1928), with the recently published* Haveth Childers Everywhere.

Mr. Joyce's Experiments
The Times Literary Supplement, 17 July 1930, p. 588

In the light of recent research it is possible to demonstrate that the prodigious difficulties of Mr. Joyce's latest work, provisionally entitled "Work in Progress," are at least the outcome of a logical and deliberate plan, even if it is impossible to follow with full understanding the details of its execution. As in "Ulysses," the key to the new work may be found in a philosophical concept. Briefly, "Work in Progress" is an attempt to realize Vico's project of "an ideal and timeless history": to create a composite image of human existence, regardless of time or space. Where language has seemed to Mr. Joyce insufficient for his purpose he has altered it. By deformation, punning and the interpolation of foreign languages he has given his English a suggestiveness, a capacity for multiple associations such as his theme demands. The narrative of "Work in Progress" is a simultaneous projection of many narratives. Externally it has to do with the history of Dublin, the myths, and facts of its origin, but into the prose texture are woven strands taken from history and myths of all time. There is no sharp definition; it is part of Mr. Joyce's plan to keep his medium fluid and amorphous. His story is no more than the main current in a stream of associations.

But while a knowledge of what Mr. Joyce is trying to do, of the necessity for his curious technique, is valuable, if only to acquit him of the charge of writing nonsense, it must be admitted that, even with this knowledge, an understanding of his work asks more of our erudition and ingenuity than it is possible for us to give. At best our appreciation of "Work in Progress" must be a relative one, according to our lights, on a plane subsidiary to that of its conception. What we chiefly see in it is not so much an attempt to pack the universe between its covers as an attempt to give language a new vitality, to restore to words some of the energy and freshness of meaning which has been worn out of them. If we are to derive aesthetic satisfaction from the work as a whole, we must approach it with something of that free expectancy of mind with which we approach music. In an article in *Transition* (No. 15) Mr. Robert McAlmon writes that Mr. Joyce "wishes to originate a flexible language that might be an esperanto of the subconscious and he wishes to believe that anybody reading his work gets a sensation of understanding, which is the understanding which music is allowed without too much explanation."

Of the two fragments from "Work in Progress" before us "Anna Livia Plurabelle" is the likelier to yield this "sensation of understanding" to the general reader, if he can approach it without prejudice and without asking "too much explanation." This story of Anna Livia (Dublin's river) is told by two old washerwomen who stand on the banks of the Liffey—no more than a stream between them at the beginning of the episode—gossiping about the owners of the clothes they are washing. They discuss Earwicker, the composite hero of "Work in Progress" and lord of Anna Livia, under one of his many aliases. But their talk is chiefly of Anna, of her domestic troubles, her love affairs, her escapades. The descriptions of her are quaint and playful. In the prose the flowing of the river and all its attributes are evoked simultaneously with the feminine qualities of the impersonation. Lack of an adequate scale of reference must mean that much of the inner significance of this fragment is lost to us. But there remains a delicate appeal to the senses which it needs no table of reference to appreciate, as in the description of Anna's escape from her nurse, when

Joyce in December 1930

the wiggly livvly, she sideslipped out by a gap in the Devil's glen while Sally her nurse was sound asleep in a sloot and feefee fiefie fell over a spillway before she found her stride and lay and wriggled in all the stagnant black pools of rainy under a fallow coo and she laughed innocefree her limbs aloft and a whole drove of maiden hawthorns blushing and looking askance upon her

—or in the typically allusive evocation of dusk with which the episode ends. The river has widened out, and the old women are so far apart that they cannot hear each other for the noise of the water:—

Can't hear with bawk of bats, all the liffeying waters of. Ho, talk save us! My foos won't moos. I feel as old as yonder elm. . . . Night! Night! My ho head halls. I feel as heavy as yonder stone. . . .

Myth envelops the gossipers, tellers of myths. One is changed to a tree, one to a stone—"Beside the rivering waters of, hitherandthithering waters of. Night!"

The other fragment, "Haveth Childers Everywhere," is more opaque generally. Ingenuity as well as an extensive knowledge of Dublin and its history are necessary to understand Earwicker's pompous recital of all that he has done for the city and for his Anna. Its implications are occasionally obvious, to Dubliners at least, as in the reference to street-names in

> in my nordsoud circulums, my eastmoreland and westlandmore, running boullowards and syddenly parading . . .

Read aloud, as Mr. Joyce's work should be, the prose of this fragment has a stateliness appropriate to its matter, in ponderous, masculine contrast to the streamlike melodies of *Anna Livia Plurabelle*.

In his September 1928 article in Criterion, *"Style and the Limitations of Speech," O'Faolain, an Irish novelist, playwright, and biographer, condemned Joyce's language: "It is not merely ahistoric—not merely the shadow of an animal that never was, the outline of a tree that never grew, for even then we might trace it to some basic reality distorted and confused—but it comes from nowhere, goes nowhere, is not part of life at all."*

Letter to the Editor
Sean O'Faolain
Criterion, 10 (October 1930): 147

DEAR SIR,

A re-reading of *Anna Livia Plurabelle,* with more pleasure than at any previous reading, convinces me that in an article which you kindly published in the *Criterion* of September, 1928, I did not do complete justice to Mr. Joyce's new prose, and with your permission I should like to add a further word to what I said in that essay. I do not think there is anything in that essay which I do not still believe, but it did not go far enough in its appreciation of the merits that do lie in Mr. Joyce's language. It becomes clear to me that a kind of distinction once properly made between prose and poetry is passing away. Prose we have always thought of as being a more explicit and direct medium than poetry, which, though at its clearest always explicit, is full of a remoter beauty, richer in 'meaning' apprehended rather than perceived and incapable of translation for those who by reason of nationality or stupidity find its language difficult or strange. Some have found it valuable to think of English prose swinging between the plain and the ornate: perhaps a more suggestive antinomy will henceforth be found between explicit prose and prose mainly suggestive. At what point the new antinomy entered into English I have not studied but it is something that historians of prose-rhythms in the nineteenth century should attempt to fix. I do not, of course, imagine that prose was

not always highly suggestive at its best, but prose written by what I may call 'poets gone wrong'—with a few exceptions (like those occasional bursts in Sir Thomas Browne and more frequent bursts in Jeremy Taylor) in the seventeenth century, is, I believe, a departure that occurred very late indeed in the history of English. This prose that conveys its 'meaning' vaguely and unprecisely, by its style rather than its words, has its delights, as music has its own particular delights proper to itself, and I have wished to say that for these half-conveyed, or not even half-conveyed suggestions of 'meaning' Mr. Joyce's prose can be tantalizingly delightful, a prose written by a poet who missed the tide, and which can be entirely charming if approached as prose from which an explicit or intellectual communication was never intended. In my article and elsewhere, I suggested that such prose is, as it were, morally deficient—being almost wholly sensuous—but that question I do not wish to re-open here.

Sincerely yours, SEAN O'FAOLAIN

The British translator and critic Stuart Gilbert met Joyce in Paris in 1927, and the two became close friends. He collaborated with Joyce in translating Ulysses *into French and with Joyce's assistance wrote* James Joyce's Ulysses, *an influential early study of the novel. When* New Experiment *reprinted the opening pages of* Work in Progress (Finnegans Wake, *pp. 3–29), Gilbert provided this comment and explication.*

A Footnote to Work in Progress
Stuart Gilbert
New Experiment (Cambridge), No. 7 (Spring 1931): 30–33

For his *Work in Progress* James Joyce employs at once a new literary form and a new technique of words; hence the difficulties in its perusal. The form of *Work in Progress* (so far as can be judged from that portion of the work—a little more than half—which has so far been published) may be likened to a carefully planned and exactly ordered fantasia, based on a set of ancient but abiding folk-tunes. For it is the paradox of this work to be at once fantastic and extremely symmetrical; nothing could be further from the super-realist 'free writing,' yet a reader's first impression is one of confusion, a vivid welter of ideas and free associations. A baroque superstructure hides the steel frame beneath.

The effect is one of polyphony; themes flow one above the other as in a fugue; the printed words represent a series of cross-sections, chords. Syllabic sounds are treated as units which can be moulded or reassembled so as to convey a host of meanings in a single vocable. A slight vowel change may suffice to add the required nuance, or—and this is where the plain reader is apt to stumble—the basic word or root is sometimes deformed out of easy recognition.

Ulysses was the epic of a day; *Work in Progress* is a nocturne, the stuff of dreams. The time dimension falls into abeyance, as in dreams; personalities far removed in time are merged in each other and, similarly, the scene of action is at once specific and world-wide.

The passage now reprinted in *Experiment* is taken from the opening pages of *Work in Progress* and was originally published in *transition*, No. 1 (April 1927). Its texture is comparatively simple and its humour exoteric. In the first paragraph we discover the gigantic protagonist, the strong man of any situation, a Vercingetorix, Adam, Sitric Silkenbeard (the Danish King of Duboin), Noah, Dunlop of the Tyres, Peter the Great, the 'Boss' of a big modern brewery, newspaper, etc. Two of his noncenames are Here Comes Everybody and H. C. Earwicker (*alias* Persse O' Reilly). The initials H.C.E., once familiar as those of a pompous minister in Gladstonian times (Hugh Childers Erskine), often serve to indicate his presence, as in *Hic cubat edilis*. One of his many avatars is the Hill of Howth, near Dublin (there is an allusion to this in the word 'Whooth?') Besides him we find Anna Livia Plurabelle, his river wife, the eternal feminine, one of whose vehicles is the Dublin Liffey; A.L.P. is a gay little old woman who trips along to a lilt of rollicking dactyls. . . . Satirists, moralists, reformers, all alike are mocked by the phantoms of their meliorism; the primal matter, a Proteus, contrives to slip through their fingers and leave them gaping at panther, snake or watery mirage upon the barren beach of Pharos . . . it was left to the author of *Work in Progress* to weave a spell to bind the old man of the tides, a grotesquery corrival with the cosmic harlequinade. . . .

—reprinted from *James Joyce: The Critical Heritage*

Stuart, who had reviewed Tales Told of Shem and Shaun *in the November 1929* transition, *here returned to access Joyce's* Work in Progress.

Mr. Joyce's Word Creatures
Michael Stuart
Symposium, 2 (October 1931): 459–467

Thus far the Dubliner has given life to three Universals in *Work in Progress*: the Word-River in the Fragment entitled *Anna Livia Plurabelle,* the Word-Insect in *The Ondt and the Gracehoper,* and the Word-City in *Haveth Childers Everywhere.* These three Fragments correspond to the three principal characters of the universal history which *Work in Progress* is intended to be. The names under which these three heroes occur most frequently in the story are Anna Livia Plurabelle, Earwicker (H. C. E. or Here Comes Everybody), and Shem and Shaun, a duel personality born from the marriage of A. L. P. and H. C. E.

We may note from the subjoined analysis of the verbal elements in *The Ondt and the Gracehoper,* selected because of its brevity and effectiveness, the following significant points. The language of this Fragment consists of a mosaic of seventeen tongues, English serving as the basic element with which the other idioms are interwoven. Names of insects and insect-members, references to Egyptian religious symbolism, and to the four principles of the development of human society as laid down by the Italian jurist, Vico, are the material from which the author creates his fable. The tone of this Fragment is satiric to the point of ribaldry; the impression of the whole is that of some airy Word-Creature ready to take wing.

A word on the plan of *Work in Progress* is relevant to the poetic problem set for himself by the author, affording simultaneously a view of the writer's general development. The Dubliner's art witnesses a steady progression from the Individual to the Universal. Indeed, the spiritual essence of scholasticism is so deeply imbedded in the roots of his soul that it manifests itself in his mature works in an all-pervading fashion. All of the self-created complexities in *Ulysses* and *Work in Progress* resulting in ornamentation of structure, language, and character-creation arise undoubtedly from a compelling soul-need familiar to theologians of weaving a rich network of detail around the thread of an idea, a trait most noticeable in Gothic architecture and in the work of medieval book-illuminators. There is not a similar case in modern literature in which the problem inherited by scholasticism from ancient philosophy is resurrected to such a vigorous life as in the works of Mr. Joyce. We may note something of this fact in the three stages of his creative activity: the tendency to describe flesh-and-blood individuals as in *Dubliners, Exiles,* and *The Portrait* with the significant occurrence of unity of time and place in *Exiles;* secondly, the tendency to universalize by suggesting as in *Ulysses* the existence of the aggregate, the City, and beyond the City, humanity; and lastly, as in *Work in Progress,* the tendency to disregard the life-story of individuals now merely named and remembered as the shadows of a dream 'in the palace of dim night' to create Universals as the characters of his story. In *Ulysses* as in Mr. Joyce's last work the reader often becomes aware that the action is being revealed through the mind of one of the characters, creating simultaneously the double effect of the subjective

Joyce in 1933

and the objective, so that a familiarity with each of these vast Gothic structures gives one the sense of some omnipresent Aristotelian divinity thinking his world into creation.

In *Work in Progress* the author has set himself the task of writing a miniature *universal* history as recalled by a sleeping Dubliner in a series of dreams lasting from about eight o'clock in the evening till four in the morning. Here, in a nutshell, is the whole scheme of the work. The chief poetic problem in this nocturnal world history is the creation of Universals. Unless *The Ondt and the Gracehoper* suggests a winged creature and *Anna Livia Plurabelle* a flowing river, the author has failed. It is the author's intention that the Creature or Thing embodied in each Fragment shall not be a description of an insect or a river but the verbal image of the Thing or Creature named. With Joyce the Word is life-giving, the Word is laughter-making (not the situation or character description as with Rabelais or Cervantes), the Word is the all-in-all. A parallel to this magic evocative power of the word is to be found only in the Egyptian *Book of the Dead* and the *Popol Vuh* of the Central Americans. According to the followers of Osiris, not only the proper word, but also the manner, the tone in which words were pro-

nounced meant success or failure for the soul seeking life eternal. In reading *Work in Progress* it is the tone of the voice, the manner of pronouncing aloud each word that will unlock to the reader the meanings of a word or a phrase.

The Ondt and the Gracehoper is a variation of the fable about the industrious ant, the champion of time, and the lazy, light-headed grasshopper, the champion of space. The contention between the two insects is interpreted according to tradition, although the sympathies of the author are evidently on the side of the 'gracehoper . . . who was always jigging a jog, hoppy on akkant of his joyicity. . . . making ungraceful overtures to Floh and Luse and Bienie and Vespatilla. . . . or . . . striking up funny funereels with Besterfather Zeuts, the Aged One . . . .' And, of course, 'the impossible gracehoper' comes to the sad end of the 'spindhrift,' 'sans mantis, sans shoeshooe, feather weighed animule, actually and presumptuably sinctifying chonic o' despair. . . ,' The assiduous ant, 'boundlessly blissified,' reproves the Gracehoper, 'a darkener of the threshold.' Today as ever fables are written to point a moral for the human kind. Here (inter alia) the ant may stand as the symbol of any contemporary antagonistic to the time-spirit, whether a writer of 'volumes immense' or philosopher or worldwide genius who cannot 'beat time. . . .'

–reprinted from *James Joyce: The Critical Heritage*

Bridson reviewed the first English edition of Two Tales of Shem and Shaun, *which omitted the fragment "The Muddest Thick That Was Ever heard Dump" that had been included in the 1929 Paris edition* Tales Told of Shem and Shaun.

Views and Review
D. G. Bridson
New English Weekly, 5 January 1933, pp. 281–282

This is the third selection of Mr. Joyce's *Work in Progress* to be published in this country. First of all came *Anna Livia Plurabelle*, which is probably the best of the three. Then came *Haveth Childers Everywhere*, which has the appearance of being slightly more ambiguous. Now we have *Two Tales of Shem and Shaun*, which are nearer, perhaps, to the first than the second.

A great deal has been said about Mr. Joyce's later work, and a great deal more has probably been written. The number of honest folk who regard him as a genial-minded maniac, however, must still be far in excess of the number who do not. Yet it is surely time that an intelligent interest be taken in unusual work which has been published for an odd five years. . . . The obvious fact is that 'Work in Progress' (at least, those fragments of it which have appeared in England) should not be referred, as literature, to any other published literature at all. The approach to its appreciation should be rather through its music than through its sense.

But before proceeding to any consideration of its musical qualities it were advisable to consider Joyce's aim in writing the book in the first place. And it must here be stated that his expressed wish is that 'what I am doing should not be judged until it is completed.' But it is also permissible to quote his further remark that the fragments have 'a certain independent life of their own.' Accordingly it seems fair to suppose that so long as we do not concern ourselves with the contributory qualities of the fragments, but are rather content to examine them for the qualities common to every page of them published thus far, we shall be on ground which is fairly safe. The quality most obviously apparent is a seeming obscurity. A first reading of the opening sentence of 'The Mookse and the Gripes,' for instance, may suggest that the sentence is wholly devoid of meaning.—'Eins within a space and a weary wide space it wast ere wohned a Mookse.' But if the meaning is not at once apparent, it is there nevertheless. A child, indeed, would probably find little or no difficulty in the matter: what it did not understand, it would certainly take for granted. If the sentence is anyway apprehensible, it most obviously is possessed of a meaning. Now precisely how long it took Mr. Joyce to twist his fifteen words to their final shape, we do not know. But twenty pages of similar work, he assures us, employed him for twelve hundred hours. The full understanding (taking understanding to mean a coincidence of the reader's evoked flow of ideas with that of the author considering his work) would occupy the reader for the best part of his life. Every word, as a matter of fact, would have to be assessed on a varying number of planes of meaning,—the number sometimes being as many as ten or a dozen. Mr. Joyce's explanation of a typical phrase, as related by Mr. Sisley Huddleston, is this. 'His commentary was illuminating. I have no desire to misrepresent him, but as I remember he would take such a phrase as "Phœnix culpa," and would then explain. Now here you have a suggestion of *felix culpa*—the blessed sin of the early Church fathers—that is to say, the downfall of Adam and Eve which brought Christ into the world; and you have the suggestion, not only of the Garden of Eden, but of Phœnix Park in Dublin, and of Irish history with its wrongs and crimes, and you have the eternal way of a man with a maid, and you have . . .' Let that suffice for an explanation of Fiendish Park, muddy chrushmess, the Mookse and the Gripes, and the Ondt and the Grace-hoper. The fact remains, that the closer the application to the text, the more and more words appear in their own original sense,—each with more rings of association than there are about Saturn. But the book holds more than

acrostics, and the reader is well advised to disregard the meaning entirely for a while. That the 'aim' of the work is a process of enlarging and revitalising the language, we have the author's assurance. But the work is more than a mine for philologists.

Gerard Manly Hopkins once remarked, it will be remembered, that however awkward his verse might appear, it had only to be read with the ear to be appreciated. And the fact that Mr. Joyce has recorded a reading of the last four pages of *Anna Livia Plurabelle* is significant. To many, indeed, the recent broadcasting of the record brought an understanding of the work which they never before imagined possible. For whatever the value of his telescoped words, his associated ideas, his parallel planes of meaning,—the fact remains that the most important feature of Mr. Joyce's recent prose for the plain reader is its superb musical cadence.

For a full enjoyment of the *Two Tales,* then, the reader must empty his mind of all prejudice and opinion, reading the book for the first time impersonally. His first reading will at least supply him with a proper pronunciation (and this is important) for such unusual words as archunsitslike, infairioriboos, ishallassoboundbewilso-thoutoosezit, pulladeftkiss and oxtrabeeforeness. And no longer so likely as before to trip over words whose unusual 'shape' at first confused him, the reader is in a fair way to begin his real appreciation. . . . And now, reading the book *aloud,* the full beauty of the rhythm and the peculiar turn of the words is (or certainly ought to be) at once apparent and enjoyed. There is nothing in these *Two Tales* so lovely, perhaps, as the ending of *Anna Livia,* but there is a humour no less rich and an idiom no less fascinating. As the mind relaxes before the flow of the words, a succession of images is called up much as is the cinematic flow of images in a dream. The words call up ideas which are mentally visualised as either objects or events, each fading away into other patterns more complicated and surprising at every reading. For the words becoming ever more familiar to him, the associated ideas which they hold within themselves are loosed ever more freely and generously, until the reader's mind is almost overwhelmed by the visual imagery evoked. Then it is that the meaning begins to appear in its final simplicity. And always there is the superlative beauty of the ono-matopœic and lyrical prose for accompaniment. It is this music, in fact, which is alone able to induce that mental quietude and detachment necessary to a full appreciation of the imagery.

The reading of these fragments is an experience not to be paralleled by the reading of any other book which has yet been published. The beauty of pure sound might be roughly paralleled in the reading of Homer (say) where the reader's knowledge of Greek was negligible: but such a reading would give none of the rich associations or imagery of the reading of Joyce. To *understand* the work,—that is to understand it consciously and of intent,—is hardly worth our trouble, if it is in our power to do so.

It will be argued, of course, as it has been argued already, that such a peculiarly aesthetic experience as the reading of *Work in Progress* entails is not worth our enjoying. But where the results of the reading are so incontestably delightful as are the results of a sympathetic reading of either *Anna Livia* or *Shem and Shaun,* we have small need to concern ourselves with the ethics of appreciation. That Mr. Joyce is a sincere artist as well as a genius goes without saying. That he thinks it worth his while to write the prose he does, should be our justification sufficient for reading it. Where our reading delights us, we have small cause to complain in any case.

Two Tales of Shem and Shaun is a book not only to buy; it is a book to enjoy and a book to memorise. Essentially it is a book to recite. . . .

—reprinted from *James Joyce: The Critical Heritage*

Jolas's transition *ceased publication after three years in 1930 but began again in 1932 and resumed the publication of* Work in Progress. *In the February 1933 issue* transition *published a fragment that corresponds to pages 219–259 of* Finnegans Wake.

Marginalia to James Joyce's *Work in Progress*
Eugene Jolas
transition, No. 22 (February 1933): 101–105

I.

No collectivist system, whatever its ultimate economic and political aspect, will be able to destroy two essential entities of man: the saint and the genius. The dogma of sociological interpretation in the creative sphere—based on the belief that the creator is essentially an instrument for bringing about melioristic utopias—is inadmissible, for the scissions in man go beyond all attempts at uniformisation. It is in the two forces of the genius and the saint that all the extreme possibilities of the human personality are incorporated. They represent the synthetic functions of life.

II.

The principal criterion of genius is the capacity to construct a mythological world. In creating the saga of Anna Livia Plurabelle, James Joyce has given us the modern idea of Magna Mater, the superoccidental vision of the Anatolian Cybele, of the Egyptian Rhea. In the fragment being published in this number of

Transition, he presents the modern saga of the infancy of mankind.

III.

Every effort to force the work of James Joyce into a literary-historic mould has heretofore been a failure. By the time the critics has caught up with ULYSSES, identified it, and neatly pigeon-holed it into the category of naturalism, his new work had already progressed beyond all academis sign-posts, having no reference-point other than a *visionary* quality of invention. *Work in Progress* is, if we must indulge in identification, anti-naturalist, and, on the positive side, mythological. For it is primarily the story of mankind and the universe. The first mantic myth written in our age. A cosmography in hierophantic terms.

IV.

The Anamyth of Childhood begins with the presentation of the various characters, or rather, of the amalgam of characters with which the book deals. There is Hump, the protagonist, the symbol of the male principle, the Besterfather, the Titan of the Scandinavian sagas, known previously under other names, such as Here Comes Everybody, H. C. Earwigger, Lipoleums, or plain He. In the present instalment we also trace him again as Meisther Wikingson and Heer Assassor Neelson. Then there is Ann, better known as Anna Livia Plurabelle, *das Ewig' Weibliche,* the Great Mother. Alongside of the minor characters, the Customers of the inn whose conversation, hacked into fragmentary dialogues, we listened to in the beginning of the book, are re-introduced. Glugg and Chuff, the sons of the house, also known under the names of Shem and Shaun, confront the seven girls, the Floras, with whose doings at "lighting up o'clock sharp" we are specifically concerned.

V.

An "argument" representing once more symbolically the Mookse and the Gripes—this time in the antithesis of Chuffy and Glugger—begins the description of the story. Its basis is the manichean principle of light and darkness. Quickly the scene shifts to the sketch of the Floras. We watch the kinematics of the seven colors of the rainbow, a theme which reoccurs, under numerous guises and hieroglyphs, throughout this fragment. Taking as his startingpoint the Irish children's game "The Angels and the Devils", the author builds a richly-textured word-pageant, in which we see pass the legend of all the children of the world, past, present and future, during which we hear Joycian versions of children's songs from many languages, such as "Sur le Pont d'Avignon", "Little Bo-Peep", "Mary had a little Lamb" etc.

VI.

The dramatic background of the events is an inn near Dublin. It is dusk and the children are playing in front of the house. The angels and the devils of their game become huge mythic figures passing down pre-history and history. The children have tried to remember their lessons. Glugg's scholastic achievements are rather meagre. Then it is time to go to bed, they rush into the house, the door crashes to. *Beifall*. They say their prayers to the "Loud", in the zoo nearby in Phoenix Park the animals move with nocturnal sounds, the customers in the inn continue swapping stories.

VII.

Thomistic and gnostic elements are dovetailed into the text. The paradisaical fall and the birth of sin give the keynote to the story, the struggle between Ahriman and Ozmud resounds, "for felix is as culpas does". The spirit of evil, the arch fiend, the apostate angel, is presented with a plethora of names taken from the folklore of the ages. He is Aguiliarept, the Joycian nomenclature for the more classical Aghatharept. When "they fleurelly to Nebnos", we watch the change of the noun Fleuretty into a verb. Rofocale is changed into Rosocale. We see the four elements: air, earth, sun and water, fit into the evocation of the four evangelists: "He askit of the hoothed fireshield, but it was untergone into the matthued heaven. He soughed it from the luft, but that bore ne mark ne message. He luked upon the bloomingrund where barely his corns were growning. At last he listed back to beckline how she pranked alone so johntily". The seven sacraments, baptism, confirmation, eucharist, confession, priests' consecration, extreme unction and marriage, are humourously described: "He dove his head into Wat Murrey, gave Stewart Ryall a puck on the plexus, wrestled a hurry-come-union with the Gille Beg, wiped all his sinses, martial and menial, out of Shrove Sunday ManFearsome, excremuncted as freely as any frothblower into MacIsaac, had a belting bout, chaste to chaste, with McAdoo about nothing, and childhood's age being aye the shamleast, inbraced himself for any time untellable with what hunger over from the MasSiccaries of the Breeks". In the passage beginning "Ukalepe. Loathers' Leave etc", we have the author's version of the *Theodicee ex consensu gentium* synthesized with the Odyssean pilgrimage.

VIII.

A new development of Mr. Joyce's linguistic experiments can be noted in this fragment. His attempt to reproduce the language of children is particularly felici-

tous. In the girls' address to Shaun, we notice grammatical deformations that approach infantile stammering. He attempts a primitive syntax: "He possible he sooth to say notwithstanding he gaining fish considerable to look most prophitable out of smily skibluh eye"; "Is you zealous of mes?"; "He relation belong this remarkable moliman." That he is following the most modern philological researches can be deduced from the passage: 'But up tighty in the front, down again the loose, drim and drumming on her back, and a pop from her whistle what is that, o holytroopers?" This is a picaresque illustration of the theory expressed by Sir Richard Paget in his "The Nature of Human Speech" (At the Clarendon Press, S.P.E. Tract No. XXII) in which the acoustics of speech is studied from a new angle. We have here again a reference to the rainbow motif, it being in this particular passage an attempt to sound-describe the word heliotropes from the viewpoint of Sir Richard Paget's idea of gesture.

IX.

Notabene: we might observe here, the re-occurrence of Mr. Joyce's preoccupation with the irrationalism of numbers. Seven, being the symbolism of space-time, emerges here—as it does throughout the book–in the seven colors of the rainbow, (the seven names of the Floras), while four, the number of mystic space, can be found in numerous allusions, such as the passage: "No more turdenskaulds. (No more thunder), Free leaves for ebribadies (Free love for everybody), "all tinsammon in the yord (All canned goods in the earth), with harm and aches till Farther alters (with ham and eggs till the end of the world.)

X.

Into the mythological texture the author sometimes weaves bits of autobiographical material, making particular allusion to the tragedy of exile. "Allwhile preying in his mind he swure etc" is a re-statement of the famous maxim of Dedalus' in the *Portrait of the Artist as a Young Man*: silence, exile and cunning. Bruce here is a reference to the story of Scotland's Robert Bruce and the spider, silence being in this case identified with patience. Coriolanus refers to the tale of the exiled Roman, and Macchievalli is the illustration of cunning. Paname-Turricum indicates the author's stay in Paris and Zurich. Laurentius O'Toole is the native saint of Dublin who died at Eure (France). This is the hint in: *Euro pra nobis*.

XI.

The mythological symbolisms used include numerous past and living references. From the Egyptian Book of the Dead has come: "Your head has been touched by the god Enel-Rah and your face has been brightened by the goddess Aruc-Ituc". The deformations of the original terms are once more in line with the color-motif. An American negro song occurs in the passage of Meisther Wikingson, still the gigantic, pneumatic figure he always is in the book: "It's his last lap, Gigantic, fare him weal!" This is from the Louisville (Ky.) negro song composed by some vagabond singer after the sinking of the Titanic: "It's yer las' trip, Titanic, fare thee well". In giving a picture of the night, the author says: "Was even ere awhile. Now conticinium. The time of lying together will come and the wildering of the nicht till cockee doodle aubens Aurore". This is a flection of the five Roman watches of the night: vespers, conticinium, concubium, intempestas noctis, gallicinium and aura ante lucano.

XII.

In this passage of *Work in Progress,* the author returns once more to Vico's cyclical conception of history. "The same renew". The triune evolution: theocratic, heroic and human, is the basis of the work. The fear felt by primitive man is still in us. The thunder-motif

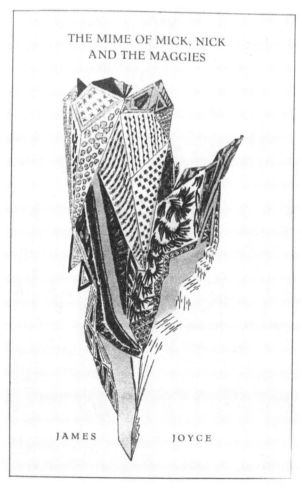

Dust jacket designed by Lucia Joyce for a fragment from Work in Progress *published in June 1934 by the Servire Press in The Hague*

in the invocation to the "Loud" is based on Vico. It is, however, obvious, that Mr. Joyce is not in the least interested in demonstrating any theory. He is merely following a vision of his own: the sense of the pre-historic and the historic as one great stream. It is interesting, in this connection, to observe that M. Lévy-Bruhl, the French sociologist, has come to some definite confirmations in his own researches. The primitive mentality, accordingly to him, is characterized chiefly by the pre-logical function of the mind. He finds–as did Vico–that the basic emotion which impelled man to create his gods and myths, is fear, or rather, apprehension. In his recent book *"Le Surnaturel et la Nature dans la Mentalité primitive"* M. Lévy-Bruhl develops the idea still further. The German metaphysician Martin Heidegger has also found apprehension to be man's principal impulse.

XIII.

An inkling of the author's most definite belief can be found in the final prayer. He looks at the universe with cosmic humor, creating a world of symbols, building a "witchman's funnominal world".

Stonier, who had reviewed the fragments Anna Livia Plurabelle *and* Haveth Childers Everywhere *in the 28 June 1930 issue of* New Statesman, *here comments on* The Mime of Mick, Nick and the Maggies (Finnegans Wake, *pp. 219–259).*

Joyce Without End
G. W. Stonier
The New Statesman and Nation, 8 (22 September 1934): 364

A common experience of dreams is the multiple activity of the mind. The dreamer, in the middle of some conversation from the previous day, suddenly realises that he is in America; he is confronted with one person and knows himself to be in the presence of another; a landscape, which appears to be green, leaves him with the sensation of red; and so on. There is no contradiction in such impressions, but only the smooth working of the mind on several planes at once. And since dreams are always convincing, these impressions, though they may not coalesce, make a whole.

I am reminded of this phenomenon by the appearance of another fragment from *Work in Progress.* One cannot read far in Mr. Joyce's new book without discovering that its whole method is based on dreams. The characters are at the same time persons and landmarks of Dublin; every scene is played on a revolving stage; and the individual words of Mr. Joyce's prose convey two or more simultaneous meanings, which strike the imagination at different levels. He plays on our sub-consciousness in a multitude of ways, now echoing a forgotten passage, now half-suggesting a thought while our attention is directed elsewhere. The fact no *single* meaning can be extracted from any paragraph has probably disturbed readers more than the actual difficulty of his verbal inventions. There is only one way of reading the later Joyce, and that is to go by the sound and the rhythm, which are simple enough, and let the meanings look after themselves. We must read passively, but at the same time Mr. Joyce expects of his reader the sort of acuteness which will spot a *double entendre*. If a music-hall audience can appreciate sexual jokes in this way, there is no reason why educated readers should not be capable of catching the allusions, historical and topical, which are embedded in *Work in Progress*. We may miss a good deal—Mr. Joyce's fond-

CATALOGUE
OF A
COLLECTION CONTAINING
MANUSCRIPTS & RARE EDITIONS OF JAMES JOYCE
A FEW MANUSCRIPTS OF WALT WHITMAN
AND TWO DRAWINGS BY WILLIAM BLAKE
Belonging to Miss Sylvia Beach
and offered for sale at her shop
SHAKESPEARE AND COMPANY
12, RUE DE L'ODÉON, 12
PARIS-VIᵉ

Cover for the 1935 catalogue for the sale held to raise money for Beach's bookstore

ness for Dublin and modern languages may baffle the outsider—but what emerges is slapstick raised to the status of art; and, indeed, as a master of ribald poetry, Mr. Joyce has few equals in literature.

The Mime of Mick, Nick and the Maggies begins, then, in a Dublin theatre—"Every evening at lighting up o'clock sharp and until further notice in Feenichts Playhouse (bar and conveniences always open)." A number of characters are introduced after the manner of the newspaper serial—"and now read on here"—but most of them do not reappear. The playhouse fades; it is perhaps a summer evening, and the fairies and gnomes and principals of pantomime jig through the dusk, ending on a tableau.

The flossies all and the mossies all they drooped upon her draped brimfall. The bowknots, the showlots, they wilted into woeblots. The pearlagraph, the pearlagraph, knew whitchly whether to weep or laugh. For always down in Carolinas lovely Dinahs vaunt their view.

Painting of Joyce by Jacques Emile Blanche, 1935 (National Portrait Gallery, London [NPG 3883])

Bits of nursery rhyme, doggerel, popular songs waft them away. Dublin becomes Eden; from a chorus of sprites whose names spell the word Raynbow we come to the house of Amanti and the names of advertisers. So it goes on, at a good pace, this mad midsummer night's dream. If there is a mime at all, after the first few pages, it is the mime of words, which tumble into strange postures and dance through catalogues of colours, sweetmeats, bawdy prayers, Dublin slang, till at last "by deep request" the curtain drops. In the meantime, as usual, Mr. Joyce has given us a bit of everything from Adam to Mademoiselle of Armentières, and however difficult an exercise it might prove for the precis-writer, this "cosmological fairy-tale" is rich in satire and pure magic. The delight which one finds in words like "mother-in-lieu," or such a phrase as "making a bolderdash for lubberty of speech," is sharper than the ordinary pleasures of prose. The scenes, the landscapes and characters of Mr. Joyce's fantasy are squeezed into animated words.

Reading the fifty pages of this new "fragment"—so carefully written and written over—we are reminded, with awe and almost with horror, of the parent work, that vast snowball trundling down some hidden slope, of which this is merely a chip thrown into the sky. How many thousand *Micks* and *Anna Livias* has it gathered up in its course? And when will it reach the bottom? The reviewer foresees a day when he, too, will be expected to go out with a search party, ice-axe and Vico in hand, to examine the new landmark and scratch his initials in the ice. Meanwhile, he is content with a crystal or two.

The Mime of Mick, Nick and the Maggies, though not so good as *Anna Livia Plurabelle,* is a fair specimen of its author's prose. It contains, by the way, for those who have the true crossword mind, scriptural references on pages 3, 7 and 32, etc.; an acrostic on p. 16; advertisements of skin foods and hair tonics (reversed) on p. 38; a quotation from *Ulysses* on p. 34; and rhymes and ribaldry *partout.*

Work in Progress is "a compendium, an encyclopedia of the entire mental life of a man of genius," a definition which Wilhelm Schlegel posited, more than a hundred years ago, for the novel of the future.

– Eugène Jolas, "Homage to the Mythmaker,"
transition, no. 27 (May 1938)

Reviews of *Finnegans Wake*

Published on 4 May 1939, sixteen years after Ulysses, *the completed* Finnegans Wake *puzzled the public and most critics, but it also had its defenders, who saw in the work more than just a linguistic tour de force and responded not only to its humor, imagery, and musical cadences but also to its perceived meaning and the encyclopedic learning it represented. In his early review in* The New York Times *Padraic Colum put the case succinctly: "We have novels that give us greatly a three dimensional world: here is a narrative that gives a new dimension." A few months after the publication of* Finnegans Wake, *World War II broke out and the prospects for a favorable reception of the book were diminished.*

Rosenfeld wrote another review of the novel, "James Joyce: Charlatan or Genius?," in the July 1939 issue of American Mercury. *In that article he concludes that "what seems gibberish at first glance, ultimately resolves itself into conglomerates of meanings.* Finnegans Wake, *even more so than* Ulysses, *is a book by Joyce for Joyce and other writers. However it be regarded, it remains an amazing performance; and whatever its fate, it seems likely to fertilize other talents, provoke other minds, for generations to come."*

James Joyce's Jabberwocky
Paul Rosenfeld
The Saturday Review of Literature, (6 May 1939): 10–11

Long heralded and eagerly awaited, the new, two-hundred-thousand-word novel by the illustrious author of *Ulysses* proves to be a work not unlike *The Making of Americans* by Gertrude Stein and *Towards a Better Life* by Kenneth Burke. It is one of the latter-day abstract fictions in which the writing is not so much about something as that something itself. As in its relatives, in *Finnegans Wake* the style, the essential qualities and movement of the words, their rhythmic and melodic sequences, and the emotional color of the page are the main representatives of the author's thought and feeling. The accepted significations of the words are secondary.

Indeed, in the case of this new volume, the language approaches a condition of privacy. It is composed to a great extent of sonorous neologisms reassembling syllables and whisps of words derived from Irish, English, and American dialects and languages as related to English as Norse, French, German, and Italian are; and of portmanteau-words, etymological puns, Hibernicisms, and other humorous ambiguities. In some instances, these neologisms reveal themselves as clever and economical concentrations of two or more meanings. In many others,

Joyce with Sylvia Beach and Adrienne Monnier in Shakespeare and Company, May 1938

they remain unintelligible, and the author's drift is entirely elusive.

Yet it is possible that in future years this new language of Joyce's will grow less private. It must be remembered that at the time of its first publication, "Ulysses" also contained a large number of expressions which seemed unintelligible and which have now come to make clear sense: and this circumstance, even in the face of the fact that "Finnegans Wake" differs more completely from "Ulysses" than that book differed from works in the tradition of realistic fiction, emboldens one to believe that the newcomer may come to speak more distinctly to us than it does at present. Even now, certain pages, passages, indeed whole chapters of it make or appear to make sense: and in any case seem to convey their author's ideas and his characteristic boundlessly bitter, boundlessly sad, and still humorous feeling. One of them is the initial chapter, which loosely adheres to the old narrative form. It causes us to conceive the situation of a man who has "fallen" or believes himself to have "fallen," either physically or morally, and

during a thunderstorm lies drunkenly asleep in the Phoenix Park in Dublin by the banks of the Liffey. Another is the final chapter of Part I, the famous 'Anna Livia Plurabelle' chapter. It is a sort of gongoristic and onomatopeic prose-poem about life symbolized as a girl and the course and flow of a river. Still others are the drunken epithalamium in Part II, the Swiftian sections of Part III, and almost the whole of the brief and relatively lucid final portion, with its feeling of a sad awakening.

And as a whole the book conveys or seems to convey a meaning. To begin with, the narrative plunges us into some manner of timeless reality, in which the selves of the Norse founders of Dublin and the subject of the narrative (possibly H. C. Earwicker, an imaginery Dublin postman of the 1900s, possibly Here Comes Everybody or even the author himself) and the egos of Sir Tristram and of Dean Swift are contemporaneous and even interchangeable. This vague realm is haunted by shadows of certain archetypes in the human mind: mist-giants (Jute and Mutt), Michael and Satan (The Mookse and The

Eugène Jolas and Joyce in the late 1930s (photograph by Giselle Freund)

Gripes); the perfection of the number Four; above all by a bisexual deity whose masculine principle is symbolized by a mountain (Howth) and an elmtree, while its feminine one is symbolized by waterways, and which appears in human pairs such as Adam and Eve, Tristram and Yseult, Swift and Vanessa, and the "hero" and his "Annie." The narrative reflects their relations and lets us hear their alternative voices.

And this timeless reality appears to be the scene of some evolutionary process. Interfused in substance though they are, the four parts are distinct and represent a progress. The first has a mythological atmosphere, the second an heroic and theological one (there is a suggestion of heroic drama and of theological volumes and their commentaries), the third a rationalistic and human character (a fable and a liberal sermon figure here), while the fourth is full of suggestions of preparations for action and creation.

Now, these four stages correspond to the four periods of human evolution according to the eighteenth-century Italian philosopher Giambattista Vico, whose name, like that of Giordano Bruno, appears throughout the book in various disguises. Vico cherished many quaint ideas besides the idea that human-

ity developed progressively on theorcratic, philosophic, rationalistic, and creative levels: for example, the idea that primitive man, who originally was promiscuous, was scared into caves by thunder which seemed to him to express the anger of the heavens, and in these caves developed monogamatic ties and morality. Hence, several writers have adopted the hypothesis that precisely as "Ulysses" represents a serio-comic reindividuation of the form of the "Odyssey," "Finnegans Wake" represents a serio-comic reindividuation of Vico's mould. And, taking this hypothesis in connection with certain other circumstances: (1) the timeless reality; (2) the title, which is derived from an Irish ballad celebrating Finnegan's fall and death-like trance till the word "whisky" restored him; and (3) the suggestion of sleeping and waking and the circumstance that the language suggests the operations of the mind during slumber under conditions of strain and discomfort—we arrive at the following conclusion. It is that in all likelihood *Finnegans Wake* represents sleep half-satirically conceived as a recapitulation of the process by which life organized itself and society developed; and particularly the action of the mind of a sleeping individual whose monogamitic inclinations are struggling to harmonize themselves with vagabond and ascetic ones. This would not prevent its being a half-tender and half-savagely blasphemous picture, much in Joyce's spirit, of human life as a drunken dream.

Yet in the face of the wit and mysterious poetry with which the book is strewn, and all the reasons for foreseeing its future greater intelligibility, we close it without a great feeling of enthusiasm. Livelier, more ingenious, and denser of verbal texture than Gertrude Stein's and Kenneth Burke's somewhat similar productions it distinctly is. The Jabberwocky-like "ballads of Perce Oreille" interspersed amid the prose are certainly delightful. But for all its evidences of Joyce's profound philology, his style lacks the strong root-feeling of the language. It is cold and cerebral in comparison with that of a veritable 'radical' like Gerard Manley Hopkins. The pressure of passion and driving necessity frequently seems absent. And too often we have the sense of repletion and a mark overshot.

FINNEGANS WAKE

by
James Joyce

1939
London: Faber & Faber Limited
New York: The Viking Press

Title page for Joyce's last work published in his lifetime

The Progress of Mr Joyce

The Times Literary Supplement, (6 May 1939): 265–266

Few, if any, books of our time have been so much discussed before publication as Mr. James Joyce's "Finnegans Wake"–the book which was described during its sixteen years of gestation as "Work in Progress." Here we were to have something even more Joycean than the Joyce of "Ulysses"–the quintessence, the *ne plus ultra* of that style and that method which have had so considerable an influence upon contemporary literature. Mr. Joyce is perhaps easily first among the literary innovators of to-day who have deliberately turned their backs on tradition in the conviction that life as it is honestly seen by perceptive minds to-day demands for its expression a new technique–in his case even a new vocabulary and a new grammar. For a generation to whose intellectuals it seemed inevitable that the poetic methods of Tennyson should give way to the methods of Mr. T. S. Eliot and later Mr. Auden, and that the drama which had passed quite easily from Pinero to Shaw should move on to Pirandello or Eugene O'Neill, it seemed equally necessary that fiction should find a new model in Mr. Joyce.

It has often been said of Mr. Joyce that he was a writer in revolt against the conditions that prevailed in his country–religious, social, intellectual. But that might equally have been said thirty years ago about Mr. Shaw or Mr. Wells, who have little in common with him. Revolt has no significance unless it has a positive and constructive side to it–and Mr. Shaw and Mr. Wells were concerned about social or moral reconstruction, which is utterly alien to Mr. Joyce's purpose in literature. On the contrary, "Finnegans Wake" shows him as almost savagely satisfied with the thrilling spectacle of life as he sees it in all its sordidness, its restless emotionalism, its inconsequence, its somnambulant absurdity. He does not desire to reform it, but to gratify his creative spirit in the expression of his impressions of it. His constructive purpose is to find a way satisfactory to himself of expressing the movement of life as he sees it, changing its texture and hue from moment to moment, a flux of sensations whose reality cannot be appreciated without a sense of the flux. To achieve his end he thinks it necessary to rid himself of traditional literary methods which, in his opinion, lend themselves to the very falsities of apprehension abjured by him. His task is that of expressionism in Croce's sense of the term–it consists on the creative side in the clarifying to himself of his own impressions of life, the intuitive shaping of the stream of ideas into a whole, and afterwards translating the inner expression into words.

Words–strange, violent, fabulous words–are his joy and his banc. It is in the process of translating his vision into language that Mr. Joyce becomes so baffling. It is not merely that he has introduced strange words into his vocabulary. Doughty, to some extent in "Arabia Deserta," and far more in "Dawn in Britain," faced his readers with the difficulties of an obsolete vocabulary and an unusual syntax. But in other respects his methods conformed to literary traditions—there was nothing revolutionary there—we felt ourselves getting nearer to and not farther from an ancient way of living. But Mr. Joyce has turned everything upside down. He has twisted ordinary words into something different merely because he seems to like them better in Jabberwockian form. Far-fetched literary, philosophical, journalistic, or music-hall references which have leapt into his mind thrust themselves into the middle of his nouns and adjectives. His language twists and turns with every vivid idea that interrupts his own thought and must needs be reproduced for the reader. The result is what the sur-realists appear to aim at—an uprush of words and images from the subconscious imagination—we hear shouts of laughter or lamentation, shrieks of gaiety and sorrow, low mutterings of reflection, explosions, yet all set down with a kind of cold-blooded matter-of-factness so far as the translator, namely the author, is concerned.

A sympathetic and patient reader can get stimulation and entertainment out of such literature. But he will only get from it a fraction of what was in Mr. Joyce's mind. There is only one person who can fully understand and appreciate this stupendous work, or can tell us truly how splendid it is or is not; and that person is Mr. Joyce himself. For in turning his back on the language of communication which we know and inventing a new language of expression he has presented insuperable obstacles to complete understanding. It is true, we are not required to understand in the sense that we could understand a logical thesis or a plain narrative. The comprehension asked of us is rather that with which we should expect to appreciate music, whose notes and chords do not profess to carry a precise meaning, yet in combination may produce in us both emotional and intellectual results. But even if we accept "Finnegans Wake" in this sense, it is still the case that the notation is unfamiliar, the scales alien. Mr. Joyce is of course abundantly justified if he is content with the satisfaction of art for art's sake, and a splendid audience of one. But in so far as he aims at communication—and why else publish a book?—how serious a drawback that he should require a method which interposes such barriers between his most appreciative readers and his own fertile mind.

Review of *Finnegans Wake*
Padraic Colum
The New York Times, 7 May 1939, pp. l, 14

How, in two thousand words or less, is one to review a book which even a cursory examination shows to be unprecedented, a book of considerable length by a thoughtful and tremendously equipped man who has spent sixteen years writing it? The only thing one can do is to indicate the value of the work and to show a way of approaching it with lessened perplexity. I say *lessened* perplexity, for a certain perplexity cannot wholly be removed from a reading of it and the present reviewer freely acknowledges that there is much in the book that he is still seeking explanation for.

Language, nothing less than the problem of conveying meaning through words, is the first term we have to discuss in connection with "Finnegans Wake." Let us get away from the book for a moment and begin by saying that writing today—I mean what can be described as imaginative writing—is dissociated from the value-making word: that is, it is writing, passing from the brain through the hand to the paper without ever coming out on the lips to be words that a man would say in passion or merriment. I am not speaking now of magazine writing, but of the writing of authors of status—John Galsworthy, for instance. As I write this sentence I see the title of a moving picture before me: it is "The Lone Ranger"; I think that there is more verbal creation in these words than in chapters of Galsworthy's. "Ranger" is a real word, holding a sense of distance, suggesting mountains; "lone" beside it makes the distance inner. There are great writers today who do not put us off with destitute words: Yeats's "The dolphin-torn, the gong-tormented sea" are value-making words.

The problem of the writer of today is to possess real words, not ectoplasmic words, and to know how to order them. They must move for him like pigeons in flight that make a shadow on the grass, not like corn popping. And so all serious writers of English today look to James Joyce, who has proved himself the most learned, the most subtle, the most thorough-going exponent of the value-making word. From his early days Joyce has exercised his imagination and intellect upon the significance of words, the ordering of words. We have the youth of "Portrait of the Artist as a Young Man" meditating upon a sentence he had read:

". . . A day of dappled seaborne clouds."

The phrase and the day and the scene harmonized in a chord. Words. Was it their colors? He allowed them to glow and fade, hue after hue: sunrise gold, the russet and green of apple orchards, azure of waves, the grayfringed fleece of clouds. No, it was not their colors: it was the poise and balance of the period itself.

Joyce approached the problem of the word not only as a writer but as a musician, a linguist, a man trained in acholastic philosophy in which definition and rigorous literalness are insisted on. And this concern with the word has brought him far as a literary technician. All writers are concerned with process, with trying to pass from what can be described to what can be activated. Most of us leave it at the stage of description. "He sat there and listened to the music"; "Sitting there, he listened to the music." So we write, but we know very well that this sort of writing gives us nothing of the process—a man responding to music. Joyce, in his later books anyway, wants to deal only with processes. In "Portrait of the Artist" some one looks at the algebraic signs on a blackboard: he writes of "the Morris dance" of these signs. In that phrase a historical process is presented: we have the activism of algebra, its Saracenic origin, the decline of the civilization it came out of to the point when Europe knew only its remnants as dancers and buffoons.

Accept what looks like Volapük on the pages, I would say to one who has got "Finnegans Wake," and turn to the last section in the first part, the section that begins "O tell me all about Anna Livia!" This section has been published and discussed; readers interested in literary development have an idea of what it is about. The reader who is not looking for usual connotations, for logical structure, can find something delightful here: he can experience the child's surprise at flowing water and all that goes on beside it:

> She sideslipped out by a gap in the Devil's glen while Sally, her nurse, was sound asleep in a sloot and, feefee fiefie, fell over a spillway before she found her stride and lay and wriggled in all the stagnant black pools of rainy under a fallow coo and she laughed innocfree with her limbs aloft and a whole drove of maiden hawthorns blushing and looking askance upon her.

It is about the Liffey, Dublin's river, Anna Livia. Anna Livia is also a woman; the women washing clothes on the banks are talking about her as a woman. It may entertain the reader who begins here casually to pick out the names of the world's rivers that are used in this narrative of Anna's bedding. "O, passmore that and oxus another!" Her ravisher is the man from overseas, the Viking founder of Dublin. "In a gabbard he barqued it, the boat of life, from the harbourless Ivernikan Okean, till he spied the loom

of her landfall and loosed two croakers from under the titilt, the gran Phenician rover." The croakers are the ravens of Odin; the Phenician suggests the hero Finn (who appears as Finnegan) as well as these first voyagers along the Atlantic, the Phoenicians. The story told in this episode is not local; it is the myth of river-civilizations. As the water flows night descends, death takes the place of life, the gossiping washerwomen are metamorphosed into a stone and a tree. And here we have a passage that has the evocativeness of music:

> A tale told of Shaun or Shem? All Livia's daughtersons. Dark hawks hear us. Night! Night! My ho head halls. I feel as heavy as yonder stone. Tell me of John or Shaun? Who were Shem and Shaun the living sons or daughters of? Night now! Tell me, tell me, tell me, tell me, elm. Night night. Tehmetale of stem or stone. Beside the rivering waters of, hitherandthithering waters of. Night!

On the tale of Anna Livia, the riverwoman, like flotsam and jetsam, are carried the names and deeds of remembered people, and histories and legends. A reading of this episode will give one, I think, a sense of Joyce's idiom and of the direction of this formidably original book.

The last chapter is about resurrection, the resurrection of the dead. Here let me inform the reader that the general idea of "Finnegans Wake" is in the philosophy of the seventeenth-century Italian Vico. History, according to Vico, goes from savagery to corruption which is death, and then to a new beginning: its figures are Polyphemus in his cave, Achilles on the battlefield, Caesar with his imperium, Nero playing the lyre and falling under the swords of his guards. Then the rude beginnings of a civilization. This last chapter is the one that I should recommend the inadequately instructed reader to turn to after the Anna Livia episode.

It begins with a sacred word three times repeated "Sandhyas! Sandhyas! Sandhyas!" Then, instead of the trumpet, we have the radio call:

> Calling all downs. Calling all downs to dayne. Array! Surrection. Eireweeker to the wohld bludyn world. O rally, O rally, O rally! Phlenxity, O rally! To what lifelike thyne of the bird can be. Seek you somany matters. Haze sea east to Osseania. Here!

"Dayne," of course, suggests daylight: also the Viking origin of the hero. One of his names is Earwicker, but the name of his country, Eire, is now inserted. "Phlenxity" suggests the phoenix, the bird of resurrection, and the mind is carried back to the fall of Earwicker, that occasion of sin that was in a garden in the Phoenix Park. The book ends:

My leaves have drifted from me. All. But one clings still. I'll bear it on me. To remind me of. Lff. So soft this morning ours. Yes. Carry me along, taddy, like you done through the toy fair. If I seen him bearing down on me under whitespread wings like he'd come from Arkangels, I sink I'd die down over his feet, humbly, dumbly, only to washup. Yes, tid. There's where. First. We pass through grass behush and bush to. Wish! A gull. Gulls. Far calls. Coming, far! End here. Us then. Finn, again! Take bussofthee, mememoree! Till thousandsthee. Lps. The keys to. Given! A way a lone a loved a long the.

"Lff," I take it, is Lif out of Eddas who survives Ragnarok and begins again the cycle of history. The keys suggest St. Peter. "Me" and "memories" are contained in the idea of the resurrection of the body. But why, it will be asked, has James Joyce to manufacture words of this sort, and who, in the name of Finnegan, are the people in his book?

Perhaps this is the place for me to insert two glosses of my own. Where I grew up in Ireland there were several boys who had uncles whose name was Manus. For many years I had the notion that the name was exclusively avuncular, that it was the property of the uncles. Then I learned that the Irish Manus was taken from the Scandinavian Magnus: thereupon a portion of Irish-Scandinavian history became real and present for me. Later I learned that the Scandinavian Magnus was from Carlus Magnus, Charlemagne, and the Carlovingian Empire became dimly seen, heard, felt, personified in some way; something remained of it in villages I knew, and the expression of that something would add to the present content of literature. To express it one would have to use words which, belonging to the present, could at the same time evoke the past.

Again, I got into a train, say, at Buffalo: men, women and children are in the coaches, reading, dozing, looking on the scenes they pass; I do not know where they come from or where they are going to. For a moment they are abstract human beings. One feels them as neither acting nor acted upon. But to evoke this feeling of actlessness one would have to form a language that would be removed from normal language which is about actions. In a minute, of course, one personalizes them, discovering that this is a salesman and the other is a teacher going to Florida. All the same, each has a life that cannot be expressed in the language of action; all the same, each has a life that has been molded by the mountain and the river, by Polyphemus, Achilles, Caesar and Nero.

Well, cursorily speaking, this is what "Finnegans Wake" is about. It is history made present through these vasty figures who sum up the race, who are also the mountain and the river of the land. The figures are not representational but are like figures in a tapestry that emerge, merge with each other and with natural objects. One sees Tristan become the Duke of Wellington, or St. Patrick. Anna Livia becomes Swift's Vanessa. The title of the book is from an Irish-American vaudeville song. It was a song about a hod-carrier who fell off his wall, who was thought to be dead, who was given a wake, and who, at the mention of whisky, resurrected himself. But the name Finnegan is the same as that of the national hero, Finn MacCool. And Finn means "the fair-haired" and so might stand for all Nordic heroes.

He has fallen like Adam and like Humpty-Dumpty; he is accused of a crime that is said to have taken place in a garden, in Phoenix (for the purpose of the charge, Fiendish Park); he justifies himself by telling how he created a civilization for his Anna Livia. He is the boss-man in any situation and so he can be referred to as Adam or the Duke of Wellington or Daniel O'Connell. His woman is the river, but she is also the Little Annie Rooney of the song. And the man is Earwicker, but he is most often written of as H. C. E. or Here Comes Everybody. His sons as Shem the Penman and Jaunty Jaun; they are also Cain and Abel, the angel Michael and Satan.

Having read the Anna Livia episode and the Resurrection episode, the reader knows enough of the idiom and the plan to begin with the first chapter. Even if he does not understand all that is on any one page he will find sentences lovely in their freshness and their beauty and sentences that one can chuckle over for months. We have novels that give us greatly a three dimensional world: here is a narrative that gives a new dimension.

A journalist, a magazine editor, and a novelist, Malcolm Muggeridge was a controversial critic, the author of The Sun Never Sets: The Story of England in the Nineteen Thirties *(1940).*

Review of *Finnegans Wake*
Malcolm Muggeridge
Time and Tide, 20 May 1939, pp. 654–656

Mr. James Joyce's *Finnegans Wake* faces the reviewer with peculiar difficulties. In the first place he cannot read it, only battle through a page or so at a time without pleasure or profit. This would not, in itself, matter so much; but he does not know what the book is about. The dust-cover, which might be expected to help, says nothing except that *Finnegans Wake* has taken sixteen years to write, that it has been "more talked about and written about during the period of its composition than any

Joyce was on the cover of Time *again in 8 May 1939. In the article, it is pointed out that Nathaniel Hawthorne, more than one-hundred years before* Finnegans Wake, *wrote down in his notebook his idea for a work similar to Joyce's: "To write a dream which shall resemble the real course of a dream, with all its inconsistency, its strange tranformations . . . with nevertheless a leading idea running through the whole. Up to this old age of the world, no such thing has ever been written."*
(*photograph by Giselle Freund; TimePix*)

previous work of English literature," and that it would inevitably be "the most important event of any season in which it appeared." Previous works of English literature which have been talked and written about during the period of their composition, are not specified. Beyond arousing a faint curiosity as to what they may be, the effect of the dust-cover is negative.

Thus defeated by book and blurb, it is natural to cast a surreptitious eye at what other reviewers have had to say. Here, too, the result is disappointing. They have all hedged, except perhaps Mr. Gogarty, who pronounces the book "the most colossal leg-pull in literature since McPherson's *Ossian,*" and explains it as being Mr. Joyce's revenge for past neglect–if so surely a somewhat laborious one. The usual line is that Mr. Joyce is a great writer, that for reasons best known to himself he has evolved a curious way of writing which bears little

resemblance to the English language as commonly used, that so painstaking an effort is not to be dismissed out of hand, and that in any case gramophone records of passages from *Finnegans Wake* recited by Mr. Joyce have been found by competent persons to be delectable.

If *Finnegans Wake* had been published in the form of gramophone records, these would, presumably, have been sent to musical critics, who would than have given their opinion of the sound they produced when played. As, however, it has been published as a book, with printed, numbered pages like any other, and intended to be read, the excellence or otherwise of gramophone records made from it and reproducing the author's perhaps finely modulated voice, seems neither here nor there.

Considered as a book, and considering the object of a book to be by means of written symbols to convey the author's emotions or thoughts to the reader, *Finnegans Wake* must be pronounced a complete fiasco. Such a word as "bababadalgharaghtakamminarronnkonn-bronntonnerronntuonnthunntrovarrhounawnskawntoo-hoohoordenenthurnuk!" is not merely senseless, it is absurd. How many mornings Mr. Joyce devoted to coining this particular word, I do not know; perhaps it only took him one morning, or just an hour or so; but in any case he was wasting his time as surely as, more surely than, a village idiot trying to catch a sunbeam.

Idiocy has its charm; the distracted utterances of a dislocated mind seem to bear some relation to one another, to suggest a dim coherence like a faded picture; "Come o'er the bourn, Bessy to me," or, "Pillicock sat on Pillicock-hill," have an odd poignancy, relevance even, when poor Tom says them, but only because he was supposed to be mad. Imagine a sane Poor Tom, imagine him arriving at

> Still through the hawthorn blows the cold wind;
> Says suum, mun, ha, no, nonny.
> Dolphin my boy, my boy, sessa ! let him trot by.

after sixteen laborious years, and that is *Finnegans Wake.*

To discover coherence in incoherence, form in formlessness, light in darkness, has been an everlasting pursuit. Mr. Joyce has reversed the process, look-

> The end of [*Finnegans Wake*], like the end of *Ulysses,* is the best part of it, and no one can read it . . . without receiving an impression of a strange sorrow and mourning over life. It is curiously simple and direct.
>
> Edwin Muir, review of *Finnegans Wake*
> *Listener,* 21 (11 May 1939): 1013

ing for incoherence in coherence, formlessness in form, darkness in light. Words instead of straining to contain what has been dimly understood, to signify truth, strain to confuse. They desert experience and understanding, and signify only chaos, in the process inevitably disintegrating, ceasing to be words at all. Language which emerged from confused, meaningless sound, returns to its origins–painstakingly, laboriously returns, taking sixteen years over the process.

Here and there in *Finnegans Wake,* it is true, a mood may be sensed, an association of images or of words detected; but these are occasional flashes of coherence in an ocean of incoherence; mistakes, it almost seems, failures in Mr. Joyce's method. The effect of the whole is of impenetrable and despairing darkness–

> The logos of somewome to that base anything, when most characteristically mantissa minus, comes to nullum in the endth: orso, here is nowet badder than the sin of Aha with his cosin Lil, verswayed on coverswised, and all that's consecants and contangincies till Perperp stops repippinghim since her redtangles are all abscissan for limitsing this tendency of our Frivulteeny Sexuagesima to expense herselfs as sphere as possible, paradismic perimutter, in all directions on the bend of the unbridalled, the infinisissimals of her facets manier and manier . . .

That the creator of Bloom in *Ulysses* should end by writing such gibberish, a kind of erudite baby-talk is a striking example of the necessity in a writer, however talented, of a unifying view of life if his imagination is to continue to be productive. Life washes round us, turbulent, incomprehensible; and up to a point it is possible to accept its turbulence and incomprehensibility. Why, after all, should there be any unity, any oneness? Why not just a chaos, chaotic waves inanely lapping round each chaotic soul? Then there comes a point when such a view is insupportable. It cannot be–passion starting up and dying down, life starting up and dying down, as aimlessly as Vesuvius. When this point is reached, either some integrating principle must be found, or defeat must be accepted. Defeat means escaping from reality, some form or other of falsification–Let there be darkness! instead of, Let there be light! Among the many forms this cry–Let there be darkness!–has taken in a time when it is particularly prevalent, posterity will note as one of the strangest Mr. Joyce's successful essay in incomprehensibility, running to 628 pages, and entitled for no apparent reason *Finnegans Wake.*

Brooklyn-born writer, critic, and memoirist, Kazin at the age of twenty-seven wrote a landmark study of modern American fiction, On Native Grounds: An Interpretation of Modern American Prose Literature *(1942). In* The Inmost Leaf: A Selection of Essays *(1955) Kazin celebrated Joyce for being "an outlaw to the very end."*

Review of *Finnegans Wake*
Alfred Kazin
New York Herald Tribune, 21 May 1939, p. 4

Finnegans Wake is James Joyce's fourth book of fiction, and the first in which he does not formally appear as a character. Whether as the boyish 'I' who peers through the first stories in *Dubliners,* or the gangling, desperately proud Stephen Dedalus who bestrides *A Portrait of the Artist as a Young Man* and *Ulysses,* Joyce has played the paramount role in his own fiction. In a very real sense his books have been the saga of James Joyce; they have offered a confession, staggering in its concentrated intensity of the mind of Stephen Dedalus as agonist and lay priest, intellectual and lover, infidel and poet.

All writers, we say, are conditioned by their youth; they get their subject from youth's grievance, Joyce has been obsessed by his youth to the exclusion of all else. The world has always been for him the Ireland he has not seen for thirty years; God has always been the cultivated, inexorable, rather sadly remote God who presides over the Dublin intelligentsia. His subject has always been the Dublin of 1900–10; the people he knew in it, the superstitions and aspirations they shared, his universe. He has turned round and round in that universe as Dante suffered in the sight of God. Like the great Catholic spirits of the Middle Ages, Joyce has accepted the common experience of mankind as an abstraction. It is something he has known and pondered by instinct, a symbol among the paraphernalia of man's fate.

Alone among the artists of our time, therefore, perhaps alone in Europe since Beethoven wrote those last quartets that climax man's quarrel with life, Joyce has slowly and with relentless patience assumed the overpowering importance of his soul and written as if the world were well lost for art. Through blindness, war, poverty, neglect, the cackling of those who do not understand, Joyce has followed his *métier.* Yet remarkable as his accomplishment has been, the terrifying isolation that has made him the writer he is seems today even more significant. For it has brought him, through one of those cycles that spell the biography of genius, from the longings of *Dubliners,* the limpid beauty of *Portrait of the Artist as a Young Man,* the herculean comedy of *Ulysses,* to the nightmare of darkness and immolation. That is *Finnegans Wake.*

No one has yet described *Finnegans Wake*. What we have had is an effort to fix the intention of the work, and none of the many interpretations and essays in Joycean exegesis that I have seen has gone beyond the rudimentary summary Edmund Wilson offered eight years ago in *Axel's Castle*. We know that the book presents a Dublin night, as *Ulysses* presents a Dublin day. The hero is a Norwegian living in Dublin, Humphrey Chimpden Earwicker (H.C.E., or Here Comes Everybody), who has been at various times a postman, a worker in Guinness's Brewery, an assistant in a shop. He is married and the father of several children, but he has been carrying on a flirtation with a girl named Anna Livia. As the book opens ('riverrun, past Eve and Adam's from swerve of shore to pen of bay, brings us by a commodius vicus of recirculation back to Howth Castle and Environs'), he is slowly falling asleep, and the great dream that is *Finnegans Wake* begins.

Now Joyce has tried not to describe the dream, but to present it. The conscious will is not only to capture the unconscious, but it is to anatomize it. Sleep is a great marsh of conscience, of desire; it is a corridor of fear in which men utter the words that were never spoken, resolve the hopes that were never offered. The sleeper is always alone, and though he may not figure in his dream, life spills out in his mind in a staggering and frightful confusion. A song may turn into a woman's face, an enemy assume the devil's horns. For Joyce sleep has no relation to time or space; it is a great void into which the names, the places, the objects, the associations, the tricks and caprices of mind, the whole stalking phantasmagoria of consciousness, filter through. It is as if a God were looking at life not as a chapter in history, or as a tableau of conduct, but as something stupendous in its disorganization, a clutching of many hands, a blind and mangled effort to rise from the slime, the great desire to assume identity.

But with this, Joyce (and this, I think, is the central drive of the book) has made of sleep an instrument of satire. Sleep not only reverses normal daily consciousness; it mocks it. Just as a child who has been cruelly hurt by some elder will dream of conquest and revenge, so for the mature mind sleep is the assertion of its dignity. The dream may often seem distorted, and even more agonizing than life, but it is a disordered formulation of the desire for order. In Earwicker's sleep, life becomes not only astonishingly fluid, but brilliantly free. The will has full dominion; what has been restrained by law or shamed by custom suddenly breaks loose. There are no longer any castes, any bars; there is, above all, no conscious morality.

So Earwicker, dreaming of Phoenix Park in Dublin (where he made love to Anna Livia), is thrown into a world in which Wellington leaps out of his statue, the sol-

diers' monuments are dissolved into an army of fusiliers, the clothes he was wearing turn into goat and sheep skin, the desire for Anna Livia, the shame at desiring Anna Livia, is spun into a whirling carnival of fear and exaltation. For a moment the sleep rouses, sleep is shaken off, the language is stilted, legal, chill ('a baser meaning has been read into these characters the literal sense of which decency can safely scarcely hint'); but then the tempo slackens, sleep has taken possession again, the dream returns to that crucial evening in Phoenix Park. Earwicker's longing at this moment is to justify himself; it is not true, one hears him saying, he did nothing wrong. But the dream has confused the dreamer; fusiliers and Anna Livia are interchanged; the intervals of sense are blended. Thus we read: 'He lay at one time under the ludicrous imputation of annoying Welsh fusiliers in the people's park. Hay, hay, hay! Hoq, hoq, hoq! Faun and Flora on the lea love that little old joq. To any one who knew and loved the Christlikeness of the big clean minded giant H. C. Earwicker throughout his excellency's long vice-freegal existence the mere suggestion of him as a lust sleuth nosing for trouble in a boobytrap rings particularly preposterous.'

But how, you will ask, can Joyce know a dream? The answer, of course, is that he can't. In reality *Finnegans Wake* is a stupendous improvisation, a great pun. Even in sleep one cannot imagine an Irish-Norwegian brewer remembering words in a language he has never read, perhaps never heard. Yet Joyce sprinkles the book with agglomerations out of seventeen or eighteen languages. When we read 'quidam, if he did not exist it would be necessary quoniam to invent him,' the brilliant play on Voltaire's aphorism has no relation to Earwicker's conscious or unconscious experience. It is the sleep, in truth, not of one man, but of a drowsing humanity. All cultures have relation to it, all minds, all languages nourish its night speech. The brilliance of Joyce's display can seem almost too resplendent; we feel ourselves in the presence of a nature so superior in kind that the effect is blinding. Words take on dozens of associations, all equally firm, real, clever; the punning becomes a galvanic needle on the sloth and fat of conventional language and thinking.

But what, I ask you, are you going to do with 'As the lion in our teargarten remembers the nenuphar of his Nile (shall Ariuz forget Arioun or Boghas the baregams of the Marmarazalles from Marmeniere?). It may be, tots wearsense full a naggin twentyg have sigilposted what. . . .' Or that wonderful word on page 3, two lines long, which begins 'bababadalgharaghtakamminarronnonkonnbronntonner,' etc? As one tortures one's way through *Finnegans Wake,* an impression grows that Joyce has lost his hold on human life. Obsessed by a spaceless and timeless void, he has outrun himself. We begin to feel that his very freedom to say anything has become a compulsion to say nothing. He is not speculating on anything man may possibly know; he has created a world of his own, that night world in which all men are masters and all men dupes, and he has lost his way in it. For extraordinary a feat of language and insight and learning as *Finnegnas Wake* is, what may we expect to follow it? The denigration has been too complete; after this twisting, howling, stumbling murk, language so convulsed, meaning so emptied, there is nothing. This is night and this is sleep; and there is also the day. For it is always frightening to remember that sleep is an approximation of death.

While professing admiration for Joyce, the English poet and novelist Richard Aldington believes that Joyce has gone too far into his own mind to be accessible to the reader.

Review of *Finnegans Wake*

Richard Aldington

The Atlantic Monthly, 163 (June 1939): n.p.

Mr. James Joyce is an author whose work must be approached with respect. *A Portrait of the Artist* was a great advance on *Dubliners,* but all his previous work was eclipsed by *Ulysses*, one of the most remarkable literary achievements of this century.

Finnegans Wake has been in progress for seventeen years, and at least four excerpts from it have been previously published. Readers have thus had time to make themselves familiar with the peculiar style Mr. Joyce has seen fit to adopt. And if these fragments seemed meaningless, there was at least a hope that the complete work would prove otherwise. Common honesty compels this reviewer to state that he is unable to explain either the subject or the meaning (if any) of Mr. Joyce's book; and that, having spent several hours a day for more than a fortnight in wretched toil over these 628 pages, he has no intention of wasting one more minute of precious life over Mr. Joyce's futile inventions, tedious ingenuities, and verbal freaks.

Such a book is either impudent or insolent; impudent, if it is merely an elaborate hoax; insolent, if it is serious and the author really thinks that the world has either time or inclination to master a new system of Jabberwock English merely to read one book.

The problem of *what* Mr. Joyce has to say in *Finnegans Wake* may be left to those who have time and energy to waste. The reader who takes up this book for the first time will at once be involved into the problem of *how* he says it. Mr. Joyce claims that he understands and can explain every syllable of the book. Doubtless, but who cares? Readers are not interested in what the author's words mean to him, but in what they mean to them. And what Mr. Joyce has written is 628 pages of pedantic nonsense. Prodigious toil and a wonderful mind have been wasted on the production of this book, which is Balzac's unknown masterpiece of words. It consists of enormous wodges of 'portmanteau words'—there is one sentence (pages 126–139) over 400 lines long—of Jabberwock words, involving punning plays on proverbs, popular sayings, clichés, nursery rhymes, slang, quotations and allusions, pigeon English, alliterative jingles, slang, foreign languages, and honorificabilitudinitatibus words. This heavy compost is frequently infected with that lecherous suggestiveness of which Mr. Joyce is a master, which was defended in *Ulysses* as germane to the characters, but which here seems to have no purpose more interesting than the author's morose delectation.

Finnegan 'lived in the broadest way immarginable in his rushlit toofarback for messuages before joshuan judges had given us numbers or Helveticus committed deuteronomy. . . .' 'Margin,' you see is telescoped with 'imaginable,' 'Leviticus' with 'Helvetius,' and so on. Who cares? Sometimes the puns are agonizing, as Willingdone's (Wellington's) 'pulluponeasyan wartrews'—i.e., Peloponnesian War trews.

Let it be well understood that these are not awkward bits picked out with mean intent, but that the whole book is written in this—must it be called?—style.

Alice in Wonderland definitions: e.g., 'brandnewburger,' page 265. Footnote: 'A viking vernacular expression still used in Summerhill district for a jerryhatted man of forty who puts two fingers into his boiling souplate and licks them in turn to find out if there is enough mushroom catsup in the mutton broth.' Verb sap.

Alliterative jingles: page 250. 'Lel lols for libelman libling his lore. Lolo Lolo liēbermann you loved to be leaving Libnius. . . .' So what?

Nursery rhymes: page 511.

Pretty polysyllables: page 1. 'Bababadalgharaghtakamminarronnkonnbronntonnerronn tuonnthunntrovarrhounawnskawntoohoohooordenenthurnuk!' (Accuracy of spelling not guaranteed.)

Such are the main ingredients of this ghastly stodge, repeated over and over again. The boredom endured in the penance of reading this book is something one would not inflict on any human being, but far be it from me to discourage any reader who prefers to use a perfectly good five-dollar bill to buy *Finnegans Wake* rather than to light a cigarette with it. (The latter course will give more lasting satisfaction.)

Translated into native Tasmanian, this book should have a well deserved sale.

Review of *Finnegans Wake*
The Irish Times, 3 June 1939, p. 7

The writing of "Finnegans Wake" took sixteen years, short enough, perhaps, beside the stretch of time that could be spent in trying to understand it. For it must be said at once that this way, at least, Mr. Joyce gives full measure to the reader. Nothing moves, or appears or is said as ever before in any book. It is endlessly exciting in its impenetrability. Beside it even his own "Ulysses" is simplicity itself. Around that work a vast and still uncompleted literature of explanation has grown up, which has made its author a legend that even "Finnegans Wake" may not diminish. He will continue to enjoy his sheltered existence in the region of the unknown; for the attempts to explain "Finnegan," which are sure to come, are likely to do nothing more than add to the mystery of Mr. Joyce.

The work is described as a novel, and, although in their essence all the stories of the world may be there, there is no single story that one can grasp. It may be a novel to end novels; for, if there is shape at all, it is the shape of a superb annihilation as—of some gigantic thing let loose to destroy what we had come to regard as a not unnecessary part of civilisation. One feels its power, the kind of gleaming genius behind it, but no communication of anything is achieved, perhaps simply because it is just not intended.

Quotation Unavailing

One way of attempting to give a sense of its indefinable quality would be to quote passages which seem, after much pondering of them, to have a meaning and some relation to a plan. But on second thoughts it becomes clear that this method would not help; for, although such passages would be part of the whole of the book, they would not be part of any whole that the book contains, since it is compact only of chaos and the shape of things all smashed and gone. There are moments of beauty, the measured sounds of lyrical prose which beat upon the ear, but which do not come into the understanding and always an airy gesture beyond the words which make it, as if Mr. Joyce had greatly enjoyed doing all this despite the torture of sixteen years' labour that it took. Yet pleasure never altogether reaches to the reader; he is faced with an acute bewilderment from the beginning, which is no beginning, to the end, which is no end.

The Convolutions of a Dream

And what of the middle portion of this work of art? There is no middle either. It passes in one night,

and the significance of night is upon it. It is the endless folding and unfolding of a dream. It makes its own space in which to have unlimited freedom to complicate itself. It is something alive only in its sleep, and from it comes a muttering beneath hundreds of thousands of subconscious words. The life that can leap from a page is never here, but there is another kind of energy, a fierce fluency which becomes a mockery of itself. There is the author's curious erudition at work upon a vast vocabulary, beating words out of their accustomed shapes into a flux which envelops the reader, who, used to other ways of writing, finds himself resenting this power to bewilder him.

The reader begins to reject constructively the formlessness which is all around him; he tries to find a way out, to relate to some kind of plan of his own, even one of these embedded pages. There are lingering lovely passages like flickers of gold. By following the small light they give there may be real illumination a little further on. But the light fails, and he is left to wander round and round in the maze.

The Author's Game

The author appears to be doing something which has no relation to the reader of a work of fiction; nothing coherent comes out of all these words; it is a game which only Mr. Joyce can play, for he alone knows the rules, if there are any. He will take a word and twist and turn it, and chase it up and down through every language that he knows—English, French, German, Gaelic, Latin, Greek, Dutch, Sanscrit, Esperante. The sounds of words in infinite variety fascinate him.

One thinks of an arrangement of sounds, of music, and gropes towards another kind of clue, feeling that an emotional effect may be produced and an appeal to the imagination achieved by reading bits of it aloud to oneself, a method for which the Dublin accent has been recommended. But this second method of approach also has only a momentary success. One has been trying to make meaning with the sounds, but it has died away, for there was no logical sequence in the words which made them. Time and space and identity as we have known them are here no more.

To What Purpose?

Detaching oneself from the book one tries to come to grips with the purpose of Mr. Joyce in writing "Finnegans Wake," for there must have been some purpose behind all those sixteen years of labour. It can be only one of two things. It can be that he was engaged all that time on the compilation of a new and wonderful work on English, and that his notion of giving it the semblance of a form which baffles us, permits him to try out the results of his experiments with words without coming too close to the form of a dictionary of outlandish usage. He is learned and subtle in the ways of words, and he may have considered it necessary to do this service for the language, so as to release it from the clogging effects of conventional accumulation and its tyranny over mind in the constriction which it has reached. Or he may have thought of taking up the duty neglected by the academicians of adjusting language generally to the new speeds of earth and air.

Thus, we may be face to face in "Finnegans Wake" with one of the great milestones of literature, and in this book a new language may have been born. If so, it will be necessary to learn it for ourselves without assistance, because to ask Mr. Joyce for a key to it would be to ask him to surrender all claims for "Finnegans Wake" to be considered a work of art. As such, this is its chosen expression. We may come to learn the language only by first realising what the book is about. And that is where Mr. Joyce has the advantage over the reader.

The "Gigantic Hoax" Theory

This is one conception of "Finnegans's Wake," but there is another which, unfortunately, is perilously on the edge of what already has been suggested as an explanation of the work–that it is simply a gigantic hoax which it has taken sixteen years to perpetrate, and this alternative viewpoint, or suspicion, arises because one finds in the book such an undercurrent of the Dublin material already employed in "Ulysses."

It was in Dublin that Mr. Joyce learned how to let language run away with him in an attempt to set down the only life he has ever come to know. It would seem that every sight and sound and word of Dublin must go on releasing itself as in a river of memory flowing, and that every device of language must be employed to get the immense joke that it is for him out of his consciousness. To name but a few of these we have rhyming slang, analogical formation, onomatopoeia, puns in seven languages, spoonerisms, mergers, echoes and a great deal of pure nonsense; but the essential material of all, no matter what language they may flow into or out of, is Dublin.

A Dublin Flood

The slang and speech of Dublin are everything to him. His obsession could conceivably be made the starting point of an attempt to recover English to livelier expression, but the experiment here seems to lack the necessary enlargement of a theme. It continually turns back upon itself, suggesting nothing bigger, for all its bulk and torrential flow by times, than the inescapable quality of the Dublin that Mr. Joyce has made for himself. His is as one submerged by his material, and not even "silence, exile and cunning" have given him escape.

In the second view the book would appear to be a mere tortured piece of self-analysis and as something in the nature of a private document, laboriously penned for the author's amusement possibly, but not for the public gaze. It would be better in that case that it should be taken as having no meaning beyond what it may hold for Mr. Joyce himself, and that it should not be regarded as anything so serious as an attempt to destroy the medium of rational expression, since here, to begin with, there was nothing to express, the author having come to complete fatigue in creativeness.

The extent to which "Finnegans Wake" may begin to influence the English language will be the measure of its reality and the only proper test of its importance. The writer may come to it to dig for words amidst the ruins of the novel, but the form of "Ulysses" and the content of it which could be imitated are not here. This book could be imitated only by Mr. Joyce himself. It may appear, therefore, in the ultimate view, that, although after "Ulysses" he had no more to say, in "Finnegans Wake" he went on saying it.

In her Life and Literature *column, Mary Colum discussed several books, including* Finnegans Wake *and Pearl Buck's* The Chinese Novel. *She began her review, "It would be difficult to find two ideals of novel writing more opposed to each other than those represented in Joyce's* Finnegan's Wake *and Mrs. Buck's theorizing on the Chinese novel."*

The Old and the New
Mary M. Colum
The Forum and Century, 102 (October 1939): 158, 163

. . . Joyce's *Finnegans Wake* represents, for good or for ill, the very last word, up to the present and maybe for a long time in the future, in the development of the novel. It is a step further in the revelation, in the understanding of Man the Unknown, the most unknown creature in the universe, than any we have had up to the present.

Finnegans Wake will be read by people who have an avid interest in what goes on in the mind and the emotions; it will be read by people interested in the renewal of language, in the sounds of language, and in the fantastic, unexpected word and idea associations that take place in the mind; it will be read by

> Such a book as *Finnegans Wake* is a natural and logical development from the theories and productions of the French poet, Arthur Rimbaud.
>
> – Mary Colum, "The Old and the New," p. 162

people interested in such things as the racial mind and the racial experience. But it will be read especially by those who have followed the way literature has been going for the past seventy years, for it represents the perfectly logical development of that way, and its influence will stretch far beyond the narrow circle of those who read the book. But I do not believe that that narrow circle will embrace more than a couple of thousand or that a single one of them will comprehend it totally—except, perhaps, some lonely and persistent reader on the banks of the Liffey who can retire indefinitely to an attic with a bottle of whisky under one arm and a musical instrument of some kind under the other, to read of and ponder on an Earwicker who is himself and who contains all the past and future that is in himself.

Finnegans Wake is the revelation of the goings on in that part of the mind which contains the raw and confused materials of consciousness, and the events of the whole book take place in the minds of people who are in a state of dream, whether sleeping or waking. As we spend at least one third of our lives in sleep and over two thirds of it in some state of dream, it is fitting that some writer should devote himself to exploring what takes place in our minds and emotions during those periods; it is fitting, if we are to give any allegiance to the modern conception of literature as an attempt to portray the whole of man.

. . . .

At the end of her article, Colum's discussion of Enid Starkie's biography Arthur Rimbaud *brings her back to Joyce's work.*

DREAMS INTO WORDS

The vision of America that is in "Le Bateau Ivre" was shared by many imaginative Europeans; something of it is in the preface to Eugene Jolas' *I Have Seen Monsters and Angels:*

> I would suddenly find myself catapulted into an incredible dream-America, a real-unreal ambiance. . . . Influenced by my reading of the lives and adventures of Columbus, Cortez, Pizzaro, I saw myself the

Joyce, circa 1940 (photograph by Man Ray; Library of Congress, Prints and Photographs Division [LC-USZ62-41466])

leader of a great army that succeeded after heroic battles in defeating enemy hordes on the Pan-American continent.

Eugene Jolas, as a good disciple of the author of *Finnegan's Wake,* as a good disciple of Rimbaud, believes that dreams, waking or sleeping, have a prophetic significance.

> The word-or-object symbols of the dream reproduce the conflict between the lower and the higher forces. The clash between the irrational forces of the past and the cosmological forces of the future can be seen in the new sense of time which the night life reveals to us.

Now the difference between the old and the very modern literature is precisely in this concern with time—this modern concern which has obsessed the philosophers as well as the poets and the novelists. This new formulation of time and the significance of dream brings me back to *Finnegan's Wake.* But I have to confess that, like every other reader of the book, I do not yet completely comprehend it. If there are enough readers of this department interested, I will return to it in a later article, when I know more about it.

Illness and Death

By the end of December 1939, the Joyces moved from Paris to Saint-Gérand-le-Puy, a small village near Vichy, where they stayed for a year before departing for neutral Switzerland. With his wife, Nora, son, and grandson, Joyce arrived in Zurich in mid December 1940. Joyce's daughter, Lucia, was not able to travel with them; she was being treated for mental illness in Pornichet in Brittany. About three weeks after their arrival in Zurich, Joyce was suddenly hospitalized on 10 January 1941 with acute abdominal pains. The next day, he was operated on for a perforated duodenal ulcer. Although the operation appeared to be successful, Joyce died on 13 January 1941, just a few weeks short of his fifty-ninth birthday. He is buried in Fluntern Cemetery near the zoological gardens just outside of Zurich. Nora Joyce died on 10 April 1951 and is buried beside him. In 1981 Milton Hebald's sculpture of Joyce smoking a cigarette with legs crossed was dedicated at the present grave site.

Obituaries about Joyce, including those written for The New York Times *and* New York Herald Tribune, *often acknowledged his achievement in* Ulysses *while overlooking the significance of* Finnegans Wake.

James Joyce Dies; Wrote 'Ulysses'
The New York Times, 13 January 1941

Irish Author of Book Banned
for Years Here and in England
Stricken in Zurich at 58

LITERARY INFLUENCE WIDE

Scholar and Innovator Hailed
and Attacked for Odd Style
and 'New Language'

ZURICH, Switzerland, Monday, Jan. 13 (AP)— James Joyce, Irish author whose "Ulysses" was the center of one of the most bitter literary controversies of modern times, died in a hospital here early today despite the efforts of doctors to save him by blood transfusions. He would have been 59 years old Feb. 2.

Joyce underwent an intestinal operation Saturday afternoon at the Schwesternhaus von Rotenkreuz Hospital. For a time he appeared to be recovering. Only yesterday his son reported him to have been cheerful and apparently out of danger.

Joyce in Switzerland near the end of his life (Collection of Dr. Giedion and Carola Gideon-Welcker)

In "How to Read Finnegans Wake," an article published in the November/December 1940 issue of New Horizons, *Walter Rybert offers advice.*

The first requirement in reading *Finnegans Wake* is a revision in reading habits. Be "given time to read" is one, or "take it easy." It can't be done while hanging on a strap or sitting in a railway station. You've got to be where you won't be ashamed to laugh out loud, murmur "ah!" or satisfy the desire to read something of what you've just discovered to an appreciative listener, preferably feminine. An easy chair, nothing else will do, are essentials. A pint of grog will be helpful.

During the afternoon, however, the writer suffered a sudden relapse and sank rapidly. He died at 2:15 A. M. (8:15 P. M., Eastern standard time.)

His wife and son were at the hospital when he died.

Hailed and Belittled by Critics

The status of James Joyce as a writer never could be determined in his lifetime. In the opinion of some critics, notably Edmund Wilson, he deserved to rank with the great innovators of literature as one whose influence upon other writers of his time was incalculable. On the other hand, there were critics like Max Eastman who gave him a place with Gertrude Stein and T. S. Eliot among the "Unintelligibles" and there was Professor Irving Babbitt of Harvard who dismissed his most widely read novel, 'Ulysses," as one which only could have been written "in an advanced stage of psychic disintegration."

Originally published in 1922, "Ulysses" was not legally available in the United States until eleven years later, when United States Judge John Munro Woolsey handed down his famous decision to the effect that the book was not obscene. Hitherto the book had been smuggled in and sold at high prices by "bookleggers" and a violent critical battle had raged around it.

Judge Woolsey's Decision

"'Ulysses' is not an easy book to read or understand," Judge Woolsey wrote. "But there has been much written about it, and in order properly to approach the consideration of it it is advisable to read a number of other books which have now become its satellites. The study of 'Ulysses' is therefore a heavy task.

"The reputation of 'Ulysses' in the literary world, however, warranted my taking such time as was necessary to enable me to satisfy myself as to the intent with which the book was written, for, of course, in any case where a book is claimed to be obscene it must first be determined whether the intent with which it was written was what is called, according to the usual phrase, pornographic, that is, written for the purpose of exploiting obscenity.

"If the conclusion is that the book is pornographic that is the end of the inquiry . . . but in 'Ulysses,' in spite of its unusual frankness, I do not detect anywhere the leer of the sensualist. I hold, therefore, that it is not pornographic."

On the passages dealing with sex, Judge Woolsey paused to remark that the reader must not forget that "the characters are Celtic and the time is Spring." His decision was hailed as one of the most civilized ever pro-

pounded by an American judge. After he had admitted "Ulysses" to the country, there was a rush to buy the almost immediately available authorized and uncensored edition published by Random House. Since then the book, unlike many another once banned by the censor and then forgotten, has been read widely; less for the passages once objected to then for the book as a whole.

Although Joyce appeared in many of his writings, notably "A Portrait of the Artist as a Young Man" and "Ulysses," as Stephen Dedalus, many details of his life are missing. The most comprehensive study is Herbert Gorman's biography published in 1940.

Was Born in Dublin

The writer was born Feb. 2, 1882, in Dublin, Ireland, the son of John Stanislaus Joyce (The Simon Dedalus of "Ulysses" whom Bloom hears singing in the Ormond bar) and Mary Murray Joyce. His father supposedly had one of the finest tenor voices in Ireland. James Joyce had an equally fine voice.

The Joyce family was not prosperous and it was large. James stood out among his brothers and sisters and, at the age of 9, is supposed to have written an attack on Tim Healy, the anti-Parnellite, which was printed but of which no known copy exists. Since he was literary it was decided to give him an education and he was sent first to Clongowes Wood College, then to Belvedere College, also in Ireland, and later he received his Bachelor of Arts degree from the Royal University in Dublin.

He was an amazing scholar, and an independent and solitary figure. When he was 17 he read Ibsen's plays and wrote an essay for the Fortnightly Review about the author of "The Doll's House." Dissatisfied with the English translations, Joyce learned Norwegian when he was 19 years old so that he might read his literary god in the original. At the same time he was reading and studying Dante, all the Elizaethan poets, St. Thomas Aquinas and Aristotle.

In those days, according to Padraic Colum, who knew him at the Royal University (later reorganized as the National University), Joyce was a tall, slender young man with "a Dantesque face and steely blue eyes," who sauntered along the street in a peaked tennis cap, soiled tennis shoes, carrying an ashplant for a cane. Stephen Dedalus carries a similar cane in "Ulysses" and frequently talks with it! He loved to sing and recite poetry in his fine tenor voice, but he spoke harshly and used "many of the unprintable words he got printed in 'Ulysses.'"

Conceit and arrogance were his characteristics. When he first met Yeats he remarks:

"We have met too late: you are too old to be influenced by me."

Joyce's death mask, which was commissioned by Carola Gideon-Welcker and cast by the sculptor Paul Speck (courtesy of the Patrick and Beatrice Haggerty Museum of Art, Marquette University)

AE (George Russell) recognized his "keen and cold intelligence," but told the young man, "I'm afraid you have not enough chaos in you to make a world."

Joyce was in continuous rebellion against Ireland and its life and said: "When the soul of a man is born in this country there are nets flung at it to hold it back from flight."

The words are Stephen Dedalus's in "A Portrait of the Artist as a Young Man," but it was Joyce speaking, and, at the age of 20, he left Ireland for Paris where he intended, and for a time pretended, to study medicine.

At this time he started the stories that were eventually published as "Dubliners" (this book was later publicly burned in a Dublin public square) and started his first novel. This, the "Portrait of the Artist" was ten years in the writing. His first published work—except for the forgotten attack on Tim Healy—was "Chamber Music," a collection of Elizabethan-like verses, which were printed in 1907.

It was at this time that he met Nora Barnacle, "a sleek blonde beauty" from Galway, the daughter of

Thomas and Ann Healy Barnacle. They soon went to the Continent to live (their marriage was not regularized until twenty-seven years later, when they visited a London registry office to legalize the status of their two children, George and Lucia). In Trieste, where they settled after some wandering, Joyce taught English at the Berlitz School and the Commercial Academy. He knew seventeen languages, ancient and modern, including Arabic, Sanskrit and Greek.

"Dubliners" Issued in 1914

In 1914 "Dubliners" was published in London. In the same year he also finished his novel "Portrait of the Artist as a Young Man."

When war was declared Joyce and his wife, who were British citizens, were in Austria. He was forced out of his job as a teacher, and the couple moved to Zurich.

While living in Zurich Joyce began to suffer from a severe ocular illness and eventually underwent at least ten operations on his eyes. For years he was almost totally blind and much of his later writing was done with red crayon on huge white sheets of paper.

"Ulysses" was begun under this difficult situation. Much of it was published by Margaret Anderson in The Little Review, the magazine which Otto Kahn, New York banker, once subsidized for his Greenwich Village friends. Chapters appeared between March, 1918, and August, 1920, when the Society for the Suppression of Vice had The Review stopped by court order.

After the war the Joyces returned to Trieste, where they lived with Stanislaus Joyce, the author's brother. Then, in 1919, they went to Paris, where they made their home until the next war sent them again to Zurich to occupy the house they had known in 1914.

In 1922 Joyce's greatest book, "Ulysses," was published in Paris. Great Britain, Ireland and the United States banned the book.

For many years after "Ulysses" was done Joyce worked on what he called "Work in Progress." Much of it appeared in Transition, the magazine published in the Nineteen Twenties in Paris by Eugene Jolas. In May, 1939, it was published as "Finnegan's Wake." a book "distinguished" by such "words" as Goragorridgeorballyedpushkalsom, to name one of the simpler ones, and many puns. In it Mr. Joyce suggested the book was the work of "a too pained whitelwit laden with the loot of learning."

During all his years as a writer Joyce was carefully protected by his wife, who once said she cared for him despite "his necessity to write those books no one can understand." His conversation was clear, never anything like his writing, and his wit as keen.

Joyce's son, George Joyce, married the former Miss Helen Castor of Long Branch, N. J. They had one son, Stephen James Joyce. James Joyce and his wife made their home with his son for many years before the present war.

* * *

James Joyce Is Dead at Zurich; Irish Author of 'Ulysses' Was 58

New York Herald Tribune, 13 January 1941

Writer, Until Recently Marooned without Funds in France and Dependent on U. S. Embassy's Help, Fails to Rally After Operation

By The Associated Press

ZURICH, Switzerland,–Jan. 13 (Monday)–James Joyce, Irish author whose "Ulysses" was the center of one of the most bitter literary controversies of modern times, died in a hospital here early today despite the efforts of doctors to save him by blood transfusions. He would have been 59 years old Feb. 2.

Joyce underwent an intestinal operation Saturday afternoon at the Schwesternhaus von Rotenkreus Hospital. For a time he appeared to be recovered. Only yesterday his son reported him cheerful and apparently out of danger.

But during the afternoon the writer suffered a sudden relapse and sank rapidly. He died at 2:15 a. m. (8:15 p. m. Eastern standard time). His wife and son were at the hospital when he died.

Was Isolated in France

Word that James Joyce had reached Switzerland with most of his family reached New York only last week. Previously he had been isolated in France unable to get any funds from outside. Royalties on "Finnegans Wake," his latest book, could not reach him from the United States nor from Great Britain.

Robert N. Kastor, of 300 Central Park West, whose daughter is the wife of Joyce's son, said last night that since the German occupation of France, Joyce had been reduced to painful straits. He had been unable, Mr. Kastor said, to engage in any literary work, the complicated routine of mere existence taking up his entire time. He was virtually on the dole at the American Embassy.

Until Mr. Kastor, Padraic Colum, poet and dramatist, and a few other friends of the author formed a committee to aid him, his future was precarious indeed. On hearing of his arrival in Switzerland, the committee forwarded funds there and was confident that the worst was over. Mr. Kastor and Mr. Colum were discussing the situation with some optimism last night when they got word of Joyce's death. They had already called a meeting of their committee for today. Mr. Kastor said he believed that Joyce's daughter, Lucia, still was in the occupied area of France.

Provoked Storm of Controversy

Not since the appearance in book form in the middle of the nineteenth century of Gustave Flaubert's "Madame Bovary" had a literary work provoked such a storm of controversy, of praise and pillorying, as did the "Ulysses" of James Joyce. Where Flaubert sought a scrupulously truthful portrayal of life, Joyce attempted what his admirers and interpreters called a stream-of-consciousness portrayal of what went on in the human mind, consciously and unconsciously–and in the human body, too.

"Ulysses," the writing of which occupied him through seven years, during nearly four of which Europe was engaged in the World War, was his major work. Intermittently through intervals between semi-blindness and operations on his eyes he later wrote what was promised as his real magnum opus, which he called "Finnegans Wake." But when it appeared in the spring of 1989, after seventeen years of promise, most of the critics frankly confessed they didn't know what it was about. "Lewis Gannett could only report that 'the book seems to have no relation to literature, which is one of the arts of communication." William McFee commented that "to any intelligent reader who gives all he has to a study of the new work, it appears that something has slipped in the artist's mind. . . . One of the greatest masters of the English language seems to sit in darkness, mumbling unintelligibly to himself."

Through the post-war 1920's, an experimental decade in literature, Joyce was the idol of many a modern writer and reader. To hear them sing his praises, his "Ulysses" had created a new art form, revolutionized literature. The book was the story of one day in the life of a Jewish advertisement solicitor in Dublin, one Leopold Bloom, and purported to set down his every act and thought through twenty-four hours. Its 700-odd pages concluded with, what went through the head of Mrs. Bloom after Leopold got to sleep that night, a torrent of 25,000 words without even a punctuation mark to break the flow.

Most of the "little four-letter words" of Anglo Saxon previously considered "unprintable" were among those

25,000 and it was that chapter, more than any of the others, which caused the book to be banned for short or long periods in various countries.

Brought Out as Book in 1922

First brought out in book form in Paris in 1922, it was not until 1933 that the book was legally admitted into the United States when a decision of Federal Judge John Munro Woolsey, who had studied it for five months, and who found it a sincere work of art which had accomplished "with astonishing success" a venture into a new literary genre. As to the charges that it was obscene, Judge Woolsey found that while in places it might be "somewhat emetic," to some readers, "nowhere does it pretend to be an aphrodisiac."

Long before Judge Woolsey's decision opened legal doors to the Joyceian masterpiece, it had been read by thousands of Americans, most of whom had got their copies in Paris in the "good old days" of the 1920's. Meanwhile Joyce admirers outdid one another trying to clear up the "obscure" passages of the master for the less clairvoyant. There was, however, but one "key" to "Ulysses" which had the author's approval and aid, the exegetical commentary by Stuart Gilbert called "James Joyce's Ulysses."

Before "Ulysses" got into the courts and thus into the newspapers, the circle of Joyce readers was a limited one. But already, in his native Dublin, one of his books, "Dubliners," had been publicly burned and most of his others were on Ireland's Index.

Joyce was born in Dublin Feb. 2, 1882, the son of John and Mary Murray Joyce, who were relatively well to do. It was the Jesuits who gave the boy his early education. He attended Clongowes Wood College, Belvedere College and the Royal University, Dublin, from which he received his Bachelor of Arts degree. Then, for awhile, he studied medicine at the University of Paris, but turned aside from making that his career. He then studied to become an opera singer, as he had a fine tenor voice, but again he changed his mind, went home to Dublin, and wrote.

An accomplished linguist he had set himself to learn Norwegian in order to take his Ibsen straight. At nineteen he wrote an essay on Ibsen for "The Fortnightly Review" which the author of "The Doll's House" so liked that he wrote Joyce of his appreciation. Joyce followed this up in 1901 with "The Day of the Rabblemen," an essay on the literary situation in Dublin in which he expressed his view that an artist should live apart from the mass of the people. Then came his first book of poetry, "Chamber Music," much of it since put to melodies.

Statue of James Joyce by Milton Hebald dedicated at Fluntern Cemetery in Zürich in 1981 (courtesy of Lucretia Joyce Lyons)

Two Books Follow

"Dubliners" followed and the "Portrait of the Artist as a Young Man," both far more intelligible to the average reader than "Ulysses." He also wrote a play, "Exiles." Years later, in 1925, it was produced in New York by the Neighborhood Players, in Grand Street.

In 1904, after his marriage, Joyce went abroad as a teacher of languages.

Upon his return to Dublin in 1912 he opened a motion-picture theater, the first, in Ireland, but that venture soon collapsed. So he returned to the Continent, settling first at Trieste and then, upon the outbreak of the war, in Zurich, Switzerland. He was at work on "Ulysses." One day a friend visited him. "I have been working hard all day," Joyce remarked. The friend supposed he must have made considerable progress with the manuscript; but, no, Joyce said, the day's work had consisted of completing to his full satisfaction two sentences. The two sentences were: "Perfume of embraces all him assailed. With hungered flesh obscurely he mutely craved to adore."

These, compared to many other Joyceian phrases, were lucid indeed. The ten languages that he knew all had a way of creeping into his writings in England, along with some tongue hitherto unknown to any literature, but which some researchers sought to trace back to the Jabberwocky of Lewis Carroll, and the later transpositions that are known as Spoonerisms after the English professor who delighted in that particular form of playing on words.

But some of Joyce's conglomerations of sesquipedalian verbiage transcended all the known tongues of the earth, though his most ardent supporters insisted that if one knew enough, thought enough and tried sufficiently, the meaning of all his pages would be clear. But even those who understood "ineluctable modality of the visible" confessed themselves stumped when the master poured forth such neo-Chaucerian paragraphs as the following:

"I made praharfeast upon acorpolous and fastbroke down in Neederthorpe. I let faireviews in on Slobodens but ranked Pothgardes round wrathmindsers: I bathandbaddened on mendicity and I corocured off the unoculated."

Gave Advice to Reader

In "Finnegans Wake" Joyce advised the reader how properly to approach his work. He recommended that the reader "sing in the chorias to the ethur."

"In the heliotropical noughttime following a fade of transformed Tuff," he continued, "and, pending its viseversion, a metenergic reglow of beaming Batt, the bairdboard bombardment screen, if tastefully taut guranium satin, tends to teleframe and step up to the charge of a light barricade."

After the war Joyce settled in Paris. With his wife, their son, George, and their daughter, Lucia, he took an apartment near the Eiffel Tower and there, while the controversy raged over "Ulysses," he began the slow work of getting "Finnegan's Wake" out of his system. It was interrupted often by his eye afflictions. Once he was confined to a darkened room for several months. Over other long periods his sight was so bad that he was obliged to do his writing in large scrawls with a red pencil. In Paris and in Switzerland he underwent a dozen operations, first on one eye, then on the other. Once a doctor told him he would soon be blind for life, but an operation by an American ophthalmologist living in Paris, the late Dr. Louis Borsch, improved his vision shortly thereafter.

In 1931 Joyce and his wife traveled from Paris to London where they visited a registry office and twenty-seven years after their first announced marriage in Dublin, went through the marriage ceremony again. Joyce, as always, said nothing. His attorney merely explained that

"for testamentary reasons it was thought well that the parties should be married according to English law." Some months later—on Feb. 15, 1932—Joyce became a grandfather through the birth of a son to his daughter-in-law, Mrs. George Joyce, who was American-born, the former Helene Fleischmann. The child was named Stephen James Joyce.

A first installment of "Ulysses," the work upon which Joyce must stand or fall in literature, appeared in the United States in "The Little Review," edited by Margaret Anderson, in 1918, the manuscript having been sent to her by Ezra Pound. Promptly the post office pounced upon it as indecent, seized and burned all copies it could get its hands on. But the installments continued, the magazine being distributed by express. In 1920 John S. Sumner, of the Society for the Prevention of Vice, had Miss Anderson and her co-editor, Jane Heap, indicted, and in 1921 they were found guilty of publishing indecent matter by the Court of General Sessions, fined $50 each and fingerprinted as criminals. Then an American expatriate, Sylvia Beach, had the book printed in France, calling the publishing firm Shakespeare & Co. First copies, brought to Paris from the printers at Dijon, sold for as high as $30. Copies were seized in England, Ireland and the United States, one whole edition being destroyed by the British.

The book was translated into French, German, Spanish and Japanese. Twenty thousand copies in English were sold in Paris, mostly to American and English tourists. Customs officials both in England and the United States seized and confiscated what copies they discovered. One publisher printed the book and put it out in the United States, thereby beginning a series of lawsuits.

It was not until 1933 that the decision of Judge Woolsey made the book generally available in this country. The decision was upheld in 1934 by the United States Circuit Court of Appeals, but not without a dissenting vote.

"I hold," said Judge Woolsey's opinion, "that 'Ulysses' is a sincere and honest book and I think that the criticisms of it are entirely disposed of by its rationale. Furthermore, 'Ulysses' is an amazing tour de force when one considers the success which has been in the main achieved with such a difficult objective as Joyce set for himself. As I have stated, 'Ulysses' is not an easy book to read; it is brilliant and dull, intelligible and obscure by turns. In many places it seems to me to be disgusting, but although it contains many words usually considered dirty I have not found anything that I consider to be dirt for dirt's sake. Each word of the book contributes like a bit of mosaic to the detail of the picture which Joyce is seeking to construct for his readers. If one does not wish to associate with such folk as Joyce describes, that is one's own choice.

"The words which are criticized as dirty are old Saxon words known to almost all men and in venture, to many women, and are such words as would be naturally and habitually used, I believe, by the types of folk whose life, physical and mental, Joyce is seeking to describe. In respect of the recurrent emergencies of theme of sex in the minds of his characters, it must always be remembered that his locale was Celtic and his season spring."

In "Ulysses" which has many parallels with the classic "Odyssey," the principal character, Bloom, has breakfast, goes to work, attends a funeral, lunches, shops, visits the public baths and a library, meets friends, sits on the dunes by the sea and later, in company with a young man named Stephen Dedalus, goes to Dublin's red-light district. The book ends with Mrs. Bloom's long silent soliloquy as she lies awake abed, after the husband, to whom she has been unfaithful, had gone to sleep. Joyce tried to record not only every act but every thought of the principal characters through the one day he chose to present in their little world, the day of June 16, 1904.

Tributes

Thornton Wilder is an American novelist and playwright. Some critics have argued that his Pulitzer Prize-winning, three-act play The Skin of Our Teeth *(1942), which portrays a five-thousand-year history of man, was inspired by* Finnegans Wake.

James Joyce, 1882–1941
Thornton Wilder
Poetry, 57 (1940–1941): 370–374

During thirty-five years of self-imposed exile James Joyce never ceased from the contemplation of Dublin. From Trieste, from Rome, from Zürich, earning his living in the appalling treadmill of the Berlitz schools, night after night he relived the Dublin of 1900, its sights and sounds and smells and inhabitants—bound to Dublin in love and hate, parallel, irreconcilable, each emotion whipping on its contrary; a love that could only briefly make peace with the hatred through the operation of the comic spirit; a hatred that could only intermittently make peace with the love through the intensity of artistic creation. This unresolved love and hate recurred in every aspect of his life: it went out towards his youth, towards the religion in which he was brought up, towards the rôle of artist, towards the phenomenon of language itself. It compelled him to destroy and to extoll; to annihilate through analysis and to make live through passionate comprehension.

The price that must be paid for a love that cannot integrate its hate is sentimentality; the price that must be paid for a hate that cannot integrate its love is, variously, empty rhetoric, insecurity of taste, and the sterile refinements of an intellect bent on destruction.

Between these perils Joyce won some great triumphs.

* * *

Like Cervantes, he groped confusedly for his subject and his form. The history of a writer is his search for his own subject, his myth-theme, hidden from him, but prepared for him in every hour of his life, his *Gulliver's Travels,* his *Robinson Crusoe.* Like Cervantes, unsuccessful, Joyce tried poetry and drama. Knowing the incomparable resources of his prose rhythms one is astonished at these verses,—a watery musicality, a pinched ventriloqual voice. Knowing the vital dialogues in *Dubliners* and that electrifying scene, the quarrel at the Christmas dinnertable, in *A Portrait of the Artist as a Young Man,* one is astonished at the woodenness of his play *Exiles.*

Like Cervantes, he turned with greater success to short narratives, and like him found in the dimensions of the long book, his form and his theme.

Portrait by Paul Joyce, the grandson of Joyce's brother Charles, of Joyce sitting beneath a portrait of his father (courtesy of Paul Joyce)

Remembering Joyce

The Martello Tower, in which Joyce stayed in September 1904, was opened as a museum in 1962 (courtesy of Lucretia Joyce Lyons)

The front and back of the Irish ten-pound bill with the opening line of Finnegans Wake *on the back*

7 Eccles Street, the Bloom residence, shortly before it was razed, and the James Joyce Centre, 35 North Great George's Street, which features the original door removed from Bloom's address. The Joyce Centre was officially opened on 10 June 1996 (courtesy of Giuliana and Joshua Chapman).

Memorial to Joyce in St. Stephen's Green (courtesy of Lucretia Joyce Lyons)

Statue of James Joyce located on Earl Street N. in Dublin (courtesy of Faith Steinberg)

* * *

Ulysses brought a new method into literature, the interior monologue. The century-long advance of realism now confronted this task: the realistic description of consciousness. To realism, mind is a bladder, a stream of fleeting odds and ends of image and association. Joyce achieved this method with a mastery and fullness of illustration that effaces any question of precursors. He alone has been able to suggest the apparent incoherence and triviality of this incessant woolgathering, and yet to impose upon it a coördination beyond itself, in art. With what consternation the Masters would have beheld this sight. Shakespeare reserved divagation for Juliet's nurse, Jane Austen for Miss Bates. Hamlet's interior monologue is based upon the assumption that for a short time the human mind may pursue its idea in purity. Yet all art is convention, even the inner monologue. Joyce's discovery has the character of necessity, a Twentieth Century necessity, and again it was wrung from him by the operation of his love and hate. There is destruction in that it saps the dignity of the mind; there is profound sympathy in the uses to which he put it for characterization. With it he explores three souls, Stephen Dedalus and the Blooms; one failure and two great triumphs.

* * *

Dedalus is confessedly autobiographical; how can unreconciled love and hate make a self-portrait? Here the price is paid, sentimentality. Dedalus extends his bleeding heart, not without complacency; he mocks himself for it, but even in the mockery we surprise the sob of an Italian tenor. The miracle of the book is Leopold Bloom, Joyce's anti-self, *l'homme moyen sensuel,* and his wife, Marion,—transcendent confirmations of the method itself. If we could surprise the interior monologue of any person—it seems to affirm—we would be obliged to enlarge the famous aphorism: to understand that much is not only to forgive that much; it is to extend to another person that suspension of objective judgment which we accord to ourselves; a homage to the life-force itself in the play of consciousness relegating all questions of approval or disapproval.

* * *

Ulysses exemplifies, as a technical problem, the mastery of the long book,—where Proust and so many others have failed. This has been achieved, perilously, by a resort to curious architectural devices and by the play of the comic spirit,—these Chinese boxes of complicated schematization: each chapter marked by one color; each chapter representing an organ in the human body; each under the sign of a theological virtue and its allied vice; each bearing a relation,—partly as parody, partly for emotion—to a correspond-

ing book of the *Odyssey.* At first glance how unlike the abounding creativity of the great books,—of Rabelais, Cervantes and Dante—are these devious ingenuities and buried cross-references; and yet *Ulysses* has the climate of the great books. It circulates in the resources of the style, equal to every mood and to every game; in the lofty requirement that the reader give his whole attention to every word; in the omnipresence of a surpassingly concrete Dublin; in the humanity of the characters; and in the earnestness of an element that one can only call "confessional."

* * *

After *Ulysses,* Joyce went through a period of disorganization: the search for the new subject; the increasing threat to his eyesight.

One day a friend sent him a postcard picturing the Bay of Dublin and Howth Head,—that promontory in which Celt and Dane and Saxon have always seen the outline of a sleeper's head. Joyce resolved to write the thoughts of that sleeping man. For seventeen years he worked on *Finnegans Wake,* peering over the page with fading vision, elaborating its complexities, like some ancient illuminator fashioning the traceries of the Book of Kells. A book in sleep-language,—the inner monologue unlocked to still greater possibilities of apparent incoherence and hence requiring a still more elaborate schematic scaffolding. Those who have deciphered even a small part of the work have glimpsed the grandeur of the plan: the sleeper reliving the history of mankind and identifying himself with the heroes and sinners of the world's myth literature; his thoughts influenced by the stars that pass over his head and couched in a language which reproduces the talking-on-two-levels characteristic of sleep; a language in which all the tongues of the world have coalesced into a pâte, the barriers between them having become imperceptible at that level; the sleeper wrestling all night with the problem of original sin, with the sense of guilt acquired from offenses which his waking self knows nothing of. Towards dawn, his enemies mastered, identifying himself with Finn, the ancient Irish hero, he awakes to a new day in the eternal cyclic revolutions of lives and civilizations. Finn! Again wake!

We cannot know yet whether hate has buried this conception under the debris of language analyzed to dust or whether love through identification with human history, through the laughter of the comic genius, and through the incomparable musicality of its style, has won its greatest triumph of all.

Joyce recommended this work to the world as his greatest, and it may be that when we come to know it, our gratitude for so many excellences in the earlier books will be exceeded by all that we owe him for this one.

This essay was republished in James Joyce: Two Decades of Criticism *(1948).*

My Friend James Joyce

Eugene Jolas

Partisan Review, 8 (March–April 1941): 82–93

To those who knew him intimately, James Joyce was a human being of great warmth and charm, although, at first approach, his personality could seem almost forbidding. In fact, it took him some time to accept an easy comradeship in social intercourse. He often appeared to be on his guard, an attitude that was particularly noticeable during the period of excessive curiosity concerning him that followed the publication of *Ulysses.* But once he had given his friendship, nothing could swerve him from his granitic loyalty. He was never an ebullient man. His moments of silence and introspection frequently weighed, even, on his immediate surroundings. Then a profound pessimism, that seemed to hold him prisoner within himself, made him quite inaccessible to outsiders. Usually, however, among his intimates, there finally came a festive pause, when he would begin to dance and sing, or engage in barbed thrusts of wit; when he would show flashes of gaiety and humor that could, on occasion, approach a kind of delirium.

He was never an easy conversationalist, and had a tendency to monosyllabic utterances. He did not relish being questioned directly on any subject. He never gave any interviews, and I was always careful not to quote him for publication. When he was in the mood, his talk, given in his mellifluous Dublin speech, was a ripple of illuminating ideas and words. Once he had left his anarchic and misanthropic taciturnity, he could enjoy the companionship of his friends, on whom, in some ways, he was very dependent, with a demonstration of good fellowship that brought out another facet of his nature. He eschewed all esotericism in his talk. Nor was he interested in high-flown abstractions, but was engrossed rather by the drama of human relations, human behavior, human thought and customs. The range of subjects he enjoyed discussing was a wide one: poetry prodigiously remembered and faultlessly recited; music and musicians, especially singing, of which his technical knowledge was astonishing; the theater, where his preferences went to Ibsen, Hauptmann, Scribe; the various liturgies; education; anthropology; philology; and certain sciences, particularly physics, geometry, and mathematics. He was little interested in pure politics and economics, although he followed events faithfully.

I am conscious of difficulty in writing about him, for he was often amused by the articles that concerned his private life. He seemed to resent the constant macabre preoccupations with the condition of his eyes. Once, when I read a particularly inept piece about his personal habits, written in German, he said: "What are they writing about? *Es ist eben nichts zu malen.*" (There really is nothing to paint, anyway.) During the fourteen years of our association–which coincided with the writing of *Work in Progress,* or *Finnegans Wake*–I had many opportunities to observe his kindliness, his humor, his pathos. I saw his stoicism before fate. I saw him in moments of insouciance and in moments of distress. In spite of the frailty of his physique, there was certain toughness in him which saw him through the ups and downs of his destiny. This tenacity was part of his honesty of conviction, his horror of cheap compromise, his fanatic belief in his own intellectual powers. His being was compact and fashioned by a will of steel. He was a man of deep tolerance and objected to all denigrations of friends, or enemies, in his presence.

I met James Joyce for the first time in 1924, three years before I launched *transition.* It was at a rather dull banquet given at the Restaurant Marguéry in honor of Valéry Larbaud, his first French friend and translator. (By a curious turn of fate, Larbaud was the last French writer Joyce saw anything of. While in Vichy, during the war, he went frequently to visit the now incurably ill author of *Barnabooth.*) Joyce was beaming in the aureole of *Ulysses,* and in a happy mood, when I was introduced to him. He thanked me courteously for something I had written about the book in a literary column I was then conducting for the Paris edition of the *Chicago Tribune.* We did not meet again until early in 1927, when I was preparing *transition* with Elliot Paul. We had approached Miss Sylvia Beach, his publisher, to ask her for a manuscript from Joyce, but with very little hope that anything would be forthcoming. Miss Beach consulted him, and within a few days we had the manuscript in our hands.

On a Sunday afternoon, in the winter of 1927, Joyce invited Mlle Adrienne Monnier, Miss Sylvia Beach, my wife, Elliot Paul, and me to his home in the Square Robiac to listen to his reading of the manuscript in question. We listened to the Waterloo scene, which subsequently appeared in the first issue of the review. His voice was resonantly musical, and at times a smile went over his face, as he read a particularly exhilarating passage. After he had finished, he said: "What do you think of it? Did you like it?" We were all stirred by his verbal fantasy, excited, even, but puzzled. It was not easy to reply with conven-

Poster for Mary Ellen Bute's 1965 movie Passages from Finnegans Wake, *a surrealistic presentation based on Mary Manning's play of the same title. The dialogue is taken directly from the book; explanatory subtitles are provided (courtesy of Kit Smyth Basquin).*

tional phrases. There was no precedent in literature for judging this fragment with its structure of multiple planes and its novelty of a polysynthetic language. Some weeks later, he let me read the entire manuscript. It was not more than one hundred and twenty pages long and had been written, he said, within a few weeks during a stay on the Riviera in 1922. Yet it was already complete in itself, organically compressed, containing the outline of the entire saga. Even the title had been chosen, he indicated, but only he and Mrs. Joyce knew it. It was still a primitive version, to which he had already begun to add numberless paragraphs, phrases, words. In a moment of confidence he told me something about the genesis of the idea. His admirer, Miss Harriet Weaver–who, some years before, like a Maecenas of other days, had made it possible for the struggling writer to be freed of financial worry–had asked him what book he was planning to write after *Ulysses*. He replied that now *Ulysses* was done he considered himself as a man without a job. "I am like a tailor who would like to try his hand at making a new-style suit," he continued. "Will you order one?" Miss Weaver handed him a pamphlet written by a village priest in England and giving a description of a giant's grave found in the parish lot. "Why not try the story of this giant?" she asked jokingly. The giant's narrative became the story of Finn McCool, or *Finnegans Wake*.

The first issues of *transition* containing installments from what was then known as *Work in Progress*–Joyce told me that his provisional title was the invention of Ford Madox Ford, who had previously published a fragment in his *transatlantic review*–brought forth a fanfare of sensational outbursts. The confused critics in France, England, and America snorted, for the most part, their violent disapproval. Miss Weaver herself regretfully wrote Miss Beach she feared Joyce was wasting his genius; an opinion which disturbed Joyce profoundly, for, after all, it was for her that the "tailor" was working. His friend Larbaud said he regarded the work as a *divertissement philologique* and of no great importance in Joyce's creative evolution. H. G. Wells wrote him that he still had a number of books to write and could not give the time to attempt to decipher Joyce's experiment. Ezra Pound attacked it in a letter and urged him to put it in the "family album," together with his poems. Only Edmund Wilson was intelligently sympathetic. After a while the reactions become more and more vehement, even personal, and on the whole journalistically stereotyped. Joyce continued working at his vision.

We saw a good deal of him during those years. Our office was not very far from his home, near the

Eiffel Tower, and his urbane presence amid the disorder of our primitive hotel room was always a welcome one. All his friends collaborated then in the preparations of the fragments destined for *transition:* Stuart Gilbert, Padraic Colum, Elliot Paul, Robert Sage, Helen and Giorgio Joyce, and others. He worked with painstaking care, almost with pedantry. He had invented an intricate system of symbols permitting him to pick out the new words and paragraphs he had been writing down for years, and which referred to the multiple characters in his creation. He would work for weeks, often late at night, with the help of one or the other of his friends. It seemed almost a collective composition in the end, for he let his friends participate in his inventive zeal, as they searched through numberless notebooks with mysterious reference points to be inserted in the text. When finished, the proof looked as if a coal-heaver's sooty hands had touched it. Once the work was done, we would dine with him at his favorite restaurant, the *Trianons,* where he liked the atmosphere and cuisine, and where he was sure to find his dry, golden Chablis, or, if the evening grew more hilarious than usual, an excellent Pommery champagne. His nearly whispered conversations never had any nuance of scatology, and whenever one of the more Rabelaisian of his companions would indulge in some too robust *gauloiserie,* he would deftly, almost impatiently, lead the dialogue into other channels. Sometimes he would bring with him a page he had written and hand it around the table with a gesture of polite modesty. He never explained his work, save through indirection.

At that time Joyce's family life was closely knit and happy, and his humor was a natural manifestation of this ambience. It did not yet have that mordant quality which it acquired in later years, after great sorrow had entered his home circle. And yet, even then, it was rather what André Breton has called somewhere *un humour noir.* Later, he grew more asocial. But his friends succeeded in cheering him up. Once he celebrated, on the same day, his fiftieth birthday and the tenth anniversary of the publication of *Ulysses.* The events were hardly noticed by the literary world, which was then discovering social realism and considered Joyce outmoded. On that occasion, we gave a small dinner at our home in Paris attended by Mrs. Joyce, Thomas McGreevy, Samuel Beckett, Lucy and Paul Léon, Helen and Giorgio Joyce, and others. The birthday cake was decorated with an ingenious candy replica of a copy of *Ulysses,* in its blue jacket. Called on to cut the cake, Joyce looked at it a moment and said : "*Accipite et manducate ex hoc omnes: Hoc est enim corpus meum.*" The

talk at the table turned on the subject of popular sayings. Someone expressed a suspicion of all of them and gave voice to his dislike for the adage: *in vino veritas,* which he held to be untrue and bromidic. Joyce agreed warmly and added: "it should really be: *in riso veritas;* for nothing so reveals us as our laughter." He was always astonished that so few people had commented on the comic spirit in his writings.

I was preparing a short homage to him in *transition* and had, among other features, ordered a sketch of Joyce by the Spanish artist, César Abin. The result was an impressing study of a distinguished *homme de lettres,* with a pen in hand, his own volumes reverentially piled beside him. But Joyce would have none of it and insisted on giving the cartoonist precise instructions for the design and execution of the job. He wanted it, first of all, to look like a question mark, because friends had told him once that his figure resembled a question mark, when seen standing meditatively on a street corner. For more than two weeks he kept adding new suggestions, until he was finally satisfied with it. He asked to be drawn with a battered old derby hung with spider webs and bearing a ticket on which was inscribed the fatal number 13. He asked that a star be put on the tip of his nose, in memory of a criticaster's description of him as a "blue-nosed comedian"; that his feet be suspended perilously over a globe called Ireland, on which only Dublin was visible; that he have patches on the knees of his trousers; that out of his pockets there should emerge the manuscript of a song entitled: "Let me like a soldier fall." For his "luck," his "fate," had already started down the somber path it never left again. It was as though he had a premonition of the immense trials that lay before him. It was during this period that he suggested that we plan a *bal de la purée*—which is French slang for general insolvency—since the depression was beginning to be felt in Paris more and more. The gayest of the guests was Joyce himself, who finally inveigled all the ladies present to give him the first prize for his costume: that of an old Irish stage character famous once as *Handy Andy.*

At that time, the sudden death of his father came to him as a profound shock. He had never made any bones about his great affection for his father, and the autobiographical elements of his work reveal this in numberless symbolical and mythological allusions. *Ulysses* was man in search of his father, and *Finnegans Wake* is once again the expression of that filial quest. In those days, Joyce dreamed much about him, and one evening he said suddenly: "I hear my father talking to me. I wonder where he is." Sometimes he would tell picaresque tales of his father's wit, and the last one I remember was one

Images of an Artist

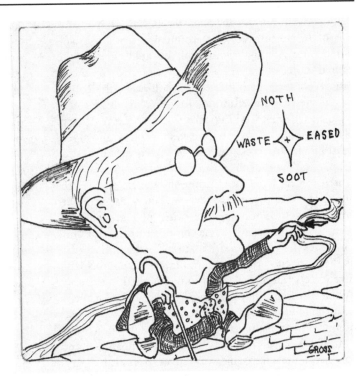

Portrait of Joyce on ceramic tile by Ciceil Gross. The compass points are from Finnegans Wake *and relate to the river Liffey depicted in the background (courtesy of Ciceil Gross).*

Woodcut of Joyce by Hannah Thomas, 1956 (Library of Congress, Prints and Photographs Division [FP xx T457 D1])

Etching of Joyce by Alessandro Fargnoli, April 2000 (courtesy of Alessandro Fargnoli)

Portraits of Joyce by Carl Arrington (Collection of Nicholas Fargnoli)

"Joyce in the Park," by Ciceil and Murray Gross after Georges Seurat (courtesy of Ciceil and Murray Gross)

that concerned his father's reaction in Dublin to a minuscule sketch of Joyce made by Brancusi. It was merely a geometrical spiral study symbolizing the ear. "Well, Jim hasn't changed much," said his father on seeing the portrait.

During the summer and fall of 1931, Joyce's daughter Lucia suffered a nervous collapse, and we spent several months with the Joyce family in a little frontier town in the mountains of Austria. Joyce had not been writing for some time, partly because of the intense worry he felt over his daughter's condition, partly because of the general mood of inertia caused by the depression. So we took long walks together along the swirling mountain river Ill near by, or we climbed the wooded hills. He had a deep love for mountains and rivers, because, he said, "They are the phenomena that will remain when all the peoples and their governments will have vanished." Yet he was not at all a nature romantic. He was rather a man of the megapolis. Toward dusk, after a siesta, he would go walking again. Eight o'clock was the hour he had set for himself many decades before as the time for his first glass of wine of the day. That summer he evolved a sort of ritual which, to me, had an almost grotesque fascination. At half past seven, he would race suddenly for the railroad station, where the Paris-Vienna Express was due to stop for ten minutes each day. He would quietly walk up and down the platform. "Over on those tracks there," he said one evening, "the fate of *Ulysses* was decided in 1915." He referred to the fact that in this Austrian town of the border he had almost been prevented by some jinx from crossing into Switzerland during the first World War. When the train finally came in, he rushed to the nearest car in order to examine the French, German, and Yugo-Slav inscriptions, palped the letters with the sensitive fingers of defective vision. Then he would ask me questions about the persons getting on or off the train. He would try to listen to their conversations. His fine ear for dialectal nuances in German often astonished me. When the train continued on its way into the usually foggy night, he stood on the platform waving his hat, as if he had just bid god-speed to a dear friend. With eight o'clock approaching, he almost skipped back to the hotel for his first draught of *Tischwein*–or, as Mrs. Joyce, who thought the drink of rather inferior quality, used to say, *dishwine*.

After a while I started making preparations for a new issue of *transition,* and this stimulated him to work. He attacked the problem with savage energy. "How difficult it is to put pen to paper again," he said one evening. "Those first sentences have cost me a great deal of pain." But gradually the task was in

hand. It was to be known later as *The Mime of Mick Nick and the Maggies.* He wrote steadily on this fragment during those frenetic months, constantly interrupted by moments of anxiety about the health of his daughter, and by his own resultant nervousness. At his hotel, where we would work in the afternoon, he gave me a densely written foolscap sheet beginning with the words: "Every evening at lighting up o'clock sharp and until further notice. . . ." which I typed for him. After a few pages had thus been transcribed, we began to look through the notebooks–which he lugged around on all his travels–and the additions, set down years before for a still unwritten text he had merely outlined in his mind, became more and more numerous. The manuscript grew into thirty pages and was not yet finished. He never changed a single word. There was always a certain inevitability, an almost volcanic affirmativeness, about his primal choice of words. To me, his deformations seemed to grow more daring. He added ceaselessly, like a worker in mosaic, enriching his original pattern with ever new inventions.

"There really is no coincidence in this book," he said during one of our walks. "I might easily have written this story in the traditional manner. . . . Every novelist knows the recipe. . . . It is not very difficult to follow a simple, chronological scheme which the critics will understand. . . . But I, after all, am trying to tell the story of this Chapelizod family in a new way. . . . Time and the river and the mountain are the real heroes of my book. . . . Yet the elements are exactly what every novelist might use: man and woman, birth, childhood, night, sleep, marriage, prayer, death. . . . There is nothing paradoxical about this. . . . Only I am trying to build many planes of narrative with a single esthetic purpose. . . . Did you ever read Laurence Sterne . . . ?"

We read Goethe's *Farbenlehre,* but he finally said he could use nothing from it. He was interested in a comic version of the theodicy, and he asked me to get one of the Jesuits near by to give me an Augustinian text. There was a famous Jesuit school in the town, and he occasionally reminisced about his Dublin days with the fathers. But his anti-religious convictions were unshakable. I had come back from a talk with his daughter, who seemed to be interested in knowing something about Catholic dogma. Joyce, on hearing this, grew suddenly quite violent and said: "Why should a young woman bother her head about such things? Buddha and Confucius and all the others were not able to understand anything about it. We know nothing, and never shall know anything. . . ." He discussed Vico's theory of the origin of language. The conception of the cyclical evolution of civilizations born from each other like the phoenix from the ashes haunted him. He began to speculate on the new physics, and the theory of the expanding universe. And, while walking with him, I always had the impression that he was not really in an Austrian frontier town but in Dublin, and that everything he thought and wrote was about his native land.

He completed the *Mime* in Zürich, after our return there. We used to take a motorboat in the late afternoon and go out on the lake. Or else we would go walking up hill to the Zoo, where one evening he suddenly quoted to me the magnificent nocturne of Phoenix Park, with the verbal magic of animal sounds dying off in the gathering night. Or else we would walk up and down the *Bahnhofstrasse,* and I would think of his poem about this street. He would talk about his World War experiences in the Swiss town and chat about old friends, especially his English friend, Frank Budgen, who was his companion in those days. Then we would dine at the *Kronenhalle,* which he now preferred to the more colorful *Zum Pfauen* that had been his *Stammlokal* in the old days. His guests were the few friends he had in Zürich: Dr. Bernard Fehr, of the University; Dr. Borach, and Mr. Edouard Brauchbar, English pupils during the first world war; Dr. and Mrs S. Giedion. He was very fond of the Swiss *fondant* wine from the Valais, and we often left the restaurant in a grape-happy mood.

A British clipping came saying that Joyce was trying to revive Swift's *little language* to Stella. "Not at all," said Joyce to me. "I am using a *Big Language.*" He said one evening: "I have discovered that I can do anything with language I want." His linguistic memory was extraordinary. He seemed constantly *à l'affût,* always to be listening rather than talking. "Really, it is not I who am writing this crazy book," he said in his whimsical way one evening. "It is you, and you, and you, and that man over there, and that girl at the next table." One day I found him in a Zürich teashop laughing quietly to himself. "Did you win *le gros lot?*" I asked. He said he had asked the waitress for a glass of lemon squash. The somewhat obtuse Swiss girl looked puzzled. Then she had an inspiration: "Oh, you mean *Lebensquatsch?*" she stammered. (Her German neologism might be translated by: life's piffle!) Joyce retained all such scraps of conversations, lopped-off syllables said in moments of inertia or fatigue, *jeux de mots,* alcoholically deformed words, slips of the tongue–all the verbal grotesques and fantasies which he heard issuing in unconscious moments. His knowledge of French, German, modern Greek, and especially Italian stood him in good stead, and he added constantly to that stock of information by studying Hebrew, Russian, Japanese, Chinese, Finnish, and other tongues. At the bottom of his vocabulary was also an immense command of Anglo-Irish words that only seem like neologisms to us today, because they have, for the most part,

become obsolete. His revival of these will some day interest the philologists. Language to him was a social as well as a subjective process. He was deeply interested in the experiments of the French Jesuit, Jousse, and the English philogist, Paget, and *Finnegans Wake* is full of strange applications of their gesture theory. He often talked with a derisive smile of the auxiliary languages, among them Esperanto and Ido.

Back in Paris he became more and more absorbed by meditations on the imaginative creation. He read Coleridge and was interested in the distinction he made between imagination and fancy. He wondered if he himself had imagination. As the political horizon in Europe grew more threatening, his high Olympian neutrality asserted itself more and more. In those days I remember reading to him a German translation from a speech by Radek in which the Russian attacked *Ulysses,* at the Congress of Kharkov, as being without a social conscience. "Well," said Joyce, "all the characters in my books belong to the lower middle classes, and even the working class; and they are all quite poor." He began to read *Wuthering Heights.* "This woman had pure imagination," he said. "Kipling had it, too, and certainly Yeats." His admiration for the Irish poet was very great. A recent commentator, asserting that Joyce lacked reverence for the logos in poetry, inferred that he had little regard for Yeats. I can assure the gentleman that this was not true. Joyce often recited Yeats's poems to us from memory. "No surrealist poet can equal this for imagination," he said. Once, when Yeats spoke over the radio, he invited us to listen in with him. I read *The Vision* to him, and he was deeply absorbed by the colossal conception, only regretting that "Yeats did not put all this into a creative work." At Yeats's death he sent a wreath to his grave at Antibes, and his emotion on hearing of the poet's passing was moving to witness. He always denied, too, that he had said to Yeats that he was too old to be influenced by him.

Joyce had a passion for the irrational manifestation of life. Yet there was nothing in common between his attitude and that of the surrealists and psychoanalysts. Nor did his experiments have anything to do with those of the German romantics who explored the mysticism of the individual world. Joyce was an intensely conscious observer of the unconscious drama. During walks in Paris, we often talked about dreams. Sometimes I related to him my own dreams, which, during the prewar years, began to take on a strangely fantastic, almost apocalyptic, silhouette. He was always eager to discuss them, because they interested him as images of the nocturnal universe. He himself, he said, dreamed relatively little, but, when he did, his dreams were usually related to ideas, personal and mythic, with which he was occupied in his waking hours. He was very much attracted by Dunn's theory of *serialism,* and I read to him that author's brilliant *A Theory with Time,* which Joyce regarded highly. He told me one of his dreams, and subsequent events seemed to confirm Dunn's mutidimensional conceptions. He was walking through a big city and met three men who called themselves Minos, Eaque, and Rhadamante. They suddenly broke off their conversation with him and became threatening. He had to run to escape from their screams of obloquy. Three weeks later I noticed a feature story in the *Paris-Soir* to the effect that the police were looking for a crank who was sending explosives through the mails. This fanatic signed himself: Minos, Eaque, Rhadamante, the judges of Hell. One of Joyce's less complicated dreams, however, caused considerable chuckling each time he thought of it. This was a dream the climax of which was the titanic figure of Molly Bloom, seated on the side of a high hill. "As for you, James Joyce, I've had enough of you," she shouted. His reply he never remembered.

Some six months before *Work in Progress* was scheduled to appear, there was an amusing incident in connection with its title, then still known only to Mr. and Mrs. Joyce. Often he had challenged his friends to guess it. He even made a permanent offer to pay one thousand francs in cash to the person who would guess it. We all tried: Stuart Gilbert, Herbert Gorman, Samuel Beckett, Paul Léon, and I, but we failed miserably. One summer night, while dining on the terrace of Fouquet's, Joyce repeated his offer. The Riesling was especially good that night, and we were in high spirits. Mrs. Joyce began an Irish song about Mr. Flannigan and Mrs. Shannigan. Joyce looked startled and urged her to stop. This she did, but, when he saw no harm had been done, he very distinctly, as a singer does it, made the lip motions which seemed to indicate F and W. My wife's guess was *Fairy's Wake.* Joyce looked astonished and said "Brava! But something is missing." For a few days we mulled over it. One morning I knew it was *Finnegans Wake,* although it was only an intuition. That evening I suddenly threw the words into the air. Joyce blanched. Slowly he set down the wineglass he held. "Ah, Jolas, you've taken something out of me," he said, almost sadly. When we parted that night, he embraced me, danced a few of his intricate steps, and asked: "How would you like to have the money?" I replied: "In sous." The following morning, during my absence from home, he arrived with a bag filled with ten-franc pieces. He gave them to my daughters with instructions to serve them to me at lunch. So it was *Finnegans Wake.* All those present were sternly enjoined by Joyce not to reveal it, and we kept it a secret until he made the official announcement at his birthday dinner on the following February second.

The reception given this labor of seventeen years was to be a disappointing one. Among the few whose analysis struck him as being comprehensive and conscientious were, in rough order of his appreciation, William Troy's essay in *Partisan Review,* Harry Levin's article in *New Directions,* Edmund Wilson's essays in the *New Republic,* Alfred Kazin's review in the *New York Herald-Tribune,* and Padraic Colum's piece in the *New York Times,* as well as one or two from England and Scotland. From Ireland there was little reaction, and the reception in France, on which he had counted so much, was lamentable. This state of affairs was a source of deep depression during the last year of his life and was responsible, more than anything else, for the fact that he was completely indifferent to any suggestion for a future work.

For Joyce himself, *Finnegans Wake* had prophetic significance. Finn MacCool, the Finnish-Norwegian-Irish hero of the tale, seemed to him to be coming alive again after the publication of the book, and, in a letter from France I received from him last spring, he said: ". . . It is strange, however, that after publication of my book, Finland came into the foreground suddenly. First by awarding of the Nobel Prize to a Finnish writer, and then by the political door. The most curious comment I have received on the book is a symbolical one from Helsinki, where, as foretold by the prophet, the Finn again wakes, and volunteer Buckleys are hurrying from all sides to shoot that Russian general. . . ." "Prophetic, too, were the last pages of my book, . . ." he added in this same letter. The last pages, that had cost him such profound anguish at the time of their writing. "I felt so completely exhausted," he told me when it was done, "as if all the blood had run out of my brain. I sat for a long while on a street bench, unable to move. . . ."

"And it's old and old it's sad and old it's sad and weary I go back to you, my cold father, my cold, mad father, my cold mad feary father, till the near sight of the mere size of him, the moyles and moyles of it, moananoaning, makes me seasilt saltsick and I rush, my only, into your arms. . . ."

There was no turning back after these lines, my friend. You knew it well. Adew!

For Further Reading and Reference

LETTERS

Letters of James Joyce, volume 1, edited by Stuart Gilbert (London: Faber & Faber / New York: Viking, 1957); revised and edited by Richard Ellmann (New York: Viking, 1966); volumes 2 and 3, edited by Ellmann (London: Faber & Faber / New York: Viking, 1966);

Selected Letters of James Joyce, edited by Ellmann (New York: Viking, 1975; London: Faber & Faber, 1975).

BIBLIOGRAPHIES

Robert Martin Adams, "The Bent Knife Blade: Joyce in the 1960s," *Partisan Review,* 29 (1962): 507–518;

Maurice Beebe, Phillip Herring, and A. Walton Litz, compilers, "Criticism of James Joyce: A Selected Checklist," *Modern Fiction Studies,* 15 (1969): 105–182;

Bernard Benstock, "The James Joyce Industry: A Reassessment," in *Yeats, Joyce, and Beckett: New Light on Three Modern Irish Writers,* edited by Kathleen McGrory and John Unterecker (Lewisburg, Pa.: Bucknell University Press, 1976), pp. 118–132;

Alan M. Cohn, "Joyce Bibliographies: A Survey," *American Book Collector,* 15, no. 10 (1965): 11–16;

Thomas E. Connolly, comp., *The Personal Library of James Joyce: A Descriptive Bibliography* (Buffalo, N.Y.: University Bookstore, University of Buffalo, 1957);

Robert H. Deming, ed., *A Bibliography of James Joyce Studies* (Lawrence: University of Kansas Libraries, 1964); revised and enlarged edition (Boston: G. K. Hall, 1977);

Sidney Feshbach and William Herman, "The History of Joyce Criticism and Scholarship," in *A Companion to Joyce Studies,* edited by Zack Bowen and James F. Carens (Westport, Conn. & London: Greenwood Press, 1984), pp. 727–780;

Tetsumaro Hayashi, ed., *James Joyce: Research Opportunities and Dissertation Abstracts* (Jefferson, N.C.: McFarland, 1985);

A. Walton Litz, "Joyce," in *The English Novel: Select Bibliographical Guides,* edited by A. E. Dyson (London & New York: Oxford University Press, 1974), pp. 349–369;

H. Marshall McLuhan, "A Survey of Joyce Criticism," *Renascence,* 4 (1951): 12–18;

Alan Parker, *James Joyce: A Bibliography of His Writings, Critical Material, and Miscellanea* (Boston: F. W. Faxon, 1948);

Thomas Jackson Rice, *James Joyce: A Guide to Research* (New York & London: Garland, 1982);

John J. Slocum and Herbert Cahoon, eds., *A Bibliography of James Joyce (1882–1941)* (New Haven: Yale University Press, 1953);

Thomas F. Staley, *An Annotated Critical Bibliography of James Joyce* (New York: St. Martin's Press, 1989; London, U.K.: Harvester Wheatsheaf, 1989);

Staley, "James Joyce," in *Anglo-Irish Literature: A Review of Research,* edited by Richard J. Finneran (New York: Modern Language Association, 1976), pp. 366–435;

Staley, "James Joyce," in *Recent Research on Anglo-Irish Writers: A Supplement to Anglo-Irish Literature: A Review of Research,* edited by Richard J. Finneran (New York: Modern Language Association, 1983), pp. 181–202;

William White, "James Joyce," in *New Cambridge Bibliography of English Literature,* volume 4 (Cambridge: Cambridge University Press, 1972), pp. 444–471.

SELECTED BIOGRAPHIES AND BIOGRAPHICAL SOURCES

Robert Martin Adams, *Surface and Symbol: The Consistency of James Joyce's* Ulysses (New York: A Galaxy Book, 1967), p. 256;

Chester G. Anderson, *James Joyce and His World* (London: Thames & Hudson, 1967; New York: Viking, 1968);

Margaret Anderson, *My Thirty Years War* (New York: Covici-Friede, 1930);

Sylvia Beach, *Shakespeare and Company* (New York: Harcourt, 1959); edition with introduction by James Laughlin (Lincoln: University of Nebraska Press, 1991);

Morris Beja, *James Joyce: A Literary Life* (Columbus: Ohio State University Press, 1992);

Silvio Benco, "James Joyce in Trieste," *Bookman,* 72 (December 1930): 375–380;

Louis Berrone, *James Joyce in Padua,* edited, translated, and with an introduction by Berrone (New York: Random House, 1977);

Rosa Maria Bosinelli, Paola Pugliatti, and Romana Zacchi, eds., *Myriadminded Man: Jottings on Joyce* (Bologna: Editrice, 1986);

Bruce S. J. Bradley, *James Joyce's Schooldays,* foreword by Richard Ellmann (Dublin: Gill & Macmillan, 1982; New York: St. Martin's Press, 1982);

Alessandro Francini Bruni, *Joyce intimo spogliato in piazza* (Trieste: La Editoriale Libraria, 1992); translated and republished in *Portraits of the Artist in Exile: Recollections of James Joyce by Europeans,* edited by Willard Potts (Seattle: University of Washington Press, 1997);

Frank Budgen, *James Joyce and the Making of* Ulysses (London: Greyson, 1934; New York: Harrison Smith & Robert Haas, 1934);

Budgen, "Mr. Joyce," in *Myselves When Young* (London & New York: Oxford University Press, 1970);

Hubert Foss, ed., *The Joyce Book* (London: Sylvan & H. Milford, Oxford University Press, 1933);

John Francis Byrne, *Silent Years: An Autobiography, With Memoirs of James Joyce and Our Ireland* (New York: Farrar, Strauss & Young, 1953);

Sandy Campbell, "Mrs Joyce in Zürich," *Harper's Bazaar* (October 1952);

Mary Colum, *Life and the Dream* (New York: Doubleday, 1947); revised with additional material (Chester Springs, Pa.: Dufour, 1966);

Colum, "A Little Knowledge of Joyce," *Saturday Review of Literature,* 33 (29 April 1950): 11–12;

Colum, "Portrait of James Joyce," *Dublin Magazine,* 7 (April–June 1932): 40–48;

Mary Colum and Padraic Colum, *Our Friend James Joyce* (Garden City, N.Y.: Doubleday, 1958);

Peter Costello, *James Joyce: The Years of Growth 1882–1915* (New York: Pantheon, 1992);

Costello, *Leopold Bloom: A Biography* (Dublin: Gill & Macmillan, 1981);

Constantine Curran, *James Joyce Remembered* (New York & London: Oxford University Press, 1968);

Curran, "When James Joyce Lived in Dublin," *Vogue,* 109 (May 1947): 144–149;

Alice Curtayne, "Portrait of the Artist as a Brother: an Interview with James Joyce's Sister," *Critic,* 21 (1963): 43–47;

Stan Gebler Davies, *James Joyce: A Portrait of the Artist* (London: Davis-Poynter, 1975; New York: Stein & Day, 1975);

Hugh J. Dawson, "Thomas MacGreevy and Joyce," *James Joyce Quarterly,* 25 (Spring 1988): 305–321;

Le Donne di Giacomo: Il Mondo Femminile nella Trieste di James Joyce / The Female World in James Joyce's Trieste (Trieste: Hammerle Editori, 1999);

Leon Edel, *James Joyce: The Last Journey* (New York: Gotham Book Mart, 1947);

Richard Ellmann, *James Joyce* (New York: Oxford University Press, 1959; revised, 1982);

Ellmann, *Ulysses on the Liffey* (New York: Oxford University Press, 1972; London: Faber & Faber, 1972);

Ellmann, ed., *Giacomo Joyce,* notes and introduction by Ellmann (New York: Viking, 1968; London: Faber & Faber, 1968);

Ellmann and Edmund L. Epstein, "James Augustine Aloysius Joyce," in *A Companion to Joyce Studies,* edited by Zack Bowen and James F. Carens (Westport, Conn.: Greenwood Press, 1984): pp. 3–37;

Nohan D. Fabricant, "The Ocular History of James Joyce," in *Thirteen Famous Patients* (Philadelphia: Chilton, 1960);

Thomas Faerber and Markus Luchsinger, *Joyce in Zurich* (Zurich: Unionsverlag, 1988);

A. Nicholas Fargnoli and Michael Patrick Gillespie, *James Joyce From A to Z* (New York: Facts on File, 1995);

Noel Riley Fitch, *Sylvia Beach and the Lost Generation: Literary Paris in the Twenties and Thirties* (New York: Norton, 1983);

Gisèle Freund, *Trois Jours avec Joyce* (Paris: Denoël, 1982);

Freund and V. P. Carleton, *James Joyce in Paris: His Final Years,* preface by Simone de Beauvoir (New York: Harcourt, Brace & World, 1965; London: Cassell, 1965);

Carola Giedeon-Welcker, *In Memoriam James Joyce* (Zürich: Fretz & Wasmuth, 1941);

Giedeon-Welcker, "James Joyce in Zurich," in *The Golden Horizon,* edited, with an introduction, by Cyril Connolly (London: Weidenfeld & Nicolson, 1953; New York: University Books, 1955), pp. 383–387;

Louis Gillet, *Stèle pour James Joyce* (Marseille: Éditions du Sagittaire, 1941); translated, with an introduction, by Georges Markow-Totevy as *Claybook for James Joyce,* preface by Leon Edel (New York: Abelard-Schuman, 1958);

Oliver St. John Gogarty, *As I Was Going Down Sackville Street: A Phantasy in Fact* (London: Cowan, 1937; New York: Reynal & Hitchcock, 1937), pp. 293–295;

Gogarty, "The Joyce I Knew," obituary, *Saturday Review of Literature,* 23 (25 January 1941);

Gogarty, *It Isn't This Time of Year at All! An Unpremeditated Autobiography* (Garden City: Doubleday, 1954);

Gogarty, *Mourning Became Mrs. Spendlove and Other Portraits, Grave and Gay* (New York: Creative Age, 1948);

Gogarty, "They Think They Know Joyce," *Saturday Review of Literature,* 33 (18 March 1950): 8–9, 35–37;

Gogarty, "The Tower: Fact and Fiction," *Irish Times* (16 June 1962): 11;

Herbert S. Gorman, *James Joyce: A Definitive Biography* (London: John Lane, 1941);

Gorman, *James Joyce: His First Forty Years* (New York: B. W. Huebsch, 1924; London: Geoffrey Bles, 1926);

David Hayman, "Shadow of his Mind: The Papers of Lucia Joyce," in *James Joyce: The Centennial Symposium,* edited by Morris Beja (Urbana: University of Illinois Press, 1986);

Kees van Hoek, "Mrs. James Joyce," *Irish Times* (12 November 1949);

Louis Hyman, *The Jews of Ireland: From Earliest Times to the Year 1910* (Jerusalem: Israel Universities Press / London: Jewish Historical Society of England, 1972);

Vivien Igoe, *James Joyce's Dublin Houses* (London: Mandarin, 1990);

Maria Jolas, ed., *A James Joyce Yearbook* (Paris: Transition Press, 1949);

Stanislaus Joyce, *The Dublin Diary of Stanislaus Joyce,* edited by George H. Healy (London: Faber & Faber, 1962; Ithaca, N.Y.: Cornell University Press, 1962); revised as *The Complete Dublin Diary of Stanislaus Joyce* (Ithaca, N.Y.: Cornell University Press, 1971);

Joyce, "The Joyces," *Listener* (London), 41(26 May 1949): 896;

Joyce, *My Brother's Keeper: James Joyce's Early Years,* edited, with an introduction and notes, by Ellman, preface by T. S. Eliot (New York: Viking, 1958);

Joyce, "Ricordi di James Joyce," *Litterature,* 5 (July/September 1941): 25–35, (October/December 1941): 23–35; translated from Italian by Ellsworth Mason as *Recollections of James Joyce* (New York: The James Joyce Society, 1950);

Richard M. Kain, "An Interview with Carla Giedeon-Welcker and Maria Jolas," *James Joyce Quarterly,* 11 (Winter 1974): 94–112;

Hugh Kenner, *Dublin's Joyce* (London: Chatto & Windus, 1955; Bloomington: Indiana University Press, 1956), pp. 226–227;

Paul Léon, "In Memory of Joyce," *Poésie,* 5 (1942): 35;

Harry Levin, *James Joyce: A Critical Introduction* (Norfolk, Conn.: New Directions Books, 1941; London: Faber & Faber, 1944);

Jane Lidderdale, "Lucia Joyce at St. Andrew's," *James Joyce Broadsheet,* 10 (February 1983): 3;

Lidderdale and Mary Nicholson, *Dear Miss Weaver: Harriet Shaw Weaver, 1876–1961* (New York: Viking, 1970; London: Faber & Faber, 1970);

Hugh MacDiarmid, *In Memoriam James Joyce* (Glasgow: Maclellan, 1955);

Brenda Maddox, *Nora: The Real Life of Molly Bloom* (Boston: Houghton Mifflin, 1988);

Marvin Magalaner and Richard M. Kain, *Joyce: The Man, The Work, The Reputation* (New York: New York University Press, 1956);

Robert McAlmon, *Being Geniuses Together: An Autobiography* (London: Secker & Warburg, 1938); revised and republished, with supplementary chapters by Kay Boyle, as *Being Geniuses Together, 1920–1930* (Garden City, N.Y.: Doubleday, 1968);

John McCourt, *The Years of Bloom: James Joyce in Trieste 1904–1920* (Madison: University of Wisconsin Press, 2000);

Dougald McMillan, *Transition: The History of a Literary Era, 1927–1938* (London: Calder & Boyers, 1975; New York: Braziller, 1976), pp. 179–231;

Jacques Mercanton, "The Hours of James Joyce," translated by Lloyd C. Parks, *Kenyon Review,* 24 (1962): 700–730; 25 (1963): 93–118;

Jeffrey Meyers, "James and Nora Joyce," in *Married to Genius* (London: London Magazine Editions, 1977; New York: Barnes & Noble, 1977);

E. H. Mikhail, ed., *James Joyce: Interviews and Recollections,* foreword by Frank Delaney (London: Macmillan, 1990; New York: St. Martin's Press, 1990);

Frank Nino, "Souvenirs sur James Joyce," *La Table Ronde* (Paris) (23 November 1947): 1671–1693;

Lucie Noël, *James Joyce and Paul L. Léon: The Story of a Friendship* (New York: Gotham Book Mart, 1950);

Edna O'Brien, *James Joyce* (New York: Viking Penguin, 1999);

Ulick O'Connor, ed., *The Joyce We Knew: Memoirs by Eugene Sheehy, Will G. Fallon, Padraic Colum, Arthur Power* (Cork, Ireland: Mercier, 1967);

Padraic O'Laoi, *Nora Barnacle Joyce: A Portrait* (Galway: Kenny Bookshop and Art Galleries, 1982);

David Pierce, *James Joyce's Ireland* (New Haven: Yale University Press, 1992);

Gianni Pinguentini, *James Joyce in Italia* (Verona: Linotipia veronese di Ghidini e Fiorini, 1963);

Harry J. Pollack, "The Girl Joyce Did Not Marry," *James Joyce Quarterly,* 4 (Summer 1967): 255–257;

Willard Potts, ed., *Portraits of the Artist in Exile: Recollections of James Joyce by Europeans* (Seattle: University of Washington Press, 1979);

Ezra Pound, *Conversations with James Joyce,* edited by Clive Hart (London: Millington, 1974);

Pound, *Pound/Joyce: The Letters of Ezra Pound to James Joyce,* with Pound's *Essays on Joyce,* edited, with commentary, by Forrest Read (New York: New Directions, 1967; London: Faber & Faber, 1968);

Arthur Power, *Conversations With James Joyce,* edited by Clive Hart (New York: Barnes & Noble, 1974; London: Millington, 1974);

Benjamin L. Reid, *The Man From New York: John Quinn and His Friends* (New York: Oxford University Press, 1968);

Mary T. Reynolds, "Joyce and Nora: The Indispensable Countersign," *Sewanee Review,* 72 (Winter 1964): 29–64;

Myra Russel, ed., *James Joyce's Chamber Music: The Lost Settings,* with an introduction by Russel (Bloomington: Indiana University Press, 1993);

Robert Scholes and Richard M. Kain, eds., *The Workshop of Daedalus* (Evanston, Ill.: Northwestern University Press, 1965);

Eugene Sheehy, *May It Please The Court* (Dublin: Fallon, 1951);

Philippe Soupault, "Composition of Place: Joyce and Trieste," *Modern British Literature,* 5 (1980): 3–9;

Soupault, *Souvenirs de James Joyce* (Alger: Charlot, 1943);

Thomas Staley, "James Joyce in Trieste," *Georgia Review,* 16 (October 1962): 446–449;

Staley and Randolph Lewis, eds., *Reflections on James Joyce: Stuart Gilbert's Paris Journal* (Austin: University of Texas Press, 1993);

Kevin Sullivan, *Joyce Among the Jesuits* (New York: Columbia University Press, 1958);

Italo Svevo, *James Joyce: A Lecture Delivered in Milan in 1927,* translated by Stanislaus Joyce (New York: New Directions, 1950);

William York Tindall, *The Joyce Country* (University Park: Pennsylvania State University Press, 1960); enlarged edition (New York: Schocken Books, 1966);

Louis J. Walsh, "With Joyce and Kettle at U.C.D.," *Irish Digest,* 12 (June 1942): 27–29.

GENERAL CRITICISM, CONTEXT, AND INTERPRETATION

Robert M. Adams, *James Joyce: Common Sense and Beyond* (New York: Random House, 1966);

Alison Armstrong, *The Joyce of Cooking: Food and Drink from James Joyce's Dublin* (Barrytown, N.Y.: Station Hill, 1986);

Derek Attridge, *The Cambridge Companion to James Joyce* (Cambridge & New York: Cambridge University Press, 1990);

Attridge and Daniel Ferrer, eds., *Post-structuralist Joyce: Essays from the French* (Cambridge & New York: Cambridge University Press, 1984);

Jacques Aubert, *Introduction à l'esthetique de James Joyce* (Paris: Didier, 1973);

Ruth Bauerle, ed., *The James Joyce Songbook* (New York: Garland, 1982);

Sylvia Beach, *Catalogue of a Collection Containing Manuscripts and Rare Editions of James Joyce, Etc.* (Paris: Shakespeare, 1935);

Maurice Beebe, "James Joyce: Barnacle Goose and Lapwin," *PMLA*, 81 (June 1956): 302–320;

Beebe, "Joyce and Stephen Dedalus: The Problem of Autobiography," in *A James Joyce Miscellany,* edited by Marvin Magalaner (Carbondale: Southern Illinois University Press, 1959);

Morris Beja, *Epiphany in the Modern Novel* (Seattle: University of Washington Press, 1971);

Beja and Shari Benstock, *Coping with Joyce: Essay from the Copenhagen Symposium* (Columbus: Ohio State University Press, 1989);

Bernard Benstock, *James Joyce* (New York: Ungar, 1985);

Benstock, *The Seventh of Joyce* (Bloomington: Indiana University Press, 1982; Brighton: Harvester, 1982);

Benstock, ed., *Critical Essays on James Joyce* (Boston, Mass.: G. K. Hall, 1985);

Bernard Benstock and Shari Benstock, *Who's He When He's At Home: A James Joyce Directory* (Urbana: University of Illinois Press, 1980);

Victor Bérard, *Les Phéneciens dans l'Odyssée* (Paris, 1902);

Bruce Bidwell with Linda Heffer, *The Joycean Way* (Dublin: Wolfhound, 1981);

Sydney Bolt, *A Preface to James Joyce* (London & New York: Longman, 1981);

Zack Bowen and James F. Carens, eds., *A Companion to Joyce Studies* (Westport, Conn.: Greenwood, 1984);

Ernest A. Boyd, *Ireland's Literary Renaissance* (Dublin: Maunsel, 1916; New York: John Lane, 1916);

Edward Brandabur, *A Scrupulous Meanness: A Study of Joyce's Early Work* (Urbana: University of Illinois Press, 1971);

Sheldon Brivic, *Joyce Between Freud and Jung* (Port Washington, N.Y. / London: Kennikat Press, 1980);

Brivic, *Joyce the Creator* (Madison: University of Wisconsin Press, 1985);

Brivic, *The Veil of Signs: Joyce, Lacan, and Perception* (Urbana: University of Illinois Press, 1991);

Dennis Brown, *Intertextual Dynamics within the Literary Group–Joyce, Lewis, Eliot, and Pound: The Men of 1914* (New York: St. Martin's Press, 1991);

Richard Brown, *James Joyce and Sexuality* (Cambridge & New York: Cambridge University Press, 1985);

Phyllis Carey and Ed Jewinski, eds., *Re: Joyce'N Beckett* (New York: Fordham University Press, 1992);

Hélène Cixous, *L'Exil de James Joyce, ou l'Art du Remplacement* (Paris: Bernard Grasset, 1968); translated as *The Exile of James Joyce,* by Sally A. J. Purcell (New York: David Lewis, 1972);

Cixous, *Readings: The Poetics of Blanchot, Joyce, Kafka, Kleist, Lispector, and Tsvetayeva,* edited, translated, and introduction by Verena Andermatt (Minneapolis: University of Minnesota Press, 1991);

Jackson I. Cope, *Joyce's Cities: Archaeologies of the Soul* (Baltimore & London: Johns Hopkins University Press, 1981);

Stelio Crise, *Epiphanies & Phadographs: James Joyce e Trieste* (Milano: All'insegna del Pesce d'Oro, 1967);

Benedetto Croce, *Filosofia di Giambattista Vico* (Bari: G. Laterza & Figli, 1911); translated as *The Philosophy of Giambattista Vico,* by R. G. Collingwood (New York: Macmillan, 1913; London: H. Latimer, 1913);

Richard K. Cross, *Flaubert and Joyce: The Rite of Fiction* (Princeton: Princeton University Press, 1971);

Reed Way Dasenbrock, *Imitating the Italians: Wyatt, Spenser, Synge, Pound, Joyce* (Baltimore: Johns Hopkins University Press, 1991);

Frank Delaney, *James Joyce's Odyssey: A Guide to the Dublin of Ulysses* (London: Hodder & Stoughton, 1981; New York: Holt, Rinehart & Winston, 1982);

Richard H. Demming, *James Joyce: The Critical Heritage,* 2 volumes (London: Routledge & Kegan Paul, 1970; New York: Barnes & Noble, 1970);

Charles Duff, *James Joyce and the Plain Reader* (London: Harmsworth, 1932);

Edouard Dujardin, *Les Laruiers sont coupés* (Paris: A. Messein, 1924);

Dujardin, *Le Monologue intérieur: son apparition, ses origines, sa place dans l'oeuvre de James Joyce* (Paris, 1931);

Janet E. Dunleavy, ed., *Reviewing Classics of Joyce Criticism* (Urbana & Chicago: University of Illinois Press, 1991);

Dunleavy, Melvin J. Friedman, and Michael Patrick Gillespie, eds., *Joycean Occasions: Essays from the Milwaukee James Joyce Conference* (Newark: University of Delaware Press, 1991; London & Cranberry, N.J.: Associated University Presses, 1991);

Umberto Eco, *Poetiche di Joyce* (Milano: Bompiani, 1982); translated as *The Aesthetics of Chaosmos: The Middle Ages of James Joyce,* by Ellen Esrock (Tulsa, Okla.: University of Tulsa Press, 1982);

Richard Ellmann, *The Consciousness of Joyce* (London: Faber & Faber, 1977; Toronto & New York: Oxford University Press, 1977);

Ellmann, *James Joyce's Tower* (Dun Laoghaire: Eastern Regional Tourism Organisation, 1969);

Richard Finneran, *Recent Research on Anglo-Irish Writers* (New York: Modern Language Association of America, 1983);

Finneran, ed., *Anglo-Irish Literature: A Review of Research* (New York: Modern Language Association of America, 1976);

John Garvin, *James Joyce's Disunited Kingdom and the Irish Dimension* (Dublin: Gill & MacMillan, 1976; New York: Barnes & Noble, 1976);

Bernard Gheerbrandt, *James Joyce—sa vie, son oeuvre, son rayonnment* (Paris: Librarie la Hune, 1949);

Stuart Gilbert, "The Latin Background of James Joyce's Art," *Horizon* (London), 10 (1944);

Michael Patrick Gillespie, *Inverted Volumes Improperly Arranged: James Joyce and His Trieste Library* (Ann Arbor: University of Michigan Research Press, 1980);

Gillespie, *Reading the Book of Himself: Narrative Strategies in the Works of James Joyce* (Columbus: Ohio State University Press, 1989);

Seon Givens, ed., *James Joyce: Two Decades of Criticism* (New York: Vanguard, 1948; with new introduction, 1963);

Louis Golding, *James Joyce* (London: Butterworth, 1933);

Arnold Goldman, *The Joyce Paradox: Form and Freedom in His Fiction* (Evanston, Ill.: Northwestern University Press, 1966; London: Routledge & Kegan Paul, 1966);

John Gordon, *James Joyce's Metamorphoses* (Dublin: Gill & Macmillan / Totowa, N.J.: Barnes & Noble, 1981);

Michael Groden, ed., *The James Joyce Archive,* 63 volumes (New York: Garland, 1977);

John J. Gross, *James Joyce* (New York: Viking, 1970; London: Fontana, 1971);

Margaret Mills Harper, *The Aristocracy of Art in Joyce and Wolfe* (Baton Rouge & London: Louisiana State University Press, 1990);

Suzette A. Henke, *James Joyce and the Politics of Desire* (New York & London: Routledge, 1990);

Henke and Elaine Unkeless, eds., *Women in Joyce* (Urbana & Chicago: University of Illinois Press, 1982);

Cheryl Herr, *Joyce's Anatomy of Culture* (Urbana & Chicago: University of Illinois Press, 1986);

Phillip F. Herring, *Joyce's Uncertainty Principle* (Princeton: Princeton University Press, 1987);

Matthew J. C. Hodgart, *James Joyce: A Student's Guide* (London & Boston: Routledge, 1978);

Hodgart and Mabel P. Worthington, *Song in the Works of James Joyce* (New York: University of Columbia Press, 1959);

Eileen Lanouette Hughes, "The Mystery Lady of *Giacomo Joyce*," *Life* (19 February 1968): 54+;

Patricia Hutchins, *James Joyce's Dublin* (London: Grey Walls Press, 1950);

Hutchins, *James Joyce's World* (London: Methuen, 1957);

Richard M. Kain, *Dublin in the Age of William Butler Yeats and James Joyce* (Norman: University of Oklahoma Press, 1962; Newton Abbott, U.K.: David & Charles, 1972);

Hugh Kenner, *Joyce's Voices* (Berkeley, Los Angeles & London: University of California Press, 1978);

Kenner, *The Stoic Comedians: Flaubert, Joyce, and Beckett* (Boston: Beacon, 1962);

R. B. Kershner, *Joyce, Bakhtin, and Popular Literature: Chronicles of Disorder* (Chapel Hill & London: University of North Carolina Press, 1989);

Charles Lamb, *Adventures of Ulysses,* edited, with introduction and notes, by John Cooke (Dublin: Browne & Nolan, 1892);

Valéry Larbaud, "James Joyce," *Nouvelle Revue Francaise* (Paris), April 1922;

Larbaud, "A Propos de James Joyce," *Nouvelle Revue Francaise* (Paris), January 1925;

F. R. Leavis, "James Joyce and the Revolution of the Word," *Scrutiny*, 2 (1933): 193–201;

Geert Lernout, *The French Joyce* (Ann Arbor: University of Michigan Press, 1990);

Wyndham Lewis, "An analysis of the mind of James Joyce," *Time and Western Man* (New York, 1928);

A. Walton Litz, *James Joyce* (New York: Twayne, 1966; revised edition, 1972);

Corinna del Greco Lobner, "James Joyce's Dublin," *Twentieth Century Studies*, 4 (November 1970): 6–25;

Lobner, *James Joyce's Italian Connection: The Poetics of the Word* (Iowa City: University of Iowa Press, 1989);

J. B. Lyons, *James Joyce and Medicine* (Dublin: Dolmen Press, 1973);

Colin MacCabe, *James Joyce and the Revolution of the Word* (London: Macmillan, 1978; New York: Barnes & Noble, 1979);

MacCabe, ed., *James Joyce: New Perspectives* (Brighton, U.K.: Harvester, 1982; Bloomington: Indiana University Press, 1982);

Tony Malone, *Joyce's Parlor Music* (Maginni Enterprises, 1994);

Marvin Magalaner, "James Mangan and Joyce's Dedalus Family," *Philosophical Quarterly*, 31 (October 1952): 363–371;

Magalaner, *Time of Apprenticeship: the Fiction of the Young James Joyce* (New York & London: Abelard-Schuman, 1959);

Vicki Mahaffey, *Reauthorizing Joyce* (Cambridge & New York: Cambridge University Press, 1988);

Dominic Manganiello, *Joyce's Politics* (London: Routledge & Kegan Paul, 1980);

Timothy Martin, *Joyce and Wagner: A Study of Influence* (Cambridge: Cambridge University Press, 1991);

Jean-Jacques Mayoux, *James Joyce* (Paris: Gallimard, 1965);

W. J. McCormack and Alistair Stead, *James Joyce & Modern Literature* (London & Boston: Routledge & Kegan Paul, 1982);

H. Marshall McLuhan, "James Joyce: Trivial and Quadrivial," *Thought* (1953);

McLuhan, "Joyce, Aquinas, and the Poetic Process," *Renascence*, 4 (1951);

Giorgio Melchiori, *The Tightrope Walkers* (London: Routledge & Kegan Paul, 1956);

Vivian Mercier, "Joyce and the Irish Tradition of Parody," in *The Irish Comic Tradition* (Oxford: Clarendon Press, 1962), pp. 210–236;

J. Mitchell Morse, *The Sympathetic Alien: James Joyce and Catholicism* (New York: New York University Press, 1959);

Ira B. Nadel, *Joyce and the Jews: Culture and Texts* (Iowa City: University of Iowa Press, 1989);

William T. Noon, *Joyce and Aquinas* (New Haven, Conn.: Yale University Press, 1957);

Darcy O'Brien, *The Conscience of James Joyce* (Princeton: Princeton University Press, 1967);

Michael O'Shea, *James Joyce and Heraldry* (Albany: State University of New York Press, 1986);

Patrick Parrinder, *James Joyce* (Cambridge: Cambridge University Press, 1984);

Charles Peake, *James Joyce: The Citizen and the Artist* (Stanford, Cal.: Stanford University Press, 1977);

Richard F. Peterson, *James Joyce Revisited* (New York: Twayne, 1992);

Peterson, Alan M. Cohn, and Edmund L. Epstein, eds., *Work in Progress: Joyce Centenary Essays* (Carbondale: Southern Illinois University Press, 1983);

Jean-Michel Rabaté, *Joyce upon the Void: The Genesis of Doubt* (New York: St. Martin's Press, 1991);

Mary T. Reynolds, *Joyce and Dante: The Shaping Imagination* (Princeton: Princeton University Press, 1981);

Reynolds, "Joyce's Villanelle and D'Annunzio's Sonnet Sequence," *Journal of Modern Fiction,* 5 (February 1976): 19–45;

John Paul Riquelme, *Teller and Tale in Joyce's Fiction: Oscillating Perspectives* (Baltimore: Johns Hopkins University Press, 1983);

Alan Roughley, *James Joyce and Critical Theory: An Introduction* (Ann Arbor: University of Michigan Press, 1991);

John Ryan, ed., *A Bash in the Tunnel: James Joyce by the Irish* (London & Brighton: Clifton Books, 1970);

Robert E. Scholes and Richard M. Kain, eds., *The Workshop of Daedalus* (Evanston, Ill.: Northwestern University Press, 1965);

Beryl Scholssman, *Joyce's Catholic Comedy of Language* (Madison: University of Wisconsin Press, 1985);

Bonnie Kime Scott, *James Joyce* (Atlantic Highlands, N.J.: Humanities Press, 1987);

Scott, *Joyce and Feminism* (Bloomington: Indiana University Press, 1984);

Scott, ed., *New Alliances in Joyce Studies: "When it's Aped to Foul a Delfian"* (Newark: University of Delaware Press; London & Toronto: Associated University Presses, 1988);

Fritz Senn, *Joyce's Dislocutions: Essays on Reading as Translation,* edited by John Paul Riquelme (Baltimore: Johns Hopkins University Press, 1984);

Peter Spielberg, *James Joyce's Manuscripts and Letters at the University of Buffalo* (Buffalo: University of Buffalo Press, 1962);

Thomas Staley, ed., *James Joyce Today: Essays on the Major Works* (Bloomington: Indiana University Press, 1966);

L. A. G. Strong, *The Sacred River: An Approach to Joyce* (London: Methuen, 1949);

Stanley Sultan, *Eliot, Joyce & Company* (New York & Oxford: Oxford University Press, 1987);

William York Tindall, *James Joyce: His Way of Interpreting the Modern World* (New York: Scribners, 1950);

Tindall, *A Reader's Guide to James Joyce* (New York: Noonday, 1959);

William Troy, "Stephen Dedalus and James Joyce," *Nation,* 138 (14 February 1934): 187–188;

B. J. Tysdahl, *Joyce and Ibsen: A Study in Literary Influence* (Oslo: Norwegian Universities Press; New York: Humanities Press, 1968);

Donald Phillip Verene, ed., *Vico and Joyce* (Albany: State University of New York Press, 1987);

Albert Wachtel, *The Cracked Lookingglass: James Joyce and the Nightmare of History* (Selinsgrove: Susquehanna University Press, 1992);

Katie Wales, *The Language of James Joyce* (New York: St. Martin's Press, 1992);

Edmund Wilson, "James Joyce," *Axel's Castle: A Study in the Imaginative Literature of 1870–1930* (New York & London: Scribners, 1931).

CRITICISM AND INTERPRETATION BY WORK

DUBLINERS

James R. Baker, "Ibsen, Joyce and Living Dead: A Study of *Dubliners*," in *A James Joyce Miscellany*, third series, edited by Marvin Magalaner (Carbondale, Ill.: Southern Illinois University Press, 1962), pp. 18–32;

Baker and Thomas F. Staley, eds., *James Joyce's* Dubliners: *A Critical Handbook* (Belmont, Cal.: Wadsworth, 1969);

Joseph E. Baker, "The Trinity in Joyce's 'Grace,'" *James Joyce Quarterly*, 2 (Summer 1965): 299–303;

Rick Barney and others, "Analyzing 'Araby' as Story and Discourse: A Summary of the MURGE Project," *James Joyce Quarterly*, 18 (Spring 1981): 237–255;

Warren Beck, *Joyce's Dubliners: Substance, Vision, and Art* (Durham, N.C.: Duke University Press, 1969);

Karl Beckson, "Moore's *The Untilled Field* and Joyce's *Dubliners:* The Short Story's Intricate Maze," *English Literature in Transition*, 15 (1972): 291–304;

Morris Beja, ed., *James Joyce,* Dubliners *and* A Portrait of the Artist as a Young Man: *A Casebook* (London: Macmillan, 1973);

Bernard Benstock, "Arabesques: Third Position of Concord," *James Joyce Quarterly*, 5 (Fall 1967): 30–39;

Benstock, "Joyce's Rheumatics: The Holy Ghost in *Dubliners*," *Southern Review*, 14 (January 1978): 1–15;

Joseph L. Blotner, "Ivy Day in the Committee Room," *Perspective*, 9 (Summer 1957): 210–217;

Zack Bowen, "Hungarian Politics in 'After the Race,'" *James Joyce Quarterly*, 7 (Winter 1969): 138–139;

Bowen, "Joyce's Prophylactic Paralysis: Exposure in *Dubliners*," *James Joyce Quarterly*, 19 (Spring 1982): 257–275;

Robert Boyle, "Swiftian Allegory and Dantean Parody in Joyce's 'Grace,'" *James Joyce Quarterly*, 7 (Fall 1969): 11–21;

Boyle, "'Two Gallants' and 'Ivy Day in the Committee Room,'" *James Joyce Quarterly*, 1 (Fall 1963): 3–9;

Harold Brodbar, "A Religious Allegory: Joyce's 'A Little Cloud,'" *Midwest Quarterly*, 2 (Spring 1961): 221–227;

Richard Carpenter, "The Witch Maria," *James Joyce Review*, 3 (February 1959): 3–7;

Warren Carrier, "*Dubliners:* Joyce's Dantean Vision," *Renascence,* 17 (1965): 211–215;

Margaret Chestnutt, "Joyce's *Dubliners:* History, Ideology, and Social Reality," *Eire-Ireland,* 14 (1979): 93–105;

Ben L. Collins, "Joyce's Use of Yeats and of Irish History: A Reading of 'A Mother,'" *Eire-Ireland,* 5 (September 1970): 45–66;

Thomas E. Connolly, "Joyce's 'The Sisters': A Pennyworth of Snuff," *College English,* 27 (December 1965): 189–195;

Connolly, "Marriage Divination in Joyce's 'Clay,'" *Studies in Short Fiction,* 3 (Spring 1966): 293–299;

John William Corrington, "Isolation as Motif in 'A Painful Case,'" *James Joyce Quarterly,* 3 (Spring 1966): 182–191;

Concepcion D. Dadufalza, "The Quest of the Chalice-Bearer in James Joyce's 'Araby,'" *Diliman Review,* 7 (July 1959): 317–325;

Joseph K. Davis, "The City as Radical Order: James Joyce's *Dubliners,*" *Studies in the Literary Imagination,* 3 (October 1970): 79–96;

Robert Adams Day, "Joyce's Gnomons, Lenehan and the Persistence of an Image," *Novel: A Forum on Fiction,* 14 (Fall 1980): 5–19;

Richard Ellmann, "Backgrounds of 'The Dead,'" *Kenyon Review,* 20 (Autumn 1958): 507–528;

Monroe Engel, "*Dubliners* and Exotic Expectation," in *Twentieth-Century Literature in Retrospective,* edited by Reuben A. Brower (Cambridge, Mass.: Harvard University Press, 1971), pp. 3–26;

Edmund L. Epstein, "Hidden Imagery in James Joyce's 'Two Gallants,'" *James Joyce Quarterly,* 7 (Summer 1970): 369–370;

Sidney Feshbach, "Death in 'An Encounter,'" *James Joyce Quarterly,* 2 (Winter 1965): 82–89;

Therese Fischer, "From Reliable to Unreliable Narrator: Rhetorical Changes in Joyce's 'The Sisters,'" *James Joyce Quarterly,* 9 (Fall 1971): 85–92;

John Freimarck, "'Araby': A Quest for Meaning," *James Joyce Quarterly,* 7 (Summer 1970): 366–368;

Freimarck, "Missing Pieces in Joyce's *Dubliners,*" *Twentieth-Century Literature,* 24 (Winter 1978): 239–257;

Marilyn French, "Missing Pieces in Joyce's *Dubliners,*" *Twentieth-Century Literature,* 24 (1978): 443–472;

Grattan Freyer, "A Reader's Report on *Dubliners,*" *James Joyce Quarterly,* 10 (Summer 1973): 445–457;

Gerhard Friedrich, "Bret Harte as a Source for James Joyce's 'The Dead,'" *Philological Quarterly,* 33 (October 1954): 442–444;

Friedrich, "The Gnomic Clue to James Joyce's *Dubliners,*" *Modern Language Notes,* 72 (1957): 421–424;

Friedrich, "The Perspective of Joyce's *Dubliners,*" *College English,* 26 (1965): 421–426;

Hans Walter Gabler, "Preface," in *James Joyce's Dubliners: A Facsimile of Drafts and Manuscripts* (New York: Garland, 1978);

Peter Garrett, ed., *Twentieth-Century Interpretations of* Dubliners: *A Collection of Critical Essays* (Englewood Cliffs, N.J.: Prentice-Hall, 1968);

Brewster Ghiselin, "The Unity of Joyce's *Dubliners*," *Accent,* 16 (Spring/Summer 1956): 75–88, 196–213;

Don Gifford and Robert J. Seidman, *Notes for Joyce: Dubliners and Portrait of the Artist* (New York: E. P. Dutton, 1967);

Michael Patrick Gillespie, "Aesthetic Evolution: The Shaping Forces Behind Dubliners," *Language and Style,* 19 (Spring 1987): 149–163;

Michael Groden, "Preface," in *Dubliners: A Facsimile of Proofs for the 1910 Edition* (New York: Garland, 1977);

Groden, "Preface," in *Dubliners: A Facsimile of Proofs for the 1914 Edition* (New York: Garland, 1977);

John V. Hagopian, "Counterparts," in *Insight II: Analyses of Modern British Literature,* edited by Hagopian (Frankfurt: Hirschgraben, 1964), pp. 201–206;

Maurice Harmon, "Little Chandler and Byron's 'First Poem,'" *Threshold,* 17 (1962): 59–61;

Clive Hart, ed., *James Joyce's* Dubliners: *Critical Essays* (New York: Viking, 1969 / London: Faber & Faber, 1969);

John Raymond Hart, "Moore on Joyce: the Influence of *The Untilled Field* on *Dubliners,*" *Dublin Magazine,* 10 (Summer 1973): 61–76;

James D. Johnson, "Joyce's 'Araby' and *Romans* VII and VIII," *American Notes & Queries,* 13 (September 1974);

Stanislaus Joyce, "The Background to *Dubliners,*" *Listener,* 51 (March 1954): 526–527;

Elaine M. Kefauer, "Swift's Clothing Philosophy in *A Tale of a Tub* and Joyce's 'Grace,'" *James Joyce Quarterly,* 5 (Winter 1968): 162–165;

John V. Kelleher, "Irish History and Mythology in James Joyce's 'The Dead,'" *Review of Politics,* 27 (July 1965): 414–433;

Sister Eileen Kennedy, "Moore's *The Untilled Field* and Joyce's *Dubliners,*" *Eire-Ireland,* 5 (Autumn 1970): 81–89;

George Knox, "Michael Furey: Symbol-Name in Joyce's 'The Dead,'" *Western Humanities Review,* 13 (Spring 1959): 221–222;

Howard Lachtman, "The Magic Lantern Business: James Joyce's Ecclesiastical Satire in Dubliners," *James Joyce Quarterly,* 7 (Winter 1969): 82–92;

Richard Levin and Charles Shattuck, "First Flight to Ithaca: A New Reading of Joyce's *Dubliners,*" *Accent,* 4 (Winter 1944): 75–99;

C. C. Loomis Jr., "Structure and Sympathy in Joyce's 'The Dead,'" *PMLA,* 75 (March 1960): 149–151;

J. B. Lyons, "Animadversions on Paralysis as a Symbol in 'The Sisters,'" *James Joyce Quarterly,* 11 (Spring 1974): 257–265;

Andrew Lytle, "A Reading of Joyce's 'The Dead,'" *Sewanee Review,* 77 (Spring 1966): 193–216;

Donagh MacDonagh, "Joyce and 'The Lass of Aughrim,'" *Hibernia,* 31 (June 1967): 21;

MacDonagh "Joyce, Nietzsche, and Hauptmann in James Joyce's 'A Painful Case,'" *PMLA*, 68 (March 1953): 95–102;

MacDonagh, "'The Sisters' of James Joyce," *University of Kansas City Review*, 18 (Summer 1952): 255–261;

Jerome Mandel, "Medieval Romance and the Structure of 'Araby,'" *James Joyce Quarterly*, 13 (Winter 1976): 234–237;

William T. Moynihan, ed., *Joyce's "The Dead,"* (Boston: Allyn & Bacon, 1965);

F. X. Newman, "The Land of Ooze: Joyce's 'Grace' and the *Book of Job*," *Studies in Short Fiction*, 4 (Fall 1966): 70–79;

Carl Niemeyer, "'Grace' and Joyce's Method of Parody," *College English*, 27 (December 1965): 196–201;

William T. Noon, "Joyce's 'Clay': An Interpretation," *College English*, 17 (November 1955): 93–95;

Margot Norris, "Narration under a Blindfold: Reading Joyce's 'Clay,'" *PMLA*, 102 (1987): 206–215;

Brendan P. O'Hehir, "Structural Symbol in Joyce's 'The Dead,'" *Twentieth-Century Literature*, 3 (April 1957): 3–13;

Michael J. O'Neill, "Joyce's Use of Memory in 'A Mother,'" *Modern Language Notes*, 74 (March 1959): 226–230;

Frank Ormsby and John Cronin, "'A Very Fine Piece of Writing:' 'Ivy Day in the Committee Room,'" *Eire-Ireland*, 7 (Summer 1972): 84–94;

Vincent P. Pecora, "'The Dead' and the Generosity of the Word," *PMLA*, 101 (March 1986): 233–245;

Margot Peters, "The Phonological Structure of James Joyce's 'Araby,'" *Language and Style*, 6 (Spring 1973): 135–144;

Mary Power, "The Naming of Kathleen Kearney," *Journal of Modern Literature*, 5 (September 1976): 532–534;

Robert P. Roberts, "'Araby' and the Palimpsest of Criticism; or, Through a Glass Eye Darkly," *Antioch Review*, 26 (Winter 1966/1967): 469–489;

Bruce A. Rosenberg, "The Crucifixion in the 'The Boarding House,'" *Studies in Short Fiction*, 5 (Fall 1967): 44–53;

James Ruoff, "'A Little Cloud': Joyce's Portrait of a Would-be Artist," *Research Studies of the State College of Washington*, 25 (September 1957): 256–271;

Epifano San Juan Jr., *James Joyce and the Craft of Fiction: An Interpretation of* Dubliners (Rutherford, N. J.: Fairleigh Dickinson University Press, 1972);

Hugo Schmidt, "A Commentary on 'Clay,'" in *Elements of Fiction* (New York: Oxford University Press, 1968), pp. 66–77;

Schmidt, "Hauptmann's Michael Kramer and Joyce's 'The Dead,'" *PMLA*, 80 (March 1965): 141–142;

Robert Scholes, "Further Observations on the Text of *Dubliners*," *Studies in Bibliography*, 17 (1964): 107–122;

Scholes, "Grant Richards to James Joyce," *Studies in Bibliography*, 16 (1963): 139–160;

Scholes, "Semiotic Approaches to a Fictional Text: 'Joyce's Eveline,'" *James Joyce Quarterly*, 16 (Fall 1978/Winter 1979): 65–80;

Scholes, "Some Observations on the Text of *Dubliners*: 'The Dead,'" *Studies in Bibliography*, 15 (1962): 191–205;

Fritz Senn, "'He Was Too Scrupulous Always': Joyce's 'The Sisters,'" *James Joyce Quarterly*, 2 (Winter 1965): 66–72;

Senn, "Not Too Scrupulous Always," *James Joyce Quarterly*, 4 (Spring 1967): 244;

Clarice Short, "Joyce's 'A Little Cloud,'" *Modern Language Notes*, 72 (April 1957): 275–278;

Thomas F. Smith, "Color and Light in 'The Dead,'" *James Joyce Quarterly*, 2 (Summer 1965): 304–313;

James J. Sosnoski, "*Story and Discourse* and the Practice of Literary Criticism: 'Araby,' A Test Case," *James Joyce Quarterly*, 18 (Spring 1981): 255–267;

Thomas F. Staley, "Moral Responsibility in Joyce's 'Clay,'" *Renascence*, 18 (Spring 1966): 124–128;

William B. Stein, "Joyce's 'Araby': Paradise Lost," *Perspective*, 12 (Spring 1962): 215–222;

Stein, "Joyce's 'The Sisters,'" *Explicator*, 21 (September 1962), item 2;

Frederick C. Stern, "'Parnell Is Dead': 'Ivy Day in the Committee Room,'" *James Joyce Quarterly*, 10 (Winter 1973): 228–239;

Donald T. Torchiana, *Backgrounds for Joyce's* Dubliners (Boston: Allen & Unwin, 1986);

Torchiana, "The Ending of 'The Dead': I Follow Saint Patrick," *James Joyce Quarterly*, 18 (Winter 1981): 123–133;

Torchiana, "Joyce's 'After the Race,' The Race of Castlebar, and Dun Laoghaire," *Eire-Ireland*, 6 (Fall 1971): 119–128;

Torchiana, "Joyce's 'Eveline' and the Blessed Margaret Mary Alacoque," *James Joyce Quarterly*, 6 (Fall 1968): 22–28;

Torchiana, "Joyce's 'Two Gallants': A Walk Through the Ascendancy," *James Joyce Quarterly*, 6 (Winter 1968): 115–127;

Torchiana, "The Opening of *Dubliners:* A Reconsideration," *Irish University Review*, 1 (Spring 1971): 149–160;

Lionel Trilling, "Characterization in 'The Dead,'" in *The Experience of Literature* (New York: Holt, Rinehart & Winston, 1967), pp. 228–231;

Joseph C. Voelker, "'He Lumped the Emancipates Together': More Analogues for Joyce's Mr. Duffy," *James Joyce Quarterly*, 18 (Fall 1980): 23–35;

Burton A. Waisbren and Florence L. Walzl, "Paresis and the Priest: James Joyce's Symbolic Use of Syphilis in 'The Sisters,'" *Annals of Internal Medicine*, 80 (June 1974): 758–762;

Florence L. Walzl, "A Date in Joyce's 'The Sisters,'" *Texas Studies in Literature and Language*, 2 (Summer 1962): 183–187;

Walzl, "*Dubliners:* Women in Irish Society," in *Women in Joyce*, edited by Suzette Henke and Elaine Unkeless (Urbana, Ill.: University of Illinois Press, 1982), pp. 31–56;

Walzl, "Gabriel and Michael: The Conclusion of 'The Dead,'" *James Joyce Quarterly*, 4 (Fall 1966): 17–31;

Walzl, "Joyce's 'Clay': Fact and Fiction," *Explicator*, 20 (February 1962), item 46;

Walzl, "Joyce's 'The Sisters': A Development," *James Joyce Quarterly*, 10 (Summer 1973): 375–421;

Walzl, "The Life Chronology of *Dubliners*," *James Joyce Quarterly*, 14 (Summer 1977): 408–415;

Walzl, "The Liturgy of the Epiphany Seasons and the Epiphanies of Joyce," *PMLA,* 80 (September 1965): 436–450;

Walzl, "Patterns of Paralysis in Joyce's *Dubliners,*" *College English,* 22 (1961): 519–520;

David F. Ward, "The Race Before the Story: James Joyce and the Gordon Bennett Cup Automobile Race," *Eire-Ireland,* 2 (Summer 1967): 27–35;

Charles D. Wright, "Melancholy Duffy and Sanguine Sinico: Humors in 'A Painful Case,'" *James Joyce Quarterly,* 3 (Spring 1966): 171–180.

A PORTRAIT OF THE ARTIST AS A YOUNG MAN

Chester G. Anderson, "The Sacrificial Butter," *Accent,* 12 (1952): 3–13;

Anderson, ed., *A Portrait of the Artist as a Young Man: Text, Criticism, and Notes* (New York: Viking, 1968);

Robert J. Andreach, "James Joyce," in *Studies in Structure: The Stages of the Spiritual Life of Four Modern Authors* (New York: Fordham University Press, 1964), pp. 40–71;

James S. Atherton, "Introduction" and "Notes," in *A Portrait of the Artist as a Young Man* (London: Heinemann, 1964), pp. ix-xxii; 239–258;

Maurice Beebe, "Joyce and Aquinas: The Theory of Aesthetics," *Philological Quarterly,* 36 (January 1957): 20–35;

Beebe, "The *Portrait* as Portrait: Joyce and Impressionism," *Irish Renaissance Annual,* volume one, edited by Zack Bowen (Newark: University of Delaware Press, 1980); pp. 13–31;

Morris Beja, "James Joyce: The Bread of Everyday Life," in *Epiphany in the Modern Novel* (Seattle: University of Washington Press, 1971); pp. 71–111;

Beja, ed., *James Joyce:* Dubliners *and* A Portrait of the Artist as a Young Man: *A Casebook* (London: Macmillan, 1973);

Bernard Benstock, "The Temptation of St. Stephen: A View of the Villanelle," *James Joyce Quarterly,* 14 (Fall 1976): 31–38;

Wayne C. Booth, "The Problem of Distance in *A Portrait of the Artist,*" in *The Rhetoric of Fiction* (Chicago: University of Chicago Press, 1961), pp. 324–336;

Elizabeth F. Boyd, "Joyce's Hell Fire Sermons," *Modern Language Notes,* 75 (1960): 561–571;

Homer Obed Brown, *James Joyce's Early Fiction: The Biography of Form* (Cleveland, Ohio: Case Western Reserve University, 1972);

Jerome H. Buckley, "Portrait of James Joyce as a Young Aesthete," in *Season of Youth: The Bildungsroman From Dickens to Golding* (Cambridge, Mass.: Harvard University Press, 1974); pp. 225–247;

Kenneth Burke, "Fact, Inference, and Proof in the Analysis of Literary Symbolism," in *Terms for Order,* edited by Stanley Edgar Hyman (Bloomington: Indiana University Press, 1964), pp. 145–172;

Joseph A. Buttigieg, *A Portrait of the Artist in Different Perspective* (Athens: Ohio University Press, 1987);

Thomas E. Connolly, "Kinesis and Stasis: Structural Rhythm in Joyce's *Portrait of the Artist*," *Dublin Universtiy Review*, 3 (1966): 21–30;

Connolly, ed., *Joyce's Portrait: Criticism and Critiques* (New York: Appleton-Century-Crofts, 1962);

James Doherty, "Joyce and *Hell Opened to Christians:* The Edition He Used for His Hell Sermons," *Modern Philology*, 61 (1963): 110–119;

Maud Ellmann, "Disremembering Dedalus: *A Portrait of the Artist as a Young Man*," in *Untying the Text: A Poststructuralist Reader,* edited by Robert Young (Boston: Routledge & Kegan Paul, 1981);

Edmund L. Epstein, *The Ordeal of Stephen Dedalus: The Conflict of the Generations in James Joyce's* A Portrait of the Artist as a Young Man (Carbondale: Southern Illinois University Press, 1971);

Joseph Feehan, ed., *Dedalus on Crete: Essays on the Implications of Joyce's* Portrait (Los Angeles: St. Thomas More Guild, Immaculate Heart College, 1957);

Sidney Feshbach, "A Slow and Dark Birth: A Study of the Organization of *A Portrait of the Artist as a Young Man*," *James Joyce Quarterly*, 4 (1967): 289–300;

Diane Fortuna, "The Labyrinth as Controlling Image in Joyce's *A Portrait of the Artist as Young Man*," *Bulletin of the New York Public Library,* 76 (1972): 120–180;

Hans Walter Gabler, "The Christmas Dinner Scene, Parnell's Death, and the Genesis of *A Portrait of the Artist as a Young Man*," *James Joyce Quarterly,* 13 (1975): 27–38;

Gabler, "The Seven Lost Years of *A Portrait of the Artist as a Young Man*," in *Approaches to Joyce's* Portrait: *Ten Essays,* edited by Thomas F. Staley and Bernard Benstock (Pittsburgh, Pa: University of Pittsburgh Press, 1976), pp. 25–60;

Don Gifford and Robert J. Seidman, *Joyce Annotated: Notes For* Dubliners *and* A Portrait of The Artist As a Young Man, revised and enlarged edition (Berkeley, Los Angeles & London: University of California Press, 1982);

Elliot B. Gose Jr., "Destruction and Creation in *A Portrait of the Artist as a Young Man*," *James Joyce Quarterly*, 22 (Spring 1985): 259–270;

Nathan Halper, *The Early James Joyce* (New York: Columbia University Press, 1973);

Leslie Hancock, *Word Index to James Joyce's* Portrait of the Artist (Carbondale: Southern Illinois University Press, 1967);

John Edward Hardy, "Joyce's *Portrait:* The Flight of the Serpent," in *Man in the Modern Novel* (Seattle: University of Washington Press, 1964), pp. 67–81;

David Hayman, "*A Portrait of the Artist as a Young Man* and *L'Education Sentimentale:* The Structural Affinities," *Orbis Litterarum,* 19 (1964): 161–175;

David E. Jones, "The Essence of Beauty in James Joyce's Aesthetics," *James Joyce Quarterly*, 10 (Spring 1973): 291–311;

Hugh Kenner, "The *Portrait* in Perspective," in *James Joyce: Two Decades of Criticism,* edited by Seon Givens (New York: Vanguard, 1948; with a new introduction by Givens, 1963) pp. 132–174;

R. B. Kershner Jr., "Time and Language in Joyce's *Portrait*," *ELH*, 43 (1976): 604–619;

Stephen R. Kuder, "James Joyce and Ignatius of Loyola: The Spiritual Exercises in *A Portrait of the Artist*," *Christianity and Literature*, 31 (1982): 48–57;

Jon Lanham, "The Genre of *A Portrait of the Artist as a Young Man* and 'the rhythm of its structure,'" *Genre*, 10 (1977): 77–102;

Lee T. Lemon, "*A Portrait of the Artist as a Young Man:* Motif as Motivation and Structure," *Modern Fiction Studies*, 12 (1966/1967): 441–452;

Ilse Dusoir Lind, "*The Way of All Flesh* and *A Portrait of the Artist as a Young Man:* A Comparison," *Victorian Newsletter*, 9 (Spring 1956): 7–10;

F. C. McGrath, "Laughing in His Sleeve: The Sources of Stephen's Aesthetics," *James Joyce Quarterly*, 23 (Spring 1986): 259–275;

William E. Morris and Clifford A. Nault, eds., *Portraits of an Artist: A Casebook on James Joyce's* A Portrait of the Artist as a Young Man (New York: Odyssey, 1962);

James Naremore, "Style as Meaning in *A Portrait of the Artist*," *James Joyce Quarterly*, 4 (Summer 1967): 331–342;

Grant H. Redford, "The Role of Structure in Joyce's *Portrait*," *Modern Fiction Studies*, 4 (1958): 21–30;

John Paul Riquelme, "Pretexts for Reading and for Writing: Title, Epigraph, and Journal in *A Portrait of the Artist as a Young Man*," *James Joyce Quarterly*, 18 (Spring 1981): 301–321;

Charles Rossman, "Stephen Dedalus and the Spiritual-Heroic Refrigeration Apparatus: Art and Life in Joyce's *Portrait*," in *Forms of Modern British Fiction*, edited by Alan W. Friedman (Austin: University of Texas Press, 1975), pp. 101–131;

Louis D. Rubin, "A Portrait of a Highly Visible Artist," in *The Teller In the Tale* (Seattle: University of Washington Press, 1967); pp. 141–177;

Robert S. Ryf, *A New Approach to Joyce: The Portrait of the Artist as a Guide Book* (Berkeley & Los Angeles: University of California Press, 1962);

Robert Scholes, "Joyce and Epiphany: The Key to the Labyrinth?" *Sewanee Review*, 72 (Winter 1964): 65–77;

Scholes, "Stephen Dedalus: Poet or Esthete?" *PMLA*, 79 (1964): 484–489;

Scholes and Richard M. Kain, eds., *The Workshop of Daedalus: James Joyce and the Raw Materials for* A Portrait of the Artist as a Young Man (Evanston, Ill.: Northwestern University Press, 1965);

Mark Schorer, "Technique as Discovery," *Hudson Review*, 1 (1948): 67–87;

William M. Schutte, ed., *Twentieth Century Interpretations of* A Portrait of the Artist as a Young Man: *A Collection of Critical Essays* (Englewood Cliffs, N.J.: Prentice-Hall, 1968);

Evert Sprinchorn, "Joyce: *A Portrait of the Artist as a Young Man:* A Portrait of the Artist as Achilles," in *Approaches to the Twentieth Century Novel*, edited by John Unterecker (New York: Crowell, 1965), pp. 9–50;

John Bristow Smith, *Imagery and the Mind of Stephen Dedalus: A Computer-Assisted Study of Joyce's* A Portrait of the Artist as a Young Man (Lewisburg, Pa.: Bucknell University Press, 1980);

Thomas F. Staley and Bernard Benstock, eds., *Approach to Joyce's* Portrait: *Ten Essays* (Pittsburgh: University of Pittsburgh Press, 1976);

Harvey P. Sucksmith, *James Joyce:* A Portrait of the Artist as a Young Man (London: Arnold, 1973);

James R. Thrane, "Joyce's Sermon on Hell: Its Sources and Its Background," *Modern Philology,* 57 (1960): 172–198;

Thomas F. Van Laan, "The Meditative Structure of Joyce's *Portrait,*" *James Joyce Quarterly,* 1 (Spring 1964): 3–13.

EXILES

Robert M. Adams, "Light on Joyce's *Exiles?* A New MS, a Curious Analogue, and Some Speculations," *Studies in Bibliography,* 17 (1964): 83–105;

Adams, "The Manuscript of James Joyce's Play," *Yale University Library Gazette,* 39 (July 1964): 30–41;

D. J. F. Aitken, "Dramatic Archetypes in Joyce's Exiles," *Modern Fiction Studies,* 4 (1958): 26–37;

Bernard Bandler, "Joyce's *Exiles,*" *Hound and Horn,* 6 (1933): 266–285;

Ruth Bauerle, "Bertha's Role in *Exiles,*" in *Women in Joyce,* edited by Suzette Henke and Elaine Unkeless (Urbana: University of Illinois Press, 1982), pp. 108–131;

Bauerle, *A Word List to James Joyce's* Exiles (New York & London: Garland, 1981);

Michael Beausang, "In the Name of the Law: Marital Freedom and Justice in *Exiles,*" in *"Scribble" 1: Genèse des textes,* edited by Claude Jacquet (Paris: Lettres Modernes, 1988), pp. 39–55;

Bernard Benstock, "*Exiles,* Ibsen and the Play's Function in the Joyce Canon," *Forum,* 11 (1970): 42–52;

Benstock, "*Exiles:* 'Paradox Lust' and 'Lost Paladays,'" *ELH,* 36 (1969): 739–756;

Zack Bowen, "*Exiles:* The Confessional Mode," *James Joyce Quarterly,* 29 (Spring 1992): 581–586;

Edward Brandabur, "Exiles," in *A Scrupulous Meanness* (Urbana: University of Illinois Press, 1971), pp. 127–158;

Sheldon R. Brivic, "Structure and Meaning in Joyce's *Exiles,*" *James Joyce Quarterly,* 6 (1968): 29–52;

Carole Browne and Leo Knuth, "James Joyce's *Exiles:* The Ordeal of Richard Rowan," *James Joyce Quarterly,* 17 (1979): 7–20;

Earl John Clark, "James Joyce's *Exiles,*" *James Joyce Quarterly,* 6 (Fall 1968): 69–78;

John M. Clark, "Writing *Jerusalem* Backwards: William Blake in *Exiles,*" *James Joyce Quarterly,* 26 (Winter 1989): 183–197;

Padraic Colum, "Introduction," in *Exiles* (New York: Viking, 1951), pp. 7–11;

Frank R. Cunningham, "Joyce's *Exiles:* A Problem of Dramatic Stasis," *Modern Drama,* 12 (1970): 399–407;

Theo Q. Dombrowski, "Joyce's *Exiles:* The Problem of Love," *James Joyce Quarterly,* 15 (1978): 118–127;

James W. Douglass, "James Joyce's *Exiles:* A Portrait of the Artist," *Renascence,* 15 (1963): 82–87;

Simon Evans, *The Penetration of* Exiles, *Wake Newslitter,* monograph no. 9 (Colchester, U.K.: Wake Newslitter Press, 1984);

James T. Farrell, "*Exiles* and Ibsen," in *James Joyce: Two Decades of Criticism,* edited by Seon Givens (New York: Vanguard, 1948), pp. 95–131;

Francis Fergusson, "*Exiles* and Ibsen's Work," *Hound and Horn,* 5 (1932): 345–353;

Fergusson, "A Reading of *Exiles,*" in *Exiles* Joyce (Norfolk, Conn.: New Directions, 1945), pp. v–xviii;

William R. Ferris, "Rebellion Matured: Joyce's *Exiles,*" *Eire-Ireland,* 4 (1969): 73–81;

Louis Golding, *James Joyce* (London: Butterworth, 1933), pp. 69–82;

Kenneth Grose, *James Joyce* (London: M. Evans, 1975), pp. 36–41;

Maurice Harmon, "Richard Rowan, His Own Scapegoat," *James Joyce Quarterly,* 3 (1965): 34–40;

Dean H. Keller, "Linati's Translations of *Exiles:* An Unnoticed Appearance," *James Joyce Quarterly,* 10 (Spring 1973): 265;

Hugh Kenner, "Joyce's *Exiles,*" *Hudson Review,* 5 (1952): 389–403;

Archie K. Loss, "Presences and Visions in *Exiles, A Portrait of the Artist,* and *Ulysses,*" *James Joyce Quarterly,* 13 (Spring 1976): 148–162;

Celeste Loughman, "Bertha, Victress, in Joyce's *Exiles,*" *James Joyce Quarterly,* 19 (Fall 1981): 69–72;

Vivienne Koch Macleod, "The Influence of Ibsen on Joyce," *PMLA,* 60 (1945): 879–898;

Macleod, "The Influence of Ibsen on Joyce: Addendum," *PMLA,* 62 (1947): 573–580;

John MacNicholas, *James Joyce's* Exiles: *A Textual Companion* (New York & London: Garland, 1979);

MacNicholas, "Joyce's *Exiles:* The Argument for Doubt," *James Joyce Quarterly,* 11 (Fall 1973): 33–40;

MacNicholas, "The Stage History of *Exiles,*" *James Joyce Quarterly,* 19 (Fall 1981): 9–26;

R. A. Maher, "James Joyce's *Exiles:* The Comedy of Discontinuity," *James Joyce Quarterly,* 9 (1972): 461–474;

Timothy P. Martin, "Wagner's *Tannhauser* in *Exiles:* A Further Source," *James Joyce Quarterly,* 19 (Fall 1981): 73–76;

Deena P. Metzger, "Variations on a Theme: A Study of *Exiles* by James Joyce and *The Great God Brown* by Eugene O'Neill," *Modern Drama,* 8 (1965): 174–184;

Virginia Moseley, "Aye to Aye," in *Joyce and the Bible* (Dekalb: Northern Illinois University Press, 1967), pp. 45–56;

Moseley, "Joyce's *Exiles* and the Prodigal Son," *Modern Drama,* 1 (1959): 218–227;

Sandra Manoogian Pearce, "'Like a stone': Joyce's Eucharistic Imagery in *Exiles,*" *James Joyce Quarterly,* 29 (Spring 1992): 587–591;

Ezra Pound, "Mr. James Joyce and the Modern Stage," *Drama,* 6 (1916): 122–132;

Mary T. Reynolds, "Dante in Joyce's *Exiles,*" *James Joyce Quarterly,* 18 (Fall 1980): 35–44;

John Rodker, Israel Solon, Samuel A. Tannebaum, and Jane Heap, "*Exiles:* A Discussion of James Joyce's Plays," *Little Review,* 5 (1919): 20–27;

Brian Schaffer, "Kindred by Choice: Joyce's *Exiles* and Goethe's *Elective Affinities,*" *James Joyce Quarterly,* 26 (Winter 1989): 199–212;

Myron Schwartzman, "A Successful *Exiles* in New York," *James Joyce Quarterly,* 14 (Summer 1977): 361–362;

Elliott M. Simon, "James Joyce's *Exiles* and the Tradition of the Edwardian Problem Play," *Modern Drama,* 20 (March 1977): 21–35;

William York Tindall, *A Reader's Guide to James Joyce* (New York: Noonday, 1959), pp. 104–122;

Bjorn Tysdahl, "Joyce's *Exiles* and Ibsen," *Orbis Literrarum,* 19 (1964): 176–186;

Joseph Voelker, "The Beastly Incertitudes: Doubt, Difficulty, and Discomfiture in James Joyce's *Exiles,*" *Journal of Modern Literature,* 14 (1988): 499–516;

Stephen Watt, *Joyce, O'Casey and the Irish Popular Theatre* (Syracuse, N.Y.: Syracuse University Press, 1991);

Roland von Weber, "On and About Joyce's *Exiles,*" in *James Joyce Yearbook,* edited by Maria Jolas (Paris: Transition, 1949), pp. 47–67;

Raymond Williams, "The *Exiles* of James Joyce," *Politics and Letters,* 1 (1948): 13–21.

ULYSSES

Hermione de Almeida, *Byron and Joyce Through Homer:* Don Juan *and* Ulysses (New York: Columbia University Press, 1981);

Bruce Arnold, *The Scandal of* Ulysses (London: Sinclair-Stevenson, 1991);

Craig Wallace Barrow, *Montage in James Joyce's* Ulysses (Madrid & Potomac, Md.: Studia Humanitatis, 1980);

Ruth Bauerle, "A Sober Drunken Speech: Stephen's Parodies in 'The Oxen of the Sun,'" *James Joyce Quarterly,* 5 (Fall 1967): 40–46;

Bernard Benstock, *Narrative Con/Texts in* Ulysses (Urbana & Chicago: University of Illinois Press, 1991);

R. P. Blackmur, "The Jew in Search of a Son: Joyce's *Ulysses,*" in *Eleven Essays in the European Novel,* edited by Blackmur (New York: Harcourt, Brace & World, 1964), pp. 27–47;

Harry Blamires, *The Bloomsday Book: A Guide Through Joyce's* Ulysses (London: Methuen, 1966); revised as *The New Bloomsday Book* (London: Routledge, 1988);

Louis Bonnerot, ed., *Ulysses: Cinquante Ans Après* (Paris: Didier, 1974);

Zack Bowen, *Musical Allusions in the Works of James Joyce: Early Poetry Through* Ulysses (Albany: State University of New York Press, 1974);

Bowen, Ulysses *as a Comic Novel* (Syracuse, N.Y.: Syracuse University Press, 1989);

Frank Budgen, *James Joyce and the Making of* Ulysses (Bloomington: Indiana University Press, 1960);

James Van Dyck Card, *An Anatomy of "Penelope"* (Rutherford, N.J.: Fairleigh Dickinson University Press, 1984; London & Toronto: Associated University Presses, 1984);

Paul P. J. van Caspel, *Bloomers on the Liffey: Eisegetical Readings of James Joyce's* Ulysses, *Part II* (Groningen, Netherlands: Veenstra Visser, 1980; revised and enlarged, Baltimore: Johns Hopkins University Press, 1986);

Jackson I. Cope, "The Rythmic Gesture: Image and Aesthetic in Joyce's *Ulysses*," *ELH,* 29 (1962): 67–89;

S. Foster Damon, "The Odyssey in Dublin; with a Postscript, 1947," in *James Joyce: Two Decades of Criticism,* edited by Seon Givens (New York: Vanguard, 1948; revised edition, 1963), pp. 203–242;

Robert Adams Day, "Joyce's Waste Land and Eliot's Unknown God," in *Literary Monographs,* volume four, edited by Eric Rothstein (Madison: University of Wisconsin Press, 1971), pp. 139–210; 218–226;

Clive Driver, ed., *Ulysses: A Facsimile of the Manuscript,* 3 volumes (New York: Octagon, 1975);

Edward Duncan, "Unsubstantial Father: A Study of the *Hamlet* Symbolism in Joyce's *Ulysses*," *University of Toronto Quarterly,* 19 (1950): 126–140;

T. S. Eliot, "*Ulysses,* Order, and Myth," *Dial,* 75 (November 1923): 480–483;

William Empson, "The Theme of *Ulysses*," *Kenyon Review,* 18 (1956): 26–52;

Saul Field and Morton P. Levitt, *Bloomsday: An Interpretation of James Joyce's* Ulysses (Greenwich, Conn.: New York Graphic Society, 1972);

Monika Fludernik, "Narrative and Its Development in *Ulysses*," *Journal of Narrative Technique,* 16 (Winter 1986): 15–40;

Marilyn French, *The Book as World: James Joyce's* Ulysses (Cambridge, Mass.: Harvard University Press, 1976);

Melvin J. Friedman, "James Joyce: The Full Development of the Method," in *Stream of Consciousness: A Study of Literary Method* (New Haven: Yale University Press, 1955), pp. 210–243;

David Fuller, *James Joyce's* Ulysses (New York: St. Martin's Press, 1992);

Hans Walter Gabler, "The Synchrony and Diachrony of Texts: Practice and Theory of the Critical Edition of James Joyce's *Ulysses*," in *Text: Transactions of the Society of Textual Scholarship* (New York: AMS Press, 1981), pp. 305–326;

Philip Gaskell, "Joyce, *Ulysses,* 1992," in *From Writer to Reader: Studies in Editorial Method* (New York: Oxford University Press, 1978), pp. 213–244;

Don Gifford with Robert J. Seidman, *Notes for Joyce: An Annotation of James Joyce's* Ulysses (New York: Dutton, 1974; revised and enlarged edition, Berkeley: University of California Press, 1988);

Stuart Gilbert, *James Joyce's "Ulysses": A Study* (London: Faber & Faber, 1930; revised and slightly enlarged edition, 1952; revised again, New York: Knopf, 1952);

Richard Gill, "The 'Corporal Works of Mercy' as a Moral Pattern in Joyce's *Ulysses*," *Twentieth Century Literature,* 9 (1963): 17–21;

Michael Patrick Gillespie, "Certitude and Circularity: the Search for *Ulysses*," *Studies in the Novel,* 22 (Summer 1990): 216–230;

Gillespie, "Redrawing the Artist as a Young Man," in *Joyce's* Ulysses: *The Larger Perspective,* edited by Robert Neuman and Weldon Thornton (Newark: University of Delaware Press, 1987), pp. 123–140;

Gillespie, "A Swift Reading of *Ulysses*," *Texas Studies in Literature and Language,* 27 (Summer 1985): 178–190;

Gillespie, "Wagner in the Ormond Bar: Operatic Elements in the 'Sirens' Episode of *Ulysses*," *Irish Renaissance Annual,* 4 (1983): 157–173;

Gillespie, "Why Does One Re-Read *Ulysses*?": *Assessing the 1984* Ulysses, edited by C. George Sandulescu and Clive Hart (Gerrards Cross, Bucks, U.K.: Colin Smythe, 1986; Totowa, N.J.: Barnes & Noble, 1986), pp. 43–57;

S. L. Goldberg, *The Classical Temper: A Study of James Joyce's* Ulysses (London: Chatto & Windus, 1961);

Elliott B. Gose Jr., *The Transformation Process in Joyce's* Ulysses (Toronto: University of Toronto Press, 1980);

Roy K. Gottfried, *The Art of Joyce's Syntax in* Ulysses (Athens: University of Georgia Press, 1980);

Michael Groden, Ulysses *in Progress* (Princeton: Princeton University Press, 1977);

John Halperin, *The Art of James Joyce: Method and Design in Ulysses and Finnegans Wake* (London: Oxford University Press, 1961);

Miles Lawrence Hanley, *Word Index to James Joyce's* Ulysses (Madison: University of Wisconsin Press, 1937);

Marguerite Harkness, *The Aesthetics of Dedalus and Bloom* (Lewisburg, Pa.: Bucknell University Press, 1984; London & Toronto: Associated University Presses, 1984);

Clive Hart, *James Joyce's* Ulysses (Sydney: Sydney University Press, 1968);

Hart and A. M. Leo Knuth, *A Topographical Guide to James Joyce's* Ulysses (Colchester, U.K.: Wake Newslitter Press, 1975; revised edition, Colchester, U.K.: University of Essex, 1981);

Hart and David Hayman, eds., *James Joyce's* Ulysses: *Critical Essays* (Berkeley & Los Angeles: University of California Press, 1974);

David Hayman, "Forms of Folly in Joyce: A Study of Clowning in *Ulysses*," *ELH,* 34 (1967): 260–283;

Hayman, Ulysses: *The Mechanics of Meaning* (Englewood Cliffs, N.J.: Prentice-Hall, 1970; revised and expanded edition, Madison: University of Wisconsin Press, 1982);

Arthur Heine, "Shakespeare in James Joyce," *Shakespeare Association Bulletin,* 24 (1949): 56–70;

Suzette Henke, *Joyce's Moraculous Sindbook: A Study of* Ulysses (Columbus: Ohio State University Press, 1978);

Phillip F. Herring, "The Bedsteadfastness of Molly Bloom," *Modern Fiction Studies,* 15 (1969): 49–61;

Herring, "Toward an Historical Molly Bloom," *ELH,* 45 (1978): 501–521;

John Porter Houston, *Joyce and Prose: An Exploration of the Language of* Ulysses (Lewisburg, Pa.: Bucknell University Press, 1989);

Robert Humphrey, "Joyce's Daedal Network," in *Stream of Consciousness in the Modern Novel* (Berkeley & Los Angeles: University of California Press, 1954), pp. 87–99;

Louis Hyman, "Some Aspects of the Jewish Background of *Ulysses*," in *The Jews of Ireland: From the Earliest Times to the Year 1910* (Jerusalem: Israel Universities Press / London: Jewish Historical Society of England, 1972), pp. 167–192;

Robert Janusko, *The Sources and Structures of James Joyce's "Oxen"* (Ann Arbor: University of Michigan Research Press, 1983);

Carl Gustave Jung, "*Ulysses:* a Monologue," reprinted in *The Spirit of Man, Art, and Literature,* volume 15 of Bollingen Series 20: *The Collected Works of Jung,* edited by Herbert Head, Michael Fordham, and Gerhard Adler, translated by R. F. C. Hall (New York: Pantheon, 1966), pp. 109–134;

Richard M. Kain, *Fabulous Voyager: James Joyce's* Ulysses (Chicago: University of Chicago Press, 1947);

Harold Kaplan, "Stoom: The Universal Comedy of James Joyce," in *The Passive Voice: An Approach to Modern Fiction* (Athens: Ohio University Press, 1966), pp. 43–91;

Hugh Kenner, *Ulysses* (London: Allen & Unwin, 1980; revised edition, Baltimore & London: Johns Hopkins University Press, 1987);

Kenner, "Who's He When He's at Home?," in *Light Rays: James Joyce and Modernism,* edited by Heyward Ehrlich (New York: New Horizon, 1984), pp. 58–69;

Chong-Keon Kim, *James Joyce:* Ulysses *and Literary Modernism* (Seoul, Korea: Tamgu Dang, 1985);

Valery Larbaud, "James Joyce," *Nouvelle Revue Français,* 1 (April 1922): 385–409;

Karen Lawrence, *The Odyssey of Style in* Ulysses (Princeton: Princeton University Press, 1981);

Jennifer Schiffer Levine, "Originality and Repetition in *Finnegans Wake* and *Ulysses,*" *PMLA,* 94 (1979): 106–120;

A. Walton Litz, "The Genre of *Ulysses,*" in *The Theory of the Novel,* edited by John Halperin (New York: Oxford University Press, 1974), pp. 109–120;

Litz, *The Art of James Joyce: Method and Design in* Ulysses *and* Finnegans Wake (London: Oxford University Press, 1961);

Helen H. Macaré, *A* Ulysses *Phrasebook* (Portola Valley, Cal.: Woodside Priory, 1981);

James H. Maddox Jr., *Joyce's* Ulysses *and the Assault upon Character* (London: Harvester, 1978; New Brunswick, N.J.: Rutgers University Press, 1978);

Richard E. Madtes, *The "Ithaca" Chapter of Joyce's* Ulysses (Ann Arbor: University of Michigan Research Press, 1983);

Augustine Martin, "Novelist and City: The Technical Challenge," in *The Irish Writer and the City,* edited by Maurice Harmon (Gerrards Cross, Bucks, U.K.: Colin Smythe, 1984; Totowa, N.J.: Barnes & Noble, 1984), pp. 37–51;

Michael Mason, *James Joyce:* Ulysses (London: Arnold, 1972);

Mason, "Why Is Leopold Bloom a Cuckold," *ELH,* 44 (Spring 1977): 171–188;

Patrick A. McCarthy, Ulysses: *Portals of Discovery* (Boston: Twayne, 1990);

Patrick McGee, *Paperspace: Style as Ideology in Joyce's* Ulysses (Lincoln & London: University of Nebraska Press, 1988);

James McMichael, Ulysses *and Justice* (Princeton: Princeton University Press, 1991);

Giorgio Melchiori, ed., *Joyce in Rome: The Genesis of* Ulysses (Rome: Bulzoni, 1984);

J. Mitchell Morse, "Molly Bloom Revisited," in *A James Joyce Miscellany,* edited by Marvin Magalaner (Carbondale: Southern Illinois University Press, 1959);

Vladimir Vladimirovich Nabokov, *Lectures on Ulysses: Facsimile of the Manuscript* (Bloomfield Hills, Mich.: Bruccoli Clark, 1980);

Robert A. Newman and Weldon Thornton, eds., *Joyce's* Ulysses: *The Larger Perspective* (Newark: University of Delaware Press, 1987; London & Toronto: Associated University Presses, 1987);

R. W. Owen, *James Joyce and the Beginnings of* Ulysses (Ann Arbor: University of Michigan Research Press, 1983);

Ezra Pound, "James Joyce et Pécuchet," 1922, translated by Fred Bornhauser, *Shenandoah,* 32 (1952), 9–20;

Mary Power, "The Discovery of Ruby," *James Joyce Quarterly,* 18 (Winter 1981): 115–121;

Mario Praz, "James Joyce," in *James Joyce, Thomas Stearns Eliot: Due Maestri Dei Moderni* (Turin: Edizioni Rai Radiotelevisione Italiana, 1967), pp. 3–82;

John Henry Raleigh, *The Chronicle of Leopold and Molly Bloom: Ulysses as Narrative* (Berkeley & Los Angeles: University of California Press, 1977);

Charles Rossman, ed., *Studies in the Novel: A Special Issue on Editing* Ulysses, 22 (Summer 1990): 113–269;

C. George Sandulescu, *The Joycean Monologue: A Study of Character and Monologue in Joyce's* Ulysses *Against the Background of Literary Tradition* (Colchester, U.K.: Wake Newslitter Press, 1979);

Sandulescu and Clive Hart, eds., *Assessing the 1984* Ulysses (Gerrards Cross, U.K.: Colin Smythe; Totowa, N.J.: Barnes & Noble, 1986);

William Schutte, *Index of Recurrent Elements in James Joyce's* Ulysses (Carbondale: Southern Illinois University Press, 1982);

Schutte, *Joyce and Shakespeare: A Study in the Meaning of* Ulysses (New Haven: Yale University Press, 1957);

Michael Seidel, *Epic Geography: James Joyce's* Ulysses (Princeton: Princeton University Press, 1976);

Mark Shechner, *Joyce in Nighttown: A Psychoanalytic Inquiry into* Ulysses (Berkeley & Los Angeles: University of California Press, 1974);

Paul Jordan Smith, *A Key to the* Ulysses *of James Joyce* (Chicago: Covici, 1927);

Thomas F. Staley, ed., Ulysses: *Fifty Years* (Bloomington: Indiana University Press, 1974);

Staley and Bernard Benstock, eds., *Approaches to* Ulysses: *Ten Essays* (Pittsburgh: University of Pittsburgh Press, 1970);

William B. Stanford, *The* Ulysses *Theme: A Study in the Adaptability of a Traditional Hero* (Oxford: Blackwell, 1954; revised 1963); revised (New York: Barnes & Noble, 1968); with a new foreword by Charles Boer (Dallas: Spring Publications, 1992);

Erwin R. Steinberg, *The Stream of Consciousness and Beyond in* Ulysses (Pittsburgh: University of Pittsburgh Press, 1973);

Wolfhard Steppe with Hans Walter Gabler, *A Handlist to James Joyce's* Ulysses (New York & London: Garland, 1985);

Stanley Sultan, *The Argument of* Ulysses (Columbus: Ohio State University Press, 1964);

Sultan, Ulysses, The Waste Land, *and Modernism: A Jubilee Study* (Port Washington, N.Y.: Kennikat Press, 1977);

Brook Thomas, *James Joyce's* Ulysses: *A Book of Many Happy Returns* (Baton Rouge: Louisiana State University Press, 1982);

Lawrance R. Thompson, *A Comic Principle in Sterne-Meredith-Joyce* (Oslo: University of Oslo British Institute, 1954; Norwood, Pa.: Norwood Editions, 1978);

Weldon Thornton, *Allusions in* Ulysses: *An Annotated List* (Chapel Hill: University of North Carolina Press, 1968);

Philip Toynbee, "A Study of James Joyce's *Ulysses,*" in *James Joyce: Two Decades of Criticism,* edited by Seon Givens (New York: Vanguard, 1948; revised, 1963), pp. 243–284;

Lindsey Tucker, *Stephen and Bloom at Life's Feast: Alimentary Symbolism and the Creative Process in James Joyce's* Ulysses (Columbus: Ohio State University Press, 1984);

Alick West, "James Joyce: *Ulysses,*" in *Crisis and Criticism and Selected Literary Essays* (London: Lawrence & Wishart, 1975), pp. 143–180;

Edmund L. Wilson, "James Joyce," in *Axel's Castle: A Study of the Imaginative Literature of 1870–1930* (New York: Scribners, 1931), pp. 191–236;

David G. Wright, *Ironies in* Ulysses (Savage, Md.: Barnes & Noble, 1991).

FINNEGANS WAKE

James S. Atherton, *The Books at the Wake: A Study of Literary Allusions in James Joyce's* Finnegans Wake (New York: Viking, 1960);

Samuel Beckett, *Our Examination Round His Factification for Incamination of* "Work in Progress," second edition (Northampton, U.K.: John Dickens & Conner, 1962);

Michael H. Begnal and Grace Eckley, *Narrator and Character in* Finnegans Wake (Lewisburg, Pa.: Bucknell University Press, 1975);

Begnal and Fritz Senn, eds., *A Conceptual Guide to* Finnegans Wake (University Park: Pennsylvania State University Press, 1974);

Bernard Benstock, *Joyce-Again's Wake: An Analysis of* Finnegans Wake (Seattle: University of Washington Press, 1965);

John Bishop, *Joyce's Book of the Dark:* Finnegans Wake (Madison: University of Wisconsin Press, 1986);

Frances Motz Boldereff, *Hermes to His Son Thoth: Being Joyce's Use of Giordano Bruno in* Finnegans Wake (Woodward, Pa.: Classic Nonfiction Library, 1968);

Boldereff, *Reading* Finnegans Wake (New York: Barnes & Noble, 1959);

Helmut Bonheim, *Joyce's Benefictions* (Berkeley: University of California Press, 1964);

Bonheim, *A Lexicon of the German in* Finnegans Wake (Berkeley & Los Angeles: University of California Press, 1967);

Robert S. J. Boyle, *"Finnegans Wake,* Page 185: An Explication," *James Joyce Quarterly,* 4 (1966): 3–16;

Boyle, *James Joyce's Pauline Vision: A Catholic Exposition* (Carbondale & Edwardsville: Southern Illinois University Press, 1978);

Boyle, "Miracle in Black Ink: A Glance at Joyce's Use of His Eucharistic Image," *James Joyce Quarterly,* 10 (1972): 47–60;

Boyle, "Worshipper of the Word: James Joyce and the Trinity," in *A Starchamber Quiry: A James Joyce Centennial Volume, 1882–1982* (New York & London: Methuen, 1982);

Arthur T. Broes, "More People at the Wake (Contd.)," *A Wake Newslitter,* 4 (1967): 25–30;

Norman O. Brown, *Life Against Death: The Psychoanalytic Meaning of History* (Middletown, Conn.: Wesleyan University Press, 1959);

Anthony Burgess, *Here Comes Everybody: An Introduction to James Joyce for the Ordinary Reader* (London: Faber & Faber, 1965); published as *Re Joyce* (New York: Norton, 1965); revised with new foreword by Burgess (Feltham, U.K.: Hamlyn, 1982);

Burgess, *Joysprick* (London: Deutsch, 1973);

Burgess, *A Shorter* Finnegans Wake (London: Faber & Faber, 1966);

Joseph Campbell and Henry Morton Robinson, *A Skeleton Key to* Finnegans Wake (New York: Harcourt, Brace, 1944);

Craig Carver, "James Joyce and the Theory of Magic," *James Joyce Quarterly,* 15 (1978): 201–214;

Vincent John Cheng, *Shakespeare and Joyce: A Study of* Finnegans Wake (University Park & London: Pennsylvania State University Press, 1984);

Dounia Bunis Christiani, *Scandinavian Elements of* Finnegans Wake (Evanston, Ill.: Northwestern University Press, 1965);

Thomas E. Connolly, ed., *Scribbledehobble: The Ur-Workbook for* Finnegans Wake (Evanston, Ill.: Northwestern University Press, 1961);

Jack P. Dalton and Clive Hart, eds., *Twelve and a Tilly: Essays on the Occasion of the 25th Anniversary of* Finnegans Wake (Evanston, Ill.: Northwestern University Press, 1965; London: Faber & Faber, 1966);

Seamus Deane, ed., *Finnegans Wake* (New York: Penguin, 1992);

Kimberly J. Devlin, *Wandering and Return in* Finnegans Wake (Princeton: Princeton University Press, 1990);

Barbara DiBernard, *Alchemy and* Finnegans Wake (Albany: State Univerity of New York, 1980);

William F. Dohman, "'Chilly Spaces': Wyndham Lewis as Ondt," *James Joyce Quarterly,* 11 (Summer 1974): 368–386;

Grace Eckley, *Children's Lore in* Finnegans Wake (Syracuse: Syracuse University Press, 1985);

E. L. Epstein, "Chance, Doubt, Coincidence and the Prankquean's Riddle," *A Wake Newslitter,* 6 (February 1969): 3–7;

A. Nicholas Fargnoli, "A-taufing in the *Wake:* Joyce's Baptismal Motif," *James Joyce Quarterly,* 20 (Spring 1983): 293–305;

Michael Patrick Gillespie, "An Inquisition of Chapter Seven of *Finnegans Wake,*" *Renascence,* 35 (Winter 1983): 138–151;

Gillespie, "Lurking ad the Litter: *Finnegans Wake* 110.27–112.30" in *New Alliances in Joyce Studies: "When it's Aped to Foul a Delfian,"* edited by Bonnie Kime Scott (Newark: University of Delaware Press, 1988), pp. 230–237;

Gillespie, "Raiding fur Bugginers: *Finnegans Wake,* 611.04–613.04," *James Joyce Quarterly,* 24 (Spring 1987): 319–330;

Gillespie, "'When is a man not a man': Deconstructive and Reconstructive Impulses in *Finnegans Wake,*" *International Fiction Review,* 18 (1991): 1–14;

Adaline Glasheen, *A Census of Finnegans Wake* (London: Faber & Faber, 1956);

Glasheen, *A Second Census of Finnegans Wake* (Evanston: Northwestern University Press, 1963);

Glasheen, *A Third Census of Finnegans Wake: An Index of the Characters and Their Roles* (Berkeley: University of California Press, 1977);

Clive Hart, *A Concordance to* Finnegans Wake (Minneapolis: University of Minnesota Press, 1963);

Hart, *Structure and Motif in* Finnegans Wake (London: Faber & Faber, 1962; Evanston, Ill.: Northwestern University Press, 1962);

Hart and Fritz Senn, eds., *A Wake Digest* (Sydney: Sydney University Press, 1968; University Park: Pennsylvania State Press, 1968; London: Methuen, 1968);

David Hayman, "Nodality and the Infra-Structure of *Finnegans Wake,*" *James Joyce Quarterly,* 16 (Fall 1978/Winter 1979): 135–150;

Hayman, ed., *A First-Draft Version of* Finnegans Wake (Austin: University of Texas Press, 1963);

Ronald J. Koch, "Giordano Bruno and *Finnegans Wake,*" *James Joyce Quarterly,* 9 (1971): 225–249;

A. Walton Litz, *The Art of James Joyce: Method and Design in* Ulysses *and* Finnegans Wake (New York: Oxford University Press, 1961);

Patrick A. McCarthy, *The Riddles of* Finnegans Wake (Rutherford, N.J.: Fairleigh Dickinson University Press; London & Toronto: Associated University Presses, 1980);

McCarthy, ed., *Critical Essays on James Joyce's* Finnegans Wake (New York: G. K. Hall, 1992);

Roland McHugh, *Annotations to* Finnegans Wake (Baltimore & London: Johns Hopkins University Press, 1980; revised, 1991);

McHugh, *The* Finnegans Wake *Experience* (Dublin: Irish Academic Press, 1981; Berkeley & Los Angeles: University of California Press, 1981);

McHugh, *The Sigla of* Finnegans Wake (Austin: University of Texas Press, 1976; London: Arnold, 1976);

Louis O. Mink, *A* Finnegans Wake *Gazetteer* (Bloomington & London: Indiana University Press, 1978);

Margot C. Norris, *The Decentered Universe of "Finnegans Wake": A Structuralist Analysis* (Baltimore: Johns Hopkins University Press, 1977);

Riana O'Dwyer, "Czarnowski and *Finnegans Wake:* A Study of the Cult of the Hero," *James Joyce Quarterly,* 17 (Spring 1980): 281–291;

Brendan O'Hehir, *A Gaelic Lexicon for* Finnegans Wake and Glossary for Joyce's Other Works (Los Angeles & Berkeley: University of California Press, 1967);

O'Hehir and John Dillon, *A Classical Lexicon for* Finnegans Wake (Berkeley: University of California Press, 1977);

George Otte, "Time and Space (With the Emphasis on the Conjunction): Joyce's Response to Lewis," *James Joyce Quarterly,* 22 (Spring 1985): 297–306;

Danis Rose and John O'Hanlon, *Understanding* Finnegans Wake: *A Guide to the Narrative of James Joyce's Masterpiece* (New York & London: Garland, 1982);

C. George Sandulescu, *The Language of the Devil: Texture and Archetype in* Finnegans Wake (Gerrads Cross, U.K.: Colin Smythe; Chester Springs, Pa.: Dufour Editions, 1987);

Margaret C. Solomon, *Eternal Geomater: The Sexual Universe of* Finnegans Wake (Carbondale & Edwardsville: Southern Illinois University Press, 1969);

Solomon, "Sham Rocks: Shem's Answer to the First Riddle of the Universe," *A Wake Newslitter,* 7 (1970), 67–72;

William York Tindall, *A Reader's Guide to* Finnegans Wake (New York: Farrar, Straus & Giroux, 1969);

Mark L. Troy, *Mummeries of Resurrection: The Cycle of Osiris in* Finnegans Wake (Uppsala: University of Uppsala, 1976);

Pierre Vitoux, "Aristotle, Berkeley, and Newman [Newton] in 'Proteus' and *Finnegans Wake,*" *James Joyce Quarterly,* 18 (Winter 1981): 161–175;

Edmund Wilson, "The Dream of H. C. Earwicker," in *The Wound and the Bow* (Boston: Houghton Mifflin, 1941).

CATALOGUES AND COLLECTIONS

Catherine Fahy, *The James Joyce-Paul Le'on Papers in The National Library of Ireland, A Catalogue* (Dublin: National Library of Ireland, 1992);

Michael Patrick Gillespie with Erick Bradford Stocker, *James Joyce's Trieste Library: A Catalogue of Materials* (Austin: Humanities Research Center, University of Texas, 1986);

Phillip F. Herring, *Joyce's Notes and Early Drafts for* Ulysses: *Selections from the Buffalo Collections* (Charlottesville: University Press of Virginia, 1977);

Herring, *Joyce's Ulysses Notesheets in the British Museum* (Charlottesville: University Press of Virginia, 1972);

Steven Lund, *James Joyce: Letters, Manuscripts, and Photographs at Southern Illinois University* (Troy, N.Y.: Whitston, 1983);

Arthur Mizener, *The Cornell Joyce Collection, given to Cornell University by William G. Mennen* (Ithaca, N.Y.: Cornell University Press, 1958);

Dave Oliphant and Thomas Zigal, eds., *Joyce at Texas: Essays on the James Joyce Materials at the Humanities Research Center* (Austin: Humanities Research Center/University of Texas, 1983);

Robert E. Scholes, *The Cornell Joyce Collection: a Catalogue* (Ithaca, N.Y.: Cornell University Press, 1961).

SELECTED DOCUMENTARIES AND THEATRICAL AND MOTION-PICTURE ADAPTATIONS

See also the "Current JJ Checklist" in the *James Joyce Quarterly;*

Kim Evans, director, "James Joyce" in *The Modern World: Ten Great Writers,* volume 7, 60-minute videocassette (1988);

Enrico Frattaroli, fluidofiumericorsi, for reciting voices, soprano, midi device, and percussion;

Donald Freed, *Is He Still Dead?,* play, New Haven, Conn., Long Wharf Theater (1990);

Tom Gallacher, *Mr J Is Leaving Paris,* play (1982);

"James Joyce: A Concise Biography," in *The Famous Author Series,* a 60-minute videocassette (1996);

Burgess Meredith, director, *James Joyce's Women,* adapted and performed by Fionnula Flanagan (1979);

Pat Murphy, director, *Nora* (1999), motion-picture biography of Joyce's wife, Nora Barnacle, written by Brenda Maddox (1999);

Michael Pearce, director, *James Joyce's Women,* motion picture (MCA Home Video, 1985);

Tom Stoppard, *Travesties,* play, London, Aldwych Theatre, Royal Shakespeare Company; revised, London, Barbicon, Royal Shakespeare Company (16 October 1993).

DUBLINERS

Murray Boren, music, and Glen Nelson, libretto, *The Dead,* one-act opera, New York, 1993;

Jack Hofsiss, director, *The Dead,* adapted by Richard Nelson, music by Shaun Davey, New York, Playwrights Horizons 28, October 1999;

John Huston, director, *The Dead,* motion picture, 1987.

FINNEGANS WAKE

Stephen J. Albert, *Riverrun,* four-movement orchestral work, 1983;

Albert, *To Wake the Dead,* song cycle, 1978;

Albert, *Tree Stone,* song cycle, 1983–1984;

John Buller, *The Mime of Mick, Nick and the Maggies: On Part 2 of Finnegans Wake by James Joyce,* for soprano, tenor, baritone, chorus, and narrator, 1978;

Mary Ellen Bute, *Passages from* Finnegans Wake, motion picture, 1965;

John Cage, *Roaratorio: An Irish Circus on* Finnegans Wake, combination of selected passages from *Finnegans Wake* and recordings of traditional Irish music, 1979;

Cage, excerpt in *The Wonderful Widow of Eighteen Springs,* for mezzosoprano, 1942;

Jean Erdman, *The Coach With the Six Insides,* allegorical play, music by Teiji Ito, 1962;

Zenon Fajfer, director, *Finnegans Make,* performed by Zenkasi Theatre Company at the Polish Cultural Institute, London, 1996;

Ciceil L. Gross, director, *Nine Characters in Search of a Wake,* play, Gotham Book Mart, New York City, 2 February 1997;

Andre Hodier, *Anna Livia Plurabelle: A Jazz Cantata,* 1970;

Tod Machover, *Soft Morning, City!,* London, St. John's Smith Square, 20 May 1980;

Mary Manning, *Passages from* Finnegans Wake *by James Joyce: A Free Adaptation for the Theatre,* 1955; made into a motion picture by Mary Ellen Bute;

Roger Marsh, *"Not a soul but ourselves. . . . ,"* ; San Diego, 29 November 1977;

Harry Partch, excerpt in *Isobel and Annah the Allmaziful,* for two flutes and kithara, 1944;

The Pilobolus Dance Theater, *Rejoyce: A Pilobolus, Finnegans Wake,* 1993;

Margaret Rogers, *A Babble of Earwigs, or Sinnegan with Finnegan,* a chorale, 1987;

Humphrey Searle, excerpts in *The Riverrun,* for speakers and orchestra, 1951;

Ten 28/Process, "Installation/Performance/Exhibition: *FW* II.4 (12: 383–399)," 8–11 October 1993, Tranway Theatre, Glasgow;

"A Painful Case," Michael Voysey, adaptor, and John Lynch, director, RTE (Irish Television), 1985.

A PORTRAIT OF THE ARTIST AS A YOUNG MAN

Luciano Berio, excerpt in *Epifanie,* for female vocal and orchestra, 1959–1961; revised in 1965;

Luigi Dallapiccola, excerpt in *Requiescant,* for chorus and orchestra, 1957–1958;

Mátyás Seiber, *Three Fragments,* for speaker, chorus, ensemble, 1957;

Joseph Strick, director, *A Portrait of the Artist as a Young Man,* motion picture, 1979.

ULYSSES

George Antheil, excerpt in *Extract: Mr Bloom and the Cyclops,* an unfinished opera, 1925–1926;

Luciano Berio, excerpt in *Thema* (Omaggio a Joyce), two-track tape, 1958;

Dermot Bolger, *A Dublin Bloom: An Original Free Adaptation of James Joyce's Ulysses,* play, 1995;

Cathie Boyd, director, *Parallel Lines,* Transverse Theatre, Edinburgh, August, 1996;

Anthony Burgess, *The Blooms of Dublin,* musical, 1982 (for the Joyce centenary broadcast by BBC radio);

Circe, dramatic adaption of episode 15 of *Ulysses,* 1983;

Ian Graham, *James Joyce: The Trials of Ulysses,* documentary, 2000;

Mátyás Seiber, for tenor, chorus, and orchestra, 1946–1947;

Joseph Strick, director, *Ulysses,* motion picture, 1967;

Anna Zapparoli and Mario Borciani, musical adaptation of Molly Bloom's monologue, chapter 18, Penelope, of *Ulysses,* 2000.

JOURNALS

The Abiko Quarterly (Literary Rag)

A "Finnegans Wake" Circular (1985–1992)

Hypermedia Joyce Studies, http: //www.2street.com/joyce/ email:hjs@2street.com;

James Joyce Broadsheet

James Joyce Literary Supplement

James Joyce Newsletter

James Joyce Review (1957–1959)

James Joyce Quarterly

Joyce Studies Annual

A Wake Newslitter (1962–1980, 1982–1984)

SPECIAL ISSUES

Envoy, James Joyce Special Number, edited by Brian O'Nolan, 5 (May 1951);

Journal of Modern Literature, special issue, *Joyce and the Joyceans,* 22 (Winter 1998/1999);

Joyce Studies Annual, (1990–1995); includes a James Joyce checklist of new editions and translations, secondary sources with references to reviews, musical settings, theatrical productions, readings, motion pictures, and miscellaneous information;

Ellen Carol Jones, ed., *Modern Fiction Studies: Feminist Readings of Joyce,* 35 (Autumn 1989).

ORGANIZATIONS

American Friends of James Joyce, contact Gerry O'Beirne, e-mail: gobeirn@ggk.com, phone: (212) 372–1394, fax: (212) 372–8394;

FWAKE-L, mailing list, subscribe to: listserv@listserv.hea.ie with following message: subscribe FWAKE-L firstname lastname;

International James Joyce Foundation, contact International James Joyce Foundation, Department of English, Ohio State University, 164 West 17th Avenue, Columbus, OH 43210;

James Joyce Centre, contact James Joyce Centre, 35 North Great George's Street, Dublin 1, Ireland;

The James Joyce Museum, contact Curator, The James Joyce Museum, The Joyce Tower, Sandycove, County Dublin, Ireland;

James Joyce Society, contact A. Nicholas Fargnoli, President, James Joyce Society, 26 Varick Court, Rockville Centre, NY 11570;

J-JOYCE, mailing list, subscribe to: listproc@lists.utah.edu with following message: subscribe j-joyce firstname lastname.

PAPERS

For a complete list of libraries and a detailed index of James Joyce holdings, see *James Joyce's Manuscripts: An Index,* compiled by Michael Groden (New York: Garland, 1980). Listed here are libraries holding or housing significant Joyce material: British Library (London; formerly British Museum); Cornell University (Ithaca, N.Y.); Harvard University (Cambridge, Mass.); Princeton University (Princeton, N.J.); Rosenbach Foundation (Philadelphia, Pa.); Southern Illinois University (Carbondale, Ill.); State University of New York at Buffalo (Buffalo, N.Y.); University of Texas (Austin, Tex.); Yale University (New Haven, Conn.).

Cumulative Index

Dictionary of Literary Biography, Volumes 1-247
Dictionary of Literary Biography Yearbook, 1980-2000
Dictionary of Literary Biography Documentary Series, Volumes 1-19
Concise Dictionary of American Literary Biography, Volumes 1-7
Concise Dictionary of British Literary Biography, Volumes 1-8
Concise Dictionary of World Literary Biography, Volumes 1-4

Cumulative Index

DLB before number: *Dictionary of Literary Biography,* Volumes 1-247
Y before number: *Dictionary of Literary Biography Yearbook, 1980-2000*
DS before number: *Dictionary of Literary Biography Documentary Series,* Volumes 1-19
CDALB before number: *Concise Dictionary of American Literary Biography,* Volumes 1-7
CDBLB before number: *Concise Dictionary of British Literary Biography,* Volumes 1-8
CDWLB before number: *Concise Dictionary of World Literary Biography,* Volumes 1-4

A

Aakjær, Jeppe 1866-1930 . . . . .DLB-214

Abbey, Edwin Austin 1852-1911 . . . . . . .DLB-188

Abbey, Maj. J. R. 1894-1969 . . . . .DLB-201

Abbey Press DLB-49

The Abbey Theatre and Irish Drama,
1900-1945 .DLB-10

Abbot, Willis J. 1863-1934 . . . . .DLB-29

Abbott, Jacob 1803-1879 . . . . .DLB-1, 243

Abbott, Lee K. 1947- DLB-130

Abbott, Lyman 1835-1922 . . . . .DLB-79

Abbott, Robert S. 1868-1940 . . . . . . .DLB-29, 91

Abe Kōbō 1924-1993 . . . . .DLB-182

Abelard, Peter circa 1079-1142? DLB-115, 208

Abelard-Schuman .DLB-46

Abell, Arunah S. 1806-1888 . . . . .DLB-43

Abell, Kjeld 1901-1961 . . . . .DLB-214

Abercrombie, Lascelles 1881-1938 . . . . . . .DLB-19

Aberdeen University Press Limited DLB-106

Abish, Walter 1931- DLB-130, 227

Ablesimov, Aleksandr Onisimovich
1742-1783 . . . . .DLB-150

Abraham à Sancta Clara 1644-1709 . . . . . .DLB-168

Abrahams, Peter
1919- DLB-117, 225; CDWLB-3

Abrams, M. H. 1912- DLB-67

Abramson, Jesse 1904-1979 . . . . .DLB-241

Abrogans circa 790-800 . . . . .DLB-148

Abschatz, Hans Aßmann von
1646-1699 . . . . .DLB-168

Abse, Dannie 1923- DLB-27, 245

Abutsu-ni 1221-1283 . . . . .DLB-203

Academy Chicago Publishers DLB-46

Accius circa 170 B.C.-circa 80 B.C. DLB-211

Accrocca, Elio Filippo 1923- DLB-128

Ace Books DLB-46

Achebe, Chinua 1930- DLB-117; CDWLB-3

Achtenberg, Herbert 1938- DLB-124

Ackerman, Diane 1948- DLB-120

Ackroyd, Peter 1949- DLB-155, 231

Acorn, Milton 1923-1986 . . . . .DLB-53

Acosta, Oscar Zeta 1935?- DLB-82

Acosta Torres, José 1925- DLB-209

Actors Theatre of Louisville DLB-7

Adair, Gilbert 1944- DLB-194

Adair, James 1709?-1783? DLB-30

Adam, Graeme Mercer 1839-1912 . . . . . . .DLB-99

Adam, Robert Borthwick II 1863-1940 . . .DLB-187

Adame, Leonard 1947- DLB-82

Adameşteanu, Gabriel 1942- DLB-232

Adamic, Louis 1898-1951 . . . . .DLB-9

Adams, Abigail 1744-1818 . . . . .DLB-200

Adams, Alice 1926-1999 . . . . DLB-234, Y-86

Adams, Bertha Leith (Mrs. Leith Adams,
Mrs. R. S. de Courcy Laffan)
1837?-1912 .DLB-240

Adams, Brooks 1848-1927 . . . . .DLB-47

Adams, Charles Francis, Jr. 1835-1915 . . . .DLB-47

Adams, Douglas 1952- Y-83

Adams, Franklin P. 1881-1960 . . . . .DLB-29

Adams, Hannah 1755-1832 . . . . .DLB-200

Adams, Henry 1838-1918 . . . . DLB-12, 47, 189

Adams, Herbert Baxter 1850-1901 . . . . . . .DLB-47

Adams, J. S. and C. [publishing house] DLB-49

Adams, James Truslow
1878-1949 . . . . DLB-17; DS-17

Adams, John 1735-1826 . . . . .DLB-31, 183

Adams, John 1735-1826 and
Adams, Abigail 1744-1818 . . . . .DLB-183

Adams, John Quincy 1767-1848 . . . . .DLB-37

Adams, Léonie 1899-1988 . . . . .DLB-48

Adams, Levi 1802-1832 . . . . .DLB-99

Adams, Samuel 1722-1803 . . . . .DLB-31, 43

Adams, Sarah Fuller Flower
1805-1848 . . . . .DLB-199

Adams, Thomas 1582 or 1583-1652 . . . . .DLB-151

Adams, William Taylor 1822-1897 . . . . . . .DLB-42

Adamson, Sir John 1867-1950 . . . . .DLB-98

Adcock, Arthur St. John 1864-1930 . . . . . .DLB-135

Adcock, Betty 1938- DLB-105

"Certain Gifts" .DLB-105

Adcock, Fleur 1934- DLB-40

Addison, Joseph 1672-1719 . . .DLB-101; CDBLB-2

Ade, George 1866-1944 . . . . .DLB-11, 25

Adeler, Max (see Clark, Charles Heber)

Adonias Filho 1915-1990 . . . . .DLB-145

Adorno, Theodor W. 1903-1969 . . . . . . .DLB-242

Advance Publishing Company DLB-49

Ady, Endre 1877-1919 . . . . . . DLB-215; CDWLB-4

AE 1867-1935 . . . . .DLB-19; CDBLB-5

Ælfric circa 955-circa 1010 . . . . .DLB-146

Aeschines
circa 390 B.C.-circa 320 B.C. DLB-176

Aeschylus 525-524 B.C.-456-455 B.C.
. . . . DLB-176; CDWLB-1

Afro-American Literary Critics:
An Introduction DLB-33

After Dinner Opera Company Y-92

Agassiz, Elizabeth Cary 1822-1907 . . . . . .DLB-189

Agassiz, Louis 1807-1873 . . . . .DLB-1, 235

Agee, James
1909-1955 . . . . .DLB-2, 26, 152; CDALB-1

The Agee Legacy: A Conference at the University
of Tennessee at Knoxville Y-89

Aguilera Malta, Demetrio 1909-1981 . . . .DLB-145

Ai 1947- DLB-120

Aichinger, Ilse 1921- DLB-85

Aidoo, Ama Ata 1942- DLB-117; CDWLB-3

Aiken, Conrad
1889-1973 . . . . .DLB-9, 45, 102; CDALB-5

Aiken, Joan 1924- DLB-161

Aikin, Lucy 1781-1864 . . . . .DLB-144, 163

Ainsworth, William Harrison 1805-1882 . .DLB-21

Aistis, Jonas 1904-1973 . . . . . DLB-220; CDWLB-4

Aitken, George A. 1860-1917 . . . . .DLB-149

Aitken, Robert [publishing house] DLB-49

Akenside, Mark 1721-1770 . . . . .DLB-109

Akins, Zoë 1886-1958 . . . . .DLB-26

Aksahov, Sergei Timofeevich
1791-1859 . . . . .DLB-198

Akutagawa, Ryūnsuke 1892-1927 . . . . . . .DLB-180

Alabaster, William 1568-1640 . . . . .DLB-132

Alain de Lille circa 1116-1202/1203 . . . . .DLB-208

Alain-Fournier 1886-1914 . . . . .DLB-65

Alanus de Insulis (see Alain de Lille)

Alarcón, Francisco X. 1954- DLB-122

Alarcón, Justo S. 1930- DLB-209

Alba, Nanina 1915-1968 . . . . DLB-41

Albee, Edward 1928- DLB-7; CDALB-1

Albert the Great circa 1200-1280 . . . . . . DLB-115

Albert, Octavia 1853-ca. 1889 . . . . DLB-221

Alberti, Rafael 1902-1999 . . . . DLB-108

Albertinus, Aegidius circa 1560-1620 . . . . DLB-164

Alcaeus born circa 620 B.C. DLB-176

Alcott, Bronson 1799-1888 . . . . DLB-1, 223

Alcott, Louisa May 1832-1888
. . . DLB-1, 42, 79, 223, 239; DS-14; CDALB-3

Alcott, William Andrus 1798-1859 . . . . DLB-1, 243

Alcuin circa 732-804 . . . . DLB-148

Alden, Beardsley and Company DLB-49

Alden, Henry Mills 1836-1919 . . . . DLB-79

Alden, Isabella 1841-1930 . . . . DLB-42

Alden, John B. [publishing house] DLB-49

Aldington, Richard
1892-1962 . . . . .DLB-20, 36, 100, 149

Aldis, Dorothy 1896-1966 . . . . DLB-22

Aldis, H. G. 1863-1919 . . . . DLB-184

Aldiss, Brian W. 1925- DLB-14

Aldrich, Thomas Bailey
1836-1907 . . . . .DLB-42, 71, 74, 79

Alegría, Ciro 1909-1967 . . . . DLB-113

Alegría, Claribel 1924- DLB-145

Aleixandre, Vicente 1898-1984 . . . . DLB-108

Aleksandravičius, Jonas (see Aistis, Jonas)

Aleksandrov, Aleksandr Andreevich
(see Durova, Nadezhda Andreevna)

Aleramo, Sibilla 1876-1960 . . . . DLB-114

Alexander, Cecil Frances 1818-1895 . . . . . DLB-199

Alexander, Charles 1868-1923 . . . . DLB-91

Alexander, Charles Wesley
[publishing house] DLB-49

Alexander, James 1691-1756 . . . . DLB-24

Alexander, Lloyd 1924- DLB-52

Alexander, Sir William, Earl of Stirling
1577?-1640 . . . . DLB-121

Alexie, Sherman 1966- DLB-175, 206

Alexis, Willibald 1798-1871 . . . . DLB-133

Alfred, King 849-899 . . . . DLB-146

Alger, Horatio, Jr. 1832-1899 . . . . DLB-42

Algonquin Books of Chapel Hill DLB-46

Algren, Nelson
1909-1981 . . . . .DLB-9; Y-81, Y-82; CDALB-1

Nelson Algren: An International
Symposium Y-00

Allan, Andrew 1907-1974 . . . . DLB-88

Allan, Ted 1916- DLB-68

Allbeury, Ted 1917- DLB-87

Alldritt, Keith 1935- DLB-14

Allen, Ethan 1738-1789 . . . . DLB-31

Allen, Frederick Lewis 1890-1954 . . . . . DLB-137

Allen, Gay Wilson 1903-1995 . . . .DLB-103; Y-95

Allen, George 1808-1876 . . . . DLB-59

Allen, George [publishing house] DLB-106

Allen, George, and Unwin Limited DLB-112

Allen, Grant 1848-1899 . . . . .DLB-70, 92, 178

Allen, Henry W. 1912- Y-85

Allen, Hervey 1889-1949 . . . . DLB-9, 45

Allen, James 1739-1808 . . . . DLB-31

Allen, James Lane 1849-1925 . . . . DLB-71

Allen, Jay Presson 1922- DLB-26

Allen, John, and Company DLB-49

Allen, Paula Gunn 1939- DLB-175

Allen, Samuel W. 1917- DLB-41

Allen, Woody 1935- DLB-44

Allende, Isabel 1942- DLB-145; CDWLB-3

Alline, Henry 1748-1784 . . . . DLB-99

Allingham, Margery 1904-1966 . . . . DLB-77

Allingham, William 1824-1889 . . . . DLB-35

Allison, W. L. [publishing house] DLB-49

The *Alliterative Morte Arthure and the Stanzaic
Morte Arthur* circa 1350-1400 . . . . DLB-146

Allott, Kenneth 1912-1973 . . . . DLB-20

Allston, Washington 1779-1843 . . . . . DLB-1, 235

Almon, John [publishing house] DLB-154

Alonzo, Dámaso 1898-1990 . . . . DLB-108

Alsop, George 1636-post 1673 . . . . DLB-24

Alsop, Richard 1761-1815 . . . . DLB-37

Altemus, Henry, and Company DLB-49

Altenberg, Peter 1885-1919 . . . . DLB-81

Althusser, Louis 1918-1990 . . . . DLB-242

Altolaguirre, Manuel 1905-1959 . . . . DLB-108

Aluko, T. M. 1918- DLB-117

Alurista 1947- DLB-82

Alvarez, A. 1929- DLB-14, 40

Alver, Betti 1906-1989 . . . . . DLB-220; CDWLB-4

Amadi, Elechi 1934- DLB-117

Amado, Jorge 1912- DLB-113

Ambler, Eric 1909-1998 . . . . DLB-77

American Conservatory Theatre DLB-7

American Fiction and the 1930s DLB-9

American Humor: A Historical Survey
East and Northeast
South and Southwest
Midwest
West DLB-11

The American Library in Paris Y-93

American News Company DLB-49

The American Poets' Corner: The First
Three Years (1983-1986) Y-86

American Publishing Company DLB-49

American Stationers' Company DLB-49

American Sunday-School Union DLB-49

American Temperance Union DLB-49

American Tract Society DLB-49

The American Trust for the
British Library Y-96

The American Writers Congress
(9-12 October 1981) Y-81

The American Writers Congress: A Report
on Continuing Business Y-81

Ames, Fisher 1758-1808 . . . . DLB-37

Ames, Mary Clemmer 1831-1884 . . . . DLB-23

Amiel, Henri-Frédéric 1821-1881 . . . . . . .DLB-217

Amini, Johari M. 1935- DLB-41

Amis, Kingsley 1922-1995
. . . . . . DLB-15, 27, 100, 139, Y-96; CDBLB-7

Amis, Martin 1949- DLB-194

Ammianus Marcellinus
circa A.D. 330-A.D. 395 . . . . DLB-211

Ammons, A. R. 1926- DLB-5, 165

Amory, Thomas 1691?-1788 . . . . DLB-39

Anania, Michael 1939- DLB-193

Anaya, Rudolfo A. 1937- DLB-82, 206

Ancrene Riwle circa 1200-1225 . . . . DLB-146

Andersch, Alfred 1914-1980 . . . . DLB-69

Andersen, Benny 1929- DLB-214

Anderson, Alexander 1775-1870 . . . . DLB-188

Anderson, David 1929- DLB-241

Anderson, Frederick Irving 1877-1947 . . . DLB-202

Anderson, Margaret 1886-1973 . . . . . DLB-4, 91

Anderson, Maxwell 1888-1959 . . . . . . .DLB-7, 228

Anderson, Patrick 1915-1979 . . . . DLB-68

Anderson, Paul Y. 1893-1938 . . . . DLB-29

Anderson, Poul 1926- DLB-8

Anderson, Robert 1750-1830 . . . . DLB-142

Anderson, Robert 1917- DLB-7

Anderson, Sherwood
1876-1941 . . . . . DLB-4, 9, 86; DS-1; CDALB-4

Andreae, Johann Valentin 1586-1654 . . . . DLB-164

Andreas Capellanus
flourished circa 1185 . . . . DLB-208

Andreas-Salomé, Lou 1861-1937 . . . . DLB-66

Andres, Stefan 1906-1970 . . . . DLB-69

Andreu, Blanca 1959- DLB-134

Andrewes, Lancelot 1555-1626 . . . . .DLB-151, 172

Andrews, Charles M. 1863-1943 . . . . .DLB-17

Andrews, Miles Peter ?-1814 . . . . DLB-89

Andrian, Leopold von 1875-1951 . . . . DLB-81

Andrić, Ivo 1892-1975 . . . . . .DLB-147; CDWLB-4

Andrieux, Louis (see Aragon, Louis)

Andrus, Silas, and Son DLB-49

Andrzejewski, Jerzy 1909-1983 . . . . DLB-215

Angell, James Burrill 1829-1916 . . . . DLB-64

Angell, Roger 1920- DLB-171, 185

Angelou, Maya 1928- DLB-38; CDALB-7

Anger, Jane flourished 1589 . . . . DLB-136

Angers, Félicité (see Conan, Laure)

Anglo-Norman Literature in the Development
of Middle English Literature DLB-146

The Anglo-Saxon Chronicle circa 890-1154 . . DLB-146

The "Angry Young Men" DLB-15

Angus and Robertson (UK) Limited DLB-112

Anhalt, Edward 1914-2000 . . . . DLB-26

Anners, Henry F. [publishing house] DLB-49

Annolied between 1077 and 1081 . . . . DLB-148

Annual Awards for *Dictionary of Literary Biography*
Editors and Contributors Y-98, Y-99, Y-00

Anselm of Canterbury 1033-1109 . . . . . . .DLB-115

Anstey, F. 1856-1934 . . . . DLB-141, 178

Anthony, Michael 1932- DLB-125

Anthony, Piers 1934- DLB-8

Anthony, Susanna 1726-1791 . . . . .DLB-200

Antin, David 1932- DLB-169

Antin, Mary 1881-1949 . . . . .DLB-221; Y-84

Anton Ulrich, Duke of Brunswick-Lüneburg
1633-1714 . . . . .DLB-168

Antschel, Paul (see Celan, Paul)

Anyidoho, Kofi 1947- DLB-157

Anzaldúa, Gloria 1942- DLB-122

Anzengruber, Ludwig 1839-1889 . . . . . . .DLB-129

Apess, William 1798-1839 . . . . DLB-175, 243

Apodaca, Rudy S. 1939- DLB-82

Apollonius Rhodius third century B.C. . . .DLB-176

Apple, Max 1941- DLB-130

Appleton, D., and Company DLB-49

Appleton-Century-Crofts DLB-46

Applewhite, James 1935- DLB-105

Applewood Books DLB-46

Apuleius circa A.D. 125-post A.D. 164
. . . . .DLB-211; CDWLB-1

Aquin, Hubert 1929-1977 . . . . .DLB-53

Aquinas, Thomas 1224 or 1225-1274 . . . .DLB-115

Aragon, Louis 1897-1982 . . . . .DLB-72

Aralica, Ivan 1930- DLB-181

Aratus of Soli
circa 315 B.C.-circa 239 B.C. DLB-176

Arbasino, Alberto 1930- DLB-196

Arbor House Publishing Company DLB-46

Arbuthnot, John 1667-1735 . . . . .DLB-101

Arcadia House DLB-46

Arce, Julio G. (see Ulica, Jorge)

Archer, William 1856-1924 . . . . .DLB-10

Archilochhus
mid seventh century B.C.E. DLB-176

The Archpoet circa 1130?-? DLB-148

Archpriest Avvakum (Petrovich)
1620?-1682 . . . . .DLB-150

Arden, John 1930- DLB-13, 245

Arden of Faversham .DLB-62

Ardis Publishers Y-89

Ardizzone, Edward 1900-1979 . . . . .DLB-160

Arellano, Juan Estevan 1947- DLB-122

The Arena Publishing Company DLB-49

Arena Stage DLB-7

Arenas, Reinaldo 1943-1990 . . . . .DLB-145

Arendt, Hannah 1906-1975 . . . . .DLB-242

Arensberg, Ann 1937- Y-82

Arghezi, Tudor 1880-1967 . . .DLB-220; CDWLB-4

Arguedas, José María 1911-1969 . . . . .DLB-113

Argueta, Manlio 1936- DLB-145

Arias, Ron 1941- DLB-82

Arishima, Takeo 1878-1923 . . . . .DLB-180

Aristophanes circa 446 B.C.-circa 386 B.C.
. . . . DLB-176; CDWLB-1

Aristotle 384 B.C.-322 B.C.
. . . . DLB-176; CDWLB-1

Ariyoshi Sawako 1931-1984 . . . . .DLB-182

Arland, Marcel 1899-1986 . . . . .DLB-72

Arlen, Michael 1895-1956 . . . . DLB-36, 77, 162

Armah, Ayi Kwei 1939- . . . DLB-117; CDWLB-3

Armantrout, Rae 1947- DLB-193

Der arme Hartmann ?-after 1150 . . . . . . .DLB-148

Armed Services Editions DLB-46

Armstrong, Martin Donisthorpe
1882-1974 . . . . .DLB-197

Armstrong, Richard 1903- DLB-160

Arndt, Ernst Moritz 1769-1860 . . . . .DLB-90

Arnim, Achim von 1781-1831 . . . . .DLB-90

Arnim, Bettina von 1785-1859 . . . . .DLB-90

Arnim, Elizabeth von (Countess Mary
Annette Beauchamp Russell)
1866-1941 . . . . .DLB-197

Arno Press DLB-46

Arnold, Edward [publishing house] DLB-112

Arnold, Edwin 1832-1904 . . . . .DLB-35

Arnold, Edwin L. 1857-1935 . . . . .DLB-178

Arnold, Matthew
1822-1888 . . . . .DLB-32, 57; CDBLB-4

Preface to *Poems* (1853) DLB-32

Arnold, Thomas 1795-1842 . . . . .DLB-55

Arnott, Peter 1962- DLB-233

Arnow, Harriette Simpson 1908-1986 . . . . . .DLB-6

Arp, Bill (see Smith, Charles Henry)

Arpino, Giovanni 1927-1987 . . . . .DLB-177

Arreola, Juan José 1918- DLB-113

Arrian circa 89-circa 155 . . . . .DLB-176

Arrowsmith, J. W. [publishing house] DLB-106

The Art and Mystery of Publishing:
Interviews Y-97

Arthur, Timothy Shay
1809-1885 . . . . .DLB-3, 42, 79; DS-13

The Arthurian Tradition and
Its European Context DLB-138

Artmann, H. C. 1921-2000 . . . . .DLB-85

Arvin, Newton 1900-1963 . . . . .DLB-103

Asch, Nathan 1902-1964 . . . . .DLB-4, 28

Ascham, Roger 1515 or 1516-1568 . . . . . .DLB-236

Ash, John 1948- DLB-40

Ashbery, John 1927- DLB-5, 165; Y-81

Ashbridge, Elizabeth 1713-1755 . . . . .DLB-200

Ashburnham, Bertram Lord
1797-1878 . . . . .DLB-184

Ashendene Press DLB-112

Asher, Sandy 1942- Y-83

Ashton, Winifred (see Dane, Clemence)

Asimov, Isaac 1920-1992 . . . . .DLB-8; Y-92

Askew, Anne circa 1521-1546 . . . . .DLB-136

Aspazija 1865-1943 . . . . . . .DLB-220; CDWLB-4

Asselin, Olivar 1874-1937 . . . . .DLB-92

The Association of American Publishers Y-99

The Association for Documentary Editing . . . Y-00

Astley, William (see Warung, Price)

Asturias, Miguel Angel
1899-1974 . . . . DLB-113; CDWLB-3

At Home with Albert Erskine Y-00

Atheneum Publishers DLB-46

Atherton, Gertrude 1857-1948 . . . . . DLB-9, 78, 186

Athlone Press DLB-112

Atkins, Josiah circa 1755-1781 . . . . .DLB-31

Atkins, Russell 1926- DLB-41

Atkinson, Louisa 1834-1872 . . . . .DLB-230

The Atlantic Monthly Press DLB-46

Attaway, William 1911-1986 . . . . .DLB-76

Atwood, Margaret 1939- DLB-53

Aubert, Alvin 1930- DLB-41

Aubert de Gaspé, Phillipe-Ignace-François
1814-1841 . . . . .DLB-99

Aubert de Gaspé, Phillipe-Joseph
1786-1871 . . . . .DLB-99

Aubin, Napoléon 1812-1890 . . . . .DLB-99

Aubin, Penelope
1685-circa 1731 . . . . .DLB-39

Preface to *The Life of Charlotta
du Pont* (1723) DLB-39

Aubrey-Fletcher, Henry Lancelot (see Wade, Henry)

Auchincloss, Louis 1917- DLB-2, 244; Y-80

Auden, W. H. 1907-1973 . . .DLB-10, 20; CDBLB-6

Audio Art in America: A Personal Memoir . . . Y-85

Audubon, John Woodhouse
1812-1862 . . . . .DLB-183

Auerbach, Berthold 1812-1882 . . . . .DLB-133

Auernheimer, Raoul 1876-1948 . . . . .DLB-81

Augier, Emile 1820-1889 . . . . .DLB-192

Augustine 354-430 . . . . .DLB-115

Responses to Ken Auletta Y-97

Aulus Cellius
circa A.D. 125-circa A.D. 180? DLB-211

Austen, Jane
1775-1817 . . . . .DLB-116; CDBLB-3

Auster, Paul 1947- DLB-227

Austin, Alfred 1835-1913 . . . . .DLB-35

Austin, Jane Goodwin 1831-1894 . . . . . . .DLB-202

Austin, Mary 1868-1934 . . . . . DLB-9, 78, 206, 221

Austin, William 1778-1841 . . . . .DLB-74

Australie (Emily Manning)
1845-1890 . . . . .DLB-230

Author-Printers, 1476–1599 . . . . .DLB-167

Author Websites Y-97

Authors and Newspapers Association DLB-46

Authors' Publishing Company DLB-49

Avallone, Michael 1924-1999 . . . . Y-99

Avalon Books DLB-46

Avancini, Nicolaus 1611-1686 . . . . .DLB-164

Avendaño, Fausto 1941- DLB-82

Averroëö 1126-1198 . . . . .DLB-115

Avery, Gillian 1926- DLB-161

Avicenna 980-1037 .... DLB-115

Avison, Margaret 1918- DLB-53

Avon Books DLB-46

Avyžius, Jonas 1922-1999............ DLB-220

Awdry, Wilbert Vere 1911-1997....... DLB-160

Awoonor, Kofi 1935- DLB-117

Ayckbourn, Alan 1939- DLB-13, 245

Aymé, Marcel 1902-1967 .... DLB-72

Aytoun, Sir Robert 1570-1638 .... DLB-121

Aytoun, William Edmondstoune
    1813-1865.................. DLB-32, 159

B

B. V. (see Thomson, James)

Babbitt, Irving 1865-1933 .... DLB-63

Babbitt, Natalie 1932- DLB-52

Babcock, John [publishing house]....... DLB-49

Babits, Mihály 1883-1941... DLB-215; CDWLB-4

Babrius circa 150-200 ....DLB-176

Baca, Jimmy Santiago 1952- DLB-122

Bache, Benjamin Franklin 1769-1798 ..... DLB-43

Bacheller, Irving 1859-1950 .... DLB-202

Bachmann, Ingeborg 1926-1973 .... DLB-85

Bačinskaitė-Bučienė, Salomėja (see Nėris, Salomėja)

Bacon, Delia 1811-1859 .... DLB-1, 243

Bacon, Francis
    1561-1626 .... DLB-151, 236; CDBLB-1

Bacon, Sir Nicholas circa 1510-1579 ..... DLB-132

Bacon, Roger circa 1214/1220-1292 ..... DLB-115

Bacon, Thomas circa 1700-1768 .... DLB-31

Bacovia, George
    1881-1957........... DLB-220; CDWLB-4

Badger, Richard G., and Company DLB-49

Bagaduce Music Lending Library.......... Y-00

Bage, Robert 1728-1801 .... DLB-39

Bagehot, Walter 1826-1877........... DLB-55

Bagley, Desmond 1923-1983 .... DLB-87

Bagley, Sarah G. 1806-1848 .... DLB-239

Bagnold, Enid 1889-1981 ...DLB-13, 160, 191, 245

Bagryana, Elisaveta
    1893-1991 ....DLB-147; CDWLB-4

Bahr, Hermann 1863-1934......... DLB-81, 118

Bailey, Abigail Abbot 1746-1815........ DLB-200

Bailey, Alfred Goldsworthy 1905- DLB-68

Bailey, Francis [publishing house]....... DLB-49

Bailey, H. C. 1878-1961 .... DLB-77

Bailey, Jacob 1731-1808 .... DLB-99

Bailey, Paul 1937- DLB-14

Bailey, Philip James 1816-1902.......... DLB-32

Baillargeon, Pierre 1916-1967.......... DLB-88

Baillie, Hugh 1890-1966............. DLB-29

Baillie, Joanna 1762-1851 .... DLB-93

Bailyn, Bernard 1922- DLB-17

Bainbridge, Beryl 1933- DLB-14, 231

Baird, Irene 1901-1981 .... DLB-68

Baker, Augustine 1575-1641 .... DLB-151

Baker, Carlos 1909-1987 .... DLB-103

Baker, David 1954- DLB-120

Baker, Herschel C. 1914-1990 .... DLB-111

Baker, Houston A., Jr. 1943- DLB-67

Baker, Nicholson 1957- DLB-227

Baker, Samuel White 1821-1893 .... DLB-166

Baker, Thomas 1656-1740 .... DLB-213

Baker, Walter H., Company
    ("Baker's Plays") DLB-49

The Baker and Taylor Company....... DLB-49

Bakhtin, Mikhail Mikhailovich
    1895-1975.................... DLB-242

Balaban, John 1943- DLB-120

Bald, Wambly 1902- DLB-4

Balde, Jacob 1604-1668 .... DLB-164

Balderston, John 1889-1954 .... DLB-26

Baldwin, James
    1924-1987......DLB-2, 7, 33; Y-87; CDALB-1

Baldwin, Joseph Glover 1815-1864 .... DLB-3, 11

Baldwin, Louisa (Mrs. Alfred Baldwin)
    1845-1925 .... DLB-240

Baldwin, Richard and Anne
    [publishing house] DLB-170

Baldwin, William circa 1515-1563 ..... DLB-132

Bale, John 1495-1563 .... DLB-132

Balestrini, Nanni 1935- DLB-128, 196

Balfour, Sir Andrew 1630-1694 .... DLB-213

Balfour, Arthur James 1848-1930...... DLB-190

Balfour, Sir James 1600-1657 .... DLB-213

Ballantine Books................... DLB-46

Ballantyne, R. M. 1825-1894 .... DLB-163

Ballard, J. G. 1930- DLB-14, 207

Ballard, Martha Moore 1735-1812 ..... DLB-200

Ballerini, Luigi 1940- DLB-128

Ballou, Maturin Murray
    1820-1895 ....DLB-79, 189

Ballou, Robert O. [publishing house] DLB-46

Balzac, Honoré de 1799-1855 .... DLB-119

Bambara, Toni Cade
    1939- DLB-38, 218; CDALB-7

Bamford, Samuel 1788-1872 .... DLB-190

Bancroft, A. L., and Company......... DLB-49

Bancroft, George 1800-1891... DLB-1, 30, 59, 243

Bancroft, Hubert Howe 1832-1918 ...DLB-47, 140

Bandelier, Adolph F. 1840-1914 .... DLB-186

Bangs, John Kendrick 1862-1922 .....DLB-11, 79

Banim, John 1798-1842........DLB-116, 158, 159

Banim, Michael 1796-1874 .... DLB-158, 159

Banks, Iain 1954- DLB-194

Banks, John circa 1653-1706............ DLB-80

Banks, Russell 1940- DLB-130

Bannerman, Helen 1862-1946 .... DLB-141

Bantam Books DLB-46

Banti, Anna 1895-1985..............DLB-177

Banville, John 1945- DLB-14

Banville, Théodore de 1823-1891 ....DLB-217

Baraka, Amiri
    1934- DLB-5, 7, 16, 38; DS-8; CDALB-1

Barańczak, Stanisław 1946- DLB-232

Baratynsky, Evgenii Abramovich
    1800-1844 .... DLB-205

Barbauld, Anna Laetitia
    1743-1825........... DLB-107, 109, 142, 158

Barbeau, Marius 1883-1969 .... DLB-92

Barber, John Warner 1798-1885........ DLB-30

Bàrberi Squarotti, Giorgio 1929- DLB-128

Barbey d'Aurevilly, Jules-Amédée
    1808-1889 .... DLB-119

Barbier, Auguste 1805-1882 ....DLB-217

Barbilian, Dan (see Barbu, Ion)

Barbour, John circa 1316-1395 .... DLB-146

Barbour, Ralph Henry 1870-1944 .... DLB-22

Barbu, Ion 1895-1961...... DLB-220; CDWLB-4

Barbusse, Henri 1873-1935............ DLB-65

Barclay, Alexander circa 1475-1552 ..... DLB-132

Barclay, E. E., and Company........... DLB-49

Bardeen, C. W. [publishing house]...... DLB-49

Barham, Richard Harris 1788-1845 ..... DLB-159

Barich, Bill 1943- DLB-185

Baring, Maurice 1874-1945............ DLB-34

Baring-Gould, Sabine
    1834-1924 .... DLB-156, 190

Barker, A. L. 1918- DLB-14, 139

Barker, Arthur, Limited DLB-112

Barker, George 1913-1991 .... DLB-20

Barker, Harley Granville 1877-1946 ...... DLB-10

Barker, Howard 1946- DLB-13, 233

Barker, James Nelson 1784-1858 .... DLB-37

Barker, Jane 1652-1727............. DLB-39, 131

Barker, Lady Mary Anne 1831-1911 .... DLB-166

Barker, William circa 1520-after 1576 ... DLB-132

Barkov, Ivan Semenovich 1732-1768 .... DLB-150

Barks, Coleman 1937- DLB-5

Barlach, Ernst 1870-1938 .... DLB-56, 118

Barlow, Joel 1754-1812............... DLB-37

The Prospect of Peace (1778) DLB-37

Barnard, John 1681-1770 .... DLB-24

Barne, Kitty (Mary Catherine Barne)
    1883-1957 .... DLB-160

Barnes, A. S., and Company DLB-49

Barnes, Barnabe 1571-1609 .... DLB-132

Barnes, Djuna 1892-1982 .... DLB-4, 9, 45

Barnes, Jim 1933- DLB-175

Barnes, Julian 1946- DLB-194; Y-93

Barnes, Margaret Ayer 1886-1967 .... DLB-9

Barnes, Peter 1931- DLB-13, 233

Barnes, William 1801-1886 .... DLB-32

Barnes and Noble Books DLB-46

Barnet, Miguel 1940- DLB-145

Barney, Natalie 1876-1972 .... DLB-4

Barnfield, Richard 1574-1627 . . . . DLB-172

Baron, Richard W.,
    Publishing Company DLB-46

Barr, Amelia Edith Huddleston
    1831-1919 . . . . DLB-202, 221

Barr, Robert 1850-1912 . . . . DLB-70, 92

Barral, Carlos 1928-1989 . . . . DLB-134

Barrax, Gerald William 1933- DLB-41, 120

Barrès, Maurice 1862-1923 . . . . DLB-123

Barrett, Eaton Stannard 1786-1820 . . . . . . DLB-116

Barrie, J. M.
    1860-1937 . . . . . . DLB-10, 141, 156; CDBLB-5

Barrie and Jenkins DLB-112

Barrio, Raymond 1921- DLB-82

Barrios, Gregg 1945- DLB-122

Barry, Philip 1896-1949 . . . . DLB-7, 228

Barry, Robertine (see Françoise)

Barry, Sebastian 1955- DLB-245

Barse and Hopkins DLB-46

Barstow, Stan 1928- DLB-14, 139

Barth, John 1930- DLB-2, 227

Barthelme, Donald
    1931-1989 . . . . DLB-2, 234; Y-80, Y-89

Barthelme, Frederick 1943- DLB-244; Y-85

Bartholomew, Frank 1898-1985 . . . . DLB-127

Bartlett, John 1820-1905 . . . . DLB-1, 235

Bartol, Cyrus Augustus 1813-1900 . . . . DLB-1, 235

Barton, Bernard 1784-1849 . . . . DLB-96

Barton, John ca. 1610-1675 . . . . DLB-236

Barton, Thomas Pennant 1803-1869 . . . . . DLB-140

Bartram, John 1699-1777 . . . . DLB-31

Bartram, William 1739-1823 . . . . DLB-37

Basic Books DLB-46

Basille, Theodore (see Becon, Thomas)

Bass, Rick 1958- DLB-212

Bass, T. J. 1932- Y-81

Bassani, Giorgio 1916- DLB-128, 177

Basse, William circa 1583-1653 . . . . DLB-121

Bassett, John Spencer 1867-1928 . . . . DLB-17

Bassler, Thomas Joseph (see Bass, T. J.)

Bate, Walter Jackson 1918-1999 . . . . . DLB-67, 103

Bateman, Christopher
    [publishing house] DLB-170

Bateman, Stephen circa 1510-1584 . . . . . . DLB-136

Bates, H. E. 1905-1974 . . . . DLB-162, 191

Bates, Katharine Lee 1859-1929 . . . . DLB-71

Batiushkov, Konstantin Nikolaevich
    1787-1855 . . . . DLB-205

Batsford, B. T. [publishing house] DLB-106

Battiscombe, Georgina 1905- DLB-155

The Battle of Maldon circa 1000 . . . . DLB-146

Baudelaire, Charles 1821-1867 . . . . DLB-217

Bauer, Bruno 1809-1882 . . . . DLB-133

Bauer, Wolfgang 1941- DLB-124

Baum, L. Frank 1856-1919 . . . . DLB-22

Baum, Vicki 1888-1960 . . . . DLB-85

Baumbach, Jonathan 1933- Y-80

Bausch, Richard 1945- DLB-130

Bausch, Robert 1945- DLB-218

Bawden, Nina 1925- DLB-14, 161, 207

Bax, Clifford 1886-1962 . . . . DLB-10, 100

Baxter, Charles 1947- DLB-130

Bayer, Eleanor (see Perry, Eleanor)

Bayer, Konrad 1932-1964 . . . . DLB-85

Baynes, Pauline 1922- DLB-160

Baynton, Barbara 1857-1929 . . . . DLB-230

Bazin, Hervé 1911-1996 . . . . DLB-83

Beach, Sylvia 1887-1962 . . . . DLB-4; DS-15

Beacon Press DLB-49

Beadle and Adams DLB-49

Beagle, Peter S. 1939- Y-80

Beal, M. F. 1937- Y-81

Beale, Howard K. 1899-1959 . . . . DLB-17

Beard, Charles A. 1874-1948 . . . . DLB-17

A Beat Chronology: The First Twenty-five
    Years, 1944-1969 . . . . DLB-16

Periodicals of the Beat Generation DLB-16

The Beats in New York City DLB-237

The Beats in the West DLB-237

Beattie, Ann 1947- DLB-218; Y-82

Beattie, James 1735-1803 . . . . DLB-109

Beatty, Chester 1875-1968 . . . . DLB-201

Beauchemin, Nérée 1850-1931 . . . . DLB-92

Beauchemin, Yves 1941- DLB-60

Beaugrand, Honoré 1848-1906 . . . . DLB-99

Beaulieu, Victor-Lévy 1945- DLB-53

Beaumont, Francis circa 1584-1616
    and Fletcher, John 1579-1625
    . . . . DLB-58; CDBLB-1

Beaumont, Sir John 1583?-1627 . . . . DLB-121

Beaumont, Joseph 1616-1699 . . . . DLB-126

Beauvoir, Simone de 1908-1986 . . . . DLB-72; Y-86

Becher, Ulrich 1910- DLB-69

Becker, Carl 1873-1945 . . . . DLB-17

Becker, Jurek 1937-1997 . . . . DLB-75

Becker, Jurgen 1932- DLB-75

Beckett, Samuel 1906-1989
    . . . . DLB-13, 15, 233; Y-90; CDBLB-7

Beckford, William 1760-1844 . . . . DLB-39

Beckham, Barry 1944- DLB-33

Becon, Thomas circa 1512-1567 . . . . DLB-136

Becque, Henry 1837-1899 . . . . DLB-192

Beddoes, Thomas 1760-1808 . . . . DLB-158

Beddoes, Thomas Lovell 1803-1849 . . . . . DLB-96

Bede circa 673-735 . . . . DLB-146

Beecher, Catharine Esther 1800-1878 . . DLB-1, 243

Beecher, Henry Ward 1813-1887 . . . . . DLB-3, 43

Beer, George L. 1872-1920 . . . . DLB-47

Beer, Johann 1655-1700 . . . . DLB-168

Beer, Patricia 1919-1999 . . . . DLB-40

Beerbohm, Max 1872-1956 . . . . DLB-34, 100

Beer-Hofmann, Richard 1866-1945 . . . . . . DLB-81

Beers, Henry A. 1847-1926 . . . . DLB-71

Beeton, S. O. [publishing house] DLB-106

Bégon, Elisabeth 1696-1755 . . . . DLB-99

Behan, Brendan
    1923-1964 . . . . DLB-13, 233; CDBLB-7

Behn, Aphra 1640?-1689 . . . . DLB-39, 80, 131

Behn, Harry 1898-1973 . . . . DLB-61

Behrman, S. N. 1893-1973 . . . . DLB-7, 44

Belaney, Archibald Stansfeld (see Grey Owl)

Belasco, David 1853-1931 . . . . DLB-7

Belford, Clarke and Company DLB-49

Belinsky, Vissarion Grigor'evich
    1811-1848 . . . . DLB-198

Belitt, Ben 1911- DLB-5

Belknap, Jeremy 1744-1798 . . . . DLB-30, 37

Bell, Adrian 1901-1980 . . . . DLB-191

Bell, Clive 1881-1964 . . . . DS-10

Bell, Daniel 1919- DLB-246

Bell, George, and Sons DLB-106

Bell, Gertrude Margaret Lowthian
    1868-1926 . . . . DLB-174

Bell, James Madison 1826-1902 . . . . DLB-50

Bell, Madison Smartt 1957- DLB-218

Bell, Marvin 1937- DLB-5

Bell, Millicent 1919- DLB-111

Bell, Quentin 1910-1996 . . . . DLB-155

Bell, Robert [publishing house] DLB-49

Bell, Vanessa 1879-1961 . . . . DS-10

Bellamy, Edward 1850-1898 . . . . DLB-12

Bellamy, John [publishing house] DLB-170

Bellamy, Joseph 1719-1790 . . . . DLB-31

La Belle Assemblée 1806-1837 . . . . DLB-110

Bellezza, Dario 1944-1996 . . . . DLB-128

Belloc, Hilaire 1870-1953 . . . . DLB-19, 100, 141, 174

Belloc, Madame (see Parkes, Bessie Rayner)

Bellonci, Maria 1902-1986 . . . . DLB-196

Bellow, Saul
    1915- DLB-2, 28; Y-82; DS-3; CDALB-1

Belmont Productions DLB-46

Bels, Alberts 1938- DLB-232

Belševica, Vizma 1931- DLB-232; CDWLB-4

Bemelmans, Ludwig 1898-1962 . . . . DLB-22

Bemis, Samuel Flagg 1891-1973 . . . . DLB-17

Bemrose, William [publishing house] DLB-106

Ben no Naishi 1228?-1271? DLB-203

Benchley, Robert 1889-1945 . . . . DLB-11

Bencúr, Matej (see Kukučín, Martin)

Benedetti, Mario 1920- DLB-113

Benedict, Pinckney 1964- DLB-244

Benedict, Ruth 1887-1948 . . . . DLB-246

Benedictus, David 1938- DLB-14

Benedikt, Michael 1935- DLB-5

Benediktov, Vladimir Grigor'evich
    1807-1873 . . . . DLB-205

Benét, Stephen Vincent
1898-1943 . . . . DLB-4, 48, 102

Benét, William Rose 1886-1950 . . . . DLB-45

Benford, Gregory 1941- Y-82

Benjamin, Park 1809-1864 . . . . DLB-3, 59, 73

Benjamin, S. G. W. 1837-1914 . . . . DLB-189

Benjamin, Walter 1892-1940 . . . . DLB-242

Benlowes, Edward 1602-1676 . . . . DLB-126

Benn Brothers Limited DLB-106

Benn, Gottfried 1886-1956 . . . . DLB-56

Bennett, Arnold
1867-1931 . . . . DLB-10, 34, 98, 135; CDBLB-5

Bennett, Charles 1899-1995 . . . . DLB-44

Bennett, Emerson 1822-1905 . . . . DLB-202

Bennett, Gwendolyn 1902- DLB-51

Bennett, Hal 1930- DLB-33

Bennett, James Gordon 1795-1872 . . . . DLB-43

Bennett, James Gordon, Jr. 1841-1918 . . . . DLB-23

Bennett, John 1865-1956 . . . . DLB-42

Bennett, Louise 1919- DLB-117; CDWLB-3

Benni, Stefano 1947- DLB-196

Benoit, Jacques 1941- DLB-60

Benson, A. C. 1862-1925 . . . . DLB-98

Benson, E. F. 1867-1940 . . . . DLB-135, 153

Benson, Jackson J. 1930- DLB-111

Benson, Robert Hugh 1871-1914 . . . . DLB-153

Benson, Stella 1892-1933 . . . . DLB-36, 162

Bent, James Theodore 1852-1897 . . . . DLB-174

Bent, Mabel Virginia Anna ?-? DLB-174

Bentham, Jeremy 1748-1832 . . . . DLB-107, 158

Bentley, E. C. 1875-1956 . . . . DLB-70

Bentley, Phyllis 1894-1977 . . . . DLB-191

Bentley, Richard [publishing house] DLB-106

Benton, Robert 1932- and Newman,
David 1937- DLB-44

Benziger Brothers DLB-49

Beowulf circa 900-1000 or 790-825
. . . . DLB-146; CDBLB-1

Berent, Wacław 1873-1940 . . . . DLB-215

Beresford, Anne 1929- DLB-40

Beresford, John Davys
1873-1947 . . . . DLB-162, 178, 197

"Experiment in the Novel" (1929) DLB-36

Beresford-Howe, Constance 1922- DLB-88

Berford, R. G., Company DLB-49

Berg, Stephen 1934- DLB-5

Bergengruen, Werner 1892-1964 . . . . DLB-56

Berger, John 1926- DLB-14, 207

Berger, Meyer 1898-1959 . . . . DLB-29

Berger, Thomas 1924- DLB-2; Y-80

Berkeley, Anthony 1893-1971 . . . . DLB-77

Berkeley, George 1685-1753 . . . . DLB-31, 101

The Berkley Publishing Corporation DLB-46

Berlin, Lucia 1936- DLB-130

Berman, Marshall 1940- DLB-246

Bernal, Vicente J. 1888-1915 . . . . DLB-82

Bernanos, Georges 1888-1948 . . . . DLB-72

Bernard, Harry 1898-1979 . . . . DLB-92

Bernard, John 1756-1828 . . . . DLB-37

Bernard of Chartres circa 1060-1124? . . . DLB-115

Bernard of Clairvaux 1090-1153 . . . . . . DLB-208

The Bernard Malamud Archive at the
Harry Ransom Humanities
Research Center. Y-00

Bernard Silvestris
flourished circa 1130-1160 . . . . DLB-208

Bernari, Carlo 1909-1992 . . . . DLB-177

Bernhard, Thomas
1931-1989 . . . . DLB-85, 124; CDWLB-2

Bernstein, Charles 1950- DLB-169

Berriault, Gina 1926-1999 . . . . DLB-130

Berrigan, Daniel 1921- DLB-5

Berrigan, Ted 1934-1983 . . . . DLB-5, 169

Berry, Wendell 1934- DLB-5, 6, 234

Berryman, John 1914-1972 . . . . DLB-48; CDALB-1

Bersianik, Louky 1930- DLB-60

Berthelet, Thomas [publishing house] DLB-170

Berto, Giuseppe 1914-1978 . . . . DLB-177

Bertolucci, Attilio 1911- DLB-128

Berton, Pierre 1920- DLB-68

Bertrand, Louis "Aloysius"
1807-1841 . . . . DLB-217

Besant, Sir Walter 1836-1901 . . . . . . DLB-135, 190

Bessette, Gerard 1920- DLB-53

Bessie, Alvah 1904-1985 . . . . DLB-26

Bester, Alfred 1913-1987 . . . . DLB-8

Besterman, Theodore 1904-1976 . . . . DLB-201

The Bestseller Lists: An Assessment Y-84

Bestuzhev, Aleksandr Aleksandrovich
(Marlinsky) 1797-1837 . . . . DLB-198

Bestuzhev, Nikolai Aleksandrovich
1791-1855 . . . . DLB-198

Betham-Edwards, Matilda Barbara (see Edwards,
Matilda Barbara Betham-)

Betjeman, John
1906-1984 . . . . DLB-20; Y-84; CDBLB-7

Betocchi, Carlo 1899-1986 . . . . DLB-128

Bettarini, Mariella 1942- DLB-128

Betts, Doris 1932- DLB-218; Y-82

Beùkoviù, Matija 1939- DLB-181

Beveridge, Albert J. 1862-1927 . . . . DLB-17

Beverley, Robert circa 1673-1722 . . . . . DLB-24, 30

Bevilacqua, Alberto 1934- DLB-196

Bevington, Louisa Sarah 1845-1895 . . . . . DLB-199

Beyle, Marie-Henri (see Stendhal)

Białoszewski, Miron 1922-1983 . . . . DLB-232

Bianco, Margery Williams 1881-1944 . . . DLB-160

Bibaud, Adèle 1854-1941 . . . . DLB-92

Bibaud, Michel 1782-1857 . . . . DLB-99

Bibliographical and Textual Scholarship
Since World War II Y-89

Bichsel, Peter 1935- DLB-75

Bickerstaff, Isaac John 1733-circa 1808 . . . . DLB-89

Biddle, Drexel [publishing house] DLB-49

Bidermann, Jacob
1577 or 1578-1639 . . . . DLB-164

Bidwell, Walter Hilliard 1798-1881 . . . . . . DLB-79

Bienek, Horst 1930- DLB-75

Bierbaum, Otto Julius 1865-1910 . . . . DLB-66

Bierce, Ambrose 1842-1914?
. . . . . . DLB-11, 12, 23, 71, 74, 186; CDALB-3

Bigelow, William F. 1879-1966 . . . . DLB-91

Biggle, Lloyd, Jr. 1923- DLB-8

Bigiaretti, Libero 1905-1993 . . . . DLB-177

Bigland, Eileen 1898-1970 . . . . DLB-195

Biglow, Hosea (see Lowell, James Russell)

Bigongiari, Piero 1914- DLB-128

Billinger, Richard 1890-1965 . . . . DLB-124

Billings, Hammatt 1818-1874 . . . . DLB-188

Billings, John Shaw 1898-1975 . . . . DLB-137

Billings, Josh (see Shaw, Henry Wheeler)

Binding, Rudolf G. 1867-1938 . . . . DLB-66

Bingay, Malcolm 1884-1953 . . . . DLB-241

Bingham, Caleb 1757-1817 . . . . DLB-42

Bingham, George Barry 1906-1988 . . . . . . DLB-127

Bingham, Sallie 1937- DLB-234

Bingley, William [publishing house] DLB-154

Binyon, Laurence 1869-1943 . . . . DLB-19

Biographia Brittanica DLB-142

Biographical Documents I Y-84

Biographical Documents II Y-85

Bioren, John [publishing house] DLB-49

Bioy Casares, Adolfo 1914- DLB-113

Bird, Isabella Lucy 1831-1904 . . . . DLB-166

Bird, Robert Montgomery 1806-1854 . . . DLB-202

Bird, William 1888-1963 . . . . DLB-4; DS-15

Birken, Sigmund von 1626-1681 . . . . DLB-164

Birney, Earle 1904- DLB-88

Birrell, Augustine 1850-1933 . . . . DLB-98

Bisher, Furman 1918- DLB-171

Bishop, Elizabeth
1911-1979 . . . . DLB-5, 169; CDALB-6

Bishop, John Peale 1892-1944 . . . . . . DLB-4, 9, 45

Bismarck, Otto von 1815-1898 . . . . DLB-129

Bisset, Robert 1759-1805 . . . . DLB-142

Bissett, Bill 1939- DLB-53

Bitzius, Albert (see Gotthelf, Jeremias)

Bjørnvig, Thorkild 1918- DLB-214

Black, David (D. M.) 1941- DLB-40

Black, Walter J. [publishing house] DLB-46

Black, Winifred 1863-1936 . . . . DLB-25

The Black Aesthetic: Background DS-8

Black Theaters and Theater Organizations in
America, 1961-1982:
A Research List DLB-38

Black Theatre: A Forum [excerpts] DLB-38

Blackamore, Arthur 1679-? DLB-24, 39

Blackburn, Alexander L. 1929- Y-85

Blackburn, Paul 1926-1971 . . . . DLB-16; Y-81

Blackburn, Thomas 1916-1977 . . . . DLB-27

Blackmore, R. D. 1825-1900 . . . . DLB-18

Blackmore, Sir Richard 1654-1729. . . . . . DLB-131

Blackmur, R. P. 1904-1965 . . . . DLB-63

Blackwell, Basil, Publisher DLB-106

Blackwood, Algernon Henry
1869-1951 . . . . DLB-153, 156, 178

Blackwood, Caroline 1931-1996 . . . . . DLB-14, 207

Blackwood, William, and Sons, Ltd. DLB-154

Blackwood's Edinburgh Magazine
1817-1980 . . . . DLB-110

Blades, William 1824-1890 . . . . DLB-184

Blaga, Lucian 1895-1961 . . . . DLB-220

Blagden, Isabella 1817?-1873 . . . . DLB-199

Blair, Eric Arthur (see Orwell, George)

Blair, Francis Preston 1791-1876 . . . . DLB-43

Blair, James circa 1655-1743. . . . . DLB-24

Blair, John Durburrow 1759-1823 . . . . DLB-37

Blais, Marie-Claire 1939- DLB-53

Blaise, Clark 1940- DLB-53

Blake, George 1893-1961. . . . . DLB-191

Blake, Lillie Devereux 1833-1913 . . . DLB-202, 221

Blake, Nicholas 1904-1972 . . . . DLB-77
(see Day Lewis, C.)

Blake, William
1757-1827 . . . . DLB-93, 154, 163; CDBLB-3

The Blakiston Company DLB-49

Blandiana, Ana 1942- DLB-232; CDWLB-4

Blanchot, Maurice 1907- DLB-72

Blanckenburg, Christian Friedrich von
1744-1796. . . . . DLB-94

Blaser, Robin 1925- DLB-165

Blaumanis, Rudolfs 1863-1908 . . . . DLB-220

Bleasdale, Alan 1946- DLB-245

Bledsoe, Albert Taylor 1809-1877 . . . . . DLB-3, 79

Bleecker, Ann Eliza 1752-1783 . . . . DLB-200

Blelock and Company DLB-49

Blennerhassett, Margaret Agnew
1773-1842 . . . . DLB-99

Bles, Geoffrey [publishing house]. DLB-112

Blessington, Marguerite, Countess of
1789-1849 . . . . DLB-166

The Blickling Homilies circa 971 . . . . DLB-146

Blind, Mathilde 1841-1896 . . . . DLB-199

Blish, James 1921-1975. . . . . DLB-8

Bliss, E., and E. White
[publishing house] DLB-49

Bliven, Bruce 1889-1977 . . . . DLB-137

Blixen, Karen 1885-1962 . . . . DLB-214

Bloch, Robert 1917-1994 . . . . DLB-44

Block, Lawrence 1938- DLB-226

Block, Rudolph (see Lessing, Bruno)

Blondal, Patricia 1926-1959 . . . . DLB-88

Bloom, Harold 1930- DLB-67

Bloomer, Amelia 1818-1894 . . . . DLB-79

Bloomfield, Robert 1766-1823 . . . . DLB-93

Bloomsbury Group DS-10

Blotner, Joseph 1923- DLB-111

Blount, Thomas 1618?-1679 . . . . DLB-236

Bloy, Léon 1846-1917 . . . . DLB-123

Blume, Judy 1938- DLB-52

Blunck, Hans Friedrich 1888-1961 . . . . . . DLB-66

Blunden, Edmund 1896-1974 . . . DLB-20, 100, 155

Blundeville, Thomas 1522?-1606 . . . . DLB-236

Blunt, Lady Anne Isabella Noel
1837-1917 . . . . DLB-174

Blunt, Wilfrid Scawen 1840-1922 . . . . DLB-19, 174

Bly, Nellie (see Cochrane, Elizabeth)

Bly, Robert 1926- DLB-5

Blyton, Enid 1897-1968 . . . . DLB-160

Boaden, James 1762-1839 . . . . DLB-89

Boas, Frederick S. 1862-1957 . . . . DLB-149

The Bobbs-Merrill Archive at the
Lilly Library, Indiana University Y-90

Boborykin, Petr Dmitrievich 1836-1921 . . DLB-238

The Bobbs-Merrill Company DLB-46

Bobrov, Semen Sergeevich
1763?-1810 . . . . DLB-150

Bobrowski, Johannes 1917-1965 . . . . DLB-75

The Elmer Holmes Bobst Awards in Arts
and Letters Y-87

Bodenheim, Maxwell 1892-1954 . . . . . . DLB-9, 45

Bodenstedt, Friedrich von 1819-1892 . . . . DLB-129

Bodini, Vittorio 1914-1970. . . . . DLB-128

Bodkin, M. McDonnell 1850-1933 . . . . . . DLB-70

Bodley, Sir Thomas 1545-1613 . . . . DLB-213

Bodley Head DLB-112

Bodmer, Johann Jakob 1698-1783 . . . . . . DLB-97

Bodmershof, Imma von 1895-1982 . . . . . . DLB-85

Bodsworth, Fred 1918- DLB-68

Boehm, Sydney 1908- DLB-44

Boer, Charles 1939- DLB-5

Boethius circa 480-circa 524 . . . . DLB-115

Boethius of Dacia circa 1240-? DLB-115

Bogan, Louise 1897-1970 . . . . DLB-45, 169

Bogarde, Dirk 1921- DLB-14

Bogdanovich, Ippolit Fedorovich
circa 1743-1803 . . . . DLB-150

Bogue, David [publishing house] DLB-106

Böhme, Jakob 1575-1624 . . . . DLB-164

Bohn, H. G. [publishing house] DLB-106

Bohse, August 1661-1742. . . . . DLB-168

Boie, Heinrich Christian 1744-1806. . . . . . DLB-94

Bok, Edward W. 1863-1930 . . . . . . DLB-91; DS-16

Boland, Eavan 1944- DLB-40

Boldrewood, Rolf (Thomas Alexander Browne)
1826?-1915 . . . . DLB-230

Bolingbroke, Henry St. John, Viscount
1678-1751 . . . . DLB-101

Böll, Heinrich
1917-1985 . . . . DLB-69; Y-85; CDWLB-2

Bolling, Robert 1738-1775 . . . . DLB-31

Bolotov, Andrei Timofeevich
1738-1833 . . . . DLB-150

Bolt, Carol 1941- DLB-60

Bolt, Robert 1924-1995 . . . . DLB-13, 233

Bolton, Herbert E. 1870-1953 . . . . DLB-17

Bonaventura DLB-90

Bonaventure circa 1217-1274 . . . . DLB-115

Bonaviri, Giuseppe 1924- DLB-177

Bond, Edward 1934- DLB-13

Bond, Michael 1926- DLB-161

Boni, Albert and Charles
[publishing house] DLB-46

Boni and Liveright. DLB-46

Bonner, Marita 1899-1971 . . . . DLB-228

Bonner, Paul Hyde 1893-1968. . . . . DS-17

Bonner, Sherwood (see McDowell, Katharine
Sherwood Bonner)

Robert Bonner's Sons DLB-49

Bonnin, Gertrude Simmons (see Zitkala-Ša)

Bonsanti, Alessandro 1904-1984 . . . . DLB-177

Bontemps, Arna 1902-1973 . . . . DLB-48, 51

The Book Arts Press at the University
of Virginia. Y-96

The Book League of America DLB-46

Book Publishing Accounting: Some Basic
Concepts Y-98

Book Reviewing in America: I. Y-87

Book Reviewing in America: II Y-88

Book Reviewing in America: III Y-89

Book Reviewing in America: IV Y-90

Book Reviewing in America: V. Y-91

Book Reviewing in America: VI Y-92

Book Reviewing in America: VII Y-93

Book Reviewing in America: VIII. Y-94

Book Reviewing in America and the
Literary Scene Y-95

Book Reviewing and the
Literary Scene Y-96, Y-97

Book Supply Company DLB-49

The Book Trade History Group Y-93

The Book Trade and the Internet Y-00

The Booker Prize. Y-96

Address by Anthony Thwaite,
Chairman of the Booker Prize Judges
Comments from Former Booker
Prize Winners Y-86

The Books of George V. Higgins:
A Checklist of Editions and Printings Y-00

Boorde, Andrew circa 1490-1549 . . . . DLB-136

Boorstin, Daniel J. 1914- DLB-17

Booth, Franklin 1874-1948. . . . . DLB-188

Booth, Mary L. 1831-1889 . . . . DLB-79

Booth, Philip 1925- Y-82

Booth, Wayne C. 1921- DLB-67

Booth, William 1829-1912. . . . . DLB-190

Borchardt, Rudolf 1877-1945. . . . . DLB-66

Borchert, Wolfgang 1921-1947 . . . . . DLB-69, 124

Borel, Pétrus 1809-1859. . . . . DLB-119

Borges, Jorge Luis
1899-1986 . . . . . . DLB-113; Y-86; CDWLB-3

Börne, Ludwig 1786-1837 . . . . DLB-90

Bornstein, Miriam 1950- DLB-209

Borowski, Tadeusz
1922-1951 . . . . DLB-215; CDWLB-4

Borrow, George 1803-1881 . . . . . DLB-21, 55, 166

Bosch, Juan 1909- DLB-145

Bosco, Henri 1888-1976 . . . . DLB-72

Bosco, Monique 1927- DLB-53

Bosman, Herman Charles 1905-1951 . . . . DLB-225

Bostic, Joe 1908-1988 . . . . DLB-241

Boston, Lucy M. 1892-1990 . . . . DLB-161

Boswell, James
1740-1795 . . . . DLB-104, 142; CDBLB-2

Boswell, Robert 1953- DLB-234

Bote, Hermann
circa 1460-circa 1520 . . . . DLB-179

Botev, Khristo 1847-1876 . . . . DLB-147

Botta, Anne C. Lynch 1815-1891 . . . . DLB-3

Botto, Ján (see Krasko, Ivan)

Bottome, Phyllis 1882-1963 . . . . DLB-197

Bottomley, Gordon 1874-1948 . . . . DLB-10

Bottoms, David 1949- DLB-120; Y-83

Bottrall, Ronald 1906- DLB-20

Bouchardy, Joseph 1810-1870 . . . . DLB-192

Boucher, Anthony 1911-1968 . . . . DLB-8

Boucher, Jonathan 1738-1804 . . . . DLB-31

Boucher de Boucherville, George
1814-1894 . . . . DLB-99

Boudreau, Daniel (see Coste, Donat)

Bourassa, Napoléon 1827-1916 . . . . DLB-99

Bourget, Paul 1852-1935 . . . . DLB-123

Bourinot, John George 1837-1902 . . . . DLB-99

Bourjaily, Vance 1922- DLB-2, 143

Bourne, Edward Gaylord
1860-1908 . . . . DLB-47

Bourne, Randolph 1886-1918 . . . . DLB-63

Bousoño, Carlos 1923- DLB-108

Bousquet, Joë 1897-1950 . . . . DLB-72

Bova, Ben 1932- Y-81

Bovard, Oliver K. 1872-1945 . . . . DLB-25

Bove, Emmanuel 1898-1945 . . . . DLB-72

Bowen, Elizabeth
1899-1973 . . . . DLB-15, 162; CDBLB-7

Bowen, Francis 1811-1890 . . . . DLB-1, 59, 235

Bowen, John 1924- DLB-13

Bowen, Marjorie 1886-1952 . . . . DLB-153

Bowen-Merrill Company DLB-49

Bowering, George 1935- DLB-53

Bowers, Bathsheba 1671-1718 . . . . DLB-200

Bowers, Claude G. 1878-1958 . . . . DLB-17

Bowers, Edgar 1924-2000 . . . . DLB-5

Bowers, Fredson Thayer
1905-1991 . . . . .DLB-140; Y-80, 91

Bowles, Paul 1910-1999 . . . . . DLB-5, 6, 218; Y-99

Bowles, Samuel III 1826-1878 . . . . DLB-43

Bowles, William Lisles 1762-1850 . . . . . . DLB-93

Bowman, Louise Morey 1882-1944 . . . . . DLB-68

Boyd, James 1888-1944 . . . . DLB-9; DS-16

Boyd, John 1919- DLB-8

Boyd, Thomas 1898-1935 . . . . DLB-9; DS-16

Boyd, William 1952- DLB-231

Boyesen, Hjalmar Hjorth
1848-1895 . . . . .DLB-12, 71; DS-13

Boyle, Kay 1902-1992 . . . . .DLB-4, 9, 48, 86; Y-93

Boyle, Roger, Earl of Orrery 1621-1679 . . . DLB-80

Boyle, T. Coraghessan 1948- DLB-218; Y-86

Božić, Mirko 1919- DLB-181

Brackenbury, Alison 1953- DLB-40

Brackenridge, Hugh Henry
1748-1816 . . . . .DLB-11, 37

Brackett, Charles 1892-1969 . . . . DLB-26

Brackett, Leigh 1915-1978 . . . . DLB-8, 26

Bradburn, John [publishing house] DLB-49

Bradbury, Malcolm 1932-2000 . . . . . .DLB-14, 207

Bradbury, Ray 1920- DLB-2, 8; CDALB-6

Bradbury and Evans DLB-106

Braddon, Mary Elizabeth
1835-1915 . . . . .DLB-18, 70, 156

Bradford, Andrew 1686-1742 . . . . DLB-43, 73

Bradford, Gamaliel 1863-1932 . . . . DLB-17

Bradford, John 1749-1830 . . . . DLB-43

Bradford, Roark 1896-1948 . . . . DLB-86

Bradford, William 1590-1657 . . . . DLB-24, 30

Bradford, William III 1719-1791 . . . . . DLB-43, 73

Bradlaugh, Charles 1833-1891 . . . . DLB-57

Bradley, David 1950- DLB-33

Bradley, Ira, and Company DLB-49

Bradley, J. W., and Company DLB-49

Bradley, Katherine Harris (see Field, Michael)

Bradley, Marion Zimmer 1930-1999 . . . . . DLB-8

Bradley, William Aspenwall 1878-1939 . . . DLB-4

Bradshaw, Henry 1831-1886 . . . . DLB-184

Bradstreet, Anne
1612 or 1613-1672 . . . . . . DLB-24; CDABL-2

Bradūnas, Kazys 1917- DLB-220

Bradwardine, Thomas circa
1295-1349 . . . . DLB-115

Brady, Frank 1924-1986 . . . . DLB-111

Brady, Frederic A. [publishing house] DLB-49

Bragg, Melvyn 1939- DLB-14

Brainard, Charles H. [publishing house] . . DLB-49

Braine, John 1922-1986 . DLB-15; Y-86; CDBLB-7

Braithwait, Richard 1588-1673 . . . . DLB-151

Braithwaite, William Stanley
1878-1962 . . . . DLB-50, 54

Braker, Ulrich 1735-1798 . . . . DLB-94

Bramah, Ernest 1868-1942 . . . . DLB-70

Branagan, Thomas 1774-1843 . . . . DLB-37

Branch, William Blackwell 1927- DLB-76

Branden Press DLB-46

Branner, H.C. 1903-1966 . . . . DLB-214

Brant, Sebastian 1457-1521 . . . . .DLB-179

Brassey, Lady Annie (Allnutt)
1839-1887 . . . . DLB-166

Brathwaite, Edward Kamau
1930- DLB-125; CDWLB-3

Brault, Jacques 1933- DLB-53

Braun, Matt 1932- DLB-212

Braun, Volker 1939- DLB-75

Brautigan, Richard
1935-1984 . . . . DLB-2, 5, 206; Y-80, Y-84

Braxton, Joanne M. 1950- DLB-41

Bray, Anne Eliza 1790-1883 . . . . DLB-116

Bray, Thomas 1656-1730 . . . . DLB-24

Brazdžionis, Bernardas 1907- DLB-220

Braziller, George [publishing house] DLB-46

The Bread Loaf Writers' Conference 1983 . . . Y-84

Breasted, James Henry 1865-1935 . . . . DLB-47

Brecht, Bertolt
1898-1956 . . . . .DLB-56, 124; CDWLB-2

Bredel, Willi 1901-1964 . . . . DLB-56

Bregendahl, Marie 1867-1940 . . . . DLB-214

Breitinger, Johann Jakob 1701-1776 . . . . . DLB-97

Bremser, Bonnie 1939- DLB-16

Bremser, Ray 1934- DLB-16

Brennan, Christopher 1870-1932 . . . . DLB-230

Brentano, Bernard von 1901-1964 . . . . . . DLB-56

Brentano, Clemens 1778-1842 . . . . DLB-90

Brentano's DLB-49

Brenton, Howard 1942- DLB-13

Breslin, Jimmy 1929-1996 . . . . DLB-185

Breton, André 1896-1966 . . . . DLB-65

Breton, Nicholas circa 1555-circa 1626 . . . DLB-136

The Breton Lays
1300-early fifteenth century DLB-146

Brewer, Luther A. 1858-1933 . . . . .DLB-187

Brewer, Warren and Putnam DLB-46

Brewster, Elizabeth 1922- DLB-60

Breytenbach, Breyten 1939- DLB-225

Bridge, Ann (Lady Mary Dolling Sanders
O'Malley) 1889-1974 . . . . DLB-191

Bridge, Horatio 1806-1893 . . . . DLB-183

Bridgers, Sue Ellen 1942- DLB-52

Bridges, Robert
1844-1930 . . . . DLB-19, 98; CDBLB-5

The Bridgewater Library DLB-213

Bridie, James 1888-1951 . . . . DLB-10

Brieux, Eugene 1858-1932 . . . . DLB-192

Brigadere, Anna 1861-1933 . . . . DLB-220

Bright, Mary Chavelita Dunne (see Egerton, George)

Brimmer, B. J., Company DLB-46

Brines, Francisco 1932- DLB-134

Brink, André 1935- DLB-225

Brinley, George, Jr. 1817-1875 . . . . DLB-140

Brinnin, John Malcolm 1916-1998 . . . . . . DLB-48

Brisbane, Albert 1809-1890 . . . . DLB-3

Brisbane, Arthur 1864-1936 . . . . DLB-25

British Academy DLB-112

The British Critic 1793-1843 . . . . .DLB-110

The British Library and the Regular
    Readers' Group Y-91

British Literary Prizes Y-98

*The British Review and London Critical
    Journal 1811-1825* DLB-110

British Travel Writing, 1940-1997 . . . . . . .DLB-204

Brito, Aristeo 1942- DLB-122

Brittain, Vera 1893-1970 . . . . .DLB-191

Brizeux, Auguste 1803-1858 . . . . .DLB-217

Broadway Publishing Company DLB-46

Broch, Hermann
    1886-1951 . . . . .DLB-85, 124; CDWLB-2

Brochu, André 1942- DLB-53

Brock, Edwin 1927- DLB-40

Brockes, Barthold Heinrich 1680-1747 . . . .DLB-168

Brod, Max 1884-1968 . . . . .DLB-81

Brodber, Erna 1940- DLB-157

Brodhead, John R. 1814-1873 . . . . .DLB-30

Brodkey, Harold 1930-1996 . . . . .DLB-130

Brodsky, Joseph 1940-1996 . . . . Y-87

Brodsky, Michael 1948- DLB-244

Broeg, Bob 1918- DLB-171

Brøgger, Suzanne 1944- DLB-214

Brome, Richard circa 1590-1652 . . . . .DLB-58

Brome, Vincent 1910- DLB-155

Bromfield, Louis 1896-1956 . . . . . . .DLB-4, 9, 86

Bromige, David 1933- DLB-193

Broner, E. M. 1930- DLB-28

Bronk, William 1918-1999 . . . . .DLB-165

Bronnen, Arnolt 1895-1959 . . . . .DLB-124

Brontë, Anne 1820-1849 . . . . .DLB-21, 199

Brontë, Charlotte
    1816-1855 . . . . . .DLB-21, 159, 199; CDBLB-4

Brontë, Emily
    1818-1848 . . . . . . DLB-21, 32, 199; CDBLB-4

Brook, Stephen 1947- DLB-204

Brook Farm 1841-1847 . . . . .DLB-223

Brooke, Frances 1724-1789 . . . . .DLB-39, 99

Brooke, Henry 1703?-1783 . . . . .DLB-39

Brooke, L. Leslie 1862-1940 . . . . .DLB-141

Brooke, Margaret, Ranee of Sarawak
    1849-1936 .DLB-174

Brooke, Rupert
    1887-1915 . . . . .DLB-19, 216; CDBLB-6

Brooker, Bertram 1888-1955 . . . . .DLB-88

Brooke-Rose, Christine 1923- DLB-14, 231

Brookner, Anita 1928- DLB-194; Y-87

Brooks, Charles Timothy 1813-1883 . . .DLB-1, 243

Brooks, Cleanth 1906-1994 . . . . . . .DLB-63; Y-94

Brooks, Gwendolyn
    1917-2000 . . . . . . .DLB-5, 76, 165; CDALB-1

Brooks, Jeremy 1926- DLB-14

Brooks, Mel 1926- DLB-26

Brooks, Noah 1830-1903 . . . . .DLB-42; DS-13

Brooks, Richard 1912-1992 . . . . .DLB-44

Brooks, Van Wyck
    1886-1963 . . . . .DLB-45, 63, 103

Brophy, Brigid 1929-1995 . . . . .DLB-14

Brophy, John 1899-1965 . . . . .DLB-191

Brossard, Chandler 1922-1993 . . . . .DLB-16

Brossard, Nicole 1943- DLB-53

Broster, Dorothy Kathleen 1877-1950 . . . .DLB-160

Brother Antoninus (see Everson, William)

Brotherton, Lord 1856-1930 . . . . .DLB-184

Brougham and Vaux, Henry Peter Brougham,
    Baron 1778-1868 . . . . .DLB-110, 158

Brougham, John 1810-1880 . . . . .DLB-11

Broughton, James 1913-1999 . . . . .DLB-5

Broughton, Rhoda 1840-1920 . . . . .DLB-18

Broun, Heywood 1888-1939 . . . . . . .DLB-29, 171

Brown, Alice 1856-1948 . . . . .DLB-78

Brown, Bob 1886-1959 . . . . .DLB-4, 45

Brown, Cecil 1943- DLB-33

Brown, Charles Brockden
    1771-1810 . . . . .DLB-37, 59, 73; CDALB-2

Brown, Christy 1932-1981 . . . . .DLB-14

Brown, Dee 1908- Y-80

Brown, Frank London 1927-1962 . . . . . . .DLB-76

Brown, Fredric 1906-1972 . . . . .DLB-8

Brown, George Mackay
    1921-1996 . . . . DLB-14, 27, 139

Brown, Harry 1917-1986 . . . . .DLB-26

Brown, Larry 1951- DLB-234

Brown, Marcia 1918- DLB-61

Brown, Margaret Wise 1910-1952 . . . . . . .DLB-22

Brown, Morna Doris (see Ferrars, Elizabeth)

Brown, Oliver Madox 1855-1874 . . . . . . .DLB-21

Brown, Sterling 1901-1989 . . . . . . .DLB-48, 51, 63

Brown, T. E. 1830-1897 . . . . .DLB-35

Brown, Thomas Alexander (see Boldrewood, Rolf)

Brown, Warren 1894-1978 . . . . .DLB-241

Brown, William Hill 1765-1793 . . . . .DLB-37

Brown, William Wells
    1814-1884 . . . . .DLB-3, 50, 183

Browne, Charles Farrar 1834-1867 . . . . . .DLB-11

Browne, Frances 1816-1879 . . . . .DLB-199

Browne, Francis Fisher 1843-1913 . . . . . . .DLB-79

Browne, Howard 1908-1999 . . . . .DLB-226

Browne, J. Ross 1821-1875 . . . . .DLB-202

Browne, Michael Dennis 1940- DLB-40

Browne, Sir Thomas 1605-1682 . . . . . . .DLB-151

Browne, William, of Tavistock
    1590-1645 .DLB-121

Browne, Wynyard 1911-1964 . . . . . . .DLB-13, 233

Browne and Nolan DLB-106

Brownell, W. C. 1851-1928 . . . . .DLB-71

Browning, Elizabeth Barrett
    1806-1861 . . . . .DLB-32, 199; CDBLB-4

Browning, Robert
    1812-1889 . . . . .DLB-32, 163; CDBLB-4

Introductory Essay: *Letters of Percy
    Bysshe Shelley* (1852) DLB-32

Brownjohn, Allan 1931- DLB-40

Brownson, Orestes Augustus
    1803-1876 . . . . .DLB-1, 59, 73, 243

Bruccoli, Matthew J. 1931- DLB-103

Bruce, Charles 1906-1971 . . . . .DLB-68

John Edward Bruce: Three Documents DLB-50

Bruce, Leo 1903-1979 . . . . .DLB-77

Bruce, Mary Grant 1878-1958 . . . . .DLB-230

Bruce, Philip Alexander 1856-1933 . . . . . . .DLB-47

Bruce Humphries [publishing house] DLB-46

Bruce-Novoa, Juan 1944- DLB-82

Bruckman, Clyde 1894-1955 . . . . .DLB-26

Bruckner, Ferdinand 1891-1958 . . . . .DLB-118

Brundage, John Herbert (see Herbert, John)

Brutus, Dennis
    1924- DLB-117, 225; CDWLB-3

Bryan, C. D. B. 1936- DLB-185

Bryant, Arthur 1899-1985 . . . . .DLB-149

Bryant, William Cullen
    1794-1878 . . . . .DLB-3, 43, 59, 189; CDALB-2

Bryce Echenique, Alfredo
    1939- DLB-145; CDWLB-3

Bryce, James 1838-1922 . . . . .DLB-166, 190

Bryden, Bill 1942- DLB-233

Brydges, Sir Samuel Egerton 1762-1837 . . .DLB-107

Bryskett, Lodowick 1546?-1612 . . . . .DLB-167

Buchan, John 1875-1940 . . . . .DLB-34, 70, 156

Buchanan, George 1506-1582 . . . . .DLB-132

Buchanan, Robert 1841-1901 . . . . . . .DLB-18, 35

"The Fleshly School of Poetry and Other
    Phenomena of the Day" (1872), by
    Robert Buchanan DLB-35

"The Fleshly School of Poetry: Mr. D. G.
    Rossetti" (1871), by Thomas Maitland
    (Robert Buchanan) DLB-35

Buchman, Sidney 1902-1975 . . . . .DLB-26

Buchner, Augustus 1591-1661 . . . . .DLB-164

Büchner, Georg 1813-1837 . . .DLB-133; CDWLB-2

Bucholtz, Andreas Heinrich 1607-1671 . . .DLB-168

Buck, Pearl S. 1892-1973 . . .DLB-9, 102; CDALB-7

Bucke, Charles 1781-1846 . . . . .DLB-110

Bucke, Richard Maurice 1837-1902 . . . . . .DLB-99

Buckingham, Joseph Tinker 1779-1861 and
    Buckingham, Edwin 1810-1833 . . . . . .DLB-73

Buckler, Ernest 1908-1984 . . . . .DLB-68

Buckley, William F., Jr. 1925- DLB-137; Y-80

Buckminster, Joseph Stevens
    1784-1812 . . . . .DLB-37

Buckner, Robert 1906- DLB-26

Budd, Thomas ?-1698 . . . . .DLB-24

Budrys, A. J. 1931- DLB-8

Buechner, Frederick 1926- Y-80

Buell, John 1927- DLB-53

Bufalino, Gesualdo 1920-1996 . . . . .DLB-196

Buffum, Job [publishing house] DLB-49

Bugnet, Georges 1879-1981 . . . . .DLB-92

Buies, Arthur 1840-1901 . . . . .DLB-99

Building the New British Library
   at St Pancras Y-94

Bukowski, Charles 1920-1994 . . . DLB-5, 130, 169

Bulatović, Miodrag
   1930-1991 . . . . DLB-181; CDWLB-4

Bulgarin, Faddei Venediktovich
   1789-1859 . . . . DLB-198

Bulger, Bozeman 1877-1932 . . . . .DLB-171

Bullein, William
   between 1520 and 1530-1576 . . . . DLB-167

Bullins, Ed 1935- DLB-7, 38

Bulwer, John 1606-1656 . . . . DLB-236

Bulwer-Lytton, Edward (also Edward Bulwer)
   1803-1873 . . . . DLB-21

"On Art in Fiction "(1838) DLB-21

Bumpus, Jerry 1937- Y-81

Bunce and Brother DLB-49

Bunner, H. C. 1855-1896 . . . . .DLB-78, 79

Bunting, Basil 1900-1985 . . . . DLB-20

Buntline, Ned (Edward Zane Carroll Judson)
   1821-1886 . . . . DLB-186

Bunyan, John 1628-1688 . . . . . DLB-39; CDBLB-2

Burch, Robert 1925- DLB-52

Burciaga, José Antonio 1940- DLB-82

Bürger, Gottfried August 1747-1794 . . . . . . DLB-94

Burgess, Anthony
   1917-1993 . . . . DLB-14, 194; CDBLB-8

The Anthony Burgess Archive at
   the Harry Ransom Humanities
   Research Center Y-98

Anthony Burgess's 99 Novels:
   An Opinion Poll .Y-84

Burgess, Gelett 1866-1951 . . . . DLB-11

Burgess, John W. 1844-1931 . . . . DLB-47

Burgess, Thornton W. 1874-1965 . . . . DLB-22

Burgess, Stringer and Company DLB-49

Burick, Si 1909-1986 . . . . .DLB-171

Burk, John Daly circa 1772-1808 . . . . DLB-37

Burk, Ronnie 1955- DLB-209

Burke, Edmund 1729?-1797 . . . . DLB-104

Burke, James Lee 1936- DLB-226

Burke, Kenneth 1897-1993 . . . . DLB-45, 63

Burke, Thomas 1886-1945 . . . . DLB-197

Burley, Dan 1907-1962 . . . . DLB-241

Burlingame, Edward Livermore
   1848-1922 . . . . DLB-79

Burnet, Gilbert 1643-1715 . . . . DLB-101

Burnett, Frances Hodgson
   1849-1924 . . . . DLB-42, 141; DS-13, 14

Burnett, W. R. 1899-1982 . . . . DLB-9, 226

Burnett, Whit 1899-1973 and
   Martha Foley 1897-1977 . . . . DLB-137

Burney, Fanny 1752-1840 . . . . DLB-39

Dedication, *The Wanderer* (1814) DLB-39

Preface to *Evelina* (1778) DLB-39

Burns, Alan 1929- DLB-14, 194

Burns, John Horne 1916-1953 . . . . .Y-85

Burns, Robert 1759-1796 . . . . . DLB-109; CDBLB-3

Burns and Oates DLB-106

Burnshaw, Stanley 1906- DLB-48

Burr, C. Chauncey 1815?-1883 . . . . DLB-79

Burr, Esther Edwards 1732-1758 . . . . DLB-200

Burroughs, Edgar Rice 1875-1950 . . . . DLB-8

Burroughs, John 1837-1921 . . . . DLB-64

Burroughs, Margaret T. G. 1917- DLB-41

Burroughs, William S., Jr. 1947-1981 . . . . . DLB-16

Burroughs, William Seward 1914-1997
   . . . . DLB-2, 8, 16, 152, 237; Y-81, Y-97

Burroway, Janet 1936- DLB-6

Burt, Maxwell Struthers
   1882-1954 . . . . DLB-86; DS-16

Burt, A. L., and Company DLB-49

Burton, Hester 1913- DLB-161

Burton, Isabel Arundell 1831-1896 . . . . . . DLB-166

Burton, Miles (see Rhode, John)

Burton, Richard Francis
   1821-1890 . . . . DLB-55, 166, 184

Burton, Robert 1577-1640 . . . . DLB-151

Burton, Virginia Lee 1909-1968 . . . . DLB-22

Burton, William Evans 1804-1860 . . . . . . DLB-73

Burwell, Adam Hood 1790-1849 . . . . DLB-99

Bury, Lady Charlotte 1775-1861 . . . . DLB-116

Busch, Frederick 1941- DLB-6, 218

Busch, Niven 1903-1991 . . . . DLB-44

Bushnell, Horace 1802-1876 . . . . .DS-13

Bussieres, Arthur de 1877-1913 . . . . DLB-92

Butler, Charles ca. 1560-1647 . . . . DLB-236

Butler, Guy 1918- DLB-225

Butler, E. H., and Company DLB-49

Butler, Josephine Elizabeth 1828-1906 . . . DLB-190

Butler, Juan 1942-1981 . . . . DLB-53

Butler, Judith 1956- DLB-246

Butler, Octavia E. 1947- DLB-33

Butler, Pierce 1884-1953 . . . . DLB-187

Butler, Robert Olen 1945- DLB-173

Butler, Samuel 1613-1680 . . . . DLB-101, 126

Butler, Samuel 1835-1902 . . . . DLB-18, 57, 174

Butler, William Francis 1838-1910 . . . . . . DLB-166

Butor, Michel 1926- DLB-83

Butter, Nathaniel [publishing house] DLB-170

Butterworth, Hezekiah 1839-1905 . . . . DLB-42

Buttitta, Ignazio 1899- DLB-114

Butts, Mary 1890-1937 . . . . DLB-240

Buzzati, Dino 1906-1972 . . . . .DLB-177

Byars, Betsy 1928- DLB-52

Byatt, A. S. 1936- DLB-14, 194

Byles, Mather 1707-1788 . . . . DLB-24

Bynneman, Henry
   [publishing house] DLB-170

Bynner, Witter 1881-1968 . . . . DLB-54

Byrd, William circa 1543-1623 . . . . .DLB-172

Byrd, William II 1674-1744 . . . . DLB-24, 140

Byrne, John Keyes (see Leonard, Hugh)

Byron, George Gordon, Lord
   1788-1824 . . . . DLB-96, 110; CDBLB-3

Byron, Robert 1905-1941 . . . . DLB-195

C

Caballero Bonald, José Manuel
   1926- DLB-108

Cabañero, Eladio 1930- DLB-134

Cabell, James Branch 1879-1958 . . . . . .DLB-9, 78

Cabeza de Baca, Manuel 1853-1915 . . . . . DLB-122

Cabeza de Baca Gilbert, Fabiola
   1898- DLB-122

Cable, George Washington
   1844-1925 . . . . .DLB-12, 74; DS-13

Cable, Mildred 1878-1952 . . . . DLB-195

Cabrera, Lydia 1900-1991 . . . . DLB-145

Cabrera Infante, Guillermo
   1929- DLB-113; CDWLB-3

Cadell [publishing house] DLB-154

Cady, Edwin H. 1917- DLB-103

Caedmon flourished 658-680 . . . . DLB-146

Caedmon School circa 660-899 . . . . DLB-146

Cafés, Brasseries, and Bistros DS-15

Cage, John 1912-1992 . . . . DLB-193

Cahan, Abraham 1860-1951 . . . . . . DLB-9, 25, 28

Cain, George 1943- DLB-33

Cain, James M. 1892-1977 . . . . DLB-226

Caird, Mona 1854-1932 . . . . .DLB-197

Čaks, Aleksandrs
   1901-1950 . . . . DLB-220; CDWLB-4

Caldecott, Randolph 1846-1886 . . . . DLB-163

Calder, John (Publishers), Limited DLB-112

Calderón de la Barca, Fanny
   1804-1882 . . . . DLB-183

Caldwell, Ben 1937- DLB-38

Caldwell, Erskine 1903-1987 . . . . DLB-9, 86

Caldwell, H. M., Company DLB-49

Caldwell, Taylor 1900-1985 . . . . .DS-17

Calhoun, John C. 1782-1850 . . . . DLB-3

Cǎlinescu, George 1899-1965 . . . . DLB-220

Calisher, Hortense 1911- DLB-2, 218

A Call to Letters and an Invitation
   to the Electric Chair,
   by Siegfried Mandel DLB-75

Callaghan, Mary Rose 1944- DLB-207

Callaghan, Morley 1903-1990 . . . . DLB-68

Callahan, S. Alice 1868-1894 . . . . . .DLB-175, 221

Callaloo Y-87

Callimachus circa 305 B.C.-240 B.C. DLB-176

Calmer, Edgar 1907- DLB-4

Calverley, C. S. 1831-1884 . . . . DLB-35

Calvert, George Henry 1803-1889 . . . . . DLB-1, 64

Calvino, Italo 1923-1985 . . . . DLB-196

Cambridge, Ada 1844-1926 . . . . DLB-230

Cambridge Press DLB-49

Cambridge Songs (Carmina Cantabrigensia)
   circa 1050 . . . . DLB-148

Cambridge University Press DLB-170

Camden, William 1551-1623. . . . . DLB-172

Camden House: An Interview with
James Hardin. Y-92

Cameron, Eleanor 1912- DLB-52

Cameron, George Frederick
1854-1885 . . . . .DLB-99

Cameron, Lucy Lyttelton 1781-1858 . . . . .DLB-163

Cameron, Peter 1959- DLB-234

Cameron, William Bleasdell 1862-1951 . . .DLB-99

Camm, John 1718-1778 . . . . .DLB-31

Camon, Ferdinando 1935- DLB-196

Camp, Walter 1859-1925 . . . . .DLB-241

Campana, Dino 1885-1932 . . . . .DLB-114

Campbell, Bebe Moore 1950- DLB-227

Campbell, Gabrielle Margaret Vere
(see Shearing, Joseph, and Bowen, Marjorie)

Campbell, James Dykes 1838-1895 . . . . . .DLB-144

Campbell, James Edwin 1867-1896 . . . . . . .DLB-50

Campbell, John 1653-1728. . . . . .DLB-43

Campbell, John W., Jr. 1910-1971 . . . . .DLB-8

Campbell, Roy 1901-1957 . . . . .DLB-20, 225

Campbell, Thomas 1777-1844 . . . . . .DLB-93, 144

Campbell, William Wilfred 1858-1918 . . . .DLB-92

Campion, Edmund 1539-1581. . . . . .DLB-167

Campion, Thomas
1567-1620 . . . . .DLB-58, 172; CDBLB-1

Campton, David 1924- DLB-245

Camus, Albert 1913-1960 . . . . .DLB-72

The Canadian Publishers' Records
Database Y-96

Canby, Henry Seidel 1878-1961 . . . . . . .DLB-91

Candelaria, Cordelia 1943- DLB-82

Candelaria, Nash 1928- DLB-82

Canetti, Elias
1905-1994 . . . . DLB-85, 124; CDWLB-2

Canham, Erwin Dain 1904-1982. . . . . . .DLB-127

Canitz, Friedrich Rudolph Ludwig von
1654-1699 . . . . .DLB-168

Cankar, Ivan 1876-1918. . . . . DLB-147; CDWLB-4

Cannan, Gilbert 1884-1955 . . . . DLB-10, 197

Cannan, Joanna 1896-1961 . . . . .DLB-191

Cannell, Kathleen 1891-1974. . . . . .DLB-4

Cannell, Skipwith 1887-1957 . . . . .DLB-45

Canning, George 1770-1827. . . . . .DLB-158

Cannon, Jimmy 1910-1973 . . . . .DLB-171

Cano, Daniel 1947- DLB-209

Cantú, Norma Elia 1947- DLB-209

Cantwell, Robert 1908-1978 . . . . .DLB-9

Cape, Jonathan, and Harrison Smith
[publishing house] DLB-46

Cape, Jonathan, Limited DLB-112

Čapek, Karel 1890-1938 . . . . DLB-215; CDWLB-4

Capen, Joseph 1658-1725. . . . . .DLB-24

Capes, Bernard 1854-1918. . . . . .DLB-156

Capote, Truman 1924-1984
. . . . . DLB-2, 185, 227; Y-80, Y-84; CDALB-1

Caproni, Giorgio 1912-1990 . . . . .DLB-128

Caragiale, Mateiu Ioan 1885-1936. . . . . . .DLB-220

Cardarelli, Vincenzo 1887-1959. . . . . . . .DLB-114

Cárdenas, Reyes 1948- DLB-122

Cardinal, Marie 1929- DLB-83

Carew, Jan 1920- DLB-157

Carew, Thomas 1594 or 1595-1640. . . . .DLB-126

Carey, Henry circa 1687-1689-1743. . . . . .DLB-84

Carey, M., and Company DLB-49

Carey, Mathew 1760-1839. . . . . DLB-37, 73

Carey and Hart DLB-49

Carlell, Lodowick 1602-1675. . . . . .DLB-58

Carleton, William 1794-1869. . . . . .DLB-159

Carleton, G. W. [publishing house]. DLB-49

Carlile, Richard 1790-1843 . . . . DLB-110, 158

Carlson, Ron 1947- DLB-244

Carlyle, Jane Welsh 1801-1866 . . . . .DLB-55

Carlyle, Thomas
1795-1881 . . . . .DLB-55, 144; CDBLB-3

"The Hero as Man of Letters: Johnson,
Rousseau, Burns" (1841) [excerpt] DLB-57

The Hero as Poet. Dante;
Shakspeare (1841) DLB-32

Carman, Bliss 1861-1929. . . . . .DLB-92

Carmina Burana circa 1230 . . . . .DLB-138

Carnero, Guillermo 1947- DLB-108

Carossa, Hans 1878-1956 . . . . .DLB-66

Carpenter, Humphrey
1946- DLB-155; Y-84, Y-99

The Practice of Biography III: An Interview
with Humphrey Carpenter Y-84

Carpenter, Stephen Cullen ?-1820?. DLB-73

Carpentier, Alejo
1904-1980. . . . . .DLB-113; CDWLB-3

Carr, Marina 1964- DLB-245

Carrier, Roch 1937- DLB-53

Carrillo, Adolfo 1855-1926 . . . . .DLB-122

Carroll, Gladys Hasty 1904- DLB-9

Carroll, John 1735-1815. . . . . .DLB-37

Carroll, John 1809-1884 . . . . .DLB-99

Carroll, Lewis
1832-1898 . . . . . . DLB-18, 163, 178; CDBLB-4

The Lewis Carroll Centenary Y-98

Carroll, Paul 1927- DLB-16

Carroll, Paul Vincent 1900-1968. . . . . . . .DLB-10

Carroll and Graf Publishers DLB-46

Carruth, Hayden 1921- DLB-5, 165

Carryl, Charles E. 1841-1920 . . . . .DLB-42

Carson, Anne 1950- DLB-193

Carswell, Catherine 1879-1946 . . . . .DLB-36

Cărtărescu, Mirea 1956- DLB-232

Carter, Angela 1940-1992 . . . . DLB-14, 207

Carter, Elizabeth 1717-1806 . . . . .DLB-109

Carter, Henry (see Leslie, Frank)

Carter, Hodding, Jr. 1907-1972 . . . . .DLB-127

Carter, John 1905-1975 . . . . .DLB-201

Carter, Landon 1710-1778 . . . . .DLB-31

Carter, Lin 1930- Y-81

Carter, Martin 1927-1997. . . . DLB-117; CDWLB-3

Carter, Robert, and Brothers. DLB-49

Carter and Hendee DLB-49

Cartwright, Jim 1958- DLB-245

Cartwright, John 1740-1824. . . . . .DLB-158

Cartwright, William circa 1611-1643 . . . .DLB-126

Caruthers, William Alexander 1802-1846. . .DLB-3

Carver, Jonathan 1710-1780. . . . . .DLB-31

Carver, Raymond
1938-1988 . . . . DLB-130; Y-83, Y-88

First Strauss "Livings" Awarded to Cynthia
Ozick and Raymond Carver
An Interview with Raymond Carver Y-83

Cary, Alice 1820-1871 . . . . .DLB-202

Cary, Joyce 1888-1957. . . .DLB-15, 100; CDBLB-6

Cary, Patrick 1623?-1657 . . . . .DLB-131

Casey, Juanita 1925- DLB-14

Casey, Michael 1947- DLB-5

Cassady, Carolyn 1923- DLB-16

Cassady, Neal 1926-1968 . . . . DLB-16, 237

Cassell and Company DLB-106

Cassell Publishing Company. DLB-49

Cassill, R. V. 1919- DLB-6, 218

Cassity, Turner 1929- DLB-105

Cassius Dio circa 155/164-post 229. . . . . .DLB-176

Cassola, Carlo 1917-1987. . . . . .DLB-177

The Castle of Perserverance circa 1400-1425. .DLB-146

Castellano, Olivia 1944- DLB-122

Castellanos, Rosario
1925-1974 . . . . .DLB-113; CDWLB-3

Castillo, Ana 1953- DLB-122, 227

Castillo, Rafael C. 1950- DLB-209

Castlemon, Harry (see Fosdick, Charles Austin)

Čašule, Kole 1921- DLB-181

Caswall, Edward 1814-1878 . . . . .DLB-32

Catacalos, Rosemary 1944- DLB-122

Cather, Willa
1873-1947 . . . .DLB-9, 54, 78; DS-1; CDALB-3

Catherine II (Ekaterina Alekseevna), "The Great,"
Empress of Russia 1729-1796 . . . . . . .DLB-150

Catherwood, Mary Hartwell 1847-1902 . . .DLB-78

Catledge, Turner 1901-1983 . . . . .DLB-127

Catlin, George 1796-1872. . . . . .DLB-186, 189

Cato the Elder 234 B.C.-149 B.C. DLB-211

Cattafi, Bartolo 1922-1979. . . . . .DLB-128

Catton, Bruce 1899-1978 . . . . .DLB-17

Catullus circa 84 B.C.-54 B.C.
. . . . DLB-211; CDWLB-1

Causley, Charles 1917- DLB-27

Caute, David 1936- DLB-14, 231

Cavendish, Duchess of Newcastle,
Margaret Lucas 1623-1673. . . . . .DLB-131

Cawein, Madison 1865-1914. . . . . .DLB-54

Caxton, William [publishing house] DLB-170

The Caxton Printers, Limited DLB-46

Caylor, O. P. 1849-1897 . . . . DLB-241

Cayrol, Jean 1911- DLB-83

Cecil, Lord David 1902-1986 . . . . DLB-155

Cela, Camilo José 1916- Y-89

Celan, Paul 1920-1970 . . . . . . DLB-69; CDWLB-2

Celati, Gianni 1937- DLB-196

Celaya, Gabriel 1911-1991 . . . . DLB-108

A Celebration of Literary Biography Y-98

Céline, Louis-Ferdinand 1894-1961 . . . . . . DLB-72

The Celtic Background to Medieval English
   Literature DLB-146

Celtis, Conrad 1459-1508 . . . . DLB-179

Center for Bibliographical Studies and
   Research at the University of
   California, Riverside Y-91

The Center for the Book in the Library
   of Congress Y-93

Center for the Book Research Y-84

Centlivre, Susanna 1669?-1723 . . . . DLB-84

The Centre for Writing, Publishing and
   Printing History at the University
   of Reading Y-00

The Century Company DLB-49

Cernuda, Luis 1902-1963 . . . . DLB-134

Cervantes, Lorna Dee 1954- DLB-82

Ch., T. (see Marchenko, Anastasiia Iakovlevna)

Chaadaev, Petr Iakovlevich
   1794-1856 . . . . DLB-198

Chacel, Rosa 1898- DLB-134

Chacón, Eusebio 1869-1948 . . . . DLB-82

Chacón, Felipe Maximiliano 1873-? DLB-82

Chadwick, Henry 1824-1908 . . . . DLB-241

Chadwyck-Healey's Full-Text Literary Databases:
   Editing Commercial Databases of
   Primary Literary Texts Y-95

Challans, Eileen Mary (see Renault, Mary)

Chalmers, George 1742-1825 . . . . DLB-30

Chaloner, Sir Thomas 1520-1565 . . . . DLB-167

Chamberlain, Samuel S. 1851-1916 . . . . . . DLB-25

Chamberland, Paul 1939- DLB-60

Chamberlin, William Henry 1897-1969 . . . DLB-29

Chambers, Charles Haddon 1860-1921 . . . DLB-10

Chambers, María Cristina (see Mena, María Cristina)

Chambers, Robert W. 1865-1933 . . . . . . DLB-202

Chambers, W. and R.
   [publishing house] DLB-106

Chamisso, Albert von 1781-1838 . . . . DLB-90

Champfleury 1821-1889 . . . . DLB-119

Chandler, Harry 1864-1944 . . . . DLB-29

Chandler, Norman 1899-1973 . . . . DLB-127

Chandler, Otis 1927- DLB-127

Chandler, Raymond
   1888-1959 . . . . DLB-226; DS-6; CDALB-5

Raymond Chandler Centenary Tributes
   from Michael Avallone, James Ellroy,
   Joe Gores, and William F. Nolan Y-88

Channing, Edward 1856-1931 . . . . DLB-17

Channing, Edward Tyrrell
   1790-1856 . . . . DLB-1, 59, 235

Channing, William Ellery
   1780-1842 . . . . DLB-1, 59, 235

Channing, William Ellery II
   1817-1901 . . . . DLB-1, 223

Channing, William Henry
   1810-1884 . . . . DLB-1, 59, 243

Chaplin, Charlie 1889-1977 . . . . DLB-44

Chapman, George
   1559 or 1560-1634 . . . . DLB-62, 121

Chapman, John DLB-106

Chapman, Olive Murray 1892-1977 . . . . . DLB-195

Chapman, R. W. 1881-1960 . . . . DLB-201

Chapman, William 1850-1917 . . . . DLB-99

Chapman and Hall DLB-106

Chappell, Fred 1936- DLB-6, 105

   "A Detail in a Poem" DLB-105

Chappell, William 1582-1649 . . . . DLB-236

Charbonneau, Jean 1875-1960 . . . . DLB-92

Charbonneau, Robert 1911-1967 . . . . DLB-68

Charles, Gerda 1914- DLB-14

Charles, William [publishing house] DLB-49

Charles d'Orléans 1394-1465 . . . . DLB-208

Charley (see Mann, Charles)

Charteris, Leslie 1907-1993 . . . . DLB-77

Chartier, Alain circa 1385-1430 . . . . . . DLB-208

Charyn, Jerome 1937- Y-83

Chase, Borden 1900-1971 . . . . DLB-26

Chase, Edna Woolman 1877-1957 . . . . . . DLB-91

Chase, Mary Coyle 1907-1981 . . . . DLB-228

Chase-Riboud, Barbara 1936- DLB-33

Chateaubriand, François-René de
   1768-1848 . . . . DLB-119

Chatterton, Thomas 1752-1770 . . . . DLB-109

Essay on Chatterton (1842), by
   Robert Browning DLB-32

Chatto and Windus DLB-106

Chatwin, Bruce 1940-1989 . . . . DLB-194, 204

Chaucer, Geoffrey
   1340?-1400 . . . . DLB-146; CDBLB-1

Chauncy, Charles 1705-1787 . . . . DLB-24

Chauveau, Pierre-Joseph-Olivier
   1820-1890 . . . . DLB-99

Chávez, Denise 1948- DLB-122

Chávez, Fray Angélico 1910- DLB-82

Chayefsky, Paddy 1923-1981 . . . . . DLB-7, 44; Y-81

Cheesman, Evelyn 1881-1969 . . . . DLB-195

Cheever, Ezekiel 1615-1708 . . . . DLB-24

Cheever, George Barrell 1807-1890 . . . . . DLB-59

Cheever, John 1912-1982
   . . . . . DLB-2, 102, 227; Y-80, Y-82; CDALB-1

Cheever, Susan 1943- Y-82

Cheke, Sir John 1514-1557 . . . . DLB-132

Chelsea House DLB-46

Chênedollé, Charles de 1769-1833 . . . . . DLB-217

Cheney, Ednah Dow 1824-1904 . . . . . DLB-1, 223

Cheney, Harriet Vaughn 1796-1889 . . . . . DLB-99

Chénier, Marie-Joseph 1764-1811 . . . . . . DLB-192

Chernyshevsky, Nikolai Gavrilovich
   1828-1889 . . . . DLB-238

Cherry, Kelly 1940- Y-83

Cherryh, C. J. 1942- Y-80

Chesebro', Caroline 1825-1873 . . . . DLB-202

Chesney, Sir George Tomkyns
   1830-1895 . . . . DLB-190

Chesnut, Mary Boykin 1823-1886 . . . . . DLB-239

Chesnutt, Charles Waddell
   1858-1932 . . . . DLB-12, 50, 78

Chesson, Mrs. Nora (see Hopper, Nora)

Chester, Alfred 1928-1971 . . . . DLB-130

Chester, George Randolph 1869-1924 . . . DLB-78

The Chester Plays circa 1505-1532;
   revisions until 1575 . . . . DLB-146

Chesterfield, Philip Dormer Stanhope,
   Fourth Earl of 1694-1773 . . . . DLB-104

Chesterton, G. K. 1874-1936
   . . . DLB-10, 19, 34, 70, 98, 149, 178; CDBLB-6

Chettle, Henry circa 1560-circa 1607 . . . . DLB-136

Cheuse, Alan 1940- DLB-244

Chew, Ada Nield 1870-1945 . . . . DLB-135

Cheyney, Edward P. 1861-1947 . . . . DLB-47

Chiara, Piero 1913-1986 . . . . DLB-177

Chicano History DLB-82

Chicano Language DLB-82

Child, Francis James 1825-1896 . . . DLB-1, 64, 235

Child, Lydia Maria 1802-1880 . . . . . DLB-1, 74, 243

Child, Philip 1898-1978 . . . . DLB-68

Childers, Erskine 1870-1922 . . . . DLB-70

Children's Book Awards and Prizes DLB-61

Children's Illustrators, 1800-1880 . . . . . . DLB-163

Childress, Alice 1920-1994 . . . . DLB-7, 38

Childs, George W. 1829-1894 . . . . DLB-23

Chilton Book Company DLB-46

Chin, Frank 1940- DLB-206

Chinweizu 1943- DLB-157

Chitham, Edward 1932- DLB-155

Chittenden, Hiram Martin 1858-1917 . . . . DLB-47

Chivers, Thomas Holley 1809-1858 . . . . . . DLB-3

Cholmondeley, Mary 1859-1925 . . . . DLB-197

Chomsky, Noam 1928- DLB-246

Chopin, Kate 1850-1904 . . . DLB-12, 78; CDALB-3

Chopin, Rene 1885-1953 . . . . DLB-92

Choquette, Adrienne 1915-1973 . . . . DLB-68

Choquette, Robert 1905- DLB-68

Chrétien de Troyes
   circa 1140-circa 1190 . . . . DLB-208

Christensen, Inger 1935- DLB-214

The Christian Publishing Company DLB-49

Christie, Agatha
   1890-1976 . . . . DLB-13, 77, 245; CDBLB-6

Christine de Pizan
   circa 1365-circa 1431 . . . . DLB-208

Christus und die Samariterin circa 950 . . . . . DLB-148

Christy, Howard Chandler 1873-1952 . . . DLB-188

Chulkov, Mikhail Dmitrievich
  1743?-1792........................DLB-150

Church, Benjamin 1734-1778...........DLB-31

Church, Francis Pharcellus 1839-1906 ....DLB-79

Church, Peggy Pond 1903-1986 ....DLB-212

Church, Richard 1893-1972...........DLB-191

Church, William Conant 1836-1917 ......DLB-79

Churchill, Caryl 1938- DLB-13

Churchill, Charles 1731-1764..........DLB-109

Churchill, Winston 1871-1947.........DLB-202

Churchill, Sir Winston
  1874-1965 ....DLB-100; DS-16; CDBLB-5

Churchyard, Thomas 1520?-1604.......DLB-132

Churton, E., and Company...........DLB-106

Chute, Marchette 1909-1994 ....DLB-103

Ciardi, John 1916-1986 ....DLB-5; Y-86

Cibber, Colley 1671-1757..............DLB-84

Cicero
  106 B.C.-43 B.C........ DLB-211, CDWLB-1

Cima, Annalisa 1941- DLB-128

Čingo, Živko 1935-1987 ....DLB-181

Cioran, E. M. 1911-1995..............DLB-220

Čipkus, Alfonsas (see Nyka-Niliūnas, Alfonsas)

Cirese, Eugenio 1884-1955............DLB-114

Cīrulis, Jānis (see Bels, Alberts)

Cisneros, Sandra 1954- DLB-122, 152

City Lights Books DLB-46

Cixous, Hélène 1937- DLB-83, 242

Clampitt, Amy 1920-1994 ....DLB-105

Clancy, Tom 1947- DLB-227

Clapper, Raymond 1892-1944..........DLB-29

Clare, John 1793-1864 ....DLB-55, 96

Clarendon, Edward Hyde, Earl of
  1609-1674 ....DLB-101

Clark, Alfred Alexander Gordon (see Hare, Cyril)

Clark, Ann Nolan 1896- DLB-52

Clark, C. E. Frazer Jr. 1925- DLB-187

Clark, C. M., Publishing Company.......DLB-46

Clark, Catherine Anthony 1892-1977 .....DLB-68

Clark, Charles Heber 1841-1915........DLB-11

Clark, Davis Wasgatt 1812-1871 ....DLB-79

Clark, Eleanor 1913- DLB-6

Clark, J. P. 1935- DLB-117; CDWLB-3

Clark, Lewis Gaylord 1808-1873....DLB-3, 64, 73

Clark, Walter Van Tilburg
  1909-1971 ....DLB-9, 206

Clark, William (see Lewis, Meriwether)

Clark, William Andrews Jr. 1877-1934 ...DLB-187

Clarke, Austin 1896-1974............DLB-10, 20

Clarke, Austin C. 1934- DLB-53, 125

Clarke, Gillian 1937- DLB-40

Clarke, James Freeman
  1810-1888 ....DLB-1, 59, 235

Clarke, Lindsay 1939- DLB-231

Clarke, Marcus 1846-1881.............DLB-230

Clarke, Pauline 1921- DLB-161

Clarke, Rebecca Sophia 1833-1906 ....DLB-42

Clarke, Robert, and Company DLB-49

Clarkson, Thomas 1760-1846 ....DLB-158

Claudel, Paul 1868-1955 ....DLB-192

Claudius, Matthias 1740-1815 ....DLB-97

Clausen, Andy 1943- DLB-16

Clawson, John L. 1865-1933 ....DLB-187

Claxton, Remsen and Haffelfinger DLB-49

Clay, Cassius Marcellus 1810-1903.......DLB-43

Cleage, Pearl 1948- DLB-228

Cleary, Beverly 1916- DLB-52

Cleary, Kate McPhelim 1863-1905 ......DLB-221

Cleaver, Vera 1919-   and
  Cleaver, Bill 1920-1981..............DLB-52

Cleland, John 1710-1789 ....DLB-39

Clemens, Samuel Langhorne (Mark Twain)
  1835-1910 ....DLB-11, 12, 23, 64, 74,
                      186, 189; CDALB-3

Mark Twain on Perpetual Copyright Y-92

Clement, Hal 1922- DLB-8

Clemo, Jack 1916- DLB-27

Clephane, Elizabeth Cecilia
  1830-1869 ....DLB-199

Cleveland, John 1613-1658 ....DLB-126

Cliff, Michelle 1946- DLB-157; CDWLB-3

Clifford, Lady Anne 1590-1676.........DLB-151

Clifford, James L. 1901-1978 ....DLB-103

Clifford, Lucy 1853?-1929..... DLB-135, 141, 197

Clifton, Lucille 1936- DLB-5, 41

Clines, Francis X. 1938- DLB-185

Clive, Caroline (V) 1801-1873..........DLB-199

Clode, Edward J. [publishing house] DLB-46

Clough, Arthur Hugh 1819-1861 ....DLB-32

Cloutier, Cécile 1930- DLB-60

Clouts, Sidney 1926-1982 ....DLB-225

Clutton-Brock, Arthur 1868-1924 ....DLB-98

Coates, Robert M. 1897-1973...... DLB-4, 9, 102

Coatsworth, Elizabeth 1893- DLB-22

Cobb, Charles E., Jr. 1943- DLB-41

Cobb, Frank I. 1869-1923 ....DLB-25

Cobb, Irvin S. 1876-1944........DLB-11, 25, 86

Cobbe, Frances Power 1822-1904.......DLB-190

Cobbett, William 1763-1835 .... DLB-43, 107

Cobbledick, Gordon 1898-1969 ....DLB-171

Cochran, Thomas C. 1902- DLB-17

Cochrane, Elizabeth 1867-1922 ......DLB-25, 189

Cockerell, Sir Sydney 1867-1962........DLB-201

Cockerill, John A. 1845-1896...........DLB-23

Cocteau, Jean 1889-1963...............DLB-65

Coderre, Emile (see Jean Narrache)

Coe, Jonathan 1961- DLB-231

Coetzee, J. M. 1940- DLB-225

Coffee, Lenore J. 1900?-1984...........DLB-44

Coffin, Robert P. Tristram 1892-1955.....DLB-45

Coghill, Mrs. Harry (see Walker, Anna Louisa)

Cogswell, Fred 1917- DLB-60

Cogswell, Mason Fitch 1761-1830.......DLB-37

Cohen, Arthur A. 1928-1986...........DLB-28

Cohen, Leonard 1934- DLB-53

Cohen, Matt 1942- DLB-53

Colbeck, Norman 1903-1987...........DLB-201

Colden, Cadwallader 1688-1776 ......DLB-24, 30

Colden, Jane 1724-1766 ....DLB-200

Cole, Barry 1936- DLB-14

Cole, George Watson 1850-1939 ....DLB-140

Colegate, Isabel 1931- DLB-14, 231

Coleman, Emily Holmes 1899-1974 ....DLB-4

Coleman, Wanda 1946- DLB-130

Coleridge, Hartley 1796-1849 ....DLB-96

Coleridge, Mary 1861-1907 ....DLB-19, 98

Coleridge, Samuel Taylor
  1772-1834 ....DLB-93, 107; CDBLB-3

Coleridge, Sara 1802-1852.............DLB-199

Colet, John 1467-1519 ....DLB-132

Colette 1873-1954 ....DLB-65

Colette, Sidonie Gabrielle (see Colette)

Colinas, Antonio 1946- DLB-134

Coll, Joseph Clement 1881-1921 ....DLB-188

Collier, John 1901-1980...............DLB-77

Collier, John Payne 1789-1883 ....DLB-184

Collier, Mary 1690-1762 ....DLB-95

Collier, P. F. [publishing house]..........DLB-49

Collier, Robert J. 1876-1918.............DLB-91

Collin and Small DLB-49

Collingwood, W. G. 1854-1932 ....DLB-149

Collins, An floruit circa 1653...........DLB-131

Collins, Isaac [publishing house] DLB-49

Collins, Merle 1950- DLB-157

Collins, Mortimer 1827-1876 ....DLB-21, 35

Collins, Tom (see Furphy, Joseph)

Collins, Wilkie
  1824-1889 ....DLB-18, 70, 159; CDBLB-4

Collins, William 1721-1759 ....DLB-109

Collins, William, Sons and Company DLB-154

Collis, Maurice 1889-1973.............DLB-195

Collyer, Mary 1716?-1763? DLB-39

Colman, Benjamin 1673-1747 ....DLB-24

Colman, George, the Elder 1732-1794.....DLB-89

Colman, George, the Younger
  1762-1836 ....DLB-89

Colman, S. [publishing house]...........DLB-49

Colombo, John Robert 1936- DLB-53

Colquhoun, Patrick 1745-1820 ....DLB-158

Colter, Cyrus 1910- DLB-33

Colum, Padraic 1881-1972.............DLB-19

Columella fl. first century A.D.........DLB-211

Colvin, Sir Sidney 1845-1927 ....DLB-149

Colwin, Laurie 1944-1992....... DLB-218; Y-80

Comden, Betty 1919- and
  Green, Adolph 1918- DLB-44

Come to Papa.........................Y-99

Comi, Girolamo 1890-1968 ....DLB-114

The Comic Tradition Continued
[in the British Novel] DLB-15

Commager, Henry Steele 1902-1998 .....DLB-17

The Commercialization of the Image of
Revolt, by Kenneth Rexroth DLB-16

Community and Commentators: Black
Theatre and Its Critics DLB-38

Commynes, Philippe de
circa 1447-1511...................DLB-208

Compton-Burnett, Ivy 1884?-1969.......DLB-36

Conan, Laure 1845-1924 ....DLB-99

Concord History and Life DLB-223

Concord Literary History of a Town....DLB-223

Conde, Carmen 1901- DLB-108

Conference on Modern Biography.........Y-85

Congreve, William
1670-1729 ....DLB-39, 84; CDBLB-2

Preface to *Incognita* (1692) DLB-39

Conkey, W. B., Company DLB-49

Conn, Stewart 1936- DLB-233

Connell, Evan S., Jr. 1924- DLB-2; Y-81

Connelly, Marc 1890-1980.........DLB-7; Y-80

Connolly, Cyril 1903-1974............DLB-98

Connolly, James B. 1868-1957 ....DLB-78

Connor, Ralph 1860-1937 ....DLB-92

Connor, Tony 1930- DLB-40

Conquest, Robert 1917- DLB-27

Conrad, John, and Company.........DLB-49

Conrad, Joseph
1857-1924.... DLB-10, 34, 98, 156; CDBLB-5

Conroy, Jack 1899-1990.................Y-81

Conroy, Pat 1945- DLB-6

Considine, Bob 1906-1975 ....DLB-241

The Consolidation of Opinion: Critical
Responses to the Modernists DLB-36

Consolo, Vincenzo 1933- DLB-196

Constable, Archibald, and Company DLB-154

Constable, Henry 1562-1613 ....DLB-136

Constable and Company Limited.......DLB-112

Constant, Benjamin 1767-1830 ....DLB-119

Constant de Rebecque, Henri-Benjamin de
(see Constant, Benjamin)

Constantine, David 1944- DLB-40

Constantin-Weyer, Maurice 1881-1964 ...DLB-92

Contempo Caravan: Kites in a Windstorm ...Y-85

A Contemporary Flourescence of Chicano
Literature Y-84

Continental European Rhetoricians,
1400-1600......................DLB-236

The Continental Publishing Company....DLB-49

Conversations with Editors Y-95

Conversations with Publishers I: An Interview
with Patrick O'Connor Y-84

Conversations with Publishers II: An Interview
with Charles Scribner III..............Y-94

Conversations with Publishers III: An Interview
with Donald Lamm Y-95

Conversations with Publishers IV: An Interview
with James Laughlin..................Y-96

Conversations with Rare Book Dealers I: An
Interview with Glenn Horowitz........Y-90

Conversations with Rare Book Dealers II: An
Interview with Ralph Sipper Y-94

Conversations with Rare Book Dealers
(Publishers) III: An Interview with
Otto Penzler.....................Y-96

The Conversion of an Unpolitical Man,
by W. H. Bruford DLB-66

Conway, Moncure Daniel
1832-1907....................DLB-1, 223

Cook, David C., Publishing Company....DLB-49

Cook, Ebenezer circa 1667-circa 1732.....DLB-24

Cook, Edward Tyas 1857-1919 ....DLB-149

Cook, Eliza 1818-1889 ....DLB-199

Cook, Michael 1933- DLB-53

Cooke, George Willis 1848-1923 ....DLB-71

Cooke, Increase, and Company DLB-49

Cooke, John Esten 1830-1886 ....DLB-3

Cooke, Philip Pendleton 1816-1850.... DLB-3, 59

Cooke, Rose Terry 1827-1892 ....DLB-12, 74

Cook-Lynn, Elizabeth 1930- DLB-175

Coolbrith, Ina 1841-1928 ....DLB-54, 186

Cooley, Peter 1940- DLB-105

"Into the Mirror" DLB-105

Coolidge, Clark 1939- DLB-193

Coolidge, George [publishing house] DLB-49

Coolidge, Susan (see Woolsey, Sarah Chauncy)

Cooper, Anna Julia 1858-1964 ....DLB-221

Cooper, Edith Emma (see Field, Michael)

Cooper, Giles 1918-1966 ....DLB-13

Cooper, J. California 19??- DLB-212

Cooper, James Fenimore
1789-1851..........DLB-3, 183; CDALB-2

Cooper, Kent 1880-1965 ....DLB-29

Cooper, Susan 1935- DLB-161

Cooper, Susan Fenimore 1813-1894.....DLB-239

Cooper, William [publishing house].....DLB-170

Coote, J. [publishing house] DLB-154

Coover, Robert 1932- DLB-2, 227; Y-81

Copeland and Day DLB-49

Ćopić, Branko 1915-1984.............DLB-181

Copland, Robert 1470?-1548 ....DLB-136

Coppard, A. E. 1878-1957 ....DLB-162

Coppée, François 1842-1908 ....DLB-217

Coppel, Alfred 1921- Y-83

Coppola, Francis Ford 1939- DLB-44

Copway, George (Kah-ge-ga-gah-bowh)
1818-1869 ....DLB-175, 183

Corazzini, Sergio 1886-1907..........DLB-114

Corbett, Richard 1582-1635..........DLB-121

Corbière, Tristan 1845-1875..........DLB-217

Corcoran, Barbara 1911- DLB-52

Cordelli, Franco 1943- DLB-196

Corelli, Marie 1855-1924 ....DLB-34, 156

Corle, Edwin 1906-1956................Y-85

Corman, Cid 1924- DLB-5, 193

Cormier, Robert 1925-2000 ... DLB-52; CDALB-6

Corn, Alfred 1943- DLB-120; Y-80

Cornford, Frances 1886-1960.........DLB-240

Cornish, Sam 1935- DLB-41

Cornish, William circa 1465-circa 1524 .. DLB-132

Cornwall, Barry (see Procter, Bryan Waller)

Cornwallis, Sir William, the Younger
circa 1579-1614 ....DLB-151

Cornwell, David John Moore (see le Carré, John)

Corpi, Lucha 1945- DLB-82

Corrington, John William
1932-1988 ....DLB-6, 244

Corrothers, James D. 1869-1917 ....DLB-50

Corso, Gregory 1930- DLB-5, 16, 237

Cortázar, Julio 1914-1984....DLB-113; CDWLB-3

Cortéz, Carlos 1923- DLB-209

Cortez, Jayne 1936- DLB-41

Corvinus, Gottlieb Siegmund
1677-1746 ....DLB-168

Corvo, Baron (see Rolfe, Frederick William)

Cory, Annie Sophie (see Cross, Victoria)

Cory, William Johnson 1823-1892......DLB-35

Coryate, Thomas 1577?-1617.......DLB-151, 172

Ćosić, Dobrica 1921- DLB-181; CDWLB-4

Cosin, John 1595-1672...........DLB-151, 213

Cosmopolitan Book Corporation........DLB-46

Costain, Thomas B. 1885-1965 ....DLB-9

Coste, Donat 1912-1957..............DLB-88

Costello, Louisa Stuart 1799-1870.......DLB-166

Cota-Cárdenas, Margarita 1941- DLB-122

Cotten, Bruce 1873-1954 ....DLB-187

Cotter, Joseph Seamon, Sr. 1861-1949 ....DLB-50

Cotter, Joseph Seamon, Jr. 1895-1919 ....DLB-50

Cottle, Joseph [publishing house] DLB-154

Cotton, Charles 1630-1687...........DLB-131

Cotton, John 1584-1652.............DLB-24

Cotton, Sir Robert Bruce 1571-1631.....DLB-213

Coulter, John 1888-1980 ....DLB-68

Cournos, John 1881-1966..............DLB-54

Courteline, Georges 1858-1929 ....DLB-192

Cousins, Margaret 1905-1996 ....DLB-137

Cousins, Norman 1915-1990 ....DLB-137

Couvreur, Jessie (see Tasma)

Coventry, Francis 1725-1754 ....DLB-39

Dedication, *The History of Pompey
the Little* (1751) DLB-39

Coverdale, Miles 1487 or 1488-1569 ....DLB-167

Coverly, N. [publishing house]..........DLB-49

Covici-Friede DLB-46

Coward, Noel
1899-1973.........DLB-10, 245; CDBLB-6

Coward, McCann and Geoghegan.......DLB-46

Cowles, Gardner 1861-1946 . . . . .DLB-29

Cowles, Gardner "Mike" Jr.
1903-1985 . . . . DLB-127, 137

Cowley, Abraham 1618-1667 . . . . . .DLB-131, 151

Cowley, Hannah 1743-1809 . . . . .DLB-89

Cowley, Malcolm
1898-1989 . . . . DLB-4, 48; Y-81, Y-89

Cowper, William 1731-1800 . . . . . . .DLB-104, 109

Cox, A. B. (see Berkeley, Anthony)

Cox, James McMahon 1903-1974 . . . . . . .DLB-127

Cox, James Middleton 1870-1957 . . . . . . .DLB-127

Cox, Leonard ca. 1495-ca. 1550 . . . . . . .DLB-236

Cox, Palmer 1840-1924 . . . . .DLB-42

Coxe, Louis 1918-1993 . . . . .DLB-5

Coxe, Tench 1755-1824 . . . . .DLB-37

Cozzens, Frederick S. 1818-1869 . . . . . . .DLB-202

Cozzens, James Gould
1903-1978 . . . . .DLB-9; Y-84; DS-2; CDALB-1

James Gould Cozzens—A View from Afar Y-97

James Gould Cozzens Case Re-opened Y-97

James Gould Cozzens: How to Read Him Y-97

Cozzens's *Michael Scarlett* Y-97

James Gould Cozzens Symposium and
Exhibition at the University of
South Carolina, Columbia Y-00

Crabbe, George 1754-1832 . . . . .DLB-93

Crace, Jim 1946- DLB-231

Crackanthorpe, Hubert 1870-1896 . . . . . .DLB-135

Craddock, Charles Egbert (see Murfree, Mary N.)

Cradock, Thomas 1718-1770 . . . . .DLB-31

Craig, Daniel H. 1811-1895 . . . . .DLB-43

Craik, Dinah Maria 1826-1887 . . . . . .DLB-35, 136

Cramer, Richard Ben 1950- DLB-185

Cranch, Christopher Pearse
1813-1892 . . . . .DLB-1, 42, 243

Crane, Hart 1899-1932 . . . . .DLB-4, 48; CDALB-4

Crane, R. S. 1886-1967 . . . . .DLB-63

Crane, Stephen
1871-1900 . . . . . . .DLB-12, 54, 78; CDALB-3

Crane, Walter 1845-1915 . . . . .DLB-163

Cranmer, Thomas 1489-1556 . . . . . .DLB-132, 213

Crapsey, Adelaide 1878-1914 . . . . .DLB-54

Crashaw, Richard 1612 or 1613-1649 . . . .DLB-126

Craven, Avery 1885-1980 . . . . .DLB-17

Crawford, Charles 1752-circa 1815 . . . . . . .DLB-31

Crawford, F. Marion 1854-1909 . . . . .DLB-71

Crawford, Isabel Valancy 1850-1887 . . . . . .DLB-92

Crawley, Alan 1887-1975 . . . . .DLB-68

Crayon, Geoffrey (see Irving, Washington)

Creamer, Robert W. 1922- DLB-171

Creasey, John 1908-1973 . . . . .DLB-77

Creative Age Press DLB-46

Creech, William [publishing house] DLB-154

Creede, Thomas [publishing house] DLB-170

Creel, George 1876-1953 . . . . .DLB-25

Creeley, Robert 1926- . . .DLB-5, 16, 169; DS-17

Creelman, James 1859-1915 . . . . .DLB-23

Cregan, David 1931- DLB-13

Creighton, Donald Grant 1902-1979 . . . . .DLB-88

Cremazie, Octave 1827-1879 . . . . .DLB-99

Crémer, Victoriano 1909?- DLB-108

Crescas, Hasdai circa 1340-1412? DLB-115

Crespo, Angel 1926- DLB-134

Cresset Press DLB-112

Cresswell, Helen 1934- DLB-161

Crèvecoeur, Michel Guillaume Jean de
1735-1813 . . . . .DLB-37

Crewe, Candida 1964- DLB-207

Crews, Harry 1935- DLB-6, 143, 185

Crichton, Michael 1942- Y-81

A Crisis of Culture: The Changing Role
of Religion in the New Republic DLB-37

Crispin, Edmund 1921-1978 . . . . .DLB-87

Cristofer, Michael 1946- DLB-7

Crnjanski, Miloš
1893-1977 . . . . .DLB-147; CDWLB-4

Crocker, Hannah Mather 1752-1829 . . . . .DLB-200

Crockett, David (Davy)
1786-1836 . . . . .DLB-3, 11, 183

Croft-Cooke, Rupert (see Bruce, Leo)

Crofts, Freeman Wills 1879-1957 . . . . .DLB-77

Croker, John Wilson 1780-1857 . . . . .DLB-110

Croly, George 1780-1860 . . . . .DLB-159

Croly, Herbert 1869-1930 . . . . .DLB-91

Croly, Jane Cunningham 1829-1901 . . . . . .DLB-23

Crompton, Richmal 1890-1969 . . . . .DLB-160

Cronin, A. J. 1896-1981 . . . . .DLB-191

Cros, Charles 1842-1888 . . . . .DLB-217

Crosby, Caresse 1892-1970 . . . . .DLB-48

Crosby, Caresse 1892-1970
and Crosby, Harry
1898-1929 . . . . .DLB-4; DS-15

Crosby, Harry 1898-1929 . . . . .DLB-48

Crosland, Camilla Toulmin
(Mrs. Newton Crosland)
1812-1895 . . . . .DLB-240

Cross, Gillian 1945- DLB-161

Cross, Victoria 1868-1952 . . . . .DLB-135, 197

Crossley-Holland, Kevin 1941- DLB-40, 161

Crothers, Rachel 1878-1958 . . . . .DLB-7

Crowell, Thomas Y., Company DLB-49

Crowley, John 1942- Y-82

Crowley, Mart 1935- DLB-7

Crown Publishers .DLB-46

Crowne, John 1641-1712 . . . . .DLB-80

Crowninshield, Edward Augustus
1817-1859 . . . . .DLB-140

Crowninshield, Frank 1872-1947 . . . . .DLB-91

Croy, Homer 1883-1965 . . . . .DLB-4

Crumley, James 1939- DLB-226; Y-84

Cruse, Mary Anne 1825?-1910 . . . . .DLB-239

Cruz, Victor Hernández 1949- DLB-41

Csokor, Franz Theodor 1885-1969 . . . . . . .DLB-81

Csoóri, Sándor 1930- DLB-232; CDWLB-4

Cuala Press DLB-112

Cullen, Countee
1903-1946 . . . . .DLB-4, 48, 51; CDALB-4

Culler, Jonathan D. 1944- DLB-67, 246

Cullinan, Elizabeth 1933- DLB-234

The Cult of Biography
Excerpts from the Second Folio Debate:
"Biographies are generally a disease of
English Literature" – Germaine Greer,
Victoria Glendinning, Auberon Waugh,
and Richard Holmes Y-86

Cumberland, Richard 1732-1811 . . . . .DLB-89

Cummings, Constance Gordon
1837-1924 . . . . .DLB-174

Cummings, E. E.
1894-1962 . . . . .DLB-4, 48; CDALB-5

Cummings, Ray 1887-1957 . . . . .DLB-8

Cummings and Hilliard DLB-49

Cummins, Maria Susanna
1827-1866 . . . . .DLB-42

Cumpián, Carlos 1953- DLB-209

Cunard, Nancy 1896-1965 . . . . .DLB-240

Cundall, Joseph [publishing house] DLB-106

Cuney, Waring 1906-1976 . . . . .DLB-51

Cuney-Hare, Maude 1874-1936 . . . . .DLB-52

Cunningham, Allan 1784-1842 . . . . .DLB-116, 144

Cunningham, J. V. 1911- DLB-5

Cunningham, Peter F.
[publishing house] DLB-49

Cunquiero, Alvaro 1911-1981 . . . . .DLB-134

Cuomo, George 1929- Y-80

Cupples, Upham and Company DLB-49

Cupples and Leon DLB-46

Cuppy, Will 1884-1949 . . . . .DLB-11

Curiel, Barbara Brinson 1956- DLB-209

Curll, Edmund [publishing house] DLB-154

Currie, James 1756-1805 . . . . .DLB-142

Currie, Mary Montgomerie Lamb Singleton,
Lady Currie
(see Fane, Violet)

Cursor Mundi circa 1300 . . . . .DLB-146

Curti, Merle E. 1897- DLB-17

Curtis, Anthony 1926- DLB-155

Curtis, Cyrus H. K. 1850-1933 . . . . .DLB-91

Curtis, George William
1824-1892 . . . . .DLB-1, 43, 223

Curzon, Robert 1810-1873 . . . . .DLB-166

Curzon, Sarah Anne 1833-1898 . . . . .DLB-99

Cushing, Harvey 1869-1939 . . . . .DLB-187

Custance, Olive (Lady Alfred Douglas)
1874-1944 . . . . .DLB-240

Cynewulf circa 770-840 . . . . .DLB-146

Czepko, Daniel 1605-1660 . . . . .DLB-164

Czerniawski, Adam 1934- DLB-232

D

Dabit, Eugène 1898-1936 . . . . .DLB-65

Daborne, Robert circa 1580-1628 . . . . .DLB-58

Dąbrowska, Maria
   1889-1965 . . . . DLB-215; CDWLB-4

Dacey, Philip 1939- DLB-105

"Eyes Across Centuries: Contemporary
   Poetry and 'That Vision Thing,'" DLB-105

Dach, Simon 1605-1659 . . . . DLB-164

Daggett, Rollin M. 1831-1901 . . . . DLB-79

D'Aguiar, Fred 1960- DLB-157

Dahl, Roald 1916-1990 . . . . DLB-139

Dahlberg, Edward 1900-1977 . . . . DLB-48

Dahn, Felix 1834-1912 . . . . DLB-129

Dal', Vladimir Ivanovich (Kazak Vladimir
   Lugansky) 1801-1872 . . . . DLB-198

Dale, Peter 1938- DLB-40

Daley, Arthur 1904-1974 . . . . .DLB-171

Dall, Caroline Healey 1822-1912 . . . . . DLB-1, 235

Dallas, E. S. 1828-1879 . . . . DLB-55

   From The Gay Science (1866) DLB-21

The Dallas Theater Center. DLB-7

D'Alton, Louis 1900-1951 . . . . DLB-10

Daly, Carroll John 1889-1958 . . . . DLB-226

Daly, T. A. 1871-1948 . . . . DLB-11

Damon, S. Foster 1893-1971 . . . . DLB-45

Damrell, William S. [publishing house] . . . DLB-49

Dana, Charles A. 1819-1897 . . . . DLB-3, 23

Dana, Richard Henry, Jr.
   1815-1882 . . . . DLB-1, 183, 235

Dandridge, Ray Garfield DLB-51

Dane, Clemence 1887-1965 . . . . .DLB-10, 197

Danforth, John 1660-1730 . . . . DLB-24

Danforth, Samuel, I 1626-1674 . . . . DLB-24

Danforth, Samuel, II 1666-1727 . . . . DLB-24

Dangerous Years: London Theater,
   1939-1945 . . . . DLB-10

Daniel, John M. 1825-1865. . . . . DLB-43

Daniel, Samuel 1562 or 1563-1619 . . . . . . DLB-62

Daniel Press DLB-106

Daniells, Roy 1902-1979 . . . . DLB-68

Daniels, Jim 1956- DLB-120

Daniels, Jonathan 1902-1981 . . . . DLB-127

Daniels, Josephus 1862-1948 . . . . DLB-29

Daniel, Sarah 1957- DLB-245

Danilevsky, Grigorii Petrovich
   1829-1890 . . . . DLB-238

Dannay, Frederic 1905-1982 and
   Manfred B. Lee 1905-1971 . . . . DLB-137

Danner, Margaret Esse 1915- DLB-41

Danter, John [publishing house] DLB-170

Dantin, Louis 1865-1945 . . . . DLB-92

Danzig, Allison 1898-1987 . . . . .DLB-171

D'Arcy, Ella circa 1857-1937 . . . . DLB-135

Darke, Nick 1948- DLB-233

Darley, Felix Octavious Carr 1822-1888 . DLB-188

Darley, George 1795-1846 . . . . DLB-96

Darmesteter, Madame James
   (see Robinson, A. Mary F.)

Darwin, Charles 1809-1882 . . . . .DLB-57, 166

Darwin, Erasmus 1731-1802. . . . . DLB-93

Daryush, Elizabeth 1887-1977 . . . . DLB-20

Dashkova, Ekaterina Romanovna
   (née Vorontsova) 1743-1810 . . . . DLB-150

Dashwood, Edmée Elizabeth Monica de la Pasture
   (see Delafield, E. M.)

Daudet, Alphonse 1840-1897 . . . . DLB-123

d'Aulaire, Edgar Parin 1898- and
   d'Aulaire, Ingri 1904- DLB-22

Davenant, Sir William 1606-1668 . . . DLB-58, 126

Davenport, Guy 1927- DLB-130

Davenport, Marcia 1903-1996 . . . . .DS-17

Davenport, Robert ?-? DLB-58

Daves, Delmer 1904-1977 . . . . DLB-26

Davey, Frank 1940- DLB-53

Davidson, Avram 1923-1993 . . . . DLB-8

Davidson, Donald 1893-1968 . . . . DLB-45

Davidson, John 1857-1909 . . . . DLB-19

Davidson, Lionel 1922- DLB-14

Davidson, Robyn 1950- DLB-204

Davidson, Sara 1943- DLB-185

Davie, Donald 1922- DLB-27

Davie, Elspeth 1919- DLB-139

Davies, Sir John 1569-1626 . . . . .DLB-172

Davies, John, of Hereford 1565?-1618 . . . DLB-121

Davies, Peter, Limited DLB-112

Davies, Rhys 1901-1978 . . . . DLB-139, 191

Davies, Robertson 1913- DLB-68

Davies, Samuel 1723-1761 . . . . DLB-31

Davies, Thomas 1712?-1785 . . . . . . DLB-142, 154

Davies, W. H. 1871-1940 . . . . .DLB-19, 174

Daviot, Gordon 1896?-1952 . . . . DLB-10
   (see also Tey, Josephine)

Davis, Arthur Hoey (see Rudd, Steele)

Davis, Charles A. 1795-1867 . . . . DLB-11

Davis, Clyde Brion 1894-1962 . . . . DLB-9

Davis, Dick 1945- DLB-40

Davis, Frank Marshall 1905-? DLB-51

Davis, H. L. 1894-1960 . . . . DLB-9, 206

Davis, John 1774-1854 . . . . DLB-37

Davis, Lydia 1947- DLB-130

Davis, Margaret Thomson 1926- DLB-14

Davis, Ossie 1917- DLB-7, 38

Davis, Paxton 1925-1994 . . . . .Y-89

Davis, Rebecca Harding 1831-1910 . . DLB-74, 239

Davis, Richard Harding 1864-1916
   . . . . .DLB-12, 23, 78, 79, 189; DS-13

Davis, Samuel Cole 1764-1809 . . . . DLB-37

Davis, Samuel Post 1850-1918 . . . . DLB-202

Davison, Peter 1928- DLB-5

Davydov, Denis Vasil'evich
   1784-1839 . . . . DLB-205

Davys, Mary 1674-1732 . . . . DLB-39

   Preface to The Works of
      Mrs. Davys (1725) DLB-39

DAW Books DLB-46

Dawson, Ernest 1882-1947 . . . . DLB-140

Dawson, Fielding 1930- DLB-130

Dawson, Sarah Morgan 1842-1909 . . . . . DLB-239

Dawson, William 1704-1752. . . . . DLB-31

Day, Angel flourished 1583-1599 . . . .DLB-167, 236

Day, Benjamin Henry 1810-1889 . . . . DLB-43

Day, Clarence 1874-1935 . . . . DLB-11

Day, Dorothy 1897-1980 . . . . DLB-29

Day, Frank Parker 1881-1950 . . . . DLB-92

Day, John circa 1574-circa 1640 . . . . DLB-62

Day, John [publishing house] DLB-170

Day, The John, Company DLB-46

Day Lewis, C. 1904-1972 . . . . DLB-15, 20
   (see also Blake, Nicholas)

Day, Mahlon [publishing house] DLB-49

Day, Thomas 1748-1789. . . . . DLB-39

Dazai Osamu 1909-1948 . . . . DLB-182

Deacon, William Arthur 1890-1977 . . . . . DLB-68

Deal, Borden 1922-1985. . . . . DLB-6

de Angeli, Marguerite 1889-1987 . . . . DLB-22

De Angelis, Milo 1951- DLB-128

De Bow, James Dunwoody Brownson
   1820-1867 .DLB-3, 79

de Bruyn, Günter 1926- DLB-75

de Camp, L. Sprague 1907-2000. . . . . DLB-8

De Carlo, Andrea 1952- DLB-196

De Casas, Celso A. 1944- DLB-209

Dechert, Robert 1895-1975. . . . . .DLB-187

Dee, John 1527-1608 or 1609 . . . . . DLB-136, 213

Deeping, George Warwick 1877-1950 . . . DLB 153

Defoe, Daniel
   1660-1731. . . . . . . DLB-39, 95, 101; CDBLB-2

   Preface to Colonel Jack (1722) DLB-39

   Preface to The Farther Adventures of
      Robinson Crusoe (1719) DLB-39

   Preface to Moll Flanders (1722) DLB-39

   Preface to Robinson Crusoe (1719) DLB-39

   Preface to Roxana (1724) DLB-39

de Fontaine, Felix Gregory 1834-1896 . . . DLB-43

De Forest, John William 1826-1906 . . DLB-12, 189

DeFrees, Madeline 1919- DLB-105

   "The Poet's Kaleidoscope: The Element
      of Surprise in the Making of
      the Poem" DLB-105

DeGolyer, Everette Lee 1886-1956 . . . . . .DLB-187

de Graff, Robert 1895-1981 . . . . .Y-81

de Graft, Joe 1924-1978 . . . . .DLB-117

De Heinrico circa 980? DLB-148

Deighton, Len 1929- DLB-87; CDBLB-8

DeJong, Meindert 1906-1991 . . . . DLB-52

Dekker, Thomas
   circa 1572-1632 . . . . . DLB-62, 172; CDBLB-1

Delacorte, Jr., George T. 1894-1991 . . . . . DLB-91

Delafield, E. M. 1890-1943 . . . . DLB-34

Delahaye, Guy 1888-1969 . . . . DLB-92

de la Mare, Walter
   1873-1956. . . . . . DLB-19, 153, 162; CDBLB-6

Deland, Margaret 1857-1945 . . . . .DLB-78

Delaney, Shelagh 1939- DLB-13; CDBLB-8

Delano, Amasa 1763-1823 . . . . .DLB-183

Delany, Martin Robinson 1812-1885. . . . .DLB-50

Delany, Samuel R. 1942- DLB-8, 33

de la Roche, Mazo 1879-1961 . . . . .DLB-68

Delavigne, Jean François Casimir
   1793-1843 . . . . .DLB-192

Delbanco, Nicholas 1942- DLB-6, 234

Del Castillo, Ramón 1949- DLB-209

De León, Nephtal 1945- DLB-82

Delgado, Abelardo Barrientos 1931- DLB-82

Del Giudice, Daniele 1949- DLB-196

De Libero, Libero 1906-1981. . . . . .DLB-114

DeLillo, Don 1936- DLB-6, 173

de Lisser H. G. 1878-1944 . . . . .DLB-117

Dell, Floyd 1887-1969 . . . . .DLB-9

Dell Publishing Company DLB-46

delle Grazie, Marie Eugene 1864-1931 . . . .DLB-81

Deloney, Thomas died 1600 . . . . .DLB-167

Deloria, Ella C. 1889-1971. . . . . .DLB-175

Deloria, Vine, Jr. 1933- DLB-175

del Rey, Lester 1915-1993 . . . . .DLB-8

Del Vecchio, John M. 1947- DS-9

Del'vig, Anton Antonovich 1798-1831. . . .DLB-205

de Man, Paul 1919-1983 . . . . .DLB-67

DeMarinis, Rick 1934- DLB-218

Demby, William 1922- DLB-33

Deming, Philander 1829-1915 . . . . .DLB-74

Deml, Jakub 1878-1961 . . . . .DLB-215

Demorest, William Jennings 1822-1895. . . .DLB-79

De Morgan, William 1839-1917 . . . . .DLB-153

Demosthenes 384 B.C.-322 B.C. DLB-176

Denham, Henry [publishing house] DLB-170

Denham, Sir John 1615-1669. . . . . . . .DLB-58, 126

Denison, Merrill 1893-1975 . . . . .DLB-92

Denison, T. S., and Company DLB-49

Dennery, Adolphe Philippe 1811-1899 . . .DLB-192

Dennie, Joseph 1768-1812 . . . . . DLB-37, 43, 59, 73

Dennis, John 1658-1734. . . . . .DLB-101

Dennis, Nigel 1912-1989 . . . . . . .DLB-13, 15, 233

Denslow, W. W. 1856-1915 . . . . .DLB-188

Dent, J. M., and Sons. DLB-112

Dent, Tom 1932-1998 . . . . .DLB-38

Denton, Daniel circa 1626-1703. . . . . . . .DLB-24

DePaola, Tomie 1934- DLB-61

Department of Library, Archives, and Institutional
   Research, American Bible Society Y-97

De Quille, Dan 1829-1898. . . . . .DLB-186

De Quincey, Thomas
   1785-1859 . . . . .DLB-110, 144; CDBLB-3

"Rhetoric" (1828; revised, 1859)
   [excerpt]. DLB-57

Derby, George Horatio 1823-1861 . . . . . .DLB-11

Derby, J. C., and Company. DLB-49

Derby and Miller. DLB-49

De Ricci, Seymour 1881-1942 . . . . .DLB-201

Derleth, August 1909-1971 . . . . . . .DLB-9; DS-17

Derrida, Jacques 1930- DLB-242

The Derrydale Press DLB-46

Derzhavin, Gavriil Romanovich
   1743-1816 .DLB-150

Desaulniers, Gonsalve 1863-1934 . . . . . . .DLB-92

Desbordes-Valmore, Marceline
   1786-1859 .DLB-217

Deschamps, Emile 1791-1871. . . . . .DLB-217

Deschamps, Eustache 1340?-1404. . . . . . .DLB-208

Desbiens, Jean-Paul 1927- DLB-53

des Forêts, Louis-Rene 1918- DLB-83

Desiato, Luca 1941- DLB-196

Desnica, Vladan 1905-1967 . . . . .DLB-181

DesRochers, Alfred 1901-1978. . . . . .DLB-68

Desrosiers, Léo-Paul 1896-1967. . . . . . . .DLB-68

Dessi, Giuseppe 1909-1977 . . . . .DLB-177

Destouches, Louis-Ferdinand
   (see Céline, Louis-Ferdinand)

De Tabley, Lord 1835-1895 . . . . .DLB-35

Deutsch, André, Limited DLB-112

Deutsch, Babette 1895-1982 . . . . .DLB-45

Deutsch, Niklaus Manuel (see Manuel, Niklaus)

Deveaux, Alexis 1948- DLB-38

The Development of the Author's Copyright
   in Britain. DLB-154

The Development of Lighting in the Staging
   of Drama, 1900-1945 . . . . .DLB-10

"The Development of Meiji Japan" DLB-180

De Vere, Aubrey 1814-1902 . . . . .DLB-35

Devereux, second Earl of Essex, Robert
   1565-1601 .DLB-136

The Devin-Adair Company. DLB-46

De Vinne, Theodore Low 1828-1914 . . . .DLB-187

Devlin, Anne 1951- DLB-245

De Voto, Bernard 1897-1955. . . . . .DLB-9

De Vries, Peter 1910-1993. . . . . . . .DLB-6; Y-82

Dewdney, Christopher 1951- DLB-60

Dewdney, Selwyn 1909-1979. . . . . .DLB-68

Dewey, John 1859-1952. . . . . .DLB-246

Dewey, Orville 1794-1882 . . . . .DLB-243

Dewey, Thomas B. 1915-1981 . . . . .DLB-226

DeWitt, Robert M., Publisher DLB-49

DeWolfe, Fiske and Company DLB-49

Dexter, Colin 1930- DLB-87

de Young, M. H. 1849-1925 . . . . .DLB-25

Dhlomo, H. I. E. 1903-1956 . . . . . . DLB-157, 225

Dhuoda circa 803-after 843 . . . . .DLB-148

The Dial 1840-1844 . . . . .DLB-223

The Dial Press. .DLB-46

Diamond, I. A. L. 1920-1988 . . . . .DLB-26

Dibble, L. Grace 1902-1998. . . . . .DLB-204

Dibdin, Thomas Frognall 1776-1847 . . . . .DLB-184

Di Cicco, Pier Giorgio 1949- DLB-60

Dick, Philip K. 1928-1982 . . . . .DLB-8

Dick and Fitzgerald DLB-49

Dickens, Charles 1812-1870
   . . . . . . .DLB-21, 55, 70, 159, 166; CDBLB-4

Dickey, James 1923-1997
   . . . . DLB-5, 193; Y-82, Y-93, Y-96;
                                      DS-7, DS-19; CDALB-6

James Dickey Tributes. Y-97

The Life of James Dickey: A Lecture to
   the Friends of the Emory Libraries,
   by Henry Hart Y-98

Dickey, William 1928-1994. . . . . .DLB-5

Dickinson, Emily
   1830-1886 . . . . DLB-1, 243; CDWLB-3

Dickinson, John 1732-1808 . . . . .DLB-31

Dickinson, Jonathan 1688-1747 . . . . .DLB-24

Dickinson, Patric 1914- DLB-27

Dickinson, Peter 1927- DLB-87, 161

Dicks, John [publishing house]. DLB-106

Dickson, Gordon R. 1923- DLB-8

Dictionary of Literary Biography Yearbook Awards
   . . . . Y-92, Y-93, Y-97, Y-98, Y-99, Y-00

The Dictionary of National Biography. DLB-144

Didion, Joan 1934-
   . . . . . DLB-2, 173, 185; Y-81, Y-86; CDALB-6

Di Donato, Pietro 1911- DLB-9

Die Fürstliche Bibliothek Corvey Y-96

Diego, Gerardo 1896-1987 . . . . .DLB-134

Digges, Thomas circa 1546-1595. . . . . . .DLB-136

The Digital Millennium Copyright Act:
   Expanding Copyright Protection in
   Cyberspace and Beyond Y-98

Dillard, Annie 1945- Y-80

Dillard, R. H. W. 1937- DLB-5, 244

Dillingham, Charles T., Company DLB-49

The Dillingham, G. W., Company DLB-49

Dilly, Edward and Charles
   [publishing house] DLB-154

Dilthey, Wilhelm 1833-1911 . . . . .DLB-129

Dimitrova, Blaga 1922- . . . DLB-181; CDWLB-4

Dimov, Dimitr 1909-1966 . . . . .DLB-181

Dimsdale, Thomas J. 1831?-1866 . . . . . . .DLB-186

Dinescu, Mircea 1950- DLB-232

Dinesen, Isak (see Blixen, Karen)

Dingelstedt, Franz von 1814-1881 . . . . . . .DLB-133

Dintenfass, Mark 1941- Y-84

Diogenes, Jr. (see Brougham, John)

Diogenes Laertius circa 200. . . . . .DLB-176

DiPrima, Diane 1934- DLB-5, 16

Disch, Thomas M. 1940- DLB-8

Disney, Walt 1901-1966 . . . . .DLB-22

Disraeli, Benjamin 1804-1881 . . . . .DLB-21, 55

D'Israeli, Isaac 1766-1848 . . . . .DLB-107

Ditlevsen, Tove 1917-1976. . . . . .DLB-214

Ditzen, Rudolf (see Fallada, Hans)

Dix, Dorothea Lynde 1802-1887. . . . . .DLB-1, 235

Dix, Dorothy (see Gilmer, Elizabeth Meriwether)

Dix, Edwards and Company. DLB-49

Dix, Gertrude circa 1874-? DLB-197

Dixie, Florence Douglas 1857-1905. . . . . . .DLB-174

Dixon, Ella Hepworth
  1855 or 1857-1932 . . . . DLB-197

Dixon, Paige (see Corcoran, Barbara)

Dixon, Richard Watson 1833-1900 . . . . . . DLB-19

Dixon, Stephen 1936- DLB-130

Dmitriev, Ivan Ivanovich 1760-1837. . . . . DLB-150

Dobell, Bertram 1842-1914. . . . . DLB-184

Dobell, Sydney 1824-1874 . . . . DLB-32

Dobie, J. Frank 1888-1964 . . . . DLB-212

Döblin, Alfred 1878-1957 . . . . DLB-66; CDWLB-2

Dobson, Austin 1840-1921 . . . . DLB-35, 144

Doctorow, E. L.
  1931- DLB-2, 28, 173; Y-80; CDALB-6

Documents on Sixteenth-Century
  Literature DLB-167, 172

Dodd, Anne [publishing house] DLB-154

Dodd, Mead and Company DLB-49

Dodd, Susan M. 1946- DLB-244

Dodd, William E. 1869-1940 . . . . DLB-17

Doderer, Heimito von 1896-1968. . . . . . . DLB-85

Dodge, B. W., and Company. DLB-46

Dodge, Mary Abigail 1833-1896 . . . . DLB-221

Dodge, Mary Mapes
  1831?-1905. . . . . DLB-42, 79; DS-13

Dodge Publishing Company. DLB-49

Dodgson, Charles Lutwidge (see Carroll, Lewis)

Dodsley, R. [publishing house] DLB-154

Dodsley, Robert 1703-1764. . . . . DLB-95

Dodson, Owen 1914-1983 . . . . DLB-76

Dodwell, Christina 1951- DLB-204

Doestick, Q. K. Philander, P. B.
  (see Thomson, Mortimer)

Doheny, Carrie Estelle 1875-1958 . . . . . . DLB-140

Doherty, John 1798?-1854 . . . . DLB-190

Doig, Ivan 1939- DLB-206

Doinaş, Ştefan Augustin 1922- DLB-232

Domínguez, Sylvia Maida 1935- DLB-122

Donahoe, Patrick [publishing house] DLB-49

Donald, David H. 1920- DLB-17

The Practice of Biography VI: An
  Interview with David Herbert Donald. . . . Y-87

Donaldson, Scott 1928- DLB-111

Doni, Rodolfo 1919- DLB-177

Donleavy, J. P. 1926- DLB-6, 173

Donnadieu, Marguerite (see Duras, Marguerite)

Donne, John
  1572-1631. . . . . DLB-121, 151; CDBLB-1

Donnelley, R. R., and Sons Company DLB-49

Donnelly, Ignatius 1831-1901. . . . . DLB-12

Donohue and Henneberry DLB-49

Donoso, José 1924-1996 . . . . DLB-113; CDWLB-3

Doolady, M. [publishing house] DLB-49

Dooley, Ebon (see Ebon)

Doolittle, Hilda 1886-1961 . . . . DLB-4, 45

Doplicher, Fabio 1938- DLB-128

Dor, Milo 1923- DLB-85

Doran, George H., Company. DLB-46

Dorgelès, Roland 1886-1973. . . . . DLB-65

Dorn, Edward 1929-1999. . . . . DLB-5

Dorr, Rheta Childe 1866-1948. . . . . DLB-25

Dorris, Michael 1945-1997 . . . . .DLB-175

Dorset and Middlesex, Charles Sackville,
  Lord Buckhurst, Earl of 1643-1706 . . . .DLB-131

Dorst, Tankred 1925- DLB-75, 124

Dos Passos, John 1896-1970
  . . . . DLB-4, 9; DS-1, DS-15; CDALB-5

John Dos Passos: Artist Y-99

John Dos Passos: A Centennial
  Commemoration .Y-96

Dostoevsky, Fyodor 1821-1881 . . . . DLB-238

Doubleday and Company DLB-49

Dougall, Lily 1858-1923. . . . . DLB-92

Doughty, Charles M.
  1843-1926 . . . . DLB-19, 57, 174

Douglas, Lady Alfred (see Custance, Olive)

Douglas, Gavin 1476-1522 . . . . DLB-132

Douglas, Keith 1920-1944 . . . . DLB-27

Douglas, Norman 1868-1952 . . . . DLB-34, 195

Douglass, Frederick 1818-1895
  . . . . DLB-1, 43, 50, 79, 243; CDALB-2

Douglass, William circa 1691-1752. . . . . . DLB-24

Dourado, Autran 1926- DLB-145

Dove, Arthur G. 1880-1946 . . . . DLB-188

Dove, Rita 1952- DLB-120; CDALB-7

Dover Publications DLB-46

Doves Press DLB-112

Dowden, Edward 1843-1913 . . . . DLB-35, 149

Dowell, Coleman 1925-1985 . . . . DLB-130

Dowland, John 1563-1626 . . . . .DLB-172

Downes, Gwladys 1915- DLB-88

Downing, J., Major (see Davis, Charles A.)

Downing, Major Jack (see Smith, Seba)

Dowriche, Anne
  before 1560-after 1613 . . . . .DLB-172

Dowson, Ernest 1867-1900 . . . . DLB-19, 135

Doxey, William [publishing house] DLB-49

Doyle, Sir Arthur Conan
  1859-1930 . . .DLB-18, 70, 156, 178; CDBLB-5

Doyle, Kirby 1932- DLB-16

Doyle, Roddy 1958- DLB-194

Drabble, Margaret
  1939- DLB-14, 155, 231; CDBLB-8

Drach, Albert 1902- DLB-85

Dragojević, Danijel 1934- DLB-181

Drake, Samuel Gardner 1798-1875. . . . . . DLB-187

The Dramatic Publishing Company. DLB-49

Dramatists Play Service DLB-46

Drant, Thomas early 1540s?-1578 . . . . . . DLB-167

Draper, John W. 1811-1882 . . . . DLB-30

Draper, Lyman C. 1815-1891 . . . . DLB-30

Drayton, Michael 1563-1631 . . . . DLB-121

Dreiser, Theodore 1871-1945
  . . . . . . .DLB-9, 12, 102, 137; DS-1; CDALB-3

Dresser, Davis 1904-1977. . . . . DLB-226

Drewitz, Ingeborg 1923-1986. . . . . DLB-75

Drieu La Rochelle, Pierre 1893-1945 . . . . . DLB-72

Drinker, Elizabeth 1735-1807 . . . . DLB-200

Drinkwater, John
  1882-1937 . . . . .DLB-10, 19, 149

Droste-Hülshoff, Annette von
  1797-1848 . . . . DLB-133; CDWLB-2

The Drue Heinz Literature Prize
  Excerpt from "Excerpts from a Report
  of the Commission," in David
  Bosworth's The Death of Descartes
  An Interview with David Bosworth. Y-82

Drummond, William, of Hawthornden
  1585-1649 . . . . DLB-121, 213

Drummond, William Henry
  1854-1907 . . . . DLB-92

Druzhinin, Aleksandr Vasil'evich
  1824-1864 . . . . DLB-238

Dryden, Charles 1860?-1931 . . . . .DLB-171

Dryden, John
  1631-1700 . . . . . . DLB-80, 101, 131; CDBLB-2

Držić, Marin
  circa 1508-1567 . . . . . . .DLB-147; CDWLB-4

Duane, William 1760-1835. . . . . DLB-43

Dubé, Marcel 1930- DLB-53

Dubé, Rodolphe (see Hertel, François)

Dubie, Norman 1945- DLB-120

Dubois, Silvia 1788 or 1789?-1889 . . . . . . DLB-239

Du Bois, W. E. B.
  1868-1963 . . . .DLB-47, 50, 91, 246; CDALB-3

Du Bois, William Pène 1916-1993 . . . . DLB-61

Dubrovina, Ekaterina Oskarovna
  1846-1913 . . . . DLB-238

Dubus, Andre 1936-1999 . . . . DLB-130

Ducange, Victor 1783-1833 . . . . DLB-192

Du Chaillu, Paul Belloni 1831?-1903 . . . . DLB-189

Ducharme, Réjean 1941- DLB-60

Dučić, Jovan 1871-1943 . . . . .DLB-147; CDWLB-4

Duck, Stephen 1705?-1756 . . . . DLB-95

Duckworth, Gerald, and Company
  Limited. DLB-112

Duclaux, Madame Mary (see Robinson, A. Mary F.)

Dudek, Louis 1918- DLB-88

Duell, Sloan and Pearce DLB-46

Duerer, Albrecht 1471-1528 . . . . .DLB-179

Duff Gordon, Lucie 1821-1869 . . . . DLB-166

Dufferin, Helen Lady, Countess of Gifford
  1807-1867. DLB-199

Duffield and Green. DLB-46

Duffy, Maureen 1933- DLB-14

Dufief, Nicholas Gouin 1776-1834 . . . . . .DLB-187

Dugan, Alan 1923- DLB-5

Dugard, William [publishing house]. DLB-170

Dugas, Marcel 1883-1947. . . . . DLB-92

Dugdale, William [publishing house] DLB-106

Duhamel, Georges 1884-1966 . . . . DLB-65

Dujardin, Edouard 1861-1949 . . . . .DLB-123

Dukes, Ashley 1885-1959 . . . . .DLB-10

Dumas, Alexandre *père* 1802-1870 . . . . .DLB-119, 192

Dumas, Alexandre *fils* 1824-1895. . . . . . .DLB-192

Dumas, Henry 1934-1968 . . . . .DLB-41

du Maurier, Daphne 1907-1989 . . . . .DLB-191

Du Maurier, George 1834-1896. . . . .DLB-153, 178

Dunbar, Paul Laurence
1872-1906 . . . . .DLB-50, 54, 78; CDALB-3

Dunbar, William
circa 1460-circa 1522. . . . . .DLB-132, 146

Duncan, Norman 1871-1916 . . . . .DLB-92

Duncan, Quince 1940- DLB-145

Duncan, Robert 1919-1988 . . . . . . .DLB-5, 16, 193

Duncan, Ronald 1914-1982. . . . . .DLB-13

Duncan, Sara Jeannette 1861-1922 . . . . . .DLB-92

Dunigan, Edward, and Brother DLB-49

Dunlap, John 1747-1812 . . . . .DLB-43

Dunlap, William 1766-1839 . . . . . . .DLB-30, 37, 59

Dunn, Douglas 1942- DLB-40

Dunn, Harvey Thomas 1884-1952 . . . . . .DLB-188

Dunn, Stephen 1939- DLB-105

"The Good, The Not So Good" DLB-105

Dunne, Finley Peter 1867-1936 . . . . . .DLB-11, 23

Dunne, John Gregory 1932- Y-80

Dunne, Philip 1908-1992 . . . . .DLB-26

Dunning, Ralph Cheever 1878-1930 . . . . . . .DLB-4

Dunning, William A. 1857-1922 . . . . .DLB-17

Dunsany, Lord (Edward John Moreton
Drax Plunkett, Baron Dunsany)
1878-1957 . . . . DLB-10, 77, 153, 156

Duns Scotus, John circa 1266-1308 . . . . . .DLB-115

Dunton, John [publishing house] DLB-170

Dunton, W. Herbert 1878-1936. . . . . . . .DLB-188

Dupin, Amantine-Aurore-Lucile (see Sand, George)

Durand, Lucile (see Bersianik, Louky)

Duranti, Francesca 1935- DLB-196

Duranty, Walter 1884-1957 . . . . .DLB-29

Duras, Marguerite 1914-1996 . . . . .DLB-83

Durfey, Thomas 1653-1723 . . . . .DLB-80

Durova, Nadezhda Andreevna
(Aleksandr Andreevich Aleksandrov)
1783-1866 . . . . .DLB-198

Durrell, Lawrence 1912-1990
. . . . DLB-15, 27, 204; Y-90; CDBLB-7

Durrell, William [publishing house]. DLB-49

Dürrenmatt, Friedrich
1921-1990 . . . . . . .DLB-69, 124; CDWLB-2

Duston, Hannah 1657-1737 . . . . .DLB-200

Dutt, Toru 1856-1877 . . . . .DLB-240

Dutton, E. P., and Company DLB-49

Duvoisin, Roger 1904-1980 . . . . .DLB-61

Duyckinck, Evert Augustus
1816-1878 . . . . .DLB-3, 64

Duyckinck, George L. 1823-1863 . . . . .DLB-3

Duyckinck and Company DLB-49

Dwight, John Sullivan 1813-1893 . . . .DLB-1, 235

Dwight, Timothy 1752-1817 . . . . .DLB-37

Dybek, Stuart 1942- DLB-130

Dyer, Charles 1928- DLB-13

Dyer, Sir Edward 1543-1607 . . . . .DLB-136

Dyer, George 1755-1841 . . . . .DLB-93

Dyer, John 1699-1757 . . . . .DLB-95

Dyk, Viktor 1877-1931. . . . . .DLB-215

Dylan, Bob 1941- DLB-16

E

Eager, Edward 1911-1964 . . . . .DLB-22

Eagleton, Terry 1943- DLB-242

Eames, Wilberforce 1855-1937 . . . . .DLB-140

Earle, Alice Morse 1853-1911 . . . . .DLB-221

Earle, James H., and Company DLB-49

Earle, John 1600 or 1601-1665 . . . . .DLB-151

Early American Book Illustration,
by Sinclair Hamilton DLB-49

Eastlake, William 1917-1997 . . . . .DLB-6, 206

Eastman, Carol ?- DLB-44

Eastman, Charles A. (Ohiyesa)
1858-1939 . . . . .DLB-175

Eastman, Max 1883-1969 . . . . .DLB-91

Eaton, Daniel Isaac 1753-1814. . . . . .DLB-158

Eaton, Edith Maude 1865-1914. . . . . . . .DLB-221

Eaton, Winnifred 1875-1954 . . . . .DLB-221

Eberhart, Richard 1904- DLB-48; CDALB-1

Ebner, Jeannie 1918- DLB-85

Ebner-Eschenbach, Marie von
1830-1916 . . . . .DLB-81

Ebon 1942- DLB-41

E-Books Turn the Corner Y-98

Ecbasis Captivi circa 1045 . . . . .DLB-148

Ecco Press DLB-46

Eckhart, Meister circa 1260-circa 1328 . . .DLB-115

The Eclectic Review 1805-1868 . . . . .DLB-110

Eco, Umberto 1932- DLB-196, 242

Edel, Leon 1907-1997. . . . . .DLB-103

Edes, Benjamin 1732-1803 . . . . .DLB-43

Edgar, David 1948- DLB-13, 233

Edgeworth, Maria
1768-1849 . . . . DLB-116, 159, 163

The Edinburgh Review 1802-1929 . . . . .DLB-110

Edinburgh University Press. DLB-112

The Editor Publishing Company. DLB-49

Editorial Institute at Boston University Y-00

Editorial Statements DLB-137

Edmonds, Randolph 1900- DLB-51

Edmonds, Walter D. 1903-1998 . . . . .DLB-9

Edschmid, Kasimir 1890-1966. . . . . .DLB-56

Edson, Russell 1935- DLB-244

Edwards, Amelia Anne Blandford
1831-1892 . . . . .DLB-174

Edwards, Dic 1953- DLB-245

Edwards, Edward 1812-1886. . . . . .DLB-184

Edwards, James [publishing house] DLB-154

Edwards, Jonathan 1703-1758 . . . . .DLB-24

Edwards, Jonathan, Jr. 1745-1801 . . . . . . .DLB-37

Edwards, Junius 1929- DLB-33

Edwards, Matilda Barbara Betham
1836-1919 . . . . .DLB-174

Edwards, Richard 1524-1566 . . . . .DLB-62

Edwards, Sarah Pierpont 1710-1758. . . . .DLB-200

Effinger, George Alec 1947- DLB-8

Egerton, George 1859-1945. . . . . .DLB-135

Eggleston, Edward 1837-1902 . . . . .DLB-12

Eggleston, Wilfred 1901-1986 . . . . .DLB-92

Eglītis, Anšlavs 1906-1993 . . . . .DLB-220

Ehrenreich, Barbara 1941- DLB-246

Ehrenstein, Albert 1886-1950 . . . . .DLB-81

Ehrhart, W. D. 1948- DS-9

Ehrlich, Gretel 1946- DLB-212

Eich, Günter 1907-1972 . . . . .DLB-69, 124

Eichendorff, Joseph Freiherr von
1788-1857 . . . . .DLB-90

Eifukumon'in 1271-1342 . . . . .DLB-203

1873 Publishers' Catalogues DLB-49

Eighteenth-Century Aesthetic
Theories DLB-31

Eighteenth-Century Philosophical
Background. .DLB-31

Eigner, Larry 1926-1996 . . . . .DLB-5, 193

Eikon Basilike 1649 . . . . .DLB-151

Eilhart von Oberge
circa 1140-circa 1195. . . . . .DLB-148

Einhard circa 770-840 . . . . .DLB-148

Eiseley, Loren 1907-1977 . . . . DS-17

Eisenberg, Deborah 1945- DLB-244

Eisenreich, Herbert 1925-1986 . . . . .DLB-85

Eisner, Kurt 1867-1919 . . . . .DLB-66

Eklund, Gordon 1945- Y-83

Ekwensi, Cyprian
1921- DLB-117; CDWLB-3

Elaw, Zilpha circa 1790-? DLB-239

Eld, George [publishing house] DLB-170

Elder, Lonne III 1931- DLB-7, 38, 44

Elder, Paul, and Company DLB-49

The Electronic Text Center and the Electronic
Archive of Early American Fiction at the
University of Virginia Library Y-98

Eliade, Mircea 1907-1986. . . .DLB-220; CDWLB-4

Elie, Robert 1915-1973. . . . . .DLB-88

Elin Pelin 1877-1949. . . . . . . DLB-147; CDWLB-4

Eliot, George
1819-1880 . . . . .DLB-21, 35, 55; CDBLB-4

Eliot, John 1604-1690 . . . . .DLB-24

Eliot, T. S. 1888-1965
. . . . DLB-7, 10, 45, 63, 245; CDALB-5

T. S. Eliot Centennial Y-88

Eliot's Court Press DLB-170

Elizabeth I 1533-1603 . . . . .DLB-136

Elizabeth of Nassau-Saarbrücken
after 1393-1456 . . . . .DLB-179

Elizondo, Salvador 1932- DLB-145

Elizondo, Sergio 1930- DLB-82

Elkin, Stanley 1930-1995 . . . .DLB-2, 28, 218; Y-80

Elles, Dora Amy (see Wentworth, Patricia)

Ellet, Elizabeth F. 1818?-1877 . . . . DLB-30

Elliot, Ebenezer 1781-1849 . . . . DLB-96, 190

Elliot, Frances Minto (Dickinson)
1820-1898 . . . . DLB-166

Elliott, Charlotte 1789-1871 . . . . DLB-199

Elliott, George 1923- DLB-68

Elliott, George P. 1918-1980 . . . . DLB-244

Elliott, Janice 1931- DLB-14

Elliott, Sarah Barnwell 1848-1928 . . . . . . DLB-221

Elliott, Thomes and Talbot DLB-49

Elliott, William 1788-1863 . . . . DLB-3

Ellis, Alice Thomas (Anna Margaret Haycraft)
1932- DLB-194

Ellis, Edward S. 1840-1916 . . . . DLB-42

Ellis, Frederick Staridge
[publishing house] DLB-106

The George H. Ellis Company DLB-49

Ellis, Havelock 1859-1939 . . . . DLB-190

Ellison, Harlan 1934- DLB-8

Ellison, Ralph
1914-1994 . . . . DLB-2, 76, 227; Y-94; CDALB-1

Ellmann, Richard 1918-1987 . . . . . .DLB-103; Y-87

Ellroy, James 1948- DLB-226; Y-91

Elyot, Thomas 1490?-1546 . . . . DLB-136

Emanuel, James Andrew 1921- DLB-41

Emecheta, Buchi 1944- DLB-117; CDWLB-3

Emendations for *Look Homeward, Angel* Y-00

The Emergence of Black Women Writers DS-8

Emerson, Ralph Waldo 1803-1882
. . . . DLB-1, 59, 73, 183, 223; CDALB-2

Ralph Waldo Emerson in 1982 . . . . Y-82

Emerson, William 1769-1811 . . . . DLB-37

Emerson, William 1923-1997 . . . . Y-97

Emin, Fedor Aleksandrovich
circa 1735-1770 . . . . DLB-150

Empedocles fifth century B.C. DLB-176

Empson, William 1906-1984 . . . . DLB-20

Enchi Fumiko 1905-1986 . . . . DLB-182

"Encounter with the West" DLB-180

The End of English Stage Censorship,
1945-1968 . . . . DLB-13

Ende, Michael 1929-1995 . . . . DLB-75

Endō Shūsaku 1923-1996 . . . . DLB-182

Engel, Marian 1933-1985 . . . . DLB-53

Engels, Friedrich 1820-1895 . . . . DLB-129

Engle, Paul 1908- DLB-48

English, Thomas Dunn 1819-1902 . . . . . . DLB-202

English Composition and Rhetoric (1866),
by Alexander Bain [excerpt] DLB-57

The English Language: 410 to 1500 . . . . . DLB-146

Ennius 239 B.C.-169 B.C. DLB-211

Enright, D. J. 1920- DLB-27

Enright, Elizabeth 1909-1968 . . . . DLB-22

Epic and Beast Epic DLB-208

Epictetus circa 55-circa 125-130 . . . . .DLB-176

Epicurus 342/341 B.C.-271/270 B.C. DLB-176

Epps, Bernard 1936- DLB-53

Epstein, Julius 1909- and
Epstein, Philip 1909-1952 . . . . DLB-26

Equiano, Olaudah
circa 1745-1797 . . . . DLB-37, 50; DWLB-3

Olaudah Equiano and Unfinished Journeys:
The Slave-Narrative Tradition and
Twentieth-Century Continuities, by
Paul Edwards and Pauline T.
Wangman DLB-117

The E-Researcher: Possibilities and Pitfalls . . . Y-00

Eragny Press DLB-112

Erasmus, Desiderius 1467-1536 . . . . DLB-136

Erba, Luciano 1922- DLB-128

Erdrich, Louise
1954- DLB-152, 175, 206; CDALB-7

Erichsen-Brown, Gwethalyn Graham
(see Graham, Gwethalyn)

Eriugena, John Scottus circa 810-877 . . . . DLB-115

Ernst, Paul 1866-1933 . . . . DLB-66, 118

Ershov, Petr Pavlovich
1815-1869 . . . . DLB-205

Erskine, Albert 1911-1993 . . . . Y-93

Erskine, John 1879-1951 . . . . DLB-9, 102

Erskine, Mrs. Steuart ?-1948 . . . . DLB-195

Ertel', Aleksandr Ivanovich
1855-1908 . . . . DLB-238

Ervine, St. John Greer 1883-1971 . . . . DLB-10

Eschenburg, Johann Joachim 1743-1820 . . . DLB-97

Escoto, Julio 1944- DLB-145

Esdaile, Arundell 1880-1956 . . . . DLB-201

Eshleman, Clayton 1935- DLB-5

Espriu, Salvador 1913-1985 . . . . DLB-134

Ess Ess Publishing Company DLB-49

Essex House Press DLB-112

Essop, Ahmed 1931- DLB-225

Esterházy, Péter 1950- DLB-232; CDWLB-4

Estes, Eleanor 1906-1988 . . . . DLB-22

Estes and Lauriat DLB-49

Estleman, Loren D. 1952- DLB-226

Eszterhas, Joe 1944- DLB-185

Etherege, George 1636-circa 1692 . . . . . . DLB-80

Ethridge, Mark, Sr. 1896-1981 . . . . DLB-127

Ets, Marie Hall 1893- DLB-22

Etter, David 1928- DLB-105

Ettner, Johann Christoph 1654-1724 . . . . DLB-168

Eupolemius flourished circa 1095 . . . . . . DLB-148

Euripides circa 484 B.C.-407/406 B.C.
. . . . .DLB-176; CDWLB-1

Evans, Augusta Jane 1835-1909 . . . . DLB-239

Evans, Caradoc 1878-1945 . . . . DLB-162

Evans, Charles 1850-1935 . . . . DLB-187

Evans, Donald 1884-1921 . . . . DLB-54

Evans, George Henry 1805-1856 . . . . DLB-43

Evans, Hubert 1892-1986 . . . . DLB-92

Evans, M., and Company DLB-46

Evans, Mari 1923- DLB-41

Evans, Mary Ann (see Eliot, George)

Evans, Nathaniel 1742-1767 . . . . DLB-31

Evans, Sebastian 1830-1909 . . . . DLB-35

Evaristi, Marcella 1953- DLB-233

Everett, Alexander Hill 1790-1847 . . . . . . DLB-59

Everett, Edward 1794-1865 . . . . . . DLB-1, 59, 235

Everson, R. G. 1903- DLB-88

Everson, William 1912-1994 . . . . .DLB-5, 16, 212

Ewart, Gavin 1916-1995 . . . . DLB-40

Ewing, Juliana Horatia 1841-1885 . . . DLB-21, 163

The Examiner 1808-1881 . . . . DLB-110

Exley, Frederick 1929-1992 . . . . . . .DLB-143; Y-81

von Eyb, Albrecht 1420-1475 . . . . .DLB-179

Eyre and Spottiswoode DLB-106

Ezera, Regīna 1930- DLB-232

Ezzo ?-after 1065 . . . . DLB-148

F

Faber, Frederick William 1814-1863 . . . . . DLB-32

Faber and Faber Limited DLB-112

Faccio, Rena (see Aleramo, Sibilla)

Fagundo, Ana María 1938- DLB-134

Fair, Ronald L. 1932- DLB-33

Fairfax, Beatrice (see Manning, Marie)

Fairlie, Gerard 1899-1983 . . . . DLB-77

Fallada, Hans 1893-1947 . . . . DLB-56

Fancher, Betsy 1928- Y-83

Fane, Violet 1843-1905 . . . . DLB-35

Fanfrolico Press DLB-112

Fanning, Katherine 1927 . . . . .DLB-127

Fanshawe, Sir Richard 1608-1666 . . . . . . DLB-126

Fantasy Press Publishers DLB-46

Fante, John 1909-1983 . . . . .DLB-130; Y-83

Al-Farabi circa 870-950 . . . . DLB-115

Farabough, Laura 1949- DLB-228

Farah, Nuruddin 1945- DLB-125; CDWLB-3

Farber, Norma 1909-1984 . . . . DLB-61

Farigoule, Louis (see Romains, Jules)

Farjeon, Eleanor 1881-1965 . . . . DLB-160

Farley, Harriet 1812-1907 . . . . DLB-239

Farley, Walter 1920-1989 . . . . DLB-22

Farmborough, Florence 1887-1978 . . . . . . DLB-204

Farmer, Penelope 1939- DLB-161

Farmer, Philip José 1918- DLB-8

Farnaby, Thomas 1575?-1647 . . . . DLB-236

Farningham, Marianne (see Hearn, Mary Anne)

Farquhar, George circa 1677-1707 . . . . . . DLB-84

Farquharson, Martha (see Finley, Martha)

Farrar, Frederic William 1831-1903 . . . . . DLB-163

Farrar and Rinehart DLB-46

Farrar, Straus and Giroux DLB-46

Farrell, J. G. 1935-1979 . . . . DLB-14

Farrell, James T. 1904-1979 . . . DLB-4, 9, 86; DS-2

Fast, Howard 1914- DLB-9

Faulkner, George [publishing house] DLB-154

Faulkner, William 1897-1962
. . .DLB-9, 11, 44, 102; DS-2; Y-86; CDALB-5

William Faulkner Centenary Y-97

"Faulkner 100–Celebrating the Work,"
University of South Carolina, Columbia . Y-97

Impressions of William Faulkner. Y-97

Faulkner and Yoknapatawpha Conference,
Oxford, Mississippi. Y-97

Faulks, Sebastian 1953- DLB-207

Fauset, Jessie Redmon 1882-1961 . . . . .DLB-51

Faust, Irvin 1924- DLB-2, 28, 218; Y-80

Fawcett, Edgar 1847-1904 . . . . .DLB-202

Fawcett, Millicent Garrett 1847-1929 . . . . .DLB-190

Fawcett Books DLB-46

Fay, Theodore Sedgwick 1807-1898 . . . . .DLB-202

Fearing, Kenneth 1902-1961 . . . . .DLB-9

Federal Writers' Project. DLB-46

Federman, Raymond 1928- Y-80

Fedorov, Innokentii Vasil'evich
(see Omulevsky, Innokentii Vasil'evich)

Feiffer, Jules 1929- DLB-7, 44

Feinberg, Charles E. 1899-1988. . . . DLB-187; Y-88

Feind, Barthold 1678-1721 . . . . .DLB-168

Feinstein, Elaine 1930- DLB-14, 40

Feiss, Paul Louis 1875-1952 . . . . .DLB-187

Feldman, Irving 1928- DLB-169

Felipe, Léon 1884-1968 . . . . .DLB-108

Fell, Frederick, Publishers DLB-46

Felltham, Owen 1602?-1668 . . . . . . .DLB-126, 151

Felman, Soshana 1942- DLB-246

Fels, Ludwig 1946- DLB-75

Felton, Cornelius Conway 1807-1862 . .DLB-1, 235

Fenn, Harry 1837-1911 . . . . .DLB-188

Fennario, David 1947- DLB-60

Fenner, Dudley 1558?-1587? DLB-236

Fenno, Jenny 1765?-1803. . . . . .DLB-200

Fenno, John 1751-1798. . . . . .DLB-43

Fenno, R. F., and Company. DLB-49

Fenoglio, Beppe 1922-1963 . . . . .DLB-177

Fenton, Geoffrey 1539?-1608. . . . . .DLB-136

Fenton, James 1949- DLB-40

Ferber, Edna 1885-1968. . . . . .DLB-9, 28, 86

Ferdinand, Vallery III (see Salaam, Kalamu ya)

Ferguson, Sir Samuel 1810-1886 . . . . .DLB-32

Ferguson, William Scott 1875-1954 . . . . . .DLB-47

Fergusson, Robert 1750-1774 . . . . .DLB-109

Ferland, Albert 1872-1943 . . . . .DLB-92

Ferlinghetti, Lawrence
1919- DLB-5, 16; CDALB-1

Fermor, Patrick Leigh 1915- DLB-204

Fern, Fanny (see Parton, Sara Payson Willis)

Ferrars, Elizabeth 1907- DLB-87

Ferré, Rosario 1942- DLB-145

Ferret, E., and Company DLB-49

Ferrier, Susan 1782-1854 . . . . .DLB-116

Ferril, Thomas Hornsby 1896-1988 . . . . .DLB-206

Ferrini, Vincent 1913- DLB-48

Ferron, Jacques 1921-1985. . . . . .DLB-60

Ferron, Madeleine 1922- DLB-53

Ferrucci, Franco 1936- DLB-196

Fetridge and Company DLB-49

Feuchtersleben, Ernst Freiherr von
1806-1849 . . . . .DLB-133

Feuchtwanger, Lion 1884-1958 . . . . .DLB-66

Feuerbach, Ludwig 1804-1872 . . . . .DLB-133

Feuillet, Octave 1821-1890. . . . . .DLB-192

Feydeau, Georges 1862-1921. . . . . .DLB-192

Fichte, Johann Gottlieb 1762-1814. . . . . . .DLB-90

Ficke, Arthur Davison 1883-1945 . . . . . . .DLB-54

Fiction Best-Sellers, 1910-1945. . . . . .DLB-9

Fiction into Film, 1928-1975: A List of Movies
Based on the Works of Authors in
British Novelists, 1930-1959 . . . . .DLB-15

Fiedler, Leslie A. 1917- DLB-28, 67

Field, Barron 1789-1846. . . . . .DLB-230

Field, Edward 1924- DLB-105

Field, Michael
(Katherine Harris Bradley [1846-1914]
and Edith Emma Cooper
[1862-1913]) DLB-240

"The Poetry File". DLB-105

Field, Eugene
1850-1895 . . . . DLB-23, 42, 140; DS-13

Field, John 1545?-1588 . . . . .DLB-167

Field, Marshall, III 1893-1956. . . . . .DLB-127

Field, Marshall, IV 1916-1965 . . . . .DLB-127

Field, Marshall, V 1941- DLB-127

Field, Nathan 1587-1619 or 1620. . . . . . . .DLB-58

Field, Rachel 1894-1942. . . . . .DLB-9, 22

A Field Guide to Recent Schools of American
Poetry Y-86

Fielding, Helen 1958- DLB-231

Fielding, Henry
1707-1754 . . . . . . .DLB-39, 84, 101; CDBLB-2

"Defense of Amelia" (1752) DLB-39

From The History of the Adventures of
Joseph Andrews (1742). DLB-39

Preface to Joseph Andrews (1742). DLB-39

Preface to Sarah Fielding's The Adventures
of David Simple (1744). DLB-39

Preface to Sarah Fielding's Familiar Letters
(1747) [excerpt] DLB-39

Fielding, Sarah 1710-1768. . . . . .DLB-39

Preface to The Cry (1754) DLB-39

Fields, Annie Adams 1834-1915 . . . . . . .DLB-221

Fields, James T. 1817-1881. . . . . .DLB-1, 235

Fields, Julia 1938- DLB-41

Fields, Osgood and Company DLB-49

Fields, W. C. 1880-1946 . . . . .DLB-44

Fifty Penguin Years Y-85

Figes, Eva 1932- DLB-14

Figuera, Angela 1902-1984 . . . . .DLB-108

Filmer, Sir Robert 1586-1653. . . . . .DLB-151

Filson, John circa 1753-1788. . . . . .DLB-37

Finch, Anne, Countess of Winchilsea
1661-1720 . . . . .DLB-95

Finch, Robert 1900- DLB-88

Findley, Timothy 1930- DLB-53

Finlay, Ian Hamilton 1925- DLB-40

Finley, Martha 1828-1909 . . . . .DLB-42

Finn, Elizabeth Anne (McCaul)
1825-1921 . . . . .DLB-166

Finnegan, Seamus 1949- DLB-245

Finney, Jack 1911-1995 . . . . .DLB-8

Finney, Walter Braden (see Finney, Jack)

Firbank, Ronald 1886-1926 . . . . .DLB-36

Firmin, Giles 1615-1697. . . . . .DLB-24

First Edition Library/Collectors'
Reprints, Inc.. Y-91

Fischart, Johann
1546 or 1547-1590 or 1591 . . . . .DLB-179

Fischer, Karoline Auguste Fernandine
1764-1842 . . . . .DLB-94

Fischer, Tibor 1959- DLB-231

Fish, Stanley 1938- DLB-67

Fishacre, Richard 1205-1248 . . . . .DLB-115

Fisher, Clay (see Allen, Henry W.)

Fisher, Dorothy Canfield 1879-1958 . . .DLB-9, 102

Fisher, Leonard Everett 1924- DLB-61

Fisher, Roy 1930- DLB-40

Fisher, Rudolph 1897-1934 . . . . .DLB-51, 102

Fisher, Steve 1913-1980. . . . . .DLB-226

Fisher, Sydney George 1856-1927. . . . . . .DLB-47

Fisher, Vardis 1895-1968. . . . . .DLB-9, 206

Fiske, John 1608-1677 . . . . .DLB-24

Fiske, John 1842-1901 . . . . .DLB-47, 64

Fitch, Thomas circa 1700-1774. . . . . .DLB-31

Fitch, William Clyde 1865-1909 . . . . .DLB-7

FitzGerald, Edward 1809-1883 . . . . .DLB-32

Fitzgerald, F. Scott 1896-1940
. . . . .DLB-4, 9, 86, 219; Y-81, Y-92;
DS-1, 15, 16; CDALB-4

F. Scott Fitzgerald Centenary
Celebrations Y-96

F. Scott Fitzgerald Inducted into the American
Poets' Corner at St. John the Divine;
Ezra Pound Banned Y-99

"F. Scott Fitzgerald: St. Paul's Native Son
and Distinguished American Writer":
University of Minnesota Conference,
29-31 October 1982 . . . . Y-82

First International F. Scott Fitzgerald
Conference Y-92

Fitzgerald, Penelope 1916- DLB-14, 194

Fitzgerald, Robert 1910-1985. . . . . Y-80

Fitzgerald, Thomas 1819-1891. . . . . .DLB-23

Fitzgerald, Zelda Sayre 1900-1948. . . . . . . Y-84

Fitzhugh, Louise 1928-1974 . . . . .DLB-52

Fitzhugh, William circa 1651-1701. . . . . . .DLB-24

Flagg, James Montgomery 1877-1960 . . . .DLB-188

Flanagan, Thomas 1923- Y-80

Flanner, Hildegarde 1899-1987. . . . . DLB-48

Flanner, Janet 1892-1978. . . . . DLB-4

Flannery, Peter 1951- DLB-233

Flaubert, Gustave 1821-1880 . . . . DLB-119

Flavin, Martin 1883-1967 . . . . DLB-9

Fleck, Konrad
(flourished circa 1220) DLB-138

Flecker, James Elroy 1884-1915 . . . . . . DLB-10, 19

Fleeson, Doris 1901-1970 . . . . DLB-29

Fleißer, Marieluise 1901-1974. . . . . . . DLB-56, 124

Fleischer, Nat 1887-1972 . . . . DLB-241

Fleming, Abraham 1552?-1607 . . . . DLB-236

Fleming, Ian 1908-1964 . . DLB-87, 201; CDBLB-7

Fleming, Paul 1609-1640 . . . . DLB-164

Fleming, Peter 1907-1971 . . . . DLB-195

Fletcher, Giles, the Elder 1546-1611 . . . . . DLB-136

Fletcher, Giles, the Younger
1585 or 1586-1623 . . . . DLB-121

Fletcher, J. S. 1863-1935 . . . . DLB-70

Fletcher, John (see Beaumont, Francis)

Fletcher, John Gould 1886-1950. . . . . . DLB-4, 45

Fletcher, Phineas 1582-1650 . . . . DLB-121

Flieg, Helmut (see Heym, Stefan)

Flint, F. S. 1885-1960 . . . . DLB-19

Flint, Timothy 1780-1840 . . . . DLB-73, 186

Flores-Williams, Jason 1969- DLB-209

Florio, John 1553?-1625 . . . . .DLB-172

Fo, Dario 1926- Y-97

Foix, J. V. 1893-1987 . . . . DLB-134

Foley, Martha (see Burnett, Whit, and Martha Foley)

Folger, Henry Clay 1857-1930 . . . . DLB-140

Folio Society DLB-112

Follen, Charles 1796-1840. . . . . DLB-235

Follen, Eliza Lee (Cabot) 1787-1860 . . . DLB-1, 235

Follett, Ken 1949- DLB-87; Y-81

Follett Publishing Company DLB-46

Folsom, John West [publishing house] DLB-49

Folz, Hans
between 1435 and 1440-1513. . . . . . .DLB-179

Fontane, Theodor
1819-1898. . . . . DLB-129; CDWLB-2

Fontes, Montserrat 1940- DLB-209

Fonvisin, Denis Ivanovich
1744 or 1745-1792 . . . . DLB-150

Foote, Horton 1916- DLB-26

Foote, Mary Hallock
1847-1938. . . . . DLB-186, 188, 202, 221

Foote, Samuel 1721-1777. . . . . DLB-89

Foote, Shelby 1916- DLB-2, 17

Forbes, Calvin 1945- DLB-41

Forbes, Ester 1891-1967 . . . . DLB-22

Forbes, Rosita 1893?-1967 . . . . DLB-195

Forbes and Company DLB-49

Force, Peter 1790-1868 . . . . DLB-30

Forché, Carolyn 1950- DLB-5, 193

Ford, Charles Henri 1913- DLB-4, 48

Ford, Corey 1902-1969. . . . . DLB-11

Ford, Ford Madox
1873-1939. . . . . . . DLB-34, 98, 162; CDBLB-6

Ford, J. B., and Company. DLB-49

Ford, Jesse Hill 1928-1996 . . . . DLB-6

Ford, John 1586-? DLB-58; CDBLB-1

Ford, R. A. D. 1915- DLB-88

Ford, Richard 1944- DLB-227

Ford, Worthington C. 1858-1941. . . . . . . DLB-47

Fords, Howard, and Hulbert DLB-49

Foreman, Carl 1914-1984 . . . . DLB-26

Forester, C. S. 1899-1966 . . . . DLB-191

Forester, Frank (see Herbert, Henry William)

Forman, Harry Buxton 1842-1917 . . . . . . DLB-184

Fornés, María Irene 1930- DLB-7

Forrest, Leon 1937-1997 . . . . DLB-33

Forster, E. M.
1879-1970 . . . . DLB-34, 98, 162, 178, 195;
DS-10; CDBLB-6

Forster, Georg 1754-1794 . . . . DLB-94

Forster, John 1812-1876 . . . . DLB-144

Forster, Margaret 1938- DLB-155

Forsyth, Frederick 1938- DLB-87

Forten, Charlotte L. 1837-1914 . . . . . . DLB-50, 239

Charlotte Forten: Pages from
her Diary DLB-50

Fortini, Franco 1917- DLB-128

Fortune, Mary ca. 1833-ca. 1910 . . . . DLB-230

Fortune, T. Thomas 1856-1928 . . . . DLB-23

Fosdick, Charles Austin 1842-1915 . . . . . DLB-42

Foster, Genevieve 1893-1979 . . . . DLB-61

Foster, Hannah Webster 1758-1840 . . .DLB-37, 200

Foster, John 1648-1681 . . . . DLB-24

Foster, Michael 1904-1956 . . . . DLB-9

Foster, Myles Birket 1825-1899 . . . . DLB-184

Foucault, Michel 1926-1984 . . . . DLB-242

Foulis, Robert and Andrew / R. and A.
[publishing house] DLB-154

Fouqué, Caroline de la Motte
1774-1831. . . . . DLB-90

Fouqué, Friedrich de la Motte
1777-1843 . . . . DLB-90

Four Seas Company DLB-46

Four Winds Press DLB-46

Fournier, Henri Alban (see Alain-Fournier)

Fowler and Wells Company DLB-49

Fowles, John
1926- DLB-14, 139, 207; CDBLB-8

Fox, John 1939- DLB-245

Fox, John, Jr. 1862 or 1863-1919 . . . DLB-9; DS-13

Fox, Paula 1923- DLB-52

Fox, Richard K. [publishing house] DLB-49

Fox, Richard Kyle 1846-1922. . . . . DLB-79

Fox, William Price 1926- DLB-2; Y-81

Foxe, John 1517-1587 . . . . DLB-132

Fraenkel, Michael 1896-1957 . . . . DLB-4

France, Anatole 1844-1924 . . . . DLB-123

France, Richard 1938- DLB-7

Francis, C. S. [publishing house]. DLB-49

Francis, Convers 1795-1863 . . . . DLB-1, 235

Francis, Dick 1920- DLB-87

Francis, Sir Frank 1901-1988 . . . . DLB-201

Francis, Jeffrey, Lord 1773-1850. . . . . . . .DLB-107

François 1863-1910. . . . . DLB-92

François, Louise von 1817-1893 . . . . DLB-129

Franck, Sebastian 1499-1542 . . . . .DLB-179

Francke, Kuno 1855-1930 . . . . DLB-71

Frank, Bruno 1887-1945 . . . . DLB-118

Frank, Leonhard 1882-1961 . . . . DLB-56, 118

Frank, Melvin (see Panama, Norman)

Frank, Waldo 1889-1967 . . . . DLB-9, 63

Franken, Rose 1895?-1988 . . . . . .DLB-228, Y-84

Franklin, Benjamin
1706-1790 . . . . DLB-24, 43, 73, 183; CDALB-2

Franklin, James 1697-1735 . . . . DLB-43

Franklin, Miles 1879-1954 . . . . DLB-230

Franklin Library DLB-46

Frantz, Ralph Jules 1902-1979 . . . . DLB-4

Franzos, Karl Emil 1848-1904 . . . . DLB-129

Fraser, G. S. 1915-1980 . . . . DLB-27

Fraser, Kathleen 1935- DLB-169

Frattini, Alberto 1922- DLB-128

Frau Ava ?-1127 . . . . DLB-148

Fraunce, Abraham 1558?-1592 or 1593 . . DLB-236

Frayn, Michael 1933- DLB-13, 14, 194, 245

Frederic, Harold
1856-1898 . . . . DLB-12, 23; DS-13

Freeling, Nicolas 1927- DLB-87

Freeman, Douglas Southall
1886-1953 . . . . .DLB-17; DS-17

Freeman, Legh Richmond 1842-1915 . . . . DLB-23

Freeman, Mary E. Wilkins
1852-1930 . . . . .DLB-12, 78, 221

Freeman, R. Austin 1862-1943. . . . . DLB-70

Freidank circa 1170-circa 1233 . . . . DLB-138

Freiligrath, Ferdinand 1810-1876 . . . . . . DLB-133

Frémont, John Charles 1813-1890 . . . . . . DLB-186

Frémont, John Charles 1813-1890 and
Frémont, Jessie Benton 1834-1902. . . DLB-183

French, Alice 1850-1934 . . . . .DLB-74; DS-13

French Arthurian Literature DLB-208

French, David 1939- DLB-53

French, Evangeline 1869-1960 . . . . DLB-195

French, Francesca 1871-1960 . . . . DLB-195

French, James [publishing house] DLB-49

French, Samuel [publishing house] DLB-49

Samuel French, Limited DLB-106

Freneau, Philip 1752-1832 . . . . .DLB-37, 43

Freni, Melo 1934- DLB-128

Freshfield, Douglas W. 1845-1934 . . . . . .DLB-174

Freytag, Gustav 1816-1895. . . . . DLB-129

Fried, Erich 1921-1988 . . . . DLB-85

Friedan, Betty 1921- DLB-246

Friedman, Bruce Jay 1930- DLB-2, 28, 244

Friedrich von Hausen circa 1171-1190. . . .DLB-138

Friel, Brian 1929- DLB-13

Friend, Krebs 1895?-1967? DLB-4

Fries, Fritz Rudolf 1935- DLB-75

Fringe and Alternative Theater in
    Great Britain DLB-13

Frisch, Max
    1911-1991 . . . . .DLB-69, 124; CDWLB-2

Frischlin, Nicodemus 1547-1590 . . . . .DLB-179

Frischmuth, Barbara 1941- DLB-85

Fritz, Jean 1915- DLB-52

Froissart, Jean circa 1337-circa 1404. . . . .DLB-208

Fromentin, Eugene 1820-1876 . . . . .DLB-123

Frontinus circa A.D. 35-A.D. 103/104 . . . .DLB-211

Frost, A. B. 1851-1928 . . . . .DLB-188; DS-13

Frost, Robert
    1874-1963 . . . . .DLB-54; DS-7; CDALB-4

Frothingham, Octavius Brooks
    1822-1895 . . . . .DLB-1, 243

Froude, James Anthony
    1818-1894 . . . . DLB-18, 57, 144

Fruitlands 1843-1844 . . . . .DLB-223

Fry, Christopher 1907- DLB-13

Fry, Roger 1866-1934 . . . . DS-10

Fry, Stephen 1957- DLB-207

Frye, Northrop 1912-1991 . . . . DLB-67, 68, 246

Fuchs, Daniel 1909-1993 . . . . . DLB-9, 26, 28; Y-93

Fuentes, Carlos 1928- DLB-113; CDWLB-3

Fuertes, Gloria 1918- DLB-108

Fugard, Athol 1932- DLB-225

The Fugitives and the Agrarians:
    The First Exhibition Y-85

Fujiwara no Shunzei 1114-1204 . . . . .DLB-203

Fujiwara no Tameaki 1230s?-1290s? DLB-203

Fujiwara no Tameie 1198-1275 . . . . .DLB-203

Fujiwara no Teika 1162-1241 . . . . .DLB-203

Fulbecke, William 1560-1603? DLB-172

Fuller, Charles H., Jr. 1939- DLB-38

Fuller, Henry Blake 1857-1929 . . . . .DLB-12

Fuller, John 1937- DLB-40

Fuller, Margaret (see Fuller, Sarah)

Fuller, Roy 1912-1991 . . . . .DLB-15, 20

Fuller, Samuel 1912- DLB-26

Fuller, Sarah 1810-1850
    . . . . .DLB-1, 59, 73, 183, 223, 239; CDALB-2

Fuller, Thomas 1608-1661 . . . . .DLB-151

Fullerton, Hugh 1873-1945 . . . . .DLB-171

Fullwood, William flourished 1568 . . . . . .DLB-236

Fulton, Alice 1952- DLB-193

Fulton, Len 1934- Y-86

Fulton, Robin 1937- DLB-40

Furbank, P. N. 1920- DLB-155

Furman, Laura 1945- Y-86

Furness, Horace Howard
    1833-1912 . . . . .DLB-64

Furness, William Henry
    1802-1896 . . . . .DLB-1, 235

Furnivall, Frederick James
    1825-1910 . . . . .DLB-184

Furphy, Joseph
    (Tom Collins) 1843-1912 . . . . .DLB-230

Furthman, Jules 1888-1966 . . . . .DLB-26

Furui Yoshikichi 1937- DLB-182

Fushimi, Emperor 1265-1317 . . . . .DLB-203

Futabatei, Shimei
    (Hasegawa Tatsunosuke)
    1864-1909 . . . . .DLB-180

The Future of the Novel (1899), by
    Henry James .DLB-18

Fyleman, Rose 1877-1957 . . . . .DLB-160

G

Gadda, Carlo Emilio 1893-1973 . . . . .DLB-177

Gaddis, William 1922-1998 . . . . .DLB-2, Y-99

Gág, Wanda 1893-1946 . . . . .DLB-22

Gagarin, Ivan Sergeevich 1814-1882 . . . . .DLB-198

Gagnon, Madeleine 1938- DLB-60

Gaine, Hugh 1726-1807 . . . . .DLB-43

Gaine, Hugh [publishing house] DLB-49

Gaines, Ernest J.
    1933- DLB-2, 33, 152; Y-80; CDALB-6

Gaiser, Gerd 1908-1976 . . . . .DLB-69

Gaitskill, Mary 1954- DLB-244

Galarza, Ernesto 1905-1984 . . . . .DLB-122

Galaxy Science Fiction Novels DLB-46

Gale, Zona 1874-1938 . . . . DLB-9, 228, 78

Galen of Pergamon 129-after 210 . . . . . . .DLB-176

Gales, Winifred Marshall 1761-1839 . . . . .DLB-200

Gall, Louise von 1815-1855 . . . . .DLB-133

Gallagher, Tess 1943- DLB-120, 212, 244

Gallagher, Wes 1911- DLB-127

Gallagher, William Davis 1808-1894 . . . . . .DLB-73

Gallant, Mavis 1922- DLB-53

Gallegos, María Magdalena 1935- DLB-209

Gallico, Paul 1897-1976 . . . . DLB-9, 171

Gallop, Jane 1952- DLB-246

Galloway, Grace Growden 1727-1782 . . . .DLB-200

Gallup, Donald 1913- DLB-187

Galsworthy, John 1867-1933
    . . . . . .DLB-10, 34, 98, 162; DS-16; CDBLB-5

Galt, John 1779-1839 . . . . .DLB-99, 116

Galton, Sir Francis 1822-1911 . . . . .DLB-166

Galvin, Brendan 1938- DLB-5

Gambit DLB-46

Gamboa, Reymundo 1948- DLB-122

Gammer Gurton's Needle DLB-62

Gan, Elena Andreevna (Zeneida R-va)
    1814-1842 . . . . .DLB-198

Gannett, Frank E. 1876-1957 . . . . .DLB-29

Gao Xingjian 1940- Y-00

Gaos, Vicente 1919-1980 . . . . .DLB-134

García, Andrew 1854?-1943 . . . . .DLB-209

García, Lionel G. 1935- DLB-82

García, Richard 1941- DLB-209

García-Camarillo, Cecilio 1943- DLB-209

García Lorca, Federico 1898-1936 . . . . . .DLB-108

García Márquez, Gabriel
    1928- DLB-113; Y-82; CDWLB-3

Gardam, Jane 1928- DLB-14, 161, 231

Garden, Alexander circa 1685-1756 . . . . . .DLB-31

Gardiner, John Rolfe 1936- DLB-244

Gardiner, Margaret Power Farmer
    (see Blessington, Marguerite, Countess of)

Gardner, John
    1933-1982 . . . . .DLB-2; Y-82; CDALB-7

Garfield, Leon 1921-1996 . . . . .DLB-161

Garis, Howard R. 1873-1962 . . . . .DLB-22

Garland, Hamlin 1860-1940 . . DLB-12, 71, 78, 186

Garneau, Francis-Xavier 1809-1866 . . . . . .DLB-99

Garneau, Hector de Saint-Denys
    1912-1943 . . . . .DLB-88

Garneau, Michel 1939- DLB-53

Garner, Alan 1934- DLB-161

Garner, Hugh 1913-1979 . . . . .DLB-68

Garnett, David 1892-1981 . . . . .DLB-34

Garnett, Eve 1900-1991 . . . . .DLB-160

Garnett, Richard 1835-1906 . . . . .DLB-184

Garrard, Lewis H. 1829-1887 . . . . .DLB-186

Garraty, John A. 1920- DLB-17

Garrett, George
    1929- DLB-2, 5, 130, 152; Y-83

Fellowship of Southern Writers Y-98

Garrett, John Work 1872-1942 . . . . .DLB-187

Garrick, David 1717-1779 . . . . .DLB-84, 213

Garrison, William Lloyd
    1805-1879 . . . . .DLB-1, 43, 235; CDALB-2

Garro, Elena 1920-1998 . . . . .DLB-145

Garth, Samuel 1661-1719 . . . . .DLB-95

Garve, Andrew 1908- DLB-87

Gary, Romain 1914-1980 . . . . .DLB-83

Gascoigne, George 1539?-1577 . . . . .DLB-136

Gascoyne, David 1916- DLB-20

Gaskell, Elizabeth Cleghorn
    1810-1865 . . . . . .DLB-21, 144, 159; CDBLB-4

Gaspey, Thomas 1788-1871 . . . . .DLB-116

Gass, William H. 1924- DLB-2, 227

Gates, Doris 1901- DLB-22

Gates, Henry Louis, Jr. 1950- DLB-67

Gates, Lewis E. 1860-1924 . . . . .DLB-71

Gatto, Alfonso 1909-1976 . . . . .DLB-114

Gault, William Campbell 1910-1995 . . . . .DLB-226

Gaunt, Mary 1861-1942 . . . . DLB-174, 230

Gautier, Théophile 1811-1872 . . . . .DLB-119

Gauvreau, Claude 1925-1971 . . . . .DLB-88

The Gawain-Poet
    flourished circa 1350-1400 . . . . .DLB-146

Gay, Ebenezer 1696-1787 . . . . .DLB-24

Gay, John 1685-1732 . . . . .DLB-84, 95

Gayarré, Charles E. A. 1805-1895 . . . . . . DLB-30

Gaylord, Charles [publishing house] DLB-49

Gaylord, Edward King 1873-1974 . . . . . . DLB-127

Gaylord, Edward Lewis 1919- DLB-127

Geda, Sigitas 1943- DLB-232

Geddes, Gary 1940- DLB-60

Geddes, Virgil 1897- DLB-4

Gedeon (Georgii Andreevich Krinovsky)
    circa 1730-1763 . . . . DLB-150

Gee, Maggie 1948- DLB-207

Gee, Shirley 1932- DLB-245

Geßner, Salomon 1730-1788 . . . . DLB-97

Geibel, Emanuel 1815-1884 . . . . DLB-129

Geiogamah, Hanay 1945- DLB-175

Geis, Bernard, Associates DLB-46

Geisel, Theodor Seuss 1904-1991 . . . DLB-61; Y-91

Gelb, Arthur 1924- DLB-103

Gelb, Barbara 1926- DLB-103

Gelber, Jack 1932- DLB-7, 228

Gelinas, Gratien 1909- DLB-88

Gellert, Christian Füerchtegott
    1715-1769 . . . . DLB-97

Gellhorn, Martha 1908-1998 . . . . Y-82, Y-98

Gems, Pam 1925- DLB-13

Genet, Jean 1910-1986 . . . . DLB-72; Y-86

Genette, Gérard 1930- DLB-242

Genevoix, Maurice 1890-1980 . . . . DLB-65

Genovese, Eugene D. 1930- DLB-17

Gent, Peter 1942- Y-82

Geoffrey of Monmouth
    circa 1100-1155 . . . . DLB-146

George, Henry 1839-1897 . . . . DLB-23

George, Jean Craighead 1919- DLB-52

George, W. L. 1882-1926 . . . . DLB-197

George III, King of Great Britain and Ireland
    1738-1820 . . . . DLB-213

George V. Higgins to Julian Symons Y-99

Georgslied 896? DLB-148

Gerber, Merrill Joan 1938- DLB-218

Gerhardie, William 1895-1977 . . . . DLB-36

Gerhardt, Paul 1607-1676 . . . . DLB-164

Gérin, Winifred 1901-1981 . . . . DLB-155

Gérin-Lajoie, Antoine 1824-1882 . . . . DLB-99

German Drama 800-1280 . . . . DLB-138

German Drama from Naturalism
    to Fascism: 1889-1933 . . . . DLB-118

German Literature and Culture from Charlemagne
    to the Early Courtly Period
    . . . . DLB-148; CDWLB-2

German Radio Play, The DLB-124

German Transformation from the Baroque
    to the Enlightenment, The DLB-97

The Germanic Epic and Old English
    Heroic Poetry: *Widsith, Waldere,*
    and *The Fight at Finnsburg* DLB-146

Germanophilism, by Hans Kohn DLB-66

Gernsback, Hugo 1884-1967 . . . . DLB-8, 137

Gerould, Katharine Fullerton
    1879-1944 . . . . DLB-78

Gerrish, Samuel [publishing house] DLB-49

Gerrold, David 1944- DLB-8

The Ira Gershwin Centenary Y-96

Gerson, Jean 1363-1429 . . . . DLB-208

Gersonides 1288-1344 . . . . DLB-115

Gerstäcker, Friedrich 1816-1872 . . . . DLB-129

Gerstenberg, Heinrich Wilhelm von
    1737-1823 . . . . DLB-97

Gervinus, Georg Gottfried
    1805-1871 . . . . DLB-133

Geston, Mark S. 1946- DLB-8

Al-Ghazali 1058-1111 . . . . DLB-115

Gibbings, Robert 1889-1958 . . . . DLB-195

Gibbon, Edward 1737-1794 . . . . DLB-104

Gibbon, John Murray 1875-1952 . . . . DLB-92

Gibbon, Lewis Grassic (see Mitchell, James Leslie)

Gibbons, Floyd 1887-1939 . . . . DLB-25

Gibbons, Reginald 1947- DLB-120

Gibbons, William ?-? DLB-73

Gibson, Charles Dana
    1867-1944 . . . . DLB-188; DS-13

Gibson, Graeme 1934- DLB-53

Gibson, Margaret 1944- DLB-120

Gibson, Margaret Dunlop 1843-1920 . . . . . DLB-174

Gibson, Wilfrid 1878-1962 . . . . DLB-19

Gibson, William 1914- DLB-7

Gide, André 1869-1951 . . . . DLB-65

Giguère, Diane 1937- DLB-53

Giguère, Roland 1929- DLB-60

Gil de Biedma, Jaime 1929-1990 . . . . DLB-108

Gil-Albert, Juan 1906- DLB-134

Gilbert, Anthony 1899-1973 . . . . DLB-77

Gilbert, Sir Humphrey 1537-1583 . . . . . . DLB-136

Gilbert, Michael 1912- DLB-87

Gilbert, Sandra M. 1936- DLB-120, 246

Gilchrist, Alexander 1828-1861 . . . . DLB-144

Gilchrist, Ellen 1935- DLB-130

Gilder, Jeannette L. 1849-1916 . . . . DLB-79

Gilder, Richard Watson 1844-1909 . . . DLB-64, 79

Gildersleeve, Basil 1831-1924 . . . . DLB-71

Giles of Rome circa 1243-1316 . . . . DLB-115

Giles, Henry 1809-1882 . . . . DLB-64

Gilfillan, George 1813-1878 . . . . DLB-144

Gill, Eric 1882-1940 . . . . DLB-98

Gill, Sarah Prince 1728-1771 . . . . DLB-200

Gill, William F., Company DLB-49

Gillespie, A. Lincoln, Jr. 1895-1950 . . . . . DLB-4

Gilliam, Florence ?-? DLB-4

Gilliatt, Penelope 1932-1993 . . . . DLB-14

Gillott, Jacky 1939-1980 . . . . DLB-14

Gilman, Caroline H. 1794-1888 . . . . DLB-3, 73

Gilman, Charlotte Perkins 1860-1935 . . . DLB-221

Gilman, W. and J. [publishing house] DLB-49

Gilmer, Elizabeth Meriwether 1861-1951 . . DLB-29

Gilmer, Francis Walker 1790-1826 . . . . DLB-37

Gilroy, Frank D. 1925- DLB-7

Gimferrer, Pere (Pedro) 1945- DLB-134

Gingrich, Arnold 1903-1976 . . . . .DLB-137

Ginsberg, Allen
    1926-1997 . . . .DLB-5, 16, 169, 237; CDALB-1

Ginzburg, Natalia 1916-1991 . . . . .DLB-177

Ginzkey, Franz Karl 1871-1963 . . . . DLB-81

Gioia, Dana 1950- DLB-120

Giono, Jean 1895-1970 . . . . DLB-72

Giotti, Virgilio 1885-1957 . . . . DLB-114

Giovanni, Nikki 1943- . . . DLB-5, 41; CDALB-7

Gipson, Lawrence Henry 1880-1971 . . . . .DLB-17

Girard, Rodolphe 1879-1956 . . . . DLB-92

Giraudoux, Jean 1882-1944 . . . . DLB-65

Gissing, George 1857-1903 . . . . . .DLB-18, 135, 184

The Place of Realism in Fiction (1895) DLB-18

Giudici, Giovanni 1924- DLB-128

Giuliani, Alfredo 1924- DLB-128

Glackens, William J. 1870-1938 . . . . DLB-188

Gladstone, William Ewart
    1809-1898 . . . . .DLB-57, 184

Glaeser, Ernst 1902-1963 . . . . DLB-69

Glancy, Diane 1941- DLB-175

Glanville, Brian 1931- DLB-15, 139

Glapthorne, Henry 1610-1643? DLB-58

Glasgow, Ellen 1873-1945 . . . . DLB-9, 12

Glasier, Katharine Bruce 1867-1950 . . . . . DLB-190

Glaspell, Susan 1876-1948 . . . . . .DLB-7, 9, 78, 228

Glass, Montague 1877-1934 . . . . DLB-11

Glassco, John 1909-1981 . . . . DLB-68

Glauser, Friedrich 1896-1938 . . . . DLB-56

F. Gleason's Publishing Hall DLB-49

Gleim, Johann Wilhelm Ludwig
    1719-1803 . . . . DLB-97

Glendinning, Victoria 1937- DLB-155

The Cult of Biography
    Excerpts from the Second Folio Debate:
    "Biographies are generally a disease of
    English Literature" Y-86

Glinka, Fedor Nikolaevich 1786-1880 . . . . DLB-205

Glover, Richard 1712-1785 . . . . DLB-95

Glück, Louise 1943- DLB-5

Glyn, Elinor 1864-1943 . . . . DLB-153

Gnedich, Nikolai Ivanovich 1784-1833 . . . DLB-205

Gobineau, Joseph-Arthur de
    1816-1882 . . . . DLB-123

Godber, John 1956- DLB-233

Godbout, Jacques 1933- DLB-53

Goddard, Morrill 1865-1937 . . . . .DLB-25

Goddard, William 1740-1817 . . . . DLB-43

Godden, Rumer 1907-1998 . . . . DLB-161

Godey, Louis A. 1804-1878 . . . . DLB-73

Godey and McMichael DLB-49

Godfrey, Dave 1938- DLB-60

Godfrey, Thomas 1736-1763 . . . . .DLB-31

Godine, David R., Publisher DLB-46

Godkin, E. L. 1831-1902 . . . . .DLB-79

Godolphin, Sidney 1610-1643 . . . . .DLB-126

Godwin, Gail 1937- DLB-6, 234

Godwin, M. J., and Company DLB-154

Godwin, Mary Jane Clairmont
　　1766-1841 . . . . .DLB-163

Godwin, Parke 1816-1904 . . . . .DLB-3, 64

Godwin, William 1756-1836
　　. . . . . .DLB-39, 104, 142, 158, 163; CDBLB-3

Preface to *St. Leon* (1799) DLB-39

Goering, Reinhard 1887-1936 . . . . .DLB-118

Goes, Albrecht 1908- DLB-69

Goethe, Johann Wolfgang von
　　1749-1832 . . . . .DLB-94; CDWLB-2

Goetz, Curt 1888-1960 . . . . .DLB-124

Goffe, Thomas circa 1592-1629 . . . . .DLB-58

Goffstein, M. B. 1940- DLB-61

Gogarty, Oliver St. John 1878-1957 . . . .DLB-15, 19

Gogol, Nikolai Vasil'evich 1809-1852 . . . .DLB-198

Goines, Donald 1937-1974 . . . . .DLB-33

Gold, Herbert 1924- DLB-2; Y-81

Gold, Michael 1893-1967 . . . . .DLB-9, 28

Goldbarth, Albert 1948- DLB-120

Goldberg, Dick 1947- DLB-7

Golden Cockerel Press DLB-112

Golding, Arthur 1536-1606 . . . . .DLB-136

Golding, Louis 1895-1958 . . . . .DLB-195

Golding, William
　　1911-1993 . . . . .DLB-15, 100; Y-83; CDBLB-7

Goldman, Emma 1869-1940 . . . . .DLB-221

Goldman, William 1931- DLB-44

Goldring, Douglas 1887-1960 . . . . .DLB-197

Goldsmith, Oliver 1730?-1774
　　. . . . . .DLB-39, 89, 104, 109, 142; CDBLB-2

Goldsmith, Oliver 1794-1861 . . . . .DLB-99

Goldsmith Publishing Company DLB-46

Goldstein, Richard 1944- DLB-185

Gollancz, Sir Israel 1864-1930 . . . . .DLB-201

Gollancz, Victor, Limited DLB-112

Gombrowicz, Witold
　　1904-1969 . . . . .DLB-215; CDWLB-4

Gómez-Quiñones, Juan 1942- DLB-122

Gomme, Laurence James
　　[publishing house] DLB-46

Goncharov, Ivan Aleksandrovich
　　1812-1891 . . . . .DLB-238

Goncourt, Edmond de 1822-1896 . . . . . . .DLB-123

Goncourt, Jules de 1830-1870 . . . . .DLB-123

Gonzales, Rodolfo "Corky" 1928- DLB-122

González, Angel 1925- DLB-108

Gonzalez, Genaro 1949- DLB-122

Gonzalez, Ray 1952- DLB-122

Gonzales-Berry, Erlinda 1942- DLB-209

　　"Chicano Language" DLB-82

González de Mireles, Jovita
　　1899-1983 . . . . .DLB-122

González-T., César A. 1931- DLB-82

Goodbye, Gutenberg? A Lecture at the
　　New York Public Library,
　　18 April 1995, by Donald Lamm Y-95

Goodis, David 1917-1967 . . . . .DLB-226

Goodison, Lorna 1947- DLB-157

Goodman, Allegra 1967- DLB-244

Goodman, Paul 1911-1972 . . . . .DLB-130, 246

The Goodman Theatre DLB-7

Goodrich, Frances 1891-1984 and
　　Hackett, Albert 1900-1995 . . . . .DLB-26

Goodrich, Samuel Griswold
　　1793-1860 . . . . .DLB-1, 42, 73, 243

Goodrich, S. G. [publishing house] DLB-49

Goodspeed, C. E., and Company DLB-49

Goodwin, Stephen 1943- Y-82

Googe, Barnabe 1540-1594 . . . . .DLB-132

Gookin, Daniel 1612-1687 . . . . .DLB-24

Goran, Lester 1928- DLB-244

Gordimer, Nadine 1923- DLB-225; Y-91

Gordon, Adam Lindsay 1833-1870 . . . . . .DLB-230

Gordon, Caroline
　　1895-1981 . . . . . . .DLB-4, 9, 102; DS-17; Y-81

Gordon, Giles 1940- DLB-14, 139, 207

Gordon, Helen Cameron, Lady Russell
　　1867-1949 . . . . .DLB-195

Gordon, Lyndall 1941- DLB-155

Gordon, Mary 1949- DLB-6; Y-81

Gordone, Charles 1925-1995 . . . . .DLB-7

Gore, Catherine 1800-1861 . . . . .DLB-116

Gore-Booth, Eva 1870-1926 . . . . .DLB-240

Gores, Joe 1931- DLB-226

Gorey, Edward 1925-2000 . . . . .DLB-61

Gorgias of Leontini
　　circa 485 B.C.-376 B.C. DLB-176

Görres, Joseph 1776-1848 . . . . .DLB-90

Gosse, Edmund 1849-1928 . . . . .DLB-57, 144, 184

Gosson, Stephen 1554-1624 . . . . .DLB-172

The Schoole of Abuse (1579) DLB-172

Gotlieb, Phyllis 1926- DLB-88

Go-Toba 1180-1239 . . . . .DLB-203

Gottfried von Straßburg
　　died before 1230 . . . . . . .DLB-138; CDWLB-2

Gotthelf, Jeremias 1797-1854 . . . . .DLB-133

Gottschalk circa 804/808-869 . . . . .DLB-148

Gottsched, Johann Christoph
　　1700-1766 . . . . .DLB-97

Götz, Johann Nikolaus 1721-1781 . . . . . . .DLB-97

Goudge, Elizabeth 1900-1984 . . . . .DLB-191

Gough, John B. 1817-1886 . . . . .DLB-243

Gould, Wallace 1882-1940 . . . . .DLB-54

Govoni, Corrado 1884-1965 . . . . .DLB-114

Gower, John circa 1330-1408 . . . . .DLB-146

Goyen, William 1915-1983 . . . .DLB-2, 218; Y-83

Goytisolo, José Augustín 1928- DLB-134

Gozzano, Guido 1883-1916 . . . . .DLB-114

Grabbe, Christian Dietrich 1801-1836 . . . .DLB-133

Gracq, Julien 1910- DLB-83

Grady, Henry W. 1850-1889 . . . . .DLB-23

Graf, Oskar Maria 1894-1967 . . . . .DLB-56

Graf Rudolf
　　between circa 1170 and circa 1185 . . .DLB-148

Graff, Gerald 1937- DLB-246

Grafton, Richard [publishing house] DLB-170

Grafton, Sue 1940- DLB-226

Graham, Frank 1893-1965 . . . . .DLB-241

Graham, George Rex 1813-1894 . . . . .DLB-73

Graham, Gwethalyn 1913-1965 . . . . .DLB-88

Graham, Jorie 1951- DLB-120

Graham, Katharine 1917- DLB-127

Graham, Lorenz 1902-1989 . . . . .DLB-76

Graham, Philip 1915-1963 . . . . .DLB-127

Graham, R. B. Cunninghame
　　1852-1936 . . . . .DLB-98, 135, 174

Graham, Shirley 1896-1977 . . . . .DLB-76

Graham, Stephen 1884-1975 . . . . .DLB-195

Graham, W. S. 1918- DLB-20

Graham, William H. [publishing house] . . .DLB-49

Graham, Winston 1910- DLB-77

Grahame, Kenneth
　　1859-1932 . . . . .DLB-34, 141, 178

Grainger, Martin Allerdale 1874-1941 . . . .DLB-92

Gramatky, Hardie 1907-1979 . . . . .DLB-22

Grand, Sarah 1854-1943 . . . . .DLB-135, 197

Grandbois, Alain 1900-1975 . . . . .DLB-92

Grandson, Oton de circa 1345-1397 . . . . .DLB-208

Grange, John circa 1556-? DLB-136

Granich, Irwin (see Gold, Michael)

Granovsky, Timofei Nikolaevich
　　1813-1855 . . . . .DLB-198

Grant, Anne MacVicar 1755-1838 . . . . . . .DLB-200

Grant, Duncan 1885-1978 . . . . .DS-10

Grant, George 1918-1988 . . . . .DLB-88

Grant, George Monro 1835-1902 . . . . .DLB-99

Grant, Harry J. 1881-1963 . . . . .DLB-29

Grant, James Edward 1905-1966 . . . . .DLB-26

Grass, Günter 1927- . . .DLB-75, 124; CDWLB-2

Grasty, Charles H. 1863-1924 . . . . .DLB-25

Grau, Shirley Ann 1929- DLB-2, 218

Graves, John 1920- Y-83

Graves, Richard 1715-1804 . . . . .DLB-39

Graves, Robert 1895-1985
　　. . .DLB-20, 100, 191; DS-18; Y-85; CDBLB-6

Gray, Alasdair 1934- DLB-194

Gray, Asa 1810-1888 . . . . .DLB-1, 235

Gray, David 1838-1861 . . . . .DLB-32

Gray, Simon 1936- DLB-13

Gray, Thomas 1716-1771 . . . . .DLB-109; CDBLB-2

Grayson, Richard 1951- DLB-234

Grayson, William J. 1788-1863 . . . . .DLB-3, 64

The Great Bibliographers Series Y-93

The Great Modern Library Scam.......... Y-98

The Great War and the Theater, 1914-1918
[Great Britain] DLB-10

The Great War Exhibition and Symposium at
the University of South Carolina....... Y-97

Grech, Nikolai Ivanovich 1787-1867 ..... DLB-198

Greeley, Horace 1811-1872 ...... DLB-3, 43, 189

Green, Adolph (see Comden, Betty)

Green, Anna Katharine
1846-1935 .... DLB-202, 221

Green, Duff 1791-1875 .... DLB-43

Green, Elizabeth Shippen 1871-1954 .... DLB-188

Green, Gerald 1922- DLB-28

Green, Henry 1905-1973 .... DLB-15

Green, Jonas 1712-1767............... DLB-31

Green, Joseph 1706-1780............... DLB-31

Green, Julien 1900-1998............ DLB-4, 72

Green, Paul 1894-1981..........DLB-7, 9; Y-81

Green, T. and S. [publishing house] DLB-49

Green, Thomas Hill 1836-1882 .... DLB-190

Green, Timothy [publishing house] DLB-49

Greenaway, Kate 1846-1901........... DLB-141

Greenberg: Publisher DLB-46

Green Tiger Press................... DLB-46

Greene, Asa 1789-1838............... DLB-11

Greene, Belle da Costa 1883-1950 ...... DLB-187

Greene, Benjamin H.
[publishing house] DLB-49

Greene, Graham 1904-1991
...........DLB-13, 15, 77, 100, 162, 201, 204;
Y-85, Y-91; CDBLB-7

Greene, Robert 1558-1592 ..... DLB-62, 167

Greene, Robert Bernard (Bob) Jr.
1947- DLB-185

Greenfield, George 1917-2000.............. Y-00

Greenhow, Robert 1800-1854 .... DLB-30

Greenlee, William B. 1872-1953....... DLB-187

Greenough, Horatio 1805-1852 ...... DLB-1, 235

Greenwell, Dora 1821-1882 .... DLB-35, 199

Greenwillow Books DLB-46

Greenwood, Grace (see Lippincott, Sara Jane Clarke)

Greenwood, Walter 1903-1974...... DLB-10, 191

Greer, Ben 1948- DLB-6

Greflinger, Georg 1620?-1677.......... DLB-164

Greg, W. R. 1809-1881 .... DLB-55

Greg, W. W. 1875-1959 .... DLB-201

Gregg, Josiah 1806-1850.......... DLB-183, 186

Gregg Press....................... DLB-46

Gregory, Isabella Augusta Persse, Lady
1852-1932 .... DLB-10

Gregory, Horace 1898-1982........... DLB-48

Gregory of Rimini circa 1300-1358 ..... DLB-115

Gregynog Press................... DLB-112

Greiffenberg, Catharina Regina von
1633-1694 .... DLB-168

Greig, Noël 1944- DLB-245

Grenfell, Wilfred Thomason
1865-1940.................... DLB-92

Gress, Elsa 1919-1988 .... DLB-214

Greve, Felix Paul (see Grove, Frederick Philip)

Greville, Fulke, First Lord Brooke
1554-1628 ....DLB-62, 172

Grey, Sir George, K.C.B. 1812-1898 .... DLB-184

Grey, Lady Jane 1537-1554 .... DLB-132

Grey Owl 1888-1938 .... DLB-92; DS-17

Grey, Zane 1872-1939 .... DLB-9, 212

Grey Walls Press DLB-112

Griboedov, Aleksandr Sergeevich
1795?-1829.................... DLB-205

Grier, Eldon 1917- DLB-88

Grieve, C. M. (see MacDiarmid, Hugh)

Griffin, Bartholomew flourished 1596 ....DLB-172

Griffin, Gerald 1803-1840 .... DLB-159

The Griffin Poetry Prize.................. Y-00

Griffith, Elizabeth 1727?-1793........ DLB-39, 89

Preface to *The Delicate Distress* (1769) DLB-39

Griffith, George 1857-1906............DLB-178

Griffiths, Ralph [publishing house]...... DLB-154

Griffiths, Trevor 1935- DLB-13, 245

Griggs, S. C., and Company........... DLB-49

Griggs, Sutton Elbert 1872-1930........ DLB-50

Grignon, Claude-Henri 1894-1976....... DLB-68

Grigorovich, Dmitrii Vasil'evich
1822-1899 .... DLB-238

Grigson, Geoffrey 1905- DLB-27

Grillparzer, Franz
1791-1872 .... DLB-133; CDWLB-2

Grimald, Nicholas
circa 1519-circa 1562 .... DLB-136

Grimké, Angelina Weld 1880-1958 ... DLB-50, 54

Grimké, Sarah Moore 1792-1873 .... DLB-239

Grimm, Hans 1875-1959 .... DLB-66

Grimm, Jacob 1785-1863 .... DLB-90

Grimm, Wilhelm
1786-1859............ DLB-90; CDWLB-2

Grimmelshausen, Johann Jacob Christoffel von
1621 or 1622-1676..... DLB-168; CDWLB-2

Grimshaw, Beatrice Ethel 1871-1953 .....DLB-174

Grindal, Edmund 1519 or 1520-1583.... DLB-132

Griswold, Rufus Wilmot 1815-1857.... DLB-3, 59

Grosart, Alexander Balloch 1827-1899 ... DLB-184

Gross, Milt 1895-1953 .... DLB-11

Grosset and Dunlap DLB-49

Grossman, Allen 1932- DLB-193

Grossman Publishers DLB-46

Grosseteste, Robert circa 1160-1253..... DLB-115

Grosvenor, Gilbert H. 1875-1966....... DLB-91

Groth, Klaus 1819-1899............. DLB-129

Groulx, Lionel 1878-1967............. DLB-68

Grove, Frederick Philip 1879-1949 ...... DLB-92

Grove Press DLB-46

Grubb, Davis 1919-1980 .... DLB-6

Gruelle, Johnny 1880-1938............. DLB-22

von Grumbach, Argula
1492-after 1563? DLB-179

Grymeston, Elizabeth
before 1563-before 1604 .... DLB-136

Gryphius, Andreas
1616-1664 ....DLB-164; CDWLB-2

Gryphius, Christian 1649-1706........ DLB-168

Guare, John 1938- DLB-7

Guerra, Tonino 1920- DLB-128

Guest, Barbara 1920- DLB-5, 193

Guèvremont, Germaine 1893-1968 ...... DLB-68

Guidacci, Margherita 1921-1992 .... DLB-128

Guide to the Archives of Publishers, Journals,
and Literary Agents in North American
Libraries........................... Y-93

Guillén, Jorge 1893-1984 .... DLB-108

Guilloux, Louis 1899-1980............. DLB-72

Guilpin, Everard
circa 1572-after 1608? DLB-136

Guiney, Louise Imogen 1861-1920 ...... DLB-54

Guiterman, Arthur 1871-1943 .... DLB-11

Günderrode, Caroline von 1780-1806 .... DLB-90

Gundulić, Ivan 1589-1638 ...DLB-147; CDWLB-4

Gunn, Bill 1934-1989 .... DLB-38

Gunn, James E. 1923- DLB-8

Gunn, Neil M. 1891-1973.............. DLB-15

Gunn, Thom 1929- DLB-27; CDBLB-8

Gunnars, Kristjana 1948- DLB-60

Günther, Johann Christian
1695-1723.................... DLB-168

Gurik, Robert 1932- DLB-60

Gustafson, Ralph 1909- DLB-88

Gütersloh, Albert Paris 1887-1973 ...... DLB-81

Guthrie, A. B., Jr. 1901-1991 .... DLB-6, 212

Guthrie, Ramon 1896-1973 .... DLB-4

The Guthrie Theater DLB-7

Guthrie, Thomas Anstey
(see Anstey, FC)

Gutzkow, Karl 1811-1878............. DLB-133

Guy, Ray 1939- DLB-60

Guy, Rosa 1925- DLB-33

Guyot, Arnold 1807-1884................DS-13

Gwynne, Erskine 1898-1948 .... DLB-4

Gyles, John 1680-1755 .... DLB-99

Gysin, Brion 1916- DLB-16

H

H.D. (see Doolittle, Hilda)

Habermas, Jürgen 1929- DLB-242

Habington, William 1605-1654 .... DLB-126

Hacker, Marilyn 1942- DLB-120

Hackett, Albert (see Goodrich, Frances)

Hacks, Peter 1928- DLB-124

Hadas, Rachel 1948- DLB-120

Hadden, Briton 1898-1929............. DLB-91

Hagedorn, Friedrich von 1708-1754 ..... DLB-168

Hagelstange, Rudolf 1912-1984 .... DLB-69

Haggard, H. Rider
1856-1925 . . . . .DLB-70, 156, 174, 178

Haggard, William 1907-1993 . . . . Y-93

Hagy, Alyson 1960- DLB-244

Hahn-Hahn, Ida Gräfin von
1805-1880 . . . . .DLB-133

Haig-Brown, Roderick 1908-1976 . . . . . . .DLB-88

Haight, Gordon S. 1901-1985 . . . . .DLB-103

Hailey, Arthur 1920- DLB-88; Y-82

Haines, John 1924- DLB-5, 212

Hake, Edward flourished 1566-1604 . . . . .DLB-136

Hake, Thomas Gordon 1809-1895 . . . . . . .DLB-32

Hakluyt, Richard 1552?-1616 . . . . .DLB-136

Halas, František 1901-1949 . . . . .DLB-215

Halbe, Max 1865-1944 . . . . .DLB-118

Halberstam, David 1934- DLB-241

Haldane, J. B. S. 1892-1964 . . . . .DLB-160

Haldeman, Joe 1943- DLB-8

Haldeman-Julius Company DLB-46

Haldone, Charlotte 1894-1969 . . . . .DLB-191

Hale, E. J., and Son DLB-49

Hale, Edward Everett
1822-1909 . . . . .DLB-1, 42, 74, 235

Hale, Janet Campbell 1946- DLB-175

Hale, Kathleen 1898- DLB-160

Hale, Leo Thomas (see Ebon)

Hale, Lucretia Peabody 1820-1900 . . . . . . .DLB-42

Hale, Nancy
1908-1988 . . . . DLB-86; DS-17; Y-80, Y-88

Hale, Sarah Josepha (Buell)
1788-1879 . . . . .DLB-1, 42, 73, 243

Hale, Susan 1833-1910 . . . . .DLB-221

Hales, John 1584-1656 . . . . .DLB-151

Halévy, Ludovic 1834-1908 . . . . .DLB-192

Haley, Alex 1921-1992 . . . . . . .DLB-38; CDALB-7

Haliburton, Thomas Chandler
1796-1865 . . . . .DLB-11, 99

Hall, Anna Maria 1800-1881 . . . . .DLB-159

Hall, Donald 1928- DLB-5

Hall, Edward 1497-1547 . . . . .DLB-132

Hall, Halsey 1898-1977 . . . . .DLB-241

Hall, James 1793-1868 . . . . .DLB-73, 74

Hall, Joseph 1574-1656 . . . . .DLB-121, 151

Hall, Radclyffe 1880-1943 . . . . .DLB-191

Hall, Samuel [publishing house] DLB-49

Hall, Sarah Ewing 1761-1830 . . . . .DLB-200

Hall, Stuart 1932- DLB-242

Hallam, Arthur Henry 1811-1833 . . . . . . .DLB-32

On Some of the Characteristics of Modern
Poetry and On the Lyrical Poems of
Alfred Tennyson (1831) DLB-32

Halleck, Fitz-Greene 1790-1867 . . . . .DLB-3

Haller, Albrecht von 1708-1777 . . . . .DLB-168

Halliday, Brett (see Dresser, Davis)

Halliwell-Phillipps, James Orchard
1820-1889 . . . . .DLB-184

Hallmann, Johann Christian
1640-1704 or 1716? DLB-168

Hallmark Editions DLB-46

Halper, Albert 1904-1984 . . . . .DLB-9

Halperin, John William 1941- DLB-111

Halstead, Murat 1829-1908 . . . . .DLB-23

Hamann, Johann Georg 1730-1788 . . . . . . .DLB-97

Hamburger, Michael 1924- DLB-27

Hamilton, Alexander 1712-1756 . . . . .DLB-31

Hamilton, Alexander 1755?-1804 . . . . .DLB-37

Hamilton, Cicely 1872-1952 . . . . .DLB-10, 197

Hamilton, Edmond 1904-1977 . . . . .DLB-8

Hamilton, Elizabeth 1758-1816 . . . . .DLB-116, 158

Hamilton, Gail (see Corcoran, Barbara)

Hamilton, Gail (see Dodge, Mary Abigail)

Hamilton, Hamish, Limited DLB-112

Hamilton, Ian 1938- DLB-40, 155

Hamilton, Janet 1795-1873 . . . . .DLB-199

Hamilton, Mary Agnes 1884-1962 . . . . . .DLB-197

Hamilton, Patrick 1904-1962 . . . . . . .DLB-10, 191

Hamilton, Virginia 1936- DLB-33, 52

Hammett, Dashiell
1894-1961 . . . . . . .DLB-226; DS-6; CDALB-5

The Glass Key and Other Dashiell Hammett
Mysteries Y-96

Dashiell Hammett: An Appeal in *TAC* Y-91

Hammon, Jupiter 1711-died between
1790 and 1806 . . . . .DLB-31, 50

Hammond, John ?-1663 . . . . .DLB-24

Hamner, Earl 1923- DLB-6

Hampson, John 1901-1955 . . . . .DLB-191

Hampton, Christopher 1946- DLB-13

Handel-Mazzetti, Enrica von 1871-1955 . . .DLB-81

Handke, Peter 1942- DLB-85, 124

Handlin, Oscar 1915- DLB-17

Hankin, St. John 1869-1909 . . . . .DLB-10

Hanley, Clifford 1922- DLB-14

Hanley, James 1901-1985 . . . . .DLB-191

Hannah, Barry 1942- DLB-6, 234

Hannay, James 1827-1873 . . . . .DLB-21

Hano, Arnold 1922- DLB-241

Hansberry, Lorraine
1930-1965 . . . . .DLB-7, 38; CDALB-1

Hansen, Martin A. 1909-1955 . . . . .DLB-214

Hansen, Thorkild 1927-1989 . . . . .DLB-214

Hanson, Elizabeth 1684-1737 . . . . .DLB-200

Hapgood, Norman 1868-1937 . . . . .DLB-91

Happel, Eberhard Werner 1647-1690 . . . .DLB-168

The Harbinger 1845-1849 . . . . .DLB-223

Harcourt Brace Jovanovich DLB-46

Hardenberg, Friedrich von (see Novalis)

Harding, Walter 1917- DLB-111

Hardwick, Elizabeth 1916- DLB-6

Hardy, Thomas
1840-1928 . . . . . . .DLB-18, 19, 135; CDBLB-5

"Candour in English Fiction" (1890) DLB-18

Hare, Cyril 1900-1958 . . . . .DLB-77

Hare, David 1947- DLB-13

Hargrove, Marion 1919- DLB-11

Häring, Georg Wilhelm Heinrich
(see Alexis, Willibald)

Harington, Donald 1935- DLB-152

Harington, Sir John 1560-1612 . . . . .DLB-136

Harjo, Joy 1951- DLB-120, 175

Harkness, Margaret (John Law)
1854-1923 . . . . .DLB-197

Harley, Edward, second Earl of Oxford
1689-1741 . . . . .DLB-213

Harley, Robert, first Earl of Oxford
1661-1724 . . . . .DLB-213

Harlow, Robert 1923- DLB-60

Harman, Thomas flourished 1566-1573 . .DLB-136

Harness, Charles L. 1915- DLB-8

Harnett, Cynthia 1893-1981 . . . . .DLB-161

Harper, Edith Alice Mary (see Wickham, Anna)

Harper, Fletcher 1806-1877 . . . . .DLB-79

Harper, Frances Ellen Watkins
1825-1911 . . . . .DLB-50, 221

Harper, Michael S. 1938- DLB-41

Harper and Brothers DLB-49

Harpur, Charles 1813-1868 . . . . .DLB-230

Harraden, Beatrice 1864-1943 . . . . .DLB-153

Harrap, George G., and Company
Limited DLB-112

Harriot, Thomas 1560-1621 . . . . .DLB-136

Harris, Alexander 1805-1874 . . . . .DLB-230

Harris, Benjamin ?-circa 1720 . . . . .DLB-42, 43

Harris, Christie 1907- DLB-88

Harris, Frank 1856-1931 . . . . .DLB-156, 197

Harris, George Washington
1814-1869 .DLB-3, 11

Harris, Joel Chandler
1848-1908 . . . . .DLB-11, 23, 42, 78, 91

Harris, Mark 1922- DLB-2; Y-80

Harris, Wilson 1921- DLB-117; CDWLB-3

Harrison, Mrs. Burton
(see Harrison, Constance Cary)

Harrison, Charles Yale 1898-1954 . . . . . . .DLB-68

Harrison, Constance Cary 1843-1920 . . . .DLB-221

Harrison, Frederic 1831-1923 . . . . . . .DLB-57, 190

"On Style in English Prose" (1898) DLB-57

Harrison, Harry 1925- DLB-8

Harrison, James P., Company DLB-49

Harrison, Jim 1937- Y-82

Harrison, Mary St. Leger Kingsley
(see Malet, Lucas)

Harrison, Paul Carter 1936- DLB-38

Harrison, Susan Frances 1859-1935 . . . . . .DLB-99

Harrison, Tony 1937- DLB-40, 245

Harrison, William 1535-1593 . . . . .DLB-136

Harrison, William 1933- DLB-234

Harrisse, Henry 1829-1910 . . . . .DLB-47

The Harry Ransom Humanities
Research Center at the University
of Texas at Austin Y-00

Harryman, Carla 1952- DLB-193

Harsdörffer, Georg Philipp 1607-1658 . . . DLB-164

Harsent, David 1942- DLB-40

Hart, Albert Bushnell 1854-1943 . . . . DLB-17

Hart, Anne 1768-1834 . . . . DLB-200

Hart, Elizabeth 1771-1833 . . . . DLB-200

Hart, Julia Catherine 1796-1867 . . . . DLB-99

The Lorenz Hart Centenary Y-95

Hart, Moss 1904-1961 . . . . DLB-7

Hart, Oliver 1723-1795 . . . . DLB-31

Hart-Davis, Rupert, Limited DLB-112

Harte, Bret 1836-1902
. . . . DLB-12, 64, 74, 79, 186; CDALB-3

Harte, Edward Holmead 1922- DLB-127

Harte, Houston Harriman 1927- DLB-127

Hartlaub, Felix 1913-1945 . . . . DLB-56

Hartleben, Otto Erich 1864-1905 . . . . DLB-118

Hartley, L. P. 1895-1972 . . . . DLB-15, 139

Hartley, Marsden 1877-1943 . . . . DLB-54

Hartling, Peter 1933- DLB-75

Hartman, Geoffrey H. 1929- DLB-67

Hartmann, Sadakichi 1867-1944 . . . . DLB-54

Hartmann von Aue
circa 1160-circa 1205 . . . DLB-138; CDWLB-2

Harvey, Gabriel 1550?-1631 . . . . DLB-167, 213, 236

Harvey, Jean-Charles 1891-1967 . . . . DLB-88

Harvill Press Limited DLB-112

Harwood, Lee 1939- DLB-40

Harwood, Ronald 1934- DLB-13

Hašek, Jaroslav 1883-1923 . . DLB-215; CDWLB-4

Haskins, Charles Homer 1870-1937 . . . . . . DLB-47

Haslam, Gerald 1937- DLB-212

Hass, Robert 1941- DLB-105, 206

Hastings, Michael 1938- DLB-233

Hatar, Győző 1914- DLB-215

The Hatch-Billops Collection DLB-76

Hathaway, William 1944- DLB-120

Hauff, Wilhelm 1802-1827 . . . . DLB-90

A Haughty and Proud Generation (1922),
by Ford Madox Hueffer DLB-36

Haugwitz, August Adolph von
1647-1706 . . . . DLB-168

Hauptmann, Carl 1858-1921 . . . . DLB-66, 118

Hauptmann, Gerhart
1862-1946 . . . . DLB-66, 118; CDWLB-2

Hauser, Marianne 1910- Y-83

Havel, Václav 1936- DLB-232; CDWLB-4

Havergal, Frances Ridley 1836-1879 . . . . DLB-199

Hawes, Stephen 1475?-before 1529 . . . . . DLB-132

Hawker, Robert Stephen 1803-1875 . . . . . . DLB-32

Hawkes, John
1925-1998 . . . . DLB-2, 7, 227; Y-80, Y-98

John Hawkes: A Tribute Y-98

Hawkesworth, John 1720-1773 . . . . DLB-142

Hawkins, Sir Anthony Hope (see Hope, Anthony)

Hawkins, Sir John 1719-1789 . . . . . DLB-104, 142

Hawkins, Walter Everette 1883-? DLB-50

Hawthorne, Nathaniel
1804-1864 . . . DLB-1, 74, 183, 223; CDALB-2

Hawthorne, Nathaniel 1804-1864 and
Hawthorne, Sophia Peabody
1809-1871 . . . . DLB-183

Hawthorne, Sophia Peabody
1809-1871 . . . . DLB-183, 239

Hay, John 1835-1905 . . . . DLB-12, 47, 189

Hayashi, Fumiko 1903-1951 . . . . DLB-180

Haycox, Ernest 1899-1950 . . . . DLB-206

Haycraft, Anna Margaret (see Ellis, Alice Thomas)

Hayden, Robert
1913-1980 . . . . DLB-5, 76; CDALB-1

Haydon, Benjamin Robert
1786-1846 . . . . DLB-110

Hayes, John Michael 1919- DLB-26

Hayley, William 1745-1820 . . . . DLB-93, 142

Haym, Rudolf 1821-1901 . . . . DLB-129

Hayman, Robert 1575-1629 . . . . DLB-99

Hayman, Ronald 1932- DLB-155

Hayne, Paul Hamilton 1830-1886 . . . DLB-3, 64, 79

Hays, Mary 1760-1843 . . . . DLB-142, 158

Hayward, John 1905-1965 . . . . DLB-201

Haywood, Eliza 1693?-1756 . . . . DLB-39

From the Dedication, Lasselia (1723) DLB-39

From The Tea-Table DLB-39

From the Preface to The Disguis'd
Prince (1723) DLB-39

Hazard, Willis P. [publishing house] DLB-49

Hazlitt, William 1778-1830 . . . . DLB-110, 158

Hazzard, Shirley 1931- Y-82

Head, Bessie
1937-1986 . . . . DLB-117, 225; CDWLB-3

Headley, Joel T. 1813-1897 . . DLB-30, 183; DS-13

Heaney, Seamus
1939- DLB-40; Y-95; CDBLB-8

Heard, Nathan C. 1936- DLB-33

Hearn, Lafcadio 1850-1904 . . . . . . DLB-12, 78, 189

Hearn, Mary Anne (Marianne Farningham,
Eva Hope) 1834-1909 . . . . DLB-240

Hearne, John 1926- DLB-117

Hearne, Samuel 1745-1792 . . . . DLB-99

Hearne, Thomas 1678?-1735 . . . . DLB-213

Hearst, William Randolph 1863-1951 . . . . DLB-25

Hearst, William Randolph, Jr.
1908-1993 . . . . DLB-127

Heartman, Charles Frederick
1883-1953 . . . . DLB-187

Heath, Catherine 1924- DLB-14

Heath, Roy A. K. 1926- DLB-117

Heath-Stubbs, John 1918- DLB-27

Heavysege, Charles 1816-1876 . . . . DLB-99

Hebbel, Friedrich
1813-1863 . . . . DLB-129; CDWLB-2

Hebel, Johann Peter 1760-1826 . . . . DLB-90

Heber, Richard 1774-1833 . . . . DLB-184

Hébert, Anne 1916-2000 . . . . DLB-68

Hébert, Jacques 1923- DLB-53

Hecht, Anthony 1923- DLB-5, 169

Hecht, Ben 1894-1964 . . . . DLB-7, 9, 25, 26, 28, 86

Hecker, Isaac Thomas 1819-1888 . . . . DLB-1, 243

Hedge, Frederic Henry
1805-1890 . . . . DLB-1, 59, 243

Hefner, Hugh M. 1926- DLB-137

Hegel, Georg Wilhelm Friedrich
1770-1831 . . . . DLB-90

Heidish, Marcy 1947- Y-82

Heißenbüttel, Helmut 1921-1996 . . . . DLB-75

Heike monogatari DLB-203

Hein, Christoph 1944- DLB-124; CDWLB-2

Hein, Piet 1905-1996 . . . . DLB-214

Heine, Heinrich 1797-1856 . . . DLB-90; CDWLB-2

Heinemann, Larry 1944- DS-9

Heinemann, William, Limited DLB-112

Heinesen, William 1900-1991 . . . . DLB-214

Heinlein, Robert A. 1907-1988 . . . . DLB-8

Heinrich Julius of Brunswick
1564-1613 . . . . DLB-164

Heinrich von dem Türlîn
flourished circa 1230 . . . . DLB-138

Heinrich von Melk
flourished after 1160 . . . . DLB-148

Heinrich von Veldeke
circa 1145-circa 1190 . . . . DLB-138

Heinrich, Willi 1920- DLB-75

Heinse, Wilhelm 1746-1803 . . . . DLB-94

Heinz, W. C. 1915- DLB-171

Heiskell, John 1872-1972 . . . . DLB-127

Hejinian, Lyn 1941- DLB-165

Heliand circa 850 . . . . DLB-148

Heller, Joseph
1923-1999 . . . . DLB-2, 28, 227; Y-80, Y-99

Heller, Michael 1937- DLB-165

Hellman, Lillian 1906-1984 . . . . . DLB-7, 228; Y-84

Hellwig, Johann 1609-1674 . . . . DLB-164

Helprin, Mark 1947- Y-85; CDALB-7

Helwig, David 1938- DLB-60

Hemans, Felicia 1793-1835 . . . . DLB-96

Hemenway, Abby Maria 1828-1890 . . . . DLB-243

Hemingway, Ernest 1899-1961
. . . . . . DLB-4, 9, 102, 210; Y-81, Y-87, Y-99;
DS-1, DS-15, DS-16; CDALB-4

The Hemingway Centenary Celebration at the
JFK Library Y-99

Ernest Hemingway: A Centennial
Celebration Y-99

The Ernest Hemingway Collection at the
John F. Kennedy Library Y-99

Ernest Hemingway's Reaction to James Gould
Cozzens Y-98

Ernest Hemingway's Toronto Journalism
Revisited: With Three Previously
Unrecorded Stories Y-92

Falsifying Hemingway Y-96

Hemingway: Twenty-Five Years Later Y-85

Not Immediately Discernible . . . but Eventually
    Quite Clear: The *First Light* and *Final Years*
    of Hemingway's Centenary Y-99

Hemingway Salesmen's Dummies Y-00

Second International Hemingway Colloquium:
    Cuba Y-98

Hémon, Louis 1880-1913 . . . . DLB-92

Hempel, Amy 1951- DLB-218

Hemphill, Paul 1936- Y-87

Hénault, Gilles 1920- DLB-88

Henchman, Daniel 1689-1761 . . . . DLB-24

Henderson, Alice Corbin 1881-1949 . . . . . . DLB-54

Henderson, Archibald 1877-1963 . . . . DLB-103

Henderson, David 1942- DLB-41

Henderson, George Wylie 1904- DLB-51

Henderson, Zenna 1917-1983 . . . . DLB-8

Henisch, Peter 1943- DLB-85

Henley, Beth 1952- Y-86

Henley, William Ernest 1849-1903 . . . . . . DLB-19

Henning, Rachel 1826-1914 . . . . DLB-230

Henningsen, Agnes 1868-1962 . . . . DLB-214

Henniker, Florence 1855-1923 . . . . DLB-135

Henry, Alexander 1739-1824 . . . . DLB-99

Henry, Buck 1930- DLB-26

Henry VIII of England 1491-1547 . . . . . . DLB-132

Henry of Ghent
    circa 1217-1229 - 1293 . . . . DLB-115

Henry, Marguerite 1902-1997 . . . . DLB-22

Henry, O. (see Porter, William Sydney)

Henry, Robert Selph 1889-1970 . . . . DLB-17

Henry, Will (see Allen, Henry W.)

Henryson, Robert
    1420s or 1430s-circa 1505 . . . . DLB-146

Henschke, Alfred (see Klabund)

Hensley, Sophie Almon 1866-1946 . . . . . . DLB-99

Henson, Lance 1944- DLB-175

Henty, G. A. 1832?-1902 . . . . DLB-18, 141

Hentz, Caroline Lee 1800-1856 . . . . DLB-3

Heraclitus
    flourished circa 500 B.C. DLB-176

Herbert, Agnes circa 1880-1960 . . . . DLB-174

Herbert, Alan Patrick 1890-1971 . . . . . DLB-10, 191

Herbert, Edward, Lord, of Cherbury
    1582-1648 . . . . DLB-121, 151

Herbert, Frank 1920-1986 . . . . . . DLB-8; CDALB-7

Herbert, George 1593-1633 . . DLB-126; CDBLB-1

Herbert, Henry William 1807-1858 . . . . . DLB-3, 73

Herbert, John 1926- DLB-53

Herbert, Mary Sidney, Countess of Pembroke
    (see Sidney, Mary)

Herbert, Zbigniew
    1924-1998 . . . . DLB-232; CDWLB-4

Herbst, Josephine 1892-1969 . . . . DLB-9

Herburger, Gunter 1932- DLB-75, 124

Hercules, Frank E. M. 1917-1996 . . . . DLB-33

Herder, Johann Gottfried 1744-1803 . . . . . . DLB-97

Herder, B., Book Company DLB-49

Heredia, José-María de 1842-1905 . . . . . . DLB-217

Herford, Charles Harold 1853-1931 . . . . . DLB-149

Hergesheimer, Joseph 1880-1954 . . . . . . DLB-9, 102

Heritage Press DLB-46

Hermann the Lame 1013-1054 . . . . DLB-148

Hermes, Johann Timotheus
    1738-1821 . . . . DLB-97

Hermlin, Stephan 1915-1997 . . . . DLB-69

Hernández, Alfonso C. 1938- DLB-122

Hernández, Inés 1947- DLB-122

Hernández, Miguel 1910-1942 . . . . DLB-134

Hernton, Calvin C. 1932- DLB-38

Herodotus circa 484 B.C.-circa 420 B.C.
    . . . . DLB-176; CDWLB-1

Heron, Robert 1764-1807 . . . . DLB-142

Herr, Michael 1940- DLB-185

Herrera, Juan Felipe 1948- DLB-122

Herrick, E. R., and Company DLB-49

Herrick, Robert 1591-1674 . . . . DLB-126

Herrick, Robert 1868-1938 . . . . DLB-9, 12, 78

Herrick, William 1915- Y-83

Herrmann, John 1900-1959 . . . . DLB-4

Hersey, John 1914-1993 . . . DLB-6, 185; CDALB-7

Hertel, François 1905-1985 . . . . DLB-68

Hervé-Bazin, Jean Pierre Marie (see Bazin, Hervé)

Hervey, John, Lord 1696-1743 . . . . DLB-101

Herwig, Georg 1817-1875 . . . . DLB-133

Herzog, Emile Salomon Wilhelm
    (see Maurois, André)

Hesiod eighth century B.C. DLB-176

Hesse, Hermann
    1877-1962 . . . . DLB-66; CDWLB-2

Hessus, Helius Eobanus 1488-1540 . . . . . . DLB-179

Hewat, Alexander circa 1743-circa 1824 . . . DLB-30

Hewitt, John 1907- DLB-27

Hewlett, Maurice 1861-1923 . . . . DLB-34, 156

Heyen, William 1940- DLB-5

Heyer, Georgette 1902-1974 . . . . DLB-77, 191

Heym, Stefan 1913- DLB-69

Heyse, Paul 1830-1914 . . . . DLB-129

Heytesbury, William
    circa 1310-1372 or 1373 . . . . DLB-115

Heyward, Dorothy 1890-1961 . . . . DLB-7

Heyward, DuBose 1885-1940 . . . . . . DLB-7, 9, 45

Heywood, John 1497?-1580? DLB-136

Heywood, Thomas
    1573 or 1574-1641 . . . . DLB-62

Hibbs, Ben 1901-1975 . . . . DLB-137

Hichens, Robert S. 1864-1950 . . . . DLB-153

Hickey, Emily 1845-1924 . . . . DLB-199

Hickman, William Albert 1877-1957 . . . . . DLB-92

Hicks, Granville 1901-1982 . . . . DLB-246

Hidalgo, José Luis 1919-1947 . . . . DLB-108

Hiebert, Paul 1892-1987 . . . . DLB-68

Hieng, Andrej 1925- DLB-181

Hierro, José 1922- DLB-108

Higgins, Aidan 1927- DLB-14

Higgins, Colin 1941-1988 . . . . DLB-26

Higgins, George V.
    1939-1999 . . . . DLB-2; Y-81, Y-98, Y-99

George V. Higgins to Julian Symons Y-99

Higginson, Thomas Wentworth
    1823-1911 . . . . DLB-1, 64, 243

Highwater, Jamake 1942?- DLB-52; Y-85

Hijuelos, Oscar 1951- DLB-145

Hildegard von Bingen 1098-1179 . . . . DLB-148

Das Hildesbrandslied
    circa 820 . . . . DLB-148; CDWLB-2

Hildesheimer, Wolfgang
    1916-1991 . . . . DLB-69, 124

Hildreth, Richard 1807-1865 . . . DLB-1, 30, 59, 235

Hill, Aaron 1685-1750 . . . . DLB-84

Hill, Geoffrey 1932- DLB-40; CDBLB-8

Hill, George M., Company DLB-49

Hill, "Sir" John 1714?-1775 . . . . DLB-39

Hill, Lawrence, and Company,
    Publishers DLB-46

Hill, Leslie 1880-1960 . . . . DLB-51

Hill, Susan 1942- DLB-14, 139

Hill, Walter 1942- DLB-44

Hill and Wang DLB-46

Hillberry, Conrad 1928- DLB-120

Hillerman, Tony 1925- DLB-206

Hilliard, Gray and Company DLB-49

Hills, Lee 1906- DLB-127

Hillyer, Robert 1895-1961 . . . . DLB-54

Hilton, James 1900-1954 . . . . DLB-34, 77

Hilton, Walter died 1396 . . . . DLB-146

Hilton and Company DLB-49

Himes, Chester 1909-1984 . . . DLB-2, 76, 143, 226

Hindmarsh, Joseph [publishing house] . . . DLB-170

Hine, Daryl 1936- DLB-60

Hingley, Ronald 1920- DLB-155

Hinojosa-Smith, Rolando 1929- DLB-82

Hinton, S. E. 1948- CDALB-7

Hippel, Theodor Gottlieb von
    1741-1796 . . . . DLB-97

Hippocrates of Cos flourished circa 425 B.C.
    . . . . DLB-176; CDWLB-1

Hirabayashi, Taiko 1905-1972 . . . . DLB-180

Hirsch, E. D., Jr. 1928- DLB-67

Hirsch, Edward 1950- DLB-120

Hoagland, Edward 1932- DLB-6

Hoagland, Everett H., III 1942- DLB-41

Hoban, Russell 1925- DLB-52; Y-90

Hobbes, Thomas 1588-1679 . . . . DLB-151

Hobby, Oveta 1905- DLB-127

Hobby, William 1878-1964 . . . . DLB-127

Hobsbaum, Philip 1932- DLB-40

Hobson, Laura Z. 1900- DLB-28

Hobson, Sarah 1947- DLB-204

Hoby, Thomas 1530-1566 . . . . DLB-132

Hoccleve, Thomas
    circa 1368-circa 1437 . . . . DLB-146

Hochhuth, Rolf 1931- DLB-124

Hochman, Sandra 1936- DLB-5

Hocken, Thomas Morland
    1836-1910. DLB-184

Hodder and Stoughton, Limited. DLB-106

Hodgins, Jack 1938- DLB-60

Hodgman, Helen 1945- DLB-14

Hodgskin, Thomas 1787-1869 . . . . DLB-158

Hodgson, Ralph 1871-1962 . . . . DLB-19

Hodgson, William Hope
    1877-1918. . . . . DLB-70, 153, 156, 178

Hoe, Robert III 1839-1909. . . . . DLB-187

Hoeg, Peter 1957- DLB-214

Højholt, Per 1928- DLB-214

Hoffenstein, Samuel 1890-1947 . . . . DLB-11

Hoffman, Charles Fenno 1806-1884. . . . . . DLB-3

Hoffman, Daniel 1923- DLB-5

Hoffmann, E. T. A.
    1776-1822. . . . . DLB-90; CDWLB-2

Hoffman, Frank B. 1888-1958 . . . . DLB-188

Hoffman, William 1925- DLB-234

Hoffmanswaldau, Christian Hoffman von
    1616-1679. DLB-168

Hofmann, Michael 1957- DLB-40

Hofmannsthal, Hugo von
    1874-1929. . . . . .DLB-81, 118; CDWLB-2

Hofstadter, Richard 1916-1970. . . . . . DLB-17, 246

Hogan, Desmond 1950- DLB-14

Hogan, Linda 1947- DLB-175

Hogan and Thompson DLB-49

Hogarth Press. DLB-112

Hogg, James 1770-1835. . . . . DLB-93, 116, 159

Hohberg, Wolfgang Helmhard Freiherr von
    1612-1688. DLB-168

von Hohenheim, Philippus Aureolus
    Theophrastus Bombastus (see Paracelsus)

Hohl, Ludwig 1904-1980 . . . . DLB-56

Holbrook, David 1923- DLB-14, 40

Holcroft, Thomas 1745-1809 . . . . DLB-39, 89, 158

    Preface to *Alwyn* (1780) DLB-39

Holden, Jonathan 1941- DLB-105

    "Contemporary Verse Story-telling" DLB-105

Holden, Molly 1927-1981 . . . . DLB-40

Hölderlin, Friedrich 1770-1843 DLB-90; CDWLB-2

Holiday House DLB-46

Holinshed, Raphael died 1580 . . . . DLB-167

Holland, J. G. 1819-1881 . . . . DS-13

Holland, Norman N. 1927- DLB-67

Hollander, John 1929- DLB-5

Holley, Marietta 1836-1926 . . . . DLB-11

Hollinghurst, Alan 1954- DLB-207

Hollingsworth, Margaret 1940- DLB-60

Hollo, Anselm 1934- DLB-40

Holloway, Emory 1885-1977 . . . . DLB-103

Holloway, John 1920- DLB-27

Holloway House Publishing Company . . . DLB-46

Holme, Constance 1880-1955 . . . . DLB-34

Holmes, Abraham S. 1821?-1908. . . . . . . DLB-99

Holmes, John Clellon 1926-1988 . . . . .DLB-16, 237

    "Four Essays on the Beat Generation" DLB-16

Holmes, Mary Jane 1825-1907 . . . . . DLB-202, 221

Holmes, Oliver Wendell
    1809-1894 . . . . . . DLB-1, 189, 235; CDALB-2

Holmes, Richard 1945- DLB-155

The Cult of Biography
    Excerpts from the Second Folio Debate:
    "Biographies are generally a disease of
    English Literature". Y-86

Holmes, Thomas James 1874-1959. . . . . . DLB-187

Holroyd, Michael 1935- DLB-155; Y-99

Holst, Hermann E. von 1841-1904 . . . . . DLB-47

Holt, Henry, and Company DLB-49

Holt, John 1721-1784 . . . . DLB-43

Holt, Rinehart and Winston DLB-46

Holtby, Winifred 1898-1935 . . . . DLB-191

Holthusen, Hans Egon 1913- DLB-69

Hölty, Ludwig Christoph Heinrich
    1748-1776 . . . . DLB-94

Holub, Miroslav
    1923-1998 . . . . DLB-232; CDWLB-4

Holz, Arno 1863-1929 . . . . DLB-118

Home, Henry, Lord Kames
    (see Kames, Henry Home, Lord)

Home, John 1722-1808. . . . . DLB-84

Home, William Douglas 1912- DLB-13

Home Publishing Company DLB-49

Homer circa eighth-seventh centuries B.C.
    . . . . .DLB-176; CDWLB-1

Homer, Winslow 1836-1910 . . . . DLB-188

Homes, Geoffrey (see Mainwaring, Daniel)

Honan, Park 1928- DLB-111

Hone, William 1780-1842. . . . . .DLB-110, 158

Hongo, Garrett Kaoru 1951- DLB-120

Honig, Edwin 1919- DLB-5

Hood, Hugh 1928- DLB-53

Hood, Mary 1946- DLB-234

Hood, Thomas 1799-1845 . . . . DLB-96

Hook, Theodore 1788-1841 . . . . DLB-116

Hooker, Jeremy 1941- DLB-40

Hooker, Richard 1554-1600. . . . . DLB-132

Hooker, Thomas 1586-1647. . . . . DLB-24

hooks, bell 1952- DLB-246

Hooper, Johnson Jones 1815-1862 . . . . . DLB-3, 11

Hope, Anthony 1863-1933 . . . . DLB-153, 156

Hope, Christopher 1944- DLB-225

Hope, Eva (see Hearn, Mary Anne)

Hope, Laurence (Adela Florence
    Cory Nicolson) 1865-1904. . . . . DLB-240

Hopkins, Ellice 1836-1904 . . . . DLB-190

Hopkins, Gerard Manley
    1844-1889 . . . . . . DLB-35, 57; CDBLB-5

Hopkins, John (see Sternhold, Thomas)

Hopkins, John H., and Son DLB-46

Hopkins, Lemuel 1750-1801. . . . . DLB-37

Hopkins, Pauline Elizabeth 1859-1930. . . . DLB-50

Hopkins, Samuel 1721-1803 . . . . DLB-31

Hopkinson, Francis 1737-1791 . . . . DLB-31

Hopper, Nora (Mrs. Nora Chesson)
    1871-1906. DLB-240

Hoppin, Augustus 1828-1896. . . . . DLB-188

Hora, Josef 1891-1945 . . . . . .DLB-215; CDWLB-4

Horace 65 B.C.-8 B.C. DLB-211; CDWLB-1

Horgan, Paul 1903-1995. . . . . .DLB-102, 212; Y-85

Horizon Press. DLB-46

Hornby, C. H. St. John 1867-1946 . . . . . DLB-201

Hornby, Nick 1957- DLB-207

Horne, Frank 1899-1974. . . . . DLB-51

Horne, Richard Henry (Hengist)
    1802 or 1803-1884. . . . . DLB-32

Horney, Karen 1885-1952 . . . . DLB-246

Hornung, E. W. 1866-1921 . . . . DLB-70

Horovitz, Israel 1939- DLB-7

Horton, George Moses 1797?-1883?. DLB-50

Horváth, Ödön von 1901-1938 . . . . . DLB-85, 124

Horwood, Harold 1923- DLB-60

Hosford, E. and E. [publishing house] DLB-49

Hoskens, Jane Fenn 1693-1770? DLB-200

Hoskyns, John 1566-1638 . . . . DLB-121

Hosokawa Yūsai 1535-1610 . . . . DLB-203

Hostovský, Egon 1908-1973 . . . . DLB-215

Hotchkiss and Company DLB-49

Hough, Emerson 1857-1923 . . . . DLB-9, 212

Houghton, Stanley 1881-1913 . . . . DLB-10

Houghton Mifflin Company DLB-49

Household, Geoffrey 1900-1988 . . . . DLB-87

Housman, A. E. 1859-1936 . . . DLB-19; CDBLB-5

Housman, Laurence 1865-1959 . . . . DLB-10

Houston, Pam 1962- DLB-244

Houwald, Ernst von 1778-1845 . . . . DLB-90

Hovey, Richard 1864-1900 . . . . DLB-54

Howard, Donald R. 1927-1987. . . . . DLB-111

Howard, Maureen 1930- Y-83

Howard, Richard 1929- DLB-5

Howard, Roy W. 1883-1964 . . . . DLB-29

Howard, Sidney 1891-1939 . . . . .DLB-7, 26

Howard, Thomas, second Earl of Arundel
    1585-1646 . . . . DLB-213

Howe, E. W. 1853-1937. . . . . DLB-12, 25

Howe, Henry 1816-1893 . . . . DLB-30

Howe, Irving 1920-1993. . . . . DLB-67

Howe, Joseph 1804-1873 . . . . DLB-99

Howe, Julia Ward 1819-1910 . . . . DLB-1, 189, 235

Howe, Percival Presland 1886-1944. . . . . DLB-149

Howe, Susan 1937- DLB-120

Howell, Clark, Sr. 1863-1936. . . . . DLB-25

Howell, Evan P. 1839-1905 . . . . DLB-23

Howell, James 1594?-1666 . . . . .DLB-151

Howell, Soskin and Company DLB-46

Howell, Warren Richardson
 1912-1984 . . . . .DLB-140

Howells, William Dean 1837-1920
 . . . . .DLB-12, 64, 74, 79, 189; CDALB-3

Introduction to Paul Laurence Dunbar,
 Lyrics of Lowly Life (1896) DLB-50

Howitt, Mary 1799-1888 . . . . .DLB-110, 199

Howitt, William 1792-1879 and
 Howitt, Mary 1799-1888 . . . . .DLB-110

Hoyem, Andrew 1935- DLB-5

Hoyers, Anna Ovena 1584-1655 . . . . . . .DLB-164

Hoyos, Angela de 1940- DLB-82

Hoyt, Henry [publishing house] DLB-49

Hoyt, Palmer 1897-1979 . . . . .DLB-127

Hrabal, Bohumil 1914-1997 . . . . .DLB-232

Hrabanus Maurus 776?-856 . . . . .DLB-148

Hronský, Josef Cíger 1896-1960 . . . . . . .DLB-215

Hrotsvit of Gandersheim
 circa 935-circa 1000 . . . . .DLB-148

Hubbard, Elbert 1856-1915 . . . . .DLB-91

Hubbard, Kin 1868-1930 . . . . .DLB-11

Hubbard, William circa 1621-1704 . . . . . .DLB-24

Huber, Therese 1764-1829 . . . . .DLB-90

Huch, Friedrich 1873-1913 . . . . .DLB-66

Huch, Ricarda 1864-1947 . . . . .DLB-66

Huck at 100: How Old Is
 Huckleberry Finn? Y-85

Huddle, David 1942- DLB-130

Hudgins, Andrew 1951- DLB-120

Hudson, Henry Norman 1814-1886 . . . . . .DLB-64

Hudson, Stephen 1868?-1944 . . . . .DLB-197

Hudson, W. H. 1841-1922 . . . . . DLB-98, 153, 174

Hudson and Goodwin DLB-49

Huebsch, B. W. [publishing house] DLB-46

Oral History: B. W. Huebsch Y-99

Hueffer, Oliver Madox 1876-1931 . . . . . . .DLB-197

Hugh of St. Victor circa 1096-1141 . . . . . .DLB-208

Hughes, David 1930- DLB-14

Hughes, Dusty 1947- DLB-233

Hughes, John 1677-1720 . . . . .DLB-84

Hughes, Langston 1902-1967
 . . . . .DLB-4, 7, 48, 51, 86, 228; CDALB-5

Hughes, Richard 1900-1976 . . . . .DLB-15, 161

Hughes, Ted 1930-1998 . . . . .DLB-40, 161

Hughes, Thomas 1822-1896 . . . . . . .DLB-18, 163

Hugo, Richard 1923-1982 . . . . .DLB-5, 206

Hugo, Victor 1802-1885 . . . . . . DLB-119, 192, 217

Hugo Awards and Nebula Awards DLB-8

Hull, Richard 1896-1973 . . . . .DLB-77

Hulme, T. E. 1883-1917 . . . . .DLB-19

Hulton, Anne ?-1779? DLB-200

Humboldt, Alexander von 1769-1859 . . . . .DLB-90

Humboldt, Wilhelm von 1767-1835 . . . . . . .DLB-90

Hume, David 1711-1776 . . . . .DLB-104

Hume, Fergus 1859-1932 . . . . .DLB-70

Hume, Sophia 1702-1774 . . . . .DLB-200

Hume-Rothery, Mary Catherine
 1824-1885 . . . . .DLB-240

Humishuma (see Mourning Dove)

Hummer, T. R. 1950- DLB-120

Humorous Book Illustration DLB-11

Humphrey, Duke of Gloucester
 1391-1447 .DLB-213

Humphrey, William 1924-1997 . . .DLB-6, 212, 234

Humphreys, David 1752-1818 . . . . .DLB-37

Humphreys, Emyr 1919- DLB-15

Huncke, Herbert 1915-1996 . . . . .DLB-16

Huneker, James Gibbons 1857-1921 . . . . . .DLB-71

Hunold, Christian Friedrich 1681-1721 . . .DLB-168

Hunt, Irene 1907- DLB-52

Hunt, Leigh 1784-1859 . . . . DLB-96, 110, 144

Hunt, Violet 1862-1942 . . . . .DLB-162, 197

Hunt, William Gibbes 1791-1833 . . . . .DLB-73

Hunter, Evan 1926- Y-82

Hunter, Jim 1939- DLB-14

Hunter, Kristin 1931- DLB-33

Hunter, Mollie 1922- DLB-161

Hunter, N. C. 1908-1971 . . . . .DLB-10

Hunter-Duvar, John 1821-1899 . . . . .DLB-99

Huntington, Henry E. 1850-1927 . . . . . .DLB-140

Huntington, Susan Mansfield
 1791-1823 .DLB-200

Hurd and Houghton DLB-49

Hurst, Fannie 1889-1968 . . . . .DLB-86

Hurst and Blackett DLB-106

Hurst and Company DLB-49

Hurston, Zora Neale
 1901?-1960 . . . . .DLB-51, 86; CDALB-7

Husson, Jules-François-Félix (see Champfleury)

Huston, John 1906-1987 . . . . .DLB-26

Hutcheson, Francis 1694-1746 . . . . .DLB-31

Hutchinson, Ron ?- DLB-245

Hutchinson, R. C. 1907-1975 . . . . .DLB-191

Hutchinson, Thomas 1711-1780
 . . . . .DLB-30, 31

Hutchinson and Company
 (Publishers) Limited DLB-112

Hutton, Richard Holt 1826-1897 . . . . .DLB-57

von Hutton, Ulrich 1488-1523 . . . . .DLB-179

Huxley, Aldous 1894-1963
 . . . . .DLB-36, 100, 162, 195; CDBLB-6

Huxley, Elspeth Josceline
 1907-1997 . . . . .DLB-77, 204

Huxley, T. H. 1825-1895 . . . . .DLB-57

Huyghue, Douglas Smith 1816-1891 . . . . . .DLB-99

Huysmans, Joris-Karl 1848-1907 . . . . .DLB-123

Hwang, David Henry
 1957- DLB-212, 228

Hyde, Donald 1909-1966 and
 Hyde, Mary 1912- DLB-187

Hyman, Trina Schart 1939- DLB-61

I

Iavorsky, Stefan 1658-1722 . . . . .DLB-150

Iazykov, Nikolai Mikhailovich
 1803-1846 .DLB-205

Ibáñez, Armando P. 1949- DLB-209

Ibn Bajja circa 1077-1138 . . . . .DLB-115

Ibn Gabirol, Solomon
 circa 1021-circa 1058 . . . . .DLB-115

Ibuse, Masuji 1898-1993 . . . . .DLB-180

Ichijō Kanera
 (see Ichijō Kaneyoshi)

Ichijō Kaneyoshi (Ichijō Kanera)
 1402-1481 .DLB-203

The Iconography of Science-Fiction Art DLB-8

Iffland, August Wilhelm 1759-1814 . . . . . . .DLB-94

Ignatow, David 1914-1997 . . . . .DLB-5

Ike, Chukwuemeka 1931- DLB-157

Ikkyū Sōjun 1394-1481 . . . . .DLB-203

Iles, Francis (see Berkeley, Anthony)

Illich, Ivan 1926- DLB-242

The Illustration of Early German Literar
 Manuscripts, circa 1150-circa 1300 . . .DLB-148

Illyés, Gyula 1902-1983 . . . . . DLB-215; CDWLB-4

Imbs, Bravig 1904-1946 . . . . .DLB-4

Imbuga, Francis D. 1947- DLB-157

Immermann, Karl 1796-1840 . . . . .DLB-133

Inchbald, Elizabeth 1753-1821 . . . . . . .DLB-39, 89

Inge, William 1913-1973 . . . . .DLB-7; CDALB-1

Ingelow, Jean 1820-1897 . . . . .DLB-35, 163

Ingersoll, Ralph 1900-1985 . . . . .DLB-127

The Ingersoll Prizes Y-84

Ingoldsby, Thomas (see Barham, Richard Harris)

Ingraham, Joseph Holt 1809-1860 . . . . .DLB-3

Inman, John 1805-1850 . . . . .DLB-73

Innerhofer, Franz 1944- DLB-85

Innis, Harold Adams 1894-1952 . . . . .DLB-88

Innis, Mary Quayle 1899-1972 . . . . .DLB-88

Inō Sōgi 1421-1502 . . . . .DLB-203

Inoue Yasushi 1907-1991 . . . . .DLB-181

International Publishers Company DLB-46

Interviews:

Anastas, Benjamin Y-98

Baker, Nicholson Y-00

Bank, Melissa Y-98

Bernstein, Harriet Y-82

Betts, Doris Y-82

Bosworth, David Y-82

Bottoms, David Y-83

Bowers, Fredson Y-80

Burnshaw, Stanley Y-97

Carpenter, Humphrey Y-84, Y-99

Carr, Virginia Spencer Y-00

Carver, Raymond Y-83

Cherry, Kelly Y-83

Coppel, Alfred Y-83

Cowley, Malcolm Y-81

Davis, Paxton Y-89

De Vries, Peter Y-82

Dickey, James Y-82

Donald, David Herbert. Y-87

Ellroy, James Y-91

Fancher, Betsy Y-83

Faust, Irvin Y-00

Fulton, Len Y-86

Garrett, George. Y-83

Greenfield, George Y-91

Griffin, Bryan Y-81

Guilds, John Caldwell. Y-92

Hardin, James Y-92

Harrison, Jim Y-82

Hazzard, Shirley Y-82

Higgins, George V. Y-98

Hoban, Russell Y-90

Holroyd, Michael Y-99

Horowitz, Glen Y-90

Jakes, John Y-83

Jenkinson, Edward B. Y-82

Jenks, Tom Y-86

Kaplan, Justin Y-86

King, Florence. Y-85

Klopfer, Donald S. Y-97

Krug, Judith Y-82

Lamm, Donald Y-95

Laughlin, James Y-96

Lindsay, Jack Y-84

Mailer, Norman Y-97

Manchester, William Y-85

McCormack, Thomas Y-98

McNamara, Katherine Y-97

Mellen, Joan Y-94

Menaher, Daniel. Y-97

Mooneyham, Lamarr Y-82

Nosworth, David Y-82

O'Connor, Patrick Y-84, Y-99

Ozick, Cynthia Y-83

Penner, Jonathan Y-83

Pennington, Lee Y-82

Penzler, Otto. Y-96

Plimpton, George Y-99

Potok, Chaim Y-84

Prescott, Peter S. Y-86

Rabe, David Y-91

Rallyson, Carl. Y-97

Rechy, John Y-82

Reid, B. L. Y-83

Reynolds, Michael Y-95, Y-99

Schlafly, Phyllis. Y-82

Schroeder, Patricia Y-99

Schulberg, Budd Y-81

Scribner, Charles III. Y-94

Sipper, Ralph Y-94

Staley, Thomas F. Y-00

Styron, William Y-80

Toth, Susan Allen. Y-86

Tyler, Anne Y-82

Vaughan, Samuel Y-97

Von Ogtrop, Kristin Y-92

Wallenstein, Barry Y-92

Weintraub, Stanley. Y-82

Williams, J. Chamberlain Y-84

Editors, Conversations with Y-95

Interviews on E-Publishing. Y-00

Irving, John 1942- DLB-6; Y-82

Irving, Washington 1783-1859
    . . . . DLB-3, 11, 30, 59, 73, 74,
                         183, 186; CDALB-2

Irwin, Grace 1907- DLB-68

Irwin, Will 1873-1948. . . . . DLB-25

Iser, Wolfgang 1926- DLB-242

Isherwood, Christopher
    1904-1986 . . . . DLB-15, 195; Y-86

The Christopher Isherwood Archive,
    The Huntington Library Y-99

Ishiguro, Kazuo 1954- DLB-194

Ishikawa Jun 1899-1987 . . . . DLB-182

The Island Trees Case: A Symposium on
    School Library Censorship
    An Interview with Judith Krug
    An Interview with Phyllis Schlafly
    An Interview with Edward B. Jenkinson
    An Interview with Lamarr Mooneyham
    An Interview with Harriet Bernstein Y-82

Islas, Arturo 1938-1991 . . . . DLB-122

Issit, Debbie 1966- DLB-233

Ivanišević, Drago 1907-1981. . . . . DLB-181

Ivaska, Astrīde 1926- DLB-232

Ivers, M. J., and Company DLB-49

Iwaniuk, Wacław 1915- DLB-215

Iwano, Hōmei 1873-1920 . . . . DLB-180

Iwaszkiewicz, Jaroslav 1894-1980. . . . . . . DLB-215

Iyayi, Festus 1947- DLB-157

Izumi, Kyōka 1873-1939. . . . . DLB-180

J

Jackmon, Marvin E. (see Marvin X)

Jacks, L. P. 1860-1955 . . . . DLB-135

Jackson, Angela 1951- DLB-41

Jackson, Charles 1903-1968 . . . . DLB-234

Jackson, Helen Hunt
    1830-1885 . . . . DLB-42, 47, 186, 189

Jackson, Holbrook 1874-1948 . . . . DLB-98

Jackson, Laura Riding 1901-1991. . . . . . . DLB-48

Jackson, Shirley
    1916-1965 . . . . DLB-6, 234; CDALB-1

Jacob, Naomi 1884?-1964. . . . . DLB-191

Jacob, Piers Anthony Dillingham
    (see Anthony, Piers)

Jacob, Violet 1863-1946 . . . . DLB-240

Jacobi, Friedrich Heinrich 1743-1819 . . . . . DLB-94

Jacobi, Johann Georg 1740-1841. . . . . DLB-97

Jacobs, George W., and Company DLB-49

Jacobs, Harriet 1813-1897. . . . . DLB-239

Jacobs, Joseph 1854-1916 . . . . DLB-141

Jacobs, W. W. 1863-1943. . . . . DLB-135

Jacobsen, Jørgen-Frantz 1900-1938. . . . . . DLB-214

Jacobsen, Josephine 1908- DLB-244

Jacobson, Dan 1929- DLB-14, 207, 225

Jacobson, Howard 1942- DLB-207

Jacques de Vitry circa 1160/1170-1240. . . DLB-208

Jæger, Frank 1926-1977. . . . . DLB-214

Jaggard, William [publishing house]. DLB-170

Jahier, Piero 1884-1966 . . . . DLB-114

Jahnn, Hans Henny 1894-1959 . . . . . DLB-56, 124

Jakes, John 1932- Y-83

Jakobson, Roman 1896-1982 . . . . DLB-242

James, Alice 1848-1892. . . . . DLB-221

James, C. L. R. 1901-1989 . . . . DLB-125

James, George P. R. 1801-1860 . . . . DLB-116

James, Henry 1843-1916
    . . . . . . DLB-12, 71, 74, 189; DS-13; CDALB-3

James, John circa 1633-1729. . . . . DLB-24

James, M. R. 1862-1936 . . . . DLB-156, 201

James, Naomi 1949- DLB-204

James, P. D. 1920-   . . DLB-87; DS-17; CDBLB-8

James VI of Scotland, I of England
    1566-1625 . . . . DLB-151, 172

Ane Schort Treatise Conteining Some Revlis
    and Cautelis to Be Obseruit and Eschewit
    in Scottis Poesi (1584) DLB-172

James, Thomas 1572?-1629 . . . . DLB-213

James, U. P. [publishing house] DLB-49

James, Will 1892-1942 . . . . DS-16

Jameson, Anna 1794-1860 . . . . DLB-99, 166

Jameson, Fredric 1934- DLB-67

Jameson, J. Franklin 1859-1937 . . . . DLB-17

Jameson, Storm 1891-1986. . . . . DLB-36

Jančar, Drago 1948- DLB-181

Janés, Clara 1940- DLB-134

Janevski, Slavko 1920- DLB-181; CDWLB-4

Janvier, Thomas 1849-1913 . . . . DLB-202

Jaramillo, Cleofas M. 1878-1956. . . . . DLB-122

Jarman, Mark 1952- DLB-120

Jarrell, Randall 1914-1965 . DLB-48, 52; CDALB-1

Jarrold and Sons. DLB-106

Jarry, Alfred 1873-1907. . . . . DLB-192

Jarves, James Jackson 1818-1888 . . . . DLB-189

Jasmin, Claude 1930- DLB-60

Jaunsudrabiņš, Jānis 1877-1962. . . . . DLB-220

Jay, John 1745-1829 . . . . DLB-31

Jean de Garlande (see John of Garland)

Jefferies, Richard 1848-1887. . . . . DLB-98, 141

Jeffers, Lance 1919-1985. . . . . DLB-41

Jeffers, Robinson
1887-1962 . . . . .DLB-45, 212; CDALB-4

Jefferson, Thomas
1743-1826 . . . . .DLB-31, 183; CDALB-2

Jégé 1866-1940. . . . . .DLB-215

Jelinek, Elfriede 1946- DLB-85

Jellicoe, Ann 1927- DLB-13, 233

Jemison, Mary circa 1742-1833 . . . . .DLB-239

Jenkins, Dan 1929- DLB-241

Jenkins, Elizabeth 1905- DLB-155

Jenkins, Robin 1912- DLB-14

Jenkins, William Fitzgerald (see Leinster, Murray)

Jenkins, Herbert, Limited. DLB-112

Jennings, Elizabeth 1926- DLB-27

Jens, Walter 1923- DLB-69

Jensen, Johannes V. 1873-1950 . . . . .DLB-214

Jensen, Merrill 1905-1980 . . . . .DLB-17

Jensen, Thit 1876-1957. . . . . .DLB-214

Jephson, Robert 1736-1803 . . . . .DLB-89

Jerome, Jerome K. 1859-1927 . . . .DLB-10, 34, 135

Jerome, Judson 1927-1991 . . . . .DLB-105

Jerrold, Douglas 1803-1857 . . . . .DLB-158, 159

Jesse, F. Tennyson 1888-1958 . . . . .DLB-77

Jewel, John 1522-1571 . . . . .DLB-236

Jewett, John P., and Company. DLB-49

Jewett, Sarah Orne 1849-1909 . . . .DLB-12, 74, 221

The Jewish Publication Society DLB-49

Jewitt, John Rodgers 1783-1821 . . . . .DLB-99

Jewsbury, Geraldine 1812-1880 . . . . .DLB-21

Jewsbury, Maria Jane 1800-1833 . . . . .DLB-199

Jhabvala, Ruth Prawer 1927- DLB-139, 194

Jiménez, Juan Ramón 1881-1958. . . . . . . .DLB-134

Jin, Ha 1956- DLB-244

Joans, Ted 1928- DLB-16, 41

Jōha 1525-1602 . . . . .DLB-203

Johannis de Garlandia (see John of Garland)

John, Errol 1924-1988 . . . . .DLB-233

John, Eugenie (see Marlitt, E.)

John of Dumbleton
circa 1310-circa 1349. . . . . .DLB-115

John of Garland (Jean de Garlande, Johannis de
Garlandia) circa 1195-circa 1272 . . . . .DLB-208

Johns, Captain W. E. 1893-1968 . . . . .DLB-160

Johnson, Mrs. A. E. ca. 1858-1922 . . . . . .DLB-221

Johnson, Amelia (see Johnson, Mrs. A. E.)

Johnson, B. S. 1933-1973 . . . . .DLB-14, 40

Johnson, Benjamin [publishing house]. DLB-49

Johnson, Benjamin, Jacob, and
Robert [publishing house] DLB-49

Johnson, Charles 1679-1748. . . . . .DLB-84

Johnson, Charles R. 1948- DLB-33

Johnson, Charles S. 1893-1956 . . . . . . .DLB-51, 91

Johnson, Denis 1949- DLB-120

Johnson, Diane 1934- Y-80

Johnson, Dorothy M. 1905–1984 . . . . . . .DLB-206

Johnson, E. Pauline (Tekahionwake)
1861-1913 . . . . .DLB-175

Johnson, Edgar 1901-1995. . . . . .DLB-103

Johnson, Edward 1598-1672 . . . . .DLB-24

Johnson, Fenton 1888-1958 . . . . .DLB-45, 50

Johnson, Georgia Douglas 1886-1966 . . . . .DLB-51

Johnson, Gerald W. 1890-1980 . . . . .DLB-29

Johnson, Greg 1953- DLB-234

Johnson, Helene 1907-1995 . . . . .DLB-51

Johnson, Jacob, and Company. DLB-49

Johnson, James Weldon
1871-1938 . . . . .DLB-51; CDALB-4

Johnson, John H. 1918- DLB-137

Johnson, Joseph [publishing house] DLB-154

Johnson, Linton Kwesi 1952- DLB-157

Johnson, Lionel 1867-1902. . . . . .DLB-19

Johnson, Nunnally 1897-1977 . . . . .DLB-26

Johnson, Owen 1878-1952. . . . . .Y-87

Johnson, Pamela Hansford 1912- DLB-15

Johnson, Pauline 1861-1913. . . . . .DLB-92

Johnson, Ronald 1935-1998 . . . . .DLB-169

Johnson, Samuel 1696-1772 . . . DLB-24; CDBLB-2

Johnson, Samuel
1709-1784 . . . . .DLB-39, 95, 104, 142, 213

Johnson, Samuel 1822-1882. . . . . .DLB-1, 243

Johnson, Susanna 1730-1810 . . . . .DLB-200

Johnson, Terry 1955- DLB-233

Johnson, Uwe 1934-1984. . . . . .DLB-75; CDWLB-2

Johnston, Annie Fellows 1863-1931. . . . . . .DLB-42

Johnston, Basil H. 1929- DLB-60

Johnston, David Claypole 1798?-1865. . . .DLB-188

Johnston, Denis 1901-1984 . . . . .DLB-10

Johnston, Ellen 1835-1873 . . . . .DLB-199

Johnston, George 1913- DLB-88

Johnston, Sir Harry 1858-1927 . . . . .DLB-174

Johnston, Jennifer 1930- DLB-14

Johnston, Mary 1870-1936. . . . . .DLB-9

Johnston, Richard Malcolm 1822-1898 . . . .DLB-74

Johnstone, Charles 1719?-1800? DLB-39

Johst, Hanns 1890-1978 . . . . .DLB-124

Jolas, Eugene 1894-1952 . . . . .DLB-4, 45

Jones, Alice C. 1853-1933 . . . . .DLB-92

Jones, Charles C., Jr. 1831-1893 . . . . .DLB-30

Jones, D. G. 1929- DLB-53

Jones, David 1895-1974 . . .DLB-20, 100; CDBLB-7

Jones, Diana Wynne 1934- DLB-161

Jones, Ebenezer 1820-1860 . . . . .DLB-32

Jones, Ernest 1819-1868. . . . . .DLB-32

Jones, Gayl 1949- DLB-33

Jones, George 1800-1870 . . . . .DLB-183

Jones, Glyn 1905- DLB-15

Jones, Gwyn 1907- DLB-15, 139

Jones, Henry Arthur 1851-1929 . . . . .DLB-10

Jones, Hugh circa 1692-1760 . . . . .DLB-24

Jones, James 1921-1977 . . . . . . .DLB-2, 143; DS-17

James Jones Papers in the Handy Writers'
Colony Collection at the University of
Illinois at Springfield Y-98

The James Jones Society Y-92

Jones, Jenkin Lloyd 1911- DLB-127

Jones, John Beauchamp 1810-1866 . . . . . .DLB-202

Jones, LeRoi (see Baraka, Amiri)

Jones, Lewis 1897-1939 . . . . .DLB-15

Jones, Madison 1925- DLB-152

Jones, Major Joseph
(see Thompson, William Tappan)

Jones, Marie 1955- DLB-233

Jones, Preston 1936-1979. . . . . .DLB-7

Jones, Rodney 1950- DLB-120

Jones, Thom 1945- DLB-244

Jones, Sir William 1746-1794 . . . . .DLB-109

Jones, William Alfred 1817-1900 . . . . .DLB-59

Jones's Publishing House. DLB-49

Jong, Erica 1942- DLB-2, 5, 28, 152

Jonke, Gert F. 1946- DLB-85

Jonson, Ben
1572?-1637 . . . . .DLB-62, 121; CDBLB-1

Jordan, June 1936- DLB-38

Joseph and George. Y-99

Joseph, Jenny 1932- DLB-40

Joseph, Michael, Limited DLB-112

Josephson, Matthew 1899-1978 . . . . .DLB-4

Josephus, Flavius 37-100. . . . . .DLB-176

Josiah Allen's Wife (see Holley, Marietta)

Josipovici, Gabriel 1940- DLB-14

Josselyn, John ?-1675 . . . . .DLB-24

Joudry, Patricia 1921- DLB-88

Jovine, Giuseppe 1922- DLB-128

Joyaux, Philippe (see Sollers, Philippe)

Joyce, Adrien (see Eastman, Carol)

Joyce, James 1882-1941
. . . . .DLB-10, 19, 36, 162, 247; CDBLB-6

James Joyce Centenary: Dublin, 1982 . . . . . . .Y-82

James Joyce Conference. Y-85

A Joyce (Con)Text: Danis Rose and the
Remaking of *Ulysses*. Y-97

The New *Ulysses*. .Y-84

Jozsef, Attila 1905-1937 . . . . .DLB-215; CDWLB-4

Judd, Orange, Publishing Company DLB-49

Judd, Sylvester 1813-1853 . . . . .DLB-1, 243

Judith circa 930 . . . . .DLB-146

Julian of Norwich
1342-circa 1420. . . . . .DLB-1146

Julius Caesar
100 B.C.-44 B.C.. . . . . . . .DLB-211; CDWLB-1

June, Jennie
(see Croly, Jane Cunningham)

Jung, Franz 1888-1963. . . . . .DLB-118

Jünger, Ernst 1895- DLB-56; CDWLB-2

Der jüngere Titurel circa 1275 . . . . .DLB-138

Jung-Stilling, Johann Heinrich
1740-1817 . . . . .DLB-94

Justice, Donald 1925- Y-83

Juvenal circa A.D. 60-circa A.D. 130
. . . . DLB-211; CDWLB-1

The Juvenile Library
(see Godwin, M. J., and Company)

K

Kacew, Romain (see Gary, Romain)

Kafka, Franz 1883-1924 . . . . . DLB-81; CDWLB-2

Kahn, Roger 1927- DLB-171

Kaikō Takeshi 1939-1989 . . . . DLB-182

Kaiser, Georg 1878-1945 . . . . DLB-124; CDWLB-2

Kaiserchronik circca 1147 . . . . DLB-148

Kaleb, Vjekoslav 1905- DLB-181

Kalechofsky, Roberta 1931- DLB-28

Kaler, James Otis 1848-1912 . . . . DLB-12

Kames, Henry Home, Lord
1696-1782 . . . . DLB-31, 104

Kamo no Chōmei (Kamo no Nagaakira)
1153 or 1155-1216 . . . . DLB-203

Kamo no Nagaakira (see Kamo no Chōmei)

Kampmann, Christian 1939-1988 . . . . DLB-214

Kandel, Lenore 1932- DLB-16

Kanin, Garson 1912-1999 . . . . DLB-7

Kant, Hermann 1926- DLB-75

Kant, Immanuel 1724-1804 . . . . DLB-94

Kantemir, Antiokh Dmitrievich
1708-1744 . . . . DLB-150

Kantor, MacKinlay 1904-1977 . . . . DLB-9, 102

Kanze Kōjirō Nobumitsu 1435-1516 . . . . DLB-203

Kanze Motokiyo (see Zeimi)

Kaplan, Fred 1937- DLB-111

Kaplan, Johanna 1942- DLB-28

Kaplan, Justin 1925- DLB-111; Y-86

The Practice of Biography V:
An Interview with Justin Kaplan Y-86

Kaplinski, Jaan 1941- DLB-232

Kapnist, Vasilii Vasilevich 1758?-1823 . . . DLB-150

Karadžić, Vuk Stefanović
1787-1864 . . . . .DLB-147; CDWLB-4

Karamzin, Nikolai Mikhailovich
1766-1826 . . . . DLB-150

Karinthy, Frigyes 1887-1938 . . . . DLB-215

Karsch, Anna Louisa 1722-1791 . . . . DLB-97

Kasack, Hermann 1896-1966 . . . . DLB-69

Kasai, Zenzō 1887-1927 . . . . DLB-180

Kaschnitz, Marie Luise 1901-1974 . . . . DLB-69

Kassák, Lajos 1887-1967 . . . . DLB-215

Kaštelan, Jure 1919-1990 . . . . DLB-147

Kästner, Erich 1899-1974 . . . . DLB-56

Katenin, Pavel Aleksandrovich
1792-1853 . . . . DLB-205

Kattan, Naim 1928- DLB-53

Katz, Steve 1935- Y-83

Kauffman, Janet 1945- DLB-218; Y-86

Kauffmann, Samuel 1898-1971 . . . . DLB-127

Kaufman, Bob 1925- DLB-16, 41

Kaufman, George S. 1889-1961 . . . . DLB-7

Kavanagh, P. J. 1931- DLB-40

Kavanagh, Patrick 1904-1967 . . . . DLB-15, 20

Kawabata, Yasunari 1899-1972 . . . . DLB-180

Kaye-Smith, Sheila 1887-1956 . . . . DLB-36

Kazin, Alfred 1915-1998 . . . . DLB-67

Keane, John B. 1928- DLB-13

Keary, Annie 1825-1879 . . . . DLB-163

Keary, Eliza 1827-1918 . . . . DLB-240

Keating, H. R. F. 1926- DLB-87

Keatley, Charlotte 1960- DLB-245

Keats, Ezra Jack 1916-1983 . . . . DLB-61

Keats, John 1795-1821 . . . DLB-96, 110; CDBLB-3

Keble, John 1792-1866 . . . . DLB-32, 55

Keckley, Elizabeth 1818?-1907 . . . . DLB-239

Keeble, John 1944- Y-83

Keeffe, Barrie 1945- DLB-13, 245

Keeley, James 1867-1934 . . . . DLB-25

W. B. Keen, Cooke and Company DLB-49

Keillor, Garrison 1942- Y-87

Keith, Marian 1874?-1961 . . . . DLB-92

Keller, Gary D. 1943- DLB-82

Keller, Gottfried
1819-1890 . . . . DLB-129; CDWLB-2

Kelley, Edith Summers 1884-1956 . . . . DLB-9

Kelley, Emma Dunham ?-? DLB-221

Kelley, William Melvin 1937- DLB-33

Kellogg, Ansel Nash 1832-1886 . . . . DLB-23

Kellogg, Steven 1941- DLB-61

Kelly, George 1887-1974 . . . . DLB-7

Kelly, Hugh 1739-1777 . . . . DLB-89

Kelly, Piet and Company DLB-49

Kelly, Robert 1935- DLB-5, 130, 165

Kelman, James 1946- DLB-194

Kelmscott Press DLB-112

Kemble, E. W. 1861-1933 . . . . DLB-188

Kemble, Fanny 1809-1893 . . . . DLB-32

Kemelman, Harry 1908- DLB-28

Kempe, Margery circa 1373-1438 . . . . DLB-146

Kempner, Friederike 1836-1904 . . . . DLB-129

Kempowski, Walter 1929- DLB-75

Kendall, Claude [publishing company] DLB-46

Kendall, Henry 1839-1882 . . . . DLB-230

Kendall, May 1861-1943 . . . . DLB-240

Kendell, George 1809-1867 . . . . DLB-43

Kenedy, P. J., and Sons DLB-49

Kenkō circa 1283-circa 1352 . . . . DLB-203

Kennan, George 1845-1924 . . . . DLB-189

Kennedy, Adrienne 1931- DLB-38

Kennedy, John Pendleton 1795-1870 . . . . . . DLB-3

Kennedy, Leo 1907- DLB-88

Kennedy, Margaret 1896-1967 . . . . DLB-36

Kennedy, Patrick 1801-1873 . . . . DLB-159

Kennedy, Richard S. 1920- DLB-111

Kennedy, William 1928- DLB-143; Y-85

Kennedy, X. J. 1929- DLB-5

Kennelly, Brendan 1936- DLB-40

Kenner, Hugh 1923- DLB-67

Kennerley, Mitchell [publishing house] . . . DLB-46

Kenny, Maurice 1929- DLB-175

Kent, Frank R. 1877-1958 . . . . DLB-29

Kenyon, Jane 1947-1995 . . . . DLB-120

Keough, Hugh Edmund 1864-1912 . . . . .DLB-171

Keppler and Schwartzmann DLB-49

Ker, John, third Duke of Roxburghe
1740-1804 . . . . DLB-213

Ker, N. R. 1908-1982 . . . . DLB-201

Kerlan, Irvin 1912-1963 . . . . .DLB-187

Kermode, Frank 1919- DLB-242

Kern, Jerome 1885-1945 . . . . .DLB-187

Kerner, Justinus 1776-1862 . . . . DLB-90

Kerouac, Jack
1922-1969 . . DLB-2, 16, 237; DS-3; CDALB-1

The Jack Kerouac Revival Y-95

"Re-meeting of Old Friends":
The Jack Kerouac Conference Y-82

Kerouac, Jan 1952-1996 . . . . DLB-16

Kerr, Charles H., and Company DLB-49

Kerr, Orpheus C. (see Newell, Robert Henry)

Kesey, Ken 1935- . . . DLB-2, 16, 206; CDALB-6

Kessel, Joseph 1898-1979 . . . . DLB-72

Kessel, Martin 1901- DLB-56

Kesten, Hermann 1900- DLB-56

Keun, Irmgard 1905-1982 . . . . DLB-69

Key and Biddle DLB-49

Keynes, Sir Geoffrey 1887-1982 . . . . DLB-201

Keynes, John Maynard 1883-1946 . . . . . . .DS-10

Keyserling, Eduard von 1855-1918 . . . . . . DLB-66

Khan, Ismith 1925- DLB-125

Khaytov, Nikolay 1919- DLB-181

Khemnitser, Ivan Ivanovich
1745-1784 . . . . DLB-150

Kheraskov, Mikhail Matveevich
1733-1807 . . . . DLB-150

Khomiakov, Aleksei Stepanovich
1804-1860 . . . . DLB-205

Khristov, Boris 1945- DLB-181

Khvoshchinskaia, Nadezhda Dmitrievna
1824-1889 . . . . DLB-238

Khvostov, Dmitrii Ivanovich
1757-1835 . . . . DLB-150

Kidd, Adam 1802?-1831 . . . . DLB-99

Kidd, William [publishing house] DLB-106

Kidder, Tracy 1945- DLB-185

Kiely, Benedict 1919- DLB-15

Kieran, John 1892-1981 . . . . .DLB-171

Kiggins and Kellogg DLB-49

Kiley, Jed 1889-1962 . . . . DLB-4

Kilgore, Bernard 1908-1967 . . . . .DLB-127

Killens, John Oliver 1916- DLB-33

Killigrew, Anne 1660-1685 . . . . DLB-131

Killigrew, Thomas 1612-1683 . . . . .DLB-58

Kilmer, Joyce 1886-1918 . . . . .DLB-45

Kilroy, Thomas 1934- DLB-233

Kilwardby, Robert circa 1215-1279 . . . . .DLB-115

Kimball, Richard Burleigh 1816-1892 . . . .DLB-202

Kincaid, Jamaica 1949-
. . . . . . DLB-157, 227; CDALB-7; CDWLB-3

King, Charles 1844-1933 . . . . .DLB-186

King, Clarence 1842-1901 . . . . .DLB-12

King, Florence 1936. . . . . Y-85

King, Francis 1923- DLB-15, 139

King, Grace 1852-1932 . . . . .DLB-12, 78

King, Harriet Hamilton 1840-1920 . . . . .DLB-199

King, Henry 1592-1669 . . . . .DLB-126

King, Solomon [publishing house] DLB-49

King, Stephen 1947- DLB-143; Y-80

King, Susan Petigru 1824-1875 . . . . .DLB-239

King, Thomas 1943- DLB-175

King, Woodie, Jr. 1937- DLB-38

Kinglake, Alexander William
1809-1891 . . . . .DLB-55, 166

Kingsley, Charles
1819-1875 . . . . DLB-21, 32, 163, 178, 190

Kingsley, Henry 1830-1876 . . . . .DLB-21, 230

Kingsley, Mary Henrietta 1862-1900. . . . .DLB-174

Kingsley, Sidney 1906- DLB-7

Kingsmill, Hugh 1889-1949. . . . . .DLB-149

Kingsolver, Barbara
1955- DLB-206; CDALB-7

Kingston, Maxine Hong
1940- DLB-173, 212; Y-80; CDALB-7

Kingston, William Henry Giles
1814-1880 . . . . .DLB-163

Kinnan, Mary Lewis 1763-1848. . . . . . . .DLB-200

Kinnell, Galway 1927- DLB-5; Y-87

Kinsella, Thomas 1928- DLB-27

Kipling, Rudyard 1865-1936
. . . . .DLB-19, 34, 141, 156; CDBLB-5

Kipphardt, Heinar 1922-1982 . . . . .DLB-124

Kirby, William 1817-1906 . . . . .DLB-99

Kircher, Athanasius 1602-1680 . . . . .DLB-164

Kireevsky, Ivan Vasil'evich 1806-1856 . . .DLB-198

Kireevsky, Petr Vasil'evich 1808-1856 . . .DLB-205

Kirk, Hans 1898-1962 . . . . .DLB-214

Kirk, John Foster 1824-1904 . . . . .DLB-79

Kirkconnell, Watson 1895-1977. . . . . .DLB-68

Kirkland, Caroline M.
1801-1864 . . . . DLB-3, 73, 74; DS-13

Kirkland, Joseph 1830-1893. . . . . .DLB-12

Kirkman, Francis [publishing house] DLB-170

Kirkpatrick, Clayton 1915- DLB-127

Kirkup, James 1918- DLB-27

Kirouac, Conrad (see Marie-Victorin, Frère)

Kirsch, Sarah 1935- DLB-75

Kirst, Hans Hellmut 1914-1989. . . . . .DLB-69

Kiš, Danilo 1935-1989 . . . . . .DLB-181; CDWLB-4

Kita Morio 1927- DLB-182

Kitcat, Mabel Greenhow 1859-1922 . . . . .DLB-135

Kitchin, C. H. B. 1895-1967 . . . . .DLB-77

Kittredge, William 1932- DLB-212, 244

Kiukhel'beker, Vil'gel'm Karlovich
1797-1846. . . . . .DLB-205

Kizer, Carolyn 1925- DLB-5, 169

Klabund 1890-1928 . . . . .DLB-66

Klaj, Johann 1616-1656 . . . . .DLB-164

Klappert, Peter 1942- DLB-5

Klass, Philip (see Tenn, William)

Klein, A. M. 1909-1972 . . . . .DLB-68

Kleist, Ewald von 1715-1759 . . . . .DLB-97

Kleist, Heinrich von
1777-1811. . . . . .DLB-90; CDWLB-2

Klinger, Friedrich Maximilian
1752-1831. . . . . .DLB-94

Klíma, Ivan 1931- DLB-232; CDWLB-4

Kliushnikov, Viktor Petrovich
1841-1892 . . . . .DLB-238

Oral History Interview with Donald S.
Klopfer Y-97

Klopstock, Friedrich Gottlieb
1724-1803 . . . . .DLB-97

Klopstock, Meta 1728-1758 . . . . .DLB-97

Kluge, Alexander 1932- DLB-75

Knapp, Joseph Palmer 1864-1951 . . . . . . .DLB-91

Knapp, Samuel Lorenzo 1783-1838 . . . . . .DLB-59

Knapton, J. J. and P.
[publishing house] DLB-154

Kniazhnin, Iakov Borisovich
1740-1791 . . . . .DLB-150

Knickerbocker, Diedrich (see Irving, Washington)

Knigge, Adolph Franz Friedrich Ludwig,
Freiherr von 1752-1796 . . . . .DLB-94

Knight, Charles, and Company. DLB-106

Knight, Damon 1922- DLB-8

Knight, Etheridge 1931-1992. . . . . .DLB-41

Knight, John S. 1894-1981. . . . . .DLB-29

Knight, Sarah Kemble 1666-1727. . . . .DLB-24, 200

Knight-Bruce, G. W. H. 1852-1896. . . . . .DLB-174

Knister, Raymond 1899-1932 . . . . .DLB-68

Knoblock, Edward 1874-1945 . . . . .DLB-10

Knopf, Alfred A. 1892-1984 . . . . Y-84

Knopf, Alfred A. [publishing house] DLB-46

Knopf to Hammett: The Editoral
Correspondence Y-00

Knorr von Rosenroth, Christian
1636-1689 . . . . .DLB-168

"Knots into Webs: Some Autobiographical
Sources," by Dabney Stuart DLB-105

Knowles, John 1926- DLB-6; CDALB-6

Knox, Frank 1874-1944 . . . . .DLB-29

Knox, John circa 1514-1572. . . . . .DLB-132

Knox, John Armoy 1850-1906. . . . . .DLB-23

Knox, Lucy 1845-1884 . . . . .DLB-240

Knox, Ronald Arbuthnott 1888-1957 . . . . .DLB-77

Knox, Thomas Wallace 1835-1896. . . . . . .DLB-189

Kobayashi Takiji 1903-1933 . . . . .DLB-180

Kober, Arthur 1900-1975. . . . . .DLB-11

Kobiakova, Aleksandra Petrovna
1823-1892 . . . . .DLB-238

Kocbek, Edvard 1904-1981 . . . DLB-147; CDWB-4

Koch, Howard 1902- DLB-26

Koch, Kenneth 1925- DLB-5

Kōda, Rohan 1867-1947. . . . . .DLB-180

Koenigsberg, Moses 1879-1945 . . . . .DLB-25

Koeppen, Wolfgang 1906-1996. . . . . .DLB-69

Koertge, Ronald 1940- DLB-105

Koestler, Arthur 1905-1983 . . . . . . Y-83; CDBLB-7

Kohn, John S. Van E. 1906-1976 and
Papantonio, Michael 1907-1978. . . . . .DLB-187

Kokoschka, Oskar 1886-1980 . . . . .DLB-124

Kolb, Annette 1870-1967 . . . . .DLB-66

Kolbenheyer, Erwin Guido
1878-1962 . . . . .DLB-66, 124

Kolleritsch, Alfred 1931- DLB-85

Kolodny, Annette 1941- DLB-67

Kol'tsov, Aleksei Vasil'evich
1809-1842 . . . . .DLB-205

Komarov, Matvei circa 1730-1812. . . . . .DLB-150

Komroff, Manuel 1890-1974 . . . . .DLB-4

Komunyakaa, Yusef 1947- DLB-120

Koneski, Blaže 1921-1993 . . . DLB-181; CDWLB-4

Konigsburg, E. L. 1930- DLB-52

Konparu Zenchiku 1405-1468? DLB-203

Konrád, György 1933- DLB-232; CDWLB-4

Konrad von Würzburg
circa 1230-1287 . . . . .DLB-138

Konstantinov, Aleko 1863-1897. . . . . . . .DLB-147

Konwicki, Tadeusz 1926- DLB-232

Kooser, Ted 1939- DLB-105

Kopit, Arthur 1937- DLB-7

Kops, Bernard 1926?- DLB-13

Kornbluth, C. M. 1923-1958. . . . . .DLB-8

Körner, Theodor 1791-1813 . . . . .DLB-90

Kornfeld, Paul 1889-1942 . . . . .DLB-118

Kosinski, Jerzy 1933-1991 . . . . DLB-2; Y-82

Kosmač, Ciril 1910-1980 . . . . .DLB-181

Kosovel, Srečko 1904-1926 . . . . .DLB-147

Kostrov, Ermil Ivanovich 1755-1796 . . . . .DLB-150

Kotzebue, August von 1761-1819 . . . . .DLB-94

Kotzwinkle, William 1938- DLB-173

Kovačić, Ante 1854-1889. . . . . .DLB-147

Kovič, Kajetan 1931- DLB-181

Kozlov, Ivan Ivanovich 1779-1840. . . . . . .DLB-205

Kraf, Elaine 1946- Y-81

Kramer, Jane 1938- DLB-185

Kramer, Mark 1944- DLB-185

Kranjčević, Silvije Strahimir
1865-1908 . . . . .DLB-147

Krasko, Ivan 1876-1958. . . . . .DLB-215

Krasna, Norman 1909-1984 . . . . .DLB-26

Kraus, Hans Peter 1907-1988. . . . . .DLB-187

Kraus, Karl 1874-1936. . . . . .DLB-118

Krauss, Ruth 1911-1993 . . . . DLB-52

Kreisel, Henry 1922- DLB-88

Krestovsky V. (see Khvoshchinskaia,
    Nadezhda Dmitrievna)

Krestovsky, Vsevolod Vladimirovich
    1839-1895 . . . . DLB-238

Kreuder, Ernst 1903-1972. . . . . DLB-69

Krėvė-Mickevičius, Vincas 1882-1954 . . . DLB-220

Kreymborg, Alfred 1883-1966 . . . . DLB-4, 54

Krieger, Murray 1923- DLB-67

Krim, Seymour 1922-1989 . . . . DLB-16

Kristensen, Tom 1893-1974 . . . . DLB-214

Kristeva, Julia 1941- DLB-242

Krleža, Miroslav 1893-1981 . . DLB-147; CDWLB-4

Krock, Arthur 1886-1974 . . . . DLB-29

Kroetsch, Robert 1927- DLB-53

Kross, Jaan 1920- DLB-232

Krúdy, Gyula 1878-1933 . . . . DLB-215

Krutch, Joseph Wood
    1893-1970. . . . . DLB-63, 206

Krylov, Ivan Andreevich
    1769-1844. . . . . DLB-150

Kubin, Alfred 1877-1959 . . . . DLB-81

Kubrick, Stanley 1928-1999 . . . . DLB-26

Kudrun circa 1230-1240 . . . . DLB-138

Kuffstein, Hans Ludwig von
    1582-1656 . . . . DLB-164

Kuhlmann, Quirinus 1651-1689 . . . . DLB-168

Kuhnau, Johann 1660-1722 . . . . DLB-168

Kukol'nik, Nestor Vasil'evich
    1809-1868 . . . . DLB-205

Kukučín, Martin
    1860-1928 . . . . DLB-215; CDWLB-4

Kumin, Maxine 1925- DLB-5

Kuncewicz, Maria 1895-1989 . . . . DLB-215

Kundera, Milan 1929- DLB-232; CDWLB-4

Kunene, Mazisi 1930- DLB-117

Kunikida, Doppo 1869-1908 . . . . DLB-180

Kunitz, Stanley 1905- DLB-48

Kunjufu, Johari M. (see Amini, Johari M.)

Kunnert, Gunter 1929- DLB-75

Kunze, Reiner 1933- DLB-75

Kupferberg, Tuli 1923- DLB-16

Kurahashi Yumiko 1935- DLB-182

Kureishi, Hanif 1954- DLB-194, 245

Kürnberger, Ferdinand 1821-1879 . . . . . DLB-129

Kurz, Isolde 1853-1944 . . . . DLB-66

Kusenberg, Kurt 1904-1983 . . . . DLB-69

Kushchevsky, Ivan Afanas'evich
    1847-1876 . . . . DLB-238

Kushner, Tony 1956- DLB-228

Kuttner, Henry 1915-1958 . . . . DLB-8

Kyd, Thomas 1558-1594 . . . . DLB-62

Kyffin, Maurice circa 1560?-1598 . . . . DLB-136

Kyger, Joanne 1934- DLB-16

Kyne, Peter B. 1880-1957 . . . . DLB-78

Kyōgoku Tamekane 1254-1332 . . . . DLB-203

L

L. E. L. (see Landon, Letitia Elizabeth)

Laberge, Albert 1871-1960 . . . . DLB-68

Laberge, Marie 1950- DLB-60

Labiche, Eugène 1815-1888 . . . . DLB-192

Labrunie, Gerard (see Nerval, Gerard de)

La Capria, Raffaele 1922- DLB-196

Lacombe, Patrice
    (see Trullier-Lacombe, Joseph Patrice)

Lacretelle, Jacques de 1888-1985 . . . . . . DLB-65

Lacy, Ed 1911-1968 . . . . DLB-226

Lacy, Sam 1903- DLB-171

Ladd, Joseph Brown 1764-1786 . . . . DLB-37

La Farge, Oliver 1901-1963 . . . . DLB-9

Laffan, Mrs. R. S. de Courcy (see Adams,
    Bertha Leith)

Lafferty, R. A. 1914- DLB-8

La Flesche, Francis 1857-1932. . . . . DLB-175

Laforge, Jules 1860-1887 . . . . DLB-217

Lagorio, Gina 1922- DLB-196

La Guma, Alex
    1925-1985 . . . . DLB-117, 225; CDWLB-3

Lahaise, Guillaume (see Delahaye, Guy)

Lahontan, Louis-Armand de Lom d'Arce,
    Baron de 1666-1715? DLB-99

Laing, Kojo 1946- DLB-157

Laird, Carobeth 1895- Y-82

Laird and Lee DLB-49

Lalić, Ivan V. 1931-1996 . . . . DLB-181

Lalić, Mihailo 1914-1992 . . . . DLB-181

Lalonde, Michèle 1937- DLB-60

Lamantia, Philip 1927- DLB-16

Lamartine, Alphonse de 1790-1869 . . . . . DLB-217

Lamb, Lady Caroline 1785-1828 . . . . . . DLB-116

Lamb, Charles
    1775-1834 . . . . DLB-93, 107, 163; CDBLB-3

Lamb, Mary 1764-1874. . . . . DLB-163

Lambert, Betty 1933-1983 . . . . DLB-60

Lamming, George 1927- . . DLB-125; CDWLB-3

L'Amour, Louis 1908-1988 . . . . DLB-206; Y-80

Lampman, Archibald 1861-1899 . . . . DLB-92

Lamson, Wolffe and Company DLB-49

Lancer Books DLB-46

Landesman, Jay 1919- and
    Landesman, Fran 1927- DLB-16

Landolfi, Tommaso 1908-1979. . . . . .DLB-177

Landon, Letitia Elizabeth 1802-1838 . . . . DLB-96

Landor, Walter Savage 1775-1864 . . . . DLB-93, 107

Landry, Napoléon-P. 1884-1956. . . . . DLB-92

Lane, Charles 1800-1870 . . . . DLB-1, 223

Lane, F. C. 1885-1984 . . . . DLB-241

Lane, John, Company DLB-49

Lane, Laurence W. 1890-1967 . . . . DLB-91

Lane, M. Travis 1934- DLB-60

Lane, Patrick 1939- DLB-53

Lane, Pinkie Gordon 1923- DLB-41

Laney, Al 1896-1988 . . . . .DLB-4, 171

Lang, Andrew 1844-1912. . . . . . .DLB-98, 141, 184

Langevin, André 1927- DLB-60

Langgässer, Elisabeth 1899-1950 . . . . DLB-69

Langhorne, John 1735-1779 . . . . DLB-109

Langland, William
    circa 1330-circa 1400 . . . . DLB-146

Langton, Anna 1804-1893 . . . . DLB-99

Lanham, Edwin 1904-1979. . . . . DLB-4

Lanier, Sidney 1842-1881 . . . . DLB-64; DS-13

Lanyer, Aemilia 1569-1645 . . . . DLB-121

Lapointe, Gatien 1931-1983 . . . . DLB-88

Lapointe, Paul-Marie 1929- DLB-88

Larcom, Lucy 1824-1893 . . . . DLB-221, 243

Lardner, John 1912-1960 . . . . .DLB-171

Lardner, Ring 1885-1933
    . . . . DLB-11, 25, 86, 171; DS-16; CDALB-4

Lardner 100: Ring Lardner
    Centennial Symposium Y-85

Lardner, Ring, Jr. 1915-2000 . . . . . . .DLB-26, Y-00

Larkin, Philip 1922-1985 . . . . . DLB-27; CDBLB-8

La Roche, Sophie von 1730-1807 . . . . DLB-94

La Rocque, Gilbert 1943-1984 . . . . DLB-60

Laroque de Roquebrune, Robert
    (see Roquebrune, Robert de)

Larrick, Nancy 1910- DLB-61

Larsen, Nella 1893-1964. . . . . DLB-51

La Sale, Antoine de
    circa 1386-1460/1467 . . . . DLB-208

Lasch, Christopher 1932-1994 . . . . DLB-246

Lasker-Schüler, Else 1869-1945 . . . . . DLB-66, 124

Lasnier, Rina 1915- DLB-88

Lassalle, Ferdinand 1825-1864 . . . . DLB-129

Latham, Robert 1912-1995. . . . . DLB-201

Lathrop, Dorothy P. 1891-1980 . . . . DLB-22

Lathrop, George Parsons 1851-1898 . . . . . DLB-71

Lathrop, John, Jr. 1772-1820. . . . . DLB-37

Latimer, Hugh 1492?-1555. . . . . DLB-136

Latimore, Jewel Christine McLawler
    (see Amini, Johari M.)

Latymer, William 1498-1583 . . . . DLB-132

Laube, Heinrich 1806-1884 . . . . DLB-133

Laud, William 1573-1645 . . . . DLB-213

Laughlin, James 1914-1997 . . . . .DLB-48; Y-96

James Laughlin Tributes. Y-97

Conversations with Publishers IV:
    An Interview with James Laughlin Y-96

Laumer, Keith 1925- DLB-8

Lauremberg, Johann 1590-1658 . . . . DLB-164

Laurence, Margaret 1926-1987. . . . . DLB-53

Laurentius von Schnüffis 1633-1702 . . . . DLB-168

Laurents, Arthur 1918- DLB-26

Laurie, Annie (see Black, Winifred)

Laut, Agnes Christiana 1871-1936 . . . . . . DLB-92

Lauterbach, Ann 1942- DLB-193

Lautreamont, Isidore Lucien Ducasse, Comte de 1846-1870 . . . . DLB-217

Lavater, Johann Kaspar 1741-1801 . . . . DLB-97

Lavin, Mary 1912-1996 . . . . DLB-15

Law, John (see Harkness, Margaret)

Lawes, Henry 1596-1662 . . . . DLB-126

Lawless, Anthony (see MacDonald, Philip)

Lawless, Emily (The Hon. Emily Lawless) 1845-1913 DLB-240

Lawrence, D. H. 1885-1930 . . . . . DLB-10, 19, 36, 98, 162, 195; CDBLB-6

Lawrence, David 1888-1973 . . . . DLB-29

Lawrence, Jerome 1915- and Lee, Robert E. 1918-1994 . . . . DLB-228

Lawrence, Seymour 1926-1994 . . . . Y-94

Lawrence, T. E. 1888-1935 . . . . DLB-195

Lawson, George 1598-1678 . . . . DLB-213

Lawson, Henry 1867-1922 . . . . DLB-230

Lawson, John ?-1711 . . . . DLB-24

Lawson, John Howard 1894-1977 . . . . . . DLB-228

Lawson, Louisa Albury 1848-1920 . . . . . DLB-230

Lawson, Robert 1892-1957 . . . . DLB-22

Lawson, Victor F. 1850-1925 . . . . DLB-25

Layard, Sir Austen Henry 1817-1894 . . . . DLB-166

Layton, Irving 1912- DLB-88

LaZamon flourished circa 1200 . . . . DLB-146

Lazarević, Laza K. 1851-1890 . . . . DLB-147

Lazarus, George 1904-1997 . . . . DLB-201

Lazhechnikov, Ivan Ivanovich 1792-1869 . . . . DLB-198

Lea, Henry Charles 1825-1909 . . . . DLB-47

Lea, Sydney 1942- DLB-120

Lea, Tom 1907- DLB-6

Leacock, John 1729-1802 . . . . DLB-31

Leacock, Stephen 1869-1944 . . . . DLB-92

Lead, Jane Ward 1623-1704 . . . . DLB-131

Leadenhall Press DLB-106

Leakey, Caroline Woolmer 1827-1881 . . . DLB-230

Leapor, Mary 1722-1746 . . . . DLB-109

Lear, Edward 1812-1888 . . . . . . DLB-32, 163, 166

Leary, Timothy 1920-1996 . . . . DLB-16

Leary, W. A., and Company DLB-49

Léautaud, Paul 1872-1956 . . . . DLB-65

Leavis, F. R. 1895-1978 . . . . DLB-242

Leavitt, David 1961- DLB-130

Leavitt and Allen DLB-49

Le Blond, Mrs. Aubrey 1861-1934 . . . . . . DLB-174

le Carré, John 1931- DLB-87; CDBLB-8

Lécavelé, Roland (see Dorgeles, Roland)

Lechlitner, Ruth 1901- DLB-48

Leclerc, Félix 1914- DLB-60

Le Clézio, J. M. G. 1940- DLB-83

Lectures on Rhetoric and Belles Lettres (1783), by Hugh Blair [excerpts] DLB-31

Leder, Rudolf (see Hermlin, Stephan)

Lederer, Charles 1910-1976 . . . . DLB-26

Ledwidge, Francis 1887-1917 . . . . DLB-20

Lee, Dennis 1939- DLB-53

Lee, Don L. (see Madhubuti, Haki R.)

Lee, George W. 1894-1976 . . . . DLB-51

Lee, Harper 1926- DLB-6; CDALB-1

Lee, Harriet (1757-1851) and Lee, Sophia (1750-1824) DLB-39

Lee, Laurie 1914-1997 . . . . DLB-27

Lee, Li-Young 1957- DLB-165

Lee, Manfred B. (see Dannay, Frederic, and Manfred B. Lee)

Lee, Nathaniel circa 1645-1692 . . . . DLB-80

Lee, Sir Sidney 1859-1926 . . . . DLB-149, 184

Lee, Sir Sidney, "Principles of Biography," in *Elizabethan and Other Essays* DLB-149

Lee, Vernon 1856-1935 . . . . DLB-57, 153, 156, 174, 178

Lee and Shepard DLB-49

Le Fanu, Joseph Sheridan 1814-1873 . . . . DLB-21, 70, 159, 178

Leffland, Ella 1931- Y-84

le Fort, Gertrud von 1876-1971 . . . . DLB-66

Le Gallienne, Richard 1866-1947 . . . . DLB-4

Legaré, Hugh Swinton 1797-1843 . . . DLB-3, 59, 73

Legaré, James M. 1823-1859 . . . . DLB-3

The Legends of the Saints and a Medieval Christian Worldview DLB-148

Léger, Antoine-J. 1880-1950 . . . . DLB-88

Le Guin, Ursula K. 1929- DLB-8, 52; CDALB-6

Lehman, Ernest 1920- DLB-44

Lehmann, John 1907- DLB-27, 100

Lehmann, John, Limited DLB-112

Lehmann, Rosamond 1901-1990 . . . . DLB-15

Lehmann, Wilhelm 1882-1968 . . . . DLB-56

Leiber, Fritz 1910-1992 . . . . DLB-8

Leibniz, Gottfried Wilhelm 1646-1716 . . . . DLB-168

Leicester University Press DLB-112

Leigh, W. R. 1866-1955 . . . . DLB-188

Leinster, Murray 1896-1975 . . . . DLB-8

Leiser, Bill 1898-1965 . . . . DLB-241

Leisewitz, Johann Anton 1752-1806 . . . . . . DLB-94

Leitch, Maurice 1933- DLB-14

Leithauser, Brad 1943- DLB-120

Leland, Charles G. 1824-1903 . . . . DLB-11

Leland, John 1503?-1552 . . . . DLB-136

Lemay, Pamphile 1837-1918 . . . . DLB-99

Lemelin, Roger 1919- DLB-88

Lemercier, Louis-Jean-Népomucène 1771-1840 . . . . DLB-192

Le Moine, James MacPherson 1825-1912 . . . . DLB-99

Lemon, Mark 1809-1870 . . . . DLB-163

Le Moyne, Jean 1913- DLB-88

Lemperly, Paul 1858-1939 . . . . DLB-187

L'Engle, Madeleine 1918- DLB-52

Lennart, Isobel 1915-1971 . . . . DLB-44

Lennox, Charlotte 1729 or 1730-1804 . . . . DLB-39

Lenox, James 1800-1880 . . . . DLB-140

Lenski, Lois 1893-1974 . . . . DLB-22

Lentricchia, Frank 1940- DLB-246

Lenz, Hermann 1913-1998 . . . . DLB-69

Lenz, J. M. R. 1751-1792 . . . . DLB-94

Lenz, Siegfried 1926- DLB-75

Leonard, Elmore 1925- DLB-173, 226

Leonard, Hugh 1926- DLB-13

Leonard, William Ellery 1876-1944 . . . . . . DLB-54

Leonowens, Anna 1834-1914 . . . . DLB-99, 166

LePan, Douglas 1914- DLB-88

Lepik, Kalju 1920-1999 . . . . DLB-232

Leprohon, Rosanna Eleanor 1829-1879 . . . . DLB-99

Le Queux, William 1864-1927 . . . . DLB-70

Lermontov, Mikhail Iur'evich 1814-1841 . . . . DLB-205

Lerner, Max 1902-1992 . . . . DLB-29

Lernet-Holenia, Alexander 1897-1976 . . . . DLB-85

Le Rossignol, James 1866-1969 . . . . DLB-92

Lescarbot, Marc circa 1570-1642 . . . . DLB-99

LeSeur, William Dawson 1840-1917 . . . . . DLB-92

LeSieg, Theo. (see Geisel, Theodor Seuss)

Leskov, Nikolai Semenovich 1831-1895 . . DLB-238

Leslie, Doris before 1902-1982 . . . . DLB-191

Leslie, Eliza 1787-1858 . . . . DLB-202

Leslie, Frank 1821-1880 . . . . DLB-43, 79

Leslie, Frank, Publishing House DLB-49

Leśmian, Bolesław 1878-1937 . . . . DLB-215

Lesperance, John 1835?-1891 . . . . DLB-99

Lessing, Bruno 1870-1940 . . . . DLB-28

Lessing, Doris 1919- DLB-15, 139; Y-85; CDBLB-8

Lessing, Gotthold Ephraim 1729-1781 . . . . DLB-97; CDWLB-2

Lettau, Reinhard 1929- DLB-75

Letter from Japan Y-94, Y-98

Letter from London Y-96

Letter to [Samuel] Richardson on *Clarissa* (1748), by Henry Fielding DLB-39

A Letter to the Editor of *The Irish Times* Y-97

Lever, Charles 1806-1872 . . . . DLB-21

Lever, Ralph ca. 1527-1585 . . . . DLB-236

Leverson, Ada 1862-1933 . . . . DLB-153

Levertov, Denise 1923-1997 . . . . DLB-5, 165; CDALB-7

Levi, Peter 1931- DLB-40

Levi, Primo 1919-1987 . . . . DLB-177

Lévi-Strauss, Claude 1908- DLB-242

Levien, Sonya 1888-1960 . . . . DLB-44

Levin, Meyer 1905-1981 . . . . . . DLB-9, 28; Y-81

Levine, Norman 1923- DLB-88

Levine, Philip 1928- DLB-5

Levis, Larry 1946- DLB-120

Levy, Amy 1861-1889 . . . . DLB-156, 240

Levy, Benn Wolfe 1900-1973 . . . . . . .DLB-13; Y-81

Lewald, Fanny 1811-1889. . . . . DLB-129

Lewes, George Henry 1817-1878 . . . . DLB-55, 144

"Criticism In Relation To
Novels" (1863) DLB-21

The Principles of Success in Literature
(1865) [excerpt] DLB-57

Lewis, Agnes Smith 1843-1926. . . . . .DLB-174

Lewis, Alfred H. 1857-1914 . . . . DLB-25, 186

Lewis, Alun 1915-1944. . . . . DLB-20, 162

Lewis, C. Day (see Day Lewis, C.)

Lewis, C. S.
1898-1963 . . . . . DLB-15, 100, 160; CDBLB-7

Lewis, Charles B. 1842-1924 . . . . DLB-11

Lewis, Henry Clay 1825-1850 . . . . DLB-3

Lewis, Janet 1899-1999. . . . . .Y-87

Lewis, Matthew Gregory
1775-1818 . . . . .DLB-39, 158, 178

Lewis, Meriwether 1774-1809 and
Clark, William 1770-1838 . . . . . DLB-183, 186

Lewis, Norman 1908- DLB-204

Lewis, R. W. B. 1917- DLB-111

Lewis, Richard circa 1700-1734. . . . . DLB-24

Lewis, Sinclair
1885-1951 . . . . . DLB-9, 102; DS-1; CDALB-4

Sinclair Lewis Centennial Conference Y-85

Lewis, Wilmarth Sheldon 1895-1979 . . . . DLB-140

Lewis, Wyndham 1882-1957 . . . . DLB-15

Lewisohn, Ludwig 1882-1955 . . DLB-4, 9, 28, 102

Leyendecker, J. C. 1874-1951 . . . . DLB-188

Lezama Lima, José 1910-1976 . . . . DLB-113

L'Heureux, John 1934- DLB-244

Libbey, Laura Jean 1862-1924 . . . . DLB-221

The Library of America DLB-46

The Licensing Act of 1737 . . . . DLB-84

Lichfield, Leonard I [publishing house] . . .DLB-170

Lichtenberg, Georg Christoph 1742-1799 . . DLB-94

The Liddle Collection. Y-97

Lieb, Fred 1888-1980 . . . . .DLB-171

Liebling, A. J. 1904-1963 . . . . .DLB-4, 171

Lieutenant Murray (see Ballou, Maturin Murray)

Lighthall, William Douw 1857-1954. . . . . DLB-92

Lilar, Françoise (see Mallet-Joris, Françoise)

Lili'uokalani, Queen 1838-1917 . . . . DLB-221

Lillo, George 1691-1739 . . . . DLB-84

Lilly, J. K., Jr. 1893-1966 . . . . DLB-140

Lilly, Wait and Company. DLB-49

Lily, William circa 1468-1522 . . . . DLB-132

Limited Editions Club DLB-46

Limón, Graciela 1938- DLB-209

Lincoln and Edmands. DLB-49

Lindesay, Ethel Forence
(see Richardson, Henry Handel)

Lindsay, Alexander William, Twenty-fifth Earl
of Crawford 1812-1880 . . . . DLB-184

Lindsay, Sir David circa 1485-1555 . . . . . DLB-132

Lindsay, Jack 1900- Y-84

Lindsay, Lady (Caroline Blanche Elizabeth Fitzroy
Lindsay) 1844-1912 . . . . DLB-199

Lindsay, Vachel 1879-1931. . . . DLB-54; CDALB-3

Linebarger, Paul Myron Anthony
(see Smith, Cordwainer)

Link, Arthur S. 1920-1998 . . . . DLB-17

Linn, Ed 1922-2000 . . . . DLB-241

Linn, John Blair 1777-1804 . . . . DLB-37

Lins, Osman 1924-1978 . . . . DLB-145

Linton, Eliza Lynn 1822-1898 . . . . DLB-18

Linton, William James 1812-1897. . . . . . DLB-32

Lintot, Barnaby Bernard
[publishing house] DLB-170

Lion Books DLB-46

Lionni, Leo 1910-1999 . . . . DLB-61

Lippard, George 1822-1854 . . . . DLB-202

Lippincott, J. B., Company DLB-49

Lippincott, Sara Jane Clarke 1823-1904 . . . DLB-43

Lippmann, Walter 1889-1974. . . . . DLB-29

Lipton, Lawrence 1898-1975 . . . . DLB-16

Liscow, Christian Ludwig 1701-1760 . . . . . DLB-97

Lish, Gordon 1934- DLB-130

Lisle, Charles-Marie-René Leconte de
1818-1894 . . . . DLB-217

Lispector, Clarice
1925-1977. . . . . .DLB-113; CDWLB-3

A Literary Archaelogist Digs On: A Brief
Interview with Michael Reynolds by
Michael Rogers Y-99

The Literary Chronicle and Weekly Review
1819-1828 . . . . DLB-110

Literary Documents: William Faulkner
and the People-to-People Program Y-86

Literary Documents II: *Library Journal*
Statements and Questionnaires from
First Novelists Y-87

Literary Effects of World War II
[British novel]. DLB-15

Literary Prizes Y-00

Literary Prizes [British]. DLB-15

Literary Research Archives: The Humanities
Research Center, University of Texas. . . . Y-82

Literary Research Archives II: Berg Collection
of English and American Literature of
the New York Public Library. Y-83

Literary Research Archives III:
The Lilly Library. Y-84

Literary Research Archives IV:
The John Carter Brown Library Y-85

Literary Research Archives V:
Kent State Special Collections Y-86

Literary Research Archives VI: The Modern
Literary Manuscripts Collection in the
Special Collections of the Washington
University Libraries. Y-87

Literary Research Archives VII:
The University of Virginia Libraries Y-91

Literary Research Archives VIII:
The Henry E. Huntington Library Y-92

Literary Research Archives IX:
Special Collections at Boston University . . Y-99

The Literary Scene and Situation and . . . Who
(Besides Oprah) Really Runs American
Literature? Y-99

Literary Societies Y-98, Y-99, Y-00

"Literary Style" (1857), by William
Forsyth [excerpt] DLB-57

Literatura Chicanesca: The View From
Without DLB-82

Literature at Nurse, or Circulating Morals (1885),
by George Moore. DLB-18

Littell, Eliakim 1797-1870 . . . . DLB-79

Littell, Robert S. 1831-1896 . . . . DLB-79

Little, Brown and Company. DLB-49

Little Magazines and Newspapers DS-15

The Little Review 1914-1929. . . . . .DS-15

Littlewood, Joan 1914- DLB-13

Lively, Penelope 1933- DLB-14, 161, 207

Liverpool University Press. DLB-112

The Lives of the Poets DLB-142

Livesay, Dorothy 1909- DLB-68

Livesay, Florence Randal 1874-1953 . . . . . DLB-92

"Living in Ruin," by Gerald Stern DLB-105

Livings, Henry 1929-1998 . . . . DLB-13

Livingston, Anne Howe 1763-1841 . . .DLB-37, 200

Livingston, Myra Cohn 1926-1996 . . . . . . DLB-61

Livingston, William 1723-1790. . . . . DLB-31

Livingstone, David 1813-1873 . . . . DLB-166

Livingstone, Douglas 1932-1996 . . . . DLB-225

Livy 59 B.C.-A.D. 17 . . . . . . .DLB-211; CDWLB-1

Liyong, Taban lo (see Taban lo Liyong)

Lizárraga, Sylvia S. 1925- DLB-82

Llewellyn, Richard 1906-1983 . . . . DLB-15

Lloyd, Edward [publishing house] DLB-106

Lobel, Arnold 1933- DLB-61

Lochhead, Liz 1947- DLB-245

Lochridge, Betsy Hopkins (see Fancher, Betsy)

Locke, David Ross 1833-1888 . . . . DLB-11, 23

Locke, John 1632-1704. . . . . .DLB-31, 101, 213

Locke, Richard Adams 1800-1871 . . . . . . DLB-43

Locker-Lampson, Frederick
1821-1895 . . . . DLB-35, 184

Lockhart, John Gibson
1794-1854. . . . . DLB-110, 116 144

Lockridge, Ross, Jr. 1914-1948. . . . .DLB-143; Y-80

Locrine and Selimus DLB-62

Lodge, David 1935- DLB-14, 194

Lodge, George Cabot 1873-1909 . . . . DLB-54

Lodge, Henry Cabot 1850-1924. . . . . DLB-47

Lodge, Thomas 1558-1625. . . . . .DLB-172

From *Defence of Poetry* (1579) DLB-172

Loeb, Harold 1891-1974. . . . . DLB-4

Loeb, William 1905-1981. . . . . .DLB-127

Lofting, Hugh 1886-1947 . . . . DLB-160

Logan, Deborah Norris 1761-1839 . . . . . . DLB-200

Logan, James 1674-1751 . . . . .DLB-24, 140

Logan, John 1923- DLB-5

Logan, Martha Daniell 1704?-1779 . . . . . .DLB-200

Logan, William 1950- DLB-120

Logau, Friedrich von 1605-1655 . . . . . . .DLB-164

Logue, Christopher 1926- DLB-27

Lohenstein, Daniel Casper von
 1635-1683 . . . . .DLB-168

Lomonosov, Mikhail Vasil'evich
 1711-1765. . . . . .DLB-150

London, Jack
 1876-1916 . . . . .DLB-8, 12, 78, 212; CDALB-3

The London Magazine 1820-1829 . . . . .DLB-110

Long, David 1948- DLB-244

Long, H., and Brother DLB-49

Long, Haniel 1888-1956 . . . . .DLB-45

Long, Ray 1878-1935. . . . . .DLB-137

Longfellow, Henry Wadsworth
 1807-1882 . . . . . . .DLB-1, 59, 235; CDALB-2

Longfellow, Samuel 1819-1892 . . . . .DLB-1

Longford, Elizabeth 1906- DLB-155

Longinus circa first century DLB-176

Longley, Michael 1939- DLB-40

Longman, T. [publishing house] DLB-154

Longmans, Green and Company DLB-49

Longmore, George 1793?-1867 . . . . .DLB-99

Longstreet, Augustus Baldwin
 1790-1870. . . . . DLB-3, 11, 74

Longworth, D. [publishing house] DLB-49

Lonsdale, Frederick 1881-1954 . . . . .DLB-10

A Look at the Contemporary Black Theatre
 Movement. DLB-38

Loos, Anita 1893-1981. . . . .DLB-11, 26, 228; Y-81

Lopate, Phillip 1943- Y-80

López, Diana
 (see Isabella, Ríos)

López, Josefina 1969- DLB-209

Loranger, Jean-Aubert 1896-1942 . . . . . . .DLB-92

Lorca, Federico García 1898-1936. . . . . . .DLB-108

Lord, John Keast 1818-1872. . . . . .DLB-99

The Lord Chamberlain's Office and Stage
 Censorship in England DLB-10

Lorde, Audre 1934-1992 . . . . .DLB-41

Lorimer, George Horace 1867-1939 . . . . . .DLB-91

Loring, A. K. [publishing house] DLB-49

Loring and Mussey DLB-46

Lorris, Guillaume de (see *Roman de la Rose*)

Lossing, Benson J. 1813-1891 . . . . .DLB-30

Lothar, Ernst 1890-1974 . . . . .DLB-81

Lothrop, D., and Company. DLB-49

Lothrop, Harriet M. 1844-1924. . . . . .DLB-42

Loti, Pierre 1850-1923 . . . . .DLB-123

Lotichius Secundus, Petrus 1528-1560. . . .DLB-179

Lott, Emeline ?-? DLB-166

Louisiana State University Press Y-97

The Lounger, no. 20 (1785), by Henry
 Mackenzie DLB-39

Lounsbury, Thomas R. 1838-1915 . . . . . . .DLB-71

Louÿs, Pierre 1870-1925 . . . . .DLB-123

Lovelace, Earl 1935- DLB-125; CDWLB-3

Lovelace, Richard 1618-1657. . . . . .DLB-131

Lovell, Coryell and Company DLB-49

Lovell, John W., Company DLB-49

Lover, Samuel 1797-1868 . . . . .DLB-159, 190

Lovesey, Peter 1936- DLB-87

Lovinescu, Eugen
 1881-1943 . . . . .DLB-220; CDWLB-4

Lovingood, Sut
 (see Harris, George Washington)

Low, Samuel 1765-? DLB-37

Lowell, Amy 1874-1925. . . . . .DLB-54, 140

Lowell, James Russell 1819-1891
 . . . . . .DLB-1, 11, 64, 79, 189, 235; CDALB-2

Lowell, Robert 1917-1977. . .DLB-5, 169; CDALB-7

Lowenfels, Walter 1897-1976. . . . . .DLB-4

Lowndes, Marie Belloc 1868-1947. . . . . . .DLB-70

Lowndes, William Thomas 1798-1843 . . .DLB-184

Lownes, Humphrey [publishing house]. . .DLB-170

Lowry, Lois 1937- DLB-52

Lowry, Malcolm 1909-1957. . . .DLB-15; CDBLB-7

Lowther, Pat 1935-1975. . . . . .DLB-53

Loy, Mina 1882-1966 . . . . .DLB-4, 54

Lozeau, Albert 1878-1924 . . . . .DLB-92

Lubbock, Percy 1879-1965. . . . . .DLB-149

Lucan A.D. 39-A.D. 65 . . . . .DLB-211

Lucas, E. V. 1868-1938 . . . . . . .DLB-98, 149, 153

Lucas, Fielding, Jr. [publishing house] DLB-49

Luce, Clare Booth 1903-1987 . . . . .DLB-228

Luce, Henry R. 1898-1967 . . . . .DLB-91

Luce, John W., and Company. DLB-46

Lucian circa 120-180 . . . . .DLB-176

Lucie-Smith, Edward 1933- DLB-40

Lucilius circa 180 B.C.-102/101 B.C. DLB-211

Lucini, Gian Pietro 1867-1914 . . . . .DLB-114

Lucretius circa 94 B.C.-circa 49 B.C.
 . . . . .DLB-211; CDWLB-1

Luder, Peter circa 1415-1472 . . . . .DLB-179

Ludlum, Robert 1927- Y-82

Ludus de Antichristo circa 1160 . . . . .DLB-148

Ludvigson, Susan 1942- DLB-120

Ludwig, Jack 1922- DLB-60

Ludwig, Otto 1813-1865 . . . . .DLB-129

Ludwigslied 881 or 882 . . . . .DLB-148

Luera, Yolanda 1953- DLB-122

Luft, Lya 1938- DLB-145

Lugansky, Kazak Vladimir
 (see Dal', Vladimir Ivanovich)

Lukács, Georg (see Lukács, György)

Lukács, György
 1885-1971 . . . . . . .DLB-215, 242; CDWLB-4

Luke, Peter 1919- DLB-13

Lummis, Charles F. 1859-1928 . . . . .DLB-186

Lupton, F. M., Company. DLB-49

Lupus of Ferrières
 circa 805-circa 862. . . . . .DLB-148

Lurie, Alison 1926- DLB-2

Lustig, Arnošt 1926- DLB-232

Luther, Martin 1483-1546 . . . DLB-179; CDWLB-2

Luzi, Mario 1914- DLB-128

L'vov, Nikolai Aleksandrovich 1751-1803 . .DLB-150

Lyall, Gavin 1932- DLB-87

Lydgate, John circa 1370-1450. . . . . .DLB-146

Lyly, John circa 1554-1606 . . . . .DLB-62, 167

Lynch, Patricia 1898-1972 . . . . .DLB-160

Lynch, Richard flourished 1596-1601 . . . .DLB-172

Lynd, Robert 1879-1949 . . . . .DLB-98

Lyon, Matthew 1749-1822. . . . . .DLB-43

Lyotard, Jean-François 1924-1998 . . . . . . .DLB-242

Lysias circa 459 B.C.-circa 380 B.C. DLB-176

Lytle, Andrew 1902-1995 . . . . .DLB-6; Y-95

Lytton, Edward
 (see Bulwer-Lytton, Edward)

Lytton, Edward Robert Bulwer
 1831-1891. . . . . .DLB-32

M

Maass, Joachim 1901-1972. . . . . .DLB-69

Mabie, Hamilton Wright 1845-1916 . . . . . .DLB-71

Mac A'Ghobhainn, Iain (see Smith, Iain Crichton)

MacArthur, Charles 1895-1956. . . . .DLB-7, 25, 44

Macaulay, Catherine 1731-1791. . . . . .DLB-104

Macaulay, David 1945- DLB-61

Macaulay, Rose 1881-1958 . . . . .DLB-36

Macaulay, Thomas Babington
 1800-1859 . . . . .DLB-32, 55; CDBLB-4

Macaulay Company DLB-46

MacBeth, George 1932- DLB-40

Macbeth, Madge 1880-1965 . . . . .DLB-92

MacCaig, Norman 1910-1996 . . . . .DLB-27

MacDiarmid, Hugh
 1892-1978 . . . . .DLB-20; CDBLB-7

MacDonald, Cynthia 1928- DLB-105

MacDonald, George 1824-1905 . . . .DLB-18, 163, 178

MacDonald, John D. 1916-1986 . . . . .DLB-8; Y-86

MacDonald, Philip 1899?-1980 . . . . .DLB-77

Macdonald, Ross (see Millar, Kenneth)

Macdonald, Sharman 1951- DLB-245

MacDonald, Wilson 1880-1967. . . . . .DLB-92

Macdonald and Company (Publishers) . . .DLB-112

MacEwen, Gwendolyn 1941- DLB-53

Macfadden, Bernarr 1868-1955. . . . . .DLB-25, 91

MacGregor, John 1825-1892 . . . . .DLB-166

MacGregor, Mary Esther (see Keith, Marian)

Machado, Antonio 1875-1939 . . . . .DLB-108

Machado, Manuel 1874-1947. . . . . .DLB-108

Machar, Agnes Maule 1837-1927. . . . . . . .DLB-92

Machaut, Guillaume de
 circa 1300-1377 . . . . .DLB-208

Machen, Arthur Llewelyn Jones
 1863-1947 . . . . .DLB-36, 156, 178

MacInnes, Colin 1914-1976. . . . . .DLB-14

MacInnes, Helen 1907-1985 . . . . DLB-87

MacIntyre, Tom 1931- DLB-245

Mačiulis, Jonas (see Maironis, Jonas)

Mack, Maynard 1909- DLB-111

Mackall, Leonard L. 1879-1937 . . . . DLB-140

MacKaye, Percy 1875-1956 . . . . DLB-54

Macken, Walter 1915-1967 . . . . DLB-13

Mackenzie, Alexander 1763-1820 . . . . DLB-99

Mackenzie, Alexander Slidell
    1803-1848 . . . . DLB-183

Mackenzie, Compton 1883-1972 . . . . DLB-34, 100

Mackenzie, Henry 1745-1831 . . . . DLB-39

Mackenzie, William 1758-1828 . . . . DLB-187

Mackey, Nathaniel 1947- DLB-169

Mackey, Shena 1944- DLB-231

Mackey, William Wellington
    1937- DLB-38

Mackintosh, Elizabeth (see Tey, Josephine)

Mackintosh, Sir James 1765-1832 . . . . DLB-158

Maclaren, Ian (see Watson, John)

Macklin, Charles 1699-1797 . . . . DLB-89

MacLean, Katherine Anne 1925- DLB-8

Maclean, Norman 1902-1990 . . . . DLB-206

MacLeish, Archibald 1892-1982
    . . . . DLB-4, 7, 45, 228; Y-82; CDALB-7

MacLennan, Hugh 1907-1990 . . . . DLB-68

MacLeod, Alistair 1936- DLB-60

Macleod, Fiona (see Sharp, William)

Macleod, Norman 1906-1985 . . . . DLB-4

Mac Low, Jackson 1922- DLB-193

Macmillan and Company DLB-106

The Macmillan Company DLB-49

Macmillan's English Men of Letters,
    First Series (1878-1892) DLB-144

MacNamara, Brinsley 1890-1963 . . . . DLB-10

MacNeice, Louis 1907-1963 . . . . DLB-10, 20

MacPhail, Andrew 1864-1938 . . . . DLB-92

Macpherson, James 1736-1796 . . . . DLB-109

Macpherson, Jay 1931- DLB-53

Macpherson, Jeanie 1884-1946 . . . . DLB-44

Macrae Smith Company DLB-46

MacRaye, Lucy Betty (see Webling, Lucy)

Macrone, John [publishing house] DLB-106

MacShane, Frank 1927-1999 . . . . DLB-111

Macy-Masius DLB-46

Madden, David 1933- DLB-6

Madden, Sir Frederic 1801-1873 . . . . DLB-184

Maddow, Ben 1909-1992 . . . . DLB-44

Maddux, Rachel 1912-1983 . . . . . . DLB-234; Y-93

Madgett, Naomi Long 1923- DLB-76

Madhubuti, Haki R. 1942- DLB-5, 41; DS-8

Madison, James 1751-1836 . . . . DLB-37

Madsen, Svend Åge 1939- DLB-214

Maeterlinck, Maurice 1862-1949 . . . . DLB-192

Mafūz, Najīb 1911- Y-88

Magee, David 1905-1977 . . . . DLB-187

Maginn, William 1794-1842 . . . . . . .DLB-110, 159

Magoffin, Susan Shelby 1827-1855 . . . . . . DLB-239

Mahan, Alfred Thayer 1840-1914 . . . . DLB-47

Maheux-Forcier, Louise 1929- DLB-60

Mahin, John Lee 1902-1984 . . . . DLB-44

Mahon, Derek 1941- DLB-40

Maikov, Vasilii Ivanovich 1728-1778 . . . . DLB-150

Mailer, Norman 1923-
    . . . . DLB-2, 16, 28, 185; Y-80, Y-83, Y-97;
                                        DS-3; CDALB-6

Maillart, Ella 1903-1997 . . . . DLB-195

Maillet, Adrienne 1885-1963 . . . . DLB-68

Maillet, Antonine 1929- DLB-60

Maillu, David G. 1939- DLB-157

Maimonides, Moses 1138-1204 . . . . DLB-115

Main Selections of the Book-of-the-Month
    Club, 1926-1945 . . . . DLB-9

Main Trends in Twentieth-Century Book
    Clubs DLB-46

Mainwaring, Daniel 1902-1977 . . . . DLB-44

Mair, Charles 1838-1927 . . . . DLB-99

Maironis, Jonas
    1862-1932 . . . . DLB-220; CDWLB-4

Mais, Roger 1905-1955 . . . . DLB-125; CDWLB-3

Major, Andre 1942- DLB-60

Major, Charles 1856-1913 . . . . DLB-202

Major, Clarence 1936- DLB-33

Major, Kevin 1949- DLB-60

Major Books DLB-46

Makemie, Francis circa 1658-1708 . . . . . . DLB-24

The Making of Americans Contract Y-98

The Making of a People, by
    J. M. Ritchie DLB-66

Maksimović, Desanka
    1898-1993 . . . . .DLB-147; CDWLB-4

Malamud, Bernard 1914-1986
    . . . . . . .DLB-2, 28, 152; Y-80, Y-86; CDALB-1

Mălăncioiu, Ileana 1940- DLB-232

Malerba, Luigi 1927- DLB-196

Malet, Lucas 1852-1931 . . . . DLB-153

Mallarmé, Stéphane 1842-1898 . . . . DLB-217

Malleson, Lucy Beatrice (see Gilbert, Anthony)

Mallet-Joris, Françoise 1930- DLB-83

Mallock, W. H. 1849-1923 . . . . .DLB-18, 57

    "Every Man His Own Poet; or,
    The Inspired Singer's Recipe
    Book" (1877) DLB-35

Malone, Dumas 1892-1986 . . . . DLB-17

Malone, Edmond 1741-1812 . . . . DLB-142

Malory, Sir Thomas
    circa 1400-1410 - 1471 . . . DLB-146; CDBLB-1

Malraux, André 1901-1976 . . . . DLB-72

Malthus, Thomas Robert
    1766-1834 . . . . .DLB-107, 158

Maltz, Albert 1908-1985 . . . . DLB-102

Malzberg, Barry N. 1939- DLB-8

Mamet, David 1947- DLB-7

Mamin, Dmitrii Narkisovich 1852-1912. . DLB-238

Manaka, Matsemela 1956- DLB-157

Manchester University Press DLB-112

Mandel, Eli 1922- DLB-53

Mandeville, Bernard 1670-1733 . . . . DLB-101

Mandeville, Sir John
    mid fourteenth century DLB-146

Mandiargues, André Pieyre de 1909- . . . DLB-83

Manea, Norman 1936- DLB-232

Manfred, Frederick 1912-1994 . . . .DLB-6, 212, 227

Manfredi, Gianfranco 1948- DLB-196

Mangan, Sherry 1904-1961 . . . . DLB-4

Manganelli, Giorgio 1922-1990 . . . . DLB-196

Manilius fl. first century A.D. DLB-211

Mankiewicz, Herman 1897-1953 . . . . DLB-26

Mankiewicz, Joseph L. 1909-1993 . . . . . . DLB-44

Mankowitz, Wolf 1924-1998 . . . . DLB-15

Manley, Delarivière 1672?-1724 . . . . . . DLB-39, 80

    Preface to The Secret History, of Queen Zarah,
    and the Zarazians (1705) DLB-39

Mann, Abby 1927- DLB-44

Mann, Charles 1929-1998 . . . . Y-98

Mann, Heinrich 1871-1950 . . . . DLB-66, 118

Mann, Horace 1796-1859 . . . . DLB-1, 235

Mann, Klaus 1906-1949 . . . . DLB-56

Mann, Mary Peabody 1806-1887 . . . . DLB-239

Mann, Thomas 1875-1955 . . . DLB-66; CDWLB-2

Mann, William D'Alton 1839-1920 . . . . . .DLB-137

Mannin, Ethel 1900-1984 . . . . DLB-191, 195

Manning, Emily (see Australie)

Manning, Marie 1873?-1945 . . . . DLB-29

Manning and Loring DLB-49

Mannyng, Robert
    flourished 1303-1338 . . . . DLB-146

Mano, D. Keith 1942- DLB-6

Manor Books DLB-46

Mansfield, Katherine 1888-1923 . . . . DLB-162

Manuel, Niklaus circa 1484-1530 . . . . . . .DLB-179

Manzini, Gianna 1896-1974 . . . . .DLB-177

Mapanje, Jack 1944- DLB-157

Maraini, Dacia 1936- DLB-196

Marcel Proust at 129 and the Proust Society
    of America Y-00

Marcel Proust's Remembrance of Things Past:
    The Rediscovered Galley Proofs Y-00

March, William 1893-1954 . . . . DLB-9, 86

Marchand, Leslie A. 1900-1999 . . . . DLB-103

Marchant, Bessie 1862-1941 . . . . DLB-160

Marchant, Tony 1959- DLB-245

Marchenko, Anastasiia Iakovlevna
    1830-1880 . . . . DLB-238

Marchessault, Jovette 1938- DLB-60

Marcinkevičius, Justinas 1930- DLB-232

Marcus, Frank 1928- DLB-13

Marcuse, Herbert 1898-1979 . . . . DLB-242

Marden, Orison Swett 1850-1924 . . . . . . .DLB-137

Marechera, Dambudzo 1952-1987 . . . . DLB-157

Marek, Richard, Books DLB-46

Mares, E. A. 1938- DLB-122

Margulies, Donald 1954- DLB-228

Mariani, Paul 1940- DLB-111

Marie de France flourished 1160-1178 . . . . DLB-208

Marie-Victorin, Frère 1885-1944 . . . . DLB-92

Marin, Biagio 1891-1985 . . . . DLB-128

Marincovič, Ranko
    1913- DLB-147; CDWLB-4

Marinetti, Filippo Tommaso
    1876-1944 . . . . DLB-114

Marion, Frances 1886-1973 . . . . DLB-44

Marius, Richard C. 1933-1999 . . . . Y-85

Markevich, Boleslav Mikhailovich
    1822-1884 . . . . DLB-238

Markfield, Wallace 1926- DLB-2, 28

Markham, Edwin 1852-1940 . . . . DLB-54, 186

Markle, Fletcher 1921-1991 . . . . DLB-68; Y-91

Marlatt, Daphne 1942- DLB-60

Marlitt, E. 1825-1887 . . . . DLB-129

Marlowe, Christopher
    1564-1593 . . . . DLB-62; CDBLB-1

Marlyn, John 1912- DLB-88

Marmion, Shakerley 1603-1639 . . . . DLB-58

Der Marner before 1230-circa 1287 . . . . . . DLB-138

Marnham, Patrick 1943- DLB-204

The *Marprelate Tracts* 1588-1589 . . . . DLB-132

Marquand, John P. 1893-1960 . . . . DLB-9, 102

Marqués, René 1919-1979 . . . . DLB-113

Marquis, Don 1878-1937 . . . . DLB-11, 25

Marriott, Anne 1913- DLB-68

Marryat, Frederick 1792-1848 . . . . DLB-21, 163

Marsh, Capen, Lyon and Webb DLB-49

Marsh, George Perkins
    1801-1882 . . . . DLB-1, 64, 243

Marsh, James 1794-1842 . . . . DLB-1, 59

Marsh, Narcissus 1638-1713 . . . . DLB-213

Marsh, Ngaio 1899-1982 . . . . DLB-77

Marshall, Edison 1894-1967 . . . . DLB-102

Marshall, Edward 1932- DLB-16

Marshall, Emma 1828-1899 . . . . DLB-163

Marshall, James 1942-1992 . . . . DLB-61

Marshall, Joyce 1913- DLB-88

Marshall, Paule 1929- DLB-33, 157, 227

Marshall, Tom 1938- DLB-60

Marsilius of Padua
    circa 1275-circa 1342 . . . . DLB-115

Mars-Jones, Adam 1954- DLB-207

Marson, Una 1905-1965 . . . . DLB-157

Marston, John 1576-1634 . . . . DLB-58, 172

Marston, Philip Bourke 1850-1887 . . . . DLB-35

Martens, Kurt 1870-1945 . . . . DLB-66

Martial circa A.D. 40-circa A.D. 103
    . . . . DLB-211; CDWLB-1

Martien, William S. [publishing house] DLB-49

Martin, Abe (see Hubbard, Kin)

Martin, Catherine ca. 1847-1937 . . . . DLB-230

Martin, Charles 1942- DLB-120

Martin, Claire 1914- DLB-60

Martin, Jay 1935- DLB-111

Martin, Johann (see Laurentius von Schnüffis)

Martin, Thomas 1696-1771 . . . . DLB-213

Martin, Violet Florence (see Ross, Martin)

Martin du Gard, Roger 1881-1958 . . . . . . DLB-65

Martineau, Harriet
    1802-1876 . . . . DLB-21, 55, 159, 163, 166, 190

Martínez, Demetria 1960- DLB-209

Martínez, Eliud 1935- DLB-122

Martínez, Max 1943- DLB-82

Martínez, Rubén 1962- DLB-209

Martone, Michael 1955- DLB-218

Martyn, Edward 1859-1923 . . . . DLB-10

Marvell, Andrew
    1621-1678 . . . . DLB-131; CDBLB-2

Marvin X 1944- DLB-38

Marx, Karl 1818-1883 . . . . DLB-129

Marzials, Theo 1850-1920 . . . . DLB-35

Masefield, John
    1878-1967 . . . DLB-10, 19, 153, 160; CDBLB-5

Mason, A. E. W. 1865-1948 . . . . DLB-70

Mason, Bobbie Ann
    1940- DLB-173; Y-87; CDALB-7

Mason, William 1725-1797 . . . . DLB-142

Mason Brothers DLB-49

Massey, Gerald 1828-1907 . . . . DLB-32

Massey, Linton R. 1900-1974 . . . . DLB-187

Massinger, Philip 1583-1640 . . . . DLB-58

Masson, David 1822-1907 . . . . DLB-144

Masters, Edgar Lee
    1868-1950 . . . . DLB-54; CDALB-3

Masters, Hilary 1928- DLB-244

Mastronardi, Lucio 1930-1979 . . . . DLB-177

Matevski, Mateja 1929- . . . DLB-181; CDWLB-4

Mather, Cotton
    1663-1728 . . . . DLB-24, 30, 140; CDALB-2

Mather, Increase 1639-1723 . . . . DLB-24

Mather, Richard 1596-1669 . . . . DLB-24

Matheson, Annie 1853-1924 . . . . DLB-240

Matheson, Richard 1926- DLB-8, 44

Matheus, John F. 1887- DLB-51

Mathews, Cornelius 1817?-1889 . . . . . . DLB-3, 64

Mathews, Elkin [publishing house] DLB-112

Mathews, John Joseph 1894-1979 . . . . . . DLB-175

Mathias, Roland 1915- DLB-27

Mathis, June 1892-1927 . . . . DLB-44

Mathis, Sharon Bell 1937- DLB-33

Matković, Marijan 1915-1985 . . . . DLB-181

Matoš, Antun Gustav 1873-1914 . . . . DLB-147

Matsumoto Seichō 1909-1992 . . . . DLB-182

The Matter of England 1240-1400 . . . . . . DLB-146

The Matter of Rome early twelfth to late
    fifteenth century DLB-146

Matthew of Vendôme
    circa 1130-circa 1200 . . . . DLB-208

Matthews, Brander
    1852-1929 . . . . DLB-71, 78; DS-13

Matthews, Jack 1925- DLB-6

Matthews, Victoria Earle 1861-1907 . . . . . DLB-221

Matthews, William 1942-1997 . . . . DLB-5

Matthiessen, F. O. 1902-1950 . . . . DLB-63

Matthiessen, Peter 1927- DLB-6, 173

Maturin, Charles Robert 1780-1824 . . . . . DLB-178

Maugham, W. Somerset 1874-1965
    . . . . DLB-10, 36, 77, 100, 162, 195; CDBLB-6

Maupassant, Guy de 1850-1893 . . . . DLB-123

Mauriac, Claude 1914-1996 . . . . DLB-83

Mauriac, François 1885-1970 . . . . DLB-65

Maurice, Frederick Denison
    1805-1872 . . . . DLB-55

Maurois, André 1885-1967 . . . . DLB-65

Maury, James 1718-1769 . . . . DLB-31

Mavor, Elizabeth 1927- DLB-14

Mavor, Osborne Henry (see Bridie, James)

Maxwell, Gavin 1914-1969 . . . . DLB-204

Maxwell, H. [publishing house] DLB-49

Maxwell, John [publishing house] DLB-106

Maxwell, William 1908- DLB-218; Y-80

May, Elaine 1932- DLB-44

May, Karl 1842-1912 . . . . DLB-129

May, Thomas 1595 or 1596-1650 . . . . DLB-58

Mayer, Bernadette 1945- DLB-165

Mayer, Mercer 1943- DLB-61

Mayer, O. B. 1818-1891 . . . . DLB-3

Mayes, Herbert R. 1900-1987 . . . . DLB-137

Mayes, Wendell 1919-1992 . . . . DLB-26

Mayfield, Julian 1928-1984 . . . . DLB-33; Y-84

Mayhew, Henry 1812-1887 . . . . . . DLB-18, 55, 190

Mayhew, Jonathan 1720-1766 . . . . DLB-31

Mayne, Ethel Colburn 1865-1941 . . . . . . DLB-197

Mayne, Jasper 1604-1672 . . . . DLB-126

Mayne, Seymour 1944- DLB-60

Mayor, Flora Macdonald 1872-1932 . . . . . DLB-36

Mayrocker, Friederike 1924- DLB-85

Mazrui, Ali A. 1933- DLB-125

Mažuranić, Ivan 1814-1890 . . . . DLB-147

Mazursky, Paul 1930- DLB-44

McAlmon, Robert
    1896-1956 . . . . DLB-4, 45; DS-15

McArthur, Peter 1866-1924 . . . . DLB-92

McBride, Robert M., and Company DLB-46

McCabe, Patrick 1955- DLB-194

McCaffrey, Anne 1926- DLB-8

McCarthy, Cormac 1933- DLB-6, 143

McCarthy, Mary 1912-1989 . . . . DLB-2; Y-81

McCay, Winsor 1871-1934 . . . . DLB-22

McClane, Albert Jules 1922-1991 . . . . DLB-171

McClatchy, C. K. 1858-1936 . . . . DLB-25

McClellan, George Marion 1860-1934 . . . . DLB-50

McCloskey, Robert 1914- DLB-22

McClung, Nellie Letitia 1873-1951 . . . . . . DLB-92

McClure, Joanna 1930- DLB-16

McClure, Michael 1932- DLB-16

McClure, Phillips and Company DLB-46

McClure, S. S. 1857-1949 . . . . DLB-91

McClurg, A. C., and Company DLB-49

McCluskey, John A., Jr. 1944- DLB-33

McCollum, Michael A. 1946 . . . . Y-87

McConnell, William C. 1917- DLB-88

McCord, David 1897-1997 . . . . DLB-61

McCorkle, Jill 1958- DLB-234; Y-87

McCorkle, Samuel Eusebius
1746-1811 . . . . DLB-37

McCormick, Anne O'Hare 1880-1954 . . . . DLB-29

Kenneth Dale McCormick Tributes Y-97

McCormick, Robert R. 1880-1955 . . . . . . DLB-29

McCourt, Edward 1907-1972 . . . . DLB-88

McCoy, Horace 1897-1955 . . . . DLB-9

McCrae, John 1872-1918 . . . . DLB-92

McCullagh, Joseph B. 1842-1896 . . . . DLB-23

McCullers, Carson
1917-1967 . . . . . . DLB-2, 7, 173, 228; CDALB-1

McCulloch, Thomas 1776-1843 . . . . DLB-99

McDonald, Forrest 1927- DLB-17

McDonald, Walter 1934- DLB-105, DS-9

"Getting Started: Accepting the Regions
You Own—or Which Own You," . . . DLB-105

McDougall, Colin 1917-1984 . . . . DLB-68

McDowell, Katharine Sherwood Bonner
1849-1883 . . . . DLB-202, 239

McDowell, Obolensky DLB-46

McEwan, Ian 1948- DLB-14, 194

McFadden, David 1940- DLB-60

McFall, Frances Elizabeth Clarke
(see Grand, Sarah)

McFarlane, Leslie 1902-1977 . . . . DLB-88

McFee, William 1881-1966 . . . . DLB-153

McGahern, John 1934- DLB-14, 231

McGee, Thomas D'Arcy 1825-1868 . . . . . DLB-99

McGeehan, W. O. 1879-1933 . . . . DLB-25, 171

McGill, Ralph 1898-1969 . . . . DLB-29

McGinley, Phyllis 1905-1978 . . . . DLB-11, 48

McGinniss, Joe 1942- DLB-185

McGirt, James E. 1874-1930 . . . . DLB-50

McGlashan and Gill DLB-106

McGough, Roger 1937- DLB-40

McGrath, John 1935- DLB-233

McGrath, Patrick 1950- DLB-231

McGraw-Hill DLB-46

McGuane, Thomas 1939- DLB-2, 212; Y-80

McGuckian, Medbh 1950- DLB-40

McGuffey, William Holmes 1800-1873 . . . DLB-42

McGuinness, Frank 1953- DLB-245

McHenry, James 1785-1845 . . . . DLB-202

McIlvanney, William 1936- DLB-14, 207

McIlwraith, Jean Newton 1859-1938 . . . . . DLB-92

McIntosh, Maria Jane 1803-1878 . . . . DLB-239

McIntyre, James 1827-1906 . . . . DLB-99

McIntyre, O. O. 1884-1938 . . . . DLB-25

McKay, Claude 1889-1948 . . . . .DLB-4, 45, 51, 117

The David McKay Company DLB-49

McKean, William V. 1820-1903 . . . . DLB-23

McKenna, Stephen 1888-1967 . . . . DLB-197

The McKenzie Trust Y-96

McKerrow, R. B. 1872-1940 . . . . DLB-201

McKinley, Robin 1952- DLB-52

McKnight, Reginald 1956- DLB-234

McLachlan, Alexander 1818-1896 . . . . DLB-99

McLaren, Floris Clark 1904-1978 . . . . DLB-68

McLaverty, Michael 1907- DLB-15

McLean, John R. 1848-1916 . . . . DLB-23

McLean, William L. 1852-1931 . . . . DLB-25

McLennan, William 1856-1904 . . . . DLB-92

McLoughlin Brothers DLB-49

McLuhan, Marshall 1911-1980 . . . . DLB-88

McMaster, John Bach 1852-1932 . . . . DLB-47

McMurtry, Larry
1936- . . . DLB-2, 143; Y-80, Y-87; CDALB-6

McNally, Terrence 1939- DLB-7

McNeil, Florence 1937- DLB-60

McNeile, Herman Cyril 1888-1937 . . . . . . DLB-77

McNickle, D'Arcy 1904-1977 . . . . . . DLB-175, 212

McPhee, John 1931- DLB-185

McPherson, James Alan 1943- DLB-38, 244

McPherson, Sandra 1943- Y-86

McWhirter, George 1939- DLB-60

McWilliams, Carey 1905-1980 . . . . DLB-137

Mda, Zakes 1948- DLB-225

Mead, L. T. 1844-1914 . . . . DLB-141

Mead, Matthew 1924- DLB-40

Mead, Taylor ?- DLB-16

Meany, Tom 1903-1964 . . . . .DLB-171

Mechthild von Magdeburg
circa 1207-circa 1282 . . . . DLB-138

Medieval French Drama DLB-208

Medieval Travel Diaries DLB-203

Medill, Joseph 1823-1899 . . . . DLB-43

Medoff, Mark 1940- DLB-7

Meek, Alexander Beaufort 1814-1865 . . . . . DLB-3

Meeke, Mary ?-1816? DLB-116

Meinke, Peter 1932- DLB-5

Mejia Vallejo, Manuel 1923- DLB-113

Melanchthon, Philipp 1497-1560 . . . . . . .DLB-179

Melançon, Robert 1947- DLB-60

Mell, Max 1882-1971 . . . . DLB-81, 124

Mellow, James R. 1926-1997 . . . . DLB-111

Mel'nikov, Pavel Ivanovich 1818-1883 . . DLB-238

Meltzer, David 1937- DLB-16

Meltzer, Milton 1915- DLB-61

Melville, Elizabeth, Lady Culross
circa 1585-1640 . . . . .DLB-172

Melville, Herman
1819-1891 . . . . DLB-3, 74; CDALB-2

Memoirs of Life and Literature (1920),
by W. H. Mallock [excerpt] DLB-57

Mena, María Cristina 1893-1965 . . . DLB-209, 221

Menander 342-341 B.C.-circa 292-291 B.C.
. . . . .DLB-176; CDWLB-1

Menantes (see Hunold, Christian Friedrich)

Mencke, Johann Burckhard
1674-1732 . . . . DLB-168

Mencken, H. L. 1880-1956
. . . . .DLB-11, 29, 63, 137, 222; CDALB-4

H. L. Mencken's "Berlin, February, 1917" Y-00

Mencken and Nietzsche: An Unpublished
Excerpt from H. L. Mencken's *My Life
as Author and Editor* Y-93

Mendelssohn, Moses 1729-1786 . . . . DLB-97

Mendes, Catulle 1841-1909 . . . . .DLB-217

Méndez M., Miguel 1930- DLB-82

Mens Rea (or Something) Y-97

The Mercantile Library of New York Y-96

Mercer, Cecil William (see Yates, Dornford)

Mercer, David 1928-1980 . . . . DLB-13

Mercer, John 1704-1768 . . . . DLB-31

Meredith, George
1828-1909 . . . .DLB-18, 35, 57, 159; CDBLB-4

Meredith, Louisa Anne 1812-1895 . . DLB-166, 230

Meredith, Owen
(see Lytton, Edward Robert Bulwer)

Meredith, William 1919- DLB-5

Mergerle, Johann Ulrich
(see Abraham ä Sancta Clara)

Mérimée, Prosper 1803-1870 . . . . . . .DLB-119, 192

Merivale, John Herman 1779-1844 . . . . . . DLB-96

Meriwether, Louise 1923- DLB-33

Merlin Press DLB-112

Merriam, Eve 1916-1992 . . . . DLB-61

The Merriam Company DLB-49

Merrill, James 1926-1995 . . . . . . .DLB-5, 165; Y-85

Merrill and Baker DLB-49

The Mershon Company DLB-49

Merton, Thomas 1915-1968 . . . . . . .DLB-48; Y-81

Merwin, W. S. 1927- DLB-5, 169

Messner, Julian [publishing house] DLB-46

Mészöly, Miklós 1921- DLB-232

Metcalf, J. [publishing house] DLB-49

Metcalf, John 1938- DLB-60

The Methodist Book Concern DLB-49

Methuen and Company DLB-112

Meun, Jean de (see *Roman de la Rose*)

Mew, Charlotte 1869-1928 . . . . DLB-19, 135

Mewshaw, Michael 1943- Y-80

Meyer, Conrad Ferdinand 1825-1898 . . . DLB-129

Meyer, E. Y. 1946- DLB-75

Meyer, Eugene 1875-1959 . . . . DLB-29

Meyer, Michael 1921-2000 . . . . .DLB-155

Meyers, Jeffrey 1939- DLB-111

Meynell, Alice 1847-1922. . . . . .DLB-19, 98

Meynell, Viola 1885-1956 . . . . .DLB-153

Meyrink, Gustav 1868-1932 . . . . .DLB-81

Mézières, Philipe de circa 1327-1405 . . . . .DLB-208

Michael, Ib 1945- DLB-214

Michaëlis, Karen 1872-1950. . . . . .DLB-214

Michaels, Leonard 1933- DLB-130

Micheaux, Oscar 1884-1951 . . . . .DLB-50

Michel of Northgate, Dan
    circa 1265-circa 1340. . . . . .DLB-146

Micheline, Jack 1929-1998. . . . . .DLB-16

Michener, James A. 1907?-1997. . . . . .DLB-6

Micklejohn, George
    circa 1717-1818 . . . . .DLB-31

Middle English Literature:
    An Introduction. DLB-146

The Middle English Lyric DLB-146

Middle Hill Press. DLB-106

Middleton, Christopher 1926- DLB-40

Middleton, Richard 1882-1911 . . . . .DLB-156

Middleton, Stanley 1919- DLB-14

Middleton, Thomas 1580-1627 . . . . .DLB-58

Miegel, Agnes 1879-1964. . . . . .DLB-56

Mieželaitis, Eduardas 1919-1997 . . . . .DLB-220

Mihailović, Dragoslav 1930- DLB-181

Mihalić, Slavko 1928- DLB-181

Mikhailov, A. (see Sheller, Aleksandr
    Konstantinovich)

Mikhailov, Mikhail Larionovich
    1829-1865 . . . . .DLB-238

Miles, Josephine 1911-1985 . . . . .DLB-48

Miles, Susan (Ursula Wyllie Roberts)
    1888-1975 . . . . .DLB-240

Miliković, Branko 1934-1961 . . . . .DLB-181

Milius, John 1944- DLB-44

Mill, James 1773-1836 . . . . .DLB-107, 158

Mill, John Stuart
    1806-1873 . . . . .DLB-55, 190; CDBLB-4

Millar, Andrew [publishing house]. DLB-154

Millar, Kenneth
    1915-1983 . . . . .DLB-2, 226; Y-83; DS-6

Millay, Edna St. Vincent
    1892-1950 . . . . .DLB-45; CDALB-4

Millen, Sarah Gertrude 1888-1968 . . . . . .DLB-225

Miller, Arthur 1915- DLB-7; CDALB-1

Miller, Caroline 1903-1992 . . . . .DLB-9

Miller, Eugene Ethelbert 1950- DLB-41

Miller, Heather Ross 1939- DLB-120

Miller, Henry
    1891-1980 . . . . .DLB-4, 9; Y-80; CDALB-5

Miller, Hugh 1802-1856 . . . . .DLB-190

Miller, J. Hillis 1928- DLB-67

Miller, James [publishing house] DLB-49

Miller, Jason 1939- DLB-7

Miller, Joaquin 1839-1913 . . . . .DLB-186

Miller, May 1899- DLB-41

Miller, Paul 1906-1991 . . . . .DLB-127

Miller, Perry 1905-1963. . . . . DLB-17, 63

Miller, Sue 1943- DLB-143

Miller, Vassar 1924-1998. . . . . .DLB-105

Miller, Walter M., Jr. 1923- DLB-8

Miller, Webb 1892-1940 . . . . .DLB-29

Millett, Kate 1934- DLB-246

Millhauser, Steven 1943- DLB-2

Millican, Arthenia J. Bates 1920- DLB-38

Milligan, Alice 1866-1953 . . . . .DLB-240

Mills and Boon DLB-112

Milman, Henry Hart 1796-1868 . . . . .DLB-96

Milne, A. A. 1882-1956 . . . . . DLB-10, 77, 100, 160

Milner, Ron 1938- DLB-38

Milner, William [publishing house] DLB-106

Milnes, Richard Monckton (Lord Houghton)
    1809-1885 . . . . .DLB-32, 184

Milton, John
    1608-1674 . . . . .DLB-131, 151; CDBLB-2

Miłosz, Czesław 1911- DLB-215; CDWLB-4

Minakami Tsutomu 1919- DLB-182

Minamoto no Sanetomo 1192-1219. . . . . .DLB-203

The Minerva Press DLB-154

Minnesang circa 1150-1280 . . . . .DLB-138

Minns, Susan 1839-1938 . . . . .DLB-140

Minor Illustrators, 1880-1914 . . . . .DLB-141

Minor Poets of the Earlier Seventeenth
    Century. DLB-121

Minton, Balch and Company DLB-46

Mirbeau, Octave 1848-1917. . . . . . .DLB-123, 192

Mirk, John died after 1414?. DLB-146

Miron, Gaston 1928- DLB-60

A Mirror for Magistrates DLB-167

Mishima Yukio 1925-1970. . . . . .DLB-182

Mitchel, Jonathan 1624-1668. . . . . .DLB-24

Mitchell, Adrian 1932- DLB-40

Mitchell, Donald Grant
    1822-1908 . . . . .DLB-1, 243; DS-13

Mitchell, Gladys 1901-1983. . . . . .DLB-77

Mitchell, James Leslie 1901-1935. . . . . . . .DLB-15

Mitchell, John (see Slater, Patrick)

Mitchell, John Ames 1845-1918. . . . . .DLB-79

Mitchell, Joseph 1908-1996 . . . . . . DLB-185; Y-96

Mitchell, Julian 1935- DLB-14

Mitchell, Ken 1940- DLB-60

Mitchell, Langdon 1862-1935 . . . . .DLB-7

Mitchell, Loften 1919- DLB-38

Mitchell, Margaret 1900-1949 . . .DLB-9; CDALB-7

Mitchell, S. Weir 1829-1914 . . . . .DLB-202

Mitchell, W. J. T. 1942- DLB-246

Mitchell, W. O. 1914- DLB-88

Mitchison, Naomi Margaret (Haldane)
    1897-1999 . . . . .DLB-160, 191

Mitford, Mary Russell 1787-1855. . . .DLB-110, 116

Mitford, Nancy 1904-1973. . . . . .DLB-191

Mittelholzer, Edgar
    1909-1965 . . . . DLB-117; CDWLB-3

Mitterer, Erika 1906- DLB-85

Mitterer, Felix 1948- DLB-124

Mitternacht, Johann Sebastian
    1613-1679 . . . . .DLB-168

Miyamoto, Yuriko 1899-1951 . . . . .DLB-180

Mizener, Arthur 1907-1988 . . . . .DLB-103

Mo, Timothy 1950- DLB-194

Modern Age Books DLB-46

"Modern English Prose" (1876),
    by George Saintsbury DLB-57

The Modern Language Association of America
    Celebrates Its Centennial Y-84

The Modern Library. DLB-46

"Modern Novelists – Great and Small" (1855),
    by Margaret Oliphant DLB-21

"Modern Style" (1857), by Cockburn
    Thomson [excerpt] DLB-57

The Modernists (1932),
    by Joseph Warren Beach. DLB-36

Modiano, Patrick 1945- DLB-83

Moffat, Yard and Company DLB-46

Moffet, Thomas 1553-1604. . . . . .DLB-136

Mohr, Nicholasa 1938- DLB-145

Moix, Ana María 1947- DLB-134

Molesworth, Louisa 1839-1921 . . . . .DLB-135

Möllhausen, Balduin 1825-1905 . . . . .DLB-129

Molnár, Ferenc
    1878-1952 . . . . .DLB-215; CDWLB-4

Molnár, Miklós (see Mészöly, Miklós)

Momaday, N. Scott
    1934- DLB-143, 175; CDALB-7

Monkhouse, Allan 1858-1936 . . . . .DLB-10

Monro, Harold 1879-1932. . . . . .DLB-19

Monroe, Harriet 1860-1936. . . . . .DLB-54, 91

Monsarrat, Nicholas 1910-1979 . . . . .DLB-15

Montagu, Lady Mary Wortley
    1689-1762 . . . . .DLB-95, 101

Montague, C. E. 1867-1928 . . . . .DLB-197

Montague, John 1929- DLB-40

Montale, Eugenio 1896-1981. . . . . .DLB-114

Montalvo, José 1946-1994. . . . . .DLB-209

Monterroso, Augusto 1921- DLB-145

Montesquiou, Robert de 1855-1921 . . . . .DLB-217

Montgomerie, Alexander
    circa 1550?-1598. . . . . .DLB-167

Montgomery, James 1771-1854 . . . . . .DLB-93, 158

Montgomery, John 1919- DLB-16

Montgomery, Lucy Maud
    1874-1942 . . . . .DLB-92; DS-14

Montgomery, Marion 1925- DLB-6

Montgomery, Robert Bruce (see Crispin, Edmund)

Montherlant, Henry de 1896-1972 . . . . . .DLB-72

The Monthly Review 1749-1844 . . . . .DLB-110

Montigny, Louvigny de 1876-1955 . . . . . .DLB-92

Montoya, José 1932- DLB-122

Moodie, John Wedderburn Dunbar
   1797-1869 . . . . DLB-99

Moodie, Susanna 1803-1885 . . . . DLB-99

Moody, Joshua circa 1633-1697 . . . . DLB-24

Moody, William Vaughn 1869-1910 . . . DLB-7, 54

Moorcock, Michael 1939- DLB-14, 231

Moore, Catherine L. 1911- DLB-8

Moore, Clement Clarke 1779-1863 . . . . DLB-42

Moore, Dora Mavor 1888-1979 . . . . DLB-92

Moore, George 1852-1933 . . . . DLB-10, 18, 57, 135

Moore, Lorrie 1957- DLB-234

Moore, Marianne
   1887-1972 . . . . DLB-45; DS-7; CDALB-5

Moore, Mavor 1919- DLB-88

Moore, Richard 1927- DLB-105

Moore, T. Sturge 1870-1944 . . . . DLB-19

Moore, Thomas 1779-1852 . . . . DLB-96, 144

Moore, Ward 1903-1978 . . . . DLB-8

Moore, Wilstach, Keys and Company DLB-49

Moorehead, Alan 1901-1983 . . . . DLB-204

Moorhouse, Geoffrey 1931- DLB-204

The Moorland-Spingarn Research
   Center DLB-76

Moorman, Mary C. 1905-1994 . . . . DLB-155

Mora, Pat 1942- DLB-209

Moraga, Cherríe 1952- DLB-82

Morales, Alejandro 1944- DLB-82

Morales, Mario Roberto 1947- DLB-145

Morales, Rafael 1919- DLB-108

Morality Plays: *Mankind* circa 1450-1500 and
   Everyman circa 1500 . . . . DLB-146

Morante, Elsa 1912-1985 . . . . DLB-177

Morata, Olympia Fulvia 1526-1555 . . . . . DLB-179

Moravia, Alberto 1907-1990 . . . . DLB-177

Mordaunt, Elinor 1872-1942 . . . . DLB-174

Mordovtsev, Daniil Lukich 1830-1905 . . . DLB-238

More, Hannah
   1745-1833 . . . . DLB-107, 109, 116, 158

More, Henry 1614-1687 . . . . DLB-126

More, Sir Thomas
   1477 or 1478-1535 . . . . DLB-136

Moreno, Dorinda 1939- DLB-122

Morency, Pierre 1942- DLB-60

Moretti, Marino 1885-1979 . . . . DLB-114

Morgan, Berry 1919- DLB-6

Morgan, Charles 1894-1958 . . . . DLB-34, 100

Morgan, Edmund S. 1916- DLB-17

Morgan, Edwin 1920- DLB-27

Morgan, John Pierpont 1837-1913 . . . . . . DLB-140

Morgan, John Pierpont, Jr. 1867-1943 . . . DLB-140

Morgan, Robert 1944- DLB-120

Morgan, Sydney Owenson, Lady
   1776?-1859 . . . . DLB-116, 158

Morgner, Irmtraud 1933- DLB-75

Morhof, Daniel Georg 1639-1691 . . . . . . DLB-164

Mori, Ōgai 1862-1922 . . . . DLB-180

Móricz, Zsigmond 1879-1942 . . . . DLB-215

Morier, James Justinian
   1782 or 1783?-1849 . . . . DLB-116

Mörike, Eduard 1804-1875 . . . . DLB-133

Morin, Paul 1889-1963 . . . . DLB-92

Morison, Richard 1514?-1556 . . . . DLB-136

Morison, Samuel Eliot 1887-1976 . . . . DLB-17

Morison, Stanley 1889-1967 . . . . DLB-201

Moritz, Karl Philipp 1756-1793 . . . . DLB-94

Moriz von Craûn circa 1220-1230 . . . . . . DLB-138

Morley, Christopher 1890-1957 . . . . DLB-9

Morley, John 1838-1923 . . . . DLB-57, 144, 190

Morris, George Pope 1802-1864 . . . . DLB-73

Morris, James Humphrey (see Morris, Jan)

Morris, Jan 1926- DLB-204

Morris, Lewis 1833-1907 . . . . DLB-35

Morris, Margaret 1737-1816 . . . . DLB-200

Morris, Richard B. 1904-1989 . . . . DLB-17

Morris, William 1834-1896
   . . . . DLB-18, 35, 57, 156, 178, 184; CDBLB-4

Morris, Willie 1934-1999 . . . . Y-80

Morris, Wright
   1910-1998 . . . . DLB-2, 206, 218; Y-81

Morrison, Arthur 1863-1945 . . . . DLB-70, 135, 197

Morrison, Charles Clayton 1874-1966 . . . . DLB-91

Morrison, Toni 1931-
   . . . . . . DLB-6, 33, 143; Y-81, Y-93; CDALB-6

Morrow, William, and Company DLB-46

Morse, James Herbert 1841-1923 . . . . DLB-71

Morse, Jedidiah 1761-1826 . . . . DLB-37

Morse, John T., Jr. 1840-1937 . . . . DLB-47

Morselli, Guido 1912-1973 . . . . DLB-177

Mortimer, Favell Lee 1802-1878 . . . . DLB-163

Mortimer, John
   1923- DLB-13, 245; CDBLB-8

Morton, Carlos 1942- DLB-122

Morton, H. V. 1892-1979 . . . . DLB-195

Morton, John P., and Company DLB-49

Morton, Nathaniel 1613-1685 . . . . DLB-24

Morton, Sarah Wentworth 1759-1846 . . . . DLB-37

Morton, Thomas circa 1579-circa 1647 . . . DLB-24

Moscherosch, Johann Michael
   1601-1669 . . . . DLB-164

Moseley, Humphrey
   [publishing house] DLB-170

Möser, Justus 1720-1794 . . . . DLB-97

Mosley, Nicholas 1923- DLB-14, 207

Moss, Arthur 1889-1969 . . . . DLB-4

Moss, Howard 1922-1987 . . . . DLB-5

Moss, Thylias 1954- DLB-120

The Most Powerful Book Review
   in America
   [*New York Times Book Review*] Y-82

Motion, Andrew 1952- DLB-40

Motley, John Lothrop
   1814-1877 . . . . DLB-1, 30, 59, 235

Motley, Willard 1909-1965 . . . . DLB-76, 143

Mott, Lucretia 1793-1880 . . . . DLB-239

Motte, Benjamin Jr. [publishing house] . . . DLB-154

Motteux, Peter Anthony 1663-1718 . . . . . . DLB-80

Mottram, R. H. 1883-1971 . . . . DLB-36

Mount, Ferdinand 1939- DLB-231

Mouré, Erin 1955- DLB-60

Mourning Dove (Humishuma) between
   1882 and 1888?-1936 . . . . DLB-175, 221

Movies from Books, 1920-1974 . . . . DLB-9

Mowat, Farley 1921- DLB-68

Mowbray, A. R., and Company,
   Limited DLB-106

Mowrer, Edgar Ansel 1892-1977 . . . . DLB-29

Mowrer, Paul Scott 1887-1971 . . . . DLB-29

Moxon, Edward [publishing house] DLB-106

Moxon, Joseph [publishing house] DLB-170

Mphahlele, Es'kia (Ezekiel)
   1919- DLB-125; CDWLB-3

Mrożek, Sławomir 1930- . . DLB-232; CDWLB-4

Mtshali, Oswald Mbuyiseni 1940- DLB-125

Mucedorus DLB-62

Mudford, William 1782-1848 . . . . DLB-159

Mueller, Lisel 1924- DLB-105

Muhajir, El (see Marvin X)

Muhajir, Nazzam Al Fitnah (see Marvin X)

Mühlbach, Luise 1814-1873 . . . . DLB-133

Muir, Edwin 1887-1959 . . . . DLB-20, 100, 191

Muir, Helen 1937- DLB-14

Muir, John 1838-1914 . . . . DLB-186

Muir, Percy 1894-1979 . . . . DLB-201

Mujū Ichien 1226-1312 . . . . DLB-203

Mukherjee, Bharati 1940- DLB-60, 218

Mulcaster, Richard
   1531 or 1532-1611 . . . . DLB-167

Muldoon, Paul 1951- DLB-40

Müller, Friedrich (see Müller, Maler)

Müller, Heiner 1929-1995 . . . . DLB-124

Müller, Maler 1749-1825 . . . . DLB-94

Muller, Marcia 1944- DLB-226

Müller, Wilhelm 1794-1827 . . . . DLB-90

Mumford, Lewis 1895-1990 . . . . DLB-63

Munby, A. N. L. 1913-1974 . . . . DLB-201

Munby, Arthur Joseph 1828-1910 . . . . . . DLB-35

Munday, Anthony 1560-1633 . . . . . . DLB-62, 172

Mundt, Clara (see Mühlbach, Luise)

Mundt, Theodore 1808-1861 . . . . DLB-133

Munford, Robert circa 1737-1783 . . . . DLB-31

Mungoshi, Charles 1947- DLB-157

Munk, Kaj 1898-1944 . . . . DLB-214

Munonye, John 1929- DLB-117

Munro, Alice 1931- DLB-53

Munro, George [publishing house] DLB-49

Munro, H. H.
   1870-1916 . . . . DLB-34, 162; CDBLB-5

Munro, Neil 1864-1930 . . . . DLB-156

Munro, Norman L. [publishing house] DLB-49

Munroe, James, and Company DLB-49

Munroe, Kirk 1850-1930 . . . . .DLB-42

Munroe and Francis DLB-49

Munsell, Joel [publishing house] DLB-49

Munsey, Frank A. 1854-1925 . . . . . . .DLB-25, 91

Munsey, Frank A., and Company DLB-49

Murakami Haruki 1949- DLB-182

Murav'ev, Mikhail Nikitich 1757-1807 . . . . .DLB-150

Murdoch, Iris 1919-1999 . . . . . .DLB-14, 194, 233; CDBLB-8

Murdoch, Rupert 1931- DLB-127

Murfree, Mary N. 1850-1922 . . . . .DLB-12, 74

Murger, Henry 1822-1861 . . . . .DLB-119

Murger, Louis-Henri (see Murger, Henry)

Murner, Thomas 1475-1537 . . . . .DLB-179

Muro, Amado 1915-1971 . . . . .DLB-82

Murphy, Arthur 1727-1805 . . . . .DLB-89, 142

Murphy, Beatrice M. 1908- DLB-76

Murphy, Dervla 1931- DLB-204

Murphy, Emily 1868-1933 . . . . .DLB-99

Murphy, Jack 1923-1980 . . . . .DLB-241

Murphy, John, and Company DLB-49

Murphy, John H., III 1916- DLB-127

Murphy, Richard 1927-1993 . . . . .DLB-40

Murray, Albert L. 1916- DLB-38

Murray, Gilbert 1866-1957 . . . . .DLB-10

Murray, Jim 1919-1998 . . . . .DLB-241

Murray, John [publishing house] DLB-154

Murry, John Middleton 1889-1957 . . . . . .DLB-149

"The Break-Up of the Novel" (1922) DLB-36

Murray, Judith Sargent 1751-1820 . . . . DLB-37, 200

Murray, Pauli 1910-1985 . . . . .DLB-41

Musäus, Johann Karl August 1735-1787 . . . .DLB-97

Muschg, Adolf 1934- DLB-75

The Music of *Minnesang* DLB-138

Musil, Robert 1880-1942 . . . . .DLB-81, 124; CDWLB-2

Muspilli circa 790-circa 850 . . . . .DLB-148

Musset, Alfred de 1810-1857 . . . . . . .DLB-192, 217

Mussey, Benjamin B., and Company DLB-49

Mutafchieva, Vera 1929- DLB-181

Mwangi, Meja 1948- DLB-125

Myers, Frederic W. H. 1843-1901 . . . . . . .DLB-190

Myers, Gustavus 1872-1942 . . . . .DLB-47

Myers, L. H. 1881-1944 . . . . .DLB-15

Myers, Walter Dean 1937- DLB-33

Mykolaitis-Putinas, Vincas 1893-1967 . . . .DLB-220

Myles, Eileen 1949- DLB-193

N

Na Prous Boneta circa 1296-1328 . . . . . . .DLB-208

Nabl, Franz 1883-1974 . . . . .DLB-81

Nabokov, Vladimir 1899-1977 . . . . DLB-2, 244; Y-80, Y-91; DS-3; CDALB-1

The Vladimir Nabokov Archive in the Berg Collection Y-91

Nabokov Festival at Cornell Y-83

Nádaši, Ladislav (see Jégé)

Naden, Constance 1858-1889 . . . . .DLB-199

Nadezhdin, Nikolai Ivanovich 1804-1856 . . . . .DLB-198

Naevius circa 265 B.C.-201 B.C. DLB-211

Nafis and Cornish DLB-49

Nagai, Kafū 1879-1959 . . . . .DLB-180

Naipaul, Shiva 1945-1985 . . . . DLB-157; Y-85

Naipaul, V. S. 1932- DLB-125, 204, 207; Y-85; CDBLB-8; CDWLB-3

Nakagami Kenji 1946-1992 . . . . .DLB-182

Nakano-in Masatada no Musume (see Nijō, Lady)

Nałkowska, Zofia 1884-1954 . . . . .DLB-215

Nancrede, Joseph [publishing house] DLB-49

Naranjo, Carmen 1930- DLB-145

Narezhny, Vasilii Trofimovich 1780-1825 .DLB-198

Narrache, Jean 1893-1970 . . . . .DLB-92

Nasby, Petroleum Vesuvius (see Locke, David Ross)

Nash, Eveleigh [publishing house] DLB-112

Nash, Ogden 1902-1971 . . . . .DLB-11

Nashe, Thomas 1567-1601? DLB-167

Nason, Jerry 1910-1986 . . . . .DLB-241

Nast, Conde 1873-1942 . . . . .DLB-91

Nast, Thomas 1840-1902 . . . . .DLB-188

Nastasijević, Momčilo 1894-1938 . . . . . . .DLB-147

Nathan, George Jean 1882-1958 . . . . .DLB-137

Nathan, Robert 1894-1985 . . . . .DLB-9

National Book Critics Circle Awards 2000 . . . Y-00

The National Jewish Book Awards Y-85

The National Theatre and the Royal Shakespeare Company: The National Companies DLB-13

Natsume, Sōseki 1867-1916 . . . . .DLB-180

Naughton, Bill 1910- DLB-13

Navarro, Joe 1953- DLB-209

Naylor, Gloria 1950- DLB-173

Nazor, Vladimir 1876-1949 . . . . .DLB-147

Ndebele, Njabulo 1948- DLB-157

Neagoe, Peter 1881-1960 . . . . .DLB-4

Neal, John 1793-1876 . . . . .DLB-1, 59, 243

Neal, Joseph C. 1807-1847 . . . . .DLB-11

Neal, Larry 1937-1981 . . . . .DLB-38

The Neale Publishing Company DLB-49

Nebel, Frederick 1903-1967 . . . . .DLB-226

Neely, F. Tennyson [publishing house] DLB-49

Negoiţescu, Ion 1921-1993 . . . . .DLB-220

Negri, Ada 1870-1945 . . . . .DLB-114

"The Negro as a Writer," by G. M. McClellan DLB-50

"Negro Poets and Their Poetry," by Wallace Thurman DLB-50

Neidhart von Reuental circa 1185-circa 1240 . . . . .DLB-138

Neihardt, John G. 1881-1973 . . . . .DLB-9, 54

Neilson, John Shaw 1872-1942 . . . . .DLB-230

Neledinsky-Meletsky, Iurii Aleksandrovich 1752-1828 . . . . .DLB-150

Nelligan, Emile 1879-1941 . . . . .DLB-92

Nelson, Alice Moore Dunbar 1875-1935 . . .DLB-50

Nelson, Antonya 1961- DLB-244

Nelson, Kent 1943- DLB-234

Nelson, Thomas, and Sons [U.K.] DLB-106

Nelson, Thomas, and Sons [U.S.] DLB-49

Nelson, William 1908-1978 . . . . .DLB-103

Nelson, William Rockhill 1841-1915 . . . . . .DLB-23

Nemerov, Howard 1920-1991 . . . . . DLB-5, 6; Y-83

Németh, László 1901-1975 . . . . .DLB-215

Nepos circa 100 B.C.-post 27 B.C. DLB-211

Nėris, Salomėja 1904-1945 . . . . .DLB-220; CDWLB-4

Nerval, Gerard de 1808-1855 . . . . .DLB-217

Nesbit, E. 1858-1924 . . . . DLB-141, 153, 178

Ness, Evaline 1911-1986 . . . . .DLB-61

Nestroy, Johann 1801-1862 . . . . .DLB-133

Neugeboren, Jay 1938- DLB-28

Neukirch, Benjamin 1655-1729 . . . . .DLB-168

Neumann, Alfred 1895-1952 . . . . .DLB-56

Neumann, Ferenc (see Molnár, Ferenc)

Neumark, Georg 1621-1681 . . . . .DLB-164

Neumeister, Erdmann 1671-1756 . . . . . . .DLB-168

Nevins, Allan 1890-1971 . . . . DLB-17; DS-17

Nevinson, Henry Woodd 1856-1941 . . . .DLB-135

The New American Library DLB-46

New Approaches to Biography: Challenges from Critical Theory, USC Conference on Literary Studies, 1990 . . . . Y-90

New Directions Publishing Corporation . . .DLB-46

A New Edition of *Huck Finn* Y-85

New Forces at Work in the American Theatre: 1915-1925 . . . . .DLB-7

New Literary Periodicals: A Report for 1987 . . . . .Y-87

New Literary Periodicals: A Report for 1988 . . . . .Y-88

New Literary Periodicals: A Report for 1989 . . . . .Y-89

New Literary Periodicals: A Report for 1990 . . . . .Y-90

New Literary Periodicals: A Report for 1991 . . . . .Y-91

New Literary Periodicals: A Report for 1992 . . . . .Y-92

New Literary Periodicals: A Report for 1993 . . . . .Y-93

The New Monthly Magazine 1814-1884 .DLB-110

The New Variorum Shakespeare Y-85

A New Voice: The Center for the Book's First
Five Years. Y-83

The New Wave [Science Fiction] DLB-8

New York City Bookshops in the 1930s and 1940s:
The Recollections of Walter Goldwater. . . Y-93

Newbery, John [publishing house] DLB-154

Newbolt, Henry 1862-1938 . . . . DLB-19

Newbound, Bernard Slade (see Slade, Bernard)

Newby, Eric 1919- DLB-204

Newby, P. H. 1918- DLB-15

Newby, Thomas Cautley
[publishing house] DLB-106

Newcomb, Charles King 1820-1894 . . . DLB-1, 223

Newell, Peter 1862-1924. . . . . DLB-42

Newell, Robert Henry 1836-1901. . . . . . . DLB-11

Newhouse, Samuel I. 1895-1979. . . . . . . DLB-127

Newman, Cecil Earl 1903-1976 . . . . DLB-127

Newman, David (see Benton, Robert)

Newman, Frances 1883-1928 . . . . Y-80

Newman, Francis William 1805-1897. . . . DLB-190

Newman, John Henry
1801-1890 . . . . DLB-18, 32, 55

Newman, Mark [publishing house]. DLB-49

Newmarch, Rosa Harriet 1857-1940. . . . . DLB-240

Newnes, George, Limited DLB-112

Newsome, Effie Lee 1885-1979. . . . . DLB-76

Newspaper Syndication of American
Humor DLB-11

Newton, A. Edward 1864-1940 . . . . DLB-140

Nexø, Martin Andersen 1869-1954 . . . . . DLB-214

Nezval, Vítěslav
1900-1958. . . . . DLB-215; CDWLB-4

Ngugi wa Thiong'o
1938- DLB-125; CDWLB-3

Niatum, Duane 1938- DLB-175

The *Nibelungenlied* and the *Klage*
circa 1200. DLB-138

Nichol, B. P. 1944- DLB-53

Nicholas of Cusa 1401-1464. . . . . DLB-115

Nichols, Beverly 1898-1983 . . . . DLB-191

Nichols, Dudley 1895-1960 . . . . DLB-26

Nichols, Grace 1950- DLB-157

Nichols, John 1940- Y-82

Nichols, Mary Sargeant (Neal) Gove
1810-1884. . . . . DLB-1, 243

Nichols, Peter 1927- DLB-13, 245

Nichols, Roy F. 1896-1973 . . . . DLB-17

Nichols, Ruth 1948- DLB-60

Nicholson, Edward Williams Byron
1849-1912. DLB-184

Nicholson, Norman 1914- DLB-27

Nicholson, William 1872-1949 . . . . DLB-141

Ní Chuilleanáin, Eiléan 1942- DLB-40

Nicol, Eric 1919- DLB-68

Nicolai, Friedrich 1733-1811. . . . . DLB-97

Nicolas de Clamanges circa 1363-1437. . . DLB-208

Nicolay, John G. 1832-1901 and
Hay, John 1838-1905. . . . . DLB-47

Nicolson, Adela Florence Cory (see Hope, Laurence)

Nicolson, Harold 1886-1968. . . . . . .DLB-100, 149

Nicolson, Nigel 1917- DLB-155

Niebuhr, Reinhold 1892-1971. . . . . .DLB-17; DS-17

Niedecker, Lorine 1903-1970 . . . . DLB-48

Nieman, Lucius W. 1857-1935 . . . . DLB-25

Nietzsche, Friedrich
1844-1900 . . . . DLB-129; CDWLB-2

Nievo, Stanislao 1928- DLB-196

Niggli, Josefina 1910- Y-80

Nightingale, Florence 1820-1910 . . . . DLB-166

Nijō, Lady (Nakano-in Masatada no Musume)
1258-after 1306 . . . . DLB-203

Nijō Yoshimoto 1320-1388. . . . . DLB-203

Nikolev, Nikolai Petrovich
1758-1815. DLB-150

Niles, Hezekiah 1777-1839 . . . . DLB-43

Nims, John Frederick 1913-1999 . . . . DLB-5

Nin, Anaïs 1903-1977 . . . . DLB-2, 4, 152

1985: The Year of the Mystery:
A Symposium. Y-85

The 1997 Booker Prize. Y-97

The 1998 Booker Prize. Y-98

Niño, Raúl 1961- DLB-209

Nissenson, Hugh 1933- DLB-28

Niven, Frederick John 1878-1944 . . . . DLB-92

Niven, Larry 1938- DLB-8

Nixon, Howard M. 1909-1983. . . . . DLB-201

Nizan, Paul 1905-1940 . . . . DLB-72

Njegoš, Petar II Petrović
1813-1851 . . . . .DLB-147; CDWLB-4

Nkosi, Lewis 1936- DLB-157

"The No Self, the Little Self, and the Poets,"
by Richard Moore DLB-105

Nobel Peace Prize

The 1986 Nobel Peace Prize: Elie Wiesel. Y-86

The Nobel Prize and Literary Politics Y-86

Nobel Prize in Literature

The 1982 Nobel Prize in Literature:
Gabriel García Márquez. Y-82

The 1983 Nobel Prize in Literature:
William Golding Y-83

The 1984 Nobel Prize in Literature:
Jaroslav Seifert. Y-84

The 1985 Nobel Prize in Literature:
Claude Simon Y-85

The 1986 Nobel Prize in Literature:
Wole Soyinka. Y-86

The 1987 Nobel Prize in Literature:
Joseph Brodsky Y-87

The 1988 Nobel Prize in Literature:
Najīb Mahfūz. Y-88

The 1989 Nobel Prize in Literature:
Camilo José Cela Y-89

The 1990 Nobel Prize in Literature:
Octavio Paz Y-90

The 1991 Nobel Prize in Literature:
Nadine Gordimer. Y-91

The 1992 Nobel Prize in Literature:
Derek Walcott Y-92

The 1993 Nobel Prize in Literature:
Toni Morrison. Y-93

The 1994 Nobel Prize in Literature:
Kenzaburō Oe Y-94

The 1995 Nobel Prize in Literature:
Seamus Heaney Y-95

The 1996 Nobel Prize in Literature:
Wisława Szymborsha. Y-96

The 1997 Nobel Prize in Literature:
Dario Fo. Y-97

The 1998 Nobel Prize in Literature:
José Saramago Y-98

The 1999 Nobel Prize in Literature:
Günter Grass Y-99

The 2000 Nobel Prize in Literature:
Gao Xingjian Y-00

Nodier, Charles 1780-1844. . . . . DLB-119

Noel, Roden 1834-1894 . . . . DLB-35

Nogami, Yaeko 1885-1985. . . . . DLB-180

Nogo, Rajko Petrov 1945- DLB-181

Nolan, William F. 1928- DLB-8

Noland, C. F. M. 1810?-1858. . . . . DLB-11

Noma Hiroshi 1915-1991. . . . . DLB-182

Nonesuch Press DLB-112

Noonan, Robert Phillipe (see Tressell, Robert)

Noonday Press. DLB-46

Noone, John 1936- DLB-14

Nora, Eugenio de 1923- DLB-134

Nordan, Lewis 1939- DLB-234

Nordbrandt, Henrik 1945- DLB-214

Nordhoff, Charles 1887-1947 . . . . DLB-9

Norman, Charles 1904-1996 . . . . DLB-111

Norman, Marsha 1947- Y-84

Norris, Charles G. 1881-1945 . . . . DLB-9

Norris, Frank
1870-1902. . . . . . . DLB-12, 71, 186; CDALB-3

Norris, Leslie 1921- DLB-27

Norse, Harold 1916- DLB-16

Norte, Marisela 1955- DLB-209

North, Marianne 1830-1890. . . . . .DLB-174

North Point Press. DLB-46

Nortje, Arthur 1942-1970 . . . . DLB-125

Norton, Alice Mary (see Norton, Andre)

Norton, Andre 1912- DLB-8, 52

Norton, Andrews 1786-1853 . . . . DLB-1, 235

Norton, Caroline 1808-1877 . . . .DLB-21, 159, 199

Norton, Charles Eliot 1827-1908 . . DLB-1, 64, 235

Norton, John 1606-1663. . . . . DLB-24

Norton, Mary 1903-1992 . . . . DLB-160

Norton, Thomas (see Sackville, Thomas)

Norton, W. W., and Company DLB-46

Norwood, Robert 1874-1932 . . . . DLB-92

Nosaka Akiyuki 1930- DLB-182

Nossack, Hans Erich 1901-1977. . . . . DLB-69

Not Immediately Discernible . . . but Eventually
Quite Clear: The *First Light* and *Final Years*
of Hemingway's Centenary. Y-99

A Note on Technique (1926), by
   Elizabeth A. Drew [excerpts]. DLB-36

Notker Balbulus circa 840-912. . . . . .DLB-148

Notker III of Saint Gall circa 950-1022 . . .DLB-148

Notker von Zweifalten ?-1095 . . . . .DLB-148

Nourse, Alan E. 1928- DLB-8

Novak, Slobodan 1924- DLB-181

Novak, Vjenceslav 1859-1905 . . . . .DLB-147

Novakovich, Josip 1956- DLB-244

Novalis 1772-1801 . . . . .DLB-90; CDWLB-2

Novaro, Mario 1868-1944. . . . . .DLB-114

Novás Calvo, Lino 1903-1983. . . . . .DLB-145

"The Novel in [Robert Browning's] 'The Ring and
   the Book'" (1912), by Henry James . . .DLB-32

The Novel of Impressionism,
   by Jethro Bithell DLB-66

Novel-Reading: *The Works of Charles Dickens,*
   The Works of W. Makepeace Thackeray
   (1879), by Anthony Trollope DLB-21

Novels for Grown-Ups Y-97

The Novels of Dorothy Richardson (1918),
   by May Sinclair DLB-36

Novels with a Purpose (1864), by
   Justin M'Carthy. DLB-21

Noventa, Giacomo 1898-1960. . . . . .DLB-114

Novikov, Nikolai
   Ivanovich 1744-1818 . . . . .DLB-150

Novomeský, Laco 1904-1976. . . . . .DLB-215

Nowlan, Alden 1933-1983. . . . . .DLB-53

Noyes, Alfred 1880-1958. . . . . .DLB-20

Noyes, Crosby S. 1825-1908 . . . . .DLB-23

Noyes, Nicholas 1647-1717 . . . . .DLB-24

Noyes, Theodore W. 1858-1946 . . . . .DLB-29

N-Town Plays circa 1468 to early
   sixteenth century DLB-146

Nugent, Frank 1908-1965 . . . . .DLB-44

Nugent, Richard Bruce 1906- DLB-151

Nušić, Branislav
   1864-1938 . . . . .DLB-147; CDWLB-4

Nutt, David [publishing house] DLB-106

Nwapa, Flora 1931-1993 . . . .DLB-125; CDWLB-3

Nye, Bill 1850-1896. . . . . .DLB-186

Nye, Edgar Wilson (Bill) 1850-1896 . . .DLB-11, 23

Nye, Naomi Shihab 1952- DLB-120

Nye, Robert 1939- DLB-14

Nyka-Niliūnas, Alfonsas 1919- DLB-220

O

Oakes Smith, Elizabeth
   1806-1893 . . . . .DLB-1, 239, 243

Oakes, Urian circa 1631-1681 . . . . .DLB-24

Oakley, Violet 1874-1961 . . . . .DLB-188

Oates, Joyce Carol 1938-   . . . DLB-2, 5, 130; Y-81

Ōba Minako 1930- DLB-182

Ober, Frederick Albion 1849-1913 . . . . . .DLB-189

Ober, William 1920-1993 . . . . Y-93

Oberholtzer, Ellis Paxson 1868-1936. . . . . .DLB-47

Obradović, Dositej 1740?-1811 . . . . .DLB-147

O'Brien, Charlotte Grace 1845-1909. . . . .DLB-240

O'Brien, Edna 1932-   . . .DLB-14, 231; CDBLB-8

O'Brien, Fitz-James 1828-1862. . . . . .DLB-74

O'Brien, Flann (see O'Nolan, Brian)

O'Brien, Kate 1897-1974 . . . . .DLB-15

O'Brien, Tim
   1946- DLB-152; Y-80; DS-9; CDALB-7

O'Casey, Sean 1880-1964 . . . . .DLB-10; CDBLB-6

Occom, Samson 1723-1792 . . . . .DLB-175

Ochs, Adolph S. 1858-1935. . . . . .DLB-25

Ochs-Oakes, George Washington
   1861-1931 . . . . .DLB-137

O'Connor, Flannery 1925-1964
   . . . . . . .DLB-2, 152; Y-80; DS-12; CDALB-1

O'Connor, Frank 1903-1966 . . . . .DLB-162

Octopus Publishing Group DLB-112

Oda Sakunosuke 1913-1947 . . . . .DLB-182

Odell, Jonathan 1737-1818 . . . . .DLB-31, 99

O'Dell, Scott 1903-1989. . . . . .DLB-52

Odets, Clifford 1906-1963 . . . . .DLB-7, 26

Odhams Press Limited. DLB-112

Odoevsky, Aleksandr Ivanovich
   1802-1839 . . . . .DLB-205

Odoevsky, Vladimir Fedorovich
   1804 or 1803-1869 . . . . .DLB-198

O'Donnell, Peter 1920- DLB-87

O'Donovan, Michael (see O'Connor, Frank)

O'Dowd, Bernard 1866-1953 . . . . .DLB-230

Ōe Kenzaburō 1935- DLB-182; Y-94

O'Faolain, Julia 1932- DLB-14, 231

O'Faolain, Sean 1900- DLB-15, 162

Off Broadway and Off-Off Broadway. DLB-7

Off-Loop Theatres. DLB-7

Offord, Carl Ruthven 1910- DLB-76

O'Flaherty, Liam 1896-1984 . . .DLB-36, 162; Y-84

Ogilvie, J. S., and Company DLB-49

Ogilvy, Eliza 1822-1912. . . . . .DLB-199

Ogot, Grace 1930- DLB-125

O'Grady, Desmond 1935- DLB-40

Ogunyemi, Wale 1939- DLB-157

O'Hagan, Howard 1902-1982 . . . . .DLB-68

O'Hara, Frank 1926-1966 . . . . .DLB-5, 16, 193

O'Hara, John
   1905-1970 . . . . . . .DLB-9, 86; DS-2; CDALB-5

John O'Hara's Pottsville Journalism Y-88

O'Hegarty, P. S. 1879-1955 . . . . .DLB-201

Okara, Gabriel 1921- DLB-125; CDWLB-3

O'Keeffe, John 1747-1833. . . . . .DLB-89

Okes, Nicholas [publishing house]. DLB-170

Okigbo, Christopher
   1930-1967 . . . . .DLB-125; CDWLB-3

Okot p'Bitek 1931-1982. . . . . .DLB-125; CDWLB-3

Okpewho, Isidore 1941- DLB-157

Okri, Ben 1959- DLB-157, 231

Olaudah Equiano and Unfinished Journeys:
   The Slave-Narrative Tradition and
   Twentieth-Century Continuities, by

Paul Edwards and Pauline T.
   Wangman DLB-117

Old English Literature:
   An Introduction DLB-146

Old English Riddles
   eighth to tenth centuries DLB-146

Old Franklin Publishing House. DLB-49

Old German Genesis and *Old German Exodus*
   circa 1050-circa 1130. . . . . .DLB-148

Old High German Charms and
   Blessings DLB-148; CDWLB-2

The *Old High German Isidor*
   circa 790-800 . . . . .DLB-148

The Old Manse .DLB-223

Older, Fremont 1856-1935 . . . . .DLB-25

Oldham, John 1653-1683. . . . . .DLB-131

Oldman, C. B. 1894-1969 . . . . .DLB-201

Olds, Sharon 1942- DLB-120

Olearius, Adam 1599-1671 . . . . .DLB-164

O'Leary, Ellen 1831-1889 . . . . .DLB-240

Oliphant, Laurence 1829?-1888. . . . . .DLB-18, 166

Oliphant, Margaret 1828-1897. . . . . . .DLB-18, 190

Oliver, Chad 1928- DLB-8

Oliver, Mary 1935- DLB-5, 193

Ollier, Claude 1922- DLB-83

Olsen, Tillie 1912 or 1913-
   . . . . .DLB-28, 206; Y-80; CDALB-7

Olson, Charles 1910-1970 . . . . . . .DLB-5, 16, 193

Olson, Elder 1909- DLB-48, 63

Omotoso, Kole 1943- DLB-125

Omulevsky, Innokentii Vasil'evich
   1836 [or 1837]-1883 . . . . .DLB-238

On Learning to Write Y-88

Ondaatje, Michael 1943- DLB-60

O'Neill, Eugene 1888-1953 . . . . .DLB-7; CDALB-5

Eugene O'Neill Memorial Theater
   Center. DLB-7

Eugene O'Neill's Letters: A Review Y-88

Onetti, Juan Carlos
   1909-1994 . . . . .DLB-113; CDWLB-3

Onions, George Oliver 1872-1961. . . . . . .DLB-153

Onofri, Arturo 1885-1928 . . . . .DLB-114

O'Nolan, Brian 1911-1966. . . . . .DLB-231

Opie, Amelia 1769-1853. . . . . .DLB-116, 159

Opitz, Martin 1597-1639 . . . . .DLB-164

Oppen, George 1908-1984. . . . . .DLB-5, 165

Oppenheim, E. Phillips 1866-1946 . . . . . .DLB-70

Oppenheim, James 1882-1932. . . . . .DLB-28

Oppenheimer, Joel 1930-1988 . . . . . . .DLB-5, 193

Optic, Oliver (see Adams, William Taylor)

Oral History: B. W. Huebsch Y-99

Oral History Interview with Donald S.
   Klopfer Y-97

Orczy, Emma, Baroness 1865-1947. . . . . . .DLB-70

Oregon Shakespeare Festival. Y-00

Origo, Iris 1902-1988. . . . . .DLB-155

Orlovitz, Gil 1918-1973 . . . . .DLB-2, 5

Orlovsky, Peter 1933- DLB-16

Ormond, John 1923- DLB-27

Ornitz, Samuel 1890-1957 . . . . DLB-28, 44

O'Rourke, P. J. 1947- DLB-185

Orten, Jiří 1919-1941 . . . . DLB-215

Ortese, Anna Maria 1914- DLB-177

Ortiz, Simon J. 1941- DLB-120, 175

Ortnit and *Wolfdietrich* circa 1225-1250. . . . DLB-138

Orton, Joe 1933-1967 . . . . DLB-13; CDBLB-8

Orwell, George
1903-1950 . . . . . DLB-15, 98, 195; CDBLB-7

The Orwell Year. Y-84

(Re-)Publishing Orwell Y-86

Ory, Carlos Edmundo de 1923- DLB-134

Osbey, Brenda Marie 1957- DLB-120

Osbon, B. S. 1827-1912. . . . . DLB-43

Osborn, Sarah 1714-1796 . . . . DLB-200

Osborne, John 1929-1994. . . . . DLB-13; CDBLB-7

Osgood, Herbert L. 1855-1918. . . . . DLB-47

Osgood, James R., and Company DLB-49

Osgood, McIlvaine and Company DLB-112

O'Shaughnessy, Arthur 1844-1881. . . . . . DLB-35

O'Shea, Patrick [publishing house] DLB-49

Osipov, Nikolai Petrovich
1751-1799 . . . . DLB-150

Oskison, John Milton 1879-1947. . . . . . . .DLB-175

Osler, Sir William 1849-1919. . . . . DLB-184

Osofisan, Femi 1946- DLB-125; CDWLB-3

Ostenso, Martha 1900-1963 . . . . DLB-92

Ostrauskas, Kostas 1926- DLB-232

Ostriker, Alicia 1937- DLB-120

Osundare, Niyi 1947- DLB-157; CDWLB-3

Oswald, Eleazer 1755-1795 . . . . DLB-43

Oswald von Wolkenstein
1376 or 1377-1445 . . . . .DLB-179

Otero, Blas de 1916-1979 . . . . DLB-134

Otero, Miguel Antonio 1859-1944 . . . . . . DLB-82

Otero, Nina 1881-1965. . . . . DLB-209

Otero Silva, Miguel 1908-1985. . . . . DLB-145

Otfried von Weißenburg
circa 800-circa 875? DLB-148

Otis, Broaders and Company. DLB-49

Otis, James (see Kaler, James Otis)

Otis, James, Jr. 1725-1783 . . . . DLB-31

Ottaway, James 1911- DLB-127

Ottendorfer, Oswald 1826-1900. . . . . DLB-23

Ottieri, Ottiero 1924- DLB-177

Otto-Peters, Louise 1819-1895 . . . . DLB-129

Otway, Thomas 1652-1685 . . . . DLB-80

Ouellette, Fernand 1930- DLB-60

Ouida 1839-1908 . . . . DLB-18, 156

Outing Publishing Company DLB-46

Outlaw Days, by Joyce Johnson DLB-16

Overbury, Sir Thomas
circa 1581-1613 . . . . DLB-151

The Overlook Press DLB-46

Overview of U.S. Book Publishing,
1910-1945 . . . . DLB-9

Ovid 43 B.C.-A.D. 17 . . . . . . DLB-211; CDWLB-1

Owen, Guy 1925- DLB-5

Owen, John 1564-1622. . . . . DLB-121

Owen, John [publishing house]. DLB-49

Owen, Peter, Limited DLB-112

Owen, Robert 1771-1858 . . . . .DLB-107, 158

Owen, Wilfred
1893-1918 . . . . DLB-20; DS-18; CDBLB-6

The Owl and the Nightingale
circa 1189-1199 . . . . DLB-146

Owsley, Frank L. 1890-1956 . . . . DLB-17

Oxford, Seventeenth Earl of, Edward
de Vere 1550-1604. . . . . .DLB-172

Ozerov, Vladislav Aleksandrovich
1769-1816. . . . . DLB-150

Ozick, Cynthia 1928- DLB-28, 152; Y-83

First Strauss "Livings" Awarded to Cynthia
Ozick and Raymond Carver
An Interview with Cynthia Ozick Y-83

P

Pace, Richard 1482?-1536 . . . . DLB-167

Pacey, Desmond 1917-1975 . . . . DLB-88

Pack, Robert 1929- DLB-5

Packaging Papa: *The Garden of Eden* Y-86

Padell Publishing Company DLB-46

Padgett, Ron 1942- DLB-5

Padilla, Ernesto Chávez 1944- DLB-122

Page, L. C., and Company. DLB-49

Page, Louise 1955- DLB-233

Page, P. K. 1916- DLB-68

Page, Thomas Nelson
1853-1922 . . . . .DLB-12, 78; DS-13

Page, Walter Hines 1855-1918. . . . . . DLB-71, 91

Paget, Francis Edward 1806-1882 . . . . . . DLB-163

Paget, Violet (see Lee, Vernon)

Pagliarani, Elio 1927- DLB-128

Pain, Barry 1864-1928 . . . . .DLB-135, 197

Pain, Philip ?-circa 1666 . . . . DLB-24

Paine, Robert Treat, Jr. 1773-1811 . . . . . . DLB-37

Paine, Thomas
1737-1809 . . . . DLB-31, 43, 73, 158; CDALB-2

Painter, George D. 1914- DLB-155

Painter, William 1540?-1594 . . . . DLB-136

Palazzeschi, Aldo 1885-1974 . . . . DLB-114

Paley, Grace 1922- DLB-28, 218

Palfrey, John Gorham 1796-1881 . . DLB-1, 30, 235

Palgrave, Francis Turner 1824-1897. . . . . . DLB-35

Palmer, Joe H. 1904-1952. . . . . .DLB-171

Palmer, Michael 1943- DLB-169

Paltock, Robert 1697-1767. . . . . DLB-39

Paludan, Jacob 1896-1975 . . . . DLB-214

Pan Books Limited DLB-112

Panama, Norman 1914- and
Frank, Melvin 1913-1988. . . . . DLB-26

Panaev, Ivan Ivanovich 1812-1862. . . . . . DLB-198

Panaeva, Avdot'ia Iakovlevna
1820-1893 . . . . DLB-238

Pancake, Breece D'J 1952-1979. . . . . DLB-130

Panduro, Leif 1923-1977 . . . . DLB-214

Panero, Leopoldo 1909-1962 . . . . DLB-108

Pangborn, Edgar 1909-1976 . . . . DLB-8

"Panic Among the Philistines": A Postscript,
An Interview with Bryan Griffin Y-81

Panizzi, Sir Anthony 1797-1879. . . . . DLB-184

Panneton, Philippe (see Ringuet)

Panshin, Alexei 1940- DLB-8

Pansy (see Alden, Isabella)

Pantheon Books DLB-46

Papadat-Bengescu, Hortensia
1876-1955 . . . . DLB-220

Papantonio, Michael (see Kohn, John S. Van E.)

Paperback Library DLB-46

Paperback Science Fiction. DLB-8

Paquet, Alfons 1881-1944. . . . . DLB-66

Paracelsus 1493-1541 . . . . .DLB-179

Paradis, Suzanne 1936- DLB-53

Páral, Vladimír, 1932- DLB-232

Pardoe, Julia 1804-1862 . . . . DLB-166

Paredes, Américo 1915-1999 . . . . DLB-209

Pareja Diezcanseco, Alfredo 1908-1993 . . DLB-145

Parents' Magazine Press. DLB-46

Parise, Goffredo 1929-1986 . . . . .DLB-177

Parisian Theater, Fall 1984: Toward
A New Baroque Y-85

Parizeau, Alice 1930- DLB-60

Parke, John 1754-1789 . . . . DLB-31

Parker, Dan 1893-1967. . . . . DLB-241

Parker, Dorothy 1893-1967 . . . . . . DLB-11, 45, 86

Parker, Gilbert 1860-1932 . . . . DLB-99

Parker, J. H. [publishing house] DLB-106

Parker, James 1714-1770 . . . . DLB-43

Parker, John [publishing house] DLB-106

Parker, Matthew 1504-1575 . . . . DLB-213

Parker, Stewart 1941-1988 . . . . DLB-245

Parker, Theodore 1810-1860 . . . . DLB-1, 235

Parker, William Riley 1906-1968. . . . . . . DLB-103

Parkes, Bessie Rayner (Madame Belloc)
1829-1925 . . . . DLB-240

Parkman, Francis
1823-1893 . . . . .DLB-1, 30, 183, 186, 235

Parks, Gordon 1912- DLB-33

Parks, Tim 1954- DLB-231

Parks, William 1698-1750. . . . . DLB-43

Parks, William [publishing house] DLB-49

Parley, Peter (see Goodrich, Samuel Griswold)

Parmenides
late sixth-fifth century B.C. DLB-176

Parnell, Thomas 1679-1718 . . . . DLB-95

Parnicki, Teodor 1908-1988. . . . . DLB-215

Parr, Catherine 1513?-1548 . . . . DLB-136

Parrington, Vernon L. 1871-1929 . . . . . DLB-17, 63

Parrish, Maxfield 1870-1966 . . . . DLB-188

Parronchi, Alessandro 1914- DLB-128

Parton, James 1822-1891 . . . . DLB-30

Parton, Sara Payson Willis
1811-1872 . . . . DLB-43, 74, 239

Partridge, S. W., and Company DLB-106

Parun, Vesna 1922- DLB-181; CDWLB-4

Pasinetti, Pier Maria 1913- DLB-177

Pasolini, Pier Paolo 1922- DLB-128, 177

Pastan, Linda 1932- DLB-5

Paston, George (Emily Morse Symonds)
1860-1936 . . . . DLB-149, 197

The Paston Letters 1422-1509 . . . . DLB-146

Pastorius, Francis Daniel
1651-circa 1720 . . . . DLB-24

Patchen, Kenneth 1911-1972 . . . . DLB-16, 48

Pater, Walter
1839-1894 . . . . DLB-57, 156; CDBLB-4

Aesthetic Poetry (1873) DLB-35

Paterson, A. B. "Banjo" 1864-1941 . . . . . DLB-230

Paterson, Katherine 1932- DLB-52

Patmore, Coventry 1823-1896 . . . . DLB-35, 98

Paton, Alan 1903-1988 . . . . DS-17

Paton, Joseph Noel 1821-1901 . . . . DLB-35

Paton Walsh, Jill 1937- DLB-161

Patrick, Edwin Hill ("Ted") 1901-1964 . . . DLB-137

Patrick, John 1906-1995 . . . . DLB-7

Pattee, Fred Lewis 1863-1950 . . . . DLB-71

Pattern and Paradigm: History as
Design, by Judith Ryan DLB-75

Patterson, Alicia 1906-1963 . . . . DLB-127

Patterson, Eleanor Medill 1881-1948 . . . . . . DLB-29

Patterson, Eugene 1923- DLB-127

Patterson, Joseph Medill 1879-1946 . . . . . . DLB-29

Pattillo, Henry 1726-1801 . . . . DLB-37

Paul, Elliot 1891-1958 . . . . DLB-4

Paul, Jean (see Richter, Johann Paul Friedrich)

Paul, Kegan, Trench, Trubner and
Company Limited DLB-106

Paul, Peter, Book Company DLB-49

Paul, Stanley, and Company Limited . . . DLB-112

Paulding, James Kirke 1778-1860 . . . . DLB-3, 59, 74

Paulin, Tom 1949- DLB-40

Pauper, Peter, Press DLB-46

Pavese, Cesare 1908-1950 . . . . DLB-128, 177

Pavić, Milorad 1929- DLB-181; CDWLB-4

Pavlov, Konstantin 1933- DLB-181

Pavlov, Nikolai Filippovich 1803-1864 . . . . . DLB-198

Pavlova, Karolina Karlovna 1807-1893 . . . . DLB-205

Pavlović, Miodrag
1928- DLB-181; CDWLB-4

Paxton, John 1911-1985 . . . . DLB-44

Payn, James 1830-1898 . . . . DLB-18

Payne, John 1842-1916 . . . . DLB-35

Payne, John Howard 1791-1852 . . . . DLB-37

Payson and Clarke DLB-46

Paz, Octavio 1914-1998 . . . . Y-90, Y-98

Pazzi, Roberto 1946- DLB-196

Peabody, Elizabeth Palmer 1804-1894 . . DLB-1, 223

Peabody, Elizabeth Palmer
[publishing house] DLB-49

Peabody, Oliver William Bourn
1799-1848 . . . . DLB-59

Peace, Roger 1899-1968 . . . . DLB-127

Peacham, Henry 1578-1644? DLB-151

Peacham, Henry, the Elder
1547-1634 . . . . DLB-172, 236

Peachtree Publishers, Limited DLB-46

Peacock, Molly 1947- DLB-120

Peacock, Thomas Love 1785-1866 . . . DLB-96, 116

Pead, Deuel ?-1727 . . . . DLB-24

Peake, Mervyn 1911-1968 . . . . DLB-15, 160

Peale, Rembrandt 1778-1860 . . . . DLB-183

Pear Tree Press DLB-112

Pearce, Philippa 1920- DLB-161

Pearson, H. B. [publishing house] DLB-49

Pearson, Hesketh 1887-1964 . . . . DLB-149

Pechersky, Andrei (see Mel'nikov, Pavel Ivanovich)

Peck, George W. 1840-1916 . . . . DLB-23, 42

Peck, H. C., and Theo. Bliss
[publishing house] DLB-49

Peck, Harry Thurston 1856-1914 . . . . . DLB-71, 91

Peden, William 1913-1999 . . . . DLB-234

Peele, George 1556-1596 . . . . DLB-62, 167

Pegler, Westbrook 1894-1969 . . . . DLB-171

Pekić, Borislav 1930-1992 . . . DLB-181; CDWLB-4

Pellegrini and Cudahy DLB-46

Pelletier, Aimé (see Vac, Bertrand)

Pemberton, Sir Max 1863-1950 . . . . DLB-70

de la Peña, Terri 1947- DLB-209

Penfield, Edward 1866-1925 . . . . DLB-188

Penguin Books [U.K.] DLB-112

Penguin Books [U.S.] DLB-46

Penn Publishing Company DLB-49

Penn, William 1644-1718 . . . . DLB-24

Penna, Sandro 1906-1977 . . . . DLB-114

Pennell, Joseph 1857-1926 . . . . DLB-188

Penner, Jonathan 1940- Y-83

Pennington, Lee 1939- Y-82

Pepys, Samuel
1633-1703 . . . . DLB-101, 213; CDBLB-2

Percy, Thomas 1729-1811 . . . . DLB-104

Percy, Walker 1916-1990 . . . . . DLB-2; Y-80, Y-90

Percy, William 1575-1648 . . . . DLB-172

Perec, Georges 1936-1982 . . . . DLB-83

Perelman, Bob 1947- DLB-193

Perelman, S. J. 1904-1979 . . . . DLB-11, 44

Perez, Raymundo "Tigre" 1946- DLB-122

Peri Rossi, Cristina 1941- DLB-145

Perkins, Eugene 1932- DLB-41

Perkoff, Stuart Z. 1930-1974 . . . . DLB-16

Perley, Moses Henry 1804-1862 . . . . DLB-99

Permabooks DLB-46

Perovsky, Aleksei Alekseevich
(Antonii Pogorel'sky) 1787-1836 . . . . . DLB-198

Perri, Henry 1561-1617 . . . . DLB-236

Perrin, Alice 1867-1934 . . . . DLB-156

Perry, Bliss 1860-1954 . . . . DLB-71

Perry, Eleanor 1915-1981 . . . . DLB-44

Perry, Henry (see Perri, Henry)

Perry, Matthew 1794-1858 . . . . DLB-183

Perry, Sampson 1747-1823 . . . . DLB-158

Persius A.D. 34-A.D. 62 . . . . DLB-211

Perutz, Leo 1882-1957 . . . . DLB-81

Pesetsky, Bette 1932- DLB-130

Pestalozzi, Johann Heinrich 1746-1827 . . . . DLB-94

Peter, Laurence J. 1919-1990 . . . . DLB-53

Peter of Spain circa 1205-1277 . . . . DLB-115

Peterkin, Julia 1880-1961 . . . . DLB-9

Peters, Lenrie 1932- DLB-117

Peters, Robert 1924- DLB-105

"Foreword to *Ludwig of Bavaria*" DLB-105

Petersham, Maud 1889-1971 and
Petersham, Miska 1888-1960 . . . . DLB-22

Peterson, Charles Jacobs 1819-1887 . . . . . . DLB-79

Peterson, Len 1917- DLB-88

Peterson, Levi S. 1933- DLB-206

Peterson, Louis 1922-1998 . . . . DLB-76

Peterson, T. B., and Brothers DLB-49

Petitclair, Pierre 1813-1860 . . . . DLB-99

Petrescu, Camil 1894-1957 . . . . DLB-220

Petronius circa A.D. 20-A.D. 66
. . . . DLB-211; CDWLB-1

Petrov, Aleksandar 1938- DLB-181

Petrov, Gavriil 1730-1801 . . . . DLB-150

Petrov, Valeri 1920- DLB-181

Petrov, Vasilii Petrovich 1736-1799 . . . . . . DLB-150

Petrović, Rastko
1898-1949 . . . . DLB-147; CDWLB-4

Petruslied circa 854? DLB-148

Petry, Ann 1908-1997 . . . . DLB-76

Pettie, George circa 1548-1589 . . . . DLB-136

Peyton, K. M. 1929- DLB-161

Pfaffe Konrad flourished circa 1172 . . . . . . DLB-148

Pfaffe Lamprecht flourished circa 1150 . . . DLB-148

Pfeiffer, Emily 1827-1890 . . . . DLB-199

Pforzheimer, Carl H. 1879-1957 . . . . DLB-140

Phaedrus circa 18 B.C.-circa A.D. 50 . . . . DLB-211

Phaer, Thomas 1510?-1560 . . . . DLB-167

Phaidon Press Limited DLB-112

Pharr, Robert Deane 1916-1992 . . . . DLB-33

Phelps, Elizabeth Stuart 1815-1852 . . . . . . DLB-202

Phelps, Elizabeth Stuart 1844-1911 . . . DLB-74, 221

Philander von der Linde
(see Mencke, Johann Burckhard)

Philby, H. St. John B. 1885-1960 . . . . DLB-195

Philip, Marlene Nourbese 1947- DLB-157

Philippe, Charles-Louis 1874-1909 . . . . . . DLB-65

Philips, John 1676-1708 . . . . DLB-95

Philips, Katherine 1632-1664 . . . . DLB-131

Phillipps, Sir Thomas 1792-1872 . . . . DLB-184

Phillips, Caryl 1958- DLB-157

Phillips, David Graham 1867-1911 . . . . . DLB-9, 12

Phillips, Jayne Anne 1952- Y-80

Phillips, Robert 1938- DLB-105

"Finding, Losing, Reclaiming: A Note
    on My Poems" DLB-105

Phillips, Sampson and Company DLB-49

Phillips, Stephen 1864-1915 . . . . DLB-10

Phillips, Ulrich B. 1877-1934 . . . . DLB-17

Phillips, Wendell 1811-1884 . . . . DLB-235

Phillips, Willard 1784-1873 . . . . DLB-59

Phillips, William 1907- DLB-137

Phillpotts, Adelaide Eden (Adelaide Ross)
    1896-1993 . . . . DLB-191

Phillpotts, Eden 1862-1960 . . . DLB-10, 70, 135, 153

Philo circa 20-15 B.C.-circa A.D. 50 . . . . . DLB-176

Philosophical Library DLB-46

Phinney, Elihu [publishing house] DLB-49

Phoenix, John (see Derby, George Horatio)

PHYLON (Fourth Quarter, 1950),
    The Negro in Literature:
    The Current Scene DLB-76

Physiologus circa 1070-circa 1150 . . . . DLB-148

Piccolo, Lucio 1903-1969 . . . . DLB-114

Pickard, Tom 1946- DLB-40

Pickering, William [publishing house] . . . DLB-106

Pickthall, Marjorie 1883-1922 . . . . DLB-92

Pictorial Printing Company DLB-49

Piercy, Marge 1936- DLB-120, 227

Pierro, Albino 1916- DLB-128

Pignotti, Lamberto 1926- DLB-128

Pike, Albert 1809-1891 . . . . DLB-74

Pike, Zebulon Montgomery
    1779-1813 . . . . DLB-183

Pillat, Ion 1891-1945 . . . . DLB-220

Pilon, Jean-Guy 1930- DLB-60

Pinckney, Eliza Lucas 1722-1793 . . . . DLB-200

Pinckney, Josephine 1895-1957 . . . . DLB-6

Pindar circa 518 B.C.-circa 438 B.C.
    . . . . DLB-176; CDWLB-1

Pindar, Peter (see Wolcot, John)

Pineda, Cecile 1942- DLB-209

Pinero, Arthur Wing 1855-1934 . . . . DLB-10

Pinget, Robert 1919-1997 . . . . DLB-83

Pinnacle Books DLB-46

Piñon, Nélida 1935- DLB-145

Pinsky, Robert 1940- Y-82

Robert Pinsky Reappointed Poet Laureate Y-98

Pinter, Harold 1930- . . . DLB-13, 245; CDBLB-8

Piontek, Heinz 1925- DLB-75

Piozzi, Hester Lynch [Thrale]
    1741-1821 . . . . DLB-104, 142

Piper, H. Beam 1904-1964 . . . . DLB-8

Piper, Watty DLB-22

Pirckheimer, Caritas 1467-1532 . . . . DLB-179

Pirckheimer, Willibald 1470-1530 . . . . . . DLB-179

Pisar, Samuel 1929- Y-83

Pisemsky, Aleksai Feofilaktovich
    1821-1881 . . . . DLB-238

Pitkin, Timothy 1766-1847 . . . . DLB-30

The Pitt Poetry Series: Poetry Publishing
    Today Y-85

Pitter, Ruth 1897- DLB-20

Pix, Mary 1666-1709 . . . . DLB-80

Pixerécourt, René Charles Guilbert de
    1773-1844 . . . . DLB-192

Plaatje, Sol T. 1876-1932 . . . . DLB-125, 225

Plante, David 1940- Y-83

Platen, August von 1796-1835 . . . . DLB-90

Plath, Sylvia
    1932-1963 . . . . DLB-5, 6, 152; CDALB-1

Plato circa 428 B.C.-348-347 B.C.
    . . . . DLB-176; CDWLB-1

Plato, Ann 1824?-? DLB-239

Platon 1737-1812 . . . . DLB-150

Platt and Munk Company DLB-46

Plautus circa 254 B.C.-184 B.C.
    . . . . DLB-211; CDWLB-1

Playboy Press DLB-46

Playford, John [publishing house] DLB-170

Plays, Playwrights, and Playgoers DLB-84

Playwrights on the Theater DLB-80

Der Pleier flourished circa 1250 . . . . DLB-138

Plenzdorf, Ulrich 1934- DLB-75

Plessen, Elizabeth 1944- DLB-75

Pletnev, Petr Aleksandrovich
    1792-1865 . . . . DLB-205

Plieksāne, Elza Rozenberga (see Aspazija)

Plieksāns, Jānis (see Rainis, Jānis)

Plievier, Theodor 1892-1955 . . . . DLB-69

Plimpton, George 1927- DLB-185, 241; Y-99

Pliny the Elder A.D. 23/24-A.D. 79 . . . . . DLB-211

Pliny the Younger
    circa A.D. 61-A.D. 112 . . . . DLB-211

Plomer, William
    1903-1973 . . . . DLB-20, 162, 191, 225

Plotinus 204-270 . . . . DLB-176; CDWLB-1

Plume, Thomas 1630-1704 . . . . DLB-213

Plumly, Stanley 1939- DLB-5, 193

Plumpp, Sterling D. 1940- DLB-41

Plunkett, James 1920- DLB-14

Plutarch
    circa 46-circa 120 . . . . . . DLB-176; CDWLB-1

Plymell, Charles 1935- DLB-16

Pocket Books DLB-46

Poe, Edgar Allan
    1809-1849 . . . . . DLB-3, 59, 73, 74; CDALB-2

Poe, James 1921-1980 . . . . DLB-44

The Poet Laureate of the United States
    Statements from Former Consultants
    in Poetry Y-86

Pogodin, Mikhail Petrovich
    1800-1875 . . . . DLB-198

Pogorel'sky, Antonii
    (see Perovsky, Aleksei Alekseevich)

Pohl, Frederik 1919- DLB-8

Poirier, Louis (see Gracq, Julien)

Poláček, Karel 1892-1945 . . . . DLB-215; CDWLB-4

Polanyi, Michael 1891-1976 . . . . DLB-100

Pole, Reginald 1500-1558 . . . . DLB-132

Polevoi, Nikolai Alekseevich
    1796-1846 . . . . DLB-198

Polezhaev, Aleksandr Ivanovich
    1804-1838 . . . . DLB-205

Poliakoff, Stephen 1952- DLB-13

Polidori, John William 1795-1821 . . . . . . DLB-116

Polite, Carlene Hatcher 1932- DLB-33

Pollard, Alfred W. 1859-1944 . . . . DLB-201

Pollard, Edward A. 1832-1872 . . . . DLB-30

Pollard, Graham 1903-1976 . . . . DLB-201

Pollard, Percival 1869-1911 . . . . DLB-71

Pollard and Moss DLB-49

Pollock, Sharon 1936- DLB-60

Polonsky, Abraham 1910-1999 . . . . DLB-26

Polotsky, Simeon 1629-1680 . . . . DLB-150

Polybius circa 200 B.C.-118 B.C. DLB-176

Pomialovsky, Nikolai Gerasimovich
    1835-1863 . . . . DLB-238

Pomilio, Mario 1921-1990 . . . . DLB-177

Ponce, Mary Helen 1938- DLB-122

Ponce-Montoya, Juanita 1949- DLB-122

Ponet, John 1516?-1556 . . . . DLB-132

Poniatowski, Elena
    1933- DLB-113; CDWLB-3

Ponsard, François 1814-1867 . . . . DLB-192

Ponsonby, William [publishing house] DLB-170

Pontiggia, Giuseppe 1934- DLB-196

Pony Stories DLB-160

Poole, Ernest 1880-1950 . . . . DLB-9

Poole, Sophia 1804-1891 . . . . DLB-166

Poore, Benjamin Perley 1820-1887 . . . . . . DLB-23

Popa, Vasko 1922-1991 . . . . . DLB-181; CDWLB-4

Pope, Abbie Hanscom 1858-1894 . . . . . . DLB-140

Pope, Alexander
    1688-1744 . . . . . . DLB-95, 101, 213; CDBLB-2

Popov, Mikhail Ivanovich
    1742-circa 1790 . . . . DLB-150

Popović, Aleksandar 1929-1996 . . . . DLB-181

Popular Library DLB-46

Porete, Marguerite ?-1310 . . . . DLB-208

Porlock, Martin (see MacDonald, Philip)

Porpoise Press DLB-112

Porta, Antonio 1935-1989 . . . . DLB-128

Porter, Anna Maria 1780-1832 . . . . . DLB-116, 159

Porter, David 1780-1843 . . . . DLB-183

Porter, Eleanor H. 1868-1920 . . . . .DLB-9

Porter, Gene Stratton (see Stratton-Porter, Gene)

Porter, Henry ?-? DLB-62

Porter, Jane 1776-1850 . . . . .DLB-116, 159

Porter, Katherine Anne 1890-1980
. . . . . .DLB-4, 9, 102; Y-80; DS-12; CDALB-7

Porter, Peter 1929- DLB-40

Porter, William Sydney
1862-1910 . . . . . . .DLB-12, 78, 79; CDALB-3

Porter, William T. 1809-1858 . . . . . . .DLB-3, 43

Porter and Coates DLB-49

Portillo Trambley, Estela 1927-1998 . . . . .DLB-209

Portis, Charles 1933- DLB-6

Posey, Alexander 1873-1908 . . . . .DLB-175

Postans, Marianne circa 1810-1865 . . . . . .DLB-166

Postl, Carl (see Sealsfield, Carl)

Poston, Ted 1906-1974 . . . . .DLB-51

Potekhin, Aleksei Antipovich 1829-1908 . .DLB-238

Potok, Chaim 1929- DLB-28, 152

A Conversation with Chaim Potok Y-84

Potter, Beatrix 1866-1943 . . . . .DLB-141

Potter, David M. 1910-1971 . . . . .DLB-17

Potter, Dennis 1935-1994 . . . . .DLB-233

The Harry Potter Phenomenon. Y-99

Potter, John E., and Company. DLB-49

Pottle, Frederick A. 1897-1987 . . . . . DLB-103; Y-87

Poulin, Jacques 1937- DLB-60

Pound, Ezra 1885-1972
. . . . .DLB-4, 45, 63; DS-15; CDALB-4

Poverman, C. E. 1944- DLB-234

Povich, Shirley 1905-1998 . . . . .DLB-171

Powell, Anthony 1905-2000 . . . DLB-15; CDBLB-7

Dawn Powell, Where Have You Been All
Our Lives? Y-97

Powell, John Wesley 1834-1902 . . . . . . .DLB-186

Powell, Padgett 1952- DLB-234

Powers, J. F. 1917-1999 . . . . .DLB-130

Powers, Jimmy 1903-1995 . . . . .DLB-241

Pownall, David 1938- DLB-14

Powys, John Cowper 1872-1963 . . . . .DLB-15

Powys, Llewelyn 1884-1939 . . . . .DLB-98

Powys, T. F. 1875-1953 . . . . .DLB-36, 162

Poynter, Nelson 1903-1978 . . . . .DLB-127

The Practice of Biography: An Interview
with Stanley Weintraub Y-82

The Practice of Biography II: An Interview
with B. L. Reid Y-83

The Practice of Biography III: An Interview
with Humphrey Carpenter Y-84

The Practice of Biography IV: An Interview with
William Manchester Y-85

The Practice of Biography VI: An Interview with
David Herbert Donald Y-87

The Practice of Biography VII: An Interview with
John Caldwell Guilds Y-92

The Practice of Biography VIII: An Interview
with Joan Mellen. Y-94

The Practice of Biography IX: An Interview
with Michael Reynolds Y-95

Prados, Emilio 1899-1962 . . . . .DLB-134

Praed, Mrs. Caroline (see Praed, Rosa)

Praed, Rosa (Mrs. Caroline Praed)
1851-1935 .DLB-230

Praed, Winthrop Mackworth 1802-1839. . .DLB-96

Praeger Publishers DLB-46

Praetorius, Johannes 1630-1680. . . . . . . .DLB-168

Pratolini, Vasco 1913-1991 . . . . .DLB-177

Pratt, E. J. 1882-1964. . . . . .DLB-92

Pratt, Samuel Jackson 1749-1814 . . . . . . .DLB-39

Preciado Martin, Patricia 1939- DLB-209

Preface to *The History of Romances* (1715), by
Pierre Daniel Huet [excerpts] DLB-39

Préfontaine, Yves 1937- DLB-53

Prelutsky, Jack 1940- DLB-61

Premisses, by Michael Hamburger DLB-66

Prentice, George D. 1802-1870 . . . . .DLB-43

Prentice-Hall DLB-46

Prescott, Orville 1906-1996 . . . . Y-96

Prescott, William Hickling
1796-1859 . . . . .DLB-1, 30, 59, 235

The Present State of the English Novel (1892),
by George Saintsbury DLB-18

Prešeren, Francè
1800-1849 . . . . DLB-147; CDWLB-4

Preston, Margaret Junkin 1820-1897 . . . . .DLB-239

Preston, May Wilson 1873-1949 . . . . .DLB-188

Preston, Thomas 1537-1598. . . . . .DLB-62

Price, Reynolds 1933- DLB-2, 218

Price, Richard 1723-1791 . . . . .DLB-158

Price, Richard 1949- Y-81

Prideaux, John 1578-1650 . . . . .DLB-236

Priest, Christopher 1943- DLB-14, 207

Priestley, J. B. 1894-1984
. . . DLB-10, 34, 77, 100, 139; Y-84; CDBLB-6

Primary Bibliography: A Retrospective Y-95

Prime, Benjamin Young 1733-1791 . . . . . . .DLB-31

Primrose, Diana floruit circa 1630 . . . . . .DLB-126

Prince, F. T. 1912- DLB-20

Prince, Nancy Gardner 1799-? DLB-239

Prince, Thomas 1687-1758. . . . . .DLB-24, 140

Pringle, Thomas 1789-1834 . . . . .DLB-225

Printz, Wolfgang Casper 1641-1717. . . . . .DLB-168

Prior, Matthew 1664-1721 . . . . .DLB-95

Prisco, Michele 1920- DLB-177

Pritchard, William H. 1932- DLB-111

Pritchett, V. S. 1900-1997 . . . . .DLB-15, 139

Probyn, May 1856 or 1857-1909 . . . . .DLB-199

Procter, Adelaide Anne 1825-1864 . . .DLB-32, 199

Procter, Bryan Waller 1787-1874 . . . . .DLB-96, 144

Proctor, Robert 1868-1903 . . . . .DLB-184

*Producing Dear Bunny, Dear Volodya: The Friendship
and the Feud* Y-97

The Profession of Authorship:
Scribblers for Bread. Y-89

Prokopovich, Feofan 1681?-1736. . . . . . .DLB-150

Prokosch, Frederic 1906-1989 . . . . .DLB-48

The Proletarian Novel. DLB-9

Pronzini, Bill 1943- DLB-226

Propertius circa 50 B.C.-post 16 B.C.
. . . . .DLB-211; CDWLB-1

Propper, Dan 1937- DLB-16

Prose, Francine 1947- DLB-234

Protagoras circa 490 B.C.-420 B.C. DLB-176

Proud, Robert 1728-1813. . . . . .DLB-30

Proust, Marcel 1871-1922 . . . . .DLB-65

Prynne, J. H. 1936- DLB-40

Przybyszewski, Stanislaw 1868-1927 . . . . .DLB-66

Pseudo-Dionysius the Areopagite floruit
circa 500 . . . . .DLB-115

Public Domain and the Violation of Texts Y-97

The Public Lending Right in America Statement by
Sen. Charles McC. Mathias, Jr. PLR and the
Meaning of Literary Property Statements on
PLR by American Writers Y-83

The Public Lending Right in the United Kingdom
Public Lending Right: The First Year in the
United Kingdom Y-83

The Publication of English
Renaissance Plays DLB-62

Publications and Social Movements
[Transcendentalism] DLB-1

Publishers and Agents: The Columbia
Connection Y-87

Publishing Fiction at LSU Press. Y-87

The Publishing Industry in 1998:
Sturm-und-drang.com Y-98

The Publishing Industry in 1999. . . . . Y-99

Pückler-Muskau, Hermann von
1785-1871. . . . . DLB-133

Pufendorf, Samuel von 1632-1694. . . . . . .DLB-168

Pugh, Edwin William 1874-1930 . . . . .DLB-135

Pugin, A. Welby 1812-1852 . . . . .DLB-55

Puig, Manuel 1932-1990 . . . . DLB-113; CDWLB-3

Pulitzer, Joseph 1847-1911 . . . . .DLB-23

Pulitzer, Joseph, Jr. 1885-1955. . . . . .DLB-29

Pulitzer Prizes for the Novel, 1917-1945 . . . .DLB-9

Pulliam, Eugene 1889-1975 . . . . .DLB-127

Purchas, Samuel 1577?-1626 . . . . .DLB-151

Purdy, Al 1918-2000 . . . . .DLB-88

Purdy, James 1923- DLB-2, 218

Purdy, Ken W. 1913-1972 . . . . .DLB-137

Pusey, Edward Bouverie 1800-1882 . . . . . .DLB-55

Pushkin, Aleksandr Sergeevich
1799-1837 .DLB-205

Pushkin, Vasilii L'vovich 1766-1830 . . . . .DLB-205

Putnam, George Palmer 1814-1872 . . . . .DLB-3, 79

Putnam, Samuel 1892-1950. . . . . .DLB-4

G. P. Putnam's Sons [U.K.]. DLB-106

G. P. Putnam's Sons [U.S.] DLB-49

A Publisher's Archives: G. P. Putnam Y-92

Puzo, Mario 1920-1999 . . . . .DLB-6

Pyle, Ernie 1900-1945 . . . . .DLB-29

Pyle, Howard 1853-1911 .... DLB-42, 188; DS-13

Pym, Barbara 1913-1980 ......DLB-14, 207; Y-87

Pynchon, Thomas 1937- DLB-2, 173

Pyramid Books.....................DLB-46

Pyrnelle, Louise-Clarke 1850-1907.......DLB-42

Pythagoras circa 570 B.C.-? DLB-176

Q

Quad, M. (see Lewis, Charles B.)

Quaritch, Bernard 1819-1899.........DLB-184

Quarles, Francis 1592-1644 ....DLB-126

The Quarterly Review 1809-1967 ......DLB-110

Quasimodo, Salvatore 1901-1968.......DLB-114

Queen, Ellery (see Dannay, Frederic, and
    Manfred B. Lee)

Queen, Frank 1822-1882 ....DLB-241

The Queen City Publishing House DLB-49

Queneau, Raymond 1903-1976 ....DLB-72

Quennell, Sir Peter 1905-1993 .....DLB-155, 195

Quesnel, Joseph 1746-1809............DLB-99

The Question of American Copyright
    in the Nineteenth Century
        Preface, by George Haven Putnam
        The Evolution of Copyright, by
            Brander Matthews
        Summary of Copyright Legislation in
            the United States, by R. R. Bowker
        Analysis of the Provisions of the
            Copyright Law of 1891, by
            George Haven Putnam
        The Contest for International Copyright,
            by George Haven Putnam
        Cheap Books and Good Books,
            by Brander Matthews.........DLB-49

Quiller-Couch, Sir Arthur Thomas
    1863-1944 ....DLB-135, 153, 190

Quin, Ann 1936-1973............DLB-14, 231

Quincy, Samuel, of Georgia ?-? DLB-31

Quincy, Samuel, of Massachusetts
    1734-1789......................DLB-31

Quinn, Anthony 1915- DLB-122

The Quinn Draft of James Joyce's
    Circe Manuscript..................Y-00

Quinn, John 1870-1924..............DLB-187

Quiñónez, Naomi 1951- DLB-209

Quintana, Leroy V. 1944- DLB-82

Quintana, Miguel de 1671-1748
    A Forerunner of Chicano Literature . DLB-122

Quintillian
    circa A.D. 40-circa A.D. 96 ....DLB-211

Quintus Curtius Rufus fl. A.D. 35 ......DLB-211

Quist, Harlin, Books................DLB-46

Quoirez, Françoise (see Sagan, Françoise)

R

R-va, Zeneida (see Gan, Elena Andreevna)

Raabe, Wilhelm 1831-1910 ....DLB-129

Raban, Jonathan 1942- DLB-204

Rabe, David 1940- DLB-7, 228

Raboni, Giovanni 1932- DLB-128

Rachilde 1860-1953 ....DLB-123, 192

Racin, Kočo 1908-1943 ....DLB-147

Rackham, Arthur 1867-1939..........DLB-141

Radauskas, Henrikas
    1910-1970...........DLB-220; CDWLB-4

Radcliffe, Ann 1764-1823 ....DLB-39, 178

Raddall, Thomas 1903- DLB-68

Radford, Dollie 1858-1920...........DLB-240

Radichkov, Yordan 1929- DLB-181

Radiguet, Raymond 1903-1923 ....DLB-65

Radishchev, Aleksandr Nikolaevich
    1749-1802.....................DLB-150

Radnóti, Miklós
    1909-1944 ....DLB-215; CDWLB-4

Radványi, Netty Reiling (see Seghers, Anna)

Rahv, Philip 1908-1973.............DLB-137

Raich, Semen Egorovich 1792-1855 .....DLB-205

Raičković, Stevan 1928- DLB-181

Raimund, Ferdinand Jakob 1790-1836 ....DLB-90

Raine, Craig 1944- DLB-40

Raine, Kathleen 1908- DLB-20

Rainis, Jānis 1865-1929..... DLB-220; CDWLB-4

Rainolde, Richard
    circa 1530-1606 ....DLB-136, 236

Rakić, Milan 1876-1938 .....DLB-147; CDWLB-4

Rakosi, Carl 1903- DLB-193

Ralegh, Sir Walter
    1554?-1618............ DLB-172; CDBLB-1

Ralin, Radoy 1923- DLB-181

Ralph, Julian 1853-1903 ....DLB-23

Ramat, Silvio 1939- DLB-128

Rambler, no. 4 (1750), by Samuel Johnson
    [excerpt] DLB-39

Ramée, Marie Louise de la (see Ouida)

Ramírez, Sergío 1942- DLB-145

Ramke, Bin 1947- DLB-120

Ramler, Karl Wilhelm 1725-1798........DLB-97

Ramon Ribeyro, Julio 1929- DLB-145

Ramos, Manuel 1948- DLB-209

Ramous, Mario 1924- DLB-128

Rampersad, Arnold 1941- DLB-111

Ramsay, Allan 1684 or 1685-1758 ....DLB-95

Ramsay, David 1749-1815 ....DLB-30

Ramsay, Martha Laurens 1759-1811 ....DLB-200

Ranck, Katherine Quintana 1942- DLB-122

Rand, Avery and Company DLB-49

Rand, Ayn 1905-1982....... DLB-227; CDALB-7

Rand McNally and Company DLB-49

Randall, David Anton 1905-1975.......DLB-140

Randall, Dudley 1914- DLB-41

Randall, Henry S. 1811-1876 ....DLB-30

Randall, James G. 1881-1953 ....DLB-17

The Randall Jarrell Symposium:
    A Small Collection of Randall Jarrells
    Excerpts From Papers Delivered at the
    Randall Jarrel Symposium Y-86

Randolph, A. Philip 1889-1979.........DLB-91

Randolph, Anson D. F.
    [publishing house] DLB-49

Randolph, Thomas 1605-1635......DLB-58, 126

Random House DLB-46

Ranlet, Henry [publishing house].......DLB-49

Ransom, Harry 1908-1976 ....DLB-187

Ransom, John Crowe
    1888-1974..........DLB-45, 63; CDALB-7

Ransome, Arthur 1884-1967 ....DLB-160

Raphael, Frederic 1931- DLB-14

Raphaelson, Samson 1896-1983........DLB-44

Rashi circa 1040-1105................DLB-208

Raskin, Ellen 1928-1984................DLB-52

Rastell, John 1475?-1536...........DLB-136, 170

Rattigan, Terence
    1911-1977.......... DLB-13; CDBLB-7

Rawlings, Marjorie Kinnan 1896-1953
    ....DLB-9, 22, 102; DS-17; CDALB-7

Rawlinson, Richard 1690-1755.........DLB-213

Rawlinson, Thomas 1681-1725 ....DLB-213

Raworth, Tom 1938- DLB-40

Ray, David 1932- DLB-5

Ray, Gordon Norton 1915-1986 ....DLB-103, 140

Ray, Henrietta Cordelia 1849-1916 ......DLB-50

Raymond, Ernest 1888-1974 ....DLB-191

Raymond, Henry J. 1820-1869.......DLB-43, 79

Michael M. Rea and the Rea Award for the
    Short Story.........................Y-97

Reach, Angus 1821-1856 ....DLB-70

Read, Herbert 1893-1968..........DLB-20, 149

Read, Herbert, "The Practice of Biography," in
    *The English Sense of Humour and
    Other Essays*......................DLB-149

Read, Martha Meredith DLB-200

Read, Opie 1852-1939 ....DLB-23

Read, Piers Paul 1941- DLB-14

Reade, Charles 1814-1884 ....DLB-21

Reader's Digest Condensed Books.......DLB-46

Readers Ulysses Symposium Y-97

Reading, Peter 1946- DLB-40

Reading Series in New York City...........Y-96

The Reality of One Woman's Dream:
    The de Grummond Children's
    Literature Collection Y-99

Reaney, James 1926- DLB-68

Rebhun, Paul 1500?-1546..............DLB-179

Rèbora, Clemente 1885-1957 ....DLB-114

Rebreanu, Liviu 1885-1944 ....DLB-220

Rechy, John 1934- DLB-122; Y-82

The Recovery of Literature:
    Criticism in the 1990s: A Symposium Y-91

Redding, J. Saunders 1906-1988.......DLB-63, 76

Redfield, J. S. [publishing house] DLB-49

Redgrove, Peter 1932- DLB-40

Redmon, Anne 1943- Y-86

Redmond, Eugene B. 1937- DLB-41

Redpath, James [publishing house].......DLB-49

Reed, Henry 1808-1854 . . . . .DLB-59

Reed, Henry 1914- DLB-27

Reed, Ishmael
1938- DLB-2, 5, 33, 169, 227; DS-8

Reed, Rex 1938- DLB-185

Reed, Sampson 1800-1880 . . . . .DLB-1, 235

Reed, Talbot Baines 1852-1893 . . . . .DLB-141

Reedy, William Marion 1862-1920 . . . . . .DLB-91

Reese, Lizette Woodworth 1856-1935 . . . . .DLB-54

Reese, Thomas 1742-1796 . . . . .DLB-37

Reeve, Clara 1729-1807 . . . . .DLB-39

Preface to *The Old English Baron* (1778) DLB-39

The Progress of Romance (1785) [excerpt] DLB-39

Reeves, James 1909-1978 . . . . .DLB-161

Reeves, John 1926- DLB-88

"Reflections: After a Tornado,"
by Judson Jerome DLB-105

Regnery, Henry, Company DLB-46

Rehberg, Hans 1901-1963 . . . . .DLB-124

Rehfisch, Hans José 1891-1960 . . . . .DLB-124

Reich, Ebbe Kløvedal 1940- DLB-214

Reid, Alastair 1926- DLB-27

Reid, B. L. 1918-1990 . . . . .DLB-111; Y-83

The Practice of Biography II:
An Interview with B. L. Reid Y-83

Reid, Christopher 1949- DLB-40

Reid, Forrest 1875-1947 . . . . .DLB-153

Reid, Helen Rogers 1882-1970 . . . . .DLB-29

Reid, James ?-? .DLB-31

Reid, Mayne 1818-1883 . . . . .DLB-21, 163

Reid, Thomas 1710-1796 . . . . .DLB-31

Reid, V. S. (Vic) 1913-1987 . . . . .DLB-125

Reid, Whitelaw 1837-1912 . . . . .DLB-23

Reilly and Lee Publishing Company DLB-46

Reimann, Brigitte 1933-1973 . . . . .DLB-75

Reinmar der Alte
circa 1165-circa 1205 . . . . .DLB-138

Reinmar von Zweter
circa 1200-circa 1250 . . . . .DLB-138

Reisch, Walter 1903-1983 . . . . .DLB-44

Reizei Family DLB-203

Remarks at the Opening of "The Biographical
Part of Literature" Exhibition, by
William R. Cagle Y-98

Remarque, Erich Maria
1898-1970 . . . . .DLB-56; CDWLB-2

Remington, Frederic
1861-1909 . . . . .DLB-12, 186, 188

Reminiscences, by Charles Scribner Jr. DS-17

Renaud, Jacques 1943- DLB-60

Renault, Mary 1905-1983 . . . . Y-83

Rendell, Ruth 1930- DLB-87

Rensselaer, Maria van Cortlandt van
1645-1689 . . . . .DLB-200

Repplier, Agnes 1855-1950 . . . . .DLB-221

Representative Men and Women: A Historical
Perspective on the British Novel,
1930-1960 . . . . .DLB-15

Research in the American Antiquarian Book
Trade Y-97

Reshetnikov, Fedor Mikhailovich
1841-1871 .DLB-238

Rettenbacher, Simon 1634-1706 . . . . .DLB-168

Reuchlin, Johannes 1455-1522 . . . . .DLB-179

Reuter, Christian 1665-after 1712 . . . . . . .DLB-168

Revell, Fleming H., Company DLB-49

Reuter, Fritz 1810-1874 . . . . .DLB-129

Reuter, Gabriele 1859-1941 . . . . .DLB-66

Reventlow, Franziska Gräfin zu
1871-1918 . . . . .DLB-66

Review of Nicholson Baker's *Double Fold:
Libraries and the Assault on Paper* Y-00

Review of Reviews Office DLB-112

Review of [Samuel Richardson's] *Clarissa* (1748),
by Henry Fielding DLB-39

The Revolt (1937), by Mary Colum
[excerpts] DLB-36

Rexroth, Kenneth 1905-1982
. . . . . . DLB-16, 48, 165, 212; Y-82; CDALB-1

Rey, H. A. 1898-1977 . . . . .DLB-22

Reynal and Hitchcock DLB-46

Reynolds, G. W. M. 1814-1879 . . . . .DLB-21

Reynolds, John Hamilton 1794-1852 . . . . .DLB-96

Reynolds, Sir Joshua 1723-1792 . . . . .DLB-104

Reynolds, Mack 1917- DLB-8

A Literary Archaelogist Digs On: A Brief
Interview with Michael Reynolds by
Michael Rogers Y-99

Reznikoff, Charles 1894-1976 . . . . .DLB-28, 45

Rhett, Robert Barnwell 1800-1876 . . . . . . .DLB-43

Rhode, John 1884-1964 . . . . .DLB-77

Rhodes, James Ford 1848-1927 . . . . .DLB-47

Rhodes, Richard 1937- DLB-185

Rhys, Jean 1890-1979
. . . . DLB-36, 117, 162; CDBLB-7; CDWLB-3

Ricardo, David 1772-1823 . . . . DLB-107, 158

Ricardou, Jean 1932- DLB-83

Rice, Elmer 1892-1967 . . . . .DLB-4, 7

Rice, Grantland 1880-1954 . . . . DLB-29, 171

Rich, Adrienne 1929- DLB-5, 67; CDALB-7

Richard de Fournival
1201-1259 or 1260 . . . . .DLB-208

Richard, Mark 1955- DLB-234

Richards, David Adams 1950- DLB-53

Richards, George circa 1760-1814 . . . . . . .DLB-37

Richards, Grant [publishing house] DLB-112

Richards, I. A. 1893-1979 . . . . .DLB-27

Richards, Laura E. 1850-1943 . . . . .DLB-42

Richards, William Carey 1818-1892 . . . . . .DLB-73

Richardson, Charles F. 1851-1913 . . . . . . .DLB-71

Richardson, Dorothy M. 1873-1957 . . . . . .DLB-36

Richardson, Henry Handel
(Ethel Florence Lindesay
Robertson) 1870-1946 . . . . DLB-197, 230

Richardson, Jack 1935- DLB-7

Richardson, John 1796-1852 . . . . .DLB-99

Richardson, Samuel
1689-1761 . . . . .DLB-39, 154; CDBLB-2

Introductory Letters from the Second
Edition of *Pamela* (1741) DLB-39

Postscript to [the Third Edition of]
Clarissa (1751) DLB-39

Preface to the First Edition of
Pamela (1740) DLB-39

Preface to the Third Edition of
Clarissa (1751) [excerpt] DLB-39

Preface to Volume 1 of *Clarissa* (1747) DLB-39

Preface to Volume 3 of *Clarissa* (1748) DLB-39

Richardson, Willis 1889-1977 . . . . .DLB-51

Riche, Barnabe 1542-1617 . . . . .DLB-136

Richepin, Jean 1849-1926 . . . . .DLB-192

Richler, Mordecai 1931- DLB-53

Richter, Conrad 1890-1968 . . . . .DLB-9, 212

Richter, Hans Werner 1908- DLB-69

Richter, Johann Paul Friedrich
1763-1825 . . . . .DLB-94; CDWLB-2

Rickerby, Joseph [publishing house] DLB-106

Rickword, Edgell 1898-1982 . . . . .DLB-20

Riddell, Charlotte 1832-1906 . . . . .DLB-156

Riddell, John (see Ford, Corey)

Ridge, John Rollin 1827-1867 . . . . .DLB-175

Ridge, Lola 1873-1941 . . . . .DLB-54

Ridge, William Pett 1859-1930 . . . . .DLB-135

Riding, Laura (see Jackson, Laura Riding)

Ridler, Anne 1912- DLB-27

Ridruego, Dionisio 1912-1975 . . . . .DLB-108

Riel, Louis 1844-1885 . . . . .DLB-99

Riemer, Johannes 1648-1714 . . . . .DLB-168

Rifbjerg, Klaus 1931- DLB-214

Riffaterre, Michael 1924- DLB-67

Riggs, Lynn 1899-1954 . . . . .DLB-175

Riis, Jacob 1849-1914 . . . . .DLB-23

Riker, John C. [publishing house] DLB-49

Riley, James 1777-1840 . . . . .DLB-183

Riley, John 1938-1978 . . . . .DLB-40

Rilke, Rainer Maria
1875-1926 . . . . .DLB-81; CDWLB-2

Rimanelli, Giose 1926- DLB-177

Rimbaud, Jean-Nicolas-Arthur
1854-1891 . . . . .DLB-217

Rinehart and Company DLB-46

Ringuet 1895-1960 . . . . .DLB-68

Ringwood, Gwen Pharis 1910-1984 . . . . . .DLB-88

Rinser, Luise 1911- DLB-69

Ríos, Alberto 1952- DLB-122

Ríos, Isabella 1948- DLB-82

Ripley, Arthur 1895-1961 . . . . .DLB-44

Ripley, George 1802-1880 . . . . .DLB-1, 64, 73, 235

The Rising Glory of America:
Three Poems .DLB-37

The Rising Glory of America:
Written in 1771 (1786),
by Hugh Henry Brackenridge and
Philip Freneau DLB-37

Riskin, Robert 1897-1955 . . . . DLB-26

Risse, Heinz 1898- DLB-69

Rist, Johann 1607-1667 . . . . DLB-164

Ristikivi, Karl 1912-1977. . . . . DLB-220

Ritchie, Anna Mowatt 1819-1870 . . . . DLB-3

Ritchie, Anne Thackeray 1837-1919. . . . . . DLB-18

Ritchie, Thomas 1778-1854 . . . . DLB-43

Rites of Passage [on William Saroyan] Y-83

The Ritz Paris Hemingway Award. Y-85

Rivard, Adjutor 1868-1945. . . . . DLB-92

Rive, Richard 1931-1989 . . . . DLB-125, 225

Rivera, Marina 1942- DLB-122

Rivera, Tomás 1935-1984 . . . . DLB-82

Rivers, Conrad Kent 1933-1968. . . . . DLB-41

Riverside Press DLB-49

Rivington, Charles [publishing house] . . . DLB-154

Rivington, James circa 1724-1802 . . . . DLB-43

Rivkin, Allen 1903-1990. . . . . DLB-26

Roa Bastos, Augusto 1917- DLB-113

Robbe-Grillet, Alain 1922- DLB-83

Robbins, Tom 1936- Y-80

Roberts, Charles G. D. 1860-1943 . . . . . . DLB-92

Roberts, Dorothy 1906-1993 . . . . DLB-88

Roberts, Elizabeth Madox
  1881-1941 . . . . DLB-9, 54, 102

Roberts, James [publishing house] DLB-154

Roberts, Kenneth 1885-1957 . . . . DLB-9

Roberts, Michèle 1949- DLB-231

Roberts, Ursula Wyllie (see Miles, Susan)

Roberts, William 1767-1849 . . . . DLB-142

Roberts Brothers. DLB-49

Robertson, A. M., and Company DLB-49

Robertson, Ethel Florence Lindesay
  (see Richardson, Henry Handel)

Robertson, William 1721-1793 . . . . DLB-104

Robins, Elizabeth 1862-1952 . . . . DLB-197

Robinson, A. Mary F. (Madame James
  Darmesteter, Madame Mary
  Duclaux) 1857-1944 . . . . DLB-240

Robinson, Casey 1903-1979 . . . . DLB-44

Robinson, Edwin Arlington
  1869-1935 . . . . DLB-54; CDALB-3

Robinson, Henry Crabb 1775-1867 . . . . . DLB-107

Robinson, James Harvey 1863-1936 . . . . . DLB-47

Robinson, Lennox 1886-1958 . . . . DLB-10

Robinson, Mabel Louise 1874-1962 . . . . . DLB-22

Robinson, Marilynne 1943- DLB-206

Robinson, Mary 1758-1800 . . . . DLB-158

Robinson, Richard circa 1545-1607 . . . . . DLB-167

Robinson, Therese 1797-1870 . . . . . . DLB-59, 133

Robison, Mary 1949- DLB-130

Roblès, Emmanuel 1914-1995 . . . . DLB-83

Roccatagliata Ceccardi, Ceccardo
  1871-1919 . . . . DLB-114

Roche, Billy 1949- DLB-233

Rochester, John Wilmot, Earl of
  1647-1680 . . . . DLB-131

Rock, Howard 1911-1976. . . . . DLB-127

Rockwell, Norman Perceval 1894-1978 . . DLB-188

Rodgers, Carolyn M. 1945- DLB-41

Rodgers, W. R. 1909-1969. . . . . DLB-20

Rodney, Lester 1911- DLB-241

Rodríguez, Claudio 1934-1999. . . . . DLB-134

Rodríguez, Joe D. 1943- DLB-209

Rodríguez, Luis J. 1954- DLB-209

Rodriguez, Richard 1944- DLB-82

Rodríguez Julia, Edgardo 1946- DLB-145

Roe, E. P. 1838-1888 . . . . DLB-202

Roethke, Theodore
  1908-1963 . . . . DLB-5, 206; CDALB-1

Rogers, Jane 1952- DLB-194

Rogers, Pattiann 1940- DLB-105

Rogers, Samuel 1763-1855 . . . . DLB-93

Rogers, Will 1879-1935 . . . . DLB-11

Rohmer, Sax 1883-1959 . . . . DLB-70

Roiphe, Anne 1935- Y-80

Rojas, Arnold R. 1896-1988 . . . . DLB-82

Rolfe, Frederick William
  1860-1913 . . . . DLB-34, 156

Rolland, Romain 1866-1944. . . . . DLB-65

Rolle, Richard circa 1290-1300 - 1340 . . . DLB-146

Rölvaag, O. E. 1876-1931. . . . . DLB-9, 212

Romains, Jules 1885-1972. . . . . DLB-65

Roman, A., and Company DLB-49

Roman de la Rose: Guillaume de Lorris
  1200 to 1205-circa 1230, Jean de Meun
  1235-1240-circa 1305 . . . . DLB-208

Romano, Lalla 1906- DLB-177

Romano, Octavio 1923- DLB-122

Romero, Leo 1950- DLB-122

Romero, Lin 1947- DLB-122

Romero, Orlando 1945- DLB-82

Rook, Clarence 1863-1915 . . . . DLB-135

Roosevelt, Theodore 1858-1919. . . . . .DLB-47, 186

Root, Waverley 1903-1982 . . . . DLB-4

Root, William Pitt 1941- DLB-120

Roquebrune, Robert de 1889-1978. . . . . . DLB-68

Rorty, Richard 1931- DLB-246

Rosa, João Guimarães 1908-1967 . . . . . . DLB-113

Rosales, Luis 1910-1992. . . . . DLB-134

Roscoe, William 1753-1831 . . . . DLB-163

Danis Rose and the Rendering of *Ulysses* Y-97

Rose, Reginald 1920- DLB-26

Rose, Wendy 1948- DLB-175

Rosegger, Peter 1843-1918. . . . . DLB-129

Rosei, Peter 1946- DLB-85

Rosen, Norma 1925- DLB-28

Rosenbach, A. S. W. 1876-1952 . . . . DLB-140

Rosenbaum, Ron 1946- DLB-185

Rosenberg, Isaac 1890-1918 . . . . DLB-20, 216

Rosenfeld, Isaac 1918-1956 . . . . DLB-28

Rosenthal, Harold 1914-1999. . . . . DLB-241

Rosenthal, M. L. 1917-1996 . . . . DLB-5

Rosenwald, Lessing J. 1891-1979 . . . . . . .DLB-187

Ross, Alexander 1591-1654 . . . . DLB-151

Ross, Harold 1892-1951. . . . . .DLB-137

Ross, Leonard Q. (see Rosten, Leo)

Ross, Lillian 1927- DLB-185

Ross, Martin 1862-1915 . . . . DLB-135

Ross, Sinclair 1908- DLB-88

Ross, W. W. E. 1894-1966. . . . . DLB-88

Rosselli, Amelia 1930-1996 . . . . DLB-128

Rossen, Robert 1908-1966 . . . . DLB-26

Rossetti, Christina 1830-1894. . . DLB-35, 163, 240

Rossetti, Dante Gabriel
  1828-1882 . . . . DLB-35; CDBLB-4

Rossner, Judith 1935- DLB-6

Rostand, Edmond 1868-1918. . . . . DLB-192

Rosten, Leo 1908-1997. . . . . DLB-11

Rostenberg, Leona 1908- DLB-140

Rostopchina, Evdokiia Petrovna
  1811-1858 . . . . DLB-205

Rostovsky, Dimitrii 1651-1709 . . . . DLB-150

Rota, Bertram 1903-1966 . . . . DLB-201

  Bertram Rota and His Bookshop Y-91

Roth, Gerhard 1942- DLB-85, 124

Roth, Henry 1906?-1995 . . . . DLB-28

Roth, Joseph 1894-1939 . . . . DLB-85

Roth, Philip 1933-
  . . . . .DLB-2, 28, 173; Y-82; CDALB-6

Rothenberg, Jerome 1931- DLB-5, 193

Rothschild Family. DLB-184

Rotimi, Ola 1938- DLB-125

Routhier, Adolphe-Basile 1839-1920 . . . . DLB-99

Routier, Simone 1901-1987 . . . . DLB-88

Routledge, George, and Sons DLB-106

Roversi, Roberto 1923- DLB-128

Rowe, Elizabeth Singer 1674-1737 . . . . DLB-39, 95

Rowe, Nicholas 1674-1718 . . . . DLB-84

Rowlands, Samuel circa 1570-1630. . . . . . DLB-121

Rowlandson, Mary
  circa 1637-circa 1711. . . . . DLB-24, 200

Rowley, William circa 1585-1626 . . . . DLB-58

Rowse, A. L. 1903-1997 . . . . DLB-155

Rowson, Susanna Haswell
  circa 1762-1824 . . . . .DLB-37, 200

Roy, Camille 1870-1943 . . . . DLB-92

Roy, Gabrielle 1909-1983. . . . . DLB-68

Roy, Jules 1907- DLB-83

The G. Ross Roy Scottish Poetry Collection
  at the University of South Carolina Y-89

The Royal Court Theatre and the English
  Stage Company DLB-13

The Royal Court Theatre and the New
  Drama DLB-10

The Royal Shakespeare Company
  at the Swan Y-88

Royall, Anne 1769-1854 . . . . DLB-43

The Roycroft Printing Shop DLB-49

Royde-Smith, Naomi 1875-1964 . . . . . . .DLB-191

Royster, Vermont 1914- DLB-127

Royston, Richard [publishing house] DLB-170

Różewicz, Tadeusz 1921- DLB-232

Ruark, Gibbons 1941- DLB-120

Ruban, Vasilii Grigorevich 1742-1795 . . . .DLB-150

Rubens, Bernice 1928- DLB-14, 207

Rudd and Carleton DLB-49

Rudd, Steele (Arthur Hoey Davis). DLB-230

Rudkin, David 1936- DLB-13

Rudolf von Ems circa 1200-circa 1254 . . .DLB-138

Ruffin, Josephine St. Pierre
    1842-1924 . . . . .DLB-79

Ruganda, John 1941- DLB-157

Ruggles, Henry Joseph 1813-1906. . . . . . .DLB-64

Ruiz de Burton, María Amparo
    1832-1895 . . . . .DLB-209, 221

Rukeyser, Muriel 1913-1980 . . . . .DLB-48

Rule, Jane 1931- DLB-60

Rulfo, Juan 1918-1986 . . . . . .DLB-113; CDWLB-3

Rumaker, Michael 1932- DLB-16

Rumens, Carol 1944- DLB-40

Rummo, Paul-Eerik 1942- DLB-232

Runyon, Damon 1880-1946 . . . . .DLB-11, 86, 171

Ruodlieb circa 1050-1075. . . . . .DLB-148

Rush, Benjamin 1746-1813 . . . . .DLB-37

Rush, Rebecca 1779-?. DLB-200

Rushdie, Salman 1947- DLB-194

Rusk, Ralph L. 1888-1962. . . . . .DLB-103

Ruskin, John
    1819-1900 . . . . . .DLB-55, 163, 190; CDBLB-4

Russ, Joanna 1937- DLB-8

Russell, B. B., and Company. DLB-49

Russell, Benjamin 1761-1845 . . . . .DLB-43

Russell, Bertrand 1872-1970. . . . . .DLB-100

Russell, Charles Edward 1860-1941 . . . . . .DLB-25

Russell, Charles M. 1864-1926 . . . . .DLB-188

Russell, Fred 1906- DLB-241

Russell, George William (see AE)

Russell, Countess Mary Annette Beauchamp
    (see Arnim, Elizabeth von)

Russell, R. H., and Son DLB-49

Russell, Willy 1947- DLB-233

Rutebeuf flourished 1249-1277 . . . . .DLB-208

Rutherford, Mark 1831-1913. . . . . .DLB-18

Ruxton, George Frederick 1821-1848 . . . .DLB-186

Ryan, Michael 1946- Y-82

Ryan, Oscar 1904- DLB-68

Ryder, Jack 1871-1936. . . . . .DLB-241

Ryga, George 1932- DLB-60

Rylands, Enriqueta Augustina Tennant
    1843-1908 . . . . .DLB-184

Rylands, John 1801-1888. . . . . .DLB-184

Ryleev, Kondratii Fedorovich
    1795-1826 . . . . .DLB-205

Rymer, Thomas 1643?-1713 . . . . .DLB-101

Ryskind, Morrie 1895-1985. . . . . .DLB-26

Rzhevsky, Aleksei Andreevich
    1737-1804. . . . . .DLB-150

S

The Saalfield Publishing Company DLB-46

Saba, Umberto 1883-1957 . . . . .DLB-114

Sábato, Ernesto 1911- DLB-145; CDWLB-3

Saberhagen, Fred 1930- DLB-8

Sabin, Joseph 1821-1881 . . . . .DLB-187

Sacer, Gottfried Wilhelm 1635-1699 . . . . .DLB-168

Sachs, Hans 1494-1576 . . . . .DLB-179; CDWLB-2

Sack, John 1930- DLB-185

Sackler, Howard 1929-1982. . . . . .DLB-7

Sackville, Lady Margaret 1881-1963 . . . . .DLB-240

Sackville, Thomas 1536-1608 . . . . .DLB-132

Sackville, Thomas 1536-1608
    and Norton, Thomas 1532-1584. . . . . .DLB-62

Sackville-West, Edward 1901-1965 . . . . . .DLB-191

Sackville-West, V. 1892-1962 . . . . . .DLB-34, 195

Sadlier, D. and J., and Company. DLB-49

Sadlier, Mary Anne 1820-1903 . . . . .DLB-99

Sadoff, Ira 1945- DLB-120

Sadoveanu, Mihail 1880-1961 . . . . .DLB-220

Sáenz, Benjamin Alire 1954- DLB-209

Saenz, Jaime 1921-1986 . . . . .DLB-145

Saffin, John circa 1626-1710. . . . . .DLB-24

Sagan, Françoise 1935- DLB-83

Sage, Robert 1899-1962. . . . . .DLB-4

Sagel, Jim 1947- DLB-82

Sagendorph, Robb Hansell 1900-1970. . . .DLB-137

Sahagún, Carlos 1938- DLB-108

Sahkomaapii, Piitai (see Highwater, Jamake)

Sahl, Hans 1902- DLB-69

Said, Edward W. 1935- DLB-67

Saigyō 1118-1190. . . . . .DLB-203

Saiko, George 1892-1962. . . . . .DLB-85

St. Dominic's Press DLB-112

Saint-Exupéry, Antoine de 1900-1944 . . . .DLB-72

St. John, J. Allen 1872-1957 . . . . .DLB-188

St. Johns, Adela Rogers 1894-1988 . . . . . .DLB-29

The St. John's College Robert Graves Trust. .Y-96

St. Martin's Press. DLB-46

St. Omer, Garth 1931- DLB-117

Saint Pierre, Michel de 1916-1987 . . . . . .DLB-83

Sainte-Beuve, Charles-Augustin
    1804-1869 . . . . .DLB-217

Saints' Lives. DLB-208

Saintsbury, George 1845-1933. . . . . . DLB-57, 149

Saiokuken Sōchō 1448-1532 . . . . .DLB-203

Saki (see Munro, H. H.)

Salaam, Kalamu ya 1947- DLB-38

Šalamun, Tomaž 1941- . . .DLB-181; CDWLB-4

Salas, Floyd 1931- DLB-82

Sálaz-Marquez, Rubén 1935- DLB-122

Salemson, Harold J. 1910-1988 . . . . .DLB-4

Salinas, Luis Omar 1937- DLB-82

Salinas, Pedro 1891-1951. . . . . .DLB-134

Salinger, J. D.
    1919- DLB-2, 102, 173; CDALB-1

Salkey, Andrew 1928- DLB-125

Sallust circa 86 B.C.-35 B.C.
    . . . . DLB-211; CDWLB-1

Salt, Waldo 1914- DLB-44

Salter, James 1925- DLB-130

Salter, Mary Jo 1954- DLB-120

Saltus, Edgar 1855-1921 . . . . .DLB-202

Saltykov, Mikhail Evgrafovich
    1826-1889 . . . . .DLB-238

Salustri, Carlo Alberto (see Trilussa)

Salverson, Laura Goodman 1890-1970 . . . .DLB-92

Samain, Albert 1858-1900 . . . . .DLB-217

Sampson, Richard Henry (see Hull, Richard)

Samuels, Ernest 1903-1996 . . . . .DLB-111

Sanborn, Franklin Benjamin
    1831-1917 . . . . .DLB-1, 223

Sánchez, Luis Rafael 1936- DLB-145

Sánchez, Philomeno "Phil" 1917- DLB-122

Sánchez, Ricardo 1941-1995 . . . . .DLB-82

Sánchez, Saúl 1943- DLB-209

Sanchez, Sonia 1934- DLB-41; DS-8

Sand, George 1804-1876 . . . . .DLB-119, 192

Sandburg, Carl
    1878-1967 . . . . .DLB-17, 54; CDALB-3

Sanders, Edward 1939- DLB-16, 244

Sandoz, Mari 1896-1966 . . . . .DLB-9, 212

Sandwell, B. K. 1876-1954. . . . . .DLB-92

Sandy, Stephen 1934- DLB-165

Sandys, George 1578-1644. . . . . . . .DLB-24, 121

Sangster, Charles 1822-1893 . . . . .DLB-99

Sanguineti, Edoardo 1930- DLB-128

Sanjōnishi Sanetaka 1455-1537 . . . . .DLB-203

Sansay, Leonora ?-after 1823. . . . . .DLB-200

Sansom, William 1912-1976 . . . . .DLB-139

Santayana, George
    1863-1952 . . . . .DLB-54, 71, 246; DS-13

Santiago, Danny 1911-1988. . . . . .DLB-122

Santmyer, Helen Hooven 1895-1986 . . . . . . .Y-84

Sanvitale, Francesca 1928- DLB-196

Sapidus, Joannes 1490-1561. . . . . .DLB-179

Sapir, Edward 1884-1939 . . . . .DLB-92

Sapper (see McNeile, Herman Cyril)

Sappho circa 620 B.C.-circa 550 B.C.
    . . . . DLB-176; CDWLB-1

Saramago, José 1922- Y-98

Sardou, Victorien 1831-1908. . . . . .DLB-192

Sarduy, Severo 1937- DLB-113

Sargent, Pamela 1948- DLB-8

Saro-Wiwa, Ken 1941- DLB-157

Saroyan, William
    1908-1981 . . . . . DLB-7, 9, 86; Y-81; CDALB-7

Sarraute, Nathalie 1900-1999 . . . . DLB-83

Sarrazin, Albertine 1937-1967 . . . . DLB-83

Sarris, Greg 1952- DLB-175

Sarton, May 1912-1995 . . . . DLB-48; Y-81

Sartre, Jean-Paul 1905-1980 . . . . DLB-72

Sassoon, Siegfried
1886-1967 . . . . DLB-20, 191; DS-18

Siegfried Loraine Sassoon:
A Centenary Essay
Tributes from Vivien F. Clarke and
Michael Thorpe Y-86

Sata, Ineko 1904- DLB-180

Saturday Review Press DLB-46

Saunders, James 1925- DLB-13

Saunders, John Monk 1897-1940 . . . . DLB-26

Saunders, Margaret Marshall
1861-1947 . . . . DLB-92

Saunders and Otley DLB-106

Saussure, Ferdinand de 1857-1913 . . . . . . DLB-242

Savage, James 1784-1873 . . . . DLB-30

Savage, Marmion W. 1803?-1872 . . . . DLB-21

Savage, Richard 1697?-1743 . . . . DLB-95

Savard, Félix-Antoine 1896-1982 . . . . DLB-68

Savery, Henry 1791-1842 . . . . DLB-230

Saville, (Leonard) Malcolm 1901-1982 . . . DLB-160

Sawyer, Ruth 1880-1970 . . . . DLB-22

Sayers, Dorothy L.
1893-1957 . . . . . DLB-10, 36, 77, 100; CDBLB-6

Sayle, Charles Edward 1864-1924 . . . . . . DLB-184

Sayles, John Thomas 1950- DLB-44

Sbarbaro, Camillo 1888-1967 . . . . DLB-114

Scalapino, Leslie 1947- DLB-193

Scannell, Vernon 1922- DLB-27

Scarry, Richard 1919-1994 . . . . DLB-61

Schaefer, Jack 1907-1991 . . . . DLB-212

Schaeffer, Albrecht 1885-1950 . . . . DLB-66

Schaeffer, Susan Fromberg 1941- DLB-28

Schaff, Philip 1819-1893 . . . . DS-13

Schaper, Edzard 1908-1984 . . . . DLB-69

Scharf, J. Thomas 1843-1898 . . . . DLB-47

Schede, Paul Melissus 1539-1602 . . . . DLB-179

Scheffel, Joseph Viktor von 1826-1886 . . . DLB-129

Scheffler, Johann 1624-1677 . . . . DLB-164

Schelling, Friedrich Wilhelm Joseph von
1775-1854 . . . . DLB-90

Scherer, Wilhelm 1841-1886 . . . . DLB-129

Scherfig, Hans 1905-1979 . . . . DLB-214

Schickele, René 1883-1940 . . . . DLB-66

Schiff, Dorothy 1903-1989 . . . . DLB-127

Schiller, Friedrich
1759-1805 . . . . DLB-94; CDWLB-2

Schirmer, David 1623-1687 . . . . DLB-164

Schlaf, Johannes 1862-1941 . . . . DLB-118

Schlegel, August Wilhelm 1767-1845 . . . . DLB-94

Schlegel, Dorothea 1763-1839 . . . . DLB-90

Schlegel, Friedrich 1772-1829 . . . . DLB-90

Schleiermacher, Friedrich 1768-1834 . . . . DLB-90

Schlesinger, Arthur M., Jr. 1917- DLB-17

Schlumberger, Jean 1877-1968 . . . . DLB-65

Schmid, Eduard Hermann Wilhelm
(see Edschmid, Kasimir)

Schmidt, Arno 1914-1979 . . . . DLB-69

Schmidt, Johann Kaspar (see Stirner, Max)

Schmidt, Michael 1947- DLB-40

Schmidtbonn, Wilhelm August
1876-1952 . . . . DLB-118

Schmitz, James H. 1911- DLB-8

Schnabel, Johann Gottfried
1692-1760 . . . . DLB-168

Schnackenberg, Gjertrud 1953- DLB-120

Schnitzler, Arthur
1862-1931 . . . . DLB-81, 118; CDWLB-2

Schnurre, Wolfdietrich 1920-1989 . . . . . . DLB-69

Schocken Books DLB-46

Scholartis Press DLB-112

Scholderer, Victor 1880-1971 . . . . DLB-201

The Schomburg Center for Research
in Black Culture DLB-76

Schönbeck, Virgilio (see Giotti, Virgilio)

Schönherr, Karl 1867-1943 . . . . DLB-118

Schoolcraft, Jane Johnston 1800-1841 . . . .DLB-175

School Stories, 1914-1960 . . . . DLB-160

Schopenhauer, Arthur 1788-1860 . . . . DLB-90

Schopenhauer, Johanna 1766-1838 . . . . . . DLB-90

Schorer, Mark 1908-1977 . . . . DLB-103

Schottelius, Justus Georg 1612-1676 . . . . . DLB-164

Schouler, James 1839-1920 . . . . DLB-47

Schrader, Paul 1946- DLB-44

Schreiner, Olive
1855-1920 . . . . .DLB-18, 156, 190, 225

Schroeder, Andreas 1946- DLB-53

Schubart, Christian Friedrich Daniel
1739-1791 . . . . DLB-97

Schubert, Gotthilf Heinrich 1780-1860 . . . . DLB-90

Schücking, Levin 1814-1883 . . . . DLB-133

Schulberg, Budd 1914- DLB-6, 26, 28; Y-81

Schulte, F. J., and Company DLB-49

Schulz, Bruno 1892-1942 . . . DLB-215; CDWLB-4

Schulze, Hans (see Praetorius, Johannes)

Schupp, Johann Balthasar 1610-1661 . . . . DLB-164

Schurz, Carl 1829-1906 . . . . DLB-23

Schuyler, George S. 1895-1977 . . . . DLB-29, 51

Schuyler, James 1923-1991 . . . . DLB-5, 169

Schwartz, Delmore 1913-1966 . . . . DLB-28, 48

Schwartz, Jonathan 1938- Y-82

Schwartz, Lynne Sharon 1939- DLB-218

Schwarz, Sibylle 1621-1638 . . . . DLB-164

Schwerner, Armand 1927-1999 . . . . DLB-165

Schwob, Marcel 1867-1905 . . . . DLB-123

Sciascia, Leonardo 1921-1989 . . . . .DLB-177

Science Fantasy DLB-8

Science-Fiction Fandom and Conventions . . DLB-8

Science-Fiction Fanzines: The Time
Binders DLB-8

Science-Fiction Films DLB-8

Science Fiction Writers of America and the
Nebula Awards DLB-8

Scot, Reginald circa 1538-1599 . . . . DLB-136

Scotellaro, Rocco 1923-1953 . . . . DLB-128

Scott, Alicia Anne (Lady John Scott)
1810-1900 . . . . DLB-240

Scott, Catharine Amy Dawson
1865-1934 . . . . DLB-240

Scott, Dennis 1939-1991 . . . . DLB-125

Scott, Dixon 1881-1915 . . . . DLB-98

Scott, Duncan Campbell 1862-1947 . . . . . DLB-92

Scott, Evelyn 1893-1963 . . . . DLB-9, 48

Scott, F. R. 1899-1985 . . . . DLB-88

Scott, Frederick George 1861-1944 . . . . . . DLB-92

Scott, Geoffrey 1884-1929 . . . . DLB-149

Scott, Harvey W. 1838-1910 . . . . DLB-23

Scott, Lady Jane (see Scott, Alicia Anne)

Scott, Paul 1920-1978 . . . . .DLB-14, 207

Scott, Sarah 1723-1795 . . . . DLB-39

Scott, Tom 1918- DLB-27

Scott, Sir Walter 1771-1832
. . . . . . .DLB-93, 107, 116, 144, 159; CDBLB-3

Scott, Walter, Publishing
Company Limited DLB-112

Scott, William Bell 1811-1890 . . . . DLB-32

Scott, William R. [publishing house] DLB-46

Scott-Heron, Gil 1949- DLB-41

Scribe, Eugène 1791-1861 . . . . DLB-192

Scribner, Arthur Hawley 1859-1932 . . . . DS-13, 16

Scribner, Charles 1854-1930 . . . . DS-13, 16

Scribner, Charles, Jr. 1921-1995 . . . . Y-95

Reminiscences DS-17

Charles Scribner's Sons DLB-49; DS-13, 16, 17

Scripps, E. W. 1854-1926 . . . . DLB-25

Scudder, Horace Elisha 1838-1902 . . . . .DLB-42, 71

Scudder, Vida Dutton 1861-1954 . . . . DLB-71

Scupham, Peter 1933- DLB-40

Seabrook, William 1886-1945 . . . . DLB-4

Seabury, Samuel 1729-1796 . . . . DLB-31

Seacole, Mary Jane Grant 1805-1881 . . . . DLB-166

The Seafarer circa 970 . . . . DLB-146

Sealsfield, Charles (Carl Postl)
1793-1864 . . . . DLB-133, 186

Sears, Edward I. 1819?-1876 . . . . DLB-79

Sears Publishing Company DLB-46

Seaton, George 1911-1979 . . . . DLB-44

Seaton, William Winston 1785-1866 . . . . . DLB-43

Secker, Martin [publishing house] DLB-112

Secker, Martin, and Warburg Limited . . . DLB-112

The Second Annual New York Festival
of Mystery Y-00

Second-Generation Minor Poets of the
Seventeenth Century DLB-126

Sedgwick, Arthur George 1844-1915 . . . . . DLB-64

Sedgwick, Catharine Maria
1789-1867 . . . . .DLB-1, 74, 183, 239, 243

Sedgwick, Ellery 1872-1930 . . . . .DLB-91

Sedgwick, Eve Kosofsky 1950- DLB-246

Sedley, Sir Charles 1639-1701 . . . . .DLB-131

Seeberg, Peter 1925-1999. . . . . .DLB-214

Seeger, Alan 1888-1916 . . . . .DLB-45

Seers, Eugene (see Dantin, Louis)

Segal, Erich 1937- Y-86

Šegedin, Petar 1909- DLB-181

Seghers, Anna 1900-1983 . . . . .DLB-69; CDWLB-2

Seid, Ruth (see Sinclair, Jo)

Seidel, Frederick Lewis 1936- Y-84

Seidel, Ina 1885-1974 . . . . .DLB-56

Seifert, Jaroslav
 1901-1986 . . . . DLB-215; Y-84; CDWLB-4

Seigenthaler, John 1927- DLB-127

Seizin Press DLB-112

Séjour, Victor 1817-1874 . . . . .DLB-50

Séjour Marcou et Ferrand, Juan Victor
 (see Séjour, Victor)

Sekowski, Józef-Julian, Baron Brambeus
 (see Senkovsky, Osip Ivanovich)

Selby, Bettina 1934- DLB-204

Selby, Hubert, Jr. 1928- DLB-2, 227

Selden, George 1929-1989 . . . . .DLB-52

Selden, John 1584-1654 . . . . .DLB-213

Selected English-Language Little Magazines
 and Newspapers [France, 1920-1939] . . .DLB-4

Selected Humorous Magazines
 (1820-1950) DLB-11

Selected Science-Fiction Magazines and
 Anthologies DLB-8

Selenić, Slobodan 1933-1995 . . . . .DLB-181

Self, Edwin F. 1920- DLB-137

Self, Will 1961- DLB-207

Seligman, Edwin R. A. 1861-1939 . . . . . . .DLB-47

Selimović, Meša
 1910-1982 . . . . .DLB-181; CDWLB-4

Selous, Frederick Courteney
 1851-1917 .DLB-174

Seltzer, Chester E. (see Muro, Amado)

Seltzer, Thomas [publishing house] DLB-46

Selvon, Sam 1923-1994 . . . . .DLB-125; CDWLB-3

Semmes, Raphael 1809-1877 . . . . .DLB-189

Senancour, Etienne de 1770-1846 . . . . . . .DLB-119

Sendak, Maurice 1928- DLB-61

Seneca the Elder
 circa 54 B.C.-circa A.D. 40 . . . . .DLB-211

Seneca the Younger
 circa 1 B.C.-A.D. 65 . . . .DLB-211; CDWLB-1

Senécal, Eva 1905- DLB-92

Sengstacke, John 1912- DLB-127

Senior, Olive 1941- DLB-157

Senkovsky, Osip Ivanovich
 (Józef-Julian Sekowski, Baron Brambeus)
 1800-1858 .DLB-198

Šenoa, August 1838-1881 . . . .DLB-147; CDWLB-4

"Sensation Novels" (1863), by
 H. L. Manse .DLB-21

Sepamla, Sipho 1932- DLB-157, 225

Seredy, Kate 1899-1975 . . . . .DLB-22

Sereni, Vittorio 1913-1983 . . . . .DLB-128

Seres, William [publishing house] DLB-170

Serling, Rod 1924-1975 . . . . .DLB-26

Serote, Mongane Wally 1944- DLB-125, 225

Serraillier, Ian 1912-1994 . . . . .DLB-161

Serrano, Nina 1934- DLB-122

Service, Robert 1874-1958 . . . . .DLB-92

Sessler, Charles 1854-1935 . . . . .DLB-187

Seth, Vikram 1952- DLB-120

Seton, Elizabeth Ann 1774-1821 . . . . .DLB-200

Seton, Ernest Thompson
 1860-1942 . . . . .DLB-92; DS-13

Setouchi Harumi 1922- DLB-182

Settle, Mary Lee 1918- DLB-6

Seume, Johann Gottfried 1763-1810 . . . . . .DLB-94

Seuse, Heinrich 1295?-1366 . . . . .DLB-179

Seuss, Dr. (see Geisel, Theodor Seuss)

The Seventy-fifth Anniversary of the Armistice:
 The Wilfred Owen Centenary and
 the Great War Exhibit
 at the University of Virginia Y-93

Severin, Timothy 1940- DLB-204

Sewall, Joseph 1688-1769 . . . . .DLB-24

Sewall, Richard B. 1908- DLB-111

Sewell, Anna 1820-1878 . . . . .DLB-163

Sewell, Samuel 1652-1730 . . . . .DLB-24

Sex, Class, Politics, and Religion [in the
 British Novel, 1930-1959] DLB-15

Sexton, Anne 1928-1974 . . .DLB-5, 169; CDALB-1

Seymour-Smith, Martin 1928-1998 . . . . . .DLB-155

Sgorlon, Carlo 1930- DLB-196

Shaara, Michael 1929-1988 . . . . Y-83

Shabel'skaia, Aleksandra Stanislavovna
 1845-1921 . . . . .DLB-238

Shadwell, Thomas 1641?-1692 . . . . .DLB-80

Shaffer, Anthony 1926- DLB-13

Shaffer, Peter 1926- DLB-13, 233; CDBLB-8

Shaftesbury, Anthony Ashley Cooper,
 Third Earl of 1671-1713 . . . . .DLB-101

Shairp, Mordaunt 1887-1939 . . . . .DLB-10

Shakespeare, Nicholas 1957- DLB-231

Shakespeare, William
 1564-1616 . . . . .DLB-62, 172; CDBLB-1

The Shakespeare Globe Trust Y-93

Shakespeare Head Press DLB-112

Shakhovskoi, Aleksandr Aleksandrovich
 1777-1846 . . . . .DLB-150

Shange, Ntozake 1948- DLB-38

Shapiro, Karl 1913-2000 . . . . .DLB-48

Sharon Publications DLB-46

Sharp, Margery 1905-1991 . . . . .DLB-161

Sharp, William 1855-1905 . . . . .DLB-156

Sharpe, Tom 1928- DLB-14, 231

Shaw, Albert 1857-1947 . . . . .DLB-91

Shaw, George Bernard
 1856-1950 . . . . . . .DLB-10, 57, 190, CDBLB-6

Shaw, Henry Wheeler 1818-1885 . . . . .DLB-11

Shaw, Joseph T. 1874-1952 . . . . .DLB-137

Shaw, Irwin
 1913-1984 . . . . . .DLB-6, 102; Y-84; CDALB-1

Shaw, Mary 1854-1929 . . . . .DLB-228

Shaw, Robert 1927-1978 . . . . .DLB-13, 14

Shaw, Robert B. 1947- DLB-120

Shawn, William 1907-1992 . . . . .DLB-137

Shay, Frank [publishing house] DLB-46

Shchedrin, N. (see Saltykov, Mikhail Evgrafovich)

Shea, John Gilmary 1824-1892 . . . . .DLB-30

Sheaffer, Louis 1912-1993 . . . . .DLB-103

Shearing, Joseph 1886-1952 . . . . .DLB-70

Shebbeare, John 1709-1788 . . . . .DLB-39

Sheckley, Robert 1928- DLB-8

Shedd, William G. T. 1820-1894 . . . . .DLB-64

Sheed, Wilfred 1930- DLB-6

Sheed and Ward [U.S.] DLB-46

Sheed and Ward Limited [U.K.] DLB-112

Sheldon, Alice B. (see Tiptree, James, Jr.)

Sheldon, Edward 1886-1946 . . . . .DLB-7

Sheldon and Company DLB-49

Sheller, Aleksandr Konstantinovich
 1838-1900 . . . . .DLB-238

Shelley, Mary Wollstonecraft 1797-1851
 . . . . DLB-110, 116, 159, 178; CDBLB-3

Shelley, Percy Bysshe
 1792-1822 . . . . . .DLB-96, 110, 158; CDBLB-3

Shelnutt, Eve 1941- DLB-130

Shenstone, William 1714-1763 . . . . .DLB-95

Shepard, Clark and Brown DLB-49

Shepard, Ernest Howard 1879-1976 . . . . . .DLB-160

Shepard, Sam 1943- DLB-7, 212

Shepard, Thomas I, 1604 or 1605-1649 . . .DLB-24

Shepard, Thomas II, 1635-1677 . . . . .DLB-24

Shepherd, Luke
 flourished 1547-1554 . . . . .DLB-136

Sherburne, Edward 1616-1702 . . . . .DLB-131

Sheridan, Frances 1724-1766 . . . . .DLB-39, 84

Sheridan, Richard Brinsley
 1751-1816 . . . . .DLB-89; CDBLB-2

Sherman, Francis 1871-1926 . . . . .DLB-92

Sherman, Martin 1938- DLB-228

Sherriff, R. C. 1896-1975 . . . . . . .DLB-10, 191, 233

Sherrod, Blackie 1919- DLB-241

Sherry, Norman 1935- DLB-155

Sherry, Richard 1506-1551 or 1555 . . . . .DLB-236

Sherwood, Mary Martha 1775-1851 . . . . .DLB-163

Sherwood, Robert 1896-1955 . . . . DLB-7, 26

Shevyrev, Stepan Petrovich
 1806-1864 . . . . .DLB-205

Shiel, M. P. 1865-1947 . . . . .DLB-153

Shiels, George 1886-1949 . . . . .DLB-10

Shiga, Naoya 1883-1971 . . . . .DLB-180

Shiina Rinzō 1911-1973 . . . . .DLB-182

Shikishi Naishinnō 1153?-1201 . . . . DLB-203

Shillaber, Benjamin Penhallow
1814-1890 . . . . DLB-1, 11, 235

Shimao Toshio 1917-1986 . . . . DLB-182

Shimazaki, Tōson 1872-1943 . . . . DLB-180

Shine, Ted 1931- DLB-38

Shinkei 1406-1475 . . . . DLB-203

Ship, Reuben 1915-1975 . . . . DLB-88

Shirer, William L. 1904-1993 . . . . DLB-4

Shirinsky-Shikhmatov, Sergii Aleksandrovich
1783-1837 . . . . DLB-150

Shirley, James 1596-1666 . . . . DLB-58

Shishkov, Aleksandr Semenovich
1753-1841 . . . . DLB-150

Shockley, Ann Allen 1927- DLB-33

Shōno Junzō 1921- DLB-182

Shore, Arabella 1820?-1901 and
Shore, Louisa 1824-1895 . . . . DLB-199

Short, Peter [publishing house] DLB-170

Shorter, Dora Sigerson 1866-1918 . . . . . . DLB-240

Shorthouse, Joseph Henry 1834-1903 . . . . DLB-18

Shōtetsu 1381-1459 . . . . DLB-203

Showalter, Elaine 1941- DLB-67

Shulevitz, Uri 1935- DLB-61

Shulman, Max 1919-1988 . . . . DLB-11

Shute, Henry A. 1856-1943 . . . . DLB-9

Shuttle, Penelope 1947- DLB-14, 40

Sibbes, Richard 1577-1635 . . . . DLB-151

Sibiriak, D. (see Mamin, Dmitrii Narkisovich)

Siddal, Elizabeth Eleanor 1829-1862 . . . . DLB-199

Sidgwick, Ethel 1877-1970 . . . . DLB-197

Sidgwick and Jackson Limited DLB-112

Sidney, Margaret (see Lothrop, Harriet M.)

Sidney, Mary 1561-1621 . . . . DLB-167

Sidney, Sir Philip
1554-1586 . . . . DLB-167; CDBLB-1

An Apologie for Poetrie (the Olney
edition, 1595, of *Defence of Poesie*) DLB-167

Sidney's Press DLB-49

Sierra, Rubén 1946- DLB-122

Sierra Club Books DLB-49

Siger of Brabant circa 1240-circa 1284 . . . DLB-115

Sigourney, Lydia Huntley
1791-1865 . . . . . . .DLB-1, 42, 73, 183, 239, 243

Silkin, Jon 1930- DLB-27

Silko, Leslie Marmon 1948- DLB-143, 175

Silliman, Benjamin 1779-1864 . . . . DLB-183

Silliman, Ron 1946- DLB-169

Silliphant, Stirling 1918- DLB-26

Sillitoe, Alan 1928- DLB-14, 139; CDBLB-8

Silman, Roberta 1934- DLB-28

Silva, Beverly 1930- DLB-122

Silverberg, Robert 1935- DLB-8

Silverman, Kaja 1947- DLB-246

Silverman, Kenneth 1936- DLB-111

Simak, Clifford D. 1904-1988 . . . . DLB-8

Simcoe, Elizabeth 1762-1850 . . . . DLB-99

Simcox, Edith Jemima 1844-1901 . . . . . . DLB-190

Simcox, George Augustus 1841-1905 . . . . . DLB-35

Sime, Jessie Georgina 1868-1958 . . . . DLB-92

Simenon, Georges 1903-1989 . . . . . .DLB-72; Y-89

Simic, Charles 1938- DLB-105

"Images and 'Images,'" DLB-105

Simionescu, Mircea Horia 1928- DLB-232

Simmel, Johannes Mario 1924- DLB-69

Simmes, Valentine [publishing house] DLB-170

Simmons, Ernest J. 1903-1972 . . . . DLB-103

Simmons, Herbert Alfred 1930- DLB-33

Simmons, James 1933- DLB-40

Simms, William Gilmore
1806-1870 . . . . .DLB-3, 30, 59, 73

Simms and M'Intyre DLB-106

Simon, Claude 1913- DLB-83; Y-85

Simon, Neil 1927- DLB-7

Simon and Schuster DLB-46

Simons, Katherine Drayton Mayrant
1890-1969 . . . . Y-83

Simović, Ljubomir 1935- DLB-181

Simpkin and Marshall
[publishing house] DLB-154

Simpson, Helen 1897-1940 . . . . DLB-77

Simpson, Louis 1923- DLB-5

Simpson, N. F. 1919- DLB-13

Sims, George 1923- DLB-87; Y-99

Sims, George Robert 1847-1922 . . .DLB-35, 70, 135

Sinán, Rogelio 1904- DLB-145

Sinclair, Andrew 1935- DLB-14

Sinclair, Bertrand William 1881-1972 . . . . . DLB-92

Sinclair, Catherine 1800-1864 . . . . DLB-163

Sinclair, Jo 1913-1995 . . . . DLB-28

Sinclair, Lister 1921- DLB-88

Sinclair, May 1863-1946 . . . . DLB-36, 135

Sinclair, Upton 1878-1968 . . . . . DLB-9; CDALB-5

Sinclair, Upton [publishing house] DLB-46

Singer, Isaac Bashevis
1904-1991 . . . DLB-6, 28, 52; Y-91; CDALB-1

Singer, Mark 1950- DLB-185

Singmaster, Elsie 1879-1958 . . . . DLB-9

Sinisgalli, Leonardo 1908-1981 . . . . DLB-114

Siodmak, Curt 1902-2000 . . . . DLB-44

Sîrbu, Ion D. 1919-1989 . . . . DLB-232

Siringo, Charles A. 1855-1928 . . . . DLB-186

Sissman, L. E. 1928-1976 . . . . DLB-5

Sisson, C. H. 1914- DLB-27

Sitwell, Edith 1887-1964 . . . . . . DLB-20; CDBLB-7

Sitwell, Osbert 1892-1969 . . . . .DLB-100, 195

Skácel, Jan 1922-1989 . . . . DLB-232

Skalbe, Kārlis 1879-1945 . . . . DLB-220

Skármeta, Antonio
1940- DLB-145; CDWLB-3

Skavronsky, A. (see Danilevsky, Grigorii Petrovich)

Skeat, Walter W. 1835-1912 . . . . DLB-184

Skeffington, William
[publishing house] DLB-106

Skelton, John 1463-1529 . . . . DLB-136

Skelton, Robin 1925- DLB-27, 53

Škēma, Antanas 1910-1961 . . . . DLB-220

Skinner, Constance Lindsay
1877-1939 . . . . DLB-92

Skinner, John Stuart 1788-1851 . . . . DLB-73

Skipsey, Joseph 1832-1903 . . . . DLB-35

Skou-Hansen, Tage 1925- DLB-214

Škvorecký, Josef 1924- DLB-232; CDWLB-4

Slade, Bernard 1930- DLB-53

Slamnig, Ivan 1930- DLB-181

Slančeková, Božena (see Timrava)

Slater, Patrick 1880-1951 . . . . DLB-68

Slaveykov, Pencho 1866-1912 . . . . .DLB-147

Slaviček, Milivoj 1929- DLB-181

Slavitt, David 1935- DLB-5, 6

Sleigh, Burrows Willcocks Arthur
1821-1869 . . . . DLB-99

A Slender Thread of Hope:
The Kennedy Center Black
Theatre Project DLB-38

Slesinger, Tess 1905-1945 . . . . DLB-102

Slick, Sam (see Haliburton, Thomas Chandler)

Sloan, John 1871-1951 . . . . DLB-188

Sloane, William, Associates DLB-46

Small, Maynard and Company DLB-49

Small Presses in Great Britain and Ireland,
1960-1985 . . . . DLB-40

Small Presses I: Jargon Society Y-84

Small Presses II: The Spirit That Moves
Us Press Y-85

Small Presses III: Pushcart Press Y-87

Smart, Christopher 1722-1771 . . . . DLB-109

Smart, David A. 1892-1957 . . . . .DLB-137

Smart, Elizabeth 1913-1986 . . . . DLB-88

Smedley, Menella Bute 1820?-1877 . . . . . DLB-199

Smellie, William [publishing house] DLB-154

Smiles, Samuel 1812-1904 . . . . DLB-55

Smiley, Jane 1949- DLB-227, 234

Smith, A. J. M. 1902-1980 . . . . DLB-88

Smith, Adam 1723-1790 . . . . DLB-104

Smith, Adam (George Jerome Waldo Goodman)
1930- DLB-185

Smith, Alexander 1829-1867 . . . . DLB-32, 55

"On the Writing of Essays" (1862) DLB-57

Smith, Amanda 1837-1915 . . . . DLB-221

Smith, Betty 1896-1972 . . . . Y-82

Smith, Carol Sturm 1938- Y-81

Smith, Charles Henry 1826-1903 . . . . DLB-11

Smith, Charlotte 1749-1806 . . . . DLB-39, 109

Smith, Chet 1899-1973 . . . . .DLB-171

Smith, Cordwainer 1913-1966 . . . . DLB-8

Smith, Dave 1942- DLB-5

Smith, Dodie 1896- DLB-10

Smith, Doris Buchanan 1934- DLB-52

Smith, E. E. 1890-1965 . . . . .DLB-8

Smith, Elder and Company DLB-154

Smith, Elihu Hubbard 1771-1798 . . . . .DLB-37

Smith, Elizabeth Oakes (Prince)
(see Oakes Smith, Elizabeth)

Smith, Eunice 1757-1823 . . . . .DLB-200

Smith, F. Hopkinson 1838-1915 . . . . .DS-13

Smith, George D. 1870-1920 . . . . .DLB-140

Smith, George O. 1911-1981 . . . . .DLB-8

Smith, Goldwin 1823-1910 . . . . .DLB-99

Smith, H. Allen 1907-1976 . . . . .DLB-11, 29

Smith, Harrison, and Robert Haas
[publishing house] DLB-46

Smith, Harry B. 1860-1936 . . . . .DLB-187

Smith, Hazel Brannon 1914- DLB-127

Smith, Henry circa 1560-circa 1591 . . . . .DLB-136

Smith, Horatio (Horace) 1779-1849 . . . . . .DLB-116

Smith, Horatio (Horace) 1779-1849 and
James Smith 1775-1839 . . . . .DLB-96

Smith, Iain Crichton 1928- DLB-40, 139

Smith, J. Allen 1860-1924 . . . . .DLB-47

Smith, J. Stilman, and Company DLB-49

Smith, Jessie Willcox 1863-1935 . . . . . . .DLB-188

Smith, John 1580-1631 . . . . .DLB-24, 30

Smith, Josiah 1704-1781 . . . . .DLB-24

Smith, Ken 1938- DLB-40

Smith, Lee 1944- DLB-143; Y-83

Smith, Logan Pearsall 1865-1946 . . . . .DLB-98

Smith, Mark 1935- Y-82

Smith, Michael 1698-circa 1771 . . . . .DLB-31

Smith, Pauline 1882-1959 . . . . .DLB-225

Smith, Red 1905-1982 . . . . DLB-29, 171

Smith, Roswell 1829-1892 . . . . .DLB-79

Smith, Samuel Harrison 1772-1845 . . . . . . .DLB-43

Smith, Samuel Stanhope 1751-1819 . . . . . . .DLB-37

Smith, Sarah (see Stretton, Hesba)

Smith, Sarah Pogson 1774-1870 . . . . .DLB-200

Smith, Seba 1792-1868 . . . . .DLB-1, 11, 243

Smith, Stevie 1902-1971 . . . . .DLB-20

Smith, Sydney 1771-1845 . . . . .DLB-107

Smith, Sydney Goodsir 1915-1975 . . . . . . .DLB-27

Smith, Sir Thomas 1513-1577 . . . . .DLB-132

Smith, W. B., and Company DLB-49

Smith, W. H., and Son DLB-106

Smith, Wendell 1914-1972 . . . . .DLB-171

Smith, William flourished 1595-1597 . . . . .DLB-136

Smith, William 1727-1803 . . . . .DLB-31

A General Idea of the College of Mirania
(1753) [excerpts] DLB-31

Smith, William 1728-1793 . . . . .DLB-30

Smith, William Gardner 1927-1974 . . . . . .DLB-76

Smith, William Henry 1808-1872 . . . . . . .DLB-159

Smith, William Jay 1918- DLB-5

Smithers, Leonard [publishing house] DLB-112

Smollett, Tobias
1721-1771 . . . . .DLB-39, 104; CDBLB-2

Dedication, *Ferdinand Count
Fathom* (1753) DLB-39

Preface to *Ferdinand Count Fathom* (1753) DLB-39

Preface to *Roderick Random* (1748) DLB-39

Smythe, Francis Sydney 1900-1949 . . . . . .DLB-195

Snelling, William Joseph 1804-1848 . . . . .DLB-202

Snellings, Rolland (see Touré, Askia Muhammad)

Snodgrass, W. D. 1926- DLB-5

Snow, C. P.
1905-1980 . . . . .DLB-15, 77; DS-17; CDBLB-7

Snyder, Gary 1930- . . . DLB-5, 16, 165, 212, 237

Sobiloff, Hy 1912-1970 . . . . .DLB-48

The Society for Textual Scholarship and
TEXT Y-87

The Society for the History of Authorship,
Reading and Publishing Y-92

Soffici, Ardengo 1879-1964 . . . . .DLB-114

Sofola, 'Zulu 1938- DLB-157

Solano, Solita 1888-1975 . . . . .DLB-4

Soldati, Mario 1906-1999 . . . . .DLB-177

Šoljan, Antun 1932-1993 . . . . .DLB-181

Sollers, Philippe 1936- DLB-83

Sollogub, Vladimir Aleksandrovich
1813-1882 . . . . .DLB-198

Sollors, Werner 1943- DBL-246

Solmi, Sergio 1899-1981 . . . . .DLB-114

Solomon, Carl 1928- DLB-16

Solway, David 1941- DLB-53

Solzhenitsyn and America Y-85

Somerville, Edith Œnone 1858-1949 . . . . .DLB-135

Somov, Orest Mikhailovich
1793-1833 . . . . .DLB-198

Sønderby, Knud 1909-1966 . . . . .DLB-214

Song, Cathy 1955- DLB-169

Sono Ayako 1931- DLB-182

Sontag, Susan 1933- DLB-2, 67

Sophocles 497/496 B.C.-406/405 B.C.
. . . . DLB-176; CDWLB-1

Šopov, Aco 1923-1982 . . . . .DLB-181

Sørensen, Villy 1929- DLB-214

Sorensen, Virginia 1912-1991 . . . . .DLB-206

Sorge, Reinhard Johannes 1892-1916 . . . .DLB-118

Sorrentino, Gilbert 1929- DLB-5, 173; Y-80

Sotheby, James 1682-1742 . . . . .DLB-213

Sotheby, John 1740-1807 . . . . .DLB-213

Sotheby, Samuel 1771-1842 . . . . .DLB-213

Sotheby, Samuel Leigh 1805-1861 . . . . . . .DLB-213

Sotheby, William 1757-1833 . . . . .DLB-93, 213

Soto, Gary 1952- DLB-82

Sources for the Study of Tudor and Stuart
Drama DLB-62

Souster, Raymond 1921- DLB-88

The *South English Legendary* circa thirteenth-fifteenth
centuries DLB-146

Southerland, Ellease 1943- DLB-33

Southern, Terry 1924-1995 . . . . .DLB-2

Southern Illinois University Press Y-95

Southern Writers Between the Wars DLB-9

Southerne, Thomas 1659-1746 . . . . .DLB-80

Southey, Caroline Anne Bowles
1786-1854 . . . . .DLB-116

Southey, Robert 1774-1843 . . . . . DLB-93, 107, 142

Southwell, Robert 1561?-1595 . . . . .DLB-167

Southworth, E. D. E. N. 1819-1899 . . . . . .DLB-239

Sowande, Bode 1948- DLB-157

Sowle, Tace [publishing house] DLB-170

Soyfer, Jura 1912-1939 . . . . .DLB-124

Soyinka, Wole
1934- DLB-125; Y-86, Y-87; CDWLB-3

Spacks, Barry 1931- DLB-105

Spalding, Frances 1950- DLB-155

Spark, Muriel 1918- DLB-15, 139; CDBLB-7

Sparke, Michael [publishing house] DLB-170

Sparks, Jared 1789-1866 . . . . .DLB-1, 30, 235

Sparshott, Francis 1926- DLB-60

Späth, Gerold 1939- DLB-75

Spatola, Adriano 1941-1988 . . . . .DLB-128

Spaziani, Maria Luisa 1924- DLB-128

Special Collections at the University of Colorado
at Boulder Y-98

The Spectator 1828- DLB-110

Spedding, James 1808-1881 . . . . .DLB-144

Spee von Langenfeld, Friedrich
1591-1635 . . . . .DLB-164

Speght, Rachel 1597-after 1630 . . . . .DLB-126

Speke, John Hanning 1827-1864 . . . . .DLB-166

Spellman, A. B. 1935- DLB-41

Spence, Catherine Helen 1825-1910 . . . . .DLB-230

Spence, Thomas 1750-1814 . . . . .DLB-158

Spencer, Anne 1882-1975 . . . . .DLB-51, 54

Spencer, Charles, third Earl of Sunderland
1674-1722 . . . . .DLB-213

Spencer, Elizabeth 1921- DLB-6, 218

Spencer, George John, Second Earl Spencer
1758-1834 . . . . .DLB-184

Spencer, Herbert 1820-1903 . . . . .DLB-57

"The Philosophy of Style" (1852) DLB-57

Spencer, Scott 1945- Y-86

Spender, J. A. 1862-1942 . . . . .DLB-98

Spender, Stephen 1909-1995 . . .DLB-20; CDBLB-7

Spener, Philipp Jakob 1635-1705 . . . . . . .DLB-164

Spenser, Edmund
circa 1552-1599 . . . . .DLB-167; CDBLB-1

Envoy from *The Shepheardes Calender* DLB-167

"The Generall Argument of the
Whole Booke," from
The Shepheardes Calender DLB-167

"A Letter of the Authors Expounding
His Whole Intention in the Course
of this Worke: Which for that It Giueth
Great Light to the Reader, for the Better
Vnderstanding Is Hereunto Annexed,"
from *The Faerie Qveene* (1590) DLB-167

"To His Booke," from
The Shepheardes Calender (1579) DLB-167

"To the Most Excellent and Learned Both
    Orator and Poete, Mayster Gabriell Haruey,
    His Verie Special and Singular Good Frend
    E. K. Commendeth the Good Lyking of
    This His Labour, and the Patronage of
    the New Poete," from
    The Shepheardes Calender. DLB-167

Sperr, Martin 1944- DLB-124

Spicer, Jack 1925-1965 . . . . DLB-5, 16, 193

Spielberg, Peter 1929- Y-81

Spielhagen, Friedrich 1829-1911. . . . . . . DLB-129

"Spielmannsepen" (circa 1152-circa 1500) . . DLB-148

Spier, Peter 1927- DLB-61

Spillane, Mickey 1918- DLB-226

Spink, J. G. Taylor 1888-1962 . . . . DLB-241

Spinrad, Norman 1940- DLB-8

Spires, Elizabeth 1952- DLB-120

Spitteler, Carl 1845-1924 . . . . DLB-129

Spivak, Lawrence E. 1900- DLB-137

Spofford, Harriet Prescott
    1835-1921 . . . . DLB-74, 221

Spring, Howard 1889-1965. . . . . DLB-191

Squibob (see Derby, George Horatio)

Squier, E. G. 1821-1888 . . . . DLB-189

Stacpoole, H. de Vere 1863-1951 . . . . . . DLB-153

Staël, Germaine de 1766-1817. . . . . . DLB-119, 192

Staël-Holstein, Anne-Louise Germaine de
    (see Staël, Germaine de)

Stafford, Jean 1915-1979 . . . . .DLB-2, 173

Stafford, William 1914-1993. . . . . DLB-5, 206

Stage Censorship: "The Rejected Statement"
    (1911), by Bernard Shaw [excerpts] . . . DLB-10

Stallings, Laurence 1894-1968 . . . . .DLB-7, 44

Stallworthy, Jon 1935- DLB-40

Stampp, Kenneth M. 1912- DLB-17

Stănescu, Nichita 1933-1983. . . . . DLB-232

Stanev, Emiliyan 1907-1979 . . . . DLB-181

Stanford, Ann 1916- DLB-5

Stangerup, Henrik 1937-1998 . . . . DLB-214

Stanitsky, N. (see Panaeva, Avdot'ia Iakovlevna)

Stankevich, Nikolai Vladimirovich
    1813-1840. . . . . DLB-198

Stanković, Borisav ("Bora")
    1876-1927. . . . . .DLB-147; CDWLB-4

Stanley, Henry M. 1841-1904. . . . DLB-189; DS-13

Stanley, Thomas 1625-1678 . . . . DLB-131

Stannard, Martin 1947- DLB-155

Stansby, William [publishing house]. DLB-170

Stanton, Elizabeth Cady 1815-1902 . . . . . DLB-79

Stanton, Frank L. 1857-1927 . . . . DLB-25

Stanton, Maura 1946- DLB-120

Stapledon, Olaf 1886-1950 . . . . DLB-15

Star Spangled Banner Office. DLB-49

Stark, Freya 1893-1993. . . . . DLB-195

Starkey, Thomas circa 1499-1538 . . . . . . DLB-132

Starkie, Walter 1894-1976. . . . . DLB-195

Starkweather, David 1935- DLB-7

Starrett, Vincent 1886-1974 . . . . DLB-187

The State of Publishing. Y-97

Statements on the Art of Poetry DLB-54

Stationers' Company of London, The DLB-170

Statius circa A.D. 45-A.D. 96 . . . . DLB-211

Stead, Robert J. C. 1880-1959 . . . . DLB-92

Steadman, Mark 1930- DLB-6

The Stealthy School of Criticism (1871), by
    Dante Gabriel Rossetti. DLB-35

Stearns, Harold E. 1891-1943. . . . . DLB-4

Stebnitsky, M. (see Leskov, Nikolai Semenovich)

Stedman, Edmund Clarence 1833-1908 . . . DLB-64

Steegmuller, Francis 1906-1994 . . . . DLB-111

Steel, Flora Annie 1847-1929 . . . . . . DLB-153, 156

Steele, Max 1922- Y-80

Steele, Richard
    1672-1729 . . . . DLB-84, 101; CDBLB-2

Steele, Timothy 1948- DLB-120

Steele, Wilbur Daniel 1886-1970 . . . . DLB-86

Steere, Richard circa 1643-1721 . . . . DLB-24

Stefanovski, Goran 1952- DLB-181

Stegner, Wallace 1909-1993 . . . . .DLB-9, 206; Y-93

Stehr, Hermann 1864-1940 . . . . DLB-66

Steig, William 1907- DLB-61

Stein, Gertrude 1874-1946
    . . . . . . DLB-4, 54, 86, 228; DS-15; CDALB-4

Stein, Leo 1872-1947. . . . . DLB-4

Stein and Day Publishers DLB-46

Steinbeck, John
    1902-1968 . . . .DLB-7, 9, 212; DS-2; CDALB-5

John Steinbeck Research Center. Y-85

Steinem, Gloria 1934- DLB-246

Steiner, George 1929- DLB-67

Steinhoewel, Heinrich 1411/1412-1479. . . .DLB-179

Steloff, Ida Frances 1887-1989 . . . . DLB-187

Stendhal 1783-1842. . . . . DLB-119

Stephen Crane: A Revaluation Virginia
    Tech Conference, 1989 . . . . .Y-89

Stephen, Leslie 1832-1904 . . . . . .DLB-57, 144, 190

Stephen Vincent Benét Centenary Y-97

Stephens, A. G. 1865-1933 . . . . DLB-230

Stephens, Alexander H. 1812-1883. . . . . . DLB-47

Stephens, Alice Barber 1858-1932 . . . . . . DLB-188

Stephens, Ann 1810-1886. . . . . DLB-3, 73

Stephens, Charles Asbury 1844?-1931 . . . . DLB-42

Stephens, James 1882?-1950. . . . .DLB-19, 153, 162

Stephens, John Lloyd 1805-1852 . . . . DLB-183

Stephens, Michael 1946- DLB-234

Sterling, George 1869-1926 . . . . DLB-54

Sterling, James 1701-1763 . . . . DLB-24

Sterling, John 1806-1844. . . . . DLB-116

Stern, Gerald 1925- DLB-105

Stern, Gladys B. 1890-1973 . . . . DLB-197

Stern, Madeleine B. 1912- DLB-111, 140

Stern, Richard 1928- DLB-218; Y-87

Stern, Stewart 1922- DLB-26

Sterne, Laurence
    1713-1768 . . . . DLB-39; CDBLB-2

Sternheim, Carl 1878-1942 . . . . DLB-56, 118

Sternhold, Thomas ?-1549 and
    John Hopkins ?-1570 . . . . DLB-132

Steuart, David 1747-1824 . . . . DLB-213

Stevens, Henry 1819-1886 . . . . DLB-140

Stevens, Wallace 1879-1955 . . . DLB-54; CDALB-5

Stevenson, Anne 1933- DLB-40

Stevenson, D. E. 1892-1973 . . . . DLB-191

Stevenson, Lionel 1902-1973 . . . . DLB-155

Stevenson, Robert Louis
    1850-1894 . . . . .DLB-18, 57, 141, 156, 174;
                                                DS-13; CDBLB-5

"On Style in Literature:
    Its Technical Elements" (1885) DLB-57

Stewart, Donald Ogden
    1894-1980 . . . . DLB-4, 11, 26

Stewart, Dugald 1753-1828. . . . . DLB-31

Stewart, George, Jr. 1848-1906. . . . . DLB-99

Stewart, George R. 1895-1980 . . . . DLB-8

Stewart, Maria W. 1803?-1879 . . . . DLB-239

Stewart, Randall 1896-1964 . . . . DLB-103

Stewart and Kidd Company. DLB-46

Stickney, Trumbull 1874-1904 . . . . DLB-54

Stieler, Caspar 1632-1707 . . . . DLB-164

Stifter, Adalbert
    1805-1868 . . . . .DLB-133; CDWLB-2

Stiles, Ezra 1727-1795 . . . . DLB-31

Still, James 1906- DLB-9

Stirner, Max 1806-1856 . . . . DLB-129

Stith, William 1707-1755 . . . . DLB-31

Stock, Elliot [publishing house]. DLB-106

Stockton, Frank R.
    1834-1902 . . . . .DLB-42, 74; DS-13

Stockton, J. Roy 1892-1972 . . . . DLB-241

Stoddard, Ashbel [publishing house] DLB-49

Stoddard, Charles Warren
    1843-1909 . . . . DLB-186

Stoddard, Elizabeth 1823-1902. . . . . DLB-202

Stoddard, Richard Henry
    1825-1903 . . . . DLB-3, 64; DS-13

Stoddard, Solomon 1643-1729 . . . . DLB-24

Stoker, Bram
    1847-1912 . . . . .DLB-36, 70, 178; CDBLB-5

Stokes, Frederick A., Company DLB-49

Stokes, Thomas L. 1898-1958 . . . . DLB-29

Stokesbury, Leon 1945- DLB-120

Stolberg, Christian Graf zu 1748-1821 . . . . DLB-94

Stolberg, Friedrich Leopold Graf zu
    1750-1819. DLB-94

Stone, Herbert S., and Company DLB-49

Stone, Lucy 1818-1893. . . . . .DLB-79, 239

Stone, Melville 1848-1929 . . . . DLB-25

Stone, Robert 1937- DLB-152

Stone, Ruth 1915- DLB-105

Stone, Samuel 1602-1663 . . . . DLB-24

Stone, William Leete 1792-1844. . . . . . . DLB-202

Stone and Kimball DLB-49

Stoppard, Tom
1937- DLB-13, 233; Y-85; CDBLB-8

Playwrights and Professors DLB-13

Storey, Anthony 1928- DLB-14

Storey, David 1933- DLB-13, 14, 207, 245

Storm, Theodor 1817-1888 . . DLB-129; CDWLB-2

Story, Thomas circa 1670-1742 . . . . DLB-31

Story, William Wetmore 1819-1895 . . . DLB-1, 235

Storytelling: A Contemporary Renaissance . . . Y-84

Stoughton, William 1631-1701 . . . . DLB-24

Stow, John 1525-1605 . . . . DLB-132

Stowe, Harriet Beecher 1811-1896
. . DLB-1, 12, 42, 74, 189, 239, 243; CDALB-3

Stowe, Leland 1899- DLB-29

Stoyanov, Dimitr Ivanov (see Elin Pelin)

Strabo 64 or 63 B.C.-circa A.D. 25 . . . . . . DLB-176

Strachey, Lytton 1880-1932 . . . . . . DLB-149; DS-10

Strachey, Lytton, Preface to Eminent
Victorians DLB-149

Strahan, William [publishing house] DLB-154

Strahan and Company DLB-106

Strand, Mark 1934- DLB-5

The Strasbourg Oaths 842 . . . . DLB-148

Stratemeyer, Edward 1862-1930 . . . . DLB-42

Strati, Saverio 1924- DLB-177

Stratton and Barnard DLB-49

Stratton-Porter, Gene
1863-1924 . . . . DLB-221; DS-14

Straub, Peter 1943- Y-84

Strauß, Botho 1944- DLB-124

Strauß, David Friedrich 1808-1874 . . . . . . DLB-133

The Strawberry Hill Press DLB-154

Streatfeild, Noel 1895-1986 . . . . DLB-160

Street, Cecil John Charles (see Rhode, John)

Street, G. S. 1867-1936 . . . . DLB-135

Street and Smith DLB-49

Streeter, Edward 1891-1976 . . . . DLB-11

Streeter, Thomas Winthrop 1883-1965 . . . DLB-140

Stretton, Hesba 1832-1911 . . . . DLB-163, 190

Stribling, T. S. 1881-1965 . . . . DLB-9

Der Stricker circa 1190-circa 1250 . . . . . . DLB-138

Strickland, Samuel 1804-1867 . . . . CDWLB-99

Stringer, Arthur 1874-1950 . . . . DLB-92

Stringer and Townsend DLB-49

Strittmatter, Erwin 1912- DLB-69

Strniša, Gregor 1930-1987 . . . . DLB-181

Strode, William 1630-1645 . . . . DLB-126

Strong, L. A. G. 1896-1958 . . . . DLB-191

Strother, David Hunter 1816-1888 . . . . DLB-3

Strouse, Jean 1945- DLB-111

Stuart, Dabney 1937- DLB-105

Stuart, Jesse 1906-1984 . . . . . DLB-9, 48, 102; Y-84

Stuart, Lyle [publishing house] DLB-46

Stuart, Ruth McEnery 1849?-1917 . . . . . . DLB-202

Stubbs, Harry Clement (see Clement, Hal)

Stubenberg, Johann Wilhelm von
1619-1663 . . . . DLB-164

Studio DLB-112

The Study of Poetry (1880), by
Matthew Arnold DLB-35

Stump, Al 1916-1995 . . . . DLB-241

Sturgeon, Theodore 1918-1985 . . . . . . DLB-8; Y-85

Sturges, Preston 1898-1959 . . . . DLB-26

"Style" (1840; revised, 1859), by
Thomas de Quincey [excerpt] DLB-57

"Style" (1888), by Walter Pater DLB-57

Style (1897), by Walter Raleigh
[excerpt] DLB-57

"Style" (1877), by T. H. Wright
[excerpt] DLB-57

"Le Style c'est l'homme" (1892), by
W. H. Mallock DLB-57

Styron, William
1925- DLB-2, 143; Y-80; CDALB-6

Suárez, Mario 1925- DLB-82

Such, Peter 1939- DLB-60

Suckling, Sir John 1609-1641? DLB-58, 126

Suckow, Ruth 1892-1960 . . . . DLB-9, 102

Sudermann, Hermann 1857-1928 . . . . . . DLB-118

Sue, Eugène 1804-1857 . . . . DLB-119

Sue, Marie-Joseph (see Sue, Eugène)

Suetonius circa A.D. 69-post A.D. 122 . . . DLB-211

Suggs, Simon (see Hooper, Johnson Jones)

Sui Sin Far (see Eaton, Edith Maude)

Suits, Gustav 1883-1956 . . . . DLB-220; CDWLB-4

Sukenick, Ronald 1932- DLB-173; Y-81

Suknaski, Andrew 1942- DLB-53

Sullivan, Alan 1868-1947 . . . . DLB-92

Sullivan, C. Gardner 1886-1965 . . . . DLB-26

Sullivan, Frank 1892-1976 . . . . DLB-11

Sulte, Benjamin 1841-1923 . . . . DLB-99

Sulzberger, Arthur Hays 1891-1968 . . . . . DLB-127

Sulzberger, Arthur Ochs 1926- DLB-127

Sulzer, Johann Georg 1720-1779 . . . . DLB-97

Sumarokov, Aleksandr Petrovich
1717-1777 . . . . DLB-150

Summers, Hollis 1916- DLB-6

A Summing Up at Century's End Y-99

Sumner, Charles 1811-1874 . . . . DLB-235

Sumner, Henry A. [publishing house] DLB-49

Surtees, Robert Smith 1803-1864 . . . . DLB-21

Survey of Literary Biographies Y-00

A Survey of Poetry Anthologies,
1879-1960 . . . . DLB-54

Surveys: Japanese Literature,
1987-1995 . . . . DLB-182

Sutherland, Efua Theodora
1924-1996 . . . . DLB-117

Sutherland, John 1919-1956 . . . . DLB-68

Sutro, Alfred 1863-1933 . . . . DLB-10

Svendsen, Hanne Marie 1933- DLB-214

Swados, Harvey 1920-1972 . . . . DLB-2

Swain, Charles 1801-1874 . . . . DLB-32

Swallow Press DLB-46

Swan Sonnenschein Limited DLB-106

Swanberg, W. A. 1907- DLB-103

Swenson, May 1919-1989 . . . . DLB-5

Swerling, Jo 1897- DLB-44

Swift, Graham 1949- DLB-194

Swift, Jonathan
1667-1745 . . . . . . DLB-39, 95, 101; CDBLB-2

Swinburne, A. C.
1837-1909 . . . . DLB-35, 57; CDBLB-4

Swineshead, Richard
floruit circa 1350 . . . . DLB-115

Swinnerton, Frank 1884-1982 . . . . DLB-34

Swisshelm, Jane Grey 1815-1884 . . . . DLB-43

Swope, Herbert Bayard 1882-1958 . . . . . . DLB-25

Swords, T. and J., and Company DLB-49

Swords, Thomas 1763-1843 and
Swords, James ?-1844 . . . . DLB-73

Sykes, Ella C. ?-1939 . . . . DLB-174

Sylvester, Josuah 1562 or 1563-1618 . . . . . DLB-121

Symonds, Emily Morse (see Paston, George)

Symonds, John Addington
1840-1893 . . . . DLB-57, 144

"Personal Style" (1890) DLB-57

Symons, A. J. A. 1900-1941 . . . . DLB-149

Symons, Arthur 1865-1945 . . . . . . DLB-19, 57, 149

Symons, Julian 1912-1994 . . . . . DLB-87, 155; Y-92

Julian Symons at Eighty Y-92

Symons, Scott 1933- DLB-53

A Symposium on The Columbia History of
the Novel Y-92

Synge, John Millington
1871-1909 . . . . DLB-10, 19; CDBLB-5

Synge Summer School: J. M. Synge and the
Irish Theater, Rathdrum, County Wiclow,
Ireland Y-93

Syrett, Netta 1865-1943 . . . . DLB-135, 197

Szabó, Lőrinc 1900-1957 . . . . DLB-215

Szabó, Magda 1917- DLB-215

Szymborska, Wisława
1923- DLB-232, Y-96; CDWLB-4

T

Taban lo Liyong 1939?- DLB-125

Tabori, George 1914- DLB-245

Tabucchi, Antonio 1943- DLB-196

Taché, Joseph-Charles 1820-1894 . . . . DLB-99

Tachihara Masaaki 1926-1980 . . . . DLB-182

Tacitus circa A.D. 55-circa A.D. 117
. . . . DLB-211; CDWLB-1

Tadijanović, Dragutin 1905- DLB-181

Tafdrup, Pia 1952- DLB-214

Tafolla, Carmen 1951- DLB-82

Taggard, Genevieve 1894-1948 . . . . DLB-45

Taggart, John 1942- DLB-193

Tagger, Theodor (see Bruckner, Ferdinand)

Taiheiki late fourteenth century DLB-203

Tait, J. Selwin, and Sons DLB-49

Tait's Edinburgh Magazine 1832-1861 . . . . . DLB-110

The Takarazaka Revue Company Y-91

Talander (see Bohse, August)

Talese, Gay 1932- DLB-185

Talev, Dimitr 1898-1966 . . . . DLB-181

Taliaferro, H. E. 1811-1875 . . . . DLB-202

Tallent, Elizabeth 1954- DLB-130

TallMountain, Mary 1918-1994 . . . . DLB-193

Talvj 1797-1870 . . . . DLB-59, 133

Tamási, Áron 1897-1966 . . . . DLB-215

Tammsaare, A. H.
1878-1940 . . . . DLB-220; CDWLB-4

Tan, Amy 1952- DLB-173; CDALB-7

Tandori, Dezső 1938- DLB-232

Tanner, Thomas 1673/1674-1735 . . . . DLB-213

Tanizaki Jun'ichirō 1886-1965 . . . . DLB-180

Tapahonso, Luci 1953- DLB-175

The Mark Taper Forum DLB-7

Taradash, Daniel 1913- DLB-44

Tarbell, Ida M. 1857-1944 . . . . DLB-47

Tardivel, Jules-Paul 1851-1905 . . . . DLB-99

Targan, Barry 1932- DLB-130

Tarkington, Booth 1869-1946 . . . . DLB-9, 102

Tashlin, Frank 1913-1972 . . . . DLB-44

Tasma (Jessie Couvreur) 1848-1897 . . . . DLB-230

Tate, Allen 1899-1979 . . . . . . DLB-4, 45, 63; DS-17

Tate, James 1943- DLB-5, 169

Tate, Nahum circa 1652-1715 . . . . DLB-80

Tatian circa 830 . . . . DLB-148

Taufer, Veno 1933- DLB-181

Tauler, Johannes circa 1300-1361 . . . . DLB-179

Tavčar, Ivan 1851-1923 . . . . DLB-147

Taverner, Richard ca. 1505-1575 . . . . DLB-236

Taylor, Ann 1782-1866 . . . . DLB-163

Taylor, Bayard 1825-1878 . . . . DLB-3, 189

Taylor, Bert Leston 1866-1921 . . . . DLB-25

Taylor, Charles H. 1846-1921 . . . . DLB-25

Taylor, Edward circa 1642-1729 . . . . DLB-24

Taylor, Elizabeth 1912-1975 . . . . DLB-139

Taylor, Henry 1942- DLB-5

Taylor, Sir Henry 1800-1886 . . . . DLB-32

Taylor, Jane 1783-1824 . . . . DLB-163

Taylor, Jeremy circa 1613-1667 . . . . DLB-151

Taylor, John 1577 or 1578 - 1653 . . . . DLB-121

Taylor, Mildred D. ?- DLB-52

Taylor, Peter 1917-1994 . . . . . DLB-218; Y-81, Y-94

Taylor, Susie King 1848-1912 . . . . DLB-221

Taylor, William Howland 1901-1966 . . . DLB-241

Taylor, William, and Company DLB-49

Taylor-Made Shakespeare? Or Is "Shall I Die?" the
Long-Lost Text of Bottom's Dream? Y-85

Teasdale, Sara 1884-1933 . . . . DLB-45

Telles, Lygia Fagundes 1924- DLB-113

Temple, Sir William 1628-1699 . . . . DLB-101

Temrizov, A. (see Marchenko, Anastasia Iakovlevna)

Tench, Watkin ca. 1758-1833 . . . . DLB-230

Tenn, William 1919- DLB-8

Tennant, Emma 1937- DLB-14

Tenney, Tabitha Gilman
1762-1837 . . . . DLB-37, 200

Tennyson, Alfred
1809-1892 . . . . DLB-32; CDBLB-4

Tennyson, Frederick 1807-1898 . . . . DLB-32

Tenorio, Arthur 1924- DLB-209

Tepliakov, Viktor Grigor'evich
1804-1842 . . . . DLB-205

Terence circa 184 B.C.-159 B.C. or after
. . . . DLB-211; CDWLB-1

Terhune, Albert Payson 1872-1942 . . . . DLB-9

Terhune, Mary Virginia
1830-1922 . . . . DS-13, DS-16

Terry, Megan 1932- DLB-7

Terson, Peter 1932- DLB-13

Tesich, Steve 1943-1996 . . . . Y-83

Tessa, Delio 1886-1939 . . . . DLB-114

Testori, Giovanni 1923-1993 . . . . DLB-128, 177

Tey, Josephine 1896?-1952 . . . . DLB-77

Thacher, James 1754-1844 . . . . DLB-37

Thackeray, William Makepeace
1811-1863 . . DLB-21, 55, 159, 163; CDBLB-4

Thames and Hudson Limited DLB-112

Thanet, Octave (see French, Alice)

Thatcher, John Boyd 1847-1909 . . . . DLB-187

Thaxter, Celia Laighton 1835-1894 . . . . . DLB-239

Thayer, Caroline Matilda Warren
1785-1844 . . . . DLB-200

The Theatre Guild DLB-7

The Theater in Shakespeare's Time DLB-62

Thegan and the Astronomer
flourished circa 850 . . . . DLB-148

Thelwall, John 1764-1834 . . . . DLB-93, 158

Theocritus circa 300 B.C.-260 B.C. DLB-176

Theodorescu, Ion N. (see Arghezi, Tudor)

Theodulf circa 760-circa 821 . . . . DLB-148

Theophrastus circa 371 B.C.-287 B.C. DLB-176

Theriault, Yves 1915-1983 . . . . DLB-88

Thério, Adrien 1925- DLB-53

Theroux, Paul 1941- DLB-2, 218; CDALB-7

Thesiger, Wilfred 1910- DLB-204

They All Came to Paris DS-16

Thibaudeau, Colleen 1925- DLB-88

Thielen, Benedict 1903-1965 . . . . DLB-102

Thiong'o Ngugi wa (see Ngugi wa Thiong'o)

Third-Generation Minor Poets of the
Seventeenth Century DLB-131

This Quarter 1925-1927, 1929-1932 . . . . DS-15

Thoma, Ludwig 1867-1921 . . . . DLB-66

Thoma, Richard 1902- DLB-4

Thomas, Audrey 1935- DLB-60

Thomas, D. M. 1935- . . DLB-40, 207; CDBLB-8

D. M. Thomas: The Plagiarism
Controversy Y-82

Thomas, Dylan
1914-1953 . . . . . . DLB-13, 20, 139; CDBLB-7

The Dylan Thomas Celebration Y-99

Thomas, Edward
1878-1917 . . . . DLB-19, 98, 156, 216

Thomas, Frederick William 1806-1866 . . DLB-202

Thomas, Gwyn 1913-1981 . . . . DLB-15, 245

Thomas, Isaiah 1750-1831 . . . . . . DLB-43, 73, 187

Thomas, Isaiah [publishing house] DLB-49

Thomas, Johann 1624-1679 . . . . DLB-168

Thomas, John 1900-1932 . . . . DLB-4

Thomas, Joyce Carol 1938- DLB-33

Thomas, Lorenzo 1944- DLB-41

Thomas, R. S. 1915-2000 . . . . . DLB-27; CDBLB-8

Thomasîn von Zerclære
circa 1186-circa 1259 . . . . DLB-138

Thomasius, Christian 1655-1728 . . . . DLB-168

Thompson, Daniel Pierce 1795-1868 . . . . DLB-202

Thompson, David 1770-1857 . . . . DLB-99

Thompson, Dorothy 1893-1961 . . . . DLB-29

Thompson, E. P. 1924-1993 . . . . DLB-242

Thompson, Flora 1876-1947 . . . . DLB-240

Thompson, Francis
1859-1907 . . . . DLB-19; CDBLB-5

Thompson, George Selden (see Selden, George)

Thompson, Henry Yates 1838-1928 . . . . DLB-184

Thompson, Hunter S. 1939- DLB-185

Thompson, Jim 1906-1977 . . . . DLB-226

Thompson, John 1938-1976 . . . . DLB-60

Thompson, John R. 1823-1873 . . . . DLB-3, 73

Thompson, Lawrance 1906-1973 . . . . DLB-103

Thompson, Maurice 1844-1901 . . . . . . DLB-71, 74

Thompson, Ruth Plumly 1891-1976 . . . . . DLB-22

Thompson, Thomas Phillips 1843-1933 . . DLB-99

Thompson, William 1775-1833 . . . . DLB-158

Thompson, William Tappan
1812-1882 . . . . DLB-3, 11

Thomson, Edward William 1849-1924 . . . DLB-92

Thomson, James 1700-1748 . . . . DLB-95

Thomson, James 1834-1882 . . . . DLB-35

Thomson, Joseph 1858-1895 . . . . DLB-174

Thomson, Mortimer 1831-1875 . . . . DLB-11

Thon, Melanie Rae 1957- DLB-244

Thoreau, Henry David
1817-1862 . . . . DLB-1, 183, 223; CDALB-2

The Thoreauvian Pilgrimage: The Structure of an
American Cult DLB-223

Thorpe, Adam 1956- DLB-231

Thorpe, Thomas Bangs 1815-1878 . . . . . DLB-3, 11

Thorup, Kirsten 1942- DLB-214

Thoughts on Poetry and Its Varieties (1833),
by John Stuart Mill DLB-32

Thrale, Hester Lynch
(see Piozzi, Hester Lynch [Thrale])

Thubron, Colin 1939- DLB-204, 231

Thucydides
    circa 455 B.C.-circa 395 B.C. DLB-176

Thulstrup, Thure de 1848-1930 . . . . . . .DLB-188

Thümmel, Moritz August von
    1738-1817 . . . . .DLB-97

Thurber, James
    1894-1961 . . . . .DLB-4, 11, 22, 102; CDALB-5

Thurman, Wallace 1902-1934 . . . . .DLB-51

Thwaite, Anthony 1930- DLB-40

The Booker Prize
    Address by Anthony Thwaite,
    Chairman of the Booker Prize Judges
    Comments from Former Booker
    Prize Winners Y-86

Thwaites, Reuben Gold 1853-1913 . . . . . . .DLB-47

Tibullus circa 54 B.C.-circa 19 B.C.. . . . .DLB-211

Ticknor, George 1791-1871 . . . DLB-1, 59, 140, 235

Ticknor and Fields .DLB-49

Ticknor and Fields (revived) DLB-46

Tieck, Ludwig 1773-1853 . . . . .DLB-90; CDWLB-2

Tietjens, Eunice 1884-1944 . . . . .DLB-54

Tilghman, Christopher circa 1948 . . . . . . .DLB-244

Tilney, Edmund circa 1536-1610 . . . . . . .DLB-136

Tilt, Charles [publishing house] DLB-106

Tilton, J. E., and Company DLB-49

Time and Western Man (1927), by Wyndham
    Lewis [excerpts] DLB-36

Time-Life Books DLB-46

Times Books DLB-46

Timothy, Peter circa 1725-1782 . . . . .DLB-43

Timrava 1867-1951 . . . . .DLB-215

Timrod, Henry 1828-1867 . . . . .DLB-3

Tindal, Henrietta 1818?-1879 . . . . .DLB-199

Tinker, Chauncey Brewster 1876-1963 . . .DLB-140

Tinsley Brothers .DLB-106

Tiptree, James, Jr. 1915-1987 . . . . .DLB-8

Tišma, Aleksandar 1924- DLB-181

Titus, Edward William
    1870-1952 . . . . .DLB-4; DS-15

Tiutchev, Fedor Ivanovich 1803-1873 . . . .DLB-205

Tlali, Miriam 1933- DLB-157, 225

Todd, Barbara Euphan 1890-1976 . . . . . . .DLB-160

Todorov, Tzvetan 1939- DLB-242

Tofte, Robert
    1561 or 1562-1619 or 1620 . . . . .DLB-172

Toklas, Alice B. 1877-1967 . . . . .DLB-4

Tokuda, Shūsei 1872-1943 . . . . .DLB-180

Tolkien, J. R. R.
    1892-1973 . . . . .DLB-15, 160; CDBLB-6

Toller, Ernst 1893-1939 . . . . .DLB-124

Tollet, Elizabeth 1694-1754 . . . . .DLB-95

Tolson, Melvin B. 1898-1966 . . . . . . .DLB-48, 76

Tolstoy, Aleksei Konstantinovich
    1817-1875 . . . . .DLB-238

Tolstoy, Leo 1828-1910 . . . . .DLB-238

Tom Jones (1749), by Henry Fielding
    [excerpt] DLB-39

Tomalin, Claire 1933- DLB-155

Tomasi di Lampedusa, Giuseppe
    1896-1957 . . . . .DLB-177

Tomlinson, Charles 1927- DLB-40

Tomlinson, H. M. 1873-1958 . . . DLB-36, 100, 195

Tompkins, Abel [publishing house] DLB-49

Tompson, Benjamin 1642-1714 . . . . .DLB-24

Tomson, Graham R.
    (see Watson, Rosamund Marriott)

Ton'a 1289-1372 .DLB-203

Tondelli, Pier Vittorio 1955-1991 . . . . . . .DLB-196

Tonks, Rosemary 1932- DLB-14, 207

Tonna, Charlotte Elizabeth 1790-1846 . . .DLB-163

Tonson, Jacob the Elder
    [publishing house] DLB-170

Toole, John Kennedy 1937-1969 . . . . Y-81

Toomer, Jean 1894-1967 . . .DLB-45, 51; CDALB-4

Tor Books DLB-46

Torberg, Friedrich 1908-1979 . . . . .DLB-85

Torrence, Ridgely 1874-1950 . . . . .DLB-54

Torres-Metzger, Joseph V. 1933- DLB-122

Toth, Susan Allen 1940- Y-86

Tottell, Richard [publishing house] DLB-170

"The Printer to the Reader," (1557)
    by Richard Tottell DLB-167

Tough-Guy Literature DLB-9

Touré, Askia Muhammad 1938- DLB-41

Tourgée, Albion W. 1838-1905 . . . . .DLB-79

Tournemir, Elizaveta Sailhas de (see Tur, Evgeniia)

Tourneur, Cyril circa 1580-1626 . . . . .DLB-58

Tournier, Michel 1924- DLB-83

Tousey, Frank [publishing house] DLB-49

Tower Publications DLB-46

Towne, Benjamin circa 1740-1793 . . . . . . .DLB-43

Towne, Robert 1936- DLB-44

The Towneley Plays fifteenth and sixteenth
    centuries DLB-146

Townshend, Aurelian
    by 1583-circa 1651 . . . . .DLB-121

Toy, Barbara 1908- DLB-204

Tracy, Honor 1913- DLB-15

Traherne, Thomas 1637?-1674 . . . . .DLB-131

Traill, Catharine Parr 1802-1899 . . . . .DLB-99

Train, Arthur 1875-1945 . . . . .DLB-86; DS-16

The Transatlantic Publishing Company . . .DLB-49

The Transatlantic Review 1924-1925 . . . . DS-15

The Transcendental Club 1836-1840 . . . .DLB-223

Transcendentalism DLB-223

Transcendentalists, American DS-5

A Transit of Poets and Others: American
    Biography in 1982 . . . . Y-82

transition 1927-1938 . . . . DS-15

Translators of the Twelfth Century: Literary Issues
    Raised and Impact Created DLB-115

Travel Writing, 1837-1875 . . . . .DLB-166

Travel Writing, 1876-1909 . . . . .DLB-174

Travel Writing, 1910-1939 . . . . .DLB-195

Traven, B. 1882? or 1890?-1969? DLB-9, 56

Travers, Ben 1886-1980 . . . . .DLB-10, 233

Travers, P. L. (Pamela Lyndon)
    1899-1996 . . . . .DLB-160

Trediakovsky, Vasilii Kirillovich
    1703-1769 . . . . .DLB-150

Treece, Henry 1911-1966 . . . . .DLB-160

Trejo, Ernesto 1950- DLB-122

Trelawny, Edward John
    1792-1881 . . . . DLB-110, 116, 144

Tremain, Rose 1943- DLB-14

Tremblay, Michel 1942- DLB-60

Trends in Twentieth-Century
    Mass Market Publishing DLB-46

Trent, William P. 1862-1939 . . . . .DLB-47

Trescot, William Henry 1822-1898 . . . . . . .DLB-30

Tressell, Robert (Robert Phillipe Noonan)
    1870-1911 . . . . .DLB-197

Trevelyan, Sir George Otto
    1838-1928 . . . . .DLB-144

Trevisa, John circa 1342-circa 1402 . . . . . .DLB-146

Trevor, William 1928- DLB-14, 139

Trierer Floyris circa 1170-1180 . . . . .DLB-138

Trillin, Calvin 1935- DLB-185

Trilling, Lionel 1905-1975 . . . . .DLB-28, 63

Trilussa 1871-1950 . . . . .DLB-114

Trimmer, Sarah 1741-1810 . . . . .DLB-158

Triolet, Elsa 1896-1970 . . . . .DLB-72

Tripp, John 1927- DLB-40

Trocchi, Alexander 1925- DLB-15

Troisi, Dante 1920-1989 . . . . .DLB-196

Trollope, Anthony
    1815-1882 . . . . DLB-21, 57, 159; CDBLB-4

Trollope, Frances 1779-1863 . . . . .DLB-21, 166

Trollope, Joanna 1943- DLB-207

Troop, Elizabeth 1931- DLB-14

Trotter, Catharine 1679-1749 . . . . .DLB-84

Trotti, Lamar 1898-1952 . . . . .DLB-44

Trottier, Pierre 1925- DLB-60

Troubadours, Trobaíritz, and Trouvères . .DLB-208

Troupe, Quincy Thomas, Jr. 1943- DLB-41

Trow, John F., and Company DLB-49

Trowbridge, John Townsend 1827-1916 . .DLB-202

Truillier-Lacombe, Joseph-Patrice
    1807-1863 . . . . .DLB-99

Trumbo, Dalton 1905-1976 . . . . .DLB-26

Trumbull, Benjamin 1735-1820 . . . . .DLB-30

Trumbull, John 1750-1831 . . . . .DLB-31

Trumbull, John 1756-1843 . . . . .DLB-183

Truth, Sojourner 1797?-1883 . . . . .DLB-239

Tscherning, Andreas 1611-1659 . . . . .DLB-164

Tsubouchi, Shōyō 1859-1935 . . . . .DLB-180

Tucholsky, Kurt 1890-1935 . . . . .DLB-56

Tucker, Charlotte Maria
    1821-1893 . . . . DLB-163, 190

Tucker, George 1775-1861 . . . . .DLB-3, 30

Tucker, James 1808?-1866? DLB-230

Tucker, Nathaniel Beverley 1784-1851 . . . . .DLB-3

Tucker, St. George 1752-1827 . . . . DLB-37

Tuckerman, Frederick Goddard
    1821-1873. . . . . DLB-243

Tuckerman, Henry Theodore 1813-1871. . DLB-64

Tumas, Juozas (see Vaižgantas)

Tunis, John R. 1889-1975 . . . . .DLB-22, 171

Tunstall, Cuthbert 1474-1559 . . . . DLB-132

Tuohy, Frank 1925- DLB-14, 139

Tupper, Martin F. 1810-1889 . . . . DLB-32

Tur, Evgeniia 1815-1892 . . . . DLB-238

Turbyfill, Mark 1896- DLB-45

Turco, Lewis 1934- Y-84

Turgenev, Aleksandr Ivanovich
    1784-1845. . . . . DLB-198

Turgenev, Ivan Sergeevich 1818-1883 . . . DLB-238

Turnball, Alexander H. 1868-1918. . . . . DLB-184

Turnbull, Andrew 1921-1970 . . . . DLB-103

Turnbull, Gael 1928- DLB-40

Turner, Arlin 1909-1980 . . . . DLB-103

Turner, Charles (Tennyson)
    1808-1879. . . . . DLB-32

Turner, Ethel 1872-1958. . . . . DLB-230

Turner, Frederick 1943- DLB-40

Turner, Frederick Jackson
    1861-1932 . . . . .DLB-17, 186

Turner, Joseph Addison 1826-1868 . . . . . . DLB-79

Turpin, Waters Edward 1910-1968 . . . . . DLB-51

Turrini, Peter 1944- DLB-124

Tutuola, Amos 1920-1997 . . DLB-125; CDWLB-3

Twain, Mark (see Clemens, Samuel Langhorne)

Tweedie, Ethel Brilliana
    circa 1860-1940 . . . . .DLB-174

The 'Twenties and Berlin, by Alex Natan . DLB-66

Two Hundred Years of Rare Books and
    Literary Collections at the
    University of South Carolina. Y-00

Twombly, Wells 1935-1977 . . . . DLB-241

Twysden, Sir Roger 1597-1672. . . . . DLB-213

Tyler, Anne
    1941- DLB-6, 143; Y-82; CDALB-7

Tyler, Mary Palmer 1775-1866. . . . . DLB-200

Tyler, Moses Coit 1835-1900. . . . . . .DLB-47, 64

Tyler, Royall 1757-1826 . . . . DLB-37

Tylor, Edward Burnett 1832-1917 . . . . . . DLB-57

Tynan, Katharine 1861-1931 . . . . . DLB-153, 240

Tyndale, William circa 1494-1536 . . . . . . DLB-132

U

Uchida, Yoshika 1921-1992 . . . . .CDALB-7

Udall, Nicholas 1504-1556 . . . . DLB-62

Ugrêsić, Dubravka 1949- DLB-181

Uhland, Ludwig 1787-1862. . . . . DLB-90

Uhse, Bodo 1904-1963 . . . . DLB-69

Ujević, Augustin ("Tin") 1891-1955. . . . . DLB-147

Ulenhart, Niclas flourished circa 1600 . . . DLB-164

Ulibarrí, Sabine R. 1919- DLB-82

Ulica, Jorge 1870-1926 . . . . DLB-82

Ulivi, Ferruccio 1912- DLB-196

Ulizio, B. George 1889-1969 . . . . DLB-140

Ulrich von Liechtenstein
    circa 1200-circa 1275 . . . . DLB-138

Ulrich von Zatzikhoven
    before 1194-after 1214 . . . . DLB-138

Ulysses, Reader's Edition Y-97

Unaipon, David 1872-1967. . . . . DLB-230

Unamuno, Miguel de 1864-1936 . . . . DLB-108

Under, Marie 1883-1980
    . . . . DLB-220; CDWLB-4

Under the Microscope (1872), by
    A. C. Swinburne DLB-35

Underhill, Evelyn 1875-1941 . . . . DLB-240

Ungaretti, Giuseppe 1888-1970 . . . . DLB-114

Unger, Friederike Helene 1741-1813 . . . . DLB-94

United States Book Company DLB-49

Universal Publishing and Distributing
    Corporation DLB-46

The University of Iowa Writers' Workshop
    Golden Jubilee Y-86

The University of South Carolina Press. Y-94

University of Wales Press DLB-112

University Press of Florida. Y-00

University Press of Kansas. Y-98

University Press of Mississippi. Y-99

"The Unknown Public" (1858), by
    Wilkie Collins [excerpt] DLB-57

Uno, Chiyo 1897-1996 . . . . DLB-180

Unruh, Fritz von 1885-1970 . . . . DLB-56, 118

Unspeakable Practices II: The Festival of Vanguard
    Narrative at Brown University Y-93

Unsworth, Barry 1930- DLB-194

Unt, Mati 1944- DLB-232

The Unterberg Poetry Center of the
    92nd Street Y Y-98

Unwin, T. Fisher [publishing house] DLB-106

Upchurch, Boyd B. (see Boyd, John)

Updike, John 1932-
    . . . . .DLB-2, 5, 143, 218, 227; Y-80, Y-82;
                                    DS-3; CDALB-6

John Updike on the Internet. Y-97

Upīts, Andrejs 1877-1970 . . . . DLB-220

Upton, Bertha 1849-1912 . . . . DLB-141

Upton, Charles 1948- DLB-16

Upton, Florence K. 1873-1922 . . . . DLB-141

Upward, Allen 1863-1926 . . . . DLB-36

Urban, Milo 1904-1982 . . . . DLB-215

Urista, Alberto Baltazar (see Alurista)

Urquhart, Fred 1912- DLB-139

Urrea, Luis Alberto 1955- DLB-209

Urzidil, Johannes 1896-1976. . . . . DLB-85

The Uses of Facsimile. Y-90

Usk, Thomas died 1388 . . . . DLB-146

Uslar Pietri, Arturo 1906- DLB-113

Ussher, James 1581-1656 . . . . DLB-213

Ustinov, Peter 1921- DLB-13

Uttley, Alison 1884-1976 . . . . DLB-160

Uz, Johann Peter 1720-1796 . . . . DLB-97

V

Vac, Bertrand 1914- DLB-88

Vācietis, Ojārs 1933-1983. . . . . DLB-232

Vaičiulaitis, Antanas 1906-1992 . . . . DLB-220

Vaculík, Ludvík 1926- DLB-232

Vaičiūnaite, Judita 1937- DLB-232

Vail, Laurence 1891-1968 . . . . DLB-4

Vailland, Roger 1907-1965 . . . . DLB-83

Vaižgantas 1869-1933 . . . . DLB-220

Vajda, Ernest 1887-1954. . . . . DLB-44

Valdés, Gina 1943- DLB-122

Valdez, Luis Miguel 1940- DLB-122

Valduga, Patrizia 1953- DLB-128

Valente, José Angel 1929-2000 . . . . DLB-108

Valenzuela, Luisa 1938- DLB-113; CDWLB-3

Valeri, Diego 1887-1976 . . . . DLB-128

Valerius Flaccus fl. circa A.D. 92 . . . . DLB-211

Valerius Maximus fl. circa A.D. 31 . . . . . DLB-211

Valesio, Paolo 1939- DLB-196

Valgardson, W. D. 1939- DLB-60

Valle, Víctor Manuel 1950- DLB-122

Valle-Inclán, Ramón del 1866-1936 . . . . . DLB-134

Vallejo, Armando 1949- DLB-122

Vallès, Jules 1832-1885. . . . . DLB-123

Vallette, Marguerite Eymery (see Rachilde)

Valverde, José María 1926-1996 . . . . DLB-108

Van Allsburg, Chris 1949- DLB-61

Van Anda, Carr 1864-1945 . . . . DLB-25

van der Post, Laurens 1906-1996. . . . . . . DLB-204

Van Dine, S. S. (see Wright, Williard Huntington)

Van Doren, Mark 1894-1972 . . . . DLB-45

van Druten, John 1901-1957 . . . . DLB-10

Van Duyn, Mona 1921- DLB-5

Van Dyke, Henry 1852-1933. . . . . .DLB-71; DS-13

Van Dyke, Henry 1928- DLB-33

Van Dyke, John C. 1856-1932. . . . . DLB-186

van Gulik, Robert Hans 1910-1967 . . . . .DS-17

van Itallie, Jean-Claude 1936- DLB-7

Van Loan, Charles E. 1876-1919 . . . . . . .DLB-171

Van Rensselaer, Mariana Griswold
    1851-1934 . . . . DLB-47

Van Rensselaer, Mrs. Schuyler
    (see Van Rensselaer, Mariana Griswold)

Van Vechten, Carl 1880-1964 . . . . DLB-4, 9

van Vogt, A. E. 1912-2000. . . . . DLB-8

Vanbrugh, Sir John 1664-1726 . . . . DLB-80

Vance, Jack 1916?- DLB-8

Vančura, Vladislav
    1891-1942 . . . . .DLB-215; CDWLB-4

Vane, Sutton 1888-1963. . . . . DLB-10

Vanguard Press DLB-46

Vann, Robert L. 1879-1940 . . . . DLB-29

Vargas Llosa, Mario
1936- DLB-145; CDWLB-3

Varley, John 1947- Y-81

Varnhagen von Ense, Karl August
1785-1858 . . . . DLB-90

Varnhagen von Ense, Rahel
1771-1833 . . . . DLB-90

Varro 116 B.C.-27 B.C. DLB-211

Vasiliu, George (see Bacovia, George)

Vásquez, Richard 1928- DLB-209

Vásquez Montalbán, Manuel 1939- DLB-134

Vassa, Gustavus (see Equiano, Olaudah)

Vassalli, Sebastiano 1941- DLB-128, 196

Vaughan, Henry 1621-1695 . . . . DLB-131

Vaughan, Thomas 1621-1666 . . . . DLB-131

Vaughn, Robert 1592?-1667 . . . . DLB-213

Vaux, Thomas, Lord 1509-1556 . . . . DLB-132

Vazov, Ivan 1850-1921 . . . . . DLB-147; CDWLB-4

Véa Jr., Alfredo 1950- DLB-209

Veblen, Thorstein 1857-1929 . . . . DLB-246

Vega, Janine Pommy 1942- DLB-16

Veiller, Anthony 1903-1965 . . . . DLB-44

Velásquez-Trevino, Gloria 1949- DLB-122

Veley, Margaret 1843-1887 . . . . DLB-199

Velleius Paterculus
circa 20 B.C.-circa A.D. 30 . . . . DLB-211

Veloz Maggiolo, Marcio 1936- DLB-145

Vel'tman Aleksandr Fomich
1800-1870 . . . . DLB-198

Venegas, Daniel ?-? DLB-82

Venevitinov, Dmitrii Vladimirovich
1805-1827 . . . . DLB-205

Vergil, Polydore circa 1470-1555 . . . . . . DLB-132

Veríssimo, Erico 1905-1975 . . . . DLB-145

Verlaine, Paul 1844-1896 . . . . DLB-217

Verne, Jules 1828-1905 . . . . DLB-123

Verplanck, Gulian C. 1786-1870 . . . . DLB-59

Very, Jones 1813-1880 . . . . DLB-1, 243

Vian, Boris 1920-1959 . . . . DLB-72

Viazemsky, Petr Andreevich
1792-1878 . . . . DLB-205

Vicars, Thomas 1591-1638 . . . . DLB-236

Vickers, Roy 1888?-1965 . . . . DLB-77

Vickery, Sukey 1779-1821 . . . . DLB-200

Victoria 1819-1901 . . . . DLB-55

Victoria Press DLB-106

Vidal, Gore 1925- DLB-6, 152; CDALB-7

Vidal, Mary Theresa 1815-1873 . . . . DLB-230

Vidmer, Richards 1898-1978 . . . . DLB-241

Viebig, Clara 1860-1952 . . . . DLB-66

Viereck, George Sylvester
1884-1962 . . . . DLB-54

Viereck, Peter 1916- DLB-5

Viets, Roger 1738-1811 . . . . DLB-99

Viewpoint: Politics and Performance, by
David Edgar DLB-13

Vigil-Piñon, Evangelina 1949- DLB-122

Vigneault, Gilles 1928- DLB-60

Vigny, Alfred de
1797-1863 . . . . DLB-119, 192, 217

Vigolo, Giorgio 1894-1983 . . . . DLB-114

The Viking Press DLB-46

Vilde, Eduard 1865-1933 . . . . DLB-220

Vilinskaia, Mariia Aleksandrovna
(see Vovchok, Marko)

Villanueva, Alma Luz 1944- DLB-122

Villanueva, Tino 1941- DLB-82

Villard, Henry 1835-1900 . . . . DLB-23

Villard, Oswald Garrison
1872-1949 . . . . DLB-25, 91

Villarreal, Edit 1944- DLB-209

Villarreal, José Antonio 1924- DLB-82

Villaseñor, Victor 1940- DLB-209

Villegas de Magnón, Leonor
1876-1955 . . . . DLB-122

Villehardouin, Geoffroi de
circa 1150-1215 . . . . DLB-208

Villemaire, Yolande 1949- DLB-60

Villena, Luis Antonio de 1951- DLB-134

Villiers, George, Second Duke
of Buckingham 1628-1687 . . . . DLB-80

Villiers de l'Isle-Adam, Jean-Marie Mathias
Philippe-Auguste, Comte de
1838-1889 . . . . DLB-123, 192

Villon, François 1431-circa 1463? DLB-208

Vine Press DLB-112

Viorst, Judith ?- DLB-52

Vipont, Elfrida (Elfrida Vipont Foulds,
Charles Vipont) 1902-1992 . . . . DLB-160

Viramontes, Helena María 1954- DLB-122

Virgil 70 B.C.-19 B.C. DLB-211; CDWLB-1

Virtual Books and Enemies of Books Y-00

Vischer, Friedrich Theodor 1807-1887 . . . DLB-133

Vitruvius circa 85 B.C.-circa 15 B.C. DLB-211

Vitry, Philippe de 1291-1361 . . . . DLB-208

Vivanco, Luis Felipe 1907-1975 . . . . DLB-108

Viviani, Cesare 1947- DLB-128

Vivien, Renée 1877-1909 . . . . DLB-217

Vizenor, Gerald 1934- DLB-175, 227

Vizetelly and Company DLB-106

Voaden, Herman 1903- DLB-88

Voß, Johann Heinrich 1751-1826 . . . . DLB-90

Voigt, Ellen Bryant 1943- DLB-120

Vojnović, Ivo 1857-1929 . . . . DLB-147; CDWLB-4

Volkoff, Vladimir 1932- DLB-83

Volland, P. F., Company DLB-46

Vollbehr, Otto H. F.
1872?-1945 or 1946 . . . . DLB-187

Vologdin (see Zasodimsky, Pavel Vladimirovich)

Volponi, Paolo 1924- DLB-177

von der Grün, Max 1926- DLB-75

Vonnegut, Kurt 1922-
. . . . . . DLB-2, 8, 152; Y-80; DS-3; CDALB-6

Voranc, Prežihov 1893-1950 . . . . DLB-147

Vovchok, Marko 1833-1907 . . . . DLB-238

Voynich, E. L. 1864-1960 . . . . DLB-197

Vroman, Mary Elizabeth
circa 1924-1967 . . . . DLB-33

W

Wace, Robert ("Maistre")
circa 1100-circa 1175 . . . . DLB-146

Wackenroder, Wilhelm Heinrich
1773-1798 . . . . DLB-90

Wackernagel, Wilhelm 1806-1869 . . . . . DLB-133

Waddell, Helen 1889-1965 . . . . DLB-240

Waddington, Miriam 1917- DLB-68

Wade, Henry 1887-1969 . . . . DLB-77

Wagenknecht, Edward 1900- DLB-103

Wagner, Heinrich Leopold 1747-1779 . . . . DLB-94

Wagner, Henry R. 1862-1957 . . . . DLB-140

Wagner, Richard 1813-1883 . . . . DLB-129

Wagoner, David 1926- DLB-5

Wah, Fred 1939- DLB-60

Waiblinger, Wilhelm 1804-1830 . . . . DLB-90

Wain, John
1925-1994 . . . DLB-15, 27, 139, 155; CDBLB-8

Wainwright, Jeffrey 1944- DLB-40

Waite, Peirce and Company DLB-49

Wakeman, Stephen H. 1859-1924 . . . . . . DLB-187

Wakoski, Diane 1937- DLB-5

Walahfrid Strabo circa 808-849 . . . . DLB-148

Walck, Henry Z. DLB-46

Walcott, Derek
1930- DLB-117; Y-81, Y-92; CDWLB-3

Waldegrave, Robert [publishing house] . . . DLB-170

Waldman, Anne 1945- DLB-16

Waldrop, Rosmarie 1935- DLB-169

Walker, Alice 1900-1982 . . . . DLB-201

Walker, Alice
1944- DLB-6, 33, 143; CDALB-6

Walker, Annie Louisa (Mrs. Harry Coghill)
circa 1836-1907 . . . . DLB-240

Walker, George F. 1947- DLB-60

Walker, John Brisben 1847-1931 . . . . DLB-79

Walker, Joseph A. 1935- DLB-38

Walker, Margaret 1915- DLB-76, 152

Walker, Ted 1934- DLB-40

Walker and Company DLB-49

Walker, Evans and Cogswell Company . . . DLB-49

Wallace, Alfred Russel 1823-1913 . . . . . . DLB-190

Wallace, Dewitt 1889-1981 and
Lila Acheson Wallace 1889-1984 . . . . DLB-137

Wallace, Edgar 1875-1932 . . . . DLB-70

Wallace, Lew 1827-1905 . . . . DLB-202

Wallace, Lila Acheson
(see Wallace, Dewitt, and Lila Acheson Wallace)

Wallant, Edward Lewis
1926-1962 . . . . DLB-2, 28, 143

Waller, Edmund 1606-1687 . . . . DLB-126

Walpole, Horace 1717-1797 . . . . . DLB-39, 104, 213

Preface to the First Edition of
The Castle of Otranto (1764) DLB-39

Preface to the Second Edition of
The Castle of Otranto (1765) DLB-39

Walpole, Hugh 1884-1941 . . . . DLB-34

Walrond, Eric 1898-1966 . . . . DLB-51

Walser, Martin 1927- DLB-75, 124

Walser, Robert 1878-1956 . . . . DLB-66

Walsh, Ernest 1895-1926 . . . . DLB-4, 45

Walsh, Robert 1784-1859 . . . . DLB-59

Walters, Henry 1848-1931 . . . . DLB-140

Waltharius circa 825 . . . . DLB-148

Walther von der Vogelweide
circa 1170-circa 1230 . . . . DLB-138

Walton, Izaak
1593-1683 . . . . DLB-151, 213; CDBLB-1

Wambaugh, Joseph 1937- DLB-6; Y-83

Wand, Alfred Rudolph 1828-1891 . . . . . . DLB-188

Waniek, Marilyn Nelson 1946- DLB-120

Wanley, Humphrey 1672-1726 . . . . DLB-213

Warburton, William 1698-1779 . . . . DLB-104

Ward, Aileen 1919- DLB-111

Ward, Artemus (see Browne, Charles Farrar)

Ward, Arthur Henry Sarsfield (see Rohmer, Sax)

Ward, Douglas Turner 1930- DLB-7, 38

Ward, Mrs. Humphry 1851-1920 . . . . DLB-18

Ward, Lynd 1905-1985 . . . . DLB-22

Ward, Lock and Company DLB-106

Ward, Nathaniel circa 1578-1652 . . . . DLB-24

Ward, Theodore 1902-1983 . . . . DLB-76

Wardle, Ralph 1909-1988 . . . . DLB-103

Ware, Henry, Jr. 1794-1843 . . . . DLB-235

Ware, William 1797-1852 . . . . DLB-1, 235

Waring, Anna Letitia 1823-1910 . . . . DLB-240

Warne, Frederick, and Company [U.K.] . . . DLB-106

Warne, Frederick, and Company [U.S.] . . . DLB-49

Warner, Anne 1869-1913 . . . . DLB-202

Warner, Charles Dudley 1829-1900 . . . . . . DLB-64

Warner, Marina 1946- DLB-194

Warner, Rex 1905- DLB-15

Warner, Susan 1819-1885 . . . . DLB-3, 42, 239

Warner, Sylvia Townsend
1893-1978 . . . . DLB-34, 139

Warner, William 1558-1609 . . . . DLB-172

Warner Books DLB-46

Warr, Bertram 1917-1943 . . . . DLB-88

Warren, John Byrne Leicester (see De Tabley, Lord)

Warren, Lella 1899-1982 . . . . Y-83

Warren, Mercy Otis 1728-1814 . . . . . DLB-31, 200

Warren, Robert Penn 1905-1989
. . . . . . DLB-2, 48, 152; Y-80, Y-89; CDALB-6

Warren, Samuel 1807-1877 . . . . DLB-190

Die Wartburgkrieg circa 1230-circa 1280 . . . DLB-138

Warton, Joseph 1722-1800 . . . . DLB-104, 109

Warton, Thomas 1728-1790 . . . . DLB-104, 109

Warung, Price (William Astley)
1855-1911 . . . . DLB-230

Washington, George 1732-1799 . . . . DLB-31

Wassermann, Jakob 1873-1934 . . . . DLB-66

Wasserstein, Wendy 1950- DLB-228

Wasson, David Atwood 1823-1887 . . . DLB-1, 223

Watanna, Onoto (see Eaton, Winnifred)

Waterhouse, Keith 1929- DLB-13, 15

Waterman, Andrew 1940- DLB-40

Waters, Frank 1902-1995 . . . . DLB-212; Y-86

Waters, Michael 1949- DLB-120

Watkins, Tobias 1780-1855 . . . . DLB-73

Watkins, Vernon 1906-1967 . . . . DLB-20

Watmough, David 1926- DLB-53

Watson, James Wreford (see Wreford, James)

Watson, John 1850-1907 . . . . DLB-156

Watson, Rosamund Marriott
(Graham R. Tomson) 1860-1911 . . . . DLB-240

Watson, Sheila 1909- DLB-60

Watson, Thomas 1545?-1592 . . . . DLB-132

Watson, Wilfred 1911- DLB-60

Watt, W. J., and Company DLB-46

Watten, Barrett 1948- DLB-193

Watterson, Henry 1840-1921 . . . . DLB-25

Watts, Alan 1915-1973 . . . . DLB-16

Watts, Franklin [publishing house] DLB-46

Watts, Isaac 1674-1748 . . . . DLB-95

Waugh, Alec 1898-1981 . . . . DLB-191

Waugh, Auberon 1939-2000 . . . DLB-14, 194; Y-00

The Cult of Biography
Excerpts from the Second Folio Debate:
"Biographies are generally a disease of
English Literature" Y-86

Waugh, Evelyn
1903-1966 . . . . . DLB-15, 162, 195; CDBLB-6

Way and Williams DLB-49

Wayman, Tom 1945- DLB-53

We See the Editor at Work Y-97

Weatherly, Tom 1942- DLB-41

Weaver, Gordon 1937- DLB-130

Weaver, Robert 1921- DLB-88

Webb, Beatrice 1858-1943 and
Webb, Sidney 1859-1947 . . . . DLB-190

Webb, Frank J. ?-? DLB-50

Webb, James Watson 1802-1884 . . . . DLB-43

Webb, Mary 1881-1927 . . . . DLB-34

Webb, Phyllis 1927- DLB-53

Webb, Walter Prescott 1888-1963 . . . . DLB-17

Webbe, William ?-1591 . . . . DLB-132

Webber, Charles Wilkins 1819-1856? . . . DLB-202

Webling, Lucy (Lucy Betty MacRaye)
1877-1952 . . . . DLB-240

Webling, Peggy (Arthur Weston)
1871-1949 . . . . DLB-240

Webster, Augusta 1837-1894 . . . . . . DLB-35, 240

Webster, Charles L., and Company DLB-49

Webster, John
1579 or 1580-1634? DLB-58; CDBLB-1

John Webster: The Melbourne
Manuscript Y-86

Wassermann, Jakob 1873-1934 . . . . DLB-66

Webster, Noah
1758-1843 . . . . DLB-1, 37, 42, 43, 73, 243

Weckherlin, Georg Rodolf 1584-1653 . . . DLB-164

Wedekind, Frank
1864-1918 . . . . DLB-118; CDBLB-2

Weeks, Edward Augustus, Jr.
1898-1989 . . . . .DLB-137

Weeks, Stephen B. 1865-1918 . . . . .DLB-187

Weems, Mason Locke 1759-1825 . . . DLB-30, 37, 42

Weerth, Georg 1822-1856 . . . . DLB-129

Weidenfeld and Nicolson DLB-112

Weidman, Jerome 1913-1998 . . . . DLB-28

Weiß, Ernst 1882-1940 . . . . DLB-81

Weigl, Bruce 1949- DLB-120

Weinbaum, Stanley Grauman 1902-1935 . . DLB-8

Weintraub, Stanley 1929- DLB-111; Y82

The Practice of Biography: An Interview
with Stanley Weintraub Y-82

Weise, Christian 1642-1708 . . . . DLB-168

Weisenborn, Gunther 1902-1969 . . . . DLB-69, 124

Weiss, John 1818-1879 . . . . DLB-1, 243

Weiss, Peter 1916-1982 . . . . DLB-69, 124

Weiss, Theodore 1916- DLB-5

Weisse, Christian Felix 1726-1804 . . . . DLB-97

Weitling, Wilhelm 1808-1871 . . . . DLB-129

Welch, James 1940- DLB-175

Welch, Lew 1926-1971? DLB-16

Weldon, Fay 1931- DLB-14, 194; CDBLB-8

Wellek, René 1903-1995 . . . . DLB-63

Wells, Carolyn 1862-1942 . . . . DLB-11

Wells, Charles Jeremiah circa 1800-1879 . . DLB-32

Wells, Gabriel 1862-1946 . . . . DLB-140

Wells, H. G.
1866-1946 . . . DLB-34, 70, 156, 178; CDBLB-6

Wells, Helena 1758?-1824 . . . . DLB-200

Wells, Robert 1947- DLB-40

Wells-Barnett, Ida B. 1862-1931 . . . . . DLB-23, 221

Welty, Eudora 1909-
. . . . . DLB-2, 102, 143; Y-87; DS-12; CDALB-1

Eudora Welty: Eye of the Storyteller Y-87

Eudora Welty Newsletter Y-99

Eudora Welty's Ninetieth Birthday Y-99

Wendell, Barrett 1855-1921 . . . . DLB-71

Wentworth, Patricia 1878-1961 . . . . DLB-77

Wentworth, William Charles
1790-1872 . . . . DLB-230

Werder, Diederich von dem 1584-1657 . . DLB-164

Werfel, Franz 1890-1945 . . . . DLB-81, 124

Werner, Zacharias 1768-1823 . . . . DLB-94

The Werner Company DLB-49

Wersba, Barbara 1932- DLB-52

Wescott, Glenway 1901- DLB-4, 9, 102

Wesker, Arnold 1932- DLB-13; CDBLB-8

Wesley, Charles 1707-1788 . . . . DLB-95

Wesley, John 1703-1791 . . . . DLB-104

Wesley, Mary 1912- DLB-231

Wesley, Richard 1945- DLB-38

Wessels, A., and Company DLB-46

Wessobrunner Gebet circa 787-815 ....DLB-148

West, Anthony 1914-1988.............DLB-15

West, Cornel 1953- DLB-246

West, Dorothy 1907-1998 ....DLB-76

West, Jessamyn 1902-1984 ....DLB-6; Y-84

West, Mae 1892-1980 ....DLB-44

West, Nathanael
1903-1940 ....DLB-4, 9, 28; CDALB-5

West, Paul 1930- DLB-14

West, Rebecca 1892-1983 ....DLB-36; Y-83

West, Richard 1941- DLB-185

West and Johnson DLB-49

Westcott, Edward Noyes 1846-1898 .....DLB-202

The Western Messenger 1835-1841 ....DLB-223

Western Publishing Company...........DLB-46

Western Writers of America Y-99

The Westminster Review 1824-1914 ....DLB-110

Weston, Arthur (see Webling, Peggy)

Weston, Elizabeth Jane circa 1582-1612 ..DLB-172

Wetherald, Agnes Ethelwyn 1857-1940....DLB-99

Wetherell, Elizabeth (see Warner, Susan)

Wetherell, W. D. 1948- DLB-234

Wetzel, Friedrich Gottlob 1779-1819 .....DLB-90

Weyman, Stanley J. 1855-1928 .....DLB-141, 156

Wezel, Johann Karl 1747-1819 ....DLB-94

Whalen, Philip 1923- DLB-16

Whalley, George 1915-1983 ....DLB-88

Wharton, Edith 1862-1937
.....DLB-4, 9, 12, 78, 189; DS-13; CDALB-3

Wharton, William 1920s?- Y-80

"What You Lose on the Swings You Make Up
on the Merry-Go-Round" Y-99

Whately, Mary Louisa 1824-1889 ......DLB-166

Whately, Richard 1787-1863 ....DLB-190

From *Elements of Rhetoric* (1828;
revised, 1846) DLB-57

What's Really Wrong With Bestseller Lists .. Y-84

Wheatley, Dennis Yates 1897-1977 ....DLB-77

Wheatley, Phillis
circa 1754-1784 ....DLB-31, 50; CDALB-2

Wheeler, Anna Doyle 1785-1848? DLB-158

Wheeler, Charles Stearns 1816-1843 ...DLB-1, 223

Wheeler, Monroe 1900-1988.............DLB-4

Wheelock, John Hall 1886-1978 ....DLB-45

Wheelwright, J. B. 1897-1940..........DLB-45

Wheelwright, John circa 1592-1679 ......DLB-24

Whetstone, George 1550-1587..........DLB-136

Whetstone, Colonel Pete (see Noland, C. F. M.)

Whicher, Stephen E. 1915-1961 ....DLB-111

Whipple, Edwin Percy 1819-1886.....DLB-1, 64

Whitaker, Alexander 1585-1617 ....DLB-24

Whitaker, Daniel K. 1801-1881..........DLB-73

Whitcher, Frances Miriam
1812-1852 ....DLB-11, 202

White, Andrew 1579-1656.............DLB-24

White, Andrew Dickson 1832-1918 ......DLB-47

White, E. B. 1899-1985 ....DLB-11, 22; CDALB-7

White, Edgar B. 1947- DLB-38

White, Edmund 1940- DLB-227

White, Ethel Lina 1887-1944 ....DLB-77

White, Hayden V. 1928- DLB-246

White, Henry Kirke 1785-1806 ....DLB-96

White, Horace 1834-1916 ....DLB-23

White, Phyllis Dorothy James (see James, P. D.)

White, Richard Grant 1821-1885 ....DLB-64

White, T. H. 1906-1964 ....DLB-160

White, Walter 1893-1955 ....DLB-51

White, William, and Company DLB-49

White, William Allen 1868-1944.......DLB-9, 25

White, William Anthony Parker
(see Boucher, Anthony)

White, William Hale (see Rutherford, Mark)

Whitechurch, Victor L. 1868-1933 ....DLB-70

Whitehead, Alfred North 1861-1947 .....DLB-100

Whitehead, E. A. 1933- DLB-245

Whitehead, James 1936- Y-81

Whitehead, William 1715-1785 .....DLB-84, 109

Whitfield, James Monroe 1822-1871 ......DLB-50

Whitfield, Raoul 1898-1945............DLB-226

Whitgift, John circa 1533-1604 ....DLB-132

Whiting, John 1917-1963 ....DLB-13

Whiting, Samuel 1597-1679 ....DLB-24

Whitlock, Brand 1869-1934.............DLB-12

Whitman, Albert, and Company.........DLB-46

Whitman, Albery Allson 1851-1901 ......DLB-50

Whitman, Alden 1913-1990............... Y-91

Whitman, Sarah Helen (Power)
1803-1878 ....DLB-1, 243

Whitman, Walt
1819-1892 ....DLB-3, 64, 224; CDALB-2

Whitman Publishing Company..........DLB-46

Whitney, Geoffrey 1548 or 1552?-1601 ..DLB-136

Whitney, Isabella flourished 1566-1573...DLB-136

Whitney, John Hay 1904-1982 ....DLB-127

Whittemore, Reed 1919-1995 ....DLB-5

Whittier, John Greenleaf
1807-1892 ....DLB-1, 243; CDALB-2

Whittlesey House DLB-46

Who Runs American Literature? Y-94

Whose *Ulysses?* The Function of Editing Y-97

Wickham, Anna (Edith Alice Mary Harper)
1884-1947 ....DLB-240

Wicomb, Zoë 1948- DLB-225

Wideman, John Edgar 1941- DLB-33, 143

Widener, Harry Elkins 1885-1912.......DLB-140

Wiebe, Rudy 1934- DLB-60

Wiechert, Ernst 1887-1950.............DLB-56

Wied, Martina 1882-1957 ....DLB-85

Wiehe, Evelyn May Clowes (see Mordaunt, Elinor)

Wieland, Christoph Martin 1733-1813 ....DLB-97

Wienbarg, Ludolf 1802-1872...........DLB-133

Wieners, John 1934- DLB-16

Wier, Ester 1910- DLB-52

Wiesel, Elie
1928- DLB-83; Y-86, 87; CDALB-7

Wiggin, Kate Douglas 1856-1923 ....DLB-42

Wigglesworth, Michael 1631-1705........DLB-24

Wilberforce, William 1759-1833 ....DLB-158

Wilbrandt, Adolf 1837-1911 ....DLB-129

Wilbur, Richard
1921- DLB-5, 169; CDALB-7

Wild, Peter 1940- DLB-5

Wilde, Lady Jane Francesca Elgee
1821?-1896 ....DLB-199

Wilde, Oscar 1854-1900
.........DLB-10, 19, 34, 57, 141, 156, 190;
CDBLB-5

"The Critic as Artist" (1891) DLB-57

Oscar Wilde Conference at Hofstra
University Y-00

From "The Decay of Lying" (1889) DLB-18

"The English Renaissance of
Art" (1908) DLB-35

"L'Envoi" (1882) DLB-35

Wilde, Richard Henry 1789-1847 ......DLB-3, 59

Wilde, W. A., Company DLB-49

Wilder, Billy 1906- DLB-26

Wilder, Laura Ingalls 1867-1957 ....DLB-22

Wilder, Thornton
1897-1975........DLB-4, 7, 9, 228; CDALB-7

Thornton Wilder Centenary at Yale........Y-97

Wildgans, Anton 1881-1932 ....DLB-118

Wiley, Bell Irvin 1906-1980.............DLB-17

Wiley, John, and Sons DLB-49

Wilhelm, Kate 1928- DLB-8

Wilkes, Charles 1798-1877..............DLB-183

Wilkes, George 1817-1885 ....DLB-79

Wilkins, John 1614-1672 ....DLB-236

Wilkinson, Anne 1910-1961 ....DLB-88

Wilkinson, Christopher 1941- DLB-245

Wilkinson, Eliza Yonge
1757-circa 1813 ....DLB-200

Wilkinson, Sylvia 1940- Y-86

Wilkinson, William Cleaver 1833-1920 ...DLB-71

Willard, Barbara 1909-1994 ....DLB-161

Willard, Emma 1787-1870 ....DLB-239

Willard, Frances E. 1839-1898 ....DLB-221

Willard, L. [publishing house]...........DLB-49

Willard, Nancy 1936- DLB-5, 52

Willard, Samuel 1640-1707 ....DLB-24

Willeford, Charles 1919-1988 ....DLB-226

William of Auvergne 1190-1249 ....DLB-115

William of Conches
circa 1090-circa 1154 ....DLB-115

William of Ockham circa 1285-1347 .....DLB-115

William of Sherwood
1200/1205-1266/1271 ....DLB-115

The William Chavrat American Fiction Collection at the Ohio State University Libraries Y-92

Williams, A., and Company............ DLB-49

Williams, Ben Ames 1889-1953 .... DLB-102

Williams, C. K. 1936- DLB-5

Williams, Chancellor 1905- DLB-76

Williams, Charles 1886-1945 ...... DLB-100, 153

Williams, Denis 1923-1998............ DLB-117

Williams, Emlyn 1905-1987 ......DLB-10, 77, 245

Williams, Garth 1912-1996 .... DLB-22

Williams, George Washington
    1849-1891 .... DLB-47

Williams, Heathcote 1941- DLB-13

Williams, Helen Maria 1761-1827 ...... DLB-158

Williams, Hugo 1942- DLB-40

Williams, Isaac 1802-1865 .... DLB-32

Williams, Joan 1928- DLB-6

Williams, Joe 1889-1972............. DLB-241

Williams, John A. 1925- DLB-2, 33

Williams, John E. 1922-1994 .... DLB-6

Williams, Jonathan 1929- DLB-5

Williams, Miller 1930- DLB-105

Williams, Nigel 1948- DLB-231

Williams, Raymond 1921- ... DLB-14, 231, 242

Williams, Roger circa 1603-1683 .... DLB-24

Williams, Rowland 1817-1870......... DLB-184

Williams, Samm-Art 1946- DLB-38

Williams, Sherley Anne 1944-1999 ...... DLB-41

Williams, T. Harry 1909-1979 .... DLB-17

Williams, Tennessee
    1911-1983..... DLB-7; Y-83; DS-4; CDALB-1

Williams, Terry Tempest 1955- DLB-206

Williams, Ursula Moray 1911- DLB-160

Williams, Valentine 1883-1946 .... DLB-77

Williams, William Appleman 1921- DLB-17

Williams, William Carlos
    1883-1963 ..... DLB-4, 16, 54, 86; CDALB-4

Williams, Wirt 1921- DLB-6

Williams Brothers.................... DLB-49

Williamson, Henry 1895-1977 .... DLB-191

Williamson, Jack 1908- DLB-8

Willingham, Calder Baynard, Jr.
    1922-1995 .... DLB-2, 44

Williram of Ebersberg circa 1020-1085 .. DLB-148

Willis, Nathaniel Parker
    1806-1867......DLB-3, 59, 73, 74, 183; DS-13

Willis, Ted 1914-1992 .... DLB-245

Willkomm, Ernst 1810-1886 .... DLB-133

Willumsen, Dorrit 1940- DLB-214

Wills, Garry 1934- DLB-246

Wilmer, Clive 1945- DLB-40

Wilson, A. N. 1950- DLB-14, 155, 194

Wilson, Angus 1913-1991 ..... DLB-15, 139, 155

Wilson, Arthur 1595-1652 .... DLB-58

Wilson, August 1945- DLB-228

Wilson, Augusta Jane Evans 1835-1909 ... DLB-42

Wilson, Colin 1931- DLB-14, 194

Wilson, Edmund 1895-1972............ DLB-63

Wilson, Effingham [publishing house] ... DLB-154

Wilson, Ethel 1888-1980 .... DLB-68

Wilson, F. P. 1889-1963 .... DLB-201

Wilson, Harriet E.
    1827/1828?-1863? DLB-50, 239, 243

Wilson, Harry Leon 1867-1939 .... DLB-9

Wilson, John 1588-1667 .... DLB-24

Wilson, John 1785-1854 .... DLB-110

Wilson, John Dover 1881-1969 .... DLB-201

Wilson, Lanford 1937- DLB-7

Wilson, Margaret 1882-1973 .... DLB-9

Wilson, Michael 1914-1978 .... DLB-44

Wilson, Mona 1872-1954 .... DLB-149

Wilson, Robley 1930- DLB-218

Wilson, Romer 1891-1930 .... DLB-191

Wilson, Thomas 1524-1581 ...... DLB-132, 236

Wilson, Woodrow 1856-1924 .... DLB-47

Wimsatt, William K., Jr. 1907-1975 ...... DLB-63

Winchell, Walter 1897-1972 .... DLB-29

Winchester, J. [publishing house] DLB-49

Winckelmann, Johann Joachim
    1717-1768 .... DLB-97

Winckler, Paul 1630-1686 .... DLB-164

Wind, Herbert Warren 1916- DLB-171

Windet, John [publishing house] DLB-170

Windham, Donald 1920- DLB-6

Wing, Donald Goddard 1904-1972 ..... DLB-187

Wing, John M. 1844-1917 .... DLB-187

Wingate, Allan [publishing house] DLB-112

Winnemucca, Sarah 1844-1921 ....DLB-175

Winnifrith, Tom 1938- DLB-155

Winning an Edgar Y-98

Winsloe, Christa 1888-1944........... DLB-124

Winslow, Anna Green 1759-1780 .... DLB-200

Winsor, Justin 1831-1897 .... DLB-47

John C. Winston Company DLB-49

Winters, Yvor 1900-1968.............. DLB-48

Winterson, Jeanette 1959- DLB-207

Winthrop, John 1588-1649 .... DLB-24, 30

Winthrop, John, Jr. 1606-1676 .... DLB-24

Winthrop, Margaret Tyndal 1591-1647 .. DLB-200

Winthrop, Theodore 1828-1861 .... DLB-202

Wirt, William 1772-1834 .... DLB-37

Wise, John 1652-1725................ DLB-24

Wise, Thomas James 1859-1937....... DLB-184

Wiseman, Adele 1928- DLB-88

Wishart and Company............... DLB-112

Wisner, George 1812-1849............ DLB-43

Wister, Owen 1860-1938 ....DLB-9, 78, 186

Wister, Sarah 1761-1804............. DLB-200

Wither, George 1588-1667............ DLB-121

Witherspoon, John 1723-1794......... DLB-31

Withrow, William Henry 1839-1908 ..... DLB-99

Witkacy (see Witkiewicz, Stanisław Ignacy)

Witkiewicz, Stanisław Ignacy
    1885-1939 ....DLB-215; CDWLB-4

Wittig, Monique 1935- DLB-83

Wodehouse, P. G.
    1881-1975......... DLB-34, 162; CDBLB-6

Wohmann, Gabriele 1932- DLB-75

Woiwode, Larry 1941- DLB-6

Wolcot, John 1738-1819............. DLB-109

Wolcott, Roger 1679-1767 .... DLB-24

Wolf, Christa 1929- DLB-75; CDWLB-2

Wolf, Friedrich 1888-1953 .... DLB-124

Wolfe, Gene 1931- DLB-8

Wolfe, John [publishing house] DLB-170

Wolfe, Reyner (Reginald)
    [publishing house] DLB-170

Wolfe, Thomas
    1900-1938 .... DLB-9, 102, 229; Y-85;
                            DS-2, DS-16; CDALB-5

The Thomas Wolfe Collection at the University
    of North Carolina at Chapel Hill........ Y-97

Thomas Wolfe Centennial
    Celebration in Asheville.............. Y-00

Fire at Thomas Wolfe Memorial Y-98

The Thomas Wolfe Society Y-97

Wolfe, Tom 1931- DLB-152, 185

Wolfenstein, Martha 1869-1906........ DLB-221

Wolff, Helen 1906-1994................. Y-94

Wolff, Tobias 1945- DLB-130

Wolfram von Eschenbach
    circa 1170-after 1220 ....DLB-138; CDWLB-2

Wolfram von Eschenbach's *Parzival*:
    Prologue and Book 3 .... DLB-138

Wolker, Jiří 1900-1924............... DLB-215

Wollstonecraft, Mary
    1759-1797 ...... DLB-39, 104, 158; CDBLB-3

Wondratschek, Wolf 1943- DLB-75

Wood, Anthony à 1632-1695.......... DLB-213

Wood, Benjamin 1820-1900.......... DLB-23

Wood, Charles 1932- DLB-13

Wood, Mrs. Henry 1814-1887......... DLB-18

Wood, Joanna E. 1867-1927........... DLB-92

Wood, Sally Sayward Barrell Keating
    1759-1855.................... DLB-200

Wood, Samuel [publishing house] DLB-49

Wood, William ?-? DLB-24

The Charles Wood Affair:
    A Playwright Revived............... Y-83

Woodberry, George Edward
    1855-1930 ....DLB-71, 103

Woodbridge, Benjamin 1622-1684....... DLB-24

Woodcock, George 1912-1995.......... DLB-88

Woodhull, Victoria C. 1838-1927 .... DLB-79

Woodmason, Charles circa 1720-? DLB-31

Woodress, Jr., James Leslie 1916- DLB-111

Woods, Margaret L. 1855-1945........ DLB-240

Woodson, Carter G. 1875-1950 ....DLB-17

Woodward, C. Vann 1908-1999 ....DLB-17

Woodward, Stanley 1895-1965 . . . . DLB-171

Wooler, Thomas 1785 or 1786-1853 . . . . . DLB-158

Woolf, David (see Maddow, Ben)

Woolf, Douglas 1922-1992 . . . . DLB-244

Woolf, Leonard 1880-1969 . . . . . . DLB-100; DS-10

Woolf, Virginia 1882-1941
. . . . DLB-36, 100, 162; DS-10; CDBLB-6

Woolf, Virginia, "The New Biography," *New York Herald Tribune*, 30 October 1927 . . . . . DLB-149

Woollcott, Alexander 1887-1943 . . . . DLB-29

Woolman, John 1720-1772 . . . . DLB-31

Woolner, Thomas 1825-1892 . . . . DLB-35

Woolrich, Cornell 1903-1968 . . . . DLB-226

Woolsey, Sarah Chauncy 1835-1905 . . . . . DLB-42

Woolson, Constance Fenimore
1840-1894 . . . . DLB-12, 74, 189, 221

Worcester, Joseph Emerson
1784-1865 . . . . DLB-1, 235

Worde, Wynkyn de [publishing house] . . . DLB-170

Wordsworth, Christopher 1807-1885 . . . . DLB-166

Wordsworth, Dorothy 1771-1855 . . . . DLB-107

Wordsworth, Elizabeth 1840-1932 . . . . . . DLB-98

Wordsworth, William
1770-1850 . . . . DLB-93, 107; CDBLB-3

Workman, Fanny Bullock 1859-1925 . . . . DLB-189

The Works of the Rev. John Witherspoon
(1800-1801) [excerpts] DLB-31

A World Chronology of Important Science
Fiction Works (1818-1979) DLB-8

World Publishing Company DLB-46

World War II Writers Symposium
at the University of South Carolina,
12–14 April 1995 . . . . Y-95

Worthington, R., and Company DLB-49

Wotton, Sir Henry 1568-1639 . . . . DLB-121

Wouk, Herman 1915- Y-82; CDALB-7

Wreford, James 1915- DLB-88

Wren, Sir Christopher 1632-1723 . . . . . . DLB-213

Wren, Percival Christopher
1885-1941 . . . . DLB-153

Wrenn, John Henry 1841-1911 . . . . DLB-140

Wright, C. D. 1949- DLB-120

Wright, Charles 1935- DLB-165; Y-82

Wright, Charles Stevenson 1932- DLB-33

Wright, Frances 1795-1852 . . . . DLB-73

Wright, Harold Bell 1872-1944 . . . . DLB-9

Wright, James
1927-1980 . . . . DLB-5, 169; CDALB-7

Wright, Jay 1935- DLB-41

Wright, Louis B. 1899-1984 . . . . DLB-17

Wright, Richard
1908-1960 . . . . . DLB-76, 102; DS-2; CDALB-5

Wright, Richard B. 1937- DLB-53

Wright, Sarah Elizabeth 1928- DLB-33

Wright, Willard Huntington ("S. S. Van Dine")
1888-1939 . . . . DS-16

A Writer Talking: A Collage Y-00

Writers and Politics: 1871-1918,
by Ronald Gray DLB-66

Writers and their Copyright Holders:
the WATCH Project Y-94

Writers' Forum Y-85

Writing for the Theatre,
by Harold Pinter DLB-13

Wroth, Lawrence C. 1884-1970 . . . . DLB-187

Wroth, Lady Mary 1587-1653 . . . . DLB-121

Wurlitzer, Rudolph 1937- DLB-173

Wyatt, Sir Thomas circa 1503-1542 . . . . . DLB-132

Wycherley, William
1641-1715 . . . . DLB-80; CDBLB-2

Wyclif, John
circa 1335-31 December 1384 . . . . . . DLB-146

Wyeth, N. C. 1882-1945 . . . . DLB-188; DS-16

Wylie, Elinor 1885-1928 . . . . DLB-9, 45

Wylie, Philip 1902-1971 . . . . DLB-9

Wyllie, John Cook 1908-1968 . . . . DLB-140

Wyman, Lillie Buffum Chace
1847-1929 . . . . DLB-202

Wymark, Olwen 1934- DLB-233

Wynne-Tyson, Esmé 1898-1972 . . . . DLB-191

X

Xenophon circa 430 B.C.-circa 356 B.C. . . . DLB-176

Y

Yasuoka Shōtarō 1920- DLB-182

Yates, Dornford 1885-1960 . . . . DLB-77, 153

Yates, J. Michael 1938- DLB-60

Yates, Richard
1926-1992 . . . . DLB-2, 234; Y-81, Y-92

Yau, John 1950- DLB-234

Yavorov, Peyo 1878-1914 . . . . DLB-147

The Year in Book Publishing Y-86

The Year in Book Reviewing and the Literary
Situation Y-98

The Year in British Drama Y-99, Y-00

The Year in British Fiction Y-99, Y-00

The Year in Children's
Books Y-92–Y-96, Y-98, Y-99, Y-00

The Year in Children's Literature Y-97

The Year in Drama Y-82–Y-85, Y-87–Y-96

The Year in Fiction . . . Y-84–Y-86, Y-89, Y-94–Y-99

The Year in Fiction: A Biased View Y-83

The Year in Literary Biography . . Y-83–Y-98, Y-00

The Year in Literary Theory Y-92–Y-93

The Year in London Theatre Y-92

The Year in the Novel Y-87, Y-88, Y-90–Y-93

The Year in Poetry Y-83–Y-92, Y-94–Y-00

The Year in Science Fiction and Fantasy Y-00

The Year in Short Stories Y-87

The Year in the Short Story Y-88, Y-90–Y-93

The Year in Texas Literature Y-98

The Year in U.S. Drama Y-00

The Year in U.S. Fiction Y-00

The Year's Work in American Poetry Y-82

The Year's Work in Fiction: A Survey Y-82

Yearsley, Ann 1753-1806 . . . . DLB-109

Yeats, William Butler
1865-1939 . . . . DLB-10, 19, 98, 156; CDBLB-5

Yep, Laurence 1948- DLB-52

Yerby, Frank 1916-1991 . . . . DLB-76

Yezierska, Anzia
1880-1970 . . . . DLB-28, 221

Yolen, Jane 1939- DLB-52

Yonge, Charlotte Mary
1823-1901 . . . . DLB-18, 163

The York Cycle circa 1376-circa 1569 . . . . DLB-146

A Yorkshire Tragedy DLB-58

Yoseloff, Thomas [publishing house] DLB-46

Young, A. S. "Doc" 1919-1996 . . . . DLB-241

Young, Al 1939- DLB-33

Young, Arthur 1741-1820 . . . . DLB-158

Young, Dick 1917 or 1918 - 1987 . . . . DLB-171

Young, Edward 1683-1765 . . . . DLB-95

Young, Frank A. "Fay" 1884-1957 . . . . . . DLB-241

Young, Francis Brett 1884-1954 . . . . DLB-191

Young, Gavin 1928- DLB-204

Young, Stark 1881-1963 . . . . . . DLB-9, 102; DS-16

Young, Waldeman 1880-1938 . . . . DLB-26

Young, William
[publishing house] DLB-49

Young Bear, Ray A. 1950- DLB-175

Yourcenar, Marguerite
1903-1987 . . . . DLB-72; Y-88

"You've Never Had It So Good," Gusted by
"Winds of Change": British Fiction in the
1950s, 1960s, and After DLB-14

Yovkov, Yordan 1880-1937 . . DLB-147; CDWLB-4

Z

Zachariä, Friedrich Wilhelm 1726-1777 . . . . DLB-97

Zagajewski, Adam 1945- DLB-232

Zagoskin, Mikhail Nikolaevich
1789-1852 . . . . DLB-198

Zajc, Dane 1929- DLB-181

Zālīte, Māra 1952- DLB-232

Zamora, Bernice 1938- DLB-82

Zand, Herbert 1923-1970 . . . . DLB-85

Zangwill, Israel 1864-1926 . . . . . . DLB-10, 135, 197

Zanzotto, Andrea 1921- DLB-128

Zapata Olivella, Manuel 1920- DLB-113

Zasodimsky, Pavel Vladimirovich
1843-1912 . . . . DLB-238

Zebra Books DLB-46

Zebrowski, George 1945- DLB-8

Zech, Paul 1881-1946 . . . . DLB-56

Zeidner, Lisa 1955- DLB-120

Zeidonis, Imants 1933- DLB-232

Zeimi (Kanze Motokiyo) 1363-1443 . . . . . DLB-203

Zelazny, Roger 1937-1995 . . . . DLB-8

Zenger, John Peter 1697-1746 . . . . DLB-24, 43

Zepheria DLB-172

Zesen, Philipp von 1619-1689 . . . . DLB-164

Zhukovsky, Vasilii Andreevich
1783-1852 . . . . DLB-205

Zieber, G. B., and Company DLB-49

Ziedonis, Imants 1933- CDWLB-4

Zieroth, Dale 1946- DLB-60

Zigler und Kliphausen, Heinrich
Anshelm von 1663-1697 . . . . DLB-168

Zimmer, Paul 1934- DLB-5

Zinberg, Len (see Lacy, Ed)

Zindel, Paul 1936- DLB-7, 52; CDALB-7

Zingref, Julius Wilhelm 1591-1635. . . . . . DLB-164

Zinnes, Harriet 1919- DLB-193

Zinzendorf, Nikolaus Ludwig von
    1700-1760. . . . . DLB-168

Zitkala-Ša 1876-1938. . . . . .DLB-175

Zīverts, Mārtiņš 1903-1990. . . . . DLB-220

Zlatovratsky, Nikolai Nikolaevich
    1845-1911 . . . . DLB-238

Zola, Emile 1840-1902 . . . . DLB-123

Zolla, Elémire 1926- DLB-196

Zolotow, Charlotte 1915- DLB-52

Zschokke, Heinrich 1771-1848 . . . . DLB-94

Zubly, John Joachim 1724-1781 . . . . DLB-31

Zu-Bolton II, Ahmos 1936- DLB-41

Zuckmayer, Carl 1896-1977 . . . . DLB-56, 124

Zukofsky, Louis 1904-1978 . . . . DLB-5, 165

Zupan, Vitomil 1914-1987 . . . . DLB-181

Župančič, Oton 1878-1949 . . .DLB-147; CDWLB-4

zur Mühlen, Hermynia 1883-1951 . . . . DLB-56

Zweig, Arnold 1887-1968 . . . . DLB-66

Zweig, Stefan 1881-1942 . . . . DLB-81, 118

ISBN 0-7876-4664-4

90000

9 780787 646646